Lecture Notes in Economics and Mathematical Systems

Managing Editors: M. Beckmann and H. P. Künzi

Operations Research

197

Integer Programming and Related Areas

A Classified Bibliography 1978–1981

Compiled at the Institut für Ökonometrie und Operations Research, University of Bonn

Edited by R. von Randow

Springer-Verlag
Berlin Heidelberg New York 1982

Managing Editors
Prof. Dr. M. Beckmam
Brown University
Providence, RI 02912 USA

Prof. Dr. H. P. Künzi
Universität Zürich
CH-8090 Zürich

Editor
Dr. R. von Randow
Institut für Ökonometrie und Operations Research
Universität Bonn
Nassestr. 2, D-5300 Bonn 1

AMS Subject Classifications (1980): 05, 05A, 05B, 05C, 68, 68A, 68C
68E, 90, 90B, 90C

ISBN 978-3-540-11203-7 ISBN 978-3-642-46449-2 (eBook)
DOI 10.1007/978-3-642-46449-2

Softcover reprint of the hardcoevr 1st edition 1982
Printing and binding: Beltz Offsetdruck, Hemsbach/Bergstr.
2142/3140-543210

TABLE OF CONTENTS

PREFACE

The field of integer programming continues to be one of the most vital areas of mathematical optimization, and the flood of publications tends to become even more difficult to survey than in the past. A classified bibliography of the literature thus seems even more necessary today than it did when I started such a project in 1970 for collecting and classifying all available publications on integer programming. This pioneering work was performed by Claus Kastning during the years 1970 - 1975 in the Institut für Ökonometrie und Operations Research, Bonn, and culminated in the publication of the first volume of the classified bibliography entitled "Integer Programming and Related Areas", Lecture Notes in Economics and Mathematical Systems, Volume 128.

Work on the project was continued by Dirk Hausmann and Reinhardt Euler, and three years later the second volume was published as Lecture Notes in Economics and Mathematical Systems, Volume 160.

The present book constitutes the third volume of the bibliography and covers the period from early in 1978 to mid 1981. It contains 3924 new publications by 3075 authors and its compilation was begun by Reinhardt Euler and continued by Rabe von Randow. Its form is practically identical to that of the first two volumes, some slight changes having been made in the subject list.

Finally I would again like to thank the programmers of the Institute for their extensive programming effort.

Bonn, November 1981 Bernhard Korte

INTRODUCTORY REMARKS

This volume continues the series "Integer Programming and Related Areas: A Classified Bibliography", published as Lecture Notes in Economics and Mathematical Systems Nos. 128 and 160. It contains the publications appearing in the period from early in 1978 to mid 1981, as well as any previous publications which were not included in the first or second volume.

The following topics are covered:

- theory and methods of general integer programming ;
- combinatorial and graph theoretical optimization problems related to integer programming ;
- applications of integer programming .

A detailed list of the subjects included is given at the end of this introduction. Textbooks and proceedings volumes have been included only if they deal principally with integer programming.

PART 1 : This part comprises the alphabetical bibliography which lists all publications alphabetically by the first author and chronologically for each author, and includes the full bibliographical data plus a reference code which reflects the author's name and the year of publication. The purpose of the code is to enable the user to identify publications referenced in Part 2 and Part 3.

Bibliographical data are given as follows:

a) Textbook :

ref. code   author(s)
title. Where published: publisher(s), no. of pages. (Year).

b) Article in a journal :

ref. code author(s)
title. Journal, vol. no., pages. (Year).

c) Article in a proceedings volume :

ref. code author(s)
title. IN: Editor(s): title of the proceedings volume, pages. Where published: publisher(s). (Year).

d) Paper :

ref. code author(s)
title. Classification of the paper. Where published: publisher, no. of pages. (Year).

Publications in English, French or German appear under their original title. Titles of publications written in other languages have been translated into English and the original language indicated in brackets.

PART 2 : In this part the publications have been classified according to 51 subjects; within each subject the ordering is again alphabetical by the first author.

The subject list following these remarks contains 51 main subject headings, and for 87 further topics the corresponding subject headings have been indicated. The publications appear under all relevant headings; the references are restricted to name(s) of author(s), title and reference code, with which the full bibliographical data can be retrieved from Part 1.

PART 3 : The purpose of this part is to enable the user to locate publications for which only a coauthor's name is known. It consists of an alphabetical catalogue of all the authors appearing in Part 1, and lists for each author the reference codes of all his publications.

SUBJECT LIST

acyclic subgraph problem	→	graph theoretic results
ADJACENCY ON INTEGER POLYHEDRA		
aggregation	→	diophantine systems and aggregation
air crew scheduling	→	covering ; scheduling
ALGEBRAIC METHODS AND ALGEBRAIZATION OF PROBLEMS		
algorithm codes	→	computer codes
allocation	→	location and allocation
antiblocking	→	blocking, antiblocking, integer rounding
APPLICATIONS OF INTEGER PROGRAMMING		
approximate algorithms	→	heuristics
assembly line balancing	→	scheduling
ASSIGNMENT		
backtracking methods	→	branch and bound
balanced matrices	→	unimodular, balanced, and perfect matrices
Benders' method	→	decomposition ; mixed integer programming
bibliographies	→	surveys, bibliographies
bin packing	→	packing
bivalent programming	→	zero-one programming
BLOCKING, ANTIBLOCKING, INTEGER ROUNDING		
BOOLEAN METHODS		
BOTTLENECK PROBLEMS		
BRANCH AND BOUND		
branchings	→	graph theoretic results
chance constrained methods	→	stochastic integer programming

PART 1

ALPHABETIC BIBLIOGRAPHY

ABAE 1975 -1 ABAEV, T. G.
PROBLEM OF COMPILING AN OPTIMAL SCHEDULE FOR THE WORK OF A GROUP OF AUTOMATA STATIONS WITH DIGITAL PROGRAMMED CONTROL (RUSSIAN), THE. IN: V. I. SKURIHIN, V. E. KRAVCENKO (EDS.): AUTOMATED CONTROL SYSTEMS. PROCEEDINGS OF THE SEMINAR ON AUTOMATED CONTROL SYSTEMS AND DATA PROCESSING (RUSSIAN), KIEV 1974, 62-69. KIEV: AKAD. NAUK UKRAIN. SSR INST. KIBERNET. (1975).

ABBO 1978 -1 ABBOTT, H. L.; LIU, A. C.
EXISTENCE PROBLEM FOR COLOR CRITICAL LINEAR HYPERGRAPHS, THE. ACTA MATHEMATICA ACADEMIAE SCIENTIARUM HUNGARICAE (BUDAPEST) 32, 273-282. (1978).

ABBO 1979 -1 ABBOTT, H. L.; LIU, A. C.
BOUNDS FOR THE COVERING NUMBER OF A GRAPH. DISCRETE MATHEMATICS 25, 281-284. (1979).

ABDE 1978 -1 ABDEL-WAHAB, H. M.; KAMEDA, T.
SCHEDULING TO MINIMIZE MAXIMUM CUMULATIVE COST SUBJECT TO SERIES-PARALLEL PRECEDENCE CONSTRAINTS. OPERATIONS RESEARCH 26, 141-158. (1978).

ABDE 1980 -1 ABDEL-WAHAB, H. M.; KAMEDA, T.
ON STRICTLY OPTIMAL SCHEDULES FOR THE CUMULATIVE COST-OPTIMAL SCHEDULING PROBLEM. COMPUTING 24, 61-86. (1980).

ABDU 1980 -1 ABDUL-KADER, I.
CERTAINES PROPRIETES DES TOURNOIS AYANT UN CIRCUIT HAMILTONIEN UNIQUE. REVUE ROUMAINE DE MATHEMATIQUES PURES ET APPLIQUEES 25, 1441-1452. (1980).

ABDUA 1977 -1 ABDULAAL, M.; LEBLANC, L. J.
MULTIMODAL NETWORK EQUILIBRIUM. TECHNICAL REPORT 77013. DALLAS: SOUTHERN METHODIST UNIVERSITY, DEPARTMENT OF INDUSTRIAL ENGINEERING AND OPERATIONS RESEARCH. (1977).

ABDUA 1979 -1 ABDULAAL, M.; LEBLANC, L. J.
CONTINUOUS EQUILIBRIUM NETWORK DESIGN MODELS. TRANSPORTATION RESEARCH 13, SERIES B, 19-32. (1979).

ABEL 1979 -1 ABEL, U.; CARSTENS, H. G.; DEUBER, W.; PROEMEL, H. J.
ON HYPERGRAPHIC NETWORKS. IN: W. OETTLI, F. STEFFENS (EDS.): OPERATIONS RESEARCH VERFAHREN 32. THIRD SYMPOSIUM ON OPERATIONS RESEARCH, MANNHEIM 1978, 1-4. KOENIGSTEIN: ANTON HAIN MEISENHEIM. (1979).

ABRH 1980 -1 ABRHAM, J.; KOTZIG, A.
TRANSFORMATION OF EULER TOURS. IN: M. DEZA, I. G. ROSENBERG (EDS.): COMBINATORICS 79, PART I, 65-70. ANNALS OF DISCRETE MATHEMATICS 8. AMSTERDAM: NORTH-HOLLAND. (1980).

ACHA 1979 -1 ACHARYA, B. D.
ON THE CYCLOMATIC NUMBER OF A HYPERGRAPH. DISCRETE MATHEMATICS 27, 111-116. (1979).

ACHU 1981 -1 ACHUGBUE, J. O.; CHIN, F. Y.
BOUNDS ON SCHEDULES FOR INDEPENDENT TASKS WITH SIMILAR EXECUTION TIMES. JOURNAL OF THE ASSOCIATION FOR COMPUTING MACHINERY 28, 81-99. (1981).

ACKE 1978 -1 ACKERMAN, L. J.; LUSS, H.; BERKOWITZ, R. S.
IMPLICIT ENUMERATION ALGORITHM FOR SEQUENCING POLICIES APPLIED TO TELEPHONE SWITCHING FACILITIES, AN. IEEE TRANSACTIONS ON SYSTEMS, MAN, AND CYBERNETICS 8, NO. 4, 296-300. (1978).

ACKEA 1978 -1 ACKETA, D. M.
ON THE ENUMERATION OF MATROIDS OF RANK 2. UNIVERZITET U NOVOM SADU. ZBORNIK RADOVA PRIRODNO-MATEMATICKOG FAKULTETA (NOVI SAD) 8, 83-90. (1978).

ADAM 1980 -1 ADAM, N. R.; SURKIS, J.
PRIORITY UPDATE INTERVALS AND ANOMALIES IN DYNAMIC RATIO TYPE JOB SHOP SCHEDULING RULES. MANAGEMENT SCIENCE 26, 1227-1237. (1980).

ADAMA 1980 -1 ADAMSKI, A.
OPTIMAL DISPATCHING CONTROL OF BUS LINES. IN: K. IRACKI, K. MALANOWSKI, P. WALUKIEWICZ (EDS.): OPTIMIZATION TECHNIQUES, PART II, 334-344. LECTURE NOTES IN CONTROL AND INFORMATION SCIENCES 23. BERLIN: SPRINGER. (1980).

ADRA 1977 -1 ADRABINSKI, A.; GRABOWSKI, J.
ALGORITHM FOR SOLVING THE MACHINE SEQUENCING PROBLEM, AN. ZASTOSOWANIA MATEMATYKI 15, NO. 4, 523-542. (1977).

ADRAA 1980 -1 ADRABINSKI, A.; GRABOWSKI, J.; WODECKI, M.
ALGORITHM FOR SOLVING THE GENERAL SEQUENCING PROBLEM (POLISH), AN. PRACE NAUKOWE, INSTYTUTU MATEMATYKI, POLITECHNIKI WROCLAWSKIEJ, SERIA STUDIA I MATERIALY (WROCLAW) NO. 14 ANALIZA DYSKRETNA 15-35. (1980).

ADRAB 1977 -1 ADRABINSKI, A.; WODECKI, M.
ALGORITHM FOR SOLVING A MACHINE SEQUENCING PROBLEM WITH PARALLEL MACHINES, AN. RAPORT NR. N-27. WROCLAW: WROCLAW UNIV., INSTITUTE OF COMPUTER SCIENCE, 25 P. (1977).

AFAN 1976 -1 AFANAS'EV, JU. A.; POMANSKII, A. B.
NEW APPROACH TO THE CONSTRUCTION OF ALGORITHMS FOR THE SOLUTION OF PROBLEMS WITH DISCRETE VARIABLES (RUSSIAN), A. IN: A. JU. LEVIN (ED.): HEURISTIC OPTIMIZATION ALGORITHMS (RUSSIAN), 3-23. YAROSLAVL: JAROSLAV. GOS. UNIV. (1976).

AFANA 1978 -1 AFANAS'EV, M. JU.
EXAMPLE OF THE CYCLING OF A STOCHASTIC INTEGER ALGORITHM IN A BILEVEL MULTICOMMODITY PROBLEM (RUSSIAN), AN. IN: METHODS OF FUNCTION ANALYSIS IN MATHEMATICAL ECONOMICS (RUSSIAN), 111-114. MOSCOW: IZDAT. NAUKA. (1978).

AGAS 1975 -1 AGASHE, S. D.
NEW CHARACTERIZATION OF TREES AND CO-TREES, A. PROCEEDINGS OF THE INDIAN NATIONAL SCIENCE ACADEMY PART A 41, 305-308. (1975).

AGRA 1975 -1 AGRAWAL, S. C.
ON INTEGER SOLUTIONS TO LINEAR FRACTIONAL FUNCTIONAL PROGRAMMING PROBLEMS. ACTA CIENCIA INDICA 1, NO. 3, 203-208. (1975).

AGRA 1977 -1 AGRAWAL, S. C.
ALTERNATE METHOD ON INTEGER SOLUTIONS TO LINEAR FRACTIONAL FUNCTIONALS BY A BRANCH AND BOUND TECHNIQUE, AN. ZEITSCHRIFT FUER ANGEWANDTE MATHEMATIK UND MECHANIK 57, 52-53. (1977).

AGRAA 1978 -1 AGRAWAL, S. C.; CHAND, M.
ON INTEGER SOLUTIONS TO COMPLEMENTARY PROGRAMMING PROBLEMS WITH LINEAR FRACTIONAL OBJECTIVE FUNCTION BY A BRANCH AND BOUND TECHNIQUE. ACTA CIENCIA INDICA 4, 283-289. (1978).

AGRAA 1979 -1 AGRAWAL, S. C.; CHAND, M.
ON INTERSECTION CUTS IN FRACTIONAL INTERVAL INTEGER PROGRAMMING. ACTA CIENCIA INDICA 5, NO. 3, 140-142. (1979).

AGRAA 1980 -1 AGRAWAL, S. C.; CHAND, M.
ON INTEGER SOLUTIONS TO COMPLEMENTARY PROGRAMMING PROBLEMS WITH LINEAR FRACTIONAL OBJECTIVE FUNCTIONS. RICERCA OPERATIVA 10, NO. 13, 19-30. (1980).

AGRAB 1974 -1 AGRAWAL, S. C.; SWARUP, K.
ON INTEGER SOLUTIONS TO QUADRATIC PROGRAMS. ACTA CIENCIA INDICA 1, NO. 1, 73-78; ALSO PUBLISHED IN FOURTH ANNUAL CONVENTION OF THE OPERATIONAL RESEARCH SOCIETY OF INDIA. MADRAS: INDIAN INSTITUTE OF TECHNOLOGY. (1974).

AGUA 1973 -1 AGUADO, I. A.
DISCRETE PROGRAMMING MODEL FOR THE SEQUENCING OF TASKS IN SUGAR PRODUCING INDUSTRIES (SPANISH), A. INVESTIGACION OPERACIONAL, NO. 8, 16-22. (1973).

AHLS 1978 -1 AHLSWEDE, R.; KATONA, G. O. H.
GRAPHS WITH MAXIMAL NUMBER OF ADJACENT PAIRS OF EDGES. ACTA MATHEMATICA ACADEMIAE SCIENTIARUM HUNGARICAE 32, 97-120. (1978).

AHO 1973 -1 AHO, A. V.; HOPCROFT, J. E.; ULLMAN, J. D.
ON FINDING LOWEST COMMON ANCESTORS IN TREES. IN: FIFTH ANNUAL ACM SYMPOSIUM ON THEORY OF COMPUTING, AUSTIN 1973, 253-265. NEW YORK: ASSOCIATION FOR COMPUTING MACHINERY. (1973).

AHRE 1980 -1 AHRENS, J. H.; FINKE, G.
PRIMAL TRANSPORTATION AND TRANSSHIPMENT ALGORITHMS. ZEITSCHRIFT FUER OPERATIONS RESEARCH 24, SERIES A, 1-32. (1980).

AHREA 1978 -1 AHRENS, W.; DEHNERT, G.; GERBER, H. J.
HEURISTISCHE VERFAHREN ZUR TOURENPLANUNG BEI DER HAUSMUELLENTSORGUNG IN LAENDLICHEN REGIONEN. ZEITSCHRIFT FUER OPERATIONS RESEARCH 22, SERIE B, B85-B104. (1978).

AHUJ 1979 -1 AHUJA, V.
ALGORITHM TO CHECK NETWORK STATES FOR DEADLOCK. IBM JOURNAL OF RESEARCH AND DEVELOPMENT 23, NO. 1, 82-86. (1979).

AIEL 1977 -1 AIELLO, A.; BURATTINI, E.; MASSAROTTI, A.
REDUCIBILITY AS A TOOL TO EXTEND THE POWER OF APPROXIMATION ALGORITHMS. THE MINIMIZATION OF BOOLEAN EXPRESSIONS. REVUE FRANCAISE D'AUTOMATIQUE, D'INFORMATIQUE ET DE RECHERCHE OPERATIONELLE 11, SERIE INFORMATIQUE THEORIQUE, 75-82. (1977).

AIELA 1980 -1 AIELLO, A.; BURATTINI, E.; MASSAROTTI, A.; VENTRIGLIA, F.
'A POSTERIORI' EVALUATION OF BIN PACKING APPROXIMATION ALGORITHMS. DISCRETE APPLIED MATHEMATICS 2, 159-162. (1980).

AINO 1979 -1 AINOUCHE, A.; CHRISTOFIDES, N.
ON THE EXISTENCE OF HAMILTONIAN CIRCUITS IN UNDIRECTED GRAPHS. IC-OR-79-02. LONDON: IMPERIAL COLLEGE, DEPT. OF MANAGEMENT SCIENCE, 23 P. (1979).

AJZE 1978 -1 AJZENSHTAT, V. S.; MAXIMOVICH, E. P.
CERTAIN CLASS OF PROBLEMS OF A TRAVELLING SALESMAN (RUSSIAN). KIBERNETIKA, NO. 4, 80-83. (1978).

AKHM 1979 -1 AKHMEDOV, A.; MAJZLIN, M.; CHARYEV, G.
SOLUTION OF SOME MULTIPLE-PRODUCT PROBLEM OF INTEGER PROGRAMMING (RUSSIAN). IZVESTIJA AKADEMII NAUK TURKMENSKOI SSR, SERIJA FIZIKO-TEHNICESKIH, HIMICESKIH I GEOLOGICESKIH NAUK (ASHKHABAD) NO. 4, 113-116. (1979).

AKIY 1978 -1 AKIYAMA, J.; ERA, H.; KANEKO, K.; SAITO, T.; SATO, I.
PACKING AND COVERING IN GRAPHS (JAPANESE). IN: COMBINATORIAL STRUCTURES AND GRAPH THEORY II. PROC. SYMP. KYOTO 1977, 146-167. SURIKAISEKIKENKYUSHO KOKYUROKU NO. 333. KYOTO: KYOTO UNIVERSITY, RESEARCH INST. FOR MATH. SCIENCES. (1978).

AKIYA 1979 -1 AKIYAMA, J.; EXOO, G.; HARARY, F.
GRAPHS WITH ALL INDUCED SUBGRAPHS ISOMORPHIC, THE. MALAYSIAN MATHEMATICAL SOCIETY. BULLETIN. SECOND SERIES 2, 43-44. (1979).

AKIYA 1980 -1 AKIYAMA, J.; EXOO, G.; HARARY, F.
COVERING AND PACKING IN GRAPHS. III: CYCLIC AND ACYCLIC INVARIANTS. MATHEMATICA SLOVACA (BRATISLAVA) 30, 405-417. (1980).

AKIYB 1979 -1 AKIYAMA, J.; HAMADA, T.
DECOMPOSITIONS OF LINE GRAPHS, MIDDLE GRAPHS AND TOTAL GRAPHS OF COMPLETE GRAPHS INTO FORESTS, THE. DISCRETE MATHEMATICS 26, 203-208. (1979).

AKIYC 1979 -1 AKIYAMA, J.; HARARY, F.
GRAPH AND ITS COMPLEMENT WITH SPECIFIED PROPERTIES. I. CONNECTIVITY, A. INTERNATIONAL JOURNAL OF MATHEMATICS AND MATHEMATICAL SCIENCES 2, 223-228. (1979).

AKL 1979 -1 AKL, S. G.
LOWER BOUND ON THE MAXIMUM NUMBER OF CROSSING-FREE HAMILTON CYCLES IN A RECTILINEAR DRAWING OF K(N), A. ARS COMBINATORIA 7, 7-18. (1979).

AKL A 1978 -1 AKL, S. G.; TOUSSAINT, G. T.
FAST CONVEX HULL ALGORITHM, A. INFORMATION PROCESSING LETTERS 7, 219-222. (1978).

AKOP 1979 -1 AKOPJAN, G. C.; GALSTJAN, O. A.
CLASSES OF GRAPHS THAT ARE CRITICAL WITH RESPECT TO COVERINGS (RUSSIAN). IZVESTIJA AKADEMII NAUK ARMJANSKOI SSR, SERIJA MATEMATIKA 14, 150-153, 156. (1979).

AKSI 1974 -1 AKSIONOV, V. A.
CONCERNING THE EXTENSION OF THE 3-COLORING OF PLANAR GRAPHS (RUSSIAN). DISKRETNYI ANALIZ 26, 3-19. (1974).

AKSI 1978 -1 AKSIONOV, V. A.
ON UNIQUELY 3-COLORABLE PLANAR GRAPHS. DISCRETE MATHEMATICS 20, 209-216. (1978).

AKUL 1978 -1 AKULIC, F. E.
NET DECOMPOSITION ALGORITHM FOR THE SOLUTION OF THE MAXIMUM FLOW PROBLEM (RUSSIAN), A. VESCI AKADEMII NAVUK BSSR. SERYJA FIZIKA-MATEMATYCNYH NAVUK, NO. 1, 33-37. (1978).

ALAV 1971 -1 ALAVI, Y.; BEHZAD, M.
COMPLEMENTARY GRAPHS AND EDGE CHROMATIC NUMBERS. SIAM JOURNAL ON APPLIED MATHEMATICS 20, 161-163. (1971).

ALBA 1980 -1 ALBANO, A.; ORSINI, R.
HEURISTIC SOLUTION OF THE RECTANGULAR CUTTING STOCK PROBLEM, A. THE COMPUTER JOURNAL 23, 328-343. (1980).

ALBA 1980 -2 ALBANO, A.; ORSINI, R.
TREE SEARCH APPROACH TO THE M-PARTITION AND KNAPSACK PROBLEMS, A. THE COMPUTER JOURNAL 23, 256-261. (1980).

ALBE 1977 -1 ALBERS, S.
EINSATZPLANUNG VON FLUGZEUGBESATZUNGEN. DISSERTATION. HAMBURG: UNIV. OF HAMBURG, FACHBEREICH WIRTSCHAFTSWISSENSCHAFTEN. 326 P. (1977).

ALBE 1978 -1 ALBERS, S.
ZUR LOESUNG DES QUADRATISCHEN SET-PARTITIONING-PROBLEMS. IN: PROCEEDINGS IN OPERATIONS RESEARCH 7, 19-28. WUERZBURG: PHYSICA. (1978).

ALBE 1979 -1 ALBERS, S.
EXTENDED ALGORITHM FOR OPTIMAL PRODUCT POSITIONING, AN. EUROPEAN JOURNAL OF OPERATIONAL RESEARCH 3, 222-231. (1979).

ALBE 1980 -1 ALBERS, S.
IMPLICIT ENUMERATION ALGORITHMS FOR THE SET-PARTITIONING PROBLEM. OPERATIONS RESEARCH SPECTRUM 2, 23-32. (1980).

ALBEA 1977 -1 ALBERTSON, M. O.; BERMAN, D. M.
EVERY PLANAR GRAPH HAS AN ACYCLIC 7-COLORING. ISRAEL JOURNAL OF MATHEMATICS 28, 169-174. (1977).

ALBEB 1978 -1 ALBERTSON, M. O.; HUTCHINSON, J. P.
ON THE INDEPENDENCE RATIO OF A GRAPH. JOURNAL OF GRAPH THEORY 2, 1-8. (1978).

ALEK 1978 -1 ALEKSEEV, O. G.
APPLICATION OF BRANCH AND BOUND TO THE MINIMAX ASSIGNMENT PROBLEM (RUSSIAN). IZVESTIJA AKADEMII NAUK SSSR. TEHNICESKAJA KIBERNETIKA, NO. 5, 191-202. (1978).

ALEK 1978 -2 ALEKSEEV, O. G.
MINIMAX SCHEDULING PROBLEM, A. AVTOMATIKA I TELEMEHANIKA NO. 1, 108-111; TRANSLATED AS AUTOMATION AND REMOTE CONTROL 39, 1978, 87-89. (1978).

ALEK 1979 -1 ALEKSEEV, O. G.
PROBLEME MULTIDIMENSIONNEL DE STANDARDISATION (RUSSIAN). IZVESTIJA AKADEMII NAUK SSSR. TEHNICESKAJA KIBERNETIKA, NO. 1, 178-185. (1979).

ALEKA 1981 -1 ALEKSEEV, O. G.; BABAEV, A. A.
ON HUNGARIAN METHOD EFFICIENCY IMPROVEMENT (RUSSIAN). EKONOMIKA I MATEMATICESKIE METODY (MOSCOW) 17, NO. 1, 194-195. (1981).

ALI 1978 -1 ALI, A. I.; HELGASON, R. V.; KENNINGTON, J. L.
CONVEX COST NETWORK FLOW PROBLEM: A SURVEY OF ALGORITHMS, THE. TECHNICAL REPORT OREM 78001. DALLAS: SOUTHERN METHODIST UNIV., DEPT. OF OPERATIONS RESEARCH AND ENGINEERING MANAGEMENT, 25 P. (1978).

ALI A 1978 -1 ALI, A. I.; HELGASON, R. V.; KENNINGTON, J. L.; LALL, H. S.
PRIMAL SIMPLEX NETWORK CODES: STATE-OF-THE-ART IMPLEMENTATION TECHNOLOGY. NETWORKS 8, 315-339. (1978).

ALI A 1980 -1 ALI, A. I.; HELGASON, R. V.; KENNINGTON, J. L.; LALL, H. S.
COMPUTATIONAL COMPARISON AMONG THREE MULTICOMMODITY NETWORK FLOW ALGORITHMS. OPERATIONS RESEARCH 28, 995-1000. (1980).

ALI B 1980 -1 ALI, A. I.; KENNINGTON, J. L.
M-TRAVELLING SALEMEN PROBLEM, THE. RESEARCH REPORT CCS 381. AUSTIN: UNIV. OF TEXAS, CENTER FOR CYBERNETIC STUDIES, 20 P. (1980).

ALI B 1980 -2 ALI, A. I.; KENNINGTON, J. L.
M-TRAVELLING SALESMEN PROBLEM: A DUALITY BASED BRANCH-AND-BOUND ALGORITHM, THE. RESEARCH REPORT CCS 382. AUSTIN: UNIV. OF TEXAS, CENTER FOR CYBERNETIC STUDIES, 38 P. (1980).

ALIP 1978 -1 ALIPOV, N. V.; SHUMEJKO, N. A.
SUR UN ALGORITHME DE RESOLUTION DU PROBLEME DE CONNEXION DES FILS DE MONTAGE SOUS FORME DE CIRCUIT FERME (RUSSIAN). UPRALJAJUSHCHIE SISTEMY I MASHINY, NO. 5, 111-114. (1978).

ALLI 1981 -1 ALLINEY, S.
ALGORITHM FOR A ROUTING PROBLEM, AN. IN: R. E. BURKARD, T. ELLINGER (EDS.): METHODS OF OPERATIONS RESEARCH 40, 207-210. KOENIGSTEIN: ANTON HAIN MEISENHEIM. (1981).

ALLIA 1980 -1 ALLINEY, S.; BARNABEI, M.; PEZZOLI, L.
W-OPTIMAL ASSIGNABLE SETS AND ALLOCATION PROBLEMS. BOLLETTINO UNIONE MATEMATICA ITALIANA A (5) 17, 131-136. (1980).

ALSP 1979 -1 ALSPACH, B.
GRAPHS AND PERMUTATION GROUPS WHOSE TRANSITIVE CONSTITUENTS HAVE PRIME DEGREE. IN: ANNALS OF THE NEW YORK ACADEMY OF SCIENCES, VOL. 328, P. 12-20 (1979).

ALSP 1979 -2 ALSPACH, B.
HAMILTONIAN CYCLES IN VERTEX-TRANSITIVE GRAPHS OF ORDER 2P. IN: F. HOFFMAN, D. MAC CARTHY, R. C. MULLIN, R. G. STANTON (EDS.): PROCEEDINGS OF THE TENTH SOUTHEASTERN CONFERENCE ON COMBINATORICS, GRAPH THEORY AND COMPUTING, 131-140. CONGRESSUS NUMERANTIUM XXIII. WINNIPEG: UTILITAS. (1979).

ALSPA 1978 -1 ALSPACH, B.; PARSONS, T. D.
ISOMORPHISM OF CIRCULANT GRAPHS AND DIGRAPHS. NEW YORK (SECOND INTERNATIONAL CONFERENCE ON COMBINATORIAL MATHEMATICS), 21 P. (1978).

ALSPB 1979 -1 ALSPACH, B.; SUTCLIFFE, R. J.
VERTEX-TRANSITIVE GRAPHS OF ORDER 2P. IN: ANNALS OF THE NEW YORK ACADEMY OF SCIENCES, VOL. 319, P. 18-27 (1979).

ALT 1976 -1 ALT, A. M.
CLASS OF INTEGER OPTIMIZATION PROBLEMS (RUSSIAN), A. IN: THEORY OF OPTIMAL DECISIONS (RUSSIAN), 101-108. KIEV: AKAD. NAUK UKRAIN. SSR INST. KIBERNET. (1976).

ALTA 1980 -1 ALTAR, M.
ALGORITHM FOR THE SOLUTION OF THE DYNAMIC PRODUCTION-TRANSPORTATION PROBLEM, AN. ECONOMIC COMPUTATION AND ECONOMIC CYBERNETICS STUDIES AND RESEARCH 14, NO. 3, 31-46. (1980).

ALTR 1979 -1 ALTROGGE, G.
BEDINGUNGEN EINER ALLGEMEINEN NETZPLANSTRUKTUR. IN: PROCEEDINGS IN OPERATIONS RESEARCH 8, 54-59. WUERZBURG: PHYSICA. (1979).

ALVA 1977 -1 ALVARADO, F. L.
COMPUTATIONAL COMPLEXITY OF OPERATIONS INVOLVING PERFECT ELIMINATION OF SPARSE MATRICES. INTERNATIONAL JOURNAL OF COMPUTER MATHEMATICS 6, 69-82. (1977).

ALVAA 1977 -1 ALVAREZ, C.; DOMINGUEZ, H.; FRIEDMAN, P.
USE OF LINEAR PROGRAMMING FOR THE MACROLOCATION OF INDUSTRIAL PLANTS (SPANISH), THE. INVESTIGACION OPERACIONAL (CUBA) 21-22, 3-13. (1977).

ALY 1979 -1 ALY, A. A.; LITWHILER, D. W. JR.
POLICE BRIEFING STATIONS: A LOCATION PROBLEM. AIIE TRANSACTIONS 11, 12-22. (1979).

AMMO 1979 -1 AMMON, P.; PEEMOELLER, W.
LOESUNG GEMISCHT-GANZZAHLIGER PROBLEME MIT NETZWERKSTRUKTUR. IN: PROCEEDINGS IN OPERATIONS RESEARCH 8, 31-39. WUERZBURG: PHYSICA. (1979).

ANAS 1977 -1 ANASTASJAN, J. G.
CERTAIN PROPERTIES OF BIPARTITE HYPERGRAPHS (RUSSIAN). AKADEMIJA NAUK ARMANSKOI SSR. DOKLADY 44, NO. 2, 81-84. (1977).

ANDE 1975 -1 ANDERSEN, L. D.
EDGE-COLOURINGS OF SIMPLE AND NON-SIMPLE GRAPHS. WORKING PAPER. AARHUS: AARHUS UNIVERSITY. (1975).

ANDE 1976 -1 ANDERSEN, L. D.
ON EDGE-COLOURINGS OF NON-SIMPLE GRAPHS. PREPRINT SERIES NO. 21. AARHUS: AARHUS UNIVERSITY. (1976).

ANDE 1977 -1 ANDERSEN, L. D.
ON EDGE COLORINGS OF GRAPHS. MATHEMATICA SCANDINAVICA 40, NO. 2, 161-175. (1977).

ANDE 1978 -1 ANDERSEN, L. D.
ON EDGE-COLOURINGS OF GRAPHS. IN: J.-C. BERMOND ET AL. (EDS.): PROBLEMES COMBINATOIRES ET THEORIE DES GRAPHES. COLLOQUES INTERNATIONAUX DU CENTRE NATIONAL DE LA RECHERCHE SCIENTIFIQUE, ORSAY 1976, 3-4. PARIS: CENTRE NATIONAL DE LA RECHERCHE SCIENTIFIQUE. (1978).

ANDE 1979 -1 ANDERSEN, L. D.
LOWER BOUNDS ON THE COVER-INDEX OF A GRAPH. DISCRETE MATHEMATICS 25, 199-210. (1979).

ANDR 1977 -1 ANDRASFAI, B.
INTRODUCTORY GRAPH THEORY. ELMSFORD: PERGAMON PRESS. 268 P. (1977).

ANDRA 1978 -1 ANDREATTA, G.; BENEDETTI, M. A.; MASON, F.
TRANSPORT LINES WITH NONCONSERVATIVE FLOW (ITALIAN). RENDICONTI DEL SEMINARIO MATEMATICO DELL'UNIVERSITA DI PADOVA 60, 151-163. (1978).

ANEJ 1980 -1 ANEJA, Y. P.
INTEGER LINEAR PROGRAMMING APPROACH TO THE STEINER PROBLEM IN GRAPHS, AN. NETWORKS 10, 167-178. (1980).

ANEJA 1979 -1 ANEJA, Y. P.; AGGARWAL, V.; NAIR, K. P. K.
MAXIMIZATION OF THE VECTOR-FLOW IN MULTICOMMODITY NETWORKS. INFOR 17, 276-286. (1979).

ANEJB 1979 -1 ANEJA, Y. P.; NAIR, K. P. K.
BICRITERIA TRANSPORTATION PROBLEM. MANAGEMENT SCIENCE 25, 73-78. (1979).

ANEJB 1979 -2 ANEJA, Y. P.; NAIR, K. P. K.
TWO PROBLEMS IN MULTICOMMODITY NETWORKS. REVUE FRANCAISE D'AUTOMATIQUE, D'INFORMATIQUE ET DE RECHERCHE OPERATIONELLE 13, SERIE RECHERCHE OPERATIONELLE, 135-142. (1979).

ANEJB 1980 -1 ANEJA, Y. P.; NAIR, K. P. K.
MAXIMAL EXPECTED FLOW IN A NETWORK SUBJECT TO ARC FAILURES. NETWORKS 10, 45-57. (1980).

ANGL 1978 -1 ANGLUIN, D.
ON THE COMPLEXITY OF MINIMUM INFERENCE OF REGULAR SETS. INFORMATION AND CONTROL 39, 337-350. (1978).

ANGLA 1977 -1 ANGLUIN, D.; VALIANT, L. G.
FAST PROBABILISTIC ALGORITHMS FOR HAMILTONIAN CIRCUITS AND MATCHINGS. IN: CONFERENCE RECORD OF THE NINTH ANNUAL ACM SYMPOSIUM ON THEORY OF COMPUTING, BOULDER 1977, 30-41. NEW YORK: ASSOCIATION FOR COMPUTING MACHINERY; ALSO PUBLISHED IN JOURNAL OF COMPUTER AND SYSTEM SCIENCES 18, 1979, 155-193. (1977).

ANTO 1980 -1 ANTONA, O. D'; KUNG, J. P. S.
COHERENT ORIENTATIONS AND SERIES-PARALLEL NETWORKS. DISCRETE MATHEMATICS 32, 95-98. (1980).

ANZA 1977 -1 ANZAI, Y.
URBAN ROAD NETWORK MODELING PROBLEM - FORMULATION AND ALGORITHMS. JOURNAL OF THE OPERATIONS RESEARCH SOCIETY OF JAPAN 20, 203-230. (1977).

APPE 1977 -1 APPEL, K.; HAKEN, W.
EVERY PLANAR MAP IS FOUR COLORABLE. I. DISCHARGING. ILLINOIS JOURNAL OF MATHEMATICS 21, NO. 3, 429-490. (1977).

APPE 1977 -2 APPEL, K.; HAKEN, W.
EVERY PLANAR MAP IS FOUR COLORABLE. II. REDUCIBILITY. ILLINOIS JOURNAL OF MATHEMATICS 21, NO. 3, 491-567. (1977).

APPEA 1978 -1 APPELBE, W. F.; ITO, M. R.
SCHEDULING HEURISTICS IN A MULTIPROGRAMMING ENVIRONMENT. IEEE TRANSACTIONS ON COMPUTERS 27, 628-637. (1978).

ARAB 1966 -1 ARABEYRE, J. P.
METHODS OF CREW SCHEDULING. IN: AGIFORS SYMPOSIUM, AIR FRANCE. (1966).

ARAO 1973 -1 ARAOZ, A. A.
POLYHEDRAL NEOPOLARITIES. PH. D. DISSERTATION. WATERLOO: UNIVERSITY OF WATERLOO. (1973).

ARAOA 1979 -1 ARAOZ, J.
BLOCKING AND ANTI-BLOCKING EXTENSIONS. IN: W. OETTLI, F. STEFFENS (EDS.): OPERATIONS RESEARCH VERFAHREN 32, THIRD SYMPOSIUM ON OPERATIONS RESEARCH, MANNHEIM 1978, 5-18. KOENIGSTEIN: ANTON HAIN MEISENHEIM. (1979).

ARAOB 1977 -1 ARAOZ, J.; EDMONDS, J.; GRIFFIN, V. J.
POLARITIES GIVEN BY SYSTEMS OF BILINEAR INEQUALITIES. PAPER PRESENTED AT THE 27TH ANNUAL CONVENTION OF ASOVAC, VALENCIA VENEZUELA 1977, 14 P. (1977).

ARAOC 1981 -1 ARAOZ, J.; JOHNSON, E. L.
FACETS AND MAPPINGS FOR NON-ABELIAN GROUP PROBLEMS. RESEARCH REPORT WP 81179-OR. BONN: UNIV. BONN, INST. FUER OEKONOMETRIE UND OPERATIONS RESEARCH, ABT. OPERATIONS RESEARCH, 27 P. (1981).

ARAOC 1981 -2 ARAOZ, J.; JOHNSON, E. L.
POLYHEDRA OF ADDITIVE SYSTEM PROBLEMS. IN: R. E. BURKARD, T. ELLINGER (EDS.): METHODS OF OPERATIONS RESEARCH 40, 211-214. KOENIGSTEIN: ANTON HAIN MEISENHEIM. (1981).

ARDI 1975 -1 ARDITTI, J.-C.
CHEMINEMENTS DANS LE GRAPHE DE COMPARABILITE D'UN ARBRE. PARTITION DES SOMMETS EN CYCLES. CAHIERS DU CENTRE D'ETUDES DE RECHERCHE OPERATIONELLE 17, 111-116. (1975).

ARDI 1978 -1 ARDITTI, J.-C.
PARTIALLY ORDERED SETS AND THEIR COMPARABILITY GRAPHS, THEIR DIMENSION AND THEIR ADJACENCY. IN: J.-C. BERMOND ET AL. (EDS.): PROBLEMES COMBINATOIRES ET THEORIE DES GRAPHES, COLLOQUES INTERNATIONAUX DU CENTRE NATIONAL DE LA RECHERCHE SCIENTIFIQUE, ORSAY 1976, 5-8, PARIS: CENTRE NATIONAL DE LA RECHERCHE SCIENTIFIQUE. (1978).

ARIY 1979 -1 ARIYOSHI, H.; TSUKIYAMA, S.; SHIRAKAWA, I.; OZAKI, H.
ALGORITHMS FOR ENUMERATING ALL THE S-T CUTSETS IN O(!V!+!E!) PER CUTSET (JAPANESE). TRANSACTIONS OF THE INSTITUTE OF ELECTRONICS AND COMMUNICATION ENGINEERS OF JAPAN (TOKYO) J62-A, NO. 1, 16-23. (1979).

ARMS 1977 -1 ARMSTRONG, R. D.
EXPERIMENTS IN A MULTIPLE CHOICE MIXED INTEGER PROGRAMMING ALGORITHM. OPSEARCH 14, 215-228. (1977).

ARMS 1977 -2 ARMSTRONG, R. D.
PRIMAL SIMPLEX ALGORITHM TO SOLVE A RECTILINEAR DISTANCE FACILITY LOCATION PROBLEM, A. NAVAL RESEARCH LOGISTICS QUARTERLY 24, 619-625. (1977).

ARMSA 1979 -1 ARMSTRONG, R. D.; CHARNES, A.; PHILLIPS, F.
PAGE CUTS FOR INTEGER INTERVAL LINEAR PROGRAMMING. DISCRETE APPLIED MATHEMATICS 1, 1-14. (1979).

ARMSB 1979 -1 ARMSTRONG, R. D.; COOK, W. D.; PALACIOS-GOMEZ, F. E.
ALGORITHM FOR A NONLINEAR DISCONTINUOUS KNAPSACK PROBLEM, AN. MANAGEMENT SCIENCE 25, 884-894. (1979).

ARMSC 1979 -1 ARMSTRONG, R. D.; COOK, W. D.; SAIPE, A. L.
OPTIMAL BATCHING IN A SEMI-AUTOMATED ORDER PICKING SYSTEM. JOURNAL OF THE OPERATIONAL RESEARCH SOCIETY 30, 711-720. (1979).

ARMSD 1977 -1 ARMSTRONG, R. D.; FROME, E.
SPECIAL PURPOSE LINEAR PROGRAMMING ALGORITHM FOR OBTAINING LEAST ABSOLUTE VALUE ESTIMATORS IN A LINEAR MODEL WITH DUMMY VARIABLES. RESEARCH REPORT CCS 318. AUSTIN: UNIV. OF TEXAS, CENTER FOR CYBERNETIC STUDIES, 18 P. (1977).

ARMSE 1980 -1 ARMSTRONG, R. D.; KLINGMAN, D.; WHITMAN, D.
IMPLEMENTATION AND ANALYSIS OF A VARIANT OF THE DUAL METHOD FOR THE CAPACITATED TRANSSHIPMENT PROBLEM. EUROPEAN JOURNAL OF OPERATIONAL RESEARCH 4, 403-420. (1980).

ARMSF 1977 -1 ARMSTRONG, R. D.; SINHA, P.
CYCLIC SEPARATION SCHEDULING PROBLEM, THE. NAVAL RESEARCH LOGISTICS QUARTERLY 24, 609-618. (1977).

ARNA 1978 -1 ARNAUDOV, D. D.; JANEV, N. I.
METHOD FOR THE APPLICATION OF PARTIAL INTEGER LINEAR PROGRAMMING TO RETRIEVAL OPTIMIZATION IN MULTILEVEL INFORMATION RETRIEVAL SYSTEMS (RUSSIAN), A. PROGRAMMIROVANIE, NO.1, 51-59, 96. (1978).

AROR 1980 -1 ARORA, R. K.; RANA, S. P.
SCHEDULING IN A SEMI-ORDERED FLOW-SHOP WITHOUT INTERMEDIATE QUEUES. AIIE TRANSACTIONS 12, 263-272. (1980).

ARORA 1977 -1 ARORA, S. R.
SET PARTITIONING PROBLEM WITH LINEAR FRACTIONAL OBJECTIVE FUNCTION, A. INDIAN JOURNAL OF PURE AND APPLIED MATHEMATICS 8, 961-968. (1977).

ARORB 1977 -1 ARORA, S. R.; PURI, M. C.; SWARUP, K.
SET COVERING PROBLEM WITH LINEAR FRACTIONAL FUNCTIONAL, THE. INDIAN JOURNAL OF PURE AND APPLIED MATHEMATICS 8, 578-588. (1977).

ARRO 1979 -1 ARROWSMITH, D. K.
PERCOLATION THEORY ON MULTIROOTED DIRECTED GRAPHS. JOURNAL OF MATHEMATICAL PHYSICS 20, 101-103. (1979).
ARROA 1977 -1 ARROWSMITH, D. K.; ESSAM, J. W.
PERCOLATION THEORY ON DIRECTED GRAPHS. JOURNAL OF MATHEMATICAL PHYSICS 18, 235-238. (1977).
ARTA 1980 -1 ARTAMONOV, I. M.
SCHEDULING ALGORITHM FOR A PRODUCTION UNIT AND ESTIMATION OF SCHEDULE LENGTHS (RUSSIAN), A. MATEMATICESKIE ISSLEDOVANIJA (KISHINEV) NO. 60, 3-10, 167. (1980).
ARTE 1981 -1 ARTEMENKO, V. I.
ON ONE METHOD OF SEARCH FOR APPROXIMATE SOLUTIONS OF MIXED INTEGER LINEAR PROGRAMMING PROBLEMS (RUSSIAN). KIBERNETIKA (KIEV), NO. 1, 82-85; TRANSLATED AS CYBERNETICS. (1981).
ARTEA 1980 -1 ARTEMENKO, V. I.; SERGIENKO, I. V.
METHOD FOR SOLVING LINEAR PROGRAMMING PROBLEMS WITH BOOLEAN VARIABLES (RUSSIAN), A. DOKLADY AKADEMIJA NAUK UKRAINSKOI SSR. SERIJA A (KIEV) NO. 4, 72-75, 101. (1980).
ARTH 1980 -1 ARTHUR, J. L.; RAVINDRAN, A.
BRANCH AND BOUND ALGORITHM WITH CONSTRAINT PARTITIONING FOR INTEGER GOAL PROGRAMMING PROBLEMS, A. EUROPEAN JOURNAL OF OPERATIONAL RESEARCH 4, 421-425. (1980).
ARTZ 1979 -1 ARTZNER, P.; RADO, R.
THEOREM ON FLOW IN DIRECTED GRAPHS, A. THE JOURNAL OF THE LONDON MATHEMATICAL SOCIETY 19, 187-191. (1979).
ARUM 1980 -1 ARUMUGAM, V.; RAMANI, S.
EVALUATION OF VALUE TIME SEQUENCING RULES IN A REAL WORLD JOB SHOP. JOURNAL OF THE OPERATIONAL RESEARCH SOCIETY 31, 895-904. (1980).
ARYA 1979 -1 ARYANIN, A. N.; YAKOBSON, M. V.
SUR LA METHODE DE PARTITION DANS LES PROBLEMES D'ALLOCATION (RUSSIAN). EKONOMIKA I MATEMATICESKIE METODY 15, 68-79. (1979).
ASAN 1981 -1 ASANO, T.; KIKUCHI, S.; SAITO, N.
EFFICIENT ALGORITHM TO FIND A HAMILTONIAN CIRCUIT IN A 4-CONNECTED MAXIMAL PLANAR GRAPH, AN. IN: N. SAITO, T. NISHIZEKI (EDS.): GRAPH THEORY AND ALGORITHMS, 182-195. LECTURE NOTES IN COMPUTER SCIENCE 108. BERLIN: SPRINGER. (1981).
ASANA 1977 -1 ASANO, T.; NISHIZEKI, T.; SAITO, N.
NP-COMPLETE PROBLEMS OF FINDING A MAXIMUM CUTSET AND OF REDUCING GRAPHS TO BIPARTITE GRAPHS. SYSTEMS-COMPUTERS-CONTROLS. THE TRANSACTIONS OF THE INSTITUTE OF ELECTRONICS AND COMMUNICATION ENGINEERS OF JAPAN 8, NO. 4, 45-52. (1977).
ASANB 1978 -1 ASANO, T.; NISHIZEKI, T.; SAITO, S.
ON THE MAXIMAL BIPARTITE MATROIDS (JAPANESE). IN: COMBINATORIAL STRUCTURES AND GRAPH THEORY II. PROC. SYMP. KYOTO 1977, 168-177. SURIKAISEKIKENKYUSHO KOKYUROKU NO. 333. KYOTO: KYOTO UNIVERSITY, RESEARCH INST. FOR MATH. SCIENCES. (1978).
ASHI 1975 -1 ASHIMOV, A.; SAGYNGALIEV, K. S.
SCHEDULING OF BATCH PRODUCTION, THE. AVTOMATIKA I TELEMEHANIKA, NO. 1, 104-115; TRANSLATED AS AUTOMATION AND REMOTE CONTROL 36, 1975, 93-103. (1975).
ASPV 1979 -1 ASPVALL, B.; PLASS, M. F.; TARJAN, R. E.
LINEAR-TIME ALGORITHM FOR TESTING THE TRUTH OF CERTAIN QUANTIFIED BOOLEAN FORMULAS, A. INFORMATION PROCESSING LETTERS 8, 121-123. (1979).
ASRA 1978 -1 ASRATJAN, A. S.
CONSTRUCTION OF AN EDGE COLORING OF A SPECIAL FORM IN A BIPARTITE GRAPH, AND ITS APPLICATION IN PROBLEMS OF SCHEDULING THEORY (RUSSIAN), THE. VESTNIK MOSKOWSKOGO UNIVERSITETA. SERIJA, NO. 1, 74-81. (1978).
ASSA 1978 -1 ASSAD, A.
MULTICOMMODITY NETWORK FLOWS - A SURVEY. NETWORKS 8, 37-91. (1978).
ASSC 1979 -1 ASSCHE, A. VAN; HERROELEN, W. S.
OPTIMAL PROCEDURE FOR THE SINGLE-MODEL DETERMINISTIC ASSEMBLY LINE BALANCING PROBLEM, AN. EUROPEAN JOURNAL OF OPERATIONAL RESEARCH 3, 142-149. (1979).
ASTI 1978 -1 ASTIE-VIDAL, A.
AUTOMORPHISMES D'ARETES DES HYPERGRAPHES DES BASES D'UN MATROIDE. IN: J.-C. BERMOND ET AL. (EDS.): PROBLEMES COMBINATOIRES ET THEORIE DES GRAPHES, COLLOQUES INTERNATIONAUX DU CENTRE NATIONAL DE LA RECHERCHE SCIENTIFIQUE, ORSAY 1976, 9-11. PARIS: CENTRE NATIONAL DE LA RECHERCHE SCIENTIFIQUE. (1978).
ASTI 1978 -2 ASTIE-VIDAL, A.
GROUPES D'AUTOMORPHISMES DES GRAPHES D'INTERSECTION AUX BASES D'UN MATROIDE. IN: COLLOQUE MATHEMATIQUES DISCRETES: CODES ET HYPERGRAPHES, BRUSSELS 1978. CAHIERS DU CENTRE D'ETUDES DE RECHERCHE OPERATIONELLE 20, NO. 3-4, 235-242. (1978).
ASTI 1980 -1 ASTIE-VIDAL, A.
AUTOMORPHISM GROUP OF A MATROID, THE. IN: M. DEZA, I. G. ROSENBERG (EDS.): COMBINATORICS 79, PART II, 205-216. ANNALS OF DISCRETE MATHEMATICS 9. AMSTERDAM: NORTH-HOLLAND. (1980).
ASTI 1980 -2 ASTIE-VIDAL, A.
FACTOR GROUP OF THE AUTOMORPHISM GROUP OF A MATROID BASIS GRAPH WITH RESPECT TO THE AUTOMORPHISM GROUP OF THE MATROID. DISCRETE MATHEMATICS 32, 217-224. (1980).
ATRI 1978 -1 ATRI, G. D'
IMPROVED LOWER BOUNDS TO THE TRAVELLING SALESMAN PROBLEM. REVUE FRANCAISE D'AUTOMATIQUE, D'INFORMATIQUE ET DE RECHERCHE OPERATIONELLE 12, SERIE RECHERCHE OPERATIONELLE, 369-382. (1978).
ATRI 1978 -2 ATRI, G. D'
IMPROVED LOWER BOUNDS TO 0/1 PROBLEMS VIA LAGRANGEAN RELAXATION. IN: J. STOER (ED.): OPTIMIZATION TECHNIQUES, PROCEEDINGS OF THE 8TH IFIP CONFERENCE ON OPTIMIZATION TECHNIQUES, WUERZBURG 1977, PART 2, 190-200. LECTURE NOTES IN CONTROL AND INFORMATION SCIENCES 7. BERLIN, HEIDELBERG, NEW YORK: SPRINGER. (1978).
ATRI 1978 -3 ATRI, G. D'
PROBABILISTIC ANALYSIS OF THE KNAPSACK PROBLEM. RAPPORT DE RECHERCHE, NO. 7. PARIS: UNIV. PIERRE ET MARIE CURIE, CENTRE NATIONAL DE LA RECHERCHE SCIENTIFIQUE, 7 P. (1978).
ATRI 1979 -1 ATRI, G. D'
ANALYSE PROBABILISTE DU PROBLEME DU SAC-A-DOS. DISSERTATION. PARIS: UNIV. PARIS 6, DEPT. OF APPLIED MATHEMATICS AND COMPUTER SCIENCE. 98P. (1979).
ATRI 1980 -1 ATRI, G. D'
NOTE ON HEURISTICS FOR THE TRAVELING SALESMAN PROBLEM, A. MATHEMATICAL PROGRAMMING 19, 111-114. (1980).
ATRI 1981 -1 ATRI, G. D'
PROBABILISTIC ANALYSIS OF KNAPSACK-TYPE PROBLEMS. IN: R. E. BURKARD, T. ELLINGER (EDS.): METHODS OF OPERATIONS RESEARCH 40, 279-282. KOENIGSTEIN: ANTON HAIN MEISENHEIM. (1981).
AUSI 1980 -1 AUSIELLO, G.; MARCHETTI-SPACCAMELA, A.; PROTASI, M.
TOWARD A UNIFIED APPROACH FOR THE CLASSIFICATION OF NP-COMPLETE OPTIMIZATION PROBLEMS. THEORETICAL COMPUTER SCIENCE 12, 83-96. (1980).
AUSI 1981 -1 AUSIELLO, G.; MARCHETTI-SPACCAMELA, A.; PROTASI, M.
PROBABILISTIC ANALYSIS OF THE PERFORMANCE OF GREEDY STRATEGIES OVER DIFFERENT CLASSES OF COMBINATORIAL PROBLEMS. IN: F. GECSEG (ED.): FUNDAMENTALS OF COMPUTATION THEORY, 24-33. LECTURE NOTES IN COMPUTER SCIENCE 117. BERLIN: SPRINGER. (1981).

AVDO 1979 -1 AVDOSHIN, S. M.; BELOV, V. V.
METHODE D'ONDE GENERALISEE POUR LA RESOLUTION DES PROBLEMES EXTREMAUX SUR LES GRAPHES (RUSSIAN). AKADEMIJA NAUK SSSR. ZURNAL VYCISLITEL'NOI MATEMATIKI I MATEMATICESKOI FIZIKI 19, 739-755. (1979).

AVIS 1978 -1 AVIS, D.
TWO GREEDY HEURISTICS FOR THE WEIGHTED MATCHING PROBLEM. IN: F. HOFFMAN, D. MAC CARTHY, R. C. MULLIN, R. G. STANTON (EDS.): PROCEEDINGS OF THE NINTH SOUTHEASTERN CONFERENCE ON COMBINATORICS, GRAPH THEORY, AND COMPUTING, 65-76. CONGRESSUS NUMERANTIUM XXI. WINNIPEG: UTILITAS. (1978).

AVIS 1980 -1 AVIS, D.
NOTE ON SOME COMPUTATIONALLY DIFFICULT SET COVERING PROBLEMS. A. MATHEMATICAL PROGRAMMING 18, 138-145. (1980).

AVISA 1978 -1 AVIS, D.; CHVATAL, V.
NOTES ON BLAND'S PIVOTING RULE. MATHEMATICAL PROGRAMMING STUDY 8, 24-34. (1978).

AVON 1979 -1 AVONDO-BODINO, G.
GRAPH THEORY AND OPERATIONS RESEARCH. IN: R. J. WILSON, L. W. BEINEKE (EDS.): APPLICATIONS OF GRAPH THEORY, 223-253. LONDON, NEW YORK, SAN FRANCISCO: ACADEMIC PRESS. (1979).

AVRA 1977 -1 AVRAMESCO, A.
QUELQUES ABOUTISSEMENTS EN THEORIE DES RESEAUX. ANNALES SCIENTIFIQUES DE L'UNIVERSITE DE BESANCON. MATHEMATIQUES, NO. 10, 1-10. (1977).

AVRAA 1978 -1 AVRAMITA, G. M.
DECOMPOSITION AND SOLVING OF LARGE-SCALE PROBLEMS IN PRODUCTION SCHEDULING. ECONOMIC COMPUTATION AND ECONOMIC CYBERNETICS STUDIES AND RESEARCH 12, NO. 1, 63-76. (1978).

AVRU 1976 -1 AVRUTIK, S. V.
SUPPLEMENTARY-STEP METHOD FOR THE INVESTIGATION OF THE NEIGHBORHOOD OF A DISCRETE OPTIMUM (RUSSIAN), THE. IN: OPTIMIZATION METHODS AND OPERATIONS RESEARCH (APPLIED MATHEMATICS), WORK COLLECT. IRKUTSK, 5-10. (1976).

AXSA 1980 -1 AXSAETER, S.
ECONOMIC LOT SIZES AND VEHICLE SCHEDULING. EUROPEAN JOURNAL OF OPERATIONAL RESEARCH 4, 395-398. (1980).

AXSAA 1980 -1 AXSAETER, S.; LUNDELL, P.
MULTI-STAGE LOT SIZING IN A CASE WITH INITIAL INVENTORIES. IN: H. KOENIG, V. STEINMETZ (EDS.): METHODS OF OPERATIONS RESEARCH 38, 237-252. KOENIGSTEIN: ANTON HAIN MEISENHEIM. (1980).

AYEL 1979 -1 AYEL, J.
SUR L'EXISTENCE DE DEUX CYCLES SUPPLEMENTAIRES UNICOLORES, DISJOINTS ET DE COULEURS DIFFERENTES DANS UN GRAPHE COMPLET BICOLORE. GRENOBLE, 213 P. (1979).

AYLE 1978 -1 AYLES, P. S.; BEALE, E. M. L.; BLUES, R. C.; WILD, S. J.
MATHEMATICAL MODELS FOR THE LOCATION OF GOVERNMENT. MATHEMATICAL PROGRAMMING STUDY 9, 59-74. (1978).

BABA 1981 -1 BABAEV, A. A.; DRUGANOV, B. N.
METHOD OF BRANCH AND BOUND IN THE PROBLEM OF COMPOSING WEEKLY SCHEDULE OF STUDIES (RUSSIAN). KIBERNETIKA (KIEV), NO. 1, 63-67; TRANSLATED AS CYBERNETICS. (1981).

BABAA 1968 -1 BABAEV, DZ. A.; BABAJEVA, D. C.; ASKEROVA, L. M.
APPROXIMATIVE ALGORITHM FOR THE SOLUTION OF CONVEX INTEGER PROGRAMS (RUSSIAN), AN. VOPROSY VYCISLITEL'NOI I PRIKLADNOI MATEMATIKI, 146-156. (1968).

BABAB 1978 -1 BABAEV, DZ. A.; MAMEDOV, K. S.
AGGREGATION OF A CLASS OF SYSTEMS OF INTEGER-VALUED EQUATIONS. AKADEMIJA NAUK SSSR. ZURNAL VYCISLITEL'NOI MATEMATIKI I MATEMATICESKOI FIZIKI 18, 614-619; TRANSLATED AS U.S.S.R. COMPUTATIONAL MATHEMATICS AND MATHEMATICAL PHYSICS 18, NO. 3, 1978, 86-91. (1978).

BABAB 1978 -2 BABAEV, DZ. A.; MAMEDOV, K. S.
APPROXIMATE METHODS OF SOLUTION OF BOOLEAN PROGRAMMING PROBLEMS OF LARGE DIMENSION (RUSSIAN). IN: DZ. E. ALLAHVERDIEV (ED.): QUESTIONS OF MATHEMATICAL CYBERNETICS AND APPLIED MATHEMATICS (RUSSIAN), NO. 3, 8-16. BAKU: ELM. (1978).

BABAB 1978 -3 BABAEV, DZ. A.; MAMEDOV, K. S.
METHOD OF SOLVING A BOOLEAN PROGRAMMING PROBLEM (RUSSIAN), A. IN: DZ. E. ALLAHVERDIEV (ED.): QUESTIONS OF MATHEMATICAL CYBERNETICS AND APPLIED MATHEMATICS (RUSSIAN), NO. 3, 3-7. BAKU: ELM. (1978).

BABAC 1978 -1 BABAEV, DZ. A.; MAMEDOV, K. S.; MEKHTIEV, M. G.
METHODS OF CONSTRUCTING SUBOPTIMAL SOLUTIONS OF THE MULTIDIMENSIONAL RUCKSACK PROBLEM. ZURNAL VYCISLITELNOI MATEMATIKI I MATEMATICESKOI FIZIKI 18, NO. 6, 1443-1454; TRANSLATED AS USSR COMPUTATIONAL MATHEMATICS AND MATHEMATICAL PHYSICS 18, 1979, NO. 6, 82-91. (1978).

BABAD 1979 -1 BABAEV, DZ. A.; VELIEV, G. P.; MAMEDOV, K. S.
A PRIORI DETERMINATION OF OPTIMAL VARIABLE VALUES IN DISCRETE PROGRAMMING PROBLEMS, THE. ZURNAL VYCISLITELNOI MATEMATIKI I MATEMATICESKOI FIZIKI (MOSCOW) 19, 519-523; TRANSLATED AS USSR COMPUTATIONAL MATHEMATICS AND MATHEMATICAL PHYSICS 19, 1980, 260-264. (1979).

BABAE 1980 -1 BABAI, L.
ON THE COMPLEXITY OF CANONICAL LABELING OF STRONGLY REGULAR GRAPHS. SIAM JOURNAL ON COMPUTING 9, 212-216. (1980).

BABAF 1978 -1 BABAT, L. G.
FIXED-CHARGE PROBLEM (RUSSIAN), A. IZVESTIJA AKADEMII NAUK SSSR. TEHNICESKAJA KIBERNETIKA 3, 25-31. (1978).

BABAF 1979 -1 BABAT, L. G.
GROWTH OF COEFFICIENTS IN INTEGRAL LINEAR PROGRAMMING (RUSSIAN). IN: MATHEMATICAL METHODS OF SOLUTION OF ECONOMIC PROBLEMS, NO. 8, 34-43. MOSCOW: NAUKA. (1979).

BABI 1978 -1 BABICH, G.
EFFICIENT ALGORITHM FOR SOLVING THE RECTILINEAR LOCATION-ALLOCATION PROBLEM, AN. ENVIRONMENT AND PLANNING 10, SERIES A, 1387-1395. (1978).

BABIA 1979 -1 BABINA, N. B.
RESOURCE ALLOCATION PROBLEM WITH NONCONTRADICTORY INTERESTS (RUSSIAN), A. VESTNIK MOSKOVSKOGO UNIVERSITETA. SERIJA XV. VYCISLITEL'NAJA MATEMATIKA I KIBERNETIKA, NO. 1, 34-41 + 70. (1979).

BABU 1977 -1 BABUSHKIN, A. I.; BASHTA, A. L.; BELOV, I. S.; DUSHIN, B. I.
OPTIMIZING THE SEQUENCE OF PRODUCT ASSEMBLY. AVTOMATIKA I TELEMEHANIKA, NO. 9, 77-82; TRANSLATED AS AUTOMATION AND REMOTE CONTROL 38, 1334-1338. (1977).

BACH 1980 -1 BACHEM, A.
KOMPLEXITAETSTHEORIE IM OPERATIONS RESEARCH. ZEITSCHRIFT FUER BETRIEBSWIRTSCHAFT 50, 812-844. (1980).

BACH 1980 -2 BACHEM, A.
THEOREMS OF THE ALTERNATIVE IN COMBINATORIAL PROGRAMMING. IN: R. HENN, H. P. KUENZI, H. SCHUBERT (EDS.): METHODS OF OPERATIONS RESEARCH 36, 7-20. KOENIGSTEIN: ANTON HAIN MEISENHEIM. (1980).

BACHA 1979 -1 BACHEM, A.; GROETSCHEL, M.
NEW ASPECTS OF POLYHEDRAL THEORY. REPORT NO. 79149-OR. BONN: UNIV. BONN, INST. FUER OEKONOMETRIE UND OPERATIONS RESEARCH, 77 P. (1979).

BACHA 1981 -1 BACHEM, A.; GROETSCHEL, M.
CHARACTERIZATIONS OF ADJACENCY OF FACES OF POLYHEDRA. IN: H. KOENIG, B. KORTE, K. RITTER (EDS.): MATHEMATICAL PROGRAMMING AT OBERWOLFACH, 1-22. MATHEMATICAL PROGRAMMING STUDY 14. (1981).

BACHA 1981 -2 BACHEM, A.; GROETSCHEL, M.
HOMOGENIZATION OF POLYHEDRA. IN: R. E. BURKARD, T. ELLINGER (EDS.): METHODS OF OPERATIONS RESEARCH 40, 215-220. KOENIGSTEIN: ANTON HAIN MEISENHEIM. (1981).

BACHB 1981 -1 BACHEM, A.; JOHNSON, E. L.; SCHRADER, R.
CHARACTERIZATION OF MINIMAL INEQUALITIES FOR MIXED INTEGER PROGRAMS, A. RESEARCH REPORT WP 81197-OR. BONN: UNIV. BONN, INST. FUER OEKONOMETRIE UND OPERATIONS RESEARCH, ABT. OPERATIONS RESEARCH, 9 P. (1981).

BACHC 1979 -1 BACHEM, A.; KANNAN, R.
APPLICATIONS OF POLYNOMIAL SMITH NORMAL FORM CALCULATIONS. IN: L. COLLATZ, G. MEINARDUS, W. WETTERLING (EDS.): NUMERISCHE METHODEN BEI GRAPHENTHEORETISCHEN UND KOMBINATORISCHEN PROBLEMEN, BAND 2, OBERWOLFACH 1978, 9-21. ISNM 46, BASEL, BOSTON, STUTTGART: BIRKHAEUSER. (1979).

BACHD 1979 -1 BACHEM, A.; RANDOW, R. VON
INTEGER THEOREMS OF FARKAS LEMMA TYPE. IN: W. OETTLI, F. STEFFENS (EDS.): OPERATIONS RESEARCH VERFAHREN 32, THIRD SYMPOSIUM ON OPERATIONS RESEARCH, MANNHEIM 1978, 19-28. KOENIGSTEIN: ANTON HAIN MEISENHEIM. (1979).

BACHE 1978 -1 BACHEM, A.; SCHRADER, R.
NOTE ON A THEOREM OF JEROSLOW, A. REPORT NO. 7897-OR. BONN: UNIV. BONN, INSTITUT FUER OEKONOMETRIE UND OPERATIONS RESEARCH, 14 P. (1978).

BACHE 1979 -1 BACHEM, A.; SCHRADER, R.
DUALITY THEOREM AND MINIMAL INEQUALITIES IN MIXED INTEGER PROGRAMMING, A. ZEITSCHRIFT FUER ANGEWANDTE MATHEMATIK UND MECHANIK 59, T88-T89. (1979).

BACHE 1980 -1 BACHEM, A.; SCHRADER, R.
MINIMAL INEQUALITIES AND SUBADDITIVE DUALITY. SIAM JOURNAL ON CONTROL AND OPTIMIZATION 18, 437-443. (1980).

BACL 1979 -1 BACLAWSKI, K.; WHITE, N. L.
HIGHER ORDER INDEPENDENCE IN MATROIDS. THE JOURNAL OF THE LONDON MATHEMATICAL SOCIETY 19, NO. 2, 193-202. (1979).

BAER 1977 -1 BAER, G.
BEITRAG ZUR TRANSFORMATION GANZZAHLIGER OPTIMIERUNGSPROBLEME, EIN. ELEKTRONISCHE INFORMATIONSVERARBEITUNG UND KYBERNETIK 13, 55-60. (1977).

BAER 1978 -1 BAER, G.
THEORETISCHE FUNDIERUNG DER DISKRETEN OPTIMIERUNG MIT LOGISCHEN MITTELN, EINE. ELEKTRONISCHE INFORMATIONSVERARBEITUNG UND KYBERNETIK 14, 305-320. (1978).

BAGC 1979 -1 BAGCHI, A.; ROY, J. K.
ON V-OPTIMAL TREES. SIAM JOURNAL ON COMPUTING 8, 524-541. (1979).

BAGG 1978 -1 BAGGA, P. C.
NOTE ON EQUIVALENT JOBS FOR JOB BLOCKS IN JOB SEQUENCING PROBLEM, A. OPSEARCH 15, 114-116. (1978).

BAGGA 1979 -1 BAGGA, P. C.; KALRA, K. R.; BANSAL, S. P.
SEQUENCING UNDER REQUIRED PRECEDENCE AMONG JOBS. SCIMA (NEW DELHI) 8, NOS. 2 AND 3, 34-37. (1979).

BAIL 1979 -1 BAILEY, F. N.
COMMENTS ON "APPLICATION OF 0-1 INTEGER PROGRAMMING TO MULTITARGET TRACKING PROBLEMS". IEEE TRANSACTIONS ON AUTOMATIC CONTROL 24, 142-143. (1979).

BAILA 1980 -1 BAILEY, M. G.; GILLETT, B. E.
PARAMETRIC INTEGER PROGRAMMING ANALYSIS: A CONTRACTION APPROACH. JOURNAL OF THE OPERATIONAL RESEARCH SOCIETY 31, 257-262. (1980).

BAKE 1979 -1 BAKER, B. S.; BROWN, D. J.; KATSEFF, H. P.
LOWER BOUNDS FOR ON-LINE TWO-DIMENSIONAL PACKING ALGORITHMS. IN: CONFERENCE ON INFORMATION SCIENCES AND SYSTEMS, BALTIMORE 1979, 174-179. BALTIMORE: THE JOHNS HOPKINS UNIVERSITY. (1979).

BAKEA 1980 -1 BAKER, B. S.; COFFMAN, E. G. JR.; RIVEST, R. L.
ORTHOGONAL PACKINGS IN TWO DIMENSIONS. SIAM JOURNAL ON COMPUTING 9, 846-855. (1980).

BAKEB 1979 -1 BAKER, B. S.; SCHWARZ, J. S.
SHELF ALGORITHMS FOR TWO-DIMENSIONAL PACKING PROBLEMS. IN: CONFERENCE ON INFORMATION SCIENCES AND SYSTEMS, BALTIMORE 1979, 273-276. BALTIMORE: THE JOHNS HOPKINS UNIVERSITY. (1979).

BAKEC 1979 -1 BAKER, E.; BODIN, L. D.; FINNEGAN, W. F.; PONDER, R. J.
EFFICIENT HEURISTIC SOLUTIONS TO AN AIRLINE CREW SCHEDULING PROBLEM. AIIE TRANSACTIONS 11, 79-85. (1979).

BAKED 1980 -1 BAKER, E.; FISHER, M.
COMPUTATIONAL RESULTS FOR VERY LARGE AIR CREW SCHEDULING PROBLEMS. WORKING PAPER. CORAL GABLES: UNIV. OF MIAMI, DEPT. OF MANAGEMENT SCIENCE, 14 P. (1980).

BAKEE 1979 -1 BAKER, K. R.; BURNS, R. N.; CARTER, M. W.
STAFF SCHEDULING WITH DAY-OFF AND WORKSTRETCH CONSTRAINTS. AIIE TRANSACTIONS 11, 286-292. (1979).

BAKEF 1978 -1 BAKER, K. R.; DIXON, P.; MAGAZINE, M. J.; SILVER, E. A.
ALGORITHM FOR THE DYNAMIC LOT-SIZE PROBLEM WITH TIME-VARYING PRODUCTION CAPACITY CONSTRAINTS, AN. MANAGEMENT SCIENCE 24, 1710-1720. (1978).

BAKEG 1980 -1 BAKER, K. R.; LAWLER, E. L.; LENSTRA, J. K.; RINNOOY KAN, A. H. G.
PREEMPTIVE SCHEDULING OF A SINGLE MACHINE TO MINIMIZE MAXIMUM COST SUBJECT TO RELEASE DATES AND PRECEDENCE CONSTRAINTS. PREPRINT BW 128/80. AMSTERDAM: MATHEMATISCH CENTRUM, 7 P. (1980).

BAKEH 1980 -1 BAKER, K. R.; NUTTLE, H. L. W.
SEQUENCING INDEPENDENT JOBS WITH A SINGLE RESOURCE. NAVAL RESEARCH LOGISTICS QUARTERLY 27, 499-510. (1980).

BAKEI 1978 -1 BAKER, K. R.; SCHRAGE, L. E.
FINDING AN OPTIMAL SEQUENCE BY DYNAMIC PROGRAMMING: AN EXTENSION TO PRECEDENCE-RELATED TASKS. OPERATIONS RESEARCH 26, 111-120. (1978).

BAKEJ 1977 -1 BAKER, K. R.; SILVER, E. A.; MAGAZINE, M. J.
ALGORITHM FOR THE DYNAMIC LOT-SIZE PROBLEM WITH PRODUCTION CAPACITY CONSTRAINTS, AN. GSBA PAPER NO. 187. DURHAM: DUKE UNIVERSITY, GRADUATE SCHOOL OF BUSINESS ADMINISTRATION, 13 P. (1977).

BAKEK 1979 -1 BAKER, T. B.
ON "PROVABLE" ANALOGS OF P AND NP. MATHEMATICAL SYSTEMS THEORY 12, 213-218. (1979).

BAKH 1979 -1 BAKHSHI, H. C.; BHATIA, H. L.; PURI, M. C.
TRADE-OFF RELATIONS IN ASSIGNMENT PROBLEMS. CAHIERS DU CENTRE D'ETUDES DE RECHERCHE OPERATIONNELLE 21, 367-374. (1979).

BAKO 1975 -1 BAKO, A.
SUB-CRITICAL PATHS IN ACTIVITY NETWORK (HUNGARIAN). ALKALMAZOTT MATEMATIKAI LAPOK 1, 365-372. (1975).

BAKOA 1977 -1 BAKO, A.; KAS, P.
DETERMINING THE KTH SHORTEST PATH BY THE MATRIX METHOD (HUNGARIAN). SZIGMA. MATEMATIKAI-KOEZGAZDASAGI FOLYOIRAT 10, 61-67. (1977).

BALA 1977 -1 BALANDINA, S. V.
FORMULATION OF THE PROBLEM OF THE LOCATION OF THE COMPUTER CENTERS OF A NETWORK, AND POSSIBLE APPROACHES TO ITS SOLUTION (RUSSIAN), A. IZVESTIJA AKADEMII NAUK AZERBAIDZANSKOI SSR. SERIJA FIZIKO-TEHNICESKIH I MATEMATICESKIH NAUK, NO. 3, 68-74. (1977).

BALAA 1976 -1 BALAS, E.
DISJUNCTIVE CUT FOR SET PARTITIONING, A. WORKING PAPER 57-75-76. PITTSBURGH: CARNEGIE-MELLON UNIVERSITY. (1976).

BALAA 1979 -1 BALAS, E.
BIVALENT PROGRAMMING BY IMPLICIT ENUMERATION. IN: A. G. HOLZMAN (ED.): OPERATIONS RESEARCH SUPPORT METHODOLOGY, 467-481. NEW YORK, BASEL: DEKKER. (1979).

BALAA 1979 -2 BALAS, E.
DISJUNCTIVE PROGRAMMING. IN: P. L. HAMMER, E. L. JOHNSON, B. H. KORTE (EDS.): DISCRETE OPTIMIZATION II, 3-51. ANNALS OF DISCRETE MATHEMATICS 5, AMSTERDAM, NEW YORK, OXFORD: NORTH-HOLLAND. (1979).

BALAA 1979 -3 BALAS, E.
INTEGER AND FRACTIONAL MATCHINGS. MANAGEMENT SCIENCES RESEARCH REPORT NO. 426. PITTSBURGH: CARNEGIE-MELLON UNIV., GRADUATE SCHOOL OF INDUSTRIAL ADMINISTRATION, 18 P. (1979).

BALAA 1979 -4 BALAS, E.
SET COVERING WITH CUTTING PLANES FROM CONDITIONAL BOUNDS. IN: A. PREKOPA (ED.): SURVEY OF MATHEMATICAL PROGRAMMING, VOLUME 2, 393-422. AMSTERDAM: NORTH-HOLLAND. (1979).

BALAA 1980 -1 BALAS, E.
CUTTING PLANES FROM CONDITIONAL BOUNDS: A NEW APPROACH TO SET COVERING. MATHEMATICAL PROGRAMMING STUDY 12, 19-36. (1980).

BALAB 1977 -1 BALAS, E.; BERGTHALLER, C.
BENDERS'S METHOD REVISITED. MANAGEMENT SCIENCES RESEARCH REPORT, 401. PITTSBURGH: CARNEGIE-MELLON UNIV., GRADUATE SCHOOL OF INDUSTRIAL ADMINISTRATION, 24 P. (1977).

BALAC 1979 -1 BALAS, E.; CHRISTOFIDES, N.
RESTRICTED LAGRANGEAN APPROACH TO THE TRAVELING SALESMAN PROBLEM, A. MANAGEMENT SCIENCES RESEARCH REPORT NO. 439. PITTSBURGH: CARNEGIE-MELLON UNIV., GRADUATE SCHOOL OF INDUSTRIAL ADMINISTRATION, 41 P. (1979).

BALAD 1980 -1 BALAS, E.; HO, A. C.
SET COVERING ALGORITHMS USING CUTTING PLANES, HEURISTICS, AND SUBGRADIENT OPTIMIZATION: A COMPUTATIONAL STUDY. MATHEMATICAL PROGRAMMING STUDY 12, 37-60. (1980).

BALAE 1980 -1 BALAS, E.; JEROSLOW, R. G.
STRENGTHENING CUTS FOR MIXED INTEGER PROGRAMS. EUROPEAN JOURNAL OF OPERATIONAL RESEARCH 4, 224-234. (1980).

BALAF 1980 -1 BALAS, E.; MARTIN, C. H.
PIVOT AND COMPLEMENT - A HEURISTIC FOR 0-1 PROGRAMMING. MANAGEMENT SCIENCE 26, 86-96. (1980).

BALAG 1980 -1 BALAS, E.; MAZZOLA, J. B.
LINEARIZING NONLINEAR 0-1 PROGRAMS. RESEARCH REPORT 467. PITTSBURGH: CARNEGIE-MELLON UNIV., MANAGEMENT SCIENCE RESEARCH GROUP, 61 P. (1980).

BALAG 1980 -2 BALAS, E.; MAZZOLA, J. B.
VALID INEQUALITIES FOR 0-1 PROGRAMMING POLYTOPES. RESEARCH REPORT 468. PITTSBURGH: CARNEGIE-MELLON UNIV., MANAGEMENT SCIENCE RESEARCH GROUP, 21 P. (1980).

BALAH 1979 -1 BALAS, E.; PADBERG, M. W.
ADJACENT VERTICES OF THE ALL 0-1 PROGRAMMING POLYTOPE. REVUE FRANCAISE D'AUTOMATIQUE, D'INFORMATIQUE ET DE RECHERCHE OPERATIONELLE 13, SERIE RECHERCHE OPERATIONELLE, 3-12. (1979).

BALAH 1979 -2 BALAS, E.; PADBERG, M. W.
SET PARTITIONING - A SURVEY. IN: N. CHRISTOFIDES, A. MINGOZZI, P. TOTH, C. SANDI (EDS.): COMBINATORIAL OPTIMIZATION, 151-210. CHICHESTER, NEW YORK, BRISBANE, TORONTO: WILEY. (1979).

BALAI 1981 -1 BALAS, E.; PULLEYBLANK, W. R.
LINEAR CHARACTERIZATION OF THE PERFECTLY MATCHABLE SUBGRAPH POLYHEDRON, A. RESEARCH REPORT WP 81199-OR. BONN: UNIV. BONN, INST. FUER OEKONOMETRIE UND OPERATIONS RESEARCH, ABT. OPERATIONS RESEARCH. (1981).

BALAJ 1974 -1 BALAS, E.; SAMUELSSON, H.
FINDING A MINIMUM NODE COVER IN AN ARBITRARY GRAPH. II: THE WEIGHTED CASE. MANAGEMENT SCIENCE RESEARCH REPORT NO. 336. PITTSBURGH: CARNEGIE-MELLON UNIVERSITY. (1974).

BALAJ 1974 -2 BALAS, E.; SAMUELSSON, H.
SYMMETRIC SUBGRADIENT CUTTING PLANE METHOD FOR SET PARTITIONING, A. WORKING PAPER 5-74-75. PITTSBURGH: CARNEGIE-MELLON UNIVERSITY. (1974).

BALAK 1977 -1 BALAS, E.; ZEMEL, E.
CRITICAL CUTSETS OF GRAPHS AND CANONICAL FACETS OF SET-PACKING POLYTOPES. MATHEMATICS OF OPERATIONS RESEARCH 2, 15-19. (1977).

BALAK 1977 -2 BALAS, E.; ZEMEL, E.
SOLVING LARGE KNAPSACK PROBLEMS. REPORT. PITTSBURGH: CARNEGIE-MELLON UNIVERSITY, GRADUATE SCHOOL OF INDUSTRIAL ADMINISTRATION. (1977).

BALAK 1977 -3 BALAS, E.; ZEMEL, E.
SOLVING LARGE ZERO-ONE KNAPSACK PROBLEMS (REVISED VERSION). MANAGEMENT SCIENCE RESEARCH REPORT NO. 408. PITTSBURGH: CARNEGIE-MELLON UNIV., GRADUATE SCHOOL OF INDUSTRIAL ADMINISTRATION, 29 P. (1977).

BALAK 1978 -1 BALAS, E.; ZEMEL, E.
FACETS OF THE KNAPSACK POLYTOPE FROM MINIMAL COVERS. SIAM JOURNAL ON APPLIED MATHEMATICS 34, 119-148. (1978).

BALAK 1980 -1 BALAS, E.; ZEMEL, E.
ALGORITHM FOR LARGE ZERO-ONE KNAPSACK PROBLEMS, AN. OPERATIONS RESEARCH 28, 1130-1154. (1980).

BALL 1980 -1 BALL, M. O.
COMPLEXITY OF NETWORK RELIABILITY COMPUTATIONS. NETWORKS 10, 153-165. (1980).

BALLA 1979 -1 BALL, M. O.; BODIN, L. D.; GOLDEN, B. L.; ASSAD, A.; STATHES, C.
TRUCK FLEET ACQUISITION/ROUTING PROBLEM, A. WORKING PAPER. COLLEGE PARK: UNIV. OF MARYLAND, COLLEGE OF BUSINESS AND MANAGEMENT, 32 P. (1979).

BALLB 1979 -1 BALL, M. O.; NEMHAUSER, G. L.
MATROIDS AND A RELIABILITY ANALYSIS PROBLEM. MATHEMATICS OF OPERATIONS RESEARCH 4, 132-143. (1979).

BALLC 1980 -1 BALL, M. O.; PROVAN, J. S.
BOUNDS ON THE RELIABILITY POLYNOMIAL FOR SHELLABLE INDEPENDENCE SYSTEMS. WORKING PAPER. COLLEGE PARK: UNIV. OF MARYLAND, COLLEGE OF BUSINESS AND MANAGEMENT, 43 P. (1980).

BALU 1979 -1 BALUTA, M.; DOBRESCU, V.; PAUN, G.
ALGORITHM FOR SOLVING A COMBINATORIAL PROBLEM OF OPTIMAL SELECTION. ECONOMIC COMPUTATION AND ECONOMIC CYBERNETICS STUDIES AND RESEARCH 13, 87-95. (1979).

****

BANA 1977 -1 BANASZAK, Z.
CODING OF ROOTED TREES BY THE MAXIMAL PATH METHOD (POLISH). WROCLAW. POLITECHNIKA. WROCLAWSKA. INSTYTUT CYBERNETYKI TECHNICZNEJ. PRACE NAUKOWE. SERIA STUDIA I MATERIALY, NO. 22, GRAFY W TEOR. SYSTEM., 3-14. (1977).

BANK 1978 -1 BANK, B.
QUALITATIVE STABILITAETSUNTERSUCHUNGEN REIN- UND GEMISCHT-GANZZAHLIGER LINEARER PARAMETRISCHER OPTIMIERUNGSPROBLEME. SEMINARBERICHT 6. BERLIN: HUMBOLDT UNIV.. SEKTION MATHEMATIK. 111 P. (1978).

BANK 1980 -1 BANK, B.
STABILITY ANALYSIS IN PURE AND MIXED-INTEGER LINEAR PROGRAMMING. IN: K. IRACKI, K. MALANOWSKI, P. WALUKIEWICZ (EDS.): OPTIMIZATION TECHNIQUES, PART II, 148-153. LECTURE NOTES IN CONTROL AND INFORMATION SCIENCES 23. BERLIN: SPRINGER. (1980).

BANKA 1974 -1 BANK, B.; KLEINMAN, P.; ALONSO, A.
ON A METHOD FOR THE SOLUTION OF A SPECIAL TYPE OF INTEGER PROGRAMS WITH LINEAR CONSTRAINTS (SPANISH). INVESTIGACION OPERACIONAL, NO. 13, 34-41. (1974).

BANN 1978 -1 BANNAI, K.
HAMILTONIAN CYCLES IN GENERALIZED PETERSEN GRAPHS. JOURNAL OF COMBINATORIAL THEORY 24, SERIES B, 181-188. (1978).

BANS 1977 -1 BANSAL, S. P.
FINDING ALTERNATING MINIMUM COST PATH IN A DIRECTED NETWORK USING DYNAMIC PROGRAMMING. MICROELECTRONICS AND RELIEABILITIES 16, 231-232. (1977).

BANS 1979 -1 BANSAL, S. P.
ON LOWER BOUNDS IN PERMUTATION FLOWSHOP PROBLEMS. INTERNATIONAL JOURNAL OF PRODUCTION RESEARCH 17, 411-418. (1979).

BANS 1980 -1 BANSAL, S. P.
SINGLE MACHINE SCHEDULING TO MINIMIZE WEIGHTED SUM OF COMPLETION TIMES WITH SECONDARY CRITERION - A BRANCH AND BOUND APPROACH. EUROPEAN JOURNAL OF OPERATIONAL RESEARCH 5, 177-181. (1980).

BANSA 1977 -1 BANSAL, S. P.; BAGGA, P. C.
MINIMIZING WAITING COSTS OF A NX2 FLOWSHOP PROBLEM. SCIMA 6, 59-70. (1977).

BAPT 1979 -1 BAPTIST, P.
OPTIMALE WEGE IN ENDLICHEN GERICHTETEN GRAPHEN. PRAXIS DER MATHEMATIK 21, NO. 4, 99-105. (1979).

BARA 1980 -1 BARAHONA, F.
APPLICATION DE L'OPTIMISATION COMBINATOIRE A CERTAINS MODELES DES VERRES DE SPINS: COMPLEXITE ET SIMULATIONS. GRENOBLE: UNIV. SCIENTIFIQUE ET MEDICALE DE GRENOBLE, 73 P. (1980). (DISSERTATION)

BARA 1980 -2 BARAHONA, F.
ON THE COMPLEXITY OF MAX CUT. RAPPORT DE RECHERCHE, 186. GRENOBLE: UNIVERSITE SCIENTIFIQUE ET MEDICALE DE GRENOBLE, 8 P. (1980).

BARAA 1978 -1 BARANYAI, Z.
SOME APPLICATIONS OF EQUALIZED MATRICES. MATHEMATICAL PROGRAMMING STUDY 8, 217-225. (1978).

BARAB 1977 -1 BARAUSKAS, R. A.; VALANTINAS, I. I.
OPTIMAL CODING OF THE VERTICES OF AN UNDIRECTED GRAPH (RUSSIAN). AVTOMATIKA I VYCISLITEL'NAJA TEHNIKA , NO. 6, 1-7. (1977).

BARC 1978 -1 BARCELO, J.
STATE-OF-THE-ART SURVEY ABOUT ENUMERATIVE METHODS (SPANISH). QUESTIIO (SPAIN) 2, 51-68, 133-148. (1978).

BARD 1981 -1 BARDSWITCH, E.; HUNDERT, M.
COMBINATORIAL OPTIMIZATION APPROACH TO CYCLIC SCHEDULING OF PERSONNEL, THE. PAPER PRESENTED AT THE CORS/TIMS/ORSA MEETING, APRIL 1981, 22 P. (1981).

BARE 1980 -1 BAREFOOT, C. A.; ENTRINGER, R. C.
EXTREMAL MAXIMAL UNIQUELY HAMILTONIAN GRAPHS. JOURNAL OF GRAPH THEORY 4, 93-100. (1980).

BAREA 1969 -1 BARENBAUM, F. B.
CERTAIN TRANSPORT PROBLEM WITH A CONCAVE TARGET FUNCTION (RUSSIAN). A. MOSKOVSKII INZENERNO-STROITEL'SKII INSTITUT IM V. V. KUIBYSEVA. SBORNIK TRUDOV, NO. 62, 140-144. (1969).

BARH 1978 -1 BARHAM, A. M.; WESTWOOD, J. B.
SIMPLE HEURISTIC TO FALICITATE COURSE TIMETABLING, A. THE JOURNAL OF THE OPERATIONAL RESEARCH SOCIETY 29, 1055-1060. (1978).

BARI 1978 -1 BARI, A.; ARSHAD, M.
BRANCH AND BOUND METHOD FOR INTEGER QUADRATIC PROGRAMMING, A. PURE AND APPLIED MATHEMATIKA SCIENCES 7, 47-52. (1978).

BARIA 1979 -1 BARI, R. A.
CHROMATIC POLYNOMIALS AND THE INTERNAL AND EXTERNAL ACTIVITIES OF TUTTE. IN: J. A. BONDY, U. P. R. MURTY (EDS.): GRAPH THEORY AND RELATED TOPICS, 41-52. NEW YORK, SAN FRANCISCO, LONDON: ACADEMIC PRESS. (1979).

BARN 1980 -1 BARNABEI, M.; NICOLETTI, G.
AXIOMATIZING MATROIDS BY MEANS OF THE SET OF NONGENERATORS. BOLLETTINO UNIONE MATEMATICA ITALIANA A (5) 17, 121-127. (1980).

BARNA 1981 -1 BARNES, E. R.
ALGORITHM FOR PARTITIONING THE NODES OF A GRAPH, AN. RESEARCH REPORT 8690. YORKTOWN HEIGHTS: IBM THOMAS J. WATSON RESEARCH CENTER, 15 P. (1981).

BARNB 1979 -1 BARNES, F. W.
PACKING THE MAXIMUM NUMBER OF M X N TILES IN A LARGE P X Q RECTANGLE. DISCRETE MATHEMATICS 26, 93-100. (1979).

BARNC 1981 -1 BARNES, J. W.; VANSTON, L. K.
SCHEDULING JOBS WITH LINEAR DELAY PENALTIES AND SEQUENCE DEPENDENT SETUP COSTS. OPERATIONS RESEARCH 29, 146-160. (1981).

BARR 1980 -1 BARR, R. S.; ELAM, J.; GLOVER, F.; KLINGMAN, D.
NETWORK AUGMENTING PATH BASIS ALGORITHM FOR TRANSSHIPMENT PROBLEMS, A. IN: A. V. FIACCO, K. O. KORTANEK (EDS.): EXTREMAL METHODS AND SYSTEMS ANALYSIS, 250-274. LECTURE NOTES IN ECONOMICS AND MATHEMATICAL SYSTEMS 174. BERLIN: SPRINGER. (1980).

BARRA 1977 -1 BARR, R. S.; GLOVER, F.; KLINGMAN, D.
ALTERNATING BASIS ALGORITHM FOR ASSIGNMENT PROBLEMS, THE. MATHEMATICAL PROGRAMMING 13, 1-13. (1977).

BARRA 1978 -1 BARR, R. S.; GLOVER, F.; KLINGMAN, D.
GENERALIZED ALTERNATING PATH ALGORITHM FOR TRANSPORTATION PROBLEMS, THE. EUROPEAN JOURNAL OF OPERATIONAL RESEARCH 2, 137-144. (1978).

BARRA 1978 -2 BARR, R. S.; GLOVER, F.; KLINGMAN, D.
NEW ALTERNATING BASIS ALGORITHM FOR SEMI-ASSIGNMENT NETWORKS, A. IN: W. W. WHITE (ED.): COMPUTERS AND MATHEMATICAL PROGRAMMING, GAITHERSBURG 1976, 223-232. NBS SPECIAL PUBLICATION 502. WASHINGTON: NATIONAL BUREAU OF STANDARDS. (1978).

BARRA 1979 -1 BARR, R. S.; GLOVER, F.; KLINGMAN, D.
ENHANCEMENTS OF SPANNING TREE LABELING PROCEDURES FOR NETWORK OPTIMIZATION. INFOR 17, 16-34. (1979).

BARRA 1979 -2 BARR, R. S.; GLOVER, F.; KLINGMAN, D.
NEW OPTIMIZATION METHOD FOR LARGE-SCALE FIXED CHARGE TRANSPORTATION PROBLEMS, A. RESEARCH REPORT CCS 350. AUSTIN: UNIV. OF TEXAS, CENTER FOR CYBERNETIC STUDIES, 39 P. (1979).

BARRB 1965 -1 BARRACLOUGH, E. D.
APPLICATION OF A DIGITAL COMPUTER TO THE CONSTRUCTION OF TIME-TABLES, THE. THE COMPUTER JOURNAL 8, 136-146. (1965).

BARRC 1978 -1 BARRER, J. N.
CERTAIN PERMUTATION PROBLEMS AND THEIR RELATION TO THE ASSIGNMENT PROBLEM. WORKING PAPER, 381. BUFFALO: STATE UNIV. OF NEW YORK, SCHOOL OF MANAGEMENT, 22 P. (1978).

BARRC 1979 -1 BARRER, J. N.
BASES OF THE EXTREME POINTS OF THE ASSIGNMENT POLYTOPE. WORKING PAPER SERIES NO. 425. BUFFALO: STATE UNIV. OF NEW YORK, SCHOOL OF MANAGEMENT, 16 P. (1979).

BART 1979 -1 BARTHOLDI, J. J. III
GUARANTEED-ACCURACY ROUND-OFF ALGORITHM FOR CYCLIC SCHEDULING AND SET COVERING, A. TECHNICAL REPORT, 79-9. ANN ARBOR: UNIV. OF MICHIGAN, DEPT. OF INDUSTRIAL AND OPERATIONS ENGINEERING, 16 P. (1979).

BARTA 1980 -1 BARTHOLDI, J. J. III; ORLIN, J. B.; RATLIFF, H. D.
CYCLIC SCHEDULING VIA INTEGER PROGRAMS WITH CIRCULAR ONES. OPERATIONS RESEARCH 28, 1074-1085. (1980).

BARTB 1978 -1 BARTHOLDI, J. J. III; RATLIFF, H. D.
UNNETWORKS WITH APPLICATIONS TO IDLE TIME SCHEDULING. MANAGEMENT SCIENCE 24, 850-858. (1978).

BARTC 1978 -1 BARTNIK, W. G.
ALGORITHMES DE COUPLAGE DANS LES GRAPHES. PARIS: UNIVERSITE P. ET M. CURIE, 130 P. (1978).

BARTD 1979 -1 BARTON, R. R.; HEARN, D. W.
DECOMPOSITION TECHNIQUES FOR NONLINEAR COST MULTICOMMODITY FLOW PROBLEMS. RESEARCH REPORT, 79-2. GAINESVILLE: UNIV. OF FLORIDA, INDUSTRIAL AND SYSTEMS ENGINEERING DEPT., 29 P. (1979).

BATA 1979 -1 BATAGELJ, V.; PISANSKI, T.
ON PARTIALLY DIRECTED EULERIAN MULTIGRAPHS. INSTITUT MATHEMATIQUE. PUBLICATION. NOUVELLE SERIE 25, 16-24. (1979).

BATI 1977 -1 BATIGNE, D. R.
INTEGRAL GENERALIZED INVERSES OF INTEGRAL MATRICES. WASHINGTON: GEORGE WASHINGTON UNIV. , 44 P. (1977). (DISSERTATION)

BATY 1979 -1 BATYCKI, T.; KASPRZAK, A.
BRANCH-AND-BOUND ALGORITHM FOR DETERMINATION OF ADAPTIVE ROUTING IN SOME CLASS OF PACKET-SWITCHED COMPUTER COMMUNICATION NETWORKS, THE. SYSTEMS SCIENCE (WROCLAW) 5, 51-62. (1979).

BAUE 1981 -1 BAUER, D.; BOESCH, F.; SUFFEL, C.; TINDELL, R.
CONNECTIVITY EXTREMAL PROBLEMS AND THE DESIGN OF RELIABLE PROBABILISTIC NETWORKS. PAPER PRESENTED AT THE JOINT MEETING OF CORS, ORSA AND TIMS, TORONTO 1981, 14 P. (1981).

BAUM 1978 -1 BAUM, S.; TROTTER, L. E. JR.
FINITE CHECKABILITY FOR INTEGER ROUNDING PROPERTIES IN COMBINATORIAL PROBRAMMING PROBLEMS. REPORT NO. 78109-OR. BONN: UNIV. BONN, INSTITUT FUER OEKONOMETRIE UND OPERATIONS RESEARCH, 13 P. (1978).

BAUM 1978 -2 BAUM, S.; TROTTER, L. E. JR.
INTEGER ROUNDING FOR POLYMATROID AND BRANCHING OPTIMIZATION PROBLEMS. REPORT NO. 78120-OR. BONN: UNIV. BONN, INSTITUT FUER OEKONOMETRIE UND OPERATIONS RESEARCH, 21 P. (1978).

BAYB 1978 -1 BAYBARS, I.
NEW CHARACTERIZATION OF MAXIMAL PLANAR GRAPHS AND A GRAPH THEORETIC APPROACH TO THE FACILITIES DESIGN PROBLEM, A. LOS ANGELES (ORSA/TIMS MEETING, NOVEMBER 1978) 55 P. (1978).

BAYB 1979 -1 BAYBARS, I.
ON K-PATH HAMILTONIAN MAXIMAL PLANAR GRAPHS. PITTSBURGH: CARNEGIE-MELLON UNIV., 9 P. (1979).

BAYB 1980 -1 BAYBARS, I.
CHARACERIZATION OF HAMILTONIAN MAXIMAL PLANAR GRAPHS. PITTSBURGH: CARNEGIE-MELLON UNIV., 10 P. (1980).

BAYB 1980 -2 BAYBARS, I.
OPTIMAL ASSIGNMENT OF BROADCASTING FREQUENCIES. DRC-21-04-80. PITTSBURGH: CARNEGIE-MELLON UNIV., DESIGN RESEARCH CENTER, 17 P. (1980).

BAYBA 1979 -1 BAYBARS, I.; KORTANEK, K. O.; MIZUNO, N.
MIXED INTEGER PROGRAMMING MODEL FOR TRANSMISSION SYSTEM PLANNING IN TELECOMMUNICATIONS NETWORKS WITH GENERAL CIRCUIT REQUIREMENTS, A. PITTSBURGH: CARNEGIE-MELLON UNIV., 8 P. (1979).

BAZA 1978 -1 BAZARAA, M. S.
INFEASIBILITY PRICING ALGORITHM FOR THE MULTICOMMODITY MINIMUM COST FLOW PROBLEM, AN. COMPUTERS AND OPERATIONS RESEARCH 5, 251-262. (1978).

BAZAA 1979 -1 BAZARAA, M. S.; ELSHAFEI, A. N.
EXACT BRANCH-AND-BOUND PROCEDURE FOR THE QUADRATIC-ASSIGNMENT PROBLEM, AN. NAVAL RESEARCH LOGISTICS QUARTERLY 26, 109-121. (1979).

BAZAB 1977 -1 BAZARAA, M. S.; JARVIS, J. J.
LINEAR PROGRAMMING AND NETWORK FLOWS. NEW YORK, LONDON U.A.: WILEY, 565 P. (1977).

BAZAC 1979 -1 BAZARAA, M. S.; SHERALI, H. D.
CUTTING PLANE METHODS FOR THE QUADRATIC ASSIGNMENT PROBLEM. REPORT. ATLANTA: GEORGIA INST. OF TECHNOLOGY, SCHOOL OF INDUSTRIAL AND SYSTEMS ENGINEERING, 27 P. (1979).

BAZAC 1979 -2 BAZARAA, M. S.; SHERALI, H. D.
NEW APPROACHES FOR SOLVING THE QUADRATIC ASSIGNMENT PROBLEM. IN: W. OETTLI, F. STEFFENS (EDS.): OPERATIONS RESEARCH VERFAHREN 32. THIRD SYMPOSIUM ON OPERATIONS RESEARCH, MANNHEIM 1978, 29-46. KOENIGSTEIN: ANTON HAIN MEISENHEIM. (1979).

BAZAC 1980 -1 BAZARAA, M. S.; SHERALI, H. D.
BENDERS' PARTITIONING SCHEME APPLIED TO A NEW FORMULATION OF THE QUADRATIC ASSIGNMENT PROBLEM. NAVAL RESEARCH LOGISTICS QUARTERLY 27, 29-41. (1980).

BEAL 1979 -1 BEALE, E. M. L.
BRANCH AND BOUND METHODS FOR MATHEMATICAL PROGRAMMING SYSTEMS. IN: P. L. HAMMER, E. L. JOHNSON, B. H. KORTE (EDS.): DISCRETE OPTIMIZATION II, 201-219. ANNALS OF DISCRETE MATHEMATICS 5, AMSTERDAM, NEW YORK, OXFORD: NORTH-HOLLAND. (1979).

BEAL 1980 -1 BEALE, E. M. L.
FRACTIONAL PROGRAMMING WITH ZERO-ONE VARIABLES. IN: A. V. FIACCO, K. O. KORTANEK (EDS.): EXTREMAL METHODS AND SYSTEMS ANALYSIS, 430-432. LECTURE NOTES IN ECONOMICS AND MATHEMATICAL SYSTEMS 174. BERLIN: SPRINGER. (1980).

BECH 1979 -1 BECHTOLD, S. E.
QUANTITATIVE MODELS FOR OPTIMAL REST PERIOD SCHEDULING: A NOTE. OMEGA 7, 565-566. (1979).

BECT 1978 -1 BECTOR, C. R.; JOLLY, P. L.
PSEUDO-MONOTONIC INTEGER PROGRAMMING. IN: D. MAC CARTHY, H. C. WILLIAMS (EDS.): PROCEEDINGS OF THE SEVENTH MANITOBA CONFERENCE ON NUMERICAL MATHEMATICS AND COMPUTING, 211-218. CONGRESSUS NUMERANTIUM XX. WINNIPEG: UTILITAS. (1978).

BEDN 1979 -1 BEDNAR, L.; STROHMEIER, E.
LAGERSTANDORTOPTIMIERUNG UND FUHRPARKEINSATZPLANUNG IN DER KONSUMGUETER-INDUSTRIE. ZEITSCHRIFT FUER OPERATIONS RESEARCH 23, SERIE B, NO. 4, B89-B104. (1979).

BEEC 1979 -1 BEECHAM, A. F.; HURLEY, A. C.
SCHEDULING PROBLEM WITH A SIMPLE GRAPHICAL SOLUTION, A. JOURNAL OF THE AUSTRALIAN MATHEMATICAL SOCIETY, SERIES B 21, 486-495. (1979).

BEHZ 1965 -1 BEHZAD, M.
GRAPHS AND THEIR CHROMATIC NUMBERS. DOCTORAL THESIS. EAST LANSING: MICHIGAN STATE UNIVERSITY. (1965).

BEHZA 1967 -1 BEHZAD, M.; CHARTRAND, G.; COOPER, J. K.
COLOUR NUMBERS OF COMPLETE GRAPHS, THE. THE JOURNAL OF THE LONDON MATHEMATICAL SOCIETY 42, 226-228. (1967).

BEIN 1976 -1 BEINEKE, L. W.; FIORINI, S.
ON SMALL GRAPHS CRITICAL WITH RESPECT TO EDGE COLOURINGS. DISCRETE MATHEMATICS 16, 109-121. (1976).

BEINA 1973 -1 BEINEKE, L. W.; WILSON, R. J.
ON THE EDGE-CHROMATIC NUMBER OF A GRAPH. DISCRETE MATHEMATICS 5, 15-20. (1973).

BELE 1979 -1 BELENOVA, N. K.
FLOW PROBLEM IN A CAPACITATED NETWORK. AVTOMATIKA I TELEMEHANIKA (MOSCOW) NO. 9, 102-108; TRANSLATED AS AUTOMATION AND REMOTE CONTROL 40, 1980, 1343-1348. (1979).

BELEA 1978 -1 BELETSKIJ, S. A.
INCREASED EFFECTIVENESS OF THE DYNAMIC PROGRAMMING METHOD IN THE SOLUTION OF A CLASS OF DISCRETE OPTIMIZATION PROBLEMS (RUSSIAN). IN: COMBINATORIAL ALGORITHMS FOR OPTIMAL DECISION MAKING. AKADEMIJA NAUK UKRAINSKOI SSR. INSTITUT KIBERNETIKI (KIEV).PREPRINT NO. 10, 11-21. (1978).

BELJ 1976 -1 BELJAEVA, L. V.; ZURBENKO, N. G.; SOR, N. Z.
NONLINEAR TRANSPORTATION PROBLEM (RUSSIAN), A. IN: THEORY OF OPTIMAL DECISIONS (RUSSIAN), 83-89. KIEV: AKADEMII NAUK UKRAINSKOI. (1976).

BELL 1974 -1 BELL, D. E.
CONSTRUCTIVE GROUP RELAXATIONS FOR INTEGER PROGRAMS. DISSERTATION. CAMBRIDGE: MASSACHUSETTS INSTITUTE OF TECHNOLOGY. (1974).

BELL 1979 -1 BELL, D. E.
EFFICIENT GROUP CUTS FOR INTEGER PROGRAMS. MATHEMATICAL PROGRAMMING 17, 176-183. (1979).

BELL 1980 -1 BELL, D. E.
GROUP APPROACH TO INTEGER PROGRAMMING: AN OUTLINE OF RECENT PROGRESS, THE. IN: A. PREKOPA (ED.): STUDIES ON MATHEMATICAL PROGRAMMING, 13-18. MATHEMATICAL METHODS OF OPERATIONS RESEARCH VOL. 1. BUDAPEST: AKADEMIAI KIADO. (1980).

BELLA 1968 -1 BELL, T. E.
GRAPHICAL ANALYSIS PROCEDURES FOR SIMULATION AND SCHEDULING. UNPUBLISHED DOCTORAL THESIS. LOS ANGELES: UNIVERSITY OF CALIFORNIA. (1968).

BELO 1977 -1 BELOGLA, G. N.; SKOROBOGATOV, V. A.
AUTOMATION SYSTEM FOR THE SOLUTION OF PROBLEMS ON GRAPHS (RUSSIAN), AN. AKADEMIJA NAUK SSSR. SIBIRSKOE OTDELENIE. INSTITUT MATEMATIKI. VYCISLITEL'NYE SISTEMY. SBORNIK TRUDOV 69, 24-39. (1977).

BELOA 1974 -1 BELOV, I. S.; STOLIN, JA. I.
ALGORITHM FOR A FLOW-SHOP SCHEDULING PROBLEM (RUSSIAN), AN. IN: B. P. MITYAGIN (ED.): MATHEMATICAL ECONOMICS AND FUNCTIONAL ANALYSIS, 218-257. MOSCOW: NAUKA. (1974).

BENE 1980 -1 BENETEAU, L.
CLASSE PARTICULIERE DE MATROIDES PARFAITS, UNE. IN: M. DEZA, I. G. ROSENBERG (EDS.): COMBINATORICS 79, PART I, 229-232. ANNALS OF DISCRETE MATHEMATICS 8. AMSTERDAM: NORTH-HOLLAND. (1980).

BENH 1979 -1 BENHAMAMOUCH, D.
ALGORITHME DE DECOUPE OPTIMALE DANS R**2, UN. DISSERTATION. PARIS: UNIVERSITY OF PARIS 6, 135 P. (1979).

BENI 1981 -1 BENITO-ALONSO, M. A.; DEVAUX, P.
LOCATION AND SIZE OF DAY NURSERIES - A MULTIPLE GOAL APPROACH. EUROPEAN JOURNAL OF OPERATIONAL RESEARCH 6, 195-198. (1981).

BENS 1979 -1 BENSEMAN, B.; HALL, K.
SOLVING A PLANT LOCATION PROBLEM WITH INTEGER PROGRAMMING. NEW ZEALAND OPERATIONAL RESEARCH 7, 105-116. (1979).

BENT 1978 -1 BENTLEY, J. L.
FAST ALGORITHMS FOR CONSTRUCTING MINIMAL SPANNING TREES IN COORDINATE SPACES. INSTITUTE OF ELECTRICAL AND ELECTRONICS ENGINEERS. TRANSACTIONS ON COMPUTERS 27, NO. 2, 97-105. (1978).

BENT 1980 -1 BENTLEY, J. L.
PARALLEL ALGORITHM FOR CONSTRUCTING MINIMUM SPANNING TREES, A. JOURNAL OF ALGORITHMS 1, 51-59. (1980).

BENZ 1980 -1 BENZAKEN, C.; HAMMER, P. L.; SIMEONE, B.
GRAPHES DE CONFLIT DES FONCTIONS PSEUDO-BOOLEENNES QUADRATIQUES. IN: P. HANSEN, D. DE WERRA (EDS.): REGARDS SUR LA THEORIE DES GRAPHES, PROCEEDINGS OF THE CERISY COLLOQUIUM, 1980, 165-170. LAUSANNE: PRESSES POLYTECHNIQUES ROMANDES. (1980).

BENZ 1980 -2 BENZAKEN, C.; HAMMER, P. L.; SIMEONE, B.
SOME REMARKS ON CONFLICT GRAPHS OF QUADRATIC PSEUDO-BOOLEAN FUNCTIONS. IN: L. COLLATZ, G. MEINARDUS, W. WETTERLING (EDS.): KONSTRUKTIVE METHODEN DER FINITEN NICHTLINEAREN OPTIMIERUNG, 9-30. INTERNATIONAL SERIES OF NUMERICAL MATHEMATICS 55, BASEL: BIRKHAEUSER. (1980).

BERA 1979 -1 BERAHA, S.; KAHANE, J.
IS THE FOUR-COLOR CONJECTURE ALMOST FALSE? JOURNAL OF COMBINATORIAL THEORY 27, SERIES B, 1-12. (1979).

BERE 1979 -1 BERENGUER, X.
CHARACTERIZATION OF LINEAR ADMISSIBLE TRANSFORMATIONS FOR THE M-TRAVELLING SALESMAN PROBLEM, A. EUROPEAN JOURNAL OF OPERATIONAL RESEARCH 3, 232-238. (1979).

BEREA 1978 -1 BERESNEV, V. L.; ZAIKINA, G. M.
PROGRAMME DE L'ALGORITHME DE RESOLUTION DU PROBLEME D'ASSORTIMENT OPTIMAL (RUSSIAN). UPRAVLJAEMYE SISTEMY, NO. 17, 3-12. (1978).

BERG 1973 -1 BERGE, C.
INTRODUCTION A LA THEORIE DES HYPERGRAPHES. MONTREAL: PRESSES DE L'UNIVERSITE DE MONTREAL. 110 P. (1973).

BERG 1976 -1 BERGE, C.
MULTICOLORINGS OF GRAPHS AND HYPERGRAPHS, THE. THE JOURNAL OF THE UNIVERSITY OF KUWAIT. SCIENCE 3, 1-6; ALSO PUBLISHED IN Y. ALAVI, D. R. LICK (EDS.): THEORY AND APPLICATION OF GRAPHS, PROCEEDINGS OF THE INTERNATIONAL CONFERENCE, MICHIGAN 1976, 23-36. 1978, BERLIN: SPRINGER. (1976).

BERG 1978 -1 BERGE, C.
MULTICOLORING OF A GRAPH. MATHEMATICAL PROGRAMMING STUDY 8, 226-234. (1978).

BERG 1978 -2 BERGE, C.
MULTICOLORINGS. IN: A. HAJNAL, V. T. SOS (EDS.): COMBINATORICS, VOLUME I, 121-134. COLLOQUIA MATHEMATICA SOCIETATIS JANOS BOLYAI 18. AMSTERDAM: NORTH-HOLLAND. (1978).

BERG 1978 -3 BERGE, C.
RESULTATS RECENTS SUR CERTAINES CLASSES D'HYPERGRAPHES QUI GENERALISENT LES GRAPHES BIPARTIS. CAHIERS DU CENTRE D'ETUDES DE RECHERCHE OPERATIONELLE 20, 243-278. (1978).

BERG 1979 -1 BERGE, C.
MULTICOLORINGS OF GRAPHS AND HYPERGRAPHS. IN: A. RAMACHANDRA RAO (ED.): PROCEEDINGS OF THE SYMPOSIUM ON GRAPH THEORY, CALCUTTA 1976, 1-9. ISI (INDIAN STATISTICAL INSTITUTE) LECTURE NOTES 4. CALCUTTA: MACMILLAN OF INDIA. (1979).

BERG 1979 -2 BERGE, C.
PACKING PROBLEMS AND HYPERGRAPH THEORY: A SURVEY. IN: P. L. HAMMER, E. L. JOHNSON, B. H. KORTE (EDS.): DISCRETE OPTIMIZATION I, 3-37. ANNALS OF DISCRETE MATHEMATICS 4. AMSTERDAM, NEW YORK, OXFORD: NORTH-HOLLAND. (1979).

BERG 1979 -3 BERGE, C.
PACKING PROBLEMS. IN: PROCEEDINGS OF THE FIRST FRANCO-SOUTHEAST ASIAN MATHEMATICAL CONFERENCE, NANYANG UNIVERSITY, SINGAPORE 1979. SOUTHEAST ASIAN BULLETIN OF MATHEMATICS 1979, SPECIAL ISSUE, 26-35. (1979).

BERG 1979 -4 BERGE, C.
REGULARIZABLE GRAPHS. IN: A. RAMACHANDRA RAO (ED.): PROCEEDINGS OF THE SYMPOSIUM ON GRAPH THEORY, CALCUTTA 1976, 90-102. ISI (INDIAN STATISTICAL INSTITUTE) LECTURE NOTES 4. CALCUTTA: MACMILLAN OF INDIA. (1979).

BERG 1980 -1 BERGE, C.
BALANCED MATRICES AND PROPERTY (G). MATHEMATICAL PROGRAMMING STUDY 12, 163-175. (1980).

BERGA 1978 -1 BERGE, C.; HOFFMAN, A. J.
MULTICOLORATIONS DANS LES HYPERGRAPHES UNIMODULAIRES ET MATRICES DONT LES COEFFICIENTS SONT DES ENSEMBLES. IN: J.-C. BERMOND ET AL. (EDS.): PROBLEMES COMBINATOIRES ET THEORIE DES GRAPHES, COLLOQUES INTERNATIONAUX DU CENTRE NATIONAL DE LA RECHERCHE SCIENTIFIQUE, ORSAY 1976, 27-30. PARIS: CENTRE NATIONAL DE LA RECHERCHE SCIENTIFIQUE. (1978).

BERGB 1978 -1 BERGE, C.; VERGNAS, M. LAS
ON THE EXISTENCE OF SUBGRAPHS WITH DEGREE CONSTRAINTS. NEDERLANDSE AKADEMIE VAN WETENSCHAPPEN, INDAGATIONES MATHEMATICAE 40, 165-176. (1978).

BERK 1978 -1 BERKOWITZ, H. W.
RESTRICTED EULERIAN CIRCUITS IN DIRECTED GRAPHS. COLLOQUIUM MATHEMATICUM 39, 185-188. (1978).

BERL 1974 -1 BERLIN, V. G.
APPROXIMATE METHOD FOR SOLVING THE SIMPLEST PROBLEM OF SCHEDULING THEORY (RUSSIAN). AN. AVTOMATIKA I TELEMEHANIKA, NO. 8, 102-108; TRANSLATED AS AUTOMATION AND REMOTE CONTROL 35, 1974, 1299-1305. (1974).

BERM 1978 -1 BERMAN, D. M.
CRITICAL GRAPHS FOR ACYCLIC COLORINGS. CANADIAN MATHEMATICAL BULLETIN 21, NO. 1, 115-116. (1978).

BERMA 1977 -1 BERMAN, G.; COLIJN, A. W.
COMPUTER REPRESENTATION OF BOOLEAN AND PSEUDO-BOOLEAN FUNCTIONS. A. IN: F. HOFFMAN ET AL. (EDS.): PROCEEDINGS OF THE EIGHTH SOUTHEASTERN CONFERENCE ON COMBINATORICS, GRAPH THEORY, AND COMPUTING, BATON ROUGE 1977, 163-181. CONGRESSUS NUMERANTIUM XIX, WINNIPEG: UTILITAS MATHEMATICA. (1977).

BERMB 1980 -1 BERMAN, K. A.
PROOF OF TUTTE'S TRINITY THEOREM AND A NEW DETERMINANT FORMULA. A. SIAM JOURNAL ON ALGEBRAIC AND DISCRETE METHODS 1, 64-69. (1980).

BERMC 1981 -1 BERMAN, O.; LARSON, R. C.; ODONI, A. R.
DEVELOPMENTS IN NETWORK LOCATION WITH MOBILE AND CONGESTED FACILITIES. EUROPEAN JOURNAL OF OPERATIONAL RESEARCH 6, 104-116. (1981).

BERMD 1978 -1 BERMOND, J. C.
HAMILTONIAN GRAPHS. IN: L. W. BEINEKE, R. J. WILSON (EDS.): SELECTED TOPICS IN GRAPH THEORY, 127-168. LONDON, NEW YORK, SAN FRANCISCO: ACADEMIC PRESS. (1978).

BERME 1979 -1 BERMOND, J. C.; GERMA, A.; HEYDEMANN, M. C.
HAMILTONIAN CYCLES IN STRONG PRODUCTS OF GRAPHS. CANADIAN MATHEMATICAL BULLETIN 22, 305-309. (1979).

BERMF 1978 -1 BERMOND, J. C.; GERMA, A.; HEYDEMANN, M. C.; SOTTEAU, D.
HYPERGRAPHES HAMILTONIENS. IN: J.-C. BERMOND ET AL. (EDS.): PROBLEMES COMBINATOIRES ET THEORIE DES GRAPHES, COLLOQUES INTERNATIONAUX DU CENTRE NATIONAL DE LA RECHERCHE SCIENTIFIQUE, ORSAY 1976, 39-43. PARIS: CENTRE NATIONAL DE LA RECHERCHE SCIENTIFIQUE. (1978).

BERMG 1979 -1 BERMOND, J. C.; SIMOES-PEREIRA, J. M. S.; ZAMFIRESCU, C. M.
ON NONHAMILTONIAN HOMOGENEOUSLY TRACEABLE DIGRAPHS. MATHEMATICA JAPONICA 24, 423-426. (1979).

BERMH 1981 -1 BERMOND, J. C.; THOMASSEN, C.
CYCLES IN DIGRAPHS - A SURVEY. JOURNAL OF GRAPH THEORY 5, 1-44. (1981).

BERS 1973 -1 BERSHCHANSKII, JA. M.
METHOD FOR THE MINIMIZATION OF THE RESOURCE LEVEL IN A PROBLEM OF NETWORK PLANNING (RUSSIAN), A. SBORNIK TRUDOV INSTITUT PROBLEM UPRAVLENINA, VYP. 3 ISSLED. I OPTIMIZACIJA SLOZN. MNOGOSVJAZ. SISTEM, 51-56, 147. (1973).

BERS 1973 -2 BERSHCHANSKII, JA. M.
ON THE CONVERGENCE OF A MODIFICATION OF THE CUTTING PLANE METHOD (RUSSIAN). SBORNIK TRUDOV INSTITUT PROBLEM UPRAVLENINA, VYP. 3 ISSLED. I OPTIMIZACIJA SLOZN. MNOGOSVJAZ. SISTEM, 71-76, 148. (1973).

BERT 1980 -1 BERTOLAZZI, P.; LEPORELLI, C.; LUCERTINI, M.
ALTERNATIVE GROUP RELAXATION OF INTEGER PROGRAMMING PROBLEMS. IN: K. IRACKI, K. MALANOWSKI, P. WALUKIEWICZ (EDS.): OPTIMIZATION TECHNIQUES, PART II, 154-159. LECTURE NOTES IN CONTROL AND INFORMATION SCIENCES 23. BERLIN: SPRINGER. (1980).

BERTA 1979 -1 BERTONI, A.; MAURI, G.; TORELLI, M.
THREE EFFICIENT ALGORITHMS FOR COUNTING PROBLEMS. INFORMATION PROCESSING LETTERS 8, 50-53. (1979).

BERTB 1980 -1 BERTOSSI, A. A.
ON THE COMPLEXITY OF SCHEDULING JOBS ON DEDICATED RESOURCES TO MINIMIZE SET-UP COSTS. INFORMATION PROCESSING LETTERS 10, 173-177. (1980).

BERTC 1979 -1 BERTSEKAS, D. P.
ALGORITHMS FOR NONLINEAR MULTICOMMODITY NETWORK FLOW PROBLEMS. IN: A. BENSOUSSAN, J. L. LIONS (EDS.): INTERNATIONAL SYMPOSIUM ON SYSTEMS OPTIMIZATION AND ANALYSIS, ROCQUENCOURT 1978, 210-224. LECTURE NOTES IN CONTROL AND INFORMATION SCIENCE 14. BERLIN: SPRINGER. (1979).

BERTC 1980 -1 BERTSEKAS, D. P.
CLASS OF OPTIMAL ROUTING ALGORITHMS FOR COMMUNICATION NETWORKS. A. RESEARCH REPORT. CAMBRIDGE, MA: MASSACHUSETTS INST. OF TECHNOLOGY, LABORATORY FOR INFORMATION AND DECISION SYSTEMS, 12 P. (1980).

****

BERTD 1980 -1 BERTSEKAS, D. P.; GAFNI, E. M.
PROJECTION METHODS FOR VARIATIONAL INEQUALITIES WITH APPLICATION TO THE TRAFFIC ASSIGNMENT PROBLEM. LIDS-P-1043. CAMBRIDGE: MASS. INST. OF TECHNOLOGY, LABORATORY FOR INFORMATION AND DECISION SYSTEMS, 33 P. (1980).

BERTE 1979 -1 BERTSEKAS, D. P.; GAFNI, E. M.; VASTOLA, K. S.
VALIDATION OF ALGORITHMS FOR OPTIMAL ROUTING OF FLOW IN NETWORKS. IN: PROCEEDINGS OF THE 1978 IEEE CONFERENCE ON DECISION AND CONTROL, INCLUDING THE 17TH SYMPOSIUM ON ADAPTIVE PROCESSES, SAN DIEGO 1979, 220-227. NEW YORK: THE INSTITUTE OF ELECTRICAL AND ELECTRONICS ENGINEERS, INC. (1979).

BESH 1979 -1 BESHARA, S. B.; MAGAZINE, M. J.
MYOPIC HEURISTICS FOR SINGLE MACHINE SCHEDULING PROBLEMS. WORKING PAPER NO. 126. WATERLOO: UNIV. OF WATERLOO, DEPT. OF MANAGEMENT SCIENCES, 20 P. (1979).

BESS 1978 -1 BESSONOV, JU. E.; SKOROBOGATOV, V. A.
APPLICATION OF RELATIVE PARTITIONINGS FOR SEARCHING FOR CLIQUES (RUSSIAN). AKADEMIJA NAUK SSSR. SIBIRSKOE OTDELENIE. INSTITUT MATEMATIKI. VYCISLITEL'NYE SISTEMY. SBORNIK TRUDOV. NO. 77, 24-33 + 114-115. (1978).

BEST 1979 -1 BESTWICK, P. F.; LOCKYER, K. G.
PRACTICAL APPROACH TO PRODUCTION SCHEDULING, A. INTERNATIONAL JOURNAL OF PRODUCTION RESEARCH 17, 95-109. (1979).

BEYE 1979 -1 BEYER, T.; JONES, W.; MITCHELL, S.
LINEAR ALGORITHMS FOR ISOMORPHISM OF MAXIMAL OUTERPLANAR GRAPHS. JOURNAL OF THE ASSOCIATION FOR COMPUTING MACHINERY 26, 603-610. (1979).

BHAS 1980 -1 BHASKARAN, S.
OVERHAUL SCHEDULING OF NEW ZEALAND POWER GENERATORS. NEW ZEALAND OPERATIONAL RESEARCH 8, 23-32. (1980).

BHAT 1980 -1 BHAT, K. V. S.
ON THE COMPLEXITY OF TESTING A GRAPH FOR N-CUBE. INFORMATION PROCESSING LETTERS 11, 16-19. (1980).

BHATA 1979 -1 BHAT, K. V. S.; KINARIWALA, B.
ALGORITHM FOR THE N X N OPTIMUM ASSIGNMENT PROBLEM, AN. NORDISK TIDSKRIFT FOR INFORMATIONSBEHANDLING 19, 289-296. (1979).

BHATB 1977 -1 BHATIA, H. L.
TIME MINIMIZING ASSIGNMENT PROBLEMS. SCIMA 6, 75-83. (1977).

BHATB 1978 -1 BHATIA, H. L.
SOLID TRANSPORTATION PROBLEM IN LINEAR FRACTIONAL PROGRAMMING. REVUE BELGE DE STATISTIQUE, D'INFORMATIQUE ET DE RECHERCHE OPERATIONELLE 18, NO. 4, 35-50. (1978).

BHATB 1979 -1 BHATIA, H. L.
NOTE ON A ZERO-ONE MINIMIZING TRANSPORTATION PROBLEM, A. NEW ZEALAND OPERATIONAL RESEARCH 7, 159-165. (1979).

BHATC 1978 -1 BHATIA, H. L.; SWARUP, K.; PURI, M. C.
PROCEDURE FOR TIME MINIMIZATION TRANSPORTATION PROBLEM, A. INDIAN JOURNAL OF PURE AND APPLIED MATHEMATICS 8, 920-929. (1978).

BHATC 1979 -1 BHATIA, H. L.; SWARUP, K.; PURI, M. C.
TIME ENUMERATION TECHNIQUE FOR TIME-COST TRADE-OFF IN A TRANSPORTATION PROBLEM. CAHIERS DU CENTRE D'ETUDES DE RECHERCHE OPERATIONNELLE 21, 63-75. (1979).

BHATD 1979 -1 BHATNAGAR, V. L.; DAS, G.; MEHTA, O. P.
N-JOB, 2-MACHINE FLOW JOB SHOP SCHEDULING PROBLEM HAVING MINIMUM TOTAL WAITING TIME FOR ALL JOBS. PURE AND APPLIED MATHEMATIKA SCIENCES 10, 81-88. (1979).

BIAN 1980 -1 BIANCO, L.; CINI, M.; GRIPPO, L.
STRATEGIC APPROACH TO AIR TRAFFIC CONTROL, A. IN: K. IRACKI, K. MALANOWSKI, P. WALUKIEWICZ (EDS.): OPTIMIZATION TECHNIQUES, PART II, 345-355. LECTURE NOTES IN CONTROL AND INFORMATION SCIENCES 23. BERLIN: SPRINGER. (1980).

BIANA 1978 -1 BIANCO, L.; NICOLETTI, B.; RICCIARDELLI, S.
ALGORITHM FOR OPTIMAL SEQUENCING OF AIRCRAFT IN THE NEAR TERMINAL AREA, AN. IN: J. STOER (ED.): OPTIMIZATION TECHNIQUES, PROCEEDINGS OF THE 8TH IFIP CONFERENCE ON OPTIMIZATION TECHNIQUES, WUERZBURG 1977, PART 2, 443-453. LECTURE NOTES IN CONTROL AND INFORMATION SCIENCES 7. BERLIN, HEIDELBERG, NEW YORK: SPRINGER. (1978).

BIANB 1981 -1 BIANCO, L.; RICCIARDELLI, S.
MINIMIZING MEAN WEIGHTED COMPLETION TIME IN ONE MACHINE SCHEDULING PROBLEM. IN: R. E. BURKARD, T. ELLINGER (EDS.): METHODS OF OPERATIONS RESEARCH 40, 231-234. KOENIGSTEIN: ANTON HAIN MEISENHEIM. (1981).

BIES 1977 -1 BIESS, G.; JAENICKE, W.; MEISSLER, H. G.
ALGORITHMUS ZUR BESTIMMUNG ALLER ELEMENTARKREISE EINES GERICHTETEN GRAPHEN, EIN. WISSENSCHAFTLICHE ZEITSCHRIFT DER TECHNISCHEN HOCHSCHULE CARL SCHORLEMMER LEUNA-MERSEBURG 19, NO. 1, 103-111. (1977).

BIGA 1978 -1 BIGALKE, A.
KOMBINATORISCHER BEWEIS DES SATZES VON R. L. FORD UND D. R. FULKERSON, EIN. ARCHIV DER MATHEMATIK 30, NO. 1, 110-112. (1978).

BIGAA 1979 -1 BIGALKE, A.; JUNG, H. A.
UEBER HAMILTONSCHE KREISE UND UNABHAENGIGE ECKEN IN GRAPHEN. MONATSHEFTE FUER MATHEMATIK 88, 195-210. (1979).

BIGAB 1979 -1 BIGALKE, A.; KOEHLER, N.
ANTIGERICHTETE HAMILTONLINIEN IN VOLLSTAENDIG GERICHTETEN GRAPHEN. ABHANDLUNGEN AUS DEM MATHEMATISCHEN SEMINAR DER UNIVERSITAET HAMBURG 48, 114-117. (1979).

BIGG 1972 -1 BIGGS, N.
EDGE COLOURING PROBLEM, AN. THE AMERICAN MATHEMATICAL MONTHLY 79, 1018-1020. (1972).

BIGG 1977 -1 BIGGS, N.
COLOURING SQUARE LATTICE GRAPHS. BULLETIN OF THE LONDON MATHEMATICAL SOCIETY 9, NO. 1, 54-56. (1977).

BIGG 1979 -1 BIGGS, N.
ON THE ALGEBRA OF GRAPH TYPES. IN: J. A. BONDY, U. P. R. MURTY (EDS.): GRAPH THEORY AND RELATED TOPICS, 81-89. NEW YORK, SAN FRANCISCO, LONDON: ACADEMIC PRESS. (1979).

BIGG 1979 -2 BIGGS, N.
RESONANCE AND RECONSTRUCTION. IN: B. BOLLOBAS (ED.): SURVEYS IN COMBINATORICS, PROCEEDINGS OF THE 7TH BRITISH COMBINATORIAL CONFERENCE, 1-21. LONDON MATHEMATICAL SOCIETY LECTURE NOTE SERIES 38. CAMBRIDGE, LONDON, NEW YORK, MELBOURNE: CAMBRIDGE UNIVERSITY PRESS. (1979).

BIGH 1979 -1 BIGHAM, P. E.; MOGG, J. M.
CONVERGING BRANCH MULTI-STAGE PRODUCTION SCHEDULES WITH FINITE PRODUCTION RATES AND START-UP DELAYS. JOURNAL OF THE OPERATIONAL RESEARCH SOCIETY 30, 737-746. (1979).

BIGH 1979 -2 BIGHAM, P. E.; MOGG, J. M.
LOWER BOUND SOLUTIONS TO MULTI-STAGE PRODUCTION SCHEDULING PROBLEMS WITH STARTUP DELAYS. AIIE TRANSACTIONS 11, 313-318. (1979).

BIJL 1975 -1 BIJLSMA, S. J.
ON MINIMAL-TIME SHIP ROUTING. DISSERTATION. DELFT: UNIVERSITY OF TECHNOLOGY. (1975).

BIKO 1978 -1 BIKOV, V. M.
ASSIGNMENT PROBLEM WITH A DISCONTINUOUS TARGET FUNCTION (RUSSIAN), AN. KIBERNETIKA, NO. 1, 139-140. (1978).

BIKO 1978 -2 BIKOV, V. M.
IMPROVING THE EFFICIENCY OF THE LOCAL OPTIMIZATION METHODS FOR SOME CLASSES OF INTEGER PROGRAMMING PROBLEMS (RUSSIAN). DOKLADY AKADEMII NAUK UKRAINSKOI SSR SERIJA A. FIZIKO-MATEMATICESKIE I TEHNICESKIE NAUKI, NO. 1, 60-62. (1978).

BIKOA 1978 -1 BIKOV, V. M.; SERGIENKO, I. V.
METHOD OF SOLVING PROBLEMS OF DISCRETE PROGRAMMING APPROXIMATELY (RUSSIAN), A. KIBERNETIKA (KIEV), NO. 3, 75-80. (1978).

BILL 1978 -1 BILLIONNET, A.
MODELE ADAPTANT LES POLITIQUES DE PERSONNEL AUX BESOINS PREVISIONNELS. REVUE FRANCAISE D'AUTOMATIQUE, D'INFORMATIQUE ET DE RECHERCHE OPERATIONELLE 12, SERIE RECHERCHE OPERATIONELLE, 41-59. (1978).

BILL 1978 -2 BILLIONNET, A.
TRANSFORMATION DU PROBLEME DE PARTITIONNEMENT EN UN PROBLEME D'ENSEMBLE STABLE DE POIDS MAXIMAL. REVUE FRANCAISE D'AUTOMATIQUE, D'INFORMATIQUE ET DE RECHERCHE OPERATIONELLE 12, SERIE RECHERCHE OPERATIONELLE, 319-323. (1978).

BILLA 1977 -1 BILLSTEIN, N.; RADERMACHER, F. J.
TIME-COST OPTIMIZATION. IN: A. ANGERMANN ET AL. (EDS.): FIRST SYMPOSIUM ON OPERATIONS RESEARCH, HEIDELBERG 1976. METHODS OF OPERATIONS RESEARCH 27, 274-294. MEISENHEIM: ANTON HAIN. (1977).

BINZ 1978 -1 BINZ, J. C.
HAMILTONWEGE IN RECHTECKIGEN UND QUADERFOERMIGEN GITTERGRAPHEN. ELEMENTE DER MATHEMATIK 33, NO. 2, 39-42. (1978).

BIRD 1976 -1 BIRD, R.
PROGRAMS AND MACHINES. AN INTRODUCTION TO THE THEORY OF COMPUTING. LONDON, NEW YORK U.A.: WILEY, 214 P. (1976). (WILEY SERIES IN COMPUTING)

BIRO 1980 -1 BIRO, M.
EFFICIENT METHOD APPLYING INCOMPLETE ORDERING FOR SOLVING THE BINARY KNAPSACK PROBLEM. IN: K. IRACKI, K. MALANOWSKI, P. WALUKIEWICZ (EDS.): OPTIMIZATION TECHNIQUES, PART II, 160-169. LECTURE NOTES IN CONTROL AND INFORMATION SCIENCES 23. BERLIN: SPRINGER. (1980).

BITR 1979 -1 BITRAN, G. R.
THEORY AND ALGORITHMS FOR LINEAR MULTIPLE OBJECTIVE PROGRAMS WITH ZERO-ONE VARIABLES. MATHEMATICAL PROGRAMMING 17, 362-390. (1979).

BITRA 1977 -1 BITRAN, G. R.; HAX, A. C.
ON THE SOLUTION OF CONVEX KNAPSACK PROBLEMS WITH BOUNDED VARIABLES. TECHNICAL REPORT NO. 129. CAMBRIDGE: MASSACHUSETTS INSTITUTE OF TECHNOLOGY, OPERATIONS RESEARCH CENTER. (1977).

BITRB 1980 -1 BITRAN, G. R.; LAWRENCE, K. D.
LOCATING SERVICE OFFICES : A MULTICRITERIA APPROACH. OMEGA 8, 201-206. (1980).

BITRC 1979 -1 BITRAN, G. R.; SEMPOLINSKI, D. E.; SHAPIRO, J. F.
INVERSE OPTIMIZATION: AN APPLICATION TO THE CAPACITATED PLANT LOCATION PROBLEM. WORKING PAPER OR 091-79. CAMBRIDGE: MASSACHUSETTS INST. OF TECHNOLOGY, OPERATIONS RESEARCH CENTER, 29 P. (1979).

BITRD 1981 -1 BITRAN, G. R.; YANASSE, H. H.
COMPUTATIONAL COMPLEXITY OF THE CAPACITATED LOT SIZE PROBLEM. RESEARCH REPORT. CAMBRIDGE, MA: MASSACHUSETTS INST. OF TECHNOLOGY. (1981).

BIXB 1979 -1 BIXBY, R. E.
ON REID'S CHARACTERIZATION OF THE TERNARY MATROIDS. JOURNAL OF COMBINATORIAL THEORY 26, SERIES B, 174-204. (1979).

BIXBA 1979 -1 BIXBY, R. E.; CUNNINGHAM, W. H.
MATROIDS, GRAPHS, AND 3-CONNECTIVITY. IN: J. A. BONDY, U. P. R. MURTY (EDS.): GRAPH THEORY AND RELATED TOPICS, 91-103. NEW YORK, SAN FRANCISCO, LONDON: ACADEMIC PRESS. (1979).

BIXBA 1980 -1 BIXBY, R. E.; CUNNINGHAM, W. H.
CONVERTING LINEAR PROGRAMS TO NETWORK PROBLEMS. MATHEMATICS OF OPERATIONS RESEARCH 5, 321-357. (1980).

BIXBB 1978 -1 BIXBY, R. E.; WANG, D.-L.
ALGORITHM FOR FINDING HAMILTONIAN CIRCUITS IN CERTAIN GRAPHS, AN. MATHEMATICAL PROGRAMMING STUDY 8, 35-49. (1978).

BJOE 1980 -1 BJOERNER, A.
SOME MATROID INEQUALITIES. DISCRETE MATHEMATICS 31, 101-103. (1980).

BLAI 1974 -1 BLAIR, C. E.
EXTENSIONS OF SUBADDITIVE FUNCTIONS USED IN CUTTING PLANE THEORY. MANAGEMENT SCIENCE RESEARCH REPORT NO. 360. PITTSBURGH: CARNEGIE-MELLON UNIVERSITY. (1974).

BLAI 1975 -1 BLAIR, C. E.
MINIMAL INEQUALITIES FOR MIXED-INTEGER PROGRAMS. MANAGEMENT SCIENCE RESEARCH REPORT NO. 363. PITTSBURGH: CARNEGIE-MELLON UNIVERSITY. (1975).

BLAI 1975 -2 BLAIR, C. E.
TOPICS IN INTEGER PROGRAMMING. PITTSBURGH: CARNEGIE-MELLON UNIV.; AND ANN ARBOR: XEROX UNIV. MICROFILMS,1978, 25 P. (1975). (DISSERTATION)

BLAI 1980 -1 BLAIR, C. E.
FACIAL DISJUNCTIVE PROGRAMS AND SEQUENCES OF CUTTING-PLANES. DISCRETE APPLIED MATHEMATICS 2, 173-180. (1980).

BLAIA 1976 -1 BLAIR, C. E.; JEROSLOW, R. G.
CONVERSE FOR DISJUNCTIVE CONSTRAINTS, A. MANAGEMENT SCIENCE RESEARCH REPORT NO. 393. PITTSBURGH: CARNEGIE-MELLON UNIVERSITY, GRADUATE SCHOOL OF INDUSTRIAL ADMINISTRATION. (1976).

BLAIA 1980 -1 BLAIR, C. E.; JEROSLOW, R. G.
VALUE FUNCTION OF AN INTEGER PROGRAM, THE. RESEARCH REPORT MS-80-12. ATLANTA: GEORGIA INSTITUTE OF TECHNOLOGY, 51 P. (1980).

BLAIA 1981 -1 BLAIR, C. E.; JEROSLOW, R. G.
EXACT PENALTY METHOD FOR MIXED-INTEGER PROGRAMS, AN. MATHEMATICS OF OPERATIONS RESEARCH 6, 14-18. (1981).

BLAN 1978 -1 BLAND, R. G.
ELEMENTARY VECTORS AND TWO POLYHEDRAL RELAXATIONS. MATHEMATICAL PROGRAMMING STUDY 8, 159-166. (1978).

BLAN 1978 -2 BLAND, R. G.
PIVOTING IN ORIENTED MATROIDS. IN: J.-C. BERMOND ET AL. (EDS.): PROBLEMES COMBINATOIRES ET THEORIE DES GRAPHES. COLLOQUES INTERNATIONAUX DU CENTRE NATIONAL DE LA RECHERCHE SCIENTIFIQUE, ORSAY 1976, 47. PARIS: CENTRE NATIONAL DE LA RECHERCHE SCIENTIFIQUE. (1978).

BLANA 1979 -1 BLAND, R. G.; HUANG, H.-C.; TROTTER, L. E. JR.
GRAPHICAL PROPERTIES RELATED TO MINIMAL IMPERFECTION. DISCRETE MATHEMATICS 27, 11-22. (1979).

BLANB 1979 -1 BLAND, R. G.; VERGNAS, M. LAS
MINTY COLORINGS AND ORIENTATIONS OF MATROIDS. IN: A. GEWIRTZ, L. V. QUINTAS (EDS.): SECOND INTERNATIONAL CONFERENCE ON COMBINATORIAL MATHEMATICS, 86-92. ANNALS OF THE NEW YORK ACADEMY OF SCIENCES, VOLUME 319. NEW YORK: THE NEW YORK ACADEMY OF SCIENCES. (1979).

BLAS 1978 -1 BLASS, A.
GRAPHS WITH UNIQUE MAXIMAL CLUMPINGS. JOURNAL OF GRAPH THEORY 2, 19-24. (1978).

BLAZ 1978 -1 BLAZEWICZ, J.
COMPLEXITY OF COMPUTER SCHEDULING ALGORITHMS UNDER RESOURCE CONSTRAINTS. FOUNDATIONS OF CONTROL ENGINEERING 3, 51-57. (1978).

BLAZ 1978 -2 BLAZEWICZ, J.
SCHEDULING WITH DEADLINES IN MULTIPROCESSOR SYSTEMS. IN: M. ARATO, E. KNUTH (EDS.): SELECTED PAPERS ON OPERATING SYSTEMS: THEORY AND PRACTICE. LECTURES DELIVERED AT THE VISEGRAD WINTER SCHOOL, VISEGRAD 1978, 227-238. BUDAPEST: SZAMITOGEPALKALMAZASI KUTATO INTEZET. (1978).

BLAZ 1979 -1 BLAZEWICZ, J.
DEADLINE SCHEDULING OF TASKS WITH READY TIMES AND RESOURCE CONSTRAINTS. INFORMATION PROCESSING LETTERS 8, 60-63. (1979).

BLAZ 1979 -2 BLAZEWICZ, J.
SCHEDULING TASKS ON PARALLEL PROCESSORS UNDER RESOURCE CONSTRAINTS TO MINIMIZE MEAN FINISHING TIME. IN: W. OETTLI, F. STEFFENS (EDS.): OPERATIONS RESEARCH VERFAHREN 35, THIRD SYMPOSIUM ON OPERATIONS RESEARCH, MANNHEIM 1978, 67-72. KOENIGSTEIN: ANTON HAIN MEISENHEIM. (1979).

BLAZ 1980 -1 BLAZEWICZ, J.
SCHEDULING TO MINIMIZE MEAN WEIGHTED INFORMATION LOSS. RESEARCH REPORT. POZNAN: TECHNICAL UNIVERSITY, INSTITUTE OF CONTROL ENGINEERING, 19 P. (1980).

BLAZ 1981 -1 BLAZEWICZ, J.
SOLVING THE RESOURCE CONSTRAINED DEADLINE SCHEDULING PROBLEM VIA REDUCTION TO THE NETWORK FLOW PROBLEM. EUROPEAN JOURNAL OF OPERATIONAL RESEARCH 6, 75-79. (1981).

BLAZA 1980 -1 BLAZEWICZ, J.; LENSTRA, J. K.; RINNOOY KAN, A. H. G.
SCHEDULING SUBJECT TO RESOURCE CONSTRAINTS: CLASSIFICATION AND COMPLEXITY. RESEARCH REPORT 8018/O. ROTTERDAM: ERASMUS UNIV., ECONOMETRIC INST., 16 P. (1980).

BLAZB 1978 -1 BLAZEWICZ, J.; WEGLARZ, J.
DETERMINISTIC TASK SCHEDULING PROBLEM ON PROCESSORS OF COMPUTER SYSTEMS WITH ALLOWANCE FOR ADDITIONAL RESOURCES (POLISH). ARCHIWUM AUTOMATYKI I TELEMECHANIKI (WARSAW) 23, 485-509. (1978).

BLAZB 1978 -2 BLAZEWICZ, J.; WEGLARZ, J.
SCHEDULING TO MEET DEADLINES WITH RESOURCE CONSTRAINTS - COMPLEXITY RESULTS. TANULMANYOK. MTA SZAMITASTECHNIKAI ES AUTOMATIZALASI KUTATO INTEZET BUDAPEST, NO. 87, 5-19. (1978).

BLAZB 1979 -1 BLAZEWICZ, J.; WEGLARZ, J.
SCHEDULING UNDER RESOURCE CONSTRAINTS - ACHIEVEMENTS AND PROSPECTS. IN: M. ARATO, A. BUTRIMENKO, E. GELENBE (EDS.): PERFORMANCE OF COMPUTER SYSTEMS, 181-199. AMSTERDAM: NORTH-HOLLAND. (1979).

BOAS 1977 -1 BOASSON, L.; COURCELLE, B.; NIVAT, M.
NEW COMPLEXITY MEASURE FOR LANGUAGES, A. RAPPORT DE RECHERCHE NO. 255. LE CHESNAY: INSTITUT DE RECHERCHE D'INFORMATIQUE ET D'AUTOMATIQUE, 10 P. (1977).

BODI 1979 -1 BODIN, L. D.; BERMAN, L.
MODEL FOR THE CLASSIFICATION OF RAIL FREIGHT CARS, A. FRA-OPPD-79-18. COLLEGE PARK: UNIV. OF MARYLAND, COLLEGE OF BUSINESS MANAGEMENT, 102 P. (1979).

BODI 1979 -2 BODIN, L. D.; BERMAN, L.
ROUTING AND SCHEDULING OF SCHOOL BUSES BY COMPUTER. TRANSPORTATION SCIENCE 13, 113-129. (1979).

BODIA 1978 -1 BODIN, L. D.; KURSH, S. J.
COMPUTER-ASSISTED SYSTEM FOR THE ROUTING AND SCHEDULING OF STREET SWEEPERS, A. OPERATIONS RESEARCH 26, 525-537. (1978).

BODIA 1979 -1 BODIN, L. D.; KURSH, S. J.
DETAILED DESCRIPTION OF A COMPUTER SYSTEM FOR THE ROUTING AND SCHEDULING OF STREET SWEEPERS, A. COMPUTERS AND OPERATIONS RESEARCH 6, 181-198. (1979).

BODIB 1981 -1 BODIN, L. D.; ROSENFIELD, D. B.; KYDES, A. S.
SCHEDULING AND ESTIMATION TECHNIQUES FOR TRANSPORTATION PLANNING. COMPUTERS AND OPERATIONS RESEARCH 8, 25-38. (1981).

BODIC 1979 -1 BODIN, L. D.; SEXTON, T. R.
SUBSCRIBER DIAL-A-RIDE PROBLEM, THE. RESEARCH REPORT UMCP-UMTA-1-79. WASHINGTON: U.S. DEPT. OF TRANSPORTATION, URBAN MASS TRANSPORTATION ADMINISTRATION, OFFICE OF BUS. AND PARATRANSIT TECHNOLOGY, 47 P. (1979).

BODR 1979 -1 BODRIK, A. G.
SOLUTION OF SOME PRODUCTION PLANNING PROBLEMS (RUSSIAN). KIEVSKII GOSUDARSTVENNYI UNIVERSITET. ISSLEDOVANIE OPERACII ASU, NO. 13, 50-54 + 133. (1979).

BOEB 1978 -1 BOEBION, J.; ALMAR, A.; PUN, L.
SCHEDULING METHOD SYNCHRONIZING TWO LINES OF ACTIVITIES AND MINIMIZING WAITING AND PASS-TIME. INTERNATIONAL JOURNAL OF PRODUCTION RESEARCH 16, 321-335. (1978).

BOEH 1964 -1 BOEHM, C.; SANTOLINI, A.
QUASI-DECISION ALGORITHM FOR THE P-EQUIVALENCE OF TWO MATRICES, A. ICC BULLETIN 3, 57-69. (1964).

BOEN 1979 -1 BOENCHENDORF, K.
HEURISTIKEN FUER DAS N !1! PREC ! SUM(WI*CI) REIHENFOLGEPROBLEM. IN: W. OETTLI, F. STEFFENS (EDS.): OPERATIONS RESEARCH VERFAHREN 32, THIRD SYMPOSIUM ON OPERATIONS RESEARCH, MANNHEIM 1978, 47-53. KOENIGSTEIN: ANTON HAIN MEISENHEIM. (1979).

BOEN 1981 -1 BOENCHENDORF, K.
SUBGRADIENT-LIKE HEURISTIC METHODS. IN: R. E. BURKARD, T. ELLINGER (EDS.): METHODS OF OPERATIONS RESEARCH 40, 235-238. KOENIGSTEIN: ANTON HAIN MEISENHEIM. (1981).

BOFF 1979 -1 BOFFEY, T. B.; EDMOND, E. D.; HINXMAN, A. I.; PURSGLOVE, C. J.
TWO APPROACHES TO SCHEDULING CONTAINER SHIPS WITH AN APPLICATION TO THE NORTH ATLANTIC ROUTE. JOURNAL OF THE OPERATIONAL RESEARCH SOCIETY 30, 413-426. (1979).

BOFFA 1979 -1 BOFFEY, T. B.; HINXMAN, A. I.
SOLVING THE OPTIMAL NETWORK PROBLEM. EUROPEAN JOURNAL OF OPERATIONAL RESEARCH 3, 386-393. (1979).

BOFI 1976 -1 BOFILL, A.; DIAZ, A.
SENSITIVITY ANALYSIS FOR THE TRANSPORTATION PROBLEM IN LINEAR PROGRAMMING (SPANISH). INVESTIGACION OPERACIONAL, NO. 19, 15-27. (1976).

BOHE 1977 -1 BOHEME, G.
ANWENDUNGSORIENTIERTE MATHEMATIK. BD. 4: AKTUELLE ANWENDUNGEN DER MATHEMATIK. BERLIN, HEIDELBERG, NEW YORK: SPRINGER, 258 P. (1977).

BOKI 1980 -1 BOKINGE, U.; HASSELSTROEM, D.
IMPROVED VEHICLE SCHEDULING IN PUBLIC TRANSPORT THROUGH SYSTEMATIC CHANGES IN THE TIME-TABLE. EUROPEAN JOURNAL OF OPERATIONAL RESEARCH 5, 388-395. (1980).

****

BOLL 1978 -1 BOLLOBAS, B.; ELDRIDGE, S. E.
PACKINGS OF GRAPHS AND APPLICATIONS TO COMPUTATIONAL COMPLEXITY. JOURNAL OF COMBINATORIAL THEORY 25, SERIES B, 105-124. (1978).

BOLLA 1978 -1 BOLLOBAS, B.; HOBBS, A. M.
HAMILTONIAN CYCLES IN REGULAR GRAPHS. IN: B. BOLLOBAS (ED.): ADVANCES IN GRAPH THEORY, 43-48. ANNALS OF DISCRETE MATHEMATICS 3. AMSTERDAM: NORTH-HOLLAND. (1978).

BOLLB 1979 -1 BOLLOBAS, B.; MANVEL, B.
OPTIMAL VERTEX PARTITIONS. THE BULLETIN OF THE LONDON MATHEMATICAL SOCIETY 11, 113-116. (1979).

BOLLC 1976 -1 BOLLOBAS, B.; SAUER, N.
UNIQUELY COLOURABLE GRAPHS WITH LARGE GIRTH. CANADIAN JOURNAL OF MATHEMATICS 6, 1340-1344. (1976).

BOLS 1972 -1 BOLSHAKOV, I. A.; BRIKKER, B. I.
"QUASIDIAGONALISATION" FOR INTEGER QUADRATIC PROGRAMS (RUSSIAN). MAT. MET. RESH. EKON. SADAC 3, M. NAUKA, 137-145. (1972).

BOLW 1979 -1 BOLWELL, S. G.; KARWAN, M. H.
EFFICIENT USE OF SURROGATE DUALITY IN 0-1 INTEGER PROGRAMMING. RESEARCH REPORT 79-5. AMHERST: STATE UNIV. OF NEW YORK AT BUFFALO, DEPT. OF INDUSTRIAL ENGINEERING, 28 P. (1979).

BOLW 1979 -2 BOLWELL, S. G.; KARWAN, M. H.
HYBRID SURROGATE DUAL-CUTTING PLANE APPROACH TO INTEGER PROGRAMMING, A. RESEARCH REPORT NO. 79-6. AMHERST: STATE UNIV. OF NEW YORK AT BUFFALO, DEPT. OF INDUSTRIAL ENGINEERING, 21 P. (1979).

BOND 1972 -1 BONDY, J. A.
VARIATIONS ON THE HAMILTONIAN THEME. CANADIAN MATHEMATICAL BULLETIN 15, 57-62. (1972).

BOND 1976 -1 BONDY, J. A.
DICONNECTED ORIENTATIONS AND A CONJECTURE OF LAS VERGNAS. JOURNAL OF THE LONDON MATHEMATICAL SOCIETY 14, 277-282. (1976).

BOND 1977 -1 BONDY, J. A.
CYCLES IN DIGRAPHS. IN: F. HOFFMAN ET AL. (EDS.): PROCEEDINGS OF THE EIGHTH SOUTHEASTERN CONFERENCE ON COMBINATORICS, GRAPH THEORY, AND COMPUTING, BATON ROUGE 1977, 91-98. CONGRESSUS NUMERANTIUM XIX, WINNIPEG: UTILITAS MATHEMATICA. (1977).

BOND 1978 -1 BONDY, J. A.
HAMILTON CYCLES IN GRAPHS AND DIGRAPHS. IN: F. HOFFMAN, D. MAC CARTHY, R. C. MULLIN, R. G. STANTON (EDS.): PROCEEDINGS OF THE NINTH SOUTHEASTERN CONFERENCE ON COMBINATORICS, GRAPH THEORY, AND COMPUTING, 3-28. CONGRESSUS NUMERANTIUM XXI. WINNIPEG: UTILITAS. (1978).

BOND 1978 -2 BONDY, J. A.
REMARK ON TWO SUFFICIENT CONDITIONS FOR HAMILTONIAN CYCLES, A. DISCRETE MATHEMATICS 22, 191-193. (1978).

BONDA 1978 -1 BONDY, J. A.; HEMMINGER, R. L.
RECONSTRUCTION BY ENUMERATION: SOME APPLICATIONS OF A COUNTING THEOREM BY THE GRAPH RECONSTRUCTION PROBLEM. IN: J.-C. BERMOND ET AL. (EDS.): PROBLEMES COMBINATOIRES ET THEORIE DES GRAPHES, COLLOQUES INTERNATIONAUX DU CENTRE NATIONAL DE LA RECHERCHE SCIENTIFIQUE, ORSAY 1976, 51-55. PARIS: CENTRE NATIONAL DE LA RECHERCHE SCIENTIFIQUE. (1978).

BONDB 1980 -1 BONDY, J. A.; SIMONOVITS, M.
LONGEST CYCLES IN 3-CONNECTED 3-REGULAR GRAPHS. CANADIAN JOURNAL OF MATHEMATICS 32, 987-992. (1980).

BONG 1979 -1 BONGIOVANNI, G.
PROPERTY OF STRUCTURAL NUMBERS AND CUT SETS, A. CALCOLO 16, 1-3. (1979).

BONU 1979 -1 BONUCCELLI, M. A.; BOVET, D. P.
MINIMUM NODE DISJOINT PATH COVERING FOR CIRCULAR-ARC GRAPHS. INFORMATION PROCESSING LETTERS 8, 159-161. (1979).

BOOK 1979 -1 BOOK, R. V.
POLYNOMIAL SPACE AND TRANSITIVE CLOSURE. SIAM JOURNAL ON COMPUTING 8, 434-439. (1979).

BOOKA 1980 -1 BOOKBINDER, J. H.; SETHI, S. P.
DYNAMIC TRANSPORTATION PROBLEM: A SURVEY, THE. NAVAL RESEARCH LOGISTICS QUARTERLY 27, 65-87. (1980).

BOOL 1980 -1 BOOLER, J. M. P.
SOLUTION OF A RAILWAY LOCOMOTIVE SCHEDULING PROBLEM, THE. JOURNAL OF THE OPERATIONAL RESEARCH SOCIETY 31, 943-948. (1980).

BOOT 1978 -1 BOOTH, K. S.
ISOMORPHISM TESTING FOR GRAPHS, SEMIGROUPS, AND FINITE AUTOMATA ARE POLYNOMIALLY EQUIVALENT PROBLEMS. SIAM JOURNAL ON COMPUTING 7, 273-279. (1978).

BOOT 1980 -1 BOOTH, K. S.
DOMINATING SETS IN CHORDAL GRAPHS. CS-80-34. WATERLOO: UNIV. OF WATERLOO, COMPUTER SCIENCE DEPT., 10 P. (1980).

BORO 1977 -1 BOROHOVIC, R. E.; ZENIN, F. B.; ZENINA, JA. A.
ALGORITHM FOR THE COMPILATION OF A SCHEDULE UNDER THE CONDITIONS OF AN AUTOMATIC CONTROL SYSTEM (RUSSIAN), AN. IN: V. A. ZOZIKASVILI, N. M. ANGERT (EDS.): DATA TRANSMISSION IN AUTOMATIC CONTROL SYSTEMS (RUSSIAN), 71-81 + 99. KISHINEV: IZDAT. "STIINCA". (1977).

BORT 1977 -1 BORTOT, P.
SOME PROPERTIES OF A SET OF NON LINEAR BOOLEAN INEQUATIONS. IN: BEREANU, B.; IOSIFESCU, M.; POPESCU, G. (EDS.): PROCEEDINGS OF THE FIFTH CONFERENCE ON PROBABILITY THEORY, BRASOV, ROMANIA 1974, 355-360. BUCURESTI: AKADEMEI REPUBLICII SOCIALISTE ROMANIA. (1977).

BOSA 1973 -1 BOSAK, J.; FIAMCHIK, I.
CHROMATIC INDEX OF HAMILTONIAN GRAPHS. MATEMATICKY CASOPIS 23, 88-94. (1973).

BOUL 1978 -1 BOULALA, M.
ETUDE DU POLYTOPE ASSOCIE AUX STABLES D'UN GRAPHE ET CARACTERISATION DANS LE CAS DES GRAPHES SERIE-PARALLELES. GRENOBLE: UNIVERSITE SCIENTIFIQUE ET MEDICALE DE GRENOBLE, 90 P. (1978). (DISSERTATION)

BOULA 1979 -1 BOULALA, M.; UHRY, J.-P.
POLYTOPE DES INDEPENDANTS D'UN GRAPHE SERIE-PARALLELE. DISCRETE MATHEMATICS 27, 225-243. (1979).

BOUR 1978 -1 BOURI, V. K.
SOLUTION TECHNIQUE FOR THE TOTAL COST RECTILINEAR DISTANCE SINGLE FACILITY LOCATION PROBLEM, A. NEW YORK (ORSA/TIMS MEETING, MAY 1978) (1978).

BOUW 1980 -1 BOUWSMA, W.; HARARY, F.
ON THE COLOR PARTITIONS OF A GRAPH. ELEMENTE DER MATHEMATIK 35, NO. 3, 49-55. (1980).

BOVE 1980 -1 BOVET, D. P.; PETRINI, M.
EVALUATION OF SCHEDULING ALGORITHMS FOR RESOURCES WITH HIGH SET-UP TIME. EUROPEAN JOURNAL OF OPERATIONAL RESEARCH 5, 182-192. (1980).

BOYC 1980 -1 BOYCE, D. E.; JANSON, B. N.
DISCRETE TRANSPORTATION NETWORK DESIGN PROBLEM WITH COMBINED TRIP DISTRIBUTION AND ASSIGNMENT, A. TRANSPORTATION RESEARCH 14, PART B, 147-154. (1980).

BOYCA 1979 -1 BOYCE, D. E.; SOBERANES, J. L.
SOLUTIONS TO THE OPTIMAL NETWORK DESIGN PROBLEM WITH SHIPMENTS RELATED TO TRANSPORTATION COST. TRANSPORTATION RESEARCH 13, SERIES B, 65-80. (1979).

BOYCB 1978 -1 BOYCE, S.; MORTON, T. E.
BOTTLENECK HORIZONS FOR ONE MACHINE SEQUENCING WITH PRECEDENCE CONSTRAINTS (REVISED VERSION). WORKING PAPER 8-77-78. PITTSBURGH: CARNEGIE-MELLON UNIV. GRADUATE SCHOOL OF INDUSTRIAL ADMINISTRATION, 18 P. (1978).

BOYCC 1977 -1 BOYCE, W. M.
IMPROVED PROGRAM FOR THE FULL STEINER TREE PROBLEM, AN. ACM TRANSACTIONS ON MATHEMATICAL SOFTWARE 3, 359-385. (1977).

BOYCD 1978 -1 BOYCE, W. M.; GAREY, M. R.; JOHNSON, D. S.
NOTE ON BISECTING MINIMUM SPANNING TREES, A. NETWORKS 8, 187-192. (1978).

BOYE 1968 -1 BOYER, D. D.; HUNT, D. J.
MODIFIED SIMPLEX ALGORITHM FOR SOLVING THE MULTICOMMODITY FLOW PROBLEM, A. SERIAL T-211. WASHINGTON: THE GEORGE WASHINGTON UNIVERSITY LOGISTICS RESEARCH PROJECT, SEPTEMBER 1968. (1968).

BOZY 1979 -1 BOZYIGIT, M.; PAKER, Y.
FIXED ROUTING PROBLEM IN LARGE AND HIGH CONNECTIVITY NETWORKS, A. THE COMPUTER JOURNAL 22, 246-250. (1979).

BRAC 1974 -1 BRACE, A.; DAYKIN, D. E.
PSEUDO-MATCHINGS OF A BIPARTITE GRAPH. PROCEEDINGS OF THE AMERICAN MATHEMATICAL SOCIETY 42, 28-32. (1974).

BRAD 1975 -1 BRADLEY, G. H.; BROWN, G. G.; GRAVES, G.
COMPARISON OF STORAGE STRUCTURE FOR PRIMAL NETWORK CODES, A. PAPER PRESENTED AT THE ORSA/TIMS CONFERENCE CHICAGO 1975. (1975).

BRADA 1978 -1 BRADLEY, R. C. JR.
REMARK ON NONCOLORABLE CUBIC GRAPHS, A. JOURNAL OF COMBINATORIAL THEORY 24, SERIES B, 311-317. (1978).

BRADB 1977 -1 BRADLEY, S. P.; HAX, A. C.; MAGNANTI, T. L.
APPLIED MATHEMATICAL PROGRAMMING. READING, AMSTERDAM U.A.: ADDISON-WESLEY, 735 P. (1977).

BRAE 1979 -1 BRAESS, D.; KOCH, G.
ON THE EXISTENCE OF EQUILIBRIA IN ASYMMETRICAL MULTICLASS-USER TRANSPORTATION NETWORKS. TRANSPORTATION SCIENCE 13, 56-63. (1979).

BRAN 1978 -1 BRANDT, A.; INTRATOR, J.
FAST ALGORITHMS FOR LONG TRANSPORTATION PROBLEMS. COMPUTERS AND OPERATIONS RESEARCH 5, 263-272. (1978).

BRANA 1978 -1 BRANMAN, J.
SHORT COMMUNICATION. A NOTE ON PIVOTING IN TRANSPORTATION CODES. EUROPEAN JOURNAL OF OPERATIONAL RESEARCH 5, 377-379. (1978).

BRAU 1978 -1 BRAUN, H.
LITERATUR UEBER GRAPHEN-ISOMORPHIE, EINDEUTIGE STRUKTURBENENNUNG UND VERWANDTE THEMEN. UNPUBLISHED REPORT. ZUERICH: UNIVERSITAET ZUERICH, INSTITUT FUER ORGANISCHE CHEMIE. (1978).

BREE 1978 -1 BREE, D. S.; LAGEWEG, B. J.; LENSTRA, J. K.; RINNOOY KAN, A. H. G.; VANBEZOUWEN, G.
HIERARCHICAL CLUSTERING SCHEME FOR ASYMMETRIC MATRICES, A. BW 88/78. AMSTERDAM: MATHEMATISCH CENTRUM, 26 P. (1978).

BREG 1975 -1 BREGMEN, L. M.; ROMANOVSKII, I. V.
ALLOCATION AND OPTIMIZATION IN ASSIGNMENT PROBLEMS (RUSSIAN). ISSLEDOVANIE OPERACII I STATISTICESKOE MODELIROVANIE (LENINGRAD), NO. 3, 137-162, 210-211. (1975).

BREI 1979 -1 BREITBARD, Y.; LEWIS, F. D.
COMBINED COMPLEXITY CLASSES FOR FINITE FUNCTIONS. REVUE FRANCAISE D'AUTOMATIQUE, D'INFORMATIQUE ET DE RECHERCHE OPERATIONELLE 13, SERIE INFORMATIQUE THEORIQUE, 87-97. (1979).

BREL 1979 -1 BRELAZ, D.
NEW METHODS TO COLOR THE VERTICES OF A GRAPH. COMMUNICATIONS OF THE ACM 22, 251-256. (1979).

BRES 1980 -1 BRESKO, D.; CAREY, M.; HENDRICKSON, C.; OPPENHEIM, I.
BOUNDS ON EXPECTED NETWORKS PERFORMANCE WITH UNRELIABLE LINKS. DRAFT. PITTSBURGH: CARNEGIE-MELLON UNIV., 27 P. (1980).

BRIC 1978 -1 BRICKER, D. L.; CHANG, T.-S.
SURROGATE DUAL FOR THE SIMPLE PLANT LOCATION PROBLEMS, A. SCIMA 7, 16-26. (1978).

BRIN 1980 -1 BRINI, A.
CLASS OF RANK-INVARIANTS FOR PERFECT MATROID DESIGNS, A. EUROPEAN JOURNAL OF COMBINATORICS 1, 33-38. (1980).

BROE 1979 -1 BROERE, I.
GRAPHTHEORETIC COLORING PROBLEMS (AFRIKAANS). DIE SUID-AFRIKAANSE AKADEMIE VIR WETENSKAP EN KUNS. TYDSKRIF VIR NATUURWETENSKAPPE 19, 2-11. (1979).

BROEA 1979 -1 BROERE, I.; MYNHARDT, C. M.
REMARKS ON THE CRITICAL GRAPH CONJECTURE. DISCRETE MATHEMATICS 26, 209-212. (1979).

BRON 1979 -1 BRONSTEIN, M. L.; KIM, K. V.
ELIMINATION ON THE POSSIBILITY OF CYCLING IN THE PRIMAL NETWORK METHOD (RUSSIAN). EKONOMIKA I MATEMATICESKIE METODY 15, NO. 2, 408-412. (1979).

BROO 1941 -1 BROOKS, R. L.
ON COLOURING THE NODES OF A NETWORK. PROCEEDINGS OF THE CAMBRIDGE PHILOSOPHICAL SOCIETY 37, 194-197. (1941).

BROU 1979 -1 BROUWER, A. E.; SCHRIJVER, A.
UNIFORM HYPERGRAPHS. IN: A. SCHRIJVER (ED.): PACKING AND COVERING IN COMBINATORICS, 39-73. MATHEMATICAL CENTRE TRACTS 106, AMSTERDAM: MATHEMATISCH CENTRUM. (1979).

BROW 1980 -1 BROWN, G. G.; GEOFFRION, A. M.; BRADLEY, G. H.
PRODUCTION AND SALES PLANNING WITH LIMITED SHARED TOOLING AT THE KEY OPERATION. WORKING PAPER 300. LOS ANGELES: UNIV. OF CALIFORNIA, WESTERN MANAGEMENT SCIENCE INST., 26 P. (1980).

BROWA 1981 -1 BROWN, G. G.; GRAVES, G. W.
REAL-TIME DISPATCH OF PETROLEUM TANK TRUCKS. MANAGEMENT SCIENCE 27, 19-31. (1981).

BROWB 1979 -1 BROWN, J. R.
KNAPSACK SHARING PROBLEM, THE. OPERATIONS RESEARCH 27, 341-355. (1979).

BROWB 1979 -2 BROWN, J. R.
PREVENTING REDUNDANT SOLUTIONS IN PARTIAL ENUMERATION ALGORITHMS. MATHEMATICAL PROGRAMMING 16, 177-189. (1979).

BROWB 1979 -3 BROWN, J. R.
SHARING PROBLEM, THE. OPERATIONS RESEARCH 27, 324-340. (1979).

BROWC 1979 -1 BROWN, M. R.
PARTIAL ANALYSIS OF RANDOM HEIGHT-BALANCED TREES, A. SIAM JOURNAL ON COMPUTING 8, 33-41. (1979).

BROWD 1979 -1 BROWN, M. R.; TARJAN, R. E.
FAST MERGING ALGORITHM, A. JOURNAL OF THE ASSOCIATION FOR COMPUTING MACHINERY 26, 211-226. (1979).

BROWE 1978 -1 BROWN, W. G.; ERDOES, P.; SIMONOVITS, M.
ON MULTIGRAPH EXTREMAL PROBLEMS. IN: J.-C. BERMOND ET AL. (EDS.): PROBLEMES COMBINATOIRES ET THEORIE DES GRAPHES, COLLOQUES INTERNATIONAUX DU CENTRE NATIONAL DE RECHERCHE SCIENTIFIQUE, ORSAY 1976, 63-66. PARIS: CENTRE NATIONAL DE LA RECHERCHE SCIENTIFIQUE. (1978).

BROWF 1978 -1 BROWNE, J.; PROPP, J. G.; TIBREWALA, R.
CONDITIONS FOR OPTIMAL SCHEDULING CONSECUTIVE WORK PERIODS. NEW YORK: ORSA/TIMS MEETING. 8 P. (1978).

BRUA 1978 -1 BRUALDI, R. A.
CHROMATIC INDEX OF THE GRAPH OF THE ASSIGNMENT POLYTOPE, THE. IN: B. BOLLOBAS (ED.): ADVANCES IN GRAPH THEORY, 49-54. ANNALS OF DISCRETE MATHEMATICS 3. AMSTERDAM: NORTH-HOLLAND. (1978).

BRUA 1979 -1 BRUALDI, R. A.
DIAGONAL HYPERGRAPH OF A MATRIX (BIPARTITE GRAPH), THE. DISCRETE MATHEMATICS 27, 127-147. (1979).

BRUAA 1980 -1 BRUALDI, R. A.; HARARY, F.; MILLER, Z.
BIGRAPHS VERSUS DIGRAPHS VIA MATRICES. JOURNAL OF GRAPH THEORY 4, 51-73. (1980).

BRUC 1973 -1 BRUCKER, P.
ERSTELLUNG VON CPM-NETZPLAENEN, DIE. DISKUSSIONSBEITRAEGE NR. 12. REGENSBURG: UNIV. REGENSBURG, FACHBEREICH WIRTSCHAFTSWISSENSCHAFTEN 11 P. (1973).

BRUC 1973 -2 BRUCKER, P.
ON HU'S "CUTTING THE LONGEST QUEUE"-ALGORITHM. DISKUSSIONSBEITRAEGE NR. 14. REGENSBURG: UNIV. REGENSBURG, FACHBEREICH WIRTSCHAFTSWISSENSCHAFTEN 4 P. (1973).

BRUC 1978 -1 BRUCKER, P.
APPROXIMATIVE VERFAHREN ZUR LOESUNG VON DISKRETEN OPTIMIERUNGSPROBLEMEN. IN: J. MUEHLBACHER (ED.): DATENSTRUKTUREN, GRAPHEN, ALGORITHMEN. DRITTE FACHTAGUNG UEBER GRAPHENTHEORETISCHE KONZEPTE DER INFORMATIK, LINZ 1977, 263-273. MUENCHEN, WIEN: HANSER. (1978).

BRUC 1979 -1 BRUCKER, P.
NP-COMPLETE OPERATIONS RESEARCH PROBLEMS AND APPROXIMATION ALGORITHMS. ZEITSCHRIFT FUER OPERATIONS RESEARCH 23, SERIE A, 73-94. (1979).

BRUC 1981 -1 BRUCKER, P.
CHINESE POSTMAN PROBLEM FOR MIXED GRAPHS, THE. IN: H. NOLTEMEYER (ED.): GRAPHTHEORETIC CONCEPTS IN COMPUTER SCIENCE, 354-366. LECTURE NOTES IN COMPUTER SCIENCE 100. BERLIN: SPRINGER. (1981).

BRUC 1981 -2 BRUCKER, P.
ON JOB-SHOP SCHEDULING WITH UNIT-TIME TASKS. IN: R. E. BURKARD, T. ELLINGER (EDS.): METHODS OF OPERATIONS RESEARCH 40, 243-246. KOENIGSTEIN: ANTON HAIN MEISENHEIM. (1981).

BRUN 1975 -1 BRUNO, J.
ON TASK SCHEDULING WITH A (USUALLY) FINITE PLANNING HORIZON. IN: PROCEEDINGS OF THE 1975 CONFERENCE ON INFORMATION SCIENCES AND SYSTEMS, BALTIMORE 1975, 152-155. BALTIMORE: THE JOHNS HOPKINS UNIVERSITY: DEPARTMENT OF ELECTRICAL ENGINEERING. (1975).

BRUNA 1978 -1 BRUNO, J.; DOWNEY, P.
COMPLEXITY OF TASK SEQUENCING WITH DEADLINES, SET-UP TIMES AND CHANGEOVER COSTS. SIAM JOURNAL ON COMPUTING 7, 393-404. (1978).

BRUNB 1981 -1 BRUNO, J.; DOWNEY, P.; FREDERICKSON, G. N.
SEQUENCING TASKS WITH EXPONENTIAL SERVICE TIMES TO MINIMIZE THE EXPECTED FLOW TIME OR MAKESPAN. JOURNAL OF THE ASSOCIATION FOR COMPUTING MACHINERY 28, 100-113. (1981).

BRUNC 1976 -1 BRUNO, J.; GONZALEZ, T.
SCHEDULING INDEPENDENT TASKS WITH RELEASE DATES AND DUE DATES ON PARALLEL MACHINES. TECHNICAL REPORT 213. UNIVERSITY PARK: PENNSYLVANIA STATE UNIVERSITY, COMPUTER SCIENCE DEPARTMENT. (1976).

BRUND 1980 -1 BRUNO, J.; JONES, J. W., III; SO, K.
DETERMINISTIC SCHEDULING WITH PIPELINED PROCESSORS. IEEE TRANSACTIONS ON COMPUTERS 29, 308-316. (1980).

BRUNE 1978 -1 BRUNO, J.; SETHI, R.
TASK SEQUENCING IN A BATCH ENVIRONMENT WITH SETUP TIMES. FOUNDATIONS OF CONTROL ENGINEERING 3, NO. 3, 105-117. (1978).

BRUNF 1970 -1 BRUNO, J.; WEINBERG, L.
PRINCIPAL PARTITION AND PRINCIPAL MINORS OF A MATROID, WITH APPLICATIONS. IN: A. GEWIRTZ, L. V. QUINTAS (EDS.): INTERNATIONAL CONFERENCE ON COMBINATORIAL MATHEMATICS, 49-65. ANNALS OF THE NEW YORK ACADEMY OF SCIENCES, VOLUME 165, ARTICLE 1. NEW YORK: THE NEW YORK ACADEMY OF SCIENCES. (1970).

BRUT 1969 -1 BRUTER, C.
SUR DIFFERENTS PROBLEMES POSES EN THEORIE DES MATROIDES. PUBLICATIONS DE L'INSTITUT DE STATISTIQUE DE L'UNIVERSITE DE PARIS 18, NO. 3, 1-96. (1969).

BRUY 1979 -1 BRUYNEEL, G.
SOME APPLICATIONS OF MINIMAL BALANCED SETS IN GRAPH THEORY. IN: W. OETTLI, F. STEFFENS (EDS.): OPERATIONS RESEARCH VERFAHREN 32, THIRD SYMPOSIUM ON OPERATIONS RESEARCH, MANNHEIM 1978, 55-61. KOENIGSTEIN: ANTON HAIN MEISENHEIM. (1979).

BRYA 1978 -1 BRYANT, V.; DAWSON, J. E.
DESIGNS AND CIRCUIT BASES. ARCHIV DER MATHEMATIK (BASEL) 30, 665-671. (1978).

BRYAA 1980 -1 BRYANT, V.; PERFECT, H.
INDEPENDENCE THEORY IN COMBINATORICS. AN INTRODUCTORY ACCOUNT WITH APPLICATIONS TO GRAPHS AND TRANSVERSALS. LONDON, NEW YORK: CHAPMAN AND HALL, 144 P. (1980). (CHAPMAN AND HALL MATHEMATICS SERIES)

BRYL 1975 -1 BRYLAWSKI, T.
AFFINE REPRESENTATION FOR TRANSVERSAL GEOMETRIES, AN. STUDIES IN APPLIED MATHEMATICS 54, NO. 2, 143-160. (1975).

BRYL 1977 -1 BRYLAWSKI, T.
THE BROKEN-CIRCUIT COMPLEX. TRANSACTIONS OF THE AMERICAN MATHEMATICAL SOCIETY 234, 417-433. (1977).

BRYL 1979 -1 BRYLAWSKI, T.
INTERSECTION THEORY FOR EMBEDDINGS OF MATROIDS INTO UNIFORM GEOMETRIES. STUDIES IN APPLIED MATHEMATICS 61, 211-244. (1979).

BRYLA 1978 -1 BRYLAWSKI, T.; KELLY, D. G.
MATROIDS AND COMBINATORIAL GEOMETRIES. IN: G.-C. ROTA (ED.): STUDIES IN COMBINATORICS, 179-217. MAA STUDIES IN MATHEMATICS 17. WASHINGTON (D. C.): MATHEMATICAL ASSOCIATION OF AMERICA. (1978).

BRYLA 1980 -1 BRYLAWSKI, T.; KELLY, D. G.
MATROIDS AND COMBINATORIAL GEOMETRIES. CHAPEL HILL: UNIV. OF NORTH CAROLINA, DEPT. OF MATHEMATICS, 149 P. (1980). (CAROLINA LECTURE SERIES)

BRYLB 1976 -1 BRYLAWSKI, T.; LUCAS, D.
UNIQUELY REPRESENTABLE COMBINATORIAL GEOMETRIES. IN: ACCADEMIA NAZIONALE DEI LINCEI (ED.): COLLOQUIO INTERNAZIONALE SULLE TEORIE COMBINATORIE CON LA COLLABORAZIONE DELLA AMERICAN MATHEMATICAL SOCIETY, TOMO I, ROMA 1973, 83-104. ROMA: ACCADEMIA NAZIONALE DEI LINCEI. (1976).

BRYLC 1980 -1 BRYLAWSKI, T.; OXLEY, J. G.
SEVERAL IDENTITIES FOR THE CHARACTERISTIC POLYNOMIAL OF A COMBINATORIAL GEOMETRY. DISCRETE MATHEMATICS 31, 161-170. (1980).

****

BRZE 1980 -1 BRZEZINSKI, J.
PREEMPTIVE SCHEDULING OF PROCESSORS WITH PRIVATE MEMORIES. FOUNDATIONS OF CONTROL ENGINEERING (POZNAN) 5, NO. 2, 55-69. (1980).

BUCC 1977 -1 BUCCI, G.; GOLINELLI, S.
DISTRIBUTED STRATEGY FOR RESOURCE ALLOCATION IN INFORMATION NETWORKS, A. IN: E. MORLET, D. RIBBENS (EDS.): INTERNATIONAL COMPUTING SYMPOSIUM 1977. PROCEEDINGS OF THE FIFTH SYMPOSIUM HELD AT LIEGE 1977, 345-356. AMSTERDAM, NEW YORK, OXFORD: NORTH-HOLLAND. (1977).

BUCK 1980 -1 BUCKINGHAM, M. A.
CIRCLE GRAPHS. DISSERTATION. NEW YORK: COURANT INSTITUTE OF MATHEMATICAL SCIENCES, 142 P. (1980).

BUCKA 1974 -1 BUCKLEY, D. J.
TRANSPORTATION AND TRAFFIC THEORY. NEW YORK, LONDON, AMSTERDAM: ELSEVIER, 816 P. (1974). (PROCEEDINGS OF THE SIXTH INTERNAT. SYMPOSIUM, SYDNEY, 1974)

BUCKA 1979 -1 BUCKLEY, D. J.
TRAFFIC ASSIGNMENT IN A TWO-DIMENSIONAL CONTINUOUS REPRESENTATION OF A TRAFFIC NETWORK WITH FLOW-DEPENDENT SPEEDS. TRANSPORTATION RESEARCH 13, SERIES B, 167-179. (1979).

BUCKB 1979 -1 BUCKLEY, F.; HOFFMAN, A. J.
ON THE MIXED ACHROMATIC NUMBER AND OTHER FUNCTIONS OF GRAPHS. IN: J. A. BONDY, U. P. R. MURTY (EDS.): GRAPH THEORY AND RELATED TOPICS, 105-119. NEW YORK, SAN FRANCISCO, LONDON: ACADEMIC PRESS. (1979).

BUHR 1978 -1 BUHR, J.
FOUR METHODS FOR MONTHLY CREW ASSIGNMENT - A COMPARISON OF EFFICIENCY -. VANCOUVER (18. AGIFORS SYMPOSIUM, SEPTEMBER 1978) 32 P. (1978).

BULF 1975 -1 BULFIN, R. L.
MAN-MACHINE TASK ALLOCATION PROBLEM WITH SEQUENCING CONSIDERATIONS, THE. DOCTORAL DISSERTATION. ATLANTA: GEORGIA INSTITUTE OF TECHNOLOGY, 145 P. (1975).

BULFA 1980 -1 BULFIN, R. L.; PARKER, R. G.
SCHEDULING JOBS ON TWO FACILITIES TO MINIMIZE MAKESPAN. MANAGEMENT SCIENCE 26, 202-214. (1980).

BULFB 1979 -1 BULFIN, R. L.; PARKER, R. G.; SHETTY, C. M.
COMPUTATIONAL RESULTS WITH A BRANCH-AND-BOUND ALGORITHM FOR THE GENERAL KNAPSACK PROBLEM. NAVAL RESEARCH LOGISTICS QUARTERLY 26, 41-46. (1979).

BULI 1978 -1 BULICHEV, S. F.; VOLCHENKOV, S. G.
OPTIMAL PLANE PACKINGS OF TREES (RUSSIAN). IN: HEURISTIC ALGORITHMS OF OPTIMIZATION, 36-68, JAROSLAV. GOS. UNIV., YAROSLAVL. (1978).

BULT 1976 -1 BULTEAU, R.
COLORATION DANS LES GRAPHES, MULTIGRAPHES ET HYPERGRAPHES. MONS: UNIVERSITE DE L'ETAT. (1976).

BURD 1972 -1 BURDET, C.-A.
ALGEBRA AND GEOMETRY OF INTEGER PROGRAMMING CUTS: A COMBINED APPROACH, THE. PITTSBURGH: CARNEGIE-MELLON UNIVERSITY, GRADUATE SCHOOL OF INDUSTRIAL ADMINISTRATION. (1972).

BURDA 1974 -1 BURDET, C.-A.; JOHNSON, E. L.
LINEARLY CONSTRAINED GROUP MINIMIZATION. TALK AT THE ORSA/TIMS MEETING IN SAN JUAN, OCTOBER 1974. (1974).

BURDB 1979 -1 BURDJUK, V. J.; DEINEKO, V. G.
SOLVABLE CASES OF THE TRAVELLING SALESMAN PROBLEM WITH SEVERAL SALESMEN (RUSSIAN). IN: THEORY OF OPTIMAL DECISIONS, 3-9, 108. KIEV: AKADEMIJA NAUK UKRAINSKOI SSR, INSTITUT KIBERNETIKI. (1979).

BURJ 1977 -1 BURJAN, S. B.; SEROV, S. S.; UZDEMIR, A. P.
METHOD FOR SOLVING THE PARAMETRIC PROBLEM OF FINDING CIRCULATION OF MINIMAL COST IN A NETWORK. AVTOMATIKA I TELEMEHANIKA, NO. 6, 73-84; TRANSLATED AS AUTOMATION AND REMOTE CONTROL 38, 1977, 834-844. (1977).

BURK 1975 -1 BURKARD, R. E.
KOMBINATORISCHE OPTIMIERUNG IN HALBGRUPPEN. IN: R. BULIRSCH, W. OETTLI, J. STOER (EDS.): OPTIMIZATION AND OPTIMAL CONTROL, 2-17. BERLIN, HEIDELBERG, NEW YORK: SPRINGER. (1975).

BURK 1978 -1 BURKARD, R. E.
GENERAL HUNGARIAN METHOD FOR THE ALGEBRAIC TRANSPORTATION PROBLEM, A. DISCRETE MATHEMATICS 22, 219-232. (1978).

BURK 1978 -2 BURKARD, R. E.
NUMERICAL INVESTIGATIONS ON QUADRATIC ASSIGNMENT PROBLEMS. NAVAL RESEARCH LOGISTICS QUARTERLY 25, 129-148. (1978).

BURK 1978 -3 BURKARD, R. E.
QUADRATIC ASSIGNMENT PROBLEMS: SUBOPTIMAL METHODS. URBINO: SUMMER SCHOOL IN COMBINATORIAL OPTIMIZATION, 28 P. (1978).

BURK 1979 -1 BURKARD, R. E.
ON THE USE OF ALGEBRAIC OBJECTIVE FUNCTIONS IN COMBINATORIAL PROGRAMMING. REPORT 79-3. KOELN: UNIV. KOELN, MATHEMATISCHES INSTITUT, 18 P. (1979).

BURK 1979 -2 BURKARD, R. E.
REMARKS ON SOME SCHEDULING PROBLEMS WITH ALGEBRAIC OBJECTIVE FUNCTIONS. IN: W. OETTLI, F. STEFFENS (EDS.): OPERATIONS RESEARCH VERFAHREN 32. THIRD SYMPOSIUM ON OPERATIONS RESEARCH, MANNHEIM 1978, 63-77. KOENIGSTEIN: ANTON HAIN MEISENHEIM. (1979).

BURK 1979 -3 BURKARD, R. E.
TRAVELLING SALESMAN AND ASSIGNMENT PROBLEMS: A SURVEY. IN: P. L. HAMMER, E. L. JOHNSON, B. H. KORTE (EDS.): DISCRETE OPTIMIZATION I, 193-215. ANNALS OF DISCRETE MATHEMATICS 4. AMSTERDAM, NEW YORK, OXFORD: NORTH-HOLLAND. (1979).

BURK 1979 -4 BURKARD, R. E.
UEBER EINE ANWENDUNG ALGEBRAISCHER TRANSPORTPROBLEME BEI REIHENFOLGEPROBLEMEN. IN: L. COLLATZ, G. MEINARDUS, W. WETTERLING (EDS.): NUMERISCHE METHODEN BEI GRAPHENTHEORETISCHEN UND KOMBINATORISCHEN PROBLEMEN, BAND 2, OBERWOLFACH 1978, 22-36. ISNM 46. BASEL, BOSTON, STUTTGART: BIRKHAEUSER. (1979).

BURK 1980 -1 BURKARD, R. E.
SUBGRADIENT METHODS IN COMBINATORIAL OPTIMIZATION. IN: U. PAPE (ED.): DISCRETE STRUCTURES AND ALGORITHMS, 141-152. MUENCHEN: HANSER. (1980).

BURKA 1980 -1 BURKARD, R. E.; DERIGS, U.
ASSIGNMENT AND MATCHING PROBLEMS: SOLUTION METHODS WITH FORTRAN-PROGRAMS. BERLIN, HEIDELBERG, NEW YORK: SPRINGER, 148 P. (1980). (LECTURE NOTES IN ECONOMICS AND MATHEMATICAL SYSTEMS, 184)

BURKB 1981 -1 BURKARD, R. E.; FINCKE, U.
ON RANDOM QUADRATIC BOTTLENECK ASSIGNMENT PROBLEMS. RESEARCH REPORT 81-2. KOELN: UNIV. ZU KOELN, MATHEMATISCHES INST., 7 P. (1981).

BURKC 1978 -1 BURKARD, R. E.; FROEHLICH, K.
SOME REMARKS ON 3-DIMENSIONAL ASSIGNMENT PROBLEMS (EXTENDED ABSTRACT). KOELN: UNIV. KOELN, MATHEMATISCHES INSTITUT, 5 P. (1978).

BURKD 1981 -1 BURKARD, R. E.; HAMACHER, H.
MINIMAL COST FLOWS IN REGULAR MATROIDS. IN: H. KOENIG, B. KORTE, K. RITTER (EDS.): MATHEMATICAL PROGRAMMING AT OBERWOLFACH, 32-47. MATHEMATICAL PROGRAMMING STUDY 14. (1981).

BURKE 1981 -1 BURKARD, R. E.; HAMACHER, H.; TIND, J.
ON ABSTRACT DUALITY IN MATHEMATICAL PROGRAMMING. RESEARCH REPORT 81-4. KOELN: UNIV. ZU KOELN, MATHEMATISCHES INST., 22 P. (1981).

BURKF 1980 -1 BURKARD, R. E.; HAMMER, P. L.
NOTE ON HAMILTONIAN SPLIT GRAPHS, A. JOURNAL OF COMBINATORIAL THEORY 28, SERIES B, 245-248. (1980).

BURKG 1980 -1 BURKARD, R. E.; KEIDING, H.; KRARUP, J.; PRUZAN, P. M.
RELATIONSHIP BETWEEN OPTIMALITY AND EFFICIENCY IN MULTICRITERIA 0-1 PROGRAMMING PROBLEMS, A. RESEARCH REPORT 80-10. KOELN: UNIV. ZU KOELN, MATHEMATISCHES INST., 10 P. (1980).

BURKH 1980 -1 BURKARD, R. E.; KRARUP, J.; PRUZAN, P. M.
EFFICIENCY AND OPTIMALITY IN MINISUM, MINIMAX 0-1 PROGRAMMING PROBLEMS. RESEARCH REPORT 80-9. KOELN: UNIV. ZU KOELN, MATHEMATISCHES INST., 26 P. (1980).

BURKI 1979 -1 BURKARD, R. E.; NEWGER, E.
OPTIMALE ROHHOLZAUSFORMUNG. 86/2. GRAZ: RECHENZENTRUM GRAZ, 156 P. (1979).

BURKJ 1980 -1 BURKARD, R. E.; ZIMMERMANN, U.
COMBINATORIAL OPTIMIZATION IN LINEARLY ORDERED SEMIMODULES: A SURVEY. RESEARCH REPORT 80-12. KOELN: UNIV. ZU KOELN, MATHEMATISCHES INST., 58 P. (1980).

BURKJ 1980 -2 BURKARD, R. E.; ZIMMERMANN, U.
WEAKLY ADMISSIBLE TRANSFORMATIONS FOR SOLVING ALGEBRAIC ASSIGNMENT AND TRANSPORTATION PROBLEMS. MATHEMATICAL PROGRAMMING STUDY 12, 1-18. (1980).

BURL 1980 -1 BURLET, M.; UHRY, J.-P.
PARITY GRAPHS. RESEARCH REPORT. GRENOBLE: UNIVERSITE SCIENTIFIQUE ET MEDICALE DE GRENOBLE, 43 P. (1980).

BURM 1976 -1 BURMAN, D.
OPERATOR SCHEDULING SYSTEM, AN. PHILADELPHIA (49. ORSA-MEETING + TIMS, MARCH/APRIL 1976) 16 P. (1976).

BURN 1978 -1 BURNESS, G. C.; MILLER, D. M.
LOCATION OF CRASH FIRE FIGHTING FACILITIES AT AIRPORTS. PITTSBURGH: U.S. STEEL CORP. 18 P. (1978).

BURNA 1978 -1 BURNS, F.; ROOKER, J.
THREE-STAGE FLOW-SHOPS WITH RECESSIVE SECOND STAGE. OPERATIONS RESEARCH 26, 207-208. (1978).

BURNB 1978 -1 BURNS, R. N.
MANPOWER SCHEDULING WITH VARIABLE DEMANDS AND ALTERNATE WEEKENDS OFF. INFOR 16, 101-111. (1978).

BURO 1979 -1 BUROSCH, G.; DREWS, K.-D.
UEBER DIE UNABHAENGIGKEITSZAHL UND ZERLEGUNGSZAHL EINES GRAPHEN. ROSTOCKER MATHEMATISCHES KOLLOQUIUM, NO. 11, 13-24. (1979).

BURR 1976 -1 BURR, S. A.; ERDOES, P.
EXTREMAL RAMSEY THEORY FOR GRAPHS. UTILITAS MATHEMATICA 9, 247-258. (1976).

BURS 1979 -1 BURSCHEID, H. J.
ZUR VORGABE GERICHTETER KANTEN VON VERGLEICHBARKEITSGRAPHEN. MATHEMATISCHE NACHRICHTEN 91, 321-325. (1979).

BURSA 1976 -1 BURSHTEJN, M. I.
CHROMATIC NUMBER OF PLANAR HYPERGRAPHS (RUSSIAN), THE. SAKHARTHVELOS SSR MECNIEREBATHA AKADEMII MOAMBE 84, 45-48. (1976).

BURSA 1979 -1 BURSHTEJN, M. I.
EVERY 4-VALENT GRAPH HAS AN ACYCLIC 5-COLORING (RUSSIAN). SOOBSCENIJA AKADEMII NAUK GRUZINSKOI SSR 93, 21-24. (1979).

BURSA 1979 -2 BURSHTEJN, M. I.
NOTE ON EDGE-COLORING OF TRIVALENT GRAPHS (RUSSIAN), A. SOOBSHCHENIJA AKADEMII NAUK GRUZINSKOI SSR (TBILISI) 94, 277-280. (1979).

BUSO 1978 -1 BUSOLINI, D. T.
ON A PROBLEM OF C. C. CHEN AND D. E. DAYKIN. JOURNAL OF COMBINATORIAL THEORY 24, SERIES B, 286-289. (1978).

BUSO 1978 -2 BUSOLINI, D. T.
2 COLORED TRIANGLES IN EDGE COLORED COMPLETE GRAPHS. JOURNAL OF COMBINATORIAL THEORY 24, SERIES B, 365-366. (1978).

BUTA 1975 -1 BUTAN, E. I.; NECVAL, N. A.
ALGORITHMS FOR THE OPERATIONAL CONTROL OF ARRIVAL FLOWS IN A TRANSPORTATION NETWORK (RUSSIAN). UPRAVLENIE SLOZN. SISKMAMI VYP. 2, 116-125. (1975).

BUTZ 1980 -1 BUTZ, L.
CHARACTERIZATIONS OF CONNECTIVITY IN ROW COLUMN DESIGNS. REPORT NO. 80153-OR. BONN: UNIV. BONN, INST. FUER OEKONOMETRIE UND OPERATIONS RESEARCH, 19 P. (1980).

BUTZ 1981 -1 BUTZ, L.
UEBER DIE ZUSAMMENHANGSEIGENSCHAFT IN VERSUCHSPLAENEN MIT MEHRFACHER BLOCKBILDUNG: EINE KOMBINATORISCHE ANALYSE. RESEARCH REPORT NO. 81178-OR. BONN: UNIV. OF BONN, INSTITUT FUER OEKONOMETRIE UND OPERATIONS RESEARCH, 209 P. (1981).

BUTZ 1982 -1 BUTZ, L.
CONNECTIVITY IN MULTI-FACTOR DESIGNS: A COMBINATORIAL APPROACH. BERLIN: HELDERMANN VERLAG (SERIES: RESEARCH AND EDUCATION IN MATHEMATICS). (1982).

BUZY 1978 -1 BUZYCKII, P. L.; VOTJAKOV, A. A.
ALGORITHMIC CRITERION OF OPTIMALITY IN INTEGER PROGRAMMING, AN. IZVESTIJA AKADEMII NAUK SSSR. TEHNICESKAJA KIBERNETIKA, NO. 4, 15-23; TRANSLATED AS ENGINEERING CYBERNETICS 16, 1978, 10-17. (1978).

CABO 1977 -1 CABOT, A. V.; HARNETT, D. L.
INTRODUCTION TO MANAGMENT SCIENCE, AN. READING, AMSTERDAM U.A.: ADDISON-WESLEY, 524 P. (1977).

CAHI 1978 -1 CAHIT, I.; CAHIT, R.
TRANSFORMATIONS ON SPANNING TREES. JOURNAL OF THE INSTITUTE OF MATHEMATICS AND ITS APPLICATIONS 21, 353-358. (1978).

CAIE 1978 -1 CAIE, J.; LINDEN, J.; MAXWELL, W.
SOLUTION OF A MACHINE LOAD PLANNING PROBLEM. TECHNICAL REPORT, 396. ITHACA: CORNELL UNIV., COLLEGE OF ENGINEERING, 13 P. (1978).

CAIE 1980 -1 CAIE, J.; LINDEN, J.; MAXWELL, W.
SOLUTION OF A SINGLE STAGE MACHINE LOAD PLANNING PROBLEM. OMEGA 8, 355-360. (1980).

CAIEA 1979 -1 CAIE, J.; LINDEN, J.; OATS, Q.; MAXWELL, W.
HIERARCHICAL MACHINE LOAD PLANNING. TECHNICAL REPORT, 416. ITHACA: CORNELL UNIV., COLLEGE OF ENGINEERING, 22 P. (1979).

CALA 1980 -1 CALAMAI, P.; CHARALAMBOUS, C.
SOLVING MULTIFACILITY LOCATION PROBLEMS INVOLVING EUCLIDEAN DISTANCES. NAVAL RESEARCH LOGISTICS QUARTERLY 27, 609-620. (1980).

CALV 1980 -1 CALVILLO, G.
CONCAVITY AND INTERSECTION PROPERTIES FOR INTEGRAL POLYHEDRA, THE. IN: M. DEZA, I. G. ROSENBERG (EDS.): COMBINATORICS 79, PART I, 221-228. ANNALS OF DISCRETE MATHEMATICS 8. AMSTERDAM: NORTH-HOLLAND. (1980).

CAME 1978 -1 CAMERINI, P. M.
MIN-MAX SPANNING TREE PROBLEM AND SOME EXTENSIONS, THE. INFORMATION PROCESSING LETTERS 7, 10-14. (1978).

CAMEA 1975 -1 CAMERINI, P. M.; FRATTA, L.; MAFFIOLI, F.
TRAVELLING SALESMAN PROBLEM: HEURISTICALLY GUIDED SEARCH AND MODIFIED GRADIENT TECHNIQUES. REPORT. MILANO: POLITECNICO DI MILANO, INSTITUTO DI ELETTRONICA. (1975).

CAMEA 1979 -1 CAMERINI, P. M.; FRATTA, L.; MAFFIOLI, F.
NOTE ON FINDING OPTIMUM BRANCHINGS, A. NETWORKS 9, 309-312. (1979).

CAMEA 1980 -1 CAMERINI, P. M.; FRATTA, L.; MAFFIOLI, F.
K BEST SPANNING ARBORESCENCES OF A NETWORK, THE. NETWORKS 10, 91-109. (1980).

CAMEA 1980 -2 CAMERINI, P. M.; FRATTA, L.; MAFFIOLI, F.
RANKING ARBORESCENCES IN O(KM LOG N) TIME. EUROPEAN JOURNAL OF OPERATIONAL RESEARCH 4, 235-242. (1980).

CAMEB 1980 -1 CAMERINI, P. M.; GALBIATI, G.; MAFFIOLI, F.
COMPLEXITY OF SPANNING TREE PROBLEMS: PART I. EUROPEAN JOURNAL OF OPERATIONAL RESEARCH 5, 346-352. (1980).

CAMEC 1978 -1 CAMERINI, P. M.; MAFFIOLI, F.
EXACT AND HEURISTIC METHODS FOR NP-HARD MATROID PROBLEMS. IN: J.-C. BERMOND ET AL. (EDS.): PROBLEMES COMBINATOIRES ET THEORIE DES GRAPHES. COLLOQUES INTERNATIONAUX DU CENTRE NATIONAL DE LA RECHERCHE SCIENTIFIQUE, ORSAY 1976, 71-72. PARIS: CENTRE NATIONAL DE LA RECHERCHE SCIENTIFIQUE. (1978).

CAMEC 1978 -2 CAMERINI, P. M.; MAFFIOLI, F.
HEURISTICALLY GUIDED ALGORITHM FOR K-PARITY MATROID PROBLEMS. DISCRETE MATHEMATICS 21, 103-116. (1978).

CAMEC 1979 -1 CAMERINI, P. M.; MAFFIOLI, F.
POLYNOMIAL BOUNDING FOR NP-HARD PROBLEMS. IN: A. PREKOPA (ED.): SURVEY OF MATHEMATICAL PROGRAMMING, VOLUME 2, 319-324. AMSTERDAM: NORTH-HOLLAND. (1979).

CAMEC 1980 -1 CAMERINI, P. M.; MAFFIOLI, F.
POLYNOMIAL BOUNDING FOR NP-HARD PROBLEMS. MATHEMATICAL PROGRAMMING STUDY 12, 115-119. (1980).

CAMEC 1980 -2 CAMERINI, P. M.; MAFFIOLI, F.
WEIGHTED SATISFIABILITY PROBLEMS AND SOME IMPLICATIONS. IN: K. IRACKI, K. MALANOWSKI, P. WALUKIEWICZ (EDS.): OPTIMIZATION TECHNIQUES, PART II, 170-175. LECTURE NOTES IN CONTROL AND INFORMATION SCIENCES 23. BERLIN: SPRINGER. (1980).

CAMED 1979 -1 CAMERON, K.; EDMONDS, J.
ALGORITHMS FOR OPTIMUM ANTICHAINS. IN: F. HOFFMAN, D. MAC CARTHY, R. C. MULLIN, R. G. STANTON (EDS.): PROCEEDINGS OF THE TENTH SOUTHEASTERN CONFERENCE ON COMBINATORICS, GRAPH THEORY AND COMPUTING, 229-240. CONGRESSUS NUMERANTIUM XXIII. WINNIPEG: UTILITAS. (1979).

CAMEE 1975 -1 CAMERON, P. J.
ON GROUPS OF DEGREE N AND N-1, AND HIGHLY SYMMETRIC EDGE COLOURINGS. THE JOURNAL OF THE LONDON MATHEMATICAL SOCIETY 9, 385-391. (1975).

CAMI 1975 -1 CAMION, P.
HAMILTONIAN CHAINS IN SELF COMPLEMENTARY GRAPHS. CAHIERS DU CENTRE D'ETUDES DE RECHERCHE OPERATIONELLE 17, 173-184. (1975).

CANI 1978 -1 CANI, P. DE
NOTE ON THE TWO-DIMENSIONAL RECTANGULAR CUTTING-STOCK PROBLEM, A. THE JOURNAL OF THE OPERATIONAL RESEARCH SOCIETY 29, 703-706. (1978).

CARL 1976 -1 CARLITZ, L.
SET PARTITIONS. FIBONACCI QUARTERLY 14, 327-342. (1976).

CARLA 1979 -1 CARLSON, R. C.; JUCKER, J. V.; KROPP, D. H.
LESS NERVOUS MRP SYSTEMS: A DYNAMIC ECONOMIC LOT-SIZING APPROACH. MANAGEMENT SCIENCE 25, 754-761. (1979).

CARLB 1979 -1 CARLSON, R. C.; SHUKLA, P. R.
ROBUSTNESS OF THE INTERACTIVE ALGORITHM FOR MULTICRITERION ZERO-ONE VARIABLE PROBLEMS UNDER PROBABILISTIC TRADEOFFS. TECHNICAL REPORT, 79-3. STANFORD: STANFORD UNIV., DEPT. OF INDUSTRIAL ENGINEERING AND ENGINEERING MANAGEMENT, 14 P. (1979).

CARLC 1979 -1 CARLSON, R. C.; SHUKLA, P. R.; BAUM, S.
INTERACTIVE SOLUTION OF DISCRETE MULTICRITERION PROBLEMS: AN ALGORITHM AND COMPUTATIONAL RESULTS FOR THE BINARY VARIABLE CASE. TECHNICAL REPORT NO. 79-2. STANFORD: STANFORD UNIV., DEPT. OF INDUSTRIAL ENGINEERING AND ENGINEERING MANAGEMENT, 24 P. (1979).

CARN 1978 -1 CARNEIRO RIBEIRO, C. DA C.; MACULAN, N.
NETWORK EXPANSION PROBLEM, A. RIO DE JANEIRO: UNIV. FEDERAL DO RIO DE JANEIRO, 13 P. (1978).

CARP 1977 -1 CARPANETO, G.; TOTH, P.
NEW ALGORITHM FOR THE TRAVELLING SALESMAN PROBLEM WITH DUEDATES, A. IN: M. ROUBENS (ED.): ADVANCES IN OPERATIONS RESEARCH, PROCEEDINGS OF EURO II, THE SECOND EUROPEAN CONGRESS ON OPERATIONS RESEARCH, STOCKHOLM 1976, 95-102. AMSTERDAM, NEW YORK, OXFORD: NORTH-HOLLAND. (1977).

CARR 1979 -1 CARRE, B.
GRAPHS AND NETWORKS. OXFORD: CLARENDON PRESS, 277 P. (1979). (OXFORD APPLIED MATHEMATICS AND COMPUTING SCIENCE SERIES)

CART 1979 -1 CARTER, M. W.
FINAL EXAMINATION SCHEDULING FOR CORRESPONDENCE STUDENTS. RESEARCH REPORT CORR 79-7. WATERLOO: UNIV. OF WATERLOO, DEPT. OF COMBINATORICS AND OPTIMIZATION, 17 P. (1979).

CART 1980 -1 CARTER, M. W.
INDEFINITE ZERO-ONE QUADRATIC PROBLEM, THE. RESEARCH REPORT CORR 80-25. WATERLOO: FACULTY OF MATHEMATICS, 50 P. (1980).

CARTA 1978 -1 CARTER, P. L.; REMUS, W. E.; JENICKE, L. O.
PRODUCTION SCHEDULING DECISION RULES IN CHANGING AND NON-LINEAR ENVIRONMENTS. INTERNATIONAL JOURNAL OF PRODUCTION RESEARCH 16, 493-496. (1978).

CAST 1972 -1 CASTAGNA, F.; PRINS, G.
EVERY GENERALISED PETERSEN GRAPH HAS A TAIT COLOURING. PACIFIC JOURNAL OF MATHEMATICS 40, 53-58. (1972).

CASTA 1975 -1 CASTELLANI, G.
EXPLICIT SOLUTION FOR A CLASS OF ALLOCATION PROBLEMS. IN: G. LEITMANN, A. MARZOLLO (EDS.): MULTICRITERIA DECISION MAKING, 351-386. VIENNA: SPRINGER. (1975).

CASTB 1979 -1 CASTELLANI, G.; GIANNESSI, F.
DECOMPOSITION OF MATHEMATICAL PROGRAMS BY MEANS OF THEOREMS OF ALTERNATIVE FOR LINEAR AND NONLINEAR SYSTEMS. IN: A. PREKOPA (ED.): SURVEY OF MATHEMATICAL PROGRAMMING, VOLUME 2, 423-440. AMSTERDAM: NORTH-HOLLAND. (1979).

CATL 1978 -1 CATLIN, P. A.
ANOTHER BOUND ON THE CHROMATIC NUMBER OF A GRAPH. DISCRETE MATHEMATICS 24, 1-6. (1978).

CATL 1978 -2 CATLIN, P. A.
BOUND ON THE CHROMATIC NUMBER OF A GRAPH, A. DISCRETE MATHEMATICS 22, 81-84. (1978).

CATL 1979 -1 CATLIN, P. A.
BROOKS' GRAPH-COLORING THEOREM AND THE INDEPENDENCE NUMBER. JOURNAL OF COMBINATORIAL THEORY 27, SERIES B, 42-48. (1979).

****

CATL 1979 -2 CATLIN, P. A.
HAJOS' GRAPH-COLORING CONJECTURE: VARIATIONS AND COUNTEREXAMPLES. JOURNAL OF COMBINATORIAL THEORY 26, SERIES B, 268-274. (1979).

CATL 1979 -3 CATLIN, P. A.
SUBGRAPHS WITH TRIANGULAR COMPONENTS. DISCRETE MATHEMATICS 27, 149-170. (1979).

CATL 1979 -4 CATLIN, P. A.
SURVEY OF EXTENSIONS OF BROOKS' GRAPH COLORING THEOREM. IN: F. HARARY (ED.): TOPICS IN GRAPH THEORY. ANNALS OF THE NEW YORK ACADEMY OF SCIENCES 328, 95-99. NEW YORK: THE NEW YORK ACADEMY OF SCIENCES. (1979).

CAVA 1975 -1 CAVANAGH, R. A.
AIRLINE CREW SCHEDULING. PRESENTED AT XII TIMS INTERNATIONAL MEETING, KYOTO 1975. (1975).

CAZA 1978 -1 CAZANESCU, V.-E.; RUDEANU, S.
INDEPENDENT SETS AND KERNELS IN GRAPHS AND HYPERGRAPHS. UNIV. NATION. ZAIRE, ANN. FAC. SCI., MATH.-PHYS. 4, 37-66. (1978).

CHAC 1979 -1 CHACHRA, V.; GHARE, P. M.; MOORE, J. M.
APPLICATIONS OF GRAPH THEORY ALGORITHMS. NEW YORK, OXFORD: NORTH-HOLLAND, 421 P. (1979).

CHAI 1978 -1 CHAIKEN, J. M.; DORMONT, P.
PATROL CAR ALLOCATION MODEL: BACKGROUND, A. MANAGEMENT SCIENCE 24, 1280-1290. (1978).

CHAI 1978 -2 CHAIKEN, J. M.; DORMONT, P.
PATROL CAR ALLOCATION MODEL: CAPABILITIES AND ALGORITHMS, A. MANAGEMENT SCIENCE 24, 1291-1300. (1978).

CHAL 1977 -1 CHALKOV, V. D.
EFFECTIVE APPROXIMATE ALGORITHM FOR THE SOLUTION OF THE TRAVELLING SALESMAN PROBLEM (BULGARIAN), AN. GODISNIK NA VISSITE UCEBNI ZAVEDENIJA. PRILOZNA MATEMATIKA (SOFIA) 11, NO. 4, 177-189. (1977).

CHAL 1978 -1 CHALKOV, V. D.
APPROXIMATE ALGORITHM FOR SOLVING THE TRAVELLING SALESMAN PROBLEM WITH GROUPED POINTS (BULGARIAN). GODISNIK NA VISSITE UCEBNI ZAVEDENIJA, PRILOZNA MATEMATIKA (SOFIA) 14, NO. 4, 73-80. (1978).

CHALA 1981 -1 CHALMET, L. G.; FRANCIS, R. L.; KOLEN, A.
FINDING EFFICIENT SOLUTIONS FOR RECTILINEAR DISTANCE LOCATION PROBLEMS EFFICIENTLY. EUROPEAN JOURNAL OF OPERATIONAL RESEARCH 6, 117-124. (1981).

CHALB 1977 -1 CHALMET, L. G.; GELDERS, L. F.
LAGRANGIAN RELAXATIONS FOR A GENERALIZED ASSIGNMENT-TYPE PROBLEM. IN: M. ROUBENS (ED.): ADVANCES IN OPERATIONS RESEARCH, PROCEEDINGS OF EURO II, THE SECOND EUROPEAN CONGRESS ON OPERATIONS RESEARCH, STOCKHOLM 1976, 103-110. AMSTERDAM, NEW YORK, OXFORD: NORTH-HOLLAND. (1977).

CHALC 1981 -1 CHALMET, L. G.; LAWPHONGPANICH, S.
EFFICIENT SOLUTIONS FOR POINT-OBJECTIVE DISCRETE FACILITY LOCATION PROBLEMS. IN: J. N. MORSE (ED.): ORGANIZATIONS: MULTIPLE AGENTS WITH MULTIPLE CRITERIA, 56-71. LECTURE NOTES IN ECONOMICS AND MATHEMATICAL SYSTEMS 190. BERLIN: SPRINGER. (1981).

CHAM 1979 -1 CHAMBER, M. T.
MINIMAL CUTSETS FROM UNDIRECTED NETWORK DUALS. MILWAUKEE (ORSA/TIMS MEETING, OCTOBER 1979) 13 P. (1979).

CHAN 1979 -1 CHAN, A. W.; FRANCIS, R. L.
SOME LAYOUT PROBLEMS ON THE LINE WITH INTERDISTANCE CONSTRAINTS AND COSTS. OPERATIONS RESEARCH 27, 952-971. (1979).

CHANA 1979 -1 CHANDRA, A.; VRAT, P.
INVESTIGATIONS ON SINGLE FACILITY LOCATION PROBLEM WITH MIXED MODE OF TRAVEL. JOURNAL OF THE INDIAN INSTITUTE OF ENGINEERS, MECHANICAL ENGINEERING DIVISION 60, NO. 2, 41-46. (1979).

CHANB 1978 -1 CHANDRA, A. K.; HIRSCHBERG, D. S.; WONG, C. K.
BIN PACKING WITH GEOMETRIC CONSTRAINTS IN COMPUTER NETWORK DESIGN. OPERATIONS RESEARCH 26, 760-772. (1978).

CHANC 1978 -1 CHANDRA, A. K.; MARKOWSKY, G.
ON THE NUMBER OF PRIME IMPLICANTS. DISCRETE MATHEMATICS 24, 7-11. (1978).

CHAND 1979 -1 CHANDRA, S.; CHANDRAMOHAN, M.
DUALITY IN MIXED INTEGER NONCONVEX AND NONDIFFERENTIABLE PROGRAMMING. ZEITSCHRIFT FUER ANGEWANDTE MATHEMATIK UND MECHANIK 59, 205-209. (1979).

CHAND 1979 -2 CHANDRA, S.; CHANDRAMOHAN, M.
IMPROVED BRANCH AND BOUND METHOD FOR MIXED INTEGER LINEAR FRACTIONAL PROGRAMS, AN. ZEITSCHRIFT FUER ANGEWANDTE MATHEMATIK UND MECHANIK 59, 575-577. (1979).

CHAND 1980 -1 CHANDRA, S.; CHANDRAMOHAN, M.
ALL INTEGER METHOD FOR INTEGER CONVEX PROGRAMS, AN. MATHEMATISCHE OPERATIONSFORSCHUNG UND STATISTIK 11, SERIES OPTIMIZATION, 85-93. (1980).

CHAND 1980 -2 CHANDRA, S.; CHANDRAMOHAN, M.
NOTE ON INTEGER LINEAR FRACTIONAL PROGRAMMING, A. NAVAL RESEARCH LOGISTICS QUARTERLY 27, 171-174. (1980).

CHANE 1981 -1 CHANDRASEKARAN, R.; ANEJA, Y. P.; NAIR, K. P. K.
MINIMAL COST-RELIABILITY RATIO SPANNING TREE. RESEARCH REPORT. RICHARDSON, TEXAS: UNIV. OF TEXAS AT DALLAS, SCHOOL OF ADMINISTRATION AND MANAGEMENT, 13 P. (1981).

CHANF 1978 -1 CHANDRASEKARAN, R.; DAUGHETY, A.
PROBLEMS OF LOCATION ON TREES. DISCUSSION PAPER NO. 357. EVANSTON: NORTHWESTERN UNIV., CENTER FOR MATHEMATICAL STUDIES IN ECONOMICS AND MANAGMENT SCIENCE, 23 P. (1978).

CHANF 1981 -1 CHANDRASEKARAN, R.; DAUGHETY, A.
LOCATION ON TREE NETWORKS: P-CENTRE AND N-DISPERSION PROBLEMS. MATHEMATICS OF OPERATIONS RESEARCH 6, 50-57. (1981).

CHANG 1980 -1 CHANDRASEKARAN, R.; PACCA, M. J. A. P.
WEIGHTED MIN-MAX LOCATION PROBLEMS: POLYNOMIALLY BOUNDED ALGORITHMS. OPSEARCH 17, 172-180. (1980).

CHANH 1978 -1 CHANDRASEKARAN, R.; TAMIR, A.
POLYNOMIALLY BOUNDED ALGORITHMS FOR LOCATING P-CENTERS ON A TREE. DISCUSSION PAPER NO. 358. EVANSTON: NORTHWESTERN UNIV., CENTER FOR MATHEMATICAL STUDIES IN ECONOMICS AND MANAGMENT SCIENCE, 19 P. (1978).

CHANH 1980 -1 CHANDRASEKARAN, R.; TAMIR, A.
O((N LOG P)**2) ALGORITHM FOR THE CONTINUOUS P-CENTER PROBLEM ON A TREE, AN. SIAM JOURNAL ON ALGEBRAIC AND DISCRETE METHODS 1, 370-375. (1980).

CHANI 1978 -1 CHANG, Q. L.
PROBLEM OF SCHEDULING PRODUCTION SO AS TO MINIMIZE LATE DELIVERIES (CHINESE), THE. KNOWLEDGE AND PRACTICE OF MATHEMATICS, NO. 2, 47-49. (1978).

CHAO 1979 -1 CHAO, C. Y.; WHITEHEAD, E. G. JR.
CHROMATICITY OF SELF-COMPLEMENTARY GRAPHS. ARCHIV DER MATHEMATIK (BASEL) 32, 295-304. (1979).

CHAR 1961 -1 CHARNES, A.; COOPER, W. W.
MULTICOPY TRAFFIC NETWORK MODELS. IN: R. HERMAN (ED.): THEORY OF TRAFFIC FLOW, 85-96. AMSTERDAM: ELSEVIER. (1961).

CHARA 1977 -1 CHARNES, A.; COOPER, W. W.; LEWIS, K. A.; NELSON, A.; NIEHAUS, R. J.
NONLINEAR GOAL-ARC NETWORK EXTENSION OF THE MULTI-LEVEL COHERENCE MODEL FOR EEO, A. RESEARCH REPORT CCS 296. AUSTIN: UNIV. OF TEXAS, CENTER FOR CYBERNETIC STUDIES, 29 P. (1977).

CHARB 1978 -1 CHARNES, A.; DUFFA, S.; RYAN, M. J.
DEGENERACY AND THE MORE-FOR-LESS PARADOX. RESEARCH REPORT CCS 325. AUSTIN: UNIV. OF TEXAS, CENTER FOR CYBERNETIC STUDIES, 7 P. (1978).

CHARC 1977 -1 CHARTRAND, G.
GRAPHS AS MATHEMATICAL MODELS. BOSTON: PRINDLE, WEBER & SCHMIDT, 294 P. (1977).

CHARD 1969 -1 CHARTRAND, G.; FRECHEN, J. B.
ON THE CHROMATIC NUMBER OF PERMUTATION GRAPHS. IN: F. HARARY (ED.): PROOF TECHNIQUES IN GRAPH THEORY, 21-24. NEW YORK: ACADEMIC PRESS. (1969).

CHARE 1979 -1 CHARTRAND, G.; GOULD, R. J.; KAPOOR, S. F.
ON HOMOGENEOUSLY TRACEABLE NONHAMILTONIAN GRAPHS. IN: A. GEWIRTZ, L. V. QUINTAS (EDS.): SECOND INTERNATIONAL CONFERENCE ON COMBINATORIAL MATHEMATICS, 130-135. ANNALS OF THE NEW YORK ACADEMY OF SCIENCES, VOLUME 319. NEW YORK: THE NEW YORK ACADEMY OF SCIENCES. (1979).

CHARF 1979 -1 CHARTRAND, G.; GOULD, R. J.; POLIMENI, A. D.
NOTE ON LOCALLY CONNECTED AND HAMILTONIAN-CONNECTED GRAPHS, A. ISRAEL JOURNAL OF MATHEMATICS 33, 5-8. (1979).

CHAT 1979 -1 CHATY, G.; CHEIN, M.
ORDERED MATCHING AND MATCHINGS WITHOUT ALTERNATING CYCLES IN BIPARTITE GRAPHS. UTILITAS MATHEMATICA 16, 183-187. (1979).

CHEB 1976 -1 CHEBOTAREV, A. S.; SAFRANSKII, V. V.
PROBLEM OF SCHEDULING A COMPLEX OF PERFORMANCES THAT IS REPRESENTED BY A RESOURCE NETWORK MODEL OF SPECIAL FORM (RUSSIAN), THE. IN: G. P. POSPELOV (ED.): THE PROGRAMMED METHOD OF CONTROL (RUSSIAN), NO. 3, 19-28. MOSCOW: AKADEMIJA NAUK SSSR. (1976).

CHEL 1976 -1 CHELNOKOV, V. M.
GRAPHS WITH AN EXTREMAL NUMBER OF TREES, HAMILTONIAN CYCLES AND CIRCUITS (RUSSIAN). IN: STUDIES IN DISCRETE OPTIMIZATION (RUSSIAN), 424-443. MOSCOW: IZDAT. "NAUKA". (1976).

CHEN 1979 -1 CHEN, C. C.
ON THE STRUCTURE OF COMPLETE GRAPHS WITHOUT ALTERNATING CYCLES. DISCRETE MATHEMATICS 28, 1-5. (1979).

CHENA 1978 -1 CHEN, D.-S.
SIMPLE ALGORITHM FOR A WORKFORCE SCHEDULING MODEL, A. AIIE TRANSACTIONS 10, 244-251. (1978).

CHENB 1979 -1 CHEN, I.-N.; CHEN, P. Y.; FENG, T.
ASSOCIATIVE PROCESSING OF NETWORK FLOW PROBLEMS. INSTITUTE OF ELECTRICAL AND ELECTRONICS ENGINEERS. TRANSACTIONS ON COMPUTERS 28, 184-190. (1979).

CHENC 1976 -1 CHEN, K.-Y.
NETWORK APPROACH TO THE CAPACITATED LOT-SIZE PROBLEM, A. UNPUBLISHED MANUSCRIPT. PHILADELPHIA: UNIVERSITY OF PENNSYLVANIA, THE WHARTON SCHOOL. (1976).

CHEND 1975 -1 CHEN, N.-F.
ANALYSIS OF SCHEDULING ALGORITHMS IN MULTIPROCESSOR COMPUTING SYSTEMS, AN. DOCTORAL DISSERTATION. URBANA-CHAMPAIGN: UNIVERSITY OF ILLINOIS, 74 P. (1975).

CHENE 1978 -1 CHEN, R.; CROWDER, H. P.; JOHNSON, E. L.
SOLVING THE INSTALLATION SCHEDULING PROBLEM USING MIXED INTEGER LINEAR PROGRAMMING. IBM SYSTEMS JOURNAL 17, NO. 1, 82-91. (1978).

CHENF 1973 -1 CHEN, Y. H.
MATHEMATICAL MODELING OF WATER AND SEDIMENT ROUTING IN NATURAL CHANNELS. PH. D. DISSERTATION. FORT COLLINS: COLORADO STATE UNIVERSITY. (1973).

CHER 1979 -1 CHERENKOV, A. P.
INTEGRAL RESOURCE ALLOCATION PROBLEM (RUSSIAN), AN. AKADEMIJA NAUK SSSR. ZURNAL VYCISLITEL'NOI MATEMATIKI I MATEMATICESKOI FIZIKI 19, 776-779 + 800. (1979).

CHERA 1977 -1 CHERKASSKII, B. V.
O((N**2)*(P**0.5)) ALGORITHM FOR CONSTRUCTING THE MAXIMUM FLOW IN A NETWORK (RUSSIAN), AN. EHKONOMIKA I MATEMATICHESKIE METODY, NO. 7, 117-125. MOSCOW: "NAUKA". (1977).

CHERA 1977 -2 CHERKASSKII, B. V.
SOLUTION OF A PROBLEM OF MULTIPRODUCT FLOWS IN A NETWORK (RUSSIAN). EKONOMIKA I MATEMATICESKIE METODY 13, 143-151. (1977).

CHERB 1978 -1 CHERNIKOVA, N. V.
NON-NEGATIVE INTEGER SOLUTIONS OF A SYSTEM OF LINEAR EQUATIONS AND SOME QUESTIONS OF LINEAR INTEGER PROGRAMMING (RUSSIAN). KIEVSKII GOSUDARSTVENNYI UNIVERSITET. ISSLEDOVANIE OPERACII I ASU, NO. 12, 70-77 + 132. (1978).

CHERC 1970 -1 CHERNYSHEV, JU. O.
REDUCTION OF CERTAIN OPTIMAL PROBLEMS OF DISCRETE AUTOMATA DIAGNOSTICS TO THE SOLUTION OF PROBLEMS OF FLOWS IN NETWORKS (RUSSIAN). IN: METHODS AND MEDIA OF ENGINEERING CYBERNETICS (RUSSIAN), 3-9. RIGA: RIZSK. POLITEHN. INST. (1970).

CHERC 1974 -1 CHERNYSHEV, JU. O.
REDUCTION OF THE BIVALENT PROGRAMMING PROBLEM TO THE TRANSPORT PROBLEM (RUSSIAN), THE. METODY I MODELI UPRAVLENIJA 8, 3-10 + 128. (1974).

CHERC 1977 -1 CHERNYSHEV, JU. O.
OPTIMIZATION METHODS FOR COMBINATIONAL DEVICES (RUSSIAN). MOSCOW: IZDAT. "SOVETSKOE RADIO", 158 P. (1977).

CHERD 1977 -1 CHERNYSHEV, JU. O.; OSTROUH, E. N.
POSSIBILITY OF REDUCING A CERTAIN CLASS OF LINEAR PROGRAMMING PROBLEMS TO PROBLEMS OF TRANSPORT TYPE (RUSSIAN), THE. IN: G. E. PUHOV (ED.): MATHEMATICAL SIMULATION AND THE THEORY OF ELECTRICAL CIRCUITS (RUSSIAN) 15, 81-87. KIEV: NAUKOVA DUMKA. (1977).

CHERE 1978 -1 CHERVAK, JU. JU.
RECURRENCE ALGORITHM FOR THE METHOD OF CUTS AND THE METHOD OF BRANCH-AND-BOUND (RUSSIAN), A. EKONOMIKA I MATEMATICESKIE METODY 14, 1002-1005. (1978).

CHEU 1978 -1 CHEUNG, T.-Y.
STEPPING-STONE PARALLEL-CUT METHOD FOR INTEGER PROGRAMMING, A. IN: W. W. WHITE (ED.): COMPUTERS AND MATHEMATICAL PROGRAMMING, GAITHERSBURG 1976, 31-37. NBS SPECIAL PUBLICATION 502. WASHINGTON: NATIONAL BUREAU OF STANDARDS. (1978).

CHEU 1980 -1 CHEUNG, T.-Y.
COMPUTATIONAL COMPARISON OF EIGHT METHODS FOR THE MAXIMUM NETWORK FLOW PROBLEM. ACM TRANSACTIONS ON MATHEMATICAL SOFTWARE 6, 1-16. (1980).

CHEU 1980 -2 CHEUNG, T.-Y.
MULTIFACILITY LOCATION PROBLEM WITH RECTILINEAR DISTANCE BY THE MINIMUM-CUT APPROACH. ASSOCIATION FOR COMPUTING MACHINERY TRANSACTIONS ON MATHEMATICAL SOFTWARE 6, 387-390. (1980).

CHIE 1964 -1 CHIEN, R. T.; GOMORY, R. E.; HU, T. C.
COMMUNICATION NETWORKS.,IEEE TRANSACTIONS ON CIRCUIT THEORY 11, 19-22. (1964).

CHIN 1978 -1 CHIN, F. Y.; HOUCK, D. J.
ALGORITHMS FOR UPDATING MINIMAL SPANNING TREES. JOURNAL OF COMPUTER AND SYSTEM SCIENCES 16, 333-344. (1978).

CHOU 1979 -1 CHOU, T.-W. J.
ALGORITHMS FOR THE SOLUTION OF SYSTEMS OF LINEAR DIOPHANTINE EQUATIONS. MADISON: UNIV. OF WISCONSIN-MADISON, 118 P. (1979). (DISSERTATION)

CHOUA 1978 -1 CHOUKHMANE, E.-A.
HEURISTIQUE POUR LE PROBLEME DE L'ARBRE DE STEINER, UNE. REVUE FRANCAISE D'AUTOMATIQUE, D'INFORMATIQUE ET DE RECHERCHE OPERATIONELLE 12, SERIE RECHERCHE OPERATIONELLE, 207-212. (1978).

CHRI 1979 -1 CHRISTEN, C. A.; SELKOW, S. M.
SOME PERFECT COLORING PROPERTIES OF GRAPHS. JOURNAL OF COMBINATORIAL THEORY 27, SERIES B, 49-59. (1979).

CHRIA 1971 -1 CHRISTIE, A.
MULTI-DIMENSIONAL SCHEDULING ALGORITHMS. DISSERTATION. OXFORD: OXFORD UNIVERSITY. (1971).

CHRIB 1971 -1 CHRISTOFIDES, N.
OPTIMUM TRAVERSAL OF A GRAPH, THE. REPORT 71/16. LONDON: IMPERIAL COLLEGE OF SCIENCE. (1971).

CHRIB 1979 -1 CHRISTOFIDES, N.
TRAVELLING SALESMAN PROBLEM, THE. IN: N. CHRISTOFIDES, A. MINGOZZI, P. TOTH, C. SANDI (EDS.): COMBINATORIAL OPTIMIZATION, 131-150. CHICHESTER, NEW YORK, BRISBANE, TORONTO: WILEY. (1979).

CHRIC 1979 -1 CHRISTOFIDES, N.; AINOUCHE, A.
BOUNDS ON THE CONNECTIVITY AND THE INDEPENDENCE NUMBER OF A GRAPH. IC-OR-79-03. LONDON: IMPERIAL COLLEGE, DEPT. OF MANAGEMENT SCIENCE, 20 P. (1979).

CHRID 1979 -1 CHRISTOFIDES, N.; HEWINS, R. D.; SALKIN, G. R.
GRAPH THEORETIC APPROACHES TO FOREIGN EXCHANGE OPERATIONS. IN: N. CHRISTOFIDES, A. MINGOZZI, P. TOTH, C. SANDI (EDS.): COMBINATORIAL OPTIMIZATION, 409-420. CHICHESTER, NEW YORK, BRISBANE, TORONTO: WILEY. (1979).

CHRIE 1979 -1 CHRISTOFIDES, N.; HEY, A.
GRAPH COVERING RELAXATIONS OF THE SET-COVERING PROBLEM - PART 1. IC-OR-79-04. LONDON: IMPERIAL COLLEGE, DEPT. OF MANAGEMENT SCIENCE, 32 P. (1979).

CHRIF 1978 -1 CHRISTOFIDES, N.; MINGOZZI, A.; THOTH, P.
EXACT ALGORITHMS FOR THE VEHICLE ROUTING PROBLEM. IMPERIAL COLLEGE LONDON, 41 P. (1978).

CHRIG 1979 -1 CHRISTOFIDES, N.; MINGOZZI, A.; TOTH, P.
LOADING PROBLEMS. IN: N. CHRISTOFIDES, A. MINGOZZI, P. TOTH, C. SANDI (EDS.): COMBINATORIAL OPTIMIZATION, 339-370. CHICHESTER, NEW YORK, BRISBANE, TORONTO: WILEY. (1979).

CHRIG 1979 -2 CHRISTOFIDES, N.; MINGOZZI, A.; TOTH, P.
VEHICLE ROUTING PROBLEM, THE. IN: N. CHRISTOFIDES, A. MINGOZZI, P. TOTH, C. SANDI (EDS.): COMBINATORIAL OPTIMIZATION, 315-338. CHICHESTER, NEW YORK, BRISBANE, TORONTO: WILEY. (1979).

CHRIG 1980 -1 CHRISTOFIDES, N.; MINGOZZI, A.; TOTH, P.
CONTRIBUTIONS TO THE QUADRATIC ASSIGNMENT PROBLEM. EUROPEAN JOURNAL OF OPERATIONAL RESEARCH 4, 243-247. (1980).

CHRIG 1980 -2 CHRISTOFIDES, N.; MINGOZZI, A.; TOTH, P.
DYNAMIC LOADING AND UNLOADING OF LIQUIDS INTO TANKS. OPERATIONS RESEARCH 28, 633-649. (1980).

CHRIH 1978 -1 CHRISTOFIDES, N.; WHITLOCK, C.
GRAPH CONNECTIVITY AND VULNERABILITY, A SURVEY. LONDON: IMPERIAL COLLEGE, DEPT. OF MANAGEMENT SCIENCE, 52 P. (1978).

CHRIH 1978 -2 CHRISTOFIDES, N.; WHITLOCK, C.
LP-BASED TSP ALGORITHM, AN. REPORT 78-79. LONDON: IMPERIAL COLLEGE, DEPARTMENT OF MANAGEMENT SCIENCE. (1978).

CHU 1974 -1 CHU, Y. C.; TIEN, F.; MA, Z. F.; CAI, M. C.
ON THE CHARACTERIZATION OF AN EXTREME FLOW IN A TWO-COMMODITY NETWORK FLOW PROBLEM. SCIENTIA SINICA 17, 729-736. (1974).

CHUN 1980 -1 CHUNG, F. R. K.
ON THE COVERINGS OF GRAPHS. DISCRETE MATHEMATICS 30, 89-94. (1980).

CHUNA 1978 -1 CHUNG, F. R. K.; GRAHAM, R. L.
ON UNIVERSAL GRAPHS. MURRAY HILL: BELL LABORATORIES, 10 P. (1978).

CHUNB 1978 -1 CHUNG, F. R. K.; HWANG, F. K.
LOWER BOUND FOR THE STEINER TREE PROBLEM, A. SIAM JOURNAL ON APPLIED MATHEMATICS 34, 27-36. (1978).

CHUNC 1979 -1 CHUNG, S.-J.
NOTE ON THE COMPLEXITY OF LCP: THE LCP IS NP-COMPLETE, A. TECHNICAL REPORT NO. 79-2. ANN ARBOR: UNIV. OF MICHIGAN, DEPT. OF INDUSTRIAL AND OPERATIONS ENGINEERING, 9 P. (1979).

CHUNC 1979 -2 CHUNG, S.-J.
NP-COMPLETE ADJACENCY DECISION PROBLEMS ON SOME 0-1 CONVEX POLYTOPE. TECHNICAL REPORT 79-3. ANN ARBOR: UNIV. OF MICHIGAN, DEPT. OF INDUSTRIAL AND OPERATIONS ENGINEERING, 29 P. (1979).

CHUNC 1980 -1 CHUNG, S.-J.
ADJACENCY ON THE 0-1 EDGE COVERING PROBLEM. RESEARCH REPORT 80-1. ANN ARBOR: UNIV. OF MICHIGAN, DEPT. OF INDUSTRIAL AND OPERATIONS ENGINEERING, 36 P. (1980).

CHUNC 1980 -2 CHUNG, S.-J.
STRUCTURAL COMPLEXITY OF ADJACENCY ON 0-1 CONVEX POLYTOPES. DISSERTATION. ANN ARBOR: UNIV. OF MICHIGAN, DEPT. OF INDUSTRIAL AND OPERATIONS ENGINEERING, 115 P. (1980).

CHUND 1978 -1 CHUNGPHAISAN, V.
CONSTRUCTION OF HAMILTONIAN GRAPHS AND BIGRAPHS WITH PRESCRIBED DEGREES. JOURNAL OF COMBINATORIAL THEORY 24, SERIES B, 154-163. (1978).

CHUR 1978 -1 CHURCH, R. L.; GARFINKEL, R. S.
LOCATING AN OBNOXIOUS FACILITY ON A NETWORK. TRANSPORTATION SCIENCE 12, 107-118. (1978).

CHVA 1979 -1 CHVATAL, V.
GREEDY HEURISTIC FOR THE SET-COVERING PROBLEM, A. MATHEMATICS OF OPERATIONS RESEARCH 4, 233-235. (1979).

CHVA 1980 -1 CHVATAL, V.
HARD KNAPSACK PROBLEMS. OPERATIONS RESEARCH 28, 1402-1411. (1980).

CHVAA 1979 -1 CHVATAL, V.; GRAHAM, R. L.; PEROLD, A. F.; WHITESIDES, S. H.
COMBINATORIAL DESIGNS RELATED TO THE STRONG PERFECT GRAPH CONJECTURE. DISCRETE MATHEMATICS 26, 83-92. (1979).

CIOB 1977 -1 CIOBANU, G.
BRANCH-AND-BOUND ALGORITHM TO SOLVE AN ASSEMBLY LINE BALANCING PROBLEM, A. ECONOMIC COMPUTATION AND ECONOMIC CYBERNETICS STUDIES AND RESEARCH 11, NO. 4, 69-79. (1977).

CIOB 1981 -1 CIOBANU, G.
ON FEASIBLE SOLUTIONS FOR PROJECT SCHEDULING PROBLEM. IN: R. E. BURKARD, T. ELLINGER (EDS.): METHODS OF OPERATIONS RESEARCH 40, 247-250. KOENIGSTEIN: ANTON HAIN MEISENHEIM. (1981).

CIOBA 1978 -1 CIOBOTARU, S.
ON THE ENUMERATION OF HAMILTONIAN ROADS AND CIRCUITS IN CERTAIN PARTIAL GRAPHS OF K(N). REVUE ROUMAINE DE MATHEMATIQUES PURES ET APPLIQUEES 23, 1487-1496. (1978).

CIOF 1979 -1 CIOFFI, G.; JULIO, S. DE; LUCERTINI, M.
OPTIMAL DECOMPOSITION OF SEQUENTIAL MACHINES VIA INTEGER NON-LINEAR PROGRAMMING: A COMPUTATIONAL ALGORITHM. DIGITAL PROCESSES 5, 27-41. (1979).

CIUR 1979 -1 CIUREA, E.
DEUX REMARQUES SUR LE FLOT DYNAMIQUE MAXIMAL DE COUT MINIMAL. REVUE FRANCAISE D'AUTOMATIQUE, D'INFORMATIQUE ET DE RECHERCHE OPERATIONELLE 13, SERIE RECHERCHE OPERATIONELLE, 303-306. (1979).

CIUR 1979 -2 CIUREA, E.
SUR LES FLOTS DYNAMIQUES. ANALELE STIINTIFICE ALE UNIVERSITATII "AL. I. CUZA" DIN IASI. SERIA NOUA. SECTIUNEA IA MATEMATICA 25, SUPPL., 73-77. (1979).

CLAR 1980 -1 CLARK, G. M.; RANGANATHAN, A. N.
RESOURCE ALLOCATION ALGORITHM (ALCOT) FOR CONTROLLING MINE DRAINAGE POLLUTION, A. OPERATIONS RESEARCH 28, 867-888. (1980).

CLARA 1980 -1 CLARK, L.; ENTRINGER, R. C.; JACKSON, D. E.
MINIMUM GRAPHS WITH COMPLETE K-CLOSURE. DISCRETE MATHEMATICS 30, 95-102. (1980).

CLAU 1978 -1 CLAUS, A.
SIMULTANEOUS ENUMERATION APPROACH TO THE TRAVELLING SALESMAN PROBLEM, A. STUDIES IN APPLIED MATHEMATICS 58, NO. 2, 159-163. (1978).

CLAUA 1981 -1 CLAUS, A.; KRAETZIG, S.
OPTIMAL PLANNING OF NETWORK STRUCTURES WITHIN AN EXCHANGE AREA. EUROPEAN JOURNAL OF OPERATIONAL RESEARCH 7, 67-76. (1981).

CLAUB 1980 -1 CLAUSEN, J.; HANSEN, L. A.
FINDING K EDGE-DISJOINT SPANNING TREES OF MINIMUM TOTAL WEIGHT IN A NETWORK: AN APPLICATION OF MATROID THEORY. MATHEMATICAL PROGRAMMING STUDY 13, 88-101. (1980).

CLEE 1979 -1 CLEEF, H. J.; GAUL, W.
STOCHASTIC FLOW PROBLEM. PREPRINT NO. 317. BONN: UNIV. BONN, SONDERFORSCHUNGSBEREICH 72, 48 P. (1979).

CLEE 1981 -1 CLEEF, H. J.; GAUL, W.
FLOWS IN GRAPHS AND STOCHASTIC PROGRAMMING. IN: R. E. BURKARD, T. ELLINGER (EDS.): METHODS OF OPERATIONS RESEARCH 40, 251-254. KOENIGSTEIN: ANTON HAIN MEISENHEIM. (1981).

CLIM 1981 -1 CLIMACO, J. C. N.; MARTINS, E. Q. V.
ON THE DETERMINATION OF THE NONDOMINATED PATHS IN A MULTIOBJECTIVE NETWORK PROBLEM. IN: R. E. BURKARD, T. ELLINGER (EDS.): METHODS OF OPERATIONS RESEARCH 40, 255-258. KOENIGSTEIN: ANTON HAIN MEISENHEIM. (1981).

CLOC 1976 -1 CLOCOTICI, V.
SOME RELATIONS BETWEEN BASES AND CIRCUITS OF A MATROID. IN: PROCEEDINGS OF THE INSTITUTE OF MATHEMATICS IASI, 1974, 37-40. BUCHAREST: EDITURA ACAD. R. P. R. (1976).

COBH 1963 -1 COBHAM, A.; NORTH, J. H.
EXTENSION OF THE INTEGER PROGRAMMING APPROACH TO THE MINIMIZATION OF BOOLEAN FUNCTIONS. RESEARCH REPORT RAND CORPORATION 915, IBM. (1963).

COBI 1981 -1 COBIAN, J. M.; RUIZ C., M.
OPTIMIZATION MODEL FOR THE PLANNING OF ELECTRICAL DISTRIBUTION NETWORKS, AN. IN: R. E. BURKARD, T. ELLINGER (EDS.): METHODS OF OPERATIONS RESEARCH 40, 259-264. KOENIGSTEIN: ANTON HAIN MEISENHEIM. (1981).

COCK 1978 -1 COCKAYNE, E. J.; HARTNELL, B. L.; HEDETNIEMI, S. T.
LINEAR ALGORITHM FOR DISJOINT MATCHINGS IN TREES, A. DISCRETE MATHEMATICS 21, 129-136. (1978).

COCKA 1978 -1 COCKAYNE, E. J.; HEDETNIEMI, S. T.
DISJOINT CLIQUES IN REGULAR GRAPHS OF DEGREE SEVEN AND EIGHT. JOURNAL OF COMBINATORIAL THEORY 24, SERIES B, 233-237. (1978).

COEL 1981 -1 COELHO, J. D.
LOCATIONAL SURPLUS MAXIMIZATION APPROACH TO PUBLIC FACILITY LOCATION, A. IN: R. E. BURKARD, T. ELLINGER (EDS.): METHODS OF OPERATIONS RESEARCH 40, 265-270. KOENIGSTEIN: ANTON HAIN MEISENHEIM. (1981).

COFF 1978 -1 COFFMAN, E. G. JR.
DETERMINISTIC SEQUENCING: COMPLEXITY AND OPTIMAL ALGORITHMS. IN: M. ARATO, E. KNUTH (EDS.): SELECTED PAPERS ON OPERATING SYSTEMS: THEORY AND PRACTICE. LECTURES DELIVERED AT THE VISEGRAD WINTER SCHOOL, VISEGRAD 1978, 159-194. BUDAPEST: SZAMITOGEPALKALMAZASI KUTATO INTEZET. (1978).

COFFA 1977 -1 COFFMAN, E. G. JR.; CODY, R. A.; JOHNSON, D. B.
ANALYSIS OF A BIN-PACKING ALGORITHM FOR REDUCING ACCESS TIMES ON DRUM-LIKE STORAGE DEVICES. FOUNDATIONS OF CONTROL ENGINEERING 2, NO. 3, 119-130. (1977).

COFFB 1978 -1 COFFMAN, E. G. JR.; GAREY, M. R.; JOHNSON, D. S.
APPLICATION OF BIN-PACKING TO MULTIPROCESSOR SCHEDULING, AN. SIAM JOURNAL ON COMPUTING 7, 1-17. (1978).

COFFC 1980 -1 COFFMAN, E. G. JR.; GAREY, M. R.; JOHNSON, D. S.; TARJAN, R. E.
PERFORMANCE BOUNDS FOR LEVEL-ORIENTATED TWO-DIMENSIONAL PACKING ALGORITHMS. SIAM JOURNAL ON COMPUTING 9, 808-826. (1980).

COFFD 1979 -1 COFFMAN, E. G. JR.; JOHNSON, D. B.; LEUNG, J. Y.-T.
EFFICIENT ALGORITHM FOR ALLOCATING PAGED, DRUM-LIKE STORAGE, AN. NORDISK TIDSKRIFT FOR INFORMATIONSBEHANDLING 18, 52-66. (1979).

COFFE 1976 -1 COFFMAN, E. G. JR.; LABETOULLE, J.
SCHEDULING TO MINIMIZE MEAN NUMBER IN SYSTEM. IN: PROCEEDINGS OF THE NINTH HAWAII INTERNATIONAL CONFERENCE ON SYSTEM SCIENCES, HONOLULU 1976, 119-121. NORTH HOLLYWOOD: WESTERN PERIODICALS. (1976).

COFFF 1977 -1 COFFMAN, E. G. JR.; LEUNG, J. Y.-T.; SLUTZ, D.
ON THE OPTIMALITY OF FIRST-FIT AND LEVEL ALGORITHMS FOR PARALLEL MACHINE ASSIGNMENT AND SEQUENCING. IN: PROCEEDINGS OF THE 1977 INTERNATIONAL CONFERENCE ON PARALLEL PROCESSING, WAYNE STATE UNIVERSITY, DETROIT 1977, 95-99. NEW YORK: IEEE. (1977).

COFFF 1978 -1 COFFMAN, E. G. JR.; LEUNG, J. Y.-T.; SLUTZ, D.
ON THE OPTIMALITY OF FAST HEURISTICS FOR SCHEDULING AND STORAGE ALLOCATION PROBLEMS. FOUNDATIONS OF CONTROL ENGINEERING 3, NO. 4, 161-169. (1978).

COFFG 1977 -1 COFFMAN, E. G. JR.; LEUNG, J. Y.-T.; TING, D. W.
BIN-PACKING PROBLEMS AND THEIR APPLICATIONS IN STORAGE AND PROCESSOR ALLOCATION. IN: K. M. CHANDY, M. REISER (EDS.): COMPUTER PERFORMANCE, 327-339. AMSTERDAM: NORTH-HOLLAND. (1977).

COFFG 1978 -1 COFFMAN, E. G. JR.; LEUNG, J. Y.-T.; TING, D. W.
BIN-PACKING: MAXIMIZING THE NUMBER OF PIECES PACKED. ACTA INFORMATICA 9, 263-271. (1978).

COFFH 1976 -1 COFFMAN, E. G. JR.; SETHI, R.
GENERALIZED BOUND ON LPT SEQUENCING, A. REVUE FRANCAISE D'AUTOMATIQUE, D'INFORMATIQUE ET DE RECHERCHE OPERATIONELLE 10, SERIE RECHERCHE OPERATIONELLE, SUPPLEMENT, 17-25. (1976).

COGI 1979 -1 COGIS, O.; HABIB, M.
NOMBRE DE SAUTS ET GRAPHES SERIE-PARALLELES. REVUE FRANCAISE D'AUTOMATIQUE, D'INFORMATIQUE ET DE RECHERCHE OPERATIONELLE 13, SERIE INFORMATIQUE THEORIQUE, 3-18. (1979).

COHE 1978 -1 COHEN, A. I.
ALGORITHM FOR SCHEDULING SURFACE COAL MINES, AN (REVISED VERSION). PALO ALTO: SYSTEMS CONTROL, INC., 17 P. (1978).

COLB 1978 -1 COLBOURN, C. J.
BIBLIOGRAPHY OF THE GRAPH ISOMORPHISM PROBLEM, A. TECHNICAL REPORT NO. 123/78. TORONTO: UNIVERSITY OF TORONTO, DEPARTMENT OF COMPUTER SCIENCE. (1978).

COLB 1979 -1 COLBOURN, C. J.
COMPLEXITY OF SYMMETRIZING MATRICES, THE. INFORMATION PROCESSING LETTERS 9, 108-109. (1979).

COLBA 1979 -1 COLBOURN, C. J.; READ, R. C.
ORDERLY ALGORITHMS FOR GENERATING RESTRICTED CLASSES OF GRAPHS. JOURNAL OF GRAPH THEORY 3, 187-195. (1979).

COLBB 1978 -1 COLBOURN, M. J.; COLBOURN, C. J.
GRAPH ISOMORPHISM AND SELF-COMPLEMENTARY GRAPHS. ACM SIGACT NEWS 10, 25-29. (1978).

COLI 1973 -1 COLIJN, A. W.
PSEUDO-BOOLEAN PROGRAMMING. PH. D. THESIS. WATERLOO: UNIVERSITY OF WATERLOO, DEPARTMENT OF COMBINATORICS AND OPTIMIZATION. (1973).

COLL 1978 -1 COLLIER, J. B.; SCHMEICHEL, E. F.
SYSTEMATIC SEARCHES FOR HYPOHAMILTONIAN GRAPHS. NETWORKS 8, 193-200. (1978).

COLLA 1978 -1 COLLINS, M.; COOPER, L.; HELGASON, R. V.; KENNINGTON, J. L.; LEBLANC, L. J.
SOLVING THE PIPE NETWORK ANALYSIS PROBLEM USING OPTIMIZATION TECHNIQUES. MANAGEMENT SCIENCE 24, 747-760. (1978).

COLLB 1977 -1 COLLOMB, P.; GONDRAN, M.
ALGORITHME EFFICACE POUR UN ARBRE DE CLASSIFICATIONS, UN. REVUE FRANCAISE D'AUTOMATIQUE, D'INFORMATIQUE ET DE RECHERCHE OPERATIONELLE 11, SERIE RECHERCHE OPERATIONELLE, 31-49. (1977).

COMB 1979 -1 COMBOT, J.-P.; MASON, L. G.
OPTIMAL SWITCH-CONCENTRATOR LOCATION FOR A TELEPHONE NETWORK. INSTITUTE OF ELECTRICAL AND ELECTRONICS ENGINEERS. TRANSACTIONS ON COMMUNICATIONS 27, 36-44. (1979).

COMP 1975 -1 COMPANYS, R.
COMBINATORIAL PROGRAMMING: APPLICATION TO JOB SCHEDULING IN AN ORDINATOR WITH DISC OPERATIVE SYSTEM (SPANISH). IN: SYMPOSIA MATHEMATICA XV. CONVEGO DI INFORMATIA TEORICA, INDAM, ROMA 1973, 83-107. LONDON: ACADEMIC PRESS. (1975).

CONL 1978 -1 CONLEY, W.
SIMPLIFYING THE TEACHING OF INTEGER PROGRAMMING. IN:INT. J. MATH. EDUC. SCI. TECHNOL. VOL. 9, NO. 3, P. 355-359 (1978).

CONLA 1977 -1 CONLEY, W.; TRACY, D. S.
INTEGER PROGRAMMING WITH A COMPUTER: A STATISTICAL APPROACH. WINDSOR: UNIV. OF WINDSOR, 5 P. (1977).

CONN 1971 -1 CONNER, J. L.
SEQUENCE PROGRAMMING: A HEURISTIC ALGORITHM FOR THE SOLUTION OF LARGE GENERAL JOB SHOP SCHEDULING PROBLEMS. UNPUBLISHED DOCTORAL THESIS. CHICAGO: ILLINOIS INSTITUTE OF TECHNOLOGY. (1971).

CONN 1972 -1 CONNER, J. L.
HEURISTIC METHOD FOR SOLVING JOBSHOP SEQUENCING PROBLEMS, A. PRODUCTION AND INVENTORY MANAGEMENT 13, NO. 1, 54-68. (1972).

CONN 1973 -1 CONNER, J. L.
INTERACTIVE MANUFACTURING SCHEDULING AND CONTROL SYSTEM. IN: PROCEEDINGS OF THE APICS INTERNATIONAL TECHNICAL CONFERENCE, 66-74. (1973).

CONN 1973 -2 CONNER, J. L.
INTERACTIVE PRODUCTION CONTROL IN CAPACITY LIMITED SHOP. TECHNICAL PAPER MS 73-975. SOCIETY OF MANUFACTURING ENGINEERS. (1973).

CONR 1978 -1 CONRADT, D.
EFFIZIENTE IMPLEMENTIERUNG DES VERFAHRENS VON EDMONDS ZUR BESTIMMUNG EINES MAXIMALEN MATCHING, EINE. BERICHT 78-18. BERLIN: TECHNISCHE UNIV. BERLIN, FACHBEREICH INFORMATIK, 72 P. (1978).

CONR 1979 -1 CONRADT, D.
VERGLEICH AUSGEWAEHLTER MATCHING-ALGORITHMEN. IN: M. NAGL, H.-J. SCHNEIDER (EDS.): GRAPHS, DATA STRUCTURES, ALGORITHMS. PROCEEDINGS OF THE WORKSHOP WG 78 ON GRAPHTHEORETIC CONCEPTS IN COMPUTER SCIENCE, ERLANGEN 1978, 95-115. MUENCHEN, WIEN: HANSER. (1979).

COOK 1980 -1 COOK, W. D.; SAIPE, A. L.; SEIFORD, L. M.
PRODUCTION RUNS FOR MULTIPLE PRODUCTS: THE FULL-CAPACITY HEURISTIC. JOURNAL OF THE OPERATIONAL RESEARCH SOCIETY 31, 405-412. (1980).

COOKA 1979 -1 COOK, W. D.; SHIELDS, W. S.
ASSIGNMENT OF MILITARY OFFICERS TO GROUPS: A MULTI-ATTRIBUTE TEAM BALANCING PROBLEM. INFOR 17, 114-123. (1979).

COOP 1977 -1 COOPER, L.; BHAT, U. N.; LEBLANC, L. J.
INTRODUCTION TO OPERATIONS RESEARCH MODELS. PHILADELPHIA, LONDON, TORONTO: SAUNDERS, 404 P. (1977).

COOPA 1977 -1 COOPER, L.; KENNINGTON, J. L.
STEADY-STATE ANALYSIS OF NONLINEAR RESISTIVE ELECTRICAL NETWORKS USING OPTIMIZATION TECHNIQUES. TECHNICAL REPORT IEOR 77012. DALLAS: SOUTHERN METHODIST UNIVERSITY, DEPARTMENT OF INDUSTRIAL ENGINEERING AND OPERATIONS RESEARCH. (1977).

COOPB 1979 -1 COOPER, M. W.
IMPROVED ALGORITHM FOR NON-LINEAR INTEGER PROGRAMMING, AN. COMPUTERS AND MATHEMATICS WITH APPLICATIONS 5, 145-152. (1979).

COOPB 1979 -2 COOPER, M. W.
SURVEY OF METHODS FOR PURE NONLINEAR INTEGER PROGRAMMING, A. TECHNICAL REPORT OREM 79005. DALLAS: SOUTHERN METHODIST UNIV., DEPT. OF OPERATIONS RESEARCH AND ENGINEERING MANAGEMENT, 12 P. (1979).

COPP 1980 -1 COPPINS, R. J.; PENTICO, D. W.
SCHEDULING THE NATIONAL FOOTBALL LEAGUE. WORKING PAPER. RICHMOND: VIRGINIA COMMONWEALTH UNIVERSITY, SCHOOL OF BUSINESS, 15 P. (1980).

CORD 1979 -1 CORDOVIL, R.
CONTRIBUTIONS A LA THEORIE DES GEOMETRIES COMBINATOIRES: GEOMETRIES SIMPLICIALES, COMPATIBILITE DES EXTENSIONS. DISSERTATION. PARIS: UNIVERSITY OF PARIS 6, 62 P. (1979).

CORD 1980 -1 CORDOVIL, R.
REPRESENTATION OVER A FIELD OF FULL SIMPLICIAL MATROIDS. EUROPEAN JOURNAL OF COMBINATORICS 1, 201-205. (1980).

CORD 1980 -2 CORDOVIL, R.
SUR L'EVALUATION T(M;2,0) DU POLYNOME DE TUTTE D'UN MATROIDE ET UNE CONJECTURE DE B. GRUENBAUM RELATIVE AUX ARRANGEMENTS DE DROITES DU PLAN. EUROPEAN JOURNAL OF COMBINATORICS 1, 317-322. (1980).

CORDA 1979 -1 CORDOVIL, R.; VERGNAS, M. LAS
GEOMETRIES SIMPLICIALES UNIMODULAIRES. DISCRETE MATHEMATICS 26, 213-217. (1979).

CORK 1978 -1 CORKINDALE, D.
HOW TO CUT TRANSPORTATION COSTS WHILE MAINTAINING SERVICE LEVELS. INTERNATIONAL JOURNAL OF PHYSICAL DISTRIBUTION AND MATERIALS MANAGEMENT 8, NO. 6, 315-330. (1978).

CORL 1980 -1 CORLEY, H. W.; GOLNABI, H.
MINIMAX TREES, PATHS, AND CUT SETS. WORKING PAPER. ARLINGTON: UNIV. OF TEXAS, DEPT. OF INDUSTRIAL ENGINEERING, 14 P. (1980).

CORN 1978 -1 CORNEIL, D. G.; WOODWARD, M. E.
COMPARISON AND EVALUATION OF GRAPH THEORETICAL CLUSTERING TECHNIQUES, A. INFOR 16, 74-89. (1978).

CORNA 1978 -1 CORNUEJOLS, G.
ANALYSIS OF ALGORITHMS FOR A CLASS OF LOCATION PROBLEMS. TECHNICAL REPORT 382. ITHACA: CORNELL UNIV., SCHOOL OF OPERATIONS RESEARCH AND INDUSTRIAL ENGINEERING, 127 P. (1978).

CORNA 1979 -1 CORNUEJOLS, G.
DEGREE SEQUENCES OF RANDOM GRAPHS. W.P. 36-79-80. PITTSBURGH: CARNEGIE-MELLON UNIV., GRADUATE SCHOOL OF INDUSTRIAL ADMINISTRATION, 13 P. (1979).

CORNB 1979 -1 CORNUEJOLS, G.; FISHER, M. L.; NEMHAUSER, G. L.
ON "LOCATION OF BANK ACCOUNTS TO OPTIMIZE FLOAT: AN ANALYTIC STUDY OF EXACT AND APPROXIMATE ALGORITHMS". MANAGEMENT SCIENCE 25, 808-809. (1979).

CORNC 1980 -1 CORNUEJOLS, G.; NEMHAUSER, G. L.; WOLSEY, L. A.
CANONICAL REPRESENTATION OF SIMPLE PLANT LOCATION PROBLEMS AND ITS APPLICATIONS, A. SIAM JOURNAL ON ALGEBRAIC AND DISCRETE METHODS 1, 261-272. (1980).

CORNC 1980 -2 CORNUEJOLS, G.; NEMHAUSER, G. L.; WOLSEY, L. A.
WORST-CASE AND PROBABILISTIC ANALYSIS OF ALGORITHMS FOR A LOCATION PROBLEM. OPERATIONS RESEARCH 28, 847-858. (1980).

CORND 1980 -1 CORNUEJOLS, G.; PULLEYBLANK, W. R.
MATCHING PROBLEM WITH SIDE CONDITIONS, A. DISCRETE MATHEMATICS 29, 135-159. (1980).

CORND 1980 -2 CORNUEJOLS, G.; PULLEYBLANK, W. R.
PERFECT TRIANGLE-FREE 2-MATCHINGS. MATHEMATICAL PROGRAMMING STUDY 13, 1-7. (1980).

CORND 1980 -3 CORNUEJOLS, G.; PULLEYBLANK, W. R.
TRAVELLING SALESMAN POLYTOPE AND (0,2)-MATCHINGS, THE. RESEARCH REPORT 80172-OR. BONN: UNIV. BONN, INST. FUER OEKONOMETRIE UND OPERATIONS RESEARCH, 35 P. (1980).

CORND 1981 -1 CORNUEJOLS, G.; PULLEYBLANK, W. R.
CRITICAL GRAPHS, MATCHINGS AND TOURS - A HIERARCHY OF RELAXATIONS FOR THE TRAVELLING SALESMAN PROBLEM. RESEARCH REPORT WP 81198-OR. BONN: UNIV. BONN, INST. FUER OEKONOMETRIE UND OPERATIONS RESEARCH, ABT. OPERATIONS RESEARCH. (1981).

CORNE 1979 -1 CORNUEJOLS, G.; THIZY, J.-M.
SOME FACETS OF THE SIMPLE PLANT LOCATION POLYTOPE. WORKING PAPER 39-79-80. PITTSBURGH: CARNEGIE-MELLON UNIV., 16 P. (1979).

CORNE 1980 -1 CORNUEJOLS, G.; THIZY, J.-M.
LOCATION PROBLEMS, SET COVERING PROBLEMS AND THE GREEDY ALGORITHM. WORKING PAPER 25-80-81. PITTSBURGH: CARNEGIE-MELLON UNIV., 24 P. (1980).

CORO 1977 -1 COROMINAS, A.; COMPANYS, R.
GENERALISED BRANCH AND BOUND PROCEDURE (SPANISH), A. QUESTIIO 1, 49-62. (1977).

CORT 1978 -1 CORT, J. D.
COMPLEXITY OF COMBINATORIAL PROBLEMS (SPANISH). QUESTIIO (SPAIN) 2, 35-49. (1978).

COUR 1965 -1 COURTILLOT, M.
SUR LA RESOLUTION DES PROGRAMMES A SOLUTIONS ENTIERES. REVUE FRANC. TRAITEMENT INFORMAT. CHIFFRES 8, NO. 2, 81-94. (1965).

COX 1980 -1 COX, J. T.
TIME CONSTANT OF FIRST-PASSAGE PERCOLATION ON THE SQUARE LATTICE, THE. ADVANCES IN APPLIED PROBABILITY 12, 864-879. (1980).

CRAM 1979 -1 CRAMER, J.; POLLATSCHEK, M. A.
CANDIDATE TO JOB ALLOCATION PROBLEM WITH A LEXICOGRAPHIC OBJECTIVE. MANAGEMENT SCIENCE 25, 466-473. (1979).

CRAMA 1977 -1 CRAMER, M.; PONSSARD, J.-P.
ORDONNANCEMENT DES MOUVEMENTS DE TRESORERIE. REVUE FRANCAISE D'AUTOMATIQUE, D'INFORMATIQUE ET DE RECHERCHE OPERATIONELLE 11, SERIE RECHERCHE OPERATIONELLE, 393-404. (1977).

CRAP 1970 -1 CRAPO, H. H.
ERECTING GEOMETRIES. IN: A. GEWIRTZ, L. V. QUINTAS (EDS.): INTERNATIONAL CONFERENCE ON COMBINATORIAL MATHEMATICS, 89-92. ANNALS OF THE NEW YORK ACADEMY OF SCIENCES, VOLUME 165, ARTICLE 1. NEW YORK: THE NEW YORK ACADEMY OF SCIENCES. (1970).

CROI 1979 -1 CROITORU, C.
ON A DISCRETE MAX-MIN PROBLEM. ANALELE STIINTIFICE ALE UNIVERSITATII "AL. I. CUZA" DIN IASI. SERIA NOUA. SECTIUNEA I A MATEMATICA 25, 159-161. (1979).

CROI 1980 -1 CROITORU, C.
ON APPROXIMATE ALGORITHMS FOR COMBINATORIAL LINEAR MAXIMIZATION PROBLEMS. ZEITSCHRIFT FUER OPERATIONS RESEARCH 24, SERIES A, 171-175. (1980).

CROW 1978 -1 CROWDER, H. P.
CLUSTER ANALYSIS: AN APPLICATION OF LAGRANGIAN RELAXATION. IBM RESEARCH REPORT, 7371. YORKTOWN HEIGHTS: IBM RESEARCH CENTER, 16 P. (1978).

CROWA 1978 -1 CROWDER, H. P.; DEMBO, R. S.; MULVEY, J. M.
REPORTING COMPUTATIONAL EXPERIMENTS IN MATHEMATICAL PROGRAMMING. MATHEMATICAL PROGRAMMING 15, 316-329. (1978).

CROWB 1979 -1 CROWDER, H. P.; PADBERG, M. W.
SOLVING LARGE-SCALE SYMMETRIC TRAVELLING SALESMAN PROBLEMS TO OPTIMALITY. IBM RESEARCH REPORT, 7743. YORKTOWN HEIGHTS: IBM RESEARCH CENTER, 21 P. (1979).

CRUM 1979 -1 CRUM, R. L.; KLINGMAN, D.; TAVIS, L. A.
STRATEGIC MANAGEMENT OF MULTINATIONAL COMPANIES: NETWORK-BASED PLANNING SYSTEMS. RESEARCH REPORT CCS 360. AUSTIN: UNIV. OF TEXAS, CENTER FOR CYBERNETIC STUDIES, 25 P. (1979).

CRUS 1979 -1 CRUSE, A. B.
ON REMOVING A VERTEX FROM THE ASSIGNMENT POLYTOPE. LINEAR ALGEBRA AND ITS APPLICATIONS 26, 45-57. (1979).

CRUY 1978 -1 CRUYSSEN, P. VAN DER; RIJCKAERT, M. J.
HEURISTIC FOR THE ASYMMETRIC TRAVELLING SALESMAN PROBLEM. THE JOURNAL OF THE OPERATIONAL RESEARCH SOCIETY 29, 697-701. (1978).

CSER 1978 -1 CSERNY, L.
FORMULATION OF THE TIME-TABLE PROBLEM AND THE EXAMINATION OF ITS CONSISTENT SOLUTIONS. II (HUNGARIAN). THE. INFORMACIO-ELEKTRONIKA 13, 356-359. (1978).

CSIM 1965 -1 CSIMA, J.
INVESTIGATIONS ON A TIME-TABLE PROBLEM. PH. D. THESIS. TORONTO: TORONTO UNIVERSITY. (1965).

CULL 1980 -1 CULL, P.
TOURS OF GRAPHS, DIGRAPHS, AND SEQUENTIAL MACHINES. IEEE TRANSACTIONS ON COMPUTERS C-29, 50-54. (1980).

CULLA 1980 -1 CULLEN, F. H.; JARVIS, J. J.; RATLIFF, H. D.
SET PARTITIONING BASED HEURISTICS FOR INTERACTIVE ROUTING. RESEARCH REPORT J-80-1. ATLANTA: GEORGIA INST. OF TECHNOLOGY, SCHOOL OF INDUSTRIAL AND SYSTEMS ENGINEERING, 44 P. (1980).

CUMM 1977 -1 CUMMINGS, L. J.; WALLIS, W. D.
TRANSVERSAL ALGORITHM FOR REGULAR SQUARE INCIDENCE MATRICES, A. IN: F. HOFFMAN ET AL. (EDS.): PROCEEDINGS OF THE EIGHTH SOUTHEASTERN CONFERENCE ON COMBINATORICS, GRAPH THEORY, AND COMPUTING, BATON ROUGE 1977, 213-226. CONGRESSUS NUMERANTIUM XIX, WINNIPEG: UTILITAS MATHEMATICA. (1977).

CUNI 1979 -1 CUNINGHAME-GREEN, R. A.
MINIMAX ALGEBRA. BERLIN, HEIDELBERG, NEW YORK: SPRINGER, 258 P. (1979). (LECTURE NOTES IN ECONOMICS AND MATHEMATICAL SYSTEMS, 166)

CUNI 1981 -1 CUNINGHAME-GREEN, R. A.
INTEGER PROGRAMMING BY LONG DIVISION. DISCRETE APPLIED MATHEMATICS 3, 19-26. (1981).

CUNN 1979 -1 CUNNINGHAM, W. H.
BINARY MATROID SUMS. THE QUARTERLY JOURNAL OF MATHEMATICS 30, 271-281. (1979).

CUNN 1979 -2 CUNNINGHAM, W. H.
THEORETICAL PROPERTIES OF A NETWORK SIMPLEX METHOD. MATHEMATICS OF OPERATIONS RESEARCH 4, 196-208. (1979).

CUNN 1981 -1 CUNNINGHAM, W. H.
CLASS OF LINEAR PROGRAMS CONVERTIBLE TO NETWORK PROBLEMS, A. RESEARCH REPORT NO. 81204-OR. BONN: UNIV. BONN, INSTITUT FUER OEKONOMETRIE UND OPERATIONS RESEARCH, ABT. OPERATIONS RESEARCH, 6 P. (1981).

CUNN 1981 -2 CUNNINGHAM, W. H.
ON MATROID CONNECTIVITY. JOURNAL OF COMBINATORIAL THEORY, SERIES B 30, 94-99. (1981).

CUNN 1981 -3 CUNNINGHAM, W. H.
POLYHEDRA FOR COMPOSED INDEPENDENCE SYSTEMS. RESEARCH REPORT NO. 81203-OR. BONN: UNIV. BONN, INSTITUT FUER OEKONOMETRIE UND OPERATIONS RESEARCH, ABT. OPERATIONS RESEARCH, 15 P. (1981).

CUNN 1981 -4 CUNNINGHAM, W. H.
TESTING MEMBERSHIP IN MATROID POLYHEDRA. RESEARCH REPORT NO. 81207-OR. BONN: UNIV. BONN, INSTITUT FUER OEKONOMETRIE UND OPERATIONS RESEARCH, ABT. OPERATIONS RESEARCH, 21 P. (1981).

CUNN 1982 -1 CUNNINGHAM, W. H.
DECOMPOSITION OF SUBMODULAR FUNCTIONS. RESEARCH REPORT NO. 82213-OR. BONN: UNIV. BONN, INSTITUT FUER OEKONOMETRIE UND OPERATIONS RESEARCH, ABT. OPERATIONS RESEARCH. (1982).

CUNNA 1980 -1 CUNNINGHAM, W. H.; EDMONDS, J.
COMBINATORIAL DECOMPOSITION THEORY, A. CANADIAN JOURNAL OF MATHEMATICS 32, 734-765. (1980).

CUNNB 1981 -1 CUNNINGHAM, W. H.; KLINCEWICZ, J. G.
ON CYCLING IN THE NETWORK SIMPLEX METHOD. RESEARCH REPORT NO. 178. OTTAWA: CARLETON UNIV., DEPT. OF MATHEMATICS AND STATISTICS, 33 P. (1981).

CUNNC 1978 -1 CUNNINGHAM, W. H.; MARSH, A. B. III
PRIMAL ALGORITHM FOR OPTIMUM MATCHING, A. MATHEMATICAL PROGRAMMING STUDY 8, 50-72. (1978).

CUNT 1978 -1 CUNTO, E.
SCHEDULING BOATS TO SAMPLE OIL WELLS IN LAKE MARACAIBO. OPERATIONS RESEARCH 26, 183-196. (1978).

CUTL 1980 -1 CUTLER, M.
EFFICIENT SPECIAL CASE ALGORITHMS FOR THE N-LINE PLANAR TRAVELING SALESMAN PROBLEM. NETWORKS 10, 183-196. (1980).

CUTLA 1978 -1 CUTLER, M.; SHILOACH, Y.
PERMUTATION LAYOUT. NETWORKS 8, 253-278. (1978).

CVET 1972 -1 CVETKOVIC, D. M.
CHROMATIC NUMBER AND THE SPECTRUM OF A GRAPH. INSTITUT MATHEMATIQUE. PUBLICATIONES. NOUVELLE SERIE 14, 25-38. (1972).

CVETA 1979 -1 CVETKOVIC, D. M.; DOOB, M.; SACHS, H.
SPECTRA OF GRAPHS. THEORY AND APPLICATION. NEW YORK, SAN FRANCISCO, LONDON: ACADEMIC PRESS, 368 P. (1979). (PURE AND APPLIED MATHEMATICS)

CZAP 1977 -1 CZAPNIK, J.
ALGORITHM FOR RESOURCE ALLOCATION IN MULTIPROGRAMMING SYSTEMS (POLISH), AN. PODSTAWY STEROWANIA 7, NO. 1, 25-32. (1977).

DALB 1980 -1 DALBERTO, L. M.
PRACTICAL SOLUTION APPROACHES TO THE CAPACITATED PLANT LOCATION PROBLEM. ALLENTOWN: AIR PRODUCTS AND CHEMICALS, INC., 11 P. (1980).

DAMM 1978 -1 DAMM, E.
SHORTEST PATH IN A RECTANGULAR GRID, THE. IN: PROGR. CYBERN. SYST. RES. 4, SYMPOSIUM, VIENNA 1978, 511-515. (1978).

DANG 1979 -1 DANG VAN UYEN
AGGREGATION OF AN INTEGER PROGRAMMING MODEL (SLOVAK). EKONOMICKO-MATEMATICKY OBZOR 15, 44-61. (1979).

DANG 1979 -2 DANG VAN UYEN
SOLUTION TO A CLASS OF MIXED INTEGER PROGRAMMING PROBLEMS WITH 0-1 AND AND CONTINUOUS VARIABLES (CZECHOSLOVAKIAN), A. EKONOMICKO-MATEMATICKY OBZOR 15, 443-454. (1979).

DANI 1978 -1 DANIEL, R. C.
GENERALISATION OF VARIABLE UPPER BOUNDING AND GENERALISED UPPER BOUNDING, A. EUROPEAN JOURNAL OF OPERATIONAL RESEARCH 2, 202-206. (1978).

DANI 1978 -2 DANIEL, R. C.
REDUCING COMPUTATIONAL EFFORT IN SOLVING A HARD INTEGER PROGRAM. SIGMAP BULLETIN 25, 39-44. (1978).

DANIA 1979 -1 DANIEL, R. C.; JEFFREYS, M.
UNBOUNDEDNESS IN INTEGER AND DISCRETE PROGRAMMING L. P. RELAXATIONS. JOURNAL OF THE OPERATIONAL RESEARCH SOCIETY 30, 1119-1128. (1979).

DANT 1979 -1 DANTZIG, G. B.; HARVEY, R. P.; LANSDOWNE, Z. F.; ROBINSON, D. W.; MAIER, S. F.
FORMULATING AND SOLVING THE NETWORK DESIGN PROBLEM BY DECOMPOSITION. TRANSPORTATION RESEARCH 13, SERIES B, 5-17. (1979).

DAR- 1978 -1 DAR-EL, E. M.
MIXED-MODEL ASSEMBLY LINE SEQUENCING PROBLEMS. OMEGA 6, NO. 4, 313-323. (1978).

DAR-A 1980 -1 DAR-EL, E. M.; KARNI, R.
HYBRID ALGORITHM FOR INDEPENDENT TASK PARALLEL MACHINE SCHEDULING, A. OMEGA 8, 239-242. (1980).

DAR-B 1979 -1 DAR-EL, E. M.; RUBINOVITCH, Y.
MUST - A MULTIPLE SOLUTIONS TECHNIQUE FOR BALANCING SINGLE MODEL ASSEMBLY LINES. MANAGEMENT SCIENCE 25, 1105-1114. (1979).

DAS 1978 -1 DAS, G.
EQUIVALENT-JOBS FOR JOB-BLOCKS FOR 'N-JOB, 3-MACHINE' SEQUENCING PROBLEMS. PURE AND APPLIED MATHEMATIKA SCIENCES 7, 35-40. (1978).

DAS A 1978 -1 DAS, K. S.; TEOREY, T. J.
EFFICIENT JOB SCHEDULING ALGORITHM FOR MIXED TURNAROUND AND DEADLINE APPLICATIONS, AN. INFORMATION SCIENCES 16, NO. 2, 137-150. (1978).

DAS B 1978 -1 DAS, S.; PANDIT, S. N. N.
COMPUTATION OF A NEW LOWER BOUND: SEQUENCING N JOBS ON M PARALLEL PROCESSORS. OPSEARCH 15, 1-11. (1978).

DAS C 1978 -1 DAS, S. R.; SHENG, C. L.
STRONG CONNECTIVITY IN SYMMETRIC GRAPHS AND GENERATION OF MAXIMAL MINIMALLY STRONGLY CONNECTED SUBGRAPHS. INFORMATION SCIENCES 14, NO. 3, 181-187. (1978).

DAS D 1978 -1 DAS, S. R.; SHENG, C. L.; CHEN, Z.
ALGORITHM FOR FINDING ALL MAXIMAL COMPLETE SUBGRAPHS AND AN ESTIMATE OF THE ORDER OF COMPUTATIONAL COMPLEXITY, AN. COMPUTERS AND ELECTRICAL ENGINEERING 5, 365-368. (1978).

DAS E 1979 -1 DAS, S. R.; SHENG, C. L.; CHEN, Z.; LIN, T.
MAGNITUDE ORDERING OF DEGREE COMPLEMENTS OF CERTAIN NODE PAIRS IN AN UNDIRECTED GRAPH AND AN ALGORITHM TO FIND A CLASS OF MAXIMAL SUBGRAPHS. COMPUTERS AND ELECTRICAL ENGINEERING 6, NO. 3, 139-151. (1979).

DASA 1980 -1 DASARATHY, B.; WHITE, L. J.
MAXMIN LOCATION PROBLEM, A. OPERATIONS RESEARCH 28, 1385-1401. (1980).

DATH 1978 -1 DATHE, M.
ZUR LOESUNG DES ZUORDNUNGSPROBLEMS BEI ZWEI ZIELGROESSEN. ZEITSCHRIFT FUER OPERATIONS RESEARCH 22, SERIE B, B105-B118. (1978).

DAVI 1979 -1 DAVIO, M.; THAYSE, A.
ALGORITHMS FOR MINIMAL-LENGTH SCHEDULES. PHILIPS JOURNAL OF RESEARCH 34, 26-47. (1979).

DAVIA 1968 -1 DAVIS, R. D.
ON THE DELIVERY PROBLEM AND SOME RELATED TOPICS. PH. D. THESIS. EVANSTON: NORTHWESTERN UNIVERSITY. (1968).

DAVIB 1978 -1 DAVIS, R. P.; MILLER, D. M.
MODEL FOR DETERMINING MACHINE REQUIREMENTS IN A MULTISTAGE MANUFACTURING SYSTEM WITH DISCRETELY DISTRIBUTED DEMAND, A. APPLIED MATHEMATICAL MODELING 2, NO. 2, 119-122. (1978).

DAVIC 1979 -1 DAVIS, R. P.; WYSK, R. A.; KIMBLER, D. L.
TOOL-CHANGE SCHEDULING MODEL FOR MACHINING CENTRES, A. APPLIED MATHEMATICAL MODELLING 3, 285-288. (1979).

DAWS 1980 -1 DAWSON, J. E.
NOTE ON SOME ALGORITHMS FOR MATROIDS, A. JOURNAL OF MATHEMATICAL ANALYSIS AND APPLICATIONS 75, 611-615. (1980).

DAWS 1980 -2 DAWSON, J. E.
OPTIMAL MATROID BASES: AN ALGORITHM BASED ON COCIRCUITS. THE QUARTERLY JOURNAL OF MATHEMATICS. OXFORD. SERIES (2) 31, NO. 121, 65-69. (1980).

DE 1977 -1 DE, P.; MORTON, T. E.
MAKESPAN SCHEDULING FOR UNEQUAL PARALLEL PROCESSORS (REVISED VERSION). W.P. NO. 18-76-77. PITTSBURGH: CARNEGIE-MELLON UNIV., GRADUATE SCHOOL OF INDUSTRIAL ADMINISTRATION, 21 P. (1977).

DEAK 1981 -1 DEAK, I.; HOFFER, J.; MAYER, J.; NEMETH, A.; POTECZ, B.; PREKOPA, A.; STRAZICKY, B.
OPTIMAL DAILY SCHEDULING OF THE ELECTRICITY PRODUCTION IN HUNGARY. IN: R. E. BURKARD, T. ELLINGER (EDS.): METHODS OF OPERATIONS RESEARCH 40, 283-286. KOENIGSTEIN: ANTON HAIN MEISENHEIM. (1981).

DEAR 1979 -1 DEARING, P. M.; NEWRUCK, F. C.
CAPACITATED BOTTLENECK FACILITY LOCATION PROBLEM, A. MANAGEMENT SCIENCE 25, 1093-1104. (1979).

DEBA 1979 -1 DEBANNE, J. G.
NETWORK BASED REGIONAL ENERGY PLANNING MODELS - AN EVOLUTIONARY EXPOSE. WORKING PAPER 79-8. OTTAWA: UNIV. OF OTTAWA, FACULTY OF ADMINISTRATION, 32 P. (1979).

DEBO 1977 -1 DEBOWY, J.
ALGORITHM FOR OPTIMAL PARTITIONING OF A GRAPH, AN. ZASTOSOWANIA MATEMATYKI 16, 63-71. (1977).

DECK 1977 -1 DECKRO, R. F.
MULTIPLE OBJECTIVE DISTRICTING: A GENERAL HEURISTIC APPROACH USING MULTIPLE CRITERIA. OPERATIONAL RESEARCH QUARTERLY 28, 953-961. (1977).

DEFR 1978 -1 DEFRENNE, A.
TIMETABLING PROBLEM: A SURVEY, THE. CAHIERS DU CENTRE D'ETUDES DE RECHERCHE OPERATIONELLE 20, 171-182. (1978).

DEHA 1979 -1 DEHAAN, A.
SOLUTION OF A GENERALIZED CUTTING-STOCK PROBLEM BY MPSX/MIP, THE. REPORT 7932/O. ROTTERDAM: ERASMUS UNIV. ROTTERDAM, ECONOMETRIC INSTITUTE, 12 P. (1979).

DEJO 1978 -1 DEJON, B.
SPATIAL INTERACTION NETWORK FLOW MODELS. IN: PROCEEDINGS IN OPERATIONS RESEARCH 7, 377-386. WUERZBURG: PHYSICA. (1978).

DELA 1979 -1 DELATTRE, M.; HANSEN, P.
CLUSTER ANALYSIS AND GRAPH COLORING. IN: A. PREKOPA (ED.): SURVEY OF MATHEMATICAL PROGRAMMING, VOLUME 2, 325-332. AMSTERDAM: NORTH-HOLLAND. (1979).

DELF 1975 -1 DELFINO, W. C. D.
OPTIMAL DESIGN OF WATER DISTRIBUTION PIPELINE NETWORKS. DOCTORAL DISSERTATION. CLEVELAND: CASE WESTERN RESERVE UNIVERSITY, 134 P. (1975).

DELP 1976 -1 DELPORTE, C. M.; THOMAS, L. J.
LOT SIZE AND SEQUENCING FOR N PRODUCTS ON ONE FACILITY. PAPER PRESENTED AT THE SPECIAL INTEREST CONFERENCE ON THE THEORY AND APPLICATIONS OF SCHEDULING, ORLANDO. (1976).

DEMB 1974 -1 DEMBO, R. S.
NOTE ON CONSTRAINT PAIRING IN INTEGER LINEAR PROGRAMMING, A. WORKING PAPER. WATERLOO: UNIVERSITY OF WATERLOO, DEPARTMENT OF MANAGEMENT SCIENCE. (1974).

DEMBA 1980 -1 DEMBO, R. S.; HAMMER, P. L.
REDUCTION ALGORITHM FOR KNAPSACK PROBLEMS, A. IN: R. HENN, H. P. KUENZI, H. SCHUBERT (EDS.): METHODS OF OPERATIONS RESEARCH 36, 49-60. KOENIGSTEIN: ANTON HAIN MEISENHEIM. (1980).

DEMBB 1978 -1 DEMBO, R. S.; KLINCEWICZ, J. G.
APPROXIMATE SECOND-ORDER ALGORITHM FOR NETWORK FLOW PROBLEMS WITH CONVEX SEPARABLE COSTS, AN. WORKING PAPER SERIES B - TECHNICAL 21. NEW HAVEN: YALE UNIV., SCHOOL OF ORGANIZATION AND MANAGMENT, 36 P. (1978).

DEMBB 1979 -1 DEMBO, R. S.; KLINCEWICZ, J. G.
SCALED REDUCED GRADIENT ALGORITHM FOR NETWORK FLOW PROBLEMS WITH CONVEX SEPARABLE COSTS, A (REVISED VERSION). SERIES NO. 21. NEW HAVEN: YALE SCHOOL OF ORGANIZATION AND MANAGEMENT, 35 P. (1979).

DEMBC 1980 -1 DEMBOWSKI, F. L.; SCHWARZ, L.
INTEGER PROGRAMMING APPROACH TO SCHOOL DISTRICT FINANCIAL MANAGEMENT, AN. SOCIO-ECONOMIC PLANNING SCIENCES (OXFORD) 14, NO. 3, 147-153. (1980).

DEMI 1978 -1 DEMIDENKO, V. M.
ON THE OPTIMIZATION OF THE VALUE V(A,T) ON THE SET OF CYCLES (RUSSIAN). VESCI AKADEMII NAVUK BSSR. SERYJA FIZIKA-MATEMATYCNYH NAVUK (MINSK), NO. 1, 21-26, 139. (1978).

DEMI 1979 -1 DEMIDENKO, V. M.
TRAVELING SALESMAN PROBLEM WITH NON-SYMMETRIC MATRICES (RUSSIAN). VESCI AKADEMII NAVUK BSSR. SERYJA FIZIKA-MATEMATYCNYH NAVUK, NO. 1, 29-35. (1979).

DEMI 1980 -1 DEMIDENKO, V. M.
SPECIAL CASES OF THE TRAVELLING SALESMAN PROBLEM WITH A SYMMETRIC MATRIX (RUSSIAN). DOKLADY AKADEMII NAUK BSSR (MINSK) 24, NO. 2, 105-108, 188. (1980).

DEMIA 1979 -1 DEMING, R. W.
INDEPENDENCE NUMBERS OF GRAPHS - AN EXTENSION OF THE KOENIG-EGERVARY THEOREM. DISCRETE MATHEMATICS 27, 23-33. (1979).

DEMJ 1965 -1 DEMJANOV, B. F.; KHUDJAKOV, L. JU.
SOLUTION OF INTEGER QUADRATIC PROGRAMS (RUSSIAN), THE. PRIKLADNAJA MATEMATIKA I MEHANIKA 29, 158-161. (1965).

DEMM 1969 -1 DEMMY, W. S.
MULTI-COMMODITY FLOWS IN GENERALIZED NETWORKS. MEMORANDUM REPORT NO. 9. DAYTON: AIR FORCE LOGISTICS COMMAND, ADVANCED LOGISTICS SYSTEMS CENTER HEADQUARTERS. (1969).
DEMP 1968 -1 DEMPSTER, M. A. H.
ON THE GOTLIEB-CSIMA TIME-TABLING ALGORITHM. CANADIAN JOURNAL OF MATHEMATICS 20, 103-119. (1968).
DENA 1977 -1 DENARDO, E. V.
PERIODS OF CONNECTED NETWORKS AND POWER OF NONNEGATIVE MATRICES. MATHEMATICS OF OPERATIONS RESEARCH 2, 20-24. (1977).
DENAA 1978 -1 DENARDO, E. V.; FOX, B. L.
BUCKETS, SHORTEST PATHS, AND INTEGER PROGRAMMING. IN: M. L. PUTERMAN (ED.): DYNAMIC PROGRAMMING AND ITS APPLICATIONS, 249-254. NEW YORK, SAN FRANCISCO, LONDON: ACADEMIC PRESS. (1978).
DENAA 1979 -1 DENARDO, E. V.; FOX, B. L.
SHORTEST-ROUTE METHODS: 1. REACHING, PRUNING, AND BUCKETS. OPERATIONS RESEARCH 27, 161-186. (1979).
DENAA 1980 -1 DENARDO, E. V.; FOX, B. L.
ENFORCING CONSTRAINTS ON EXPANDED NETWORKS. OPERATIONS RESEARCH 28, 1213-1218. (1980).
DEO 1979 -1 DEO, N.
MINIMUM-LENGTH FUNDAMENTAL CYCLE SET. INSTITUTE OF ELECTRICAL AND ELECTRONICS ENGINEERS. TRANSACTIONS ON CIRCUITS AND SYSTEMS 26, 894-895. (1979).
DERI 1978 -1 DERIGS, U.
DUALITY AND THE ALGEBRAIC MATCHING PROBLEM. IN: R. HENN, P. KALL, H. KOENIG, B. KORTE, O. KRAFFT ET AL. (EDS.): OPERATIONS RESEARCH VERFAHREN 28. SECOND SYMPOSIUM ON OPERATIONS RESEARCH, AACHEN 1977, 253-264. MEISENHEIM: HAIN. (1978).
DERI 1979 -1 DERIGS, U.
DUALITY AND ADMISSIBLE TRANSFORMATIONS IN COMBINATORIAL OPTIMIZATION. ZEITSCHRIFT FUER OPERATIONS RESEARCH 23, SERIE A, 251-267. (1979).
DERI 1979 -2 DERIGS, U.
GENERALIZED HUNGARIAN METHOD FOR SOLVING MINIMUM WEIGHT PERFECT MATCHING PROBLEMS WITH ALGEBRAIC OBJECTIVE, A. DISCRETE APPLIED MATHEMATICS 1, 167-180. (1979).
DERI 1979 -3 DERIGS, U.
SHORTEST AUGMENTING PATH METHOD FOR SOLVING MINIMAL PERFECT MATCHING PROBLEMS, A. REPORT 79-06. KOELN: UNIV. KOELN, MATHEMATISCHES INSTITUT, 15 P. (1979).
DERI 1980 -1 DERIGS, U.
CARDINALITY MATCHING PROBLEM - METHODS AND COMPUTATION, THE. IN: P. HANSEN, D. DE WERRA (EDS.): REGARDS SUR LA THEORIE DES GRAPHES, PROCEEDINGS OF THE CERISY COLLOQUIUM, 1980, 199-204. LAUSANNE: PRESSES POLYTECHNIQUES ROMANDES. (1980).
DERI 1980 -2 DERIGS, U.
ENGPASS-ZIELFUNKTION UND ZEIT/KOSTEN - TRADE-OFFS BEIM TRANSPORTPROBLEM. KOELN: UNIVERSITAET KOELN, 203 P. (1980). (DISSERTATION)
DERI 1980 -3 DERIGS, U.
LOESUNG MINIMALER PERFEKTER MATCHINGPROBLEME MITTELS KUERZESTER ERWEITERNDER PFADE, DIE. IN: H. KOENIG, V. STEINMETZ (EDS.): METHODS OF OPERATIONS RESEARCH 37, 265-276. KOENIGSTEIN: ANTON HAIN MEISENHEIM. (1980).
DERI 1980 -4 DERIGS, U.
METHODEN ZUR LOESUNG DES BOTTLENECK-TRANSPORTPROBLEMS. IN: PROCEEDINGS IN OPERATIONS RESEARCH 9, 457-465. WUERZBURG: PHYSICA. (1980).
DERI 1980 -5 DERIGS, U.
ON TWO METHODS FOR SOLVING THE BOTTLENECK MATCHING PROBLEM. IN: K. IRACKI, K. MALANOWSKI, P. WALUKIEWICZ (EDS.): OPTIMIZATION TECHNIQUES, PART II, 176-184. LECTURE NOTES IN CONTROL AND INFORMATION SCIENCES 23. BERLIN: SPRINGER. (1980).
DERI 1981 -1 DERIGS, U.
F-FACTORS, PERFECT MATCHINGS AND RELATED CONCEPTS. IN: H. NOLTEMEYER (ED.): GRAPHTHEORETIC CONCEPTS IN COMPUTER SCIENCE, 388-403. LECTURE NOTES IN COMPUTER SCIENCE 100, BERLIN: SPRINGER. (1981).
DERI 1981 -2 DERIGS, U.
ON SOME EXPERIMENTS WITH A COMPOSITE HEURISTIC FOR SOLVING TRAVELLING SALESMAN PROBLEMS. IN: R. E. BURKARD, T. ELLINGER (EDS.): METHODS OF OPERATIONS RESEARCH 40, 287-290. KOENIGSTEIN: ANTON HAIN MEISENHEIM. (1981).
DERIA 1980 -1 DERIGS, U.; HESKE, A.
COMPUTATIONAL STUDY ON SOME METHODS FOR SOLVING THE CARDINALITY MATCHING PROBLEM, A. ANGEWANDTE INFORMATIK, NO. 4, 149-154. (1980).
DERIB 1979 -1 DERIGS, U.; KAZAKIDIS, G.
ON TWO METHODS FOR SOLVING MINIMAL PERFECT MATCHING PROBLEMS. KOELN: UNIV. KOELN, INDUSTRIESEMINAR, 15 P. (1979).
DERIC 1978 -1 DERIGS, U.; ZIMMERMANN, U.
DUALITY PRINCIPLES IN ALGEBRAIC LINEAR PROGRAMMING. REPORT 78-6. KOELN: UNIV. KOELN, MATHEMATISCHES INSTITUT, 20 P. (1978).
DERIC 1979 -1 DERIGS, U.; ZIMMERMANN, U.
AUGMENTING PATH METHOD FOR SOLVING LINEAR BOTTLENECK TRANSPORTATION PROBLEMS, AN. COMPUTING 22, 1-15. (1979).
DESC 1948 -1 DESCARTES, B.
NETWORK COLOURINGS. THE MATHEMATICAL GAZETTE 32, 67-69. (1948).
DESCA 1979 -1 DESCHAMPS, J.; LAPSCHER, F.
PRESENTATION ET OPTIMISATION D'UN PROGRAMME DE RECHERCHE DES DECOMPOSITIONS DISJOINTES D'UNE FONCTION BOOLEENNE: EXTENSION AUX FONCTIONS BOOLEENNES GENERALES. ACADEMIE DE LA REPUBLIQUE POPULAIRE ROUMAINE. REVUE ROUMAINE DE MATHEMATIQUES PURES ET APPLIQUEES 24, 893-911. (1979).
DESP 1974 -1 DESPONTIN, M.; OUDHEUSDEN, D. VAN; HANSEN, P.
CHOIX DE MEDIAS PAR PROGRAMMATION QUADRATIQUE EN VARIABLES 0-1. ACTES DU COLLOQUE DE L'AFCET, AIDE A LA DECISION 1, 1-8. (1974).
DESR 1978 -1 DESROCHES, S.; LAPORTE, G.; ROUSSEAU, J.-M.
HOREX: A COMPUTER PROGRAM FOR THE CONSTRUCTION OF EXAMINATION SCHEDULES. INFOR 16, 294-298. (1978).
DESRA 1980 -1 DESROSIERS, J.; FERLAND, J. A.; ROUSSEAU, J.-M.; LAPALME, G.; CHAPLEAU, L.
SCHOOL BUSING SYSTEM, A. CENTRE DE RECHERCHE SUR LES TRANSPORT-PUBLICATION, 164. MONTREAL: UNIV. DE MONTREAL, CENTRE DE RECHERCHE SUR LES TRANSPORTS, 35 P. (1980).
DESS 1981 -1 DESSOUKY, M. I.; DEOGUN, J. S.
SEQUENCING JOBS WITH UNEQUAL READY TIMES TO MINIMIZE MEAN FLOW TIME. SIAM JOURNAL ON COMPUTING 10, 192-202. (1981).
DESSA 1978 -1 DESSOUKY, M. I.; LARSON, R. E.
SYMMETRY AND OPTIMALITY PROPERTIES OF THE SINGLE MACHINE PROBLEM. AIIE TRANSACTIONS 10, 170-175. (1978).
DESSB 1975 -1 DESSOUKY, M. I.; LIEBMAN, J. S.; PHILLIPS, S. JR.; HOGG, G. L.
CUT-SEARCH TO THE MAXIMAL-FLOW MINIMAL-CUT PROBLEM. UNPUBLISHED MANUSCRIPT. UNIVERSITY OF ILLINOIS AT URBANA-CHAMPAIGN, DEPARTMENT OF CIVIL ENGINEERING. (1975).

***

DEWD 1977 -1 DEWDNEY, A. K.; HARARY, F.
ON THE CHROMATIC NUMBERS OF A SIMPLICIAL COMPLEX. J. COMBINATORICS INFORMATION SYST. SCI. 2, NO. 1, 28-35. (1977).

DEWE 1977 -1 DEWESS, G.
LOESUNG EINES MASCHINENBELEGUNGSPROBLEMS DURCH NETZPLANUNG MIT RESSOURCENBESCHRAENKUNG. IN: GRAPHENTHEORIE UND DEREN ANWENDUNGEN. INTERNATIONALES KOLLOQUIUM, OBERHOF 1977, 61-66. ILMENAU: TECHNISCHE HOCHSCHULE ILMENAU UND MATHEMATISCHE GESELLSCHAFT DER DDR. (1977).

DEWI 1979 -1 DEWITT, H. K.; KRIEGER, M. M.
EXPECTED LENGTH OF SHORTEST PATHS AND ALGORITHM BEHAVIOR. IN: F. HOFFMAN, D. MAC CARTHY, R. C. MULLIN, R. G. STANTON (EDS.): PROCEEDINGS OF THE TENTH SOUTHEASTERN CONFERENCE ON COMBINATORICS, GRAPH THEORY AND COMPUTING, 367-380. CONGRESSUS NUMERANTIUM XXIII. WINNIPEG: UTILITAS. (1979).

DHAL 1978 -1 DHALL, S. K.; LIU, C. L.
ON A REAL-TIME SCHEDULING PROBLEM. OPERATIONS RESEARCH 26, 127-140. (1978).

DHAV 1978 -1 DHAVALE, D.; AGGARWAL, S.
INVESTIGATION OF MULTIPRODUCT, MULTIMACHINE PRODUCTION SCHEDULING AND INVENTORY CONTROL OF A FLOW-SHOP SYSTEM, AN. INTERNATIONAL JOURNAL OF PRODUCTION RESEARCH 6, 477-492. (1978).

DIAL 1979 -1 DIAL, R.; GLOVER, F.; KARNEY, D.; KLINGMAN, D.
COMPUTATIONAL ANALYSIS OF ALTERNATIVE ALGORITHMS AND LABELING TECHNIQUES FOR FINDING SHORTEST PATH TREES, A. NETWORKS 9, 215-250. (1979).

DIAL 1980 -1 DIAL, R.; GLOVER, F.; KARNEY, D.; KLINGMAN, D.
SHORTEST PATH FOREST WITH TOPOLOGICAL ORDERING: AN ALGORITHM DESCRIPTION IN SDL. TRANSPORTATION RESEARCH 14B, 343-348. (1980).

DIAZ 1978 -1 DIAZ, J. A.
SOLVING MULTIOBJECTIVE TRANSPORTATION PROBLEMS. EKONOMICKO MATEMATICKY OBZOR 14, 267-274. (1978).

DIAZ 1979 -1 DIAZ, J. A.
FINDING A COMPLETE DESCRIPTION OF ALL EFFICIENT SOLUTIONS IN A MULTIOBJECTIVE TRANSPORTATION PROBLEM. EKONOMICKO-MATEMATICKY OBZOR 15, 62-73. (1979).

DIEN 1979 -1 DIENES, I.; KOVACS, L. B.
MAXIMUM TRANSITIVE PATHS AND THEIR APPLICATION TO A GEOLOGICAL PROBLEM SETTING UP STRATIGRAPHIC UNITS. IN: A. PREKOPA (ED.): SURVEY OF MATHEMATICAL PROGRAMMING, VOLUME 2, 441-454. AMSTERDAM: NORTH-HOLLAND. (1979).

DINE 1976 -1 DINESCU, C.
OPTIMAL ELEMENTARY PATHS IN NETWORKS WITH CIRCUITS. ANALELE UNIVERSITATII BUCURESTI. STIINTELE NATURI 25, 7-14. (1976).

DINEA 1978 -1 DINESCU, C.; SAVULESCU, B.
NEW RESULTS IN THE FLOW TRANSPORT PROBLEM. ANALELE UNIVERSITATII BUCURESTI. MATEMATICA 27, 21-35. (1978).

DINEA 1979 -1 DINESCU, C.; SAVULESCU, B.
ABOUT THE DETERMINATION OF MAXIMUM FLOW IN A NETWORK. IN: A. PREKOPA (ED.): SURVEY OF MATHEMATICAL PROGRAMMING, VOLUME 2, 239-244. AMSTERDAM: NORTH-HOLLAND. (1979).

DINI 1976 -1 DINIC, E. A.
SOLUTION OF TWO ASSIGNMENT PROBLEMS (RUSSIAN), THE. IN: A. A. FRIDMAN (ED.): STUDIES IN DISCRETE OPTIMIZATION (RUSSIAN), 333-348. MOSCOW: IZDAT. "NAUKA". (1976).

DINIA 1976 -1 DINIC, E. A.; KARZANOV, A. V.; LOMONOSOV, M. V.
STRUCTURE OF A SYSTEM OF MINIMAL EDGE CUTS OF A GRAPH (RUSSIAN), THE. IN: STUDIES IN DISCRETE OPTIMIZATION (RUSSIAN), 290-306. MOSCOW: IZDAT. "NAUKA". (1976).

DINIB 1978 -1 DINIC, E. A.; ZAICEV, M. A.
GENERATION OF MARKED TREES AND SEPARABLE NETWORKS (RUSSIAN). IN: I. A. FARADZEV (ED.): ALGORITHMIC STUDIES IN COMBINATORICS (RUSSIAN), INTERNATIONAL COLLOQUIUM ON COMBINATORICS AND GRAPH THEORY, ORSAY 1976, 100-107 + 186. MOSCOW: IZDAT. "NAUKA". (1978).

DINIB 1978 -2 DINIC, E. A.; ZAICEV, M. A.
LINEAR ORDERING AND GENERATION OF TREES (RUSSIAN). IN: I. A. FARADZEV (ED.): ALGORITHMIC STUDIES IN COMBINATORICS (RUSSIAN), INTERNATIONAL COLLOQUIUM ON COMBINATORICS AND GRAPH THEORY, ORSAY 1976, 85-99 + 186. MOSCOW: IZDAT. "NAUKA". (1978).

DION 1978 -1 DIONNE, R.
ETUDE ET EXTENSION D'UN ALGORITHME DE MURCHLAND. OPERATIONS RESEARCH 26, 132-146. (1978).

DIONA 1979 -1 DIONNE, R.; FLORIAN, M.
EXACT AND APPROXIMATE ALGORITMS FOR OPTIMAL NETWORK DESIGN. NETWORKS 9, 37-59. (1979).

DIRA 1973 -1 DIRAC, G. A.
NOTE ON HAMILTON CIRCUITS AND HAMILTON PATHS. MATHEMATISCHE ANNALEN 206, 139-147. (1973).

DIRA 1978 -1 DIRAC, G. A.
HAMILTON CIRCUITS AND LONG CIRCUITS. IN: B. BOLLOBAS (ED.): ADVANCES IN GRAPH THEORY, 75-92. ANNALS OF DISCRETE MATHEMATICS 3. AMSTERDAM: NORTH-HOLLAND. (1978).

DIRU 1980 -1 DIRUF, G.
KUNDENZEITSCHRANKEN IN DER COMPUTERGESTUETZTEN TOURENPLANUNG. ZEITSCHRIFT FUER OPERATIONS RESEARCH SERIE B (PRAXIS) 24, 207-220. (1980).

DJOK 1970 -1 DJOKOVIC, D. Z.
ISOMORPHISM PROBLEM FOR A SPECIAL CLASS OF GRAPHS. ACTA MATHEMATICA ACADEMIAE SCIENTIARUM HUNGARICAE 21, 267-270. (1970).

DJUK 1977 -1 DJUKANOV, V. G.
LIST REPRESENTATION FOR THE MACHINE SOLUTION OF AN ILL-POSED TRANSPORT PROBLEM (RUSSIAN). AKADEMIJA NAUK UKRAINOI SSR INSTITUTI KIBERNETIKI, 36-49. (1977).

DOBK 1978 -1 DOBKIN, D. P.; LIPTON, R. J.
LOWER BOUND OF 1/2*N**2 ON LINEAR SEARCH PROGRAMS FOR THE KNAPSACK PROBLEM. JOURNAL OF COMPUTER AND SYSTEM SCIENCES 16, 413-418. (1978).

DOBK 1979 -1 DOBKIN, D. P.; LIPTON, R. J.
ON THE COMPLEXITY OF COMPUTATIONS UNDER VARYING SETS OF PRIMITIVES. JOURNAL OF COMPUTER AND SYSTEM SCIENCES 18, 86-91. (1979).

DOBKA 1978 -1 DOBKIN, D. P.; LIPTON, R. J.; REISS, S. P.
EXCURSIONS INTO GEOMETRY. RESEARCH REPORT, 71. NEW HAVEN: YALE UNIV., DEPT. OF COMPUTER SCIENCE, 123 P. (1978).

DODO 1977 -1 DODONOV, A. G.; CHERNYSHEV, JU. O.; SADOVOI, N. N.; SHCHETININ, A. M.
SOLUTION OF THE ASSIGNMENT PROBLEM BY REDUCING IT TO THE PROBLEM OF FINDING THE OPTIMAL PATH ON A GRAPH (RUSSIAN). ELEKTRIKAI MODELIROVANI, NO. 15, 77-80. (1977).

DODU 1975 -1 DODU, J. C.
MODELE D'OPTIMISATION A LONG TERME D'UN RESEAU DE TRANSPORT. ELECTRICITE DE FRANCE: BULLETIN DE LA DIRECTION DES ETUDES ET RECHERCHES, SERIE C, MATHEMATIQUES, INFORMATIQUE, NO. 2, 43-56. (1975).

DODU 1978 -1 DODU, J. C.
MODELE DYNAMIQUE D'OPTIMISATION A LONG TERME D'UN RESEAU DE TRANSPORT D'ENERGIE ELECTRIQUE. REVUE FRANCAISE D'AUTOMATIQUE, D'INFORMATIQUE ET DE RECHERCHE OPERATIONELLE 12, SERIE RECHERCHE OPERATIONELLE, 141-167. (1978).

DOGR 1978 -1 DOGRAMACI, A.; SURKIS, J.
LIMITATIONS OF A PARALLEL PROCESSOR SCHEDULING ALGORITHM. INTERNATIONAL JOURNAL OF PRODUCTION RESEARCH 16, 83-85. (1978).

DOGR 1979 -1 DOGRAMACI, A.; SURKIS, J.
EVALUATION OF A HEURISTIC FOR SCHEDULING INDEPENDENT JOBS ON PARALLEL IDENTICAL PROCESSORS. MANAGEMENT SCIENCE 25, 1208-1216. (1979).

DOKU 1979 -1 DOKUCAEV, V. N.
ANALYSIS OF A NETWORK MODEL OF DELIVERY CONTROL (RUSSIAN). EKONOMIKA I MATEMATICESKIE METODY 15, 774-782. (1979).

DOLL 1980 -1 DOLL, C. L.
QUICK AND DIRTY VEHICLE ROUTING PROCEDURE. INTERFACES 10, 84-85. (1980).

DOMB 1977 -1 DOMB, C.
GENERALIZATION OF THE KOENIGSBERG BRIDGES PROBLEM, A. MATHEMATICAL PROCEEDINGS OF THE CAMBRIDGE PHILOSOPHICAL SOCIETY 82, 1-4. (1977).

DOMS 1978 -1 DOMSCHKE, W.; ENGELE, E.
MOEGLICHKEITEN DER TRANSFORMATION EINES VERKEHRSNETZES IN EIN DAZU DUALES NETZ ZUM ZWECKE VON KAPAZITAETSUNTERSUCHUNGEN. ANGEWANDTE INFORMATIK 20, NO. 10, 432-437. (1978).

DONA 1979 -1 DONALDSON, J. L.
MINKOWSKI REDUCTION OF INTEGRAL MATRICES. MATHEMATICS OF COMPUTATION 33, 201-216. (1979).

DORF 1979 -1 DORFMAN, V. A.
POLYHEDRON FOR A PROBLEM OF ORDERING TASKS AT A MACHINE (RUSSIAN). IN: CONTROL OF TECHNICAL AND ORGANIZATIONAL SYSTEMS BY APPLICATION OF COMPUTER TECHNOLOGY, 139-145, 229. MOSCOW: NAUKA. (1979).

DORH 1977 -1 DORHOUT, B.
EXPERIMENTS WITH SOME ALGORITHMS FOR THE LINEAR ASSIGNMENT PROBLEM. BW 39/77. AMSTERDAM: MATHEMATISCH CENTRUM, 21 P. (1977).

DOUM 1978 -1 DOUMEINGTS, G.; PUN, L.; MONDAIN, M.; BREUIL, D.
DECISION-MAKING SYSTEMS FOR PRODUCTION CONTROL PLANNING AND SCHEDULING. INTERNATIONAL JOURNAL OF PRODUCTION RESEARCH 16, 137-152. (1978).

DOWL 1980 -1 DOWLING, T. A.
ON THE INDEPENDENT SET NUMBERS OF A FINITE MATROID. IN: M. DEZA, I. G. ROSENBERG (EDS.): COMBINATORICS 79, PART I, 21-28. ANNALS OF DISCRETE MATHEMATICS 8. AMSTERDAM: NORTH-HOLLAND. (1980).

DOWLA 1976 -1 DOWLING, T. A.; KELLY, D. G.
ELEMENTARY STRONG MAPS BETWEEN COMBINATORIAL GEOMETRIES. IN: ACCADEMIA NAZIONALE DEI LINCEI (ED.): COLLOQUIO INTERNAZIONALE SULLE TEORIE COMBINATORIE CON LA COLLABORAZIONE DELLA AMERICAN MATHEMATICAL SOCIETY, TOMO II, ROMA 1973, 121-152. ROMA: ACCADEMIA NAZIONALE DEI LINCEI. (1976).

DOYE 1975 -1 DOYEN, J.; VANDIEST, V.
GRAPHES HYPOHAMILTONIENS. CAHIERS DU CENTRE D'ETUDES DE RECHERCHE OPERATIONELLE 17, 191-192. (1975).

DOYL 1978 -1 DOYLE, T. E.; MOORE, T. G.; SACKETT, R. A.
BENDER'S DECOMPOSITION APPROACH TO SCHEDULING SWITCHING SYSTEM REPLACEMENTS AND EQUIPMENT REUSE. LOS ANGELES (ORSA/TIMS MEETING, NOVEMBER 1978) 22 P. (1978).

DRAG 1976 -1 DRAGAN, I.
NETWORK FLOW MODEL FOR SOLVING A COOPERATIVE GAME, A. SYMPOSIA MATHEMATICA, 9. BOLOGNA: ISTITUTO NAZIONALE DI ALTA MATEMATICA, P. 215-277 (1976).

DREY 1977 -1 DREYFUS, S. E.; LAW, A. M.
ART AND THEORY OF DYNAMIC PROGRAMMING, THE. NEW YORK, SAN FRANCISCO, LONDON: ACADEMIC PRESS, 284 P. (1977). (MATHEMATICS IN SCIENCE AND ENGINEERING, 130)

DREZ 1978 -1 DREZNER, Z.; WESOLOWSKY, G. O.
FACILITY LOCATION ON A SPHERE. THE JOURNAL OF THE OPERATIONAL RESEARCH SOCIETY 29, 997-1004. (1978).

DREZ 1978 -2 DREZNER, Z.; WESOLOWSKY, G. O.
NEW METHOD FOR THE MULTIFACILITY MINIMAX LOCATION PROBLEM, A. THE JOURNAL OF THE OPERATIONAL RESEARCH SOCIETY 29, 1095-1101. (1978).

DREZ 1978 -3 DREZNER, Z.; WESOLOWSKY, G. O.
TRAJECTORY METHOD FOR THE OPTIMIZATION OF THE MULTI-FACILITY LOCATION PROBLEM WITH LP DISTANCES, A. MANAGEMENT SCIENCE 24, 1507-1514. (1978).

DREZ 1980 -1 DREZNER, Z.; WESOLOWSKY, G. O.
OPTIMAL LOCATION OF A FACILITY RELATIVE TO AREA DEMANDS. NAVAL RESEARCH LOGISTICS QUARTERLY 27, 199-206. (1980).

DREZ 1980 -2 DREZNER, Z.; WESOLOWSKY, G. O.
SINGLE FACILITY L(P)-DISTANCE MINIMAX LOCATION. SIAM JOURNAL ON ALGEBRAIC AND DISCRETE METHODS 1, 315-321. (1980).

DRIS 1977 -1 DRISCOLL, W. C.; EMMONS, H.
SCHEDULING PRODUCTION ON ONE MACHINE WITH CHANGEOVER COSTS. AIIE TRANSACTIONS 9, 388-395. (1977).

DRIS 1979 -1 DRISCOLL, W. C.; EMMONS, H.
VEHICLE ROUTING FOR MINIMUM COST. WORKING PAPER. YOUNGSTOWN: YOUNGSTOWN STATE UNIV., 17 P. (1979).

DROE 1977 -1 DROESBEKE, F.; BERCKMANS, A.
TRANSPORTATION PROBLEM WITH CAPACITIES AND MIXED CONSTRAINTS, THE. IN: M. ROUBENS (ED.): ADVANCES IN OPERATIONS RESEARCH. PROCEEDINGS OF EURO II, THE SECOND EUROPEAN CONGRESS ON OPERATIONS RESEARCH, STOCKHOLM 1976, 135-142. AMSTERDAM, NEW YORK, OXFORD: NORTH-HOLLAND. (1977).

DROEA 1978 -1 DROESBEKE, F.; FRENNE, A. DE
ETUDE DES BORNES DU NOMBRE CHROMATIQUE D'UN GRAPHE. II. IN: J.-C. BERMOND ET AL. (EDS.): PROBLEMES COMBINATOIRES ET THEORIE DES GRAPHES, COLLOQUES INTERNATIONAUX DU CENTRE NATIONAL DE LA RECHERCHE SCIENTIFIQUE, ORSAY 1976, 113-116. PARIS: CENTRE NATIONAL DE LA RECHERCHE SCIENTIFIQUE. (1978).

DUBE 1979 -1 DUBE, R.; ELSAYED, E. A.
MULTI-MACHINE LABOR ASSIGNMENT FOR VARIABLE OPERATOR SERVICE TIMES, A. COMPUTERS AND OPERATIONS RESEARCH 6, 147-154. (1979).

DUBO 1979 -1 DUBOIS, D.; BEL, G.; LLIBRE, M.
SET OF METHODS IN TRANSPORTATION NETWORK SYNTHESIS AND ANALYSIS, A. JOURNAL OF THE OPERATIONAL RESEARCH SOCIETY 30, 797-808. (1979).

DUBOA 1978 -1 DUBOIS, D.; PRADE, H.
ALGORITHMES DE PLUS COURTS CHEMINS POUR TRAITER DES DONNEES FLOUES. REVUE FRANCAISE D'AUTOMATIQUE, D'INFORMATIQUE ET DE RECHERCHE OPERATIONELLE 12, SERIE RECHERCHE OPERATIONELLE, 213-227. (1978).

DUCA 1980 -1 DUCA, D.
ON THE HIERARCHY OF THE EXTREMAL SOLUTIONS OF A FRACTIONAL PROGRAMMING PROBLEM (ROMANIAN). STUDII SI CERCETARI MATEMATICE 32, 179-185. (1980).

DUCH 1973 -1 DUCHAMP, A.
SUR LA STRUCTURE DES REPRESENTATIONS D'UN MATROIDE TRANSVERSAL. COMPTES RENDUS HEBDOMADAIRES DES SEANCES DE L'ACADEMIE DES SCIENCES PARIS. SERIES A ET B 276. A719-A722. (1973).

DUCH 1980 -1 DUCHAMP, A.
FORMES BILINEAIRES SYMETRIQUES SUR UN ESPACE VECTORIEL DE DIMENSION FINIE SUR LE CORPS A DEUX ELEMENTS. APPLICATIONS AUX MATROIDES BINAIRES. IN: M. DEZA, I. G. ROSENBERG (EDS.): COMBINATORICS 79, PART II. 269-276. ANNALS OF DISCRETE MATHEMATICS 9. AMSTERDAM: NORTH-HOLLAND. (1980).

DUCHA 1978 -1 DUCHET, P.
COLORATIONS TRANSITIVES DES GRAPHES. IN: COLLOQUE MATHEMATIQUES DISCRETES: CODES ET HYPERGRAPHES, BRUSSELS 1978. CAHIERS DU CENTRE D'ETUDES DE RECHERCHE OPERATIONELLE 20, NO. 3-4. 363-371. (1978).

DUEC 1977 -1 DUECK, W.
DISKRETE OPTIMIERUNG. BRAUNSCHWEIG: VIEWEG. 139 P. (1977). (REIHE WISSENSCHAFT)

DUER 1978 -1 DUERRE, K.
APPROXIMATE ALGORITHMS FOR COLORING LARGE GRAPHS. IN: J. MUEHLBACHER (ED.): DATENSTRUKTUREN, GRAPHEN, ALGORITHMEN. DRITTE FACHTAGUNG UEBER GRAPHENTHEORETISCHE KONZEPTE DER INFORMATIK, LINZ 1977. 191-203. MUENCHEN, WIEN: HANSER. (1978).

DUFF 1978 -1 DUFF, I. S.; REID, J. K.
IMPLEMENTATION OF TARJAN'S ALGORITHM FOR THE BLOCK TRIANGULARIZATION OF A MATRIX, AN. ACM TRANSACTIONS ON MATHEMATICAL SOFTWARE 4. 137-147. (1978).

DULA 1980 -1 DULAC, G.; FERLAND, J. A.; FORGUES, P. A.
SCHOOL BUS ROUTES GENERATOR IN URBAN SURROUNDINGS. COMPUTERS AND OPERATIONS RESEARCH 7. 199-213. (1980).

DUMA 1977 -1 DUMAS, M. B.
BRANCH BIAS HEURISTIC SCHEDULING OF THE GENERAL JOB SHOP. SCIMA 6. 33-46. (1977).

DUMA 1978 -1 DUMAS, M. B.
BOUND CUTOFF HEURISTIC SCHEDULING OF THE GENERAL JOB SHOP. SCIMA 7. 1-15. (1978).

DUMI 1979 -1 DUMITRU, V.
INTEGER NONLINEAR PROGRAMMING VIA SUMT TECHNIQUES. IN: W. OETTLI, F. STEFFENS (EDS.): OPERATIONS RESEARCH VERFAHREN 32. THIRD SYMPOSIUM ON OPERATIONS RESEARCH, MANNHEIM 1978. 79-87. KOENIGSTEIN: ANTON HAIN MEISENHEIM. (1979).

DUMIA 1979 -1 DUMITRU, V.; LUBAN, F.
MEMBERSHIP FUNCTIONS, SOME MATHEMATICAL PROGRAMMING MODELS AND PRODUCTION SCHEDULING. PREPRINT LCCE-CO-15-70. BUCURESTI: ACADEMIA DE STUDII ECONOMICE, LABORATOARELE CATEDREI DE CIBERNETICA ECONOMICA. 34 P. (1979).

DUMIA 1980 -1 DUMITRU, V.; LUBAN, F.
MATHEMATICAL PROGRAMMING REAL VARIABLE MODELS FOR INTEGER AND MIXED-INTEGER PROBLEMS. ECONOMIC COMPUTATION AND ECONOMIC CYBERNETICS STUDIES AND RESEARCH 14, NO. 3. 69-80. (1980).

DUNC 1979 -1 DUNCAN, I. B.; NOBLE, B. M.
ALLOCATION OF SPECIALTIES TO HOSPITALS IN A HEALTH DISTRICT, THE. JOURNAL OF THE OPERATIONAL RESEARCH SOCIETY 30. 953-964. (1979).

DUNS 1978 -1 DUNSMUIR, A. M.
SIMPLE ALLOCATION ALGORITHM IN PRODUCTION PLANNING, A. THE JOURNAL OF THE OPERATIONAL RESEARCH SOCIETY 29. 443-448. (1978).

DUNSA 1976 -1 DUNSTAN, F. D. J.
MATROIDS AND SUBMODULAR FUNCTIONS. QUARTERLY JOURNAL OF MATHEMATICS 27, NO. 107. 339-348. (1976).

DUPR 1979 -1 DUPRE, R.; HUCKERT, K.
NAEHERUNGSVERFAHREN FUER MASCHINENBELEGUNGSPROBLEME, EIN. IN: H. SPAETH (ED.): AUSGEWAEHLTE OPERATIONS RESEARCH SOFTWARE IN FORTRAN. 67-86. MUENCHEN: OLDENBOURG. (1979).

DUTT 1981 -1 DUTTON, R. D.; BINGHAM, R. C.
NEW GRAPH COLOURING ALGORITHM, A. THE COMPUTER JOURNAL 24. 85-86. (1981).

DUUR 1970 -1 DUUREN, A. VAN; VERANTVOORT, J.
JOB-SHOP SCHEDULING. IN: PROCEEDINGS OF THE SYMPOSIUM ON INTERACTIVE COMPUTER GRAPHICS. 25-48. DELFT. (1970).

EA 1978 -1 EA, K.
EXTENSION DU PROBLEME DU VOYAGEUR DE COMMERCE: LE PROBLEME DU RAMASSAGE SCOLAIRE, UNE. GRENOBLE. 95 P. (1978).

EARL 1968 -1 EARLY, S.
EVALUATING A TIME-TABLING ALGORITHM BASED ON GRAPH-RECOLOURING. D. PHIL THESIS. OXFORD: OXFORD UNIVERSITY. (1968).

EBER 1977 -1 EBERT, J.
OPERATOR-ALGORITHMEN AUF MATRIZEN-DARSTELLUNGEN VON GRAPHEN. MUENSTER: RECHENZENTRUM, UNIV. MUENSTER. 132 P. (1977). (SCHRIFTENREIHE, 25)

EBER 1980 -1 EBERT, J.
FINDING SPANNING FORESTS: A PROBLEM OF DATA MANIPULATION. IN: U. PAPE (ED.): DISCRETE STRUCTURES AND ALGORITHMS. 115-130. MUENCHEN: HANSER. (1980).

ECKE 1977 -1 ECKER, K.
ORGANISATION VON PARALLELEN PROZESSEN. THEORIE DETERMINISTISCHER SCHEDULES. MANNHEIM, WIEN, ZUERICH: BIBLIOGRAPHISCHES INSTITUT. 280 P. (1977). (REIHE INFORMATIK, 23)

ECKS 1977 -1 ECKSTEIN, D. M.; ALTON, D. A.
PARALLEL GRAPH PROCESSING USING DEPTH-FIRST SEARCH. IN: E. A. ASHCROFT ET AL. (EDS.): PROCEEDINGS OF A CONFERENCE ON THEORETICAL COMPUTER SCIENCE, WATERLOO 1977. 21-29. WATERLOO: UNIVERSITY OF WATERLOO. (1977).

EDMO 1979 -1 EDMONDS, J.
MATROID INTERSECTION. IN: P. L. HAMMER, E. L. JOHNSON, B. H. KORTE (EDS.): DISCRETE OPTIMIZATION I. 39-49. ANNALS OF DISCRETE MATHEMATICS 4. AMSTERDAM, NEW YORK, OXFORD: NORTH-HOLLAND. (1979).

EDMOA 1978 -1 EDMONDS, J.; JOHNSON, E. L.; LOCKHART, S. C.
BLOSSOM I: A COMPUTER CODE FOR THE MATCHING PROBLEM. WATERLOO: UNIV. OF WATERLOO. 116 P. (1978).

EDWA 1980 -1 EDWARDS, C. S.
BRANCH AND BOUND ALGORITHM FOR THE KOOPMANS-BECKMANN QUADRATIC ASSIGNMENT PROBLEM, A. MATHEMATICAL PROGRAMMING STUDY 13.35-52. (1980).

EDWAA 1980 -1 EDWARDS, G. R.
APPROACH TO THE CREW SCHEDULING PROBLEM, AN. NEW ZEALAND OPERATIONAL RESEARCH 8. 153-172. (1980).

EHNE 1976 -1 EHNERT, G.
SOME REMARKS ON AN ALGORITHM FOR TESTING PLANAR GRAPHS. IN: M. BOROWIECKI, Z. SKUPIEN, L. SZAMKOLOWICZ (EDS.): GRAPHS, HYPERGRAPHS AND BLOCK SYSTEMS. PROCEEDINGS OF THE SYMPOSIUM ON COMBINATORIAL ANALYSIS, ZIELONA GORA 1976. 53-55. ZIELONA GORA. (1976).

EHRE 1976 -1 EHRENFEUCHT, A.; HURSCH, J. L. JR.; MORGENSTERN, C.
GROWTH NUMBER AND COLORABILITY OF GRAPHS II. NOTICES OF THE AMERICAN MATHEMATICAL SOCIETY 23. A-512. (1976).

****

EILO 1978 -1 EILON, S.; GALVAO, R. D.
SINGLE AND DOUBLE VERTEX SUBSTITUTION IN HEURISTIC PROCEDURES FOR THE P-MEDIAN PROBLEM. MANAGEMENT SCIENCE 24, 1763-1766. (1978).
EISE 1978 -1 EISELT, H.
INHOMOGENE FLUSSPROBLEME: DAS MIN-MAX THEOREM. GOETTINGEN: EICHHORN, 131 P. (1978).
EL-S 1980 -1 EL-SAWY, A. H. A.
MIXED INTEGER SCHEDULING MODEL FOR COMBINED THERMAL AND HYDROELECTRIC-PUMPED STORAGE GENERATOR SYSTEMS, A. ENERGY SYSTEMS AND POLICY 3, 337-351. (1980).
ELAM 1979 -1 ELAM, J.; GLOVER, F.; KLINGMAN, D.
STRONGLY CONVERGENT PRIMAL SIMPLEX ALGORITHM FOR GENERALIZED NETWORKS, A. MATHEMATICS OF OPERATIONS RESEARCH 4, 39-59. (1979).
ELAMA 1977 -1 ELAM, J.; KLINGMAN, D.; MULVEY, J. M.
EVALUATION OF MATHEMATICAL PROGRAMMING AND MINICOMPUTERS, AN. RESEARCH REPORT CCS 313. AUSTIN: UNIV. OF TEXAS, CENTER FOR CYBERNETIC STUDIES, 19 P. (1977).
ELKE 1979 -1 ELKEN, T. R.; FREEDMAN, H. T.; GIBSON, A. E.
POLYNOMIAL BOUND ALGORITHM FOR A NONLINEAR NETWORK ALLOCATION PROBLEM,A. NEW ORLEANS (TIMS/ ORSA MEETING, APRIL/MAY 1979) 22 P. (1979).
ELMA 1978 -1 ELMAGHRABY, S. E.
ECONOMIC LOT SCHEDULING PROBLEM (ELSP): REVIEW AND EXTENSIONS, THE. MANAGEMENT SCIENCE 24, 587-598. (1978).
ELMAA 1980 -1 ELMAGHRABY, S. E.; ELIMAM, A. A.
KNAPSACK-BASED APPROACHES TO THE MAKESPAN PROBLEM ON MULTIPLE PROCESSORS. AIIE TRANSACTIONS 12, 87-96. (1980).
ELMAB 1980 -1 ELMAGHRABY, S. E.; HERROELEN, W. S.
ON THE MEASUREMENT OF COMPLEXITY IN ACTIVITY NETWORKS. EUROPEAN JOURNAL OF OPERATIONAL RESEARCH 5, 223-234. (1980).
EMEL 1978 -1 EMELICHEV, V. A.; KRACKOVSKII, A. P.
ASYMPTOTIC PROPERTIES OF TRANSPORTATION POLYHEDRA (RUSSIAN). VESCI AKADEMII NAVUK BSSR. SERYJA FIZIKA-MATEMATYCNYH NAVUK, NO. 4, 116-118. (1978).
EMELA 1977 -1 EMELICHEV, V. A.; KRAVTSOV, M. K.; KRACKOVSKII, A. P.
BEWEIS EINER HYPOTHESE VON BOLKER (RUSSIAN). DOKLADY AKADEMII NAUK BSSR 21, 788-790. (1977).
EMELA 1977 -2 EMELICHEV, V. A.; KRAVTSOV, M. K.; KRACKOVSKII, A. P.
ON A CONJECTURE ABOUT THE MAXIMAL NUMBER OF VERTICES OF A TRANPORTATION POLYTOPE (RUSSIAN). VESCI AKADEMII NAVUK BSSR. SERYJA FIZIKA-MATEMATYCNYH NAVUK, NO. 6, 114-118. (1977).
EMELA 1978 -1 EMELICHEV, V. A.; KRAVTSOV, M. K.; KRACKOVSKII, A. P.
MINIMAL NUMBER OF VERTICES OF A NONDEGENERATE TRANSPORTATION POLYTOPE WITH A FIXED NUMBER OF FACES (RUSSIAN), THE. DOKLADY AKADEMII NAUK BSSR 22, 15-17. (1978).
EMELA 1978 -2 EMELICHEV, V. A.; KRAVTSOV, M. K.; KRACKOVSKII, A. P.
ON SOME CLASSES OF TRANSPORTATION POLYTOPES (RUSSIAN). DOKLADY AKADEMII NAUK SSSR 241, 532-535; TRANSLATED AS SOVIET MATHEMATICS DOKLADY 19, 1978, 889-893. (1978).
EMELB 1977 -1 EMELICHEV, V. A.; TRUKHANOVSKIJ, N. N.
SPECTRUM OF TRANSPORTATION POLYHEDRA (RUSSIAN), THE. VESCI AKADEMII NAVUK BSSR. SERYJA FIZIKA-MATEMATYCNYH NAVUK, NO. 5, 107-108. (1977).
EMELC 1977 -1 EMELICHEVA, V. S.; KRAVTSOV, M. K.
FACES OF A DEGENERATE TRANSPORTATION POLYHEDRON (RUSSIAN), THE. VESCI AKADEMII NAVUK BSSR. SERYJA FIZIKA-MATEMATYCNYH NAVUK, NO. 5, 23-26. (1977).
EMMO 1978 -1 EMMONS, H.
SURVEY OF STATIC JOB SHOP SCHEDULING THEORY, A. (REVISED VERSION). CLEVELAND: CASE WESTERN RESERVE UNIV., DEPT. OF OPERATIONS RESEARCH, 38 P. (1978).
ENGE 1981 -1 ENGELE, G.
SIMULTANE STANDORT- UND TOURENPLANUNG. SCHRIFTEN DES FACHBEREICHS WIRTSCHAFTS- UND ORGANISATIONSWISSENSCHAFTEN DER HOCHSCHULE DER BUNDESWEHR HAMBURG, BAND 3. KOELN: CARL HEYMANNS VERLAG, 175 P. (1981).
ENGQ 1980 -1 ENGQUIST, M.
SUCCESSIVE SHORTEST PATH ALGORITHM FOR THE ASSIGNMENT PROBLEM, A. RESEARCH REPORT CCS 375. AUSTIN: UNIV. OF TEXAS, CENTER FOR CYBERNETIC STUDIES, 31 P. (1980).
ENTR 1977 -1 ENTRINGER, R. C.; SLATER, P. J.
NOTE ON K-CRITICALLY N-CONNECTED GRAPHS, A. PROCEEDINGS OF THE AMERICAN MATHEMATICAL SOCIETY 66, NO. 2, 372-375. (1977).
EPIH 1975 -1 EPIHIN, V. V.
ESTIMATION OF THE NUMBER OF TREES OF A GRAPH (RUSSIAN). IN: METHODS OF TELETRAFFIC THEORY IN INFORMATION DISTRIBUTION SYSTEMS (RUSSIAN), 157-163. MOSCOW: IZDAT NAUKA. (1975).
ERDO 1977 -1 ERDOES, P.; ROTHSCHILD, B. L.; SINGHI, N. M.
CHARACTERIZING CLIQUES IN HYPERGRAPHS. ARS COMBINATORIA 4, 81-118. (1977).
EREM 1978 -1 EREMENKO, I. V.; PHOVELISVILI, Z. I.
APPROXIMATE AND EXACT METHOD FOR SEARCHING THE HAMILTONIAN CYCLE OF MINIMAL LENGTH (RUSSIAN), AN. SAKHARTHVELOS SSR MECNIEREBATHA AKADEMIS GAMOTHVLITHI CENTRIS SROMEBI 18, NO. 2, VOPROSY VYCIS. TEHN. I UPRAVLENIJA, 20-33. (1978).
EREM 1978 -2 EREMENKO, I. V.; PHOVELISVILI, Z. I.
ON THE QUESTION OF PERFECTING A NUMERICAL SCHEME FOR THE SOLUTION OF A TRANSPORT PROBLEM BY THE HUNGARIAN METHOD (RUSSIAN). SAKHARTHVELOS SSR MECNIEREBATHA AKADEMIS GAMOTHVLITHI CENTRIS SROMEBI 18, NO. 2, VOPROSY VYCIS. TEHN. I UPRAVLENIJA, 34-41. (1978).
ERLA 1974 -1 ERLANDER, S.; SCHEELE, S.
MATHEMATICAL PROGRAMMING MODEL FOR BUS TRAFFIC IN A NETWORK, A. IN: D. J. BUCKLEY (ED.): TRANSPORTATION AND TRAFFIC THEORY, 581-605. NEW YORK: ELSEVIER. (1974).
ERLE 1977 -1 ERLENKOTTER, D.
FACILITY LOCATION WITH PRICE-SENSITIVE DEMANDS: PRIVATE, PUBLIC AND QUASI-PUBLIC. MANAGEMENT SCIENCE 24, 378-386. (1977).
ERLE 1978 -1 ERLENKOTTER, D.
DUAL BASED PROCEDURE FOR UNCAPACITATED FACILITY LOCATION, A. OPERATIONS RESEARCH 26, 992-1009. (1978).
ERLE 1978 -2 ERLENKOTTER, D.
SHOULD CALIFORNIA AGRICULTURE RECEIVE PREFERENTIAL WATER RATES. WORKING PAPER NO. 285. LOS ANGELES: UNIV. OF CALIFORNIA, WESTERN MANAGEMENT SCIENCE INSTITUTE, 34 P. (1978).
ERLE 1981 -1 ERLENKOTTER, D.
COMPARATIVE STUDY OF APPROACHES TO DYNAMIC LOCATION PROBLEMS, A. EUROPEAN JOURNAL OF OPERATIONAL RESEARCH 6, 133-143. (1981).
ERMO 1976 -1 ERMOLEV, JU. M.; MELNIK, I. M.
SHORTEST PATHS IN STOCHASTIC GRAPHS. IN: METHODS OF OPERATIONS RESEARCH AND RELIABILITY THEORY IN SYSTEMS ANALYSIS (RUSSIAN), 59-66. KIEV: AKADEMIJA NAUK UKRAINSKOI. (1976).
EROK 1981 -1 EROKHIN, I. L.; KAPLAN, S. G.
PARTIAL SEARCH ALGORITHM FOR INTEGER PROBLEMS SOLUTION (RUSSIAN). EKONOMIKA I MATEMATICESKIE METODY (MOSCOW) 17, NO. 1, 131-140. (1981).

ERSC 1979 -1 ERSCHLER, J.; FONTAN, G.; ROUBELLAT, F.
POTENTIELS SUR UN GRAPHE NON CONJONCTIF ET ANALYSE D'UN PROBLEME D'ORDONNANCEMENT A MOYENS LIMITES. REVUE FRANCAISE D'AUTOMATIQUE, D'INFORMATIQUE ET DE RECHERCHE OPERATIONELLE 13, SERIE RECHERCHE OPERATIONELLE, 363-378. (1979).

ERSC 1980 -1 ERSCHLER, J.; FONTAN, G.; ROUBELLAT, F.
GRAPHES POTENTIELS-TACHES NON CONJONCTIFS ET PROBLEMES D'ORDONNANCEMENT. IN: P. HANSEN, D. DE WERRA (EDS.): REGARDS SUR LA THEORIE DES GRAPHES, PROCEEDINGS OF THE CERISY COLLOQUIUM, 1980, 221-226. LAUSANNE: PRESSES POLYTECHNIQUES ROMANDES. (1980).

ERSCA 1977 -1 ERSCHLER, J.; ROUBELLAT, F.
LIMITED RESOURCE SCHEDULING WITH EXECUTION TIME CONSTRAINTS. IN: M. ROUBENS (ED.): ADVANCES IN OPERATIONS RESEARCH, PROCEEDINGS OF EURO II, THE SECOND EUROPEAN CONGRESS ON OPERATIONS RESEARCH, STOCKHOLM 1976, 149-158. AMSTERDAM, NEW YORK, OXFORD: NORTH-HOLLAND. (1977).

ERSCB 1980 -1 ERSCHLER, J.; ROUBELLAT, F.; VERNHES, J. P.
CHARACTERIZING THE SET OF FEASIBLE SEQUENCES FOR N JOBS TO BE CARRIED OUT ON A SINGLE MACHINE. EUROPEAN JOURNAL OF OPERATIONAL RESEARCH 4, 189-194. (1980).

ERUS 1980 -1 ERUSALIMSKY, YA. M.; SVETLOV, G. G.
BICOUPLING POINTS, BIBRIDGES AND BIUNITS OF FLOW GRAPHS (RUSSIAN). KIBERNETIKA, NO. 1, 37-39. (1980).

ESSE 1980 -1 ESSER, F.; HARARY, F.
ON THE SPECTRUM OF A COMPLETE MULTIPARTITE GRAPH. EUROPEAN JOURNAL OF COMBINATORICS 1, 211-218. (1980).

ETCH 1978 -1 ETCHEBERRY, J.; CONCA, C.; STACCHETTI, E.
IMPLICIT ENUMERATION APPROACH FOR INTEGER PROGRAMMING USING SUBGRADIENT OPTIMIZATION, AN. PUBLICATION NO. 78/04/C. UNIVERSIDAD DE CHILE. (1978).

EULE 1979 -1 EULER, R.
ON RANK FUNCTIONS OF GENERAL INDEPENDENCE SYSTEMS (EXTENDED ABSTRACT). IN: W. OETTLI, F. STEFFENS (EDS.): OPERATIONS RESEARCH VERFAHREN 32, THIRD SYMPOSIUM ON OPERATIONS RESEARCH, MANNHEIM 1978, 89-91. KOENIGSTEIN: ANTON HAIN MEISENHEIM. (1979).

EULE 1980 -1 EULER, R.
AUGMENTING PATHS AND A CLASS OF INDEPENDENCE SYSTEMS. RESEARCH REPORT 16/80. KOELN: UNIV. ZU KOELN, MATHEMATISCHES INST., 14 P. (1980).

EULE 1980 -2 EULER, R.
ON A CLASSIFICATION OF INDEPENDENCE SYSTEMS. DISCRETE APPLIED MATHEMATICS 2, 357-360. (1980).

EULE 1980 -3 EULER, R.
RANK-AXIOMATIC CHARACTERIZATIONS OF INDEPENDENCE SYSTEMS. DISCRETE MATHEMATICS 32, 9-18. (1980).

EULE 1981 -1 EULER, R.
ON A CLASSIFICATION OF INDEPENDENCE SYSTEMS. IN: R. E. BURKARD, T. ELLINGER (EDS.): METHODS OF OPERATIONS RESEARCH 40, 299-302. KOENIGSTEIN: ANTON HAIN MEISENHEIM. (1981).

EULE 1981 -2 EULER, R.
REGULAR (2,2)-SYSTEMS. RESEARCH REPORT 81-6. KOELN: UNIV. ZU KOELN, MATHEMATISCHES INST., 30 P. (1981).

EVAN 1975 -1 EVANS, J. R.
THEORETICAL AND COMPUTATIONAL ASPECTS OF INTEGER MULTICOMMODITY NETWORK FLOW PROBLEMS. UNPUBLISHED DISSERTATION. ATLANTA: GEORGIA INSTITUTE OF TECHNOLOGY, SCHOOL OF INDUSTRIAL AND SYSTEMS ENGINEERING. (1975).

EVAN 1978 -1 EVANS, J. R.
NOTE ON THE SHORTEST SPANNING TREE PROBLEM, A. GEOGRAPHICAL ANALYSIS 10, 286-288. (1978).

EVAN 1978 -2 EVANS, J. R.
ON EQUIVALENT REPRESENTATIONS OF CERTAIN MULTICOMMODITY NETWORKS AS SINGLE COMMODITY FLOW PROBLEMS. MATHEMATICAL PROGRAMMING 15, 92-99. (1978).

EVAN 1978 -3 EVANS, J. R.
SIMPLEX METHOD FOR INTEGRAL MULTICOMMODITY NETWORKS, THE. NAVAL RESEARCH LOGISTICS QUARTERLY 25, 31-39. (1978).

EVAN 1978 -4 EVANS, J. R.
SINGLE-COMMODITY TRANSFORMATION FOR CERTAIN MULTICOMMODITY NETWORKS, A. OPERATIONS RESEARCH 26, 673-680. (1978).

EVAN 1978 -5 EVANS, J. R.
SOLVING MULTICOMMODITY TRANSPORTATION PROBLEMS THROUGH AGGREGATION. LOS ANGELES (ORSA/TIMS MEETING, NOVEMBER 1978) 20 P. (1978).

EVAN 1979 -1 EVANS, J. R.
AGGREGATION IN THE GENERALIZED TRANSPORTATION PROBLEM. COMPUTERS AND OPERATIONS RESEARCH 6, 199-204. (1979).

EVAN 1980 -1 EVANS, J. R.
REDUCING COMPUTATIONAL EFFORT IN DETECTING INTEGRAL MULTICOMMODITY NETWORKS. COMPUTERS AND OPERATIONS RESEARCH 7, 261-266. (1980).

EVANA 1978 -1 EVANS, J. R.; JARVIS, J. J.
NETWORK TOPOLOGY AND INTEGRAL MULTICOMMODITY FLOW PROBLEMS. NETWORKS 8, 107-119. (1978).

EVANB 1977 -1 EVANS, J. R.; JARVIS, J. J.; DUKE, R. A.
GRAPHIC MATROIDS AND THE MULTICOMMODITY TRANSPORTATION PROBLEM. MATHEMATICAL PROGRAMMING 13, NO. 3, 323-328. (1977).

EVANC 1978 -1 EVANS, J. R.; MARTIN, K.
NOTE ON FEASIBLE FLOWS IN LOWER-BOUNDED MULTICOMMODITY NETWORKS, A. THE JOURNAL OF THE OPERATIONAL RESEARCH SOCIETY 29, 923-927. (1978).

EVEN 1976 -1 EVEN, S.
MAX FLOW ALGORITHM OF DINIC AND KARZANOV: AN EXPOSITION, THE. HAIFA: TECHNION, DEPARTMENT OF COMPUTER SCIENCE. (1976).

EVEN 1979 -1 EVEN, S.
GRAPH ALGORITHMS. LONDON: PITMAN, 249 P. (1979). (COMPUTER SOFTWARE ENGINEERING SERIES)

EVENA 1981 -1 EVEN, S.; SHILOACH, Y.
ON-LINE EDGE-DELETION PROBLEM, AN. JOURNAL OF THE ASSOCIATION FOR COMPUTING MACHINERY 28, 1-4. (1981).

EVER 1965 -1 EVERS, G. H. E.
RELEVANT FACTORS AROUND CREW-UTILIZATION. IN: AGIFORS SYMPOSIUM, KLM. (1965).

EVERA 1977 -1 EVERSHEIM, W.; HEMGESBERG, G.
ENTWICKLUNG EINES SYSTEMS ZUR OPTIMALEN ZWEIDIMENSIONALEN VERSCHNITTOPTIMIERUNG IN DER EINZEL- UND KLEINSERIENFERTIGUNG MIT HILFE DIALOGFAEHIGER RECHENANLAGEN. OPLADEN: WESTDEUTSCHER VERLAG, 131 P. (1977). (FORSCHUNGSBER. D. LANDES NORDRHEINWESTFALEN, 2663 FACHGRUPPE MATHEMATIK, INFORMATIK)

EVST 1978 -1 EVSTIGNEEV, V. A.
LOCAL ALGORITHM FOR FINDING THE STRONGLY CONNECTED SUBGRAPHS OF DIRECTED GRAPHS (RUSSIAN), THE. ZURNAL VYCISLITEL'NOI MATEMATIKI I MATEMATICESKOI FIZIKI 18, 1345-1350. (1978).

EVST 1979 -1 EVSTIGNEEV, V. A.
LOCAL ALGORITHM FOR FINDING THE BICOMPONENTS IN A FLOW GRAPH, A. USSR COMPUTATIONAL MATHEMATICS AND MATHEMATICAL PHYSICS 18, 274-279. (1979).

****

FAAL 1979 -1 FAALAND, B. H.; HILLIER, F. S.
INTERIOR PATH METHODS FOR HEURISTIC INTEGER PROGRAMMING PROCEDURES. OPERATIONS RESEARCH 27, 1069-1087. (1979).

FABI 1979 -1 FABIAN, C.
ALGORITHM FOR INTEGER CONVEX PROGRAMMING, AN. IN: A. PREKOPA (ED.): SURVEY OF MATHEMATICAL PROGRAMMING, VOLUME 2, 455-460. AMSTERDAM: NORTH-HOLLAND. (1979).

FABI 1979 -2 FABIAN, C.
DUE-DATE RESTRICTIONS IN TRAVELLING SALESMAN PROBLEM. IN: PROCEEDINGS OF THE INTERNATIONAL SYMPOSIUM ON APPLICATIONS OF MATHEMATICS IN SYSTEM THEORY. BRASOV 1978, VOLUME II, 223-228. BRASOV: UNIVERSITY OF BRASOV. (1979).

FABI 1981 -1 FABIAN, C.
CONVEX MIXED-INTEGER NONSEPARABLE PROGRAMMING. IN: R. E. BURKARD, T. ELLINGER (EDS.): METHODS OF OPERATIONS RESEARCH 40, 303-306. KOENIGSTEIN: ANTON HAIN MEISENHEIM. (1981).

FAIG 1979 -1 FAIGLE, U.
GREEDY ALGORITHM FOR PARTIALLY ORDERED SETS, THE. DISCRETE MATHEMATICS 28, 153-159. (1979).

FAIG 1980 -1 FAIGLE, U.
GEOMETRIES ON PARTIALLY ORDERED SETS. JOURNAL OF COMBINATORIAL THEORY 28, SERIES B, 26-51. (1980).

FAIG 1981 -1 FAIGLE, U.
ON SUPERMATROIDS WITH SUBMODULAR RANK FUNCTION. IN: L. LOVASZ, V. T. SOS (EDS.): ALGEBRAIC METHODS IN GRAPH THEORY, VOL. I, 149-158. COLLOQUIA MATHEMATICA SOCIETATIS JANOS BOLYAI 25. AMSTERDAM, OXFORD,NEW YORK: NORTH-HOLLAND. (1981).

FALK 1978 -1 FALK, P. G.
EXPERIMENTS IN MIXED INTEGER LINEAR PROGRAMMING CONCURRENT TO A MANUFACTURING HIERARCHY. NEW YORK (TIMS/ORSA-MEETING, MAY 1978) 15 P. (1978).

FALK 1980 -1 FALK, P. G.
EXPERIMENTS IN MIXED INTEGER LINEAR PROGRAMMING IN A MANUFACTURING SYSTEM. OMEGA 8, 473-484. (1980).

FALL 1973 -1 FALLIK, C.
APPLICATIONS ECONOMIQUES DE LA THEORIE DES GRAPHES, EN PARTICULIER AU PROBLEME DES HORAIRES. BRUXELLES: UNIVERSITE LIBRE DE BRUXELLES. (1973).

FANE 1978 -1 FANELLI, S.
EXTENSION OF HU'S GROUP MINIMIZATION ALGORITHM, AN. CALCOLO 15, NO. 2, 197-210. (1978).

FANE 1979 -1 FANELLI, S.
ON THE USE OF THE ASYMPTOTIC ALGORITHM IN APPLIED PROBLEMS OF INTEGER LINEAR PROGRAMMING (ITALIAN). RICERCA OPERATIVA, NO. 9, 3-13. (1979).

FANI 1977 -1 FANICA, G.
TESTING FOR EQUALITY BETWEEN MAXIMUM MATCHING AND MINIMUM NODE COVERING. INFORMATION PROCESSING LETTERS 6, 199-202. (1977).

FARA 1978 -1 FARADZEV, I. A.
GENERATION OF NONISOMORPHIC GRAPHS WITH A GIVEN DISTRIBUTION OF THE DEGREES OF VERTICES (RUSSIAN). IN: I. A. FARADZEV (ED.): ALGORITHMIC STUDIES IN COMBINATORICS (RUSSIAN). INTERNATIONAL COLLOQUIUM ON COMBINATORICS AND GRAPH THEORY, ORSAY 1976, 11-19 + 185. MOSCOW: IZDAT. "NAUKA". (1978).

FARA 1978 -2 FARADZEV, I. A.
GENERATION OF THREE-CONNECTED GRAPHS AND THE ENUMERATION OF INSEPARABLE NETWORKS (RUSSIAN), THE. IN: I. A. FARADZEV (ED.): ALGORITHMIC STUDIES IN COMBINATORICS (RUSSIAN), INTERNATIONAL COLLOQUIUM ON COMBINATORICS AND GRAPH THEORY, ORSAY 1976, 67-69 + 185-186. MOSCOW: IZDAT. "NAUKA". (1978).

FARA 1978 -3 FARADZEV, I. A.
OBTAINING OF A COMPLETE LIST OF SELFCOMPLEMENTARY GRAPHS UP TO 12 VERTICES (RUSSIAN), THE. IN: I. A. FARADZEV (ED.): ALGORITHMIC STUDIES IN COMBINATORICS (RUSSIAN), INTERNATIONAL COLLOQUIUM ON COMBINATORICS AND GRAPH THEORY, ORSAY 1976, 69-75 + 186. MOSCOW: IZDAT. "NAUKA". (1978).

FARK 1981 -1 FARKAS, Z. M.
SOLUTION OF A MODIFIED TRANSPORTATION PROBLEM WITH PENALTY FUNCTION BY THE METHOD "OPTIMIZATION WITH MINIMAL INFORMATION" ("OMI"). IN: R. E. BURKARD, T. ELLINGER (EDS.): METHODS OF OPERATIONS RESEARCH 40, 85-88. KOENIGSTEIN: ANTON HAIN MEISENHEIM. (1981).

FARL 1979 -1 FARLEY, A.; HEDETNIEMI, S. T.; MITCHELL, S.; PROSKUROWSKI, A.
MINIMUM BROADCAST GRAPHS. DISCRETE MATHEMATICS 25, 189-193. (1979).

FARN 1979 -1 FARN, C.-K.; MUHLEMANN, A. P.
DYNAMIC ASPECTS OF A PRODUCTION SCHEDULING PROBLEM, THE. INTERNATIONAL JOURNAL OF PRODUCTION RESEARCH 17, 15-21. (1979).

FARR 1978 -1 FARRELL, E. J.
MATCHINGS IN LADDERS. ARS COMBINATORIA 6, 153-161. (1978).

FARR 1979 -1 FARRELL, E. J.
INTRODUCTION TO MATCHING POLYNOMIALS, AN. JOURNAL OF COMBINATORIAL THEORY 27, SERIES B, 75-86. (1979).

FARR 1979 -2 FARRELL, E. J.
MATCHING IN WHEELS. ARS COMBINATORIA 8, 109-115. (1979).

FARR 1979 -3 FARRELL, E. J.
ON A CLASS OF POLYNOMIALS OBTAINED FROM THE CIRCUITS IN A GRAPH AND ITS APPLICATION TO CHARACTERISTIC POLYNOMIALS OF GRAPHS. DISCRETE MATHEMATICS 25, 121-133. (1979).

FARR 1980 -1 FARRELL, E. J.
MATCHING POLYNOMIAL AND ITS RELATION TO THE ACYCLIC POLYNOMIAL OF A GRAPH, THE. ARS COMBINATORIA 9, 221-228. (1980).

FARR 1980 -2 FARRELL, E. J.
MATCHINGS IN COMPLETE GRAPHS AND COMPLETE BIPARTITE GRAPHS. JOURNAL OF COMBINATORICS, INFORMATION AND SYSTEM SCIENCES (DELHI) 5, 47-51. (1980).

FARR 1980 -3 FARRELL, E. J.
SPANNING TREES IN GRAPHS WITH CYCLOMATIC NUMBERS 2, 3, AND 4. JOURNAL OF COMBINATORICS, INFORMATION AND SYSTEM SCIENCES (DELHI) 5, NO. 1, 38-46. (1980).

FARR 1981 -1 FARRELL, E. J.
DEFECT-D MATCHINGS IN GRAPHS WITH CYCLOMATIC NUMBERS 0, 1 AND 2. DISCRETE MATHEMATICS 33, 259-266. (1981).

FAYA 1979 -1 FAYARD, D.; PLATEAU, G.
CONTRIBUTION A LA RESOLUTION DES PROGRAMMES MATHEMATIQUES EN NOMBRES ENTIERS. DISSERTATION. LILLE: UNIVERSITY OF LILLE 1. (1979).

FAYA 1979 -2 FAYARD, D.; PLATEAU, G.
LE PROBLEME DU KNAPSACK "BAUDRUCHE" EN VARIABLES 0-1. SEMINAIRE D'ANALYSE NUMERIQUE ET D'OPTIMISATION, VILLENEUVE D'ASCQ 1979. LILLE: UNIV. SCI. TECH., 93P. (1979).

FAYA 1979 -3 FAYARD, D.; PLATEAU, G.
PROBLEME DU KNAPSACK NON LINEAIRE EN VARIABLES 0-1, UN. ELECTRICITE DE FRANCE, BULLETIN DE LA DIRECTION DES ETUDES ET RECHERCHES, SERIE C, MATHEMATIQUES, INFORMATIQUE, NO. 2, 51-77. (1979).

FAYO 1978 -1 FAYOLLE, G.; IASNOGORODSKY, R.; MITRANI, I.
ON THE SHARING OF A PROCESSOR AMONG MANY JOB CLASSES. RAPPORT DE RECHERCHE NO. 275. LE CHESNAY: INSTITUT DE RECHERCHE D'INFORMATIQUE ET D'AUTOMATIQUE, 23 P. (1978).

FEDE 1977 -1 FEDENJA, O. A.
POLYHEDRA OF A MULTI-INDEX PLANAR TRANSPORT PROBLEM WITH A MINIMAL NUMBER OF VERTICES I (RUSSIAN), THE. VESCI AKADEMII NAVUK BSSR. SERYJA FIZIKA-MATEMATYCNYH NAVUK, NO. 5, 19-23 + 137. (1977).

FEDE 1977 -2 FEDENJA, O. A.
POLYHEDRA OF A MULTI-INDEX PLANAR TRANSPORT PROBLEM WITH A MINIMAL NUMBER OF VERTICES II (RUSSIAN), THE. VESCI AKADEMII NAVUK BSSR. SERYJA FIZIKA-MATEMATYCNYH NAVUK, NO. 6, 10-15 + 139. (1977).

FEDEA 1980 -1 FEDERGRUEN, A.; LAGEWEG, B. J.
HIERARCHICAL DISTRIBUTION MODELLING WITH ROUTING COSTS. BW 117/80. AMSTERDAM: MATHEMATISCH CENTRUM, 57 P. (1980).

FEDEB 1980 -1 FEDERGRUEN, A.; ZIPKIN, P. H.
COMBINED VEHICLE ROUTING AND INVENTORY ALLOCATION PROBLEM, A. RESEARCH WORKING PAPER, 345A. NEW YORK: COLUMBIA UNIV., GRADUATE SCHOOL OF BUSINESS, 30 P. (1980).

FEIG 1979 -1 FEIGIN, L. I.
ON THE DISTINGUISHABILITY OF OPERATIONS IN SCHEDULING. DOKLADY AKADEMII NAUK SSSR (MOSCOW) 24, NO. 1, 47-51; TRANSLATED AS SOVIET PHYSICS DOKLADY 24, 9-11. (1979).

FEIG 1979 -2 FEIGIN, L. I.
SEPARABILITE DES OPERATIONS D'ORNANNCEMENT (RUSSIAN). DOKLADY AKADEMII NAUK SSSR 244, NO. 1, 47-51. (1979).

FEIN 1979 -1 FEINBERG, I.
HEURISTIC WAREHOUSE LOCATION MODEL CONSIDERING TRANSPORTATION AND OTHER COSTS AND CAPACITY CONSTRAINTS, A. NEW ORLEANS (ORSA/TIMS MEETING, APRIL/MAY 1979) 23 P. (1979).

FELZ 1979 -1 FELZENBAUM, A.; TAMIR, A.
CYCLIC PERMUTATIONS AND NEARLY SYMMETRIC INTEGER VECTORS. LINEAR ALGEBRA AND ITS APPLICATIONS 27, 159-166. (1979).

FERL 1979 -1 FERLAND, J. A.; FLORIAN, M.
SUB-OPTIMAL ALGORITHM TO SOLVE A LARGE SCALE 0-1 PROGRAMMING PROBLEM, A. IN: A. PREKOPA (ED.): SURVEY OF MATHEMATICAL PROGRAMMING, VOLUME 2, 461-470. AMSTERDAM: NORTH-HOLLAND. (1979).

FERLA 1978 -1 FERLAND, J. A.; GIRARD, A.; LAFOND, L.
MULTICOMMODITY FLOW PROBLEM WITH VARIABLE ARCS CAPACITIES. THE JOURNAL OF THE OPERATIONAL RESEARCH SOCIETY 29, 459-467. (1978).

FERN 1977 -1 FERNANDEZ, R. R.
STOPPING RULE FOR A HEURISTIC APPROACH TO THE CUTTING STOCK PROBLEM, A. DISSERTATION. MIAMI: UNIVERSITY OF MIAMI, DEPARTMENT OF MANAGEMENT SCIENCE. (1977).

FERNA 1977 -1 FERNANDEZ, R. R.; SWART, W. W.
SYSTEM FOR SOLVING CUTTING STOCK PROBLEMS, A. ATLANTA (52. ORSA-MEETING + TIMS, NOVEMBER 1977) 21 P. (1977).

FERS 1979 -1 FERSTER, V. B.
EFFECTIVELY DECREASING ALGORITHMS OF THE CUTTING PLANE METHOD FOR THE SOLUTION OF INTEGER PROGRAMMING PROBLEMS (RUSSIAN). IN: MATHEMATICAL METHODS OF SOLUTION OF ECONOMIC PROBLEMS, NO. 8, 50-60. MOSCOW: NAUKA. (1979).

FIAL 1978 -1 FIALA, F.
VEHICLE ROUTING PROBLEM. GMD-MITTEILUNGEN, 46. ST. AUGUSTIN: GESELLSCHAFT FUER MATHEMATIK UND DATENVERARBEITUNG, 66 P. (1978).

FIALA 1977 -1 FIALA, T.
NEAR OPTIMAL ALGORITHM FOR THE THREE MACHINE PROBLEM (HUNGARIAN). ALKALMAZOTT MATEMATIKAI LAPOK 3, 389-398. (1977).

FIAM 1978 -1 FIAMCHIK, I.
ACYCLIC CHROMATIC NUMBER OF A GRAPH (RUSSIAN). MATHEMATICA SLOVACA 28, NO. 2, 139-145. (1978).

FIAMA 1970 -1 FIAMCHIK, I.; JUCOVIC, E.
COLOURING THE EDGES OF A MULTIGRAPH. ARCHIV DER MATHEMATIK 21, 446-448. (1970).

FICK 1979 -1 FICKETT, J. W.
HIGH VALENCY SUBGRAPHS OF CUBES. DISCRETE MATHEMATICS 27, 211-212. (1979).

FIDR 1978 -1 FIDRMUC, M.
SIMSCRIPT II SIMULATION OF TRAFFIC NETWORK FLOW. EKONOMICKO-MATEMATICKY OBZOR 14, 89-103. (1978).

FIED 1979 -1 FIEDLER, M.
OPTIMIERUNG UND GRAPHENTHEORIE. IN: K. LOMMATZSCH (ED.): FORTSCHRITTE IN DER MATHEMATISCHEN OPTIMIERUNG, TAGUNG BERLIN 1978, 31-37. SEMINARBERICHT NR. 15, SEKTION MATHEMATIK DER HUMBOLDT-UNIV. BERLIN. (1979).

FILO 1979 -1 FILONENKO, N. V.
APPROXIMATE SOLUTION OF PARAMETRIC INTEGER PROGRAMMING PROBLEMS. KIBERNETIKA (KIEV) NO. 5, 91-94, 155; TRANSLATED AS CYBERNETICS 15, NO. 5, 703-707. (1979).

FINK 1978 -1 FINKE, G.
UNIFIED APPROACH TO RESHIPMENT, OVERSHIPMENT AND POST-OPTIMIZATION PROBLEMS, A. IN: J. STOER (ED.): OPTIMIZATION TECHNIQUES, PROCEEDINGS OF THE 8TH IFIP CONFERENCE ON OPTIMIZATION TECHNIQUES, WUERZBURG 1977, PART 2, 201-208. LECTURE NOTES IN CONTROL AND INFORMATION SCIENCES 7, BERLIN, HEIDELBERG, NEW YORK: SPRINGER. (1978).

FINK 1981 -1 FINKE, G.
BOTTLENECK PROBLEMS WITH OVERSHIPMENTS. IN: R. E. BURKARD, T. ELLINGER (EDS.): METHODS OF OPERATIONS RESEARCH 40, 307-310. KOENIGSTEIN: ANTON HAIN MEISENHEIM. (1981).

FINKA 1978 -1 FINKE, G.; AHRENS, J. H.
VARIANT OF THE PRIMAL TRANSPORTATION ALGORITHM, A. INFOR 16, 35-46. (1978).

FINKB 1980 -1 FINKELSTEIN, JU. JU.
ABOUT THE POLYNOMIAL ALGORITHM OF EPSILON-OPTIMIZATION IN THE MULTIDIMENSIONAL KNAPSACK PROBLEM (RUSSIAN). AKADEMIJA NAUK SSSR. ZURNAL VYCISLITEL'NOI MATEMATIKI I MATEMATICESKOI FIZIKI 20, 800-802. (1980).

FINN 1979 -1 FINN, G.; HOROWITZ, E.
LINEAR TIME APPROXIMATION ALGORITHM FOR MULTIPROCESSOR SCHEDULING, A. NORDISK TIDSKRIFT FOR INFORMATIONSBEHANDLING 19, 312-320. (1979).

FIOR 1974 -1 FIORINI, S.
ON THE CHROMATIC INDEX OF SIMPLE GRAPHS. DOCTORAL THESIS. MILTON KEYNES: OPEN UNIVERSITY. (1974).

FIOR 1975 -1 FIORINI, S.
ON THE CHROMATIC INDEX OF A GRAPH, III: UNIQUELY EDGE COLOURABLE GRAPHS. THE QUARTERLY JOURNAL OF MATHEMATICS 26, THIRD SERIES, 129-140. (1975).

FIOR 1975 -2 FIORINI, S.
ON THE CHROMATIC INDEX OF OUTERPLANAR GRAPHS. JOURNAL OF COMBINATORIAL THEORY 18, SERIES B, 35-38. (1975).

FIOR 1976 -1 FIORINI, S.
GRAFO CUBICO, NON-PLANARE, UNICAMENTE TRICOLORABILE, DI VITA 5. UN. CALCOLO 13, 105-108. (1976).

FIOR 1976 -2 FIORINI, S.
ON THE GIRTH OF GRAPHS CRITICAL WITH RESPECT TO EDGE COLOURINGS. THE BULLETIN OF THE LONDON MATHEMATICAL SOCIETY 8, 81-86. (1976).

FIOR 1978 -1 FIORINI, S.
BIBLIOGRAPHIC SURVEY OF EDGE COLORINGS, A. JOURNAL OF GRAPH THEORY 2, 93-106. (1978).

FIORA 1977 -1 FIORINI, S.; WILSON, R. J.
EDGE-COLOURINGS OF GRAPHS. RESEARCH NOTES IN MATHEMATICS 16. LONDON, SAN FRANCISCO, MELBOURNE: PITMAN, 154 P. (1977).

FIORA 1978 -1 FIORINI, S.; WILSON, R. J.
EDGE-COLORINGS OF GRAPHS. IN: L. W. BEINEKE, R. J. WILSON (EDS.): SELECTED TOPICS IN GRAPH THEORY, 103-126. LONDON, NEW YORK, SAN FRANCISCO: ACADEMIC PRESS. (1978).

FISH 1978 -1 FISHER, M. L.
LAGRANGIAN RELAXATION METHODS FOR COMBINATORIAL OPTIMIZATION. URBINO (SUMMER SCHOOL IN COMBINATORIAL OPTIMIZATION) 32 P. (1978).

FISH 1978 -2 FISHER, M. L.
LAGRANGIAN RELAXATION METHODS FOR COMBINATORIAL OPTIMZATION (REVISED VERSION). 78-10-06. PHILADELPHIA: UNIV. OF PENNSYLVANIA, DEPT. OF DECISION SCIENCES, 32 P. (1978).

FISH 1978 -3 FISHER, M. L.
WORST-CASE ANALYSIS OF HEURISTICS. IN: J. K. LENSTRA, A. H. G. RINNOOY KAN, P. VAN EMDE BOAS (EDS.): INTERFACES BETWEEN COMPUTER SCIENCE AND OPERATIONS RESEARCH, AMSTERDAM 1976, 87-104. MATHEMATICAL CENTRE TRACTS 99. AMSTERDAM: MATHEMATISCH CENTRUM. (1978).

FISH 1980 -1 FISHER, M. L.
WORST-CASE ANALYSIS OF HEURISTIC ALGORITHMS. MANAGEMENT SCIENCE 26, 1-18. (1980).

FISH 1981 -1 FISHER, M. L.
LAGRANGIAN RELAXATION METHOD FOR SOLVING INTEGER PROGRAMMING PROBLEMS, THE. MANAGEMENT SCIENCE 27, 1-18. (1981).

FISHA 1978 -1 FISHER, M. L.; HOCHBAUM, D.
DATABASE LOCATION IN COMPUTER NETWORKS. DECISION SCIENCES WORKING PAPER NO. 78-03-06. PHILADELPHIA: UNIVERSITY OF PENNSYLVANIA. (1978).

FISHA 1978 -2 FISHER, M. L.; HOCHBAUM, D.
PROBABILISTIC ANALYSIS OF THE EUCLIDEAN K-MEDIAN PROBLEM. RESEARCH REPORT 78-06-03. PHILADELPHIA: UNIV. OF PENNSYLVANIA, DEPT. OF DECISION SCIENCES, 12 P. (1978).

FISHB 1978 -1 FISHER, M. L.; JAIKUMAR, R.
ALGORITHM FOR THE SPACE-SHUTTLE SCHEDULING PROBLEM, AN. OPERATIONS RESEARCH 26, 166-182. (1978).

FISHB 1978 -2 FISHER, M. L.; JAIKUMAR, R.
DECOMPOSITION ALGORITHM FOR LARGE-SCALE VEHICLE ROUTING, A. RESEARCH REPORT 78-11-05. PHILADELPHIA: UNIV. OF PENNSYLVANIA, DEPT. OF DECISION SCIENCES, 27 P. (1978).

FISHC 1978 -1 FISHER, M. L.; NEMHAUSER, G. L.; WOLSEY, L. A.
ANALYSIS OF APPROXIMATIONS FOR MAXIMIZING SUBMODULAR SET FUNCTIONS - II, AN. MATHEMATICAL PROGRAMMING STUDY 8, 73-87. (1978).

FISHC 1979 -1 FISHER, M. L.; NEMHAUSER, G. L.; WOLSEY, L. A.
ANALYSIS OF APPROXIMATIONS FOR FINDING A MAXIMUM WEIGHT HAMILTONIAN CIRCUIT, AN. OPERATIONS RESEARCH 27, 799-809. (1979).

FISHD 1975 -1 FISHER, M. L.; NORTHUP, W. D.; SHAPIRO, J. F.
USING DUALITY TO SOLVE DISCRETE OPTIMIZATION PROBLEMS: THEORY AND COMPUTATIONAL EXPERIENCE. IN: M. L. BALINSKI, P. WOLFE (EDS.): NONDIFFERENTIABLE OPTIMIZATION. MATHEMATICAL PROGRAMMING STUDY 3, 56-94. (1975).

FISK 1979 -1 FISK, J. C.; HUNG, M. S.
HEURISTIC ROUTINE FOR SOLVING LARGE LOADING PROBLEMS, A. NAVAL RESEARCH LOGISTICS QUARTERLY 26, 643-650. (1979).

FISKA 1979 -1 FISK, J. C.; MAC KEOWN, P. G.
PURE FIXED CHARGE TRANSPORTATION PROBLEM, THE. NAVAL RESEARCH LOGISTICS QUARTERLY 26, 631-641. (1979).

FISKB 1980 -1 FISK, J. C.; SOLANO, A.
PRODUCTION SCHEDULING FOR HIGH-VOLUME ASSEMBLIES - A CASE STUDY. JOURNAL OF THE OPERATIONAL RESEARCH SOCIETY 31, 781-790. (1980).

FLAM 1975 -1 FLAMENT, C.
ARETES MAXIMALES DES COCYCLES D'UN GRAPHE PREORDONNE. CENTRE DE MATHEMATIQUES SOCIALE. ECOLE PRATIQUE DES HAUTES ETUDES. MATHEMATIQUES ET SCIENCES HUMAINES, NO. 51, 5-12 + 85. (1975).

FLEI 1976 -1 FLEISCHNER, H.; HOBBS, A. M.
HAMILTONIAN CYCLES IN SQUARES OF VERTEX-UNICYCLIC GRAPHS. CANADIEN MATHEMATICAL BULLETIN 19, 169-172. (1976).

FLEIA 1978 -1 FLEISHER, J. M.; MEYER, R. R.
NEW SUFFICIENT OPTIMALITY CONDITIONS FOR INTEGER PROGRAMMING AND THEIR APPLICATION. COMMUNICATIONS OF THE ASSOCIATION FOR COMPUTING MACHINERY 21, 411-418. (1978).

FLEIA 1979 -1 FLEISHER, J. M.; MEYER, R. R.
DOUBLE-RELAXATION OPTIMALITY CONDITIONS FOR INTEGER PROGRAMMING. IN: A. PREKOPA (ED.): SURVEY OF MATHEMATICAL PROGRAMMING, VOLUME 2, 471-490. AMSTERDAM: NORTH-HOLLAND. (1979).

FLET 1980 -1 FLETCHER, J. G.
MORE GENERAL ALGORITHM FOR COMPUTING CLOSED SEMIRING COSTS BETWEEN VERTICES OF A DIRECTED GRAPH, A. COMMUNICATIONS OF THE ACM 23, 350-351. (1980).

FLOR 1975 -1 FLORIAN, M.
TRAFFIC EQUILIBRIUM MODEL OF TRAVEL BY CAR AND PUBLIC TRANSIT MODES, A. PUBLICATION NO. 216. MONTREAL: UNIVERSITE DE MONTREAL, DEPARTEMENT D'INFORMATIQUE. (1975).

FLOR 1977 -1 FLORIAN, M.
IMPROVED LINEAR APPROXIMATION ALGORITHM FOR THE NETWORK EQUILIBRIUM (PACKET SWITCHING) PROBLEM, AN. TECHNICAL REPORT. MONTREAL: UNIVERSITE DE MONTREAL, CENTRE DE RECHERCHE SUR LES TRANSPORTS. (1977).

FLORA 1976 -1 FLORIAN, M.; BUSHELL, G.; FERLAND, J. A.; GUERIN, G.; NASTANSKY, L.
ENGINE SCHEDULING PROBLEM IN A RAILWAY NETWORK, THE. INFOR 14, NO. 2, 121-138. (1976).

FLORB 1978 -1 FLORIAN, M.; LENSTRA, J. K.; RINNOOY KAN, A. H. G.
DETERMINISTIC PRODUCTION PLANNING: ALGORITHMS AND COMPLEXITY. REPORT 7825/O. ROTTERDAM: ERASMUS UNIV. ROTTERDAM, ECONOMETRIC INSTITUTE, 13 P. (1978).

FLORC 1976 -1 FLORIAN, M.; NGUYEN, S.
RECENT EXPERIENCE WITH EQUILIBRIUM METHODS FOR THE STUDY OF A CONGESTED URBAN AREA. IN: M. A. FLORIAN (ED.): TRAFFIC EQUILIBRIUM METHODS, 382-395. NEW YORK: SPRINGER. (1976).

FLORD 1977 -1 FLORIAN, M.; NGUYEN, S.; SOUMIS, F.
TWO METHODS FOR ACCELERATING AN EQUILIBRIUM TRAFFIC ASSIGNMENT ALGORITHM. TECHNICAL REPORT NO. 251. MONTREAL: UNIVERSITE DE MONTREAL, DEPARTEMENT D'INFORMATIQUE. (1977).

FLOW 1977 -1 FLOWERS, A. D.; PRESTON, S. E.
WORK FORCE SCHEDULING WITH THE SEARCH DECISION RULE. OMEGA 5, 473-479. (1977).

FOCK 1978 -1 FOCKE, J.; KLOTZLER, R.
ZUR GRUNDKONZEPTION DER DISKRETEN DYNAMISCHEN OPTIMIERUNG. WISSENSCHAFTLICHE ZEITSCHRIFT DER KARL-MARX-UNIVERSITAET LEIPZIG. MATHEMATISCH-NATURWISSENSCHAFTLICHE REIHE 27, NO. 5, 447-462. (1978).

FOLD 1977 -1 FOLDES, S.; HAMMER, P. L.
SPLIT GRAPHS. IN: F. HOFFMAN ET AL. (EDS.): PROCEEDINGS OF THE EIGHTH SOUTHEASTERN CONFERENCE ON COMBINATORICS, GRAPH THEORY, AND COMPUTING, BATON ROUGE 1977, 311-315. CONGRESSUS NUMERANTIUM XIX, WINNIPEG: UTILITAS MATHEMATICA. (1977).

FOLD 1978 -1 FOLDES, S.; HAMMER, P. L.
ON A CLASS OF MATROID-PRODUCING GRAPHS. IN: A. HAJNAL, V. T. SOS (EDS.): COMBINATORICS, VOLUME I, 331-352. COLLOQUIA MATHEMATICA SOCIETATIS JANOS BOLYAI 18. AMSTERDAM: NORTH-HOLLAND. (1978).

FOLD 1978 -2 FOLDES, S.; HAMMER, P. L.
ON SPLIT GRAPHS AND SOME RELATED QUESTIONS. IN: J.-C. BERMOND ET AL. (EDS.): PROBLEMES COMBINATOIRES ET THEORIE DES GRAPHES, COLLOQUES INTERNATIONAUX DU CENTRE NATIONAL DE LA RECHERCHE SCIENTIFIQUE, ORSAY 1976, 139-140. PARIS: CENTRE NATIONAL DE LA RECHERCHE SCIENTIFIQUE. (1978).

FOLK 1969 -1 FOLKMAN, J.; FULKERSON, D. R.
EDGE COLORINGS IN BIPARTITE GRAPHS. IN: R. C. BOSE, T. A. DOWLING (EDS.): COMBINATORIAL MATHEMATICS AND ITS APPLICATIONS, 561-577. CHAPEL HILL: UNIVERSITY OF NORTH CAROLINA PRESS. (1969).

FOLKA 1978 -1 FOLKMAN, J.; LAWRENCE, J.
ORIENTED MATROIDS. JOURNAL OF COMBINATORIAL THEORY 25, SERIES B, 199-236. (1978).

FONG 1978 -1 FONG, C. O.; SRINIVASAN, V.
MULTI-REGION DYNAMIC CAPACITY EXPANSION PROBLEM - II, THE. RESEARCH PAPER NO. 228 (REVISED). STANFORD: STANFORD UNIVERSITY, GRADUATE SCHOOL OF BUSINESS. (1978).

FONL 1977 -1 FONLUPT, J.
AFFECTATION EXPONENTIELLE ET LE PROBLEME DU PLUS COURT CHEMIN DANS UN GRAPHE, L'. IN: SEMIN. ANAL. NUMER. ANNEE 1976-1977, 2E SEMESTRE, GRENOBLE 1977, 275.1-275.36. (1977).

FONL 1979 -1 FONLUPT, J.
ON THE NUMBER OF COMPLEMENTARY BASES IN A MATROID. MATH. APPL. INFORMAT., RAPP. RECH. NO. 178, 21 P. (1979).

FONL 1980 -1 FONLUPT, J.
AFFECTATION EXPONENTIELLE ET LE PROBLEME DU PLUS COURT CHEMIN DANS UN GRAPHE, L'. RESEARCH REPORT NO. 187, MATHEMATIQUES APPLIQUEES ET INFORMATIQUE. GRENOBLE: UNIV. SCIENT. ET MED. ET INST. NAT. POLYTECH. 18 P. (1980).

FONS 1979 -1 FONSO, R.
ON A STOCHASTIC TRANSPORTATION PROBLEM (ITALIAN). IN: PROCEEDINGS OF THE FIRST AMASES MEETING, PISA 1977, 149-182. TURIN: GIAPPICHELLI. (1979).

FONT 1980 -1 FONTAN, G.
NOTION DE DOMINANCE ET SON APPLICATION A L'ETUDE DE CERTAINS PROBLEMES D'ORDONNANCEMENT. DISSERTATION. TOULOUSE: UNIVERSITY OF TOULOUSE 3, 154 P. (1980).

FONTA 1975 -1 FONTET, M.
TEST D'ISOMORPHIE DE DEUX GRAPHES PLANAIRES. IN: ACTES DES JOURNEES INFORMATIQUE ET COMBINATOIRE, BORDEAUX. (1975).

FONTA 1976 -1 FONTET, M.
LINEAR ALGORITHM FOR TESTING ISOMORPHISM OF PLANAR GRAPHS, A. IN: P. MICHAELSON, R. MILNER (EDS.): THIRD INTERNATIONAL COLLOQUIUM ON AUTOMATA, LANGUAGES AND PROGRAMMING, 411-424. EDINBURGH: EDINBURGH UNIVERSITY PRESS. (1976).

FONTA 1978 -1 FONTET, M.
ON AN ALGORITHM OF HOPCROFT AND TARJAN: A NEW TRICONNECTIVITY ALGORITHM. IN: J.-C. BERMOND ET AL. (EDS.): PROBLEMES COMBINATOIRES ET THEORIE DES GRAPHES, COLLOQUES INTERNATIONAUX DU CENTRE NATIONAL DE LA RECHERCHE SCIENTIFIQUE, ORSAY 1976, 141-144. PARIS: CENTRE NATIONAL DE LA RECHERCHE SCIENTIFIQUE. (1978).

FONTA 1979 -1 FONTET, M.
CONNECTIVITE DES GRAPHES ET AUTOMORPHISMES DES CARTES: PROPRIETES ET ALGORITHMES. PARIS. (1979).

FORT 1979 -1 FORTUNE, S.
NOTE ON SPARSE COMPLETE SETS, A. SIAM JOURNAL ON COMPUTING 8, 431-433. (1979).

FORTA 1979 -1 FORTUNE, S.; HOPCROFT, J. E.
NOTE ON RABIN'S NEAREST-NEIGHBOUR ALGORITHM, A. INFORMATION PROCESSING LETTERS 8, 20-23. (1979).

FORTB 1980 -1 FORTUNE, S.; HOPCROFT, J. E.; WYLLIE, J.
DIRECTED SUBGRAPH HOMEOMORPHISM PROBLEM, THE. THEORETICAL COMPUTER SCIENCE 10, 111-121. (1980).

FOUL 1978 -1 FOULDS, L. R.; GIBBONS, P. B.
BRANCH AND BOUND APPROACH TO THE STEINER PROBLEM IN GRAPHS, A. IN: PROCEEDINGS OF THE 14TH ANNUAL CONFERENCE OF THE OPERATIONAL RESEARCH SOCIETY OF NEW ZEALAND - THEORY, 61-70. (1978).

FOUL 1980 -1 FOULDS, L. R.; GIBBONS, P. B.
NEW ALGORITHMS FOR THE BULK, ZERO-ONE TIME MINI-MAX TRANSPORTATION MODEL. NEW ZEALAND OPERATIONAL RESEARCH 8, 109-120. (1980).

FOULA 1978 -1 FOULDS, L. R.; ROBINSON, D. F.
GRAPH THEORETIC HEURISTICS FOR THE PLANT LAYOUT PROBLEM. INTERNATIONAL JOURNAL OF PRODUCTION RESEARCH 16, 27-37. (1978).

FOUQ 1978 -1 FOUQUET, J.-L.
PROBLEMES HAMILTONIENS DANS LES PUISSANCES DE GRAPHES ORIENTES. IN: J.-C. BERMOND ET AL. (EDS.): PROBLEMES COMBINATOIRES ET THEORIE DES GRAPHES, COLLOQUES INTERNATIONAUX DU CENTRE NATIONAL DE LA RECHERCHE SCIENTIFIQUE, ORSAY 1976, 145-147. PARIS: CENTRE NATIONAL DE LA RECHERCHE SCIENTIFIQUE. (1978).

FOUQA 1978 -1 FOUQUET, J.-L.; JOLIVET, J.-L.
GRAPHES HYPOHAMILTONIENS ORIENTES. IN: J.-C. BERMOND ET AL. (EDS.): PROBLEMES COMBINATOIRES ET THEORIE DES GRAPHES, COLLOQUES INTERNATIONAUX DU CENTRE NATIONAL DE LA RECHERCHE SCIENTIFIQUE, ORSAY 1976, 149-151. PARIS: CENTRE NATIONAL DE LA RECHERCHE SCIENTIFIQUE. (1978).

FOUR 1973 -1 FOURNIER, J.-C.
INTRODUCTION A LA NOTION DE MATROIDE (GEOMETRIE COMBINATOIRE). ORSAY: UNIV. DE PARIS-SUD, DEPT. DE MATHEMATIQUE, 56 P. (1973). (PUBLICATIONS MATHEMATIQUES D'ORSAY, 79-03)

FOUR 1977 -1 FOURNIER, J.-C.
METHODE ET THEOREME GENERAL DE COLORATION DES ARETES D'UN MULTIGRAPHE. JOURNAL DE MATHEMATIQUES PURES ET APPLIQUEES 56, 437-453. (1977).

FOUR 1978 -1 FOURNIER, J.-C.
CARACTERISATION DES GRAPHES DE CORDES, UNE. COMPTES REDUS HEBDOMADAIRES DES SEANCES DE L'ACADEMIE DES SCIENCES, SERIES A ET B 286, NO. 19, A811-A813. (1978).

FOUR 1978 -2 FOURNIER, J.-C.
GRAPHES DE CORDES, HYPERGRAPHES DE CHAINES D'UN ARBRE ET MATROIDES GRAPHIQUES. IN: ACTES DU COLLOQUIUM ALGEBRE APPLIQUEE ET COMBINATOIRE, 164-171. GRENOBLE. (1978).

FOUR 1978 -3 FOURNIER, J.-C.
THEOREME GENERAL DE COLORATION, UN. IN: J.-C. BERMOND ET AL. (EDS.): PROBLEMES COMBINATOIRES ET THEORIE DES GRAPHES, COLLOQUES INTERNATIONAUX DU CENTRE NATIONAL DE LA RECHERCHE SCIENTIFIQUE, ORSAY 1976, 154-155. PARIS: CENTRE NATIONAL DE LA RECHERCHE SCIENTIFIQUE. (1978).

FOURA 1977 -1 FOURNIER, R.
GRAPHS WITH ALMOST NO COLOURING. ARS COMBINATORIA 3, 123-147. (1977).

FOX 1978 -1 FOX, B. L.; LENSTRA, J. K.; RINNOOY KAN, A. H. G.; SCHRAGE, L. E.
BRANCHING FROM THE LARGEST UPPER BOUND; FOLKLORE AND FACTS. EUROPEAN JOURNAL OF OPERATIONAL RESEARCH 2, 191-194. (1978).

FOX A 1980 -1 FOX, D. B.
OPTIMIZATION IN ENGINEERING DESIGN. WORKING PAPER. WRIGHT PATTERSON: AIR FORCE INST. OF TECHNOLOGY, DEPT. OF OPERATIONAL SCIENCES, 57 P. (1980).

FOX B 1980 -1 FOX, K. R.; GAVISH, B.; GRAVES, S. C.
N-CONSTRAINT FORMULATION OF THE (TIME-DEPENDENT) TRAVELING SALESMAN PROBLEM, AN. OPERATIONS RESEARCH 28, 1018-1021. (1980).

FRAE 1979 -1 FRAENKEL, A. S.; YESHA, Y.
COMPLEXITY OF PROBLEMS IN GAMES, GRAPHS AND ALGEBRAIC EQUATIONS. DISCRETE APPLIED MATHEMATICS 1, 15-30. (1979).

FRAE 1980 -1 FRAENKEL, A. S.; YESHA, Y.
COMPLEXITY OF SOLVING ALGEBRAIC EQUATIONS. INFORMATION PROCESSING LETTERS 10, 178-179. (1980).

FRAN 1978 -1 FRANCIS, R. L.; LOWE, T. J.; RATLIFF, H. D.
DISTANCE CONSTRAINTS FOR TREE NETWORK MULTIFACILITY LOCATION PROBLEMS. OPERATIONS RESEARCH 26, 570-596. (1978).

FRANA 1977 -1 FRANCON, J.
ON THE ANALYSIS OF ALGORITHMS FOR TREES. THEORETICAL COMPUTER SCIENCE 4, NO. 2, 155-169. (1977).

FRANB 1979 -1 FRANK, A.
COVERING BRANCHINGS. ACTA UNIVERSITATIS SZEGEDIENIS. ACTA SCIENTIARUM MATHEMATICARUM 41, 77-81. (1979).

FRANB 1979 -2 FRANK, A.
KERNEL SYSTEMS OF DIRECTED GRAPHS. ACTA SCIENTIARUM MATHEMATICARUM 41, 63-76. (1979).

FRANB 1980 -1 FRANK, A.
ALGORITHM FOR SUBMODULAR FUNCTIONS ON GRAPHS, AN. RESEARCH REPORT. BUDAPEST: RESEARCH INST. FOR TELECOMMUNICATION, 37 P. (1980).

FRANB 1980 -2 FRANK, A.
DISJOINT PATHS IN THE PLANE. WORKING PAPER. BUDAPEST: RESEARCH INSTITUTE FOR TELECOMMUNICATION, 4P. (1980).

FRANB 1980 -3 FRANK, A.
HOW TO MAKE A DIGRAPH STRONGLY CONNECTED. WORKING PAPER. BUDAPEST: RESEARCH INSTITUTE FOR TELECOMMUNICATION, 16 P. (1980).

FRANB 1980 -4 FRANK, A.
NOTE ON K-STRONGLY CONNECTED ORIENTATIONS OF AN UNDIRECTED GRAPH, A. WORKING PAPER. BUDAPEST: RESEARCH INSTITUTE FOR TELECOMMUNICATION, 4 P. (1980).

FRANB 1980 -5 FRANK, A.
ON CHAIN AND ANTICHAIN FAMILIES OF A PARTIALLY ORDERED SET. JOURNAL OF COMBINATORIAL THEORY, SERIES B 29, 176-184. (1980).

FRANB 1980 -6 FRANK, A.
ON THE ORIENTATION OF GRAPHS. JOURNAL OF COMBINATORIAL THEORY 28, SERIES B, 251-261. (1980).

FRANB 1980 -7 FRANK, A.
WEIGHTED MATROID INTERSECTION ALGORITHM, A. WORKING PAPER. BUDAPEST: RESEARCH INSTITUTE FOR TELECOMMUNICATION, 12 P. (1980).

FRANB 1981 -1 FRANK, A.
FINDING FEASIBLE VECTORS OF EDMONDS-GILES POLYHEDRA. RESEARCH REPORT NO. 81205-OR. BONN: UNIV. BONN, INSTITUT FUER OEKONOMETRIE UND OPERATIONS RESEARCH, ABT. OPERATIONS RESEARCH, 24 P. (1981).

FRANB 1981 -2 FRANK, A.
GENERALIZED POLYMATROIDS. RESEARCH REPORT NO. 81206-OR. BONN: UNIV. BONN, INSTITUT FUER OEKONOMETRIE UND OPERATIONS RESEARCH, ABT. OPERATIONS RESEARCH, 7 P. (1981).

FRANB 1981 -3 FRANK, A.
HOW TO MAKE A DIRECTED GRAPH STRONGLY CONNECTED. COMBINATORICA 1, 145-153. (1981).

FRANB 1981 -4 FRANK, A.
ON DISJOINT TREES AND ARBORESCENCES. IN: L. LOVASZ, V. T. SOS (EDS.): ALGEBRAIC METHODS IN GRAPH THEORY, VOL. I, 159-170. COLLOQUIA MATHEMATICA SOCIETATIS JANOS BOLYAI 25. AMSTERDAM, OXFORD,NEW YORK: NORTH-HOLLAND. (1981).

FRANB 1981 -5 FRANK, A.
WEIGHTED MATROID INTERSECTION ALGORITHM, A. JOURNAL OF ALGORITHMS 2, 328-336. (1981).

FRANB 1982 -1 FRANK, A.
DISJOINT PATHS IN A RECTILINEAR GRID. RESEARCH REPORT NO. 82216-OR. BONN: UNIV. BONN, INSTITUT FUER OEKONOMETRIE UND OPERATIONS RESEARCH, ABT. OPERATIONS RESEARCH, 16 P. (1982).

FRANC 1978 -1 FRANK, A.; GYARFAS, A.
DIRECTED GRAPHS AND COMPUTER PROGRAMS. IN: J.-C. BERMOND ET AL. (EDS.): PROBLEMES COMBINATOIRES ET THEORIE DES GRAPHES, COLLOQUES INTERNATIONAUX DU CENTRE NATIONAL DE LA RECHERCHE SCIENTIFIQUE, ORSAY 1976, 157-158. PARIS: CENTRE NATIONAL DE LA RECHERCHE SCIENTIFIQUE. (1978).

FRANC 1978 -2 FRANK, A.; GYARFAS, A.
HOW TO ORIENT THE EDGES OF A GRAPH. IN: A. HAJNAL, V. T. SOS (EDS.): COMBINATORICS, VOLUME I, 353-364. COLLOQUIA MATHEMATICA SOCIETATIS JANOS BOLYAI 18. AMSTERDAM: NORTH-HOLLAND. (1978).

FRAND 1982 -1 FRANK, A.; TARDOS, E.
MATROIDS FROM CROSSING FAMILIES. RESEARCH REPORT NO. 82210-OR. BONN: UNIV. BONN, INSTITUT FUER OEKONOMETRIE UND OPERATIONS RESEARCH, ABT. OPERATIONS RESEARCH, 11 P. (1982).

FRANE 1978 -1 FRANK, O.
ESTIMATION OF THE NUMBER OF CONNECTED COMPONENTS IN A GRAPH BY USING A SAMPLED SUBGRAPH. SCANDINAVIAN JOURNAL OF STATISTICS 5, 177-188. (1978).

FRANF 1976 -1 FRANKE, B.
QUADRATISCHE BOTTLENECK-ZUORDNUNGS-PROBLEME. DISSERTATION. KOELN: MATHEMATISCHES INSTITUT DER UNIVERSITAET KOELN. (1976).

FRAY 1978 -1 FRAYSSEIX, H. DE
PROPRIETES DE PARITE DES BASES D'UN MATROIDE BINAIRE. COMPTES RENDUS HEBDOMADAIRES DES SEANCES DE L'ACADEMIE DES SCIENCES PARIS, SERIES A ET B 286, A1171-A1173. (1978).

FRED 1977 -1 FREDERICKSON, G. N.
APPROXIMATION ALGORITHMS FOR NP-HARD ROUTING PROBLEMS. COLLEGE PARK: UNIV. OF MARYLAND, 92 P. (1977). (DISSERTATION)
FRED 1979 -1 FREDERICKSON, G. N.
APPROXIMATION ALGORITHMS FOR SOME POSTMAN PROBLEMS. JOURNAL OF THE ASSOCIATION FOR COMPUTING MACHINERY 26, 538-554. (1979).
FRED 1980 -1 FREDERICKSON, G. N.
PROBABILISTIC ANALYSIS FOR SIMPLE ONE- AND TWO-DIMENSIONAL BIN PACKING ALGORITHMS. INFORMATION PROCESSING LETTERS 11, 156-161. (1980).
FREDA 1976 -1 FREDERICKSON, G. N.; HECHT, M. S.; KIM, C. E.
APPROXIMATION ALGORITHMS FOR SOME ROUTING PROBLEMS. IN: PROCEEDINGS OF THE 17TH ANNUAL SYMPOSIUM ON FOUNDATION OF COMPUTER SCIENCE, 216-227. HOUSTON; ALSO PUBLISHED IN SIAM JOURNAL ON COMPUTING 7, 1978, 178-193. (1976).
FREI 1979 -1 FREIDENFELDS, J.; MAC LAUGHLIN, C. D.
HEURISTIC BRANCH-AND-BOUND ALGORITHM FOR TELEPHONE FEEDER CAPACITY EXPANSION, A. OPERATIONS RESEARCH 27, 567-582. (1979).
FREN 1975 -1 FRENNE, A. DE
PROBLEME DE COLORATION DANS LES GRAPHES ET LES HYPERGRAPHES. BRUXELLES: UNIVERSITE LIBRE DE BRUXELLES. (1975).
FRID 1976 -1 FRIDMAN, A. A.; FRUMKIN, M. A.; HMELEVSKII, JU. I.; LEVNER, E. V.
STUDY OF ALGORITHM EFFICIENCY FOR DISCRETE AND COMBINATORIAL PROBLEMS. THEORY OF PROBLEM REDUCIBILITY AND UNIVERSAL PROBLEMS (RUSSIAN). REPORT NO. GR-76060393. MOSCOW: USSR ACADEMY OF SCIENCES, CENTRAL ECONOMIC AND MATHEMATICAL INSTITUTE. (1976).
FRIDA 1975 -1 FRIDMAN, F. A.
SOLUTION OF THE KNAPSACK PROBLEM WITH SPECIAL SUPPLEMENTARY CONSTRAINTS (RUSSIAN). IN: B. P. MITJAGIN (ED.): PROCEEDINGS OF THE SIXTH WINTER SCHOOL ON MATHEMATICAL PROGRAMMING AND RELATED QUESTIONS (RUSSIAN), DROGOBYCH 1973, 244-258. MOSCOW: CENTRAL. EKONOM.-MAT. INST. AKAD. NAUK SSSR. (1975).
FRIDB 1977 -1 FRIDMAN, G. S.
TWO PROBLEMS ON THE COVERING GRAPHS (RUSSIAN). IN: K. A. BAGRINOVSKII, E. L. BERLJAND (EDS.): MODELS AND METHODS FOR THE ANALYSIS OF ECONOMIC TARGET-ORIENTED SYSTEMS (RUSSIAN), 224-271. NOVOSIBIRSK: IZDAT NAUKA SIBIRISK. (1977).
FRIE 1978 -1 FRIEDMAN, M.
COMBINATORIAL PROBLEMS IN AN ADAPTIVE PUBLIC TRANSPORTATION NETWORK. TRANSPORTATION RESEARCH 12, 305-308. (1978).
FRIEA 1980 -1 FRIESDORF, H.
FLUSSPROBLME MIT GEWICHTETEN KOSTEN. KOELN: UNIV. KOELN, MATHEMATISCHES INSTITUT, 101 P. (1980). (DIPLOMARBEIT)
FRIEB 1981 -1 FRIESEN, D. K.; DEUERMEYER, B. L.
ANALYSIS OF GREEDY SOLUTIONS FOR A REPLACEMENT PART SEQUENCING PROBLEM. MATHEMATICS OF OPERATIONS RESEARCH 6, 74-87. (1981).
FRIEC 1981 -1 FRIESZ, T.
MULTIOBJECTIVE OPTIMIZATION IN TRANSPORTATION: THE CASE OF EQUILIBRIUM NETWORK DESIGN. IN: J. N. MORSE (ED.): ORGANIZATIONS: MULTIPLE AGENTS WITH MULTIPLE CRITERIA, 116-127. LECTURE NOTES IN ECONOMICS AND MATHEMATICAL SYSTEMS 190. BERLIN: SPRINGER. (1981).
FRIED 1977 -1 FRIEZE, A. M.
ALGORITHMS FOR GENERALISATIONS OF MATROIDS. LONDON: QUEEN MARY COLLEGE, DEPT. OF COMPUTER SCIENCE AND STATISTICS, 18 P. (1977).
FRIED 1978 -1 FRIEZE, A. M.
GENERALISATION OF THE GREEDY ALGORITHM FOR INDEPENDENCE SYSTEMS, A. LONDON: QUEEN MARY COLLEGE, DEPT. OF COMPUTER SCIENCE AND STATISTICS, 17 P. (1978).
FRIED 1979 -1 FRIEZE, A. M.
APPROXIMATE ALGORITHM FOR THE M-DIMENSIONAL 0-1 KNAPSACK PROBLEM, AN. WORKING PAPER. LONDON: QUEEN MARY COLLEGE, DEPT. OF COMPUTER SCIENCE AND STATISTICS, 7 P. (1979).
FRIED 1979 -2 FRIEZE, A. M.
ON THE WORST-CASE PERFORMANCE OF SOME ALGORITHMS FOR THE ASYMMETRIC TRAVELLING SALESMAN PROBLEM. LONDON: UNIV. OF LONDON DEPT. OF COMPUTER SCIENCE AND STATISTICS, 23 P. (1979).
FRIED 1979 -3 FRIEZE, A. M.
PROBABILISTIC ANALYSIS OF SOME EUCLIDEAN CLUSTERING. LONDON: QUEEN MARY COLLEGE, DEPT. OF COMPUTER SCIENCE AND STATISTICS, 19 P. (1979).
FRIED 1979 -4 FRIEZE, A. M.
WORST-CASE ANALYSIS OF ALGORITHMS FOR TRAVELLING SALESMAN PROBLEMS. IN: W. OETTLI, F. STEFFENS (EDS.): OPERATIONS RESEARCH VERFAHREN 32, THIRD SYMPOSIUM ON OPERATIONS RESEARCH, MANNHEIM 1978, 93-112. KOENIGSTEIN: ANTON HAIN MEISENHEIM. (1979).
FRIED 1980 -1 FRIEZE, A. M.
ALGORITHM FOR ALGEBRAIC ASSIGNMENT PROBLEMS, AN. DISCRETE APPLIED MATHEMATICS 1, 253-259. (1980).
FRUM 1979 -1 FRUMKIN, M. A.
ON THE NUMBER OF NONNEGATIVE INTEGER SOLUTIONS OF A LINEAR DIOPHANTINE EQUATIONS SYSTEM. MOSKOW: ACADEMY OF SCIENCE OF THE USSR, CENTRAL ECONOMICS MATHEMATICAL INSTITUTE, 19 P. (1979).
FRUMA 1980 -1 FRUMKIN, M. A.; GENS, G. V.; HMELEVSKII, JU. I.; LEVNER, E. V.
ON COMPUTATIONAL COMPLEXITY OF OPTIMIZATION COMBINATORIAL PROBLEMS. REPORT NO. 80158-OR. BONN: UNIV. BONN, INST. FUER OEKONOMETRIE UND OPERATIONS RESEARCH, 7 P. (1980).
FUES 1977 -1 FUESTOES, L.; MESZENA, G.; SIMONNE MOSOLYGO, N.
CLUSTER ANALYSIS (HUNGARIAN). SZIGMA. MATEMATIKAI-KOEZGAZDASAGI FOLYOIRAT 10, NO. 3, 111-148. (1977).
FUJI 1977 -1 FUJISHIGE, S.
ALGORITHM FOR FINDING AN OPTIMAL INDEPENDENT LINKAGE, AN. JOURNAL OF THE OPERATIONS RESEARCH SOCIETY OF JAPAN 20, 59-75. (1977).
FUJI 1977 -2 FUJISHIGE, S.
PRIMAL APPROACH TO THE INDEPENDENT ASSIGNMENT PROBLEM, A. JOURNAL OF THE OPERATIONS RESEARCH SOCIETY OF JAPAN 20, 1-15. (1977).
FUJI 1978 -1 FUJISHIGE, S.
ALGORITHMS FOR SOLVING THE INDEPENDENT FLOW PROBLEMS. JOURNAL OF THE OPERATIONS RESEARCH SOCIETY OF JAPAN 21, 189-204. (1978).
FUJI 1979 -1 FUJISHIGE, S.
MATROID THEORY AND ITS APPLICATION TO SYSTEMS ENGINEERING PROBLEMS (JAPANESE). SYSTEMS AND CONTROL 23, 11-20. (1979).
FUJI 1980 -1 FUJISHIGE, S.
LEXICOGRAPHICALLY OPTIMAL BASE OF A POLYMATROID WITH RESPECT TO A WEIGHT VECTOR. MATHEMATICS OF OPERATIONS RESEARCH 5, 186-196. (1980).
FUJI 1980 -2 FUJISHIGE, S.
PRINCIPAL STRUCTURES OF SUBMODULAR SYSTEMS. DISCRETE APPLIED MATHEMATICS 2, 77-80. (1980).

FUJI 1981 -1 FUJISHIGE, S.
CANONICAL DECOMPOSITIONS OF SYMMETRIC SUBMODULAR SYSTEMS. IN: N. SAITO, T. NISHIZEKI (EDS.): GRAPH THEORY AND ALGORITHMS, 53-64. LECTURE NOTES IN COMPUTER SCIENCE 108. BERLIN: SPRINGER. (1981).

FUJIA 1978 -1 FUJITA, S.
APPLICATION OF MARGINAL ANALYSIS TO THE ECONOMIC LOT SCHEDULING PROBLEM, THE. AIIE TRANSACTIONS 10, 354-361. (1978).

FULK 1977 -1 FULKERSON, D. R.; HARDING, G. C.
MAXIMIZING THE MINIMUM SOURCE-SINK PATH SUBJECT TO A BUDGET CONSTRAINT. MATHEMATICAL PROGRAMMING 13, 116-118. (1977).

FULL 1978 -1 FULLER, J. A.
OPTIMAL SOLUTIONS VERSUS "GOOD" SOLUTIONS. AN ANALYSIS OF HEURISTIC DECISION MAKING. OMEGA 6, 479-484. (1978).

FUNG 1978 -1 FUNG, K. T.
ON A RESTRICTIVE SCHEDULING SCHEME. INFOR 16, 288-293. (1978).

FUSS 1979 -1 FUSSENEGGER, F.; GABOW, H. N.
COUNTING APPROACH TO LOWER BOUNDS FOR SELECTION PROBLEMS, A. JOURNAL OF THE ASSOCIATION FOR COMPUTING MACHINERY 26, 227-238. (1979).

FUTO 1977 -1 FUTO, P.
NEW MODEL AND ALGORITHM FOR CLUSTER ANALYSIS (HUNGARIAN), A. SZIGMA. MATEMATIKAI-KOEZGAZDASAGI FOLYOIRAT 10, NO. 3, 199-220. (1977).

GAAL 1978 -1 GAALMAN, G. J.
OPTIMAL AGGREGATION OF MULTI-ITEM PRODUCTION SMOOTHING MODELS. MANAGEMENT SCIENCE 24, 1733-1739. (1978).

GABA 1979 -1 GABASOV, R. F.; KOSTJUKOVA, O. I.
ON AN ALGORITHM FOR SOLVING A NETWORK DISTRIBUTOR PROBLEM. IZVESTIJA AKADEMII NAUK SSSR. TEHNICESKAJA KIBERNETIKA. (MOSCOW) NO. 2, 36-43, 220; TRANSLATED AS ENGINEERING CYBERNETICS 17, NO. 2, 19-27. (1979).

GABO 1970 -1 GABOVICH, E. J.
TRAVELLING SALESMAN PROBLEM, THE. TRUDY VYCISLITEL'NOGO CENTRA. TARTUSKII GOSUDARSTVENNYI UNIVERSITET 52. (1970).

GABO 1974 -1 GABOVICH, E. J.
EQUIVALENCY PROBLEM IN DISCRETE PROGRAMMING OVER ORDERED SEMIGROUPS, AN. SEMIGROUP FORUM 8, 69-73. (1974).

GABO 1980 -1 GABOVICH, E. J.
ON SPECTRAL THEORY IN DISCRETE PROGRAMMING. BONN: UNIV. BONN, INST. F. OEKONOMETRIE UND OPERATIONS RESEARCH, 18 P. (1980).

GABOA 1979 -1 GABOVICH, E. J.; MELAMED, I. J.
COMPUTATIONAL COMPLEXITY OF ROUTING PROBLEMS (RUSSIAN). MOSKOVSKII INSTITUT INZENEROV ZELEZNODOROZNOGO TRANSPORTA TRUDY (MOSCOW) NO. 640. PRIKLADNAJA MATEMATIKA I ZADACI ZELEZNODOROZNOGO TRANSPORTA 87-94. (1979).

GABOB 1978 -1 GABOW, H. N.
GOOD ALGORITHM FOR SMALLEST SPANNING TREES WITH A DEGREE CONSTRAINT, A. NETWORKS 8, 201-208. (1978).

GABOB 1979 -1 GABOW, H. N.
ALGORITHMIC PROOFS OF TWO RELATIONS BETWEEN CONNECTIVITY AND THE 1-FACTORS OF A GRAPH. DISCRETE MATHEMATICS 26, 33-40. (1979).

GABOC 1978 -1 GABOW, H. N.; KARIV, O.
ALGORITHMS FOR EDGE COLORING BIPARTITE GRAPHS. IN: PROCEEDINGS OF THE TENTH ANNUAL ACM SYMPOSIUM ON THEORY OF COMPUTING, SAN DIEGO, 1978, 184-192. NEW YORK: THE ASSOCIATION FOR COMPUTING MACHINERY. (1978).

GABOD 1978 -1 GABOW, H. N.; MYERS, E. W.
FINDING ALL SPANNING TREES OF DIRECTED AND UNDIRECTED GRAPHS. SIAM JOURNAL ON COMPUTING 7, 280-288. (1978).

GABOE 1979 -1 GABOW, H. N.; TARJAN, R. E.
EFFICIENT ALGORITHMS FOR SIMPLE MATROID INTERSECTION PROBLEMS. IN: ANNUAL SYMPOSIUM ON FOUNDATIONS OF COMPUTER SCIENCE, SAN JUAN 1979, 196-204. NEW YORK: INSTITUTE OF ELECTRICAL AND ELECTRONICS ENGINEERS. (1979).

GABR 1977 -1 GABRIEL, R.
PROGRAMMSTELLUNG IN SPORTLICHEN MEISTERSCHAFTEN NACH MATHEMATISCHEN MODELLEN. IN: B. BEREANU, M. IOSIFESCU, G. POPESCU (EDS.): PROCEEDINGS OF THE FIFTH CONFERENCE ON PROBABILITY THEORY, BRASOV, ROMANIA 1974, 393-400. BUCURESTI: AKADEMEI REPUBLICII SOCIALISTE ROMANIA. (1977).

GABR 1981 -1 GABRIEL, R.
LEISTUNGSVERGLEICH KOMMERZIELLER SOFTWARE ZUR LOESUNG SPEZIELLER MIXED-INTEGER-PROBLEME, EIN. ANGEWANDTE INFORMATIK, NO. 1, 21-26. (1981).

GAIT 1980 -1 GAITANIDES, M.
AUFGABENSTRUKTURPLANUNG UND FLEXIBILITAET VON PRODUKTIONSPROZESSEN. ZEITSCHRIFT FUER BETRIEBSWIRTSCHAFT 50, NO. 3, 231-243. (1980).

GAL 1978 -1 GAL, T.
DETERMINATION OF ALL NEIGHBORS OF A DEGENERATE EXTREME POINT IN POLYTOPES. DISCUSSION PAPER NR. 17. HAGEN: FERNUNIV. HAGEN, FACHBEREICH WIRTSCHAFTSWISSENSCHAFTEN, 40 P. (1978).

GALI 1975 -1 GALIL, Z.
ON THE COMPLEXITY OF REGULAR RESOLUTION AND THE DAVIS-PUTNAM PROCEDURE. IBM RESEARCH REPORT 5614. YORKTOWN HEIGHTS: IBM RESEARCH CENTER, 43 P. (1975).

GALI 1978 -1 GALIL, Z.
NEW ALGORITHM FOR THE MAXIMAL FLOW PROBLEM, A. IN: INSTITUTE OF ELECTRICAL AND ELECTRONICS ENGINEERS (ED.): 19TH ANNUAL SYMPOSIUM ON FOUNDATIONS OF COMPUTER SCIENCE, ANN ARBOR 1978, 231-245. NEW YORK: INSTITUTE OF ELECTRICAL AND ELECTRONICS ENGINEERS. (1978).

GALI 1978 -2 GALIL, Z.
ON THE THEORETICAL EFFICIENCY OF VARIOUS NETWORK FLOW ALGORITHMS. IBM RESEARCH REPORT 7320. YORKTOWN HEIGHTS: IBM RESEARCH CENTER, 9 P. (1978).

GALI 1980 -1 GALIL, Z.
FINDING THE VERTEX CONNECTIVITY OF GRAPHS. SIAM JOURNAL ON COMPUTING 9, 197-199. (1980).

GALI 1980 -2 GALIL, Z.
O(V**(5/3)E**(2/3)) ALGORITHM FOR THE MAXIMAL FLOW PROBLEM, AN. ACTA INFORMATICA 14, 221-242. (1980).

GALIA 1977 -1 GALIL, Z.; MEGIDDO, N.
FAST SELECTION ALGORITHM AND THE PROBLEM OF OPTIMUM DISTRIBUTION OF EFFORT, A. IN: E. A. ASHCROFT ET AL. (EDS.): PROCEEDINGS OF A CONFERENCE ON THEORETICAL COMPUTER SCIENCE, WATERLOO 1977, 173-181. WATERLOO: UNIVERSITY OF WATERLOO. (1977).

GALIA 1979 -1 GALIL, Z.; MEGIDDO, N.
FAST SELECTION ALGORITHM AND THE PROBLEM OF OPTIMUM DISTRIBUTION OF EFFORT, A. JOURNAL OF THE ASSOCIATION FOR COMPUTING MACHINERY 26, 58-64. (1979).

GALIB 1979 -1 GALIL, Z.; NAAMAD, A.
NETWORK FLOW AND GENERALIZED PATH COMPRESSION. IN: PROCEEDINGS OF THE 11TH ANNUAL ACM SYMPOSIUM ON THEORY OF COMPUTING, ATLANTA 1979, 13-26. NEW YORK: ASSOCIATION FOR COMPUTING MACHINERY. (1979).

GALIB 1980 -1 GALIL, Z.; NAAMAD, A.
O(EV(LOG V)**2) ALGORITHM FOR THE MAXIMAL FLOW PROBLEM, AN. JOURNAL OF COMPUTER AND SYSTEM SCIENCES 21, 203-217. (1980).

GALIC 1977 -1 GALIL, Z.; SEIFERAS, J.
SAVING SPACE IN FAST STRING-MATCHING. IBM RESEARCH REPORT 6670. YORKTOWN HEIGHTS: IBM RESEARCH CENTER, 9 P. (1977).

GALL 1977 -1 GALLAGHER, R. G.
LOOPS IN MULTICOMMODITY FLOWS. IN: PROCEEDINGS OF THE 1977 IEEE CONFERENCE ON DECISION AND CONTROL, NEW ORLEANS 1977, VOL I, 819-825. NEW YORK: IEEE. (1977).

GALLA 1958 -1 GALLAI, T.
MAXIMUM-MINIMUM SAETZE UEBER GRAPHEN. ACTA MATHEMATICA ACADEMIAE SCIENTARUM HUNGARICAE 9, 395-434. (1958).

GALLA 1961 -1 GALLAI, T.
MAXIMUM-MINIMUM SAETZE UND VERALLGEMEINERTE FAKTOREN VON GRAPHEN. ACTA MATHEMATICA ACADEMIAE SCIENTARUM HUNGARICAE 12, 131-173. (1961).

GALLB 1980 -1 GALLO, G.
REOPTIMIZATION PROCEDURES IN SHORTEST PATH PROBLEMS. RIVISTA DI MATEMATICA PER LE SCIENZE ECONOMICHE E SOCIALI (MILAN) 3, NO. 1, 3-13. (1980).

GALLC 1980 -1 GALLO, G.; HAMMER, P. L.; SIMEONE, B.
QUADRATIC KNAPSACK PROBLEMS. MATHEMATICAL PROGRAMMING STUDY 12, 132-149. (1980).

GALLD 1980 -1 GALLO, G.; SANDI, C.; SODINI, C.
ALGORITHM FOR THE MIN CONCAVE COST FLOW PROBLEM, AN. EUROPEAN JOURNAL OF OPERATIONAL RESEARCH 4, 248-255. (1980).

GALLE 1975 -1 GALLO, G.; SIMEONE, B.
NEW CUTS FOR INTEGER PROGRAMMING VIA GROUP OPTIMIZATION. PUBBLICAZIONI, SER.III, IST. APPL. CALCOLO 105, 19P. (1975).

GALLF 1979 -1 GALLO, G.; SODINI, C.
ADJACENT EXTREME FLOWS AND APPLICATION TO MIN CONCAVE COST FLOW PROBLEMS. NETWORKS 9, 95-121. (1979).

GALLF 1979 -2 GALLO, G.; SODINI, C.
CONCAVE COST MINIMIZATION ON NETWORKS. EUROPEAN JOURNAL OF OPERATIONAL RESEARCH 3, 239-249. (1979).

GALLF 1979 -3 GALLO, G.; SODINI, C.
EXTREME POINTS AND ADJACENCY RELATIONSHIP IN THE FLOW POLYTOPE. CALCOLO 15, 277-288. (1979).

GALV 1980 -1 GALVAO, R. D.
DUAL-BOUNDED ALGORITHM FOR THE P-MEDIAN PROBLEM, A. OPERATIONS RESEARCH 28, 1112-1121. (1980).

GALV 1981 -1 GALVAO, R. D.
GRAPH THEORETICAL BOUND FOR THE P-MEDIAN PROBLEM, A. EUROPEAN JOURNAL OF OPERATIONAL RESEARCH 6, 162-165. (1981).

GANS 1979 -1 GANSHIN, G. S.
OPTIMISATION D'ALGORITHMES DANS LES CLASSES DE RESEAUX (RUSSIAN). AKADEMIJA NAUK SSSR. ZURNAL VYCISLITEL'NOI MATEMATIKI I MATEMATICESKOI FIZIKI 19, 811-821. (1979).

GARC 1977 -1 GARCIA, R.; HACKBARTH, K.-D.
MATHEMATISCHES PLANUNGSMODELL FUER DIE LANGFRISTIGE KOSTENOPTIMALE GESTALTUNG VON FERNMELDENETZEN. DARMSTADT: FORSCHUNGSINSTITUT DER DEUTSCHEN BUNDESPOST, P. 709-711 (1977).

GARD 1977 -1 GARDARIN, G.
ALLOCATION DE RESSOURCES SIMULTANEMENT PARTAGEABLES AVEC RESOLUTION DU VERROU MORTEL. REVUE FRANCAISE D'AUTOMATIQUE, D'INFORMATIQUE ET DE RECHERCHE OPERATIONELLE 11, SERIE INFORMATIQUE, 107-125. (1977).

GARE 1978 -1 GAREY, M. R.; GRAHAM, R. L.; JOHNSON, D. S.
PERFORMANCE GUARANTEES FOR SCHEDULING ALGORITHMS. OPERATIONS RESEARCH 26, 3-21. (1978).

GAREA 1978 -1 GAREY, M. R.; JOHNSON, D. S.
"STRONG" NP-COMPLETENESS RESULTS: MOTIVATION, EXAMPLES AND IMPLICATIONS. JOURNAL OF THE ASSOCIATION FOR COMPUTING MACHINERY 25, 499-509. (1978).

GAREB 1980 -1 GAREY, M. R.; JOHNSON, D. S.; MILLER, G. L.; PAPADIMITRIOU, C. H.
COMPLEXITY OF COLORING CIRCULAR ARCS AND CHORDS, THE. SIAM JOURNAL ON ALGEBRAIC AND DISCRETE METHODS 1, 216-227. (1980).

GAREC 1978 -1 GAREY, M. R.; JOHNSON, D. S.; PREPARATA, F. P.; TARJAN, R. E.
TRIANGULATING A SIMPLE POLYGON. INFORMATION PROCESSING LETTERS 7, 175-179. (1978).

GARED 1978 -1 GAREY, M. R.; TARJAN, R. E.
LINEAR-TIME ALGORITHM FOR FINDING ALL FEEDBACK VERTICES, A. INFORMATION PROCESSING LETTERS 7, 274-277. (1978).

GARF 1979 -1 GARFINKEL, R. S.
BRANCH AND BOUND METHODS FOR INTEGER PROGRAMMING. IN: N. CHRISTOFIDES, A. MINGOZZI, P. TOTH, C. SANDI (EDS.): COMBINATORIAL OPTIMIZATION, 1-20. CHICHESTER, NEW YORK, BRISBANE, TORONTO: WILEY. (1979).

GARFA 1978 -1 GARFINKEL, R. S.; GILBERT, K. C.
BOTTLENECK TRAVELING SALESMAN PROBLEM: ALGORITHMS AND PROBABILISTIC ANALYSIS, THE. JOURNAL OF THE ASSOCIATION FOR COMPUTING MACHINERY 25, 435-449. (1978).

GARFB 1980 -1 GARFINKEL, R. S.; PLOTNICKI, W. J.
SOLVABLE CYCLIC SCHEDULING PROBLEM WITH SERIAL PRECEDENCE STRUCTURE, A. OPERATIONS RESEARCH 28, 1236-1240. (1980).

GARK 1979 -1 GARKAVENKO, S. I.; BERDNIKOVA, L. S.
DETERMINATION OF THE PATHS IN AN ORIENTED ACYCLICAL GRAPH. KIBERNETIKA (KIEV) NO. 4, 49-52; TRANSLATED AS CYBERNETICS 15, 489-493. (1979).

GARR 1978 -1 GARROD, N. W.; MOORES, B.
IMPLICIT ENUMERATION ALGORITHM FOR SOLVING ZERO-ONE GOAL PROGRAMMING PROBLEMS, AN. OMEGA 6, NO. 4, 374-377. (1978).

GARS 1980 -1 GARSIDE, G. R.; PINTELAS, P. E.
ALGOL 68 PACKAGE FOR IMPLEMENTING GRAPH ALGORITHMS, AN. THE COMPUTER JOURNAL 23, 237-242. (1980).

GART 1976 -1 GARTNER, N. H.; GOLDEN, B. L.; WONG, R. T.
MODELING AND OPTIMIZATION FOR TRANSPORTATION SYSTEMS PLANNING AND OPERATIONS. WORKING PAPER OR 056-76. CAMBRIDGE: MASSACHUSETTS INSTITUTE OF TECHNOLOGY, OPERATIONS RESEARCH CENTER. (1976).

GARY 1975 -1 GARY, D.
SCHEDULING TO MINIMIZE INTERACTION COSTS WITH FACILITY CONSTRAINTS. DOCTORAL DISSERTATION. NEW ORLEANS: TULANE UNIVERSITY, 123 P. (1975).

****

GATI 1978 -1 GATI, G.
LEVEL-SCHEDULING FOR SPECIAL AND GENERAL PRECEDENCE GRAPHS. IN: J. MUEHLBACHER (ED.): DATENSTRUKTUREN, GRAPHEN, ALGORITHMEN. DRITTE FACHTAGUNG UEBER GRAPHENTHEORETISCHE KONZEPTE DER INFORMATIK, LINZ 1977, 251-262. MUENCHEN, WIEN: HANSER. (1978).

GATI 1979 -1 GATI, G.
FURTHER ANNOTATED BIBLIOGRAPHY ON THE ISOMORPHISM DISEASE. JOURNAL OF GRAPH THEORY 3, 95-109. (1979).

GATT 1981 -1 GATTASS, E. A.; NEMHAUSER, G. L.
APPLICATION OF VERTEX PACKING ON INTERVAL GRAPHS TO DATA ANALYSIS IN ROAD MAINTENANCE, AN. IN: R. E. BURKARD, T. ELLINGER (EDS.): METHODS OF OPERATIONS RESEARCH 40, 315-320. KOENIGSTEIN: ANTON HAIN MEISENHEIM. (1981).

GATTA 1981 -1 GATTINGER, M.; WENZEL, G.
VERALLGEMEINERTE GERUESTE, KOZYKLEN UND ZYKLEN IN GRAPHEN. IN: R. E. BURKARD, T. ELLINGER (EDS.): METHODS OF OPERATIONS RESEARCH 40, 321-324. KOENIGSTEIN: ANTON HAIN MEISENHEIM. (1981).

GAUD 1979 -1 GAUDIOSO, M.
HEURISTIC APPROACH TO THE CUTTING STOCK PROBLEM, A. IN: W. OETTLI, F. STEFFENS (EDS.): OPERATIONS RESEARCH VERFAHREN 32, THIRD SYMPOSIUM ON OPERATIONS RESEARCH, MANNHEIM 1978, 113-118. KOENIGSTEIN: ANTON HAIN MEISENHEIM. (1979).

GAUL 1978 -1 GAUL, W.
SOME STRUCTURAL PROPERTIES OF PROJECT DIGRAPHS. JOURNAL OF COMBINATORICS, INFORMATION AND SYSTEM SCIENCES 3, 217-222. (1978).

GAULA 1978 -1 GAUL, W.; HARTUNG, J.
ZEIT- UND KOSTENOPTIMIERUNG VON BOTTLENECKWEGEN. IN: PROCEEDINGS IN OPERATIONS RESEARCH 7, 387-396. WUERZBURG: PHYSICA. (1978).

GAVI 1978 -1 GAVISH, B.
ON OBTAINING THE 'BEST' MULTIPLIERS FOR A LAGRANGEAN RELAXATION FOR INTEGER PROGRAMMING. COMPUTERS AND OPERATIONS RESEARCH 5, 55-71. (1978).

GAVIA 1978 -1 GAVISH, B.; SCHWEITZER, P.; SHLIFER, E.
ASSIGNING BUSES TO SCHEDULES IN A METROPOLITAN AREA. COMPUTERS AND OPERATIONS RESEARCH 5, 129-138. (1978).

GAVIB 1979 -1 GAVISH, B.; SHLIFER, E.
APPROACH FOR SOLVING A CLASS OF TRANSPORTATION SCHEDULING PROBLEMS, AN. EUROPEAN JOURNAL OF OPERATIONAL RESEARCH 3, 122-134. (1979).

GAVIC 1980 -1 GAVISH, B.; SRIKANTH, K.
OPTIMAL SOLUTION METHOD FOR THE MULTIPLE TRAVELLING SALESMAN PROBLEM, AN. WORKING PAPER 8027. ROCHESTER: UNIV. OF ROCHESTER, GRADUATE SCHOOL OF MANAGEMENT, 43 P. (1980).

GAVR 1977 -1 GAVRIL, F.
SOME NP-COMPLETE PROBLEMS ON GRAPHS. IN: PROCEEDINGS OF THE 1977 CONFERENCE ON INFORMATION SCIENCES AND SYSTEMS, BALTIMORE 1977, 91-95. BALTIMORE: THE JOHNS HOPKINS UNIVERSITY: DEPARTMENT OF ELECTRICAL ENGINEERING. (1977).

GAVR 1977 -2 GAVRIL, F.
TESTING FOR EQUALITY BETWEEN MAXIMUM MATCHING AND MINIMUM NODE COVERING. INFORMATION PROCESSING LETTERS, NO. 6, 199-202. (1977).

GELD 1978 -1 GELDERS, L. F.; SAMBANDAM, N.
FOUR SIMPLE HEURISTICS FOR SCHEDULING A FLOW SHOP. INTERNATIONAL JOURNAL OF PRODUCTION RESEARCH 16, 221-231. (1978).

GELL 1974 -1 GELLER, D. P.; HILTON, A. J. W.
HOW TO COLOR THE LINES OF A BIGRAPH. NETWORKS 4, 281-282. (1974).

GEN 1976 -1 GEN, M.; OKUNO, H.; SHINOFUJI, S.
OPTIMIZING METHOD IN SYSTEM RELIABILITY WITH FAILURE-MODES BY IMPLICIT ENUMERATION ALGORITHM, AN. JOURNAL OF THE OPERATIONS RESEARCH SOCIETY OF JAPAN 19, 99-116. (1976).

GEND 1977 -1 GENDREAU, M.
ETUDE SUR LA GENERATION DES RESEAUX ALEATOIRES. DOCUMENT DE TRAVAIL, 98. MONTREAL: UNIV. DE MONTREAL, DEPT.D'INFORMATIQUE, 52 P. (1977).

GENS 1977 -1 GENS, G. V.; LEVNER, E. V.
ON E-ALGORITHMS FOR UNIVERSAL DISCRETE PROBLEMS (RUSSIAN). IN: PROC IV ALL-UNION CONF. ON PROBLEMS OF THEORET. CYBERN., 95-96. NOVOSIBIRSK: INST. MAT. (1977).

GENS 1978 -1 GENS, G. V.; LEVNER, E. V.
APPROXIMATE ALGORITHMS FOR CERTAIN UNIVERSAL PROBLEMS IN SCHEDULING THEORY. IZVESTIJA AKADEMII NAUK SSSR. TEHNICESKAJA KIBERNETIKA (MOSCOW) NO. 6, 38-43; TRANSLATED AS ENGINEERING CYBERNETICS 16, NO. 6, 31-36. (1978).

GENS 1979 -1 GENS, G. V.; LEVNER, E. V.
COMPLEXITY OF APPROXIMATION ALGORITHMS FOR COMBINATORIAL PROBLEMS: A SURVEY. ABSTRACT. MOSCOW: USSR ACADEMY OF SCIENCES, CENTRAL ECONOMIC AND MATHEMATICAL INSTITUTE, 18 P. (1979).

GENS 1979 -2 GENS, G. V.; LEVNER, E. V.
COMPUTATIONAL COMPLEXITY OF APPROXIMATION ALGORITHMS FOR COMBINATORIAL PROBLEMS. IN: J. BECVAR (ED.): MATHEMATICAL FOUNDATIONS OF COMPUTER SCIENCE 1979, PROCEEDINGS OF THE 8TH SYMPOSIUM, OLOMOUC 1979, 292-300. LECTURE NOTES IN COMPUTER SCIENCE 74, BERLIN, HEIDELBERG, NEW YORK: SPRINGER. (1979).

GENS 1979 -3 GENS, G. V.; LEVNER, E. V.
EFFICIENT APPROXIMATION ALGORITHMS FOR THE INTEGER PROGRAMMING PROBLEMS OF KNAPSACK TYPE. IN: PROC. IX CONF. IFIP ON OPTIMIZATION TECHNIQUES. WARSAWA. (1979).

GENS 1979 -4 GENS, G. V.; LEVNER, E. V.
PROBLEMES D'OPTIMISATION DISCRETE ET ALGORITHMES APPROCHES EFFECTIFS (REVUE) (RUSSIAN). IZVESTIJA AKADEMII NAUK SSSR. TEHNICESKAJA KIBERNETIKA (MOSCOW), NO. 6, 9-20. (1979).

GENS 1980 -1 GENS, G. V.; LEVNER, E. V.
FAST APPROXIMATION ALGORITHMS FOR KNAPSACK TYPE PROBLEMS. IN: K. IRACKI, K. MALANOWSKI, P. WALUKIEWICZ (EDS.): OPTIMIZATION TECHNIQUES, PART II, 185-194. LECTURE NOTES IN CONTROL AND INFORMATION SCIENCES 23. BERLIN: SPRINGER. (1980).

GENSA 1978 -1 GENSCH, D. H.
INDUSTRIAL APPLICATION OF THE TRAVELING SALESMAN'S SUBTOUR PROBLEM, AN. AIIE TRANSACTIONS 10, 362-370. (1978).

GEOF 1977 -1 GEOFFRION, A. M.
AGGREGATION THEORY AND ITS APPLICATION TO MODELING IN MATHEMATICAL PROGRAMMING. WORKING PAPER NO. 278. LOS ANGELES: UNIV. OF CALIFORNIA, WESTERN MANAGEMENT SCIENCE INSTITUTE, 16 P. (1977).

GEOFA 1978 -1 GEOFFRION, A. M.; MAC BRIDE, R. D.
LAGRANGEAN RELAXATION APPLIED TO CAPACITATED FACILITY LOCATION PROBLEMS. AIIE TRANSACTIONS 10, 40-47. (1978).

GEOFB 1978 -1 GEOFFROY, D. P.; SUMNER, D. P.
UPPER BOUND ON THE SIZE OF A LARGEST CLIQUE IN A GRAPH, AN. JOURNAL OF GRAPH THEORY 2, 223-231. (1978).

GEOR 1979 -1 GEORGE, J. A.
REPORT ON THE USE OF MIXED INTEGER PROGRAMMING IN AN EVALUATION OF PLANT UPGRADING, A. NEW ZEALAND OPERATIONAL RESEARCH 7, 117-125. (1979).

GEORA 1980 -1 GEORGE, J. A.; ROBINSON, D. F.
HEURISTIC FOR PACKING BOXES INTO A CONTAINER, A. COMPUTERS AND OPERATIONS RESEARCH 7, 147-156. (1980).

GEORB 1976 -1 GEORGIEVA, N. C.
ALGORITHM FOR THE EXACT PARTITIONING OF A GRAPH WITH N VERTICES INTO TWO SUBGRAPHS (BULGARIAN). AN. GODISNIK NA VISSITE UCEBNI ZAVEDENIJA. PRILOZNA MATEMATIKA 12, NO. 3, 47-56. (1976).

GERH 1979 -1 GERHARDS, L.; LINDENBERG, W.
CLIQUE DETECTION FOR NONDIRECTED GRAPHS: TWO NEW ALGORITHMS. COMPUTING 21, 295-322. (1979).

GERL 1978 -1 GERLOVIN, E. L.; SROGOVICH, E. B.
METHODS FOR SOLVING NONLINEAR NETWORK TRANSPORTATION PROBLEMS (RUSSIAN). EKONOMIKA I MATEMATICESKIE METODY 14, 1189-1196. (1978).

GERT 1978 -1 GERTSBACH, I.; STERN, H. I.
MINIMAL RESOURCES FOR FIXED AND VARIABLE JOB SCHEDULES. OPERATIONS RESEARCH 26, 68-85. (1978).

GESS 1979 -1 GESSEL, I.; WANG, D.-L.
DEPTH-FIRST SEARCH AS A COMBINATORIAL CORRESPONDENCE. JOURNAL OF COMBINATORIAL THEORY 26, SERIES A, 308-313. (1979).

GHIU 1977 -1 GHIUS, V.
FLOWS IN ARBITRARILY TRACED, GENERALIZED GRAPHS (ROMANIAN). BULETINUL INSTITUTULUI POLITEHNIC BUCURESTI 23, 69-73. (1977).

GHOS 1978 -1 GHOSH, S.; RAY, S.; BHATTACHARYA, A.
CASE STUDY FOR OPTIMAL PLANT SIZE MIX USING INTEGER LINEAR PROGRAMMING, A. OPSEARCH 15, 35-44. (1978).

GIAN 1980 -1 GIANNESSI, F.
CONTINUED FRACTIONS AND EXPLICIT SOLUTIONS OF A PARTICULAR DISCRETE OPTIMIZATION PROBLEM. DISCRETE APPLIED MATHEMATICS 1, 261-275. (1980).

GIANA 1978 -1 GIANNESSI, F.; JURINA, L.; MAIER, G.
OPTIMAL EXCAVATION PROFILE FOR A PIPELINE FREELY RESTING ON THE SEA FLOOR. FLORENCE (4TH CONGRESS OF AIMETA, OCTOBER 1978) 26 P. (1978).

GIANB 1976 -1 GIANNESSI, F.; NICCOLUCCI, F.
CONNECTIONS BETWEEN NONLINEAR AND INTEGER PROGRAMMING PROBLEMS. IN: ISTITUTO NAZIONALE DI ALTA MATEMATICA SYMPOSIA MATHEMATICA VOL. 19, P. 161-176 (1976).

GIANC 1979 -1 GIANNESSI, F.; NICOLETTI, B.
CREW SCHEDULING PROBLEM: A TRAVELLING SALESMAN APPROACH, THE. IN: N. CHRISTOFIDES, A. MINGOZZI, P. TOTH, C. SANDI (EDS.): COMBINATORIAL OPTIMIZATION, 389-408. CHICHESTER, NEW YORK, BRISBANE, TORONTO: WILEY. (1979).

GIAND 1977 -1 GIANNESSI, G.
CONTINUED FRACTIONS AND EXPLICIT SOLUTIONS OF A PARTICULAR DISCRETE OPTIMIZATION PROBLEM. PISA: UNIV. DI PISA, DIPT. DI RICERCA OPERATIVA E SCIENZE STATISTICHE, 55 P. (1977).

GIER 1979 -1 GIERTH, G.; TERNO, J.
NICHOLSON PRINCIPLE IN DISCRETE DYNAMIC OPTIMIZATION, THE. MATHEMATISCHE OPERATIONSFORSCHUNG UND STATISTIK 10, SERIES OPTIMIZATION, 67-77. (1979).

GIK 1977 -1 GIK, E. JA.; LEVNER, E. V.
PROBLEM ON THE ANALYSIS OF CIRCULATIONS IN NETWORKS (RUSSIAN), A. EKONOMIKA I MATEMATICESKIE METODY 13, 1307-1312. (1977).

GIK A 1978 -1 GIK, Y. Y.; ZHORNITSKIY, A. B.
PROPERTIES OF CYCLIC EXTENSIONS OF FLOWS IN A NETWORK. IZVESTIJA AKADEMII NAUK SSSR. TEHNICESKAJA KIBERNETIKA, NO. 3, 38-44; TRANSLATED AS ENGINEERING CYBERNETICS 16, NO. 3, 1978, 33-40. (1978).

GILE 1978 -1 GILES, R.
FACETS AND OTHER FACES OF BRANCHING POLYHEDRA. IN: A. HAJNAL, V. T. SOS (EDS.): COMBINATORICS, VOLUME I, 401-418. COLLOQUIA MATHEMATICA SOCIETATIS JANOS BOLYAI 18. AMSTERDAM: NORTH-HOLLAND. (1978).

GILE 1979 -1 GILES, R.
ADJACENCY ON THE POSTMAN POLYHEDRON. REPORT NO. 79128-OR. BONN: UNIV. BONN, INSTITUT FUER OEKONOMETRIE UND OPERATIONS RESEARCH, 7 P. (1979).

GILE 1979 -2 GILES, R.
OPTIMUM MATCHING FORESTS (EXTENDED ABSTRACT). IN: W. OETTLI, F. STEFFENS (EDS.): OPERATIONS RESEARCH VERFAHREN 32, THIRD SYMPOSIUM ON OPERATIONS RESEARCH, MANNHEIM 1978, 119-121. KOENIGSTEIN: ANTON HAIN MEISENHEIM. (1979).

GILEA 1979 -1 GILES, R.; HAUSMANN, D.
CHARACTERIZATIONS OF ADJACENCY ON THE BRANCHING POLYHEDRON. DISCRETE MATHEMATICS 26, 219-226. (1979).

GILEB 1979 -1 GILES, R.; KANNAN, R.
CHARACTERIZATION OF THRESHOLD MATROIDS (EXTENDED ABSTRACT), A. IN: W. OETTLI, F. STEFFENS (EDS.): OPERATIONS RESEARCH VERFAHREN 32, THIRD SYMPOSIUM ON OPERATIONS RESEARCH, MANNHEIM 1978, 123-124. KOENIGSTEIN: ANTON HAIN MEISENHEIM. (1979).

GILEB 1980 -1 GILES, R.; KANNAN, R.
CHARACTERIZATION OF THRESHOLD MATROIDS, A. DISCRETE MATHEMATICS 30, 181-184. (1980).

GILEC 1980 -1 GILES, R.; OYAMA, T.; TROTTER, L. E. JR.
RELATED NECESSARY CONDITIONS FOR COMPLETING PARTIAL LATIN SQUARES. JOURNAL OF COMBINATORIAL THEORY A 29, 20-31. (1980).

GILED 1979 -1 GILES, R.; PULLEYBLANK, W. R.
TOTAL DUAL INTEGRALITY AND INTEGER POLYHEDRA. LINEAR ALGEBRA AND ITS APPLICATIONS 25, 191-196. (1979).

GILEE 1979 -1 GILES, R.; TROTTER, L. E. JR.
ON STABLE SET POLYHEDRA FOR K1,3-FREE GRAPHS. REPORT NO. 79136-OR. BONN: UNIV. BONN, INST. FUER OEKONOMETRIE UND OPERATIONS RESEARCH, 18 P. (1979).

GILL 1976 -1 GILLETT, B. E.
VEHICLE DISPATCHING: SWEEP ALGORITHM AND EXTENSIONS. PRESENTED AT THE ORSA/TIMS JOINT NATIONAL MEETING, MIAMI 1976. (1976).

GILM 1979 -1 GILMORE, P. C.
CUTTING STOCK, LINEAR PROGRAMMING, KNAPSACKING, DYNAMIC PROGRAMMING AND INTEGER PROGRAMMING, SOME INTERCONNECTIONS. IN: P. L. HAMMER, E. L. JOHNSON, B. H. KORTE (EDS.): DISCRETE OPTIMIZATION I, 217-235. ANNALS OF DISCRETE MATHEMATICS 4. AMSTERDAM, NEW YORK, OXFORD: NORTH-HOLLAND. (1979).

GIMO 1979 -1 GIMOURGINAS, C.; KARWAN, M. H.
COMPUTATIONAL RESULTS OF THE P-MEDIAN AND SET COVERING PROBLEMS FOR AN AMBULANCE LOCATION STUDY IN THE CITY OF BUFFALO. WORKING PAPER. AMHERST: STATE UNIV. OF NEW YORK, DEPT. OF INDUSTRIAL ENGINEERING, 38 P. (1979).

GION 1978 -1 GIONFRIDDO, M.
ON L(S) COLORINGS OF FINITE GRAPHS (ITALIAN). UNIONE MATEMATICA ITALIANA. BOLLETINO 15A, NO. 2, 444-454. (1978).

GION 1980 -1 GIONFRIDDO, M.
AUTOMORPHISMES COLORES ET COLORATIONS (R,S) DANS UN GRAPHE (ITALIAN). BOLLETTINO B. UNIONE MATEMATICA ITALIANA (BOLOGNA) 17, 1338-1349. (1980).
GIOR 1975 -1 GIORDANO, F. R.
HEURISTIC FOR THE CONSTRUCTION OF SURROGATE CONSTRAINTS FOR THE SOLUTION OF THE LINEAR ZERO-ONE INTEGER PROBLEM, A. DOCTORAL DISSERTATION. FAYETTEVILLE: UNIVERSITY OF ARKANSAS, 94 P. (1975).
GIRL 1980 -1 GIRLICH, E.; KOVALEV, M. M.
PROBLEMKLASSE DER NICHTLINEAREN DISKRETEN OPTIMIERUNG, EINE. WISSENSCHAFTLICHE ZEITSCHRIFT DER FRIEDRICH-SCHILLER-UNIVERSITAET JENA, MATHEMATISCH-NATURWISSENSCHAFTLICHE REIHE 29, 327-338. (1980).
GISV 1971 -1 GISVOLD, K. M.; MOE, J.
METHOD FOR NONLINEAR MIXED-INTEGER PROGRAMMING AND ITS APPLICATION TO DESIGN PROBLEMS, A. PAP. ASME, N VIBR. 117. (1971).
GIUL 1977 -1 GIULIANELLI, S.; LUCERTINI, M.
METHOD FOR REDUCING COMPUTATIONAL COMPLEXITY OF ILPC PROBLEMS, A. RICERCHE DI AUTOMATICA 8, 127-141. (1977).
GIUL 1979 -1 GIULIANELLI, S.; LUCERTINI, M.
GROUP THEORETIC METHOD FOR THE SOLUTION OF INTEGER PROGRAMMING PROBLEMS (ITALIAN). RICERCA OPERATIVA NUOVA SERIE NO. 12, 51-82. (1979).
GIZE 1980 -1 GIZELIS, A. G.; SAMOUILIDIS, J. E.
SIMPLIFIED ALGORITHM FOR THE DEPOT LOCATION PROBLEM, A. OMEGA 8, 465-472. (1980).
GLAN 1978 -1 GLANKWAHMDEE, A.; LIEBMAN, J. S.; HOGG, G. L.
UNCONSTRAINED DISCRETE NONLINEAR PROGRAMMING. URBANA: UNIV. OF ILLINOIS, DEPT. OF MECHANICAL AND INDUSTRIAL ENGINEERING, 32 P. (1978).
GLAZ 1980 -1 GLAZEBROOK, K. D.
ON SINGLE-MACHINE SEQUENCING WITH ORDER CONSTRAINTS. NAVAL RESEARCH LOGISTICS QUARTERLY 27, 123-130. (1980).
GLAZA 1981 -1 GLAZEBROOK, K. D.; GITTINS, J. C.
ON SINGLE-MACHINE SCHEDULING WITH PRECEDENCE RELATIONS AND LINEAR OR DISCOUNTED COSTS. OPERATIONS RESEARCH 29, 161-173. (1981).
GLEB 1978 -1 GLEBOV, N. I.
APPLICABILITY OF THE COORDINATE-WISE SLOPE METHOD TO SOME PROBLEMS OF CONVEX INTEGER PROGRAMMING (RUSSIAN). UPRAVLJAEMYE SISTEMY, NO. 17, 52-59 + 88. (1978).
GLEB 1978 -2 GLEBOV, N. I.
SOME CASES OF REDUCIBILITY OF JOHNSON'S M-MACHINE PROBLEM TO A PROBLEM OF TWO MACHINES (RUSSIAN). UPRAVLJAEMYE SISTEMY, NO. 17, 46-51 + 87-88. (1978).
GLIC 1978 -1 GLICKMAN, T. S.
NOTE ON MULTIPROJECT SCHEDULING TO MINIMIZE THE COST OF SUPPLEMENTAL EXTERNAL RESOURCES, A. ZEITSCHRIFT FUER OPERATIONS RESEARCH 22, SERIE A, 239-242. (1978).
GLIN 1977 -1 GLINZ, M.; MOEHRING, R. H.
REDUCTION THEOREMS FOR NETWORKS WITH GENERAL SEQUENCING RELATIONS. IN: A. ANGERMANN ET AL. (EDS.): FIRST SYMPOSIUM ON OPERATIONS RESEARCH, HEIDELBERG 1976. METHODS OF OPERATIONS RESEARCH 27, 124-162. MEISENHEIM: ANTON HAIN. (1977).
GLOV 1977 -1 GLOVER, F.
FRESH LOOK AT HEURISTIC PRINCIPLES FOR INTEGER PROGRAMMING, A. MANAGEMENT SCIENCE REPORT SERIES, 77-7. BOULDER: UNIV. OF COLORADO, GRADUATE SCHOOL OF BUSINESS ADMINISTRATION, 11 P. (1977).
GLOV 1978 -1 GLOVER, F.
PARAMETRIC BRANCH AND BOUND. OMEGA 6, NO. 2, 145-152. (1978).
GLOVA 1977 -1 GLOVER, F.; HULTZ, J.; KLINGMAN, D.
NETWORK VERSUS LINEAR PROGRAMMING ALGORITHMS AND IMPLEMENTATIONS. RESEARCH H REPORT CCS 306. AUSTIN: UNIV. OF TEXAS, CENTER FOR CYBERNETIC STUDIES, 26 P. (1977).
GLOVB 1978 -1 GLOVER, F.; HULTZ, J.; KLINGMAN, D.; STUTZ, J.
GENERALIZED NETWORKS: A FUNDAMENTAL COMPUTER-BASED PLANNING TOOL. MANAGEMENT SCIENCE 24, 1209-1220. (1978).
GLOVC 1970 -1 GLOVER, F.; KARNEY, D.; KLINGMAN, D.
DOUBLE-PRICING DUAL AND FEASIBLE START ALGORITHMS FOR THE CAPACITATED TRANSPORTATION (DISTRIBUTION) PROBLEM. CCS RESEARCH REPORT NO. 105. AUSTIN: UNIVERSITY OF TEXAS, CENTER FOR CYBERNETIC STUDIES. (1970).
GLOVC 1977 -1 GLOVER, F.; KARNEY, D.; KLINGMAN, D.
STUDY OF ALTERNATIVE RELAXATION APPROACHES FOR A MANPOWER PLANNING PROBLEM, A. RESEARCH REPORT CCS 312. AUSTIN: UNIV. OF TEXAS, CENTER FOR CYBERNETIC STUDIES, 38 P. (1977).
GLOVD 1978 -1 GLOVER, F.; KARNEY, D.; KLINGMAN, D.; RUSSELL, R.
SOLVING SINGLY CONSTRAINED TRANSSHIPMENT PROBLEMS. TRANSPORTATION SCIENCE 12, 277-297. (1978).
GLOVE 1977 -1 GLOVER, F.; KLINGMAN, D.
NETWORK APPLICATION IN INDUSTRY AND GOVERNMENT. AIIE TRANSACTIONS 9, 363-376. (1977).
GLOVE 1979 -1 GLOVER, F.; KLINGMAN, D.
O(N LOG N) ALGORITHM FOR LP KNAPSACKS WITH GUB CONSTRAINTS, A. MATHEMATICAL PROGRAMMING 17, 345-361. (1979).
GLOVE 1979 -2 GLOVER, F.; KLINGMAN, D.
SIMPLEX SON ALGORITHM FOR LP-EMBEDDED NETWORK PROBLEMS (REVISED VERSION), THE. RESEARCH REPORT CCS 317. AUSTIN: UNIV. OF TEXAS, CENTER FOR CYBERNETIC STUDIES, 46 P. (1979).
GLOVE 1980 -1 GLOVER, F.; KLINGMAN, D.
RECENT DEVELOPMENTS IN COMPUTER IMPLEMENTATION TECHNOLOGY FOR NETWORK FLOW ALGORITHMS. RESEARCH REPORT CCS 377. AUSTIN: UNIV. OF TEXAS, CENTER FOR CYBERNETIC STUDIES, 33 P. (1980).
GLOVF 1979 -1 GLOVER, F.; KLINGMAN, D.; MOTE, J.; WHITMAN, D.
COMPREHENSIVE COMPUTER EVALUATION AND ENHANCEMENT OF MAXIMUM FLOW ALGORITHMS. MANAGEMENT SCIENCE REPORT SERIES,79-1. BOULDER: UNIV. OF COLORADO, GRADUATE SCHOOL OF BUSINESS ADMINISTRATION, 75 P. (1979).
GLOVF 1979 -2 GLOVER, F.; KLINGMAN, D.; MOTE, J.; WHITMAN, D.
PRIMAL SIMPLEX VARIANT FOR THE MAXIMUM FLOW PROBLEM, A. RESEARCH REPORT CCS 362. AUSTIN: UNIV. OF TEXAS, CENTER FOR CYBERNETIC STUDIES,44 P. (1979).
GLOVF 1980 -1 GLOVER, F.; KLINGMAN, D.; MOTE, J.; WHITMAN, D.
EXTENDED ABSTRACT OF AN INDEPTH ALGORITHMIC AND COMPUTATIONAL STUDY FOR MAXIMUM FLOW PROBLEMS, AN. DISCRETE APPLIED MATHEMATICS 2, 251-254. (1980).
GLOVG 1978 -1 GLOVER, F.; MAC MILLAN, C.; KLINGMAN, D.
MODELING COMBINATORIAL MATHEMATICAL PROGRAMMING PROBLEMS BY NETFORMS: AN ILLUSTRATIVE APPLICATION. IN: O. L. MANGASARIAN, R. R. MEYER, P. M. ROBINSON (EDS.): NONLINEAR PROGRAMMING 3, 303-336. NEW YORK, SAN FRANCISCO, LONDON: ACADEMIC PRESS. (1978).
GLOVH 1976 -1 GLOVER, F.; MULVEY, J. M.
NETWORK-RELATED SCHEDULING MODELS FOR PROBLEMS WITH QUASI-ADJACENCY AND BLOCK ADJACENCY STRUCTURE. WORKING PAPER HBS 76-3. CAMBRIDGE: HARVARD UNIVERSITY, GRADUATE SCHOOL OF BUSINESS ADMINISTRATION. (1976).

***

GLOVH 1980 -1 GLOVER, F.; MULVEY, J. M.
EQUIVALENCE OF THE 0-1 INTEGER PROGRAMMING PROBLEM TO DISCRETE GENERALIZED AND PURE NETWORKS. OPERATIONS RESEARCH 28, 829-836. (1980).
GLUS 1980 -1 GLUSHKOV, V. M.; KASPSHITCKAYA, M. F.; SERGIENKO, I. V.
FORMALIZATION QUESTIONS AND SOLUTIONS OF ONE CLASS OF PROBLEMS OF DISCRETE OPTIMIZATION (RUSSIAN), THE. ZURNAL VYCISLITELNOI MATEMATIKI I MATEMATICESKOI FIZIKI. AKADEMIJA NAUK SSSR (MOSCOW) 20, NO. 6, 1384-1399. TRANSLATED AS USSR COMPUTATIONAL MATHEMATICS AND MATHEMATICAL PHYSICS. (1980).
GODA 1975 -1 GODAMBE, S. B.
MIXED-MODEL PRODUCTION SCHEDULING. DISSERTATION. CHICAGO: ILLINOIS INSTITUTE OF TECHNOLOGY, 263 P. (1975).
GODI 1969 -1 GODIN, V. B.
INTERACTIVE COMPUTER SYSTEM FOR PRODUCTION SCHEDULING, AN. UNPUBLISHED DOCTORAL THESIS. CAMBRIDGE: HARVARD UNIVERSITY, GRADUATE SCHOOL OF BUSINESS ADMINISTRATION. (1969).
GODI 1978 -1 GODIN, V. B.
INTERACTIVE SCHEDULING: HISTORICAL SURVEY AND STATE OF THE ART. AIIE TRANSACTIONS 10, 331-337. (1978).
GODS 1981 -1 GODSIL, C. D.; GUTMAN, I.
ON THE MATCHING POLYNOMIAL OF A GRAPH. IN: L. LOVASZ, V. T. SOS (EDS.): ALGEBRAIC METHODS IN GRAPH THEORY, VOL. I, 241-250. COLLOQUIA MATHEMATICA SOCIETATIS JANOS BOLYAI 25. AMSTERDAM, OXFORD,NEW YORK: NORTH-HOLLAND. (1981).
GOLD 1980 -1 GOLDBERG, H. M.
JACKSON'S CONJECTURE ON EARLIEST DUE DATE SCHEDULING. MATHEMATICS OF OPERATIONS RESEARCH 5, 460-466. (1980).
GOLDA 1979 -1 GOLDBERG, M. K.
CRITICAL GRAPHS WITH AN EVEN NUMBER OF VERTICES(RUSSIAN). SOOBSCENIJA AKADEMII NAUK GRUZINSKOI SSR (TBILISI) 94, NO. 1, 25-27. (1979).
GOLDB 1976 -1 GOLDEN, B. L.
LARGE-VEHICLE ROUTING AND RELATED COMBINATORIAL PROBLEMS. DISSERTATION. CAMBRIDGE: MASSACHUSETTS INSTITUTE OF TECHNOLOGY, OPERATIONS RESEARCH CENTER. (1976).
GOLDB 1978 -1 GOLDEN, B. L.
POINT ESTIMATION OF A GLOBAL OPTIMUM FOR LARGE COMBINATORIAL PROBLEMS. COMMUNICATIONS IN STATISTICS. SIMULATION AND COMPUTATION 7, NO. 4, 361-367. (1978).
GOLDB 1978 -2 GOLDEN, B. L.
STATISTICAL ESTIMATION IN COMBINATORIAL DECISION PROBLEMS. COLLEGE PARK: UNIV. OF MARYLAND, COLLEGE OF BUSINESS AND MANAGEMENT, 15 P. (1978).
GOLDC 1978 -1 GOLDEN, B. L.; ALT, F. B.
INTERVAL ESTIMATION OF A GLOBAL OPTIMUM FOR LARGE COMBINATORIAL PROBLEMS. COLLEGE PARK: UNIV. OF MARYLAND, COLLEGE OF BUSINESS AND MANAGEMENT, 20 P. (1978).
GOLDD 1978 -1 GOLDEN, B. L.; BALL, M. O.
SHORTEST PATHS WITH EUCLIDEAN DISTANCES: AN EXPLANATORY MODEL. NETWORKS 8, 297-314. (1978).
GOLDE 1980 -1 GOLDEN, B. L.; BODIN, L. D.; DOYLE, T.; STEWART, W. R.
APPROXIMATE TRAVELING SALESMAN ALGORITHMS. OPERATIONS RESEARCH 28, 694-711. (1980).
GOLDF 1979 -1 GOLDEN, B. L.; WONG, R. T.
CAPACITATED ARC ROUTING PROBLEMS. NEW ORLEANS (ORSA/TIMS MEETING, APRIL/MAY 1979) 19 P. (1979).
GOLDG 1977 -1 GOLDFARB, D.
STEEPEST EDGE SIMPLEX ALGORITHMS FOR NETWORK FLOW PROBLEMS. IBM RESEARCH REPORT, 6649. YORKTOWN HEIGHTS: IBM RESEARCH CENTER, 17 P. (1977).
GOLU 1976 -1 GOLUMBIC, M. C.
COMBINATORIAL MERGING. IEEE TRANSACTIONS ON COMPUTERS C-25, 1164-1167. (1976).
GOLU 1978 -1 GOLUMBIC, M. C.
TRIVIALLY PERFECT GRAPHS. DISCRETE MATHEMATICS 24, 105-107. (1978).
GOLU 1980 -1 GOLUMBIC, M. C.
ALGORITHMIC GRAPH THEORY AND PERFECT GRAPHS. NEW YORK, LONDON U.A.: ACADEMIC PRESS, 284 P. (1980). (COMPUTER SCIENCE AND APPLIED MATHEMATICS)
GOND 1977 -1 GONDRAN, M.
ALGORITHME DE COUPES EN PROGRAMMATION EN NOMBRES ENTIERS, UN. BULLETIN DE LA SOCIETE MATHEMATIQUE EN FRANCE, NO. 49-50, 93-100. (1977).
GOND 1978 -1 GONDRAN, M.
DEUX TRANSFORMATIONS IDEALES POUR REGULARISER LES PROBLEMES COMBINATOIRES. ELECTRICITE DE FRANCE: BULLETIN DE LA DIRECTION DES ETUDES ET RECHERCHES, SERIE C, MATHEMATIQUES, INFORMATIQUE, NO. 2, 33-40. (1978).
GOND 1979 -1 GONDRAN, M.
ALGORITHMES LINEAIRES POUR LES PROBLEMES DE PARTITION, DE RECOUVREMENT ET DE COUPLAGE DANS LES HYPERGRAPHES D'INTERVALLES, DES. REVUE FRANCAISE D'AUTOMATIQUE, D'INFORMATIQUE ET DE RECHERCHE OPERATIONELLE 13, SERIE RECHERCHE OPERATIONELLE, 13-21. (1979).
GOND 1979 -2 GONDRAN, M.
OPTIMISATION COMBINATOIRE. ELECTRICITE DE FRANCE: BULLETIN DE LA DIRECTION DES ETUDES ET RECHERCHES. SERIE C, MATHEMATIQUES, INFORMATIQUE, NO. 1, 5-16. (1979).
GOND 1980 -1 GONDRAN, M.
CHEMINS ET CONNEXITE. IN: P. HANSEN, D. DE WERRA (EDS.): REGARDS SUR LA THEORIE DES GRAPHES. PROCEEDINGS OF THE CERISY COLLOQUIUM, 1980, 11-28. LAUSANNE: PRESSES POLYTECHNIQUES ROMANDES. (1980).
GOND 1980 -2 GONDRAN, M.
CLASSIFICATION HIERARCHIQUE ET FLOTS DANS UN GRAPHE. BULLETIN DE LA DIRECTION DES ETUDES ET RECHERCHES. ELECTRICITE DE FRANCE, SERIE C, MATHEMATIQUES, INFORMATIQUE, NO. 1, 43-48. (1980).
GONDA 1978 -1 GONDRAN, M.; MINOUX, M.
INDEPENDANCE LINEAIRE DANS LES DIOIDES, L'. ELECTRICITE DE FRANCE: BULLETIN DE LA DIRECTION DES ETUDES ET RECHERCHES, SERIE C, MATHEMATIQUES, INFORMATIQUE, NO. 1, 67-90. (1978).
GONDA 1979 -1 GONDRAN, M.; MINOUX, M.
GRAPHES ET ALGORITHMES. PARIS: EDITIONS EYROLLES, 518 P. (1979). (COLLECTION DE LA DIRECTION DES ETUDES ET RECHERCHES D'ELECTRICITE DE FRANCE, 37)
GONZ 1977 -1 GONZALEZ, T.
OPTIMAL MEAN FINISH TIME PREEMPTIVE SCHEDULES. TECHNICAL REPORT 220. UNIVERSITY PARK: PENNSYLVANIA STATE UNIVERSITY, COMPUTER SCIENCE DEPARTMENT. (1977).
GONZ 1979 -1 GONZALEZ, T.
NOTE ON OPEN SHOP PREEMPTIVE SCHEDULES, A. IEEE TRANSACTIONS ON COMPUTERS C-28, 782-786. (1979).
GONZ 1979 -2 GONZALEZ, T.
NP-HARD SHOP PROBLEMS. CS-79-35. UNIVERSITY PARK: PENNSYLVANIA STATE UNIV., DEPT. OF COMPUTER SCIENCE, 39 P. (1979).
GONZA 1980 -1 GONZALEZ, T.; JOHNSON, D. B.
NEW ALGORITM FOR PREEMPTIVE SCHEDULING OF TREES, A. JOURNAL OF THE ASSOCIATION FOR COMPUTING MACHINERY 27, 287-312. (1980).

****

GONZB 1978 -1 GONZALEZ, T.; SAHNI, S.
FLOWSHOP AND JOBSHOP SCHEDULES: COMPLEXITY AND APPROXIMATION. OPERATIONS RESEARCH 26, 36-52. (1978).

GOOD 1978 -1 GOODMAN, J. E.; ONISHI, H.
EVEN TRIANGULATIONS OF S**3 AND THE COLORING OF GRAPHS. TRANSACTIONS OF THE AMERICAN MATHEMATICAL SOCIETY 246, 501-510. (1978).

GORA 1979 -1 GORALCIKOVA, A.; KOUBEK, V.
REDUCT-AND-CLOSURE ALGORITHM FOR GRAPHS, A. IN: J. BECVAR (ED.): MATHEMATICAL FOUNDATIONS OF COMPUTER SCIENCE 1979, PROCEEDINGS 8TH SYMPOSIUM, OLOMOUC 1979, 301-307. LECTURE NOTES IN COMPUTER SCIENCE 74. BERLIN, HEIDELBERG, NEW YORK: SPRINGER. (1979).

GORB 1980 -1 GORBUNCOV, V. V.
ALGEBRAIC APPROACH TO THE SOLUTION OF A CLASS OF EXTREMAL COMBINATORIAL PROBLEMS (RUSSIAN), AN. DOKLADY AKADEMIJA NAUK UKRAINSKOI SSR. SERIJA A (KIEV), NO. 3, 45-48, 91. (1980).

GORD 1980 -1 GORDON, M.; TORKINGTON, J. A.
ENUMERATION OF COLOURED PLANE TREES WITH A GIVEN TYPE PARTITION. DISCRETE APPLIED MATHEMATICS 2, 207-224. (1980).

GORDA 1977 -1 GORDON, V. S.; CEGOLINA, E. P.
SINGLE-STAGE PROBLEM OF THE SCHEDULING THEORY WITH A TREE-ORDERED SET OF DEMANDS (RUSSIAN), THE. VESCI AKADEMII NAVUK BSSR. SERYJA FIZIKA-MATEMATYCNYH NAVUK, NO. 4, 36-40 + 140. (1977).

GORDB 1978 -1 GORDON, V. S.; SAFRANSKII, JA. M.
OPTIMAL ORDERING UNDER SERIAL-PARALLEL PRECEDENCE CONSTRAINTS (RUSSIAN). DOKLADY AKADEMII NAUK BSSR 22, NO. 3, 244-247 + 286. (1978).

GOSP 1978 -1 GOSPODAROWICZ, A.
ON SOME PROBLEMS OF SCHEDULING THEORY (POLISH). PRZEGLAD STATYSTYCZNY, POLSKA AKADEMIA NAUK. KOMITET STATISTYKI I EKONOMETRII (WARSAW) 25, 263-274. (1978).

GOTO 1974 -1 GOTO, S.; OHTSUKI, T.
SIMPLEX ALGORITHM ON A LINEAR GRAPH - A UNIFIED VIEW OF THE EXTREMAL PATH AND CUTSET PROBLEMS ON A GRAPH, THE. ELECTRONICS AND COMMUNICATIONS IN JAPAN 57, NO. 11, 26-33. (1974).

GOTOA 1978 -1 GOTO, S.; SANGIOVANNI-VINCENTELLI, A.
NEW SHORTEST PATH UPDATING ALGORITHM, A. NETWORKS 8, 341-372. (1978).

GOUL 1981 -1 GOULD, R. J.
ON LINE GRAPHS AND THE HAMILTONIAN INDEX. DISCRETE MATHEMATICS 34, 111-118. (1981).

GOUR 1979 -1 GOURLAY, A. R.
HEURISTIC ALGORITHM FOR THE SOLUTION OF SERIATION PROBLEMS, A. APPLIED MATHEMATICAL MODELLING 3, 303-306. (1979).

GOUY 1978 -1 GOUYOU-BEAUCHAMPS, D.
ALGORITHME DE RECHERCHE DE CIRCUIT HAMILTONIEN DANS LES GRAPHES 4-CONNEXES PLANAIRES, UN. IN: J.-C. BERMOND ET AL. (EDS.): PROBLEMES COMBINATOIRES ET THEORIE DES GRAPHES, COLLOQUES INTERNATIONAUX DU CENTRE NATIONAL DE LA RECHERCHE SCIENTIFIQUE, ORSAY 1976, 185-187. PARIS: CENTRE NATIONAL DE LA RECHERCHE SCIENTIFIQUE. (1978).

GOYA 1977 -1 GOYAL, D. K.
NON-PREEMPTIVE SCHEDULING OF UNEQUAL EXECUTION TIME TASKS ON TWO IDENTICAL PROCESSORS. TECHNICAL REPORT CS-77-039. PULLMAN: WASHINGTON STATE UNIVERSITY, COMPUTER SCIENCE DEPARTMENT. (1977).

GOYAA 1978 -1 GOYAL, S. K.
NOTE ON AN EXTENSION OF JOHNSON'S RESULT ON TWO-STATE PRODUCTION SCHEDULES. NEW ZEALAND OPERATIONAL RESEARCH 6, 185-189. (1978).

GRAB 1977 -1 GRABOWSKI, J.
NEW FORMULATION AND SOLUTION OF THE SEQUENCING PROBLEM: ALGORITHM, A. ZASTOSOWANIA MATEMATYKI 15, 463-474. (1977).

GRAB 1978 -1 GRABOWSKI, J.
ALGORITHM FOR THE SOLUTION OF THE TRAVELING SALESMAN PROBLEM VIA DISJUNCTIVE GRAPHS (POLISH), AN. MATEMATYKA STOSOWANA 13, 81-98. (1978).

GRAB 1978 -2 GRABOWSKI, J.
FORMULATION AND SOLUTION OF THE SEQUENCING PROBLEM WITH PARALLEL MACHINES (POLISH). ARCHIWUM AUTOMATYKI I TELEMECHANIKI (WARSAW) 23, 91-113. (1978).

GRAB 1978 -3 GRABOWSKI, J.
FORMULATION AND SOLUTION OF THE SEQUENCING PROBLEM WITH PARALLEL MACHINES. IN: J. STOER (ED.): OPTIMIZATION TECHNIQUES, PROCEEDINGS OF THE EIGHTH IFIP CONFERENCE, WUERZBURG 1977. PART 2, 400-410. LECTURE NOTES IN CONTROL AND INFORMATION SCIENCES 6. BERLIN: SPRINGER. (1978).

GRAB 1978 -4 GRABOWSKI, J.
FORMULATION AND SOLUTION OF THE SEQUENCING PROBLEM WITH PARALLEL MACHINES. ZASTOSOWANIA MATEMATYKI (WARSAW) 16, NO. 2, 215-232. (1978).

GRAB 1979 -1 GRABOWSKI, J.
GENERALIZED PROBLEMS OF OPTIMIZATION OF SEQUENCING OPERATIONS IN DISCRETE PRODUCTION SYSTEMS (POLISH). PRACE NAUKOWE. SERIA MONOGRAFIE NO. 9. WROCLAW: INSTYTUT CYBERNETYKI TECHNICZNEJ. POLITECHNIKA WROCLAWSKA. 112 P. (1979).

GRAB 1980 -1 GRABOWSKI, J.
ON TWO-MACHINE SCHEDULING WITH RELEASE AND DUE DATES TO MINIMIZE MAXIMUM LATENESS. OPSEARCH 17, 133-154. (1980).

GRAB 1981 -1 GRABOWSKI, J.
ON FLOW-SHOP PROBLEM WITH RELEASE AND DUE DATES TO MINIMIZE MAXIMUM LATENESS. IN: R. E. BURKARD, T. ELLINGER (EDS.): METHODS OF OPERATIONS RESEARCH 40, 325-328. KOENIGSTEIN: ANTON HAIN MEISENHEIM. (1981).

GRABA 1979 -1 GRABOWSKI, J.; SKUBALSKA, E.
MAXIMAL FLOW PROBLEM IN A NETWORK WITH A VARIABLE STRUCTURE, THE. IN: PROCEEDINGS OF THE INTERNATIONAL SYMPOSIUM ON APPLICATIONS OF MATHEMATICS IN SYSTEM THEORY, BRASOV 1978, VOLUME II, 209-222. BRASOV: UNIV. OF BRASOV. (1979).

GRABA 1981 -1 GRABOWSKI, J.; SKUBALSKA, E.
MAXIMAL FLOW PROBLEM IN A NETWORK WITH A VARIABLE STRUCTURE, THE. IN: R. E. BURKARD, T. ELLINGER (EDS.): METHODS OF OPERATIONS RESEARCH 40, 329-334. KOENIGSTEIN: ANTON HAIN MEISENHEIM. (1981).

GRABB 1978 -1 GRABOWSKI, W.; LELENO, J.
PROBLEME DE SELECTION DES ITINERAIRES (POLISH). POLSKA AKADEMIA NAUK. KOMITET STATISTYKII EKONOMETRII. PRZEGLAD STATYSTYCZNY 25, NO. 2, 161-169. (1978).

GRAH 1970 -1 GRAHAM, R. L.
ON PRIMITIVE GRAPHS AND OPTIMAL VERTEX ASSIGNMENTS. IN: A. GEWIRTZ, L. V. QUINTAS (EDS.): INTERNATIONAL CONFERENCE ON COMBINATORIAL MATHEMATICS, 170-186. ANNALS OF THE NEW YORK ACADEMY OF SCIENCES, VOLUME 165, ARTICLE 1. NEW YORK: THE NEW YORK ACADEMY OF SCIENCES. (1970).

GRAH 1978 -1 GRAHAM, R. L.
COMBINATORIAL MATHEMATICS OF SCHEDULING, THE. SCIENTIFIC AMERICAN 238, NO. 3, 124-133. (1978).

****

GRAH 1978 -2 GRAHAM, R. L.
COMBINATORIAL SCHEDULING THEORY. IN: L. A. STEEN (ED.): MATHEMATICS TODAY, TWELVE INFORMAL ESSAYS, 183-211. NEW YORK, HEIDELBERG, BERLIN: SPRINGER. (1978).

GRAH 1980 -1 GRAHAM, R. L.
ON A DIOPHANTINE EQUATION ARISING IN GRAPH THEORY. EUROPEAN JOURNAL OF COMBINATORICS 1, 107-112. (1980).

GRAHA 1978 -1 GRAHAM, R. L.; LAWLER, E. L.; LENSTRA, J. K.; RINNOOY KAN, A. H. G.
OPTIMIZATION AND APPROXIMATION IN DETERMINISTIC SEQUENCING AND SCHEDULING: A SURVEY. IN: J. K. LENSTRA, A. H. G. RINNOOY KAN, P. VAN EMDE BOAS (EDS.): INTERFACES BETWEEN COMPUTER SCIENCE AND OPERATIONS RESEARCH, AMSTERDAM 1976, 169-214. MATHEMATICAL CENTRE TRACTS 99, AMSTERDAM: MATHEMATISCH CENTRUM. (1978).

GRAHA 1979 -1 GRAHAM, R. L.; LAWLER, E. L.; LENSTRA, J. K.; RINNOOY KAN, A. H. G.
OPTIMIZATION AND APPROXIMATION IN DETERMINISTIC SEQUENCING AND SCHEDULING: A SURVEY. IN: P. L. HAMMER, E. L. JOHNSON, B. H. KORTE (EDS.): DISCRETE OPTIMIZATION II, 287-326. ANNALS OF DISCRETE MATHEMATICS 5. AMSTERDAM, NEW YORK, OXFORD: NORTH-HOLLAND. (1979).

GRAHB 1978 -1 GRAHAM, R. L.; LOVASZ, L.
DISTANCE MATRIX POLYNOMIALS OF TREES. ADVANCES IN MATHEMATICS 29, 60-88. (1978).

GRAN 1979 -1 GRANDON, G. M.
OPTIMIZING HIGH SCHOOL CURRICULUM ASSIGNMENTS. SOCIO-ECONOMIC PLANNING SCIENCES 13, 141-148. (1979).

GRANA 1980 -1 GRANOT, D.; GRANOT, F.
GENERALIZED COVERING RELAXATION FOR 0-1 PROGRAMS. OPERATIONS RESEARCH 28, 1442-1449. (1980).

GRANA 1980 -2 GRANOT, D.; GRANOT, F.
MINIMAL COVERS, EXTENSIONS OF MINIMAL COVERS AND FACETS OF A POSYNOMIAL INEQUALITY IN 0-1 VARIABLES. RESEARCH PAPER. VANCOUVER: UNIV. OF BRITISH COLUMBIA, FACULTY OF COMMERCE AND BUSINESS ADMINISTRATION, 29 P. (1980).

GRANB 1979 -1 GRANOT, D.; GRANOT, F.; KALLBERG, J.
COVERING RELAXATION FOR POSITIVE 0-1 POLYNOMIAL PROGRAMS. MANAGEMENT SCIENCE 25, 264-273. (1979).

GRANC 1980 -1 GRANOT, D.; GRANOT, F.; VAESSEN, W.
ACCELERATED COVERING RELAXATION ALGORITHM FOR SOLVING 0-1 POSITIVE POLYNOMIAL PROGRAMS, AN. WORKING PAPER NO. 718. VANCOUVER: UNIV. OF BRITISH COLUMBIA, FACULTY OF COMMERCE AND BUSINESS ADMINISTRATION, 22 P. (1980).

GRAND 1978 -1 GRANOT, F.
EFFICIENT HEURISTIC ALGORITHMS FOR POSITIVE 0-1 POLYNOMIAL PROGRAMMING PROBLEMS. WORKING PAPER NO. 595. VANCOUVER: UNIV. OF BRITISH COLUMBIA, FACULTY OF COMMERCE AND BUSINESS ADMINISTRATION, 24 P. (1978).

GRANE 1980 -1 GRANT, P. W.
SOME MORE INDEPENDENCE RESULTS IN COMPLEXITY THEORY. THEORETICAL COMPUTER SCIENCE 12, 119-126. (1980).

GRAT 1972 -1 GRATZER, F. J.; STEIGLITZ, K.
HEURISTIC APPROACH TO LARGE MULTICOMMODITY FLOW PROBLEMS, A. IN: J. FOX (ED.): PROCEEDINGS OF THE SYMPOSIUM ON COMPUTER COMMUNICATIONS NETWORKS AND TELETRAFFIC, 311-324. NEW YORK: POLYTECHNIC PRESS. (1972).

GRAV 1977 -1 GRAVER, J. E.; WATKINS, M. E.
COMBINATORICS WITH EMPHASIS ON THE THEORY OF GRAPHS. NEW YORK, HEIDELBERG, BERLIN: SPRINGER, 351 P. (1977). (GRADUATES TEXTS IN MATHEMATICS, 54)

GRAVA 1979 -1 GRAVES, S. C.
ON THE DETERMINISTIC DEMAND MULTI-PRODUCT SINGLE-MACHINE LOT SCHEDULING PROBLEM. MANAGEMENT SCIENCE 25, 276-280. (1979).

GRAVB 1978 -1 GRAVES, S. C.; HAESSLER, R. W.
ON "PRODUCTION RUNS FOR MULTIPLE PRODUCTS: THE TWO-PRODUCT HEURISTIC". MANAGEMENT SCIENCE 24, 1194-1196. (1978).

GRAVC 1980 -1 GRAVES, S. C.; LAMAR, B. W.
INTEGER PROGRAMMING PROCEDURE FOR ASSEMBLY SYSTEM DESIGN PROBLEMS, AN. RESEARCH REPORT. CAMBRIDGE, MA: MASSACHUSETTS INST. OF TECHNOLOGY, ALFRED P. SLOAN SCHOOL OF MANAGEMENT, 35 P. (1980).

GREE 1980 -1 GREEN-KROTKI, J. J.
MATCHING POLYHEDRA. OTTAWA: CARLETON UNIV., DEPT. OF MATHEMATICS AND STATISTICS, 87 P. (1980).

GREEA 1980 -1 GREENBERG, H.; FELDMAN, I.
BETTER STEP-OFF ALGORITHM FOR THE KNAPSACK PROBLEM, A. DISCRETE APPLIED MATHEMATICS 2, 21-26. (1980).

GREEB 1973 -1 GREENWELL, D; KRONK, H.
UNIQUELY LINE-COLORABLE GRAPHS. CANADIAN MATHEMATICAL BULLETIN 16, 525-529. (1973).

GRES 1976 -1 GRESNEV, S. N.
THEOREMS ON THE REDUCTION OF THE PACKING OF DIGRAPH VERTICES (RUSSIAN). IN: A. JU. LEVIN (ED.): HEURISTIC OPTIMIZATION ALGORITHMS (RUSSIAN), 144-152. YAROSLAVL: JAROSLAV. GOS. UNIV. (1976).

GRIB 1978 -1 GRIBOV, A. B.
SOLUTION RECURSIVE DES PROBLEMES DE TRANSPORT DE LA PROGRAMMATION LINEAIRE (RUSSIAN). VESTNIK LENINGRADSKOGO UNIVERSITETA, NO. 19, 11-19. (1978).

GRIE 1980 -1 GRIESSHABER, R.
MODEL FOR CREW SCHEDULING FOR A SHORT HAUL FLEET. WORKING PAPER. FRANKFURT: DEUTSCHE LUFTHANSA, 10 P. (1980).

GRIG 1979 -1 GRIGGS, J. R.
EXTREMAL VALUES OF THE INTERVAL NUMBER OF A GRAPH, II. DISCRETE MATHEMATICS 28, 37-47. (1979).

GRIGA 1980 -1 GRIGGS, J. R.; WEST, D. B.
EXTREMAL VALUES OF THE INTERVAL NUMBER OF A GRAPH. SIAM JOURNAL ON ALGEBRAIC AND DISCRETE METHODS 1, 1-7. (1980).

GRIGB 1979 -1 GRIGORAS, G.
ON THE NP-COMPLETENESS OF A PROBLEM IN FINITE AUTOMATA THEORY. ANALELE STIINTIFICE ALE UNIVERSITATII "AL. I. CUZA" DIN IASI. SERIA NOUA. SECTIUNEA I A MATEMATICA 25, 171-174. (1979).

GRIGC 1977 -1 GRIGOREV, D. JU.
PROBLEM OF PATH CONNECTIONS ON GRAPHS (RUSSIAN), THE. IN: THEORETICAL APPLICATIONS OF THE METHODS OF MATHEMATICAL LOGIC, II. ZAPISKI NAUCNYH SEMINAROV LENINGRADSKOGO OTDELENIJA MATEMATICESKOGO INSTITUTA IM. V. A. STEKLOVA AKADEMII NAUK SSSR (LOMI) 68, 26-29, 143. (1977).

GRIGD 1978 -1 GRIGOREVA, N. S.; ROMANOVSKII, I. V.
PROBLEMS OF CYCLIC SCHEDULING. KIBERNETIKA, NO. 1, 75-79. (1978).

GRIGE 1978 -1 GRIGORIADIS, M. D.
ALGORITHMS FOR THE MINIMUM COST SINGLE AND MULTICOMMODITY NETWORK FLOW PROBLEMS. URBINO: SUMMER SCHOOL IN COMBINATORIAL OPTIMIZATION, 72 P. (1978).

GRIN 1977 -1 GRINSTEAD, G. M.
ON COVERINGS AND PACKINGS OF THE COMPLETE GRAPH WITH CYCLES. ARS COMBINATORIA 3, 25-37. (1977).
GROE 1979 -1 GROEFLIN, H.; LIEBLING, T. M.
CONNECTED AND ALTERNATING VECTORS POLYHEDRA AND ALGORITHMS. IBM RESEARCH REPORT, 7565. YORKTOWN HEIGHTS: IBM RESEARCH CENTER, 19 P. (1979).
GROEA 1981 -1 GROEFLIN, H.; LIEBLING, T. M.; PRODON, A.
OPTIMAL SUBTREES AND EXTENSIONS. IFOR TECHNICAL REPORT. ZURICH: EIDGENOESSISCHE TECHNISCHE HOCHSCHULE, 9 P. (1981).
GROEB 1978 -1 GROETSCHEL, M.
HYPO-HAMILTONIAN FACETS OF THE SYMMETRIC TRAVELLING SALESMAN POLYTOPE. ZEITSCHRIFT FUER ANGEWANDTE MATHEMATIK UND MECHANIK 58, T469-T471. (1978).
GROEB 1979 -1 GROETSCHEL, M.
ON MINIMAL STRONG BLOCKS. JOURNAL OF GRAPH THEORY 3, 213-219. (1979).
GROEB 1979 -2 GROETSCHEL, M.
STRONG BLOCKS AND THE OPTIMUM BRANCHING PROBLEM. IN: L. COLLATZ, G. MEINARDUS, W. WETTERLING (EDS.): NUMERISCHE METHODEN BEI GRAPHENTHEORETISCHEN UND KOMBINATORISCHEN PROBLEMEN, BAND 2, OBERWOLFACH 1978, 112-121. ISNM 46, BASEL, BOSTON, STUTTGART: BIRKHAEUSER. (1979).
GROEB 1980 -1 GROETSCHEL, M.
ON THE MONOTONE SYMMETRIC TRAVELLING SALESMAN PROBLEM: HYPOHAMILTONIAN/ HYPOTRACEABLE GRAPHS AND FACETS. MATHEMATICS OF OPERATIONS RESEARCH 5, 285-292. (1980).
GROEB 1980 -2 GROETSCHEL, M.
ON THE SYMMETRIC TRAVELLING SALESMAN PROBLEM: SOLUTION OF 120-CITY PROBLEM. MATHEMATICAL PROGRAMMING STUDY 12, 61-77. (1980).
GROEB 1981 -1 GROETSCHEL, M.
APPROACHES TO HARD COMBINATORIAL OPTIMIZATION PROBLEMS. RESEARCH REPORT NO. 79147-OR. BONN: UNIV. BONN, INST. FUER OEKONOMETRIE UND OPERATIONS RESEARCH, 89 P. (1981).
GROEC 1979 -1 GROETSCHEL, M.; HARARY, F.
GRAPHS FOR WHICH ALL STRONG ORIENTATIONS ARE HAMILTONIAN, THE. JOURNAL OF GRAPH THEORY 3, 221-223. (1979).
GROED 1981 -1 GROETSCHEL, M.; LOVASZ, L.; SCHRIJVER, A.
ELLIPSOID METHOD AND ITS CONSEQUENCES IN COMBINATORIAL OPTIMIZATION, THE. COMBINATORICA 1, 169-197. (1981).
GROED 1981 -2 GROETSCHEL, M.; LOVASZ, L.; SCHRIJVER, A.
POLYNOMIAL ALGORITHMS FOR PERFECT GRAPHS. RESEARCH REPORT WP 81176-OR. BONN: UNIV. BONN, INST. FUER OEKONOMETRIE UND OPERATIONS RESEARCH, ABT. OPERATIONS RESEARCH, 40 P. (1981).
GROEE 1979 -1 GROETSCHEL, M.; PADBERG, M. W.
ON THE SYMMETRIC TRAVELLING SALESMAN PROBLEM I: INEQUALITIES. MATHEMATICAL PROGRAMMING 16, 265-280. (1979).
GROEE 1979 -2 GROETSCHEL, M.; PADBERG, M. W.
ON THE SYMMETRIC TRAVELLING SALESMAN PROBLEM II: LIFTING THEOREMS AND FACETS. MATHEMATICAL PROGRAMMING 16, 281-302. (1979).
GROEF 1981 -1 GROETSCHEL, M.; PULLEYBLANK, W. R.
CLIQUE TREES AND THE TRAVELLING SALESMAN PROBLEM. RESEARCH REPORT WP 81196-OR. BONN: UNIV. BONN, INST. FUER OEKONOMETRIE UND OPERATIONS RESEARCH, ABT. OPERATIONS RESEARCH. (1981).
GROEF 1981 -2 GROETSCHEL, M.; PULLEYBLANK, W. R.
WEAKLY BIPARTITE GRAPHS AND THE MAX-CUT PROBLEM. RESEARCH REPORT WP 81194-OR. BONN: UNIV. BONN, INST. FUER OEKONOMETRIE UND OPERATIONS RESEARCH, ABT. OPERATIONS RESEARCH. (1981).
GROEG 1980 -1 GROETSCHEL, M.; THOMASSEN, C.; WAKABAYASHI, Y.
HYPOTRACEABLE DIGRAPHS. JOURNAL OF GRAPH THEORY 4, 377-382. (1980).
GROEH 1978 -1 GROETSCHEL, M.; WAKABAYASHI, Y.
HYPOTRACEABLE DIGRAPHS. REPORT NO. 7892-OR. BONN: UNIV. BONN, INSTITUT FUER OEKONOMETRIE UND OPERATIONS RESEARCH, 29 P. (1978).
GROEH 1980 -1 GROETSCHEL, M.; WAKABAYASHI, Y.
HYPOHAMILTONIAN DIGRAPHS. IN: R. HENN, H. P. KUENZI, H. SCHUBERT (EDS.): METHODS OF OPERATIONS RESEARCH 36, 99-120. KOENIGSTEIN: ANTON HAIN MEISENHEIM. (1980).
GROEH 1981 -1 GROETSCHEL, M.; WAKABAYASHI, Y.
ON THE STRUCTURE OF THE MONOTONE ASYMMETRIC TRAVELLING SALESMAN POLYTOPE I: HYPOHAMILTONIAN FACETS. DISCRETE MATHEMATICS 34, 43-60. (1981).
GROEH 1981 -2 GROETSCHEL, M.; WAKABAYASHI, Y.
ON THE STRUCTURE OF THE MONOTONE ASYMMETRIC TRAVELLING SALESMAN POLYTOPE II: HYPOTRACEABLE FACETS. IN: H. KOENIG, B. KORTE, K. RITTER (EDS.): MATHEMATICAL PROGRAMMING AT OBERWOLFACH, 77-97. MATHEMATICAL PROGRAMMING STUDY 14. (1981).
GROP 1977 -1 GROPPEN, V. O.
EXTREMAL PROBLEMS OF GRAPHS WITH A MINIMAX GOAL FUNCTIONAL. AVTOMATIKA I TELEMEHANIKA, NO. 6, 97-102; TRANSLATED AS AUTOMATION AND REMOTE CONTROL 38, 1977, 855-859. (1977).
GROP 1978 -1 GROPPEN, V. O.
ENHANCEMENT OF OPERATING SPEED OF RANDOMIZED ALGORITHMS FOR COMBINATORIAL PROBLEMS WITH BOOLEAN VARIABLES. AVTOMATIKA I VYCISLITELNAJA TEHNIKA (RIGA) 12, NO. 5, 54-60; TRANSLATED AS AUTOMATIC CONTROL AND COMPUTER SCIENCES 12, NO. 5, 47-52. (1978).
GROP 1978 -2 GROPPEN, V. O.
IMPROVING BRANCH-AND-BOUND METHODS FOR DISCRETE PROBLEMS WITH BOOLEAN VARIABLES. AVTOMATIKA I TELEMEHANIKA, NO. 5, 106-112; TRANSLATED AS AUTOMATION AND REMOTE CONTROL 39, 1978, 708-713. (1978).
GROS 1979 -1 GROSS, J. L.; ROSEN, R. H.
LINEAR TIME PLANARITY ALGORITHM FOR 2-COMPLEXES, A. JOURNAL OF THE ASSOCIATION FOR COMPUTING MACHINERY 26, 611-617. (1979).
GROSA 1978 -1 GROSZ, M.
GENERALIZATION OF THE ASSIGNMENT PROBLEM AND ITS SOLUTION (HUNGARIAN), THE. SZIGMA 11, 75-84. (1978).
GRUE 1978 -1 GRUENBAUM, B.; SHEPHARD, G. C.
PERFECT COLORINGS OF TRANSITIVE TILINGS AND PATTERNS IN THE PLANE. DISCRETE MATHEMATICS 20, 235-248. (1978).
GRUN 1978 -1 GRUNDMANN, W.; KRAUSE, H.
BEITRAG ZUR LOESUNG SPEZIELLER TOURENPROBLEME MIT SYMMETRISCHER ENTFERNUNGSMATRIX, EIN. WISSENSCHAFTLICHE ZEITSCHRIFT DER HOCHSCHULE FUER ARCHITEKTUR UND BAUWESEN WEIMAR 25, NO. 3, 253-256. (1978).
GRUNA 1981 -1 GRUNEWALD, F. J.; SEGAL, D.
HOW TO SOLVE A QUADRATIC EQUATION IN INTEGERS. MATHEMATICAL PROCEEDINGS OF THE CAMBRIDGE PHILOSOPHICAL SOCIETY 89, NO. 1, 1-5. (1981).
GUAN 1978 -1 GUAN, M. G.
METHOD FOR FINDING THE MINIMUM ARBORESCENCE OF THE DIRECTED GRAPHS ARISING IN THE CHANNEL DESIGN PROBLEM (CHINESE), A. ACTA MATHEMATICAE APPLAGATAE SINICA 1, NO. 3, 233-239. (1978).

GUAN 1979 -1 GUAN, M. G.
BRIEF SURVEY OF RESEARCH WORKS ON NETWORK THEORY BY CHINESE MATHEMATICIANS, A. IN: PROCEEDINGS OF THE FIRST FRANCO-SOUTHEAST ASIAN MATHEMATICAL CONFERENCE, SINGAPORE 1979, VOLUME II, 264-267. SPECIAL ISSUE B, SOUTHEAST ASIAN BULLETIN OF MATHEMATICS (SINGAPORE). (1979).

GUBA 1977 -1 GUBA, W.
MAXIMALER LOKALER ALGORITHMUS FUER KLASSEN UNVERKUERZBARER UEBERDECKUNGEN. EIN. ROSTOCKER MATHEMATISCHES KOLLOQUIUM 3, 57-68. (1977).

GUDE 1978 -1 GUDEHUS, T.
TRANSPORTMATRIX UND FASSUNGSVERMOEGEN. ZEITSCHRIFT FUER OPERATIONS RESEARCH 22, SERIE B, B219-B229. (1978).

GUEN 1979 -1 GUENOCHE, A.
ENUMERATION DE CLASSES DE PERMUTATIONS. REVUE FRANCAISE D'AUTOMATIQUE, D'INFORMATIQUE ET DE RECHERCHE OPERATIONELLE 13, SERIE RECHERCHE OPERATIONELLE, 379-390. (1979).

GUIG 1971 -1 GUIGNARD, M.
INEGALITES VALIDES DE GOMORY-JOHNSON. IN: JOURNEES DE COMBINATOIRE AFCET. (1971).

GUIG 1980 -1 GUIGNARD, M.
FRACTIONAL VERTICES, CUTS AND FACETS OF THE SIMPLE PLANT LOCATION PROBLEM. MATHEMATICAL PROGRAMMING STUDY 12, 150-162. (1980).

GUIGA 1978 -1 GUIGNARD, M.; SPIELBERG, K.
DUAL METHOD FOR THE MIXED PLANT LOCATION PROBLEM, A. (REVISED VERSION). TECHNICAL REPORT NO. 20. PHILADELPHIA: UNIV. OF PENNSYLVANIA, DEPT. OF STATISTICS, 46 P. (1978).

GUIGA 1978 -2 GUIGNARD, M.; SPIELBERG, K.
EXPERIMENTAL INTERACTIVE SYSTEM FOR INTEGER PROGRAMMING, AN. IN: COMPUTERS AND MATHEMATICAL PROGRAMMING, PROC. BICENTEN. CONF., GAITHERSBURG/MD. 1976, NBS SPEC. PUBL. 502, 328-337. (1978).

GUIGA 1979 -1 GUIGNARD, M.; SPIELBERG, K.
DIRECT DUAL APPROACH TO A TRANSSHIPMENT FORMULATION FOR MULTI-LAYER NETWORK PROBLEMS WITH FIXED CHARGES, A. TECHNICAL REPORT NO. 43. PHILDAELPHIA: UNIV. OF PENNSYLVANIA, DEPT. OF STATISTICS, 41 P. (1979).

GUIGA 1979 -2 GUIGNARD, M.; SPIELBERG, K.
DIRECT DUAL METHOD FOR THE MIXED PLANT LOCATION PROBLEM WITH SOME SIDE CONSTRAINTS, A. MATHEMATICAL PROGRAMMING 17, 198-228. (1979).

GUIGA 1979 -3 GUIGNARD, M.; SPIELBERG, K.
MAINTENANCE SCHEDULING. IN: A. PREKOPA (ED.): SURVEY OF MATHEMATICAL PROGRAMMING, VOLUME 2, 491-504. AMSTERDAM: NORTH-HOLLAND. (1979).

GUIGA 1981 -1 GUIGNARD, M.; SPIELBERG, K.
LOGICAL REDUCTION METHODS IN ZERO-ONE PROGRAMMING (MINIMAL PREFERRED VARIABLES). OPERATIONS RESEARCH 29, 49-74. (1981).

GUNN 1981 -1 GUNN, J. P.
MONOCHROMATIC MAXIMUM INDEPENDENT SETS IN K-COLORED K-GRAPHS. RESEARCH REPORT. VIENNA, VIRGINIA: NETWORK ANALYSIS CORP., 301 TOWER BUILDG., 54 P. (1981).

GUPT 1978 -1 GUPTA, J. N. D.
SEARCH ALGORITHM FOR THE TRAVELING SALESMAN PROBLEM, A. COMPUTERS AND OPERATIONS RESEARCH 5, 243-250. (1978).

GUPT 1979 -1 GUPTA, J. N. D.
IMPROVED LEXICOGRAPHIC SEARCH ALGORITHM FOR THE FLOWSHOP SCHEDULING PROBLEM, AN. COMPUTERS AND OPERATIONS RESEARCH 6, 117-120. (1979).

GUPTA 1978 -1 GUPTA, J. N. D.; REDDI, S. S.
IMPROVED DOMINANCE CONDITIONS FOR THE THREE-MACHINE FLOWSHOP SCHEDULING PROBLEM. OPERATIONS RESEARCH 26, 200-203. (1978).

GUPTB 1980 -1 GUPTA, O. K.
BRANCH AND BOUND EXPERIMENTS IN NONLINEAR INTEGER PROGRAMMING. DISSERTATION. PURDUE UNIVERSITY, SCHOOL OF INDUSTRIAL ENGINEERING. (1980).

GUPTB 1980 -2 GUPTA, O. K.
NONLINEAR INTEGER PROGRAMMING ALGORITHMS: A SURVEY. RESEARCH REPORT 8005. PULLMAN: WASHINGTON STATE UNIVERSITY, DEPT. OF BUSINESS ADMINISTRATION, 28 P. (1980).

GUPTC 1977 -1 GUPTA, R.
TIME-COST TRANSPORTATION PROBLEM. EKONOMICKO-MATEMATICKY OBZOR 13, 431-443. (1977).

GUPTC 1979 -1 GUPTA, R.
SOLVING THE GENERALIZED TRANSPORTATION PROBLEM WITH CONSTRAINTS. CAHIERS DU CENTRE D'ETUDES DE RECHERCHE OPERATIONNELLE 21, 167-181. (1979).

GUPTD 1966 -1 GUPTA, R. P.
CHROMATIC INDEX AND THE DEGREE OF A GRAPH, THE. NOTICES OF THE AMERICAN MATHEMATICAL SOCIETY 13, 719. (1966).

GUPTD 1966 -2 GUPTA, R. P.
THEOREM ON THE COVER INDEX OF AN S-GRAPH, A. NOTICES OF THE AMERICAN MATHEMATICAL SOCIETY 13, 714. (1966).

GUPTD 1978 -1 GUPTA, R. P.
EDGE-COLORATION THEOREM FOR BIPARTITE GRAPHS WITH APPLICATIONS, AN. DISCRETE MATHEMATICS 23, 229-235. (1978).

GUPTE 1976 -1 GUPTA, S. K.; TURKSON, I. B.
APPLICATION OF BRANCH AND BOUND TECHNIQUE TO PRODUCTION SCHEDULING PROBLEMS. IN: B. L. JUNEJA (ED.): PROCEEDINGS OF THE INDO-BRITISH CONFERENCE ON ENGINEERING PRODUCTION, NEW DELHI 1976, A43-A60. NEW DELHI: INDIAN INSTITUTE OF TECHNOLOGY. (1976).

GUPTF 1979 -1 GUPTA, U. I.; LEE, D. T.; LEUNG, J. Y.-T.
OPTIMAL SOLUTION FOR THE CHANNEL-ASSIGNMENT PROBLEM, AN. IEEE TRANSACTIONS ON COMPUTERS C-28, 807-810. (1979).

GURA 1978 -1 GURARI, E. M.; IBARRA, O. H.
NP-COMPLETE NUMBER-THEORETIC PROBLEM, AN. IN: CONFERENCE RECORD OF THE TENTH ANNUAL ACM SYMPOSIUM ON THEORY OF COMPUTING, SAN DIEGO 1978, 205-215. NEW YORK: ASSOCIATION FOR COMPUTING MACHINERY; ALSO PUBLISHED IN JOURNAL OF THE ASSOCIATION FOR COMPUTING MACHINERY 26, 1979, 567-581. (1978).

GUSA 1976 -1 GUSAKOV, V. J.; JAKUBOVIC, S. M.
CLASSIFICATION ALGORITHMS (RUSSIAN). AKADEMIJA NAUK SSSR. VSESOJUZNYI INSTITUT NAUCNOI I TEHNICESKOI INFORMACII. NAUCNO-TEHNICESKAJA INFORMACIJA. SERIJA 2. INFORMACIONNYE PROCESSY I SISTEMY, NO. 12, 17-22 + 39-40. (1976).

GUSF 1979 -1 GUSFIELD, D.
MATROID OPTIMIZATION WITH THE INTERLEAVING OF TWO ORDERED SETS. WORKING PAPER. BERKELEY: UNIV. OF CALIFORNIA, DEPT. OF ELECTRICAL ENGINEERING AND COMPUTER SCIENCE, 10 P. (1979).

GUST 1973 -1 GUSTAFSON, C. E.
COMPUTER ASSISTED INTERACTIVE RESOURCE SCHEDULING SYSTEM. IN: NASA SPECIAL PUBLICATION 326, FOR SYMPOSIUM ON SIGNIFICANT ACCOMPLISHMENTS IN TECHNOLOGY, NOVEMBER 1972, 143-146. (1973).

GUTM 1979 -1 GUTMAN, I.
MATCHING POLYNOMIAL, THE. IN: PROCEEDINGS OF BREMER KONFERENZ ZUR CHEMIE PART I, BREMEN 1978. MATCH, NO. 6, 75-91. (1979).

GUTT 1977 -1 GUTT, S.
INFINITE FAMILIES OF HYPOHAMILTONIAN GRAPHS. ACADEMIE ROYALE DE BELGIQUE. BULLETIN DE LA CLASSE DE SCIENCES 63, NO. 5, 432-440. (1977).
GYAR 1978 -1 GYARFAS, A.; LEHEL, J.
PACKING TREES OF DIFFERENT ORDER INTO K(N). IN: A. HAJNAL, V. T. SOS (EDS.): COMBINATORICS, VOLUME I, 463-470. COLLOQUIA MATHEMATICA SOCIETATIS JANOS BOLYAI 18. AMSTERDAM: NORTH-HOLLAND. (1978).
GYOR 1975 -1 GYORI, E.
COMPARISON OF INFINITE MATROIDS (HUNGARIAN). MATEMATIKAI LAPOK. BOLYAI JANOS MATEMATIKAI TARSULAT 26, 311-317. (1975).
HABE 1978 -1 HABENICHT, W.
ZUM EINSATZ ENUMERATIVER SCHNITTEBENENVERFAHREN IN B&B-SYSTEMEN. IN: R. HENN, P. KALL, H. KOENIG, B. KORTE, O. KRAFFT ET AL. (EDS.): OPERATIONS RESEARCH VERFAHREN 28, SECOND SYMPOSIUM ON OPERATIONS RESEARCH, AACHEN 1977, 223-234. MEISENHEIM: HAIN. (1978).
HACK 1979 -1 HACKBARTH, K.-D.
ALGORITHMEN ZUR BERECHNUNG MINIMALER DISJUNKTER WEGE IN NETZEN. IN: PROCEEDINGS IN OPERATIONS RESEARCH 8, 87-93. WUERZBURG: PHYSICA. (1979).
HACK 1979 -2 HACKBARTH, K.-D.
BERECHNUNG KANTENDISJUNKTER WEGE ZWISCHEN ZWEI KNOTEN IN EINEM GRAPHEN. IN: H. SPAETH (ED.): AUSGEWAEHLTE OPERATIONS RESEARCH SOFTWARE IN FORTRAN, 87-102. MUENCHEN: OLDENBOURG. (1979).
HACKA 1980 -1 HACKSTEIN, R.; KOCH, F.
VORTEILE EINER TERMINIERUNG VON NETZPLAENEN MITTELS MINIMALER VORGANGSDAUERN. ZEITSCHRIFT FUER OPERATIONS RESEARCH SERIE B (PRAXIS) 24, 221-238. (1980).
HADL 1979 -1 HADLOCK, F.
OPTIMUM PATHS IN LATTICE GRAPHS. IN: P. C. C. WANG (ED.): INFORMATION LINKAGE BETWEEN APPLIED MATHEMATICS AND INDUSTRY, 421-430. NEW YORK: ACADEMIC PRESS. (1979).
HADL 1979 -2 HADLOCK, F.
TREE SYSTEMS FOR NETWORK FLOW CONTROL AND ROUTING. UTILITAS MATHEMATICA 15, 261-280. (1979).
HADLA 1979 -1 HADLOCK, F.; HOFFMAN, F.
MINIMUM FLEET SIZE ROUTING PROBLEM, A. IN: D. MAC CARTHY, H. C. WILLIAMS (EDS.): PROCEEDINGS OF THE EIGHTH MANITOBA CONFERENCE ON NUMERICAL MATHEMATICS AND COMPUTING, 307-328. CONGRESSUS NUMERANTIUM XXII. WINNIPEG: UTILITAS. (1979).
HADZ 1979 -1 HADZIIVANOV, N. G.; NIKIFOROV, V. S.
ESTIMATES FOR THE NUMBER OF CLIQUES OF A GRAPH WITH A GIVEN VERTEX NUMBER OF INDEPENDENCE (RUSSIAN). SERDICA 5, 50-59. (1979).
HAEG 1979 -1 HAEGGKVIST, R.
ON F-HAMILTONIAN GRAPHS. IN: J. A. BONDY, U. P. R. MURTY (EDS.): GRAPH THEORY AND RELATED TOPICS, 219-231. NEW YORK, SAN FRANCISCO, LONDON: ACADEMIC PRESS. (1979).
HAEGA 1981 -1 HAEGGKVIST, R.; NICOGHOSSIAN, G. G.
REMARK ON HAMILTONIAN CYCLES, A. JOURNAL OF COMBINATORIAL THEORY, SERIES B 30, 118-120. (1981).
HAEM 1980 -1 HAEMERS, W. H.
EIGENVALUE TECHNIQUES IN DESIGN AND GRAPH THEORY. AMSTERDAM: MATHEMATISCH CENTRUM, 102 P. (1980). (MATHEMATICAL CENTRE TRACTS, 121)
HAES 1979 -1 HAESSIG, K.
GRAPHENTHEORETISCHE METHODEN IN DER LOGISTIK. MANUSKRIPT. ZUERICH: UNIV. ZUERICH, INSTITUT FUER OPERATIONS RESEARCH, 15 P. (1979).
HAESA 1978 -1 HAESSIG, K.; REISER, P.; STIERLIN, C.
NOTE ON PRIMAL NETWORK FLOW ALGORITHMS, A. ZEITSCHRIFT FUER OPERATIONS RESEARCH 22, SERIE A, 195-198. (1978).
HAESB 1979 -1 HAESSIG, K.; SENN, W.
ENGPAESSE, STAUSTELLEN UND GLATTE HOMOGENE STROEME IN NETZEN - EINE ALTERNATIVE ZU STECKHAN'S KONZEPT. ZEITSCHRIFT FUER OPERATIONS RESEARCH 23, SERIE A, 269-273. (1979).
HAESC 1973 -1 HAESSLER, R. W.
DEVELOPMENT OF A HEURISTIC PROCEDURE TO SOLVE A PRODUCTION SCHEDULING PROBLEM, THE. PAPER PRESENTED AT THE 44TH NATIONAL ORSA MEETING, SAN DIEGO 1973. (1973).
HAESC 1976 -1 HAESSLER, R. W.
SOME MODIFICATIONS TO THE GILMORE-GOMORY CUTTING STOCK ALGORITHM. PAPER PRESENTED AT THE JOINT NATIONAL ORSA/TIMS MEETING, MIAMI 1976. (1976).
HAESC 1979 -1 HAESSLER, R. W.
IMPROVED EXTENDED BASIC PERIOD PROCEDURE FOR SOLVING THE ECONOMIC LOT SCHEDULING PROBLEM, AN. AIIE TRANSACTIONS 11, 336-340. (1979).
HAESC 1979 -2 HAESSLER, R. W.
SOLVING A BOXCAR LOADING PROBLEM. WORKING PAPER NO. 183. ANN ARBOR: UNIV. OF MICHIGAN, GRADUATE SCHOOL OF BUSINESS ADMINISTRATION 13 P. (1979).
HAESC 1979 -3 HAESSLER, R. W.
SOLVING THE TWO-STAGE CUTTING STOCK PROBLEM. OMEGA 7, 145-151. (1979).
HAESC 1980 -1 HAESSLER, R. W.
NOTE ON COMPUTATIONAL MODIFICATIONS TO THE GILMORE-GOMORY CUTTING STOCK ALGORITHM, A. OPERATIONS RESEARCH 28, 1001-1004. (1980).
HAESD 1980 -1 HAESSLER, R. W.; TALBOT, F. B.
0-1 MODEL FOR SOLVING THE CORRUGATOR TRIM PROBLEM, A. WORKING PAPER NO. 205. ANN ARBOR: UNIV. OF MICHIGAN, GRADUSTE SCHOOL OF BUSINESS ADMINISTRATION,21 P. (1980).
HAID 1972 -1 HAIDER, S. W.
INVESTIGATION OF THE USE OF AN INTERACTIVE COMPUTER MODE FOR BALANCING PACED ASSEMBLY LINES, AN. UNPUBLISHED MASTERS THESIS. LAFAYETTE: PURDUE UNIVERSITY. (1972).
HAID 1976 -1 HAIDER, S. W.
INVESTIGATION OF THE ADVANTAGES OF USING A MAN-COMPUTER INTERACTIVE MODE FOR SCHEDULING JOB SHOPS, AN. UNPUBLISHED DOCTORAL THESIS. LAFAYETTE: PURDUE UNIVERSITY. (1976).
HAJE 1977 -1 HAJEK, P.
ARITHMETICAL COMPLEXITY OF SOME PROBLEMS IN COMPUTER SCIENCE. IN: J. GRUSKA (ED.): MATHEMATICAL FOUNDATIONS OF COMPUTER SCIENCE, TATRANSKA LOMNICA 1977, 282-287. LECTURE NOTES IN COMPUTER SCIENCE 53, BERLIN, NEW YORK: SPRINGER. (1977).
HAJO 1961 -1 HAJOS, G.
UEBER EINE KONSTRUKTION NICHT N-FAERBBARER GRAPHEN. WISSENSCHAFTLICHE ZEITSCHRIFT DER MARTIN-LUTHER-UNIVERSITAET HALLE-WITTENBERG A10, 116-117. (1961).
HAKI 1962 -1 HAKIMI, S. L.
SIMULTANEOUS FLOWS THROUGH A COMMUNICATION NETWORK. IEEE TRANSACTIONS ON CIRCUIT THEORY 9, 169-175. (1962).
HAKIA 1978 -1 HAKIMI, S. L.; SCHMEICHEL, E. F.; PIERCE, J. G.
ON P-CENTERS IN NETWORKS. TRANSPORTATION SCIENCE 12, 1-15. (1978).
HALI 1980 -1 HALIN, R.
GRAPHENTHEORIE I. DARMSTADT: WISSENSCHAFTLICHE BUCHGESELLSCHAFT, 321 P. (1980).
HALL 1978 -1 HALL, M. A.
PROPERTIES OF THE EQUILIBRIUM STATE IN TRANSPORTATION NETWORKS. TRANSPORTATION SCIENCE 12, 208-216. (1978).

HALP 1979 -1 HALPERN, J.
GENERALIZED DYNAMIC FLOWS PROBLEM, A. NETWORKS 9, 133-167. (1979).
HALP 1979 -2 HALPERN, J.
SIMPLE EDGE ELIMINATION CRITERION IN A SEARCH FOR THE CENTER OF A GRAPH, A. MANAGEMENT SCIENCE 25, 105-107. (1979).
HAMA 1979 -1 HAMACHER, H.
COMPUTATIONAL COMPARISON OF THE ALGORITHM OF KARZANOV AND THE LABELING ALGORITHM FOR THE SOLUTION OF MAXIMUM FLOW PROBLEMS, A. IN: M. NAGL, H.-J. SCHNEIDER (EDS.): GRAPHS, DATA STRUCTURES, ALGORITHMS. PROCEEDINGS OF THE WORKSHOP WG 78 ON GRAPHTHEORETIC CONCEPTS IN COMPUTER SCIENCE, ERLANGEN 1978, 117-129. MUENCHEN, WIEN: HANSER. (1979).
HAMA 1979 -2 HAMACHER, H.
NUMERICAL INVESTIGATIONS ON THE MAXIMAL FLOW ALGORITHM OF KARZANOV. COMPUTING 22, 17-29. (1979).
HAMA 1980 -1 HAMACHER, H.
ALGEBRAIC FLOWS IN REGULAR MATROIDS. DISCRETE APPLIED MATHEMATICS 2, 27-38. (1980).
HAMA 1980 -2 HAMACHER, H.
ALGEBRAISCHE FLUSSPROBLEME IN REGULAEREN MATROIDEN. DISSERTATION. KOELN: UNIV. ZU KOELN, MATHEMATISCHES INST. (1980).
HAMA 1980 -3 HAMACHER, H.
MAXIMAL ALGEBRAIC FLOWS: ALGORITHMS AND EXAMPLES. IN: U. PAPE (ED.): DISCRETE STRUCTURES AND ALGORITHMS, 153-166. MUENCHEN: HANSER. (1980).
HAMA 1980 -4 HAMACHER, H.
ON A CLASS OF EASILY SOLVABLE OPTIMAL COCIRCUIT PROBLEMS IN REGULAR MATROIDS. RESEARCH REPORT 80-15. KOELN: UNIV. ZU KOELN, MATHEMATISCHES INST., 22 P. (1980).
HAMA 1980 -5 HAMACHER, H.
OPTIMAL CUTS. RESEARCH REPORT 80-8. KOELN: UNIV. ZU KOELN, MATHEMATISCHES INST., 17 P. (1980).
HAMA 1981 -1 HAMACHER, H.
FLOWS IN REGULAR MATROIDS. KOENIGSTEIN: HAIN; CAMBRIDGE: OELGESCHALGER, GUNN & HAIN, 164 P. (1981). (MATHEMATICAL SYSTEMS IN ECONOMICS, 69)
HAMA 1981 -2 HAMACHER, H.
OPTIMAL (S,T)-CUTS. IN: H. NOLTEMEYER (ED.): GRAPHTHEORETIC CONCEPTS IN COMPUTER SCIENCE, 383-387. LECTURE NOTES IN COMPUTER SCIENCE 100, BERLIN: SPRINGER. (1981).
HAMI 1978 -1 HAMIDOUNE, Y. O.
SUR LES SOMMETS DE DEMI-DEGRE H D'UN GRAPHE FORTEMENT H-CONNEXE MINIMAL. COMPTES RENDUS HEBDOMADAIRES DES SEANCES DE L'ACADEMIE DES SCIENCES PARIS, SERIES A ET B 286, A863-A865. (1978).
HAMI 1979 -1 HAMIDOUNE, Y. O.
SUR LES PARCOURS HAMILTONIENS DANS LES GRAPHES ORIENTES. DISCRETE MATHEMATICS 26, 227-234. (1979).
HAMM 1979 -1 HAMMER, G.
RANDOMISIERTE HEURISTIKEN. IN: W. OETTLI, F. STEFFENS (EDS.): OPERATIONS RESEARCH VERFAHREN 32, THIRD SYMPOSIUM ON OPERATIONS RESEARCH, MANNHEIM 1978, 125-131. KOENIGSTEIN: ANTON HAIN MEISENHEIM. (1979).
HAMMA 1979 -1 HAMMER, P. L.
BOOLEAN ELEMENTS IN COMBINATORIAL OPTIMIZATION. IN: P. L. HAMMER, E. L. JOHNSON, B. H. KORTE (EDS.): DISCRETE OPTIMIZATION I, 51-71. ANNALS OF DISCRETE MATHEMATICS 4, AMSTERDAM, NEW YORK, OXFORD: NORTH-HOLLAND. (1979).
HAMMB 1981 -1 HAMMER, P. L.; HANSEN, P.; SIMEONE, B.
UPPER PLANES OF QUADRATIC 0-1 FUNCTIONS AND STABILITY IN GRAPHS. IN: O. L. MANGASARIAN, R. R. MEYER, P. M. ROBINSON (EDS.): NONLINEAR PROGRAMMING 4, 395-414. NEW YORK: ACADEMIC PRESS. (1981).
HAMMC 1978 -1 HAMMER, P. L.; IBARAKI, T.; SIMEONE, B.
DEGREE SEQUENCES OF THRESHOLD GRAPHS. IN: F. HOFFMAN, D. MAC CARTHY, R. C. MULLIN, R. G. STANTON (EDS.): PROCEEDINGS OF THE NINTH SOUTHEASTERN CONFERENCE ON COMBINATORICS, GRAPH THEORY, AND COMPUTING, 329-356. CONGRESSUS NUMERANTIUM XXI. WINNIPEG: UTILITAS. (1978).
HAMMD 1979 -1 HAMMER, P. L.; NGUYEN, S.
PARTIAL ORDER IN THE SOLUTION SPACE OF BIVALENT PROGRAMS, A. IN: N. CHRISTOFIDES, A. MINGOZZI, P. TOTH, C. SANDI (EDS.): COMBINATORIAL OPTIMIZATION, 94-106. CHICHESTER, NEW YORK, BRISBANE, TORONTO: WILEY. (1979).
HAMME 1979 -1 HAMMER, P. L.; PELED, U. N.; POLLATSCHEK, M. A.
ALGORITHM TO DUALIZE A REGULAR SWITCHING FUNCTION, AN. IN: IEEE TRANSACTION ON COMPUTERS, VOL. C-28, NO. 3, P. 238-243 (1979).
HAMMF 1977 -1 HAMMER, P. L.; SIMEONE, B.
SPLITTANCE OF A GRAPH, THE. RESEARCH REPORT CORR 77-39. WATERLOO: UNIV. OF WATERLOO, DEPT. OF COMBINATORICS AND OPTIMIZATION, 31 P. (1977).
HAMMG 1980 -1 HAMMERSLEY, J. M.
GENERALIZATION OF MAC DIARMID'S THEOREM FOR MIXED BERNOULLI PERCOLATION, A. MATHEMATICAL PROCEEDINGS OF THE CAMBRIDGE PHILOSOPHICAL SOCIETY 88, 167-170. (1980).
HAMMH 1978 -1 HAMMOND, P.
Q-COVERINGS AND COMPLETELY REGULAR CODES IN DISTANCE-REGULAR GRAPHS. QUARTERLY JOURNAL OF MATHEMATICS 29, NO. 113, 23-30. (1978).
HAND 1978 -1 HANDLER, G. Y.
FINDING TWO CENTERS OF A TREE: THE CONTINUOUS CASE. TRANSPORTATION SCIENCE 12, 93-106. (1978).
HAND 1979 -1 HANDLER, G. Y.
COMPLEXITY AND EFFICIENCY IN MINIMAX NETWORK LOCATION. IN: N. CHRISTOFIDES, A. MINGOZZI, P. TOTH, C. SANDI (EDS.): COMBINATORIAL OPTIMIZATION, 281-314. CHICHESTER, NEW YORK, BRISBANE, TORONTO: WILEY. (1979).
HANDA 1979 -1 HANDLER, G. Y.; MIRCHANDANI, P. B.
LOCATION ON NETWORKS - THEORY AND ALGORITHMS. CAMBRIDGE, MA: THE MIT PRESS, 233 P. (1979).
HANDB 1980 -1 HANDLER, G. Y.; ZANG, I.
DUAL ALGORITHM FOR THE CONSTRAINED SHORTEST PATH PROBLEM, A. NETWORKS 10, 293-310. (1980).
HANJ 1980 -1 HANJOUL, P.; THISSE, J.-F.
LOCALISATION SUR UN RESEAU. IN: P. HANSEN, D. DE WERRA (EDS.): REGARDS SUR LA THEORIE DES GRAPHES, PROCEEDINGS OF THE CERISY COLLOQUIUM, 1980, 253-258. LAUSANNE: PRESSES POLYTECHNIQUES ROMANDES. (1980).
HANN 1978 -1 HANNAN, E. L.
APPLICATION OF GOAL PROGRAMMING TECHNIQUES TO THE CPM PROBLEM, THE. SOCIO-ECONOMIC PLANNING SCIENCES 12, NO. 5, 267-270. (1978).
HANN 1979 -1 HANNAN, E. L.
ASSIGNMENT OF PLAYERS TO MATCHES IN A HIGH SCHOOL OR COLLEGE TENNIS MATCH. COMPUTERS AND OPERATIONS RESEARCH 6, 21-26. (1979).
HANNA 1979 -1 HANNAN, E. L.; MAC KEOWN, P. G.
MATCHING SWIMMERS TO EVENTS IN A CHAMPIONSHIP SWIMMING MEET. COMPUTERS AND OPERATIONS RESEARCH 6, 225-231. (1979).

****

HANS 1978 -1 HANSEL, K.; JAENICKE, W.; WOLIN, JU. M.
ZUR BESTIMMUNG ALLER ELEMENTARKREISE IN GERICHTETEN GRAPHEN. MATHEMATISCHE OPERATIONSFORSCHUNG UND STATISTIK 9, 427-440. (1978).

HANSA 1977 -1 HANSEN, A. B.
ON A CERTAIN CLASS OF POLYTOPES ASSOCIATED WITH INDEPENDENCE SYSTEMS. MATHEMATICA SCANDINAVICA 41, NO. 2, 225-241. (1977).

HANSB 1974 -1 HANSEN, P.
PROGRAMMES MATHEMATIQUES EN VARIABLES 0-1. DISSERTATION. BRUXELLES: FACULTE DES SCIENCES APPLIQUEES DE L'UNIVERSITE LIBRE. (1974).

HANSB 1979 -1 HANSEN, P.
METHODS OF NONLINEAR 0-1 PROGRAMMING. IN: P. L. HAMMER, E. L. JOHNSON, B. H. KORTE (EDS.): DISCRETE OPTIMIZATION II, 53-70. ANNALS OF DISCRETE MATHEMATICS 5, AMSTERDAM, NEW YORK, OXFORD: NORTH-HOLLAND. (1979).

HANSB 1979 -2 HANSEN, P.
UPPER BOUNDS FOR THE STABILITY NUMBER OF A GRAPH. REVUE ROUMAINE DE MATHEMATIQUES PURES ET APPLIQUEES 24, 1195-1199. (1979).

HANSB 1980 -1 HANSEN, P.
BORNES ET ALGORITHMES POUR LES STABLES D'UN GRAPHE. IN: P. HANSEN, D. DE WERRA (EDS.): REGARDS SUR LA THEORIE DES GRAPHES, PROCEEDINGS OF THE CERISY COLLOQUIUM, 1980, 39-54. LAUSANNE: PRESSES POLYTECHNIQUES ROMANDES. (1980).

HANSB 1980 -2 HANSEN, P.
O(M LOG D) ALGORITHM FOR SHORTEST PATHS, AN. DISCRETE APPLIED MATHEMATICS 2, 151-154. (1980).

HANSC 1978 -1 HANSEN, P.; KAUFMAN, L.; ANTOINE, M.-P.
ASSIGNMENT PROBLEM WITH SOME COMPATIBLE JOBS, THE. ANALELE STIINTIFICE ALE UNIVERSITATII "AL. I. CUZA" DIN IASI. SERIA NOUA. SECTIUNEA I A MATEMATICA 24, 175-178. (1978).

HANSD 1978 -1 HANSEN, P.; LOREA, M.
DEUX CONDITIONS DE COLORABILITE DES HYPERGRAPHES. CAHIERS DU CENTRE D'ETUDES DE RECHERCHE OPERATIONELLE 20, 405-410. (1978).

HANSE 1980 -1 HANSEN, P.; PERREUR, J.; THISSE, J.-F.
LOCATION THEORY, DOMINANCE, AND CONVEXITY: SOME FURTHER RESULTS. OPERATIONS RESEARCH 28, 1241-1250. (1980).

HANSF 1981 -1 HANSEN, P.; THISSE, J.-F.; HANJOUL, P.
SIMPLE PLANT LOCATION UNDER UNIFORM DELIVERED PRICING. EUROPEAN JOURNAL OF OPERATIONAL RESEARCH 6, 94-103. (1981).

HARA 1970 -1 HARARY, F.
COVERING AND PACKING IN GRAPHS, I. IN: A. GEWIRTZ, L. V. QUINTAS (EDS.): INTERNATIONAL CONFERENCE ON COMBINATORIAL MATHEMATICS, 198-205. ANNALS OF THE NEW YORK ACADEMY OF SCIENCES, VOLUME 165, ARTICLE 1. NEW YORK: THE NEW YORK ACADEMY OF SCIENCES. (1970).

HARA 1979 -1 HARARY, F.
STRUCTURE OF THRESHOLD GRAPHS, THE. RIVISTA DI MATEMATICA PER LE SCIENZE ECONOMICHE E SOCIALI (MILAN) 2, 169-172. (1979).

HARAA 1978 -1 HARARY, F.; KABELL, J. A.
GRAPHICAL CONFLICT I: A NEW CLASS OF EXTREMAL PROBLEMS. NEW YORK: SECOND INTERNATIONAL CONFERENCE ON COMBINATORIAL MATHEMATICS, 10 P. (1978).

HARAA 1980 -1 HARARY, F.; KABELL, J. A.
INTUITIVE APPROACH TO INTERVAL NUMBERS OF GRAPHS, AN. MATHEMATICS MAGAZINE 53, 39-44. (1980).

HARAB 1979 -1 HARARY, F.; KOMMEL, H. J.
GRAPHS WITH ONLY SELF-DUAL SIGNINGS, THE. DISCRETE MATHEMATICS 26, 235-241. (1979).

HARAC 1980 -1 HARARY, F.; KOVACS, P.
REGULAR GRAPHS WITH GIVEN GIRTH PAIR. ANN ARBOR: UNIV. OF MICHIGAN, DEPT. OF MATHEMATICS, 20 P. (1980).

HARAD 1978 -1 HARARY, F.; MARCH, L.; ROBINSON, R. W.
ON ENUMERATING CERTAIN DESIGN PROBLEMS IN TERMS OF BICOLOURED GRAPHS WITH NO ISOLATES. ENVIRONMENT AND PLANNING 5, SERIES B, 31-43. (1978).

HARAE 1979 -1 HARARY, F.; ROBINSON, R. W.
LABELED BIPARTITE BLOCKS. CANADIAN JOURNAL OF MATHEMATICS 31, 60-68. (1979).

HARB 1979 -1 HARBORTH, H.; MENGERSEN, I.
EXTREMALPROBLEM FUER MATRIZEN AUS NULLEN UND EINSEN, EIN. JOURNAL FUER DIE REINE UND ANGEWANDTE MATHEMATIK 309, 149-155. (1979).

HARP 1976 -1 HARPER, L. H.; SAVAGE, J. E.
COMPLEXITY MADE SIMPLE. IN: COLLOQUIO INTERNAZIONALE SULLE TEORIE COMBINATORIE, TOMO II, ROME 1973, 253-262. ATTI DEI CONVEGNI LINCEI, NO. 17, ROME: ACCAD. NAZ. LINCEI. (1976).

HARR 1978 -1 HARRIS, B.
NEW ALGORITHM FOR TREE MODIFICATION IN THE PRIMAL TRANSPORTATION PROBLEM, A. TRANSPORTATION SCIENCE 12, 271-276. (1978).

HARR 1979 -1 HARRIS, B.
RAPID DUAL METHOD FOR THE HITCHCOCK PROBLEM, A. ENVIRONMENT AND PLANNING 11, SERIES A, 1049-1054. (1979).

HART 1975 -1 HARTIGAN, J. A.
CLUSTERING ALGORITHMS. NEW YORK, LONDON U.A.: WILEY, 351 P. (1975). (WILEY SERIES IN PROBABILITY AND MATHEMATICAL STATISTICS)

HARTA 1976 -1 HARTLEY, R. V.
OPERATIONS RESEARCH: A MANAGERIAL EMPHASIS. PACIFIC PALISADES: GOODYEAR, 795 P. (1976).

HARTB 1977 -1 HARTMANN, K.
VERFAHREN ZUR LOESUNG GANZZAHLIGER NICHTLINEARER OPTIMIERUNGSPROBLEME. MATHEMATISCHE OPERATIONSFORSCHUNG UND STATISTIK 8, SERIES OPTIMIZATION, 633-647. (1977).

HARTC 1977 -1 HARTNELL, B. L.
CHARACTERIZATION OF UNICYCLIC GRAPHS WHICH DO NOT HAVE TWO DISJOINT MAXIMAL MATCHINGS, A. UTILITAS MATHEMATICA 11, 273-287. (1977).

HARTD 1975 -1 HARTNELL, B. L.; MILGRAM, M.
DECOMPOSITION OF K*(P), FOR P A PRIME, INTO K-CIRCUITS. CAHIERS DU CENTRE D'ETUDES DE RECHERCHE OPERATIONELLE 17, 221-224. (1975).

HARTE 1975 -1 HARTWIG, A.
ANWENDUNG DES ERWEITERUNGSPRINZIPS AUF SPEZIELLE REIHENFOLGEPROBLEME. DIPLOMARBEIT. DRESDEN: TECHNISCHE UNIVERSITAET DRESDEN. (1975).

HARTF 1978 -1 HARTWIG, A.; TERNO, J.
TRANSFORMATION VON REIHENFOLGEPROBLEMEN AUF RUNDREISEPROBLEME. MANUSKRIPT 07-08-78. DRESDEN: T. U. DRESDEN, SEKTION MATHEMATIK, 12 P. (1978).

HARV 1979 -1 HARVEY, R. T.; PATTERSON, J. H.
IMPLICIT ENUMERATION ALGORITHM FOR THE TIME/COST TRADEOFF PROBLEM IN PROJECT NETWORK ANALYSIS, AN. FOUNDATIONS OF CONTROL ENGINEERING (POZNAN) 4, NO. 3, 107-117. (1979).

HASA 1980 -1 HASANUDDIN AHMAD, S.
GROUP THEORETIC APPROACH OF INTEGER PROGRAMMING - A SURVEY. RESEARCH REPORT. JEDDAH: KING ABDUL AZIZ UNIVERSITY, DEPT. OF INDUSTRIAL ENGINEERING, 16 P. (1980).

*****

HAST 1978 -1 HASTINGS, N. A. J.; MELLO, J. M. C.
DECISION NETWORKS. CHICHESTER, NEW YORK U.A.: WILEY, 196 P. (1978).
HAUP 1980 -1 HAUPTMANN, H.
STATISTIC FOR JUDGING SOLUTIONS OF THE TRAVELLING SALESMAN PROBLEM, A. IN: R. HENN, H. P. KUENZI, H. SCHUBERT (EDS.): METHODS OF OPERATIONS RESEARCH 36, 61-72. KOENIGSTEIN: ANTON HAIN MEISENHEIM. (1980).
HAUS 1978 -1 HAUSMANN, D.
ADJAZENZCHARAKTERISIERUNGEN FUER POLYEDERECKEN IN DER KOMBINATORISCHEN OPTIMIERUNG. REPORT NO. 78125-OR. BONN: UNIV. BONN, INSTITUT FUER OEKONOMETRIE UND OPERATIONS RESEARCH, 228 P. (1978).
HAUS 1978 -2 HAUSMANN, D.
POLYNOMIALER ALGORITHMUS FUER DIE ADJAZENZUEBERPRUEFUNG AUF DEM BRANCHING-POLYEDER, EIN. IN: R. HENN, P. KALL, H. KOENIG, B. KORTE, O. KRAFFT ET AL. (EDS.): OPERATIONS RESEARCH VERFAHREN 28, SECOND SYMPOSIUM ON OPERATIONS RESEARCH, AACHEN 1977, 235-240. MEISENHEIM: HAIN. (1978).
HAUS 1979 -1 HAUSMANN, D.
COMPLEXITY OF THE TESTING OF ADJACENCY ON THE B-MATCHING POLYHEDRON. IN: W. OETTLI, F. STEFFENS (EDS.): OPERATIONS RESEARCH VERFAHREN 32, THIRD SYMPOSIUM ON OPERATIONS RESEARCH, MANNHEIM 1978, 133-141. KOENIGSTEIN: ANTON HAIN MEISENHEIM. (1979).
HAUS 1980 -1 HAUSMANN, D.
ADJACENCY ON POLYTOPES IN COMBINATORIAL OPTIMIZATION. MEISENHEIM: HAIN; CAMBRIDGE: OELGESCHLAGER, GUNN & HAIN, 237 P. (1980). (MATHEMATICAL SYSTEMS IN ECONOMICS, 49)
HAUS 1980 -2 HAUSMANN, D.
FARBKLASSEN UND PSEUDOKNOTEN FUER ADJAZENZCHARAKTERISIERUNGEN. IN: R. HENN, H. P. KUENZI, H. SCHUBERT (EDS.): METHODS OF OPERATIONS RESEARCH 36, 137-142. KOENIGSTEIN: ANTON HAIN MEISENHEIM. (1980).
HAUS 1981 -1 HAUSMANN, D.
ADJACENT VERTICES ON THE B-MATCHING POLYHEDRON. DISCRETE MATHEMATICS 33, 37-52. (1981).
HAUSA 1980 -1 HAUSMANN, D.; JENKYNS, T. A.; KORTE, B.
WORST CASE ANALYSIS OF GREEDY TYPE ALGORITHMS FOR INDEPENDENCE SYSTEMS. MATHEMATICAL PROGRAMMING STUDY 12, 120-131. (1980).
HAUSB 1979 -1 HAUSMANN, D.; KANNAN, R.; KORTE, B.
EXPONENTIELLE UNTERE KOMPLEXITAETSSCHRANKEN FUER EINE KLASSE VON KNAPSACK-PROBLEMEN. REPORT NO. 79132-OR. BONN: UNIV. BONN, INSTITUT FUER OEKONOMETRIE UND OPERATIONS RESEARCH, 5 P. (1979).
HAUSB 1979 -2 HAUSMANN, D.; KANNAN, R.; KORTE, B.
EXPONENTIELLE UNTERE KOMPLEXITAETSSCHRANKEN FUER EINE KLASSE VON KNAPSACKPROBLEMEN (EXTENDED ABSTRACT). IN: W. OETTLI, F. STEFFENS (EDS.): OPERATIONS RESEARCH VERFAHREN 32, THIRD SYMPOSIUM ON OPERATIONS RESEARCH, MANNHEIM 1978, 143-147. KOENIGSTEIN: ANTON HAIN MEISENHEIM. (1979).
HAUSB 1981 -1 HAUSMANN, D.; KANNAN, R.; KORTE, B.
EXPONENTIAL LOWER BOUNDS ON A CLASS OF KNAPSACK ALGORITHMS. MATHEMATICS OF OPERATIONS RESEARCH 6, 225-232. (1981).
HAUSC 1978 -1 HAUSMANN, D.; KORTE, B.
COLOURING CRITERIA FOR ADJACENCY ON 0-1-POLYHEDRA. MATHEMATICAL PROGRAMMING STUDY 8, 106-127. (1978).
HAUSC 1978 -2 HAUSMANN, D.; KORTE, B.
K-GREEDY ALGORITHMS FOR INDEPENDENCE SYSTEMS. ZEITSCHRIFT FUER OPERATIONS RESEARCH 22, SERIE A, 219-228. (1978).
HAUSC 1978 -3 HAUSMANN, D.; KORTE, B.
LOWER BOUNDS ON THE WORST-CASE COMPLEXITY OF SOME ORACLE ALGORITHMS. DISCRETE MATHEMATICS 24, 261-276. (1978).
HAUSC 1978 -4 HAUSMANN, D.; KORTE, B.
WORST-CASE BEHAVIOUR OF POLYNOMIAL BOUNDED ALGORITHMS FOR INDEPENDENCE SYSTEMS. ZEITSCHRIFT FUER ANGEWANDTE MATHEMATIK UND MECHANIK 58, T477-T479. (1978).
HAUSC 1980 -1 HAUSMANN, D.; KORTE, B.
COMPUTATIONAL RELATIONS BETWEEN VARIOUS DEFINITIONS OF MATROIDS AND INDEPENDENCE SYSTEMS. IN: K. IRACKI, K. MALANOWSKI, P. WALUKIEWICZ (EDS.): OPTIMIZATION TECHNIQUES, PART II, 195-198. LECTURE NOTES IN CONTROL AND INFORMATION SCIENCES 23. BERLIN: SPRINGER. (1980).
HAUSC 1980 -2 HAUSMANN, D.; KORTE, B.
RELATIVE STRENGTH OF ORACLES FOR INDEPENDENCE SYSTEMS, THE. IN: J. FREHSE, D. PALLASCHKE, U. TROTTENBERG (EDS.): SPECIAL TOPICS OF APPLIED MATHEMATICS, 195-212. AMSTERDAM: NORTH-HOLLAND. (1980).
HAUSC 1981 -1 HAUSMANN, D.; KORTE, B.
ALGORITHMIC VERSUS AXIOMATIC DEFINITIONS OF MATROIDS. IN: H. KOENIG, B. KORTE, K. RITTER (EDS.): MATHEMATICAL PROGRAMMING AT OBERWOLFACH, 98-111. MATHEMATICAL PROGRAMMING STUDY 14. (1981).
HAYE 1979 -1 HAYES, G. M. JR.
DISCRETE VARIABLE APPROACH TO MACHINE PARAMETER OPTIMIZATION, A. AIIE TRANSACTIONS 11, 155-159. (1979).
HAYEA 1979 -1 HAYES, M.
BLOCKBUSTING: OR HOW TO HANDLE COMPLEX CONSTRAINTS IN THE TRANSPORTATION TABLEAU. JOURNAL OF THE OPERATIONAL RESEARCH SOCIETY 30, 993-1004. (1979).
HAYS 1967 -1 HAYS, R.
DELIVERY PROBLEM, THE. REPORT NO. 106. PITTSBURGH: CARNEGIE INSTITUTE OF TECHNOLOGY, MANAGEMENT SCIENCE RESEARCH. (1967).
HEIC 1980 -1 HEICKEN, K.; KOENIG, W.
INTEGRATION EINES HEURISTISCH-OPTIMIERENDEN VERFAHRENS ZUR LOESUNG EINES EINDIMENSIONALEN VERSCHNITTPROBLEMS IN EINEM EDV-GESTUETZTEN PRODUKTIONSPLANUNGS- UND -STEUERUNGSSYSTEMS. OR SPEKTRUM 1, 251-259. (1980).
HEIN 1978 -1 HEINHOLD, M.
OPERATIONAL RESEARCH APPROACH TO ALLOCATION OF CLIENTS TO A CERTAIN CLASS OF SERVICE INSTITUTIONS, AN. THE JOURNAL OF THE OPERATIONAL RESEARCH SOCIETY 29, 273-276. (1978).
HEINA 1976 -1 HEINRICH, K.
PROPER 3-COLOURINGS OF K6. ARS COMBINATORIA 1, 191-213. (1976).
HEINA 1977 -1 HEINRICH, K.
PROPER COLOURINGS OF K(15). JOURNAL OF THE AUSTRALIAN MATHEMATICAL SOCIETY 24, SERIES A, NO. 4, 465-495. (1977).
HEINB 1978 -1 HEINRICH, K.; WALLIS, W. D.
HAMILTONIAN CYCLES IN CERTAIN GRAPHS. JOURNAL OF THE AUSTRALIAN MATHEMATICAL SOCIETY 26, SERIES A, NO. 1, 89-98. (1978).
HEINC 1979 -1 HEINRICH, P.
BEZIEHUNG ZWISCHEN DEN WEG-KREIS-SYSTEMEN IN EINEM GERICHTETEN GRAPHEN UND DEN UNTERDETERMINANTEN SEINER CHARAKTERISTISCHEN MATRIX, EINE. MATHEMATISCHE NACHRICHTEN 93, 7-20. (1979).

HEIND 1979 -1 HEINRICH, P.; SCHAAR, G.
UEBER ZUSAMMENHAENGENDE GRAPHEN MIT P-HAMILTONSCHER (P+1)-TER POTENZ (P >= 4). MATHEMATISCHE NACHRICHTEN 90, 225-238. (1979).

HELG 1976 -1 HELGASON, R. V.; KENNINGTON, J. L.
NETFLO PROGRAM DOCUMENTATION. TECHNICAL REPORT IEOR 76011. DALLAS: SOUTHERN METHODIST UNIVERSITY, DEPARTMENT OF INDUSTRIAL ENGINEERING AND OPERATIONS RESEARCH. (1976).

HELG 1978 -1 HELGASON, R. V.; KENNINGTON, J. L.
EFFICIENT SPECIALIZATION OF THE CONVEX SIMPLEX METHOD FOR NONLINEAR NETWORK FLOW PROBLEMS, AN. TECHNICAL REPORT IEOR 77017. DALLAS: SOUTHERN METHODIST UNIV., DEPT. OF INDUSTRIAL ENG. AND OPERATIONS RESEARCH, 26 P. (1978).

HELG 1979 -1 HELGASON, R. V.; KENNINGTON, J. L.
NEW STORAGE REDUCTION TECHNIQUE FOR THE SOLUTION OF THE GROUP PROBLEM, A. NAVAL RESEARCH LOGISTICS QUARTERLY 26, 681-687. (1979).

HELL 1981 -1 HELL, P.; KIRKPATRICK, D. G.
ON GENERALIZED MATCHING PROBLEMS. INFORMATION PROCESSING LETTERS 12, 33-35. (1981).

HELL 1981 -2 HELL, P.; KIRKPATRICK, D. G.
SCHEDULING, MATCHING, AND COLORING. IN: L. LOVASZ, V. T. SOS (EDS.): ALGEBRAIC METHODS IN GRAPH THEORY, VOL. I, 273-280. COLLOQUIA MATHEMATICA SOCIETATIS JANOS BOLYAI 25. AMSTERDAM, OXFORD,NEW YORK: NORTH-HOLLAND. (1981).

HEND 1975 -1 HENDERSON, P. B.
HEURISTIC SCHEDULING POLICIES FOR SERVICE SYSTEMS WITH QUADRATIC WAITING COSTS. IN: PROCEEDINGS OF THE 1975 CONFERENCE ON INFORMATION SCIENCES AND SYSTEMS, BALTIMORE 1975, 156-159. BALTIMORE: THE JOHNS HOPKINS UNIVERSITY: DEPARTMENT OF ELECTRICAL ENGINEERING. (1975).

HENDA 1980 -1 HENDY, M. D.; FOULDS, L. R.; PENNY, D.
PROVING PHYLOGENETIC TREES MINIMAL WITH L-CLUSTERING AND SET PARTITIONING. MATHEMATICAL BIOSCIENCES 51, 71-88. (1980).

HENR 1979 -1 HENRY-LABORDERE, A.
RESOLUTION D'UN PROGRAMME QUADRATIQUE EN VARIANTES BIVALENTES PAR DECOMPOSITION. APPLICATION AU PLACEMENT DE COMMUTATEURS DANS UN RESEAU. REVUE FRANCAISE D'AUTOMATIQUE, D'INFORMATIQUE ET DE RECHERCHE OPERATIONELLE 13, SERIE RECHERCHE OPERATIONELLE, 23-35. (1979).

HEPP 1976 -1 HEPPES, A.; MALYUSZ, K.; STAHL, J.
ON THE SOLUTION OF A SORTING PROBLEM (HUNGARIAN). ALKALMAZOTT MATEMATIKAI LAPOK 2, 233-235. (1976).

HERM 1979 -1 HERMAN, R.; PRIGOGINE, I.
TWO-FLUID APPROACH TO TOWN TRAFFIC, A. SCIENCE 204, NO. 4389, 148-151. (1979).

HERMA 1973 -1 HERMANN, P. P.
ON REDUCIBILITY AMONG COMBINATORIAL PROBLEMS. REPORT TR-113. CAMBRIDGE: MASSACHUSETTS INSTITUTE OF TECHNOLOGY, PROJECT MAC. (1973).

HESS 1977 -1 HESSELBACH, J.; WIJNANDS, J.
DYNAMISCHE PROGRAMMIERUNG - METHODIK, EDV-PROGRAMM, ANWENDUNGSBEISPIEL. BAD KREUZNACH: MAX-PLANCK-INSTITUT FUER LANDARBEIT UND LANDTECHNIK, 67 P. (1977). (ARBEITEN AUS DEM MAX-PLANCK-INSTITUT FUER LANDARBEIT UND LANDTECHNIK, HEFT A-77/1)

HETY 1974 -1 HETYEI, G.
ON SUBGRAPHS OF J-COLORABLE GRAPHS (HUNGARIAN). ACTA ACADEMIAE PAEDAGOGICAE IN CIVITATE PECS. SERIA 6. MATHEMATICA-PHYSICA-CHEMICA-TECHNICA 18, 3-12. (1974).

HETY 1975 -1 HETYEI, G.
ON THE 1-FACTORS AND THE HAMILTONIAN CIRCUITS OF COMPLETE N-COLORABLE GRAPHS (HUNGARIAN). ACTA ACADEMIAE PAEDAGOGICAE IN CIVITATE PECS. SERIA 6. MATHEMATICA-PHYSICA-CHEMICA-TECHNICA 19, 5-10. (1975).

HEYD 1980 -1 HEYDEMANN, M. C.
ON CYCLES AND PATHS IN DIGRAPHS. DISCRETE MATHEMATICS 31, 217-219. (1980).

HILL 1978 -1 HILL, E. JR.
COMPARATIVE STUDY OF VERY LARGE DATA BASES, A. BERLIN, HEIDELBERG, NEW YORK: SPRINGER, 140 P. (1978). (LECTURE NOTES IN COMPUTER SCIENCE, 59)

HILLA 1977 -1 HILLIER, F. S.
FURTHER INVESTIGATION OF EFFICIENT HEURISTIC PROCEDURES FOR INTEGER LINEAR PROGRAMMING WITH AN INTERIOR, A. TECHNICAL REPORT NO. 72. STANFORD: STANFORD UNIV., DEPT. OF OPERATIONS RESEARCH, 61 P. (1977).

HILLB 1979 -1 HILLIER, F. S.; BOLING, R. W.
ON THE OPTIMAL ALLOCATION OF WORK IN SYMMETRICALLY UNBALANCED PRODUCTION LINE SYSTEMS WITH VARIABLE OPERATING TIMES. MANAGEMENT SCIENCE 25, 721-728. (1979).

HILT 1975 -1 HILTON, A. J. W.
NOTE ON EDGE-COLOURING MULTIGRAPHS, A. IN: M. FIEDLER (ED.): ADVANCES IN GRAPH THEORY, 267-271. PRAGUE: ACADEMIA. (1975).

HILT 1977 -1 HILTON, A. J. W.
DEFINITIONS OF CRITICALITY WITH RESPECT TO EDGE-COLOURING. JOURNAL OF GRAPH THEORY 1, 61-68. (1977).

HILT 1977 -2 HILTON, A. J. W.
EMBEDDING INCOMPLETE LATIN RECTANGLES AND EXTENDING THE EDGE COLOURINGS OF GRAPHS. NANTA MATHEMATICA 10, NO. 2, 201-206. (1977).

HILT 1978 -1 HILTON, A. J. W.
DIMENSION IN LINEAR SPACES. IN: J.-C. BERMOND ET AL. (EDS.): PROBLEMES COMBINATOIRES ET THEORIE DES GRAPHES, COLLOQUES INTERNATIONAUX DU CENTRE NATIONAL DE LA RECHERCHE SCIENTIFIQUE, ORSAY 1976, 233-236. PARIS: CENTRE NATIONAL DE LA RECHERCHE SCIENTIFIQUE. (1978).

HIME 1974 -1 HIMELWRIGHT, P. E.; WILLIAMSON, J. E.
ON 1-FACTORABILITY AND EDGE-COLORABILITY OF CARTESIAN PRODUCTS OF GRAPHS. ELEMENTE DER MATHEMATIK 29, 66-67. (1974).

HIND 1979 -1 HINDELANG, T. J.; MUTH, J. F.
DYNAMIC PROGRAMMING ALGORITHM FOR DECISION CPM NETWORKS, A. OPERATIONS RESEARCH 27, 225-241. (1979).

HINDA 1977 -1 HINDERER, K.; HUEBNER, G.
IMPROVEMENT OF J. F. SHAPIRO'S TURNPIKE THEOREM FOR THE HORIZON OF FINITE STAGE DISCRETE DYNAMIC PROGRAMS, AN. IN: INFORMATION THEORY, STATISTICAL DECISION FUNCTIONS, RANDOM PROCESSES; TRANS. 7TH PRAGUE CONF., VOL. A, PRAGUE 1974, 245-257. (1977).

HINDB 1978 -1 HINDI, K. S.; BRAMELLER, A.; HAMAM, K. M.
SOLUTION OF FIXED COST TRANS-SHIPMENT PROBLEMS BY A BRANCH AND BOUND METHOD. INTERNATIONAL JOURNAL FOR NUMERICAL METHODS IN ENGINEERING 12, NO. 5, 837-851. (1978).

HINE 1978 -1 HINE, J. H.
SCHEDULING SEVERAL CLASSES OF JOBS IN A NETWORK OF SERVERS. IN: PROCEEDINGS OF THE 14TH ANNUAL CONFERENCE OF THE OPERATIONAL RESEARCH SOCIETY OF NEW ZEALAND - THEORY, 49-60. (1978).

****

HINT 1976 -1 HINTEREGGER, J.
VERBESSERTES VERFAHREN ZUR FESTSTELLUNG DER ISOMORPHIE ENDLICHER GRAPHEN, EIN. DISSERTATION. INNSBRUCK: UNIVERSITAET INNSBRUCK, INSTITUT FUER INFORMATIK UND NUMERISCHE MATHEMATIK. (1976).

HINX 1980 -1 HINXMAN, A. I.
TRIM-LOSS AND ASSORTMENT PROBLEMS: A SURVEY, THE. EUROPEAN JOURNAL OF OPERATIONAL RESEARCH 5, 8-18. (1980).

HIRA 1979 -1 HIRATA, T.; MAROUOKA, A.; KIMURA, M.
POLYNOMIAL TIME ALGORITHM TO FIND A PATH COVER OF A REDUCIBLE FLOW GRAPH (JAPANESE), A. TRANSACTIONS OF THE INSTITUTE OF ELECTRONICS AND COMMUNICATION ENGINEERS OF JAPAN (TOKYO) J62-D, NO. 6, 411-418. (1979).

HIRS 1978 -1 HIRSCHBERG, D. S.
FAST PARALLEL SORTING ALGORITHMS. COMMUNICATIONS OF THE ASSOCIATION FOR COMPUTING MACHINERY 21, 657-661. (1978).

HIRSA 1979 -1 HIRSCHBERG, D. S.; WONG, C. K.
UPPER AND LOWER BOUNDS FOR GRAPH-DIAMETER PROBLEMS WITH APPLICATION TO RECORD ALLOCATION. JOURNAL OF COMBINATORIAL THEORY 26, SERIES B, 66-74. (1979).

HITC 1968 -1 HITCHNER, L. E.
COMPARATIVE INVESTIGATION OF THE COMPUTATIONAL EFFICIENCY OF SHORTEST PATH ALGORITHMS, A. REPORT ORC 68-25. BERKELEY: UNIV. OF CALIFORNIA, OPERATIONS RESEARCH CENTER. (1968).

HO 1979 -1 HO, A. C.
WORST CASE ANALYSIS OF A CLASS OF SET COVERING HEURISTICS. RESEARCH REPORT 473. PITTSBURGH: CARNEGIE-MELLON UNIV., MANAGEMENT SCIENCE RESEARCH GROUP, 17 P. (1979).

HO A 1980 -1 HO, Y. C.; SERVI, L.; SURI, R.
CLASS OF CENTER-FREE RESOURCE ALLOCATION ALGORITHMS, A. LARGE SCALE SYSTEMS 1, NO. 1, 51-62. (1980).

HOAN 1978 -1 HOANG HAI HOC
SOLVING AN INTEGER PROGRAMMING PROBLEM. IN: J. STOER (ED.): OPTIMIZATION TECHNIQUES, PROCEEDINGS OF THE 8TH IFIP CONFERENCE ON OPTIMIZATION TECHNIQUES, WUERZBURG 1977, PART 2, 209-215. LECTURE NOTES IN CONTROL AND INFORMATION SCIENCES 7. BERLIN, HEIDELBERG, NEW YORK: SPRINGER. (1978).

HOAN 1979 -1 HOANG HAI HOC
NETWORK IMPROVEMENTS VIA MATHEMATICAL PROGRAMMING. IN: A. PREKOPA (ED.): SURVEY OF MATHEMATICAL PROGRAMMING, VOLUME 2, 245-262. AMSTERDAM: NORTH-HOLLAND. (1979).

HOBB 1979 -1 HOBBS, A. M.
HAMILTONIAN SQUARES OF CACTI. JOURNAL OF COMBINATORIAL THEORY 26, SERIES B, 50-65. (1979).

HOBB 1979 -2 HOBBS, A. M.
J-COMPONENTS, BRIDGES, AND J-FRAGMENTS. IN: J. A. BONDY, U. P. R. MURTY (EDS.): GRAPH THEORY AND RELATED TOPICS, 253-260. NEW YORK, SAN FRANCISCO, LONDON: ACADEMIC PRESS. (1979).

HOBB 1979 -3 HOBBS, A. M.
MAXIMAL HAMILTONIAN CYCLES IN SQUARES OF GRAPHS. JOURNAL OF COMBINATORIAL THEORY 26, SERIES B, 35-49. (1979).

HOCH 1979 -1 HOCHBAUM, D.
ESTABLISHING A RELATIONSHIP BETWEEN SOME HARD PROBLEMS. WORKING PAPER 67-78-79. PITTSBURGH: CARNEGIE-MELLON UNIV., GRADUATE SCHOOL OF INDUSTRIAL ADMINISTRATION, 23 P. (1979).

HOCH 1979 -2 HOCHBAUM, D.
HEURISTICS FOR THE FIXED COST MEDIAN PROBLEM. WORKING PAPER 55-78-79. PITTSBURGH: CARNEGIE-MELLON UNIV., GRADUATE SCHOOL OF INDUSTRIAL ADMINISTRATION, 24 P. (1979).

HOCH 1979 -3 HOCHBAUM, D.
PROBABILISTIC ASYMPTOTIC PROPERTIES OF SOME COMBINATORIAL GEOMETRIC PROBLEMS, THE. WORKING PAPER 30-79-80. PITTSBURGH: CARNEGIE-MELLON UNIV., GRADUATE SCHOOL OF INDUSTRIAL ADMINISTRATION, 38 P. (1979).

HOCH 1980 -1 HOCHBAUM, D.
APPROXIMATION ALGORITHMS FOR THE WEIGHTED SET COVERING AND NODE COVER PROBLEMS. WORKING PAPER 64-79-80. PITTSBURGH: CARNEGIE-MELLON UNIV., GRADUATE SCHOOL OF INDUSTRIAL ADMINISTRATION, 21 P. (1980).

HOCH 1980 -2 HOCHBAUM, D.
FAST APPROXIMATION ALGORITHMS FOR SOME INTEGER PROGRAMMING PROBLEMS. WORKING PAPER 21-80-81. PITTSBURGH: CARNEGIE-MELLON UNIV., GRADUATE SCHOOL OF INDUSTRIAL ADMINISTRATION, 30 P. (1980).

HODG 1978 -1 HODGSON, M. J.
TOWARD MORE REALISTIC ALLOCATION IN LOCATION-ALLOCATION MODELS: AN INTERACTION APPROACH. ENVIRONMENT AND PLANNING 10, SERIES A, 1273-1285. (1978).

HODG 1981 -1 HODGSON, M. J.
LOCATION OF PUBLIC FACILITIES INTERMEDIATE TO THE JOURNEY TO WORK, THE. EUROPEAN JOURNAL OF OPERATIONAL RESEARCH 6, 199-204. (1981).

HODZ 1978 -1 HODZAEV, F. Z.
PROBLEM OF SPECIFYING ASSEMBLY PROCEDURES IN A MACHINE SHOP (RUSSIAN), THE. VOPROSY KIBERNETIKI (TASHKENT) NO. 102, 46-56, 158-159. (1978).

HODZA 1978 -1 HODZINSKII, A. N.
RESULTS OF A COMPUTER EXPERIMENT IN SOLVING A TYPE OF PROBLEM IN SCHEDULING THEORY BY THE BRANCH AND BOUND METHOD AND THE DROP VECTOR METHOD (RUSSIAN). IN: PROCESSING OF SOFTWARE AND HARDWARE FOR AUTOMATIC CONTROL SYSTEMS, 17-24. KIEV: AKADEMIJA NAUK UKRAINSKOI SSR, INSTITUT KIBERNETIKI. (1978).

HOED 1978 -1 HOEDE, C.
ON CHARACTERIZATION OF HAMILTONIAN GRAPHS. IN: A. HAJNAL, V. T. SOS (EDS.): COMBINATORICS, VOLUME I, 583-592. COLLOQUIA MATHEMATICA SOCIETATIS JANOS BOLYAI 18. AMSTERDAM: NORTH-HOLLAND. (1978).

HOED 1979 -1 HOEDE, C.
ZWIEBELSTRUKTUREN EINIGER KLASSEN VON KOMBINATORISCHEN UND GRAPHENTHEORETISCHEN PROBLEMEN, DIE. IN: L. COLLATZ, G. MEINARDUS, W. WETTERLING (EDS.): NUMERISCHE METHODEN BEI GRAPHENTHEORETISCHEN UND KOMBINATORISCHEN PROBLEMEN, BAND 2, OBERWOLFACH 1978, 135-161. ISNM 46. BASEL, BOSTON, STUTTGART: BIRKHAEUSER. (1979).

HOEDA 1981 -1 HOEDE, C.; VELDMAN, H. J.
CONTRACTION THEOREMS IN HAMILTONIAN GRAPH THEORY. DISCRETE MATHEMATICS 34, 61-68. (1981).

HOEN 1979 -1 HOENEMANN, F.
STRUKTURIERUNG DISKONTINUIERLICH DISKRETER PROZESSE. WISSENSCHAFTLICHE ZEITSCHRIFT DER UNIVERSITAET DRESDEN 28, 379-381. (1979).

HOENA 1979 -1 HOENERLOH, H.
LOESUNG DES EINFACHEN MASCHINENBELEGUNGSPROBLEMS (FLOW SHOP SCHEDULING PROBLEM) MIT EINEM SPEZIELLEN RECHNER, DIE. IN: W. OETTLI, F. STEFFENS (EDS.): OPERATIONS RESEARCH VERFAHREN 35, THIRD SYMPOSIUM ON OPERATIONS RESEARCH, MANNHEIM 1978, 199-209. KOENIGSTEIN: ANTON HAIN MEISENHEIM. (1979).

HOFF 1978 -1 HOFFMAN, A. J.
ON LATTICE POLYHEDRA III: BLOCKERS AND ANTI-BLOCKERS OF LATTICE CLUTTERS. MATHEMATICAL PROGRAMMING STUDY 8, 197-207. (1978).

HOFF 1979 -1 HOFFMAN, A. J.
ROLE OF UNIMODULARITY IN APPLYING LINEAR INEQUALITIES TO COMBINATORIAL THEOREMS, THE. IN: P. L. HAMMER, E. L. JOHNSON, B. H. KORTE (EDS.): DISCRETE OPTIMIZATION I, 73-84. ANNALS OF DISCRETE MATHEMATICS 4. AMSTERDAM, NEW YORK, OXFORD: NORTH-HOLLAND. (1979).

HOFFA 1970 -1 HOFFMAN, A. J.; HOWES, L.
ON EIGENVALUES AND COLORINGS OF GRAPHS, II. IN: A. GEWIRTZ, L. V. QUINTAS (EDS.): INTERNATIONAL CONFERENCE ON COMBINATORIAL MATHEMATICS, 238-242. ANNALS OF THE NEW YORK ACADEMY OF SCIENCES, VOLUME 165, ARTICLE 1. NEW YORK: THE NEW YORK ACADEMY OF SCIENCES. (1970).

HOFR 1980 -1 HOFRI, M.
TWO-DIMENSIONAL PACKING: EXPECTED PERFORMANCE OF SIMPLE LEVEL ALGORITHMS. INFORMATION AND CONTROL 45, 1-17. (1980).

HOLL 1972 -1 HOLLOWAY, C. A.; NELSON, R. T.
INTERACTIVE PROGRAM FOR THE JOB SHOP SCHEDULING PROBLEM WITH DUE DATES, AN. TECHNICAL REPORT NO. 22. STANFORD: STANFORD UNIVERSITY, GRADUATE SCHOOL FOR BUSINESS. (1972).

HOLM 1978 -1 HOLM, S.; KLEIN, D.
NONTRIVIAL METHODS FOR POSTOPTIMAL ANALYSIS IN INTEGER LINEAR PROGRAMMING. TECHNICAL REPORT NO. 3/1978. ODENSE: ODENSE UNIVERSITY, BUSINESS ADMINISTRATION, 24 P. (1978).

HOLMA 1976 -1 HOLMBERG, G.
EXTENSIONS OF THE METHOD SUGGESTED BY GILMORE AND GOMORY FOR SOLVING CUTTING STOCK PROBLEMS. UTM-PM NR. 30. STOCKHOLM: ROYAL INST. OF TECHNOLOGY, INST. OF APPLIED MATHEMATICS, 13 P. (1976).

HOLS 1979 -1 HOLST, O.
ACCESSIBILITY AS THE OBJECTIVE OF PUBLIC TRANSPORTATION PLANNING: AN INTEGRATED TRANSPORTATION AND LAND USE MODEL. EUROPEAN JOURNAL OF OPERATIONAL RESEARCH 3, 267-282. (1979).

HOLY 1979 -1 HOLYER, I. J.; COCKAYNE, E. J.
ON THE SUM OF CARDINALITIES OF EXTREMUM MAXIMAL INDEPENDENT SETS. DISCRETE MATHEMATICS 26, 243-246. (1979).

HOME 1977 -1 HOMENKO, N. P.; LYSENKO, N. V.
NECESSARY AND SUFFICIENT CONDITIONS FOR N-COLORINGS OF GRAPHS (RUSSIAN). IN: N. P. HOMENKO (ED.): GRAPH THEORY, 107-114. KIEV: IZDANIE INST. MAT., AKAD. NAUK UKRAIN. SSR. (1977).

HOMEA 1976 -1 HOMENKO, N. P.; VIVROT, T. M.
(0,1)-MATRICES (RUSSIAN). DOKLADY AKADEMIJA NAUK UKRAINSKOI SSR SERIJA A, NO. 10, 887-890, 960. (1976).

HOMEB 1977 -1 HOMENKO, N. P.; VYVROT, T. M.
PROPERTIES OF THE MATRIX OF INDEPENDENT CYCLES OF A GRAPH (RUSSIAN). IN: N. P. HOMENKO (ED.): GRAPH THEORY, 202-209. KIEV: IZDANIE INST. MAT., AKAD. NAUK UKRAIN. SSR. (1977).

HONG 1979 -1 HONG, J. W.
ON LOWER BOUNDS OF TIME COMPLEXITY OF SOME ALGORITHMS. SCIENTIA SINICA 22, 890-900. (1979).

HONGA 1977 -1 HONG, S.; PADBERG, M. W.
ON THE SOLUTION OF TRAVELLING SALESMAN PROBLEMS. GBA WORKING PAPER, NEW YORK. (1977).

HORA 1979 -1 HORAK, P.
DIGRAPHS MAXIMAL WITH RESPECT TO CONNECTIVITY. MATHEMATICA SLOVACA (BRATISLAVA) 29, 87-90. (1979).

HORAA 1979 -1 HORAK, P.; TOVAREK, L.
ON HAMILTONIAN CYCLES OF COMPLETE N-PARTITE GRAPHS. MATHEMATICA SLOVACA 29, NO. 1, 43-47. (1979).

HORAB 1978 -1 HORAK, V.
PRACTICAL APPLICATION OF, AND CONSTRUCTION OF ALGORITHMS FOR FINITE LABELLED TREES (CZECHOSLOVAKIAN). EKONOMICKO-MATEMATICKY OBZOR 14, NO. 1, 53-71. (1978).

HORN 1980 -1 HORNE, G. J.
FINDING THE K LEAST COST PATHS IN AN ACYCLIC ACTIVITY NETWORK. JOURNAL OF THE OPERATIONAL RESEARCH SOCIETY 31, 443-448. (1980).

HORO 1978 -1 HOROWITZ, E.; SAHNI, S.
FUNDAMENTALS OF COMPUTER ALGORITHMS. POTOMAC: COMPUTER SCIENCE PRESS. (1978).

HORS 1980 -1 HORST, R.
MAXIMALE FLUESSE IN NETZWERKEN MIT KANTENGEWINNEN: VERGLEICH DREIER ALGORITHMEN. ANGEWANDTE INFORMATIK, NO. 3, 116-118. (1980).

HOSI 1980 -1 HOSIOS, A. J.; ROUSSEAU, J.-M.
HEURISTIC SCHEDULING ALGORITHM, A. JOURNAL OF THE OPERATIONAL RESEARCH SOCIETY 31, 749-754. (1980).

HOUC 1977 -1 HOUCK, D. J.; PICARD, J.-C.; QUEYRANNE, M.; VEMUGANTI, R. R.
TRAVELLING SALESMAN PROBLEM AND SHORTEST N-PATHS, THE. COLLEGE PARK: UNIVERSITY OF MARYLAND. (1977).

HOUC 1980 -1 HOUCK, D. J.; PICARD, J.-C.; QUEYRANNE, M.; VEMUGANTI, R. R.
TRAVELLING SALESMAN PROBLEM AS A CONSTRAINED SHORTEST PATH PROBLEM: THEORY AND COMPUTATIONAL EXPERIENCE, THE. OPSEARCH 17, 93-109. (1980).

HOUCA 1979 -1 HOUCK, D. J.; PITTENGER, A. O.
ANALYTIC PROOFS OF A NETWORK FEASIBILITY THEOREM AND A THEOREM OF FULKERSON. LINEAR ALGEBRA AND ITS APPLICATIONS 24, 151-156. (1979).

HOWO 1979 -1 HOWORKA, E.
ON METRIC PROPERTIES OF CERTAIN CLIQUE GRAPHS. JOURNAL OF COMBINATORIAL THEORY 27, SERIES B, 67-74. (1979).

HRAM 1979 -1 HRAMOVA, N. K.
SOME GENERALIZATIONS OF THE CUTTING PLANE METHOD (RUSSIAN). VESTNIK LENINGRADSKOGO UNIVERSITETA. MATEMATIKA, MEHANIKA, ASTRONOMIJA 2, 116-117 + 122. (1979).

HSU 1980 -1 HSU, C.; WILHELM, W. E.
FLOW SHOP SEQUENCING WITH PROBABILISTIC PROCESSING TIMES. WORKING PAPER SERIES NO. 1980-003. COLUMBUS: OHIO STATE UNIV., DEPT. OF INDUSTRIAL AND SYSTEMS ENGINEERING, 22 P. (1980).

HSU A 1979 -1 HSU, W.-L.
HOW TO COLOR CLAW-FREE PERFECT GRAPHS. TECHNICAL REPORT NO. 435. ITHACA: CORNELL UNIV., SCHOOL OF OPERATIONS RESEARCH, 12 P. (1979).

HSU A 1980 -1 HSU, W.-L.
ON THE GENERAL FEASIBILITY TEST OF SCHEDULING LOT SIZES FOR SEVERAL PRODUCTS ON ONE MACHINE. RESEARCH REPORT 8017. LOUVAIN: CENTER FOR OPERATIONS RESEARCH AND ECONOMETRICS (CORE), 23 P. (1980).

HSU B 1979 -1 HSU, W.-L.; NEMHAUSER, G. L.
ALGORITHMS FOR MINIMUM COVERINGS BY CLIQUES AND MAXIMUM CLIQUES IN CLAW-FREE PERFECT GRAPHS. TECHNICAL REPORT NO. 418. ITHACA: CORNELL UNIV. SCHOOL OF OPERATIONS RESEARCH, 17 P. (1979).

HSU B 1979 -2 HSU, W.-L.; NEMHAUSER, G. L.
EASY AND HARD BOTTLENECK LOCATION PROBLEMS. DISCRETE APPLIED MATHEMATICS 1, 209-215. (1979).

HU 1979 -1 HU, T. C.; KLEITMAN, D. J.; TAMAKI, J. K.
BINARY TREES OPTIMUM UNDER VARIOUS CRITERIA. SIAM JOURNAL ON APPLIED MATHEMATICS 37, 246-256. (1979).

HU A 1980 -1 HU, T. C.; RUSKEY, F.
CIRCULAR CUTS IN A NETWORK. MATHEMATICS OF OPERATIONS RESEARCH 5, 422-434. (1980).
HUAN 1976 -1 HUANG, H.-C.
INVESTIGATIONS ON COMBINATORIAL OPTIMIZATION. DISSERTATION. TECHNICAL REPORT NO. 308. ITHACA: CORNELL UNIVERSITY, DEPARTMENT OF OPERATIONS RESEARCH. (1976).
HUANA 1980 -1 HUANG, H.-C.; TROTTER, L. E. JR.
TECHNIQUE FOR DETERMINING BLOCKING AND ANTIBLOCKING POLYHEDRAL DESCRIPTIONS, A. MATHEMATICAL PROGRAMMING STUDY 12, 197-205. (1980).
HUCK 1980 -1 HUCKERT, K.
ZUR ANWENDUNG DER BENDERSSCHEN PARTITIONSMETHODE AUF JOB-SHOP-PROBLEME. IN: H. KOENIG, V. STEINMETZ (EDS.): METHODS OF OPERATIONS RESEARCH 38, 329-344. KOENIGSTEIN: ANTON HAIN MEISENHEIM. (1980).
HUCKA 1980 -1 HUCKERT, K.; RHODE, R.; ROGLIN, O.; WEBER, R.
ON THE INTERACTIVE SOLUTION TO A MULTICRITERIA SCHEDULING PROBLEM. ZEITSCHRIFT FUER OPERATIONS RESEARCH 24, SERIES A, 47-60. (1980).
HUDS 1977 -1 HUDSON, P. D.
IMPROVING THE BRANCH AND BOUND ALGORITHMS FOR THE KNAPSACK PROBLEM. RESEARCH REPORT. BELFAST: QUEEN'S UNIVERSITY. (1977).
HUET 1978 -1 HUET, G.
ALGORITHM TO GENERATE THE BASIS OF SOLUTIONS TO HOMOGENEOUS LINEAR DIOPHANTINE EQUATIONS, AN. RAPPORT DE RECHERCHE NO. 274. LE CHESNAY: INSTITUT DE RECHERCHE D'INFORMATIQUE ET D'AUTOMATIQUE, 10 P. (1978).
HULM 1978 -1 HULME, B.; WISNIEWSKI, J. A.
COMPARISON OF SHORTEST PATH ALGORITHMS APPPLIED TO SPARSE GRAPHS, A. SAND 78-1411. ALBUQUERQUE: SANDIA LABORATORIES, 43 P. (1978).
HULT 1978 -1 HULTZ, J.; KLINGMAN, D.
SOLVING SINGULARLY CONSTRAINED GENERALIZED NETWORK PROBLEMS. APPLIED MATHEMATICS AND OPTIMIZATION 4, NO. 2, 103-119. (1978).
HUNG 1980 -1 HUNG, M. S.; ROM, W. O.
SOLVING THE ASSIGNMENT PROBLEM BY RELAXATION. OPERATIONS RESEARCH 28, 969-982. (1980).
HURR 1980 -1 HURRION, R. D.
VISUAL INTERACTIVE (COMPUTER) SOLUTIONS FOR THE TRAVELLING SALESMAN PROBLEM. JOURNAL OF THE OPERATIONAL RESEARCH SOCIETY 31, 537-540. (1980).
HWAN 1978 -1 HWANG, F. K.
RECTILINEAR STEINER PROBLEM, THE. JOURNAL OF DESIGN AUTOMATION AND FAULT-TOLERANT COMPUTING 2, NO. 4, 303-310. (1978).
HWAN 1979 -1 HWANG, F. K.
O(N LOG N) ALGORITHM FOR RECTILINEAR MINIMAL SPANNING TREES, AN. JOURNAL OF THE ASSOCIATION FOR COMPUTING MACHINERY 26, 177-182. (1979).
HWANA 1978 -1 HWANG, J. S.
COMPLETE UNISEXUAL STABLE MARRIAGES. SOOCHOW JOURNAL OF MATHEMATICS AND NATURAL SCIENCES 4, 149-151. (1978).
HWANB 1977 -1 HWANG, J. S.; SHYR, H. J.
COMPLETE STABLE MARRIAGES. SOOCHOW JOURNAL OF MATHEMATICAL AND NATURAL SCIENCES 3, 41-51. (1977).
IBAR 1977 -1 IBARAKI, T.
ON THE COMPUTATIONAL EFFICIENCY OF BRANCH-AND-BOUND ALGORITHMS. JOURNAL OF THE OPERATIONS RESEARCH SOCIETY OF JAPAN 20, 16-35. (1977).
IBAR 1978 -1 IBARAKI, T.
BRANCH-AND-BOUND PROCEDURE AND STATE-SPACE REPRESENTATION OF COMBINATORIAL OPTIMIZATION PROBLEMS. INFORMATION AND CONTROL 36, 1-27. (1978).
IBAR 1978 -2 IBARAKI, T.
DEPTH-M SEARCH IN BRANCH-AND-BOUND ALGORITHMS. INTERNATIONAL JOURNAL OF COMPUTER AND INFORMATION SCIENCES 7, NO. 4, 315-344. (1978).
IBAR 1979 -1 IBARAKI, T.
THEORETICAL AND SIMULATION STUDIES ON COMPUTATIONAL PERFORMANCE OF BRANCH-AND-BOUND ALGORITHMS. IN: A. PREKOPA (ED.): SURVEY OF MATHEMATICAL PROGRAMMING, VOLUME 2, 505-524. AMSTERDAM: NORTH-HOLLAND. (1979).
IBAR 1980 -1 IBARAKI, T.
APPROXIMATE ALGORITHMS FOR THE MULTIPLE-CHOICE CONTINUOUS KNAPSACK PROBLEMS. JOURNAL OF THE OPERATIONS RESEARCH SOCIETY OF JAPAN 23, 28-63. (1980).
IBAR 1980 -2 IBARAKI, T.
NUMBER OF ADDITIONAL VARIABLES REQUIRED FOR THE INTEGER PROGRAMMING FORMULATION, THE. DISCRETE APPLIED MATHEMATICS 2, 155-158. (1980).
IBARA 1978 -1 IBARAKI, T.; HASEGAWA, T.; TERANAKA, K.; IWASE, J.
MULTIPLE-CHOICE KNAPSACK PROBLEM, THE. JOURNAL OF THE OPERATIONS RESEARCH SOCIETY OF JAPAN 21, 59-95. (1978).
IBARB 1976 -1 IBARAKI, T.; ISHII, H.; MINE, H.
ASSIGNMENT PROBLEM ON A NETWORK, AN. JOURNAL OF THE OPERATIONS RESEARCH SOCIETY OF JAPAN 19, 70-90. (1976).
IBARC 1978 -1 IBARAKI, T.; PELED, U. N.
SUFFICIENT CONDITIONS FOR GRAPHS WITH THRESHOLD NUMBER 2. KYOTO: KYOTO UNIVERSITY, DEPT. OF APPLIED MATHEMATICS AND PHYSICS, 48 P. (1978).
IBARD 1975 -1 IBARRA, O. H.; KIM, C. E.
SCHEDULING FOR MAXIMUM PROFIT. TECHNICAL REPORT. MINNEAPOLIS: UNIVERSITY OF MINNESOTA, COMPUTER SCIENCE DEPARTMENT. (1975).
ICHI 1979 -1 ICHIMORI, T.; ISHII, H.; NISHIDA, T.
MINIMAX FLOW PROBLEM, A. MATHEMATICA JAPONICAE 24, 65-71. (1979).
ICHI 1980 -1 ICHIMORI, T.; ISHII, H.; NISHIDA, T.
FINDING THE WEIGHTED MINIMAX FLOW IN A POLYNOMIAL TIME. JOURNAL OF THE OPERATIONS RESEARCH SOCIETY OF JAPAN 23, 268-271. (1980).
ICHI 1980 -2 ICHIMORI, T.; ISHII, H.; NISHIDA, T.
FLOW IN A NETWORK WITH A CHECK NODE. JOURNAL OF THE OPERATIONS RESEARCH SOCIETY OF JAPAN 23, 111-117. (1980).
ICHI 1981 -1 ICHIMORI, T.; ISHII, H.; NISHIDA, T.
WEIGHTED MINIMAX REAL-VALUED FLOWS. JOURNAL OF THE OPERATIONS RESEARCH SOCIETY OF JAPAN 24, 52-60. (1981).
ICHIA 1981 -1 ICHIMORI, T.; SHIODE, S.; ISHII, H.; NISHIDA, T.
MINIMUM SPANNING TREE WITH NORMAL VARIATES AS WEIGHTS. JOURNAL OF THE OPERATIONS RESEARCH SOCIETY OF JAPAN 24, 61-66. (1981).
IGEL 1979 -1 IGELMUND, G.; RADERMACHER, F. J.
PRESELECTIVE STRATEGIES FOR THE OPTIMIZATION OF STOCHASTIC PROJECT NETWORKS UNDER RESOURCE CONSTRAINTS (ABSTRACT). IN: W. OETTLI, F. STEFFENS (EDS.): OPERATIONS RESEARCH VERFAHREN 32. THIRD SYMPOSIUM ON OPERATIONS RESEARCH, MANNHEIM 1978, 149-150. KOENIGSTEIN: ANTON HAIN MEISENHEIM. (1979).

IGNI 1978 -1 IGNIZIO, J. P.
SOLVING LARGE SCHEDULING PROBLEMS BY MINIMIZING CONFLICT. SIMULATION 30, NO. 3, 75-79. (1978).

IKRA 1975 -1 IKRAM, M.
ON CERTAIN NEW TERMS IN SEQUENCING THEORY AND ON ALTERNATIVE OPTIMAL SEQUENCES. PURE AND APPLIED MATHEMATICAL SCIENCES 2, NO. 1, 45-50. (1975).

ILNI 1979 -1 ILNITSKIJ, A. I.
ESTIMATION OF THE TARGET FUNCTION OF A DISCRETE PROBLEM OF SCHEDULING THEORY (RUSSIAN). KIEVSKII GOSUDARSTVENNYI UNIVERSITET. ISSLEDOVANIE OPERACII ASU, NO. 13, 54-59 + 134. (1979).

IMAI 1979 -1 IMAI, M.
PARALLELIZED BRANCH AND BOUND ALGORITHM - IMPLEMENTATION AND EFFICIENCY (JAPANESE), A. TRANSACTIONS OF THE INSTITUTE OF ELECTRONICS AND COMMUNICATIONS ENGINEERS OF JAPAN (TOKYO) J62-D, NO. 6, 403-410. (1979).

INFA 1978 -1 INFANTE MACIAS, R.; PASCUAL ACOSTA, A.
SOME VARIATIONS OF THE VARIABLE DURATION PROBLEM (SPANISH). TRABAJOS DE ESTADISTICA Y DE INVESTIGACION OPERATIVA (MADRID) 29, NO. 1, 67-76. (1978).

INFAA 1979 -1 INFANTE MACIAS, R.; VARGAS GONZALEZ, L.
ESTIMATES OF THE RESOURCE REQUIREMENTS IN NETWORK OPTIMIZATION PROBLEMS. IN: E. ALARCON, C. A. BREBBIA (EDS.): APPLIED NUMERICAL MODELLING, 601-610. LONDON: PENTECH PRESS. (1979).

INST 1976 -1 INST. PROBL. UPR. (ED.).
SCHEDULING PROBLEMS IN DISCRETE PRODUCTION AND NUMERICAL SOLUTION METHODS (RUSSIAN). MOSCOW, 61 P. (1976).

INSTA 1978 -1 INSTITUT FUER OEKONOMETRIE & OPERATIONS RESEARCH
WORKSHOP ON COMBINATORIAL OPTIMIZATION. BONN, SEPTEMBER 11-13, 1978. ABSTRACTS. RESEARCH REPORT NO. 78115-OR. BONN: UNIV. BONN, INSTITUT FUER OEKONOMETRIE UND OPERATIONS RESEARCH, ABT. OPERATIONS RESEARCH, 29 P. (1978).

INSTA 1980 -1 INSTITUT FUER OEKONOMETRIE & OPERATIONS RESEARCH
IV. WORKSHOP ON COMBINATORIAL OPTIMIZATION. BONN, AUGUST 28-30, 1980. ABSTRACTS. RESEARCH REPORT NO. 80159-OR. BONN: UNIV. BONN, INSTITUT FUER OEKONOMETRIE UND OPERATIONS RESEARCH, ABT. OPERATIONS RESEARCH, 37 P. (1980).

INTR 1980 -1 INTRATOR, J.; BERREBI, M.
AUXILIARY PROCEDURES FOR SOLVING LONG TRANSPORTATION PROBLEMS. NAVAL RESEARCH LOGISTICS QUARTERLY 27, 447-452. (1980).

INTRA 1980 -1 INTRATOR, J.; ENGELBERG, A.
SENSITIVITY ANALYSIS AS A MEANS OF REDUCING THE DIMENSIONALITY OF A CERTAIN CLASS OF TRANSPORTATION PROBLEMS. NAVAL RESEARCH LOGISTICS QUARTERLY 27, 297-313. (1980).

INTRB 1978 -1 INTRATOR, J.; PAROUSH, J.
IMPROVING LOOPS AND VANISHING VARIABLES IN LONG TRANSPORTATION PROBLEMS. COMPUTERS AND OPERATIONS RESEARCH 5, 123-128. (1978).

INUK 1979 -1 INUKAI, T.; WEINBERG, L.
GRAPH-REALIZABILITY OF MATROIDS. IN: A. GEWIRTZ, L. V. QUINTAS (EDS.): SECOND INTERNATIONAL CONFERENCE ON COMBINATORIAL MATHEMATICS, 289-305. ANNALS OF THE NEW YORK ACADEMY OF SCIENCES, VOLUME 319. NEW YORK: THE NEW YORK ACADEMY OF SCIENCES. (1979).

IOSL 1978 -1 IOSLOVIC, I. V.; ROZNOVA, O. V.
MATHEMATICAL MODELS FOR THE CHOICE OF SHIPLOAD IN AVIATION TRANSPORT (RUSSIAN). IZVESTIJA AKADEMII NAUK SSSR. TEHNICESKAJA KIBERNETIKA, NO. 3, 45-51. (1978).

IRI 1978 -1 IRI, M.
PRACTICAL ALGORITHM FOR THE MENGER-TYPE GENERALIZATION OF THE INDEPENDENT ASSIGNMENT PROBLEM, A. MATHEMATICAL PROGRAMMING STUDY 8, 88-105. (1978).

IRI 1979 -1 IRI, M.
REVIEW OF RECENT WORK IN JAPAN ON PRINCIPAL PARTITIONS OF MATROIDS AND THEIR APPLICATIONS, A. IN: A. GEWIRTZ, L. V. QUINTAS (EDS.): SECOND INTERNATIONAL CONFERENCE ON COMBINATORIAL MATHEMATICS, 306-319. ANNALS OF THE NEW YORK ACADEMY OF SCIENCES, VOLUME 319. NEW YORK: THE NEW YORK ACADEMY OF SCIENCES. (1979).

IRI 1979 -2 IRI, M.
THEORY OF FLOWS IN CONTINUA AS APPROXIMATION TO FLOWS IN NETWORKS. IN: A. PREKOPA (ED.): SURVEY OF MATHEMATICAL PROGRAMMING, VOLUME 2, 263-278. AMSTERDAM: NORTH-HOLLAND. (1979).

IRI A 1981 -1 IRI, M.; FUJISHIGE, S.
USE OF MATROID THEORY IN OPERATIONS RESEARCH, CIRCUITS AND SYSTEMS THEORY. INTERNATIONAL JOURNAL OF SYSTEMS SCIENCE 12, 27-54. (1981).

IRI B 1979 -1 IRI, M.; RECSKI, A.
REFLECTION ON THE CONCEPTS OF DUAL, INVERSE AND ADJOINT NETWORKS. RESEARCH MEMORANDUM RMI 79-7, TOKYO: UNIVERSITY OF TOKYO, DEPT. OF MATHEMATICAL ENGINEERING AND INSTRUMENTATION PHYSICS, 13 P. (1979).

IRI B 1980 -1 IRI, M.; RECSKI, A.
REFLECTION ON THE CONCEPTS OF DUAL, INVERSE AND ADJOINT NETWORKS, II: TOWARDS A QUALITATIVE THEORY. RESEARCH MEMORANDUM RMI 80-1. TOKYO: UNIVERSITY OF TOKYO, DEPT. OF MATHEMATICAL ENGINEERING AND INSTRUMENTATION PHYSICS, 13 P. (1980).

IRI C 1976 -1 IRI, M.; TOMIZAWA, N.
ALGORITHM FOR FINDING AN OPTIMAL "INDEPENDENT ASSIGNMENT", AN. JOURNAL OF THE OPERATIONS RESEARCH SOCIETY OF JAPAN 19, 32-57. (1976).

ISAE 1970 -1 ISAEVA, M. N.
LARGEST POSSIBLE NUMBER OF BASIS SOLUTIONS IN THE TRANSPORT PROBLEM, (RUSSIAN), THE. TASKENSKII INSTITUT NARODNOGO HOZJAISTUWA. NAUCYNE ZAPISKI. MATEMATIKA V PRILOZENIJAH, 3-13. (1970).

ISER 1979 -1 ISERMANN, H.
ENUMERATION AF ALL EFFICIENT SOLUTIONS FOR A LINEAR MULTIPLE-OBJECTIVE TRANSPORTATION PROBLEM, THE. NAVAL RESEARCH LOGISTICS QUARTERLY 26, 123-139. (1979).

ISHI 1978 -1 ISHII, H.
NEW METHOD FINDING THE K-TH BEST PATH IN A GRAPH, A. JOURNAL OF THE OPERATIONS RESEARCH SOCIETY OF JAPAN 21, 469-476. (1978).

ISHIA 1976 -1 ISHII, H.; IBARAKI, T.; MINE, H.
PRIMAL CUTTING PLANE ALGORITHM FOR INTEGER FRACTIONAL PROGRAMMING PROBLEMS, A. JOURNAL OF THE OPERATIONS RESEARCH SOCIETY OF JAPAN 19, 228-244. (1976).

ISHIB 1979 -1 ISHII, H.; NISHIDA, T.; DAINO, A.
FRACTIONAL SET COVERING PROBLEMS. TECHNOLOGY REPORTS OF THE OSAKA UNIVERSITY 29, NO. 1492-1516, 319-326. (1979).

ISHIC 1979 -1 ISHIYAMA, Y.; ISHIZAKI, Y.; SASABE, S.; YOSHIDA, N.
MULTI-COMMODITY FLOW APPROACH TO ASSIGNMENT OF CIRCUITS IN CASE OF FAILURE IN A COMMUNICATION NETWORK. IN: A. PREKOPA (ED.): SURVEY OF MATHEMATICAL PROGRAMMING, VOLUME 3, 195-210. AMSTERDAM: NORTH-HOLLAND. (1979).

ISKA 1978 -1 ISKANDER, W.
NEAR - OPTIMAL SOLUTION TO THE DYNAMIC JOB SHOP SEQUENCING PROBLEM, A. MORGANTOWN: WEST VIRGINIA UNIV., DEPT. OF INDUSTRIAL ENGINEERING, 12 P. (1978).

ISMA 1978 -1 ISMATULLAEV, S. A.
NUMBER OF SOLUTIONS OF A SYSTEM OF DIOPHANTINE EQUATIONS (RUSSIAN), THE. DOKLADY AKADEMII NAUK UZSSR, NO. 8, 5-7. (1978).
ITAI 1978 -1 ITAI, A.
TWO-COMMODITY FLOW. JOURNAL OF THE ASSOCIATION FOR COMPUTING MACHINERY 25, 596-611. (1978).
ITAIA 1977 -1 ITAI, A.; RODEH, M.
FINDING A MINIMUM CIRCUIT IN A GRAPH. IN: CONFERENCE RECORD OF THE NINTH ANNUAL ACM SYMPOSIUM ON THEORY OF COMPUTING, BOULDER 1977, 1-10. NEW YORK: ASSOCIATION FOR COMPUTING MACHINERY; ALSO PUBLISHED IN SIAM JOURNAL ON COMPUTING 7, 1978, 413-423. (1977).
ITAIB 1978 -1 ITAI, A.; RODEH, M.; TANIMOTO, S. L.
SOME MATCHING PROBLEMS FOR BIPARTITE GRAPHS. JOURNAL OF THE ASSOCIATION FOR COMPUTING MACHINERY 25, 517-525. (1978).
ITAIC 1979 -1 ITAI, A.; SHILOACH, Y.
MAXIMUM FLOW IN PLANAR NETWORKS. SIAM JOURNAL ON COMPUTING 8, 135-150. (1979).
ITOG 1978 -1 ITOGA, S. Y.
UPPER BOUND FOR THE STABLE MARRIAGE PROBLEM, THE. THE JOURNAL OF THE OPERATIONAL RESEARCH SOCIETY 29, 811-814. (1978).
IVAN 1981 -1 IVANEK, J.; MORAVEK, J.
HEURISTIC IMPROVEMENT OF THE DYNAMIC PROGRAMMING TREATMENT OF THE TRAVELLING SALESMAN PROBLEM. EKONOMICKO-MATEMATICKY OBZOR (PRAGUE) 17, NO. 1, 12-27. (1981).
IZBI 1962 -1 IZBICKI, H.
ZULAESSIGE KANTENFAERBUNGEN VON PSEUDO-REGULAEREN GRAPHEN 3. GRADES MIT DER KANTENFARBENZAHL 3. MONATSHEFTE FUER MATHEMATIK 66, 424-430. (1962).
IZBI 1963 -1 IZBICKI, H.
ZULAESSIGE KANTENFAERBUNGEN VON PSEUDO-REGULAEREN GRAPHEN MIT MINIMALER KANTENFARBENZAHL. MONATSHEFTE FUER MATHEMATIK 67, 25-31. (1963).
IZBI 1964 -1 IZBICKI, H.
EDGE-COLORING PROBLEM, AN. IN: M. FIEDLER (ED.): PROCEEDINGS OF THE SMOLENICE SYMPOSIUM ON GRAPH THEORY, 52-62. PRAGUE: PUBLISHING HOUSE OF THE CZESCHOSLOVAKIAN ACADEMY OF SCIENCE; NEW YORK: ACADEMIC PRESS. (1964).
JACK 1979 -1 JACKSON, B.
EDGE-DISJOINT HAMILTON CYCLES IN REGULAR GRAPHS OF LARGE DEGREE. THE JOURNAL OF THE LONDON MATHEMATICAL SOCIETY 19, 13-16. (1979).
JACK 1979 -2 JACKSON, B.
HAMILTON CYCLES IN REGULAR TWO-CONNECTED GRAPHS. IN: J. A. BONDY, U. P. R. MURTY (EDS.): GRAPH THEORY AND RELATED TOPICS, 261-265. NEW YORK, SAN FRANCISCO, LONDON: ACADEMIC PRESS. (1979).
JACK 1980 -1 JACKSON, B.
HAMILTON CYCLES IN REGULAR 2-CONNECTED GRAPHS. JOURNAL OF COMBINATORIAL THEORY 29, SERIES B, 27-46. (1980).
JACKA 1977 -1 JACKSON, W.
CHARACTERIZATION OF THE REDUCIBILITY OF NON-NEGATIVE MATRICES, A. IN: F. HOFFMAN ET AL. (EDS.): PROCEEDINGS OF THE EIGHTH SOUTHEASTERN CONFERENCE ON COMBINATORICS, GRAPH THEORY, AND COMPUTING, BATON ROUGE 1977, 381-384. CONGRESSUS NUMERANTIUM XIX. WINNIPEG: UTILITAS MATHEMATICA. (1977).
JACKA 1978 -1 JACKSON, W.
CYCLES IN BIPARTITE GRAPHS. IN: F. HOFFMAN, D. MAC CARTHY, R. C. MULLIN, R. G. STANTON (EDS.): PROCEEDINGS OF THE NINTH SOUTHEASTERN CONFERENCE ON COMBINATORICS, GRAPH THEORY, AND COMPUTING, 391-394. CONGRESSUS NUMERANTIUM XXI. WINNIPEG: UTILITAS. (1978).
JACO 1979 -1 JACOBS, K.
CONTINUOUS MAX-FLOW PROBLEM, A. IN: GAME THEORY AND RELATED TOPICS, PROC. SEM., BONN AND HAGEN 1978, 301-307. AMSTERDAM: NORTH-HOLLAND. (1979).
JACOA 1977 -1 JACOBSEN, S. K.
HEURISTIC PROCEDURES FOR DYNAMIC PLANT LOCATION. THE TECHNICAL UNIVERSITY OF DENMARK, THE INSTITUTE OF MATHEMATICAL STATISTICS AND OPERATIONS RESEARCH. (1977).
JACOA 1977 -2 JACOBSEN, S. K.
HEURISTIC SOLUTIONS TO DYNAMIC PLANT LOCATION PROBLEMS. IN: M. ROUBENS (ED.): ADVANCES IN OPERATIONS RESEARCH, PROCEEDINGS OF EURO II, THE SECOND EUROPEAN CONGRESS ON OPERATIONS RESEARCH, STOCKHOLM 1976, 207-211. AMSTERDAM, NEW YORK, OXFORD: NORTH-HOLLAND. (1977).
JACOB 1980 -1 JACOBSEN, S. K.; MADSEN, O. B. G.
COMPARATIVE STUDY OF HEURISTICS FOR A TWO-LEVEL ROUTING-LOCATION PROBLEM, A. EUROPEAN JOURNAL OF OPERATIONAL RESEARCH 5, 378-387. (1980).
JACQ 1980 -1 JACQMIN, N. E.
BINARY INTEGER LINEAR PROGRAMMING: A HYBRID IMPLICIT ENUMERATION APPROACH. TECHNICAL REPORT 80-30. STANFORD: STANFORD UNIV., DEPT. OF OPERATIONS RESEARCH, 100 P. (1980).
JAEG 1973 -1 JAEGER, F.
SUR L'INDICE CHROMATIQUE DU GRAPHE REPRESENTATIF DES ARETES D'UN GRAPHE REGULIER. COMPTES RENDUS HEBDOMADAIRES DES SEANCES DE L'ACADEMIE DES SCIENCES. SERIES A 227, 237-239; ALSO PUBLISHED IN DISCRETE MATHEMATICS 9, 1974, 161-172. (1973).
JAEG 1978 -1 JAEGER, F.
ON INTERVAL HYPERGRAPHS AND NOWHERE-ZERO FLOWS IN GRAPHS. MATH. APPL. INFORMAT., RAPP. RECH. NO. 126, 1-12. (1978).
JAEG 1979 -1 JAEGER, F.
FLOWS AND GENERALIZED COLORING THEOREMS IN GRAPHS. JOURNAL OF COMBINATORIAL THEORY 26, SERIES B, 205-216. (1979).
JAEG 1979 -2 JAEGER, F.
INTERVAL MATROIDS AND GRAPHS. DISCRETE MATHEMATICS 27, 331-336. (1979).
JAEG 1979 -3 JAEGER, F.
TWO CHARACTERIZATIONS OF COGRAPHIC MATROIDS. MATH. APPL. INFORMAT., RAPP. RECH. NO. 175, 5 P. (1979).
JAFF 1980 -1 JAFFE, J. M.
ANALYSIS OF PREEMPTIVE MULTIPROCESSOR JOB SCHEDULING, AN. MATHEMATICS OF OPERATIONS RESEARCH 5, 415-421. (1980).
JAFF 1980 -2 JAFFE, J. M.
BOUNDS ON THE SCHEDULING OF TYPED TASK SYSTEMS. SIAM JOURNAL ON COMPUTING 9, 541-551. (1980).
JAFF 1980 -3 JAFFE, J. M.
EFFICIENT SCHEDULING OF TASKS WITHOUT FULL USE OF PROCESSOR RESOURCES. THEORETICAL COMPUTER SCIENCE 12, 1-17. (1980).
JAHN 1979 -1 JAHNO, V. M.
CLASS OF LINEAR DYNAMIC TIMETABLE MODELS, A. AVTOMATIKA I TELEMEHANIKA, NO. 5, 121-126; TRANSLATED AS AUTOMATION AND REMOTE CONTROL 40, 1979, 727-732. (1979).
JAIN 1979 -1 JAIN, R. C.
ON GLOBALLY MINIMIZING POINTS OF PSEUDO-BOOLEAN QUADRATIC FUNCTIONS. PURE AND APPLIED MATHEMATIKA SCIENCES 10, 57-62. (1979).

JAINA 1979 -1 JAIN, R. C.; PANNE, C. VAN DE
TRANSPORTATION-TYPE METHODS FOR THE PLANT LOCATION PROBLEM. IN: A. PREKOPA (ED.): SURVEY OF MATHEMATICAL PROGRAMMING, VOLUME 3, 211-228. AMSTERDAM: NORTH-HOLLAND. (1979).

JAKO 1973 -1 JAKOBSEN, I. T.
SOME REMARKS ON THE CHROMATIC INDEX OF A GRAPH. ARCHIV DER MATHEMATIK 24, 440-448. (1973).

JAKO 1975 -1 JAKOBSEN, I. T.
ON GRAPHS CRITICAL WITH RESPECT TO EDGE-COLOURING. IN: A. HAJNAL, R. RADO, V. T. SOS (EDS.): INFINITE AND FINITE SETS, 927-934. AMSTERDAM, LONDON: NORTH-HOLLAND. (1975).

JAKS 1981 -1 JAKSCH, H. J.
NECESSARY O-1 CONDITIONS FOR THE EXISTENCE OF SOLUTIONS OF A TWO-COMMODITY TRANSPORT PROBLEM. METHODS OF OPERATIONS RESEARCH 39, 61-86. (1981).

JAKU 1978 -1 JAKUBOWSKI, A.
STOCHASTIC MODEL OF RESOURCE ALLOCATION TO R & D ACTIVITIES UNDER COST VALUE UNCERTAINTY. IN: OPTIMIZATION TECHNIQUES, PROCEEDINGS OF THE EIGHTH IFIP CONFERENCE, WUERZBURG 1977, PART 2, 411-421. BERLIN: SPRINGER. (1978).

JAMB 1978 -1 JAMBEKAR, A. B.; STEINBERG, D. I.
COMPUTATIONAL EXPERIENCE WITH AN ALGORITHM FOR O-1 INTEGER PROGRAMMING. COMPUTERS AND MATHEMATICS WITH APPLICATIONS 4, 305-314. (1978).

JAMB 1978 -2 JAMBEKAR, A. B.; STEINBERG, D. I.
IMPLICIT ENUMERATION ALGORITHM FOR THE ALL INTEGER PROGRAMMING PROBLEM, AN. COMPUTERS AND MATHEMATICS WITH APPLICATIONS 4, 15-31. (1978).

JANB 1977 -1 JANBYH, G. F.; STOLJAROV, B. A.
OPTIMIZATION OF THE STRUCTURE OF MULTIPROGRAMMED COMPUTER SYSTEMS FOR SOLVING SETS OF DEPENDENT TASKS (RUSSIAN). AKADEMIJA NAUK LATVIISKOI SSR. AVTOMATIKA I VYCISLITEL'NAJA TEHNIKA, NO. 6, 62-69 + 95. (1977).

JANK 1978 -1 JANKO, W.
COMBINATORIAL CONSIDERATIONS ON THE OPTIMALITY OF HEURISTIC SOLUTIONS OF PROBLEMS. IN: J. MUEHLBACHER (ED.): DATENSTRUKTUREN, GRAPHEN, ALGORITHMEN. DRITTE FACHTAGUNG UEBER GRAPHENTHEORETISCHE KONZEPTE DER INFORMATIK, LINZ 1977, 215-225. MUENCHEN, WIEN: HANSER. (1978).

JANS 1981 -1 JANSON, S.
UPPER BOUND FOR THE VELOCITY OF FIRST-PASSAGE PERCOLATION, AN. JOURNAL OF APPLIED PROBABILITY 18, 256-262. (1981).

JARV 1977 -1 JARVIS, J. J.; MARTINEZ, O. M.
SENSITIVITY ANALYSIS OF MULTICOMMODITY NETWORK FLOWS, A. TRANSPORTATION SCIENCE 11, 299-306. (1977).

JARVA 1978 -1 JARVIS, J. J.; RARDIN, R. L.; UNGER, V. E.; MOORE, R. W.; SCHIMPELER, C. C.
OPTIMAL DESIGN OF REGIONAL WASTEWATER SYSTEMS: A FIXED-CHARGE NETWORK FLOW MODEL. OPERATIONS RESEARCH 26, 538-550. (1978).

JARVB 1978 -1 JARVIS, J. J.; TUFEKCI, S.
DECOMPOSITION ALGORITHM FOR FINDING THE SHORTEST PATH BETWEEN A SOURCE AND A SINK NODE, A. ATLANTA: GEORGIA INST. OF TECHNOLOGY, SCHOOL OF INDUSTRIAL AND SYSTEMS ENGINEERING, 25 P. (1978).

JARVB 1978 -2 JARVIS, J. J.; TUFEKCI, S.
DECOMPOSITION ALGORITHM FOR LOCATING MINIMAL CUTS IN A DIRECTED NETWORK, A. INDUSTRIAL AND SYSTEMS ENGINEERING REPORT SERIES NO. J-78-9. ATLANTA: GEORGIA INST. OF TECHNOLOGY, SCHOOL OF INDUSTRIAL AND SYSTEMS ENGINEERING, 32 P. (1978).

JAVD 1979 -1 JAVDEKAR, M. M.
MINIMALLY (P-7)-HAMILTONIAN GRAPHS. IN: A. RAMACHANDRA RAO (ED.): PROCEEDINGS OF THE SYMPOSIUM ON GRAPH THEORY, CALCUTTA 1976, 197-206. ISI (INDIAN STATISTICAL INSTITUTE) LECTURE NOTES 4. CALCUTTA: MACMILLAN OF INDIA. (1979).

JECH 1977 -1 JECHLITSCHKA, K.
UEBER DIE KONSTRUKTION VON STUETZHALBRAEUMEN FUER O-1-POLYEDER. WISSENSCHAFTLICHE ZEITSCHRIFT DER HUMBOLDT-UNIVERSITAET BERLIN. MATHEMATISCH-NATURWISSENSCHAFTLICHE REIHE 26, 547-554. (1977).

JEFF 1978 -1 JEFFERSON, T. R.; SCOTT, C. H.
GEOMETRIC PROGRAMMING APPLIED TO TRANSPORTATION PLANNING. OPSEARCH 15, 22-34. (1978).

JENK 1979 -1 JENKINS, L.
PARAMETRIC ANALYSIS ON A LOCATION MODEL OF MUNICIPAL RESOURCE RECOVERY. WINDSOR: UNIV. OF WINDSOR, FACULTY OF BUSINESS ADMINISTR. 33 P. (1979).

JENK 1980 -1 JENKINS, L.
COMPUTATIONAL RESULTS WITH A TECHNIQUE OF PARAMETRIC MIXED INTEGER LINEAR PROGRAMMING. RESEARCH REPORT. WINDSOR, ONTARIO: UNIV. OF WINDSOR, FACULTY OF BUSINESS ADMINISTRATION, 47 P. (1980).

JENK 1980 -2 JENKINS, L.
ONTARIO WASTE MANAGEMENT MODEL: TORONTO EXPERIENCE, THE. RESEARCH REPORT. WINDSOR, ONTARIO: UNIV. OF WINDSOR, FACULTY OF BUSINESS ADMINISTRATION, 18 P. (1980).

JENK 1980 -3 JENKINS, L.
PARAMETRIC MIXED INTEGER PROGRAMMING: A SOLID WASTE RECYCLING APPLICATION. RESEARCH REPORT. WINDSOR, ONTARIO: UNIV. OF WINDSOR, FACULTY OF BUSINESS ADMINISTRATION, 31 P. (1980).

JENKA 1977 -1 JENKYNS, T. A.
P-SYSTEMS AS INTERSECTIONS OF MATROIDS. IN: F. HOFFMAN ET AL. (EDS.): PROCEEDINGS OF THE EIGTH SOUTHEASTERN CONFERENCE ON COMBINATORICS, GRAPH THEORY, AND COMPUTING, BATON ROUGE 1977, 415-418. CONGRESSUS NUMERANTIUM XIX. WINNIPEG: UTILITAS MATHEMATICA. (1977).

JENKA 1978 -1 JENKYNS, T. A.
EFFICACY OF HEURISTICS COMBINING ENUMERATION AND THE GREEDY ALGORITHM, THE. REPORT NO. 78114-OR. BONN: UNIV. BONN, INSTITUT FUER OEKONOMETRIE UND OPERATIONS RESEARCH, 17 P. (1978).

JENKA 1979 -1 JENKYNS, T. A.
GREEDY BUT NOT-SO-STUPID ALGORITHMS. IN: F. HOFFMAN, D. MAC CARTHY, R. C. MULLIN, R. G. STANTON (EDS.): PROCEEDINGS OF THE TENTH SOUTHEASTERN CONFERENCE ON COMBINATORICS, GRAPH THEORY AND COMPUTING, 541-546. CONGRESSUS NUMERANTIUM XXIV. WINNIPEG: UTILITAS. (1979).

JENKA 1979 -2 JENKYNS, T. A.
GREEDY TRAVELLING SALESMAN'S PROBLEM, THE. NETWORKS 9, 363-373. (1979).

JENS 1980 -1 JENSEN, P. A.; BARNES, J. W.
NETWORK FLOW PROGRAMMING. NEW YORK, CHICHESTER U.A.: WILEY, 408 P. (1980).

JENSA 1981 -1 JENSEN, P. M.
BINARY FUNDAMENTAL MATROIDS. IN: L. LOVASZ, V. T. SOS (EDS.): ALGEBRAIC METHODS IN GRAPH THEORY, VOL. I, 281-296. COLLOQUIA MATHEMATICA SOCIETATIS JANOS BOLYAI 25. AMSTERDAM, OXFORD,NEW YORK: NORTH-HOLLAND. (1981).

JENSB 1978 -1 JENSEN, P. M.; KORTE, B.
COMPLEXITY OF MATROID PROPERTY ALGORITHMS. REPORT NO. 78124-OR. BONN: UNIV. BONN, INST. FUER OEKONOMETRIE UND OPERATIONS RESEARCH, 12 P. (1978).

JERO 1980 -1 JEROMIN, B.
BEMERKUNGEN ZUR LAGRANGE-RELAXATION. WISSENSCHAFTLICHE ZEITSCHRIFT DER TECHNISCHEN UNIVERSITAET DRESDEN 29, 127-130. (1980).

JEROA 1980 -1 JEROMIN, B.; KOERNER, F.
UEBER DIE CHRISTOFIDES SCHRANKE FUER DAS TRAVELING SALESMAN PROBLEM. MANUSKRIPT 07-18-80. DRESDEN: TECHNISCHE UNIV. DRESDEN, 15 P. (1980).

JEROA 1980 -2 JEROMIN, B.; KOERNER, F.
VERSCHAERFUNG DER CHRISTOFIDES SCHRANKE FUER DAS TRAVELING SALESMAN PROBLEM, EINE. MANUSKRIPT 07-17-80. DRESDEN: TECHNISCHE UNIV. DRESDEN, 14 P. (1980).

JEROB 1975 -1 JEROSLOW, R. G.
SOME STRUCTURE AND BASIS THEOREMS FOR INTEGRAL MONOIDS. PITTSBURGH: CARNEGIE-MELLON UNIVERSITY. (1975).

JEROB 1977 -1 JEROSLOW, R. G.
REPRESENTATIONS OF UNBOUNDED OPTIMIZATIONS AS INTEGER PROGRAMS. PITTSBURGH: CARNEGIE-MELLON UNIV., 16 P. (1977).

JEROB 1978 -1 JEROSLOW, R. G.
CUTTING PLANE THEORY: ALGEBRAIC METHODS. DISCRETE MATHEMATICS 23, 121-151. (1978).

JEROB 1978 -2 JEROSLOW, R. G.
CUTTING-PLANES FOR COMPLEMENTARITY CONSTRAINTS. SIAM JOURNAL ON CONTROL AND OPTIMIZATION 16, 56-62. (1978).

JEROB 1978 -3 JEROSLOW, R. G.
SOME BASIC THEOREMS FOR INTEGRAL MONOIDS. MATHEMATICS OF OPERATIONS RESEARCH 3, 145-155. (1978).

JEROB 1979 -1 JEROSLOW, R. G.
INTRODUCTION TO THE THEORY OF CUTTING-PLANES, AN. IN: P. L. HAMMER, E. L. JOHNSON, B. H. KORTE (EDS.): DISCRETE OPTIMIZATION II, 71-95. ANNALS OF DISCRETE MATHEMATICS 5, AMSTERDAM, NEW YORK, OXFORD: NORTH-HOLLAND. (1979).

JEROB 1979 -2 JEROSLOW, R. G.
MINIMAL INEQUALITIES. MATHEMATICAL PROGRAMMING 17, 1-15. (1979).

JEROB 1979 -3 JEROSLOW, R. G.
THEORY OF CUTTING-PLANES, THE. IN: N. CHRISTOFIDES, A. MINGOZZI, P. TOTH, C. SANDI (EDS.): COMBINATORIAL OPTIMIZATION, 21-72. CHICHESTER, NEW YORK, BRISBANE, TORONTO: WILEY. (1979).

JEROB 1980 -1 JEROSLOW, R. G.
CUTTING-PLANE GAME FOR FACIAL DISJUNCTIVE PROGRAMS, A. SIAM JOURNAL ON CONTROL AND OPTIMIZATION 18, 264-281. (1980).

JEROB 1980 -2 JEROSLOW, R. G.
SOME INFLUENCES OF GENERALIZED AND ORDINARY CONVEXITY IN DISJUNCTIVE AND INTEGER PROGRAMMING. RESEARCH REPORT. ATLANTA: GEORGIA INST. OF TECHNOLOGY, 12 P. (1980).

JOHN 1973 -1 JOHNSON, D. S.
NEAR-OPTIMAL BIN PACKING ALGORITHMS. REPORT MAC TR-109. CAMBRIDGE: MASSACHUSETTS INSTITUTE OF TECHNOLOGY. (1973).

JOHN 1974 -1 JOHNSON, D. S.
FAST ALGORITHMS FOR BIN PACKING. JOURNAL OF COMPUTER AND SYSTEM SCIENCES 8, 272-314. (1974).

JOHNA 1974 -1 JOHNSON, D. S.; DEMERS, A.; ULLMAN, J. D.; GAREY, M. R.; GRAHAM, R. L.
WORST-CASE PERFORMANCE BOUNDS FOR SIMPLE ONE-DIMENSIONAL PACKING ALGORITHMS. SIAM JOURNAL ON COMPUTING 3, 299-325. (1974).

JOHNB 1978 -1 JOHNSON, D. S.; LENSTRA, J. K.; RINNOOY KAN, A. H. G.
COMPLEXITY OF THE NETWORK DESIGN PROBLEM, THE. NETWORKS 8, 279-285. (1978).

JOHNC 1966 -1 JOHNSON, E. I.
PROOF OF FOUR COLOURING THE EDGES OF A CUBIC GRAPH, A. THE AMERICAN MATHEMATICAL MONTHLY 73, 52-55. (1966).

JOHND 1965 -1 JOHNSON, E. L.
PROGRAMMING IN NETWORKS AND GRAPHS. ORC REPORT 65-1. BERKELEY: UNIVERSITY OF CALIFORNIA. (1965).

JOHND 1972 -1 JOHNSON, E. L.
ON SHORTEST PATHS AND SORTING. YORKTOWN HEIGHTS: IBM RESEARCH CENTER, 8 P. (1972).

JOHND 1978 -1 JOHNSON, E. L.
MATCHINGS AND BIDIRECTED GRAPHS. YORKTOWN HEIGHTS: IBM RESEARCH CENTER, 20 P. (1978).

JOHND 1978 -2 JOHNSON, E. L.
SUPPORT FUNCTIONS, BLOCKING PAIRS, AND ANTI-BLOCKING PAIRS. MATHEMATICAL PROGRAMMING STUDY 8, 167-196. (1978).

JOHND 1979 -1 JOHNSON, E. L.
ON THE GROUP PROBLEM AND A SUBADDITIVE APPROACH TO INTEGER PROGRAMMING. IN: P. L. HAMMER, E. L. JOHNSON, B. H. KORTE (EDS.): DISCRETE OPTIMIZATION II, 97-112. ANNALS OF DISCRETE MATHEMATICS 5, AMSTERDAM, NEW YORK, OXFORD: NORTH-HOLLAND. (1979).

JOHND 1979 -2 JOHNSON, E. L.
SUBADDITIVE LIFTING METHODS FOR PARTITIONING AND KNAPSACK PROBLEMS. IBM RESEARCH REPORT, 7620. YORKTOWN HEIGHTS: IBM RESEARCH CENTER, 34 P. (1979).

JOHND 1980 -1 JOHNSON, E. L.
INTEGER PROGRAMMING. FACETS, SUBADDITIVITY, AND DUALITY FOR GROUP AND SEMI-GROUP PROBLEMS. CBMS-NSF REGIONAL CONFERENCE SERIES IN APPLIED MATHEMATICS NO. 32. PHILADELPHIA: SOCIETY FOR INDUSTRIAL AND APPLIED MATHEMATICS. 68P. (1980).

JOHND 1981 -1 JOHNSON, E. L.
CHARACTERIZATION OF FACETS FOR MULTIPLE RIGHT-HAND CHOICE LINEAR PROGRAMS. IN: H. KOENIG, B. KORTE, K. RITTER (EDS.): MATHEMATICAL PROGRAMMING AT OBERWOLFACH, 112-142. MATHEMATICAL PROGRAMMING STUDY 14. (1981).

JOHND 1981 -2 JOHNSON, E. L.
ON THE GENERALITY OF THE SUBADDITIVE CHARACTERIZATION OF FACETS. MATHEMATICS OF OPERATIONS RESEARCH 6, 101-112. (1981).

JOHNE 1980 -1 JOHNSON, E. L.; PADBERG, M. W.
DEGREE-TWO INEQUALITIES, CLIQUE FACETS, AND BIPEFECT GRAPHS. REPORT NO. 80167-OR. BONN: UNIV. BONN, INST. F. OEKONOMETRIE UND OPERATIONS RESEARCH, 23 P. (1980).

JOHNF 1978 -1 JOHNSON, E. L.; POWELL, S.
INTEGER PROGRAMMING CODES. IN: H. GREENBERG (ED.): DESIGN AND IMPLEMENTATION OF OPTIMIZATION SOFTWARE, 225-240. ALPHEN AAN DEN RIJN: SIJTHOFF & NOORDHOFF. (1978).

JOHNG 1980 -1 JOHNSON, E. L.; SUHL, U.
EXPERIMENTS IN INTEGER PROGRAMMING. DISCRETE APPLIED MATHEMATICS 2, 39-56. (1980).

JOHNH 1975 -1 JOHNSON, J. G.
HEURISTIC ALGORITHM FOR THE MULTI-TERMINAL VEHICLE DISPATCH PROBLEM USING THE MODIFIED SWEEP ALGORITHM, A. PH. D. THESIS. ROLLA: UNIVERSITY OF MISSOURI. (1975).

JOHNI 1977 -1 JOHNSON, L. F.
ALGORITHMS FOR ENUMERATING THE SIMPLE CYCLES OF A DIGRAPH. IN: B. L. HARTNELL, H. C. WILLIAMS (EDS.): PROCEEDINGS OF THE SIXTH MANITOBA CONFERENCE ON NUMERICAL MATHEMATICS, 211-230. CONGRESSUS NUMERANTIUM XVIII. WINNIPEG: UTILITAS. (1977).

JOHNJ 1979 -1 JOHNSON, M.; ZOLTNERS, A. A.; SINHA, P.
ALLOCATION MODEL FOR CATALOG SPACE PLANNING, AN. MANAGEMENT SCIENCE 25, 117-129. (1979).

JOLI 1975 -1 JOLIVET, J.-L.
GRAPHES PARFAITS POUR UNE PROPRIETE P. CAHIERS DU CENTRE D'ETUDES DE RECHERCHE OPERATIONELLE 17, 253-256. (1975).

JONE 1979 -1 JONES, G. A.; WILSON, J. G.
OPTIMAL SCHEDULING OF JOBS ON A TRANSMISSION NETWORK. MANAGEMENT SCIENCE 25, 98-104. (1979).
JONK 1978 -1 JONKER, R.; DELEVE, G.; VANDERVELDE, J. A.; VOLGENANT, A.
SOLVING SYMMETRIC TRAVELING SALESMAN PROBLEMS ASYMMETRICALLY. REPORT: AE 7/78. AMSTERDAM: UNIV. VAN AMSTERDAM, INSTITUUT VOOR ACTUARIAAT & ECONOMETRIE, 5 P. (1978).
JONK 1980 -1 JONKER, R.; DELEVE, G.; VANDERVELDE, J. A.; VOLGENANT, A.
ROUNDING SYMMETRIC TRAVELING SALESMAN PROBLEMS WITH AN ASYMMETRIC ASSIGNMENT PROBLEM. OPERATIONS RESEARCH 28, 623-627. (1980).
JONKA 1980 -1 JONKER, R.; KAAS, R.; VOLGENANT, T.
DATA-DEPENDENT BOUNDS FOR HEURISTICS TO FIND A MINIMUM WEIGHT HAMILTONIAN CIRCUIT. OPERATIONS RESEARCH 28, 1219-1221. (1980).
JOVA 1973 -1 JOVANOVICH, A. D.; CHOBELJICH, S. N.
FAST ALGORITHM FOR FINDING A FOREST OF A LINEAR GRAPH. ELECTRONICS LETTERS 9, 504-505. (1973).
JOZS 1978 -1 JOZSEF, T.
SCHEDULING OF REGULAR PAIRS OF JOB-FLOWS. I. (HUNGARIAN). TANULMANYOK. MTA SZAMITASTECHNIKAI ES AUTOMATIZALASI KUTATO INTEZET BUDAPEST, NO. 82, 1-223. (1978).
JOZS 1978 -2 JOZSEF, T.
SCHEDULING OF REGULAR PAIRS OF JOB-FLOWS. II. (HUNGARIAN). TANULMANYOK. MTA SZAMITASTECHNIKAI ES AUTOMATIZALASI KUTATO INTEZET BUDAPEST, NO. 83, 1-272. (1978).
JUEL 1980 -1 JUEL, H.; LOVE, R. F.
SUFFICIENT CONDITIONS FOR OPTIMAL FACILITY LOCATIONS TO COINCIDE. TRANSPORTATION SCIENCE 14, 125-129. (1980).
JUEN 1979 -1 JUENGER, M.; WESTPHAL, H.
REVISED HUNGARIAN METHOD FOR OPTIMAL INSERTION INTO HASH TABLES, A. STANFORD: STANFORD UNIV. COMPUTER SCIENCE DEPT., 23 P. (1979).
JUNG 1978 -1 JUNG, H. A.
ON MAXIMAL CIRCUITS IN FINITE GRAPHS. IN: B. BOLLOBAS (ED.): ADVANCES IN GRAPH THEORY, 129-144. ANNALS OF DISCRETE MATHEMATICS 3. AMSTERDAM: NORTH-HOLLAND. (1978).
JUNGA 1970 -1 JUNGINGER, W.
UEBER DIE LOESUNG DES DREIDIMENSIONALEN TRANSPORTPROBLEMS. DISSERTATION. STUTTGART: UNIVERSITAET STUTTGART, 94 P. (1970).
JUNGA 1977 -1 JUNGINGER, W.
ALGORITHM FOR THE SOLUTION OF MULTI-INDEX TRANSPORTATION PROBLEMS, AN. IN: M. ROUBENS (ED.): ADVANCES IN OPERATIONS RESEARCH, PROCEEDINGS OF EURO II, THE SECOND EUROPEAN CONGRESS ON OPERATIONS RESEARCH, STOCKHOLM 1976, 229-235. AMSTERDAM, NEW YORK, OXFORD: NORTH-HOLLAND. (1977).
JUNGA 1978 -1 JUNGINGER, W.
KLASSIFIKATION DER MEHRDIMENSIONALEN TRANSPORTPROBLEME. IN: PROCEEDINGS IN OPERATIONS RESEARCH 7, 407. WUERZBURG: PHYSICA. (1978).
KAAS 1980 -1 KAAS, R.
BRANCH AND BOUND ALGORITHM FOR THE ACYCLIC SUBGRAPH PROBLEM, A. REPORT AE 20/80. AMSTERDAM: UNIV. OF AMSTERDAM, FACULTY OF ACTUARIAL SCIENCE & ECONOMETRICS, 16 O. (1980).
KABE 1980 -1 KABE, D. G.
DIRECT SOLUTIONS TO THE M-MEDIAN AND FRACTIONAL TRANSPORTATION PROBLEMS. INDUSTRIAL MATHEMATICS 30, 1-27. (1980).
KACP 1980 -1 KACPRZYK, J.; KRAWCZAK, M.
ON AN INEXACT TRANSPORTATION PROBLEM. IN: K. IRACKI, K. MALANOWSKI, P. WALUKIEWICZ (EDS.): OPTIMIZATION TECHNIQUES, PART II, 373-379. LECTURE NOTES IN CONTROL AND INFORMATION SCIENCES 23. BERLIN: SPRINGER. (1980).
KACPA 1980 -1 KACPRZYK, J.; STANCZAK, W.
OPTIMAL LOCATION OF A CENTRAL SUPPLY POINT IN URBAN REGIONS (POLISH). ARCHIWUM AUTOMATYKI I TELEMECHANIKI (WARSAW) 25, NO. 1, 109-120. (1980).
KAEM 1979 -1 KAEMPFE, H.
RATIONELLE LOESUNG DES GOZINTOPROBLEMS IM KREISFREIEN BEWERTETEN GERICHTETEN GRAPHEN UND WEITERE OEKONOMISCHE INTERPRETATIONEN, EINE. WISSENSCHAFTLICHE ZEITSCHRIFT DER TECHNISCHEN HOCHSCHULE KARL-MARX-STADT 21, 645-653. (1979).
KAER 1977 -1 KAERKES, R.
NETZPLAN THEORY. IN: A. ANGERMANN ET AL. (EDS.): FIRST SYMPOSIUM ON OPERATIONS RESEARCH. HEIDELBERG 1976. METHODS OF OPERATIONS RESEARCH 27, 1-65. MEISENHEIM: ANTON HAIN. (1977).
KAER 1979 -1 KAERKES, R.
OPTIMIZATION OF (STOCHASTIC) NETWORKS UNDER RESOURCE CONSTRAINTS (ABSTRACT). IN: W. OETTLI, F. STEFFENS (EDS.): OPERATIONS RESEARCH VERFAHREN 32, THIRD SYMPOSIUM ON OPERATIONS RESEARCH, MANNHEIM 1978, 151-152. KOENIGSTEIN: ANTON HAIN MEISENHEIM. (1979).
KAERA 1977 -1 KAERKES, R.; LEIPHOLZ, B.
GENERALIZED NETWORK FUNCTIONS IN FLOW NETWORKS. IN: A. ANGERMANN ET AL. (EDS.): FIRST SYMPOSIUM ON OPERATIONS RESEARCH, HEIDELBERG 1976. METHODS OF OPERATIONS RESEARCH 27, 225-273. MEISENHEIM: ANTON HAIN. (1977).
KAERB 1977 -1 KAERKES, R.; RADERMACHER, F. J.
PROFILES, NETWORK FUNCTIONS AND FACTORIZATION. IN: A. ANGERMANN ET AL. (EDS.): FIRST SYMPOSIUM ON OPERATIONS RESEARCH. HEIDELBERG 1976. METHODS OF OPERATIONS RESEARCH 27, 66-87. MEISENHEIM: ANTON HAIN. (1977).
KAHN 1980 -1 KAHN, J.
SOME NON-SPERNER PAVING MATROIDS. BULLETIN OF THE LONDON MATHEMATICAL SOCIETY 12, 268. (1980).
KAHNA 1980 -1 KAHN, J.; KUNG, J. P. S.
VARIETIES AND UNIVERSAL MODELS IN THE THEORY OF COMBINATORIAL GEOMETRIES. BULLETIN OF THE AMERICAN MATHEMATICAL SOCIETY, NEW SERIES 3, 857-858. (1980).
KAIN 1978 -1 KAINEN, P. C.
LONG AND SHORT WALKS IN TREES. IN: Y. ALAVI, D. R. LICK (EDS.): THEORY AND APPLICATION OF GRAPHS, PROCEEDINGS OF THE INTERNATIONAL CONFERENCE, MICHIGAN 1976; LECTURE NOTES IN MATHEMATICS 642, 309-313. BERLIN: SPRINGER. (1978).
KAJI 1979 -1 KAJITANI, Y.; UENO, S.
ON THE RANK OF CERTAIN CLASSES OF CUT-SETS AND TIE-SETS OF A GRAPH. INSTITUTE OF ELECTRICAL AND ELECTRONICS ENGINEERS. TRANSACTIONS ON CIRCUITS AND SYSTEMS 26, 666-668. (1979).
KALI 1979 -1 KALISZEWSKI, I.; WALUKIEWICZ, S.
TIGHTER EQUIVALENT FORMULATIONS OF INTEGER PROGRAMMING PROBLEMS. IN: A. PREKOPA (ED.): SURVEY OF MATHEMATICAL PROGRAMMING, VOLUME 2, 525-536. AMSTERDAM: NORTH-HOLLAND. (1979).
KALN 1965 -1 KALNINSH, YA.
NUMBER OF WAYS OF COLOURING THE BRANCHES OF A TREE AND A MULTITREE, THE. CYBERNETICS 1, 114-116. (1965).
KALR 1979 -1 KALRA, K. R.; BANSAL, S. P.
ALTERNATIVE OPTIMALS OF MAKE-SPAN IN TWO MACHINE FLOW SHOP PROBLEMS. SCIMA (NEW DELHI) 8, NOS. 2 AND 3, 24-33. (1979).

KALRA 1979 -1 KALRA, K. R.; BANSAL, S. P.; BAGGA, P. C.
MINIMIZATION OF WEIGHTED SUM OF COMPLETION TIMES WITH DUE DATES IN PERMUTATION FLOWSHOP PROBLEMS. JOURNAL OF COMBINATORICS, INFORMATION AND SYSTEM SCIENCES 4, 169-177. (1979).

KAME 1973 -1 KAMEDA, T.; TOIDA, S.
EFFICIENT ALGORITHMS FOR DETERMINING AN EXTREMAL TREE OF A GRAPH (EXTENDED ABSTRACT). IN: 14TH ANNUAL IEEE SYMPOSIUM ON SWITCHING AND AUTOMATA THEORY, IOWA CITY 1973, 12-15. NORTHRIDGE: IEEE COMPUTER SOCIETY. (1973).

KAMEA 1973 -1 KAMENAROV, S.
CERTAIN OPTIMIZATION METHODS FOR FLOWS IN NETWORKS (BULGARIAN). VISSIJA IKONOMICESKI INSTITUT "KARL MARKS" - SOFIJA. TRUDOVE, NO. 1, 179-237. (1973).

KANC 1978 -1 KANCEDAL, S. A.; MAKSIMOV, J. B.
COMPLEX OF LOT SIZE AND SCHEDULING MODELS FOR A SMALL LOT PRODUCTION. (RUSSIAN). A. EKONOMIKA I MATEMATICESKIE METODY 14, 1147-1159. (1978).

KANE 1978 -1 KANELLAKIS, P. C.
ALGORITHMS FOR A SCHEDULING APPLICATION OF THE ASYMMETRIC TRAVELING SALESMAN PROBLEM. M. A. THESIS. CAMBRIDGE: MASSACHUSETTS INSTITUTE OF TECHNOLOGY, DEPT. OF EECS. (1978).

KANEA 1980 -1 KANELLAKIS, P. C.; PAPADIMITRIOU, C. H.
LOCAL SEARCH FOR THE ASYMMETRIC TRAVELING SALESMAN PROBLEM. OPERATIONS RESEARCH 28, 1086-1099. (1980).

KANG 1977 -1 KANG, A. N. C.; LEE, R. C. T.; CHANG, C.-L.; CHANG, S. K.
STORAGE REDUCTION THROUGH MINIMAL SPANNING TREES AND SPANNING FORESTS. IEEE TRANSACTIONS ON COMPUTERS 5, 425-434. (1977).

KANN 1980 -1 KANNAN, R.
POLYNOMIAL ALGORITHM FOR THE TWO-VARIABLE INTEGER PROGRAMMING PROBLEM. A. JOURNAL OF THE ASSOCIATION FOR COMPUTING MACHINERY 27, 118-122. (1980).

KANN 1980 -2 KANNAN, R.
POLYNOMIAL-TIME AGGREGATION OF INTEGER PROGRAMMING PROBLEMS. MEMORANDUM NO. UCB/ERL M80/2. BERKELEY: UNIV. OF CALIFORNIA, COLLEGE OF EGNINEERING, 29 P. (1980).

KANN 1980 -3 KANNAN, R.
SIZE OF NUMBERS IN THE ANALYSIS OF CERTAIN ALGORITHMS, THE. TECHNICAL REPORT NO. 470. ITHACA: CORNELL UNIV., SCHOOL OF OPERATIONS RESEARCH, 91 P. (1980).

KANNA 1979 -1 KANNAN, R.; BACHEM, A.
POLYNOMIAL ALGORITHMS FOR COMPUTING THE SMITH AND HERMITE NORMAL FORMS OF AN INTEGER MATRIX. SIAM JOURNAL ON COMPUTING 8, 499-507. (1979).

KANNB 1978 -1 KANNAN, R.; KORTE, B.
APPROXIMATIVE COMBINATORIAL ALGORITHMS. REPORT NO. 78107-OR. BONN: UNIV. BONN, INSTITUT FUER OEKONOMETRIE UND OPERATONS RESEARCH, 69 P. (1978).

KANNC 1980 -1 KANNAN, R.; LIPTON, R. J.
ORBIT PROBLEM IS DECIDABLE, THE. RESEARCH PAPER. BERKELEY: UNIV. OF CALIFORNIA, COMPUTER SCIENCE DIVISION, 10 P. (1980).

KAO 1978 -1 KAO, E. P. C.
PREFERENCE ORDER DYNAMIC PROGRAM FOR A STOCHASTIC TRAVELING SALESMAN PROBLEM, A. OPERATIONS RESEARCH 26, 1033-1045. (1978).

KAO 1979 -1 KAO, E. P. C.
MULTI-PRODUCT DYNAMIC LOT-SIZE MODEL WITH INDIVIDUAL AND JOINT SET-UP COSTS, A. OPERATIONS RESEARCH 27, 279-289. (1979).

KAO 1980 -1 KAO, E. P. C.
MULTIPLE OBJECTIVE DECISION THEORETIC APPROACH TO ONE-MACHINE SCHEDULING PROBLEMS. A. COMPUTERS AND OPERATIONS RESEARCH 7, 251-260. (1980).

KAO A 1981 -1 KAO, E. P. C.; QUEYRANNE, M.
ON DYNAMIC PROGRAMMING METHODS FOR ASSEMBLY LINE BALANCING. RESEARCH REPORT. HOUSTON: UNIVERSITY OF HOUSTON, TEXAS, 27 P. (1981).

KAPA 1978 -1 KAPADIA, A. S.; HSI, B. P.
STEADY STATE WAITING TIME IN A MULTICENTER JOB SHOP. NAVAL RESEARCH LOGISTICS QUARTERLY 25, 149-154. (1978).

KAPL 1973 -1 KAPLINSKII, A. I.; CERNYSOVA, G. D.
CONSTRUCTION OF PROBABILISTIC ITERATIVE ALGORITHMS FOR THE SOLUTION OF INTEGER PROGRAMMING PROBLEMS (RUSSIAN). VORONEZSKII ORDENA LENINA GOSUDARSTVENNYI UNIVERSITET IM. LENINSKOGO KOMSOMOLA. TRUDY NAUCNO-ISSLEDOVATEL'SKOGO INSTITUTA MATEMATIKI 9, SB. RABOT PRIKL. ANAL., 34-38. (1973).

KAPP 1979 -1 KAPPAUF, C. H.; KOEHLER, G. J.
MIXED POSTMAN PROBLEM, THE. DISCRETE APPLIED MATHEMATICS 1, 89-103. (1979).

KARA 1976 -1 KARAPETJAN, I.A.
CRITICAL AND ESSENTIAL EDGES IN PERFECT GRAPHS (RUSSIAN). AKADEMIJA NAUK ARMJANSKOI SSR DOKLADY 63, 65-70. (1976).

KARE 1980 -1 KAREJAN, Z. A.; MOSESJAN, K. M.
HAMILTONIAN COMPLETION NUMBER OF A DIGRAPH (RUSSIAN), THE. AKADEMIJA NAUK ARMJANSKOI SSR, DOKLADY (EREVAN) 70, NO. 3, 129-132. (1980).

KAREA 1979 -1 KARELIN, V. P.; KALASHNIKOV, V. A.
UTILISATION DE LA METHODE DE LA PROGRAMMATION BIVALENTE POUR RESOUDRE QUELQUES PROBLEMES DE PROJET TECHNIQUE (RUSSIAN). MIKROELEKTRONIKA 8, 398-407. (1979).

KAREB 1980 -1 KARELIN, V. P.; KOVALEV, S. M.
PROBLEM OF THE PACKING OF SEVERAL KNAPSACKS (RUSSIAN), A. IZVESTIJA SEVERO-KAVKAZSKOGO NAUCNOGO CENTR VYSSEI SKOLY, SERIJA TEHNICESKIE NAUKI (ROSTOV-ON-DON) NO. 2, 21-23, 108. (1980).

KAREC 1979 -1 KARELIN, V. P.; MIRONOV, B. N.
ALGORITHMUS ZUR OPTIMALEN FAERBUNG DER ECKEN EINES GRAPHEN, DER AUF DER REALISIERUNG IN EINEM ASYNCHRONEN AUTOMATISCHEN MODELL ORIENTIERT IST (RUSSIAN). EIN. IZVESTIJA SEVERO-KAVKAZSKOGO NAUCNOGO CENTR VYSSEI SKOLY, SERIJA TEHNICESKIE NAUKI, NO. 2, 10-13. (1979).

KARI 1979 -1 KARIV, O.; HAKIMI, S. L.
ALGORITHMIC APPROACH TO NETWORK LOCATION PROBLEMS. I: THE P-CENTERS, AN. SIAM JOURNAL ON APPLIED MATHEMATICS 37, 513-538. (1979).

KARI 1979 -2 KARIV, O.; HAKIMI, S. L.
ALGORITHMIC APPROACH TO NETWORK LOCATION PROBLEMS. II: THE P-MEDIANS, AN. SIAM JOURNAL ON APPLIED MATHEMATICS 37, 539-560. (1979).

KARK 1981 -1 KARKAZIS, J.; BOFFEY, T. B.
SUBGRADIENT-BASED OPTIMAL SOLUTION METHOD FOR THE MULTICOMMODITY PROBLEM, A. IN: R. E. BURKARD, T. ELLINGER (EDS.): METHODS OF OPERATIONS RESEARCH 40, 339-344. KOENIGSTEIN: ANTON HAIN MEISENHEIM. (1981).

KARN 1978 -1 KARNEY, D.; KLINGMAN, D.
NETGEN REVISITED: A PROGRAM FOR GENERATING LARGE SCALE (UN) CAPACITATED ASSIGNMENT, TRANPORTATION, AND MINIMUM COST FLOW NETWORK PROBLEMS. RESEARCH REPORT CCS 320. AUSTIN: UNIV. OF TEXAS, CENTER FOR CYBERNETIC STUDIES, 14 P. (1978).

KARP 1975 -1 KARP, R. M.
COMPUTATIONAL COMPLEXITY OF COMBINATORIAL AND GRAPH-THEORETIC PROBLEMS. IN: THEORETICAL COMPUTER SCIENCE. CENTRO INTERNAZIONALE MATEMATICO ESTIVO, BRESSANOVE 1975, 98-184. ROME: EDIZIONI CREMONESE. (1975).

KARP 1978 -1 KARP, R. M.
CHARACTERIZATION OF THE MINIMUM CYCLE MEAN IN A DIGRAPH, A. DISCRETE MATHEMATICS 23, 309-311. (1978).

KARP 1978 -2 KARP, R. M.
PROBABILISTIC ANALYSIS OF PARTITIONING ALGORITHMS FOR THE TRAVELING-SALESMAN PROBLEM IN THE PLANE. IN: J. K. LENSTRA, A. H. G. RINNOOY KAN, P. VAN EMDE BOAS (EDS.): INTERFACES BETWEEN COMPUTER SCIENCE AND OPERATIONS RESEARCH, AMSTERDAM 1976, 141-168. MATHEMATICAL CENTRE TRACTS 99, AMSTERDAM: MATHEMATISCH CENTRUM. (1978).

KARP 1979 -1 KARP, R. M.
PATCHING ALGORITHM FOR THE NONSYMMETRIC TRAVELING-SALESMAN PROBLEM, A. SIAM JOURNAL ON COMPUTING 8, 561-573. (1979).

KARP 1980 -1 KARP, R. M.
ALGORITHM TO SOLVE THE M X N ASSIGNMENT PROBLEM IN EXPECTED TIME O(MN LOG N), AN. NETWORKS 10, 143-152. (1980).

KARPA 1981 -1 KARP, R. M.; ORLIN, J. B.
PARAMETRIC SHORTEST PATH ALGORITHMS WITH AN APPLICATION TO CYCLIC STAFFING. DISCRETE APPLIED MATHEMATICS 3, 37-46. (1981).

KARPB 1980 -1 KARP, R. M.; PAPADIMITRIOU, C. H.
ON LINEAR CHARACTERIZATIONS OF COMBINATORIAL OPTIMIZATION PROBLEMS. WORKING PAPER. BERKELEY: UNIV. OF CALIFORNIA, DEPT. OF ELECTRICAL ENGINEERING AND COMPUTER SCIENCE, 17 P. (1980).

KARW 1979 -1 KARWAN, M. H.; RARDIN, R. L.
SOME RELATIONSHIPS BETWEEN LAGRANGIAN AND SURROGATE DUALITY IN INTEGER PROGRAMMING. MATHEMATICAL PROGRAMMING 17, 320-334. (1979).

KARW 1981 -1 KARWAN, M. H.; RARDIN, R. L.
SURROGATE DUALITY IN A BRANCH-AND-BOUND PROCEDURE. NAVAL RESEARCH LOGISTICS QUARTERLY 28, 93-103. (1981).

KARWA 1980 -1 KARWAN, M. H.; VILLARREAL, B.
FATHOMING TOURS IN (MIXED) INTEGER LINEAR PROGRAMMING. WORKING PAPER. BUFFALO:STATE UNIV. OF NEW YORK AT BUFFALO, 26 P. (1980).

KARZ 1976 -1 KARZANOV, A. V.
ECONOMICAL REALIZATION OF THE EDMONDS ALGORITHMS FOR MATCHING MAXIMAL POWER AND MAXIMAL WEIGHT (RUSSIAN). IN: STUDIES IN DISCRETE OPTIMIZATION (RUSSIAN), 306-327. MOSCOW: IZDAT. "NAUKA". (1976).

KARZA 1978 -1 KARZANOV, A. V.; DINIC, E. A.
BOOLEAN OPTIMIZATION PROBLEM WITH CONSTRAINTS OF A SPECIAL TYPE (RUSSIAN), A. PREPRINT. MOSCOW: ALL-UNION INSTITUTE OF SYSTEM RESEARCH. (1978).

KAS 1977 -1 KAS, P.
ON PROBLEMS OF PREEMPTIVE SCHEDULING INTERPRETED BY NETWORK FLOW PROBLEMS (HUNGARIAN). ALKALMAZOTT MATEMATIKAI LAPOK 3, 131-138. (1977).

KAS 1979 -1 KAS, P.
ON A SPECIAL TYPE OF JOB SEQUENCING PROBLEM. IN: A. PREKOPA (ED.): SURVEY OF MATHEMATICAL PROGRAMMING, VOLUME 2, 279-284. AMSTERDAM: NORTH-HOLLAND. (1979).

KASA 1978 -1 KASAI, T.; KURODA, K.
GRAPH THEORETICAL CONSIDERATION ON INTERFERENCE BETWEEN SIMULTANEOUS TWO-COMMODITY FLOWS IN A DIRECTED NETWORK. BULLETIN OF UNIVERSITY OF OSAKA PREFECTURE. SERIES A. ENGINEERING AND NATURAL SCIENCES 27, 23-27. (1978).

KASS 1978 -1 KASSAY, F.
SENSITIVITY ANALYSIS OF A TRANSPORTATION PROBLEM. A CHANGE OF OBJECTIVE FUNCTION COEFFICIENTS-C(IJ) (CZECHOSLOVAKIAN). EKONOMICKO-MATEMATICKY OBZOR 14, 188-198. (1978).

KAST 1977 -1 KASTEV, S. B.
SOLUTION OF A GENERALIZED PROBLEM OF SET PARTITIONING (RUSSIAN). KIBERNETIKA, NO. 5, 115-120. (1977).

KATK 1977 -1 KATKHANOV, M. N.; BURLAKOV, E. A.; SAFRONOV, V. V.
OPTIMIZATION ALGORITHM OF THE TOLERANCES ON PARAMETERS OF THE ELEMENTS OF A COMPLEX SYSTEM (RUSSIAN). AVTOMATIKA I VYCISLITEL'NAJA TEHNIKA, NO. 3, 49-53. (1977).

KATO 1978 -1 KATOH, N.
O(KN**2) ALGORITHM FOR OBTAINING THE K-TH SHORTEST SIMPLE PATHS IN AN UNDIRECTED GRAPH WITH NON-NEGATIVE ARC LENGTH (JAPANESE), AN. TRANSACTIONS OF INSTITUTE OF ELECTRONICS AND COMMUNICATION ENGINEERS OF JAPAN 61-A, 1199-1206. (1978).

KATOA 1979 -1 KATOH, N.; IBARAKI, T.; MINE, H.
ALGORITHMS FOR A VARIANT OF THE RESOURCE ALLOCATION PROBLEM. JOURNAL OF THE OPERATIONS RESEARCH SOCIETY OF JAPAN 22, 287-300. (1979).

KATOA 1979 -2 KATOH, N.; IBARAKI, T.; MINE, H.
POLYNOMIAL TIME ALGORITHM FOR THE RESOURCE ALLOCATION PROBLEM WITH A CONVEX OBJECTIVE FUNCTION, A. OPERATIONAL RESEARCH SOCIETY JOURNAL 30, 449-455. (1979).

KATOA 1980 -1 KATOH, N.; IBARAKI, T.; MINE, H.
NOTES ON THE PROBLEM OF THE ALLOCATION OF RESOURCES TO ACTIVITIES IN DISCRETE QUANTITIES. JOURNAL OF THE OPERATIONAL RESEARCH SOCIETY 31, 595-598. (1980).

KATS 1980 -1 KATS, V. B.; MIKHAJLETSKIJ, Z. N.
SOLUTION EXACTE D'UN PROBLEME D'ORDONNANCEMENT OPTIMAL D'UN PROCESSUS CYCLIQUE (RUSSIAN). AVTOMATIKA I TELEMEHANIKA (MOSCOW) NO. 3, 187-190; TRANSLATED AS AUTOMATION AND REMOTE CONTROL. (1980).

KATSA 1979 -1 KATSNEL'SON, M. B.; KHRANOVICH, I. L.
TRANSPORT PROBLEM ON A NETWORK WITH AMPLIFICATION IN THE ARCS. I. THE SOLUTION METHOD. AVTOMATIKA I TELEMEHANIKA, NO. 1, 98-109; TRANSLATED AS AUTOMATION AND REMOTE CONTROL 40, 77-86. (1979).

KATZ 1979 -1 KATZ, I. N.; COOPER, L.
FACILITY LOCATION IN THE PRESENCE OF FORBIDDEN REGIONS, I: FORMULATION, AND THE CASE OF EUCLIDEAN DISTANCE WITH ONE FORBIDDEN CIRCLE. REPORT NO. SSM 7908. ST. LOUIS: WASHINGTON UNIV., DEPT. OF SYSTEMS SCIENCE AND MATHEMATICS, 16 P. (1979).

KAUF 1978 -1 KAUFMAN, L.; BROECKX, F.
ALGORITHM FOR THE QUADRATIC ASSIGNMENT PROBLEM USING BENDERS DECOMPOSITION, AN. EUROPEAN JOURNAL OF OPERATIONAL RESEARCH 2, 207-211. (1978).

KAUF 1981 -1 KAUFMAN, L.; BROECKX, F.
CENTER LOCATION PROBLEM WITH AN INVESTMENT CONSTRAINT, A. IN: R. E. BURKARD, T. ELLINGER (EDS.): METHODS OF OPERATIONS RESEARCH 40, 345-350. KOENIGSTEIN: ANTON HAIN MEISENHEIM. (1981).

KAUFA 1977 -1 KAUFMAN, L.; EEDE, M. VANDEN; HANSEN, P.
PLANT AND WAREHOUSE LOCATION PROBLEM, A. OPERATIONAL RESEARCH QUARTERLY 28, 547-554. (1977).

KAUFB 1980 -1 KAUFMAN, L.; PLASTRIA, F.
GENERALISATION OF THE WEBER LOCATION PROBLEM, A. CSOOTW/142. BRUSSEL: VRIJE UNIV. BRUSSEL, CENTRUM VOOR STATISTIEK EN OPERATIONEEL ONDERZOEK, 14 P. (1980).

KAUFC 1972 -1 KAUFMAN, M. T.
ANOMALIES IN SCHEDULING UNIT-TIME TASKS. TECHNICAL REPORT 34. STANFORD: STANFORD ELECTRONIC LABORATORY. (1972).
KAUFD 1977 -1 KAUFMANN, A.; HENRY-LABORDERE, A.
INTEGER AND MIXED PROGRAMMING. THEORY AND APPLICATIONS. MATHEMATICS IN SCIENCE AND ENGINEERING 137. NEW YORK, SAN FRANCISCO, LONDON: ACADEMIC PRESS, 379 P. (1977).
KAUFE 1977 -1 KAUFMANN, A.; PICHAT, E.
METHODES MATHEMATIQUES NON NUMERIQUES ET LEURS ALGORITHMES. TOME 1 ALGORITHMES DE RECHERCHE DES ELEMENTS MAXIMAUX. PARIS, NEW YORK U.A.: MASSON, 189 P. (1977).
KAUFE 1977 -2 KAUFMANN, A.; PICHAT, E.
METHODES MATHEMATIQUES NON NUMERIQUES ET LEURS ALGORITHMES. TOME 2 ALGORITHMES DE RECHERCHE DE CHEMINS ET PROBLEMS ASSOCIES. PARIS, NEW YORK U.A.: MASSON, 159 P. (1977).
KAZA 1974 -1 KAZAKOVA, M. F.
PROBLEM OF FINDING THE PARETO OPTIMA IN A POLYMATRIX TRAVELLING SALESMAN PROBLEM (RUSSIAN), THE. EKONOMIKA I MATEMATICESKIE METODY, SUPPLEMENT TO NO. 5, 55-61. (1974).
KEIT 1979 -1 KEITH, E. G.
OPERATOR SCHEDULING. AIIE TRANSACTIONS 11, 37-41. (1979).
KELA 1978 -1 KELAHAN, R. C.; GADDY, J. L.
APPLICATION OF THE ADAPTIVE RANDOM SEARCH TO DISCRETE AND MIXED INTEGER OPTIMIZATION. INTERNATIONAL JOURNAL FOR NUMERICAL METHODS IN ENGINEERING 12, 289-298. (1978).
KELL 1979 -1 KELLER, H.; MUELLER, W.
OPTIMIERUNG DES SCHUELERNAHVERKEHRS DURCH GEMISCHT GANZZAHLIGE PROGRAMMIERUNG. ZEITSCHRIFT FUER OPERATIONS RESEARCH 23, SERIE B, NO. 4, B105-B122. (1979).
KELM 1976 -1 KELMANS, A. K.
OPERATIONS OVER GRAPHS THAT INCREASE THE NUMBER OF THEIR TREES (RUSSIAN). IN: A. A. FRIDMAN (ED.): STUDIES IN DISCRETE OPTIMIZATION (RUSSIAN), 406-424. MOSCOW: IZDAT. "NAUKA". (1976).
KELM 1980 -1 KELMANS, A. K.
CONCEPT OF A VERTEX IN A MATROID AND 3-CONNECTED GRAPHS. JOURNAL OF GRAPH THEORY 4, 13-19. (1980).
KELM 1981 -1 KELMANS, A. K.
CONCEPT OF A VERTEX IN A MATROID, THE NON-SEPARATING CYCLES OF A GRAPH AND A NEW CRITERION FOR GRAPH PLANARITY, THE. IN: L. LOVASZ, V. T. SOS (EDS.): ALGEBRAIC METHODS IN GRAPH THEORY, VOL. I, 345-388. COLLOQUIA MATHEMATICA SOCIETATIS JANOS BOLYAI 25. AMSTERDAM, OXFORD,NEW YORK: NORTH-HOLLAND. (1981).
KELT 1978 -1 KELTON, W. D.; LAW, A. M.
MEAN-TIME COMPARISON OF ALGORITHMS FOR THE ALL-PAIRS SHORTEST-PATH PROBLEM WITH ARBITRARY ARC LENGTHS, A. NETWORKS 8, 97-106. (1978).
KEMP 1979 -1 KEMPER, F. M.
ALGORITHM FOR FORMATION OF THE ESSENTIAL CONSTRAINTS OF A TRANSPORT PROBLEM WITH PROHIBITIONS (RUSSIAN), AN. IN: MATEMATICHESKIE METODY RESHENIYA EHKONOMICHESKIKH ZADACH (MOSCOW), NO. 8, 126-134. (1979).
KENN 1978 -1 KENNINGTON, J. L.
SURVEY OF LINEAR COST MULTICOMMODITY NETWORK FLOWS, A. OPERATIONS RESEARCH 26, 209-236. (1978).
KENNA 1976 -1 KENNINGTON, J. L.; SHALABY, M.
EFFECTIVE SUBGRADIENT PROCEDURE FOR MINIMAL COST MULTICOMMODITY FLOW PROBLEMS, AN. TECH. REPORTS IEOR 750010. DALLAS: SOUTHERN METHODIST UNIVERSITY, DEPARTMENT OF INDUSTRIAL ENGINEERING AND OPERATIONS RESEARCH, 23 P. (1976).
KEOW 1978 -1 KEOWN, A. J.; MARTIN, J. D.
CAPITAL BUDGETING IN THE PUBLIC SECTOR: A ZERO-ONE GOAL PROGRAMMING APPROACH. FINANCIAL MANAGEMENT 7, NO. 2, 21-27. (1978).
KEOWA 1980 -1 KEOWN, A. J.; TAYLOR, B. W. III
CHANCE-CONSTRAINED INTEGER GOAL PROGRAMMING MODEL FOR CAPITAL BUDGETING IN THE PRODUCTION AREA, A. JOURNAL OF THE OPERATIONAL RESEARCH SOCIETY 31, 579-590. (1980).
KERG 1980 -1 KERGALL, Y.
CHAINES DE LONGUEUR MAXIMUM D'UN ARBRE. INFORMATIQUE ET SCIENCES HUMAINES 10, NO. 43, 31-43. (1980).
KERI 1978 -1 KERI, G.
ON THE POSSIBILITY OF CYCLING IN THE SIMPLEX ALGORITHM APPLIED TO THE TRANSPORTATION PROBLEM (HUNGARIAN). ALKALMAZOTT MATEMATIKAI LAPOK (BUDAPEST) 4, 193-196. (1978).
KERI 1981 -1 KERI, G.
ON THE REDUCTION OF A BIPARTITE GRAPH TO IRREDUCIBLE COMPONENTS. IN: L. LOVASZ, V. T. SOS (EDS.): ALGEBRAIC METHODS IN GRAPH THEORY, VOL. I, 389-398. COLLOQUIA MATHEMATICA SOCIETATIS JANOS BOLYAI 25. AMSTERDAM, OXFORD,NEW YORK: NORTH-HOLLAND. (1981).
KEST 1980 -1 KESTEN, H.
ON THE TIME CONSTANT AND PATH LENGTH OF FIRST-PASSAGE PERCOLATION. ADVANCES IN APPLIED PROBABILITY 12, 848-863. (1980).
KESTA 1978 -1 KESTENBAND, B. C.; YOUNG, H. P.
MATROID DESIGNS OF PRIME POWER INDEX. JOURNAL OF COMBINATORIAL THEORY 24, SERIES A, 211-234. (1978).
KEVO 1978 -1 KEVORKIAN, A. K.
GENERAL TOPOLOGICAL RESULTS ON THE CONSTRUCTION OF A MINIMUM ESSENTIAL SET OF A DIGRAPH. FORT COLLINS: SYMPOSIUM ON COMBINATORIAL MATHEMATICS AND OPTIMAL DESIGN, 29 P. (1978).
KEVO 1979 -1 KEVORKIAN, A. K.
GRAPH-THEORETIC CHARACTERIZATION OF THE MATRIX PROPERTY OF FULL IRREDUCIBILITY WITHOUT USING A TRANSVERSAL. JOURNAL OF GRAPH THEORY 3, 151-174. (1979).
KHAD 1977 -1 KHADZHIIVANOV, N. G.
GRAPH INEQUALITES (RUSSIAN). COMPTES RENDUS DE L'ACADEMIE BULGARE DES SCIENCES (SOFIA) 30, NO. 6, 793-800. (1977).
KHADA 1978 -1 KHADZHIIVANOV, N. G.; NIKIFOROV, V. S.
INEGALITE DE NORDHAUS-STEWART-MOON-MOSER (RUSSIAN). SERDICA 4, 344-350. (1978).
KHAK 1978 -1 KHAKIMOV, A.
ADVANTAGE OF THE OPERATIVE METHOD OF MANAGING A TRANSPORTATION SYSTEM BETWEEN TWO POINTS (RUSSIAN). DOKLADY AKADEMII NAUK TADZIKSKOI SSR 21, 16-19. (1978).
KHAN 1974 -1 KHAN, A. W.
ON SEQUENCING ORDERED MATRIX FLOWSHOP PROBLEMS. DISSERTATION. LUBBOCK: TEXAS TECHNOLOGICAL UNIVERSITY, 88 P. (1974).
KHAT 1979 -1 KHATOR, S.; MOODIE, C.
MACHINE LOADING PROCEDURE WHICH CONSIDERS PART COMPLEXITY AND MACHINE CAPABILITY, A. INTERNATIONAL JOURNAL OF PRODUCTION RESEARCH 17, 33-44. (1979).
KHRA 1979 -1 KHRANOVICH, I. L.
TRANSPORT PROBLEM ON A NETWORK WITH AMPLIFICATION IN THE ARCS. II. EFFECT OF PERTURBATIONS IN THE INITIAL DATA. AVTOMATIKA I TELEMEHANIKA, NO. 2, 90-99; TRANSLATED AS AUTOMATION AND REMOTE CONTROL 40, 225-233. (1979).

KHUM 1978 -1 KHUMAWALA, B. M.; NEEBE, A. W.
NOTE ON WARSZAWSKI'S MULTI-COMMODITY LOCATION PROBLEM, A. THE JOURNAL OF THE OPERATIONAL RESEARCH SOCIETY 29, 171-172. (1978).

KHUMA 1979 -1 KHUMAWALA, B. M.; STEINBERG, E.
EFFICIENT HEURISTIC FOR THE SINGLE SOURCE USER CAPACITATED WAREHOUSE LOCATION PROBLEM, AN. THE LOGISTICS AND TRANSPORTATION REVIEW 15, 517-526. (1979).

KIKU 1980 -1 KIKUNO, T.; YOSHIDA, N.; KAKUDA, Y.
NP-COMPLETENESS OF SOME TYPE OF P-CENTER PROBLEM. DISCRETE APPLIED MATHEMATICS 2, 361-363. (1980).

KIKUA 1979 -1 KIKUST, P. B.
ORGANIZATION OF SORTING IN THE SEARCH FOR THE MAXIMUM CLIQUE OF A GRAPH (RUSSIAN). LATVIISKII MATEMATICESKII EZEGODNIK (RIGA), NO. 23, 147-150, 274. (1979).

KIM 1976 -1 KIM, C.
ANALYSIS OF THE EXPECTED PERFORMANCE OF ALGORITHMS FOR THE PARTITION PROBLEM. COMPUTER SCIENCE TECHNICAL REPORT. COLLEGE PARK: UNIVERSITY OF MARYLAND. (1976).

KIM A 1975 -1 KIM, C. E.
APPROXIMATION ALGORITHMS FOR SOME P-COMPLETE SCHEDULING PROBLEMS. DISSERTATION. MINNEAPOLIS: UNIVERSITY OF MINNESOTA, 110 P. (1975).

KIME 1979 -1 KIMEMIA, J.; GERSHWIN, S. B.
NETWORK FLOW OPTIMIZATION IN FLEXIBLE MANUFACTURING SYSTEMS. IN: PROCEEDINGS OF THE 1978 IEEE CONFERENCE ON DECISION AND CONTROL, INCLUDING THE 17TH SYMPOSIUM ON ADAPTIVE PROCESSES, SAN DIEGO 1979, 633-639. NEW YORK: THE INSTITUTE OF ELECTRICAL AND ELECTRONICS ENGINEERS, INC. (1979).

KINB 1980 -1 KINBER, E. B.
POLYNOMIAL ALGORITHM FOR FINDING MINIMAL VERTEX COVERINGS FOR A CLASS OF PLANAR GRAPHS (RUSSIAN), A. IZVESTIJA VYSSIH UCEBNYH ZAVEDENII MATEMATIKA (KAZAN) NO. 1, 75-77. (1980).

KING 1979 -1 KING, J. R.
SCHEDULING AND THE PROBLEM OF COMPUTATIONAL COMPLEXITY. OMEGA 7, 233-240. (1979).

KINGA 1980 -1 KING, J. R.; SPACHIS, A. S.
HEURISTICS FOR FLOW-SHOP SCHEDULING. INTERNATIONAL JOURNAL OF PRODUCTION RESEARCH 18, 345-358. (1980).

KINGA 1980 -2 KING, J. R.; SPACHIS, A. S.
SCHEDULING: BIBLIOGRAPHY AND REVIEW. INTERNATIONAL JOURNAL OF PHYSICAL DISTRIBUTION AND MATERIALS MANAGEMENT (U.K.) 10, NO. 3, 100-132. (1980).

KINN 1977 -1 KINNEY, J. M.
ALMOST TRACEABLE GRAPHS AND TRACEABILITY. UNIVERSITY: UNIVERSITY OF MISSISSIPPI, 78 P. (1977). (DISSERTATION)

KIRK 1976 -1 KIRKPATRICK, D.
DETERMINING GRAPH PROPERTIES FROM MATRIX REPRESENTATIONS. IN: R. L. CONSTABLE (ED.): SIXTH ANNUAL ACM SYMPOSIUM ON THEORY OF COMPUTING, SEATTLE 1974, 84-90. NEW YORK: ASSOCIATION FOR COMPUTING MACHINERY. (1976).

KIRKA 1978 -1 KIRKPATRICK, D. G.; HELL, P.
ON THE COMPLEXITY OF A GENERALIZED MATCHING PROBLEM. IN: CONFERENCE RECORD OF THE TENTH ANNUAL ACM SYMPOSIUM ON THEORY OF COMPUTING, SAN DIEGO 1978, 240-245. NEW YORK: ASSOCIATION FOR COMPUTING MACHINERY. (1978).

KISE 1978 -1 KISE, H.; IBARAKI, T.; MINE, H.
SOLVABLE CASE OF THE ONE-MACHINE SCHEDULING PROBLEM WITH READY AND DUE TIMES, A. OPERATIONS RESEARCH 26, 121-126. (1978).

KISE 1979 -1 KISE, H.; IBARAKI, T.; MINE, H.
PERFORMANCE ANALYSIS OF SIX APPROXIMATION ALGORITHMS FOR THE ONE-MACHINE MAXIMUM LATENESS SCHEDULING PROBLEM WITH READY TIMES. JOURNAL OF THE OPERATIONS RESEARCH SOCIETY OF JAPAN 22, 205-224. (1979).

KISEA 1979 -1 KISE, H.; KABATA, M.; UNO, M.; IBARAKI, T.; MINE, H.
APPROXIMATION ALGORITHM FOR THE PARALLEL-MACHINE MAXIMUM LATENESS SCHEDULING PROBLEM WITH READY TIME CONSTRAINT. HONOLULU (14TH INTERNATIONAL TIMS MEETING, JUNE 1979) 10 P. (1979).

KISEB 1978 -1 KISE, H.; UNO, M.
ONE-MACHINE SCHEDULING PROBLEMS WITH EARLIEST START AND DUE TIME CONSTRAINTS. MEMOIRS OF THE FACULTY OF INDUSTRIAL ARTS, KYOTO TECHNICAL UNIVERSITY, SCIENCE AND TECHNOLOGY 27, 25-34. (1978).

KISEC 1979 -1 KISE, H.; UNO, M.; KABATA, M.
APPROXIMATION ALGORITHMS FOR IDENTICAL PARALLEL-MACHINE SCHEDULING PROBLEMS WITH READY TIMES AND PRECEDENCE CONSTRAINTS. MEMOIRS OF THE FACULTY OF INDUSTRIAL ARTS, KYOTO TECHNICAL UNIVERSITY, SCIENCE AND TECHNOLOGY 28, 64-72. (1979).

KIVI 1979 -1 KIVISTIK, L. A.
SOLUTION OF INTEGER PROGRAMMING PROBLEMS WITH ADDITIONAL ALTERNATIVE CONDITIONS (RUSSIAN), THE. IZVESTIJA AKADEMII NAUK ESTONSKOJ SSR, FIZIKA, MATEMATIKA (TALLIN) 28, 181-186. (1979).

KIVI 1980 -1 KIVISTIK, L. A.
DISCRETE MATHEMATICAL PROGRAMMING PROBLEMS WITH SEPARABLE FUNCTIONS (RUSSIAN). IZVESTIJA AKADEMII NAUK ESTONSKOI SSR, SERIJA FIZIKA-MATEMATIKA (TALLIN) 29, NO. 2, 120-126, 229. (1980).

KLAP 1980 -1 KLAPKA, J.; DVORAK, J.
MORE EFFICIENT COMPUTATION OF OPTIMAL LOT SIZES IN A MULTISTAGE PRODUCTION PROCESS (CZECHOSLOVAKIAN), A. EKONOMICKO-MATEMATICKY OBZOR 16, 179-189. (1980).

KLAS 1979 -1 KLASTORIN, T. D.
EFFECTIVE SUBGRADIENT ALGORITHM FOR THE GENERALIZED ASSIGNMENT PROBLEM, AN. COMPUTERS AND OPERATIONS RESEARCH 6, 155-164. (1979).

KLAS 1979 -2 KLASTORIN, T. D.
ON THE MAXIMAL COVERING LOCATION PROBLEM AND THE GENERALIZED ASSIGNMENT PROBLEM. MANAGEMENT SCIENCE 25, 107-112. (1979).

KLEE 1979 -1 KLEE, V.
COMBINATORIAL OPTIMIZATION: WHAT IS THE STATE OF THE ART? IN: P. C. C. WANG (ED.): INFORMATION LINKAGE BETWEEN APPLIED MATHEMATICS AND INDUSTRY, 71-136. NEW YORK: ACADEMIC PRESS. (1979).

KLEE 1980 -1 KLEE, V.
COMBINATORIAL OPTIMIZATION: WHAT IS THE STATE OF THE ART? MATHEMATICS OF OPERATIONS RESEARCH 5, 1-26. (1980).

KLEEA 1979 -1 KLEE, V.; LARMAN, D.
USE OF FLOYD'S ALGORITHM TO FIND SHORTEST RESTRICTED PATHS. IN: P. L. HAMMER, E. L. JOHNSON, B. H. KORTE (EDS.): DISCRETE OPTIMIZATION I, 237-249. ANNALS OF DISCRETE MATHEMATICS 4, AMSTERDAM, NEW YORK, OXFORD: NORTH-HOLLAND. (1979).

KLEI 1973 -1 KLEIMANN, P.
INHOMOGENEOUS MODELS OF ALLOCATION WITH FIXED SURCHARGES OF TWO CLASSES (RUSSIAN). EKONOMIKA I MATEMATICESKIE METODY 9, 753-756. (1973).

KLEIA 1980 -1 KLEIN, D.; HANNAN, E. L.
BRANCH AND BOUND ALGORITHM FOR THE MULTIPLE OBJECTIVE ZERO-ONE LINEAR PROGRAMMING PROBLEM, A. WORKING PAPER 79-2. WASHINGTON (ORSA/TIMS MEETING, MAY 1980) 26 P. (1980).

KLEIB 1979 -1 KLEIN, D.; HOLM, S.
INTEGER PROGRAMMING POST-OPTIMAL ANALYSIS WITH CUTTING PLANES. MANAGEMENT SCIENCE 25, 64-72. (1979).

KLEIC 1980 -1 KLEINDORFER, P. R.; LIEBER, Z.
EXISTENCE CONDITIONS FOR THE PRODUCTION SCHEDULING AND EMPLOYMENT SMOOTHING PROBLEM. INFOR 18, 62-67. (1980).

KLEID 1975 -1 KLEITMAN, D. J.
ALGORITHMS. ADVANCES IN MATHEMATICS 16, 233-245. (1975).

KLEIE 1972 -1 KLEITMAN, D. J.; CLAUS, A.
LARGE SCALE MULTICOMMODITY FLOW PROBLEM: TELPAK, A. IN: J. FOX (ED.): PROCEEDINGS OF THE SYMPOSIUM ON COMPUTER COMMUNICATIONS NETWORKS AND TELETRAFFIC, 335-338. NEW YORK: POLYTECHNIC PRESS. (1972).

KLEM 1978 -1 KLEMYSEV, O. F.
SOME COVERING PROBLEMS (ALGORITHMS WITH POWER ESTIMATES). IZVESTIJA AKADEMII NAUK SSSR. TEHNICESKAJA KIBERNETIKA, NO. 4, 205-208; TRANSLATED AS ENGINEERING CYBERNETICS 16, 1978, 155-159. (1978).

KLET 1979 -1 KLETIN, V. A.
ANALYSE DE L'EFFICACITE DES ALGORITHMES COMBINATOIRES DE RECHERCHE DES ARBRES EXTREMAUX SUR LES GRAPHES ORIENTES PONDERES (RUSSIAN). AVTOMATIKA I TELEMEHANIKA 11, 134-141. (1979).

KLIN 1979 -1 KLINGMAN, D.; MOTE, J.
MULTI-PERIOD PRODUCTION, DISTRIBUTION, AND INVENTORY PLANNING MODEL, A. RESEARCH REPORT CCS 364. AUSTIN: UNIV. OF TEXAS, CENTER FOR CYBERNETIC STUDIES, 42 P. (1979).

KLIN 1979 -2 KLINGMAN, D.; MOTE, J.
SOLUTION APPROACHES FOR NETWORK FLOW PROBLEMS WITH MULTIPLE CRITERIA. RESEARCH REPORT CCS 363. AUSTIN: UNIV. OF TEXAS, CENTER FOR CYBERNETIC STUDIES, 39 P. (1979).

KLINA 1978 -1 KLINGMAN, D.; MOTE, J.; WHITMAN, D.
IMPROVING FLOW MANAGEMENT AND CONTROL VIA IMPROVING SHORTEST PATH ANALYSIS. RESEARCH REPORT CCS 322. AUSTIN: UNIV. OF TEXAS, CENTER FOR CYBERNETIC STUDIES, 57 P. (1978).

KLUY 1979 -1 KLUYVER, C. A. DE
SOLVING THE MULTI-INDEX TRANSPORTATION PROBLEM BY DECOMPOSITION. ECONOMIC COMPUTATION AND ECONOMIC CYBERNETICS STUDIES AND RESEARCH 13, 85-105. (1979).

KLUYA 1980 -1 KLUYVER, C. A. DE; WHYTE, A. G. D.
FOREST HARVEST SCHEDULING IN FIJI: A COMPARATIVE CASE STUDY OF LINEAR PROGRAMMING, HEURISTIC AND DECOMPOSITION TECHNIQUES. NEW ZEALAND OPERATIONAL RESEARCH 8, 33-72. (1980).

KNAU 1979 -1 KNAUER, B.
SIMPLE ALGORITHM FOR MAXIMUM MATCHING OF GRAPHS, A. IN: L. COLLATZ, G. MEINARDUS, W. WETTERLING (EDS.): NUMERISCHE METHODEN BEI GRAPHENTHEORETISCHEN UND KOMBINATORISCHEN PROBLEMEN, BAND 2, OBERWOLFACH 1978, 184-194. ISNM 46, BASEL, BOSTON, STUTTGART: BIRKHAEUSER. (1979).

KNOE 1980 -1 KNOEDEL, W.
O(N**3) ALGORITHM FOR THE DECOMPOSITION OF A DIGRAPH, AN. IN: U. PAPE (ED.): DISCRETE STRUCTURES AND ALGORITHMS, 131-140. MUENCHEN: HANSER. (1980).

KNOE 1981 -1 KNOEDEL, W.
BIN PACKING ALGORITHM WITH COMPLEXITY O(N LOG N) AND PERFORMANCE 1 IN THE STOCHASTIC LIMIT, A. IN: J. GRUSKA, M. CHYTIL (EDS.): MATHEMATICAL FOUNDATIONS OF COMPUTER SCIENCE 1981, 369-378. LECTURE NOTES IN COMPUTER SCIENCE 118. BERLIN: SPRINGER. (1981).

KNUT 1974 -1 KNUTH, D.
POSTSCRIPT ABOUT NP-HARD PROBLEMS. ACM SIGACT NEWS 6, 15-16. (1974).

KNUTA 1977 -1 KNUTH, E.
ON THE SOLVABILITY OF RESOURCE ALLOCATION PROBLEMS (HUNGARIAN). ALKALMAZOTT MATEMATIKAI LAPOK 3, 27-63. (1977).

KOBA 1979 -1 KOBAYASHI, T.
COMBINATORIAL PROBLEMS AND THEIR ALGORITHMS IN OPERATIONS RESEARCH (JAPANESE). SYSTEMS AND CONTROL 23, 29-36. (1979).

KOCH 1979 -1 KOCH, E.
RAMIFICATIONS OF MATCHING THEORY. WATERLOO: UNIV. OF WATERLOO, 178 P. + APPENDIX (1979). (DISSERTATION)

KOCHA 1979 -1 KOCH, R.
ZUR LOESUNG ZWEIDIMENSIONALER ZUSCHNITTPROBLEME DURCH DIE ERZEUGUNG GUENSTIGER ZUSCHNITTVARIANTEN. WISSENSCHAFTLICHE ZEITSCHRIFT DER TECHNISCHEN HOCHSCHULE "OTTO VON GUERICKE" 23, 623-625. (1979).

KOCHB 1981 -1 KOCHMAN, G. A.; MAC CALLUM, C. J. JR.
FACILITY LOCATION MODELS FOR PLANNING A TRANSATLANTIC COMMUNICATIONS NETWORK. EUROPEAN JOURNAL OF OPERATIONAL RESEARCH 6, 205-211. (1981).

KOEH 1979 -1 KOEHLER, A. B.; MAC CLURE, R. H.
USE OF ARCS AND NODES FOR THE DETERMINATION OF CRITICAL PATHS IN PERT/CPM NETWORKS, THE. DECISION SCIENCES 10, 329-333. (1979).

KOEHA 1978 -1 KOEHLER, N.
BEWERTETE BAEUME. ARCHIV DER MATHEMATIK 30, NO. 1, 104-109. (1978).

KOEN 1981 -1 KOENE, J.
MAXIMAL FLOW THROUGH A PROCESSING NETWORK WITH THE SOURCE AS THE ONLY PROCESSING NODE. IN: R. E. BURKARD, T. ELLINGER (EDS.): METHODS OF OPERATIONS RESEARCH 40, 357-360. KOENIGSTEIN: ANTON HAIN MEISENHEIM. (1981).

KOER 1979 -1 KOERNER, F.
BEMERKUNGEN ZUM RUCKSACKPROBLEM. INFORMATIONEN 07-14-79. DRESDEN: TECHNISCHE UNIV. DRESDEN, 8 P. (1979).

KOER 1979 -2 KOERNER, F.
SORTIERUNG DER VERZWEIGUNGSREIHENFOLGE, DIE. INFORMATIONEN 07-13-79. DRESDEN: TECHNISCHE UNIV. DRESDEN, 9 P. (1979).

KOER 1979 -3 KOERNER, F.
STRUKTURUNTERSUCHUNGEN AM ALGORITHMUS VON KORTE, KRELLE UND OBERHOFER. INFORMATIONEN 07-12-79. DRESDEN: TECHNISCHE UNIV. DRESDEN, 10 P. (1979).

KOER 1980 -1 KOERNER, F.
EFFEKTIVER BRANCH AND BOUND ALGORITHMUS FUER DAS ISING PROBLEM, EIN. INFORMATIONEN 07-19-80. DRESDEN: TECH. UNIV. DRESDEN, SEKTION MATHEMATIK, 12 P. (1980).

KOER 1980 -2 KOERNER, F.
UEBER DAS DISKRETE QUADRATISCHE OPTIMIERUNGSPROBLEM. MANUSKRIPT 07-11-80. DRESDEN: TECHNISCHE UNIV. DRESDEN, 16 P. (1980).

KOER 1980 -3 KOERNER, F.
ZUR SUBTORELIMINATION BEIM TRAVELING SALESMAN PROBLEM. MANUSKRIPT 07-13-80. DRESDEN: TECHNISCHE UNIV. DRESDEN, 15 P. (1980).

KOH 1977 -1 KOH, K. M.
ON THE STABILITY NUMBER OF A GRAPH. NANYANG UNIVERSITY, NANTA MATHEMATICA 10, 53-57. (1977).

KOH A 1979 -1 KOH, K. M.; TAN, T.; ROGERS, D. G.
TWO THEOREMS ON GRACEFUL TREES. DISCRETE MATHEMATICS 25, 141-148. (1979).

****

KOKH 1977 -1 KOKHOV, V. O.; LAZARJEV, V. O.; SHAMAJEVA, O. YU.
EFFECTIVE ALGORITHM FOR THE RECOGNITION OF THE ISOMORPHISM OF DIRECTED GRAPHS (UKRAINIAN). AUTOMATYKA, NO. 6, 46-54. (1977).

KOLA 1980 -1 KOLASINSKA, E.
ON A MINIMUM CYCLE BASIS OF A GRAPH. ZASTOSOWANIA MATEMATYKI (WARSAW) 16, 631-639. (1980).

KOLC 1976 -1 KOLCOV, V. N.
DECOMPOSITION OF A BIPARTITE GRAPH INTO A MINIMAL NUMBER OF PLANE SUBGRAPHS (RUSSIAN). IN: A. JU. LEVIN (ED.): HEURISTIC OPTIMIZATION ALGORITHMS (RUSSIAN), 153-157. YAROSLAVL: JAROSLAV. GOS. UNIV. (1976).

KOLE 1979 -1 KOLEN, A.
COMPLEXITY OF LOCATION PROBLEMS ON NETWORKS. AFDELING TOEGEPASTE WISKUNDE BW 107/79. AMSTERDAM: MATHEMATISCH CENTRUM, 17 P. (1979).

KOLE 1979 -2 KOLEN, A.
ON "A CUT APPROACH TO THE RECTILINEAR DISTANCE FACILITY LOCATION PROBLEM" BY J.-C. PICARD AND H.D. RATLIFF. BW 103/79. AMSTERDAM: MATHEMATISCH CENTRUM, 10 P. (1979).

KOLE 1979 -3 KOLEN, A.
P-MEDIAN PROBLEM WITH MUTUAL COMMUNICATION ON A TREE, THE. AFDELING MATHEMATISCHE BESLISKUNDE BW 114/79. AMSTERDAM: MATHEMATISCH CENTRUM, 11 P. (1979).

KOLE 1980 -1 KOLEN, A.
DUALITY AND THE NONLINEAR ROUND-TRIP L-CENTER AND COVERING PROBLEMS ON A TREE. BW 123/80. AMSTERDAM: MATHEMATISCH CENTRUM, 19 P. (1980).

KOLEA 1981 -1 KOLESNIKOV, V. V.
ON A PROBLEM SOLUTION OF MACHINE PROCESSING SCHEDULE UNDER ORDINARY GRAPH (RUSSIAN). EKONOMIKA I MATEMATICESKIE METODY (MOSCOW) 17, NO. 1, 121-130. (1981).

KOMA 1979 -1 KOMAR, J.; LOS, J.
KOENIG THEOREM IN THE INFINITE CASE (EXTENDED ABSTRACT). IN: W. OETTLI, F. STEFFENS (EDS.): OPERATIONS RESEARCH VERFAHREN 32, THIRD SYMPOSIUM ON OPERATIONS RESEARCH, MANNHEIM 1978, 153-155. KOENIGSTEIN: ANTON HAIN MEISENHEIM. (1979).

KOMAA 1977 -1 KOMATSU, M.; OUCHI, Y.; NAKANISHI, H.; SANADA, H.; TEZUKA, Y.
OPTIMUM ROUTE ASSIGNMENT THEOREM AND ITS APPLICATION TO ADAPTIVE ROUTING PROCEDURE IN MESSAGE SWITCHING NETWORKS. ELECTRONICS AND COMMUNICATIONS IN JAPAN 60, NO. 12, 78-86. (1977).

KONO 1971 -1 KONONENKO, A. M.
TRANSPORTATION POLYTOPES OF ORDER 2 X N (RUSSIAN). IN: PROCEEDINGS OF THE FOURTH WINTER SCHOOL ON MATHEMATICAL PROGRAMMING AND RELATED QUESTIONS (RUSSIAN), DROGOBYCH 1971, 66-70. MOSCOW: MOSKOV. INZ.-STROITEL. INST. (1971).

KONOA 1978 -1 KONONENKO, A. M.; TRUKHANOVSKIJ, N. N.
ENUMERATION DES ARBRES MAXIMAUX D'UNE CLASSE DE GRAPHES BIPARTIS (RUSSIAN). VESCI AKADEMII NAVUK BSSR. SERYJA FIZIKA-MATEMATYCNYH NAVUK, NO. 6, 111-113. (1978).

KONOA 1978 -2 KONONENKO, A. M.; TRUKHANOVSKIJ, N. N.
POLYEDRES DE TRANSPORT AVEC UN NOMBRE MAXIMAL DE SOMMETS (RUSSIAN). VESCI AKADEMII NAVUK BSSR. SERYJA FIZIKA-MATEMATYCNYH NAVUK, NO. 5, 23-28. (1978).

KONOA 1979 -1 KONONENKO, A. M.; TRUKHANOVSKIJ, N. N.
CLASSES DE POLYEDRES DE TRANSPORT AVEC UN NOMBRE MAXIMAL DE SOMMETS (RUSSIAN). VESCI AKADEMII NAVUK BSSR. SERYJA FIZIKA-MATEMATYCNYH NAVUK, NO. 5, 123-125. (1979).

KONV 1978 -1 KONVALINA, J.; KOSLOSKI, R. M.
COMBINATORIAL ALGORITHM FOR GENERATING CYCLIC QUASI-HADAMARD MATRICES, A. UTILITAS MATHEMATICA 14, 269-277. (1978).

KONY 1978 -1 KONYA, I.; SOMOGYI, P.; SZABADOS, T.
METHOD OF TIME-TABLE CONSTRUCTION BY COMPUTER, A. PERIODICA POLYTECHNICA, ELECTRICAL ENGINEERING (BUDAPEST) 22, 171-181. (1978).

KORB 1977 -1 KORBUT, A. A.; SIGAL, I. H.; FINKELSTEIN, JU. JU.
BRANCH AND BOUND METHOD. A SURVEY OF THEORY, ALGORITHMS, PROGRAMS AND APPLICATIONS (RUSSIAN), THE. MATHEMATISCHE OPERATIONSFORSCHUNG UND STATISTIK SERIES OPTIMIZATION 8, 253-280. (1977).

KORB 1979 -1 KORBUT, A. A.; SIGAL, I. H.; FINKELSTEIN, JU. JU.
EFFECTIVENESS OF COMBINATORIAL METHODS IN DISCRETE PROGRAMMING (RUSSIAN), THE. IN: CURRENT STATE OF THE THEORY OF OPERATIONS RESEARCH, 283-310. MOSCOW: NAUKA. (1979).

KORC 1977 -1 KORCHEMKIN, M. B.
DECOMPOSITION OF NETWORK PROBLEMS BY THE METHOD OF SEPARATING AND GROUPING SIMPLE CIRCUITS (RUSSIAN). IN: K. A. BAGRINOVSKII, E. L. BERLJAND (EDS.): MODELS AND METHODS FOR THE ANALYSIS OF ECONOMIC TARGET-ORIENTED SYSTEMS (RUSSIAN), 47-51. NOVOSIBIRSK: IZDAT. "NAUKA" SIBIRSK. OTDEL. (1977).

KORC 1979 -1 KORCHEMKIN, M. B.
PIECEWISE SOLUTION OF A CERTAIN CLASS OF TRANSPORTATION PROBLEMS, THE. EESTI NSV TEADUSTE AKADEEMIA TOIMETISED. IZVESTIJA AKADEMII NAUK ESTONSKOI SSR. SERIJA FIZIKA-MATEMATIKA (TALLIN) 28, NO. 4, 317-324. (1979).

KORF 1978 -1 KORFHAGE, R. R.
SIGMA-POLYNOMIALS AND GRAPH COLORING. JOURNAL OF COMBINATORIAL THEORY 24, SERIES B, 137-153. (1978).

KORH 1979 -1 KORHONEN, P.
ALGORITHM FOR TRANSFORMING A SPANNING TREE INTO A STEINER TREE, AN. IN: A. PREKOPA (ED.): SURVEY OF MATHEMATICAL PROGRAMMING, VOLUME 2, 349-358. AMSTERDAM: NORTH-HOLLAND. (1979).

KORM 1975 -1 KORMAN, S. M.
GRAPH COLOURING AND RELATED PROBLEMS IN OPERATIONS RESEARCH. PH. D. THESIS. LONDON: IMPERIAL COLLEGE. (1975).

KORM 1979 -1 KORMAN, S. M.
GRAPH-COLOURING PROBLEM, THE. IN: N. CHRISTOFIDES, A. MINGOZZI, P. TOTH, C. SANDI (EDS.): COMBINATORIAL OPTIMIZATION, 211-236. CHICHESTER, NEW YORK, BRISBANE, TORONTO: WILEY. (1979).

KORN 1978 -1 KORNBLUM, D. F.
"GREEDY" ALGORITHMS FOR SOME LATTICE POLYHEDRA PROBLEMS. IN: F. HOFFMAN, D. MAC CARTHY, R. C. MULLIN, R. G. STANTON (EDS.): PROCEEDINGS OF THE NINTH SOUTHEASTERN CONFERENCE ON COMBINATORICS, GRAPH THEORY, AND COMPUTING, 437-456. CONGRESSUS NUMERANTIUM XXI. WINNIPEG: UTILITAS. (1978).

KORN 1978 -2 KORNBLUM, D. F.
GREEDY ALGORITHMS FOR SOME OPTIMIZATION PROBLEMS ON A LATTICE POLYHEDRON. NEW YORK: CITY UNIV. OF NEW YORK, 81 P. (1978). (DISSERTATION)

KORNA 1978 -1 KORNIENKO, N. M.; METELSKIJ, N. N.
DESCRIPTION OF PARTIAL ORDERINGS OF FEASIBLE SOLUTIONS OF INTEGER LINEAR PROGRAMMING PROBLEMS (RUSSIAN). DOKLADY AKADEMII NAUK BSSR 22, NO. 3, 208-211. (1978).

KORNB 1977 -1 KORNILOVA, L. E.; NGUYEN VAN VI
TRANSPORTATION PROBLEM WITH RESPECT TO THE TIME CRITERION (RUSSIAN). ISSLEDOVANIE OPERACIJ I ASU 9, 50-60 + 121. (1977).

KORNB 1977 -2 KORNILOVA, L. E.; NGUYEN VAN VI
TRANSPORTATION PROBLEM WITH RESPECT TO THE TIME CRITERION WITH AN ADDITIONAL CONSTRAINT (RUSSIAN). ISSLEDOVANIE OPERACIJ I ASU 9, 60-66 + 121. (1977).

KORNB 1977 -3 KORNILOVA, L. E.; NGUYEN VAN VI
TWO NONSTATIONARY NETWORK PROBLEMS (RUSSIAN). ISSLEDOVANIE OPERACII I ASU VYP. 10, 102-108, 142. (1977).
KORNC 1978 -1 KORNILOVA, L. E.; VOITISHIN, YU. V.
CERTAIN PROPERTIES OF ANTICHAINS OF PARTIALLY ORDERED SETS (RUSSIAN). KIBERNETIKA, NO. 5, 90-91. (1978).
KORO 1966 -1 KOROBKOV, V. K.; KRICHEVSKII, R. E.
ALGORITHMS FOR THE TRAVELING SALESMAN PROBLEM (RUSSIAN). IN: MATHEMATICAL MODELS AND METHODS OF OPTIMAL PLANNING, 106-108. NOVOSIBIRSK: NAUKA. (1966).
KORS 1977 -1 KORSHUNOV, A. D.
SOLUTION OF A PROBLEM OF P. ERDOES AND A. RENYI ON HAMILTONIAN CYCLES IN NON-ORIENTED GRAPHS (RUSSIAN). DISKRETNYI ANALIZ, NO. 31, METODY DISKRET. ANAL. V TEORII UPRAVLJAJUSCIH SISTEM, 17-56 + 90. (1977).
KORT 1980 -1 KORTANEK, K. O.; YAMASAKI, M.
EQUALITIES IN TRANSPORTATION PROBLEMS AND CHARACTERIZATIONS OF OPTIMAL SOLUTIONS. NAVAL RESEARCH LOGISTICS QUARTERLY 27, 589-596. (1980).
KORTA 1979 -1 KORTE, B.
APPROXIMATIVE ALGORITHMS FOR DISCRETE OPTIMIZATION PROBLEMS. IN: P. L. HAMMER, E. L. JOHNSON, B. H. KORTE (EDS.): DISCRETE OPTIMIZATION I, 85-120. ANNALS OF DISCRETE MATHEMATICS 4, AMSTERDAM, NEW YORK, OXFORD: NORTH-HOLLAND. (1979).
KORTA 1979 -2 KORTE, B.
GANZZAHLIGE PROGRAMMIERUNG. IN: M. J. BECKMANN, G. MENGES, R. SELTEN (EDS.): HANDWOERTERBUCH DER MATHEMATISCHEN WIRTSCHAFTSWISSENSCHAFTEN, BAND 3, 45-62. WIESBADEN: GABLER. (1979).
KORTA 1981 -1 KORTE, B.
MATROID PROPERTIES AND MATROID ORACLES. RESEARCH REPORT WP 81200-OR. BONN: UNIV. BONN, INST. FUER OEKONOMETRIE UND OPERATIONS RESEARCH, ABT. OPERATIONS RESEARCH. (1981).
KORTA 1981 -2 KORTE, B.
MATROIDS AND INDEPENDENCE SYSTEMS. RESEARCH REPORT WP 79148-OR. BONN: UNIV. BONN, INST. FUER OEKONOMETRIE UND OPERATIONS RESEARCH, ABT. OPERATIONS RESEARCH, 44 P. (1981).
KORTB 1981 -1 KORTE, B.; LOVASZ, L.
MATHEMATICAL STRUCTURES UNDERLYING GREEDY ALGORITHMS. IN: F. GECSEG (ED.): FUNDAMENTALS OF COMPUTATION THEORY, 205-209. LECTURE NOTES IN COMPUTER SCIENCE 117. BERLIN: SPRINGER. (1981).
KORTC 1979 -1 KORTE, B.; MONMA, C. L.
SOME REMARKS ON A CLASSIFICATION OF ORACLE-TYPE-ALGORITHMS. IN: L. COLLATZ, G. MEINARDUS, W. WETTERLING (EDS.): NUMERISCHE METHODEN BEI GRAPHENTHEORETISCHEN UND KOMBINATORISCHEN PROBLEMEN, BAND 2, OBERWOLFACH 1978, 195-215. ISNM 46, BASEL, BOSTON, STUTTGART: BIRKHAEUSER. (1979).
KORTD 1981 -1 KORTE, B.; SCHRADER, R.
ON THE EXISTENCE OF FAST APPROXIMATION SCHEMES. IN: O. L. MANGASARIAN, R. R. MEYER, P. M. ROBINSON (EDS.): NONLINEAR PROGRAMMING 4, 415-438. NEW YORK: ACADEMIC PRESS. (1981).
KORTD 1981 -2 KORTE, B.; SCHRADER, R.
SURVEY ON ORACLE TECHNIQUES, A. IN: J. GRUSKA, M. CHYTIL (EDS.): MATHEMATICAL FOUNDATIONS OF COMPUTER SCIENCE 1981, 61-77. LECTURE NOTES IN COMPUTER SCIENCE 118. BERLIN: SPRINGER. (1981).
KORZ 1978 -1 KORZAN, B.
ELEMENTS OF THE THEORY OF GRAPHS AND NETWORKS. METHODS AND APPLICATIONS (POLISH). WARSAW: WYDAWNICTWA NAUKOWO-TECHNICZNE, 279 P. (1978).
KOSA 1978 -1 KOSARAJU, S. R.
INSERTIONS AND DELETIONS IN ONE-SIDED HEIGHT-BALANCED TREES. COMMUNICATIONS OF THE ASSOCIATION FOR COMPUTING MACHINERY 21, 226-227. (1978).
KOSO 1978 -1 KOSOVSKII, N. K.
KOLMOGOROV'S SUBRECURSIVE ALGORITHMIC COMPLEXITY (RUSSIAN). VESTNIK LENINGRADSKOGO UNIVERSITETA, MATEMATIKA, MEHANIKA, ASTRONOMIJA, NO. 19, 54-59 + 150. (1978).
KOST 1979 -1 KOSTJUKOVA, O. I.
DUAL SUPPORT METHOD FOR SOLVING A MINIMAL COST FLOW PROBLEM ON A GENERALIZED NETWORK. AVTOMATIKA I TELEMEHANIKA, NO. 5, 104-113; TRANSLATED AS AUTOMATION AND REMOTE CONTROL 40, 1979, 713-721. (1979).
KOSTA 1977 -1 KOSTOCHKA, A. V.; MAZUROVA, N. P.
ESTIMATION DANS LA THEORIE DU COLORIAGE DES GRAPHES (RUSSIAN), UNE. AKADEMIJA NAUK SSSR. SIBIRSKOE OTDELENIE. INSTITUT MATEMATIKI. DISKETNYI ANALIZ. SBORNIK TRUDOV, NO. 30, 23-29. (1977).
KOSTB 1980 -1 KOSTREVA, M. M.
ADAPTIVE ESTIMATES IMPROVE BINARY PROGRAMMING. GMR-3217. WARREN: GENERAL MOTORS RESEARCH LABORATORIES, 18 P. (1980).
KOTZ 1975 -1 KOTZIG, A.
TRANSFORMATIONS OF EDGE-COLOURINGS OF GRAPHS. DISCRETE MATHEMATICS 11, 391-399. (1975).
KOTZ 1977 -1 KOTZIG, A.
CHANGE GRAPHS OF EDGE-COLOURINGS OF PLANAR CUBIC GRAPHS. JOURNAL OF COMBINATORIAL THEORY 22, SERIES B, 26-30. (1977).
KOTZA 1978 -1 KOTZIG, A.; LABELLE, J.
STRONGLY HAMILTONIAN GRAPHS. UTILITAS MATHEMATICA 14, 99-116. (1978).
KOTZA 1979 -1 KOTZIG, A.; LABELLE, J.
QUELQUES PROBLEMES OUVERTS CONCERNANT LES GRAPHES FORTEMENT HAMILTONIENS. LES ANNALES DES SCIENCES MATHEMATIQUES DU QUEBEC 3, 95-106. (1979).
KOU 1978 -1 KOU, L.; MARKOWSKY, G.; BERMAN, L.
FAST ALGORITHM FOR STEINER TREES, A. IBM RESEARCH REPORT, 7390. YORKTOWN HEIGHTS: IBM RESEARCH CENTER, 8 P. (1978).
KOUB 1981 -1 KOUBEK, V.; RIHA, A.
MAXIMUM K-FLOW IN A NETWORK, THE. IN: J. GRUSKA, M. CHYTIL (EDS.): MATHEMATICAL FOUNDATIONS OF COMPUTER SCIENCE 1981, 389-397. LECTURE NOTES IN COMPUTER SCIENCE 118. BERLIN: SPRINGER. (1981).
KOVA 1979 -1 KOVALEV, M. M.
POLYHEDRAL SEMIMATROIDS (RUSSIAN). VESCI AKADEMII NAVUK BSSR. SERYJA FIZIKA-MATEMATYCNYH NAVUK, NO. 3, 8-12. (1979).
KOVA 1980 -1 KOVALEV, M. M.
ANALYSIS OF THE GREEDY ALGORITHM FOR CONVEX INTEGER PROGRAMMING (RUSSIAN). VESCI AKADEMII NAVUK BSSR. SERYJA FIZIKA-MATEMATYCNYH NAVUK (MINSK) NO. 2, 69-75. (1980).
KOVA 1980 -2 KOVALEV, M. M.
PARTIAL ORDER METHOD (RUSSIAN). DOKLADY AKADEMII NAUK BSSR (MINSK) 24, NO. 2, 113-116. (1980).
KOVAA 1978 -1 KOVALEV, M. M.; GIRLICH, E.
EXACT NUMBER OF VERTICES OF POLYHEDRA IN THE CONDITIONS OF THE STANDARDIZATION PROBLEM (RUSSIAN), THE. VESCI AKADEMII NAVUK BSSR. SERYJA FIZIKA-MATEMATYCNYH NAVUK, NO. 2, 16-21 + 138. (1978).

KOVAB 1979 -1 KOVALEV, M. M.; ISACHENKO, A. N.
SEMIMATROIDE. IN: PROCEEDINGS OF THE 24. INT. WISS. KOLL. TECHNISCHE HOCHSCHULE ILMENAU, DDR, 1979, 57-59. (1979).

KOVAC 1978 -1 KOVALEV, M. M.; ISACHENKO, A. N.; NGUEN NGIA
LINEARISATION DES PROBLEMES COMBINATOIRES D'OPTIMISATION (RUSSIAN). DOKLADY AKADEMII NAUK BSSR 22, NO. 10, 869-872. (1978).

KOWA 1977 -1 KOWALCZYK, Z.
TRYING TO APPLY MATHEMATICAL PROGRAMMING TO THE PROBLEM OF CHOOSING AN OPTIMAL PROJECT VARIANT (POLISH). ZESZYTY NAUKOWE POLITEHNIKI GDANSKIEJ. BUDOWNICTWO LADOWE, NO. 31, 137-156. (1977).

KOZE 1978 -1 KOZEN, D.
CLIQUE PROBLEM EQUIVALENT TO GRAPH ISOMORPHISM, A. IN: SIGACT NEWS 10, 2 (1978), P. 50-52 (1978).

KOZEA 1979 -1 KOZERACKAJA, L. N.
MODIFICATION OF MC CLUSKEY'S ALGORITHM (RUSSIAN), A. ISSLEDOVANIE OPERACII I ASU (KIEV), NO. 14, 66-74, 135. (1979).

KOZL 1977 -1 KOZLOV, M. K.; SHAFRANSKIJ, V. V.
TIME SCHEDULING OF OPERATIUN COMPLEXES WITH LIMITED INTENSITIES OF EXECUTION OF COMPONENT OPERATIONS. IZVESTIJA AKADEMII NAUK SSSR. TEHNICESKAJA KIBERNETIKA NO.5, 38-43; TRANSLATED AS ENGINEERING CYBERNETICS 15, 1977, 25-30. (1977).

KOZU 1977 -1 KOZUHAROV, A. N.; LARICHEV, O. I.
MULTI-TEST ASSIGNMENT PROBLEM. AVTOMATIKA I TELEMEHANIKA, NO. 7, 71-88; TRANSLATED AS AUTOMATION AND REMOTE CONTROL 38, 1977, 1004-1018. (1977).

KOZU 1979 -1 KOZUHAROV, A. N.; LARICHEV, O. I.
MULTIPLE CRITERIA ASSIGNMENT PROBLEM: COMBINING THE COLLECTIVE CRITERION WITH INDIVIDUAL PREFERENCES. MATHEMATIQUES ET SCIENCES HUMAINES (PARIS), NO. 68, 63-77, 87. (1979).

KRAC 1978 -1 KRACKOVSKII, A. P.
FORMULA FOR THE MAXIMUM NUMBER OF VERTICES OF A TRANSPORTATION POLYTOPE (RUSSIAN), A. VESCI AKADEMII NAVUK BSSR. SERYJA FIZIKA-MATEMATYCNYH NAVUK, NO. 1, 105-106. (1978).

KRAC 1979 -1 KRACKOVSKII, A. P.
ASYMPTOTIC PROBLEM OF BOLKER (RUSSIAN), AN. VESCI AKADEMII NAVUK BSSR. SERYJA FIZIKA-MATEMATYCNYH NAVUK (MINSK), NO. 2, 118-120, 142. (1979).

KRACA 1979 -1 KRACKOVSKII, A. P.; EMELICHEV, V. A.
ESTIMATION OF THE UPPER LIMIT FOR THE TRANSPORT POLYTOPE DIAMETER (RUSSIAN). DOKLADY AKADEMII NAUK BSSR 23, 297-299 + 380. (1979).

KRAF 1981 -1 KRAFFT, O.
NOTE ON A SPECIAL TRANSPORTATION PROBLEM, A. METHODS OF OPERATIONS RESEARCH 39, 97-102. (1981).

KRAP 1978 -1 KRAPIVA, A. J.
ON CONSTRUCTING THE MINIMUM CUTTING-OFF SET OF THE GRAPH (RUSSIAN). KIBERNETIKA, NO. 4, 150-151. (1978).

KRAR 1978 -1 KRARUP, J.; PRUZAN, P. M.
COMPUTER-AIDED LAYOUT DESIGN. MATHEMATICAL PROGRAMMING STUDY 9, 75-94. (1978).

KRAR 1979 -1 KRARUP, J.; PRUZAN, P. M.
SELECTED FAMILIES OF LOCATION PROBLEMS. IN: P. L. HAMMER, E. L. JOHNSON, B. H. KORTE (EDS.): DISCRETE OPTIMIZATION II, 327-387. ANNALS OF DISCRETE MATHEMATICS 5, AMSTERDAM, NEW YORK, OXFORD: NORTH-HOLLAND. (1979).

KRAR 1980 -1 KRARUP, J.; PRUZAN, P. M.
IMPACT OF DISTANCE ON LOCATION PROBLEMS, THE. EUROPEAN JOURNAL OF OPERATIONAL RESEARCH 4, 256-269. (1980).

KRAR 1981 -1 KRARUP, J.; PRUZAN, P. M.
REDUCIBILITY OF MINIMAX TO MINISUM 0-1 PROGRAMMING PROBLEMS. EUROPEAN JOURNAL OF OPERATIONAL RESEARCH 6, 125-132. (1981).

KRARA 1981 -1 KRARUP, J.; PRUZAN, P. M.; BURKARD, R. E.
EFFICIENCY AND OPTIMALITY IN MINISUM, MINIMAX 0-1 PROGRAMMING PROBLEMS. IN: R. E. BURKARD, T. ELLINGER (EDS.): METHODS OF OPERATIONS RESEARCH 40, 361-366. KOENIGSTEIN: ANTON HAIN MEISENHEIM. (1981).

KRARB 1980 -1 KRARUP, J.; WALUKIEWICZ, S.
RELATIONS AMONG INTEGER PROGRAMS. IN: K. IRACKI, K. MALANOWSKI, P. WALUKIEWICZ (EDS.): OPTIMIZATION TECHNIQUES, PART II, 199-210. LECTURE NOTES IN CONTROL AND INFORMATION SCIENCES 23. BERLIN: SPRINGER. (1980).

KRAU 1979 -1 KRAUS, V.
USE OF MARKOV CHAINS IN SOLVING INTEGER OPTIMIZATION PROBLEMS (CZECHOSLOVAKIAN), THE. EKONOMICKO-MATEMATICKY OBZOR 15, 134-146. (1979).

KRAUA 1977 -1 KRAUSE, H.
MOEGLICHKEITEN ZUR LOESUNG VON ZWEISTUFIGEN TRANSPORTPROBLEMEN. WISSENSCHAFTLICHE ZEITSCHRIFT DER HOCHSCHULE FUER ARCHITEKTUR UND BAUWESEN IN WEIMAR 24, 445-449. (1977).

KRAV 1979 -1 KRAVETS, V. L.
CONCERNING THE SOLUTION OF A CLASS OF COVERING PROBLEMS BY DISCRETE OPTIMIZATION METHODS (RUSSIAN). KIBERNETIKA, NO. 4, 70-74. (1979).

KRAVA 1973 -1 KRAVTSOV, M. K.
DIFFERENCE METHOD FOR SOLVING THE ASSIGNMENT PROBLEM (RUSSIAN), A. VESCI AKADEMII NAVUK BSSR. SERYJA FIZIKA-MATEMATYCNYH NAVUK, NO. 5, 56-62 + 137. (1973).

KRAVA 1973 -2 KRAVTSOV, M. K.
ON THE QUESTION OF LOWERING THE DIMENSION OF A TRANSPORT PROBLEM (RUSSIAN). VESCI AKADEMII NAVUK BSSR, SERYJA FIZIKA-MATEMATYCNYH NAVUK 2, 59-62, 136. (1973).

KRAVA 1979 -1 KRAVTSOV, M. K.
(D-2)-DIMENSIONAL FACES OF A TRANSPORT POLYHEDRON OF DIMENSION D (RUSSIAN). VESCI AKADEMII NAVUK BSSR. SERYJA FIZIKA-MATEMATYCNYH NAVUK, NO. 3, 5-8. (1979).

KRAVB 1979 -1 KRAVTSOV, M. K.; EMELICHEV, V. A.
ESTIMATION PAR EXCES DU DIAMETRE D'UN POLYEDRE DE TRANSPORT (RUSSIAN). VESCI AKADEMII NAVUK BSSR. SERYJA FIZIKA-MATEMATYCNYH NAVUK, NO. 5, 121-123. (1979).

KRAVB 1979 -2 KRAVTSOV, M. K.; EMELICHEV, V. A.
UPPER BOUND FOR THE DIAMETER OF A TRANSPORT POLYTOPE (RUSSIAN). VESCI AKADEMII NAVUK BSSR (MINSK), SERYJA FIZIKA-MATEMATYCNYH NAVUK, 5, NO. 5, 121-123, 143. (1979).

KRAVC 1979 -1 KRAVTSOV, M. K.; KORZNIKOV, A. D.
ENUMERATION PROBLEMS ON TRUNCATED TRANSPORT POLYTOPES (RUSSIAN). VESCI AKADEMII NAVUK BSSR. SERYJA FIZIKA-MATEMATYCNYH NAVUK, NO. 4, 12-19. (1979).

KREI 1979 -1 KREININ, M. I.; NIKONOV, V. A.; SAVICKAJA, T. I.
SOLUTION OF A PROBLEM OF JOB-SHOP LOADING (RUSSIAN). IN: COMPUTATIONAL METHODS AND COMPUTER SOFTWARE, 76-83. KAZAN: KAZAN. UNIV. (1979).

KRES 1980 -1 KRESS, M.; TAMIR, A.
USE OF JACOBI'S LEMMA IN UNIMODULARITY THEORY, THE. MATHEMATICAL PROGRAMMING 18, 344-348. (1980).

KRIC 1978 -1 KRICHEL, R.
ANALYSE EINES RECHNERMODELLS DURCH RUECKFUEHRUNG AUF EIN 3-MASCHINEN- FLOW-SHOP-PROBLEM. ANGEWANDTE INFORMATIK 20, 258-267. (1978).

KRIS 1975 -1 KRISHNAMOORTHY, M. S.
NP-HARD PROBLEM IN BIPARTITE GRAPHS, AN. SIGACT NEWS 7, 26. (1975).

KRISA 1979 -1 KRISHNAMOORTHY, M. S.; DEO, N.
COMPLEXITY OF THE MINIMUM-DUMMY-ACTIVITIES PROBLEM IN A PERT NETWORK. NETWORKS 9, 189-194. (1979).

KRISA 1979 -2 KRISHNAMOORTHY, M. S.; DEO, N.
NODE-DELETION NP-COMPLETE PROBLEMS. SIAM JOURNAL ON COMPUTING 8, 619-625. (1979).

KRISB 1979 -1 KRISHNAMOORTHY, M. S.; SAKSENA, J. P.
ALGEBRA OF PROJECT NETWORKS. IN: PRODUCTIVITY VOL. 20 NO. 2, P. 205-218 (1979).

KRIV 1979 -1 KRIVONOZKO, V. E.; PROPOI, A. I.
METHOD FOR THE SOLUTION OF DYNAMIC TRANSPORTATION PROBLEMS. AVTOMATIKA I TELEMEHANIKA (MOSCOW) NO. 12, 133-145; TRANSLATED AS AUTOMATION AND REMOTE CONTROL 40, NO. 12, PART 2, 1817-1827. (1979).

KRON 1974 -1 KRONK, H.; RADLOWSKI, M.; FRANEN, B.
ON THE LINE CHROMATIC NUMBER OF TRIANGLE-FREE GRAPHS. GRAPH THEORY NEWSLETTER 3, NO. 3, 3. (1974).

KROU 1980 -1 KROUZEK, J.
ON THE DEVELOPMENT OF EFFICIENT PRODUCTION SCHEDULING AND CONTROL MODELS. EKONOMICKO-MATEMATICKY OBZOR 16, 171-178. (1980).

KUBA 1978 -1 KUBALE, M.; DABROWSKI, J.
EMPIRICAL COMPARISON OF EFFICIENCY OF SOME GRAPH COLOURING ALGORITHMS. ARCHIWUM AUTOMATYKI I TELEMECHANIKI 23, 129-139. (1978).

KUBO 1975 -1 KUBO, H.; OKINO, N.
NEW SOLUTION OF THE SYMMETRIC TRAVELLING SALESMAN PROBLEM, A. MEMOIRS OF THE FACULTY OF ENGINEERING, HOKKAIDO UNIVERSITY 14, 21-31. (1975).

KUBO 1975 -2 KUBO, H.; OKINO, N.
PRACTICAL APPROACHES TO THE TRAVELLING SALESMAN PROBLEM (JAPANESE). JOURNAL OF THE JAPANESE SOCIETY OF PRECISION ENGINEERING 41, 426-430. (1975).

KUBO 1976 -1 KUBO, H.; OKINO, N.
NEW PRACTICAL SOLUTION FOR LARGE-SCALE TRAVELING SALESMAN PROBLEMS (JAPANESE), A. JOURNAL OF THE OPERATIONS RESEARCH SOCIETY OF JAPAN 19, 272-285. (1976).

KUBOA 1977 -1 KUBO, N.; TSUKIYAMA, S.; SHIRAKAWA, I.; ARIYOSHI, H.
ALGORITHM FOR FINDING A MAXIMAL CUT, AN. ELECTRONICS AND COMMUNICATIONS IN JAPAN 60, NO. 4, 30-37. (1977).

KUBOB 1980 -1 KUBOKAWA, S.; SOSHIRODA, M.
SCHEDULING PROCEDURES FOR SPECIAL ORDER ITEMS IN A TWO-STAGE LOT PRODUCTION SYSTEM. INTERNATIONAL JOURNAL OF PRODUCTION RESEARCH 18, 43-56. (1980).

KUCE 1981 -1 KUCERA, L.
MAXIMUM FLOW IN PLANAR NETWORKS. IN: J. GRUSKA, M. CHYTIL (EDS.): MATHEMATICAL FOUNDATIONS OF COMPUTER SCIENCE 1981, 418-422. LECTURE NOTES IN COMPUTER SCIENCE 118. BERLIN: SPRINGER. (1981).

KUCH 1978 -1 KUCHARCZYK, J.
METHODS OF CLUSTER ANALYSIS AND THEIR ALGORITHMS IN THE PROGRAMMING LANGUAGE ALGOL 60. 1: HIERARCHICAL AGGLOMERATIVE METHODS. RAPORT NR. N-36. WROCLAW: WROCLAW UNIV., INSTITUE OF COMPUTER SCIENCE 31 P. (1978).

KUCH 1978 -2 KUCHARCZYK, J.
METHODS OF CLUSTER ANALYSIS AND THEIR ALGORITHMS IN THE PROGRAMMING LANGUAGE ALGOL 60. 3: METHODS BASED ON A GIVEN ORDERING OF OBJECTS. RAPORT NR. N-39. WROCLAW: WROCLAW UNIV., INSTITUTE OF COMPUTER SCIENCE, 23 P. (1978).

KUCH 1978 -3 KUCHARCZYK, J.
METHODS OF CLUSTER ANALYSIS AND THEIR REALIZATION IN THE PROGRAMMING LANGUAGE ALGOL 60. 2: HIERARCHICAL DIVISIVE METHODS DUE TO HUBERT. RAPORT NR. N-38. WROCLAW: WROCLAW UNIV., INSTITUTE OF COMPUTER SCIENCE, 16 P. (1978).

KUHN 1977 -1 KUHN, H. W.
PATHFIX: AN ALGORITHM FOR COMPUTING TRAFFIC EQUILIBRIA. IN: PROCEEDINGS OF THE 1977 IEEE CONFERENCE ON DECISION AND CONTROL, NEW ORLEANS 1977, VOL. I, 831-834. NEW YORK: IEEE. (1977).

KUKS 1978 -1 KUKSA, A. I.; LAPTIN, J. P.
DYNAMIC PROGRAMMING IN THE NETWORK PROBLEM FOR OBTAINING THE SHORTEST SCHEDULE. KIBERNETIKA, NO. 1, 111-113. (1978).

KULK 1978 -1 KULKARNI, K. H.
MINIMALLY LOCALLY 1-CONNECTED GRAPHS. BULLETIN OF THE AUSTRALIAN MATHEMATICAL SOCIETY 19, 77-80. (1978).

KUMA 1979 -1 KUMAR, S.
MAXIMUM RELIABILITY ROUTE SUBJECT TO M IMPROVEMENTS IN A NONDIRECTED NETWORK. IEEE TRANSACTIONS ON RELIABILITY R-28, 127-128. (1979).

KUMAA 1979 -1 KUMAR, S.; SHARMA, J.; RAY, L. M.
NEW TECHNIQUE FOR MULTIDIMENSIONAL CAPACITY EXPANSION PROJECTS, A. COMPUTERS AND ELECTRICAL ENGINEERING 6, 35-39. (1979).

KUND 1981 -1 KUNDE, M.
NONPREEMPTIVE LP-SCHEDULING ON HOMOGENEOUS MULTIPROCESSOR SYSTEMS. SIAM JOURNAL ON COMPUTING 10, 151-173. (1981).

KUNDA 1979 -1 KUNDU, S.
INTERMEDIATE-VALUE THEOREM FOR OPTIMUM TREE VALUATION, AN. INFORMATION PROCESSING LETTERS 8, 141-145. (1979).

KUNG 1978 -1 KUNG, J. P. S.
ALPHA FUNCTION OF A MATROID. I. TRANSVERSAL MATROIDS, THE. STUDIES IN APPLIED MATHEMATICS 58, NO. 3, 263-275. (1978).

KUNG 1978 -2 KUNG, J. P. S.
ALTERNATING BASIS EXCHANGES IN MATROIDS. PROCEEDINGS OF THE AMERICAN MATHEMATICAL SOCIETY 71, 355-358. (1978).

KUNG 1978 -3 KUNG, J. P. S.
BIMATROIDS AND INVARIANTS. ADVANCES IN MATHEMATICS 30, NO. 3, 238-249. (1978).

KUNG 1980 -1 KUNG, J. P. S.
ON SPECIALIZATIONS OF MATROIDS. STUDIES IN APPLIED MATHEMATICS 62, 183-187. (1980).

KUPC 1976 -1 KUPCOV, L. P.; SEROV, S. S.
SEARCH FOR THE COMPLETE OPTIMAL SOLUTION IN AN INTEGER LINEAR PROGRAMMING PROBLEM (RUSSIAN), THE. IN: CONTROL PROBLEMS IN TECHNOLOGY, ECONOMICS AND BIOLOGY (RUSSIAN), 109-121, 225. MOSCOW: NAUKA. (1976).

KURB 1980 -1 KURBEL, K.
PRINCIPLES OF SOFTWARE DESIGN FOR QUANTITATIVE METHODS: AN APPLICATION TO LOT SIZE PLANNING, SEQUENCING, AND SCHEDULING. IN: H. KOENIG, V. STEINMETZ (EDS.): METHODS OF OPERATIONS RESEARCH 38, 355-370. KOENIGSTEIN: ANTON HAIN MEISENHEIM. (1980).

****

KURE 1977 -1 KUREJCHIK, V. M.
APPLICATION OF STRUCTURAL NUMBERS TO THE CONSTRUCTION OF INDEPENDENT SUBSETS OF THE SET OF VERTICES OF A GRAPH (RUSSIAN). IZVESTIJA AKADEMII NAUK SSSR. TEHNICESKAJA KIBERNETIKA, NO. 6, 126-131. (1977).

KURE 1979 -1 KUREJCHIK, V. M.
ALGORITHME POUR DETERMINER LES SOUS-ENSEMBLES EXTERIEUREMENT STABLES EN SE BASANT SUR LES NOMBRES STRUCTURAUX (RUSSIAN). IZVESTIJA VYSSIH UCEBNYH ZAVEDENII. ELEKTROMEHANIKA, NO. 7, 577-581. (1979).

KUREA 1979 -1 KUREJCHIK, V. M.; LITVINENKO, V. A.
DETERMINATION OF THE CLIQUES OF A SYMMETRIC GRAPH (RUSSIAN). SEVERO-KAVKAZSKOGO NAUCNOGO CENTRA VYSSEI SKOLY. IZVESTIJA. SERIJA TEHNICESKIE NAUKI, NO. 2, 13-16. (1979).

KURI 1976 -1 KURISU, T.
TWO-MACHINE SCHEDULING UNDER REQUIRED PRECEDENCE AMONG JOBS. JOURNAL OF THE OPERATIONS RESEARCH SOCIETY OF JAPAN 19, 1-13. (1976).

KURI 1977 -1 KURISU, T.
THREE-MACHINE SCHEDULING PROBLEM WITH PRECEDENCE CONSTRAINTS. JOURNAL OF THE OPERATIONS RESEARCH SOCIETY OF JAPAN 20, 231-242. (1977).

KURI 1977 -2 KURISU, T.
TWO-MACHINE SCHEDULING UNDER ARBITRARY PRECEDENCE CONSTRAINTS. JOURNAL OF THE OPERATIONS RESEARCH SOCIETY OF JAPAN 20, 113-131. (1977).

KURI 1979 -1 KURISU, T.
SINGLE-MACHINE SEQUENCING WITH PRECEDENCE CONSTRAINTS AND DEFERRAL COSTS. JOURNAL OF THE OPERATIONS RESEARCH SOCIETY OF JAPAN 22, 1-15. (1979).

KURIA 1975 -1 KURIYAMA, S.; SHIMOSAKON, T.; NOSE, T.; TOKIOKA, H.
APPLICATION OF DYNAMIC PROGRAMMING TO OBTAIN AN OPTIMAL INVENTORY TRANSPORTATION SYSTEM FOR SEASONAL GOODS (AN N-STATION INVENTORY TRANSSHIPMENT MODEL) (JAPANESE). AN. MEMOIRS OF THE OSAKA INSTITUTE OF TECHNOLOGY. SERIES A. SCIENCE AND TECHNOLOGY 20, NO. 2, 191-220. (1975).

KUSH 1981 -1 KUSHNER, D. D.; DAVIS, K. R.
COST ANALYSIS OF FOUR ASSIGNMENT HEURISTICS IN DYNAMIC LINE BALANCING. RESEARCH REPORT. ATLANTA: GEORGIA STATE UNIV., DEPT. OF QUANTITATIVE METHODS, 46 P. (1981).

KUZO 1979 -1 KUZDRALL, P. J.; MELNYK, S. A.; PIPER, C. J.
COMPARATIVE ANALYSIS OF LOT-SIZING ALGORITHM PERFORMANCE, A. WORKING PAPER. LONDON: UNIV. OF WESTERN ONTARIO, SCHOOL OF BUSINESS ADMINSTRATION, 17 P. (1979).

KUZJ 1979 -1 KUZJURIN, N. N.
QUELQUES ESTIMATIONS RECURRENTES ET ASYMPTOTIQUES DANS LE PROBLEME DE RECOUVREMENTS (RUSSIAN). AKADEMIJA NAUK SOJUZA SSR. MATEMATICESKIE ZAMETKI 26, 603-611. (1979).

KUZN 1976 -1 KUZNETSOV, V. A.
METHOD FOR THE SOLUTION OF A TRANSPORTATION-PRODUCTION PROBLEM OF A SPECIAL FORM (RUSSIAN), A. PRIMENENIE MATEMATIKI V EKONOMIKE, NO. 11, 13-23. (1976).

KUZNA 1978 -1 KUZNETSOV, V. F.
SOLUTION OF AN INTEGER-VALUED PROBLEM OF DISTRIBUTION OF RESOURCES IN THE CASE OF RENEWAL OPERATIONS. IZVESTIJA AKADEMII NAUK SSSR. TEHNICESKAJA KIBERNETIKA (MOSCOW) NO. 6, 33-37; TRANSLATED AS ENGINEERING CYBERNETICS 16, NO. 6, 26-30. (1978).

LABA 1977 -1 LABADIE, J. W.; MORROW, D. M.; CHEN, Y. H.
HEURISTIC MULTIDIMENSIONAL DYNAMIC PROGRAMMING ALGORITHM FOR URBAN STORMWATER MANAGEMENT. ATLANTA (52. ORSA-MEETING + TIMS, NOVEMBER 1977) 37 P. (1977).

LABE 1978 -1 LABETOULLE, J.; LAWLER, E. L.; LENSTRA, J. K.; RINNOOY KAN, A. H. G.
PREEMPTIVE SCHEDULING OF UNIFORM MACHINES (PRELIMINARY DRAFT). URBINO: SUMMER SCHOOL IN COMBINATORIAL OPTIMIZATION, 18 P. (1978).

LABE 1979 -1 LABETOULLE, J.; LAWLER, E. L.; LENSTRA, J. K.; RINNOOY KAN, A. H. G.
PREEMPTIVE SCHEDULING OF UNIFORM MACHINES SUBJECT TO RELEASE DATES. BW 99/79. AMSTERDAM: MATHEMATISCH CENTRUM, 19 P. (1979).

LADE 1979 -1 LADERMAN, J. D.
COMPUTATIONAL COMPLEXITY: ALGORITHMS WITH FEWEST OPERATIONS. IN: P. R. MEYER (ED.): PAPERS IN MATHEMATICS, 45-53. ANNALS OF THE NEW YORK ACADEMY OF SCIENCES 321, NEW YORK: NEW YORK ACADEMY OF SCIENCES. (1979).

LAGE 1977 -1 LAGEWEG, B. J.; LENSTRA, J. K.; RINNOOY KAN, A. H. G.
JOB-SHOP SCHEDULING BY IMPLICIT ENUMERATION. MANAGEMENT SCIENCE 24, 441-450. (1977).

LAGE 1978 -1 LAGEWEG, B. J.; LENSTRA, J. K.; RINNOOY KAN, A. H. G.
GENERAL BOUNDING SCHEME FOR THE PERMUTATION FLOW-SHOP PROBLEM, A. OPERATIONS RESEARCH 26, 53-67. (1978).

LAGE 1979 -1 LAGEWEG, B. J.; LENSTRA, J. K.; RINNOOY KAN, A. H. G.
MINIMIZING MAXIMUM LATENESS ON ONE MACHINE: ALGORITHMS AND APPLICATIONS. IN: N. CHRISTOFIDES, A. MINGOZZI, P. TOTH, C. SANDI (EDS.): COMBINATORIAL OPTIMIZATION, 371-388. CHICHESTER, NEW YORK, BRISBANE, TORONTO: WILEY. (1979).

LAGO 1973 -1 LAGOSHA, B. A.
DETERMINATION OF OPTIMAL ROUTES FOR FREIGHTSHIPS (SPANISH). INVESTIGACION OPERACIONAL, NO. 9, 35-42. (1973).

LAHR 1979 -1 LAHRICHI, A.
COUTS MOYENS DE CIRCUITS HAMILTONIENS DE K(N). REVUE FRANCAISE D'AUTOMATIQUE, D'INFORMATIQUE ET DE RECHERCHE OPERATIONELLE 13, SERIE RECHERCHE OPERATIONELLE, 199-204. (1979).

LAHR 1979 -2 LAHRICHI, A.
ORDONNANCEMENTS; LA NOTION DE PARTIE OBLIGATOIRE ET SON APPLICATION AUX PROBLEMES CUMULATIFS. DISSERTATION. PARIS: UNIVERSITY OF PARIS 6. (1979).

LAKS 1978 -1 LAKSHMINARAYAN, S.; LAKSHMANAN, R.; PAPINEAU, R. L.; ROCHETTE, R.
OPTIMAL SINGLE MACHINE SCHEDULING WITH EARLINESS AND TARDINESS PENALTIES. OPERATIONS RESEARCH 26, 1079-1082. (1978).

LAKS 1979 -1 LAKSHMINARAYAN, S.; LAKSHMANAN, R.; PAPINEAU, R. L.; ROCHETTE, R.
ORDER PRESERVING ALLOCATION OF JOBS TO TWO NON-IDENTICAL PARALLEL MACHINES: A SOLVABLE CASE OF THE MAXIMUM CUT PROBLEM. INFOR 17, 230-241. (1979).

LAM 1975 -1 LAM, S.
WORST CASE ANALYSIS OF MULTIPROCESSOR SCHEDULING ALGORITHMS. UNIVERSITY PARK: PENNSYLVANIA STATE UNIV., 118 P. (1975). (DISSERTATION)

LAM A 1975 -1 LAM, S.; SETHI, R.
WORST CASE ANALYSIS OF THE COFFMAN-GRAHAM SCHEDULING ALGORITHM. IN: PROCEEDINGS OF THE 1975 CONFERENCE ON INFORMATION SCIENCES AND SYSTEMS, BALTIMORE 1975, 160-165. BALTIMORE: THE JOHNS HOPKINS UNIVERSITY: DEPARTMENT OF ELECTRICAL ENGINEERING. (1975).

LAMB 1979 -1 LAMBRECHT, M. R.; VANDERVEKEN, H.
HEURISTIC PROCEDURES FOR THE SINGLE OPERATION, MULTI-ITEM LOADING PROBLEM. AIIE TRANSACTIONS 11, 319-326. (1979).

LAMB 1979 -2 LAMBRECHT, M. R.; VANDERVEKEN, H.
PRODUCTION SCHEDULING AND SEQUENCING FOR MULTI-STAGE PRODUCTION SYSTEMS. OPERATIONS RESEARCH-SPEKTRUM 1, 103-114. (1979).

LAND 1979 -1 LAND, A.
SOLUTION OF SOME 100-CITY TRAVELLING SALESMAN PROBLEMS, THE. WORKING PAPER. LONDON: LONDON SCHOOL OF ECONOMICS, 20 P. (1979).

****

LANDA 1979 -1 LAND, A.; POWELL, S.
COMPUTER CODES FOR PROBLEMS OF INTEGER PROGRAMMING. IN: P. L. HAMMER, E. L. JOHNSON, B. H. KORTE (EDS.): DISCRETE OPTIMIZATION II, 221-269. ANNALS OF DISCRETE MATHEMATICS 5. AMSTERDAM, NEW YORK, OXFORD: NORTH-HOLLAND. (1979).

LANDB 1979 -1 LANDAUER, C.
REPRESENTATIONS OF MATROIDS. IN: J. A. BONDY, U. P. R. MURTY (EDS.): GRAPH THEORY AND RELATED TOPICS, 267-275. NEW YORK, SAN FRANCISCO, LONDON: ACADEMIC PRESS. (1979).

LANG 1980 -1 LANGE, E.
INTERAKTIVES SYSTEM ZUR LINEAREN PROGRAMMIERUNG BEI MEHRFACHEN ZIELEN UND GANZZAHLIGKEITSBEDINGUNGEN, EIN. ANGEWANDTE INFORMATIK, NO. 7, 266-270. (1980).

LANS 1981 -1 LANSDOWNE, Z. F.
RAIL FREIGHT TRAFFIC ASSIGNMENT. TRANSPORTATION RESEARCH 15A, 183-190. (1981).

LAPA 1978 -1 LAPAUGH, A. S.; RIVEST, R. L.
SUBGRAPH HOMOMORPHISM PROBLEM, THE. IN: PROCEEDINGS OF THE TENTH ANNUAL ACM SYMPOSIUM ON THEORY OF COMPUTING, SAN DIEGO 1978, 40-50. NEW YORK: ASSOCIATION FOR COMPUTING MACHINERY. (1978).

LAPO 1978 -1 LAPORTE, G.
SERIATION PROBLEM AND THE TRAVELLING SALESMAN PROBLEM, THE. JOURNAL OF COMPUTATIONAL AND APPLIED MATHEMATICS 4, 259-268. (1978).

LAPOA 1978 -1 LAPORTE, G.; BIRON, J.; NOBERT, Y.
ROTATING SCHEDULES. MONTREAL: ECOLE DES HAUTES ETUDES COMMERCIALES, 17 P. (1978).

LAPOB 1979 -1 LAPORTE, G.; NOBERT, Y.
EXACT ALGORITHM FOR MINIMIZING DELIVERY AND OPERATING COSTS IN DEPOT LOCATION, AN. RAPPORT DE RECHERCHE, 79-03. MONTREAL: ECOLE DES HAUTES ETUDES COMMERCIALES, 20 P. (1979).

LAPOB 1980 -1 LAPORTE, G.; NOBERT, Y.
CUTTING PLANES ALGORITHM FOR THE M-SALESMEN PROBLEM, A. JOURNAL OF THE OPERATIONAL RESEARCH SOCIETY 31, 1017-1024. (1980).

LAPOB 1981 -1 LAPORTE, G.; NOBERT, Y.
EXACT ALGORITHM FOR MINIMIZING ROUTING AND OPERATING COSTS IN DEPOT LOCATION, AN. EUROPEAN JOURNAL OF OPERATIONAL RESEARCH 6, 224-226. (1981).

LAPOC 1980 -1 LAPORTE, G.; NOBERT, Y.; BIRON, J.
ROTATING SCHEDULES. EUROPEAN JOURNAL OF OPERATIONAL RESEARCH 4, 24-30. (1980).

LAPOD 1981 -1 LAPORTE, G.; NORBERT, Y.; MERCURE, H.
MULTI-DEPOT TRAVELLING SALESMAN PROGRAM, THE. IN: R. E. BURKARD, T. ELLINGER (EDS.): METHODS OF OPERATIONS RESEARCH 40, 367-370. KOENIGSTEIN: ANTON HAIN MEISENHEIM. (1981).

LAPS 1978 -1 LAPSHIN, S. V.
DYNAMIC FORECASTING OF JOB SEQUENCING AND SIZE IN SERIAL PRODUCTION. AVTOMATIKA I TELEMEHANIKA (MOSCOW), NO. 5, 154-161; TRANSLATED AS AUTOMATION AND REMOTE CONTROL 39, NO. 5, PART 2, 749-755. (1978).

LAPT 1978 -1 LAPTIN, J. P.
COMPARISON OF CERTAIN METHODS OF COMPUTING THE LOWER BOUNDS OF SHORTEST SCHEDULES. KIBERNETIKA (KIEV) NO. 5, 74-78; TRANSLATED AS CYBERNETICS 14, 1979, 721-726. (1978).

LARS 1980 -1 LARSON, R. C.; LI, V. O. K.
FINDING MINIMUM RECTILINEAR DISTANCE PATHS IN THE PRESENCE OF BARRIERS. WASHINGTON (ORSA/TIMS MEETING, MAY 1980) 27 P. (1980).

LARSA 1980 -1 LARSON, R. C.; SADIQ, G.
FACILITY LOCATIONS WITH THE L(1) METRIC IN THE PRESENCE OF BARRIERS TO TRAVEL. WORKING PAPER OR 099-80. CAMBRIDGE, MA: MASSACHUSETTS INST. OF TECHNOLOGY, OPERATIONS RESEARCH CENTER, 19 P. (1980).

LARSB 1978 -1 LARSON, R. E.; DESSOUKY, M. I.
HEURISTIC PROCEDURES FOR THE SINGLE MACHINE PROBLEM TO MINIMIZE MAXIMUM LATENESS. AIIE TRANSACTIONS 10, 176-183. (1978).

LASH 1979 -1 LASHKARI, R. S.; JAISINGH, S. C.
EFFICIENT ALGORITHM FOR QUADRATIC ASSIGNMENT PROBLEM, AN. WINDSOR: UNIV. OF WINDSOR, DEPT. OF INDUSTRIAL ENGINEERING, 17 P. (1979).

LASH 1980 -1 LASHKARI, R. S.; JAISINGH, S. C.
HEURISTIC APPROACH TO QUADRATIC ASSIGNMENT PROBLEM, A. JOURNAL OF THE OPERATIONAL RESEARCH SOCIETY 31, 845-850. (1980).

LASK 1971 -1 LASKER, R.; HARE, W.
CHROMATIC NUMBERS OF CERTAIN GRAPHS. THE JOURNAL OF THE LONDON MATHEMATICAL SOCIETY 4, 489-492. (1971).

LASZ 1978 -1 LASZLO, C.
FORMULATION OF THE TIME-TABLE PROBLEM AND THE EXAMINATION OF ITS CONSISTENT SOLUTIONS I (HUNGARIAN), THE. INFORMACIO ELEKTRONIKA 13, 307-313. (1978).

LATU 1973 -1 LATUSKIEWICZ, J.
ALGORITHM FOR EXAMINING WHETHER A GRAPH IS A HAMILTONIAN GRAPH. II (POLISH), AN. ZESZYTY NAUK. UNIW. LODZ. NAUKI MAT. PZYROD. SER. II ZESZYT 50 CYBERNET., 139-144. (1973).

LAUF 1980 -1 LAUFER, P. J.
ON STRONGLY HAMILTONIAN COMPLETE BIPARTITE GRAPHS. ARS COMBINATORIA 9, 43-46. (1980).

LAUR 1978 -1 LAURIERE, J. L.
LANGUAGE AND A PROGRAM FOR STATING AND SOLVING COMBINATORIAL PROBLEMS. A. ARTIFICIAL INTELLIGENCE 1, 29-127. (1978).

LAVA 1979 -1 LAVALLEE, I.
RECTANGLES MAXIMAUX DANS UNE RELATION BINAIRE QUELCONQUE. IN: W. OETTLI, F. STEFFENS (EDS.): OPERATIONS RESEARCH VERFAHREN 32, THIRD SYMPOSIUM ON OPERATIONS RESEARCH, MANNHEIM 1978, 157-171. KOENIGSTEIN: ANTON HAIN MEISENHEIM. (1979).

LAWI 1979 -1 LAWIS, R. T.; PARKER, R. G.
BIN PACKING, MULTI-PROCESSOR SCHEDULING, AND GRAPH COLORING. WORKING PAPER. ATLANTA: GEORGIA INST. OF TECHNOLOGY, 17 P. (1979).

LAWL 1977 -1 LAWLER, E. L.
FAST APPROXIMATION ALGORITHMS FOR KNAPSACK PROBLEMS. IN: PROC. OF THE 18TH ANNUAL SYMPOSIUM ON FOUNDATIONS OF COMPUTER SCIENCE, 206-213. NEW YORK: INSTITUTE OF ELECTRICAL AND ELECTRONICS ENGINEERS, INC. (1977).

LAWL 1978 -1 LAWLER, E. L.
FAST APPROXIMATION ALGORITHMS FOR KNAPSACK PROBLEMS. IN: J. K. LENSTRA, A. H. G. RINNOOY KAN, P. VAN EMDE BOAS (EDS.): INTERFACES BETWEEN COMPUTER SCIENCE AND OPERATIONS RESEARCH. AMSTERDAM 1976, 109-139. MATHEMATICAL CENTRE TRACTS 99, AMSTERDAM: MATHEMATISCH CENTRUM. (1978).

LAWL 1979 -1 LAWLER, E. L.
EFFICIENT IMPLEMENTATION OF DYNAMIC PROGRAMMING ALGORITHMS FOR SEQUENCING PROBLEMS. AFDELING MATHEMATISCHE BESLISKUNDE BW 106/79. AMSTERDAM: MATHEMATISCH CENTRUM, 16 P. (1979).

LAWL 1979 -2 LAWLER, E. L.
FAST APPROXIMATION ALGORITHMS FOR KNAPSACK PROBLEMS. MATHEMATICS OF OPERATIONS RESEARCH 4, 339-356. (1979).

LAWL 1979 -3 LAWLER, E. L.
PREEMPTIVE SCHEDULING OF UNIFORM PARALLEL MACHINES TO MINIMIZE THE WEIGHTED NUMBER OF LATE JOBS. AFDELING MATHEMATISCHE BESLISKUNDE BW 105/79. AMSTERDAM: MATHEMATISCH CENTRUM, 20 P. (1979).

LAWL 1979 -4 LAWLER, E. L.
SHORTEST PATH AND NETWORK FLOW ALGORITHMS. IN: P. L. HAMMER, E. L. JOHNSON, B. H. KORTE (EDS.): DISCRETE OPTIMIZATION I, 251-263. ANNALS OF DISCRETE MATHEMATICS 4, AMSTERDAM, NEW YORK, OXFORD: NORTH-HOLLAND. (1979).

LAWL 1980 -1 LAWLER, E. L.
INTRODUCTION TO POLYMATROIDAL NETWORK FLOWS, AN. AFDELING MATHEMATISCHE BELISKUNDE BW 129/80. AMSTERDAM: MATHEMATISCH CENTRUM, 16 P. (1980).

LAWLA 1978 -1 LAWLER, E. L.; LABETOULLE, J.
ON PREEMPTIVE SCHEDULING OF UNRELATED PARALLEL PROCESSORS BY LINEAR PROGRAMMING. JOURNAL OF THE ASSOCIATION FOR COMPUTING MACHINERY 25, 612-619. (1978).

LAWLB 1980 -1 LAWLER, E. L.; LENSTRA, J. K.; RINNOOY KAN, A. H. G.
GENERATING ALL MAXIMAL INDEPENDENT SETS: NP-HARDNESS AND POLYNOMIAL-TIME ALGORITHMS. SIAM JOURNAL ON COMPUTING 9, 558-565. (1980).

LAWLB 1981 -1 LAWLER, E. L.; LENSTRA, J. K.; RINNOOY KAN, A. H. G.
MINIMIZING MAXIMUM LATENESS IN A TWO-MACHINE OPEN SHOP. MATHEMATICS OF OPERATIONS RESEARCH 6, 153-158. (1981).

LAWLC 1980 -1 LAWLER, E. L.; MARTEL, C. U.
COMPUTING MAXIMAL "POLYMATROIDAL" NETWORK FLOWS. RESEARCH REPORT UCB/ERL M80/52. BERKELEY: UNIV. OF CALIFORNIA, ELECTRONICS RESEARCH LABORATORY, 32 P. (1980).

LAWLC 1981 -1 LAWLER, E. L.; MARTEL, C. U.
SCHEDULING PERIODICALLY OCCURRING TASKS ON MULTIPLE PROCESSORS. INFORMATION PROCESSING LETTERS 12, 9-12. (1981).

LAWLD 1978 -1 LAWLER, E. L.; SIVAZLIAN, B. D.
MINIMIZATION OF TIME-VARYING COSTS IN SINGLE-MACHINE SCHEDULING. OPERATIONS RESEARCH 26, 563-569. (1978).

LAWR 1980 -1 LAWRENCE, J.; WEINBERG, L.
UNIONS OF ORIENTED MATROIDS. IN: M. DEZA, I. G. ROSENBERG (EDS.): COMBINATORICS 79, PART I, 29-34. ANNALS OF DISCRETE MATHEMATICS 8. AMSTERDAM: NORTH-HOLLAND. (1980).

LAWRA 1981 -1 LAWRENCE, S.; LAWRENCE, K.; REEVES, G.
MULTIPLE GOAL MODEL FOR ALLOCATION OF TEACHING PERSONNEL, A. IN: J. N. MORSE (ED.): ORGANIZATIONS: MULTIPLE AGENTS WITH MULTIPLE CRITERIA, 222-231. LECTURE NOTES IN ECONOMICS AND MATHEMATICAL SYSTEMS 190. BERLIN: SPRINGER. (1981).

LAWRB 1973 -1 LAWRIE, N.; VEITCH, H.
TIME-TABLING IN SECONDARY SCHOOLS - A STUDY OF MANUAL AND COMPUTER METHODS. GLASGOW: UNIVERSITY OF STRATHCLYDE. (1973).

LE 1979 -1 LE CONG THANH
ON THE PROBLEM OF FINDING SHORTEST PATHS IN FINITE GRAPHS (RUSSIAN). ELEKTRONISCHE INFORMATIONSVERARBEITUNG UND KYBERNETIK 15, 445-453. (1979).

LEBE 1977 -1 LEBEDEV, V. YU.
SCHEME FOR SOLVING A PARTIALLY INTEGER-VALUED PROBLEM OF MATHEMATICAL PROGRAMMING, A. USSR COMPUTATIONAL MATHEMATICS AND MATHEMATICAL PHYSICS 17, NO. 5, 86-91. (1977).

LEBEA 1978 -1 LEBEDEVA, T. T.
APPLICATION OF THE DIRECTING VICINITY METHOD FOR SOLVING PARTIALLY INTEGRAL PROBLEMS OF LINEAR PROGRAMMING (RUSSIAN). IN: PROCESSING OF SOFTWARE AND HARDWARE FOR AUTOMATIC CONTROL SYSTEMS, 31-38. KIEV: AKADEMIJA NAUK UKRAINSKOI SSR. INSTITUT KIBERNETIKI. (1978).

LEBEB 1978 -1 LEBEDEVA, T. T.; SERGIENKO, I. V.
METHOD OF DIRECTED VICINITIES (RUSSIAN), THE. DOKLADY AKADEMIJA NAUK UKRAINSKOI SSR, SERIJA A, FIZIKO-MATEMATICESKIE I TEHNICESKIE NAUKI (KIEV) NO. 8, 741-744. (1978).

LEBEC 1978 -1 LEBEDINSKAJA, N. B.
MINIMIZATION OF MAXIMUM PENALTY IN THE CASE OF PREEMPTION OF JOBS (RUSSIAN). ZAPINSKI NAUCNYH SEMINAROV LENINGRADSKOGO OTDELENIJA MATEMATICESKOGO INSTITUTA IM. V. A. STEKLOVA (LOMI) 80, 117-124, 267-268; TRANSLATED AS JOURNAL OF SOVIET MATHEMATICS. (1978).

LEBL 1979 -1 LEBLANC, L. J.; ABDULAAL, M.
EFFICIENT DUAL APPROACH TO THE URBAN ROAD NETWORK DESIGN PROBLEM, AN. COMPUTERS AND MATHEMATICS WITH APPLICATIONS 5, 11-19. (1979).

LEBL 1979 -2 LEBLANC, L. J.; ABDULAAL, M.
OPTIMIZATION METHODS FOR DESIGN OF MULTIMODEL NETWORKS. IN: RESEARCH DIRECTIONS IN COMPUTER CONTROL OF URBAN TRAFFIC SYSTEMS, PUBL. BY: AMERICAN SOCIETY OF CIVIL ENGINEERS, P. 149-164 (1979).

LEBLA 1976 -1 LEBLANC, L. J.; MORLOK, E. K.
ANALYSIS AND COMPARISON OF BEHAVIORAL ASSUMPTIONS IN TRAFFIC ASSIGNMENT, AN. IN: M. A. FLORIAN (ED.): TRAFFIC EQUILIBRIUM METHODS, 413-425. NEW YORK: SPRINGER. (1976).

LECL 1978 -1 LECLERC, B.
MATROIDES SUR UN ENSEMBLE PREORDONNE. BASES MINIMALES, CIRCUITS ET COCIRCUITS, PARTIES COMMENCANTES. ACADEMIE DES SCIENCES SERIE A-B 6, A301-A304. (1978).

LEDI 1979 -1 LEDIN, M. I.
CLASS OF HOMOGENEOUS RESOURCE-ALLOCATION PROBLEMS (RUSSIAN), A. EKONOMIKA I MATEMATICESKIE METODY 15, 572-581. (1979).

LEE 1978 -1 LEE, D. T.; PREPARATA, F. P.
ALL NEAREST-NEIGHBOUR PROBLEM FOR CONVEX POLYGONS, THE. INFORMATION PROCESSING LETTERS 7, 189-192. (1978).

LEE A 1979 -1 LEE, S. M.
GOAL PROGRAMMING METHODS FOR MULTIPLE OBJECTIVE INTEGER PROGRAMS. NORCROSS: AMERICAN INSTITUTE OF INDUSTRIAL ENGINEERS, 28 P. (1979). (OR MONOGRAPH SERIES, 2)

LEE B 1978 -1 LEE, S. M.; CLAYTON, R. E.; TAYLOR, B. W. III
GOAL PROGRAMMING APPROACH TO MULTI-PERIOD PRODUCTION LINE SCHEDULING, A. COMPUTERS AND OPERATIONS RESEARCH 5, 205-211. (1978).

LEE C 1979 -1 LEE, S. M.; FRANZ, L. S.
OPTIMIZING THE LOCATION-ALLOCATION PROBLEM WITH MULTIPLE OBJECTIVES. INTERNATIONAL JOURNAL OF PHYSICAL DISTRIBUTION AND MATERIALS MANAGEMENT (U.K.) 9, NO. 6, 245-255. (1979).

LEE D 1979 -1 LEE, S. M.; FRANZ, L. S.; WYNNE, A. J.
OPTIMIZING STATE PATROL MANPOWER ALLOCATION. JOURNAL OF THE OPERATIONAL RESEARCH SOCIETY 30, 885-896. (1979).

LEE E 1981 -1 LEE, S. M.; GREEN, G. I.; KIM, C. S.
MULTIPLE CRITERIA MODEL FOR THE LOCATION-ALLOCATION PROBLEM, A. COMPUTERS AND OPERATIONS RESEARCH 8, 1-8. (1981).

LEE F 1977 -1 LEE, S. M.; MORRIS, R. L.
INTEGER GOAL PROGRAMMING METHODS. NORTH HOLLAND/TIMS STUDIES IN THE MANAGEMENT SCIENCES 6, 273-289. (1977).

LEFK 1978 -1 LEFKOVITCH, L. P.
CLUSTER GENERATION AND GROUPING USING MATHEMATICAL PROGRAMMING. MATHEMATICAL BIOSCIENCES 41, 91-110. (1978).

LEGG 1977 -1 LEGGETT, E. W.
TOOLS AND TECHNIQUES FOR CLASSIFYING NP-HARD PROBLEMS. COLUMBUS: OHIO STATE UNIVERSITY, 113 P. (1977). (DISSERTATION)

LEHM 1979 -1 LEHMAN, A.
ON THE WIDTH-LENGTH INEQUALITY. MATHEMATICAL PROGRAMMING 16, 245-259. (1979).

LEIG 1979 -1 LEIGHTON, F. T.
GRAPH COLORING ALGORITHM FOR LARGE SCHEDULING PROBLEMS, A. JOURNAL OF RESEARCH OF THE NATIONAL BUREAU OF STANDARDS 84, 489-506. (1979).

LEIP 1978 -1 LEIPAELAE, T.
ON THE SOLUTIONS OF STOCHASTIC TRAVELING SALESMAN PROBLEMS. EUROPEAN JOURNAL OF OPERATIONAL RESEARCH 2, 291-297. (1978).

LENS 1981 -1 LENSTRA, H. W. JR.
INTEGER PROGRAMMING WITH A FIXED NUMBER OF VARIABLES. RESEARCH REPORT 81-03. AMSTERDAM: UNIV. VAN AMSTERDAM, MATHEMATISCH INSTITUUT, 20 P. (1981).

LENSA 1973 -1 LENSTRA, J. K.; RINNOOY KAN, A. H. G.
TOWARDS A BETTER ALGORITHM FOR THE JOB-SHOP SCHEDULING PROBLEM - I. REPORT BN22. AMSTERDAM: MATHEMATISCH CENTRUM. (1973).

LENSA 1976 -1 LENSTRA, J. K.; RINNOOY KAN, A. H. G.
NOTE ON THE EXPECTED PERFORMANCE OF BRANCH-AND-BOUND ALGORITHMS, A. AFDELING MATHEMATISCHE BESLISKUNDE BW 63/76. AMSTERDAM. (1976).

LENSA 1978 -1 LENSTRA, J. K.; RINNOOY KAN, A. H. G.
COMPLEXITY OF SCHEDULING UNDER PRECEDENCE CONSTRAINTS. OPERATIONS RESEARCH 26, 22-35. (1978).

LENSA 1978 -2 LENSTRA, J. K.; RINNOOY KAN, A. H. G.
COMPUTATIONAL COMPLEXITY OF DISCRETE OPTIMIZATION PROBLEMS. IN: J. K. LENSTRA, A. H. G. RINNOOY KAN, P. VAN EMDE BOAS (EDS.): INTERFACES BETWEEN COMPUTER SCIENCE AND OPERATIONS RESEARCH, AMSTERDAM 1976, 63-85. MATHEMATICAL CENTRE TRACTS 99. AMSTERDAM: MATHEMATISCH CENTRUM. (1978).

LENSA 1978 -3 LENSTRA, J. K.; RINNOOY KAN, A. H. G.
ON THE EXPECTED PERFORMANCE OF BRANCH-AND-BOUND ALGORITHMS. OPERATIONS RESEARCH 26, 347-349. (1978).

LENSA 1979 -1 LENSTRA, J. K.; RINNOOY KAN, A. H. G.
CHARACTERIZATION OF LINEAR ADMISSIBLE TRANSFORMATIONS FOR THE M-TRAVELLING SALESMAN PROBLEM: A RESULT OF BERENGUER, A. EUROPEAN JOURNAL OF OPERATIONAL RESEARCH 3, 250-252. (1979).

LENSA 1979 -2 LENSTRA, J. K.; RINNOOY KAN, A. H. G.
COMPLEXITY OF PACKING, COVERING AND PARTITIONING PROBLEMS. IN: A. SCHRIJVER (ED.): PACKING AND COVERING IN COMBINATORICS, 275-291. MATHEMATICAL CENTRE TRACTS 106. AMSTERDAM: MATHEMATISCH CENTRUM. (1979).

LENSA 1979 -3 LENSTRA, J. K.; RINNOOY KAN, A. H. G.
COMPLEXITY OF VEHICLE ROUTING AND SCHEDULING PROBLEMS. AFDELING MATHEMATISCHE BESLISKUNDE BW 111/79. AMSTERDAM: MATHEMATISCH CENTRUM, 11 P. (1979).

LENSA 1979 -4 LENSTRA, J. K.; RINNOOY KAN, A. H. G.
COMPUTATIONAL COMPLEXITY OF DISCRETE OPTIMIZATION PROBLEMS. IN: P. L. HAMMER, E. L. JOHNSON, B. H. KORTE (EDS.): DISCRETE OPTIMIZATION I, 121-140. ANNALS OF DISCRETE MATHEMATICS 4. AMSTERDAM, NEW YORK, OXFORD: NORTH-HOLLAND. (1979).

LENSA 1980 -1 LENSTRA, J. K.; RINNOOY KAN, A. H. G.
COMPLEXITY RESULTS FOR SCHEDULING CHAINS ON A SINGLE MACHINE. EUROPEAN JOURNAL OF OPERATIONAL RESEARCH 4, 270-275. (1980).

LENSA 1980 -2 LENSTRA, J. K.; RINNOOY KAN, A. H. G.
INTRODUCTION A L'ORDONNANCEMENT DE PLUSIEURS MACHINES. IN: P. HANSEN, D. DE WERRA (EDS.): REGARDS SUR LA THEORIE DES GRAPHES, PROCEEDINGS OF THE CERISY COLLOQUIUM, 1980, 81-96. LAUSANNE: PRESSES POLYTECHNIQUES ROMANDES. (1980).

LENSA 1980 -3 LENSTRA, J. K.; RINNOOY KAN, A. H. G.
INTRODUCTION TO MULTIPROCESSOR SCHEDULING, AN. AFDELING MATHEMATISCHE BESLISKUNDE BW 121/80. AMSTERDAM: MATHEMATISCH CENTRUM, 18 P. (1980).

LENSA 1980 -4 LENSTRA, J. K.; RINNOOY KAN, A. H. G.
RECURSIVE APPROACH TO THE IMPLEMENTATION OF ENUMERATION METHODS, A. AFDELING MATHEMATISCHE BESLISKUNDE BW 116/80. AMSTERDAM: MATHEMATISCH CENTRUM, 18 P. (1980).

LENSA 1980 -5 LENSTRA, J. K.; RINNOOY KAN, A. H. G.
THEORIE DE LA COMPLEXITE DE CALCUL APPLIQUEE AUX PROBLEMES DE COUPLAGE, RECOUVREMENT ET PARTITIONNEMENT. IN: P. HANSEN, D. DE WERRA (EDS.): REGARDS SUR LA THEORIE DES GRAPHES, PROCEEDINGS OF THE CERISY COLLOQUIUM, 1980, 65-80. LAUSANNE: PRESSES POLYTECHNIQUES ROMANDES. (1980).

LEON 1978 -1 LEONARDI, G.
OPTIMUM FACILITY LOCATION BY ACCESSIBILITY MAXIMIZING. ENVIRONMENT AND PLANNING 10, SERIES A, 1287-1305. (1978).

LEONA 1973 -1 LEONT'EV, V. K.
STUDY OF AN ALGORITHM FOR SOLVING TRAVELING SALESMAN PROBLEM (RUSSIAN). AKADEMIJA NAUK SSSR. ZURNAL VYCISLITEL'NOI MATEMATIKI I MATEMATICESKOI FIZIKI 13, 1228-1236. (1973).

LEONA 1978 -1 LEONT'EV, V. K.
NUMBER OF OPTIMAL PLANS IN THE PROBLEM OF ASSIGNMENTS (RUSSIAN), THE. PROBLEMY KIBERNETIKI, NO. 34, 259-264 + 272. (1978).

LEONA 1979 -1 LEONT'EV, V. K.
DISCRETE EXTREMAL PROBLEMS (RUSSIAN). IN: R. V. GAMKRELIDZE (ED.): THEORY OF PROBABILITY. MATHEMATICAL STATISTICS. THEORETICAL CYBERNETICS, 39-101. MOSCOW: VINITI. (1979).

LERO 1977 -1 LEROUX, A.
GRAPHES DE TRANSFERT ET LA NOTION DE GRAPHE INVERSE, LES. REVUE FRANCAISE D'AUTOMATIQUE, D'INFORMATIQUE ET DE RECHERCHE OPERATIONELLE 11, SERIE RECHERCHE OPERATIONELLE, 379-392. (1977).

LESC 1980 -1 LESCH, J.; LESCH, M.; SCHMEICHEL, I.
VERFAHREN ZUR ERMITTLUNG DER MAXIMALEN STABILEN MENGEN IN EINEM UNGERICHTETEN GRAPHEN, EIN. ELEKTRONISCHE INFORMATIONSVERARBEITUNG UND KYBERNETIK 16, 63-68. (1980).

LESN 1977 -1 LESNIAK-FOSTER, L. M.
ON CRITICALLY HAMILTONIAN GRAPHS. ACTA MATHEMATICA ACADEMIAE SCIENTIARUM HUNGARICAE 29, 255-258. (1977).

LESN 1978 -1 LESNIAK-FOSTER, L. M.
ON N-DISTANT HAMILTONIAN LINE GRAPHS. AEQUATIONES MATHEMATICAE 17, 141-147. (1978).

LESNA 1977 -1 LESNIAK-FOSTER, L. M.; STRAIGHT, H. J.
COCHROMATIC NUMBER OF A GRAPH, THE. ARS COMBINATORIA 3, 39-45. (1977).

LEUN 1977 -1 LEUNG, J. Y.-T.
FAST ALGORITHMS FOR PACKING PROBLEMS. UNIVERSITY PARK: PENNSYLVANIA STATE UNIV., 159 P. (1977). (DISSERTATION)

LEUNA 1980 -1 LEUNG, J. Y.-T.; MERRILL, M. L.
NOTE ON PREEMPTIVE SCHEDULING OF PERIODIC, REAL-TIME TASKS, A. INFORMATION PROCESSING LETTERS 11, 115-118. (1980).

LEV 1978 -1 LEV, B.; SOYSTER, A. L.
INTEGER PROGRAMMING WITH BOUNDED VARIABLES VIA CANONICAL SEPARATION. THE JOURNAL OF THE OPERATIONAL RESEARCH SOCIETY 29, 477-488. (1978).

LEVI 1978 -1 LEVIN, G. M.; TANAEV, V. S.
DECOMPOSITION METHODS OF OPTIMIZATION OF PROJECT SOLUTIONS (RUSSIAN). MINSK: IZDAT. "NAUKA I TEHNIKA", 240 P. (1978).

LEVIA 1975 -1 LEVIN, M. I.
NETWORKS WITH A COMPLEX TECHNOLOGICAL CHARACTERISTICS (RUSSIAN). EKONOMIKA I MATEMATICESKIE METODY 11, 945-952. (1975).

LEVIB 1980 -1 LEVIN, M. S.
ON EFFICIENT SOLUTION OF SOME PROBLEMS OF THE NETWORK SCHEDULE THEORY (RUSSIAN). KIBERNETIKA, NO. 1, 131-135. (1980).

LEVIC 1978 -1 LEVIN, M. S.; LEVNER, E. V.
EFFECTIVE SOLUTION OF THE BELLMAN-JOHNSON PROBLEM ON A TREE-LIKE NETWORK, AN. AVTOMATIKA I TELEMEHANIKA, NO. 10, 110-118; TRANSLATED AS AUTOMATION AND REMOTE CONTROL 39, 1978, 1497-1504. (1978).

LEVID 1979 -1 LEVIN, V. I.
BLOCK LOGICAL CONSTRUCTIONS IN SOME PROBLEMS OF DISCRETE OPTIMIZATION. FOUNDATIONS OF CONTROL ENGINEERING (POZNAN) 4, 127-131. (1979).

LEVID 1979 -2 LEVIN, V. I.
METHODE STRUCTURELLE ET LOGIQUE D'OPTIMISATION COMBINATOIRE, EN PRESENCE DE CONSTRAINTES (RUSSIAN). AKADEMIJA NAUK LATVIISKOI SSR. AVTOMATIKA I VYCISLITEL'NAJA TEHNIKA, NO. 5, 48-55. (1979).

LEVID 1979 -3 LEVIN, V. I.
STRUCTURAL AND LOGICAL METHODS OF COMBINATORIAL OPTIMIZATION. AVTOMATIKA I VYCHISLITELNAJA TEHNIKA (RIGA), NO. 1, 45-92; TRANSLATED AS AUTOMATIC CONTROL AND COMPUTER SCIENCES 13, 1979, 40-46. (1979).

LEVIE 1977 -1 LEVITIN, E. S.; HRANOVIC, I. L.
ESTIMATE OF THE INFLUENCE OF ERRORS IN THE ORIGINAL DATA ON THE ACCURACY OF THE SOLUTION OF THE PROBLEM OF THE OPTIMAL DISTRIBUTION OF FLOWS ON A NETWORK (RUSSIAN), AN. EKONOMIKA I MATEMATICESKIE METODY, NO. 7, 126-142. (1977).

LEVN 1971 -1 LEVNER, E. V.
SCHEDULING PROBLEM THAT CAN BE REDUCED TO A SHORTEST PATH PROBLEM (RUSSIAN), A. IN: PROCEEDINGS OF THE FOURTH WINTER SCHOOL ON MATHEMATICAL PROGRAMMING AND RELATED QUESTIONS (RUSSIAN), DROGOBYCH 1971, 93-98. MOSCOW: MOSKOV. INZ.-STROITEL. INST. (1971).

LEVN 1976 -1 LEVNER, E. V.
PARAMETRIC MODEL OF NETWORK PLANNING (RUSSIAN), A. IN: A. A. FRIDMAN (ED.): STUDIES IN DISCRETE OPTIMIZATION (RUSSIAN), 382-394. MOSCOW: IZDAT. "NAUKA". (1976).

LEVNA 1978 -1 LEVNER, E. V.; GENS, G. V.
DISCRETE OPTIMIZATION PROBLEMS AND EFFICIENT APPROXIMATION ALGORITHMS (RUSSIAN). MOSCOW: USSR ACADEMY OF SCIENCES, CENTRAL ECONOMIC AND MATHEMATICAL INSTITUTE. (1978).

LEVY 1980 -1 LEVY, L.; GOLDEN, B. L.; ASSAD, A.
FLEET SIZE AND MIX VEHICLE ROUTING PROBLEM, THE. WORKING PAPER MS/S 80-011. COLLEGE PARK: UNIV. OF MARYLAND, COLLEGE OF BUSINESS AND MANAGEMENT, 37 P. (1980).

LEWI 1961 -1 LEWIS, G. F.
SCHOOL TIME-TABLE, THE. LONDON: CAMBRIDGE UNIVERSITY PRESS. (1961).

LEWIA 1978 -1 LEWIS, H. R.; CHRISTOS, H. P.
EFFICIENCY OF ALGORITHMS, THE. SCIENTIFIC AMERICAN 238, NO. 1, 96-109. (1978).

LEWIB 1978 -1 LEWIS, H. R.; PAPADIMITRIOU, C. H.
EFFICACITE DES ALGORITHMES, L'. POUR LA SCIENCE 5, 62-75. (1978).

LEWIC 1978 -1 LEWIS, J. M.
ON THE COMPLEXITY OF THE MAXIMUM SUBGRAPH PROBLEM. IN: PROCEEDINGS OF THE TENTH ANNUAL ACM SYMPOSIUM ON THEORY OF COMPUTING, SAN DIEGO, 1978, 265-274. NEW YORK: THE ASSOCIATION FOR COMPUTING MACHINERY. (1978).

LEWID 1980 -1 LEWIS, J. M.; YANNAKAKIS, M.
NODE-DELETION PROBLEM FOR HEREDITARY PROPERTIES IS NP-COMPLETE, THE. JOURNAL OF COMPUTER AND SYSTEM SCIENCES 20, 219-230. (1980).

LI 1977 -1 LI, H. F.
SCHEDULING TREES IN PARALLEL/PIPELINED PROCESSING ENVIRONMENTS. IEEE TRANSACTIONS ON COMPUTERS 26, NO. 11, 1101-1112. (1977).

LI A 1977 -1 LI, W.-X.
CONNECTIVITY OF COMPLEMENTARY GRAPHS (CHINESE), THE. KEXUE TONGBAO 22, NO. 2, 78. (1977).

LI A 1979 -1 LI, W.-X.
OPTIMAL ALLOCATION OF EXPERIMENTS WITH TIME DELAY OF FOUR PERIODS (CHINESE). ACTA MATHEMATICA SINICA 22, 261-275. (1979).

LIAN 1980 -1 LIANG, F. M.
LOWER BOUND FOR ON-LINE BIN PACKING, A. INFORMATION PROCESSING LETTERS 10, 76-79. (1980).

LIBU 1977 -1 LIBURA, M.
SENSITIVITY ANALYSIS OF SOLUTIONS OF THE INTEGER KNAPSACK PROBLEM (POLISH). ARCHIWUM AHTOMATYKI I TELEMECHANIKI 22, NO. 3, 313-322. (1977).

LIBU 1977 -2 LIBURA, M.
SENSITIVITY PROBLEMS OF INTEGER PROGRAMMING SOLUTIONS. ARCHIWUM AUTOMATYCKI I TELEMECHANIKI 22, NO. 3, 299-311. (1977).

LIBU 1981 -1 LIBURA, M.
INTEGER PROGRAMMING PROBLEMS WITH INEXACT OBJECTIVE FUNCTION. IN: R. E. BURKARD, T. ELLINGER (EDS.): METHODS OF OPERATIONS RESEARCH 40, 371-374. KOENIGSTEIN: ANTON HAIN MEISENHEIM. (1981).

LICK 1975 -1 LICK, D. R.
ACYCLIC COLOR FUNCTIONS ON GRAPHS. RIVISTA DI MATEMATICA DELLA UNIVERSITA DI PARMA 1, 135-141. (1975).

LIEB 1977 -1 LIEBERHERR, K.
INFORMATIONSVERDICHTUNG VON MODELLEN IN DER AUSSAGENLOGIK UND DAS P = NP-PROBLEM. ZUERICH: EIDGENOESSISCHE TECHNISCHE HOCHSCHULE, 145 P. (1977). (DISSERTATION ETH 5941)

LIEB 1980 -1 LIEBERHERR, K.
P-OPTIMAL HEURISTICS. THEORETICAL COMPUTER SCIENCE 10, 123-131. (1980).

LIEB 1981 -1 LIEBERHERR, K.
PROBABILISTIC COMBINATORIAL OPTIMIZATION. IN: J. GRUSKA, M. CHYTIL (EDS.): MATHEMATICAL FOUNDATIONS OF COMPUTER SCIENCE 1981, 423-432. LECTURE NOTES IN COMPUTER SCIENCE 118. BERLIN: SPRINGER. (1981).

LIEBA 1977 -1 LIEBMAN, J. S.; CHANARATNA, V.; KHACHATURIAN, N.
DISCRETE OPTIMIZATION IN STRUCTURAL DESIGN. IN: PROCEEDINGS OF THE SYMPOSIUM ON APPLICATION OF COMPUTER METHODS IN ENGINEERING VOL. 1, (ED. L. C. WELLFORD, JR.) P. 553-562 (1977).

LIES 1979 -1 LIESEGANG, D. G.
"TUBE-PASSING PROBLEM" AND THE TRAVELLING SALESMAN PROBLEM, THE. IN: A. PREKOPA (ED.): SURVEY OF MATHEMATICAL PROGRAMMING, VOLUME 2, 537-544. AMSTERDAM: NORTH-HOLLAND. (1979).

LIFS 1980 -1 LIFSCHITZ, V.
EFFICIENCY OF AN ALGORITHM OF INTEGER PROGRAMMING: A PROBABILISTIC ANALYSIS, THE. PROCEEDINGS OF THE AMERICAN MATHEMATICAL SOCIETY 79, 72-76. (1980).

LIHO 1976 -1 LIHOLAT, N. A.
PROBLEM ON THE COVERING OF A GRAPH BY A MINIMAL POWER SET (RUSSIAN), A. IN: STUDIES IN CONTEMPORARY PROBLEMS OF SUMMABILITY AND APPROXIMATION OF FUNCTIONS AND THEIR APPLICATIONS (RUSSIAN), 139-143, 165. DNEPROPETROVSK: GOS. UNIVERSITY. (1976).

LIIT 1978 -1 LIITTSCHWAGER, J. M.; WANG, C.
INTEGER PROGRAMMING SOLUTION OF A CLASSIFICATION PROBLEM. MANAGEMENT SCIENCE 24, 1515-1525. (1978).

LIKH 1974 -1 LIKHACHEV, V. M.
SEARCH ALGORITHM FOR THE MINIMUM NUMBER OF VERTICES IN AN ORIENTED GRAPH THROUGH WHICH PASS ALL CIRCUITS OF THE GRAPH. IZVESTIJA AKADEMII NAUK SSR. TEHNICESKAJA KIBERNETIKA, NO. 1, 162-165; TRANSLATED AS ENGINEERING CYBERNETICS 12, 1974, 131-134. (1974).

LIN 1980 -1 LIN, K.-S.
SCHEDULING WITH PARALLEL MACHINES TO MINIMIZE TOTAL JOB TARDINESS. WASHINGTON (ORSA/TIMS MEETING, MAY 1980) 10 P. (1980).

LIND 1978 -1 LINDSTROEM, B.
ON THE CHROMATIC NUMBER OF REGULAR MATROIDS. JOURNAL OF COMBINATORIAL THEORY 24, SERIES B, 370-373. (1978).

LIND 1979 -1 LINDSTROEM, B.
NON-REGULAR SIMPLICIAL MATROIDS. DISCRETE MATHEMATICS 28, 101-102. (1979).

LING 1978 -1 LINGURAJ, B. P.; WOLFE, H.
HEURISTIC METHOD FOR OBTAINING AN INTEGER SOLUTION TO A FACILITY DESIGN OPTIMIZATION PROBLEM, A. OPERATIONS RESEARCH 26, 171-182. (1978).

LINI 1980 -1 LINIS, V. K.; MAKSIM, M. S.
NUMBER OF TRANSPORT FACILITIES NECESSARY FOR FULFILLMENT OF A TRAFFIC SCHEDULE (RUSSIAN), THE. MATEMATICESKIE ISSLEDOVANIJA (KISHINEV) NO. 60, 115-122, 171. (1980).

LINK 1979 -1 LINKS, G.; RUBIN, D. S.
FINITE PRIMAL CUTTING PLANE ALGORITHMS FOR INTEGER PROGRAMS. SIAM JOURNAL ON CONTROL AND OPTIMIZATION 17, 47-55. (1979).

LINT 1976 -1 LINT, J. H. VAN
RECENT DEVELOPMENTS IN COMBINATORICS (DUTCH). NIEUW ARCHIEF VOOR WISKUNDE 24, 215-225. (1976).

LIOU 1978 -1 LIOUVILLE, B.
PROBLEME DU VOYAGEUR DE COMMERCE DANS UN PRODUIT CARTESIEN DE DEUX GRAPHES, LE. REVUE FRANCAISE D'AUTOMATIQUE, D'INFORMATIQUE ET DE RECHERCHE OPERATIONELLE 12, SERIE RECHERCHE OPERATIONELLE, 263-275. (1978).

LIPT 1978 -1 LIPTON, R. J.; MILLER, R. E.
BATCHING METHOD FOR COLORING PLANAR GRAPHS, A. INFORMATION PROCESSING LETTERS 7, 185-188. (1978).

LIPTA 1979 -1 LIPTON, R. J.; TARJAN, R. E.
SEPARATOR THEOREM FOR PLANAR GRAPHS, A. SIAM JOURNAL ON APPLIED MATHEMATICS 36, 177-189. (1979).

LITV 1970 -1 LITVAK, B. G.; RAPPOPORT, A. M.
CONDITIONS FOR THE REDUCIBILITY OF LINEAR PROGRAMMING PROBLEMS TO TRANSPORTATION PROBLEMS (RUSSIAN). MOSKOVSKII GOSUDARSTVENNYI UNIVERSITET. MEHANIKO-MATEMATICESKII FAKUL'TET. MATEMATICESKIE VOPROSY UPRAVLENIJA PROIZVODSTVOM 2, 122-135. (1970).

LITVA 1977 -1 LITVINOV, V. N.
APPROACH TO THE SOLUTION OF THE PROBLEM OF THE MINIMIZATION OF THE LENGTH OF A CONNNECTING NET IN THE PLACING OF GEOMETRIC OBJECTS (RUSSIAN), AN. AKADEMIJA NAUK UKRAINSKOI SSR. INSTITUT KIBERNETIKI. PREPRINT NO. 32, RAZMESCENIE GEOM. OV'EKT. I VOPROSY OPTIMAL. PROEKTIR., 12-18. (1977).

LITW 1979 -1 LITWHILER, D. W. JR.; ALY, A. A.
LARGE REGION LOCATION PROBLEMS. COMPUTERS AND OPERATIONS RESEARCH 6, 1-12. (1979).

LITW 1980 -1 LITWHILER, D. W. JR.; ALY, A. A.
STEINER'S PROBLEM AND FAGNANO'S RESULT ON THE SPHERE. MATHEMATICAL PROGRAMMING 18, 286-290. (1980).

LIU 1977 -1 LIU, C. L.
DETERMINISTIC JOB SCHEDULING IN COMPUTING SYSTEMS. IN: H. BEILNER, E. GELENBE (EDS.): MODELLING AND PERFORMANCE EVALUATION OF COMPUTER SYSTEMS. PROCEEDINGS OF THE SECOND INTERNATIONAL WORKSHOP, STRESA 1976, 241-254. AMSTERDAM, NEW YORK, OXFORD: NORTH-HOLLAND. (1977).

LIU 1977 -2 LIU, C. L.
ELEMENTS OF DISCRETE MATHEMATICS. NEW YORK, DUESSELDORF: MCGRAW-HILL, 294 P. (1977). (MACGRAW-HILL COMPUTER SCIENCE SERIES)

LIU A 1974 -1 LIU, J. W. S.; LIU, C. L.
BOUNDS ON SCHEDULING ALGORITHMS FOR HETEROGENEOUS COMPUTING SYSTEMS. IN: J. R. ROSENFELD (ED.): INFORMATION PROCESSING 74. PROCEEDINGS OF THE IFIP CONGRESS, STOCKHOLM 1974, 349-353. AMSTERDAM, LONDON: NORTH-HOLLAND. (1974).

LIU B 1978 -1 LIU, Y. P.
MODULO-2 PROGRAMMING AND PLANAR EMBEDDINGS (CHINESE). ACTA MATHEMATICAE APPLAGATAE SINICA (PEKING) 1, 321-329. (1978).

LIU C 1980 -1 LIU, Z. H.; MA, Z. F.; ZHU, Y. J.; CAI, M. C.
MINIMUM SPANNING TREES WITH DEGREE CONSTRAINTS (CHINESE). ACTA MATHEMATICAE APPLAGATAE SINICA (PEKING) 3, 1-12. (1980).

LIVJ 1980 -1 LIVJANT, R. Z.
ON THE NEIGHBORHOOD OF INTEGRAL VERTICES OF CERTAIN POLYHEDRA (RUSSIAN). VESTNIK LENINGRADSKOGO UNIVERSITETA, MATEMATIKA MEHANIKA ASTRONOMIJA (LENINGRAD) NO. 2, 9-12, 123. (1980).

LIVS 1968 -1 LIVSHIC, E. M.
ANALYSIS OF ALGORITHMS FOR NETWORK MODEL OPTIMIZATION (RUSSIAN). EKONOMIKA I MATEMATICESKIE METODY 4, 768-775. (1968).

LIVS 1969 -1 LIVSHIC, E. M.
PERFORMANCE BOUNDS FOR APPROXIMATE SOLUTIONS OF OPTIMIZATION NETWORK PROBLEMS (RUSSIAN). IN: PROC. I WINTER SCHOOL ON MATH. PROGRAMMING, BOOK 3, 477-497. MOSCOW: USSR ACADEMY OF SCIENCES, CENTRAL ECONOMIC AND MATHEMATICAL INSTITUTE. (1969).

LIVSA 1972 -1 LIVSHIC, E. M.; RUBLINECKII, V. I.
ON RELATIVE COMPLEXITY OF DISCRETE OPTIMIZATION PROBLEMS (RUSSIAN). VYCISLITEL'NAJA MATEMATIKA I VYCISLITEL'NAJA TEHNIKA 3, 78-95. (1972).

LJUB 1978 -1 LJUBCHENKO, G. G.
NUMERICAL GRAPHS (RUSSIAN). IN: A. N. SARKOVSKII (ED.): THEORETICAL AND APPLIED QUESTIONS OF DIFFERENTIAL EQUATIONS AND ALGEBRA, 169-173, 267. KIEV: NAUKOVA DUMKA. (1978).

LJUBA 1977 -1 LJUBOVICKII, L. V.
PROPERTIES OF THE BASIS MATRICES OF A CLASS OF POLYHEDRA (RUSSIAN). UPRAVLJAEMYE SISTEMY (NOVOSIBIRSK), NO. 16, 73-80, 83. (1977).

LLOY 1981 -1 LLOYD, E. L.
COFFMAN-GRAHAM SCHEDULING OF UET TASK SYSTEMS WITH 0-1 RESOURCES. INFORMATION PROCESSING LETTERS 12, 40-45. (1981).

LOCK 1978 -1 LOCKETT, A. G.; MUHLEMANN, A. P.
PROBLEM OF AGGREGATE SCHEDULING. AN APPLICATION OF GOAL PROGRAMMING, A. INTERNATIONAL JOURNAL OF PRODUCTION RESEARCH 16, 127-135. (1978).

LODI 1976 -1 LODISH, C. M.
ASSIGNING SALESMEN TO MAXIMIZE PROFIT. JOURNAL OF MARKETING RESEARCH 4, 440-444. (1976).

LOIZ 1980 -1 LOIZOU, G.
ON A CYCLE FINDING ALGORITHM. INFORMATION PROCESSING LETTERS 11, 33-36. (1980).

LOKI 1979 -1 LOKIN, F. C. J.
PROCEDURES FOR TRAVELLING SALESMAN PROBLEMS WITH ADDITIONAL CONSTRAINTS. EUROPEAN JOURNAL OF OPERATIONAL RESEARCH 3, 135-141. (1979).

LOMO 1978 -1 LOMONOSOV, M. V.
ON THE SYSTEM OF FLOWS IN A NETWORK. PROBLEMY PEREDACI INFORMACII 14, NO. 4, 60-73; TRANSLATED AS PROBLEMS OF INFORMATION TRANSMISSION 14, NO. 4, 280-290. (1978).

LONG 1980 -1 LONGYEAR, J. Q.
CIRCUIT BASIS IN BINARY MATROIDS, THE. JOURNAL OF NUMBER THEORY 12, 71-76. (1980).

LORE 1978 -1 LOREA, M.
HYPERGRAPHES ET MATROIDES. IN: J.-C. BERMOND ET AL. (EDS.): PROBLEMES COMBINATOIRES ET THEORIE DES GRAPHES, COLLOQUES INTERNATIONAUX DU CENTRE NATIONAL DE LA RECHERCHE SCIENTIFIQUE, ORSAY 1976, 279-280. PARIS: CENTRE NATIONAL DE LA RECHERCHE SCIENTIFIQUE. (1978).

LORE 1978 -2 LOREA, M.
MATROIDES SUR LES ENSEMBLES D'ARETES D'HYPERGRAPHES. CAHIERS DU CENTRE D'ETUDES DE RECHERCHE OPERATIONELLE 20, 127-136. (1978).

LORE 1979 -1 LOREA, M.
ON MATROIDAL FAMILIES. DISCRETE MATHEMATICS 28, 103-106. (1979).

LOS 1979 -1 LOS, M.
DISCRETE-CONVEX PROGRAMMING APPROACH TO THE SIMULTANEOUS OPTIMIZATION OF LAND USE AND TRANSPORTATION, A. TRANSPORTATION RESEARCH 13, SERIES B, 33-48. (1979).

LOS A 1981 -1 LOS, M.; NGUYEN, S.
SPATIAL ALLOCATION ON A NETWORK WITH CONGESTION. TRANSPORTATION RESEARCH 15B, 113-126. (1981).

LOUL 1979 -1 LOULOU, R.; MICHAELIDES, E.
NEW GREEDY-LIKE HEURISTICS FOR THE MULTIDIMENSIONAL 0-1 KNAPSACK PROBLEM. OPERATIONS RESEARCH 27, 1101-1114. (1979).

LOVA 1975 -1 LOVASZ, L.
COMBINATORIAL MINIMAX THEOREMS (HUNGARIAN). MATEMATIKAI LAPOK. BOLYAI JANOS MATEMATIKAI TARSULAT 26, 209-264. (1975).

LOVA 1976 -1 LOVASZ, L.
CHROMATIC NUMBER OF HYPERGRAPHS AND LINEAR ALGEBRA. CONSILIUM INSTITUTI MATHEMATICI. ACADEMIAE SCIENTIARUM HUNGARICAE. STUDIA SCIENTARUM MATHEMATICARUM HUNGARICA 11, 113-114. (1976).

LOVA 1976 -2 LOVASZ, L.
GRAPH THEORY AND INTEGER PROGRAMMING (HUNGARIAN). MATEMATIKAI LAPOK 27, 69-86. (1976).

LOVA 1977 -1 LOVASZ, L.
FLATS IN MATROIDS AND GEOMETRIC GRAPHS. IN: P. J. CAMERON (ED.): COMBINATORIAL SURVEYS, 45-86. LONDON: ACADEMIC PRESS. (1977).

LOVA 1977 -2 LOVASZ, L.
HOMOLOGY THEORY FOR SPANNING TREES OF A GRAPH, A. ACTA MATHEMATICA ACADEMIAE SCIENTIARIUM HUNGARICAE 30, 241-251. (1977).

LOVA 1978 -1 LOVASZ, L.
SOME FINITE BASIS THEOREMS ON GRAPH THEORY. IN: A. HAJNAL, V. T. SOS (EDS.): COMBINATORICS, VOLUME II, 717-730. COLLOQUIA MATHEMATICA SOCIETATIS JANOS BOLYAI 18. AMSTERDAM: NORTH-HOLLAND. (1978).

LOVA 1979 -1 LOVASZ, L.
GRAPH THEORY AND INTEGER PROGRAMMING. IN: P. L. HAMMER, E. L. JOHNSON, B. H. KORTE (EDS.): DISCRETE OPTIMIZATION I, 141-158. ANNALS OF DISCRETE MATHEMATICS 4. AMSTERDAM, NEW YORK, OXFORD: NORTH-HOLLAND. (1979).

LOVA 1979 -2 LOVASZ, L.
ON DETERMINANTS, MATCHINGS, AND RANDOM ALGORITHMS. IN: L. BUDACH (ED.): FUNDAMENTALS OF COMPUTATION THEORY FCT '79, 565-574. BERLIN: AKADEMIE-VERLAG. (1979).

LOVA 1979 -3 LOVASZ, L.
SELECTING INDEPENDENT LINES FROM A FAMILY OF LINES IN A SPACE. WORKING PAPER. SZEGED: BOLYAI INSTITUTE, 20 P. (1979).

LOVA 1979 -4 LOVASZ, L.
TOPOLOGICAL AND ALGEBRAIC METHODS IN GRAPH THEORY. IN: J. A. BONDY, U. P. R. MURTY (EDS.): GRAPH THEORY AND RELATED TOPICS, 1-14. NEW YORK, SAN FRANCISCO, LONDON: ACADEMIC PRESS. (1979).

LOVA 1980 -1 LOVASZ, L.
MATROID MATCHING AND SOME APPLICATIONS. JOURNAL OF COMBINATORIAL THEORY 28, SERIES B, 208-236. (1980).

LOVA 1980 -2 LOVASZ, L.
MATROIDS AND SPERNER'S LEMMA. EUROPEAN JOURNAL OF COMBINATORICS 1, 65-66. (1980).

LOVA 1981 -1 LOVASZ, L.
BOUNDING THE INDEPENDENCE NUMBER OF A GRAPH. REPORT NO. 81175-OR. BONN: UNIV. BONN, INST. FUER OEKONOMETRIE UND OPERATIONS RESEARCH, 16 P. (1981).

LOVA 1981 -2 LOVASZ, L.
MATROID MATCHING PROBLEM, THE. IN: L. LOVASZ, V. T. SOS (EDS.): ALGEBRAIC METHODS IN GRAPH THEORY, VOL. II, 495-518. COLLOQUIA MATHEMATICA SOCIETATIS JANOS BOLYAI 25. AMSTERDAM, OXFORD, NEW YORK: NORTH-HOLLAND. (1981).

LOVE 1976 -1 LOVE, R. F.; JUEL, H.
PROPERTIES AND SOLUTION METHODS FOR LARGE LOCATION-ALLOCATION PROBLEMS. TECHNICAL SUMMER REPORT NO. 1634. MADISON: UNIVERSITY OF WISCONSIN, MATHEMATICS RESEARCH CENTER. (1976).

LOVEA 1978 -1 LOVE, R. F.; MORRIS, J. G.
ON CONVEXITY PROOFS IN LOCATION THEORY. NAVAL RESEARCH LOGISTICS QUARTERLY 25, 179-182. (1978).

LOVEB 1978 -1 LOVE, R. R. JR; VEMUGANTI, R. R.
SINGLE-PLANT MOLD ALLOCATION PROBLEM WITH CAPACITY AND CHANGEOVER RESTRICTIONS, THE. OPERATIONS RESEARCH 26, 159-165. (1978).

LOWE 1978 -1 LOWE, T. J.
EFFICIENT SOLUTIONS IN MULTIOBJECTIVE TREE NETWORK LOCATION PROBLEMS. TRANSPORTATION SCIENCE 12, 298-316. (1978).

LOWEA 1979 -1 LOWE, T. J.; FRANCIS, R. L.; REINHARDT, E. W.
GREEDY NETWORK FLOW ALGORITHM FOR A WAREHOUSE LEASING PROBLEM, A. AIIE TRANSACTIONS 11, 170-182. (1979).

LOWEB 1978 -1 LOWE, T. J.; THORNTON, V. D.; FRANCIS, R. L.
LAYOUT OF DIVISIBLE ACTIVITIES ON THE LINE, THE. AIIE TRANSACTIONS 10, 58-69. (1978).

LOZA 1978 -1 LOZANO-PEREZ, T.; WESLEY, M. A.
ALGORITHM FOR PLANNING COLLISION-FREE PATHS AMONGST POLYHEDRAL OBSTACLES, AN. IBM RESEARCH REPORT, 7171. YORKTOWN HEIGHTS: IBM RESEARCH CENTER, 21 P. (1978).

LOZO 1979 -1 LOZOVANU, D. D.
OPTIMAL OUTGOING TREES IN DIGRAPHS (RUSSIAN). IZVESTIYA AKADEMII NAUK MOLDAVSKOJ SSR (KISHINEV), SERIYA FIZIKO-TEKHNICHESKIKH I MATEMATICHESKIKH NAUK, NO. 2, 14-22, 94. (1979).

LOZO 1981 -1 LOZOVANU, D. D.
OPTIMUM SUBGRAPHS IN A WEIGHTED DIGRAPH (RUSSIAN). KIBERNETIKA (KIEV), NO. 2, 16-19; TRANSLATED AS CYBERNETICS. (1981).

LOZOA 1980 -1 LOZOVANU, D. D.; ZAMBICKII, D. K.
PROBLEM OF OPTIMAL PLACEMENT OF A NETWORK SOURCE ENSURING A FLOW OF MINIMAL COST (RUSSIAN). THE. MATEMATICESKIE ISSLEDOVANIJA (KISHINEV) NO. 60, 75-83, 170. (1980).

LU 1970 -1 LU, M. T.
COMPUTERIZED AIRLINE CREW SCHEDULING SYSTEM, A. PH. D. THESIS. MINNEAPOLIS: UNIVERSITY OF MINNESOTA. (1970).

LUBA 1979 -1 LUBAN, F.; DUMITRU, V.
ON THE JOB SHOP SCHEDULING BY MATHEMATICAL PROGRAMMING. ECONOMIC COMPUTATION AND ECONOMIC CYBERNETICS STUDIES AND RESEARCH, NO. 4, 69-84. (1979).

LUCC 1976 -1 LUCCHESI, C.
MINIMAX EQUALITY FOR DIRECTED GRAPHS, A. WATERLOO: UNIV. OF WATERLOO, DEPT. OF COMPUTER SCIENCE, 111 P. (1976). (DISSERTATION)

LUCCA 1978 -1 LUCCHESI, C.; YOUNGER, D. H.
MINIMAX THEOREM FOR DIRECTED GRAPHS, A. THE JOURNAL OF THE LONDON MATHEMATICAL SOCIETY 17, 369-374. (1978).

LUCE 1979 -1 LUCERTINI, M.; MARCHETTI-SPACCAMELA, A.
APPROXIMATE SOLUTIONS OF AN INTEGER LINEAR PROGRAMMING PROBLEM WITH RESOURCE VARIATIONS. IN: MODELLING AND OPTIMIZATION OF COMPLEX SYSTEMS, PROC. IFIP-TC 7 WORKING CONF., NOVOSIBIRSK 1978, 207-219. LECTURE NOTES IN CONTROL AND INFORMATION SCIENCES 18. BERLIN: SPRINGER. (1979).

LUDW 1979 -1 LUDWIG, R.
ZUR LOESUNG GROSSER STANDORTPROBLEME. IN: W. OETTLI, F. STEFFENS (EDS.): OPERATIONS RESEARCH VERFAHREN 35, THIRD SYMPOSIUM ON OPERATIONS RESEARCH, MANNHEIM 1978, 263-269. KOENIGSTEIN: ANTON HAIN MEISENHEIM. (1979).

LUEK 1975 -1 LUEKER, G. S.
EFFICIENT ALGORITHMS FOR CHORDAL GRAPHS AND INTERVAL GRAPHS. PRINCETON: PRINCETON UNIV., 190 P. (1975). (DISSERTATION)

LUEK 1978 -1 LUEKER, G. S.
MAXIMIZATION PROBLEMS ON GRAPHS WITH EDGE WEIGHTS CHOSEN FROM A NORMAL DISTRIBUTION. TECHNICAL REPORT, 115. IRVINE: UNIV. OF CALIFORNIA, DEPT. OF INFORMATION AND COMPUTER SCIENCE, 20 P. (1978).

LUEK 1979 -1 LUEKER, G. S.
OPTIMIZATION PROBLEMS ON GRAPHS WITH INDEPENDENT RANDOM EDGE WEIGHTS. TECHNICAL REPORT NO. 131. IRVINE: UNIVERSITY OF CALIFORNIA, DEPARTMENT OF INFORMATION AND COMPUTER SCIENCE. (1979).

LUEKA 1979 -1 LUEKER, G. S.; BOOTH, K. S.
LINEAR TIME ALGORITHM FOR DECIDING INTERVAL GRAPH ISOMORPHISM, A. JOURNAL OF THE ASSOCIATION FOR COMPUTING MACHINERY 26, 183-195. (1979).

LUGA 1979 -1 LUGACHEV, M. I.
PROBLEM OF DISTRIBUTION AND ORDERING IN PRODUCTION SCHEDULING (RUSSIAN), A. EKONOMIKA I MATEMATICESKIE METODY 15, 177-183. (1979).

LUGAA 1979 -1 LUGACHEV, M. I.; SHUBINA, L. Y.
OPERATIVE PLANNING PROBLEM FOR A DISCRETE PRODUCTION PROCESS WITH REGARD TO EQUIPMENT READJUSTMENT (RUSSIAN), AN. IN: INVESTIGATIONS ON MATHEMATICAL ECONOMICS AND ADJACENT QUESTIONS, WORK COLLECTION. MOSCOW, 45-52. (1979).

LUKO 1977 -1 LUKO, G.
TRUTH FUNCTIONS AND PROBLEMS IN GRAPH COLORING. ACTA CYBERNETICA 3, NO. 4, 327-333. (1977).

LUSS 1980 -1 LUSS, H.
NETWORK FLOW APPROACH FOR CAPACITY EXPANSION PROBLEMS WITH TWO FACILITY TYPES, A. NAVAL RESEARCH LOGISTICS QUARTERLY 27, 597-608. (1980).

LYON 1979 -1 LYON, G.
BATCH SCHEDULING FROM SHORT LISTS. INFORMATION PROCESSING LETTERS 8, 57-59. (1979).

LYSK 1980 -1 LYSKA, W.; MUELLER, H.
ALGORITHMUS ZUR LOESUNG EINER KLASSE LINEARER 0-1 OPTIMIERUNGSAUFGABEN MIT SPEZIELLER STRUKTUR, EIN. MATHEMATISCHE OPERATIONSFORSCHUNG UND STATISTIK, SERIES OPTIMIZATION 11, 435-446. (1980).

MA 1980 -1 MA, Z. F.; LIU, Z. H.; CAI, M. C.
OPTIMUM RESTRICTED BASE OF A MATROID. IN: M. DEZA, I. G. ROSENBERG (EDS.): COMBINATORICS 79, PART II, 253-258. ANNALS OF DISCRETE MATHEMATICS 9. AMSTERDAM: NORTH-HOLLAND. (1980).

MAAM 1981 -1 MAAMOUN, M.
PARITE DES CYCLES CONTENANT DES SOMMETS SPECIFIES D'UN GRAPHE. DISCRETE MATHEMATICS 34, 145-152. (1981).

MAC 1978 -1 MAC BRIDE, R. D.; YORMARK, J. S.
PARAMETRIC QUADRATIC INTEGER PROGRAMMING AGAINST ONE CONSTRAINT. WORKING PAPER NO. 9. LOS ANGELES: UNIV. OF SOUTHERN CALIFORNIA, GRADUATE SCHOOL OF BUSINESS ADMINISTRATION, 33 P. (1978).

MAC 1980 -1 MAC BRIDE, R. D.; YORMARK, J. S.
FINDING ALL SOLUTIONS FOR A CLASS OF PARAMETRIC QUADRATIC INTEGER PROGRAMMING PROBLEMS. MANAGEMENT SCIENCE 26, 784-795. (1980).

MAC 1980 -2 MAC BRIDE, R. D.; YORMARK, J. S.
IMPLICIT ENUMERATION ALGORITHM FOR QUADRATIC INTEGER PROGRAMMING, AN. MANAGEMENT SCIENCE 26, 282-296. (1980).

MAC A 1978 -1 MAC CARTHY, P. J.
MATCHINGS IN GRAPHS III: INFINITE GRAPHS. IN: Y. ALAVI, D. R. LICK (EDS.): THEORY AND APPLICATION OF GRAPHS, PROCEEDINGS OF THE INTERNATIONAL CONFERENCE, MICHIGAN 1976, 384-393. LECTURE NOTES IN MATHEMATICS 642, BERLIN: SPRINGER. (1978).

MAC A 1978 -2 MAC CARTHY, P. J.
MATCHINGS IN INFINITE GRAPHS. CZECHOSLOVAKIAN MATHEMATICAL JOURNAL 28, NO. 2, 245-251. (1978).

MAC A 1979 -1 MAC CARTHY, P. J.
CHARACTERIZATION OF STRICT MATCHING MATROIDS, A. THE QUARTERLY JOURNAL OF MATHEMATICS. OXFORD. SECOND SERIES 30, NO. 118, 191-196. (1979).

MAC B 1978 -1 MAC DIARMID, C.
BLOCKING, ANTIBLOCKING AND PAIRS OF MATROIDS AND POLYMATROIDS. JOURNAL OF COMBINATORIAL THEORY 25, SERIES B, 313-325. (1978).

MAC B 1979 -1 MAC DIARMID, C.
DETERMINING THE CHROMATIC NUMBER OF A GRAPH. SIAM JOURNAL ON COMPUTING 8, 1-14. (1979).

MAC B 1980 -1 MAC DIARMID, C.
CLUTTER PERCOLATION AND RANDOM GRAPHS. MATHEMATICAL PROGRAMMING STUDY 13, 17-25. (1980).

MAC B 1980 -2 MAC DIARMID, C.
PERCOLATION ON SUBSETS OF THE SQUARE LATTICE. JOURNAL OF APPLIED PROBABILITY 17, 278-283. (1980).

MAC B 1981 -1 MAC DIARMID, C.
GENERAL PERCOLATION AND RANDOM GRAPHS. ADVANCES IN APPLIED PROBABILITY 13, 40-60. (1981).

MAC C 1980 -1 MAC DONALD, G. W.; HODGSON, T. J.
INTERACTIVE SCHEDULING OF A GENERALIZED FLOWSHOP. RESEARCH REPORT 80-16. GAINESVILLE: UNIV. OF FLORIDA, DEPT. OF INDUSTRIAL AND SYSTEMS ENGINEERING, 41 P. (1980).

MAC D 1978 -1 MAC ELIECE, R. J.; RODEMICH, E. R.; RUMSEY, H. C. JR.
LOVASZ BOUND AND SOME GENERALIZATIONS, THE. JOURNAL OF COMBINATORIAL INFORMATION SYSTEM SCIENCE 3, 134-152. (1978).

MAC E 1975 -1 MAC GINNIS, L. F.
APPROXIMATE AND EXACT SOLUTION PROCEDURES FOR A CLASS OF FACILITIES LOCATION PROBLEMS. DISSERTATION. RALEIGH: NORTH CAROLINA STATE UNIVERSITY AT RALEIGH, 171 P. (1975).

MAC E 1978 -1 MAC GINNIS, L. F.
IMPLEMENTATION AND TESTING OF A PRIMAL-DUAL ALGORITHM FOR ASSIGNMENT PROBLEM. INDUSTRIAL AND SYSTEMS ENGINEERING REPORTS SERIES, NO. J -78-31. ATLANTA: GEORGIA INSTITUTE OF TECHNOLOGY, 29 P. (1978).

MAC F 1978 -1 MAC GINNIS, L. F.; CULVER, W. D.; DEANE, R. H.
ONE- AND TWO-PHASE HEURISTICS FOR WORKFORCE SCHEDULING. COMPUTERS AND INDUSTRIAL ENGINEERING 2, NO. 1, 7-15. (1978).

MAC G 1978 -1 MAC GINNIS, L. F.; WHITE, J. A.
SINGLE FACILITY RECTILINEAR LOCATION PROBLEM WITH MULTIPLE CRITERIA, A. TRANSPORTATION SCIENCE 12, 217-231. (1978).

MAC H 1979 -1 MAC GREGOR, J. J.
RELATIONAL CONSISTENCY ALGORITHMS AND THEIR APPLICATION IN FINDING SUBGRAPH AND GRAPH ISOMORPHISMS. INFORMATION SCIENCES 19, 229-250. (1979).

MAC I 1978 -1 MAC KEOWN, P. G.
SOME COMPUTATIONAL RESULTS OF USING THE AHRENS-FINKE METHOD FOR HANDLING DEGENERACY IN FIXED CHARGE TRANSPORTATION PROBLEMS. MATHEMATICAL PROGRAMMING 15, 355-359. (1978).

MAC I 1980 -1 MAC KEOWN, P. G.
SOLVING INCREMENTAL QUANTITY DISCOUNTED TRANSPORTATION PROBLEMS BY VERTEX RANKING. NAVAL RESEARCH LOGISTICS QUARTERLY 27, 437-446. (1980).

MAC J 1980 -1 MAC KEOWN, P. G.; SINHA, P.
EASY SOLUTION FOR A SPECIAL CLASS OF FIXED CHARGE PROBLEMS, AN. NAVAL RESEARCH LOGISTICS QUARTERLY 27, 621-624. (1980).

MAC K 1978 -1 MAC MASTER, C. L.
ANALYSIS OF ALGORITHMS FOR THE DUTCH NATIONAL FLAG PROBLEM, AN. COMMUNICATIONS OF THE ASSOCIATION FOR COMPUTING MACHINERY 21, 842-846. (1978).

MACH 1978 -1 MACHTEY, M.; WINKLMANN, K.; YOUNG, P.
SIMPLE GODEL NUMBERINGS, ISOMORPHISMS, AND PROGRAMMING PROPERTIES. SIAM JOURNAL ON COMPUTING 7, 39-60. (1978).

MACK 1978 -1 MACK, H. L.; SMITH, L. D.
SCHEDULING WITH LIST PROCESSING AND PROBLEM ORIENTED DATA STRUCTURES: AN ITINERANT TEACHER EXAMPLE. EUROPEAN JOURNAL OF OPERATIONAL RESEARCH 2, 175-184. (1978).

MADE 1979 -1 MADER, W.
CONNECTIVITY AND EDGE-CONNECTIVITY IN FINITE GRAPHS. IN: B. BOLLOBAS (ED.): SURVEYS IN COMBINATORICS, PROCEEDINGS OF THE 7TH BRITISH COMBINATORIAL CONFERENCE, 66-95. LONDON MATHEMATICAL SOCIETY LECTURE NOTE SERIES 38, CAMBRIDGE, LONDON, NEW YORK, MELBOURNE: CAMBRIDGE UNIVERSITY PRESS. (1979).

MADE 1979 -2 MADER, W.
REDUKTIONSMETHODE FUER DEN KANTENZUSAMMENHANG IN GRAPHEN, EINE. MATHEMATISCHE NACHRICHTEN 93, 187-204. (1979).

MADE 1979 -3 MADER, W.
ZUR STRUKTUR MINIMAL N-FACH ZUSAMMENHAENGENDER GRAPHEN. ABHANDLUNGEN AUS DEM MATHEMATISCHEN SEMINAR DER UNIVERSITAET HAMBURG 49, 49-69. (1979).

MADS 1980 -1 MADSEN, O. B. G.
CUTTING SEQUENCING ALGORITHM, A. IN: K. IRACKI, K. MALANOWSKI, P. WALUKIEWICZ (EDS.): OPTIMIZATION TECHNIQUES, PART II, 388-396. LECTURE NOTES IN CONTROL AND INFORMATION SCIENCES 23. BERLIN: SPRINGER. (1980).

MAFF 1978 -1 MAFFIOLI, F.
DISCREET CHARM OF MATROID PROBLEMS, THE. URBINO: SUMMER SCHOOL ON COMBINATORIAL OPTIMIZATION, 39 P. (1978).

MAFF 1979 -1 MAFFIOLI, F.
COMPLEXITY OF COMBINATORIAL OPTIMIZATION ALGORITHMS AND THE CHALLENGE OF HEURISTICS, THE. IN: N. CHRISTOFIDES, A. MINGOZZI, P. TOTH, C. SANDI (EDS.): COMBINATORIAL OPTIMIZATION, 107-130. CHICHESTER, NEW YORK, BRISBANE, TORONTO: WILEY. (1979).

MAFF 1980 -1 MAFFIOLI, F.
COUPLAGES ET MATROIDES. IN: P. HANSEN, D. DE WERRA (EDS.): REGARDS SUR LA THEORIE DES GRAPHES, PROCEEDINGS OF THE CERISY COLLOQUIUM, 1980, 97-110. LAUSANNE: PRESSES POLYTECHNIQUES ROMANDES. (1980).

MAGA 1979 -1 MAGAZINE, M. J.; OGUZ, O.
FULLY POLYNOMIAL APPROXIMATE ALGORITHM FOR THE 0-1 KNAPSACK PROBLEM, A. (REVISED VERSION). WORKING PAPER NO. 114. WATERLOO: UNIV. OF WATERLOO, DEPT. OF MANAGMENT SCIENCES, 11 P. (1979).

MAGAA 1979 -1 MAGAZINE, M. J.; WEE, T. S.
GENERALIZATION OF BIN-PACKING HEURISTICS TO THE LINE BALANCING PROBLEM, THE. WORKING PAPER NO. 128. WATERLOO: UNIV. OF WATERLOO, DEPT. OF MANAGEMENT SCIENCES, 33 P. (1979).

MAGG 1974 -1 MAGGU, P. L.; ALAM, M. S.; IKRAM, M.
ON CERTAIN TYPE OF SEQUENCING PROBLEM WITH N JOBS AND M MACHINES. PURE AND APPLIED MATHEMATIKA SCIENCES 1, NO. 2, 55-59. (1974).

MAGGA 1977 -1 MAGGU, P. L.; DAS, G.
EQUIVALENT JOBS FOR JOB BLOCKS IN JOB SEQUENCING. OPSEARCH 14, 277-281. (1977).

MAGGA 1979 -1 MAGGU, P. L.; DAS, G.
ON THE CONCEPT OF DUALITY IN SEQUENCING THEORY. PURE AND APPLIED MATHEMATIKA SCIENCES 9, 55-64. (1979).

MAGGA 1979 -2 MAGGU, P. L.; DAS, G.
SHORT NOTE ON THE PAPER: "EQUIVALENT JOBS FOR JOB-BLOCKS IN JOB SEQUENCING" (OPSEARCH 14, 1977, 277-281). PURE AND APPLIED MATHEMATIKA SCIENCES 9, 53-54. (1979).

MAGGB 1974 -1 MAGGU, P. L.; IKRAM, M.; ALAM, M. S.
ON CERTAIN THEOREMS IN SEQUENCING THEORY. PURE AND APPLIED MATHEMATIKA SCIENCES 1, NO. 2, 60-62. (1974).

MAGN 1979 -1 MAGNANTI, T. L.; WONG, R. T.
ACCELERATING BENDERS DECOMPOSITION: ALGORITHMIC ENHANCEMENTS AND MODEL SELECTION CRITERIA. WORKING PAPER OR 093-79. CAMBRIDGE: MASSACHUSETTS INST. OF TECHNOLOGY, OPERATIONS RESEARCH CENTER, 36 P. (1979).

MAGR 1978 -1 MAGRUPOVA, D. A.
MATRIX-DIAGONAL METHOD OF SOLVING A CLASS OF TRANSPORT PROBLEMS OF LINEAR PROGRAMMING (RUSSIAN), THE. VOPROSY KIBERNETIKI. AKADEMIJA NAUK UZBEKSKOI SSR, NO. 102, 65-74 + 159. (1978).

MAGRA 1976 -1 MAGRUPOW, T. M.
NEW APPROACH TO THE CONSTRUCTION OF A MINIMAL TREE (RUSSIAN), A. VOPROSY KIBERNETIKI. AKADEMIJA NAUK UZBESKOI SSR (TASHKENT) 85, 3-12. (1976).

MAHR 1978 -1 MAHR, B.
STRATEGIES AND ARITHMETIC COMPLEXITY OF PATHALGORITHMS. IN: J. MUEHLBACHER (ED.): DATENSTRUKTUREN, GRAPHEN, ALGORITHMEN. DRITTE FACHTAGUNG UEBER GRAPHENTHEORETISCHE KONZEPTE DER INFORMATIK, LINZ 1977, 169-177. MUENCHEN, WIEN: HANSER. (1978).

MAHR 1981 -1 MAHR, B.
BIRD'S-EYE VIEW TO PATH PROBLEMS, A. IN: H. NOLTEMEYER (ED.): GRAPHTHEORETIC CONCEPTS IN COMPUTER SCIENCE, 335-353. LECTURE NOTES IN COMPUTER SCIENCE 100. BERLIN: SPRINGER. (1981).

MAIE 1977 -1 MAIER, D.; STORER, J. A.
NOTE ON THE COMPLEXITY OF THE SUPERSTRING PROBLEM, A. REPORT NO. 233. PRINCETON: PRINCETON UNIVERSITY, COMPUTER SCIENCE LABORATORY. (1977).

MAIEA 1969 -1 MAIER, S.
MULTI-ITEM NETWORK FLOW MODEL WITH CAPACITY CONSTRAINTS, A. TECH. REPORT 69-14. STANFORD: STANFORD UNIVERSITY, OPERATIONS RESEARCH HOUSE. (1969).

MAIEA 1975 -1 MAIER, S.
SOLVING THE TRAFFIC ASSIGNMENT AND SUB-AREA FOCUSING PROBLEMS BY GEOGRAPHIC DECOMPOSITION. WORKING PAPER NO. 155. DURHAM: DUKE UNIVERSITY, GRADUATE SCHOOL OF BUSINESS ADMINISTRATION. (1975).

MAIR 1979 -1 MAIRS, T. G.
ON A PRODUCTION ALLOCATION AND DISTRIBUTION PROBLEM. NEW ORLEANS (ORSA/TIMS MEETING, APRIL/MAY 1979) 11 P. (1979).

MAIRA 1978 -1 MAIRS, T. G.; WAKEFIELD, G. W.; JOHNSON, E. L.; SPIELBERG, K.
ON A PRODUCTION ALLOCATION AND DISTRIBUTION PROBLEM. MANAGEMENT SCIENCE 24, 1622-1630. (1978).

MAJE 1980 -1 MAJER, A. B.
METHODE DE DESCENTE PAR COORDONNEES POUR UNE CLASSE DE PROBLEMES DE PROGRAMMATION ENTIERE ET NON LINEAIRE (RUSSIAN). AVTOMATIKA I VYCISLITELNAJA TEHNIKA (RIGA) NO. 4, 65-67; TRANSLATED AS AUTOMATIC CONTROL AND COMPUTER SCIENCES. (1980).

MAKA 1978 -1 MAKAROV, G. D.; LIHOLAT, N. A.
EXTREMAL PROBLEM ON GRAPHS (RUSSIAN), AN. KIEVSKII GOSUDARSTVENNYI UNIVERSITET. MEZVEDOMSTVENNYI NAUCNYI SBORNIK. VYCISLITEL'NAJA I PRIKLADNAJA MATEMATIKA, NO. 34, 133-139 + 168. (1978).

MAKAA 1975 -1 MAKAROV, I. P.; YAVORSKII, V. V.
ONE GENERALIZATION OF THE TRAVELING SALESMAN PROBLEM. AVTOMATIKA I TELEMEHANIKA, NO. 4, 71-74; TRANSLATED AS AUTOMATION AND REMOTE CONTROL 36, 1975, 586-589. (1975).

MAKS 1980 -1 MAKSIM, M. S.
MINIMIZATION OF THE NUMBER OF TRANSPORT FACILITIES BY CHANGE IN THE DAYS OF FULFILLMENT OF NONDAILY TRIPS (RUSSIAN). MATEMATICESKIE ISSLEDOVANIJA (KISHINEV) NO. 60, 127-136, 172. (1980).

MAKSA 1978 -1 MAKSIMENKOV, A. V.
COMPUTER RESOURCE SCHEDULING WITH MINIMUM DISPROPORTIONS (RUSSIAN). AVTOMATIKA I VYCISLITELNAJA TEHNIKA (RIGA), NO. 4, 69-75, 94. (1978).

MAKSA 1979 -1 MAKSIMENKOV, A. V.
SCHEDULING WITH RESTRICTION ON RESOURCE USE RATE. KIBERNETIKA (KIEV) NO. 6, 91-95; TRANSLATED AS CYBERNETICS 15, NO. 6, 876-881. (1979).

MAKSB 1978 -1 MAKSIMENKOV, A. V.; SHCHERS, A. L.
SCHEDULING THE FILLING OF STANDING ORDER ASSIGNMENTS (RUSSIAN). PROGRAMMIROVANIE, NO. 1, 77-83; TRANSLATED AS PROGRAMMING AND COMPUTER SOFTWARE 4, 1978, 63-68. (1978).

MAKSC 1980 -1 MAKSIMOV, J. B.; KRIVORUCHKO, E. I.
APPLICATION OF THE BRANCH AND BOUND METHOD TO THE SOLUTION OF DISCRETE VOLUME SCHEDULING PROBLEMS (RUSSIAN). AVTOMATIZIROVANNYE SISTEMY UPRAVLENIJA I PRIBORY AVTOMATIKI (KHARKOV) NO. 54, 74-80. (1980).

MALA 1980 -1 MALASHENKO, YU. E.; STANEVICHUS, A.-J. A.
ON THE SOLUTION OF AN INTEGER PROGRAMMING PROBLEM (RUSSIAN). AKADEMIJA NAUK SSSR. ZURNAL VYCISLITEL'NOI MATEMATIKI I MATEMATICESKOI FIZIKI 20, 623-629. (1980).

MALAA 1975 -1 MALATO DE SOUSA, J. A.
ON A PROBLEM OF SHORTEST PATHS IN GRAPHS (PORTUGUESE). GAZETA DE MATEMATICA 36/37, 13-23. (1975).

MALH 1978 -1 MALHOTRA, V. M.; KUMAR, M. P.; MAHESHWARI, S. N.
O(!V!**3) ALGORITHM FOR FINDING MAXIMUM FLOWS IN NETWORKS, AN. INFORMATION PROCESSING LETTERS 7, 277-278. (1978).

MALK 1978 -1 MALKEVITCH, J.
SPANNING TREES IN POLYTOPAL GRAPHS. NEW YORK (2ND INTERNATIONAL CONFERENCE ON COMBINATORIAL MATHEMATICS) 18 P. (1978).

MALO 1978 -1 MALOJI, M. W.; UHRY, J.-P.
PRIMAL, ONE-PASS ALGORITHM FOR CONSTRUCTING A MINIMUM-WEIGHT ROOTED SPANNING ARBORESCENCE, A. EQUIIPE DE RECHERCHE OPERATIONNELLE. GRENOBLE: UNIV. SCIENTIFIQUE ET MEDICALE, MATHEMATIQUES APPLIQUEES ET INFORMATIQUE, 20 P. (1978).

MALY 1977 -1 MALYSHKO, V. V.
SOME PROPERTIES OF ARC GRAPHS (RUSSIAN). VESTNIK BELORUSSKOGO GOSUDARSTVENNOGO UNIVERSITETA IM. V. I. LENINA , SERIJA I, NO. 3, 7-9, 92. (1977).

MAME 1978 -1 MAMEDOV, K. S.
TWO-SIDED ESTIMATION OF THE OPTIMAL VALUE OF THE TARGET FUNCTION IN BOOLEAN PROGRAMMING PROBLEMS (RUSSIAN). IN: DZ. E. ALLAHVERDIEV (ED.): QUESTIONS OF MATHEMATICAL CYBERNETICS AND APPLIED MATHEMATICS (RUSSIAN), NO. 3, 17-22. BAKU: ELM. (1978).

MANC 1979 -1 MANCA, P.
ON A SIMPLE CHARACTERIZATION OF THRESHOLD GRAPHS. RIVISTA DI MATEMATICA PER LE SCIENZE ECONOMICHE E SOCIALE (MILAN) 2, 3-8. (1979).

MAND 1978 -1 MANDL, C. E.
ALGORITHMS AND COMPUTER PROGRAMS IN DETERMINISTIC NETWORK OPTIMIZATION APPLIED TO PUBLIC SYSTEMS. RESEARCH MEMORANDUM NO. 126. WIEN: INSTITUT FUER HOEHERE STUDIEN, 244 P. (1978).

MAND 1979 -1 MANDL, C. E.
APPLIED NETWORK OPTIMIZATION. LONDON, NEW YORK U.A.: ACADEMIC PRESS, 175 P. (1979).

MAND 1980 -1 MANDL, C. E.
EVALUATION AND OPTIMIZATION OF URBAN PUBLIC TRANSPORTATION NETWORKS. EUROPEAN JOURNAL OF OPERATIONAL RESEARCH 5, 396-404. (1980).

MARC 1976 -1 MARCU, D.
APPLICATION OF VECTOR SPACES TO THE CALCULATION OF THE NUMBER OF CONNECTED COMPONENTS OF A FINITE DIRECTED GRAPH (ROMANIAN). AN. STUDII SI CERCETARI MATEMATICE 28, NO. 2, 199-203. (1976).

MARC 1978 -1 MARCU, D.
SUR LA CONNEXITE SEMI-FORTE D'UN DIGRAPHE. ANALELE STIINTIFICE ALE UNIVERSITATII "AL. I. CUZA" DIN IASI. SERIA NOUA. SECTIUNEA I A MATEMATICA 24, NO. 1, 173-174. (1978).

MARC 1979 -1 MARCU, D.
METHOD FOR FINDING THE STRONG COMPONENTS OF A DIGRAPH, A. STUDIA UNIVERSITATAS BABES-BOLYAI, MATHEMATICA 24, NO. 2, 22-24. (1979).

MARC 1979 -2 MARCU, D.
METHOD FOR FINDING THE STRONGLY CONNECTED COMPONENTS OF A DIGRAPH, A. ANALELE STIINTIFICE ALE UNIVERSITATII "AL. I. CUZA" DIN IASI, SERIA NOUA, SECTIUNEA I A MATEMATICA 25, 417-418. (1979).

MARC 1979 -3 MARCU, D.
ON CERTAIN VECTOR SPACES ASSOCIATED TO THE ORIENTED FINITE GRAPHS. ANALELE STIINTIFICE ALE UNIVERSITATII "AL. I. CUZA" DIN IASI. SERIA NOUA. SECTIUNEA I A MATEMATICA 25, 175-181. (1979).

MARK 1977 -1 MARKOSJAN, A. G.; MARKOSJAN, S. E.
ALGORITHM FOR THE DECOMPOSITION OF A DIGRAPH INTO A DIFOREST (RUSSIAN). AKADEMIJA NAUK ARMJANSKOI SSR. DOKLADY 65, NO. 3, 129-131. (1977).

MARL 1979 -1 MARLIN, P. G.
APPLICATION OF THE TRANSPORTATION MODEL TO A LARGE SCALE "DISTRICTING" PROBLEM. MILWAUKEE (ORSA/TIMS MEETING, OCTOBER 1979) 19 P. (1979).

MARQ 1979 -1 MARQUEZ DIEZ CANEDO, J.; MEDINA-MORA ESCALANTE, O.
NETWORK SOLUTION TO A GENERAL VEHICLE SCHEDULING PROBLEM, A. IN: A. PREKOPA (ED.): SURVEY OF MATHEMATICAL PROGRAMMING, VOLUME 2, 285-294. AMSTERDAM: NORTH-HOLLAND. (1979).

MARS 1975 -1 MARSTEN, R. E.
USE OF THE BOXSTEP METHOD IN DISCRETE OPTIMIZATION, THE. IN: M. L. BALINSKI, P. WOLFE (EDS.): NONDIFFERENTIABLE OPTIMIZATION. MATHEMATICAL PROGRAMMING STUDY 3, 127-144. (1975).

MARSA 1980 -1 MARSTEN, R. E.; MULLER, M. R.
MIXED-INTEGER PROGRAMMING APPROACH TO AIR CARGO FLEET PLANNING, A. MANAGEMENT SCIENCE 26, 1096-1107. (1980).

MARSB 1979 -1 MARSTEN, R. E.; MULLER, M. R.; KILLION, C. L.
CREW PLANNING AT FLYING TIGER: A SUCCESSFUL APPLICATION OF INTEGER PROGRAMMING. MANAGEMENT SCIENCE 25, 1175-1183. (1979).

MART 1979 -1 MARTEL, A.
HORAIRE DE TRAVAIL OPTIMAL FARE A UNE DEMANDE ALEATOIRE: LE CAS DES JEUX OLYMPIQUES DE MONTREAL. DOCUMENT DE TRAVAIL 79-06. QUEBEC: UNIV. LAVAL, FACULTE DES SCIENCES DE L'ADMINISTRATION, 28 P. (1979).

MARTA 1975 -1 MARTELLI, A.
SOME REMARKS ON THE COMPLEXITY OF HEURISTIC SEARCH ALGORITHMS. IN: E. GELENBE, D. POTIER (EDS.): INTERNATIONAL COMPUTING SYMPOSIUM, ANTIBES 1975, 69-76. AMSTERDAM, OXFORD: NORTH-HOLLAND. (1975).

MARTB 1978 -1 MARTELLO, S.
ALGORITHM FOR FINDING A MINIMAL EQUIVALENT GRAPH OF A STRONGLY CONNECTED DIGRAPH, AN. COMPUTING 21, 183-194. (1978).

MARTC 1977 -1 MARTELLO, S.; TOTH, P.
BRANCH AND BOUND ALGORITHMS FOR THE SOLUTION OF THE GENERAL UNIDIMENSIONAL KNAPSACK PROBLEM. IN: M. ROUBENS (ED.): ADVANCES IN OPERATIONS RESEARCH, PROCEEDINGS OF EURO II, THE SECOND EUROPEAN CONGRESS ON OPERATIONS RESEARCH, STOCKHOLM 1976, 295-301. AMSTERDAM, NEW YORK, OXFORD: NORTH-HOLLAND. (1977).

MARTC 1978 -1 MARTELLO, S.; TOTH, P.
ALGORITHM 37. ALGORITHM FOR THE SOLUTION OF THE 0-1 SINGLE KNAPSACK PROBLEM. COMPUTING 21, 81-86. (1978).

MARTC 1978 -2 MARTELLO, S.; TOTH, P.
PROBLEM OF OPTIMAL CHANGE MAKING (ITALIAN), THE. RICERCA OPERATIVA 8, NO. 6, 3-16. (1978).

MARTC 1979 -1 MARTELLO, S.; TOTH, P.
FINDING A MINIMAL EQUIVALENT GRAPH OF A DIGRAPH. NEW ORLEANS (TIMS/ORSA MEETING, APRIL/MAY 1979) 21 P. (1979).

MARTC 1979 -2 MARTELLO, S.; TOTH, P.
HEURISTIC ALGORITHMS FOR THE MULTIPLE KNAPSACK PROBLEM. AMSTERDAM (THIRD EUROPEAN CONGRESS ON OPERATIONS RESEARCH, APRIL 1979) 22 P. (1979).

MARTC 1979 -3 MARTELLO, S.; TOTH, P.
0-1 KNAPSACK PROBLEM, THE. IN: N. CHRISTOFIDES, A. MINGOZZI, P. TOTH, C. SANDI (EDS.): COMBINATORIAL OPTIMIZATION, 237-280. CHICHESTER, NEW YORK, BRISBANE, TORONTO: WILEY. (1979).

MARTC 1980 -1 MARTELLO, S.; TOTH, P.
ALGORITHM FOR THE GENERALIZED ASSIGNMENT PROBLEM, AN. WASHINGTON (TIMS/ORSA MEETING, MAY 1980) 16 P. (1980).

MARTC 1980 -2 MARTELLO, S.; TOTH, P.
NOTE ON THE INGARGIOLA-KORSH ALGORITHM FOR ONE-DIMENSIONAL KNAPSACK PROBLEMS, A. OPERATIONS RESEARCH 28, 1226-1227. (1980).

MARTC 1980 -3 MARTELLO, S.; TOTH, P.
OPTIMAL AND CANONICAL SOLUTIONS OF THE CHANGE MAKING PROBLEM. EUROPEAN JOURNAL OF OPERATIONAL RESEARCH 4, 322-329. (1980).

MARTC 1980 -4 MARTELLO, S.; TOTH, P.
SOLUTION OF THE ZERO-ONE MULTIPLE KNAPSACK PROBLEM. EUROPEAN JOURNAL OF OPERATIONAL RESEARCH 4, 276-283. (1980).

MARTD 1975 -1 MARTIN-VEGA, L. A.
OPTIMAL RULES AND ALGORITHMS FOR SOME PARALLEL PROCESSOR SCHEDULING PROBLEMS. DOCTORAL DISSERTATION. GAINESVILLE: THE UNIVERSITY OF FLORIDA, 191 P. (1975).

MARTE 1977 -1 MARTIN-VEGA, L. A.; RATLIFF, H. D.
SCHEDULING RULES FOR PARALLEL PROCESSORS. AIIE TRANSACTIONS 9, 330-337. (1977).

MARTF 1979 -1 MARTINEC, I.
COMBINATORIAL ALGORITHM FOR M-TOUR TRAVELLING SALESMAN PROBLEMS (CZECHOSLOVAKIAN), A. EKONOMICKO-MATEMATICKY OBZOR 15, 320-341. (1979).

MARTG 1977 -1 MARTINOV, N. J.
3-COLORABLE PLANAR GRAPHS (RUSSIAN). SERDICA BULGARICAE MATHEMATICAE PUBLICATIONES 1, 11-16. (1977).

MARTH 1978 -1 MARTYNA, J.
STUDY OF JOB ROUTING BEHAVIOR IN AN OPERATING SYSTEM (POLISH), A. PODSTAWY STEROWANIA. POLSKA AKADEMIA NAUK. CENTRUM BADAN NAUKOWYCH W WOJ. KATOWICKIM. ZAKLAD SYSTEMOW AUTOMATYKI KOMPLEKSOWEJ 8, 445-453. (1978).

MARU 1979 -1 MARUCHECK, A. S.; ALY, A. A.
EFFICIENT ALGORITHM FOR THE LOCATION-ALLOCATION PROBLEM WITH RECTANGULAR REGIONS. AN. WORKING PAPER. NORMAN: UNIV. OF OKLAHOMA, SCHOOL OF INDUSTRIAL ENGINEERIGN, 27 P. (1979).

MARUA 1977 -1 MARUYAMA, K.; CHANG, S. K.; TANG, D. T.
GENERAL PACKING ALGORITHM FOR MULTIDIMENSIONAL RESOURCE REQUIREMENTS. A. INTERNATIONAL JOURNAL OF COMPUTER AND INFORMATION SCIENCE 6, NO. 2, 131-149. (1977).

MASC 1980 -1 MASCH, V. V.
CYCLIC METHOD OF SOLVING THE TRANSSHIPMENT PROBLEM WITH AN ADDITIONAL LINEAR CONSTRAINT, THE. NETWORKS 10, 17-31. (1980).

MASO 1981 -1 MASON, J. H.
GLUEING MATROIDS TOGETHER: A STUDY OF DILWORTH TRUNCATIONS AND MATROID ANALOGUES OF EXTERIOR AND SYMMETRIC POWERS. IN: L. LOVASZ, V. T. SOS (EDS.): ALGEBRAIC METHODS IN GRAPH THEORY, VOL. II, 519-562. COLLOQUIA MATHEMATICA SOCIETATIS JANOS BOLYAI 25. AMSTERDAM, OXFORD,NEW YORK: NORTH-HOLLAND. (1981).

MASOA 1980 -1 MASON, J. H.; OXLEY, J. G.
CIRCUIT COVERING RESULT FOR MATROIDS. A. MATHEMATICAL PROCEEDINGS OF THE CAMBRIDGE PHILOSOPHICAL SOCIETY 87, 25-27. (1980).

MATH 1978 -1 MATHAISEL, D. F. X.; MULLER, M. R.
ASSIGNMENT OF CARGO FLOWS TO AN AIRLINE NETWORK. LOS ANGELES (ORSA/TIMS MEETING, NOVEMBER 1978) 39 P. (1978).

MATHA 1979 -1 MATHON, R.
NOTE ON THE GRAPH ISOMORPHISM COUNTING PROBLEM, A. INFORMATION PROCESSING LETTERS 8, 131-132. (1979).

MATS 1977 -1 MATSUI, K.
SOME PROPERTIES FOR EQUIVALENCE CLASSES OF FLOW NETWORKS. ELECTRONICS AND COMMUNICATIONS IN JAPAN 60, NO. 3, 1-7. (1977).

MATS 1977 -2 MATSUI, K.
SUFFICIENT CONDITION FOR SYNTHESIS OF DIRECTED NETWORKS WITH TWO-COMMODITY FLOWS, A. MEMOIRS OF THE DEFENSE ACADEMY 17, NO. 3, 79-86. (1977).

MATT 1978 -1 MATTHAEUS, F.
TOURENPLANUNG - VERFAHREN ZUR EINSATZDISPOSITION VON FUHRPARKS. DARMSTADT: TOECHE-MITTLER. 244 P. (1978).

MATTA 1977 -1 MATTHEISS, T. H.; RUBIN, D. S.
SURVEY AND COMPARISON OF METHODS FOR FINDING ALL VERTICES OF CONVEX POLYHEDRAL SETS, A. TECHNICAL REPORT NO. 77-14. CHAPEL HILL: UNIV. OF NORTH CAROLINA, OPERATIONS RESEARCH AND SYSTEMS ANALYSIS, 33 P. (1977).

MATTB 1977 -1 MATTHEWS, L. R.
MATROIDS FROM GRAPHS AND DIRECTED GRAPHS. DISSERTATION. OXFORD: OXFORD UNIV. 156 P. (1977).

MATTB 1978 -1 MATTHEWS, L. R.
MATROIDS FROM DIRECTED GRAPHS. DISCRETE MATHEMATICS 24, 47-61. (1978).

MATTB 1978 -2 MATTHEWS, L. R.
NOTE ON THE MUTUAL INDEPENDENCE OF EVENTS, A. REPORT NO. 7896-OR. BONN: UNIV. BONN, INSTITUT FUER OEKONOMETRIE UND OPERATIONS RESEARCH, 7 P. (1978).

MATTB 1978 -3 MATTHEWS, L. R.
PROPERTIES OF BICIRCULAR MATROIDS. IN: J.-C. BERMOND ET AL. (EDS.): PROBLEMES COMBINATOIRES ET THEORIE DES GRAPHES, COLLOQUES INTERNATIONAUX DU CENTRE NATIONAL DE LA RECHERCHE SCIENTIFIQUE, ORSAY 1976, 289-290. PARIS: CENTRE NATIONAL DE LA RECHERCHE SCIENTIFIQUE. (1978).

MATTB 1979 -1 MATTHEWS, L. R.
DUALITY IN INDEPENDENCE SYSTEMS. IN: W. OETTLI, F. STEFFENS (EDS.): OPERATIONS RESEARCH VERFAHREN 32, THIRD SYMPOSIUM ON OPERATIONS RESEARCH, MANNHEIM 1978, 173-179. KOENIGSTEIN: ANTON HAIN MEISENHEIM. (1979).

MATTB 1979 -2 MATTHEWS, L. R.
INFINITE SUBGRAPHS AS MATROID CIRCUITS. JOURNAL OF COMBINATORIAL THEORY 27, SERIES B, 260-273. (1979).

MAUR 1981 -1 MAURER, H.
POST-OFFICE PROBLEM AND RELATED QUESTIONS, THE. IN: H. NOLTEMEYER (ED.): GRAPHTHEORETIC CONCEPTS IN COMPUTER SCIENCE, 1-19. LECTURE NOTES IN COMPUTER SCIENCE 100, BERLIN: SPRINGER. (1981).

MAURA 1979 -1 MAURER, S. B.
VERTEX COLORINGS WITHOUT ISOLATES. JOURNAL OF COMBINATORIAL THEORY 27, SERIES B, 294-319. (1979).

MAURB 1978 -1 MAURER, S. B.; SLATER, P. J.
ON K-CRITICAL N-CONNECTED GRAPHS. DISCRETE MATHEMATICS 20, 255-262. (1978).

MAURB 1979 -1 MAURER, S. B.; SLATER, P. J.
MINIMALLY 2-EDGE-CONNECTED GRAPHS. IN: A. GEWIRTZ, L. V. QUINTAS (EDS.): SECOND INTERNATIONAL CONFERENCE ON COMBINATORIAL MATHEMATICS, 377-382. ANNALS OF THE NEW YORK ACADEMY OF SCIENCES, VOLUME 319. NEW YORK: THE NEW YORK ACADEMY OF SCIENCES. (1979).

MAURC 1978 -1 MAURRAS, J. F.
GOOD ALGORITHMS, OLD IDEAS. CLAMART: ELECTRICITE DE FRANCE, DEPT. METHODES D'OPTIMISATION, 11 P. (1978).

MAVR 1979 -1 MAVRIDES, L. P.
INDIRECT METHOD FOR THE GENERALIZED K-MEDIAN PROBLEM APPLIED TO LOCK-BOX LOCATION, AN. MANAGEMENT SCIENCE 25, 990-996. (1979).

MAXE 1975 -1 MAXEMCHUK, N. F.
DISPERSITY ROUTING IN STORE-AND-FORWARD NETWORKS. DOCTORAL DISSERTATION. PHILADELPHIA: UNIVERSITY OF PENNSYLVANIA, 267 P. (1975).

MAYB 1978 -1 MAYBERRY, J. P.; SAIPE, A. L.
REPLY TO GRAVES AND HAESSLER'S NOTE ON THE PAPER "PRODUCTION RUNS FOR MULTIPLE PRODUCTS: THE TWO-PRODUCT HEURISTIC". MANAGEMENT SCIENCE 24, 1197-1199. (1978).

MAZZ 1980 -1 MAZZOLA, J. B.
PROCEDURE FOR GENERATING THE CONVEX HULL OF A 0-1 PROGRAMMING POLYTOPE WITH POSITIVE COEFFICIENTS, A. RESEARCH REPORT 472. PITTSBURGH: CARNEGIE-MELLON UNIV., MANAGEMENT SCIENCE RESEARCH GROUP, 24 P. (1980).

MECH 1976 -1 MECHTA, A. J.; RIFAI, A. K.
APPLICATION OF LINEAR PROGRAMMING VS. GOAL PROGRAMMING TO ASSIGNMENT PROBLEM. AKRON BUSINESS AND ECONOMIC REVIEW 7, 52-55. (1976).

MEDG 1950 -1 MEDGYESSY, P.
SUR LA STRUCTURE DES RESEAUX FINIS, CUBIQUES ET COLORIES. MATHESIS 59, 173-176. (1950).

MEEU 1980 -1 MEEUSEN, W.
ON THE MAXIMAL NUMBER OF K-CLIQUES IN A GRAPH WITH N VERTICES (TOWARDS AN APPLICATION ON THE MEASUREMENT OF FINANCIAL CONCENTRATION). REVUE BELGE DE STATISTIQUE, D'INFORMATIQUE ET DE RECHERCHE OPERATIONELLE 20, NO. 3, 1-12. (1980).

MEGE 1978 -1 MEGEATH, J. D.
SUCCESSFUL HOSPITAL PERSONNEL SCHEDULING. INTERFACES 2, 55-61. (1978).

MEGI 1978 -1 MEGIDDO, N.
COMBINATORIAL OPTIMIZATION WITH RATIONAL OBJECTIVE FUNCTIONS. IN: PROCEEDINGS OF THE TENTH ANNUAL ACM SYMPOSIUM ON THEORY OF COMPUTING, SAN DIEGO, 1978, 1-12. NEW YORK: THE ASSOCIATION FOR COMPUTING MACHINERY. (1978).

MEGI 1978 -2 MEGIDDO, N.
COST ALLOCATION FOR STEINER TREES. NETWORKS 8, 1-6. (1978).

MEGI 1979 -1 MEGIDDO, N.
COMBINATORIAL OPTIMIZATION WITH RATIONAL OBJECTIVE FUNCTIONS. MATHEMATICS OF OPERATIONS RESEARCH 4, 414-424. (1979).

MEGIA 1979 -1 MEGIDDO, N.; GALIL, Z.
ON FULKERSON'S CONJECTURE ABOUT CONSISTENT LABELING PROCESSES. MATHEMATICS OF OPERATIONS RESEARCH 4, 265-267. (1979).

MEGIB 1978 -1 MEGIDDO, N.; TAMIR, A.
O(N TIMES LOG N) ALGORITHM FOR A CLASS OF MATCHING PROBLEMS, AN. SIAM JOURNAL ON COMPUTING 7, 154-157. (1978).

MEGIC 1979 -1 MEGIDDO, N.; TAMIR, A.; ZEMEL, E.; CHANDRASEKARAN, R.
O(N(LOG N)(LOG N)) ALGORITHM FOR THE KTH LONGEST PATH IN A TREE WITH APPLICATIONS TO LOCATION PROBLEMS, AN. DISCUSSION PAPER NO. 379. EVANSTON: NORTHWESTERN UNIV., CENTER FOR MATHEMATICAL STUDIES IN ECONOMICS AND MANAGEMENT SCIENCE, 18 P. (1979).

MEHL 1978 -1 MEHLHORN, K.
EFFIZIENTE ALGORITHMEN: EIN BEISPIEL. INFORMATIK-SPEKTRUM 2, 81-89. (1978).

MEHT 1975 -1 MEHTA, J. M.
STUDY OF PASSING IN FLOW SHOP SCHEDULING PROBLEMS, THE. DOCTORAL DISSERTATION. EAST LANSING: MICHIGAN STATE UNIVERSITY, 225 P. (1975).

MEHTA 1980 -1 MEHTA, N. K.
PERFORMANCE OF SELECTED GRAPH COLORING ALGORITHMS - EMPIRICAL RESULTS. WORKING PAPER. BETHLEHEM: LEHIGH UNIV., DEPT. OF INDUSTRIAL ENGINEERING, 21 P. (1980).

MEIR 1978 -1 MEIR, A.
ON TOTAL COVERING AND MATCHING OF GRAPHS. JOURNAL OF COMBINATORIAL THEORY 24, SERIES B, 164-168. (1978).

MEIS 1978 -1 MEISSNER, J.-D.
HEURISTISCHE PROGRAMMIERUNG. WIESBADEN: AKADEMISCHE VERLAGSGESELLSCHAFT, 270 P. (1978). (STUDIEN-TEXTE OPERATIONS RESEARCH)

MELA 1979 -1 MELAMED, I. J.; PLOTINSKIJ, Y. M.
ALGORITHME HEURISTIQUE DE RESOLUTION DU PROBLEME DE LIVRAISON GENERALISE (RUSSIAN). AVTOMATIKA I TELEMEHANIKA (MOSCOW), NO. 12, 167-172. (1979).

MELN 1978 -1 MELNIK, I. M.
INHOMOGENEOUS NETWORK TRANSPORT PROBLEM (RUSSIAN). KIBERNETIKA, NO. 2, 69-72. (1978).

MELNA 1970 -1 MELNIKOV, L. S.
CHROMATIC CLASS AND THE LOCATION OF A GRAPH ON A CLOSED SURFACE, THE. AKADEMIJA NAUK SOJUZA SSR. MATEMATICESKIE ZAMETKI 7, 671-681; TRANSLATED AS MATHEMATICAL NOTES OF THE ACADEMY OF SCIENCES OF THE USSR. 1970, 405-411. (1970).

MELNB 1976 -1 MELNIKOV, O. I.
SOLUTION OF CERTAIN BELLMAN-JOHNSON PROBLEMS WITH A (0,1)-MATRIX (RUSSIAN). VESCI AKADEMII NAVUK BSSR. SERYJA FIZIKA-MATEMATYCNYH NAVUK, NO. 4, 11-16 + 139. (1976).

MELNC 1979 -1 MELNIKOV, O. I.; SHAFRANSKII, Y. M.
PARAMETRIC PROBLEM IN SCHEDULING THEORY. KIBERNETIKA (KIEV), NO. 3, 53-57, 122; TRANSLATED AS CYBERNETICS 15, 352-357. (1979).

MEND 1970 -1 MENDELSOHN, N. S.
LINEAR DIOPHANTINE EQUATION WITH APPLICATIONS TO NON-NEGATIVE MATRICES, A. IN: A. GEWIRTZ, L. V. QUINTAS (EDS.): INTERNATIONAL CONFERENCE ON COMBINATORIAL MATHEMATICS, 287-294. ANNALS OF THE NEW YORK ACADEMY OF SCIENCES, VOLUME 165, ARTICLE 1. NEW YORK: THE NEW YORK ACADEMY OF SCIENCES. (1970).

MERC 1978 -1 MERCHANT, D. K.; NEMHAUSER, G. L.
MODEL AND AN ALGORITHM FOR THE DYNAMIC TRAFFIC ASSIGNMENT PROBLEM, A. TRANSPORTATION SCIENCE 12, 183-199. (1978).

MERC 1978 -2 MERCHANT, D. K.; NEMHAUSER, G. L.
OPTIMALITY CONDITIONS FOR A DYNAMIC TRAFFIC ASSIGNMENT MODEL. TRANSPORTATION SCIENCE 12, 200-207. (1978).

MERE 1973 -1 MEREDITH, G. H. J.
REGULAR N-VALENT, N-CONNECTED, NON-HAMILTONIAN, NON-N-EDGE-COLOURABLE GRAPHS. JOURNAL OF COMBINATORIAL THEORY 14, SERIES B, 55-60. (1973).

MEREA 1972 -1 MEREDITH, G. H. J.; LLOYD, E. K.
HAMILTONIAN GRAPHS O4 TO O7, THE. IN: D. J. A. WELSH, D. R. WOODALL (EDS.): COMBINATORICS, 229-236. OXFORD: INSTITUTE OF MATHEMATICS AND ITS APPLICATIONS. (1972).

MEREB 1978 -1 MERESSOO, T.
DECOMPOSITION METHOD FOR THE RESOURCE ALLOCATION PROBLEM (RUSSIAN), A. EESTI NSV TEADUSTE AKADEEMIA TOIMETISED. FUEUESIKA MATEMAATIKA 27, 168-173. (1978).

METE 1977 -1 METELSKIJ, N. N.; SLYK, V. A.
CONDITIONS FOR THE SOLVABILITY OF THE INTEGER LINEAR PROGRAMMING PROBLEM (RUSSIAN). VESCI AKADEMII NAVUK BSSR. SERYJA FIZIKA-MATEMATYCNYH NAVUK, NO. 5, 16-19. (1977).

MEVE 1976 -1 MEVERT, P.; SUHL, U.
ALGORITHMS AND A COMPUTATIONAL STUDY FOR THE MULTIDIMENSIONAL KNAPSACK PROBLEM. WORKING PAPER 16/1976. BERLIN: UNIVERSITAET BERLIN, FACHBEREICH 10, WE 6. (1976).

MEYE 1979 -1 MEYER, A. R.; WINKLMANN, K.
FUNDAMENTAL THEOREM OF COMPLEXITY THEORY (PRELIMINARY VERSION), THE. IN: J. W. DE BAKKER, J. VAN LEEUWEN (EDS.): FOUNDATIONS OF COMPUTER SCIENCE III, PART 1, 97-112. AMSTERDAM: MATHEMATISCH CENTRUM. (1979).

MEYEA 1981 -1 MEYER, H.
KOMPLEXITAETSPROBLEME IN GERT-NETZPLAENEN. METHODS OF OPERATIONS RESEARCH 39, 103-112. (1981).

MEYEB 1979 -1 MEYER, R. R.
EQUIVALENT CONSTRAINTS FOR DISCRETE SETS. DISCRETE APPLIED MATHEMATICS 1, 31-50. (1979).

MEYEB 1981 -1 MEYER, R. R.
THEORETICAL AND COMPUTATIONAL COMPARISON OF "EQUIVALENT" MIXED-INTEGER FORMULATIONS, A. NAVAL RESEARCH LOGISTICS QUARTERLY 28, 115-132. (1981).

MEYEC 1975 -1 MEYER, R. R.; FLEISHER, J. M.
STRONG DUALITY FOR A CLASS OF INTEGER PROGRAMS. COMPUTER SCIENCES TECHNICAL REPORT, 256. MADISON: UNIV. OF WISCONSIN-MADISON, COMPUTER SCIENCE DEPT., 6 P. (1975).

MEYED 1978 -1 MEYER, R. R.; SMITH, M. L.
ALGORITHMS FOR A CLASS OF "CONVEX" NONLINEAR INTEGER PROGRAMS. IN: W. W. WHITE (ED.): COMPUTERS AND MATHEMATICAL PROGRAMMING, 210-215. NBS SPECIAL PUBLICATION 502. WASHINGTON: NATIONAL BUREAU OF STANDARDS. (1978).

MEYEE 1980 -1 MEYER, R. R.; THAKKAR, M. V.; HALLMAN, W. P.
RATIONAL MIXED-INTEGER AND POLYHEDRAL UNION MINIMIZATION MODELS. MATHEMATICS OF OPERATIONS RESEARCH 5, 135-146. (1980).

****

MEYEF 1978 -1 MEYER, R. R.; WAGE, M. L.
ON THE POLYHEDRALITY OF THE CONVEX HULL OF THE FEASIBLE SET OF AN INTEGER PROGRAM. SIAM JOURNAL ON CONTROL AND OPTIMIZATION 16, 682-687. (1978).

MEYN 1978 -1 MEYNIEL, H.
5-COLORATIONS D'UN GRAPHE PLANAIRE FORMENT UNE CLASSE DE COMMUTATION UNIQUE, LES. JOURNAL OF COMBINATORIAL THEORY 24, SERIES B, 251-257. (1978).

MICH 1970 -1 MICHALSEN, H.
WORKING STRATEGY FOR GENERAL SCHOOL SCHEDULING, A. REGNESENTEVET NTH, SINTEF, UNIVERSITY OF NORWAY. (1970).

MIHA 1978 -1 MIHALYFFY, L.
IMPROVED METHOD OF SUCCESSIVE OPTIMA FOR THE ASSIGNMENT PROBLEM, AN. IN: J. STOER (ED.): OPTIMIZATION TECHNIQUES, PROCEEDINGS OF THE 8TH IFIP CONFERENCE ON OPTIMIZATION TECHNIQUES, WUERZBURG 1977, PART 2, 225-233. LECTURE NOTES IN CONTROL AND INFORMATION SCIENCES 7, BERLIN, HEIDELBERG, NEW YORK: SPRINGER. (1978).

MIHA 1979 -1 MIHALYFFY, L.
ON THE PROBLEM OF THE SECOND BEST ASSIGNMENT. PROBLEMS OF CONTROL AND INFORMATION THEORY 8, 257-265. (1979).

MIKH 1980 -1 MIKHALEVICH, V. S.; VOLKOVICH, V. L.; VOLOSHIN, A. F.; POSDNYAKOV, YU. M.
ALGORITHMS OF SEQUENTIAL ANALYSIS AND "SCREENING" OF VARIANTS IN DISCRETE OPTIMIZATION PROBLEMS (RUSSIAN). KIBERNETIKA, NO. 3, 76-85. (1980).

MILA 1979 -1 MILANOV, P. B.
ALGORITHME EFFECTIF DE RESOLUTION D'UN PROBLEME D'ALLOCATION DE RESSOURCES AVEC UNE FONCTION D'OBJECTIF CONVEXE (RUSSIAN). VESCI AKADEMII NAVUK BSSR. SERYJA FIZIKA-MATEMATYCNYH NAVUK, NO. 2, 127-128. (1979).

MILG 1977 -1 MILGRAM, M.; DUBUISSON, B.
ALGORITHME HEURISTIQUE DE DECOMPOSITION D'UN GRAPHE, UN. REVUE FRANCAISE D'AUTOMATIQUE, D'INFORMATIQUE ET DE RECHERCHE OPERATIONELLE 11, SERIE RECHERCHE OPERATIONELLE, 175-199. (1977).

MILI 1976 -1 MILIOTIS, P.
ALL-INTEGER ARITHMETIC LP-CUTTING PLANES CODE APPLIED TO THE TRAVELLING SALESMAN PROBLEM, AN. WORKING PAPER. LONDON: LONDON SCHOOL OF ECONOMICS. (1976).

MILI 1978 -1 MILIOTIS, P.
USING CUTTING PLANES TO SOLVE THE SYMMETRIC TRAVELING SALESMAN PROBLEM. MATHEMATICAL PROGRAMMING 15, 177-188. (1978).

MILL 1978 -1 MILLER, G. L.
ON THE N**(LOG(2)N) ISOMORPHISM TECHNIQUE. IN: PROCEEDINGS OF THE 10TH ANNUAL ACM SYMPOSIUM ON THEORY OF COMPUTING. NEW YORK: ASSOCIATION FOR COMPUTING MACHINERY. (1978).

MILL 1979 -1 MILLER, G. L.
GRAPH ISOMORPHISM, GENERAL REMARKS. JOURNAL OF COMPUTER AND SYSTEM SCIENCES 18, 128-142. (1979).

MILLA 1974 -1 MILLER, H. E.
MATHEMATICAL PROGRAMMING MODELS OF NURSE SCHEDULING AND ALLOCATION. DISSERTATION. EVANSTON: NORTHWESTERN UNIVERSITY, 138 P. (1974).

MILLB 1979 -1 MILLER, R. E.; PIPPENGER, N.; ROSENBERG, A. L.; SNYDER, L.
OPTIMAL 2,3-TREES. SIAM JOURNAL ON COMPUTING 8, 42-59. (1979).

MILLC 1975 -1 MILLER, S. D.; PAYNE, H. J.; THOMPSON, W. A.
ALGORITHM FOR TRAFFIC ASSIGNMENT ON CAPACITY CONSTRAINED TRANSPORTATION NETWORKS WITH QUEUES, AN. IN: PROCEEDINGS OF THE 1975 CONFERENCE ON INFORMATION SCIENCES AND SYSTEMS, BALTIMORE 1975, 297-302. BALTIMORE: THE JOHNS HOPKINS UNIVERSITY: DEPARTMENT OF ELECTRICAL ENGINEERING. (1975).

MILLD 1979 -1 MILLS, W. H.
COVERING DESIGNS I: COVERINGS BY A SMALL NUMBER OF SUBSETS. ARS COMBINATORIA 8, 199-315. (1979).

MINA 1980 -1 MINAEV, YU. N.
UNIFIED FORMAL-HEURISTIC ALGORITHM FOR SOLVING INTEGRAL LINEAR PROGRAMMING PROBLEM (RUSSIAN), A. KIBERNETIKA, NO. 4, 131-135. (1980).

MINI 1977 -1 MINIEKA, E.
OPTIMUM BRANCHINGS WITH A SPECIFIED NUMBER OF ARCS. CHICAGO: UNIV. OF ILLINOIS, COLLEGE OF BUSINESS ADMINISTRATION, 15 P. (1977).

MINI 1978 -1 MINIEKA, E.
OPTIMIZATION ALGORITHMS FOR NETWORKS AND GRAPHS. NEW YORK, BASEL: DEKKER, 356 P. (1978). (INDUSTRIAL ENGINEERING, 1)

MINI 1979 -1 MINIEKA, E.
CHINESE POSTMAN PROBLEM FOR MIXED NETWORKS, THE. MANAGEMENT SCIENCE 25, 643-648. (1979).

MINI 1980 -1 MINIEKA, E.
CONDITIONAL CENTERS AND MEDIANS OF A GRAPH. NETWORKS 10, 265-272. (1980).

MINIA 1975 -1 MININA, T. R.; PEREKREST, V. T.
CERTAIN WAY OF APPROXIMATING THE SOLUTIONS OF THE TRAVELING SALESMAN PROBLEM (RUSSIAN), A. DOKLADY AKADEMII NAUK SSSR 220, 31-34. (1975).

MINO 1978 -1 MINOUX, M.
ACCELERATED GREEDY ALGORITHMS FOR MAXIMIZING SUBMODULAR SET FUNCTIONS. IN: J. STOER (ED.): OPTIMIZATION TECHNIQUES, PROCEEDINGS OF THE 8TH IFIP CONFERENCE ON OPTIMIZATION TECHNIQUES, WUERZBURG 1977, PART 2, 234-243. LECTURE NOTES IN CONTROL AND INFORMATION SCIENCES 7, BERLIN, HEIDELBERG, NEW YORK: SPRINGER. (1978).

MINO 1979 -1 MINOUX, M.
GENERALIZED PATH ALGEBRAS. IN: A. PREKOPA (ED.): SURVEY OF MATHEMATICAL PROGRAMMING, VOLUME 2, 359-364. AMSTERDAM: NORTH-HOLLAND. (1979).

MINO 1980 -1 MINOUX, M.
SOLUTIONS ENTIERES ET SOLUTIONS CONTINUES DES PROBLEMES DE COUPLAGES DANS LES GRAPHES PONDERES FINIS. COMPTES RENDUS HEBDOMADAIRES DES SEANCES DE L'ACADEMIE DES SCIENCES (PARIS), SERIES A 291, NO. 5, 363-364. (1980).

MINT 1967 -1 MINTY, G. J.
THEOREM ON THREE-COLORING THE EDGES OF A TRIVALENT GRAPH, A. JOURNAL OF COMBINATORIAL THEORY 2, 164-167. (1967).

MINT 1980 -1 MINTY, G. J.
ON MAXIMAL INDEPENDENT SETS OF VERTICES IN CLAW-FREE GRAPHS. JOURNAL OF COMBINATORIAL THEORY 28, SERIES B, 284-304. (1980).

MIRC 1979 -1 MIRCHANDANI, P. B.; ODONI, A. R.
LOCATING NEW PASSENGER FACILITIES ON A TRANSPORTATION NETWORK. TRANSPORTATION RESEARCH 13, SERIES B, 113-122. (1979).

MIRC 1979 -2 MIRCHANDANI, P. B.; ODONI, A. R.
LOCATIONS OF MEDIANS ON STOCHASTIC NETWORKS. TRANSPORTATION SCIENCE 13, 85-97. (1979).

MIRCA 1980 -1 MIRCHANDANI, P. B.; OUDJIT, A.
LOCALIZING 2-MEDIANS ON PROBABILISTIC AND DETERMINISTIC TREE NETWORKS. NETWORKS 10, 329-350. (1980).

MISH 1978 -1 MISHCHENKO, A. E.; SHAFRANSKIJ, V. V.
USE OF NETWORK MODELS WITH "INTERMEDIATE" RESOURCES FOR CALENDAR-SIZE SCHEDULING OF COMPLEX JOBS (RUSSIAN), THE. IZVESTIJA AKADEMII NAUK SSSR. TEHNICESKAJA KIBERNETIKA (MOSCOW) NO. 2, 29-35. (1978).

MISHA 1980 -1 MISHRA, B. K.; DAS, C.
MINIMAX AND SYMMETRIC DUALITY FOR A NONLINEAR MIXED-INTEGER PROGRAMMING PROBLEM. OPSEARCH 17, 1-11. (1980).

MISR 1979 -1 MISRA, R. B.
ALGORITHM FOR ENUMERATING ALL SIMPLE PATHS IN A COMMUNICATION NETWORK, AN. MICROELECTRONICS AND RELIABILITY 19, 363-366. (1979).

MISRA 1981 -1 MISRA, S.; DAS, C.
THREE-DIMENSIONAL TRANSPORTATION PROBLEM WITH CAPACITY RESTRICTION. NEW ZEALAND OPERATIONAL RESEARCH 9, 47-58. (1981).

MISZ 1979 -1 MISZCZYNSKI, M. T.; STRZELEC, K. R.
OPTIMAL CUTTING ALGORITHM FOR RECTANGLE ELEMENTS. IN: A. PREKOPA (ED.): SURVEY OF MATHEMATICAL PROGRAMMING. VOLUME 2, 545-552. AMSTERDAM: NORTH-HOLLAND. (1979).

MITC 1979 -1 MITCHELL, S.; COCKAYNE, E. J.; HEDETNIEMI, S. T.
LINEAR ALGORITHMS ON RECURSIVE REPRESENTATIONS OF TREES. JOURNAL OF COMPUTER AND SYSTEM SCIENCES 18, 76-85. (1979).

MITCA 1979 -1 MITCHELL, S.; HEDETNIEMI, S. T.
LINEAR ALGORITHMS FOR EDGE-COLORING TREES AND UNICYCLIC GRAPHS. INFORMATION PROCESSING LETTERS 9, 110-112. (1979).

MITE 1979 -1 MITEV, J. G.
USE OF A NUMBER OF ADMISSIBLE SOLUTIONS OF EQUATIONS IN ALGORITHMS FOR PURELY INTEGER PROBLEMS OF LINEAR PROGRAMMING (RUSSIAN), THE. ZURNAL VYCISLITEL'NOI MATEMATIKI I MATEMATICESKOI FIZIKI 19, 1059-1061 + 1085; TRANSLATED AS USSR COMPUTATIONAL MATHEMATICS AND MATHEMATICAL PHYSICS 19, NO. 4, 279-281. (1979).

MITE 1981 -1 MITEV, J. G.
SUCCESSIVE SOLUTIONS METHOD FOR AN INTEGER OPTIMIZATIONAL PROBLEM (RUSSIAN). EKONOMIKA I MATEMATICESKIE METODY (MOSCOW) 17, NO. 1, 187-188. (1981).

MITS 1972 -1 MITSUMORI, S.
OPTIMUM PRODUCTION SCHEDULING OF MULTICOMMODITY IN FLOW LINE. IEEE TRANSACTIONS ON SYSTEMS, MAN, AND CYBERNETICS 2, 486-493. (1972).

MITS 1978 -1 MITSUMORI, S.
MINIMUM NUMBER OF VEHICLES TO MEET DYNAMIC TRANSPORTATION DEMAND. INSTITUTE OF ELECTRICAL AND ELECTRONICS ENGINEERS. TRANSACTIONS ON SYSTEMS, MAN, AND CYBERNETICS 8, NO. 2, 110-114. (1978).

MITT 1979 -1 MITTAL, B. S.; BAGGA, P. C.
FLOW SHOP SCHEDULING WITH PARALLEL MACHINES. CAHIERS DU CENTRE D'ETUDES DE RECHERCHE OPERATIONNELLE 21, 87-91. (1979).

MIYA 1981 -1 MIYAZAKI, S.
ONE MACHINE SCHEDULING PROBLEM WITH DUAL CRITERIA. JOURNAL OF THE OPERATIONS RESEARCH SOCIETY OF JAPAN 24, 37-51. (1981).

MIYAA 1980 -1 MIYAZAKI, S.; NISHIYAMA, N.
ANALYSIS FOR MINIMIZING WEIGHTED MEAN FLOW-TIME IN FLOW-SHOP SCHEDULING. JOURNAL OF THE OPERATIONS RESEARCH SOCIETY OF JAPAN 23, 118-133. (1980).

MIYAB 1978 -1 MIYAZAKI, S.; NISHIYAMA, N.; HASHIMOTO, F.
ADJACENT PAIRWISE APPROACH TO THE MEAN FLOW-TIME SCHEDULING PROBEM, AN. JOURNAL OF THE OPERATIONS RESEARCH SOCIETY OF JAPAN 21, 287-301. (1978).

MJEL 1978 -1 MJELDE, K. M.
DISCRETE RESOURCE ALLOCATION BY A BRANCH AND BOUND METHOD. THE JOURNAL OF THE OPERATIONAL RESEARCH SOCIETY 29, 1021-1023. (1978).

MJEL 1980 -1 MJELDE, K. M.
BOUNDED ALLOCATIONS OF DISCRETE AND BINARY RESOURCES. JOURNAL OF THE OPERATIONAL RESEARCH SOCIETY 31, 949-952. (1980).

MOEH 1979 -1 MOEHRING, R. H.
MINIMIZING COSTS OF RESOURCE REQUIREMENTS SUBJECT TO A FIXED COMPLETION TIME (ABSTRACT). IN: W. OETTLI, F. STEFFENS (EDS.): OPERATIONS RESEARCH VERFAHREN 32, THIRD SYMPOSIUM ON OPERATIONS RESEARCH, MANNHEIM 1978, 181-182. KOENIGSTEIN: ANTON HAIN MEISENHEIM. (1979).

MOEH 1980 -1 MOEHRING, R. H.
SCHEDULING PROBLEMS WITH A SINGULAR SOLUTION. RESEARCH REPORT. AACHEN: TECHNISCHE UNIVERSITAET, LEHRSTUHL FUER MATHEMATIK,14 P. (1980).

MOEH 1981 -1 MOEHRING, R. H.
SCHEDULING PROBLEMS WITH GENERAL PRECEDENCE AND RESOURCE CONSTRAINTS: AN ORDER-THEORETICAL APPROACH. IN: R. E. BURKARD, T. ELLINGER (EDS.): METHODS OF OPERATIONS RESEARCH 40, 375-378. KOENIGSTEIN: ANTON HAIN MEISENHEIM. (1981).

MOHA 1979 -1 MOHANTY, S. P.; RAO, D.
CHARACTERIZATION AND ENUMERATION OF HYPOTRAVERSABLE GRAPHS. BULLETIN OF THE AUSTRALIAN MATHEMATICAL SOCIETY 20, 437-445. (1979).

MOLE 1979 -1 MOLE, R. H.
SURVEY OF LOCAL DELIVERY VEHICLE ROUTING METHODOLOGY, A. JOURNAL OF THE OPERATIONAL RESEARCH SOCIETY 30, 245-252. (1979).

MOLI 1979 -1 MOLISZ, W.
OPTIMIZATION OF MULTICOMMODITY FLOWS IN A COMPUTER NETWORK (POLISH). ARCHIWUM AUTOMATYKI I TELEMECHANIKI 24, 107-122. (1979).

MOLL 1979 -1 MOLLUZZO, J. C.
SOME HAMILTONIAN COUNTEREXAMPLES. IN: F. HARARY (ED.): TOPICS IN GRAPH THEORY. ANNALS OF THE NEW YORK ACADEMY OF SCIENCES 328, 157-165. NEW YORK: THE NEW YORK ACADEMY OF SCIENCES. (1979).

MOLL 1979 -2 MOLLUZZO, J. C.
TOUGHNESS, HAMILTONIAN-CONNECTEDNESS, AND N-HAMILTONICITY. IN: A. GEWIRTZ, L. V. QUINTAS (EDS.): SECOND INTERNATIONAL CONFERENCE ON COMBINATORIAL MATHEMATICS, 402-404. ANNALS OF THE NEW YORK ACADEMY OF SCIENCES, VOLUME 319. NEW YORK: THE NEW YORK ACADEMY OF SCIENCES. (1979).

MOLN 1979 -1 MOLNAR, A.
PRACTICAL SOLUTION OF THE PLANT LOCATION PROBLEM (HUNGARIAN). SZIGMA - MATEMATIKAI-KOEZGÁZDASAGI FOLYOIRAT 12, 109-118. (1979).

MONI 1980 -1 MONIEN, B.; URMETZER, N.; VORNBERGER, O.
CONSIDERATION OF THE TRAVELLING SALESMAN PROBLEM USING THE ASSIGNMENT PROBLEM, A. IN: U. PAPE (ED.): DISCRETE STRUCTURES AND ALGORITHMS, 167-180. MUENCHEN: HANSER. (1980).

MONM 1978 -1 MONMA, C. L.
PROPERTIES AND EFFICIENT ALGORITHMS FOR CERTAIN CLASSES OF SEQUENCING PROBLEMS. REPORT NO. 78108-OR. BONN: UNIV. BONN, INSTITUT FUER OEKONOMETRIE UND OPERATIONS RESEARCH, 162 P. (1978). (DISSERTATION)

MONM 1979 -1 MONMA, C. L.
TWO-MACHINE MAXIMUM FLOW TIME PROBLEM WITH SERIES-PARALLEL PRECEDENCE CONSTRAINTS: AN ALGORITHM AND EXTENSIONS, THE. OPERATIONS RESEARCH 27, 792-798. (1979).

MONM 1980 -1 MONMA, C. L.
DISSECTION STRATEGIES FOR MULTIGRAM CODES. HOLMDEL: BELL LABORATORIES.17 P. (1980).

MONM 1980 -2 MONMA, C. L.
LINEAR-TIME ALGORITHMS FOR SCHEDULING EQUAL-LENGTH TASKS WITH DUE DATES ON PARALLEL PROCESSORS SUBJECT TO PRECEDENCE CONSTRANINTS. WORKING PAPER. HOLMDEL: BELL LABORATORIES, 17 P. (1980).

MONM 1980 -3 MONMA, C. L.
SEQUENCING TO MINIMIZE THE MAXIMUM JOB COST. OPERATIONS RESSEARCH 28, 942-951. (1980).

MONM 1981 -1 MONMA, C. L.
SEQUENCING WITH GENERAL PRECEDENCE CONSTRAINTS. DISCRETE APPLIED MATHEMATICS 3, 137-150. (1981).

MONMA 1981 -1 MONMA, C. L.; RINNOOY KAN, A. H. G.
EFFICIENTLY SOLVABLE SPECIAL CASES OF THE PERMUTATION FLOW-SHOP PROBLEM. PAPER PRESENTED AT THE CORS/ORSA/TIMS MEETING, TORONTO 1981, 28 P. (1981).

MONMB 1977 -1 MONMA, C. L.; SIDNEY, J. B.
GENERAL ALGORITHM FOR OPTIMAL JOB SEQUENCING WITH SERIES-PARALLEL PRECEDENCE CONSTRAINTS, A. TECHNICAL REPORT 347. ITHACA: CORNELL UNIVERSITY, SCHOOL OF OPERATIONS RESEARCH. (1977).

MONMC 1979 -1 MONMA, C. L.; TROTTER, L. E. JR.
ON PERFECT GRAPHS AND POLYHEDRA WITH (0,1)-VALUED EXTREME POINTS. MATHEMATICAL PROGRAMMING 17, 239-242. (1979).

MONT 1979 -1 MONTEROSSO, C. D. B.; BORNSTEIN, C. T.
HEURISTIC ALGORITHM FOR THE LOCATION AND DIMENSIONING OF WAREHOUSES, A. IN: W. OETTLI, F. STEFFENS (EDS.): OPERATIONS RESEARCH VERFAHREN 35, THIRD SYMPOSIUM ON OPERATIONS RESEARCH, MANNHEIM 1978, 315-328. KOENIGSTEIN: ANTON HAIN MEISENHEIM. (1979).

MOON 1979 -1 MOON, I. D.
DISTANCE CONSTRAINTS WITH LOWER BOUNDS FOR TREE NETWORK LOCATION PROBLEMS. WORKING PAPER NO. 79-02. NEW YORK: COLUMBIA UNIV., DEPT. OF INDUSTRIAL ENGINEERING AND OPERATIONS RESEARCH, 20 P. (1979).

MOON 1980 -1 MOON, I. D.
TREE NETWORK LOCATION PROBLEMS WITH MAXIMUM SEPARATIONS. WORKING PAPER NO. 80-52. NEW YORK: COLUMBIA UNIV., DEPT. OF INDUSTRIAL ENGINEERING & OPERATIONS RESEARCH, 21 P. (1980).

MOOR 1978 -1 MOORE, L. J.; TAYLOR, B. W. III; LEE, S. M.
ANALYSIS OF A TRANSSHIPMENT PROBLEM WITH MULTIPLE CONFLICTING OBJECTIVES. COMPUTERS AND OPERATIONS RESEARCH 5, 39-46. (1978).

MOORA 1980 -1 MOORE, T. G.
CENTRAL CUTTING PLANE ALGORITHM FOR INTEGER PROGRAMMING, A. WASHINGTON (ORSA/TIMS MEETING, MAY 1980) 32 P. (1980).

MORE 1966 -1 MORELAND, J. A.
SCHEDULING OF AIRLINE FLIGHT CREWS. M. P. THESIS. CAMBRIDGE: MASSACHUSETTS INSTITUTE OF TECHNOLOGY. (1966).

MORI 1977 -1 MORITA, K.; UMEO, H.; SUGATA, K.
COMPUTATIONAL COMPLEXITY OF L(M,N) TAPE-BOUNDED TWO-DIMENSIONAL TURING MACHINES. SYSTEMS-COMPUTERS-CONTROLS. THE TRANSACTIONS OF THE INSTITUTE OF ELECTRONICS AND COMMUNICATION ENGINEERS OF JAPAN 8, NO. 6, 17-24. (1977).

MORIA 1978 -1 MORITO, S; SALKIN, H. M.
SEARCH ENUMERATION ALGORITHM FOR A MULTIPLANT, MULTIPRODUCT SCHEDULING PROBLEM, A. IN: COMPUTERS AND MATHEMATICAL PROGRAMMING, PROC. BICENTEN. CONF., GAITHERSBURG/MD. 1976, NBS SPEC. PUBL. 502, 144-151. (1978).

MORIB 1978 -1 MORITZ, A.
MATHEMATISCHES MODELL FUER DIE ERRECHNUNG DER MINIMALEN TRANSPORTKOSTEN IM UNGARISCHEN BINNENHANDEL. ZEITSCHRIFT FUER OPERATIONS RESEARCH 22, SERIE B, B175-B183. (1978).

MORL 1980 -1 MORLOCK, M.
ZEITPLANUNG MIT EINER ERWEITERUNG VON CPM. ZEITSCHRIFT FUER ANGEWANDTE MATHEMATIK UND MECHANIK 60, 360-361. (1980).

MORO 1976 -1 MOROZOV, S. A.
ON THE PROBLEM OF FINDING THE SHORTEST CONNECTING TREE WITH CONSTRAINT (RUSSIAN). IN: CONTROL SYST., NO. 15, ACAD. SCI. USSR SIB. DEP. INST. MATH., NOVOSIBIRSK, 40-47. (1976).

MORR 1978 -1 MORRIS, J. G.
ON THE EXTENT TO WHICH CERTAIN FIXED-CHARGE DEPOT LOCATION PROBLEMS CAN BE SOLVED BY LP. THE JOURNAL OF THE OPERATIONAL RESEARCH SOCIETY 29, 71-76. (1978).

MORRA 1979 -1 MORRIS, J. G.; NORBACK, J. P.
SIMPLE APPROACH TO LINEAR FACILITY LOCATION, A (REVISED VERSION). WISCONSIN WORKING PAPER 8-78-24. MADISON: UNIV. OF WISCONSIN-MADISON, GRADUATE SCHOOL OF BUSINESS, 11 P. (1979).

MORT 1978 -1 MORTON, T. E.; BALA, G. D.
ALGORISTICS FOR SINGLE-MACHINE SEQUENCING WITH PRECEDENCE CONSTRAINTS. MANAGEMENT SCIENCE 24, 1011-1020. (1978).

MOUL 1978 -1 MOULOUD, B.
ETUDE DU POLYTOPE ASSOCIE AUX STABLES D'UN GRAPHE ET CARACTERISATION DANS LE CAS LES GRAPHES SERIE-PARALLELES. DISSERTATION. GRENOBLE: UNIVERSITE SCIENTIFIQUE ET MEDICALE, 90 P. (1978).

MOUS 1980 -1 MOUSTAKIDES, G.; BEDROSIAN, S. D.
FINDING THE GRAPH WITH THE MAXIMUM NUMBER OF SPANNING TREES. JOURNAL OF THE FRANKLIN INSTITUTE 310, NO. 6, 343-348. (1980).

MUEH 1979 -1 MUEHLBACHER, J.
F-FACTORS OF GRAPHS: A GENERALIZED MATCHING PROBLEM. INFORMATION PROCESSING LETTERS 8, 207-214. (1979).

MUEL 1978 -1 MUELLER-MERBACH, H.
IMPROVED UPPER BOUND FOR THE ZERO-ONE KNAPSACK PROBLEM; A NOTE ON THE PAPER BY MARTELLO AND TOTH, AN. EUROPEAN JOURNAL OF OPERATIONAL RESEARCH 2, 212-213. (1978).

MUEL 1978 -2 MUELLER-MERBACH, H.
KASKADENBAUMVERFAHREN ZUR LOESUNG DES "KNAPSACKPROBLEMS", EIN. ANGEWANDTE INFORMATIK 20, 494-505. (1978).

MUELA 1981 -1 MUELLER, H.
ZUR STRUKTUR UND KOMPLEXITAET DISKRETER OPTIMIERUNGSPROBLEME, DIE DURCH ERBLICHE EIGENSCHAFTEN AUF ENDLICHEN MENGENSYSTEMEN GEGEBEN SIND. STUTTGART: UNIV. STUTTGART, INST. FUER INFORMATIK, 130 P. (1981). (DISSERTATION)

MUELB 1979 -1 MUELLER, V.
ON COLORINGS OF GRAPHS WITHOUT SHORT CYCLES. DISCRETE MATHEMATICS 26, 165-176. (1979).

MUELC 1978 -1 MUELLER, V.; PELANT, J.
NUMBER OF HAMILTONIAN CIRCUITS, THE. JOURNAL OF COMBINATORIAL THEORY 24, SERIES B, 223-227. (1978).

****

MUKA 1979 -1 MUKAWA, H.; OKAMOTO, Y.; SORIMACHI, Y.; TAMAI, T.
IMPLEMENTATION OF THE HEURISTIC MIXED INTEGER PROGRAM TO THE MATHEMATICAL PROGRAMMING SYSTEM. IN: A. PREKOPA (ED.): SURVEY OF MATHEMATICAL PROGRAMMING. VOLUME 3, 37-48. AMSTERDAM: NORTH-HOLLAND. (1979).

MUKH 1975 -1 MUKHOPADHYAY, A.
TWO-PROCESSOR SCHEDULES FOR INDEPENDENT TASK SYSTEMS WITH BOUNDED EXECUTION TIMES. IN: PROCEEDINGS OF THE 1975 CONFERENCE ON INFORMATION SCIENCES AND SYSTEMS, BALTIMORE 1975, 147-151. BALTIMORE: THE JOHNS HOPKINS UNIVERSITY: DEPARTMENT OF ELECTRICAL ENGINEERING. (1975).

MULD 1979 -1 MULDER, H. M.
RAMSEY THEORY. IN: A. SCHRIJVER (ED.): PACKING AND COVERING IN COMBINATORICS, 107-117. MATHEMATICAL CENTRE TRACTS 106, AMSTERDAM: MATHEMATISCH CENTRUM. (1979).

MULV 1978 -1 MULVEY, J. M.
PIVOT STRATEGIES FOR PRIMAL-SIMPLEX NETWORK CODES. JOURNAL OF THE ASSOCIATION FOR COMPUTING MACHINERY 25, 266-270. (1978).

MULV 1978 -2 MULVEY, J. M.
TESTING OF LARGE-SCALE NETWORK OPTIMIZATION PROGRAM. MATHEMATICAL PROGRAMMING 15, 291-315. (1978).

MULV 1979 -1 MULVEY, J. M.
TESTING OF A NETWORK RELAXATION METHOD FOR 0-1 SET-PARTITIONING AND SET COVERING. IN: A. PREKOPA (ED.): SURVEY OF MATHEMATICAL PROGRAMMING. VOLUME 2, 365-378. AMSTERDAM: NORTH-HOLLAND. (1979).

MURP 1979 -1 MURPHY, F. H.; SOYSTER, A. L.
MULTIPRODUCT LOT-SIZE SCHEDULING WITH PROPORTIONAL PRODUCT DEMANDS. NAVAL RESEARCH LOGISTICS QUARTERLY 26, 97-108. (1979).

MURP 1979 -2 MURPHY, F. H.; SOYSTER, A. L.
SENSITIVITY ANALYSIS OF THE COSTS IN THE DYNAMIC LOT SIZE MODEL. AIIE TRANSACTIONS 11, 245-249. (1979).

MURPA 1978 -1 MURPHY, F. H.; STOHR, E. A.
MATHEMATICAL PROGRAMMING APPROACH TO THE SCHEDULING OF SORTING OPERATIONS, A. NAVAL RESEARCH LOGISTICS QUARTERLY 25, 155-168. (1978).

MURPB 1975 -1 MURPHY, J.
CRITICAL PATH SCHEDULING OF FULLY PROFESSIONAL ENGINEERING CURRICULA. DOCTORAL DISSERTATION. COLLEGE STATION: TEXAS A. & M. UNIVERSITY, 194 P. (1975).

MURPC 1979 -1 MURPHY, R. A.; ALLEN, R. E.
PROBLEM OF ASSIGNING SUPPLIERS TO PLANTS, A. AIIE TRANSACTIONS 11, 303-305. (1979).

MURPD 1978 -1 MURPHY, R. A.; SKITT, R. A.; SWEENEY, D. J.
HEURISTIC METHODS FOR THE MULTI-ITEM ACTIVITY SCHEDULING PROBLEM. CINCINNATI: UNIV. OF CINCINNATI, DEPT. OF QUANTITATIVE ANALYSIS, 15 P. (1978).

MURT 1981 -1 MURTY, K. G.; PERIN, C.
EDGE COVERING ALGORITHMS AND THEIR APPLICATIONS. IN: R. E. BURKARD, T. ELLINGER (EDS.): METHODS OF OPERATIONS RESEARCH 40, 379-384. KOENIGSTEIN: ANTON HAIN MEISENHEIM. (1981).

MURTA 1978 -1 MURTY, U. S. R.
APPLICATION OF RADO'S THEOREM TO DISJOINT MATCHINGS IN BIPARTITE GRAPHS, AN. JOURNAL OF THE LONDON MATHEMATICAL SOCIETY 17, NO. 2, 193-194. (1978).

MURTB 1978 -1 MURTY, U. S. R.; SIMON, I.
BETA-FUNCTION THAT IS NOT A SUM OF RANK FUNCTIONS OF MATROIDS, A. IN: J.-C. BERMOND ET AL. (EDS.): PROBLEMES COMBINATOIRES ET THEORIE DES GRAPHES. COLLOQUES INTERNATIONAUX DU CENTRE NATIONAL DE LA RECHERCHE SCIENTIFIQUE, ORSAY 1976, 305-306. PARIS: CENTRE NATIONAL DE LA RECHERCHE SCIENTIFIQUE. (1978).

MUSA 1980 -1 MUSALEM, J. S.
CONVERTING LINEAR MODELS TO NETWORK MODELS. WORKING PAPER, 299. LOS ANGELES: UNIV. OF CALIFORNIA, WESTERN MANAGEMENT SCIENCE INSTITUTE, 147 P. (1980).

MYCI 1955 -1 MYCIELSKI, J.
SUR LE COLORIAGE DES GRAPHES. COLLOQUIUM MATHEMATICUM 3, 161. (1955).

NABE 1975 -1 NABESHIMA, I.
BRANCH AND BOUND ALGORITHM FOR MULTIPROJECT SCHEDULING WITH RESOURCE CONSTRAINTS WHERE EXPLICIT SET-UP TIME EXISTS. REPORTS OF THE UNIVERSITY OF ELECTRO-COMMUNICATIONS 26, 41-49. (1975).

NABE 1976 -1 NABESHIMA, I.
NOTES ON THE ANALYTICAL RESULTS IN FLOW SHOP SCHEDULING 1. REPORTS OF THE UNIVERSITY OF ELECTRO-COMMUNICATIONS 27, 245-252. (1976).

NABE 1976 -2 NABESHIMA, I.
NOTES ON THE ANALYTICAL RESULTS IN FLOW SHOP SCHEDULING 2. REPORTS OF THE UNIVERSITY OF ELECTRO-COMMUNICATIONS 27, 253-257. (1976).

NABE 1977 -1 NABESHIMA, I.
EXTENDED BRANCH AND BOUND ALGORITHM AND ITS APPLICATION TO BIOBJECTIVE PROBLEM. REPORTS OF THE UNIVERSITY OF ELECTRO-COMMUNICATIONS 28, 67-74. (1977).

NABE 1977 -2 NABESHIMA, I.
NOTES ON THE ANALYTICAL RESULTS IN FLOW SHOP SCHEDULING 3. REPORTS OF THE UNIVERSITY OF ELECTRO-COMMUNICATIONS 28, 34-44. (1977).

NABE 1977 -3 NABESHIMA, I.
NOTES ON THE ANALYTICAL RESULTS IN FLOW SHOP SCHEDULING 4. REPORTS OF THE UNIVERSITY OF ELECTRO-COMMUNICATIONS 28, 45-55. (1977).

NABE 1977 -4 NABESHIMA, I.
NOTES ON THE ANALYTICAL RESULTS IN FLOW SHOP SCHEDULING 5. REPORTS OF THE UNIVERSITY OF ELECTRO-COMMUNICATIONS 28, 57-65. (1977).

NABE 1978 -1 NABESHIMA, I.
NOTES ON THE ANALYTICAL RESULTS IN FLOW SHOP SCHEDULING 6. REPORTS OF THE UNIVERSITY OF ELECTRO-COMMUNICATIONS 29, 21-25. (1978).

NABE 1978 -2 NABESHIMA, I.
NOTES ON THE ANALYTICAL RESULTS IN FLOW SHOP SCHEDULING 7. REPORTS OF THE UNIVERSITY OF ELECTRO-COMMUNICATIONS 29, 27-31. (1978).

NABE 1978 -3 NABESHIMA, I.
NOTES ON THE ANALYTICAL RESULTS IN FLOW SHOP SCHEDULING 8. REPORTS OF THE UNIVERSITY OF ELECTRO-COMMUNICATIONS 29, 179-186. (1978).

NABE 1979 -1 NABESHIMA, I.
NOTES ON THE ANALYTICAL RESULTS IN FLOW SHOP SCHEDULING 10. REPORTS OF THE UNIVERSITY OF ELECTRO-COMMUNICATIONS 30, 189-196. (1979).

NABE 1979 -2 NABESHIMA, I.
NOTES ON THE ANALYTICAL RESULTS IN FLOW SHOP SCHEDULING 9. REPORTS OF THE UNIVERSITY OF ELECTRO-COMMUNICATIONS 30, 51-54. (1979).

NABEA 1978 -1 NABESHIMA, I.; MARUYAMA, S.
ON N*M MEAN COMPLETION TIME FLOW SHOP PROBLEM. ANALYTICAL RESULTS, EXTENDED BRANCH AND BOUND ALGORITHM AND COMPUTATIONAL EXPERIENCE. REPORTS OF THE UNIVERSITY OF ELECTRO-COMMUNICATIONS 28, NO. 2, 219-226. (1978).

NACK 1978 -1 NACKEL, J. G.; GOLDMAN, J.; FAIRMAN, W. L.
GROUP DECISION PROCESS FOR RESOURCE ALLOCATION IN THE HEALTH SETTING. A. MANAGEMENT SCIENCE 24, 1259-1267. (1978).

NADO 1978 -1 NADDEF, D.
RANG DES COUPLAGES MAXIMUMS D'UN GRAPHE. DISSERTATION. GRENOBLE: UNIVERSITE SCIENTIFIQUE ET MEDICALE DE GRENOBLE. (1978).

NADDA 1980 -1 NADDEF, D.; PULLEYBLANK, W. R.
EAR DECOMPOSITIONS OF ELEMENTARY GRAPHS AND GF(2)-RANK OF PERFECT MATCHINGS. RESEARCH REPORT 80171-OR. BONN: UNIV. BONN, INST. FUER OEKONOMETRIE UND OPERATIONS RESEARCH, 30 P. (1980).

NADDA 1980 -2 NADDEF, D.; PULLEYBLANK, W. R.
HAMILTONICITY AND COMBINATORIAL POLYHEDRA. RAPPORT DE RECHERCHE, 195. GRENOBLE: UNIV. SCIENTIFIQUE ET MEDICALE, MATHEMATIQUES APPLIQUEES ET INFORMATIQUE, 18 P. (1980).

NADDB 1980 -1 NADDEF, D.; SBIHI, N.; TCHUENTE, M.
INDEPENDENCE SYSTEMS WITH CONTINUOUS CARDINALITY OF BASES. DISCRETE MATHEMATICS 31, 107-109. (1980).

NAEG 1977 -1 NAEGLER, G.; SIEBER, N.
ANWENDUNG DER GRAPHENTHEORIE IN DER ABLAUFPLANUNG, DIE. IN: GRAPHENTHEORIE UND DEREN ANWENDUNGEN, INTERNATIONALES KOLLOQUIUM, OBERHOF 1977, 180-188. ILMENAU: TECHNISCHE HOCHSCHULE ILMENAU UND MATHEMATISCHE GESELLSCHAFT DER DDR. (1977).

NAGE 1980 -1 NAGELHOUT, R. V.; THOMPSON, G. L.
SINGLE SOURCE TRANSPORTATION ALGORITHM, A. COMPUTERS AND OPERATIONS RESEARCH 7, 185-198. (1980).

NAGE 1980 -2 NAGELHOUT, R. V.; THOMPSON, G. L.
STUDY OF THE BOTTLENECK SINGEL SOURCE TRANSPORTATION PROBLEM, A. MANAGEMENT SCIENCES RESEARCH REPORT NO.456. PITTSBURGH: CARNEGIE-MELLON UNIV., GRADUATE SCHOOL OF INDUSTRIAL ADMINISTRATION, 28 P. (1980).

NAGE 1981 -1 NAGELHOUT, R. V.; THOMPSON, G. L.
COST OPERATOR APPROACH TO MULTISTAGE LOCATION-ALLOCATION, A. EUROPEAN JOURNAL OF OPERATIONAL RESEARCH 6, 149-161. (1981).

NAKA 1977 -1 NAKAHORI, I.; NAKAZAKI, K.; NISHIKAWA, Y.
GRAPH-THEORETIC CONSIDERATION AND ALGORITHMS FOR A MULTICOMMODITY FLOW ASSIGNMENT PROBLEM, A. ELECTRONICS AND COMMUNICATION IN JAPAN 60, NO. 2, 12-25. (1977).

NAKAA 1977 -1 NAKAMURA, T.; YAMASAKI, M.
EXTREMAL LENGTH OF AN INFINITE NETWORK WHICH IS NOT NECESSARILY LOCALLY FINITE. HIROSHIMA MATHEMATICAL JOURNAL 7, 813-826. (1977).

NAKAA 1977 -2 NAKAMURA, T.; YAMASAKI, M.
MINIMAL CUT PROBLEMS ON AN INFINITE NETWORK. HIROSHIMA MATHEMATICAL JOURNAL 7, NO. 2, 597-603. (1977).

NAKAB 1973 -1 NAKANISHI, N.
QUANTUM FIELD THEORY AND THE COLORING PROBLEM OF GRAPHS. COMMUNICATIONS IN MATHEMATICAL PHYSICS 32, 167-181. (1973).

NAKAC 1979 -1 NAKASHIMA, K.; HATTORI, Y.
EFFICIENT BOTTOM-UP ALGORITHM FOR ENUMERATING MINIMAL CUT SETS OF FAULT TREES, AN. IEEE TRANSACTIONS ON RELIABILITY R-28, 353-357. (1979).

NAMB 1979 -1 NAMBIAR, J. M.; CHALMET, L. G.
LOCATION AND VEHICLE SCHEDULING PROBLEM IN COLLECTING AND PROCESSING RUBBER, A. NEW ORLEANS (ORSA/TIMS MEETING, APRIL/MAY 1979) 20 P. (1979).

NAMBA 1981 -1 NAMBIAR, J. M.; GELDERS, L. F.; WASSENHOVE, L. N. VAN
LARGE SCALE LOCATION-ALLOCATION PROBLEM IN THE NATURAL RUBBER INDUSTRY, A. EUROPEAN JOURNAL OF OPERATIONAL RESEARCH 6, 183-189. (1981).

NAME 1979 -1 NAMEKATA, T.; TABATA, Y.; NISHIDA, T.
SEQUENTIAL ALLOCATION PROBLEM WITH TWO KINDS OF TARGETS, A. JOURNAL OF THE OPERATIONS RESEARCH SOCIETY OF JAPAN 22, 16-28. (1979).

NAND 1978 -1 NANDA, R.
SCHEDULING CREWS FOR CONTINUOUS SHIFT WORK. NEW YORK (ORSA/TIMS MEETING, MAY 1978) 18 P. (1978).

NANI 1969 -1 NANIWADA, M.
MULTICOMMODITY FLOWS IN A COMMUNICATION NETWORK. ELECTRONICS AND COMMUNICATIONS IN JAPAN 52-A, 34-41. (1969).

NARI 1979 -1 NARIHISA, H.
BOOLEAN PROGRAMMING. MEMOIRS OF THE DEFENSE ACADEMY. MATHEMATICS, PHYSICS, CHEMISTRY AND ENGINEERING 19, 5-21. (1979).

NARU 1981 -1 NARULA, S. C.
LAGRANGEAN RELAXATION IN AN HIERARCHICAL LOCATION-ALLOCATION PROBLEM. IN: R. E. BURKARD, T. ELLINGER (EDS.): METHODS OF OPERATIONS RESEARCH 40, 385-388. KOENIGSTEIN: ANTON HAIN MEISENHEIM. (1981).

NARUA 1980 -1 NARULA, S. C.; HO, C. A.
DEGREE-CONSTRAINED MINIMUM SPANNING TREE. COMPUTERS AND OPERATIONS RESEARCH 7, 239-250. (1980).

NARUB 1979 -1 NARULA, S. C.; KINDORF, J. R.
LINEAR 0-1 PROGRAMMING: A COMPARISON OF IMPLICIT ENUMERATION ALGORITHMS. COMPUTERS AND OPERATIONS RESEARCH 6, 47-51. (1979).

NARUC 1979 -1 NARULA, S. C.; OGBU, U. I.
HIERARCHICAL LOCATION ALLOCATION PROBLEM, AN. OMEGA 7, 137-143. (1979).

NARUC 1980 -1 NARULA, S. C.; OGBU, U. I.
K-PARTITE ASSIGNMENT PROBLEM, A. OMEGA 8, 118-119. (1980).

NASE 1979 -1 NASEKIN, V. J.
METHOD FOR THE SOLUTION OF MONOTONIC INTEGER LINEAR PROGRAMMING PROBLEMS, A. KIBERNETIKA (KIEV) NO. 5, 106-109, 155; TRANSLATED AS CYBERNETICS 15, NO. 5, 719-723. (1979).

NASH 1979 -1 NASH, B. W.
SIMPLIFIED ALTERNATIVE TO CURRENT AIRLINE FUEL ALLOCATION MODELS, A. MILWAUKEE (ORSA/TIMS MEETING, OCTOBER 1979) 22 P. (1979).

NATA 1979 -1 NATALI, L.; NICOLETTI, B.; SCALAS, M. R.
MANPOWER STAFFING AT AN AIRPORT: A GENERALIZED SET COVERING PROBLEM. IN: A. PREKOPA (ED.): SURVEY OF MATHEMATICAL PROGRAMMING, VOLUME 3, 279-294. AMSTERDAM: NORTH-HOLLAND. (1979).

NATAA 1978 -1 NATARAJAN, K. S.; WHITE, L. J.
OPTIMUM DOMINATION IN WEIGHTED TREES. INFORMATION PROCESSING LETTERS 7, 261-266. (1978).

NAUS 1978 -1 NAUSS, R. M.
IMPROVED ALGORITHM FOR THE CAPACITATED FACILITY LOCATION PROBLEM, AN. THE JOURNAL OF THE OPERATIONAL RESEARCH SOCIETY 29, 1195-1201. (1978).

NAUS 1978 -2 NAUSS, R. M.
0-1 KNAPSACK PROBLEM WITH MULTIPLE CHOICE CONSTRAINTS, THE. EUROPEAN JOURNAL OF OPERATIONAL RESEARCH 2, 125-131. (1978).

NAUS 1979 -1 NAUSS, R. M.
PARAMETRIC INTEGER PROGRAMMING. COLUMBIA: UNIVERSITY OF MISSOURI PRESS, 98 P. (1979). (UNIVERSITY OF MISSOURI STUDIES, 67)

NAUS 1979 -2 NAUSS, R. M.
SOLVING LOCK BOX LOCATION PROBLEMS. FINANCIAL MANAGEMENT 8, 21-31. (1979).
NAUSA 1981 -1 NAUSS, R. M.; KEELER, B. R.
MINIMIZATION OF LEASE PAYMENTS IN LEVERAGED LEASES: AN APPLICATION OF INTEGER PROGRAMMING. RESEARCH REPORT. ST. LOUIS: UNIV. OF MISSOURI, SCHOOL OF BUSINESS ADMINISTRATION. (1981).
NEBE 1976 -1 NEBESKY, L.
GENERALIZATION OF HAMILTONIAN CYCLES FOR TREES, A. CZECHOSLOVAK MATHEMATICAL JOURNAL 26(101), 596-603. (1976).
NEBE 1978 -1 NEBESKY, L.
ON PANCYCLIC LINE GRAPHS. CZECHOSLOVAK MATHEMATICAL JOURNAL 28(103), 650-655. (1978).
NEBE 1979 -1 NEBESKY, L.
ON EULERIAN SUBGRAPHS OF COMPLEMENTARY GRAPHS. CEHOSLOVACKAJA AKADEMIJA NAUK. CEHOSLOVACKII MATEMATICESKII ZURNAL 29, 298-302. (1979).
NEEB 1978 -1 NEEBE, A. W.
BRANCH AND BOUND ALGORITHM FOR THE P-MEDIAN TRANSPORTATION PROBLEM, A. THE JOURNAL OF THE OPERATIONAL RESEARCH SOCIETY 29, 989-995. (1978).
NEEBA 1981 -1 NEEBE, A. W.; KHUMAWALA, B. M.
IMPROVED ALGORITHM FOR THE MULTICOMMODITY LOCATION PROBLEM, AN. JOURNAL OF THE OPERATIONAL RESEARCH SOCIETY 32, 143-150. (1981).
NEIT 1977 -1 NEITZEL, W.
TOURENPLANUNG. PROBLEMDARSTELLUNG UND LOESUNSVERFAHREN FUER EIN-DEPOT-PROBLEME. FRANKFURT, BERN, LAS VEGAS: LANG, 235 P. (1977). (EUROPAEISCHE HOCHSCHULSCHRIFTEN, REIHE V, 184)
NEME 1977 -1 NEMETH, E.
NOTE ON A MINI-MAX PROBLEM IN SCHEDULING, A. IN: B. L. HARTNELL, H. C. WILLIAMS (EDS.): PROCEEDINGS OF THE SIXTH MANITOBA CONFERENCE ON NUMERICAL MATHEMATICS, 343-350. CONGRESSUS NUMERANTIUM XVIII. WINNIPEG: UTILITAS. (1977).
NEMH 1978 -1 NEMHAUSER, G. L.; SHEU, W.-L.
EASY AND HARD BOTTLENECK LOCATION PROBLEMS. TECHNICAL REPORT, 386. ITHACA: CORNELL UNIV., SCHOOL OF OPERATIONS RESEARCH AND INDUSTRIAL ENGINEERING, 11 P. (1978).
NEMHA 1979 -1 NEMHAUSER, G. L.; WEBER, G. M.
OPTIMAL SET PARTITIONING, MATCHINGS AND LAGRANGIAN DUALITY. NAVAL RESEARCH LOGISTICS QUARTERLY 26, 553-563. (1979).
NEMHB 1978 -1 NEMHAUSER, G. L.; WOLSEY, L. A.
MAXIMIZING SUBMODULAR SET FUNCTIONS: FORMULATIONS AND ANALYSIS OF ALGORITHMS. TECHNICAL REPORT NO. 398. ITHACA: CORNELL UNIV., SCHOOL OF OPERATION RESEARCH AND INDUSTRIAL ENGINEERING, 39 P (1978).
NEMHC 1978 -1 NEMHAUSER, G. L.; WOLSEY, L. A.; FISHER, M. L.
ANALYSIS OF APPROXIMATIONS FOR MAXIMIZING SUBMODULAR SET FUNCTIONS-1, AN. MATHEMATICAL PROGRAMMING 14, 265-294. (1978).
NENG 1980 -1 NENG, B.
ZUR ERSTELLUNG VON OPTIMALEN TRIEBFAHRZEUGLAUFPLAENEN. RESEARCH REPORT 80-17. KOELN: UNIV. ZU KOELN, MATHEMATISCHES INST., 41 P. (1980).
NENO 1979 -1 NENOV, N. D.; KHADZHIIVANOV, N. G.
SUR LES GRAPHES CONTENANT UN TRIANGLE MONOCHROMATIQUE DANS LE CAS DE COLORATION ARBITRAIRE DES ARETES AVEC DEUX COULEURS (RUSSIAN). SERDICA (SOFIA) 5, 303-305. (1979).
NEPO 1978 -1 NEPOMIASTCHY, P.
RESOLUTION D'UN PROBLEME D'ORDONNANCEMENT A RESSOURCES VARIABLES. REVUE FRANCAISE D'AUTOMATIQUE, D'INFORMATIQUE ET DE RECHERCHE OPERATIONELLE 12, SERIE RECHERCHE OPERATIONELLE, 249-261. (1978).
NESE 1979 -1 NESETRIL, J.; ROEDL, V.
SHORT PROOF OF THE EXISTENCE OF HIGHLY CHROMATIC HYPERGRAPHS WITHOUT SHORT CYCLES, A. JOURNAL OF COMBINATORIAL THEORY 27, SERIES B, 225-227. (1979).
NETT 1977 -1 NETT, E.
ON SCHEDULING ALGORITHMS FOR N-FREE TASK DEPENDENCY STRUCTURES. IN: PROCEEDINGS OF THE 1977 INTERNATIONAL CONFERENCE ON PARALLEL PROCESSING, WAYNE STATE UNIVERSITY, DETROIT 1977, 100-107. NEW YORK: IEEE. (1977).
NETT 1979 -1 NETT, E.
DETERMINISTISCHE STRATEGIEN ZUM SCHEDULING VON TASKABHAENGIGKEITSSTRUKTUREN FUER MEHRPROZESSORSYSTEME. BERICHTE DER GESELLSCHAFT FUER MATHEMATIK UND DATENVERARBEITUNG BONN 122, MUENCHEN, WIEN: OLDENBOURG, 53 P. (1979).
NEUM 1980 -1 NEUMAIER, A.
CLIQUES AND CLAWS IN EDGE-TRANSITIVE STRONGLY REGULAR GRAPHS. MATHEMATISCHE ZEITSCHRIFT 174, NO. 3, 197-202. (1980).
NEWE 1979 -1 NEWELL, G. F.
SOME ISSUES RELATING TO THE OPTIMAL DESIGN OF BUS ROUTES. TRANSPORTATION SCIENCE 13, 20-35. (1979).
NGUE 1980 -1 NGUEN, N. C.
ON ONE METHOD FOR FINDING A COMMON FORMULA OF INTEGER SOLUTIONS FOR A SYSTEM OF LINEAR INEQUALITIES (RUSSIAN). KIBERNETIKA, NO. 4, 86-90. (1980).
NGUEA 1981 -1 NGUEN, N. C.; CHERNIKOVA, N. V.
NEW ALGORITHM OF SOLUTION OF DISCRETE PROGRAMMING PROBLEM (RUSSIAN), A. ZURNAL VYCISLITELNOI MATEMATIKI I MATEMATICESKOI FIZIKI (MOSCOW) 21, 329-338; TRANSLATED AS USSR COMPUTATIONAL MATHEMATICS AND MATHEMATICAL PHYSICS. (1981).
NGUEB 1980 -1 NGUEN, N. T.
SOLVABILITY OF A SYSTEM OF LINEAR INEQUALITIES IN INTEGERS UNDER ANY VECTOR OF THE RIGHT-HAND PART (RUSSIAN), THE. UKRAINSKII MATEMATICESKII ZURNAL (KIEV) 32, NO. 4, 557-561; TRANSLATED AS UKRAINIAN MATHEMATICAL JOURNAL. (1980).
NGUY 1978 -1 NGUYEN VAN VI
TRANSPORT TIME CRITERION PROBLEM WITH ADDITIONAL LIMITATIONS. KIBERNETIKA, NO. 4, 84-88. (1978).
NGUY 1979 -1 NGUYEN VAN VI
SOME CLASSES OF PROBLEMS ON ADMISSIBLE DYNAMICAL FLOW WITH MINIMUM TIME (RUSSIAN). ISSLEDOVANIE OPERACII I ASU (KIEV), NO. 14, 35-47, 134. (1979).
NGUYA 1978 -1 NGUYEN, H. Q.
SEMIMODULAR FUNCTIONS AND COMBINATORIAL GEOMETRIES. TRANSACTIONS OF THE AMERICAN MATHEMATICAL SOCIETY 238, NO. 515, 355-383. (1978).
NGUYA 1979 -1 NGUYEN, H. Q.
WEAK CUTS OF COMBINATORIAL GEOMETRIES. TRANSACTIONS OF THE AMERICAN MATHEMATICAL SOCIETY 250, 247-262. (1979).
NGUYB 1973 -1 NGUYEN, S.
MATHEMATICAL PROGRAMMING APPROACH TO EQUILIBRIUM METHODS OF TRAFFIC ASSIGNMENT WITH FIXED DEMANDS, A. TECHNICAL REPORT. MONTREAL: UNIVERSITE DE MONTREAL, CENTRE DE RECHERCHE SUR LES TRANSPORTS. (1973).
NGUYB 1976 -1 NGUYEN, S.
UNIFIED APPROACH TO EQUILIBRIUM METHODS FOR TRAFFIC ASSIGNMENTS, A. IN: M. A. FLORIAN (ED.): TRAFFIC EQUILIBRIUM METHODS, 148-182. NEW YORK: SPRINGER. (1976).

NICH 1978 -1 NICHOLS, R. A.; BULFIN, R. L.; PARKER, R. G.
INTERACTIVE PROCEDURE FOR MINIMIZING MAKESPAN ON PARALLEL PROCESSORS, AN. INTERNATIONAL JOURNAL OF PRODUCTION RESEARCH 16, 77-81. (1978).

NICHA 1972 -1 NICHOLSON, T. A. J.; PULLEN, R. D.
COMPUTER TERMINAL SYSTEM FOR MANAGING SCHEDULES ORDERS THROUGH PLANTS, A. IN: DECISION DESIGN AND THE COMPUTER. INSTITUTION OF CHEMICAL ENGINEERS SYMPOSIUM SERIES NO. 35, LONDON: INSTITUTION OF CHEMICAL ENGINEERS. (1972).

NICO 1979 -1 NICOLAI, W.
OPTIMIERUNG SPEZIELLER GERT-NETZPLAENE. ZEITSCHRIFT FUER ANGEWANDTE MATHEMATIK UND MECHANIK 59, T108-T109. (1979).

NICO 1981 -1 NICOLAI, W.
TIME-ORIENTED ANALYSIS OF PROJECTS USING STOCHASTIC NETWORK TECHNIQUES. KOENIGSTEIN: HAIN; AND CAMBRIDGE: OELGESCHLAGER, GUNN & HAIN, 110 P. (1981). (MATHEMATICAL SYSTEMS IN ECONOMICS, 61)

NICOA 1980 -1 NICOLETTI, G.
GENERATING CRYPTOMORPHIC AXIOMATIZATIONS OF MATROIDS. IN: R. ARTZY, I. VAISMAN (EDS.): GEOMETRY AND DIFFERENTIAL GEOMETRY, HAIFA 1979, 110-113. LECTURE NOTES IN MATHEMATICS 792. BERLIN: SPRINGER. (1980).

NICU 1979 -1 NICULESCU, S.
ALGORITHM FOR FINDING THE PATHS BETWEEN TWO VERTICES OF A GRAPH (ROMANIAN), AN. STUDII SI CERCETARI MATEMATICE 31, 581-592. (1979).

NICU 1979 -2 NICULESCU, S.
ALGORITHM FOR FINDING THE PATHS BETWEEN TWO VERTICES OF A GRAPH, AN. SOVIET MATHEMATICS. DOKLADY, 31, 581-592. (1979).

NICU 1979 -3 NICULESCU, S.
ALGORITHM TO FIND HAMILTONIAN PATHS IN GRAPHS, AN. BULLETIN MATHEMATIQUE DE LA SOCIETE DES SCIENCES MATHEMATIQUES DE LA REPUBLIQUE SOCIALISTE DE ROUMANIE, NOUVELLE SERIE 23(71), 279-287. (1979).

NIEB 1978 -1 NIEBLAS, M. H.; ESPINOSA, L. P.
ASSIGNMENT OF LOCOMOTIVES TO A RAILWAY TIMETABLE: A PRACTICAL APPLICATION OF THE HUNGARIAN METHOD (SPANISH), THE. INVESTIGACION OPERACIONAL (CUBA) 23, 31-39. (1978).

NIED 1979 -1 NIEDRINGHAUS, W. P.
SCHEDULING WITHOUT QUEUEING: THE SPACE FACTORY PROBLEM. IN: CONFERENCE ON INFORMATION SCIENCES AND SYSTEMS, BALTIMORE 1979, 91-96. BALTIMORE: THE JOHNS HOPKINS UNIVERSITY. (1979).

NIEM 1980 -1 NIEMINEN, J.
ON MINIMALLY INTERCONNECTED SUBNETWORKS OF A NETWORK. CONTROL AND CYBERNETICS (WARSAW) 9, NO. 1-2, 47-52. (1980).

NIEP 1977 -1 NIEPAGE, H.-D.
GANZZAHLIGE ZENTRENMETHODE, DIE. WISSENSCHAFTLICHE ZEITSCHRIFT DER HUMBOLDT-UNIVERSITAET BERLIN, MATHEMATISCH-NATURWISSENSCHAFTLICHE REIHE 26, 571-573. (1977).

NIEP 1977 -2 NIEPAGE, H.-D.
UEBERDECKUNGSPRINZIP ZUR LOESUNG FREIER GANZZAHLIGER MINIMUMPROBLEME, EIN. WISSENSCHAFTLICHE ZEITSCHRIFT DER HUMBOLDT-UNIVERSITAET BERLIN, MATHEMATISCH-NATURWISSENSCHAFTLICHE REIHE 26, 575-581. (1977).

NIEP 1980 -1 NIEPAGE, H.-D.
LINEARISIERTE GANZZAHLIGE ZENTRENVERFAHREN. MATHEMATISCHE OPERATIONSFORSCHUNG UND STATISTIK, SERIES OPTIMIZATION 11, 421-434. (1980).

NIGM 1975 -1 NIGMATULLIN, R. G.
COMPLEXITY OF APPROXIMATE SOLUTION OF COMBINATORIAL PROBLEMS (RUSSIAN). DOKLADY AKADEMII NAUK SSSR 224, NO. 2. (1975).

NIGM 1978 -1 NIGMATULLIN, R. G.
ON APPROXIMATE ALGORITHMS WITH RESTRICTED ABSOLUTE ERROR FOR DISCRETE EXTREMUM PROBLEMS (RUSSIAN). KIBERNETIKA, NO. 1, 95-100. (1978).

NIGM 1980 -1 NIGMATULLIN, R. G.
O(M+N)-ALGORITHM FOR MATCHING MAXIMALITY RECOGNITION (RUSSIAN), AN. ROSTOCKER MATHEMATISCHES KOLLOQUIUM 13, 49-64. (1980).

NIJE 1979 -1 NIJENHUIS, A.
MINIMAL-PATH ALGORITHM FOR THE "MONEY CHANGING PROBLEM", A. AMERICAN MATHEMATICAL MONTHLY 86, 832-835. (1979).

NIJK 1981 -1 NIJKAMP, P.; SPRONK, J.
MULTIDIMENSIONAL LOCATIONAL DECISIONS AND INTERACTIVE PROGRAMMING. IN: J. N. MORSE (ED.): ORGANIZATIONS: MULTIPLE AGENTS WITH MULTIPLE CRITERIA, 248-264. LECTURE NOTES IN ECONOMICS AND MATHEMATICAL SYSTEMS 190. BERLIN: SPRINGER. (1981).

NIKO 1976 -1 NIKOGOSJAN, Z. G.
THEOREMS ON HAMILTONIAN CYCLES AND SKELETONS (RUSSIAN). MOLODOI NAUCNYI RABOTNIK 2(24), 15-20. (1976).

NIRM 1979 -1 NIRMALA, K.
COMPLEMENTARY GRAPHS AND TOTAL CHROMATIC NUMBERS. IN: A. RAMACHANDRA RAO (ED.): PROCEEDINGS OF THE SYMPOSIUM ON GRAPH THEORY, CALCUTTA 1976, 227-245. ISI (INDIAN STATISTICAL INSTITUTE) LECTURE NOTES 4. CALCUTTA: MACMILLAN OF INDIA. (1979).

NISH 1978 -1 NISHIZEKI, T.
LOWER BOUNDS ON THE CARDINALITY OF THE MAXIMUM MATCHINGS OF GRAPHS. IN: F. HOFFMAN, D. MAC CARTHY, R. C. MULLIN, R. G. STANTON (EDS.): PROCEEDINGS OF THE NINTH SOUTHEASTERN CONFERENCE ON COMBINATORICS, GRAPH THEORY, AND COMPUTING, 527-548. CONGRESSUS NUMERANTIUM XXI. WINNIPEG: UTILITAS. (1978).

NISH 1979 -1 NISHIZEKI, T.
ON THE RELATIONSHIP BETWEEN THE GENUS AND THE CARDINALITY OF THE MAXIMUM MATCHINGS OF A GRAPH. DISCRETE MATHEMATICS 25, 149-156. (1979).

NISHA 1977 -1 NISHIZEKI, T.; ASANO, T.; SAITO, N.
ON THE MAXIMAL EVEN MATROIDS. ELECTRONICS AND COMMUNICATIONS IN JAPAN 60, NO. 2, 60-66. (1977).

NJAR 1980 -1 NJARIPJA, H.
SOME NEW ESTIMATION PROBLEMS FOR PROBLEMS OF INTEGER LINEAR PROGRAMMING (RUSSIAN). IZVESTIJA AKADEMII NAUK ESTONSKOI SSR, SERIJA FIZIKA-MATEMATIKA (TALLIN) 29, NO. 2, 127-132, 229. (1980).

NORB 1979 -1 NORBACK, J. P.; LOVE, R. F.
HEURISTIC FOR THE HAMILTONIAN PATH PROBLEM IN EUCLIDEAN TWO-SPACE. JOURNAL OF THE OPERATIONAL RESEARCH SOCIETY 30, 363-368. (1979).

NORT 1979 -1 NORTHUP, W. D.; SHAPIRO, J. F.
LOGS: AN OPTIMIZATION SYSTEM FOR LOGISTICS PLANNING. WORKING PAPER OR 089-79. CAMBRIDGE: MASSACHUSETTS INST. OF TECHNOLOGY, OPERATIONS RESEARCH CENTER, 20 P. (1979).

NOSH 1978 -1 NOSHITA, K.; MASUDA, E.; MACHIDA, H.
ON THE EXPECTED BEHAVIOURS OF THE DIJKSTRA'S SHORTEST PATH ALGORITHM FOR COMPLETE GRAPHS. INFORMATION PROCESSING LETTERS 7, 237-243. (1978).

NOVO 1979 -1 NOVOKRESHCHENOVA, L. D.; EPSHTEIN, G. L.
FORMATION OF AGGREGATES IN PARALLEL SOLUTION OF A TRANSPORT PROBLEM (RUSSIAN). MOSKOVSKII INSTITUT INZENEROV ZELEZNODOROZNOGO TRANSPORTA TRUDY NO. 640 PRIKLADNAJA MATEMATIKI I ZADACI ZELEZNODOROZNOGO TRANSPORTA 147-149, 160. (1979).

NTAF 1979 -1 NTAFOS, S. C.; HAKIMI, S. L.
ON PATH COVER PROBLEMS IN DIGRAPHS AND APPLICATIONS TO PROGRAM TESTING. INSTITUTE OF ELECTRICAL AND ELECTRONICS ENGINEERS. TRANSACTIONS ON SOFTWARE ENGINEERING 5, 520-529. (1979).

NUFF 1978 -1 NUFFELEN, C. VAN
ON THE RANK OF THE ADJACENCY MATRIX. IN: J.-C. BERMOND ET AL. (EDS.): PROBLEMES COMBINATOIRES ET THEORIE DES GRAPHES. COLLOQUES INTERNATIONAUX DU CENTRE NATIONAL DE LA RECHERCHE SCIENTIFIQUE, ORSAY 1976, 321-322. PARIS: CENTRE NATIONAL DE LA RECHERCHE SCIENTIFIQUE. (1978).

NUFF 1980 -1 NUFFELEN, C. VAN
REMARKS ON THE ADJACENCY MATRIX OF A GRAPH. IN: P. HANSEN, D. DE WERRA (EDS.): REGARDS SUR LA THEORIE DES GRAPHES, PROCEEDINGS OF THE CERISY COLLOQUIUM, 1980, 275-278. LAUSANNE: PRESSES POLYTECHNIQUES ROMANDES. (1980).

NUSS 1978 -1 NUSSINO, R.; PIECZENIK, G.; GRIGGS, J. R.; KLEITMAN, D. J.
ALGORITHMS FOR LOOP MATCHINGS. SIAM JOURNAL OF APPLIED MATHEMATICS 35, 68-82. (1978).

OAKF 1966 -1 OAKFORD, A. C.
SCHOOL SCHEDULING - PRACTICE AND THEORY. JOURNAL OF EDUCATIONAL DATA PROCESSING IV 1, 16-50. (1966).

OBER 1979 -1 OBERLY, D. J.; SUMNER, D. P.
EVERY CONNECTED, LOCALLY CONNECTED NONTRIVIAL GRAPH WITH NO INDUCED CLAW IS HAMILTONIAN. JOURNAL OF GRAPH THEORY 3, 351-356. (1979).

OBERA 1981 -1 OBERSCHELP, W.
MATCHING POLYNOMIALS AND ROOK THEORY. IN: J. MERKWITZ, W. OBERSCHELP (EDS.): KOLLOQUIUM UEBER MATHEMATISCHE METHODEN DES OPERATIONS RESEARCH, AACHEN 1980, IN MEM. R. KAERKES, 105-114. METHODS OF OPERATIONS RESEARCH 42. KOENIGSTEIN: ANTON HAIN MEISENHEIM. (1981).

OECH 1981 -1 OECHSLEIN, H.
PRIMAL-DUALE VERFAHREN FUER NICHTLINEARE, INSBESONDERE FUER SCHLECHT KONDITIONIERTE NETZWERKPROBLEME. IN: R. E. BURKARD, T. ELLINGER (EDS.): METHODS OF OPERATIONS RESEARCH 40, 393-396. KOENIGSTEIN: ANTON HAIN MEISENHEIM. (1981).

OGAW 1978 -1 OGAWA, H.; NISHIZEKI, T.; SAITO, S.
METHOD FOR APPROXIMATE CALCULATION OF MAXIMUM CUTS (JAPANESE), A. IN: COMBINATORIAL STRUCTURES AND GRAPH THEORY II. PROC. SYMP. KYOTO 1977, 189-198. SURIKAISEKIKENKYUSHO KOKYUROKU NO. 333. KYOTO: KYOTO UNIVERSITY, RESEARCH INST. FOR MATH. SCIENCES. (1978).

OGUZ 1979 -1 OGUZ, O.; MAGAZINE, M. J.
POLYNOMIAL TIME APPROXIMATION ALGORITHM FOR THE MULTIDIMENSIONAL 0/1 KNAPSACK PROBLEM, A. ANKARA: MIDDLE EAST TECHNICAL UNIVERSITY, 6 P. (1979).

OHSE 1978 -1 OHSE, D.
ZEIT-UMLADE- ODER BOTTLENECK-TRANSSHIPMENTPROBLEM, DAS. IN: PROCEEDINGS IN OPERATIONS RESEARCH 7, 409-419. WUERZBURG: PHYSICA. (1978).

OHTS 1981 -1 OHTSUKI, T.
TWO DISJOINT PATH PROBLEM AND WIRE ROUTING DESIGN, THE. IN: N. SAITO, T. NISHIZEKI (EDS.): GRAPH THEORY AND ALGORITHMS, 207-216. LECTURE NOTES IN COMPUTER SCIENCE 108, BERLIN: SPRINGER. (1981).

OHUC 1979 -1 OHUCKI, A.; KAJI, I.
ALGORITHMS AND SENSITIVITY ANALYSIS FOR OPTIMAL ALLOCATION PROBLEMS HAVING QUADRATIC OBJECTIVE FUNCTIONS. SAPPORO: HOKKAIDO UNIV., DEPT. OF ELECTRICAL ENGINEERING, 25 P. (1979).

OI 1978 -1 OI, K.; SAYAMA, H.; TAKAMATSU, T.
MULTIMODALITY ANALYSIS OF A CLASS OF MULTISTAGE ALLOCATION PROBLEMS. JOURNAL OF OPTIMIZATION THEORY AND APPLICATIONS 25, 33-48. (1978).

OKAM 1979 -1 OKAMURA, K.; YAMASHINA, H.
HEURISTIC ALGORITHM FOR THE ASSEMBLY LINE MODEL-MIX SEQUENCING PROBLEM TO MINIMIZE THE RISK OF STOPPING THE CONVEYOR, A. INTERNATIONAL JOURNAL OF PRODUCTION RESEARCH 17, 233-247. (1979).

OKAW 1979 -1 OKAWA, S.; NISHITANI, Y.; HONDA, N.
BIPARTITE SUBGRAPH PROBLEMS WITH DEGREE AT MOST THREE (JAPANESE), THE. TRANSACTIONS OF THE INSTITUTE OF ELECTRONICS AND COMMUNICATION ENGINEERS OF JAPAN (TOKYO) 62-D, 348-355. (1979).

OLAR 1979 -1 OLARU, E.; SUCIU, G.
DAUERSTABILE UND KRITISCH IMPERFEKTE GRAPHEN. ANALELE UNIVERSITATII DIN TIMISOARA, SERIA STIINTE MATEMATICE (TIMISOARA) 17, NO. 1, 59-64. (1979).

OMAR 1977 -1 OMAR, A.
FINDING ALL EXTREME POINTS AND EXTREME RAYS OF A CONVEX POLYHEDRAL SET. EKONOMICKO-MATEMATICKY OBZOR 13, 331-342. (1977).

ONAG 1979 -1 ONAGA, K.; MAYEDA, W.
BOOLEAN THEORY OF NETWORK FLOWS AND METRICS AND ITS APPLICATIONS TO PARTICLE TRANSMISSION AND CLUSTERING, A. NETWORKS 9, 249-281. (1979).

ONAGA 1978 -1 ONAGA, K.; MURATA, T.
DT-POLYNOMIAL APPROACH TO DISCRETE TIME-VARYING NETWORK FLOW PROBLEMS, THE. JOURNAL OF THE FRANKLIN INSTITUTE 305, NO. 3, 161-185. (1978).

OPAT 1979 -1 OPATRNY, J.
TOTAL ORDERING PROBLEM. SIAM JOURNAL ON COMPUTING 8, 111-114. (1979).

OR 1979 -1 OR, I.; PIERSKALLA, W. P.
TRANSPORTATION LOCATION-ALLOCATION MODEL FOR REGIONAL BLOOD BANKING, A. AIIE TRANSACTIONS 11, 86-95. (1979).

OREL 1977 -1 OREL, E. N.
FINDING A SHORTEST PATH IN A GRAPH USING THE MINORANT OF THE BELLMAN FUNCTION. AVTOMATIKA I TELEMEHANIKA, NO. 2, 88-91; TRANSLATED AS AUTOMATION AND REMOTE CONTROL 38, 235-237. (1977).

ORLI 1977 -1 ORLIN, J. B.
CONTENTMENT IN GRAPH THEORY: COVERING GRAPHS WITH CLIQUES. PROCEEDINGS OF THE KONINKLIJKE NEDERLANDSE AKADEMIE VAN WETENSCHAPEN 39, NO. 5, 406-424. (1977).

ORLI 1980 -1 ORLIN, J. B.
MAXIMUM DYNAMIC NETWORK FLOWS. TECHNICAL REPORT, 173. CAMBRIDGE: MASSACHUSETTS INST. OF TECHNOLOGY, OPERATIONS RESEARCH CENTER, 34 P. (1980).

ORLI 1980 -2 ORLIN, J. B.
MINIMUM CONVEX COST DYNAMIC NETWORK FLOWS. TECHNICAL REPORT NO. 172. CAMBRIDGE: MASSACHUSETTS INSTITUTE OF TECHNOLOGY, OPERATIONS RESEARCH CENTER, 47 P. (1980).

ORLI 1981 -1 ORLIN, J. B.
COMPLEXITY OF DYNAMIC LANGUAGES AND DYNAMIC OPTIMIZATION PROBLEMS (EXTENDED ABSTRACT), THE. RESEARCH REPORT. CAMBRIDGE, MA: MASSACHUSETTS INSTITUTE OF TECHNOLOGY, SLOAN SCHOOL OF MANAGEMENT, 8 P. (1981).

ORON 1979 -1 ORON, G.
ALGORITHM FOR OPTIMIZING NON LINEAR CONSTRAINED ZERO-ONE PROBLEMS TO IMPROVE WASTEWASTER TREATMENT, AN. ENGINEERING OPTIMIZATION 4, NO. 2, 109-115. (1979).

OSKO 1975 -1 OSKOLKOV, I. O.
SIMULTANEOUS BRANCHING BY SEVERAL VARIABLES IN THE BRANCH-AND-BOUND METHOD. AVTOMATIKA I TELEMEHANIKA, NO. 4, 75-81; TRANSLATED AS AUTOMATION AND REMOTE CONTROL 36, 1975, 590-595. (1975).

OSKOA 1968 -1 OSKOLKOVA, S. E.; OSKOLKOV, I. O.
APPLICATION OF CERTAIN HEURISTIC METHODS TO THE SOLUTION OF SCHEDULING PROBLEMS (SURVEY). AVTOMATICA I TELEMEHANIKA, NO. 2, 177-184; TRANSLATED AS AUTOMATION AND REMOTE CONTROL 29. 1968, 329-335. (1968).

OSTR 1978 -1 OSTRESH, L. M. JR.
CONVERGENCE AND DESCENT IN THE FERMAT LOCATION PROBLEM. TRANSPORTATION SCIENCE 12, 153-164. (1978).

OSTR 1978 -2 OSTRESH, L. M. JR.
ON THE CONVERGENCE OF A CLASS OF ITERATIVE METHODS FOR SOLVING THE WEBER LOCATION PROBLEM. OPERATIONS RESEARCH 26, 597-609. (1978).

OSTR 1978 -3 OSTRESH, L. M. JR.
STEPWISE LOCATION-ALLOCATION PROBLEM: EXACT SOLUTIONS IN CONTINUOUS AND DISCRETE SPACES. THE. GEOGRAPHICAL ANALYSIS 10, 174-185. (1978).

OSYC 1980 -1 OSYCZKA, A.
MULTICRITERION NETWORK OPTIMIZATION PROBLEM. COMPUTING 25, 363-368. (1980).

OUBI 1978 -1 OUBINA, L.
LOCALISATION D'UNE PROPRIETE DU GRAPHE DES BASES D'UN MATROIDE BINAIRE. IN: J.-C. BERMOND ET AL. (EDS.): PROBLEMES COMBINATOIRES ET THEORIE DES GRAPHES. COLLOQUES INTERNATIONAUX DU CENTRE NATIONAL DE LA RECHERCHE SCIENTIFIQUE, ORSAY 1976, 323-324. PARIS: CENTRE NATIONAL DE LA RECHERCHE SCIENTIFIQUE. (1978).

OUDH 1980 -1 OUDHEUSDEN, D. VAN; PLASTRIA, F.
MODELE DE LOCALISATION COMME APPLICATION DE LA THEORIE DES JEUX, UN. ANNALES FACULTE DES SCIENCES, UNIVERSITE NATIONALE DU ZAIRE, SECTION MATHEMATIQUE-PHYSIQUE (KINSHASA) 4, 247-268. (1980).

OVER 1975 -1 OVERBECK-LARISCH, M.
HAMILTONISCHE LINIEN IN DIGRAPHEN. IN: L. COLLATZ, G. MEINARDUS, H. WERNER (EDS.): NUMERISCHE METHODEN BEI GRAPHENTHEORETISCHEN UND KOMBINATORISCHEN PROBLEMEN; TAGUNG DES MATHEMATISCHEN FORSCHUNGSINSTITUTES OBERWOLFACH 1974, 109-116. ISNM 29. BASEL: BIRKHAEUSER. (1975).

OVERA 1979 -1 OVERTON, M. L.; PROSKUROWSKI, A.
CANONICAL INCIDENCE MATRICES OF GRAPHS. NORDISK TIDSKRIFT FOR INFORMATIONSBEHANDLING 19, 271-273. (1979).

OXLE 1978 -1 OXLEY, J. G.
COCIRCUIT COVERINGS AND PACKINGS FOR BINARY MATROIDS. MATHEMATICAL PROCEEDINGS OF THE CAMBRIDGE PHILOSOPHICAL SOCIETY 83, 347-351. (1978).

OXLE 1978 -2 OXLEY, J. G.
COLORING, PACKING AND THE CRITICAL PROBLEM. THE QUARTERLY JOURNAL OF MATHEMATICS. SECOND SERIES 29, NO. 113, 11-22. (1978).

OXLE 1978 -3 OXLEY, J. G.
INFINITE MATROIDS AND DUALITY. IN: J.-C. BERMOND ET AL. (EDS.): PROBLEMES COMBINATOIRES ET THEORIE DES GRAPHES. COLLOQUES INTERNATIONAUX DU CENTRE NATIONAL DE LA RECHERCHE SCIENTIFIQUE, ORSAY 1976, 325-326. PARIS: CENTRE NATIONAL DE LA RECHERCHE SCIENTIFIQUE. (1978).

OXLE 1978 -4 OXLEY, J. G.
INFINITE MATROIDS. PROCEEDINGS OF THE LONDON MATHEMATICAL SOCIETY 37, NO. 2, 259-272. (1978).

OXLE 1979 -1 OXLEY, J. G.
GENERALIZATION OF A COVERING PROBLEM OF MULLIN AND STANTON FOR MATROIDS, A. IN: A. F. HORADAM, W. D. WALLIS (EDS.): COMBINATORIAL MATHEMATICS VI, 92-97. LECTURE NOTES IN MATHEMATICS 748. BERLIN: SPRINGER. (1979).

OXLE 1980 -1 OXLEY, J. G.
ON A COVERING PROBLEM OF MULLIN AND STANTON FOR BINARY MATROIDS. AEQUATIONES MATHEMATICAE 20, 104-112. (1980).

OXLE 1980 -2 OXLEY, J. G.
ON HARTFIEL AND MAXSON'S DEFINITION OF CONNECTED SETS OF A MATROID. JOURNAL OF COMBINATORIAL THEORY 28, SERIES B, 249-250. (1980).

OXLEA 1979 -1 OXLEY, J. G.; WELSH, D. J. A.
ON SOME PERCOLATION RESULTS OF J. M. HAMMERSLEY. JOURNAL OF APPLIED PROBABILITY 16, 526-540. (1979).

OXLEA 1979 -2 OXLEY, J. G.; WELSH, D. J. A.
TUTTE POLYNOMIAL AND PERCOLATION, THE. IN: J. A. BONDY, U. P. R. MURTY (EDS.): GRAPH THEORY AND RELATED TOPICS, 329-339. NEW YORK, SAN FRANCISCO, LONDON: ACADEMIC PRESS. (1979).

PABS 1978 -1 PABST, R.
VERWENDUNGSMOEGLICHKEITEN DER EXTERNEN SPEICHERMEDIEN VON EDV-ANLAGEN BEI DER LOESUNG BESTIMMTER AUFGABEN DER DISKRETEN OPTIMIERUNG. DIPLOMARBEIT. DRESDEN: TECHNISCHE UNIVERSITAET DRESDEN. (1978).

PADB 1979 -1 PADBERG, M. W.
COVERING, PACKING AND KNAPSACK PROBLEMS. IN: P. L. HAMMER, E. L. JOHNSON, B. H. KORTE (EDS.): DISCRETE OPTIMIZATION I, 265-287. ANNALS OF DISCRETE MATHEMATICS 4, AMSTERDAM, NEW YORK, OXFORD: NORTH-HOLLAND. (1979).

PADB 1979 -2 PADBERG, M. W.
NULL-EINS-ENTSCHEIDUNGSPROBLEME. IN: M. J. BECKMANN, G. MENGES, R. SELTEN (EDS.): HANDWOERTERBUCH DER MATHEMATISCHEN WIRTSCHAFTSWISSENSCHAFTEN, BAND 3, 187-230. WIESBADEN: GABLER. (1979).

PADB 1980 -1 PADBERG, M. W.
(1,K)-CONFIGURATIONS AND FACETS FOR PACKING PROBLEMS. MATHEMATICAL PROGRAMMING 18, 94-99. (1980).

PADBA 1980 -1 PADBERG, M. W.; HONG, S.
ON THE SYMMETRIC TRAVELLING SALESMAN PROBLEM: A COMPUTATIONAL STUDY. MATHEMATICAL PROGRAMMING STUDY 12, 78-107. (1980).

PADBB 1979 -1 PADBERG, M. W.; RAO, M. R.
ODD MINIMUM CUT-SETS AND B-MATCHINGS. WORKING PAPER. NEW YORK: NEW YORK UNIV., GRADUATE SCHOOL OF BUSINESS ADMINISTRATION, 29 P. (1979).

PAES 1978 -1 PAESSENS, H.
TOURENPLANUNG BEI DER MUELLSAMMLUNG IN STAEDTISCHEN BEREICHEN. IN: R. HENN, P. KALL, H. KOENIG, B. KORTE, O. KRAFFT ET AL. (EDS.): OPERATIONS RESEARCH VERFAHREN 28. SECOND SYMPOSIUM ON OPERATIONS RESEARCH, AACHEN 1977, 96-111. MEISENHEIM: HAIN. (1978).

PAGE 1978 -1 PAGET, M.
PROPRIETES DE COMPLEXITE POUR UNE FAMILLE D'ALGORITHMES DE MARKOV. REVUE FRANCAISE D'AUTOMATIQUE, D'INFORMATIQUE ET DE RECHERCHE OPERATIONELLE 12, SERIE INFORMATIQUE THEORIQUE, 15-32. (1978).

*****

PAID 1980 -1 PAIDAK, I. N.
METHOD FOR SOLVING SOME MULTICRITERIAL COMBINATORIAL PROBLEMS (RUSSIAN). EKONOMIKA I MATEMATICESKIE METODY (MOSCOW) 16, 182-185. (1980).

PALL 1978 -1 PALLOTTINO, S.; STORCHI, G.
ALGORITHM FOR DETERMINING THE FUNDAMENTAL CYCLES AND THE MAXIMAL FORESTS OF K-CONNECTED GRAPHS (ITALIAN). AN. QUADERNI, SERIE III, ISTITUTO PER LE APPLICAZIONI DEL CALCOLO "MAURO PICONE", CONSIGLIO NAZIONALE DELLE RICERCHE (ROMA) 73, 19P. (1978).

PANA 1978 -1 PANAYIOTOPOULOS, J.-C.
NEW APPROACH TO PLANT LOCATION ANALYSIS, A. INDUSTRIAL MATHEMATICS 28, NO. 2, 85-94. (1978).

PANA 1978 -2 PANAYIOTOPOULOS, J.-C.
SOLVING THE ASSIGNMENT PROBLEM IN THREE-DIMENSIONAL SPACE. INDUSTRIAL MATHEMATICS 28, NO. 2, 77-83. (1978).

PANA 1979 -1 PANAYIOTOPOULOS, J.-C.
INTEGER PROGRAMMING WITH IRREGULAR DATA SPACE. JOURNAL OF THE OPERATIONS RESEARCH SOCIETY OF JAPAN 22, 275-286. (1979).

PANAA 1979 -1 PANAYIOTOPOULOS, J.-C.; PAPOULIAS, D. B.
GENERAL PROBLEM OF M PERSONS AND N POSITIONS FOR SHORT- AND LONG-TERM DECISION-MAKING, THE. JOURNAL OF THE OPERATIONAL RESEARCH SOCIETY 30, 917-922. (1979).

PANN 1978 -1 PANNY, W.
VERFAHREN ZUR LOESUNG DES TRAVELLING-SALESMAN-PROBLEMS UNTER BESONDERER BERUECKSICHTIGUNG DER METHODE "BRANCH-AND-BOUND". DISSERTATION. WIEN: WIRTSCHAFTSUNIVERSITAET WIEN. VERBAND DER WISSENSCHAFTLICHEN GESELLSCHAFTEN OESTERREICHS, 122 P. (1978).

PANW 1978 -1 PANWALKAR, S. S.; CHARLES, D.
STATISTICAL ASPECTS OF FLOW SHOP SEQUENCING. LOS ANGELES (ORSA/TIMS MEETING, NOVEMBER 1978) 9 P. (1978).

PANWA 1979 -1 PANWALKAR, S. S.; KHAN, A. W.
ORDERED FLOW SHOP SEQUENCING PROBLEM WITH TWK TYPE DUE DATES AND TOTAL TARDINESS CRITERION, AN. JOURNAL OF THE INSTITUTE OF MATHEMATICS AND ITS APPLICATIONS 23, 367-372. (1979).

PANWB 1979 -1 PANWALKAR, S. S.; WOOLLAM, C. R.
FLOW SHOP SCHEDULING PROBLEMS WITH NO IN-PROCESS WAITING: A SPECIAL CASE. JOURNAL OF THE OPERATIONAL RESEARCH SOCIETY 30, 661-664. (1979).

PANWB 1980 -1 PANWALKAR, S. S.; WOOLLAM, C. R.
ORDERED FLOW SHOP PROBLEMS WITH NO IN-PROCESS WAITING: FURTHER RESULTS. JOURNAL OF THE OPERATIONAL RESEARCH SOCIETY 31, 1039-1044. (1980).

PAPA 1976 -1 PAPADIMITRIOU, C. H.
COMPLEXITY OF COMBINATORIAL OPTIMIZATION PROBLEMS, THE. PRINCETON: PRINCETON UNIV., 133 P. (1976). (DISSERTATION)

PAPA 1978 -1 PAPADIMITRIOU, C. H.
ADJACENCY RELATION ON THE TRAVELLING SALESMAN POLYTOPE IS NP-COMPLETE, THE. MATHEMATICAL PROGRAMMING 14, 312-324. (1978).

PAPA 1978 -2 PAPADIMITRIOU, C. H.
COMPLEXITY OF THE CAPACITATED TREE PROBLEM, THE. NETWORKS 8, 217-230. (1978).

PAPA 1980 -1 PAPADIMITRIOU, C. H.
WORST-CASE AND PROBABILISTIC ANALYSIS OF A GEOMETRIC LOCATION PROBLEM. RESEARCH PAPER. CAMBRIDGE: MASSACHUSETTS INSTITUTE OF TECHNOLOGY, LABORATORY FOR COMPUTER SCIENCE, 22 P. (1980).

PAPAA 1980 -1 PAPADIMITRIOU, C. H.; KANELLAKIS, P. C.
FLOWSHOP SCHEDULING WITH LIMITED TEMPORARY STORAGE. JOURNAL OF THE ASSOCIATION FOR COMPUTING MACHINERY 27, 533-549. (1980).

PAPAB 1978 -1 PAPADIMITRIOU, C. H.; STEIGLITZ, K.
SOME EXAMPLES OF DIFFICULT TRAVELING SALESMAN PROBLEMS. OPERATIONS RESEARCH 26, 434-443. (1978).

PAPAC 1979 -1 PAPADIMITRIOU, C. H.; YANNAKAKIS, M.
COMPLEXITY OF RESTRICTED SPANNING TREE PROBLEMS, THE. CAMBRIDGE: MASSACHUSETTS INST. OF TECHNOLOGY, 28 P. (1979).

PAPAC 1979 -2 PAPADIMITRIOU, C. H.; YANNAKAKIS, M.
SCHEDULING INTERVAL-ORDERED TASKS. SIAM JOURNAL ON COMPUTING 8, 405-409. (1979).

PAPAD 1978 -1 PAPAGEORGIOU, J. C.
GOAL PROGRAMMING MODEL FOR RESOURCE ALLOCATION IN THE SCHOOL SYSTEM OF GREECE, A. KYBERNETES 7, 229-237. (1978).

PAPE 1980 -1 PAPE, U.
HEURISTISCHES VERFAHREN ZUR ERMITTLUNG VON FAHRPLAENEN IN DER CONTAINER-SCHIFFAHRT, EIN. OPERATIONS RESEARCH - SPEKTRUM 1, 169-181. (1980).

PAPEA 1979 -1 PAPE, U.; BOHM, H.-J.; RIEGER, A.
ANWENDUNGSSYSTEM ZUR ERSTELLUNG EINES STAUPLANES FUER CONTAINERSCHIFFE, EIN. BERICHT 79-4. BERLIN: TECHNISCHE UNIV. BERLIN, FACHBEREICH 20-INFORMATIK, 60 P. (1979).

PAPEB 1979 -1 PAPE, U.; CONRADT, D.
MAXIMALES MATCHING IN GRAPHEN. IN: H. SPAETH (ED.): AUSGEWAEHLTE OPERATIONS RESEARCH SOFTWARE IN FORTRAN, 103-114. MUENCHEN: OLDENBOURG. (1979).

PAPEC 1976 -1 PAPERNOV, B. A.
FEASIBILITY OF MULTICOMMODITY FLOWS (RUSSIAN). IN: A. A. FRIDMAN (ED.): STUDIES IN DISCRETE OPTIMIZATION (RUSSIAN), 230-261. MOSCOW: IZDAT. "NAUKA". (1976).

PAPO 1976 -1 PAPOULIAS, D. B.
INVESTIGATION OF COMBINATORIAL TIME-TABLING SYSTEMS. DISSERTATION. OXFORD: OXFORD UNIVERSITY. (1976).

PAPO 1977 -1 PAPOULIAS, D. B.
ASSIGNMENT-TO-DAYS PROBLEM IN A SCHOOL TIME-TABLE, A HEURISTIC APPROACH, THE. IN: GIORNATE DI LAVORO AIRO '77, PARMA UNIVERSITY, 585-596. (1977).

PAPO 1978 -1 PAPOULIAS, D. B.
ALGORITHM FOR SCHOOL TIME-TABLING SYSTEMS (PART II), AN. RICERCA OPERATIVA, NO. 8, 59-70. (1978).

PAPO 1980 -1 PAPOULIAS, D. B.
ASSIGNMENT-TO-DAYS PROBLEM IN A SCHOOL TIME-TABLE, A HEURISTIC APPROACH, THE. EUROPEAN JOURNAL OF OPERATIONAL RESEARCH 4, 31-41. (1980).

PAPOA 1979 -1 PAPOULIAS, D. B.; PANAYIOTOPOULOS, J.-C.
CONSIDERATIONS ON THE REQUIREMENTS MATRIX OF A NON-REGULAR SCHOOL TIME-TABLE PROBLEM. EUROPEAN JOURNAL OF OPERATIONAL RESEARCH 3, 382-385. (1979).

PARK 1976 -1 PARKER, C. S.
EXPERIMENTAL INVESTIGATION OF SOME HEURISTIC STRATEGIES FOR COMPONENT PLACEMENT, AN. OPERATIONAL RESEARCH QUARTERLY 27, 71-81. (1976).

PARKA 1973 -1 PARKER, E.
EDGE COLORING NUMBERS OF SOME REGULAR GRAPHS. PROCEEDINGS OF THE AMERICAN MATHEMATICAL SOCIETY 37, 423-424. (1973).

PARS 1973 -1 PARSONS, J. E.
TRANSPORTATION PROBLEM: ANOTHER APPROXIMATION METHOD, THE. JOURNAL OF SYSTEMS MANAGEMENT, 42-43. (1973).

PART 1975 -1 PARTHASARATHY, K. R.; CHOUDUM, S. A.
INTERSECTION NUMBER OF K(4)-FREE GRAPHS, THE. CAHIERS DU CENTRE D'ETUDES DE RECHERCHE OPERATIONELLE 17, 301-306. (1975).

PARTA 1979 -1 PARTHASARATHY, K. R.; RAVINDRA, G.
VALIDITY OF THE STRONG PERFECT-GRAPH CONJECTURE FOR (K4 - E)-FREE GRAPHS, THE. JOURNAL OF COMBINATORIAL THEORY 26, SERIES B, 98-100. (1979).

PAST 1977 -1 PASTIJN, H. J. A. M.
HYBRID ALGORITHM FOR THE GENERAL MIP-PROBLEM, A. IN: M. ROUBENS (ED.): ADVANCES IN OPERATIONS RESEARCH, PROCEEDINGS OF EURO II, THE SECOND EUROPEAN CONGRESS ON OPERATIONS RESEARCH, STOCKHOLM 1976, 347-352. AMSTERDAM, NEW YORK, OXFORD: NORTH-HOLLAND. (1977).

PATE 1979 -1 PATEL, N. R.
LOCATING RURAL SOCIAL SERVICE CENTERS IN INDIA. MANAGEMENT SCIENCE 25, 22-30. (1979).

PATEA 1970 -1 PATERSON, M. S.
UNSOLVABILITY IN 3 X 3 MATRICES. IN: STUDIES IN APPLIED MATHEMATICS, 49, NO. 1, P. 105-107 (1970).

PATEA 1975 -1 PATERSON, M. S.
COMPLEXITY OF MATRIX ALGORITHMS. IN: MATHEMATICAL CENTRE TRACTS 63, P. 181-215 (1975).

PATEA 1976 -1 PATERSON, M. S.
INTRODUCTION TO BOOLEAN FUNCTION COMPLEXITY, AN. WARWICK: UNIV. OF WARWICK, DEPT. OF COMPUTER SCIENCE, P. 183-201 (1976).

PATEA 1976 -2 PATERSON, M. S.
NEW BOUNDS ON FORMULA SIZE. WARWICK: UNIV. OF WARWICK, DEPT. OF COMPUTER SCIENCE, 11 P. (1976).

PATK 1979 -1 PATKAR, V.; AGGARWAL, S.
BRANCH AND BOUND TECHNIQUE FOR INTEGER GEOMETRIC PROGRAMMING. ZEITSCHRIFT FUER ANGEWANDTE MATHEMATIK UND MECHANIK 59, 395-396. (1979).

PATT 1978 -1 PATTERSON, J. H.
BALASIAN-BASED ENUMERATION PROCEDURES: A STUDY IN COMPUTATION EFFICIENCY. IN: W. W. WHITE (ED.): COMPUTERS AND MATHEMATICAL PROGRAMMING, GAITHERSBURG 1976, 241-250. NBS SPECIAL PUBLICATION. WASHINGTON: NATIONAL BUREAU OF STANDARDS. (1978).

PATTA 1976 -1 PATTERSON, J. H.
ZERO-ONE INTEGER PROGRAMMING: A STUDY IN COMPUTATIONAL EFFICIENCY AND A STATE-OF-THE-ART SURVEY. IN: BICENT. CONF. ON. MATH. PROGR., BETHESDA 1976. (1976).

PAUL 1980 -1 PAUL, H.; LAW, S. S.; LEONG, H. K.
METHOD FOR SINGLE FACILITY MULTIPLE PRODUCTS SCHEDULING, A. JOURNAL OF THE OPERATIONAL RESEARCH SOCIETY 31, 825-832. (1980).

PAULA 1979 -1 PAUL, R. J.
PRODUCTION SCHEDULING PROBLEM IN THE GLASS-CONTAINER INDUSTRY, A. OPERATIONS RESEARCH 27, 290-302. (1979).

PAULB 1978 -1 PAUL, W. J.
KOMPLEXITAETSTHEORIE. LEITFAEDEN DER ANGEWANDTEN MATHEMATIK UND MECHANIK 39. STUTTGART: TEUBNER, 247 P. (1978).

PAUN 1979 -1 PAUN, G.
ON SOME VARIANTS OF THE TRAVELLING SALESMAN PROBLEM. A MATHEMATICAL LINGUISTIC APPROACH (ROMANIAN). STUDII SI CERCETARI MATEMATICE 31, 213-226. (1979).

PAYA 1978 -1 PAYAN, C.
COUPLAGES MAXIMAUX DISJOINTS. IN: J.-C. BERMOND ET AL. (EDS.): PROBLEMES COMBINATOIRES ET THEORIE DES GRAPHES, COLLOQUES INTERNATIONAUX DU CENTRE NATIONAL DE LA RECHERCHE SCIENTIFIQUE, ORSAY 1976, 327-329. PARIS: CENTRE NATIONAL DE LA RECHERCHE SCIENTIFIQUE. (1978).

PAYA 1978 -2 PAYAN, C.
COVERINGS BY MINIMAL TRANSVERSALS. DISCRETE MATHEMATICS 23, 273-277. (1978).

PAYA 1979 -1 PAYAN, C.
REMARKS ON CLIQUES AND DOMINATING SETS IN GRAPHS. ARS COMBINATORIA 7, 181-189 (1979).

PAYA 1980 -1 PAYAN, C.
CLASS OF THRESHOLD AND DOMISHOLD GRAPHS: EQUISTABLE AND EQUIDOMINATING GRAPHS, A. DISCRETE MATHEMATICS 29, 47-52. (1980).

PEAR 1979 -1 PEARMAN, A. D.
STRUCTURE OF THE SOLUTION SET TO NETWORK OPTIMISATION PROBLEMS, THE. TRANSPORTATION RESEARCH 13, SERIES B, 81-90. (1979).

PECK 1980 -1 PECK, G. W.
HAMILTONIAN CYCLES OF ADJACENT TRIPLES. STUDIES IN APPLIED MATHEMATICS 63, NO. 3, 275-278. (1980).

PEET 1979 -1 PEETERS, H.
EMPIRISCHER LEISTUNGSVERGLEICH DER KOMMERZIELLEN SOFTWARESYSTEME APEX III, EMPS UND MPSX-MIP/370 BEI GEMISCH-GANZZAHLIGEN OPTIMIERUNGSPROBLEMEN. REGENSBURG (DGOR-JAHRESTAGUNG 1979) 8 P. (1979).

PEGD 1979 -1 PEGDEN, C. D.; PETERSEN, C. C.
ALGORITHM (GIPC2) FOR SOLVING INTEGER PROGRAMMING PROBLEMS WITH SEPARABLE NONLINEAR OBJECTIVE FUNCTIONS, AN. NAVAL RESEARCH LOGISTICS QUARTERLY 26, 595-609. (1979).

PEGE 1975 -1 PEGELS, C. C.
COMPUTER-BASED INTERACTIVE PLANNING SYSTEM FOR SCHEDULING BLOOD COLLECTIONS, A. TRANSFUSION 15, NO. 4, 381-386. (1975).

PELE 1978 -1 PELED, U. N.
MATROIDAL GRAPHS. DISCRETE MATHEMATICS 20, 263-286. (1978).

PELEA 1981 -1 PELED, U. N.; SIMEONE, B.
BOX-THRESHOLD GRAPHS. RESEARCH REPORT. NEW YORK: COLUMBIA UNIVERSITY, DEPT. OF COMPUTER SCIENCE, 26 P. (1981).

PELEA 1981 -2 PELED, U. N.; SIMEONE, B.
POLYNOMIAL-TIME ALGORITHM FOR RECOGNIZING THRESHOLD FUNCTIONS, A. IN: R. E. BURKARD, T. ELLINGER (EDS.): METHODS OF OPERATIONS RESEARCH 40, 397-400. KOENIGSTEIN: ANTON HAIN MEISENHEIM. (1981).

PELI 1979 -1 PELIKAN, J.
ON THE SOLUTION OF A SPECIAL ASSIGNMENT PROBLEM (CZECHOSLOVAKIAN). EKONOMICKO-MATEMATICKY OBZOR 14, 468-470. (1979).

PELI 1980 -1 PELIKAN, J.
SCHEDULING WITH MINIMIZATION OF HIGH CONSUMPTION RATE OF A RESOURCE (CZECHOSLOVAKIAN). EKONOMICKO-MATEMATICKY OBZOR (PRAGUE) 16, 332-338. (1980).

PERE 1976 -1 PEREPELITSA, V. A.; SEVASTYANOV, S. V.
ON A PROBLEM OF SCHEDULING THEORY ON A NETWORK (RUSSIAN). IN: CONTROL SYST. NO. 15, 48-67. NOVOSIBIRSK: ACAD. SCI. USSR SIB. DEP. INST. MATH. (1976).

PERI 1980 -1 PERIN, C.
USER'S GUIDE TO MATCOV. TECHNICAL REPORT 80-5. ANN ARBOR: UNIV. OF MICHIGAN, DEPT. OF INDUSTRIAL AND OPERATIONS ENGINEERING, 109 P. (1980).

PERI 1981 -1 PERIN, C.
ON THE POLYTOPE OF THE 1-MATCHING/COVERING PROBLEM. TECHNICAL REPORT 81-2. ANN ARBOR: UNIV. OF MICHIGAN, DEPT. OF INDUSTRIAL AND OPERATIONS ENGINEERING, 16 P. (1981).

PERI 1981 -2 PERIN, C.
1-MATCHING/COVERING PROBLEM, THE. TECHNICAL REPORT 81-3. ANN ARBOR: UNIV. OF MICHIGAN, DEPT. OF INDUSTRIAL AND OPERATIONS ENGINEERING, 30 P. (1981).

PERL 1976 -1 PERL, J.
ON FINDING ALL SOLUTIONS OF THE PARTITIONING PROBLEM. WROCLAW TECHNICAL UNIVERSITY. SYSTEMS SCIENCE 2, NO. 4, 103-124. (1976).

PERLA 1981 -1 PERL, Y.; SCHACH, S. R.
MAX-MIN TREE PARTITIONING. JOURNAL OF THE ASSOCIATION FOR COMPUTING MACHINERY 28, 5-15. (1981).

PERLB 1981 -1 PERL, Y.; ZAKS, S.
DEFICIENT GENERALIZED FIBONACCI MAXIMUM PATH GRAPHS. DISCRETE MATHEMATICS 34, 153-164. (1981).

PERS 1973 -1 PERSHIN, O. JU.
ALGORITHM FOR SOLVING THE PROBLEM OF M CENTERS (RUSSIAN), AN. SBORNIK TRUDOV INSTITUT PROBLEM UPRAVLENINA, VYP. 3 ISSLED. I OPTIMIZACIJA SLOZN. MNOGOSVJAZ. SISTEM, 61-70, 148. (1973).

PERSA 1973 -1 PERSHIN, O. JU.; ZELCER, M. A.
SOME APPLICATIVE ASPECTS OF THE PROBLEM OF M CENTERS (RUSSIAN). SBORNIK TRUDOV INSTITUT PROBLEM UPRAVLENINA, VYP. 3 ISSLED. I OPTIMIZACIJA SLOZN. MNOGOSVJAZ. SISTEM, 84-92, 149. (1973).

PETE 1975 -1 PETERS, R. J.
MIXED INTEGER LINEAR PROGRAMMING IN PRODUCTION PLANNING (DUTCH). DISSERTATION. GRONINGEN: STATE UNIVERSITY. (1975).

PETEA 1979 -1 PETERSOHN, U.; STAHN, H.
NAEHERUNGSVERFAHREN ZUR POLYOPTIMALEN LOESUNG DES MASCHINENBELEGUNGSPROBLEMS. WISSENSCHAFTLICHE ZEITSCHRIFT DER TECHNISCHEN UNIVERSITAET DRESDEN 28, 119-124. (1979).

PETEB 1980 -1 PETERSON, B. E.
CUT-FLOW PROCEDURE FOR TRANSPORTATION NETWORK OPTIMIZATION, A. NETWORKS 10, 33-43. (1980).

PETR 1978 -1 PETROVIC, R.
RESOURCE ALLOCATION IN A SET OF NETWORKS UNDER MULTIPLE OBJECTIVES. IN: J. STOER (ED.): OPTIMIZATION TECHNIQUES, PROCEEDINGS OF THE EIGHTH IFIP CONFERENCE ON OPTIMIZATION TECHNIQUES, WUERZBURG 1977, PART 2, 244-252. LECTURE NOTES IN CONTROL AND INFORMATION SCIENCES 7. BERLIN: SPRINGER. (1978).

PEVZ 1979 -1 PEVZNER, P. A.
ON THE PROBLEM OF TWO-PRODUCT PACKING OF CUTS (RUSSIAN). MOSKOVSKII INSTITUT INZENEROV ZELEZNODOROZNOGO TRANSPORTA TRUDY NO. 640 PRIKLADNAJA MATEMATIKA I ZADACI ZELEZNODOROZNOGO TRANSPORTA 126-131. (1979).

PFAF 1976 -1 PFAFFENBERGER, R. C.; WALKER, D. A.
MATHEMATICAL PROGRAMMING FOR ECONOMICS AND BUSINESS. AMES: IOWA STATE UNIVERSITY PRESS, 462 P. (1976).

PFEI 1974 -1 PFEIFFER, F. K. JR.
SYSTEMATIC HEURISTIC APPROACH TO SCHEDULING IN THE SMALL JOB SHOP, A. DISSERTATION. AMHERST: UNIVERSITY OF MASSACHUSETTS, 184 P. (1974).

PHEL 1981 -1 PHELPS, R. I.
OPTIMAL BATCH SIZES FOR A TWO-STAGE PRODUCTION SYSTEM. JOURNAL OF THE OPERATIONAL RESEARCH SOCIETY 32, 151-154. (1981).

PHIL 1977 -1 PHILLIPS, S. JR.; DESSOUKY, M. I.
SOLVING THE PROJECT TIME/COST TRADEOFF PROBLEM USING THE MINIMAL CUT CONCEPT. MANAGEMENT SCIENCE 24, 393-400. (1977).

PHIL 1979 -1 PHILLIPS, S. JR.; DESSOUKY, M. I.
CUT SEARCH ALGORITHM WITH ARC CAPACITIES AND LOWER BOUNDS, THE. MANAGEMENT SCIENCE 25, 396-404. (1979).

PIAN 1979 -1 PIANCA, P.; VOLPENTESTA, A.; ZECCHIN, M.
ON THE SOLUTION OF A CLASS OF EXTREMAL PROBLEMS WITH INTEGER VARIABLES CONNECTED WITH THE PROBLEM OF OPTIMAL ALLOCATION AT A SERVICE CENTER (ITALIAN). IN: PROCEEDINGS OF THE FIRST AMASES MEETING, PISA 1977, 309-331. TURIN: GIAPPICHELLI. (1979).

PICA 1978 -1 PICARD, J.-C.; QUEYRANNE, M.
TIME-DEPENDENT TRAVELING SALESMAN PROBLEM AND ITS APPLICATION TO THE TARDINESS PROBLEM IN ONE-MACHINE SCHEDULING, THE. OPERATIONS RESEARCH 26, 86-110. (1978).

PICA 1980 -1 PICARD, J.-C.; QUEYRANNE, M.
ON THE STRUCTURE OF ALL MINIMUM CUTS IN A NETWORK AND APPLICATIONS. MATHEMATICAL PROGRAMMING STUDY 13, 8-16. (1980).

PICAA 1978 -1 PICARD, J.-C.; RATLIFF, H. D.
CUT APPROACH TO THE RECTILINEAR DISTANCE FACILITY LOCATION PROBLEM, A. OPERATIONS RESEARCH 26, 422-433. (1978).

PICAA 1980 -1 PICARD, J.-C.; RATLIFF, H. D.
CUT APPROACH TO A CLASS OF QUADRATIC INTEGER PROGRAMMING PROBLEMS, A. NETWORKS 10, 363-370. (1980).

PIEH 1978 -1 PIEHLER, J.
BEMERKUNGEN ZU EINER ARBEIT VON ACHOU UEBER DIE ANZAHL ZULAESSIGER LOESUNGEN EINES KNAPSACK PROBLEMS. MATHEMATISCHE OPERATIONSFORSCHUNG UND STATISTIK 9, SERIES OPTIMIZATION, 167-170. (1978).

PIEH 1978 -2 PIEHLER, J.
ZUR DREHUNG VON GOMORY-SCHNITTEN. MATHEMATISCHE OPERATIONSFORSCHUNG UND STATISTIK 9, SERIES OPTIMIZATION, 3-8. (1978).

PIEH 1979 -1 PIEHLER, J.
DIOPHANTISCHE GLEICHUNGEN IN DER GANZZAHLIGEN OPTIMIERUNG. IN: K. LOMMATZSCH (ED.): FORTSCHRITTE IN DER MATHEMATISCHEN OPTIMIERUNG, TAGUNG BERLIN 1978, 87-94. SEMINARBERICHT NR. 15, SEKTION MATHEMATIK DER HUMBOLDT-UNIV. BERLIN. (1979).

PIEH 1980 -1 PIEHLER, J.
UEBER GITTERPUNKTE IN KEGELN. WISSENSCHAFTLICHE ZEITSCHRIFT DER TECHNISCHEN HOCHSCHULE LEUNA-MERSEBURG 22, NO. 1, 80-85. (1980).

PIER 1980 -1 PIERONI, P.
DUAL DECOMPOSITION APPROACH FOR ORIENTING ONE-WAY STREETS AND LANES IN A CITY NETWORK, A. RESEARCH REPORT A-73. PISA: UNIVERSITY OF PISA, DIPARTIMENTO DI RICERCA OPERATIVA E SCIENZE STATISTICHE, 27 P. (1980).

PILI 1976 -1 PILIPOSJAN, T. E.
CERTAIN ASSIGNMENT PROBLEM (RUSSIAN), A. AKADEMIJA NAUK ARMJANSKOI SSR 5, 265-268. (1976).

PIME 1978 -1 PIMENTEL, R. F.
COMPARATIVE ANALYSIS OF SOME TECHNIQUES TO SOLVE THE GENERALIZED TRANSPORTATION PROBLEM (SPANISH). REVISTA BRASILIERA DE PESQUISA OPERACIONAL (BRAZIL) 1, NO. 1, 13-26. (1978).

❁❁

PINO 1976 -1 PINOCHET, M. R.
CENTRALIZATION AND DECENTRALIZATION OF DECISION-MAKING IN TRANSPORTATION NETWORKS. ASSOCIATION FOR COMPUTING MACHINERY. SPECIAL INTEREST GROUP ON MATHEMATICAL PROGRAMMING. NEWSLETTER 20, 54-68. (1976).

PINS 1978 -1 PINSKER, A. G.
TRANSPORTATION PROBLEM IN FUNCTION SPACES, THE. AKADEMIJA NAUK SSSR. SIBIRSKOE OTDELENIE. SIBIRSKII MATEMATICESKII ZURNAL 19, 1418-1420 + 1440; TRANSLATED AS SIBERIAN MATHEMATICAL JOURNAL 19, 1979, 1001-1003. (1978).

PINT 1978 -1 PINTO, P. A.; DANNENBERG, D. G.; KHUMAWALA, B. M.
HEURISTIC NETWORK PROCEDURE FOR THE ASSEMBLY LINE BALANCING PROBLEM, A. NAVAL RESEARCH LOGISTICS QUARTERLY 25, 299-308. (1978).

PIOT 1976 -1 PIOTROVSKI, M.
CLASS OF HAMILTONIAN GRAPHS (RUSSIAN), A. FUNCTIONES ET APPROXIMATIO COMMENTARII MATHEMATICI 3, 277-282. (1976).

PIOT 1976 -2 PIOTROVSKI, M.
SOME PROPERTIES OF HAMILTONIAN GRAPHS (RUSSIAN). FUNCTIONES ET APPROXIMATIO COMMENTARII MATHEMATICI 3, 283-286. (1976).

PIOT 1977 -1 PIOTROVSKI, M.
ON A THEOREM OF L. POSA TYPE FOR HAMILTONIAN GRAPHS (RUSSIAN). UNIWERSYTET IM. ADAMA MICKIEWICZA W POZNANIU INSTYTUT MATEMATIYCKI. FUNCTIONES ET APPROXIMATIO COMMENTARII MATHEMATICI 5, 61-63. (1977).

PIPP 1977 -1 PIPPENGER, N.
FAST SIMULATION OF COMBINATIONAL LOGIC NETWORKS BY MACHINES WITHOUT RANDOM-ACCESS STORAGE. IBM RESEARCH REPORT 6582. YORKTOWN HEIGHTS: IBM RESEARCH CENTER, 14 P. (1977).

PIPP 1977 -2 PIPPENGER, N.
ON ANOTHER BOOLEAN MATRIX. IBM RESEARCH REPORT 6914. YORKTOWN HEIGHTS: IBM RESEARCH CENTER. 11 P. (1977).

PIPPA 1979 -1 PIPPENGER, N.; FISCHER, M. J.
RELATIONS AMONG COMPLEXITY MEASURES. JOURNAL OF THE ASSOCIATION FOR COMPUTING MACHINERY 26, 361-381. (1979).

PIRY 1979 -1 PIRYANOVICH, V. A.
COMPUTER EXPERIMENTS ON SOLVING INTEGER LINEAR PROGRAMMING PROBLEMS BY LOCALLY STOCHASTIC ALGORITHMS. ZURNAL VYCISLITELNOI MATEMATIKI I MATEMATICESKOI FIZIKI 19, 79-87; TRANSLATED AS USSR COMPUTATIONAL MATHEMATICS AND MATHEMATICAL PHYSICS 19, NO. 1, 81-89. (1979).

PITA 1978 -1 PITACCO, E.
ON A GENERALIZATION OF THE TRAVELING SALESMAN PROBLEM (ITALIAN). RIVISTA DI MATEMATICA PER LE SCIENZE ECONOMICHE E SOCIALI (MILAN) 1, NO. 2, 51-66. (1978).

PITF 1979 -1 PITFIELD, D. E.; SENIOR, M.
ALGORITHM 7: OBTAINING SHADOW PRICES FROM THE NAG TRANSPORTATION PROBLEM PRIMAL. ENVIRONMENT AND PLANNING 11, SERIES A, 1069-1078. (1979).

PLAI 1976 -1 PLAISTED, D. A.
SOME POLYNOMIAL AND INTEGER DIVISIBILITY PROBLEMS ARE NP-HARD. IN: 17TH ANNUAL SYMPOSIUM ON FOUNDATIONS OF COMPUTER SCIENCE, HOUSTON 1976, 264-267. LONG BEACH: IEEE COMPUTER SOCIETY; ALSO PUBLISHED IN SIAM JOURNAL ON COMPUTING 7, 1978, 458-464. (1976).

PLAIA 1980 -1 PLAISTED, D. A.; ZAKS, S.
NP-COMPLETE MATCHING PROBLEM, AN. DISCRETE APPLIED MATHEMATICS 2, 65-72. (1980).

PLAK 1980 -1 PLAKHOTISHIN, A. M.
PROBLEM OF CONSTRUCTION SCHEDULING OF OBJECTS (RUSSIAN), A. EKONOMIKA I MATEMATICESKIE METODY (MOSCOW) 16, 972-986. (1980).

PLAN 1979 -1 PLANKE, W.
UEBER EINIGE VERBESSERUNGEN DES VERZWEIGUNGSVERFAHRENS VON DRIEBEEK IN DER GEMISCHT GANZZAHLIGEN LINEAREN OPTIMIERUNG. WISSENSCHAFTLICHE ZEITSCHRIFT DER TECHNISCHEN HOCHSCHULE "CARL SCHORLEMMER" LEUNA-MERSEBURG 21, 51-62. (1979).

PLES 1975 -1 PLESNIK, J.
SIMPLE PROOF OF THE PERFECT MATCHING THEOREM, A. MATEMATICKY CASOPIS (BRATISLAVA) 25, 185-186. (1975).

PLES 1978 -1 PLESNIK, J.
BOUNDS ON CHROMATIC NUMBERS OF MULTIPLE FACTORS OF A COMPLETE GRAPH. JOURNAL OF GRAPH THEORY 2, 9-17. (1978).

PLES 1979 -1 PLESNIK, J.
NP-COMPLETENESS OF THE HAMILTONIAN CYCLE PROBLEM IN PLANAR DIGRAPHS WITH DEGREE BOUND TWO, THE. INFORMATION PROCESSING LETTERS 8, 199-201. (1979).

PLES 1979 -2 PLESNIK, J.
REMARK ON MATCHINGS IN REGULAR GRAPHS. ACTA FACULTATIS RERUM NATURALIUM UNIVERSITATIS COMENIANAE. MATHEMATICA (BRATISLAVA) 34, 63-67. (1979).

PLES 1980 -1 PLESNIK, J.
COLORING OF GRAPHS BY PARTITIONING. MATHEMATICA SLOVACA (BRATISLAVA) 30, NO. 2, 121-126. (1980).

PLES 1980 -2 PLESNIK, J.
ON THE COMPUTATIONAL COMPLEXITY ON CENTERS LOCATING IN A GRAPH. APLIKACE MATEMATIKY (PRAGUE) 25, NO. 6, 445-452. (1980).

PLUM 1981 -1 PLUMMER, M. D.
SOME RECENT RESULTS ON CYCLE TRAVERSABILITY IN GRAPHS. REPORT NO. 81181-OR. BONN: UNIV. BONN, INST. FUER OEKONOMETRIE UND OPERATIONS RESEARCH, 9 P. (1981).

POBI 1978 -1 POBISOVA, M.
AUFGABEN UEBER DIE TEILUNG DES STANGENMATERIALS, DIE. CESKOSLOVENSKA AKADEMIE VED. APLIKACE MATEMATIKY 23, NO. 2, 98-114. (1978).

PODD 1980 -1 PODDUBNY, G. V.
OPTIMIZATIONAL PROBLEM OF TRANS-SHIPMENTS IN PORTS (RUSSIAN). EKONOMIKA I MATEMATICESKIE METODY 16, 502-510. (1980).

POGA 1978 -1 POGANY, Z.
ALGORITHM FOR SOLVING THE GENERALIZED TRANSPORTATION PROBLEM, AN. IN: J. STOER (ED.): OPTIMIZATION TECHNIQUES, PROCEEDINGS OF THE 8TH IFIP CONFERENCE ON OPTIMIZATION TECHNIQUES, WUERZBURG 1977, PART 2, 253-262. LECTURE NOTES IN CONTROL AND INFORMATION SCIENCES 7, BERLIN, HEIDELBERG, NEW YORK: SPRINGER. (1978).

POHL 1970 -1 POHL, I.
SORTING PROBLEM AND ITS COMPLEXITY, A. INTERNAL REPORT. SANTA CRUZ: UNIVERSITY OF CALIFORNIA. (1970).

POLA 1979 -1 POLANSKY, O. E.; GUTMAN, I.
ZUR WEGEMATRIX SCHLICHTER GRAPHEN. MATCH, NO. 5, 219-225. (1979).

POLE 1976 -1 POLESSKII, V. P.
LATTICE OF ISTHMUSES OF A SUMMED MATROID (RUSSIAN), THE. PROBLEMY PEREDACI INFORMACII 12, NO. 4, 95-104. (1976).

POLJ 1967 -1 POLJAK, B. T.
GENERAL METHOD FOR SOLVING EXTREMUM PROBLEMS, A. SOVIET MATHEMATICS DOKLADY 8, 593-597. (1967).

POLJA 1972 -1 POLJANSKII, S. V.
TRAVELING SALESMAN PROBLEM AND PBIB(2)-DESIGNS (RUSSIAN), THE. KOMBINATORNYI ANALIZ 2, 46-49. (1972).

POP 1974 -1 POP, P.
ON L. NEMETI'S MODEL FOR SHOP SCHEDULING (ROMANIAN). REVUE D'ANALYSE NUMERIQUE ET DE LA THEORIE DE L'APPROXIMATION 3, NO. 2, 177-186. (1974).

POPE 1979 -1 POPESCU, D.
PROPRIETES DES GRAPHES SIGNES (ROMANIAN). STUDII SI CERCETARI MATEMATICE 31, 433-452. (1979).

POPE 1979 -2 POPESCU, D.
SOME HAMILTONIAN PROPERTIES OF SOME CLASSES OF GRAPHS WHICH EXTEND PETERSEN'S GRAPH (ROMANIAN). STUDII SI CERCETARI MATEMATICE 31, 77-103. (1979).

PORO 1977 -1 POROCKII, S. M.
TWO-STEP STOCHASTIC PROBLEMS OR THE TRANSPORT TYPE. IZVESTIJA AKADEMII NAUK SSSR. TEHNICESKAJA KIBERNETIKA, NO. 2, 23-31; TRANSLATED AS ENGINEERING CYBERNETICS 15, NO. 2, 1977, 20-29. (1977).

POSN 1980 -1 POSNER, M. E.
CONTINUOUS COLLAPSING KNAPSACK PROBLEM, THE. MILWAUKEE: UNIV. OF WISCONSIN-MILWAUKEE, SCHOOL OF BUSINESS ADMINISTRATION, 16 P. (1980).

POSNA 1978 -1 POSNER, M. E.; GUIGNARD, M.
COLLAPSING 0-1 KNAPSACK PROBLEM, THE. MATHEMATICAL PROGRAMMING 15, 155-161. (1978).

POTE 1981 -1 POTEMKINA, A. V.; SHEVCHENKO, V. N.
CONSTRUCTION OF REGULAR CUTTING-OFF IN CONVEX INTEGER PROGRAMMING (RUSSIAN). EKONOMIKA I MATEMATICESKIE METODY (MOSCOW) 17, 390-393. (1981).

POTR 1979 -1 POTRZEBOWSKI, H.
BRANCH AND BOUND AS A DECOMPOSITION METHOD OF DETERMINING SCHEDULES FOR PARALLEL MACHINES (POLISH). ARCHIWUM AUTOMATYKI I TELEMEHANIKI 24, 301-313. (1979).

POTT 1980 -1 POTTS, C. N.
ADAPTIVE BRANCHING RULE FOR THE PERMUTATION FLOW-SHOP PROBLEM, AN. EUROPEAN JOURNAL OF OPERATIONAL RESEARCH 5, 19-25. (1980).

POTT 1980 -2 POTTS, C. N.
ALGORITHM FOR THE SINGLE MACHINE SEQUENCING PROBLEM WITH PRECEDENCE CONSTRAINTS, AN. MATHEMATICAL PROGRAMMING STUDY 13, 78-87. (1980).

POTT 1980 -3 POTTS, C. N.
ANALYSIS OF A HEURISTIC FOR ONE MACHINE SEQUENCING WITH RELEASE DATES AND DELIVERY TIMES. OPERATIONS RESEARCH 28, 1436-1441. (1980).

POUZ 1979 -1 POUZET, M.
NOTE SUR LE PROBLEME DE ULAM. JOURNAL OF COMBINATORIAL THEORY 27, SERIES B, 231-236. (1979).

POWE 1980 -1 POWELL, S.
ROW GENERATION METHODS. CANTERBURY: UNIVERSITY OF KENT, 18 P. (1980).

POWEA 1978 -1 POWER, L. R.
INTERNAL SORTING USING A MINIMAL TREE MERGE STRATEGY. IBM RESEARCH REPORT 7090. YORKTOWN HEIGHTS: IBM RESEARCH CENTER, 13 P. (1978).

PRAG 1954 -1 PRAGER, W.
PROBLEMS OF TRAFFIC AND TRANSPORTATION. IN: PROCEEDINGS OF THE SYMPOSIUM ON OPERATIONS RESEARCH IN BUSINESS AND INDUSTRY, 105-113. KANSAS CITY. (1954).

PRAK 1978 -1 PRAKASH, S.
ON THE MACHINE-ASSIGNMENT PROBLEM. PROCEEDINGS OF THE NATIONAL ACADEMY OF SCIENCES, INDIA. SECTION A 48, 103-110. (1978).

PRAS 1981 -1 PRASTACOS, G. P.
ALLOCATION OF A PERISHABLE PRODUCT INVENTORY. OPERATIONS RESEARCH 29, 95-107. (1981).

PRIC 1978 -1 PRICE, W. L.
ALGORITHM WHICH GENERATES THE HAMILTONIAN CIRCUITS OF A CUBIC PLANAR MAP, AN. THE JOURNAL OF THE LONDON MATHEMATICAL SOCIETY 18, NO. 2, 193-201. (1978).

PRIE 1979 -1 PRIESE, L.
TOWARDS A PRECISE CHARACTERIZATION OF THE COMPLEXITY OF UNIVERSAL AND NONUNIVERSAL TURING MACHINES. SIAM JOURNAL ON COMPUTING 8, 508-523. (1979).

PRIT 1979 -1 PRITSKER, A. A. B.
MODELING AND ANALYSIS USING Q-GERT NETWORKS. NEW YORK: WILEY, 456 P. (1979).

PROL 1978 -1 PROLL, L. G.
SIMPLE BUT EFFECTIVE TRANSFORMATION FOR A CLASS OF ILPS, A. THE JOURNAL OF THE OPERATIONAL RESEARCH SOCIETY 29, 1009-1011. (1978).

PROS 1979 -1 PROSKUROWSKI, A.
MINIMUM DOMINATING CYCLES IN 2-TREES. INTERNATIONAL JOURNAL OF COMPUTER AND INFORMATION SCIENCES 8, 405-417. (1979).

PROT 1977 -1 PROTASOV, I. V.; TRETJAK, V. P.; CHARIN, V. S.
OPTIMIZATION PROBLEM CONNECTED WITH COVERINGS (RUSSIAN), AN. ISSELDOVAMNIJA OPERACII I ASU VYP. 10, 95-98 + 142. (1977).

PROT 1979 -1 PROTASOV, I. V.; TRETJAK, V. P.; CHARIN, V. S.
ON THE COVERING PROBLEM (RUSSIAN). ISSLEDOVANIE OPERACII I ASU (KIEV) NO. 14, 61-65, 134. (1979).

PRZY 1979 -1 PRZYBYLAK, F.
CALCULATION OF A ONE-DIMENSIONAL KNAPSACK FUNCTION (POLISH). ZESZYTY NAUKOWE POLITECHNIKI SLASKIEJ. MATEMATYKA-FIZYKA (GLIWICE) NO. 35, 155-164. (1979).

PRZY 1979 -2 PRZYBYLAK, F.
GENERALIZED ONE-DIMENSIONAL KNAPSACK FUNCTION (POLISH). ZESZYTY NAUKOWE POLITECHNIKI SLASKIEJ. MATEMATYKA-FIZYKA (GLIWICE) NO. 35, 147-154. (1979).

PSAR 1978 -1 PSARAFTIS, H. N.
REAL-TIME FLEXIBLE-ROUTE SCHEDULING ALGORITHM, A. LOS ANGELES (ORSA/TIMS MEETING, NOVEMBER 1978): 28 P. (1978).

PSAR 1980 -1 PSARAFTIS, H. N.
DYNAMIC PROGRAMMING APPROACH FOR SEQUENCING GROUPS OF IDENTICAL JOBS, A. OPERATIONS RESEARCH 28, 1347-1359. (1980).

PSAR 1980 -2 PSARAFTIS, H. N.
DYNAMIC PROGRAMMING SOLUTION TO THE SINGLE VEHICLE MANY-TO-MANY IMMEDIATE REQUEST DIAL-A-RIDE PROBLEM, A. TRANSPORTATION SCIENCE 14, 130-154. (1980).

PULL 1977 -1 PULLEYBLANK, W. R.
LINEAR PROGRAMMING RELAXATION OF THE NODE PACKING PROBLEM OR 2-BICRITICAL GRAPHS AND NODE COVERS, A. CALGARY: UNIV. OF CALGARY, DEPT. OF COMPUTER SCIENCE, 24 P. (1977).

PULL 1979 -1 PULLEYBLANK, W. R.
MINIMUM NODE COVERS AND 2-BICRITICAL GRAPHS. MATHEMATICAL PROGRAMMING 17, 91-103. (1979).

PULL 1979 -2 PULLEYBLANK, W. R.
NOTE ON GRAPHS SPANNED BY EULERIAN GRAPHS, A. JOURNAL OF GRAPH THEORY 3, 309-310. (1979).

****

PULL 1979 -3 PULLEYBLANK, W. R.
POLYHEDRAL OPTIMIZATION AND THE TRAVELLING SALESMAN PROBLEM. IN: D. MAC CARTHY, H. C. WILLIAMS (EDS.): PROCEEDINGS OF THE EIGHTH MANITOBA CONFERENCE ON NUMERICAL MATHEMATICS AND COMPUTING, 51-64. CONGRESSUS NUMERANTIUM XXII. WINNIPEG: UTILITAS. (1979).

PULL 1980 -1 PULLEYBLANK, W. R.
MATCHING RANK OF HALIN GRAPHS, THE. RESEARCH REPORT NO. 80165-OR. BONN: UNIV. OF BONN, INSTITUT FUER OEKONOMETRIE UND OPERATIONS RESEARCH, 22 P. (1980).

PULL 1980 -1 PULLEYBLANK, W. R.
DUAL INTEGRALITY IN B-MATCHING PROBLEMS. MATHEMATICAL PROGRAMMING STUDY 12, 176-196. (1980).

PULL 1981 -1 PULLEYBLANK, W. R.
MATCHING RANK OF HALIN GRAPHS, THE. IN: R. E. BURKARD, T. ELLINGER (EDS.): METHODS OF OPERATIONS RESEARCH 40, 401-404. KOENIGSTEIN: ANTON HAIN MEISENHEIM. (1981).

PULL 1981 -2 PULLEYBLANK, W. R.
ON MINIMIZING SETUPS IN PRECEDENCE CONSTRAINED SCHEDULING. RESEARCH REPORT WP 81185-OR. BONN: UNIV. BONN, INST. FUER OEKONOMETRIE UND OPERATIONS RESEARCH, ABT. OPERATIONS RESEARCH, 32 P. (1981).

PULL 1981 -3 PULLEYBLANK, W. R.
TOTAL DUAL INTEGRALITY AND B-MATCHINGS. RESEARCH REPORT 81180-OR. BONN: UNIV. BONN, INST. FUER OEKONOMETRIE UND OPERATIONS RESEARCH, 6 P. (1981).

PURI 1974 -1 PURI, M. C.; SWARUP, K.
SIMPLE ENUMERATIVE METHOD FOR FIXED CHARGE PROBLEM. INDIAN JOURNAL OF PURE AND APPLIED MATHEMATICS 5, NO. 10, 894-901. (1974).

QUEY 1977 -1 QUEYRANNE, M.
PROBLEME DU VOYAGEUR DE COMMERCE A COUTS VARIABLES ET QUELQUES APPLICATIONS, LE. DISSERTATION. GRENOBLE: UNIVERSITE SCIENTIFIQUE ET MEDICALE DE GRENOBLE, 104 P. (1977).

QUIN 1976 -1 QUINTART, G.
APPLICATION DE LA THEORIE DES GRAPHES AUX PROBLEMES D'HORAIRE. MONS: UNIVERSITE DE L'ETAT. (1976).

RABI 1979 -1 RABIN, M. O.
PROBABILISTIC ALGORITHM FOR TESTING PRIMALITY. TECHNICAL REPORT. CAMBRIDGE: MASSACHUSETTS INST. OF TECHNOLOGY, 20 P. (1979).

RADE 1977 -1 RADERMACHER, F. J.
FLOATS IN PROJECT NETWORKS. IN: A. ANGERMANN ET AL. (EDS.): FIRST SYMPOSIUM ON OPERATIONS RESEARCH, HEIDELBERG 1976. METHODS OF OPERATIONS RESEARCH 27, 163-224. MEISENHEIM: ANTON HAIN. (1977).

RADE 1981 -1 RADERMACHER, F. J.
COST-DEPENDENT ESSENTIAL SYSTEMS OF ES-STRATEGIES FOR STOCHASTIC SCHEDULING PROBLEMS. IN: J. MERKWITZ, W. OBERSCHELP (EDS.): KOLLOQUIUM UEBER MATHEMATISCHE METHODEN DES OPERATIONS RESEARCH, AACHEN 1980, IN MEM. R. KAERKES, 17-32. METHODS OF OPERATIONS RESEARCH 42. KOENIGSTEIN: ANTON HAIN MEISENHEIM. (1981).

RADO 1978 -1 RADO, R.
MONOCHROMATIC PATHS IN GRAPHS. IN: B. BOLLOBAS (ED.): ADVANCES IN GRAPH THEORY, 191-194. ANNALS OF DISCRETE MATHEMATICS 3. AMSTERDAM: NORTH-HOLLAND. (1978).

RADO 1981 -1 RADO, R.
SATZ UEBER STROEMUNGEN IN GERICHTETEN GRAPHEN, EIN. IN: J. MERKWITZ, W. OBERSCHELP (EDS.): KOLLOQUIUM UEBER MATHEMATISCHE METHODEN DES OPERATIONS RESEARCH, AACHEN 1980, IN MEM. R. KAERKES, 1-4. METHODS OF OPERATIONS RESEARCH 42. KOENIGSTEIN: ANTON HAIN MEISENHEIM. (1981).

RADZ 1977 -1 RADZISZOWSKI, S.
PROGRAMMABILITY AND P = NP CONJECTURE. IN: M. KARPINSKI (ED.): FUNDAMENTALS OF COMPUTATION THEORY, POZNAN-KORNIK 1977, 494-498. LECTURE NOTES IN COMPTER SCIENCE 56. BERLIN, NEW YORK: SPRINGER; ALSO PUBLISHED IN FUNDAMENTA INFORMATICAE 2, 1978, 71-82. (1977).

RADZ 1978 -1 RADZISZOWSKI, S.
PROGRAMMABILITY AND P=NP CONJECTURE. FUNDAMENTA INFORMATICAE 2, 71-82. (1978).

RAGH 1978 -1 RAGHAVACHARI, M.; SABHARWAL, Y. P.
ON THE NUMBER OF NON-NEGATIVE INTEGRAL SOLUTIONS TO THE KNAPSACK PROBLEM. SCIMA 7, 82-87. (1978).

RAI 1980 -1 RAI, S.; AGGARWAL, K. K.
ON COMPLEMENTATION OF PATHSETS AND CUTSETS. IEEE TRANSACTIONS ON RELIABILITY 29, 139-140. (1980).

RAMA 1975 -1 RAMACHANDRA RAO, A.; BHASKARA RAO, K. P. S.
MODULARITY IN COMBINATORIAL GEOMETRIES. PROCEEDINGS OF THE INDIAN NATIONAL SCIENCE ACADEMY PART A 41, 260-263. (1975).

RAMAA 1977 -1 RAMACHANDRAN, S.
NOTE ON COLORING LINE GRAPHS THAT ARE PLANAR, A. MADURAI UNIVERSITY. JOURNAL 6, NO. 1, 105. (1977).

RAMAA 1978 -1 RAMACHANDRAN, S.
PLANAR GRAPHS WITH SQUARE OR CUBE ROOT ARE FOUR-COLOURABLE. JOURNAL OF COMBINATORIAL THEORY 24, SERIES B, 362-364. (1978).

RAMAB 1980 -1 RAMAKRISHNAN, K. G.
SOLVING TWO-COMMODITY TRANSPORTATION PROBLEMS WITH COUPLING CONSTRAINTS. JOURNAL OF THE ASSOCIATION FOR COMPUTING MACHINERY 27, 736-757. (1980).

RAMAC 1978 -1 RAMAMOORTHY, C. V.; LI, H. F.
CORRECTIONS TO: "SCHEDULING PARALLEL PROCESSABLE TASKS FOR A UNIPROCESSOR" (IEEE TRANSACTIONS ON COMPUTERS 25 (1976) NO. 5, 485-495) BY C. V. RAMAMOORTHY, T. F. FOX AND H. F. LI. IEEE TRANSACTIONS ON COMPUTERS 27, 288. (1978).

RAMAD 1980 -1 RAMANI, K. V.; RAGHURAM, G.
UTILIZATION OF TRANSPORTATION UNITS: AN OPTIMAL ALLOCATION STUDY. OPSEARCH 17, 33-40. (1980).

RAMAE 1976 -1 RAMANKULOV, S.; KUPUEV, P.
MATHEMATICAL MODEL FOR RESOURCE ALLOCATION (RUSSIAN), A. TRUDY KIRGIZKOGO GOSUDARSTVENNOGO UNIVERSITETA. SERIJA MATEMATICESKIH NAUK 12, 70-75. (1976).

RAO 1979 -1 RAO, G. S.; STONE, H. S.; HU, T. C.
ASSIGNMENT OF TASKS IN A DISTRIBUTED PROCESSOR SYSTEM WITH LIMITED MEMORY. INSTITUTE OF ELECTRICAL AND ELECTRONICS ENGINEERS. TRANSACTIONS ON COMPUTERS 28, 291-299. (1979).

RAO A 1980 -1 RAO, M. R.
NOTE ON THE MULTIPLE TRAVELING SALESMEN PROBLEM, A. OPERATIONS RESEARCH 28, 628-632. (1980).

RAO B 1980 -1 RAO, R. C.; SHAFTEL, T. L.
COMPUTATIONAL EXPERIENCE ON AN ALGORITHM FOR THE TRANSPORTATION PROBLEM WITH NONLINEAR OBJECTIVE FUNCTIONS. NAVAL RESEARCH LOGISTICS QUARTERLY 27, 145-157. (1980).

RAO B 1981 -1 RAO, R. C.; SHAFTEL, T. L.
CAPACITATED TRANSPORTATION PRODUCTION PROBLEM: COMPUTATIONAL EXPERIENCE, THE. RESEARCH REPORT 756. WEST LAFAYETTE: PURDUE UNIVERSITY, KRANNERT GRADUATE SCHOOL OF MANAGEMENT, 20 P. (1981).

RAO C 1979 -1 RAO, S. B.
SOLUTION OF THE HAMILTONIAN PROBLEM FOR SELF-COMPLEMENTARY GRAPHS. JOURNAL OF COMBINATORIAL THEORY 27, SERIES B, 13-41. (1979).

****

RAO D 1977 -1 RAO, S. B.; RAVINDRA, G.
CHARACTERIZATION OF PERFECT TOTAL GRAPHS. A. JOURNAL OF MATHEMATICAL AND PHYSICAL SCIENCES 11, NO. 1, 25-26. (1977).

RARD 1973 -1 RARDIN, R. L.
GROUP THEORETIC AND RELATED APPROACHES TO FIXED CHARGE PROBLEMS. UNPUBLISHED DISSERTATION. ATLANTA: GEORGIA INSTITUTE OF TECHNOLOGY, DEPARTMENT OF INDUSTRIAL AND SYSTEMS ENGINEERING. (1973).

RARDA 1979 -1 RARDIN, R. L.; CHOE, U.
TIGHTER RELAXATIONS OF FIXED CHARGE NETWORK FLOW PROBLEMS. REPORT SERIES J-79-18. ATLANTA: GEORGIA INST. OF TECHNOLOGY, SCHOOL OF INDUSTRIAL AND SYSTEMS ENGINEERING, 23 P. (1979).

RARDB 1978 -1 RARDIN, R. L.; LIN, B. W.
WHAT MAKES INTEGER PROGRAMMING PROBLEMS HARD TO SOLVE: AN EMPIRICAL STUDY. OPSEARCH 15, 65-77. (1978).

RARDB 1980 -1 RARDIN, R. L.; LIN, B. W.
RIP RANDOM INTEGER PROGRAMMING TEST PROBLEM GENERATOR, THE. RESEARCH REPORT J-80-16. ATLANTA: GEORGIA INSTITUTE OF TECHNOLOGY, SCHOOL OF INDUSTRIAL AND SYSTEMS ENGINEERING, 38 P. (1980).

RARDC 1979 -1 RARDIN, R. L.; ROSENTHAL, R. E.
GRAPH STRUCTURES UNDERLYING SUBMATRICES OF NETWORK FLOW TABLEAUX. TRANSPORTATION SCIENCE 13, 98-112. (1979).

RATH 1977 -1 RATHMANN, D.
ZUR LOESUNG DISKRETER OPTIMIERUNGSPROBLEME MIT GRUPPENTHEORETISCHEN ANSAETZEN. GOETTINGEN: UNIV. GOETTINGEN, FAKULTAET FUER WIRTSSCHAFTS- UND SOZIALWISSENSCHAFTEN, 242 P. (1977). (DISSERTATION)

RAUS 1975 -1 RAUSCHER, C.
EINFUEHRUNG IN DIE OPTIMIERUNG VON NETZWERKEN. SCIENTIA ELECTRICA 21, NO. 2, 29-51. (1975).

RAVI 1975 -1 RAVINDRA, G.
ON BERGE'S CONJECTURE CONCERNING PERFECT GRAPHS. PROCEEDINGS OF THE INDIAN NATIONAL SCIENCE ACADEMY PART A 41, 294-296. (1975).

RAVI 1979 -1 RAVINDRA, G.
B-GRAPHS. IN: A. RAMACHANDRA RAO (ED.): PROCEEDINGS OF THE SYMPOSIUM ON GRAPH THEORY, CALCUTTA 1976, 268-280. ISI (INDIAN STATISTICAL INSTITUTE) LECTURE NOTES 4. CALCUTTA: MACMILLAN OF INDIA. (1979).

RAVIA 1980 -1 RAVINDRAN, A.; HANLINE, D. L.
OPTIMAL LOCATION OF COAL BLENDING PLANTS BY MIXED-INTEGER PROGRAMMING. AIIE TRANSACTIONS 12, 179-185. (1980).

RAYW 1979 -1 RAYWARD-SMITH, V. J.
ON COMPUTING THE SMITH NORMAL FORM OF AN INTEGER MATRIX. ACM TRANSACTIONS ON MATHEMATICAL SOFTWARE 5, 451-456. (1979).

READ 1979 -1 READ, R. C.
ALGORITHMS IN GRAPH THEORY. IN: R. J. WILSON, L. W. BEINEKE (EDS.): APPLICATIONS OF GRAPH THEORY, 381-417. LONDON, NEW YORK, SAN FRANCISCO: ACADEMIC PRESS. (1979).

REAR 1974 -1 REARDON, K. J.
DECOMPOSITION OF DUAL-ANGULAR INTEGER PROGRAMS, WITH APPLICATIONS TO MUTLI-STAGE CAPITAL BUDGETING. DISSERTATION. STANFORD: STANFORD UNIVERSITY, 132 P. (1974).

REBI 1975 -1 REBIBO, K. K.; YEN, A. M.
AUTOMATED APPROACH TO THE ASSIGNMENT OF DRIVERS IN URBAN TRANSIT, AN. IN: PROCEEDINGS OF THE 1975 CONFERENCE ON INFORMATION SCIENCES AND SYSTEMS, BALTIMORE 1975, 303-305. BALTIMORE: THE JOHNS HOPKINS UNIVERSITY: DEPARTMENT OF ELECTRICAL ENGINEERING. (1975).

RECS 1975 -1 RECSKI, A.
APPLICATION OF MATROIDS IN THE ANALYSIS OF ELECTRICAL NETWORKS. II. (HUNGARIAN). MATEMATIKAI LAPOK. BOLYAI JANOS MATEMATIKAI TARSULAT 26, 287-303. (1975).

RECS 1978 -1 RECSKI, A.
CONTRIBUTIONS TO THE N-PORT INTERCONNECTION PROBLEM BY MEANS OF MATROIDS. IN: A. HAJNAL, V. T. SOS (EDS.): COMBINATORICS, VOLUME II, 877-892. COLLOQUIA MATHEMATICA SOCIETATIS JANOS BOLYAI 18. AMSTERDAM: NORTH-HOLLAND. (1978).

RECS 1978 -2 RECSKI, A.
DECOMPOSITIONS OF A GRAPHIC MATROID. IN: COLLOQUE MATHEMATIQUES DISCRETES: CODES ET HYPERGRAPHES, BRUSSELS 1978. CAHIERS DU CENTRE D'ETUDES DE RECHERCHE OPERATIONELLE 20, NO. 3-4, 437-442. (1978).

RECS 1978 -3 RECSKI, A.
MATROIDAL STRUCTURE OF N-PORTS. IN: A. HAJNAL, V. T. SOS (EDS.): COMBINATORICS, VOLUME II, 893-910. COLLOQUIA MATHEMATICA SOCIETATIS JANOS BOLYAI 18. AMSTERDAM: NORTH-HOLLAND. (1978).

RECS 1981 -1 RECSKI, A.
ALGORITHM TO DETERMINE WHETHER THE SUM OF SOME GRAPHIC MATROIDS IS GRAPHIC, AN. IN: L. LOVASZ, V. T. SOS (EDS.): ALGEBRAIC METHODS IN GRAPH THEORY, VOL. II, 647-656. COLLOQUIA MATHEMATICA SOCIETATIS JANOS BOLYAI 25. AMSTERDAM, OXFORD,NEW YORK: NORTH-HOLLAND. (1981).

RECSA 1980 -1 RECSKI, A.; IRI, M.
NETWORK THEORY AND TRANSVERSAL MATROIDS. DISCRETE APPLIED MATHEMATICS 2, 311-326. (1980).

REES 1980 -1 REESE, J.
STANDORT- UND BELEGUNGSPLANUNG FUER MASCHINEN IN MEHRSTUFIGEN PRODUKTIONSPROZESSEN. BERLIN, HEIDELBERG, NEW YORK: SPRINGER, 193 P. (1980).

REIB 1979 -1 REIBIGER, A.; STRAUBE, B.
UEBER DIE AXIOMATISCHE BEGRUENDUNG EINER ALLGEMEINEN NETZWERKTHEORIE. WISSENSCHAFTLICHE ZEITSCHRIFT DER TECHNISCHEN UNIVERSITAET DRESDEN 28, 399-407. (1979).

REIF 1981 -1 REIF, J. H.
MINIMUM S-T CUT OF A PLANAR UNDIRECTED NETWORK IN O(N LOG**2 N) TIME. IN: P. EVEN, O. KARIV (EDS.): AUTOMATA, LANGUAGES AND PROGRAMMING, 56-67. LECTURE NOTES IN COMPUTER SCIENCE 115. BERLIN: SPRINGER. (1981).

REIS 1979 -1 REISS, S. P.
RATIONAL SEARCH. INFORMATION PROCESSING LETTERS 8, 89-90. (1979).

REMK 1980 -1 REMKE, W.
LOESUNG EINES DREISTUFIGEN TRANSPORTPROBLEMS MIT HILFE VON SUBGRADIENTENVERFAHREN. MATHEMATISCHE OPERATIONSFORSCHUNG UND STATISTIK 11, SERIES OPTIMIZATION, 95-108. (1980).

RESI 1977 -1 RESINA, C.
PROPOSED SOLUTION METHOD FOR A CLASS OF MIXED INTEGER PROGRAMMING PROBLEMS (ITALIAN). RICERCA OPERATIVA 8, NO. 4, 3-11. (1977).

RETK 1978 -1 RETKIN, H.; MOGI, S.
SOME COMBINATORIAL IDENTITIES ON MATROIDS. IN: J.-C. BERMOND ET AL. (EDS.): PROBLEMES COMBINATOIRES ET THEORIE DES GRAPHES, COLLOQUES INTERNATIONAUX DU CENTRE NATIONAL DE LA RECHERCHE SCIENTIFIQUE, ORSAY 1976, 343-344. PARIS: CENTRE NATIONAL DE LA RECHERCHE SCIENTIFIQUE. (1978).

REVA 1980 -1 REVA, V. N.
OPTIMAL ORDERING OF THE FLOW GRAPH VERTICES (RUSSIAN). KIBERNETIKA, NO. 2, 136. (1980).

****

REVE 1981 -1 REVELLE, C.; COHON, J.; SHOBRYS, D.
MULTIPLE OBJECTIVES IN FACILITY LOCATION: A REVIEW. IN: J. N. MORSE (ED.): ORGANIZATIONS: MULTIPLE AGENTS WITH MULTIPLE CRITERIA, 320-337. LECTURE NOTES IN ECONOMICS AND MATHEMATICAL SYSTEMS 190. BERLIN: SPRINGER. (1981).

REVJ 1976 -1 REVJAKIN, A. M.
DESCRIPTION OF THE FACTORS OF COMBINATORIAL GEOMETRIES (RUSSIAN). A. KOMBINATORNYI ANALIZ. MOSKOVSKII GOSUDARSTVENNYI UNIVERSITET IM M. V. LOMONOSOVA 4, 69-72. (1976).

REVJ 1976 -2 REVJAKIN, A. M.
ONE-POINT EXTENSIONS OF COMBINATORIAL GEOMETRIES (RUSSIAN). KOMBINATORNYI ANALIZ. MOSKOVSKII GOSUDARSTVENNYI UNIVERSITET IM M. V. LOMONOSOVA 4, 64-68. (1976).

RICH 1975 -1 RICHTER, D.
UEBER DIE LOESUNG DISKRETER, NICHTLINEARER OPTIMIERUNGSAUFGABEN. DISSERTATION. BERLIN: HUMBOLDT-UNIVERSITAET. (1975).

RICHA 1979 -1 RICHTER, K.
DYNAMISCHE AUFGABEN DER DISKRETEN OPTIMIERUNG. WISSENSCHAFTLICHE ZEITSCHRIFT DER TECHNISCHEN HOCHSCHULE KARL-MARX-STADT 21, 549-557. (1979).

RIEP 1978 -1 RIEPL, R.-J.
OR-VERFAHREN IM VERKEHRSWESEN. IN: PROCEEDINGS IN OPERATIONS RESEARCH 7, 421-429. WUERZBURG: PHYSICA. (1978).

RIIV 1979 -1 RIIVES, K.
DETERMINATION OF THE VERTICES OF TRANSPORT POLYTOPES (RUSSIAN). A. TARTU RIIKLIKU UELIKOOLI TOIMETISED NO. 500 TRUDY PO MATHEMATIKE I MEHANIKE, NO. 25, 105-118. (1979).

RING 1959 -1 RINGEL, G.
FAERBUNGSPROBLEM AUF FLAECHEN UND GRAPHEN. MATHEMATISCHE MONOGRAPHIEN 2. BERLIN: VEB DEUTSCHER VERLAG DER WISSENSCHAFTEN, 132 P. (1959).

RINN 1976 -1 RINNOOY KAN, A. H. G.
MACHINE SCHEDULING PROBLEMS: CLASSIFICATION, COMPLEXITY AND COMPUTATIONS. THE HAGUE: NIJHOFF, 180 P. (1976).

RIVE 1976 -1 RIVEST, R. L.; VUILLEMIN, J.
ON THE TIME REQUIRED TO RECOGNIZE PROPERTIES OF GRAPHS FROM THEIR ADJACENCY MATRICES. IN: JOURNEES ALGORITHMIQUES (ECOLE NORMALE SUPERIEURE, PARIS 1975), 213-227. PARIS: SOCIETE MATHEMATIQUE DE FRANCE. (1976).

RIVI 1978 -1 RIVIERE, M.
RECOUVREMENT DES SOMMETS D'UN GRAPHE PLANAIRE PAR DES ARETES ET DES STABLES. CAHIERS DU CENTRE D'ETUDES DE RECHERCHE OPERATIONELLE 20, 137-146. (1978).

ROBA 1956 -1 ROBACKER, J. T.
NOTES ON LINEAR PROGRAMMING: PART XXXVII CONCERNING MULTICOMMODITY NETWORKS. REPORT RM-1799. SANTA MONICA: THE RAND CORPORATION. (1956).

ROBB 1976 -1 ROBBINS, J.
PROGRAM FOR SOLUTION OF LARGE SCALE VEHICLE ROUTING PROBLEMS, A. DISSERTATION. STILLWATER: OKLAHOMA STATE UNIVERSITY, DEPT. OF INDUSTRIAL ENGINEERING AND MANAGEMENT. (1976).

ROBI 1980 -1 ROBIN, G.
SUR UN PROBLEME D'OPTIMISATION EN NOMBRES ENTIERS. MATHEMATISCHE OPERATIONSFORSCHUNG UND STATISTIK, SERIES OPTIMIZATION 11, 403-420. (1980).

ROBIA 1980 -1 ROBINSON, D. F.; FOULDS, L. R.
DIGRAPHS: THEORY AND TECHNIQUES. NEW YORK, LONDON, PARIS: GORDON AND BREACH, 256 P. (1980).

ROBIB 1976 -1 ROBINSON, D. W.
ANALYSIS OF A SHORTEST PATH ALGORITHM FOR TRANSPORTATION APPLICATIONS. TECHNICAL REPORT. CONTROL ANALYSIS CORPORATION. (1976).

ROBIC 1980 -1 ROBINSON, G. C.; WELSH, D. J. A.
COMPUTATIONAL COMPLEXITY OF MATROID PROPERTIES, THE. MATHEMATICAL PROCEEDINGS OF THE CAMBRIDGE PHILOSOPHICAL SOCIETY 87, 29-45. (1980).

ROBID 1977 -1 ROBINSON, J. M.
DETERMINING THE K-TH SHORTEST PATH BY MATRIX METHOD (HUNGARIAN). SZIGMA 10, 75-96. (1977).

ROEC 1980 -1 ROECK, H.
SCALING TECHNIQUES FOR MINIMAL COST NETWORK FLOWS. IN: U. PAPE (ED.): DISCRETE STRUCTURES AND ALGORITHMS, 181-192. MUENCHEN: HANSER. (1980).

ROGL 1980 -1 ROGLIN, O.
SOME REMARKS ON SCHEDULING NURSING PERSONNEL. OPERATIONS RESEARCH 28, 828-829. (1980).

ROHD 1978 -1 ROHDE, M.
SET-PARTITIONING-PROBLEM - WIRTSCHAFTLICHE ANWENDUNGEN UND ALGORITHMEN -,DAS. BEITRAEGE ZUR UNTERNEHMENSFORSCHUNG, 9. BERLIN: FREIE UNIVERSITAET BERLIN, INSTITUT FUER UNTERNEHMENSFORSCHUNG, 113 P. (1978).

ROHD 1979 -1 ROHDE, M.
ENUMERATIVER ALGORITHMUS ZUR LOESUNG DES SET-PARTITIONING-PROBLEMS MIT RANDBEDINGUNGEN, EIN. IN: PROCEEDINGS IN OPERATIONS RESEARCH 8, 23-30. WUERZBURG: PHYSICA. (1979).

ROHD 1979 -2 ROHDE, M.
SET PARTITIONING MIT LINEAREN RANDBEDINGUNGEN. OPERATIONS RESEARCH-SPEKTRUM 1, 75-87. (1979).

ROHL 1978 -1 ROHL, J. S.
GENERATING PERMUTATIONS BY CHOOSING. THE COMPUTER JOURNAL 21, 302-305. (1978).

ROHLA 1978 -1 ROHLF, F. J.
PROBABILISTIC MINIMUM SPANNING TREE ALGORITHM, A. INFORMATION PROCESSING LETTERS 7, 44-48. (1978).

ROLL 1979 -1 ROLLO, J.
GROUPEMENT DES TACHES DE PRODUCTION DANS L'ORDONNANCEMENT DE LA PRODUCTION (CZECHOSLOVAKIAN). EKONOMICKO-MATEMATICKY OBZOR 15, 310-319. (1979).

ROMA 1978 -1 ROMAN, S.
PROBLEM ON MULTICOLORINGS OF GRAPHS, A. DISCRETE MATHEMATICS 22, 41-48. (1978).

ROMAA 1980 -1 ROMANI, F.
SHORTEST-PATH PROBLEM IS NOT HARDER THAN MATRIX MULTIPLICATION. INFORMATION PROCESSING LETTERS 11, 134-136. (1980).

ROME 1981 -1 ROMERO, D.
TIC MATRICES, AN EXTENSION OF THE BOTTLENECK ASSIGNMENT PROBLEM. IN: R. E. BURKARD, T. ELLINGER (EDS.): METHODS OF OPERATIONS RESEARCH 40, 405-408. KOENIGSTEIN: ANTON HAIN MEISENHEIM. (1981).

ROSA 1979 -1 ROSA, M. S.
FINDING THE PATH WITH SMALLEST AVERAGE SPEED FROM A GIVEN SOURCE TO A GIVEN DESTINATION IN A DIRECTED NETWORK WITHOUT CYCLES. REVUE BELGE DE STATISTIQUE, D'INFORMATIQUE ET DE RECHERCHE OPERATIONELLE 19, NO. 3, 44-52. (1979).

ROSE 1978 -1 ROSE, D. J.; TARJAN, R. E.
ALGORITHMIC ASPECTS OF VERTEX ELIMINATION ON DIRECTED GRAPHS. SIAM JOURNAL ON APPLIED MATHEMATICS 34, 176-197. (1978).

ROSEA 1978 -1 ROSENBERG, A. L.
NOTE ON PATHS EMBEDDED IN TREES, A. IBM RESEARCH REPORT, 7304. YORKTOWN HEIGHTS: IBM RESEARCH CENTER, 4 P. (1978).

ROSEB 1977 -1 ROSENBERG, A. L.; SNYDER, L.
BOUNDS ON THE COSTS OF DATA ENCODINGS. IBM RESEARCH REPORT 6907. YORKTOWN: IBM RESEARCH CENTER, 45 P. (1977).
ROSEB 1978 -1 ROSENBERG, A. L.; SNYDER, L.
COMPACT B-TREES. IBM RESEARCH REPORT, 7343. YORKTOWN HEIGHTS: IBM RESEARCH CENTER, 23 P. (1978).
ROSEC 1963 -1 ROSENBLATT, D.
ON THE GRAPHS OF FINITE IDEMPOTENT BOOLEAN RELATION MATRICES. JOURNAL OF RESEARCH OF THE NATIONAL BUREAU OF STANDARDS 67B, 249-256. (1963).
ROSEC 1967 -1 ROSENBLATT, D.
AGGREGATION IN MATRIX MODELS OF RESOURCE FLOWS II. BOOLEAN RELATION MATRIX METHODS. THE AMERICAN STATISTICIAN 21, 32-37. (1967).
ROSED 1979 -1 ROSENBLATT, M. J.
FACILITIES LAYOUT PROBLEM: A MULTI-GOAL APPROACH, THE. INTERNATIONAL JOURNAL OF PRODUCTION RESEARCH 17, 323-331. (1979).
ROSEE 1970 -1 ROSENFELD, M.
ON TAIT COLORING OF CUBIC GRAPHS. IN: R. K. GUY ET AL. (EDS.): COMBINATORIAL STRUCTURES AND THEIR APPLICATIONS, 373-376. NEW YORK: GORDEN AND BREACH. (1970).
ROSEF 1979 -1 ROSENFELD, P.
TESTING THE PERFORMANCE OF A HEURISTIC FOR A SCHEDULING PROBLEM WHICH HAS NO KNOWN SOLUTION TECHNIQUE. YORKTOWN HEIGHTS: IBM RESEARCH CENTER, 15 P. (1979).
ROSEG 1977 -1 ROSENTHAL, R. E.
SCHEDULING RESERVOIR RELEASES FOR MAXIMUM HYDROPOWER BENEFIT BY NONLINEAR PROGRAMMING ON A NETWORK. TECHNICAL REPORT. KNOXVILLE: UNIVERSITY OF TENNESSEE, MANAGEMENT SCIENCE PROGRAM. (1977).
ROSH 1977 -1 ROSHCHIN, G. B.
ALGORITHM FOR DETERMINING THE MINIMAL SPANNING TREE OF AN INCREASING GRAPH (RUSSIAN), AN. ZURNAL VYCISLITEL'NOI MATEMATIKI I MATEMATICESKOI FISIKI 17, 1607-1610. (1977).
ROSH 1978 -1 ROSHCHIN, G. B.
DETERMINATION OF A MINIMUM SPANNING TREE OF A GRAPH (RUSSIAN). IZVESTIJA AKADEMII NAUK SSSR TEKH. KIBERN. SSSR, NO. 1, 129-133. (1978).
ROSHA 1978 -1 ROSHCHIN, V. A.
APPROACH TO THE SOLUTION OF PARTIALLY INTEGRAL PROBLEMS OF LINEAR PROGRAMMING (RUSSIAN), AN. IN: PROCESSING OF SOFTWARE AND HARDWARE FOR AUTOMATIC CONTROL SYSTEMS, 39-43. KIEV: AKADEMIJA NAUK UKRAINSKOI SSR. INSTITUT KIBERNETIKI. (1978).
ROSI 1979 -1 ROSING, K. E.; HILLSMAN, E. L.; ROSING-VOGELAAR, H.
NOTE COMPARING OPTIMAL AND HEURISTIC SOLUTIONS TO THE P-MEDIAN PROBLEM, A. GEOGRAPHICAL ANALYSIS 11, 86-89. (1979).
ROSS 1980 -1 ROSS, G. T.; SOLAND, R. M.
BOUNDED INTERVAL GENERALIZED ASSIGNMENT MODEL, THE. NAVAL RESEARCH LOGISTICS QUARTERLY 27, 625-634. (1980).
ROSS 1980 -2 ROSS, G. T.; SOLAND, R. M.
MULTICRITERIA APPROACH TO THE LOCATION OF PUBLIC FACILITIES, A. EUROPEAN JOURNAL OF OPERATIONAL RESEARCH 4, 307-321. (1980).
ROSSA 1979 -1 ROSS, G. T.; ZOLTNERS, A. A.
WEIGHTED ASSIGNMENT MODELS AND THEIR APPLICATION. MANAGEMENT SCIENCE 25, 683-696. (1979).
ROTA 1978 -1 ROTARU, S.
DEUX METHODES DE RESOLUTION DE LA PROGRAMMATION ENTIERE (ROMANIAN). UNIVERSITATAS BABES-BOLYAI. STUDIA. MATHEMATICA 23, NO. 2, 7-15. (1978).
ROTH 1979 -1 ROTHENGATTER, W.
APPLICATION OF OPTIMAL SUBSET SELECTION TO PROBLEMS OF DESIGN AND SCHEDULING IN URBAN TRANSPORTATION NETWORKS. TRANSPORTATION RESEARCH 13, SERIES B, 49-63. (1979).
ROTHA 1970 -1 ROTHFARB, B.; FRISCH, I. T.
COMMON TERMINAL MULTICOMMODITY FLOW WITH A CONCAVE COST FUNCTION. SIAM JOURNAL ON APPLIED MATHEMATICS 18, 489-502. (1970).
ROTHB 1969 -1 ROTHSCHILD, B.; WHINSTON, A.
MULTICOMMODITY NETWORK FLOWS. WORKING PAPER. LAFAYETTE: PURDUE UNIVERSITY, KRANNERT SCHOOL. (1969).
ROUC 1979 -1 ROUCAIROL, C.
REDUCTION METHOD FOR QUADRATIC ASSIGNMENT PROBLEMS, A. IN: W. OETTLI, F. STEFFENS (EDS.): OPERATIONS RESEARCH VERFAHREN 32, THIRD SYMPOSIUM ON OPERATIONS RESEARCH, MANNHEIM 1978, 183-187. KOENIGSTEIN: ANTON HAIN MEISENHEIM. (1979).
ROUN 1980 -1 ROUNTREE, S. L. K.; GILLETT, B. E.
PARAMETRIC INTEGER LINEAR PROGRAMMING: A SYNTHESIS OF BRANCH AND BOUND WITH CUTTING PLANES. WORKING PAPER. ROLLA: UNIV. OF MISSOURI, COMPUTER SCIENCE DEPT., 15 P. (1980).
ROUX 1975 -1 ROUX, M.
NOTES SUR L'ARBRE DE LONGUEUR MINIMA. REVUE DE STATISTIQUE APPLIQUEE. CENTRE D'ENSEIGNEMENT ET DE RECHERCHE DE STATISTIQUE APPLIQUEE 23, NO. 2, 29-35. (1975).
ROWI 1977 -1 ROWICKI, A.
NOTE ON OPTIMAL PREEMPTIVE SCHEDULING OF TWO-PROCESSOR SYSTEMS, A. INFORMATION PROCESSING LETTERS 6, 25-28. (1977).
ROWI 1977 -2 ROWICKI, A.
ON OPTIMAL PREEMPTIVE SCHEDULING FOR TWO-PROCESSOR SYSTEMS. BULLETIN DE L'ACADEMIE POLONAISE DES SCIENCES. SERIE DES SCIENCES MATHEMATIQUES, ASTRONOMIQUES ET PHYSIQUES 25, 697-706. (1977).
ROWI 1978 -1 ROWICKI, A.
ON OPTIMAL PREEMPTIVE SCHEDULING OF INDEPENDENT TASKS FOR MULTIPROCESSOR SYSTEMS. BULLETIN DE L'ACADEMIE POLONAISE DES SCIENCES. SERIE DES SCIENCES MATHEMATIQUES, ASTRONOMIQUES ET PHYSIQUES 26, 643-650. (1978).
ROWI 1978 -2 ROWICKI, A.
ON THE OPTIMAL PREEMPTIVE SCHEDULING FOR MULTIPROCESSOR SYSTEM. BULLETIN DE L'ACADEMIE POLONAISE DES SCIENCES. SERIE DES SCIENCES MATHEMATIQUES, ASTRONOMIQUES ET PHYSIQUES 26, 651-660. (1978).
ROY 1978 -1 ROY, J. R.; KARLQVIST, A.
SOME NUMERICAL CONSIDERATIONS OF OPTIMAL ALLOCATION WITH GRAVITY FLOW COSTS. APPLIED MATHEMATICAL MODELLING 2, NO. 3, 177-184. (1978).
ROY A 1978 -1 ROY, M. K.
EVALUATION OF PERMUTATION ALGORITHMS. THE COMPUTER JOURNAL 21, 296-302. (1978).
ROY B 1977 -1 ROY, S.
APPLICATION OF NON-LINEAR PROGRAMMING IN POWER PLANT LOCATION PROBLEM, AN. INDIAN JOURNAL OF PURE AND APPLIED MATHEMATICS 8, 773-778. (1977).
RUBI 1978 -1 RUBIN, F.
ENUMERATING ALL SIMPLE PATHS IN A GRAPH. IEEE TRANSACTIONS ON CIRCUITS AND SYSTEMS 25, 641-642. (1978).

RUBIA 1974 -1 RUBIN, J.
SCHEDULING OF AIRLINE CREWS FOR AIRCRAFT SCHEDULES WITH FREQUENCY EXCEPTIONS. REPORT G320-2103. CAMBRIDGE: IBM CAMBRIDGE SCIENCE CENTER. (1974).

RUBIB 1980 -1 RUBINSHTEIN, M. I.; CHERKASHIN, A. M.
DISCRETE PROBLEM OF OPTIMAL RESOURCE ALLOCATION IN ACTIVITY NETWORKS. AVTOMATIKA I TELEMEHANIKA (MOSCOW) NO. 1, 146-152; TRANSLATED AS AUTOMATION AND REMOTE CONTROL 41, NO. 1(2), 116-122. (1980).

RUBIB 1980 -2 RUBINSHTEIN, M. I.; CHERKASHIN, A. M.
PROBLEME DISCRET D'ALLOCATION OPTIMALE DES RESSOURCES DANS UN COMPLEXE D'OPERATIONS EN RESEAU (RUSSIAN). AVTOMATIKA I TELEMEHANIKA (MOSCOW), NO. 1, 146-152. (1980).

RUES 1981 -1 RUESCHENDORF, L.
EQUIVALENCE OF TWO NODE CONDITIONS IN BIPARTITE GRAPHS, THE. METHODS OF OPERATIONS RESEARCH 39, 175-178. (1981).

RUHE 1979 -1 RUHE, G.
TERMINRECHNUNG DES LEINET ALS POTENTIALPROBLEM AUF EINEM GRAPH MIT PAAREN GEKOPPELTER BOEGEN, DIE. WISSENSCHAFTLICHE ZEITSCHRIFT DER TECHNISCHEN HOCHSCHULE LEIPZIG 3, 369-374. (1979).

RUIZ 1977 -1 RUIZ, J. P.; LARA, R. A.
IMPLEMENTATION ON A SMALL COMPUTER OF A SEQUENCING ALGORITHM (SPANISH), THE. INVESTIGACION OPERACIONAL (CUBA) 21-22, 137-145. (1977).

RUIZA 1979 -1 RUIZDEFCO, F.; LARRANETA, J.
LEXICOGRAPHIC ENUMERATION ALGORITHM FOR THE KNAPSACK PROBLEM, A. WORKING PAPER. SEVILLA: UNIV. DE SEVILLA, ESCUELA TECNICA SUPERIOR DE INGENIEROS INDUSTRIALES. 21 P. (1979).

RUSC 1978 -1 RUSCHITZKA, M.
ANALYTICAL TREATMENT OF POLICY FUNCTION SCHEDULERS, AN. OPERATIONS RESEARCH 26, 845-863. (1978).

RUSK 1978 -1 RUSKEY, F.
GENERATING T-ARY TREES LEXICOGRAPHICALLY. SIAM JOURNAL ON COMPUTING 7, 424-439. (1978).

RUSN 1978 -1 RUSNAK, Z.
ATTEMPT TO SOLVE THE LOCATION PROBLEM WITH WEIGHTS ON THE PLANE (POLISH), AN. PRZEGLAD STATYSTYCZNY (WARSAW) 25, 537-541. (1978).

RUSS 1979 -1 RUSSELL, R.; IGO, W.
ASSIGNMENT ROUTING PROBLEM, AN. NETWORKS 9, 1-17. (1979).

RUTK 1978 -1 RUTKAUSKAS, P.
APPROXIMATION D'UN PROCESSUS DISCRET D'ALLOCATION DE RESSOURCES PAR UN ANALOGUE CONTINU OPTIMAL (RUSSIAN). INSTITUT FIZIKI I MATEMATIKI LITOVSKOI SSR. MATEMATICESKIE METODY V SOCIAL'NYH NAUKAH. TRUDY RESPUBLIKANSKOGO NAUCNOGO SEMINARA "PROCESSY OPTIMAL'NOGO UPRAVLENIJA". IL SEKCIJA, NO. 11, 99-109. (1978).

RYAN 1980 -1 RYAN, M. J.
MORE ON THE MORE FOR LESS PARADOX IN THE DISTRIBUTION MODEL. IN: A. V. FIACCO, K. O. KORTANEK (EDS.): EXTREMAL METHODS AND SYSTEMS ANALYSIS, 275-305. LECTURE NOTES IN ECONOMICS AND MATHEMATICAL SYSTEMS 174. BERLIN: SPRINGER. (1980).

RYANA 1979 -1 RYANG, S. Y.; RYU, H. D.
NEW METHOD OF DECIDING HAMILTONIAN CIRCLES AND SPANNING PARTIAL GRAPHS, (KOREAN), A. CHO-SON IN-MIN KONG-HWA-KUK KWA-HAK-WON T'ONG-BO 27, NO. 1, 7-9. (1979).

RYU 1978 -1 RYU, H. D.
FORMULA DECIDING THE WHOLE OF THE HAMILTONIAN CIRCLE OF A GRAPH (KOREAN), A. CHO-SON IN-MIN KONG-HWA-KUK KWA-HAK-WON T'ONG-BO 26, NO. 5, 254-256. (1978).

RYU 1978 -2 RYU, H. D.
FORMULA FOR COMPLETELY DETERMINING AN EULERIAN SPANNING PATH OF A GRAPH (KOREAN), A. CHO-SON IN-MIN KONG-HWA-KUK KWA-HAK-WON T'ONG-BO 26, NO. 6, 289-290. (1978).

RYZK 1978 -1 RYZKOV, A. P.
METHODS OF SOLVING A PROBLEM OF WEIGHTED COLORING OF A GRAPH. IZVESTIJA AKADEMII NAUK SSSR. TEHNICESKAJA KIBERNETIKA, NO. 5, 119-126 + 222; TRANSLATED AS ENGINEERING CYBERNETICS 16, 1978, 89-95. (1978).

SABA 1975 -1 SABAU, A.
ON THE SOLUTION OF A TRANSPORTATION PROBLEM ON AN INTERVAL (ROMANIAN). UNIVERSITATEA DES BRASOV. LUCRARI STIINTIFICE 17, 39-41. (1975).

SACH 1976 -1 SACHS, H.
ON THE NUMBER OF SPANNING TREES. PROCEEDINGS OF THE FIFTH BRITISH COMBINATORIAL CONFERENCE, 529-535. CONGRESSUS NUMERANTIUM NO. XV. WINNIPEG: UTILITAS MATHEMATICA. (1976).

SACK 1977 -1 SACKOV, V. N.
COMBINATORIAL METHODS OF DISCRETE MATHEMATICS (RUSSIAN). MOSCOW: IZDAT. "NAUKA", 319 P. (1977).

SADO 1978 -1 SADOWSKI, R. P.; JACOBSON, R. E.
SCHEDULING ALGORITHMS FOR THE UNBALANCED PRODUCTION LINE: AN ANALYSIS AND COMPARISON. AIIE TRANSACTIONS 10, 31-39. (1978).

SADOA 1979 -1 SADOWSKI, R. P.; MEDEIROS, D. J.
EFFECT OF VARIABILITY ON THE UNBALANCED PRODUCTION LINE, THE. INTERNATIONAL JOURNAL OF PRODUCTION RESEARCH 17, 527-540. (1979).

SADY 1978 -1 SADYKOV, R. G.
OPTIMIZATION OF AN ALGORITHM FOR DEVISING A SCHEDULE OF EDUCATIONAL ACTIVITIES (RUSSIAN). IN: A. N. CEKALIN, E. V. ERMOLIN (EDS.): APPLICATION OF COMPUTERS TO THE SOLUTION OF PROBLEMS IN MATHEMATICAL PHYSICS AND AUTOMATIC CONTROL SYSTEMS (RUSSIAN), 179-197. KAZAN: IZDAT. KAZAN. UNIV. (1978).

SADY 1979 -1 SADYKOV, R. G.
ON THE SOLUTION OF AN ASSIGNMENT PROBLEM (RUSSIAN). IN: COMPUTATIONAL METHODS AND COMPUTER SOFTWARE, 88-106. KAZAN: KAZAN. UNIV. (1979).

SAED 1981 -1 SAEDT, A. P. H.
SITING OF GREEN FORAGE DRYING PLANTS FOR USE BY A LARGE NUMBER OF FARMS - A LOCATION-ALLOCATION CASE STUDY, THE. EUROPEAN JOURNAL OF OPERATIONAL RESEARCH 6, 190-194. (1981).

SAFO 1979 -1 SAFONOVA, T. E.
REALIZATION OF AN ALGORITHM FOR CONSTRUCTING AN OPTIMAL SCHEDULE WITH A STARTING POINT IN A GIVEN INTERVAL (RUSSIAN). IN: NUMERICAL METHODS AND QUESTIONS IN THE ORGANIZATION OF CALCULATIONS, 3. ZAPISKI NAUCNYH SEMINAROV LENINGRADSKOGO OTDELENIJA MATEMATICESKOGO INSTITUTA IM. V. A. STEKLOVA AKADEMII NAUK SSSR (LOMI) (LENINGRAD) 90, 194-209, 301. (1979).

SAFR 1972 -1 SAFRONENKO, V. A.
MATHEMATICAL AND ELECTRONIC SIMULATION OF THE PROBLEM OF OPTIMAL SCHEDULING (RUSSIAN). IZDAT. 'NAUKA I TEHNIKA', MINSK, 182 P. (1972).

SAHA 1975 -1 SAHA, J. L.
ON SOME PROBLEMS IN RAILWAY NETWORKS. DOCTORAL DISSERTATION. CLEVELAND: CASE WESTERN RESERVE UNIVERSITY, 93 P. (1975).

SAHAA 1979 -1 SAHA, T.
ON A TRI-CRITERION TRANSPORTATION PROBLEM. JOURNAL OF MATHEMATICAL AND PHYSICAL SCIENCES (MADRAS) 13, 507-522. (1979).

SAHL 1978 -1 SAHLING, B.-M.
VERKEHRSABLAUF IN NETZEN - EIN GRAPHENTHEORETISCHES OPTIMIERUNGSVERFAHREN. IN: R. HENN, P. KALL, H. KOENIG, B. KORTE, O. KRAFFT ET AL. (EDS.): OPERATIONS RESEARCH VERFAHREN 28, SECOND SYMPOSIUM ON OPERATIONS RESEARCH, AACHEN 1977, 112-125. MEISENHEIM: HAIN. (1978).

SAHN 1979 -1 SAHNI, S.
PREEMPTIVE SCHEDULING WITH DUE DATES. OPERATIONS RESEARCH 27, 925-934. (1979).

SAHNA 1979 -1 SAHNI, S.; CHO, Y.
COMPLEXITY OF SCHEDULING SHOPS WITH NO WAIT IN PROCESS. MATHEMATICS OF OPERATIONS RESEARCH 4, 448-457. (1979).

SAHNA 1979 -2 SAHNI, S.; CHO, Y.
NEARLY ON LINE SCHEDULING OF A UNIFORM PROCESSOR SYSTEM WITH RELEASE TIMES. SIAM JOURNAL ON COMPUTING 8, 275-285. (1979).

SAHNA 1980 -1 SAHNI, S.; CHO, Y.
SCHEDULING INDEPENDENT TASKS WITH DUE TIMES ON A UNIFORM PROCESSOR SYSTEM. JOURNAL OF THE ASSOCIATION FOR COMPUTING MACHINERY 27, 550-563. (1980).

SAHNB 1975 -1 SAHNI, S.; GONZALEZ, T.
P-COMPLETE APPROXIMATION PROBLEMS. MINNEAPOLIS: UNIV. OF MINNESOTA, COMPUTER INFORMATION AND CONTROL SCIENCES DEPT., 20 P. (1975).

SAHNC 1978 -1 SAHNI, S.; HOROWITZ, E.
COMBINATORIAL PROBLEMS: REDUCIBILITY AND APPROXIMATION. OPERATIONS RESEARCH 26, 718-759. (1978).

SAHU 1977 -1 SAHU, S.
ANALYSIS STUDIES ON SOME ASPECTS OF PLANT LAYOUT AND DESIGN. DISSERTATION. KHARAGPUR: INDIAN INSTITUTE OF TECHNOLOGY, INDUSTRIAL MANAGEMENT CENTRE. (1977).

SAKA 1978 -1 SAKAROVITCH, M.
QUELQUES THEOREMES DE DUALITE COMBINATOIRE. DISCRETE MATHEMATICS 21, 201-212. (1978).

SAKS 1978 -1 SAKSENA, J. P.
RAKE LINK MINIMISATION PROBLEM. NEW DELHI: NATIONAL PRODUCTIVITY COUNCIL, 14 P. (1978).

SAKS 1979 -1 SAKSENA, J. P.
BEAT PATROLLING IN URBAN AREAS. A CASE STUDY. EUROPEAN JOURNAL OF OPERATIONAL RESEARCH 3, 199-206. (1979).

SALC 1973 -1 SALCEDO, E.
METHODS OF PARTIAL ENUMERATION FOR THE SOLUTION OF DISCRETE OPTIMIZATION PROBLEMS (SPANISH), THE. INVESTIGACION OPERACIONAL, NO. 8, 23-26. (1973).

SALK 1975 -1 SALKIN, H. M.
INTEGER PROGRAMMING. READING, LONDON U.A.: ADDISON-WESLEY, 537 P. (1975).

SALKA 1979 -1 SALKIN, H. M.; LIN, C. H.
AGGREGATIONS OF SUBSIDIARY FIRMS FOR MINIMAL UNEMPLOYMENT COMPENSATION PAYMENTS VIA INTEGER PROGRAMMING. MANAGEMENT SCIENCE 25, 405-408. (1979).

SALZ 1979 -1 SALZBORN, F. J. M.
SCHEDULING BUS SYSTEMS WITH INTERCHANGES. ADELAIDE: UNIV. OF ADELAIDE, 36 P. (1979).

SAMP 1977 -1 SAMPATHKUMAR, E.; NEERALAGI, P. S.; VENKATACHALAM, C. V.
GENERALIZATION OF THE CHROMATIC AND LINE CHROMATIC NUMBERS OF A GRAPH, A. JOURNAL OF THE KARTNATAK UNIVERSITY. SCIENCE 22, 44-49. (1977).

SAMY 1978 -1 SAMYLOVSKII, A. I.; SUSKOV, B. G.
CONSTRUCTION OF THE CHARACTERISTIC FUNCTION OF A NON-CONVEX SET AND THE RELATED PROBLEM OF QUADRATIC INTEGER-VALUED PROGRAMMING. ZURNAL VYCISLITEL'NOI MATEMATIKI I MATEMATICESKOI FIZIKI 18, 322-337; TRANSLATED AS U.S.S.R. COMPUTATIONAL MATHEMATICS AND MATHEMATICAL PHYSICS 18, NO. 2, 1978, 38-50. (1978).

SAMY 1978 -2 SAMYLOVSKII, A. I.; SUSKOV, B. G.
NON-CONVEX SET CHARACTERISTIC FUNCTION CONSTRUCTION AND CONNECTED INTEGER QUADRATIC PROGRAMMING PROBLEM. ZURNAL VYCISLITEL'NOI MATEMATIKI I MATEMATICESKOI FIZIKI 18, 314-321. (1978).

SAND 1974 -1 SANDBERG, V. JU.
HEURISTIC ALGORITHM FOR GRAPH COLORING (RUSSIAN), A. VORONEZSKII ORDENA LENINA GOSUDARSTVENNYI UNIVERSITET IM LENINSKOGO KOMSOMOLA. TRUDY NAUCNO-ISSLEDOVATEL'SKOGO INSTITUTA MATEMATIKI, NO. 12, SB. STATEI PO PRIKL. ANAL., 58-64. (1974).

SANDA 1979 -1 SANDI, C.
SUBGRADIENT OPTIMIZATION. IN: N. CHRISTOFIDES, A. MINGOZZI, P. TOTH, C. SANDI (EDS.): COMBINATORIAL OPTIMIZATION, 73-93. CHICHESTER, NEW YORK, BRISBANE, TORONTO: WILEY. (1979).

SANDA 1980 -1 SANDI, C.
0-1 INTEGER PROGRAMMING USING SUBGRADIENT AND ELLIPSOID METHODS. PISA (INTERNATIONAL WORKSHOP ON ADVANCES IN LINEAR OPTIMIZATION ALGORITHMS AND SOFTWARE, JULY 1980) 15 P. (1980).

SANG 1970 -1 SANG, N.; FLORIAN, M.
NOTE ON LOWER BOUNDS FOR THE MACHINE SCHEDULING PROBLEM, A. PUBLICATION NO. 49. MONTREAL: UNIVERSITE DE MONTREAL, DEPARTEMENT D'INFORMATIQUE. (1970).

SANGA 1979 -1 SANGIOVANNI-VINCENTELLI, A.; BICKART, T. A.
BIPARTITE GRAPHS AND AN OPTIMAL BORDERED TRIANGULAR FORM OF A MATRIX. INSTITUTE OF ELECTRICAL AND ELECTRONICS ENGINEERS. TRANSACTIONS ON CIRCUITS AND SYSTEMS 26, 880-889. (1979).

SANI 1979 -1 SANIKIDZE, D. O.
ALGORITHM FOR FINDING THE SHORTEST COVERING USING THE COLORING OF NONORIENTED GRAPHS IN SOLVING SOME PROBLEMS OF MINIMIZATION (RUSSIAN), AN. SOOBSHCHENIJA AKADEMII NAUK GRUZINSKOI SSR (TBILISI) 95, 137-139. (1979).

SANN 1979 -1 SANNOMIYA, N.
METHOD FOR SOLVING MIXED-INTEGER LINEAR PROGRAMMING PROBLEMS WITH ANGULAR STRUCTURE, A. MEMOIRS OF THE FACULTY OF ENGINEERING. KYOTO UNIVERSITY 41, 462-473. (1979).

SAPA 1977 -1 SAPAK, O.
REPRESENTATION OF THE FINITE DIRECTED ACYCLIC GRAPH. ARCHIVUM MATHEMATICUM (BRNO) 13, 111-116. (1977).

SAPI 1975 -1 SAPIRO, A. D.
SOME ASYMPTOTIC PROPERTIES OF A CERTAIN PROBLEM IN SCHEDULING THEORY (RUSSIAN). EKONOMIKA I MATEMATICESKIE METODY 11, 1214-1216. (1975).

SAPIA 1970 -1 SAPIRO, V. R.
ON THE QUESTION OF THE STATISTICAL ESTIMATION OF VARIOUS METHODS FOR SOLVING THE TRANSPORT PROBLEM (RUSSIAN). TASKENSKII INSTITUT NARODNOGO HOZJAISTUWA. NAUCYNE ZAPISKI. MATEMATIKA V PRILOZENIJAH, 33-38. (1970).

SAPO 1978 -1 SAPOVALOVSKII, V. I.
ON A PROBLEM OF ENUMERATIVE MATHEMATICAL PROGRAMMING IN NETWORK FORMULATION (UKRAINIAN). IN: QUESTIONS OF QUALITATIVE THEORY OF DIFFERENTIAL EQUATIONS AND THEIR APPLICATIONS (UKRAINIAN), 65-66. KIEV: ACAD. SCI. UKR. SSR, INST. MATH. (1978).

SAPOA 1977 -1 SAPOZENKO, A. A.; ASRATJAN, A. S.; KUZJURIN, N. N.
SURVEY OF SOME RESULTS IN COVERING PROBLEMS (RUSSIAN), A. METODY DISKRETNOGO ANALIZA (NOVOSIBIRSK), NO. 30, 46-75. (1977).

SARC 1979 -1 SARCHIMELIYA, R. A.
ON THE REPRESENTATION OF INTEGRAL SOLUTIONS IN A DISCRETE PROGRAMMING PROBLEM (RUSSIAN). SOOBSCENIJA AKADEMII NAUK GRUZINSKOI SSR 94, 309-312. (1979).

SARV 1977 -1 SARVANOV, V. I.
APPROXIMATE SOLUTION OF A LINEAR MINIMISATION PROBLEM OVER THE SET OF CYCLIC PERMUTATIONS (RUSSIAN). VESCI AKADEMII NAVUK BSSR. SERYJA FIZIKA-MATEMATYCNYH NAVUK, NO. 6, 5-10. (1977).

SASA 1976 -1 SASAKI, M.; SAKAKIBARA, T.; MATSUI, K.
NEW CONDITION OF THE FEASIBILITY OF TWO-COMMODITY FLOWS IN A COMMUNICATION NETWORK, A. IN: PROCEEDINGS OF THE NINTH HAWAII INTERNATIONAL CONFERENCE ON SYSTEM SCIENCES, HONOLULU 1976, 80-82. NORTH HOLLYWOOD, CALIF.: WESTERN PERIODICALS. (1976).

SASAA 1979 -1 SASAKI, R.; SHINGAI, S.; TAKARAKI, K.
EXTENDED MAO & WALLINGFORD'S METHOD FOR SOLVING NONLINEAR INTEGER PROGRAMMING PROBLEMS AND ITS APPLICATION, AN. KAWASAKI: HITACHI SYSTEMS DEVELOPMENT LABORATORY, 20 P. (1979).

SASAB 1978 -1 SASAKI, R.; TSURUOKA, R.; HARUNA, L.
COMBINATORIAL OPTIMIZATION METHOD OF SYSTEMS WITH FUZZY OBJECTIVES AND UNCERTAIN PARAMETERS AND ITS APPLICATION, A. REPRINT. KAWASAKI: SYSTEMS DEVELOPMENT LABORATORY, HITACHI LTD., P. 715-719 (1978).

SATO 1978 -1 SATO, H.; KOBAYASHI, K.; HOSHI, M.
ON MAPS BETWEEN MATROIDS (JAPANESE). IN: COMBINATORIAL STRUCTURES AND GRAPH THEORY II. PROC. SYMP. KYOTO 1977, 97-145. SURIKAISEKIKENKYUSHO KOKYUROKU NO. 333. KYOTO: KYOTO UNIVERSITY, RESEARCH INST. FOR MATH. SCIENCES. (1978).

SATOA 1978 -1 SATO, I.
ON A FEW CLIQUE-GRAPH EQUATIONS. TRU MATHEMATICS 14, NO. 2, 31-36. (1978).

SAUN 1978 -1 SAUNDERS, B. D.; SCHNEIDER, H.
FLOWS ON GRAPHS APPLIED TO DIAGONAL SIMILARITY AND DIAGONAL EQUIVALENCE FOR MATRICES. DISCRETE MATHEMATICS 24, 205-220. (1978).

SAUN 1979 -1 SAUNDERS, B. D.; SCHNEIDER, H.
APPLICATIONS OF THE GORDAN-STIEMKE THEOREM IN COMBINATORIAL MATRIX THEORY. SIAM REVIEW 21, 528-541. (1979).

SAVA 1980 -1 SAVAGE, C.
MAXIMUM MATCHINGS AND TREES. INFORMATION PROCESSING LETTERS 10, 202-205. (1980).

SAVAA 1979 -1 SAVAGE, J. E.
SPACE-TIME TRADEOFFS. UDINE (SUMMER SCHOOL ON COMPUTATIONAL COMPLEXITY, JUNE 1979) 29 P. (1979).

SAVI 1976 -1 SAVITCH, W. J.
THREE HARDEST PROBLEMS. IN: K. R. APT, J. W. DE BAKKER (EDS.): FOUNDATIONS OF COMPUTER SCIENCE II, PART 2, AMSTERDAM 1976, 109-149. MATHEMATICAL CENTRE TRACTS, NO. 82. AMSTERDAM: MATHEMATISCH CENTRUM. (1976).

SAWI 1976 -1 SAWIK, T.
MINIMAL-TIME PROGRAMMING FOR MULTI-ASSORTMENT PRODUCTION (POLISH). ARCHIWUM AUTOMATYKI I TELEMECHANIKI 21, NO. 3, 327-340. (1976).

SAWI 1976 -2 SAWIK, T.
TIME-OPTIMAL PRODUCTION SCHEDULING IN THE CASE OF A TIME-VARYING SET OF AVAILABLE PRODUCTION EQUIPMENT (POLISH). ARCHIWUM AUTOMATYKI I TELEMECHANIKI 22, NO. 4, 473-486. (1976).

SAWI 1978 -1 SAWIK, T.
OPERATIONS SCHEDULING AS A CONTROL PROBLEM WITH BOOLEAN VARIABLES. PODSTAWY STEROWANIA 8, 409-416. (1978).

SAXE 1979 -1 SAXENA, P. C.; PATKAR, V.; PARKASH, O.
NOTE ON AN ALGORITHM FOR INTEGER SOLUTION TO LINEAR AND PIECEWISE LINEAR PROGRAMS, A. PURE AND APPLIED MATHEMATIKA SCIENCES 9, 31-36. (1979).

SBIH 1978 -1 SBIHI, N.
ETUDE DES STABLES DANS LES GRAPHES SANS ETOILE. GRENOBLE: UNIVERSITE SCIENTIFIQUE ET MEDICALE DE GRENOBLE, INSTITUT NATIONAL POLYTECHNIQUE, 100 P. (1978). (DISSERTATION)

SBIH 1980 -1 SBIHI, N.
ALGORITHME DE RECHERCHE D'UN STABLE DE CARDINALITE MAXIMUM DANS UN GRAPHE SANS ETOILE. DISCRETE MATHEMATICS 29, 53-76. (1980).

SCER 1974 -1 SCERBAK, A. F.; LEVIN, G. L.; VOLCEK, B. A.
CERTAIN CLASS OF OPTIMAL WORK SCHEDULING PROBLEMS (RUSSIAN), A. EKONOMIKA I MATEMATICESKIE METODY 10, 947-956. (1974).

SCHA 1974 -1 SCHABACK, R.
OPTIMIERUNGSPROBLEM AUS DER KRISTALLOGRAPHIE, EIN. IN: L. COLLATZ, W. WETTERLING (EDS.): NUMERISCHE METHODEN BEI OPTIMIERUNGSAUFGABEN 2, TAGUNG OBERWOLFACH 1973, 113-123. BASEL: BIRKHAEUSER. (1974).

SCHAA 1978 -1 SCHAEFER, A.
NETZE MIT VERTEILUNGSFAKTOREN. MEISENHEIM: HAIN, 143 P. (1978). (BEITRAEGE ZUR DATENVERARBEITUNG UND UNTERNEHMENSFORSCHUNG, 21)

SCHE 1974 -1 SCHEIM, D. E.
NUMBER OF EDGE 3-COLORINGS OF A PLANAR CUBIC GRAPH AS A PERMANENT, THE. DISCRETE MATHEMATICS 8, 377-382. (1974).

SCHEA 1979 -1 SCHEITHAUER, G.; TERNO, J.
NEW EXTENSION PRINCIPLE ALGORITHM FOR THE TRAVELING SALESMAN PROBLEM, A. MANUSKRIPT 07-21-79. DRESDEN: TECHNISCHE UNIV. DRESDEN, SEKTION MATHEMATIK, 16 P. (1979).

SCHEA 1979 -2 SCHEITHAUER, G.; TERNO, J.
TSPE - AN ALGOL PROCEDURE FOR SOLVING THE TRAVELING SALESMAN PROBLEM. MANUSKRIPT 07-32-79. DRESDEN:TECHNISCHE UNIV. DRESDEN, SEKTION MATHEMATIK, 16 P. (1979).

SCHEB 1979 -1 SCHENK, G.; THIERS, G.
COMPARISON OF SOME ALGORITHMS AND HEURISTICS FOR SOLVING THE HITCHCOCK-KOOPMANS TRANSPORTATION PROBLEM, A. REVUE BELGE DE STATISTIQUE, D'INFORMATIQUE ET DE RECHERCHE OPERATIONELLE 19, NO. 2, 36-52. (1979).

SCHI 1980 -1 SCHICK, G. J.; STROUP, J. W.
EXPERIENCE WITH A MULTI-YEAR PLANNING MODEL. DOUGLAS PAPER 6876. WASHINGTON (ORSA/TIMS MEETING, MAY 1980) 6 P. (1980).

SCHIA 1979 -1 SCHIEBEL, W.; TERNO, J.; UNGER, G.
BEITRAG ZUR KLASSIFIZIERUNG VON RUNDREISEPROBLEMEN, EIN. MATHEMATISCHE OPERATIONSFORSCHUNG UND STATISTIK 10, SERIES OPTIMIZATION, 523-528. (1979).

SCHIB 1975 -1 SCHIEBEL, W.; UNGER, G.
DUALE ENTARTUNG IN DER LINEAREN OPTIMIERUNG, TRANSPORTPROBLEM MIT ZUSAETZLICHEN NEBENBEDINGUNGEN UND RUNDREISEPROBLEM. DISSERTATION. DRESDEN: TECHNISCHE UNIVERSITAET DRESDEN. (1975).

SCHIC 1979 -1 SCHILLING, D.; ELZINGA, D. J.; COHON, J.; CHURCH, R. L.; REVELLE, C.
TEAM/FLEET MODELS FOR SIMULTANEOUS FACILITY AND EQUIPMENT SITING, THE. TRANSPORTATION SCIENCE 13, 163-175. (1979).

SCHID 1976 -1 SCHINDLER, S.
SCHEDULING GENERAL MONITOR SYSTEMS. IN: PROCEEDINGS OF THE NINTH HAWAII INTERNATIONAL CONFERENCE ON SYSTEM SCIENCES, HONOLULU 1976, 122-124. NORTH HOLLYWOOD: WESTERN PERIODICALS. (1976).

SCHL 1979 -1 SCHLUETER, E.
REIHENFOLGEMODELLE MIT PARALLELITAET ZWISCHEN BEARBEITUNGSSTYLEN UND AUFTRAEGEN. WISSENSCHAFTLICHE ZEITSCHRIFT DER TECHNISCHEN HOCHSCHULE "OTTO VON GUERICKE" 23, 631-632. (1979).

SCHM 1980 -1 SCHMERL, J. H.
RECURSIVE COLORINGS OF GRAPHS. CANADIAN JOURNAL OF MATHEMATICS 32, 821-830. (1980).

SCHMA 1978 -1 SCHMID, H. J.
GEOMETRICAL INTERPRETATION OF THE HUNGARIAN METHOD, A. DISCRETE MATHEMATICS 21, 297-308. (1978).

SCHMB 1976 -1 SCHMIDT, D. C.; DRUFFEL, L. E.
FAST BACKTRACKING ALGORITHM TO TEST DIRECTED GRAPHS FOR ISOMORPHISM USING DISTANCE MATRICES, A. JOURNAL OF THE ASSOCIATION FOR COMPUTING MACHINERY 23, 433-445. (1976).

SCHMC 1974 -1 SCHMIDT, G.; STROEHLEIN, T.
SOME ASPECTS IN THE CONSTRUCTION OF TIMETABLES. IN: J. L. ROSENFELD (ED.): INFORMATION PROCESSING '74. PROCEEDINGS OF THE IFIP CONGRESS, STOCKHOLM 1974, 516-520. AMSTERDAM, LONDON: NORTH-HOLLAND. (1974).

SCHMC 1980 -1 SCHMIDT, G.; STROEHLEIN, T.
TIMETABLE CONSTRUCTION - AN ANNOTATED BIBLIOGRAPHY. THE COMPUTER JOURNAL 23, 307-316. (1980).

SCHMD 1979 -1 SCHMIDT, R.
ON THE EXISTENCE OF UNCOUNTABLY MANY MATROIDAL FAMILIES. DISCRETE MATHEMATICS 27, 93-97. (1979).

SCHMD 1979 -2 SCHMIDT, R.
ZYKLISCHE ORIENTIERUNGEN ENDLICHER BEWERTETER GRAPHEN. MONATSHEFTE FUER MATHEMATIK 88, 253-263. (1979).

SCHME 1978 -1 SCHMITZ, P.; SCHOENLEIN, A.
LINEARE UND LINEARISIERBARE OPTIMIERUNGSMODELLE SOWIE IHRE ADV-GESTUETZTE LOESUNG. BRAUNSCHWEIG: VIEWEG, 339 P. (1978). (STUDIENBUECHER INFORMATIK)

SCHN 1978 -1 SCHNIEDERJANS, M. J.; KWAK, N. K.
SIMULATED TRANSPORTATION PROBLEM FOR IMPROVED OPERATIONAL PLANNING: AN APPLICATION IN THE TRUCKING INDUSTRY, A. COMPUTERS AND OPERATIONS RESEARCH 5, 149-156. (1978).

SCHNA 1976 -1 SCHNORR, C. P.
NETWORK COMPLEXITY AND THE BREADTH OF BOOLEAN FUNCTIONS, THE. FRANKFURT: UNIV. FRANKFURT, FACHBEREICH MATHEMATIK, 14 P. (1976).

SCHNA 1978 -1 SCHNORR, C. P.
ALGORITHM FOR TRANSITIVE CLOSURE WITH LINEAR EXPECTED TIME, AN. SIAM JOURNAL ON COMPUTING 7, 127-133. (1978).

SCHNA 1978 -2 SCHNORR, C. P.
MULTITERMINAL NETWORK FLOW AND CONNECTIVITY IN UNSYMMETRICAL NETWORKS. IN: G. AUSIELLO, C. BOEHM (EDS.): AUTOMATA, LANGUAGES AND PROGRAMMING, 425-439. NEW YORK: SPRINGER. (1978).

SCHNA 1979 -1 SCHNORR, C. P.
BOTTLENECKS AND EDGE CONNECTIVITY IN UNSYMMETRICAL NETWORKS. SIAM JOURNAL ON COMPUTING 8, 265-274. (1979).

SCHO 1978 -1 SCHOCH, M.
ERWEITERUNGSPRINZIP UND SEINE ANWENDUNG ZUR ENTWICKLUNG VON ALGORITHMEN FUER DIE LOESUNG KOMBINATORISCHER OPTIMIERUNGSAUFGABEN, DAS. MATHEMATISCHE OPERATIONSFORSCHUNG UND STATISTIK 9, 356-421. (1978).

SCHO 1979 -1 SCHOCH, M.
NEUERE ERGEBNISSE IN DER DISKRETEN OPTIMIERUNG. IN: K. LOMMATZSCH (ED.): FORTSCHRITTE IN DER MATHEMATISCHEN OPTIMIERUNG, TAGUNG BERLIN 1978, 95-107. SEMINARBERICHT NR. 15, SEKTION MATHEMATIK DER HUMBOLDT-UNIV. BERLIN. (1979).

SCHOA 1978 -1 SCHOCH, M.; LYSKA, W.
KOMBINATORISCHE ALGORITHMEN ZUR LOESUNG SPEZIELLER NICHTLINEARER 0-1 OPTIMIERUNGSAUFGABEN. MATHEMATISCHE OPERATIONSFORSCHUNG UND STATISTIK 9, SERIES OPTIMIZATION, 9-20. (1978).

SCHOA 1978 -2 SCHOCH, M.; LYSKA, W.
WEITERER KOMBINATORISCHER ALGORITHMUS FUER 0-1-OPTIMIERUNGSAUFGABEN, EIN. MATHEMATISCHE OPERATIONSFORSCHUNG UND STATISTIK 9, SERIES OPTIMIZATION, 307-320. (1978).

SCHOB 1977 -1 SCHOLZ, K.
ON SCHEDULING MULTI-PROCESSOR SYSTEMS WITH ALGEBRAICAL OBJECTIVES. REPORT 77-15. KOELN: UNIV. KOELN, MATHEMATISCHES INSTITUT, 22 P. (1977).

SCHR 1981 -1 SCHRADER, R.
APPROXIMATIONS TO CLUSTERING AND SUBGRAPH PROBLEMS ON TREES. RESEARCH REPORT NO. 81202-OR. BONN: UNIV. BONN, INSTITUT FUER OEKONOMETRIE UND OPERATIONS RESEARCH, ABT. OPERATIONS RESEARCH, 14 P. (1981).

SCHR 1981 -2 SCHRADER, R.
NOTE ON APPROXIMATION ALGORITHMS FOR GRAPH PARTITIONING PROBLEMS, A. RESEARCH REPORT WP 81187-OR. BONN: UNIV. BONN, INST. FUER OEKONOMETRIE UND OPERATIONS RESEARCH, ABT. OPERATIONS RESEARCH, 5 P. (1981).

SCHRA 1970 -1 SCHRAGE, L. E.
BOUND BASED ON THE EQUIVALENCE OF MIN-MAX-COMPLETION TIME AND MIN-MAX-LATENESS SCHEDULING OBJECTIVES, A. REPORT 7042. CHICAGO: UNIVERSITY OF CHICAGO, DEPARTMENT OF ECONOMICS AND GRADUATE SCHOOL OF BUSINESS. (1970).

SCHRB 1978 -1 SCHRAGE, L. E.; BAKER, K. R.
DYNAMIC PROGRAMMING SOLUTION OF SEQUENCING PROBLEMS WITH PRECEDENCE CONSTRAINTS. OPERATIONS RESEARCH 26, 444-449. (1978).

SCHRC 1980 -1 SCHREUDER, J. A. M.
CONSTRUCTING TIMETABLES FOR SPORT COMPETITIONS. MATHEMATICAL PROGRAMMING STUDY 13, 58-67. (1980).

SCHRC 1981 -1 SCHREUDER, J. A. M.
APPLICATION OF A LOCATION MODEL TO FIRE STATIONS IN ROTTERDAM. EUROPEAN JOURNAL OF OPERATIONAL RESEARCH 6, 212-219. (1981).

SCHRD 1978 -1 SCHRIJVER, A.
LINKING OF MATROIDS BY LINKING SYSTEMS, THE. IN: A. HAJNAL, V. T. SOS (EDS.): COMBINATORICS, VOLUME II, 973-982. COLLOQUIA MATHEMATICA SOCIETATIS JANOS BOLYAI 18. AMSTERDAM: NORTH-HOLLAND. (1978).

SCHRD 1978 -2 SCHRIJVER, A.
ON THE STRUCTURE OF DELTOIDS. IN: J.-C. BERMOND ET AL. (EDS.): PROBLEMES COMBINATOIRES ET THEORIE DES GRAPHES. COLLOQUES INTERNATIONAUX DU CENTRE NATIONAL DE LA RECHERCHE SCIENTIFIQUE, ORSAY 1976, 379-380. PARIS: CENTRE NATIONAL DE LA RECHERCHE SCIENTIFIQUE. (1978).

SCHRD 1978 -3 SCHRIJVER, A.
VERTEX-CRITICAL SUBGRAPHS OF KNESER GRAPHS. NIEUW ARCHIEF VOOR WISKUNDE, III. SERIE 26, 454-461. (1978).

SCHRD 1979 -1 SCHRIJVER, A.
FRACTIONAL PACKING AND COVERING. IN: A. SCHRIJVER (ED.): PACKING AND COVERING IN COMBINATORICS, 201-274. MATHEMATICAL CENTRE TRACTS 106. AMSTERDAM: MATHEMATISCH CENTRUM. (1979).
SCHRD 1979 -2 SCHRIJVER, A.
MATROIDS AND LINKING SYSTEMS. JOURNAL OF COMBINATORIAL THEORY 26, SERIES B, 349-369. (1979).
SCHRD 1980 -1 SCHRIJVER, A.
COUNTEREXAMPLE TO A CONJECTURE OF EDMONDS AND GILES, A. DISCRETE MATHEMATICS 32, 213-214. (1980).
SCHRD 1980 -2 SCHRIJVER, A.
MIN-MAX RELATIONS FOR DIRECTED GRAPHS. WORKING PAPER. AMSTERDAM: UNIV. VAN AMSTERDAM, INSTITUUT FOOR ACTURARIAAT EN ECONOMETRIE, 24 P. (1980). <
SCHRD 1980 -3 SCHRIJVER, A.
ON CUTTING PLANES. IN: M. DEZA, I. G. ROSENBERG (EDS.): COMBINATORICS 79, PART II, 291-296. ANNALS OF DISCRETE MATHEMATICS 9. AMSTERDAM: NORTH-HOLLAND. (1980).
SCHRE 1979 -1 SCHRIJVER, A.; SEYMOUR, P. D.
SOLUTION OF TWO FRACTIONAL PACKING PROBLEMS OF LOVASZ. DISCRETE MATHEMATICS 26, 177-184. (1979).
SCHRF 1978 -1 SCHROECK, W.
KONSTRUKTION KOSTENOPTIMALER ZERLEGUNGEN VON GRAPHEN. INTERNER BERICHT NR. II/6. BONN: UNIV. BONN, INSTITUT FUER INFORMATIK, 110 P. (1978).
SCHRG 1979 -1 SCHRUBEN, L. W.
ASSIGNMENT OF PRIMARY RESPONSE ZONES TO EMERGENCY MEDICAL UNITS. AIIE TRANSACTIONS 11, 30-36. (1979).
SCHU 1979 -1 SCHULTZ, H. K.
PRACTICAL METHOD FOR VEHICLE SCHEDULING, A. INTERFACES 9, NO. 3, 13-19. (1979).
SCHUA 1979 -1 SCHUTT, J. H.
MIXED INTEGER LINEAR PROGRAMMING FORMULATIONS FOR DISTRIBUTION NETWORKS. MILWAUKEE (ORSA/ TIMS MEETING, OCTOBER 1979) 20 P. (1979).
SCOT 1979 -1 SCOTT, C. H.; JEFFERSON, T. R.; KERDVONBUNDIT, P.
GEOMETRIC PROGRAMMING DUALITY APPLIED TO THE RESOURCE ALLOCATION PROBLEM. INFOR 17, 133-137. (1979).
SCOTA 1980 -1 SCOTT, J. L.
HEURISTIC ALGORITHM FOR EXAMINATION TIMETABLING, A. NEW ZEALAND OPERATIONAL RESEARCH 8, 103-108. (1980).
SCUL 1979 -1 SCULLI, D.
DYNAMIC ASPECTS OF LINE BALANCING. OMEGA 7, 557-561. (1979).
SEDI 1970 -1 SEDIKH, L. G.
ALGORITHM FOR THE SOLUTION OF QUADRATIC INTEGER PROGRAMS (RUSSIAN), AN. PRIMENENIE METODOV VYCISLITEL'NOI MATEMATIKI I EVM V TEHNIKO-EKONOMICESKIH RASCETAH, NO. 2, 87-93. (1970).
SEEL 1978 -1 SEELAENDER, J.
EINIGE BEMERKUNGEN ZUR BESTIMMUNG DES SCHNITTRANGS IN DER GANZZAHLIGEN LINEAREN OPTIMIERUNG. MATHEMATISCHE OPERATIONSFORSCHUNG UND STATISTIK 9, 321-334. (1978).
SEEL 1980 -1 SEELAENDER, J.
EINIGE BEMERKUNGEN ZUR BESTIMMUNG VON STABILITAETSBEREICHEN IN DER REIN GANZZAHLIGEN LINEAREN OPTIMIERUNG. MATHEMATISCHE OPERATIONSFORSCHUNG UND STATISTIK, SERIES OPTIMIZATION 11, 261-272. (1980).
SEEL 1980 -2 SEELAENDER, J.
UEBER DIE BESTIMMUNG VON STABILITAETSBEREICHEN BEI SPEZIELLEN GEMISCHT-GANZZAHLIGEN LINEAREN OPTIMIERUNGSPROBLEMEN. MATHEMATISCHE OPERATIONSFORSCHUNG UND STATISTIK, SERIES OPTIMIZATION 11, 447-454. (1980).
SEEL 1980 -3 SEELAENDER, J.
ZUR EXISTENZ VON GITTER- UND HALBGITTERPUNKTEN IN BESTIMMTEN POLYEDRISCHEN MENGEN. WISSENSCHAFTLICHE ZEITSCHRIFT DER TECHNISCHEN HOCHSCHULE LEUNA-MERSEBURG 22, NO. 1, 91-100. (1980).
SEELA 1979 -1 SEELING, R.
ZEIT-KOSTEN-OPTIMIERUNG VON NETZPLAENEN. BAUTECHNIK 56, 133-141. (1979).
SEID 1978 -1 SEIDMAN, S. B.; FOSTER, B. L.
GRAPH-THEORETIC GENERALIZATION OF THE CLIQUE CONCEPT, A. JOURNAL OF MATHEMATICS AND SOCIOLOGY 6, 139-154. (1978).
SEKI 1979 -1 SEKIGUCHI, Y.
SYNTHETICAL ANALYSIS OF ENUMERATIVE ALGORITHMS. HOKKAIDO: HOKKAIDO UNIV., DEPT. OF BUSINESS ADMINISTRATION, 32 P. (1979).
SEKI 1981 -1 SEKIGUCHI, Y.
UNIFYING FRAMEWORK OF COMBINATORIAL OPTIMIZATION ALGORITHMS: TREE PROGRAMMING AND ITS VALIDITY, A. JOURNAL OF THE OPERATIONS RESEARCH SOCIETY OF JAPAN 24, 67-94. (1981).
SELK 1978 -1 SELKOW, S. M.
NEW BOUNDS FOR THE CLIQUE NUMBER OF A GRAPH. INFORMATION PROCESSING LETTERS 7, 173-174. (1978).
SEN 1972 -1 SEN, S.
MULTICOMMODITY CONCAVE COST MINIMIZATION PROBLEM FOR COMMUNICATION NETWORKS, A. ORC 72-5. BERKELEY: UNIVERSITY OF CALIFORNIA, OPERATIONS RESEARCH CENTER. (1972).
SEN A 1980 -1 SEN, S. K.
NONNEGATIVE INTEGRAL SOLUTION OF LINEAR EQUATIONS. PROCEEDINGS OF THE INDIAN ACADEMY OF SCIENCES, SECTION A, MATHEMATICAL SCIENCES (BANGALORE) 89, 25-33. (1980).
SEND 1978 -1 SENDEROV, I. B.
MODIFIZIERUNG EINES ZUFAELLIGEN SUCHALGORITHMUS FUER DIE LOESUNG VON PROBLEMEN DER DISKRETEN PROGRAMMIERUNG (RUSSIAN), EINE. IZVESTIJA AKADEMII NAUK SSSR. TEHNICESKAJA KIBERNETIKA, NO. 4, 203-205. (1978).
SENG 1979 -1 SENGUPTA, A.; PALIT, A.
ON CLIQUE GENERATION USING BOOLEAN EQUATIONS. PROCEEDINGS OF THE INSTITUTION OF ELECTRICAL ENGINEERS. ELECTRONICS, POWER, CONTROL & SCIENCE 67, 178-180. (1979).
SENO 1977 -1 SENO, A.; FUKUNAGA, K.; KASAI, T.
ALGORITHM FOR GRAPH ISOMORPHISM, AN. BULLETIN OF THE UNIVERSITY OF OSAKA PREFECTURE, SERIES A 26, NO. 2, 61-74. (1977).
SERD 1978 -1 SERDYUKOV, A. I.
SUR QUELQUES CHEMINS EXTREMAUX DANS LES GRAPHES (RUSSIAN). UPRAVLJAEMYE SISTEMY, NO. 17, 76-79. (1978).
SERD 1978 -2 SERDYUKOV, A. I.
TRAVELING SALESMAN PROBLEM IN THE PRESENCE OF EXCLUSIONS (RUSSIAN), THE. UPRAVLJAEMYE SISTEMY, NO. 17, 80-86 + 89. (1978).
SERE 1975 -1 SEREK, M.; ZAVIACIC, V.
USE OF DISCRETE LINEAR PROGRAMMING IN THE SOLUTION OF THE PROBLEM OF PURITY OF SURFACE WATERS, THE. SBORNIK VYSOKEHO UCENI TECHNICKEHO V BRNE, NO. 1-4, 159-166. (1975).

SERG 1980 -1 SERGIENKO, I. V.; BIKOV, V. M.
METHOD FOR SOLVING A GENERALIZED KNAPSACK PROBLEM USING PARALLEL COMPUTATIONS (RUSSIAN), A. DOKLADY AKADEMIJA NAUK UKRANSKOI SSR. SERIJA A (KIEV) NO. 7, 84-87. (1980).
SERGA 1980 -1 SERGIENKO, I. V.; LEBEDEVA, T. T.; ROSHCHIN, V. A.
APPROXIMATE METHODS FOR THE SOLUTION OF DISCRETE OPTIMIZATION PROBLEMS (RUSSIAN). AKADEMIJA NAUK UKRAINSKOI SSR, ORDENA LENINA INSTITUT KIBERNETIKI. KIEV: NAUKOVA DUMKA. 274 P. (1980).
SERO 1978 -1 SEROV, S. S.
DECOMPOSITION METHOD FOR NETWORK FLOW PROBLEMS. AVTOMATIKA I TELEMEHANIKA, NO. 11, 138-148; TRANSLATED AS AUTOMATION AND REMOTE CONTROL 39, 1978, 1692-1700. (1978).
SERV 1975 -1 SERVIT, M.
HEURISTIC METHOD FOR SOLVING WEIGHTED SET COVERING PROBLEMS, A. DIGITAL PROCESSES (SWITZERLAND) 1, 177-182. (1975).
SESH 1980 -1 SESHAN, C. R.; ACHARY, K. K.
BRANCH AND BOUND ALGORITHM FOR A TRANSPORTATION TYPE PROBLEM WITH PIECEWISE LINEAR CONVEX OBJECTIVE FUNCTION, A. ZEITSCHRIFT FUER ANGEWANDTE MATHEMATIK UND MECHANIK 60, 303-308. (1980).
SESHA 1980 -1 SESHAN, C. R.; TIKEKAR, V. G.
ALGORITHMS FOR INTEGER FRACTIONAL PROGRAMMING. JOURNAL OF THE INDIAN INSTITUTE OF SCIENCE (BANGALORE) 62, NO. 2, 9-16. (1980).
SESHA 1980 -2 SESHAN, C. R.; TIKEKAR, V. G.
ON SHARMA-SWARUP ALGORITHM FOR TIME MINIMIZING TRANSPORTATION PROBLEMS. PROCEEDINGS OF THE INDIAN ACADEMY OF SCIENCES, SECTION A, MATHEMATICAL SCIENCES (BANGALORE) 89, NO. 2, 101-102. (1980).
SETH 1977 -1 SETHI, R.
ON THE COMPLEXITY OF MEAN FLOW TIME SCHEDULING. MATHEMATICS OF OPERATIONS RESEARCH 2, 320-330. (1977).
SEVA 1978 -1 SEVASTYANOV, S. V.
ON APPROXIMATE SOLUTION OF SCHEDULING PROBLEMS (RUSSIAN). METODY DISCRET. ANALYZA V SYNT. UPRAV. SYSTEM 32, 66-75. (1978).
SEVC 1975 -1 SEVCENKO, V. N.
SOLUTION OF THE ELEMENTARY INTEGER LINEAR PROGRAMMING PROBLEM (RUSSIAN), THE. UPRAVLJAEMYE SYSTEMY 14, 69-73 + 76-77. (1975).
SEWA 1978 -1 SEWARD, S. M.; PLANE, D. R.; HENDRICK, T. E.
MUNICIPAL RESOURCE ALLOCATION: MINIMIZING THE COST OF FIRE PROTECTION. MANAGEMENT SCIENCE 24, 1740-1748. (1978).
SEXT 1978 -1 SEXTON, T. R.
MULTI-VEHICLE SUBSCRIPTION PROBLEM: A HEURISTIC ALGORITHM, THE. STONY BROOK: STATE UNIV. OF NEW YORK, URBAN AND POLICY SCIENCES, 35 P. (1978).
SEXTA 1979 -1 SEXTON, T. R.; BODIN, L. D.
SINGLE VEHICLE MANY TO MANY ROUTING AND SCHEDULING PROBLEM WITH DESIRED DELIVERY TIMES, THE. STONY BROOK: STATE UNIV. OF NEW YORK, 61 P. (1979).
SEYM 1978 -1 SEYMOUR, P. D.
MATROIDS REPRESENTABLE OVER GF(3), THE. IN: J.-C. BERMOND ET AL. (EDS.): PROBLEMES COMBINATOIRES ET THEORIE DES GRAPHES, COLLOQUES INTERNATIONAUX DU CENTRE NATIONAL DE LA RECHERCHE SCIENTIFIQUE, ORSAY 1976, 381-383. PARIS: CENTRE NATIONAL DE LA RECHERCHE SCIENTIFIQUE. (1978).
SEYM 1978 -2 SEYMOUR, P. D.
TWO-COMMODITY CUT THEOREM, A. DISCRETE MATHEMATICS 23, 177-183. (1978).
SEYM 1979 -1 SEYMOUR, P. D.
MATROID REPRESENTATION OVER GF(3). JOURNAL OF COMBINATORIAL THEORY 26, SERIES B, 159-173. (1979).
SEYM 1979 -2 SEYMOUR, P. D.
ON MULTI-COLOURINGS OF CUBIC GRAPHS, AND CONJECTURES OF FULKERSON AND TUTTE. PROCEEDINGS OF THE LONDON MATHEMATICAL SOCIETY 38, 423-460. (1979).
SEYM 1979 -3 SEYMOUR, P. D.
ON ODD CUTS AND PLANE MULTICOMMODITY FLOWS. WORKING PAPER. OXFORD: MERTON COLLEGE, 28 P. (1979).
SEYM 1979 -4 SEYMOUR, P. D.
SHORT PROOF OF THE TWO-COMMODITY FLOW THEOREM, A. JOURNAL OF COMBINATORIAL THEORY 26, SERIES B, 370-371. (1979).
SEYM 1979 -5 SEYMOUR, P. D.
SUMS OF CIRCUITS. IN: J. A. BONDY, U. P. R. MURTY (EDS.): GRAPH THEORY AND RELATED TOPICS, 341-355. NEW YORK, SAN FRANCISCO, LONDON: ACADEMIC PRESS. (1979).
SEYM 1980 -1 SEYMOUR, P. D.
DECOMPOSITION OF REGULAR MATROIDS. JOURNAL OF COMBINATORIAL THEORY 28, SERIES B, 305-359. (1980).
SEYM 1980 -2 SEYMOUR, P. D.
DISJOINT PATHS IN GRAPHS. DISCRETE MATHEMATICS 29, 293-309. (1980).
SEYM 1980 -3 SEYMOUR, P. D.
FOUR-TERMINUS FLOWS. NETWORKS 10, 79-86. (1980).
SEYM 1980 -4 SEYMOUR, P. D.
ON TUTTE'S CHARACTERIZATION OF GRAPHIC MATROIDS. IN: M. DEZA, I. G. ROSENBERG (EDS.): COMBINATORICS 79, PART I, 83-90. ANNALS OF DISCRETE MATHEMATICS 8. AMSTERDAM: NORTH-HOLLAND. (1980).
SEYM 1980 -5 SEYMOUR, P. D.
PACKING AND COVERING WITH MATROID CIRCUITS. JOURNAL OF COMBINATORIAL THEORY 28, SERIES B, 237-242. (1980).
SEYM 1981 -1 SEYMOUR, P. D.
SOME APPLICATIONS OF MATROID DECOMPOSITION. IN: L. LOVASZ, V. T. SOS (EDS.): ALGEBRAIC METHODS IN GRAPH THEORY, VOL. II, 713-726. COLLOQUIA MATHEMATICA SOCIETATIS JANOS BOLYAI 25. AMSTERDAM, OXFORD,NEW YORK: NORTH-HOLLAND. (1981).
SEYMA 1978 -1 SEYMOUR, P. D.; WELSH, D. J. A.
PERCOLATION PROBABILITIES ON THE SQUARE LATTICE. IN: B. BOLLOBAS (ED.): ADVANCES IN GRAPH THEORY, 227-246. ANNALS OF DISCRETE MATHEMATICS 3. AMSTERDAM: NORTH-HOLLAND. (1978).
SGUR 1977 -1 SGUREV, V. S.; VASILEV, V. S.
DECOMPOSITION METHOD FOR THE SOLUTION OF A CLASS OF INTEGER PROGRAMMING PROBLEMS (BULGARIAN), A. PROBLEMI NA TEHNICESKATA KIBERNETIKA 6, 12-18. (1977).
SGUR 1978 -1 SGUREV, V. S.; VASILEV, V. S.
OPTIMIZATION OF A CLOSED TRANSPORT SYSTEM (BULGARIAN). PROBLEMI NA TEHNICESKATA KIBERNETIKA 8, 3-11. (1978).
SGUR 1980 -1 SGUREV, V. S.; VASILEV, V. S.
OPTIMIZATION OF A CLOSED DYNAMIC TRANSPORTATION SYSTEM WITH LIMITED CAPACITY (BULGARIAN). PROBLEMI NA TEHNICESKATA KIBERNETIKA (SOFIA) 10, 16-23. (1980).

SHAF 1978 -1 SHAFTEL, T. L.
COMPUTATIONAL EXPERIENCE ON AN ALGORITHM FOR THE TRANSPORTATION PROBLEM WITH NON-LINEAR OBJECTIVE FUNCTIONS. QUEEN'S UNIVERSITY, SCHOOL OF BUSINESS WORKING PAPER 78-18. KINGSTON: QUEEN'S UNIVERSITY, 28 P. (1978).

SHAH 1981 -1 SHAH, A. R.
OPTIMAL ASSIGNMENT OF MEDICAL GRADUATES TO PRE-REGISTRATION JOBS, AN. EUROPEAN JOURNAL OF OPERATIONAL RESEARCH 6, 393-398. (1981).

SHAK 1978 -1 SHAKHBASJAN, K. V.
STRUCTURAL SOLUTIONS IN PROBLEMS OF SCHEDULING THEORY (RUSSIAN). IN: V. N. KUBLANOVSKAJA, T. N. SMIRNOVA (EDS.): NUMERICAL METHODS AND QUESTIONS IN THE ORGANIZATION OF CALCULATIONS (RUSSIAN), 239-248 + 270. LENINGRAD: IZDAT. "NAUKA". (1978).

SHAK 1979 -1 SHAKHBASJAN, K. V.
ORDERING OF A STRUCTURAL SET OF TASKS MINIMIZING THE TOTAL PENALTY (RUSSIAN), THE. IN: NUMERICAL METHODS AND QUESTIONS IN THE ORGANIZATION OF CALCULATIONS. 3. ZAPISKI NAUCNYH SEMINAROV LENINGRADSKOGO OTDELENIJA MATEMATICESKOGO INSTITUTA IM. V. A. STEKLOVA AKADEMII NAUK SSSR (LOMI) (LENINGRAD) 90, 229-264, 302. (1979).

SHAKA 1977 -1 SHAKHBASJAN, K. V.; LEBEDINSKAJA, N. B.
MINIMIZATION OF THE TOTAL PENALTY IN THE PROBLEM OF THE PARALLEL ORDERING OF N INDEPENDENT TASKS (RUSSIAN). DOKADLY AKADEMII NAUK SSSR 237, 790-792. (1977).

SHAKA 1977 -2 SHAKHBASJAN, K. V.; LEBEDINSKAJA, N. B.
OPTIMAL SCHEDULINGS WITH GAPS FOR INDEPENDENT TASKS IN A QUEUEING SYSTEM WITH N SERVERS (RUSSIAN). ZAPISKI NAUCNYH SEMINAROV LENINGRADSKOGO OTDELENIJA MATEMATICESKOGO INSTITUTA IM. V. A. STEKLOVA AKADEMII NAUK SSSR (LOMI) 70, 205-231. (1977).

SHAM 1979 -1 SHAMIR, A.
LINEAR TIME ALGORITHM FOR FINDING MINIMUM CUTSETS IN REDUCIBLE GRAPHS, A. SIAM JOURNAL ON COMPUTING 8, 645-655. (1979).

SHAN 1949 -1 SHANNON, C. E.
THEOREM ON COLORING THE LINES OF A NETWORK, A. JOURNAL OF MATHEMATICAL PHYSICS 28, 148-151. (1949).

SHAP 1979 -1 SHAPIRO, B. I.
PROBLEME D'ALLOCATION DES RESSOURCES DANS LES CONDITIONS D'ORGANISATION DE PROJETS ET SA METHODE DE RESOLUTION NUMERIQUE (RUSSIAN). AVTOMATIKA I TELEMEHANIKA, NO. 3, 96-106. (1979).

SHAPA 1978 -1 SHAPIRO, J. F.
FUTURE DIRECTIONS OF LARGE SCALE MIXED INTEGER PROGRAMMING. WORKING PAPER OR 081-78. CAMBRIDGE: MASS. INSTITUTE OF TECHNOLOGY, OPERATIONS RESEARCH CENTER, 10 P. (1978).

SHAPA 1979 -1 SHAPIRO, J. F.
SURVEY OF LAGRANGIAN TECHNIQUES FOR DISCRETE OPTIMIZATION, A. IN: P. L. HAMMER, E. L. JOHNSON, B. H. KORTE (EDS.): DISCRETE OPTIMIZATION II, 113-138. ANNALS OF DISCRETE MATHEMATICS 5, AMSTERDAM, NEW YORK, OXFORD: NORTH-HOLLAND. (1979).

SHAPB 1980 -1 SHAPIRO, R. D.
SCHEDULING COUPLED TASKS. NAVAL RESEARCH LOGISTICS QUARTERLY 27, 489-498. (1980).

SHAR 1978 -1 SHARMA, J. K.
EXTENSIONS AND SPECIAL CASES OF TRANSPORTATION PROBLEM: A SURVEY. INDIAN JOURNAL OF PURE AND APPLIED MATHEMATICS 9, 928-940. (1978).

SHAR 1978 -2 SHARMA, J. K.
NOTE ON THE TIME MINIMIZING SOLID TRANSPORTATION PROBLEM, A. PURE AND APPLIED MATHEMATIKA SCIENCES 7, 41-42. (1978).

SHARA 1980 -1 SHARMA, J. K.; SHARMA, M. M.
ON MIXED INTEGER SOLUTIONS TO GOAL PROGRAMMING PROBLEMS. INDIAN JOURNAL OF PURE AND APPLIED MATHEMATICS 11, 314-320. (1980).

SHARB 1977 -1 SHARMA, J. K.; SWARUP, K.
TIME MINIMIZING TRANSPORTATION PROBLEMS. PROCEEDINGS OF THE INDIAN ACADEMY OF SCIENCES. SECTION A 86, NO. 6, 513-518. (1977).

SHARC 1970 -1 SHARP, J. F.; SNYDER, J. C.; GREENE, J. H.
DECOMPOSITION ALGORITHM FOR SOLVING THE MULTIFACILITY PRODUCTION-TRANSPORTATION PROBLEM WITH NONLINEAR PRODUCTION COSTS, A. ECONOMETRICA 19, 490-506. (1970).

SHCH 1976 -1 SHCHERBINA, O. A.
OPTIMAL PARTITIONING INTO BLOCKS OF A QUASIBLOCK PROBLEM OF BOOLEAN PROGRAMMING (RUSSIAN). IN: A COLLECTION OF PAPERS ON MATHEMATICAL CYBERNETICS (RUSSIAN), NO. 1, 81-89. MOSCOW: VYCISL. CENTR. AKAD. NAUK SSSR. (1976).

SHCH 1980 -1 SHCHERBINA, O. A.
SUR UN ALGORITHME LOCAL POUR LES PROBLEMES D'OPTIMISATION A VALEURS ENTIERES (RUSSIAN). ZURNAL VYCISLITELNOI MATEMATIKI I MATEMATICESKOI FIZIKI (MOSCOW) 20, 802-804; TRANSLATED AS USSR COMPUTATIONAL MATHEMATICS AND MATHEMATICAL PHYSICS. (1980).

SHEE 1977 -1 SHEE, S. C.
TABULAR ALGORITHMS FOR THE SHORTEST PATH AND LONGEST PATH. NANTA MATHEMATICA 10, NO. 2, 100-105. (1977).

SHEF 1979 -1 SHEFFI, Y.; DAGANZO, C. F.
ALGORITHM FOR NETWORK EQUILIBRATION WITH MULTINOMIAL PROBIT MODELS, AN. DRAFT. CAMBRIDGE: MASSACHUSETTS INST. OF TECHNOLOGY, CIVIL ENGINEERING DEPARTMENT, 33 P. (1979).

SHEI 1978 -1 SHEINMAN, O. K.
DUALITY IN SOME DISCRETE MINIMIZATION PROBLEMS. USPEHI MATEMATICESKIH NAUK (MOSCOW) 33, NO. 2, 211; TRANSLATED AS RUSSIAN MATHEMATICAL SURVEYS 33, NO. 2, 251-252. (1978).

SHEI 1979 -1 SHEINMAN, O. K.
GROUP-THEORETIC METHODS OF CONSTRUCTING CUTS IN INTEGER PROGRAMMING (RUSSIAN). MATEMATICHESKIE METODY RESHENIYA EHKONOMICHESKIKH ZADACH (MOSCOW), NO. 8, 44-49. MOSCOW: NAUKA. (1979).

SHEI 1980 -1 SHEINMAN, O. K.
DUALITY AND SUBADDITIVE FUNCTIONS IN INTEGER PROGRAMMING (RUSSIAN). EKONOMIKA I MATEMATICESKIE METODY 16, 808-810. (1980).

SHEN 1978 -1 SHENDEROV, I. B.
MODIFICATION OF RANDOM SEARCH FOR THE SOLUTION OF DISCRETE OPTIMIZATION PROBLEMS (RUSSIAN). IZVESTIJA AKADEMII NAUK SSSR. TEHNICESKAJA KIBERNETIKA, NO. 4, 203-205. (1978).

SHEP 1980 -1 SHEPARDSON, F.; MARSTEN, R. E.
LAGRANGEAN RELAXATION ALGORITHM FOR THE TWO DUTY PERIOD SCHEDULING PROBLEM, A. MANAGEMENT SCIENCE 26, 274-281. (1980).

SHEPA 1979 -1 SHEPHERD, R. A.; HIRSHFIELD, D. S.
SOFTWARE SUPPORT FOR COMBINATORIAL OPTIMIZATION. WORKING PAPER. ARLINGTON: KETRON INC., 15 P. (1979).

SHER 1978 -1 SHERALI, H. D.; SHETTY, C. M.
PRIMAL SIMPLEX BASED SOLUTION PROCEDURE FOR THE RECTILINEAR DISTANCE MULTIFACILITY LOCATION PROBLEM, A. THE JOURNAL OF THE OPERATIONAL RESEARCH SOCIETY 29, 373-381. (1978).

SHER 1979 -1 SHERALI, H. D.; SHETTY, C. M.
DISJUNCTIVE PROGRAMMING, POLYHEDRAL ANNEXATION TECHNIQUES AND NONDOMINATED DISJUNCTIVE CUTTING PLANES. INDUSTRIAL AND SYSTEMS ENGINEERING SERIES J-79-28. ATLANTA: GEORGIA INST. OF TECHNOLOGY, INDUSTRIAL AND SYSTEMS ENGINEERING, 26 P. (1979).

SHER 1980 -1 SHERALI, H. D.; SHETTY, C. M.
FINITELY CONVERGENT PROCEDURE FOR FACIAL DISJUNCTIVE PROGRAMS, A. REPORT SERIES J-80-19. ATLANTA: GEORGIA INST. OF TECHNOLOGY, SCHOOL OF INDUSTRIAL AND SYSTEMS ENGINEERING, 23 P. (1980).

SHER 1980 -2 SHERALI, H. D.; SHETTY, C. M.
ON THE GENERATION OF DEEP DISJUNCTIVE CUTTING PLANES. NAVAL RESEARCH LOGISTICS QUARTERLY 27, 453-476. (1980).

SHER 1980 -3 SHERALI, H. D.; SHETTY, C. M.
OPTIMIZATION WITH DISJUNCTIVE CONSTRAINTS. BERLIN, HEIDELBERG, NEW YORK: SPRINGER, 156 P. (1980). (LECTURE NOTES IN ECONOMICS AND MATHEMATICAL SYSTEMS, 181)

SHERA 1978 -1 SHERMAN, A. I.
ALGORITHM FOR THE APPROXIMATE SOLUTION OF INTEGER LINEAR PROGRAMMING PROBLEMS (RUSSIAN), AN. IN: P. COI (ED.): MATHEMATICAL METHODS AND COMPUTER SCIENCE IN MINING (RUSSIAN), 142-168 + 227. ALMA-ATA: IZDAT "NAUKA" KAZAH. SSR. (1978).

SHET 1980 -1 SHETTY, C. M.; SHERALI, H. D.
RECTILINEAR DISTANCE LOCATION-ALLOCATION PROBLEM: A SIMPLEX BASED ALGORITHM. IN: A. V. FIACCO, K. O. KORTANEK (EDS.): EXTREMAL METHODS AND SYSTEMS ANALYSIS, 442-465. LECTURE NOTES IN ECONOMICS AND MATHEMATICAL SYSTEMS 174. BERLIN: SPRINGER. (1980).

SHEV 1981 -1 SHEVCHENKO, V. N.
ON THE NUMBER OF EXTREME POINTS IN INTEGRAL PROGRAMMING (RUSSIAN). KIBERNETIKA (KIEV), NO. 2, 133-134; TRANSLATED AS CYBERNETICS. (1981).

SHIE 1979 -1 SHIER, D. R.
ON ALGORITHMS FOR FINDING THE K SHORTEST PATHS IN A NETWORK. NETWORKS 9, 195-214. (1979).

SHIEA 1980 -1 SHIER, D. R.; WITZGALL, C.
ARC TOLERANCES IN SHORTEST PATH AND NETWORK FLOW PROBLEMS. NETWORKS 10, 277-292. (1980).

SHIH 1979 -1 SHIH, WEI
BRANCH AND BOUND METHOD FOR THE MULTICONSTRAINT ZERO-ONE KNAPSACK PROBLEM, A. JOURNAL OF THE OPERATIONAL RESEARCH SOCIETY 30, 369-378. (1979).

SHIL 1979 -1 SHILOACH, Y.
EDGE-DISJOINT BRANCHING IN DIRECTED MULTIGRAPHS. INFORMATION PROCESSING LETTERS 8, 24-27. (1979).

SHIL 1979 -2 SHILOACH, Y.
MINIMUM LINEAR ARRANGEMENT ALGORITHM FOR UNDIRECTED TREES, A. SIAM JOURNAL ON COMPUTING 8, 15-32. (1979).

SHIL 1979 -3 SHILOACH, Y.
MULTI-TERMINAL 0-1 FLOW. SIAM JOURNAL ON COMPUTING 8, 422-430. (1979).

SHIL 1979 -4 SHILOACH, Y.
STRONG LINEAR ORDERINGS OF A DIRECTED NETWORK. INFORMATION PROCESSING LETTERS 8, 146-148. (1979).

SHIL 1980 -1 SHILOACH, Y.
MULTI-TERMINAL MINIMUM CUT ALGORITHM FOR PLANAR GRAPHS, A. SIAM JOURNAL ON COMPUTING 9, 219-224. (1980).

SHIL 1980 -2 SHILOACH, Y.
POLYNOMIAL SOLUTION TO THE UNDIRECTED TWO PATHS PROBLEM, A. JOURNAL OF THE ASSOCIATION FOR COMPUTING MACHINERY 27, 445-456. (1980).

SHIM 1978 -1 SHIMAMOTO, Y.
ON AN EXTENSION OF THE GRINBERG THEOREM. JOURNAL OF COMBINATORIAL THEORY 24, SERIES B, 169-180. (1978).

SHIMA 1978 -1 SHIMSHAK, D. G.; KASLIK, J. A.; BARCLAY, T. D.
EFFECTIVE HEURISTIC FOR VOGELS'S APPROXIMATION METHOD. NEW YORK (TIMS/ORSA MEETING, MAY 1978): 11 P. (1978).

SHIR 1976 -1 SHIRAKAWA, I.
SURVEY OF THE ANALYSIS OF THE COMPLEXITY OF COMBINATORIAL PROBLEMS (JAPANESE), A. SYSTEMS AND CONTROL 20, NO. 8, 395-404. (1976).

SHIRA 1979 -1 SHIRLAND, L. E.; ELLIS, P. M.
OPTIMUM LOCATION OF TRAINING CENTERS. OMEGA 7, 569-573. (1979).

SHLY 1978 -1 SHLYK, V. A.
ON THE FACES OF MASTER GOMORY POLYHEDRA (RUSSIAN). VESCI AKADEMII NAVUK BSSR. SERIJA FIZIKA-MATEMATYCNYH NAVUK, NO. 2, 5-11. (1978).

SHLY 1980 -1 SHLYK, V. A.
PROPERTY OF FACETS OF MASTER GOMORY POLYHEDRA OF CYCLICAL GROUPS (RUSSIAN), A. VESCI AKADEMII NAVUK BSSR. SERYJA FIZIKA-MATEMATYCNYH NAVUK (MINSK), NO. 2, 45-48, 141. (1980).

SHME 1978 -1 SHMELEV, V. V.
SOLVING INTEGER LINEAR PROGRAMMING PROBLEMS BY THE PENALTY FUNCTION METHOD. AVTOMATIKA I TELEMEHANIKA, NO. 11, 149-157; TRANSLATED AS AUTOMATION AND REMOTE CONTROL 39, 1978, 1700-1707. (1978).

SHOC 1979 -1 SHOCK, R. C.
EXACT ALGORITHM FOR THE SMALL SCALE TRAVELLING SALESMAN PROBLEM, AN. TRANSACTIONS OF THE ILLINOIS STATE ACADEMY OF SCIENCE 72, 73-83. (1979).

SHTU 1979 -1 SHTUIKYS, V.
ALGORITHM FOR SOLVING A PARALLEL SEQUENCING PROBLEM (RUSSIAN), AN. TEORIJA OPTIMALNYH RESENII - TRUDY SEMINARA "PROCESSY OPTIMALNOGO UPRAVLENIJA" VI (VILNIUS) SEKCIJA NO. 5, 81-94, 119. (1979).

SHUK 1979 -1 SHUKLA, P. R.; CARLSON, R. C.
ANALYSIS AND SOLUTION OF DISCRETE MULTICRITERION PROBLEMS WITH RANGED TRADEOFFS. TECHNICAL REPORT, 79-4. STANFORD: STANFORD UNIV.M DEPT. OF INDUSTRIAL ENGINEERING AND ENGINEERING MANAGEMENT, 24 P. (1979).

SHVA 1978 -1 SHVARTIN, S. M.
STUDY OF STABILITY OF TRANSPORTATION PROBLEMS (RUSSIAN). ZURNAL VYCISLITEL'NOI MATEMATIKI I MATEMATICESKOI FIZIKI 18, NO. 1, 235-240. (1978).

SIDN 1978 -1 SIDNEY, J. B.
OPTIMAL JOB-SHOP SCHEDULING WITH EARLINESS AND TARDINESS PENALTIES. WORKING PAPER 78-24. OTTAWA: UNIV. OF OTTAWA, FACULTY OF ADMINISTRATION, 7 P. (1978).

SIDN 1979 -1 SIDNEY, J. B.
TWO-MACHINE MAXIMUM FLOW TIME PROBLEM WITH SERIES PARALLEL PRECEDENCE RELATIONS, THE. OPERATIONS RESEARCH 27, 782-791. (1979).

SIEB 1979 -1 SIEBER, N.
PROBLEMS OF OPTIMIZATION IN A NETWORK MODEL. IN: A. PREKOPA (ED.): SURVEY OF MATHEMATICAL PROGRAMMING, VOLUME 2, 295-300. AMSTERDAM: NORTH-HOLLAND. (1979).

SIED 1981 -1 SIEDERSLEBEN, J.
COMBINATORIAL PROBLEMS WITH GERT NETWORKS. IN: R. E. BURKARD, T. ELLINGER (EDS.): METHODS OF OPERATIONS RESEARCH 41, 227-230. KOENIGSTEIN: ANTON HAIN MEISENHEIM. (1981).

SILV 1975 -1 SILVERI, G.
INPUT GENERATOR FOR A MAXIMAL NETWORK FLOW ALGORITHM AND AN APPLICATION TO WATER RESOURCE MANAGEMENT (ITALIAN), AN. QUADERNI, SERIE III, ISTITUTO PER LE APPLICAZIONI DEL CALCOLO "MAURO PICONE", CONSIGLIO NAZIONALE DELLE RICERCHE (ROMA) 12, 49P. (1975).

****

SIME 1978 -1 SIMEONE, B.
ASYMPTOTICALLY EXACT POLYNOMIAL ALGORITHM FOR EQUIPARTITION PROBLEMS, AN. PUBBLICAZIONI SERIE III-N. 153. ROMA: ISTITUTO PER LE APPLICAZIONI DEL CALCOLO, 14 P. (1978).

SIME 1979 -1 SIMEONE, B.
CONIC ALGORITHM FOR THE GROUP MINIMIZATION PROBLEM, A. CAHIERS DU CENTRE D'ETUDES DE RECHERCHE OPERATIONNELLE 21, 337-351. (1979).

SIME 1979 -2 SIMEONE, B.
QUADRATIC 0-1 PROGRAMMING, BOOLEAN FUNCTIONS AND GRAPHS. WATERLOO: UNIV. OF WATERLOO, 303 P. (1979). (DISSERTATION)

SIMM 1979 -1 SIMMONS, G. J.; SLATER, P. J.
GENERALIZED PETERSEN GRAPHS G(N,4) ARE HAMILTONIAN FOR ALL N NOT = 8, THE. IN: F. HOFFMAN, D. MAC CARTHY, R. C. MULLIN, R. G. STANTON (EDS.): PROCEEDINGS OF THE TENTH SOUTHEASTERN CONFERENCE ON COMBINATORICS, GRAPH THEORY AND COMPUTING, 861-872. CONGRESSUS NUMERANTIUM XXIV. WINNIPEG: UTILITAS. (1979).

SIMO 1978 -1 SIMOES-PEREIRA, J. M. S.
COMMENT ON MATROIDAL FAMILIES, A. IN: J.-C. BERMOND ET AL. (EDS.): PROBLEMES COMBINATOIRES ET THEORIE DES GRAPHES, COLLOQUES INTERNATIONAUX DU CENTRE NATIONAL DE LA RECHERCHE SCIENTIFIQUE, ORSAY 1976, 385-387. PARIS: CENTRE NATIONAL DE LA RECHERCHE SCIENTIFIQUE. (1978).

SIMOA 1975 -1 SIMON, J.
ON SOME CENTRAL PROBLEMS IN COMPUTATIONAL COMPLEXITY. ITHACA: CORNELL UNIVERSITY, 139 P. (1975). (DISSERTATION)

SIMOB 1978 -1 SIMONS, B.
FAST ALGORITHM FOR SINGLE PROCESSOR SCHEDULING, A. IN: INSTITUTE OF ELECTRICAL AND ELECTRONICS ENGINEERS (ED.): 19TH ANNUAL SYMPOSIUM ON FOUNDATIONS OF COMPUTER SCIENCE, ANN ARBOR 1978, 246-252. NEW YORK: INSTITUTE OF ELECTRICAL AND ELECTRONICS ENGINEERS. (1978).

SIMOC 1979 -1 SIMOVICI, D. A.; GRIGORAS, G.
EVEN INITIAL FEEDBACK VERTEX SET PROBLEM IS NP-COMPLETE. INFORMATION PROCESSING LETTERS 8, 64-66. (1979).

SIMS 1977 -1 SIMS, J. A.
COMPLETE CLASS OF MATROIDS, A. THE QUARTERLY JOURNAL OF MATHEMATICS , OXFORD, SECOND SERIES 28, 449-451. (1977).

SIMU 1978 -1 SIMUNDICH, T. M.
EFFICIENT ALGORITHM FOR SOLVING A STOCHASTIC, INTEGER PROGRAMMING PROBLEM ARISING IN RADIO NAVIGATION, AN. IN: J. STOER (ED.): OPTIMIZATION TECHNIQUES, PROCEEDINGS OF THE 8TH IFIP CONFERENCE ON OPTIMIZATION TECHNIQUES, WUERZBURG 1977, PART 2, 263-268. LECTURE NOTES IN CONTROL AND INFORMATION SCIENCES 7, BERLIN, HEIDELBERG, NEW YORK: SPRINGER. (1978).

SINC 1979 -1 SINCLAIR, M.
AUGMENTED LAGRANGEAN RELAXATIONS IN GENERAL MIXED INTEGER PROGRAMMING. QUAESTIONES MATHEMATICAE 3, NO. 2, 115-146. (1979).

SING 1979 -1 SINGHAL, K.; NAIR, K. P. K.
NETWORK PLANNING IN PROJECTS SUBJECT TO TECHNOLOGICAL INTERACTIONS AMONG ACTIVITY ALTERNATIVES. INFOR 17, 124-132. (1979).

SINH 1979 -1 SINHA, P.; ZOLTNERS, A. A.
MULTIPLE-CHOICE KNAPSACK PROBLEM, THE. OPERATIONS RESEARCH 27, 503-515. (1979).

SIU 1976 -1 SIU, C. L.
DETERMINISTIC JOB SCHEDULING IN COMPUTING SYSTEMS. IN: PROCEEDINGS OF THE SECOND INTERNATIONAL WORKSHOP, STRESA 1976, 241-254. AMSTERDAM. (1976).

SKUP 1974 -1 SKUPIEN, Z.
HAMILTONIAN CIRCUITS AND PATH COVERINGS OF VERTICES IN GRAPHS. COLLOQUIUM MATHEMATICUM 30, 295-316. (1974).

SKUP 1977 -1 SKUPIEN, Z.
ON EXTENDING PATH SYSTEMS AND (Q, R)-EDGE HAMILTONIAN GRAPHS. BULLETIN DE L'ACADEMIE POLONAISE DES SCIENCES. SERIE DES SCIENCES MATHEMATIQUES, ASTRONOMIQUES ET PHYSIQUES 25, 343-348. (1977).

SKUP 1978 -1 SKUPIEN, Z.
FINDING ALL MAXIMAL PATH FACTORS OF A TREE AND RELATED PROBLEMS. IN: COMBINATORICS, KESZTHELY 1976, COLLOQ. MATH. JANOS BOLYAI 18, 1031-1043. (1978).

SKUP 1979 -1 SKUPIEN, Z.
ON MAXIMAL NON-HAMILTONIAN GRAPHS. ROSTOCKER MATHEMATISCHES KOLLOQUIUM, NO. 11, 97-106. (1979).

SKUPA 1974 -1 SKUPIEN, Z.; WOJDA, A. P.
ON HIGHLY HAMILTONIAN GRAPHS. BULLETIN DE L'ACADEMIE POLONAISE DES SCIENCES 22, 463-471. (1974).

SKUPA 1975 -1 SKUPIEN, Z.; WOJDA, A. P.
EXTREMAL NON-(P, Q)-HAMILTONIAN GRAPHS. STUDIA SCIENTIARUM MATHEMATICARUM HUNGARICA 10, 323-328. (1975).

SKUR 1977 -1 SKURBA, V. V.; BELETSKIJ, S. A.
NUMERICAL METHODS IN THE SOLUTION OF THE ASSEMBLY LINE BALANCING PROBLEM. A SURVEY. KIBERNETIKA, NO. 1, 96-108; TRANSLATED AS CYBERNETICS 13, 1977, 96-108. (1977).

SLAD 1980 -1 SLADKY, K.
BOUNDS ON DISCRETE DYNAMIC PROGRAMMING RECURSION I - MODELS WITH NON-NEGATIVE MATRICES. KYBERNETIKA (PRAGUE) 16, 526-547. (1980).

SLAT 1978 -1 SLATE, L.; SPIELBERG, K.
EXTENDED CONTROL LANGUAGE OF MPSX/370 AND POSSIBLE APPLICATIONS, THE. IBM SYSTEMS JOURNAL 17, NO. 1, 64-81. (1978).

SLATA 1977 -1 SLATER, P. J.
FIBONACCI NUMBERS IN THE COUNT OF SPANNING TREES. THE FIBONACCI QUARTERLY 15, NO. 1, 11-14. (1977).

SLATA 1978 -1 SLATER, P. J.
CENTRAL PATHS IN A GRAPH. SAND78-0809J. ALBUQUERQUE: SANDIA LABORATORIES, 17 P. (1978).

SLATA 1978 -2 SLATER, P. J.
CONSTRUCTIVE CHARACTERIZATION OF TREES WITH AT LEAST K DISJOINT MAXIMUM MATCHINGS, A. JOURNAL OF COMBINATORIAL THEORY 25, SERIES B, 326-338. (1978).

SLEA 1980 -1 SLEATOR, D. D. K. D. B.
2.5 TIMES OPTIMAL ALGORITHM FOR PACKING IN TWO DIMENSIONS, A. INFORMATION PROCESSING LETTERS 10, 37-40. (1980).

SLOM 1977 -1 SLOMINSKI, L.
EFFICIENT APPROACH TO THE BOTTLENECK ASSIGNMENT PROBLEM, AN. BULLETIN DE L'ACADEMIE POLONAISE DES SCIENCES SERIE DES SCIENCES TECHNIQUES 25, NO. 4, 17-23. (1977).

SLOM 1978 -1 SLOMINSKI, L.
BOTTLENECK DISCRETE PROBLEMS. IN: J. KRARUP, ST. WALUKIEWICZ (EDS.): PROCEEDINGS POLISH-DANISH MATHEMATICAL PROGRAMMING SEMINAR, 107-123. PRACE INSTYTUTU BADAN SYSTEMOWYCH PAN 28, WARSAW. (1978).

SLOM 1979 -1 SLOMINSKI, L.
BOTTLENECK ASSIGNMENT PROBLEM: AN EFFICIENT ALGORITHM. ARCHIVUM AUTOMATYKI I TELEMECHANIKI 24, 469-482. (1979).

SLOM 1980 -1 SLOMINSKI, L.
ON EFFICIENCY OF ALGORITHMS FOR COMBINATORIAL OPTIMIZATION PROBLEMS. REPORT OMP/80. WARSAW: POLISH ACADEMY OF SCIENCES, SYSTEMS RESEARCH INSTITUTE. (1980).

SLOM 1980 -2 SLOMINSKI, L.
SYSTEMS OF REPRESENTATIVE PROBLEMS AND COMBINATORIAL FLOW NETWORKS. REPORT OMP/80. WARSAW: POLISH ACADEMY OF SCIENCES, SYSTEMS RESEARCH INSTITUTE. (1980).

SLOM 1981 -1 SLOMINSKI, L.
ON STATISTICALLY EFFICIENT ALGORITHMS FOR COMBINATORIAL OPTIMIZATION PROBLEMS. IN: R. E. BURKARD, T. ELLINGER (EDS.): METHODS OF OPERATIONS RESEARCH 40, 413-416. KOENIGSTEIN: ANTON HAIN MEISENHEIM. (1981).

SLOW 1977 -1 SLOWINSKI, R.
OPTIMAL AND HEURISTIC PROCEDURES FOR PROJECT SCHEDULING WITH MULTIPLE CONSTRAINED RESOURCES - A SURVEY. FOUNDATIONS OF CONTROL ENGINEERING 2, NO. 1, 33-49. (1977).

SLOW 1978 -1 SLOWINSKI, R.
NODE ORDERING HEURISTIC FOR NETWORK SCHEDULING UNDER MULTIPLE RESOURCE CONSTRAINTS, A. FOUNDATIONS OF CONTROL ENGINEERING 3, NO. 1, 19-27. (1978).

SLOW 1979 -1 SLOWINSKI, R.
COST-MINIMAL PREEMPTIVE SCHEDULING OF INDEPENDENT JOBS WITH RELEASE AND DUE DATES ON OPEN SHOP UNDER RESOURCE CONSTRAINTS. INFORMATION PROCESSING LETTERS 9, 233-237. (1979).

SLOWA 1978 -1 SLOWINSKI, R.; WEGLARZ, J.
SOLVING THE GENERAL PROJECT SCHEDULING PROBLEM WITH MULTIPLE CONSTRAINED RESOURCES BY MATHEMATICAL PROGRAMMING. FOUNDATIONS OF CONTROL ENGINEERING 3, NO. 1, 29-39. (1978).

SMIR 1980 -1 SMIRNOV, A. N.; SHEVCHENKO, V. N.
MARTIN'S ALGORITHM AND REGULAR CUT-OFFS FOR INTEGER LINEAR PROGRAMMING (RUSSIAN). ZURNAL VYCISLITELNOI MATEMATIKI I MATEMATICESKOI FIZIKI (MOSCOW) 20, NO. 2, 505-509, 553. (1980).

SMIT 1980 -1 SMITH, A.; CANI, P. DE
ALGORITHM TO OPTIMIZE THE LAYOUT OF BOXES IN PALLETS, AN. JOURNAL OF THE OPERATIONAL RESEARCH SOCIETY 31, 573-578. (1980).

SMITA 1978 -1 SMITH, C. A. B.
ON TUTTE'S DICHROMATE POLYNOMIAL. IN: B. BOLLOBAS (ED.): ADVANCES IN GRAPH THEORY, 247-258. ANNALS OF DISCRETE MATHEMATICS 3. AMSTERDAM: NORTH-HOLLAND. (1978).

SMITB 1978 -1 SMITH, D. R.
NEW PROOF OF THE OPTIMALITY OF THE SHORTEST REMAINING PROCESSING TIME DISCIPLINE, A. OPERATIONS RESEARCH 26, 197-199. (1978).

SMITC 1979 -1 SMITH, J. A.
APPLICATION OF SCHEDULING THEORY TO ICEBREAKING OPERATIONS, AN. GROTON: U.S. COAST GUARD RESEARCH & DEVELOPMENT CENTER, 18 P. (1979).

SMITD 1979 -1 SMITH, J. M.
USE OF QUEUEING NETWORKS AND MIXED INTEGER PROGRAMMING TO OPTIMALLY ALLOCATE RESOURCES WITHIN A LIBRARY. AMHERST: UNIV. OF MASSACHUSETTS, DEPT. OF INDUSTRIAL ENGINEERING AND OPERATIONS RESEARCH, 31 P. (1979).

SMITE 1980 -1 SMITH, J. M.; LIEBMAN, J. S.
O(N**2) HEURISTIC ALGORITHM FOR THE DIRECTED STEINER MINIMAL TREE PROBLEM, AN. APPLIED MATHEMATICAL MODELLING 4, NO. 5, 369-375. (1980).

SMITF 1979 -1 SMITH, R. L.
DEFERRAL STRATEGIES FOR A DYNAMIC COMMUNICATIONS NETWORK. NETWORKS 9, 61-87. (1979).

SMITG 1975 -1 SMITH, R. S.
TWO PHASE EMPLOYEE SCHEDULING ALGORITHM FOR OPERATIONS HAVING VARIABLE MANPOWER REQUIREMENTS WITH APPLICATIONS INVOLVING SINGLE AND COMPOSITE PLANNING CYCLES, A. DOCTORAL DISSERTATION. AMHERST: UNIVERSITY OF MASSACHUSETTS, 139 P. (1975).

SMITH 1980 -1 SMITH, T. H. C.
LIFO IMPLICIT ENUMERATION ALGORITHM FOR THE ASYMMETRIC TRAVELLING SALESMAN PROBLEM USING A ONE-ARBORESCENCE RELAXATION, A. MATHEMATICAL PROGRAMMING STUDY 12, 108-114. (1980).

SMITI 1975 -1 SMITH, T. H. C.; THOMPSON, G. L.
COMPARISON OF TWO DIFFERENT LAGRANGEAN RELAXATIONS OF THE TSP, A. MANAGEMENT SCIENCE REPORT 382. PITTSBURGH: CARNEGIE-MELLON UNIVERSITY. (1975).

SMOL 1978 -1 SMOLJAR, L. I.
MODELS OF OPERATIONAL PLANNING IN DISCRETE PRODUCTION (RUSSIAN). MOSCOW: IZDAT. "NAUKA", 320 P. (1978).

SMOR 1976 -1 SMORODINSKI, JA. A.
TREES AND THE MANY-BODY PROBLEM (RUSSIAN). IZVESTIJA VYSSIH UCEBNYH ZAVEDENII RADIOFIZICA 19, 932-941. (1976).

SMYT 1978 -1 SMYTHE, R. T.; WIERMAN, J. C.
FIRST-PASSAGE PERCOLATION ON THE SQUARE LATTICE. BERLIN, HEIDELBERG, NEW YORK: SPRINGER, 196 P. (1978). (LECTURE NOTES IN MATHEMATICS, 671)

SNIE 1979 -1 SNIEDOVICH, M.
PREFERENCE ORDER ASSEMBLY LINE PROBLEM: A COUNTER EXAMPLE. IBM RESEARCH REPORT, 7904. YORKTOWN HEIGHTS: IBM RESEARCH CENTER, 8 P. (1979).

SNIE 1979 -2 SNIEDOVICH, M.
PREFERENCE ORDER STOCHASTIC TRAVELING SALESPERSON PROBLEMS: A COUNTER EXAMPLE. IBM RESEARCH REPORT, 7905. YORKTOWN HEIGHTS: IBM RESEARCH CENTER, 8 P. (1979).

SNIE 1979 -3 SNIEDOVICH, M.
SOME COMMENTS ON PREFERENCE ORDER DYNAMIC PROGRAMMING MODELS. IBM RESEARCH REPORT, 7906. YORKTOWN HEIGHTS: IBM RESEARCH CENTER, 21 P. (1979).

SNIE 1980 -1 SNIEDOVICH, M.
PREFERENCE ORDER STOCHASTIC KNAPSACK PROBLEMS: METHODOLOGICAL ISSUES. N.R.I.M.S. TECHNICAL REPORT NO. 144. TWISK, SOUTH AFRICA. 17P. (1980).

SNIEA 1979 -1 SNIEDOVICH, M.; SMART, J. S.
DYNAMIC PROGRAMMING: AN INTERACTIVE APPROACH. IBM RESEARCH REPORT, 7858. YORKTOWN HEIGHTS: IBM RESEARCH CENTER, 10 P. (1979).

SOLO 1976 -1 SOLOMONOV, L. A.; ZHGUTOV, G. D.
APPLICATION OF THE GOMORY METHOD FOR THE CALCULATION OF AN OPTIMAL PLAN FOR PRODUCTION SHIPMENT (RUSSIAN), AN. IN: DIFFER. EQUAT. COMPUT. MATH., SARATOV, INTERUNIV. SCI. COLLECT. 6, PART I, 64-76. (1976).

SOME 1980 -1 SOMERS, J.; ADLER, I.
MAX-FLOW PROBLEM WITH PARAMETRIC CAPACITIES, THE. DISCRETE APPLIED MATHEMATICS 1, 287-300. (1980).

SONN 1978 -1 SONNTAG, H.
LINIENPLANUNG IM OEFFENTLICHEN PERSONENNAHVERKEHR. IN: PROCEEDINGS IN OPERATIONS RESEARCH 7, 430-439. WUERZBURG: PHYSICA. (1978).

SONN 1979 -1 SONNTAG, H.
HEURISTISCHES VERFAHREN ZUM ENTWURF NACHFRAGEORIENTIERTER LINIENFUEHRUNG IM OEFFENTLICHEN PERSONENNAHVERKEHR, EIN. ZEITSCHRIFT FUER OPERATIONS RESEARCH 23, SERIE B, NO. 2, B15-B31. (1979).
SONN 1979 -2 SONNTAG, H.
VERFAHREN ZUR ALTERNATIVROUTENSUCHE IN VERKEHRSNETZEN, EIN. COMPUTING 21, 323-332. (1979).
SOUM 1980 -1 SOUMIS, F.; FERLAND, J. A.; ROUSSEAU, J.-M.
MODEL FOR LARGE-SCALE AIRCRAFT ROUTING AND SCHEDULING PROBLEMS, A. TRANSPORTATION RESEARCH 14, PART B, 191-201. (1980).
SOUN 1980 -1 SOUN, Y.; TRUEMPER, K.
SINGLE COMMODITY REPRESENTATION OF MULTICOMMODITY NETWORKS. SIAM JOURNAL ON ALGEBRAIC AND DISCRETE METHODS 1, 348-358. (1980).
SOYS 1978 -1 SOYSTER, A. L.; LEV, B.; SLIVKA, W.
ZERO-ONE PROGRAMMING WITH MANY VARIABLES AND FEW CONSTRAINTS. EUROPEAN JOURNAL OF OPERATIONAL RESEARCH 2, 195-201. (1978).
SPAC 1979 -1 SPACHIS, A. S.; KING, J. R.
JOB-SHOP SCHEDULING HEURISTICS WITH LOCAL NEIGHBOURHOOD SEARCH. INTERNATIONAL JOURNAL OF PRODUCTION RESEARCH 17, 507-526. (1979).
SPAE 1978 -1 SPAETH, H.
EXPLIZITE LOESUNG DES DREIDIMENSIONALEN MINIMAX-STANDORTPROBLEMS IN DER CITY-BLOCK-DISTANZ. ZEITSCHRIFT FUER OPERATIONS RESEARCH 22, SERIE A, 229-238. (1978).
SPAE 1979 -1 SPAETH, H.
LOESUNG MULTIPLER STANDORTPROBLEME BEI GEMISCHT GERADLINIGEN UND RECHTWINKELIGEN ENTFERNUNGEN, DIE. IN: H. SPAETH (ED.): AUSGEWAEHLTE OPERATIONS RESEARCH SOFTWARE IN FORTRAN, 51-66. MUENCHEN: OLDENBOURG. (1979).
SPEL 1977 -1 SPELDE, H. G.
BOUNDS FOR THE DISTRIBUTION FUNCTION OF NETWORK VARIABLES. IN: A. ANGERMANN ET AL. (EDS.): FIRST SYMPOSIUM ON OPERATIONS RESEARCH, HEIDELBERG 1976. METHODS OF OPERATIONS RESEARCH 27, 113-123. MEISENHEIM: ANTON HAIN. (1977).
SPER 1979 -1 SPERANZA, F.
SUR LES COLORATIONS DES GRAPHES ORIENTES. UNIONE MATEMATICA ITALIANA. BOLLETINO 16A, 517-522. (1979).
SPIE 1979 -1 SPIELBERG, K.
ENUMERATIVE METHODS IN INTEGER PROGRAMMING. IN: P. L. HAMMER, E. L. JOHNSON, B. H. KORTE (EDS.): DISCRETE OPTIMIZATION II, 139-183. ANNALS OF DISCRETE MATHEMATICS 5, AMSTERDAM, NEW YORK, OXFORD: NORTH-HOLLAND. (1979).
SPIEA 1980 -1 SPIELBERG, K.; SUHL, U.
EXPERIMENTAL SOFTWARE SYSTEM FOR LARGE SCALE 0-1 PROBLEMS WITH EFFICIENT DATA STRUCTURES AND ACCESS TO MPSX/370, AN. IBM RESEARCH REPORT RC 8219. YORKTWON HEIGHTS: IBM RESEARCH CENTER, 31 P. (1980).
SRIM 1979 -1 SRIMANI, P. K.; SENGUPTA, A.
ALGEBRAIC DETERMINATION OF CIRCUITS IN A DIRECTED GRAPH. INTERNATIONAL JOURNAL OF SYSTEMS SCIENCE 10, 1409-1413. (1979).
STAH 1979 -1 STAHL, W.; DOMSCHKE, W.
VERFAHREN ZUR BESTIMMUNG OPTIMALER MASCHINENSTANDORTE BEI RECHTWINKLIGER ENTFERNUNGSMESSUNG, EIN. IN: W. OETTLI, F. STEFFENS (EDS.): OPERATIONS RESEARCH VERFAHREN 35, THIRD SYMPOSIUM ON OPERATIONS RESEARCH, MANNHEIM 1978, 495-506. KOENIGSTEIN: ANTON HAIN MEISENHEIM. (1979).
STAN 1979 -1 STANAT, D. F.; MAGO, G. A.
MINIMIZING MAXIMUM FLOWS IN LINEAR GRAPHS. NETWORKS 9, 333-361. (1979).
STANA 1978 -1 STANCU-MINASIAN, I. M.
ON THE TRANSPORTATION PROBLEM WITH MULTIPLE OBJECTIVE FUNCTIONS. BULLETIN MATHEMATIQUE DE LA SOCIETE DES SCIENCES MATHEMATIQUES DE LA REPUBLIQUE SOCIALISTE DE ROUMANIE 22, NO. 3, 315-328. (1978).
STANB 1978 -1 STANEK, W.
LOESUNG EINES SPEZIELLEN REIHENFOLGEPROBLEMS AUF DEM GEBIET DER FERTIGUNGSSTEUERUNG. WISSENSCHAFTLICHE ZEITSCHRIFT DER TECHNISCHEN HOCHSCHULE KARL-MARX-STADT 20, 489-497. (1978).
STANC 1978 -1 STANICKI, T.
TWO-CRITERION INTEGER OPTIMIZATION OF SUB-ASSEMBLY ASSIGNMENT IN THE DESIGN OF COMPLEX SYSTEMS BY THE METHOD OF VARIABLE CONSTRAINTS AND PARTIAL ENUMERATION (POLISH). PRACE NAUKOWE, INSTYTUT CYBERNETYKI TEHNICZNEJ, POLYTECHNIKA WROCLAW, SERIA KONFERENCJE (WROCLAW) NO. 18, PROJEKTOWANIE III, T. 1, 265-278. (1978).
STAP 1979 -1 STAPLES, J.
ON SOME SUBCLASSES OF WELL-COVERED GRAPHS. JOURNAL OF GRAPH THEORY 3, 197-204. (1979).
STAP 1980 -1 STAPLES, J.
OPTIMAL EVALUATIONS OF GRAPH-LIKE EXPRESSIONS. THEORETICAL COMPUTER SCIENCE 10, 297-316. (1980).
STEC 1978 -1 STECKHAN, H.
ENGPAESSE, STAUSTELLEN UND GLATTE HOMOGENE STROEME IN NETZEN. ZEITSCHRIFT FUER OPERATIONS RESEARCH 22, SERIE A, 199-218. (1978).
STEC 1979 -1 STECKHAN, H.
KONSISTENZTEST FUER BASISDATEN VON PROJEKTNETZEN. IN: PROCEEDINGS IN OPERATIONS RESEARCH 8, 49-53. WUERZBURG: PHYSICA. (1979).
STEC 1979 -2 STECKHAN, H.
NETZFLUSS-ANALYSE. IN: M. J. BECKMANN, G. MENGES, R. SELTEN (EDS.): HANDWOERTERBUCH DER MATHEMATISCHEN WIRTSCHAFTSWISSENSCHAFTEN, BAND 3, 157-174. WIESBADEN: GABLER. (1979).
STEF 1979 -1 STEFFEN, A. E.; ALY, A. A.
SINGLE FACILITY LOCATION PROBLEM AMONG RECTANGULAR REGIONS, A. IN: W. OETTLI, F. STEFFENS (EDS.): OPERATIONS RESEARCH VERFAHREN 35, THIRD SYMPOSIUM ON OPERATIONS RESEARCH, MANNHEIM 1978, 507-515. KOENIGSTEIN: ANTON HAIN MEISENHEIM. (1979).
STEI 1978 -1 STEIN, D. M.
ASYMPTOTIC, PROBABILISTIC ANALYSIS OF A ROUTING PROBLEM, AN. MATHEMATICS OF OPERATIONS RESEARCH 3, 89-102. (1978).
STEI 1978 -2 STEIN, D. M.
SCHEDULING DIAL-A-RIDE TRANSPORTATION SYSTEMS. TRANSPORTATION SCIENCE 12, 232-249. (1978).
STEIA 1980 -1 STEINBERG, E.; NAPIER, H. A.
OPTIMAL MULTI-LEVEL LOT SIZING FOR REQUIREMENTS PLANNING SYSTEMS. MANAGEMENT SCIENCE 26, 1258-1271. (1980).
STER 1978 -1 STERBOUL, F.
HYPERGRAPHES TRANSVERSAUX DES COUPLAGES. IN: J.-C. BERMOND ET AL. (EDS.): PROBLEMES COMBINATOIRES ET THEORIE DES GRAPHES, COLLOQUES INTERNATIONAUX DU CENTRE NATIONAL DE LA RECHERCHE SCIENTIFIQUE, ORSAY 1976, 393-394. PARIS: CENTRE NATIONAL DE LA RECHERCHE SCIENTIFIQUE. (1978).
STER 1978 -2 STERBOUL, F.
SUR LE NOMBRE TRANSVERSAL DES HYPERGRAPHES UNIFORMES. DISCRETE MATHEMATICS 22, 91-96. (1978).

STER 1979 -1 STERBOUL, F.
CHARACTERIZATION OF THE GRAPHS IN WHICH THE TRANSVERSAL NUMBER EQUALS THE MATCHING NUMBER. A. JOURNAL OF COMBINATORIAL THEORY 27, SERIES B, 228-229. (1979).

STERA 1981 -1 STERBOUL, F.; WERTHEIMER, D.
COMMENT CONSTRUIRE UN GRAPHE PERT MINIMAL. RAIRO RECHERCHE OPERATIONELLE 15, NO. 1, 85-98. (1981).

STERB 1976 -1 STERN, H. I.
MINIMIZING MAKESPAN FOR INDEPENDENT JOBS ON NONIDENTICAL PARALLEL MACHINES - AN OPTIMAL PROCEDURE. WORKING PAPER 2/75. BEER-SHEVA: BEN-GURION UNIVERSITY OF THE NEGEV, DEPARTMENT OF INDUSTRIAL ENGINEERING AND MANAGEMENT. (1976).

STERC 1979 -1 STERN, H. I.; DROR, M.
ROUTING ELECTRIC METER READERS. COMPUTERS AND OPERATIONS RESEARCH 6, 209-223. (1979).

STERD 1981 -1 STERN, M.
GENERALIZED MATROID LATTICES. IN: L. LOVASZ, V. T. SOS (EDS.): ALGEBRAIC METHODS IN GRAPH THEORY, VOL. II, 727-748. COLLOQUIA MATHEMATICA SOCIETATIS JANOS BOLYAI 25. AMSTERDAM, OXFORD,NEW YORK: NORTH-HOLLAND. (1981).

STEU 1979 -1 STEUDEL, H. J.
GENERATING PALLET LOADING PATTERNS: A SPECIAL CASE OF THE TWO-DIMENSIONAL CUTTING STOCK PROBLEM. MANAGEMENT SCIENCE 25, 997-1004. (1979).

STEW 1979 -1 STEWART, T. J.; ITTMANN, H. W.
TWO-STAGE OPTIMIZATION IN A TRANSPORTATION PROBLEM. JOURNAL OF THE OPERATIONAL RESEARCH SOCIETY 30, 897-904. (1979).

STEWA 1979 -1 STEWART, W. R.; GOLDEN, B. L.
VEHICLE ROUTING ALGORITHM BASED ON GENERALIZED LAGRANGE MULTIPLIERS (ROUGH DRAFT). WILLIAMSBURG: COLLEGE OF WILLIAM AND MARY, SCHOOL OF BUSINESS, 12 P. (1979).

STEWA 1980 -1 STEWART, W. R.; GOLDEN, B. L.
CHANCE-CONSTRAINED APPROACH TO THE STOCHASTIC VEHICLE ROUTING PROBLEM, A. WILLIAMSBURGH: COLLEGE OF WILLIAM AND MARY, 12 P. (1980).

STEWA 1980 -2 STEWART, W. R.; GOLDEN, B. L.
SUBSCRIBER BUS ROUTING PROBLEM, THE. IN: PROCEEDINGS OF THE 1980 IEEE INTERNATIONAL CONFERENCE ON CIRCUITS AND COMPUTERS, 4 P. (1980).

STIE 1975 -1 STIERLIN, C.
ALGORITHM FOR THE SIMULTANEOUS LOCATION OF EMERGENCY ROOMS AND OF AMBULANCE CENTERS. AN. DOCTORAL DISSERTATION. PHILADELPHIA: UNIVERSITY OF PENNSYLVANIA, 181 P. (1975).

STIN 1977 -1 STINSON, D.
DETERMINATION OF A PACKING NUMBER. ARS COMBINATORIA 3, 89-114. (1977).

STINA 1977 -1 STINSON, J. P.
HEURISTIC ALGORITHM FOR OBTAINING AN INITIAL SOLUTION FOR THE TRAVELING SALESMAN PROBLEM, A. WORKING PAPER WP-77 12. SYRACUSE: SYRACUSE UNIV., SCHOOL OF MANAGEMENT, 12 P. (1977).

STINB 1978 -1 STINSON, J. P.; DAVIS, E. W.; KHUMAWALA, B. M.
MULTIPLE RESOURCE-CONSTRAINED SCHEDULING USING BRANCH AND BOUND. AIIE TRANSACTIONS 10, 252-259. (1978).

STON 1977 -1 STONE, H. S.
MULTIPROCESSOR SCHEDULING WITH THE AID OF NETWORK FLOW ALGORITHMS. INSTITUTE OF ELECTICAL AND ELECTRONICS ENGINEERS. TRANSACTIONS ON SOFTWARE ENGINEERING 3, 85-93. (1977).

STRA 1979 -1 STRAIGHT, H. J.
PACKING TREES OF DIFFERENT SIZE INTO THE COMPLETE GRAPH. IN: F. HARARY (ED.): TOPICS IN GRAPH THEORY. ANNALS OF THE NEW YORK ACADEMY OF SCIENCES 328, 190-192. NEW YORK: THE NEW YORK ACADEMY OF SCIENCES. (1979).

STRE 1977 -1 STREET, A. P.; WALLIS, W. D.
COMBINATORIAL THEORY: AN INTRODUCTION. WINNIPEG: CHARLES BABBAGE RESEARCH CENTRE, 610 P. (1977).

STRO 1979 -1 STROEHLEIN, T.
TIGHTNESS AND FLEXIBILITY IN TIMETABLE PROBLEMS. IN: M. NAGL, H.-J. SCHNEIDER (EDS.): GRAPHS, DATA STRUCTURES, ALGORITHMS. PROCEEDINGS OF THE WORKSHOP WG 78 ON GRAPHTHEORETIC CONCEPTS IN COMPUTER SCIENCE, ERLANGEN 1978, 299-306. MUENCHEN, WIEN: HANSER. (1979).

SU 1978 -1 SU, Z.-S.; SEVCIK, K. C.
COMBINATORIAL APPROACH TO DYNAMIC SCHEDULING PROBLEMS. A. OPERATIONS RESEARCH 26, 836-844. (1978).

SUBR 1979 -1 SUBRAHMANYAM, Y. V.
SOME SPECIAL CASES OF ASSIGNMENT PROBLEMS. OPSEARCH 16, 45-47. (1979).

SUFF 1979 -1 SUFFEL, C.
SPANNING SUBGRAPHS OF EULERIAN GRAPHS, THE. IN: F. HARARY (ED.): TOPICS IN GRAPH THEORY. ANNALS OF THE NEW YORK ACADEMY OF SCIENCES 328, 193-200. NEW YORK: THE NEW YORK ACADEMY OF SCIENCES. (1979).

SUHL 1978 -1 SUHL, U.
ALGORITHM AND EFFICIENT DATA STRUCTURES FOR THE BINARY KNAPSACK PROBLEM, AN. EUROPEAN JOURNAL OF OPERATIONAL RESEARCH 2, 420-428. (1978).

SUHL 1978 -2 SUHL, U.
IMPLEMENTATIONSTECHNIKEN FUER EINEN BRANCH-AND-BOUND-ALGORITHMUS ZUR LOESUNG VON (0-1)-PROGRAMMEN. IN: PROCEEDINGS IN OPERATIONS RESEARCH 7, 497-506. WUERZBURG: PHYSICA. (1978).

SULE 1979 -1 SULE, D. R.; HARMON, B.
DETERMINATION OF COORDINATED MAINTENANCE SCHEDULING FREQUENCIES FOR A GROUP OF MACHINES. AIIE TRANSACTIONS 11, 48-53. (1979).

SULL 1980 -1 SULLIVAN, P. J.; PETERS, N.
FLEXIBLE USER-ORIENTED LOCATION-ALLOCATION ALGORITHM, A. JOURNAL OF ENVIRONMENTAL MANAGEMENT (LONDON) 10, 181-193. (1980).

SUMN 1979 -1 SUMNER, D. P.
RANDOMLY MATCHABLE GRAPHS. JOURNAL OF GRAPH THEORY 3, 183-186. (1979).

SUPR 1974 -1 SUPRUNENKO, D. A.
ON THE ASSIGNMENT PROBLEM (RUSSIAN). VESCI AKADEMII NAVUK BSSR. SERYJA FIZIKA-MATEMATYCNYH NAVUK, NO. 4, 5-10 + 138. (1974).

SURA 1975 -1 SURANYI, L.
LARGE ALPHA-CRITICAL GRAPHS WITH SMALL DEFICIENCY. ON LINE-CRITICAL GRAPHS. II. STUDIA SCIENTIARUM MATHEMATICARUM HUNGARICA 10, 397-412. (1975).

SURY 1979 -1 SURYGIN, V. A.
ESTIMATES OF THE COMPLEXITY OF NORMAL ALGORITHMS (RUSSIAN). DOKLADY AKADEMII NAUK SSSR 244, 1097-1101. (1979).

SUSH 1975 -1 SUSHKOV, Y. A.
(1,Q)-MATCHINGS. VESTNIK LENINGRADSKOGO UNIVERSITETA. MATEMATIKA 4, NO. 19, 50-55; TRANSLATED AS VESTNIK LENINGRAD UNIVERSITY, MATHEMATICS 8, 1980, 383-390. (1975).

SUZU 1978 -1 SUZUKI, H.
GENERALIZED KNAPSACK PROBLEM WITH VARIABLE COEFFICIENTS, A. MATHEMATICAL PROGRAMMING 15, 162-176. (1978).

SVEN 1978 -1 SVENSSON, A.
EQUILIBRIUM EQUATION FOR ROAD TRAFFIC, AN. TRANSPORTATION RESEARCH 12, 309-314. (1978).

SVES 1978 -1 SVESTKA, J. A.
CONTINUOUS VARIABLE REPRESENTATION OF THE TRAVELING SALESMAN PROBLEM, A. MATHEMATICAL PROGRAMMING 15, 211-213. (1978).

SWAR 1966 -1 SWARUP, K.
TRANSPORTATION TECHNIQUE IN LINEAR FRACTIONAL FUNCTIONAL PROGRAMMING. JOURNAL OF THE ROYAL NAVAL SCIENTIFIC SERVICE 21, NO. 5. (1966).

SWEE 1979 -1 SWEENEY, D. J.; MURPHY, R. A.
METHOD OF DECOMPOSITION FOR INTEGER PROGRAMS, A. OPERATIONS RESEARCH 27, 1028-1141. (1979).

SYSL 1977 -1 SYSLO, M. M.
BISECTION METHOD FOR THE TRAVELING SALESMAN PROBLEM, A. ZASTOSOWANIA MATEMATYKI 16, 59-62. (1977).

SYSL 1977 -2 SYSLO, M. M.
LINEAR TIME ALGORITHM FOR CODING OUTERPLANAR GRAPHS. RAPORT NR. N-20. WROCLAW: WROCLAW UNIV., INSTITUTE OF COMPUTER SCIENCE, 11 P. (1977).

SYSL 1977 -3 SYSLO, M. M.
ON SOME PROBLEMS RELATED TO FUNDAMENTAL CYCLE SETS OF A GRAPH. RAPORT NR. N-33. WROCLAW: WROCLAW UNIV., INSTITUTE OF COMPUTER SCINCE, 19 P. (1977).

SYSL 1978 -1 SYSLO, M. M.
ON CHARACTERIZATIONS OF CYCLE GRAPHS AND ON OTHER FAMILIES OF INTERSECTION GRAPHS. RAPORT NR. N-40. WROCLAW: WROCLAW UNIV., INSTITUTE OF COMPUTER SCIENCE, 23 P. (1978).

SYSL 1979 -1 SYSLO, M. M.
CHARACTERIZATION OF HYPERGRAPHS GENERATED BY ARBORESCENCES, A. KYBERNETIKA 15, 403-407. (1979).

SYSL 1979 -2 SYSLO, M. M.
ON CYCLE BASES OF A GRAPH. NETWORKS 9, 123-132. (1979).

SYSL 1979 -3 SYSLO, M. M.
ON THE CYCLE SPACE METHODS (EXTENDED ABSTARCT). IN: W. OETTLI, F. STEFFENS (EDS.): OPERATIONS RESEARCH VERFAHREN 32, THIRD SYMPOSIUM ON OPERATIONS RESEARCH, MANNHEIM 1978, 189-192. KOENIGSTEIN: ANTON HAIN MEISENHEIM. (1979).

SYSL 1979 -4 SYSLO, M. M.
ON THE STRUCTURE OF CYCLES IN A GRAPH. BULLETIN DE L'ACADEMIE POLONAISE DES SCIENCES. SERIE DES SCIENCES MATHEMATIQUES, ASTRONOMIQUES ET PHYSIQUES 27, 241-246. (1979).

SYSL 1979 -5 SYSLO, M. M.
ON TWO CYCLE SPACE METHODS FOR LISTING CYCLES OF A GRAPH. ROSTOCKER MATHEMATISCHES KOLLOQUIUM 11, 115-121. (1979).

SYSL 1980 -1 SYSLO, M. M.
GENERALIZATIONS OF THE STANDARD TRAVELLING SALESMAN PROBLEM. ZASTOSOWANIA MATEMATYKI (WARSAW) 16, 621-629. (1980).

SYSL 1981 -1 SYSLO, M. M.
EFFICIENT CYCLE VECTOR SPACE ALGORITHM FOR LISTING ALL CYCLES OF A PLANAR GRAPH, AN. IN: L. LOVASZ, V. T. SOS (EDS.): ALGEBRAIC METHODS IN GRAPH THEORY, VOL. II, 749-762. COLLOQUIA MATHEMATICA SOCIETATIS JANOS BOLYAI 25. AMSTERDAM, OXFORD,NEW YORK: NORTH-HOLLAND. (1981).

SYSL 1981 -2 SYSLO, M. M.
ON THE FAMILY OF ALL FUNDAMENTAL CYCLE SETS OF A GRAPH. IN: R. E. BURKARD, T. ELLINGER (EDS.): METHODS OF OPERATIONS RESEARCH 40, 417-420. KOENIGSTEIN: ANTON HAIN MEISENHEIM. (1981).

SYSLA 1976 -1 SYSLO, M. M.; IRI, M.
EFFICIENT OUTERPLANARITY TESTING. RAPORT NR. N-4. WROCLAW: WROCLAW UNIV., INSTITUTE OF COMPUTER SCIENCE, 13 P. (1976).

SYSLB 1977 -1 SYSLO, M. M.; SKUPIEN, Z.
APPLIED GRAPH THEORY. III. EULER AND HAMILTONIAN GRAPHS. THE TRAVELING SALESMAN PROBLEM (POLISH). MATEMATYKA STOSOWANA 10, 5-54. (1977).

SZAM 1976 -1 SZAMKOLOWICZ, L.
SOME REMARKS ON GRAPHICITY OF SIMPLE MATROIDS. IN: GRAPHS, HYPERGRAPHS, BLOCK SYSTEMS; PROC. SYMP. COMB. ANAL., ZIELONA GORA 1976, 283-289. (1976).

SZAM 1977 -1 SZAMKOLOWICZ, L.
SOME REMARKS ON STABLE SETS OF A HYPERGRAPH. POLITECHNIKI WROCLAWSKIEJ. INSTYTUTU MATEMATYKI. PRACE NAUKOWE SERIA STUDIA I MATERIALY (WROCLAW) 13, 27-32. (1977).

SZAM 1979 -1 SZAMKOLOWICZ, L.
ON PROBLEMS RELATED TO CHARACTERISTIC VERTICES OF GRAPHS. COLLOQUIUM MATHEMATICUM (WARSAW) 42, 367-375. (1979).

SZAM 1979 -2 SZAMKOLOWICZ, L.
SOME REMARKS ON HYPERGRAPHS OF VERTEX COVERINGS FOR SIMPLE GRAPHS WITHOUT LOOPS. R. C. MAT. (ITALY) 12, 501-510. (1979).

SZEK 1975 -1 SZEKERES, G.
NON-COLOURABLE TRIVALENT GRAPHS. IN: A. P. STREET, W. D. WALLIS (EDS.): COMBINATORIAL MATHEMATICS 3, 227-233. LECTURE NOTES IN MATHEMATICS 452. NEW YORK: SPRINGER. (1975).

SZWA 1978 -1 SZWARC, W.
DOMINANCE CONDITIONS FOR THE THREE-MACHINE FLOW-SHOP PROBLEM. OPERATIONS RESEARCH 26, 203-206. (1978).

SZWA 1979 -1 SZWARC, W.
CRITICAL PATH APPROACH IN THE FLOW-SHOP PROBLEM, THE. OPSEARCH 16, 98-102. (1979).

SZWA 1981 -1 SZWARC, W.
EXTREME SOLUTIONS OF THE TWO MACHINE FLOW-SHOP PROBLEM. NAVAL RESEARCH LOGISTICS QUARTERLY 28, 103-114. (1981).

SZWAA 1979 -1 SZWARC, W.; POSNER, M. E.
TRIDIAGONAL TRANSPORTATION PROBLEM, THE. RESEARCH REPORT. MILWAUKEE: UNIV. OF WISCONSIN, SCHOOL OF BUSINESS ADMINISTRATION, 14 P. (1979).

SZWAB 1979 -1 SZWARCFITER, J. L.
SYSTEMS OF DISTINCT REPRESENTATIVES FOR K FAMILIES OF SETS. INFORMATION PROCESSING LETTERS 9, 195-196. (1979).

SZYM 1979 -1 SZYMURA, J.
OPTIMIZATION OF THE PRODUCTION LINE SCHEDULE (POLISH). PODSTAWY STEROWANIA 9, 177-188. (1979).

TABA 1973 -1 TABAK, D.
APPLICATION OF MODERN CONTROL AND OPTIMIZATION TECHNIQUES TO TRANSPORTATION SYSTEMS. IN: C. T. LEONDES (ED.): CONTROL AND DYNAMIC SYSTEMS: ADVANCES IN THEORY AND APPLICATIONS 10, 345-434. NEW YORK, LONDON: ACADEMIC PRESS. (1973).

TABAA 1977 -1 TABATA, K.
BASIS-CONSTRAINED LINEAR PROGRAMMING PROBLEM; ITS FORMULATION AND A BRANCH-AND-BOUND SOLUTION, A. ELECTRONIC ENGINEERING OF JAPAN 97, NO. 1, 132-136. (1977).

TAGU 1978 -1 TAGUCHI, A.
MAXIMUM-FLOW PROBLEM IN DISCRETE CONTINUOUS COMPOUND SYSTEM AND ITS NUMERICAL APPROACH. JOURNAL OF THE OPERATIONS RESEARCH SOCIETY OF JAPAN 21, 245-273. (1978).

TAHA 1971 -1 TAHA, H.
HYPERBOLIC PROGRAMMING WITH BIVALENT VARIABLES. TECHNICAL REPORT 71-7. FAYETTEVILLE: UNIVERSITY OF ARKANSAS. (1971).

TAI 1979 -1 TAI, K.-C.
TREE-TO-TREE CORRECTION PROBLEM, THE. JOURNAL OF THE ASSOCIATION FOR COMPUTING MACHINERY 26, 422-433. (1979).

TAKA 1979 -1 TAKAHASHI, H.; MATSUYAMA, A.
APPROXIMATE SOLUTION FOR THE STEINER PROBLEM IN GRAPHS, AN. MATHEMATICA JAPONICA 24, 573-577. (1979).

TAKAA 1980 -1 TAKAMIZAWA, K.; NISHIZEKI, T.; SAITO, N.
ALGORITHM FOR FINDING A SHORT CLOSED SPANNING WALK IN A GRAPH, AN. NETWORKS 10, 249-264. (1980).

TAKAA 1980 -2 TAKAMIZAWA, K.; NISHIZEKI, T.; SAITO, N.
LINEAR TIME COMPUTABILITY OF COMBINATORIAL PROBLEMS ON SERIES-PARALLEL GRAPHS. TECHNICAL REPORT. SENDAI: TOHOKU UNIVERSITY, DEPT. ELECTR. COMMUN. (1980).

TAKAA 1981 -1 TAKAMIZAWA, K.; NISHIZEKI, T.; SAITO, N.
COMBINATORIAL PROBLEMS ON SERIES-PARALLEL GRAPHS. IN: N. SAITO, T. NISHIZEKI (EDS.): GRAPH THEORY AND ALGORITHMS, 79-94. LECTURE NOTES IN COMPUTER SCIENCE 108, BERLIN: SPRINGER. (1981).

TAKAA 1981 -2 TAKAMIZAWA, K.; NISHIZEKI, T.; SAITO, N.
COMBINATORIAL PROBLEMS ON SERIES-PARALLEL GRAPHS. DISCRETE APPLIED MATHEMATICS 3, 75-76. (1981).

TALA 1979 -1 TALANOV, V. A.; IL'ICEV, A. P.
THREE-INDEX TRANSPORTATION PROBLEMS AND COMPILING SCHOOL TIMETABLES (RUSSIAN). EKONOMIKA I MATEMATICESKIE METODY 15, 806-811. (1979).

TALB 1978 -1 TALBOT, F. B.; PATTERSON, J. H.
EFFICIENT INTEGER PROGRAMMING ALGORITHM WITH NETWORK CUTS FOR SOLVING RESOURCE-CONSTRAINED SCHEDULING PROBLEMS, AN. MANAGEMENT SCIENCE 24, 1163-1174. (1978).

TAMI 1979 -1 TAMIR, A.
SCHEDULING JOBS TO TWO MACHINES SUBJECT TO BATCH ARRIVAL ORDERING. NAVAL RESEARCH LOGISTICS QUARTERLY 26, 521-525. (1979).

TAMIA 1979 -1 TAMIR, A.; ZEMEL, E.
LOCATING CENTERS ON A TREE WITH DISCONTINUOUS SUPPLY AND DEMAND REGIONS. DISCUSSION PAPER, 397. EVANSTON: NORTHWESTERN UNIV., CENTER FOR MATHEMATICAL STUDIES IN ECONOMICS AND MANAGEMENT SCIENCE, 30 P. (1979).

TANG 1964 -1 TANG, D. T.
BIPATH NETWORKS AND MULTICOMMODITY FLOWS. IEEE TRANSACTIONS ON CIRCUIT THEORY 11, 468-474. (1964).

TANG 1965 -1 TANG, D. T.
COMMENTS ON FEASIBILITY CONDITIONS OF SIMULTANEOUS FLOWS IN A NETWORK. OPERATIONS RESEARCH 13, 143-146. (1965).

TANK 1978 -1 TANKO, J.
DOMINATING SCHEDULES OF STEADY JOB-FLOW PAIRS (HUNGARIAN). ALKALMAZOTT MATEMATIKAI LAPOK (BUDAPEST) 4, 271-325. (1978).

TANS 1980 -1 TANSEL, B. C.; FRANCIS, R. L.; LOWE, T. J.
BINDING INEQUALITIES FOR TREE NETWORK LOCATION PROBLEMS WITH DISTANCE CONSTRAINTS. TRANSPORTATION SCIENCE 14, 107-124. (1980).

TARJ 1974 -1 TARJAN, R. E.
TESTING GRAPH CONNECTIVITY. IN: SIXTH ANNUAL ACM SYMPOSIUM ON THEORY OF COMPUTING, SEATTLE 1974, 185-193. NEW YORK: ASSOCIATION FOR COMPUTING MACHINERY. (1974).

TARJ 1978 -1 TARJAN, R. E.
COMPLEXITY OF COMBINATORIAL ALGORITHMS. SIAM REVIEW 20, 457-492. (1978).

TARJ 1979 -1 TARJAN, R. E.
CLASS OF ALGORITHMS WHICH REQUIRE NONLINEAR TIME TO MAINTAIN DISJOINT SETS, A. JOURNAL OF COMPUTER AND SYSTEM SCIENCES 18, 110-127. (1979).

TAYL 1978 -1 TAYLOR, B. W. III; KEOWN, A. J.
PLANNING URBAN RECREATIONAL FACILITIES WITH INTEGER GOAL PROGRAMMING. THE JOURNAL OF THE OPERATIONAL RESEARCH SOCIETY 29, 751-758. (1978).

TAYLA 1975 -1 TAYLOR, P. E.
OPTIMUM MANAGEMENT OF AIR TRAFFIC BETWEEN MAJOR AIR TERMINALS, THE. DOCTORAL DISSERTATION. COLUMBUS: THE OHIO STATE UNIVERSITY, 191 P. (1975).

TAZA 1979 -1 TAZAWA, S.
CLAW-DECOMPOSITION AND EVENLY-PARTITE-CLAW-DECOMPOSITION OF COMPLETE MULTI-PARTITE GRAPHS. HIROSHIMA MATHEMATICAL JOURNAL 9, 503-531. (1979).

TCHE 1980 -1 TCHERBINA, O. A.
ON LOCAL ALGORITHM OF INTEGRAL OPTIMIZATION (RUSSIAN). AKADEMIJA NAUK SSSR. ZURNAL VYCISLITEL'NOI MATEMATIKI I MATEMATICESKOI FIZIKI 20, 802-804. (1980).

TCHEA 1978 -1 TCHERVAK, JU. JU.
RETURNING ALGORITHM OF CUTTING-OFF METHOD AND BRANCH-AND-BOUND METHOD (RUSSIAN). ECONOMICS AND THE MATHEMATICAL METHODS 5, 1002-1006. (1978).

TELE 1978 -1 TELEMTAEV, M. M.
OPTIMALITY CONDITION FOR A HAMILTONIAN CYCLE (RUSSIAN). IZVESTIJA AKADEMII NAUK KAZAHSKOI SSR, SERIJA FIZIKO MATEMATICESKAJA, NO. 3, 67-70 + 94. (1978).

TEMP 1980 -1 TEMPELMEIER, H.
BESTIMMUNG DES OPTIMALEN STANDORTS EINES AUSLIEFERUNGSLAGERS BEI ENTFERNUNGSABHAENGIGER NACHFRAGE UND NICHTLINEAREN TRANSPORTKOSTEN, DIE. ZEITSCHRIFT FUER OPERATIONS RESEARCH, SERIE B: PRAXIS 24, 167-188. (1980).

TEMPA 1971 -1 TEMPERLEY, H. N. V.; LIEB, E. H.
RELATIONS BETWEEN THE "PERCOLATION" AND "COLOURING" PROBLEM AND OTHER GRAPH-THEORETICAL PROBLEMS ASSOCIATED WITH REGULAR PLANAR LATTICES: SOME EXACT RESULTS FOR THE "PERCOLATION" PROBLEM. PROCEEDINGS OF THE ROYAL SOCIETY LONDON, SERIES A 322, NO. 1549, 251-280. (1971).

TENG 1978 -1 TENG, J. T.; HWANG, F. K.
MATRIX ALGORITHM FOR LARGER KNAPSACK PROBLEMS, A. BULLETIN OF THE INSTITUTE OF MATHEMATICS, ACADEMIA SINICA 6, 197-201. (1978).

TERA 1979 -1 TERADA, R.
POLYNOMIAL TIME ALGORITHMS FOR NP-HARD PROBLEMS WHICH ARE OPTIMAL OR NEAR-OPTIMAL WITH PROBABILITY ONE. COMPUTER SCIENCES TECHNICAL REPORT 351. MADISON: UNIV. OF WISCONSIN, COMPUTER SCIENCES DEPT., 18 P. (1979).

TERN 1978 -1 TERNO, J.
GRUNDPRINZIPIEN DER DISKRETEN OPTIMIERUNG. WISSENSCHAFTLICHE ZEITSCHRIFT DER TECHNISCHEN UNIVERSITAET DRESDEN 27, 1159-1161. (1978).

TERZ 1980 -1 TERZI, D. G.
INVESTIGATION OF DISCRETE PROGRAMMING ALGORITHMS (RUSSIAN). MATEMATICESKIE ISSLEDOVANIJA (KISHINEV) NO. 60, 153-160, 172. (1980).

THEP 1981 -1 THEPOT, J.
CLUSTER ANALYSIS FOR GRAPH COLORING. IN: R. E. BURKARD, T. ELLINGER (EDS.): METHODS OF OPERATIONS RESEARCH 40, 421-424. KOENIGSTEIN: ANTON HAIN MEISENHEIM. (1981).

THEPA 1980 -1 THEPOT, J.; LECHENAULT, G.
METHODE DE CLASSIFICATION POUR LA COLORATION DES GRAPHES. IN: P. HANSEN, D. DE WERRA (EDS.): REGARDS SUR LA THEORIE DES GRAPHES, PROCEEDINGS OF THE CERISY COLLOQUIUM, 1980, 313-316. LAUSANNE: PRESSES POLYTECHNIQUES ROMANDES. (1980).

THOM 1977 -1 THOMAS, A.
MODELS FOR OPTIMAL CAPACITY EXPANSION. PH. D. DISSERTATION. NEW HAVEN: YALE UNIVERSITY. (1977).

THOMA 1978 -1 THOMAS, G. S.; JENNINGS, J. C.; ABBOTT, P.
BLENDING PROBLEM USING INTEGER PROGRAMMING ON-LINE, A. MATHEMATICAL PROGRAMMING STUDY 9, 30-42. (1978).

THOMB 1978 -1 THOMASON, A. G.
HAMILTONIAN CYCLES AND UNIQUELY EDGE COLOURABLE GRAPHS. IN: B. BOLLOBAS (ED.): ADVANCES IN GRAPH THEORY, 259-268. ANNALS OF DISCRETE MATHEMATICS 3. AMSTERDAM: NORTH-HOLLAND. (1978).

THOMC 1974 -1 THOMASSEN, C.
GRAPHS IN WHICH EVERY PATH IS CONTAINED IN A HAMILTONIAN PATH. JOURNAL FUER DIE REINE UND ANGEWANDTE MATHEMATIK 268/269, 271-282. (1974).

THOMC 1976 -1 THOMASSEN, C.
PATHS AND CYCLES IN GRAPHS. DISSERTATION. WATERLOO: UNIVERSITY OF WATERLOO. (1976).

THOMC 1978 -1 THOMASSEN, C.
HYPOHAMILTONIAN GRAPHS AND DIGRAPHS. IN: Y. ALAVI, D. R. LICK (EDS.): THEORY AND APPLICATION OF GRAPHS, PROCEEDINGS OF THE INTERNATIONAL CONFERENCE, MICHIGAN 1976. LECTURE NOTES OF MATHEMATICS 642, 557-571. BERLIN: SPRINGER. (1978).

THOMC 1979 -1 THOMASSEN, C.
LONG CYCLES IN DIGRAPHS WITH CONSTRAINTS ON THE DEGREES. IN: B. BOLLOBAS (ED.): SURVEYS IN COMBINATORICS, PROCEEDINGS OF THE 7TH BRITISH COMBINATORIAL CONFERENCE, 211-228. LONDON MATHEMATICAL SOCIETY LECTURE NOTE SERIES 38. CAMBRIDGE, LONDON, NEW YORK, MELBOURNE: CAMBRIDGE UNIVERSITY PRESS. (1979).

THOMC 1979 -2 THOMASSEN, C.
NONSEPARATING CYCLES IN K-CONNECTED GRAPHS. PREPRINT SERIES 1979/80, NO. 1. AARHUS: AARHUS UNIVERSITET, MATEMATISK INSTITUT, 5 P. (1979).

THOMC 1980 -1 THOMASSEN, C.
HAMILTONIAN-CONNECTED TOURNAMENTS. JOURNAL OF COMBINATORIAL THEORY 28, SERIES B, 142-163. (1980).

THOMC 1980 -2 THOMASSEN, C.
2-LINKED GRAPHS. EUROPEAN JOURNAL OF COMBINATORICS 1, 371-378. (1980).

THOMC 1981 -1 THOMASSEN, C.
PLANAR CUBIC HYPOHAMILTONIAN AND HYPOTRACEABLE GRAPHS. JOURNAL OF COMBINATORIAL THEORY, SERIES B 30, 36-44. (1981).

THUE 1979 -1 THUENTE, D. J.
TWO ALGORITHMS FOR SHORTEST PATHS THROUGH MULTIPLE CRITERIA NETWORKS. IN: P. C. C. WANG (ED.): INFORMATION LINKAGE BETWEEN APPLIED MATHEMATICS AND INDUSTRY, 567-574. NEW YORK: ACADEMIC PRESS. (1979).

TIET 1978 -1 TIETZE, W.
PROBLEM DER DREIERCLIQUEN. EIN BEITRAG ZUR GRAPHENTHEORIE, DAS. ELEMENTE DER MATHEMATIK 33, 81-90. (1978).

TIMO 1976 -1 TIMOFEEV, E. A.
LOWER BOUND FOR THE TRAVELING SALESMAN PROBLEM (RUSSIAN), A. IN: A. JU. LEVIN (ED.): HEURISTIC OPTIMIZATION ALGORITHMS (RUSSIAN), 177-184. YAROSLAVL: JAROSLAV. GOS. UNIV. (1976).

TIMO 1977 -1 TIMOFEEV, E. A.
ON THE CONSTRUCTION OF AN EDGEWISE M-CONNECTED SKELETAL SUBGRAPH WITH MINIMUM LENGTH OF A MAXIMAL EDGE. SOVIET MATHEMATICS. DOKLADY 18, 563-566. (1977).

TIMO 1979 -1 TIMOFEEV, E. A.
MINMAX DOUBLY CONNECTED SUBGRAPHS AND THE TRAVELLING SALESMAN PROBLEM FOR "WEAK POINTS" (RUSSIAN). KIBERNETIKA, NO. 4, 75-79. (1979).

TIND 1979 -1 TIND, J.
BLOCKING AND ANTIBLOCKING POLYHEDRA. IN: P. L. HAMMER, E. L. JOHNSON, B. H. KORTE (EDS.): DISCRETE OPTIMIZATION I, 159-174. ANNALS OF DISCRETE MATHEMATICS 4. AMSTERDAM, NEW YORK, OXFORD: NORTH-HOLLAND. (1979).

TIND 1979 -2 TIND, J.
ON DUALITY IN NON-CONVEX AND INTEGER PROGRAMMING. IN: W. OETTLI, F. STEFFENS (EDS.): OPERATIONS RESEARCH VERFAHREN 32, THIRD SYMPOSIUM ON OPERATIONS RESEARCH, MANNHEIM 1978, 193-201. KOENIGSTEIN: ANTON HAIN MEISENHEIM. (1979).

TIND 1980 -1 TIND, J.
CERTAIN KINDS OF POLAR SETS AND THEIR RELATION TO MATHEMATICAL PROGRAMMING. MATHEMATICAL PROGRAMMING STUDY 12, 206-213. (1980).

TINDA 1978 -1 TIND, J.; WOLSEY, L. A.
ON THE USE OF PENUMBRAS IN BLOCKING AND ANTIBLOCKING THEORY. CORE DISCUSSION PAPER 7827. LOUVAIN-LA-NEUVE: CENTER FOR OPERATIONS RESEARCH & ECONOMETRICS, 17 P. (1978).

TINDA 1978 -2 TIND, J.; WOLSEY, L. A.
UNIFYING FRAMEWORK FOR DUALITY THEORY IN MATHEMATICAL PROGRAMMING, A. CORE DISCUSSION PAPER 7834. LOUVAIN-LA-NEUVE: CENTER FOR OPERATIONS RESEARCH & ECONOMETRICS, 24 P. (1978).

TINDB 1972 -1 TINDALL, J. B.
MINIMAL DISCONNECTING SETS IN DIRECTED MULTI-COMMODITY NETWORKS. UNPUBLISHED DISSERTATION. ATLANTA: GEORGIA INSTITUTE OF TECHNOLOGY, SCHOOL OF INDUSTRIAL AND SYSTEMS ENGINEERING. (1972).

TING 1979 -1 TINGLEY, G. A.
STILL ANOTHER SOLUTION METHOD FOR THE MONTHLY AIRCREW ASSIGNMENT PROBLEM. PUGNOCHIUSO (NINETEENTH ANNUAL AGIFORS SYMPOSIUM, SEPTEMBER 1979) 55 P. (1979).

TINH 1977 -1 TINHOFER, G.
ON THE ISOMORPHISMS OF STRUCTURES. UNPUBLISHED REPORT. MUENCHEN: TECHNISCHE UNIVERSITAET MUENCHEN, INSTITUT FUER STATISTIK UND UNTERNEHMENSFORSCHUNG. (1977).

TINH 1980 -1 TINHOFER, G.
GRAPHSACK PROBLEM, THE. IN: U. PAPE (ED.): DISCRETE STRUCTURES AND ALGORITHMS, 1-16. MUENCHEN: HANSER. (1980).

TISH 1977 -1 TISHYADHIGAMA, S.; POLAK, E.; KLESSIG, R.
COMPARATIVE STUDY OF SEVERAL GENERAL CONVERGENCE CONDITIONS FOR ALGORITHMS MODELED BY POINT-TO-SET MAPS, A. MEMORANDUM NO. UBC/ERL M77/78. BERKELEY: UNIV. OF CALIFORNIA, ELECTRONICS RESEARCH LABORATORY, 32 P. (1977).

TJUT 1976 -1 TJUTJUKIN, V. K.
OPTIMAL TWO-OPERATION SCHEDULING IN THE CASE OF PARALLEL-SERIAL PRODUCTION MOTION (RUSSIAN). PRIMENENIE MATEMATIKI V EKONOMIKE, NO. 11, 60-69. (1976).

TOBI 1978 -1 TOBIAS, T.
KUHN-TUCKER CONDITIONS FOR THE TWO-PHASE STOCHASTIC PROGRAMMING PROBLEM WITH INTEGRAL CONSTRAINTS (RUSSIAN). EESTI NSV TEADUSK AKADEEMIA TOIMETSET. FUEUESIKA-MATEMAATIKA 27. NO. 1, 3-8. (1978).

TOFT 1978 -1 TOFT, B.
INVESTIGATION OF COLOUR-CRITICAL GRAPHS WITH COMPLEMENTS OF LOW CONNECTIVITY, AN. IN: B. BOLLOBAS (ED.): ADVANCES IN GRAPH THEORY, 279-288. ANNALS OF DISCRETE MATHEMATICS 3. AMSTERDAM: NORTH-HOLLAND. (1978).

TOKU 1979 -1 TOKUMASU, S.; MOTOI, N.; ODAMURA, M.
SPECIAL MATCHING PROBLEM AND AN ALGORITHM FOR IT (JAPANESE), A. JOURNAL OF THE OPERATIONS RESEARCH SOCIETY OF JAPAN 22, 123-137. (1979).

TOME 1977 -1 TOMESCU, I.
SUR LES PLUS LONGUES CYCLES DANS LES GRAPHES CHROMATIQUES. BULLETIN MATHEMATIQUE DE LA SOCIETE DES SCIENCES MATHEMATIQUES DE LA REPUBLIQUE SOCIALISTE DE ROUMAINE 21(69), 433-439. (1977).

TOME 1978 -1 TOMESCU, I.
SUR LES CYCLES ELEMENTAIRES DANS LES GRAPHES ET HYPERGRAPHES K-CHROMATIQUES. CALCOLO 15. NO. 1, 1-15. (1978).

TOME 1979 -1 TOMESCU, I.
NOMBRE MAXIMAL DE COLORIAGES DES ARETES D'UN GRAPHE, LE. ACADEMIE DE LA REPUBLIQUE POPULAIRE ROUMAINE. REVUE ROUMAINE DE MATHEMATIQUES PURES ET APPLIQUEES 24, 811-816. (1979).

TOME 1979 -2 TOMESCU, I.
NOMBRE MINIMAL DE COLORATIONS D'UN HYPERGRAPHE K-CHROMATIQUE, LE. DISCRETE MATHEMATICS 25, 179-188. (1979).

TOME 1980 -1 TOMESCU, I.
SOME PROPERTIES OF IRREDUCIBLE COVERINGS BY CLIQUES OF COMPLETE MULTIPARTITE GRAPHS. JOURNAL OF COMBINATORIAL THEORY 28, SERIES B, 127-141. (1980).

TOMI 1976 -1 TOMIZAWA, N.
STRONGLY IRREDUCIBLE MATROIDS AND PRINCIPAL PARTITION OF A MATROID INTO STRONGLY IRREDUCIBLE MINORS. ELECTRONICS AND COMMUNICATIONS IN JAPAN 59, NO. 2, 1-10. (1976).

TOML 1967 -1 TOMLIN, J. A.
MATHEMATICAL PROGRAMMING MODELS FOR TRAFFIC NETWORK PROBLEMS. UNPUBLISHED DOCTORAL DISSERTATION. ADELAIDE: UNIVERSITY OF ADELAIDE, DEPARTMENT OF MATHEMATICS. (1967).

TONE 1977 -1 TONE, K.
ON OPTIMAL PATTERN FLOWS. JOURNAL OF THE OPERATIONS RESEARCH SOCIETY OF JAPAN 20, 77-93. (1977).

TONE 1979 -1 TONE, K.
ON OPTIMAL PATTERN FLOWS. IN: A. PREKOPA (ED.): SURVEY OF MATHEMATICAL PROGRAMMING, VOLUME 2, 301-318. AMSTERDAM, NEW YORK, OXFORD: NORTH-HOLLAND. (1979).

TORR 1975 -1 TORRIGIANI, M.
ON A MORE GENERAL DEFINITION OF DISTINCT MATCHINGS (ITALIAN). G. IST. ITAL. ATTUARI 38, 87-104. (1975).

TOTH 1976 -1 TOTH, P.
NEW REDUCTION ALGORITHM FOR 0-1 KNAPSACK PROBLEMS, A. PRESENTED AT THE ORSA/TIMS JOINT NATIONAL MEETING, MIAMI 1976. (1976).

TOTH 1980 -1 TOTH, P.
DYNAMIC PROGRAMMING ALGORITHMS FOR THE ZERO-ONE KNAPSACK PROBLEM. COMPUTING 25, 29-45. (1980).

TOUS 1979 -1 TOUSSAINT, G. T.
RELATIVE NEIGHBOURHOOD GRAPH OF A FINITE PLANAR SET, THE. TECHNICAL REPORT NO. SOCS 79.7. MONTREAL: MCGILL UNIV., SCHOOL OF COMPUTER SCIENCE, 32 P. (1979).

TOUS 1980 -1 TOUSSAINT, G. T.
COMMENT:"ALGORITHMS FOR COMPUTING RELATIVE NEIGHBORHOOD GRAPH" BY R. B. URQUHART. WITH A REPLY BY URQUHART. ELECTRONICS LETTERS 16,860-861. (1980).

TOUSA 1981 -1 TOUSSAINT, G. T.; MENARD, R.
FAST ALGORITHMS FOR COMPUTING THE PLANAR RELATIVE NEIGHBORHOOD GRAPH. IN: R. E. BURKARD, T. ELLINGER (EDS.): METHODS OF OPERATIONS RESEARCH 40, 425-428. KOENIGSTEIN: ANTON HAIN MEISENHEIM. (1981).

TOWN 1977 -1 TOWNSEND, W.
MINIMISING THE MAXIMUM PENALTY IN THE M-MACHINE SEQUENCING PROBLEM. OPERATIONAL RESEARCH QUARTERLY 28, 727-734. (1977).

TOYO 1978 -1 TOYODA, Y.
IMPROVEMENT IN IMPLICIT ENUMERATION (JAPANESE), AN. JOURNAL OF THE OPERATIONS RESEARCH SOCIETY OF JAPAN 21, 218-225. (1978).

TRAU 1978 -1 TRAUB, F. J.
RECENT RESULTS AND OPEN PROBLEMS IN ANALYTIC COMPUTATIONAL COMPLEXITY. IN: A. N. TIKHONOV ET AL. (EDS.): MATHEMATICAL MODELS AND NUMERICAL METHODS. PAPERS FROM THE FIFTH SEMESTER HELD AT THE STEFAN BANACH INTERNATIONAL MATHEMATICAL CENTER, WARSAW 1975, 269-272. WARSAW: POLISH SCIENTIFIC PUBLISHERS. (1978).

TREH 1978 -1 TREHEL, M.
NOTES SUR LE COUPLAGE DIRECT - COUPLAGE DANS LES COMBINAISONS. CAHIERS DU CENTRE D'ETUDES DE RECHERCHE OPERATIONELLE 20, 147-162. (1978).

TREM 1978 -1 TREMOLIERES, R.
SCHEDULING JOBS OF EQUAL DURATIONS WITH TARDINESS COSTS AND RESOURCE LIMITATIONS. THE JOURNAL OF THE OPERATIONAL RESEARCH SOCIETY 29, 229-233. (1978).

TREMA 1977 -1 TREMOLIERES, R.; AUBERT, J.-C.
DETERMINATION D'UNE FLOTTE MINIMALE ET ORDONNANCEMENT DES TACHES DANS LA LIVRAISON DU BETON PRET A L'EMPLOI. REVUE FRANCAISE D'AUTOMATIQUE, D'INFORMATIQUE ET DE RECHERCHE OPERATIONELLE 11, SERIE RECHERCHE OPERATIONELLE, 305-321. (1977).

TRIG 1978 -1 TRIGT, C. VAN
WORST-CASE ANALYSIS OF ALGORITHMS. A. SOME G. C. D. ALGORITHMS. PHILIPS JOURNAL OF RESEARCH 33, 66-77. (1978).

TRIP 1980 -1 TRIPATHY, A.
LAGRANGEAN RELAXATION APPROACH TO COURSE TIMETABLING, A. JOURNAL OF THE OPERATIONAL RESEARCH SOCIETY 31, 599-602. (1980).

TROC 1980 -1 TROCHELMANN, J.
TOURENPLANUNG FUER DAS DETERMINISTISCHE EIN-DEPOT-PROBLEM. VERKEHRSWISSENSCHAFTLICHE STUDIEN 35. GOETTINGEN: VANDENHOECK & RUPRECHT, 170 P. (1980).

TROJ 1978 -1 TROJANOWSKI, A. E.
RANKING AND LISTING ALGORITHMS FOR K-ARY TREES. SIAM JOURNAL ON COMPUTING 7, 492-509. (1978).

TROJA 1981 -1 TROJANOWSKI, M.
GRAPH THEORY AND ALGEBRAIC APPROACH TO SOLVING NETWORK CONCAVE PROBLEMS, A. IN: R. E. BURKARD, T. ELLINGER (EDS.): METHODS OF OPERATIONS RESEARCH 40, 429-432. KOENIGSTEIN: ANTON HAIN MEISENHEIM. (1981).

****

TROT 1978 -1 TROTTER, L. E. JR.; WEINBERGER, D. B.
SYMMETRIC BLOCKING AND ANTI-BLOCKING RELATIONS FOR GENERALIZED CIRCULATIONS. MATHEMATICAL PROGRAMMING STUDY 8, 141-158. (1978).

TROTA 1978 -1 TROTTER, W. T. JR.; ERDOES, P.
WHEN THE CARTESIAN PRODUCT OF DIRECTED CYCLES IS HAMILTONIAN. JOURNAL OF GRAPH THEORY 2, 137-142. (1978).

TROTB 1979 -1 TROTTER, W. T. JR.; HARARY, F.
ON DOUBLE AND MULTIPLE INTERVAL GRAPHS. JOURNAL OF GRAPH THEORY 3, 205-211. (1979).

TRUB 1977 -1 TRUBIN, V. A.
ONE-PARAMETER ALLOCATION AND UNIFICATION PROBLEMS (RUSSIAN). IN: THEORY OF OPTIMAL SOLUTIONS (RUSSIAN), 36-40. KIEV: AKAD. NAUK UKRAIN. SSR INST. KIBERNET. (1977).

TRUB 1978 -1 TRUBIN, V. A.
EFFECTIVE ALGORITHM FOR THE WEBER PROBLEM WITH RECTANGULAR METRIC (RUSSIAN). KIBERNETIKA, NO. 6, 67-79. (1978).

TRUBA 1981 -1 TRUBIN, V. A.; VOITISHIN, YU. V.
ALGORITHM FOR SOLVING A SET-DIVISION PROBLEM (RUSSIAN), AN. KIBERNETIKA (KIEV), NO. 2, 136; TRANSLATED AS CYBERNETICS. (1981).

TRUD 1976 -1 TRUDEAU, R. J.
DOTS AND LINES. KENT: KENT STATE UNIV. PRESS, 203 P. (1976).

TRUE 1978 -1 TRUEMPER, K.
ALGEBRAIC CHARACTERIZATIONS OF UNIMODULAR MATRICES. SIAM JOURNAL ON APPLIED MATHEMATICS 35, 328-332. (1978).

TRUE 1978 -2 TRUEMPER, K.
OPTIMAL FLOWS IN NONLINEAR GAIN NETWORKS. NETWORKS 8, 17-36. (1978).

TRUE 1979 -1 TRUEMPER, K.
ALPHA-BALANCED MATRICES AND GF(3)-REPRESENTABILITY OF MATROIDS. RICHARDSON: UNIV. OF TEXAS AT DALLAS, 49 P. (1979).

TRUE 1979 -2 TRUEMPER, K.
COMPLEXITY OF REPRESENTABILITY TESTS FOR MATROIDS. WORKING PAPER. RICHARDSON: UNIV. OF TEXAS, 17 P. (1979).

TRUE 1980 -1 TRUEMPER, K.
EFFICIENT TEST FOR REGULARITY OF MATROIDS, AN. WORKING PAPER. RICHARDSON: UNIV. OF TEXAS, 31 P. (1980).

TRUEA 1979 -1 TRUEMPER, K.; SOUN, Y.
MINIMAL FORBIDDEN SUBGRAPHS OF UNIMODULAR MULTICOMMODITY NETWORKS. MATHEMATICS OF OPERATIONS RESEARCH 4, 379-389. (1979).

TRUK 1979 -1 TRUKHANOVSKIJ, N. N.
CONDITIONS DE RESOLUBILITE D'UNE CLASSE DE PROBLEMES DE TRANSPORT PLANAIRES A PLUSIEURS INDICES (RUSSIAN). VESCI AKADEMII NAVUK BSSR. SERYJA FIZIKA-MATEMATYCNYH NAVUK, NO. 3, 126-127. (1979).

TRYP 1975 -1 TRYPIA, M. N.
METHODS FOR INTEGER PROGRAMMING. UNPUBLISHED PH. D. THESIS. LONDON: UNIVERSITY OF LONDON. (1975).

TRYP 1979 -1 TRYPIA, M. N.
BINARY TREE SEARCH METHOD FOR THE 0-1 LINEAR PROGRAMMING PROBLEM, A. NEW ZEALAND OPERATIONAL RESEARCH 7, 69-78. (1979).

TSAR 1977 -1 TSAROUCHIS, N.
SIMPLEX-TYPE ALGORITHM FOR A HYBRID ZERO-ONE PROGRAMMING PROBLEM, A. IN: M. ROUBENS (ED.): ADVANCES IN OPERATIONS RESEARCH, PROCEEDINGS OF EURO II, THE SECOND EUROPEAN CONGRESS ON OPERATIONS RESEARCH, STOCKHOLM 1976, 535-541. AMSTERDAM, NEW YORK, OXFORD: NORTH-HOLLAND. (1977).

TSIM 1979 -1 TSIMBALIST, E. I.; RUZAEV, E. N.; KANUNOV, A. I.
ALGORITHME DE RECHERCHE DES ISTHMES D'UN GRAPHE (RUSSIAN). IZVESTIJA VYSSHIKH UCHEBNYKH ZAVEDENIJ. RADIOELEKTRONIKA 22, 104-106. (1979).

TSUK 1980 -1 TSUKIYAMA, S.; ARIYOSHI, H.; SHIRAKAWA, I.; OZAKI, H.
ALGORITHM TO ENUMERATE ALL CUTSETS OF A GRAPH IN LINEAR TIME PER CUTSET, AN. JOURNAL OF THE ASSOCIATION FOR COMPUTING MACHINERY 27, 619-632. (1980).

TSUKA 1979 -1 TSUKIYAMA, S.; SHIRAKAWA, I.; ASAHARA, S.
ALGORITHM FOR THE VIA ASSIGNMENT PROBLEM IN MULTILAYER BACKBOARD WIRING, AN. INSTITUTE OF ELECTRICAL AND ELECTRONICS ENGINEERS. TRANSACTIONS ON CIRCUITS AND SYSTEMS 26, 369-377. (1979).

TUCK 1979 -1 TUCKER, A. C.
BERGE'S STRONG PERFECT GRAPH CONJECTURE. IN: A. GEWIRTZ, L. V. QUINTAS (EDS.): SECOND INTERNATIONAL CONFERENCE ON COMBINATORIAL MATHEMATICS, 530-535. ANNALS OF THE NEW YORK ACADEMY OF SCIENCES, VOLUME 319. NEW YORK: THE NEW YORK ACADEMY OF SCIENCES. (1979).

TUCK 1980 -1 TUCKER, A. C.
APPLIED COMBINATORICS. NEW YORK, BRISBANE U.A.: WILEY, 385 P. (1980).

TUFE 1980 -1 TUFEKCI, S.
SOLVING THE PROJECT TIME/COST TRADEOFF PROBLEM USING THE FIRST-LABELED FIRST-SCANNED MAXIMAL FLOW ALGORITHM. WORKING PAPER 80-004. SYRACUSE: SURACUSE UNIV., DEPT. OF INDUSTRIAL ENGINERING AND OPERATIONS RESEARCH, 24 P. (1980).

TUFEA 1981 -1 TUFEKCI, S.; TOLEDO, M.
COMPARISON OF DECOMPOSITION ALGORITHMS FOR SHORTEST PATH PROBLEMS, A. WORKING PAPER 81-001. SYRACUSE, N.Y.: SYRACUSE UNIVERSITY, DEPT. OF INDUSTRIAL ENGINEERING AND OPERATIONS RESEARCH, 18 P. (1981).

TURC 1981 -1 TURCHANYI, P. S.
DISTRIBUTED ROUTING ALGORITHM IN A NETWORK WITH PRIORITY CLASSES, A. IN: R. E. BURKARD, T. ELLINGER (EDS.): METHODS OF OPERATIONS RESEARCH 40, 433-436. KOENIGSTEIN: ANTON HAIN MEISENHEIM. (1981).

TURG 1978 -1 TURGEON, A.
OPTIMAL SCHEDULING OF THERMAL GENERATING UNITS. IEEE TRANSACTIONS ON AUTOMATIC CONTROL 23, NO. 6, 1000-1005. (1978).

TUTT 1960 -1 TUTTE, W. T.
NON-HAMILTONIAN GRAPH, A. CANADIAN MATHEMATICAL BULLETIN 3, 1-5. (1960).

TUTT 1961 -1 TUTTE, W. T.
ON THE COLORING OF GRAPHS. CANADIAN MATHEMATICAL BULLETIN 4, 157-160. (1961).

TUTT 1966 -1 TUTTE, W. T.
ON THE ALGEBRAIC THEORY OF GRAPH COLORINGS. JOURNAL OF COMBINATORIAL THEORY 1, 15-50. (1966).

TUTT 1977 -1 TUTTE, W. T.
ON THE SPANNING TREES OF SELF-DUAL MAPS. RESEARCH REPORT CORR 77-50. WATERLOO: UNIV. OF WATERLOO, FACULTY OF MATHEMATICS, 18 P. (1977).

TUTT 1978 -1 TUTTE, W. T.
COLOURING PROBLEMS. MATHEMATICAL INTELLIGENCER 1, 72-75. (1978).

TUTT 1979 -1 TUTTE, W. T.
ALL THE KING'S HORSES (A GUIDE TO RECONSTRUCTION). IN: J. A. BONDY, U. P. R. MURTY (EDS.): GRAPH THEORY AND RELATED TOPICS, 15-33. NEW YORK, SAN FRANCISCO, LONDON: ACADEMIC PRESS. (1979).

TUTT 1980 -1 TUTTE, W. T.
1-FACTORS AND POLYNOMIALS. EUROPEAN JOURNAL OF COMBINATORICS 1, 77-87. (1980).

TUTTA 1980 -1 TUTTE, W. T.; ADAM, A. T.
PROBLEMES DE COLORATION (HUNGARIAN). MATEMATIKAI LAPOK, BOLYAI JANOS MATEMATIKAI TARSULAT (BUDAPEST) 28, NO. 1-3, 207-214. (1980).

TYSH 1979 -1 TYSHKEVICH, R. I.
ENUMERATION OF (0,1)-MATRICES DEFINED BY THE NUMBER OF ONES IN ROWS AND COLUMNS (RUSSIAN). DOKLADY AKADEMII NAUK BSSR (MINSK) 23, 589-591. (1979).

TYSHA 1979 -1 TYSHKEVICH, R. I.; CHERNJAK, A. A.
CANONICAL DECOMPOSITION OF A GRAPH DEFINED BY THE POWERS OF ITS VERTICES (RUSSIAN). VESCI AKADEMII NAVUK BSSR, SERYJA FIZIKA-MATEMATYCNYH NAVUK 5, NO. 5, 14-26, 138. (1979).

ULA 1979 -1 ULA, N.
ANALOGUE COMPUTER SOLUTION OF CERTAIN ZERO-ONE INTEGER PROGRAMMING PROBLEMS. INTERNATIONAL JOURNAL OF ELECTRONICS 46, 555-561. (1979).

ULLR 1973 -1 ULLRICH, M.
STRUKTURUNTERSUCHUNGEN BEI SPEZIELLEN REIHENFOLGEPROBLEMEN. DISSERTATION. DRESDEN: TECHNISCHE UNIVERSITAET DRESDEN. (1973).

UNDE 1978 -1 UNDERGROUND, P.
ON GRAPHS WITH HAMILTONIAN SQUARES. DISCRETE MATHEMATICS 21, 323. (1978).

UNTE 1979 -1 UNTERAUER, K.
DYNAMIC WEIGHTED BINARY SEARCH TREES. ACTA INFORMATICA 11, 341-362. (1979).

URQU 1980 -1 URQUHART, R. B.
ALGORITHMS FOR COMPUTATION OF RELATIVE NEIGHBOURHOOD GRAPH. ELECTRONICS LETTERS 16, NO. 14, 556-557. (1980).

URSI 1975 -1 URSIC, S.
DISCRETE OPTIMIZATION ALGORITHM BASED ON BINOMIAL POLYTOPES, A. DISSERTATION. MADISON: UNIVERSITY OF WISCONSIN, 68 P. (1975).

USHA 1979 -1 USHAKOV, I. A.
METHODE APPROCHEE D'OPTIMISATION DES SYSTEMES A OBJETS REPARTIS (RUSSIAN). IZVESTIJA AKADEMII NAUK SSSR. TEHNICESKAJA KIBERNETIKA, NO. 1, 5-10. (1979).

USHAA 1977 -1 USHAKOV, I. A.; LITVAK, YE. I.
UPPER AND LOWER ESTIMATES OF PARAMETERS OF TWO-POLE NETWORKS. IZVESTIJA AKADEMII NAUK SSSR. TEHNICESKAJA KIBERNETIKA, NO. 1, 72-79; TRANSLATED AS ENGINEERING CYBERNETICS 15, 1977, 59-66. (1977).

USTY 1979 -1 USTYUZHANINOV, V. G.
QUELQUES PROPRIETES DES RECOUVREMENTS DE TABLES BINAIRES (RUSSIAN). KIBERNETIKA, NO. 4, 7-15. (1979).

UZDE 1977 -1 UZDEMIR, A. P.
DECOMPOSITION IN SOLUTION OF COMBINATORY PROBLEM OF DETERMINING MOMENTS OF INTRODUCTION OF ENTERPRISES. AVTOMATIKA I TELEMEHANIKA, NO. 10, 110-121; TRANSLATED AS AUTOMATION AND REMOTE CONTROL 38, 1977, 1519-1537. (1977).

UZDE 1977 -2 UZDEMIR, A. P.
ESTIMATION PROBLEMS IN A NUMERICAL METHOD OF SOLUTION OF DYNAMIC INDUSTRIAL PLANT LOCATION PROBLEM. AVTOMATIKA I TELEMEHANIKA, NO. 7, 105-108; TRANSLATED AS AUTOMATION AND REMOTE CONTROL 38, 1977, 1033-1038. (1977).

UZDE 1978 -1 UZDEMIR, A. P.
SOLUTION METHOD FOR A COMBINATORIAL PROBLEM IN THE PLANNING OF NEW ENTERPRISES (RUSSIAN). AVTOMATIKA I TELEMEHANIKA, NO. 10, 142-152. (1978).

UZDE 1979 -1 UZDEMIR, A. P.
DYNAMIC LOCATION OF INDUSTRIAL PLANTS I. AVTOMATIKA I TELEMEHANIKA (MOSCOW) NO. 11, 142-151; TRANSLATED AS AUTOMATION AND REMOTE CONTROL 40, NO. 11, 1671-1678. (1979).

UZDE 1979 -2 UZDEMIR, A. P.
DYNAMIC LOCATION OF INDUSTRIAL PLANTS II. AVTOMATIKA I TELEMEHANIKA (MOSCOW) NO. 12, 146-158; TRANSLATED AS AUTOMATION AND REMOTE CONTROL 40, NO. 12, PART 2, 1828-1837. (1979).

UZDEA 1978 -1 UZDEMIR, A. P.; SHMELEV, V. V.
INTEGER DYNAMIC PROBLEMS OF ECONOMIC PLANNING WITH NETWORK CONSTRAINTS. I. AVTOMATIKA I TELEMEHANIKA, NO. 7, 106-115; TRANSLATED AS AUTOMATION AND REMOTE CONTROL 39, 1978, 1025-1033. (1978).

VAIR 1978 -1 VAIRAVAN, K.
IMPROVED SCHEDULING ALGORITHM FOR THE PARALLEL EXECUTION OF TASK SYSTEMS, AN. IN: PROCEEDINGS OF THE 1978 CONFERENCE ON INFORMATION SCIENCES AND SYSTEMS, BALTIMORE 1978, 496-499. BALTIMORE: THE JOHNS HOPKINS UNIVERSITY: DEPARTMENT OF ELECTRICAL ENGINEERING. (1978).

VAJN 1980 -1 VAJNSHTEJN, A. D.
METHODE DE DICHOTOMIE DANS QUELQUES PROBLEMES MINIMAX SUR LES GRAPHES (RUSSIAN). AVTOMATIKA I TELEMEHANIKA (MOSCOW) NO. 8, 85-87; TRANSLATED AS AUTOMATION AND REMOTE CONTROL. (1980).

VALI 1979 -1 VALIANT, L. G.
COMPLEXITY OF COMPUTING THE PERMANENT, THE. THEORETICAL COMPUTER SCIENCE 8, 189-201. (1979).

VALI 1979 -2 VALIANT, L. G.
COMPLEXITY OF ENUMERATION AND RELIABILITY PROBLEMS, THE. SIAM JOURNAL ON COMPUTING 8, 410-421. (1979).

VAMO 1978 -1 VAMOS, P.
MISSING AXIOM OF MATROID THEORY IS LOST FOREVER, THE. THE JOURNAL OF THE LONDON MATHEMATICAL SOCIETY 18, 403-408. (1978).

VAND 1976 -1 VANDENMEERENDONK, H. W.
SINGLE MACHINE MULTI-PRODUCT PLANNING PROBLEMS. REPRINT SERIES NO. 207. ROTTERDAM: ERASMUS UNIV. ROTTERDAM, P. 555-562 (1976).

VANDA 1975 -1 VANDERJAGT, D. W.
EDGE-CONNECTIVITY AND LOCAL EDGE-CONNECTIVITY OF GRAPHS. MATHEMATICA (CLUJ) 17(40), 213-216. (1975).

VANDB 1979 -1 VANDERVELDE, J. A.; JONKER, R.; DELEVE, G.; VOLGENANT, A.
LOWER BOUNDS FOR TRAVELING SALESMAN PROBLEMS WITH KNOWN RELATIVE ORDER FOR A PART OF THE CITIES. REPORT AE 3/79. AMSTERDAM: UNIV. OF AMSTERDAM, FACULTY OF ACTUARIAL SCIENCE & ECONOMETRICS, 9 P. (1979).

VANDC 1980 -1 VANDERVELDE, J. A.; KAAS, R.; DELEVE, G.
STRONGER GOMORY CUTS BY MULTIDIMENSIONAL KNAPSACK PROBLEMS. MATHEMATISCHE OPERATIONSFORSCHUNG UND STATISTIK, SERIES OPTIMIZATION 11, 249-260. (1980).

VANE 1975 -1 VANEMDEN, M. H.
ANALYSIS OF COMPLEXITY, AN (2ND PRINTING). AMSTERDAM: MATHEMATISCH CENTRUM, 86 P. (1975). (MATHEMATICAL CENTRE TRACTS, 35)

VANR 1980 -1 VANROY, T. J.
CROSS DECOMPOSITION ALGORITHM FOR CAPACITATED FACILITY LOCATION. A. 80-8A. LEUVEN: KATHOLIEKE UNIV. LEUVEN. DEPT. WERKTEUIGKUNDE INDUSTRIEEL BELEID. 24 P. (1980).

VANR 1980 -2 VANROY, T. J.
CROSS DECOMPOSITION FOR INTEGER PROGRAMMING. (80-07A. LEUVEN: KATHOLIEKE UNIV. LEUVEN. DEPT. WERKTUIGKUNDE INDUSTRIEEL BELEID, 31 P. (1980).

VASI 1975 -1 VASILEV, L. N.
SPECIAL CASE OF THE ASSIGNMENT PROBLEM (RUSSIAN). A. IN: B. P. MITJAGIN (ED.): PROCEEDINGS OF THE SIXTH WINTER SCHOOL ON MATHEMATICAL PROGRAMMING AND RELATED QUESTIONS (RUSSIAN). DROGOBYCH 1973. 32-40. MOSCOW: CENTRAL. EKONOM.-MAT. INST. AKAD. NAUK SSSR. (1975).

VASIA 1979 -1 VASILEVA, E. M.; LEVIT, B. JU.; LIVSIC, V. N.
CHOICE OF OPTIMAL TRAJECTORY IN THE DEVELOPMENT OF A TURNPIKE TRANSPORTATION NETWORK (RUSSIAN). THE. EKONOMIKA I MATEMATICESKIE METODY 15, 731-746. (1979).

VEMU 1976 -1 VEMUGANTI, R. R.
ON THE FEASIBILITY OF SCHEDULING LOT SIZES FOR SEVERAL PRODUCTS ON ONE MACHINE. BALTIMORE: UNIV. OF BALTIMORE. (1976).

VEMU 1978 -1 VEMUGANTI, R. R.
ON THE FEASIBILITY OF SCHEDULING LOT SIZES FOR TWO PRODUCTS ON ONE MACHINE. MANAGEMENT SCIENCE 24, 1668-1673. (1978).

VENG 1979 -1 VENGEROV, V. N.; NIKITIN, A. S.
HEURISTIC ALGORITHM FOR CUTTING WEIGHTED GRAPHS (RUSSIAN). VESCI AKADEMII NAVUK BSSR, SERYJA FIZIKA-MATEMATYCNYH NAVUK 5, NO. 5, 26-30, 138-139. (1979).

VENGA 1975 -1 VENGEROVA, I. V.; FINKELSTEIN, JU. JU.
ON THE QUESTION OF THE EFFICIENCY OF THE BRANCH-AND-BOUND METHOD (RUSSIAN). EKONOMIKA I MATEMATICESKIE METODY 11, 186-193. (1975).

VERC 1978 -1 VERCELLIS, C.
ENUMERATIVE ALGORITHM FOR COVERING PROBLEMS. AN. A-53. PISA: UNIV. DI PISA. DIPT. DI RICERCA OPERATIVA E SCIENZE STATISTICHE, 19 P. (1978).

VERG 1978 -1 VERGIN, R. C.; LEE, T. N.
SCHEDULING RULES FOR THE MULTIPLE PRODUCT SINGLE MACHINE SYSTEM WITH STOCHASTIC DEMAND. INFOR 16, 64-73. (1978).

VERGA 1971 -1 VERGNAS, M. LAS
SUR UNE PROPRIETE DES ARBRES MAXIMAUX DANS UN GRAPHE. COMPTES RENDUS HEBDOMADAIRES DES SEANCES DE L'ACADEMIE DES SCIENCES (PARIS) 272, 1297-1300. (1971).

VERGA 1975 -1 VERGNAS, M. LAS
DEGREE-CONSTRAINED SUBGRAPHS AND MATROID THEORY. IN: A. HAJNAL, R. RADO, V. T. SOS (EDS.): INFINITE AND FINITE SETS III, 1473-1502. AMSTERDAM, LONDON: NORTH-HOLLAND. (1975).

VERGA 1978 -1 VERGNAS, M. LAS
BASES IN ORIENTED MATROIDS. JOURNAL OF COMBINATORIAL THEORY 25, SERIES B, 283-289. (1978).

VERGA 1978 -2 VERGNAS, M. LAS
EXTENSIONS PONCTUELLES COMPATIBLES D'UNE GEOMETRIE COMBINATOIRE. COMPTES RENDUS HEBDOMADAIRES DES SEANCES DE L'ACADEMIE DES SCIENCES (PARIS). SERIES A ET B, 286, NO. 21, A981-A984. (1978).

VERGA 1978 -3 VERGNAS, M. LAS
EXTENSIONS PONCTUELLES D'UNE GEOMETRIE COMBINATOIRE ORIENTEE. IN: J.-C. BERMOND ET AL. (EDS.): PROBLEMES COMBINATOIRES ET THEORIE DES GRAPHES, COLLOQUES INTERNATIONAUX DU CENTRE NATIONAL DE LA RECHERCHE SCIENTIFIQUE, INTERNATIONAL, ORSAY 1976, 265-270. PARIS: CENTRE NATIONAL DE LA RECHERCHE SCIENTIFIQUE. (1978).

VERGA 1978 -4 VERGNAS, M. LAS
SUR LES ACTIVITES DES ORIENTATIONS D'UNE GEOMETRIE COMBINATOIRE. CAHIERS DU CENTRE D'ETUDES DE RECHERCHE OPERATIONELLE 20, 293-300. (1978).

VERGA 1980 -1 VERGNAS, M. LAS
CONVEXITY IN ORIENTED MATROIDS. JOURNAL OF COMBINATORIAL THEORY, SERIES B 29, 231-243. (1980).

VERGA 1980 -2 VERGNAS, M. LAS
FUNDAMENTAL CIRCUITS AND A CHARACTERIZATION OF BINARY MATROIDS. DISCRETE MATHEMATICS 31, 327. (1980).

VERGA 1980 -3 VERGNAS, M. LAS
ON THE TUTTE POLYNOMIAL OF A MORPHISM OF MATROIDS. IN: M. DEZA, I. G. ROSENBERG (EDS.): COMBINATORICS 79, PART I, 7-20. ANNALS OF DISCRETE MATHEMATICS 8. AMSTERDAM: NORTH-HOLLAND. (1980).

VICK 1980 -1 VICKSON, R. G.
CHOOSING THE JOB SEQUENCE AND PROCESSING TIMES TO MINIMIZE TOTAL PROCESSING PLUS FLOW COST ON A SINGLE MACHINE. OPERATIONS RESEARCH 28, 1155-1167. (1980).

VICK 1980 -2 VICKSON, R. G.
TWO SINGLE MACHINE SEQUENCING PROBLEMS INVOLVING CONTROLLABLE JOB PROCESSING TIMES. AIIE TRANSACTIONS 12, 258-262. (1980).

VIDA 1978 -1 VIDAL, R. V. V.
DESIGN OF A PIPELINE ROUTE. MATHEMATICAL PROGRAMMING STUDY 9, 95-108. (1978).

VIDO 1980 -1 VIDOMENKO, V. P.
ASYMMETRY OF THE SCHEDULE PROBLEMS AND ITS EFFECT ON THE SOLUTION ACCURACY (RUSSIAN). KIBERNETIKA, NO. 1, 112-115. (1980).

VIDY 1978 -1 VIDYASANKAR, K.
COVERING THE EDGE SET OF A DIRECTED GRAPH WITH TREES. DISCRETE MATHEMATICS 24, 79-85. (1978).

VIDY 1978 -2 VIDYASANKAR, K.
MINIMUM STRONG COVER IN CIRCUIT-BALANCED GRAPHS. UTILITAS MATHEMATICA 14, 287-303. (1978).

VIDY 1980 -1 VIDYASANKAR, K.
COVERS AND STRONG COVERS IN DIRECTED BIPARTITE GRAPHS. JOURNAL OF GRAPH THEORY 4, 279-286. (1980).

VIGN 1967 -1 VIGNERON, L.
DENOMBREMENT DES COLORATIONS QUE L'ON PEUT TRACER SUR UN GRAPHE G PLANAIRE, CUBIQUE SANS ISTHME, CONNEXE, EN UTILISANT AU PLUS TROIS COULEURS D'ARETES. IN: P. ROSENSTHIEL (ED.): THEORIE DES GRAPHES, 399-400. PARIS: DUNOD. (1967).

VIGN 1978 -1 VIGNERON, L.
A PROPOS DE LA CONJECTURE DE TAIT. DEFINITION DE LA C-PARITE D'UN CYCLE BICOLORE D'ARETES; EFFETS PRODUITS PAR L'ECHANGE DES COULEURS SUR UN CYCLE DANS LE CAS OU IL EST C-PAIR ET DANS LE CAS OU IL EST C-IMPAIR. IN: J.-C. BERMOND ET AL. (EDS.): PROBLEMES COMBINATOIRES ET THEORIE DES GRAPHES, COLLOQUES INTERNATIONAUX DU CENTRE NATIONAL DE LA RECHERCHE SCIENTIFIQUE, ORSAY 1976, 411-414. PARIS: CENTRE NATIONAL DE LA RECHERCHE SCIENTIFIQUE. (1978).

VILL 1975 -1 VILLANUEVA, J. E.
SOME EXECUTION-TIME PROPERTIES OF OPTIMAL SCHEDULES IN MULTIPROCESSOR SYSTEMS. DOCTORAL DISSERTATION. AMES: IOWA STATE UNIVERSITY, 123 P. (1975).

VILLA 1978 -1 VILLARREAL, B.; KARWAN, M. H.
MULTICRITERION INTEGER LINEAR PROGRAMMING A (HYBRID) DYNAMIC PROGRAMMING RECURSIVE APPROACH. TECHNICAL REPORT NO. 78-4. AMHERST: STATE UNIV. OF NEW YORK, DEPT. OF INDUSTRIAL ENGINEERING, 43 P. (1978).

VILLA 1978 -2 VILLARREAL, B.; KARWAN, M. H.
MULTICRITERION INTEGER LINEAR PROGRAMMING: SOME EXTENSIONS. TECHNICAL REPORT NO. 78-5. AMHERST: STATE UNIV. OF NEW YORK, DEPT. OF INDUSTRIAL ENGINEERING, 31 P. (1978).

VILLA 1979 -1 VILLARREAL, B.; KARWAN, M. H.
INTERACTIVE DYNAMIC PROGRAMMING APPROACH TO MULTICRITERIA DISCRETE PROGRAMMING, AN. RESEARCH PAPER. AMHERST: STATE UNIV. OF NEW YORK AT BUFFALO, DEPT. OF INDUSTRIAL ENGINEERING, 35 P. (1979).

VILLB 1980 -1 VILLARREAL, B.; KARWAN, M. H.; ZIONTS, S.
INTERACTIVE BRANCH AND BOUND PROCEDURE FOR MULTICRITERION INTEGER LINEAR PROGRAMMING, AN. IN: MULTIPLE CRITERIA DECISION MAKING THEORY AND APPLICATION, PROC. 3. CONF. HAGEN/ KOENIGSWINTER 1979, 448-467, LECTURE NOTES IN ECONOMICS AND MATHEMATICAL SYSTEMS 177. BERLIN: SPRINGER. (1980).

VINC 1978 -1 VINCKE, P.
ORDRES ET PREORDRES TOTAUX A DISTANCE MINIMUM D'UN QUASI-ORDRE. CAHIERS DU CENTRE D'ETUDES DE RECHERCHE OPERATIONELLE 20, 451-462. (1978).

VINN 1975 -1 VINNICHENKO, N. G.
NUMBER OF EDGES OF AN N-VERTEX K-CONNECTED GRAPH WITH GIVEN STABILITY NUMBER (RUSSIAN), THE. PRIKLADNAJA MATEMATIKA I PROGRAMMIROVANIE VYP. 13, 31-36, 146. (1975).

VITA 1981 -1 VITANYI, P. M. B.
HOW WELL CAN A GRAPH BE N-COLORED? DISCRETE MATHEMATICS 34, 69-80. (1981).

VIZI 1964 -1 VIZING, V. G.
ON AN ESTIMATE OF THE CHROMATIC CLASS OF A P-GRAPH (RUSSIAN). AKADEMIJA NAUK SSSR. SIBIRSKOE OTDELENIE. INSTITUT MATEMATIKI. DISKRETNYI ANALIZ. SBORNIK TRUDOV 3, 25-30. (1964).

VIZI 1964 -2 VIZING, V. G.
ON THE CHROMATIC CLASS OF A MULTIGRAPH (RUSSIAN). IN: PROCEEDINGS OF THE THIRD SIBERIAN CONFERENCE ON MATHEMATICS AND MECHANICS, TOMSK. (1964).

VIZI 1965 -1 VIZING, V. G.
CHROMATIC CLASS OF A MULTIGRAPH, THE. KIBERNETIKA 3, 29-39; TRANSLATED AS CYBERNETICS 3. 1965, 32-41. (1965).

VIZI 1965 -2 VIZING, V. G.
CHROMATIC CLASS OF MULTIGRAPHS (RUSSIAN), THE. DISSERTATION. NOVOSIBIRSK. (1965).

VIZI 1965 -3 VIZING, V. G.
CRITICAL GRAPHS WITH A GIVEN CHROMATIC CLASS (RUSSIAN). AKADEMIJA NAUK SSSR. SIBIRSKOE OTDELENIE. INSTITUT MATEMATIKI. DISKRETNYI ANALIZ. SBORNIK TRUDOV 5, 9-17. (1965).

VIZI 1973 -1 VIZING, V. G.
OBJECT FUNCTION VALUES IN SEQUENCING PROBLEMS DOMINATED BY AN AVERAGE VALUE (RUSSIAN), THE. KIBERNETIKA, NO. 5, 76-78. (1973).

VIZI 1976 -1 VIZING, V. G.
COLORING THE VERTICES OF A GRAPH IN PRESCRIBED COLORS (RUSSIAN). DISKRETNYI ANALIZ, NO. 29, METODY DISKRET. ANAL. V TEORII KODOV I SHEM 3-10, 101. (1976).

VIZV 1976 -1 VIZVARI, B.
USE OF LAGRANGIAN MULTIPLIERS IN INTEGER PROGRAMMING ALGORITHMS (HUNGARIAN), THE. ALKALMAZOTT MATEMATIKAI LAPOK 2, 413-425. (1976).

VIZV 1977 -1 VIZVARI, B.
ON THE OPTIMAL SOLUTIONS OF DISCRETE PROGRAMMING PROBLEMS (HUNGARIAN). ALKALMAZOTT MATEMATIKAI LAPOK 3, 139-150. (1977).

VIZV 1978 -1 VIZVARI, B.
LAGRANGE MULTIPLIERS IN INTEGER PROGRAMMING. PROBLEMS OF CONTROL AND INFORMATION THEORY. PROBLEMY UPRAVLENIJA I TEORII INFORMACII 7, NO. 5, 393-406. (1978).

VLAC 1978 -1 VLACH, M.
MULTICOMMODITY LOCATION PROBLEMS. ZEITSCHRIFT FUER ANGEWANDTE MATHEMATIK UND MECHANIK 58, T495-T496. (1978).

VLAC 1979 -1 VLACH, M.
ONE-PROCESSOR SCHEDULING WITH NONUNIFORM READY TIMES. MATHEMATISCHE OPERATIONSFORSCHUNG UND STATISTIK 10, SERIES OPTIMIZATION, 93-96. (1979).

VLIE 1978 -1 VLIET, D. VAN
IMPROVED SHORTEST PATH ALGORITHMS FOR TRANSPORT NETWORKS. TRANSPORTATION RESEARCH 12, 7-20. (1978).

VOEL 1978 -1 VOELKL, N.
EINSATZ DER GANZZAHLIGEN OPTIMIERUNG IN DER TEXOGRAPHIE, EIN. IN: H. SPAETH (ED.): FALLSTUDIEN OPERATIONS RESEARCH, BAND 1, 184-202. MUENCHEN, WIEN: OLDENBOURG. (1978).

VOIN 1974 -1 VOIN, A. M.
OPTIMAL COMBINATION OF TECHNOLOGICAL OPERATIONS ON A PRODUCTION LINE (RUSSIAN). EKONOMIKA I MATEMATICESKIE METODY 10, 729-736. (1974).

VOIT 1980 -1 VOITISHIN, YU. V.
ON ONE METHOD FOR ESTIMATE CALCULATION IN THE PROBLEM OF SET PARTITIONING (RUSSIAN). KIBERNETIKA (KIEV) NO. 6, 129-130; TRANSLATED AS CYBERNETICS. (1980).

VOIT 1980 -2 VOITISHIN, YU. V.
PROBLEM ON THE MINIMAL FLOW IN THE NETWORK AND ALGORITHMS OF ITS SOLUTION (RUSSIAN), THE. KIBERNETIKA, NO. 1, 116-118. (1980).

VOLG 1978 -1 VOLGENANT, A.; JONKER, R.; DELEVE, G.
NON-OPTIMAL TRAVELING SALESMAN TRAJECTORIES 1: THE SYMMETRIC CASE (IN DUTCH). REPORT AE 11/ 78. AMSTERDAM: UNIV. VAN AMSTERDAM, INTERFACULTEIT DER ACTUARIELE WETENSCHAPPEN EN ECONOMETRIE, 9 P. (1978).

VOLP 1977 -1 VOLPENTESTA, A.
EQUI-ASSIGNED BINARY VECTORS AND EXPLICIT SOLUTIONS OF A PARTICULAR DISCRETE OPTIMIZATION PROBLEM. A-46. PISA: UNIV. DI PISA, DIPT. DI RICERHA OPERATIVA E SCIENZE STATISTICHE, 16 P. (1977).

VOLP 1978 -1 VOLPENTESTA, A.
ON THE INTEGER MULTICOMMODITY TRANSPORTATION PROBLEM. AN APPLICATION TO CREW SCHEDULING PROBLEMS. PISA: UNIV. DI PISA, DIPARTIMENTO DI RICERCA OPERATIVA E SCIENZE STATISTICHE, 15 P. (1978).

VOLP 1978 -2 VOLPENTESTA, A.
ON THE PROBLEM OF CHARACTERIZING THE OPTIMAL SET OF A PARTICULAR DISCRETE OPTIMIZATION PROBLEM. A-55. PISA: UNIV. DI PISA, DIPT. DI RICERCA OPERATIVA E SCIENZE STATISTICHE, 13 P. (1978).

VOLP 1980 -1 VOLPENTESTA, A.
EQUI-ASSIGNMENTS AND EXPLICIT SOLUTIONS OF A PARTICULAR DISCRETE OPTIMIZATION PROBLEM. DISCRETE APPLIED MATHEMATICS 2, 261-265. (1980).

VORN 1981 -1 VORNBERGER, O.
ALTERNATING CYCLE COVERS AND PATHS. IN: H. NOLTEMEYER (ED.): GRAPHTHEORETIC CONCEPTS IN COMPUTER SCIENCE, 367-378. LECTURE NOTES IN COMPUTER SCIENCE 100, BERLIN: SPRINGER. (1981).

VOSS 1980 -1 VOSS, H.-J.
GRAPHS HAVING ODD CIRCUITS WITH AT LEAST K CHORDS. ELEKTRONISCHE INFORMATIONSVERARBEITUNG UND KYBERNETIK 16, 77-86. (1980).

VOSSA 1977 -1 VOSS, H.-J.; ZULUAGA, C.
MAXIMALE GERADE UND UNGERADE KREISE IN GRAPHEN. I. WISSENSCHAFTLICHE ZEITSCHRIFT DER TECHNISCHEN HOCHSCHULE ILMENAU 23, NO. 4, 57-70. (1977).

VOUT 1980 -1 VOUTILAINEN, R.
ON THE PATTERN SEQUENCING PROBLEM - DEFINITIONS, COMPLEXITY, AND APPLICATIONS. CAMBRIDGE (FOURTH EUROPEAN CONGRESS ON OPERATIONS RESEARCH, JULY 1980) 28 P. (1980).

VRAC 1975 -1 VRACIU, G.; LUPSOIU, C.
ALGORITHM FOR DISCRETE PROGRAMMING WITH APPLICATIONS FOR PRODUCTION PROGRAMMING (ROMANIAN). ANALELE UNIVERSITATII DIN CRAIOVA, MAT. FIZ. ELECTROTEH. 3, 35-38. (1975).

WADI 1979 -1 WADIA, A. B.
GENERATION OF NODE LISTS USING SEGMENT ANALYSIS. IBM RESEARCH REPORT, 7752. YORKTOWN HEIGHTS: IBM RESEARCH CENTER, 22 P. (1979).

WAJS 1978 -1 WAJS, W.
ON A CERTAIN ALGORITHM FOR ARRANGING TIME TABLES (POLISH). SCIENTIFIC SESSION OF THE YOUNG WORKERS OF SCIENCE SZSP AGH, SCI. BULL. STANISLAW STASZIC UNIV., NO. 691, SPEC. SER.-BULL. 58, 193-200. (1978).

WALD 1975 -1 WALDMANN, O.
INTEGRATED OPERATIONAL PLANNING OF FLOW-SHOP-TYPE PRODUCTION LINES WITH REFERENCE TO A PRACTICAL APPLICATION. DISSERATION. SCHENECTADY: UNION COLLEGE AND UNIVERSITY, 230 P. (1975).

WALK 1980 -1 WALK, M.
QUALITAET EINES VERALLGEMEINERTEN TRANSPORT- UND POTENTIALPROBLEMS. MATHEMATISCHE OPERATIONSFORSCHUNG UND STATISTIK, SERIES OPTIMIZATION 11, 465-472. (1980).

WALK 1980 -2 WALK, M.
OPTIMALE PROGRAMME FUER MULTISTROEME AUF ENDLICHEN GERICHTETEN GRAPHEN. WISSENSCHAFTLICHE ZEITSCHRIFT DER FRIEDRICH-SCHILLER-UNIVERSITAET JENA, MATHEMATISCH-NATURWISSENSCHAFTLICHE REIHE 29, 319-325. (1980).

WALKA 1976 -1 WALK, M.; VERBESEK, W.
VERALLGEMEINERTE STROEME UND SPANNUNGEN UEBER ENDLICHEN GERICHTETEN GRAPHEN. IN: 21. INTERNATIONALES WISSENSCHAFTLICHES KOLLOQUIM, ILMENAU 1976, HEFT 4, 65-67. (1976).

WALKB 1977 -1 WALKUP, D. W.
MATCHINGS IN RANDOM REGULAR BIPARTITE DIGRAPHS. ST. LOUIS: WASHINGTON UNIV., DEPT. OF COMPUTER SCIENCE, 8 P. (1977).

WALKB 1977 -2 WALKUP, D. W.
MATCHINGS IN RANDOM REGULAR BIPARTITE GRAPHS. TECHNICAL REPORT. ST. LOUIS: WASHINGTON UNIVERSITY, DEPARTMENT OF COMPUTER SCIENCE. (1977).

WALKB 1979 -1 WALKUP, D. W.
ON THE EXPECTED VALUE OF A RANDOM ASSIGNMENT PROBLEM. SIAM JOURNAL ON COMPUTING 8, 440-442. (1979).

WALL 1976 -1 WALLER, D. A.
REGULAR EIGENVALUES OF GRAPHS AND ENUMERATION OF SPANNING TREES. IN: ACCADEMIA NAZIONALE DEI LINCEI (ED.): COLLOQUIO INTERNAZIONALE SULLE TEORIE COMBINATORIE CON LA COLLABORAZIONE DELLA AMERICAN MATHEMATICAL SOCIETY, TOMO I, ROMA 1973, 313-320. ROMA: ACCADEMIA NAZIONALE DEI LINCEI. (1976).

WALLA 1976 -1 WALLIS, W. D.
NUMBER OF MONOCHROMATIC TRIANGLES IN EDGE-COLOURINGS OF A COMPLETE GRAPH, THE. JOURNAL OF COMBINATORICS AND INFORMATION SYSTEM SCIENCES 1, 17-20. (1976).

WALS 1976 -1 WALSH, A. M.
POLYNOMIAL ALGORITHMS FOR CERTAIN GRAPH-THEORETIC PROBLEMS. SAN DIEGO: UNIV. OF CALIFORNIA, 88 P. (1976). (DISSERTATION)

WALSA 1975 -1 WALSH, A. M.; BURKHARD, W. A.
POLYNOMIAL ALGORITHMS FOR (3,1) GRAPHS. IN: PROCEEDINGS OF THE 1975 CONFERENCE ON INFORMATION SCIENCES AND SYSTEMS, BALTIMORE 1975, 245-248. BALTIMORE: THE JOHNS HOPKINS UNIVERSITY: DEPARTMENT OF ELECTRICAL ENGINEERING. (1975).

WALSA 1977 -1 WALSH, A. M.; BURKHARD, W. A.
EFFICIENT ALGORITHMS FOR (3,1) GRAPHS. INFORMATION SCIENCES 13, NO. 1, 1-10. (1977).

WALSB 1978 -1 WALSH, T. R. S.; WRIGHT, E. M.
K-CONNECTEDNESS OF UNLABELLED GRAPHS, THE. THE JOURNAL OF THE LONDON MATHEMATICAL SOCIETY 18, 397-402. (1978).

WALT 1979 -1 WALTHER, H.
ANWENDUNGEN DER GRAPHENTHEORIE. BRAUNSCHWEIG, WIESBADEN: VIEWEG, 239 P. (1979).

WALTA 1980 -1 WALTON, P. N.; WELSH, D. J. A.
ON THE CHROMATIC NUMBER OF BINARY MATROIDS. MATHEMATIKA (LONDON) 27, NO. 53, PART 1, 1-9. (1980).

WALU 1978 -1 WALUKIEWICZ, S.
USING PSEUDOBOOLEAN PROGRAMMING IN DECOMPOSITION METHOD. IN: J. STOER (ED.): OPTIMIZATION TECHNIQUES, PROCEEDINGS OF THE 8TH IFIP CONFERENCE ON OPTIMIZATION TECHNIQUES, WUERZBURG 1977, PART 2, 269-277. LECTURE NOTES IN CONTROL AND INFORMATION SCIENCES 7. BERLIN, HEIDELBERG, NEW YORK: SPRINGER. (1978).

WANG 1978 -1 WANG, D.-L.; WANG, P.
SOME RESULTS ABOUT THE CHVATAL CONJECTURE. DISCRETE MATHEMATICS 24, 95-101. (1978).

WANGA 1981 -1 WANG, P. Y.
TWO ALGORITHMS FOR CONSTRAINED TWO-DIMENSIONAL CUTTING STOCK PROBLEMS. RESEARCH REPORT 81-3. CATONSVILLE: UNIV. OF MARYLAND, BALTIMORE COUNTY, DEPT. OF MATHEMATICS, 20 P. (1981).

WANK 1978 -1 WANKMUELLER, F.
GRAPHENKLASSEN, BEI DENEN DAS CLIQUENPROBLEM IN POLYNOMIALER ZEIT LOESBAR IST. IN: J. MUEHLBACHER (ED.): DATENSTRUKTUREN, GRAPHEN, ALGORITHMEN. DRITTE FACHTAGUNG UEBER GRAPHENTHEORETISCHE KONZEPTE DER INFORMATIK, LINZ 1977, 287-298. MUENCHEN, WIEN: HANSER. (1978).

WANT 1979 -1 WANTULA, B. P.
ON A CERTAIN CHARACTERIZATION OF K-CONNECTED GRAPHS (POLISH). ZESZYTY NAUKOWE POLITECHNIKI SLASKIEJ 623, MATEMATYKA-FIZYKA (GLIWICE) 34, 55-56. (1979).

WARD 1952 -1 WARDROP, J. G.
SOME THEORETICAL ASPECTS OF ROAD TRAFFIC RESEARCH. IN: PROCEEDINGS OF THE INSTITUTE OF CIVIL ENGINEERING, PART II, 325-378. (1952).

WARR 1978 -1 WARREN, H. S. JR.
STATIC MAIN STORAGE PACKING PROBLEMS. ACTA INFORMATICA 9, 355-376. (1978).

WASS 1978 -1 WASSENHOVE, L. N. VAN; GELDERS, L. F.
FOUR SOLUTION TECHNIQUES FOR A GENERAL ONE MACHINE SCHEDULING PROBLEM; A COMPARATIVE STUDY. EUROPEAN JOURNAL OF OPERATIONAL RESEARCH 2, 281-290. (1978).

WASS 1980 -1 WASSENHOVE, L. N. VAN; GELDERS, L. F.
SOLVING A BICRITERION SCHEDULING PROBLEM. EUROPEAN JOURNAL OF OPERATIONAL RESEARCH 4, 42-48. (1980).

WATA 1981 -1 WATANABE, T.; AE, T.; NAKAMURA, A.
ON THE REMOVAL OF FORBIDDEN GRAPHS BY EDGE-DELETION OR BY EDGE-CONTRACTION. DISCRETE APPLIED MATHEMATICS 3, 151-153. (1981).

WATAA 1979 -1 WATANABE, T.; ASANO, T.; SAITO, N.
UPPER BOUNDS ON THE LENGTHS OF CHINESE POSTMAN WALKS IN UNDIRECTED GRAPHS (JAPANESE). TRANSACTIONS OF THE INSTITUTE OF ELECTRONICS AND COMMUNICATION ENGINEERS OF JAPAN (TOKYO) J62-D, NO. 4, 289-296. (1979).

WATK 1969 -1 WATKINS, M. E.
THEOREM ON TAIT COLORINGS WITH AN APPLICATION TO THE GENERALIZED PETERSEN GRAPHS. A. IN: F. HARARY (ED.): PROOF TECHNIQUES IN GRAPH THEORY, 171-177. NEW YORK: ACADEMIC PRESS; ALSO PUBLISHED IN JOURNAL OF COMBINATORIAL THEORY 6, 1969, 152-164. (1969).

WDOW 1977 -1 WDOWIAK, J.
DISCRETE LINEAR FRACTIONAL PROGRAMMING PROBLEM (POLISH), A. POLSKA ACADEMIA NAUK. KOMITET STATISTYKII EKONOMETRII. PRZEGLAD STATYSTYCZNY 24, 483-497. (1977).

WDOW 1978 -1 WDOWIAK, J.
DISCRETE LINEAR FRACTIONAL PROGRAMMING PROBLEM II (POLISH), A. PRZEGLAD STATYSTYCZNY 25, 133-140. (1978).

WEBB 1978 -1 WEBB, W. A.
SCHEDULING OF TRACKING TIMES FOR INTERPLANETARY SPACECRAFT ON THE DEEP SPACE NETWORK. NEW YORK(TIMS/ORSA MEETING, MAY 1978): 6 P. (1978).

WEED 1978 -1 WEEDA, P. J.
DYNAMIC PROGRAMMING FORMULATION FOR THE ONE MACHINE SEQUENCING PROBLEM, A. EUROPEAN JOURNAL OF OPERATIONAL RESEARCH 2, 298-300. (1978).

WEGL 1979 -1 WEGLARZ, J.
PROJECT SCHEDULING WITH DISCRETE AND CONTINUOUS RESOURCES. IEEE TRANSACTIONS ON SYSTEMS, MAN AND CYBERNETICS 9, 644-650. (1979).

WEGL 1980 -1 WEGLARZ, J.
MULTIPROCESSOR SCHEDULING WITH MEMORY ALLOCATION - A DETERMINISTIC APPROACH. IEEE TRANSACTIONS ON COMPUTERS 29, 703-709. (1980).

WEI- 1979 -1 WEI-XUAN, L.; ZHU-YIN, W.
ON THE FINDING OF ALL SOLUTIONS FOR THE OPTIMAL BLOCK SEARCH (CHINESE). ACTA MATHEMATICA SINICA 22, 45-53. (1979).

WEID 1977 -1 WEIDE, B.
SURVEY OF ANALYSIS TECHNIQUES FOR DISCRETE ALGORITHMS, A. COMPUTING SURVEYS 9, 291-313. (1977).

WEIN 1979 -1 WEINBERG, F.
NECESSARY AND SUFFICIENT CONDITION FOR THE AGGREGATION OF LINEAR DIOPHANTINE EQUATIONS, A. IN: A. PREKOPA (ED.): SURVEY OF MATHEMATICAL PROGRAMMING, VOLUME 2, 559-566. AMSTERDAM: NORTH-HOLLAND. (1979).

WEIN 1979 -2 WEINBERG, F.
SPECTRAL ALGORITHM FOR SEQUENTIAL AGGREGATION OF M LINEAR DIOPHANTINE CONSTRAINTS, A. ZEITSCHRIFT FUER ANGEWANDTE MATHEMATIK UND PHYSIK 30, 677-698. (1979).

WEINA 1980 -1 WEINTRAUB, A.; GONZALEZ, J.
ALGORITHM FOR THE TRAFFIC ASSIGNMENT PROBLEM, AN. NETWORKS 10, 197-210. (1980).

WELS 1971 -1 WELSH, D. J. A.
COMBINATORIAL PROBLEMS IN MATROID THEORY. IN: D. J. A. WELSH (ED.): COMBINATORIAL MATHEMATICS AND ITS APPLICATIONS, 291-306. LONDON, NEW YORK: ACADEMIC PRESS. (1971).

WELS 1978 -1 WELSH, D. J. A.
COMBINATORIAL PROBLEMS IN PERCOLATION THEORY. IN: J.-C. BERMOND ET AL. (EDS.): PROBLEMES COMBINATOIRES ET THEORIE DES GRAPHES, COLLOQUES INTERNATIONAUX DU CENTRE NATIONAL DE LA RECHERCHE SCIENTIFIQUE, ORSAY 1976, 423-425. PARIS: CENTRE NATIONAL DE LA RECHERCHE SCIENTIFIQUE. (1978).

WELS 1979 -1 WELSH, D. J. A.
COLOURING PROBLEMS AND MATROIDS. IN: B. BOLLOBAS (ED.): SURVEYS IN COMBINATORICS. PROCEEDINGS OF THE 7TH BRITISH COMBINATORIAL CONFERENCE, 229-257. LONDON MATHEMATICAL SOCIETY LECTURE NOTE SERIES 38, CAMBRIDGE, LONDON, NEW YORK, MELBOURNE: CAMBRIDGE UNIVERSITY PRESS. (1979).

WELS 1979 -2 WELSH, D. J. A.
STOCHASTIC OPTIMIZATION ON NETWORKS. IN: W. OETTLI, F. STEFFENS (EDS.): OPERATIONS RESEARCH VERFAHREN 32, THIRD SYMPOSIUM ON OPERATIONS RESEARCH, MANNHEIM 1978, 203-206. KOENIGSTEIN: ANTON HAIN MEISENHEIM. (1979).

WELS 1980 -1 WELSH, D. J. A.
COLOURINGS, FLOWS AND PRODUCTIVE GEOMETRY. NIEUW ARCHIEF VOOR WISKUNDE, III. SERIE 28, 159-176. (1980).

WERR 1972 -1 WERRA, D. DE
INVESTIGATIONS ON AN EDGE-COLORING PROBLEM. DISCRETE MATHEMATICS 1, 167-179. (1972).

WERR 1974 -1 WERRA, D. DE
NOTE ON GRAPH COLORING, A. REVUE FRANCAISE D'AUTOMATIQUE, INFORMATIQUE, RECHERCHE OPERATIONELLE, SERIE ROUGE 8, 49-53. (1974).

WERR 1976 -1 WERRA, D. DE
ERRATA TO "ON GOOD AND EQUITABLE EDGE COLORINGS" (CAHIERS DU CENTRE D'ETUDES DE RECHERCHE OPERATIONELLE 17, 1975, 417-426). CAHIERS DU CENTRE D'ETUDES DE RECHERCHE OPERATIONELLE 18, 255. (1976).

WERR 1977 -1 WERRA, D. DE
ON A MULTIPERIOD ASSIGNMENT PROBLEM. IN: M. ROUBENS (ED.): ADVANCES IN OPERATIONS RESEARCH, PROCEEDINGS OF EURO II, THE SECOND EUROPEAN CONGRESS ON OPERATIONS RESEARCH, STOCKHOLM 1976, 129-134. AMSTERDAM, NEW YORK, OXFORD: NORTH-HOLLAND. (1977).

WERR 1977 -2 WERRA, D. DE
PROGRESSIVE BALANCING IN CHROMATIC SCHEDULING. IN: T. A. BOFFEY (ED.): PROCEEDINGS OF COMBINATORIAL PROGRAMMING 77, 105-113. LIVERPOOL: UNIVERSITY OF LIVERPOOL. (1977).

WERR 1978 -1 WERRA, D. DE
GRAPHS, HYPERGRAPHS AND TIMETABLING. URBINO: SUMMER SCHOOL IN COMBINATORIAL OPTIMIZATION, 35 P. (1978).

WERR 1978 -2 WERRA, D. DE
NESTED COVERINGS IN BIPARTITE MULTIGRAPHS. WORKING PAPER 37. LAUSANNE: ECOLE POLYTECHNIQUE FEDERALE DE LAUSANNE. (1978).

WERR 1978 -3 WERRA, D. DE
ON LINE PERFECT GRAPHS. MATHEMATICAL PROGRAMMING 15, 236-238. (1978).

WERR 1978 -4 WERRA, D. DE
SOME COMMENTS ON A NOTE ABOUT TIMETABLING. INFOR 16, 90-92. (1978).

WERR 1979 -1 WERRA, D. DE
ON A CLASS OF HYPERGRAPHS OCCURRING IN CHROMATIC SCHEDULING. CAHIERS DU CENTRE D'ETUDES DE RECHERCHE OPERATIONNELLE 21, 239-245. (1979).

WERR 1979 -2 WERRA, D. DE
ON THE USE OF ALTERNATING CHAINS AND HYPERGRAPHS IN EDGE COLORING. JOURNAL OF GRAPH THEORY 3, 175-182. (1979).

WERR 1979 -3 WERRA, D. DE
OPTIMIZATION IN EDGE CHROMATIC SCHEDULING. IN: A. PREKOPA (ED.): SURVEY OF MATHEMATICAL PROGRAMMING, VOLUME 2, 379-382. AMSTERDAM: NORTH-HOLLAND. (1979).

WERR 1979 -4 WERRA, D. DE
PARTIAL COMPACTNESS IN EDGE-CHROMATIC SCHEDULING. IN: W. OETTLI, F. STEFFENS (EDS.): OPERATIONS RESEARCH VERFAHREN 32, THIRD SYMPOSIUM ON OPERATIONS RESEARCH, MANNHEIM 1978, 207-219. KOENIGSTEIN: ANTON HAIN MEISENHEIM. (1979).

WERR 1979 -5 WERRA, D. DE
REGULAR AND CANONICAL COLORINGS. DISCRETE MATHEMATICS 27, 309-316. (1979).

WERR 1980 -1 WERRA, D. DE
FANTAISIES CHROMATIQUES SUR DIVERSES PARTITIONS. IN: P. HANSEN, D. DE WERRA (EDS.): REGARDS SUR LA THEORIE DES GRAPHES, PROCEEDINGS OF THE CERISY COLLOQUIUM, 1980, 127-144. LAUSANNE: PRESSES POLYTECHNIQUES ROMANDES. (1980).

WERR 1980 -2 WERRA, D. DE
GEOGRAPHY, GAMES AND GRAPHS. DISCRETE APPLIED MATHEMATICS 2, 327-338. (1980).

WERR 1980 -3 WERRA, D. DE
OBSTRUCTIONS FOR REGULAR COLORINGS. RAPPORT NR. 80/6. COPENHAGEN: UNIV. OF COPENHAGEN, INSTIUTE OF DATALOGY, 20 P. (1980).

WERR 1980 -4 WERRA, D. DE
ORDONNANCEMENT CHROMATIQUE ET PROBLEMES DE COLORATION. O. R. WORKING PAPER 50. LAUSANNE: ECOLE POLYTECHNIQUE FEDERALE DE LAUSANNE, DEPT. DE MATHEMATIQUES, 45 P. (1980).

WERR 1981 -1 WERRA, D. DE
ON SOME CHARACTERIZATIONS OF TOTALLY UNIMODULAR MATRICES. MATHEMATICAL PROGRAMMING 20, 14-21. (1981).

WERR 1981 -2 WERRA, D. DE
REMARKS ON THE REQUIREMENT MATRIX OF SCHOOL TIMETABLE PROBLEMS AND REGULAR EMBEDDINGS OF GRAPHS. EUROPEAN JOURNAL OF OPERATIONAL RESEARCH 6, 298-301. (1981).

WERR 1981 -3 WERRA, D. DE
SOME PARTITIONING PROBLEMS FOR GRAPHS AND HYPERGRAPHS. IN: R. E. BURKARD, T. ELLINGER (EDS.): METHODS OF OPERATIONS RESEARCH 40, 291-294. KOENIGSTEIN: ANTON HAIN MEISENHEIM. (1981).

WESS 1977 -1 WESSEL, W.
SOME COLOR-CRITICAL EQUIVALENTS OF THE STRONG PERFECT GRAPH CONJECTURE. IN: GRAPHENTHEORIE UND DEREN ANWENDUNGEN, INTERNATIONALES KOLLOQUIUM, OBERHOF 1977, 300-309. ILMENAU: TECHNISCHE HOCHSCHULE ILMENAU UND MATHEMATISCHE GESELLSCHAFT DER DDR. (1977).

WEST 1978 -1 WEST, D. B.
PAIRS OF ADJACENT HAMILTONIAN CIRCUITS WITH SMALL INTERSECTION. STUDIES IN APPLIED MATHEMATICS 59, NO. 3, 245-248. (1978).

WESTA 1979 -1 WESTON, F. C. JR.
SYSTEMS/MATHEMATICAL PROGRAMMING APPROACH TO THE MULTIPLE PRODUCT MAKE-BUY DECISION, A. HONOLULU (14TH TIMS MEETING, JUNE 1979) 13 P. (1979).

WETJ 1977 -1 WETJEN, A.
COMMENTS ON: "A BRANCH AND BOUND CLUSTERING ALGORITHM" (IEEE TRANSACTIONS ON COMPUTERS C-24 (1975), NO. 9, 908-915) BY W. L. G. KOONTZ, P. M. NARENDRA AND K. FUKUNAGA. WITH A REPLY BY KOONTZ. IEEE TRANSACTIONS ON COMPUTERS 27, NO. 2, 189. (1977).

WHIT 1979 -1 WHITE, G. M.; CHAN, P.-W.
TOWARDS THE CONSTRUCTION OF OPTIMAL EXAMINATION SCHEDULES. INFOR 17, 219-229. (1979).

WHITA 1980 -1 WHITE, G. P.
EASY LOWER BOUND ON THE NUMBER OF TRUCKS NEEDED TO SERVICE A SET OF DESTINATIONS, AN. OMEGA - INTERNATIONAL JOURNAL OF MANAGEMENT SCIENCE 8, 385-387. (1980).

WHITB 1980 -1 WHITE, G. P.; SWEENEY, D. J.
USING MULTIDIMENSIONAL SCALING TO SOLVE TRAVELING SALESMAN AND MACHINE SCHEDULING PROBLEMS. COMPUTERS AND OPERATIONS RESEARCH 7, 177-184. (1980).

WHITC 1977 -1 WHITE, G. P.; WILLIAMS, T. A.
HEURISTIC SOLUTION TECHNIQUES FOR MULTIPLE TRIP TIME-CONSTRAINED TRAVELING SALESMAN PROBLEMS. ATLANTA (52. ORSA-MEETING + TIMS, NOVEMBER 1977) 15 P. (1977).

WHITD 1980 -1 WHITE, N. L.
UNIQUE EXCHANGE PROPERTY FOR BASES, A. LINEAR ALGEBRA AND ITS APPLICATIONS 31, 81-91. (1980).

WHITE 1972 -1 WHITE, W. W.
MATHEMATICAL PROGRAMMING, MULTICOMMODITY FLOWS, AND COMMUNICATION NETS. IN: J. FOX (ED.): PROCEEDINGS OF THE SYMPOSIUM ON COMPUTER COMMUNICATIONS NETWORKS AND TELETRAFFIC, 325-334. NEW YORK: POLYTECHNIC PRESS. (1972).

WHITF 1970 -1 WHITE, W. W.; WRATHALL, E.
SYSTEM FOR RAILROAD TRAFFIC SCHEDULING, A. TECHNICAL REPORT NO. 320-2993. IBM-PHILADELPHIA SCIENTIC CENTER. (1970).

WHITG 1979 -1 WHITEHOUSE, G. E.; BROWN, J. R.
GENRES: AN EXTENSION OF BROOKS ALGORITHM FOR PROJECT SCHEDULING WITH RESOURCE CONSTRAINTS. COMPUTERS AND INDUSTRIAL ENGINEERING 3, 261-268. (1979).

WHITH 1981 -1 WHITESIDES, S. H.
ALGORITHM FOR FINDING CLIQUE CUT-SETS, AN. INFORMATION PROCESSING LETTERS 12, 31-32. (1981).

WILF 1979 -1 WILF, H. S.
"WHY DON'T YOU JUST ...?" BARRIER IN DISCRETE ALGORITHMS, THE. THE AMERICAN MATHEMATICAL MONTHLY 86, 7 + 571. (1979).

WILL 1978 -1 WILLIAMS, H. P.
REFORMULATION OF TWO MIXED INTEGER PROGRAMMING PROBLEMS, THE. MATHEMATICAL PROGRAMMING 14, 325-331. (1978).

WILL 1979 -1 WILLIAMS, H. P.
ECONOMIC INTERPRETATION OF DUALITY FOR PRACTICAL MIXED INTEGER PROGRAMMING PROBLEMS, THE. IN: A. PREKOPA (ED.): SURVEY OF MATHEMATICAL PROGRAMMING, VOLUME 2, 567-586. AMSTERDAM: NORTH-HOLLAND. (1979).

WILLA 1968 -1 WILLIAMS, M. R.
GRAPH THEORY MODEL FOR THE SOLUTION OF TIMETABLES, A. PH. D. THESIS. GLASGOW: UNIVERSITY OF GLASGOW. (1968).

WILLB 1980 -1 WILLIAMSON, S. G.
TREE OF PATHS OF A GRAPH, THE. IN: M. DAUCHET, E. LILIN (EDS.): LES ARBRES EN ALGEBRE ET EN PROGRAMMATION, LILLE 1980, 241-261. VILLENEUVE D'ASCQ: UNIV. DE LILLE. (1980).

WILLC 1980 -1 WILLIE, R. R.
DETERMINING RELIABILITY CUT AND PATH SET FAMILIES FOR A CAPACITATED FLOW NETWORK. RESEARCH PAPER. HOLMDEL: BELL TELEPHONE LABORATORIES, 65 P. (1980).

WILS 1977 -1 WILSON, J. M.
METHOD FOR REDUCING COEFFICIENTS IN ZERO-ONE LINEAR INEQUALITIES, A. INTERNATIONAL JOURNAL OF MATHEMATICAL EDUCATION IN SCIENCE AND TECHNOLOGY 8, 31-35. (1977).

WILSA 1975 -1 WILSON, R. J.
SOME CONJECTURES ON EDGE-COLOURINGS OF GRAPHS. IN: M. FIEDLER (ED.): RECENT ADVANCES IN GRAPH THEORY, 525-528. PRAGUE: ACADEMIA. (1975).

WILSA 1976 -1 WILSON, R. J.
EDGE-COLORINGS OF CRITICAL GRAPHS. IN: ACCADEMIA NAZIONALE DEI LINCEI (ED.): COLLOQUIO INTERNAZIONALE SULLE TEORIE COMBINATORIE CON LA COLLABORAZIONE DELLA AMERICAN MATHEMATICAL SOCIETY, TOMO I. ROMA 1973, 309-312. ROMA: ACCADEMIA NAZIONALE DEI LINCEI. (1976).

WILSA 1978 -1 WILSON, R. J.
EDGE COLOURINGS OF GRAPHS - A SURVEY. IN: Y. ALAVI, D. R. LICK (EDS.): THEORY AND APPLICATION OF GRAPHS, PROCEEDINGS OF THE INTERNATIONAL CONFERENCE, MICHIGAN 1976, 608-619. LECTURE NOTES OF MATHEMATICS 642. BERLIN: SPRINGER. (1978).

WIN 1979 -1 WIN, S.
ON A CONJECTURE OF LAS VERGNAS CONCERNING CERTAIN SPANNING TREES IN GRAPHS. RESULTATE DER MATHEMATIK 2, 215-224. (1979).

WINO 1980 -1 WINOGRAD, S.
ARITHMETIC COMPLEXITY OF COMPUTATIONS. PHILADELPHIA: SOCIETY FOR INDUSTRIAL AND APPLIED MATHEMATICS, 93 P. (1980). (REGIONAL CONFERENCE SERIES IN APPLIED MATHEMATICS, 33)

WOEH 1979 -1 WOEHNER, W.
METHODE ZUR OPTIMALEN PLANUNG GEWISSER TRANSPORTPROZESSE IN NETZEN, EINE. WISSENSCHAFTLICHE ZEITSCHRIFT DER HOCHSCHULE FUER VERKEHRSWESEN "FRIEDRICH LIST" IN DRESDEN. DIE ANWENDUNG MATHEMATISCHER METHODEN IM TRANSPORT- UND NACHRICHTENWESEN 26, 613-616. (1979).

WOJD 1978 -1 WOJDA, A. P.
ON A CLASS OF HAMILTONIAN-TYPE NOTIONS. IN: J.-C. BERMOND ET AL. (EDS.): PROBLEMES COMBINATOIRES ET THEORIE DES GRAPHES, COLLOQUES INTERNATIONAUX DU CENTRE NATIONAL DE LA RECHERCHE SCIENTIFIQUE, ORSAY 1976, 431-434. PARIS: CENTRE NATIONAL DE LA RECHERCHE SCIENTIFIQUE. (1978).

WOJD 1978 -2 WOJDA, A. P.
STRONGLY (P,Q)-HAMILTONIAN GRAPHS (SOME RESULTS). IN: A. HAJNAL, V. T. SOS (EDS.): COMBINATORICS, VOLUME II, 1165-1168. COLLOQUIA MATHEMATICA SOCIETATIS JANOS BOLYAI 18. AMSTERDAM: NORTH-HOLLAND. (1978).

WOLL 1969 -1 WOLLMER, R. D.
DANTZIG-WOLFE DECOMPOSITION PRINCIPLE AND MINIMUM COST MULTICOMMODITY NETWORK FLOWS, THE. WORKING PAPER P-4191. SANTA MONICA: RAND COOPERATION. (1969).

WOLL 1980 -1 WOLLMER, R. D.
INVESTMENT IN STOCHASTIC MINIMUM COST GENERALIZED MULTICOMMODITY NETWORKS WITH APPLICATION TO COAL TRANSPORT. NETWORKS 10, 351-362. (1980).

WOLL 1980 -2 WOLLMER, R. D.
TWO STAGE LINEAR PROGRAMMING UNDER UNCERTAINTY WITH 0-1 INTEGER FIRST STAGE VARIABLES. MATHEMATICAL PROGRAMMING 19, 279-288. (1980).

WOLLA 1977 -1 WOLLNER, E.
ANALYSE UND SYNTHESE ZUVERLAESSIGER NETZE. TECHNISCHER BERICHT. DARMSTADT: FORSCHUNGSINSTITUT DER DEUTSCHEN BUNDESPOST, 43 P. (1977).

WOLS 1977 -1 WOLSEY, L. A.
VALID INEQUALITIES AND SUPERADDITIVITY OF 0-1 INTEGER PROGRAMS. MATHEMATICS OF OPERATIONS RESEARCH 2, 66-77. (1977).

WOLS 1979 -1 WOLSEY, L. A.
CUTTING PLANE METHODS. IN: A. G. HOLZMAN (ED.): OPERATIONS RESEARCH SUPPORT METHODOLOGY, 441-466. NEW YORK, BASEL: DEKKER. (1979).

WOLS 1980 -1 WOLSEY, L. A.
HEURISTIC ANALYSIS, LINEAR PROGRAMMING AND BRANCH AND BOUND. MATHEMATICAL PROGRAMMING STUDY 13, 121-134. (1980).

WOLS 1980 -2 WOLSEY, L. A.
MAXIMIZING REAL-VALUED SUBMODULAR FUNCTIONS: PRIMAL AND DUAL HEURISTICS FOR LOCATION PROBLEMS. RESEARCH REPORT 8019. LOUVAIN: CENTER FOR OPERATIONS RESEARCH AND ECONOMETRICS (CORE), 31 P. (1980).

WOLS 1981 -1 WOLSEY, L. A.
INTEGER PROGRAMMING DUALITY: PRICE FUNCTIONS AND SENSITIVITY ANALYSIS. MATHEMATICAL PROGRAMMING 20, 173-195. (1981).

WOLT 1979 -1 WOLTERS, J. A. M.
MINIMISING THE NUMBER OF AIRCRAFT FOR A TRANSPORTATION NETWORK. EUROPEAN JOURNAL OF OPERATIONAL RESEARCH 3, 394-402. (1979).

WONG 1979 -1 WONG, J. K.
NEW IMPLEMENTATION OF AN ALGORITHM FOR THE OPTIMAL ASSIGNMENT PROBLEM: AN IMPROVED VERSION OF MUNKRES' ALGORITHM, A. NORDISK TIDSKRIFT FOR INFORMATIONSBEHANDLING 19, 418-424. (1979).

WONGA 1978 -1 WONG, P.-K.
ON CERTAIN N-CONNECTED MATROIDS. JOURNAL FUER DIE REINE UND ANGEWANDTE MATHEMATIK 299/300, 1-6. (1978).

WONGB 1980 -1 WONG, R. T.
WORST-CASE ANALYSIS OF NETWORK DESIGN PROBLEM HEURISTICS. SIAM JOURNAL ON ALGEBRAIC AND DISCRETE METHODS 1, 51-63. (1980).

WONGB 1981 -1 WONG, R. T.
PROBABILISTIC ANALYSIS OF AN OPTIMAL NETWORK PROBLEM HEURISTIC. RESEARCH REPORT. TROY, N.Y.: RENSSELAER POLYTECHNIC INST., DEPT. OF MATHEMATICAL SCIENCES, 24 P. (1981).

WOOD 1978 -1 WOOD, D. M.
DYNAMIC PROGRAMMING SOLUTION TO A PROBLEM OF LOOM BOX SEQUENCE PLANNING, A. THE JOURNAL OF THE OPERATIONAL RESEARCH SOCIETY 29, 1159-1165. (1978).

WOODA 1974 -1 WOODALL, D. R.
APPLICATIONS OF POLYMATROIDS AND LINEAR PROGRAMMING TO TRANSVERSALS AND GRAPHS. IN: T. P. MAC DONOUGH, V. C. MAVRON (EDS.): COMBINATORICS, PROCEEDINGS OF THE BRITISH COMBINATORIAL CONFERENCE, ABERYSTWYTH 1973, 195-200. LONDON MATHEMATICAL SOCIETY LECTURE SERIES 13. LONDON: CAMBRIDGE UNIVERSITY PRESS. (1974).

WOODA 1977 -1 WOODALL, D. R.
ZEROS OF CHROMATIC POLYNOMIALS. IN: P. J. CAMERON (ED.): COMBINATORIAL SURVEYS, 199-224. LONDON: ACADEMIC PRESS. (1977).

WOODA 1978 -1 WOODALL, D. R.
MINIMAX THEOREMS IN GRAPH THEORY. IN: L. W. BEINEKE, R. J. WILSON (EDS.): SELECTED TOPICS IN GRAPH THEORY, 237-270. LONDON, NEW YORK, SAN FRANCISCO: ACADEMIC PRESS. (1978).

WUES 1978 -1 WUESTEFELD, A.
EINPARAMETRISCHE OPTIMIERUNG FUER DIE P-NORM ZIELFUNKTION BEIM TRANSPORTPROBLEM. DIPLOMARBEIT. KOELN: UNIVERSITAET KOELN, MATHEMATISCHES INSTITUT. (1978).

WUESA 1980 -1 WUESTEFELD, A.; ZIMMERMANN, U.
NONLINEAR ONE-PARAMETRIC LINEAR PROGRAMMING AND T-NORM TRANSPORTATION PROBLEMS. NAVAL RESEARCH LOGISTICS QUARTERLY 27, 187-197. (1980).

WUND 1979 -1 WUNDERATSCH, H.
DETERMINISTISCHES ZUORDNEN IN HETEROGENEN PROZESSORSYSTEMEN MIT PSEUDO-BOOLE METHODEN. ARBEITSBERICHTE DES INSTITUTS FUER MATHEMATISCHE MASCHINEN UND DATENVERARBEITUNG (INFORMATIK) DER UNIVERSITAET ERLANGEN-NUERNBERG 12, NO. 2. ERLANGEN: UNIV. ERLANGEN-NUERNBERG, 150 P. (1979).

WYSK 1980 -1 WYSK, R. A.; DAVIS, R. P.; TANCHOCO, J. M. A.
MACHINING PARAMETER OPTIMIZATION WITH LOT SIZE CONSIDERATIONS. AIIE TRANSACTIONS 12, 59-63. (1980).

YAKA 1979 -1 YAKAJITANI, Y.; UENO, S.
ON THE RANK OF CERTAIN CLASSES OF CUT-SETS AND TIE-SETS OF A GRAPH. IEEE TRANSACTIONS ON CIRCUITS AND SYSTEMS 26, 666-668. (1979).

YAMA 1976 -1 YAMAMOTO, Y.
ALGORITHM FOR FINDING A COMMON BASIS OF TWO MATROIDS, AN. KEIO ENGINEERING REPORTS 29, NO. 4, 41-51. (1976).

YAMA 1978 -1 YAMAMOTO, Y.
HELD-KARP ALGORITHM AND DEGREE-CONSTRAINED MINIMUM 1-TREES, THE. MATHEMATICAL PROGRAMMING 15, 228-231. (1978).

YAMA 1980 -1 YAMAMOTO, Y.
GROUP THEORETIC DUAL PROBLEM WITHOUT DUALITY GAPS FOR BOUNDED INTEGER PROGRAMS, A. JOURNAL OF THE OPERATIONS RESEARCH SOCIETY OF JAPAN 23, 146-155. (1980).

YANN 1978 -1 YANNAKAKIS, M.
NODE- AND EDGE-DELETION NP-COMPLETE PROBLEMS. IN: PROCEEDINGS OF THE TENTH ANNUAL ACM SYMPOSIUM ON THEORY OF COMPUTING, SAN DIEGO, 1978, 253-264. NEW YORK: THE ASSOCIATION FOR COMPUTING MACHINERY. (1978).

YANN 1979 -1 YANNAKAKIS, M.
EFFECT OF A CONNECTIVITY REQUIREMENT ON THE COMPLEXITY OF MAXIMUM SUBGRAPH PROBLEMS, THE. JOURNAL OF THE ASSOCIATION FOR COMPUTING MACHINERY 26, 618-630. (1979).

YANNA 1980 -1 YANNAKAKIS, M.; GAVRIL, F.
EDGE DOMINATING SETS IN GRAPHS. SIAM JOURNAL ON APPLIED MATHEMATICS 38, 364-372. (1980).

YAO 1979 -1 YAO, A. C.-C.
COMPLEXITY OF PATTERN MATCHING FOR A RANDOM STRING, THE. SIAM JOURNAL ON COMPUTING 8, 368-387. (1979).

YAO 1980 -1 YAO, A. C.-C.
NEW ALGORITHMS FOR BIN PACKING. JOURNAL OF THE ASSOCIATION FOR COMPUTING MACHINERY 27, 207-227. (1980).

YAO A 1979 -1 YAO, F. F.
GRAPH 2-ISOMORPHISM IS NP-COMPLETE. INFORMATION PROCESSING LETTERS 9, 68-72. (1979).

YATS 1972 -1 YATSUBOSHI, R.; HIRAYAMA, H.
ALGORITHM FOR FINDING FEASIBILITY CONDITIONS OF MULTICOMMODITY FLOWS IN A NETWORK, AN. ELECTRONICS AND COMMUNICATIONS IN JAPAN 55, NO. 6, 40-46. (1972).

YEE 1979 -1 YEE, J. R.; GOLDEN, B. L.
DETERMINING OPERATING STRATEGIES FOR PROBABILISTIC VEHICLE ROUTING (REVISED VERSION). WORKING PAPER. COLLEGE PARK: UNIV. OF MARYLAND, DEPT. OF ELECTRICAL ENGINEERING, 7 P. (1979).

YELL 1970 -1 YELLOW, P. C.
COMPUTATIONAL MODIFICATION OF THE SAVINGS METHOD OF VEHICLE SCHEDULING, A. OPERATIONAL RESEARCH QUARTERLY 21, 281-283. (1970).

YORM 1979 -1 YORMARK, J. S.
EFFICIENT FRONTIERS FOR NONLINEAR MULTIDIMENSIONAL KNAPSACK PROBLEMS. WORKING PAPER NO. 2. LOS ANGELES: UNIV. OF SOUTHERN CALIFORNIA, GRADUATE SCHOOL OF BUSINESS ADMINISTRATION, 22 P. (1979).

YOSH 1978 -1 YOSHIDA, T.; HITOMI, K.
OPTIMAL GROUP SCHEDULING ON MULTIPLE PRODUCTION STAGES. THEORETICAL ANALYSIS. TECHNOLOGY REPORTS OF THE OSAKA UNIVERSITY 28, 261-270. (1978).

YOSH 1979 -1 YOSHIDA, T.; HITOMI, K.
OPTIMAL TWO-STAGE PRODUCTION SCHEDULING WITH SETUP TIMES SEPARATED. AIIE TRANSACTIONS 11, 261-263. (1979).

YOSHA 1978 -1 YOSHIDA, T.; NAKAMURA, N.; HITOMI, K.
GROUP PRODUCTION SCHEDULING FOR MINIMUM TOTAL TARDINESS - PART (I). AIIE TRANSACTIONS 10, 157-162. (1978).

YOUN 1978 -1 YOUNG, H. P.
ON PERMUTATIONS AND PERMUTATION POLYTOPES. MATHEMATICAL PROGRAMMING STUDY 8, 128-140. (1978).

YOUNA 1979 -1 YOUNG, R. D.
BRANCH AND ROUND: AN ENUMERATIVE ALGORITHM FOR INTEGER PROGRAMS. IN: QUANTITATIVE PLANNING AND CONTROL, 9-22. NEW YORK: ACADEMIC PRESS. (1979).

YOUNB 1979 -1 YOUNGER, D. H.
FROM SHORTEST PATHS TO DIRECTED CUT TRANSVERSALS. IN: A. GEWIRTZ, L. V. QUINTAS (EDS.): SECOND INTERNATIONAL CONFERENCE ON COMBINATORIAL MATHEMATICS, 555-564. ANNALS OF THE NEW YORK ACADEMY OF SCIENCES, VOLUME 319. NEW YORK: THE NEW YORK ACADEMY OF SCIENCES. (1979).

YOUS 1978 -1 YOUSSEF, M. Y.
METHODES ET PROGRAMMES D'OPTIMISATION DANS LES PROBLEMES NON LINEAIRES DE FLOT ET DE TRANSPORT. NANCY, 108 P. (1978).

YUE 1976 -1 YUE, M. Y.
ON THE N JOB, M MACHINE SEQUENCING PROBLEM OF FLOW-SHOP. IN: K. B. HALEY (ED.): OPERATIONAL RESEARCH '75. PROCEEDINGS OF THE SEVENTH IFORS INTERNATIONAL CONFERENCE ON OPERATIONAL RESEARCH, TOKYO, KYOTO 1975, 179-200. AMSTERDAM: NORTH-HOLLAND. (1976).

YUE A 1979 -1 YUE, M. Y.; HAN, J. Y.
NEW METHOD FOR THE MXN FLOW-SHOP SEQUENCING PROBLEM (CHINESE), A. KEXUE TONGBAO 24, 821-824. (1979).

YUKH 1979 -1 YUKHIMENKO, B. I.
ON CERTAIN SOLUTION ALGORITHMS FOR PROBLEMS OF LINEAR PROGRAMMING WITH BOOLEAN VARIABLES (RUSSIAN). KIBERNETIKA, NO. 5, 141-143. (1979).

ZABE 1978 -1 ZABELLO, L. E.; FEDULOV, L. V.
METHOD FOR THE IMPROVEMENT OF ADMISSIBLE VARIANTS OF JOBS DEFINED BY A NETLIKE GRAPH (RUSSIAN), A. VESTNIK BELORUSSKOGO GOSUDARSTVENNOGO UNIVERSITETA IM. V. I. LENINA. NAUCNYI ZURNAL. SERIJA I. MATEMATIKA, FIZIKA, MEHANIKA, NO. 2, 17-19 + 93. (1978).

ZABR 1970 -1 ZABRANSKY, F.
ALUMINUM FOIL SLITTING TRIM LOSS PROBLEM; FORMULATED AS A MIXED INTEGER PROBLEM; SOLVED BY HEURISTIC PROGRAMMING. WORKING PAPER SERIES NO. 46. LONDON, ONTARIO: THE UNIVERSITY OF WESTERN ONTARIO, SCHOOL OF BUSINESS ADMINISTRATION. (1970).

ZAHO 1974 -1 ZAHORJAN, J.
PRODUCTION SCHEDULING MODEL TO DETERMINE THE MINIMAL COST TO MEET SEASONAL PRODUCT DEMAND, A. DISSERTATION. BUFFALO: STATE UNIVERSITY OF NEW YORK, 164 P. (1974).

ZAIC 1978 -1 ZAICENKO, V. A.; IVANOV, A. V.; ROZENFEL'D, M. Z.; FARADZEV, I. A.
ALGORITHM FOR CHECKING THE CANONICITY OF A PARTIALLY AUGMENTED ADJACENCY MATRIX OF A GRAPH (RUSSIAN), AN. IN: I. A. FARADZEV (ED.): ALGORITHMIC STUDIES IN COMBINATORICS (RUSSIAN). INTERNATIONAL COLLOQUIUM ON COMBINATORICS AND GRAPH THEORY, ORSAY 1976, 19-25 + 185. MOSCOW: IZDAT. "NAUKA". (1978).

ZAJT 1979 -1 ZAJTSEV, I. D.; SALYGA, V. I.; VAJNER, V. G.
SUR UN PROBLEME DE LA THEORIE DES RESEAUX DE COMMUNICATION (RUSSIAN). DOKLADY AKADEMIJA NAUK UKRAINSKOI SSR 12, SERIES A, 1035-1039. (1979).

ZAK 1977 -1 ZAK, JU. A.
ON A CLASS OF INTEGER LINEAR PROGRAMMING PROBLEMS WITH BOOLEAN VARIABLES (RUSSIAN). AKADEMIJA NAUK LATVIISKOI SSR. AVTOMATIKA I VYCISLITEL'NAJA TEHNIKA, NO. 6, 26-33. (1977).

ZAK 1978 -1 ZAK, JU. A.
ALGORITHMS FOR NONLINEAR PSEUDO-BOOLEAN PROGRAMMING. IZVESTIJA AKADEMII NAUK SSSR. TEHNICESKAJA KIBERNETIKA, NO. 5, 35-45 + 219; TRANSLATED AS ENGINEERING CYBERNETICS 16, 1978, NO. 5, 29-40. (1978).

ZAK 1978 -2 ZAK, JU. A.
CERTAIN PROPERTIES OF SCHEDULING PROBLEMS. AVTOMATIKA I TELEMEHANIKA, NO. 1, 123-132; TRANSLATED AS AUTOMATION AND REMOTE CONTROL 39, NO. 1, 99-107. (1978).

ZAKS 1978 -1 ZAKS, J.
SOME HAMILTONIAN RESULTS IN POLYTOPAL GRAPHS. IN: J.-C. BERMOND ET AL. (EDS.): PROBLEMES COMBINATOIRES ET THEORIE DES GRAPHES, COLLOQUES INTERNATIONAUX DU CENTRE NATIONAL DE LA RECHERCHE SCIENTIFIQUE, ORSAY 1976, 435-436. PARIS: CENTRE NATIONAL DE LA RECHERCHE SCIENTIFIQUE. (1978).

ZAKSA 1979 -1 ZAKS, S.; RICHARDS, D.
GENERATING TREES AND OTHER COMBINATORIAL OBJECTS LEXICOGRAPHICALLY. SIAM JOURNAL ON COMPUTING 8, 73-81. (1979).

ZAMB 1978 -1 ZAMBICKII, D. K.; LOZOVANU, D. D.
ALGORITHM FOR FINDING THE S-, P- AND R-CENTERS OF A TREE (RUSSIAN), AN. BULETINUL AKADEMIEI DE STIINCE A RSS MOLDOVENEST, NO. 1, 10-13, 94. (1978).

ZAME 1977 -1 ZAME, A.
TRANSVERSAL THEORY AND RANK FUNCTIONS. JOURNAL OF MATHEMATICAL ANALYSIS AND APPLICATIONS 57, 448-461. (1977).

ZAMF 1975 -1 ZAMFIRESCU, T.
GRAPHEN, IN WELCHEN JE ZWEI ECKPUNKTE VON EINEM LAENGSTEN WEG VERMIEDEN WERDEN. ANNALI DELL'UNIVERSITA DI FERRARA. NUOVO SERIE. SEZIONE VII. SCIENZE MATEMATICHE 21, 17-24. (1975).

ZAMF 1980 -1 ZAMFIRESCU, T.
THREE SMALL CUBIC GRAPHS WITH INTERESTING HAMILTONIAN PROPERTIES. JOURNAL OF GRAPH THEORY 4, 287-292. (1980).

ZANA 1981 -1 ZANAKIS, S.
METHOD FOR LARGE-SCALE INTEGER GOAL PROGRAMMING WITH AN APPLICATION TO A FACILITY LOCATION/ ALLOCATION PROBLEM, A. IN: J. N. MORSE (ED.): ORGANIZATIONS: MULTIPLE AGENTS WITH MULTIPLE CRITERIA, 490-498. LECTURE NOTES IN ECONOMICS AND MATHEMATICAL SYSTEMS 190. BERLIN: SPRINGER. (1981).

ZANAA 1977 -1 ZANAKIS, S.; LAWRENCE, K. D.
EFFECTIVE SHIFT ALLOCATION IN MULTIPRODUCT LINES: A MIXED INTEGER PROGRAMMING APPROACH. OPERATIONAL RESEARCH QUARTERLY 28, 1013-1021. (1977).

ZARE 1979 -1 ZARETZKY, L. S.
TRAVELLING SALESMAN AND DELIVERY PROBLEMS SOLVING BY METHOD OF STATE FUNCTIONS CORRECTION (RUSSIAN). ECONOMICS AND MATHEMATICAL METHODS 15, 194-201. (1979).

ZARY 1977 -1 ZARYAN, L. L.; LEBEDEV, S. S.; MESTETSKIJ, L. M.
SOLUTION OF INTEGER TRANSPORTATION PROBLEMS BY GENERALIZED LAGRANGE MULTIPLIERS (RUSSIAN). EKONOMIKA I MATEMATICESKIE METODY 13, 723-731. (1977).

ZEIT 1981 -1 ZEITLIN, Z.
INTEGER ALLOCATION PROBLEMS OF MIN-MAX TYPE WITH QUASICONVEX SEPARABLE FUNCTIONS. OPERATIONS RESEARCH 29, 207-211. (1981).

ZELI 1973 -1 ZELINKA, B.
EDGE-COLOURINGS OF PERMUTATION GRAPHS. MATEMATICKY CASOPIS 23, 193-198. (1973).

ZELI 1977 -1 ZELINKA, B.
REMARK ON SYSTEMS OF MAXIMAL CLIQUES OF A GRAPH, A. CZECHOSLOVAKIAN MATHEMATICAL JOURNAL 27, 617-618. (1977).

ZELI 1978 -1 ZELINKA, B.
NUMBER OF ISOMORPHISM CLASSES OF SPANNING TREES OF A GRAPH, THE. MATHEMATICA SLOVACA 28, 385-388. (1978).

ZELI 1978 -2 ZELINKA, B.
ON A PROBLEM OF R. HAEGGKVIST CONCERNING EDGE-COLOURINGS OF GRAPHS. CASOPIS PRO PESTOVANI MATEMATIKY 103, 289-290. (1978).

ZELI 1979 -1 ZELINKA, B.
EMBEDDING TREES INTO CLIQUE-BRIDGE-CLIQUE GRAPHS. CESKOSLOVENSKA AKADEMIE VED. CASOPIS PRO PESTOVANI MATEMATIKY 104, 353-356. (1979).

ZELI 1979 -2 ZELINKA, B.
SOME REMARKS ON EULERIAN GRAPHS. CZECHOSLOVAK MATHEMATICAL JOURNAL 29, 564-567. (1979).

ZELI 1979 -3 ZELINKA, B.
STRONGLY CONNECTED DIGRAPHS IN WHICH EACH EDGE IS CONTAINED IN EXACTLY TWO CYCLES. ACTA CYBERNETICA 4, 203-205. (1979).

ZELI 1980 -1 ZELINKA, B.
BASES OF CLASSES OF TREES CLOSED UNDER SUBDIVISIONS. MATHEMATICA SLOVACA (BRATISLAVA) 30, 61-64. (1980).

ZEME 1976 -1 ZEMEL, E.
ON THE FACIAL STRUCTURE OF 0-1 POLYTOPES. PH. D. DISSERTATION. PITTSBURGH: CARNEGIE-MELLON UNIVERSITY, GRADUATE SCHOOL OF INDUSTRIAL ADMINISTRATION. (1976).

ZEME 1978 -1 ZEMEL, E.
FUNCTIONS FOR MEASURING THE QUALITY OF PROXIMATE SOLUTIONS TO ZERO-ONE PROGRAMMING PROBLEMS. DISCUSSION PAPER NO. 323. EVANSTON: NORTHWESTERN UNIV., CENTER FOR MATHEMATICAL STUDIES IN ECONOMICS AND MANAGEMENT, 24 P. (1978).

ZEME 1978 -2 ZEMEL, E.
LIFTING THE FACETS OF ZERO-ONE POLYTOPES. MATHEMATICAL PROGRAMMING 15, 268-277. (1978).

ZEME 1980 -1 ZEMEL, E.
LINEAR MULTIPLE CHOICE KNAPSACK, THE. OPERATIONS RESEARCH 28, 1412-1423. (1980).

ZEPS 1980 -1 ZEPS, D. A.
EXHAUSTIVE SEARCH ALGORITHM FOR FINDING HAMILTONIAN CYCLES (RUSSIAN), AN. ELEKTRONISCHE INFORMATIONSVERARBEITUNG UND KYBERNETIK 16, 69-76. (1980).

ZERN 1976 -1 ZERNAK, A. N.
METHOD OF SOLVING QUASILINEAR INTEGER PROGRAMMING PROBLEMS (RUSSIAN), A. LENINGRADSKII GOSUDARSTVENNYI UNIVERSITET. AVTOMATIZIROVANNYE SISTEMY UPRAVLENIJA 3, 48-50 + 98. (1976).

ZIEL 1977 -1 ZIELINSKI, S.
SOLUTION OF LINEAR PROGRAMMING PROBLEMS IN ZERO-ONE VARIABLES. ZASTOSOWANIA MATEMATYKI 16, NO. 1, 123-131. (1977).

ZIJA 1979 -1 ZIJADULLAEV, N. S.; SERBULOV, A. V.
SOME PROBLEMS OF ESTIMATING THE AMOUNT OF CALCULATION INVOLVED IN PROBLEMS OF SCHEDULING THEORY (RUSSIAN). VOPROSY VYCISLITELNOI I PRIKLADNOI MATEMATIKI (TASHKENT) NO. 57, 153-163, 172. (1979).

ZIMM 1978 -1 ZIMMERMANN, U.
DUALITY AND THE ALGEBRAIC MATROID INTERSECTION PROBLEM. IN: R. HENN, P. KALL, H. KOENIG, B. KORTE, O. KRAFFT ET AL. (EDS.): OPERATIONS RESEARCH VERFAHREN 28, SECOND SYMPOSIUM ON OPERATIONS RESEARCH, AACHEN 1977, 285-296. MEISENHEIM: HAIN. (1978).
ZIMM 1978 -2 ZIMMERMANN, U.
THRESHOLD METHODS FOR BOOLEAN OPTIMIZATION PROBLEMS WITH SEPARABLE OBJECTIVES. IN: J. STOER (ED.): OPTIMIZATION TECHNIQUES, PROCEEDINGS OF THE 8TH IFIP CONFERENCE ON OPTIMIZATION TECHNIQUES, WUERZBURG 1977, PART 2, 289-298. LECTURE NOTES IN CONTROL AND INFORMATION SCIENCES 7, BERLIN, HEIDELBERG, NEW YORK: SPRINGER. (1978).
ZIMM 1979 -1 ZIMMERMANN, U.
DUALITY PRINCIPLES AND THE ALGEBRAIC TRANSPORTATION PROBLEM. IN: L. COLLATZ, G. MEINARDUS, W. WETTERLING (EDS.): NUMERISCHE METHODEN BEI GRAPHENTHEORETISCHEN UND KOMBINATORISCHEN PROBLEMEN, BAND 2, OBERWOLFACH 1978, 234-255. ISNM 46, BASEL, BOSTON, STUTTGART: BIRKHAEUSER. (1979).
ZIMM 1979 -2 ZIMMERMANN, U.
MATROID INTERSECTION PROBLEMS WITH GENERALIZED OBJECTIVES. IN: A. PREKOPA (ED.): SURVEY OF MATHEMATICAL PROGRAMMING, VOLUME 2, 383-392. AMSTERDAM: NORTH-HOLLAND. (1979).
ZIMM 1979 -3 ZIMMERMANN, U.
ON SOME EXTREMAL OPTIMIZATION PROBLEMS. EKONOMICKO-MATEMATICKY OBZOR 14, 438-442. (1979).
ZIMM 1980 -1 ZIMMERMANN, U.
DUALITY FOR ALGEBRAIC LINEAR PROGRAMMING. LINEAR ALGEBRA AND ITS APPLICATIONS 32, 9-31. (1980).
ZIMM 1980 -2 ZIMMERMANN, U.
LINEAR OPTIMIZATION FOR LINEAR AND BOTTLENECK OBJECTIVES WITH ONE NONLINEAR PARAMETER. IN: K. IRACKI, K. MALANOWSKI, P. WALUKIEWICZ (EDS.): OPTIMIZATION TECHNIQUES, PART II, 211-222. LECTURE NOTES IN CONTROL AND INFORMATION SCIENCES 23. BERLIN: SPRINGER. (1980).
ZIMM 1981 -1 ZIMMERMANN, U.
LINEAR AND COMBINATORIAL OPTIMIZATION IN ORDERED ALGEBRAIC STRUCTURES. AMSTERDAM, NEW YORK, OXFORD: NORTH-HOLLAND, 380 P. (1981). (ANNALS OF DISCRETE MATHEMATICS, 10)
ZIMM 1981 -2 ZIMMERMANN, U.
MINIMIZATION OF SOME NONLINEAR FUNCTIONS OVER POLYMATROIDAL FLOWS. RESEARCH REPORT 81-5. KOELN: UNIV. ZU KOELN, MATHEMATISCHES INST., 30 P. (1981).
ZIMM 1981 -3 ZIMMERMANN, U.
SOME REMARKS ON ALGEBRAIC PATH PROBLEMS. IN: R. E. BURKARD, T. ELLINGER (EDS.): METHODS OF OPERATIONS RESEARCH 40, 445-449. KOENIGSTEIN: ANTON HAIN MEISENHEIM. (1981).
ZIMMA 1975 -1 ZIMMERMANN, W. J.
TOPICS IN NETWORK SCHEDULING. DOCTORAL DISSERTATION. AUSTIN: THE UNIVERSITY OF TEXAS, 353 P. (1975).
ZION 1978 -1 ZIONTS, S.
INTEGER LINEAR PROGRAMMING WITH MULTIPLE OBJECTIVES. IN: D. W. BUNN, H. THOMAS (EDS.): FORMAL METHODS IN POLICY FORMULATION, 158-167. INTERDISCIPLINARY SYSTEMS RESEARCH 49. BASEL: BIRKHAEUSER. (1978).
ZION 1979 -1 ZIONTS, S.
SURVEY OF MULTIPLE CRITERIA INTEGER PROGRAMMING METHODS, A. IN: P. L. HAMMER, E. L. JOHNSON, B. H. KORTE (EDS.): DISCRETE OPTIMIZATION II, 389-398. ANNALS OF DISCRETE MATHEMATICS 5, AMSTERDAM, NEW YORK, OXFORD: NORTH-HOLLAND. (1979).
ZIPK 1979 -1 ZIPKIN, P. H.
AGGREGATION AND DISAGGREGATION IN CONVEX NETWORK PROBLEMS. RESEARCH WORKING PAPER NO. 235A. NEW YORK: COLUMBIA UNIV., GRADUATE SCHOOL OF BUSINESS, 31 P. (1979).
ZIPK 1980 -1 ZIPKIN, P. H.
BOUNDS FOR AGGREGATING NODES IN NETWORK PROBLEMS. MATHEMATICAL PROGRAMMING 19, 155-177. (1980).
ZIPK 1980 -2 ZIPKIN, P. H.
TRANSPORTATION PROBLEMS WITH AGGREGATED DESTINATIONS WHEN DEMANDS ARE UNCERTAIN. RESEARCH WORKING PAPER NO. 275A. NEW YORK: COLUMBIA UNIV., GRADUATE SCHOOL OF BUSINESS, 33 P. (1980).
ZJUZ 1979 -1 ZJUZIN-ZINCHENKO, A. A.
MEASURES OF CRITICALITY IN A NETWORK MODEL IN THE CASE OF LIMITED RESOURCES (RUSSIAN). KIBERNETIKA I VYCISLITELNAJA TEHNIKA (KIEV) NO. 44, 66-78, 115. (1979).
ZLOT 1978 -1 ZLOTOV, A. V.
COMBINATORIAL ALGORITHM FOR THE CONSTRUCTION OF A NETWORK WITH A DISCONTINUOUS COST FUNCTION (RUSSIAN), A. EKONOMIKA I MATEMATICESKIE METODY (MOSCOW) 14, NO. 4, 783-787. (1978).
ZOLT 1978 -1 ZOLTNERS, A. A.
DIRECT DESCENT BINARY KNAPSACK ALGORITHM, A. JOURNAL OF THE ASSOCIATION FOR COMPUTING MACHINERY 25, 304-311. (1978).
ZOLTA 1979 -1 ZOLTNERS, A. A.; SINHA, P.; CHONG, P. S. C.
OPTIMAL ALGORITHM FOR SALES REPRESENTATIVE TIME MANAGEMENT, AN. MANAGEMENT SCIENCE 25, 1197-1207. (1979).
ZORY 1977 -1 ZORYCHTA, K.
ON CONVERTING THE 0-1 LINEAR PROGRAMMING PROBLEM TO A SET-COVERING PROBLEM. BULLETIN DE L'ACADEMIE POLONAISE DES SCIENCES. SERIE DES SCIENCES MATHEMATIQUES, ASTRONOMIQUES ET PHYSIQUES 25, NO. 9, 919-923. (1977).
ZUEN 1979 -1 ZUENKOV, M. A.; IGNATUSHCHENKO, V. V.
APPROXIMATE METHOD OF SOLUTION OF ONE-DIMENSIONAL KNAPSACK PROBLEM. AVTOMATIKA I TELEMEHANIKA, NO. 1, 89-97; TRANSLATED AS AUTOMATION AND REMOTE CONTROL 40, 1979, 69-75. (1979).
ZUEV 1979 -1 ZUEV, YU. A.
SET-COVERING PROBLEM: THE COMBINATORIAL-LOCAL APPROACH AND BRANCH AND BOUND METHOD (RUSSIAN). AKADEMIJA NAUK SSSR. ZURNAL VYCISLITEL'NOI MATEMATIKI I MATEMATICESKOI FIZIKI 19, 1566-1576. (1979).
ZUFR 1979 -1 ZUFRYDEN, F. S.
ZIPMAP - A ZERO-ONE INTEGER PROGRAMMING MODEL FOR MARKET SEGMENTATION AND PRODUCT POSITIONING. JOURNAL OF THE OPERATIONAL RESEARCH SOCIETY 30, 63-70. (1979).
ZUSU 1974 -1 ZUSUPBAEV, A.
PRODUCTION ALLOCATION PROBLEM WITH A CONVEX SEPARABLE FUNCTIONAL (RUSSIAN), THE. IZVESTIJA AKADEMII NAUK KIRGIZKOI SSR 6, 14-20. (1974).
ZWAR 1972 -1 ZWART, P.
INTERSECTION CUTS FOR SEPARABLE PROGRAMMING. ST. LOUIS: WASHINGTON UNIVERSITY. (1972).

PART 2

SUBJECT CLASSIFICATION

BACHA 1981 -1 BACHEM, A.; GROETSCHEL, M.
CHARACTERIZATIONS OF ADJACENCY OF FACES OF POLYHEDRA.

BALAH 1979 -1 BALAS, E.; PADBERG, M. W.
ADJACENT VERTICES OF THE ALL 0-1 PROGRAMMING POLYTOPE.

CHUNC 1980 -1 CHUNG, S.-J.
ADJACENCY ON THE 0-1 EDGE COVERING PROBLEM.

CHUNC 1979 -2 CHUNG, S.-J.
NP-COMPLETE ADJACENCY DECISION PROBLEMS ON SOME 0-1 CONVEX POLYTOPE.

CHUNC 1980 -2 CHUNG, S.-J.
STRUCTURAL COMPLEXITY OF ADJACENCY ON 0-1 CONVEX POLYTOPES.

GAL 1978 -1 GAL, T.
DETERMINATION OF ALL NEIGHBORS OF A DEGENERATE EXTREME POINT IN POLYTOPES.

GALLF 1979 -3 GALLO, G.; SODINI, C.
EXTREME POINTS AND ADJACENCY RELATIONSHIP IN THE FLOW POLYTOPE.

GILE 1979 -1 GILES, R.
ADJACENCY ON THE POSTMAN POLYHEDRON.

GILEA 1979 -1 GILES, R.; HAUSMANN, D.
CHARACTERIZATIONS OF ADJACENCY ON THE BRANCHING POLYHEDRON.

HAUS 1978 -1 HAUSMANN, D.
ADJAZENZCHARAKTERISIERUNGEN FUER POLYEDERECKEN IN DER KOMBINATORISCHEN OPTIMIERUNG.

HAUS 1979 -1 HAUSMANN, D.
COMPLEXITY OF THE TESTING OF ADJACENCY ON THE B-MATCHING POLYHEDRON.

HAUS 1980 -1 HAUSMANN, D.
ADJACENCY ON POLYTOPES IN COMBINATORIAL OPTIMIZATION.

HAUS 1981 -1 HAUSMANN, D.
ADJACENT VERTICES ON THE B-MATCHING POLYHEDRON.

HAUS 1978 -2 HAUSMANN, D.
POLYNOMIALER ALGORITHMUS FUER DIE ADJAZENZUEBERPRUEFUNG AUF DEM BRANCHING-POLYEDER, EIN.

HAUS 1980 -2 HAUSMANN, D.
FARBKLASSEN UND PSEUDOKNOTEN FUER ADJAZENZCHARAKTERISIERUNGEN.

HAUSC 1978 -1 HAUSMANN, D.; KORTE, B.
COLOURING CRITERIA FOR ADJACENCY ON 0-1-POLYHEDRA.

LIVJ 1980 -1 LIVJANT, R. Z.
ON THE NEIGHBORHOOD OF INTEGRAL VERTICES OF CERTAIN POLYHEDRA (RUSSIAN).

PAPA 1976 -1 PAPADIMITRIOU, C. H.
COMPLEXITY OF COMBINATORIAL OPTIMIZATION PROBLEMS, THE.

PAPA 1978 -1 PAPADIMITRIOU, C. H.
ADJACENCY RELATION ON THE TRAVELLING SALESMAN POLYTOPE IS NP-COMPLETE, THE.

YOUN 1978 -1 YOUNG, H. P.
ON PERMUTATIONS AND PERMUTATION POLYTOPES.

ALGEBRAIC METHODS AND ALGEBRAIZATION OF PROBLEMS

****

BACHD 1979 -1 BACHEM, A.; RANDOW, R. VON
INTEGER THEOREMS OF FARKAS LEMMA TYPE.
BURK 1975 -1 BURKARD, R. E.
KOMBINATORISCHE OPTIMIERUNG IN HALBGRUPPEN.
BURK 1978 -1 BURKARD, R. E.
GENERAL HUNGARIAN METHOD FOR THE ALGEBRAIC TRANSPORTATION PROBLEM, A.
BURK 1979 -1 BURKARD, R. E.
ON THE USE OF ALGEBRAIC OBJECTIVE FUNCTIONS IN COMBINATORIAL PROGRAMMING.
BURK 1979 -2 BURKARD, R. E.
REMARKS ON SOME SCHEDULING PROBLEMS WITH ALGEBRAIC OBJECTIVE FUNCTIONS.
BURK 1979 -4 BURKARD, R. E.
UEBER EINE ANWENDUNG ALGEBRAISCHER TRANSPORTPROBLEME BEI REIHENFOLGEPROBLEMEN.
BURKC 1978 -1 BURKARD, R. E.; FROEHLICH, K.
SOME REMARKS ON 3-DIMENSIONAL ASSIGNMENT PROBLEMS (EXTENDED ABSTRACT).
BURKJ 1980 -1 BURKARD, R. E.; ZIMMERMANN, U.
COMBINATORIAL OPTIMIZATION IN LINEARLY ORDERED SEMIMODULES: A SURVEY.
BURKJ 1980 -2 BURKARD, R. E.; ZIMMERMANN, U.
WEAKLY ADMISSIBLE TRANSFORMATIONS FOR SOLVING ALGEBRAIC ASSIGNMENT AND TRANSPORTATION PROBLEMS.
CUNI 1979 -1 CUNINGHAME-GREEN, R. A.
MINIMAX ALGEBRA.
DERI 1978 -1 DERIGS, U.
DUALITY AND THE ALGEBRAIC MATCHING PROBLEM.
DERI 1979 -1 DERIGS, U.
DUALITY AND ADMISSIBLE TRANSFORMATIONS IN COMBINATORIAL OPTIMIZATION.
DERI 1979 -2 DERIGS, U.
GENERALIZED HUNGARIAN METHOD FOR SOLVING MINIMUM WEIGHT PERFECT MATCHING PROBLEMS WITH ALGEBRAIC OBJECTIVE, A.
DERIC 1978 -1 DERIGS, U.; ZIMMERMANN, U.
DUALITY PRINCIPLES IN ALGEBRAIC LINEAR PROGRAMMING.
FRIED 1980 -1 FRIEZE, A. M.
ALGORITHM FOR ALGEBRAIC ASSIGNMENT PROBLEMS, AN.
GABO 1974 -1 GABOVICH, E. J.
EQUIVALENCY PROBLEM IN DISCRETE PROGRAMMING OVER ORDERED SEMIGROUPS, AN.
GABO 1980 -1 GABOVICH, E. J.
ON SPECTRAL THEORY IN DISCRETE PROGRAMMING.
GONDA 1978 -1 GONDRAN, M.; MINOUX, M.
INDEPENDANCE LINEAIRE DANS LES DIOIDES, L'.
HAMA 1981 -1 HAMACHER, H.
FLOWS IN REGULAR MATROIDS.
HAMA 1980 -3 HAMACHER, H.
MAXIMAL ALGEBRAIC FLOWS: ALGORITHMS AND EXAMPLES.
JEROB 1975 -1 JEROSLOW, R. G.
SOME STRUCTURE AND BASIS THEOREMS FOR INTEGRAL MONOIDS.
JEROB 1978 -1 JEROSLOW, R. G.
CUTTING PLANE THEORY: ALGEBRAIC METHODS.
RATH 1977 -1 RATHMANN, D.
ZUR LOESUNG DISKRETER OPTIMIERUNGSPROBLEME MIT GRUPPENTHEORETISCHEN ANSAETZEN.
SAUN 1979 -1 SAUNDERS, B. D.; SCHNEIDER, H.
APPLICATIONS OF THE GORDAN-STIEMKE THEOREM IN COMBINATORIAL MATRIX THEORY.
SCHOB 1977 -1 SCHOLZ, K.
ON SCHEDULING MULTI-PROCESSOR SYSTEMS WITH ALGEBRAICAL OBJECTIVES.
TRUE 1978 -1 TRUEMPER, K.
ALGEBRAIC CHARACTERIZATIONS OF UNIMODULAR MATRICES.
WOLS 1977 -1 WOLSEY, L. A.
VALID INEQUALITIES AND SUPERADDITIVITY OF 0-1 INTEGER PROGRAMS.
WUES 1978 -1 WUESTEFELD, A.
EINPARAMETRISCHE OPTIMIERUNG FUER DIE P-NORM ZIELFUNKTION BEIM TRANSPORTPROBLEM.
ZIMM 1978 -1 ZIMMERMANN, U.
DUALITY AND THE ALGEBRAIC MATROID INTERSECTION PROBLEM.
ZIMM 1979 -1 ZIMMERMANN, U.
DUALITY PRINCIPLES AND THE ALGEBRAIC TRANSPORTATION PROBLEM.
ZIMM 1980 -1 ZIMMERMANN, U.
DUALITY FOR ALGEBRAIC LINEAR PROGRAMMING.
ZIMM 1981 -1 ZIMMERMANN, U.
LINEAR AND COMBINATORIAL OPTIMIZATION IN ORDERED ALGEBRAIC STRUCTURES.
ZIMM 1978 -2 ZIMMERMANN, U.
THRESHOLD METHODS FOR BOOLEAN OPTIMIZATION PROBLEMS WITH SEPARABLE OBJECTIVES.
ZIMM 1979 -3 ZIMMERMANN, U.
ON SOME EXTREMAL OPTIMIZATION PROBLEMS.

ABAE 1975 -1 ABAEV, T. G.
PROBLEM OF COMPILING AN OPTIMAL SCHEDULE FOR THE WORK OF A GROUP OF AUTOMATA STATIONS WITH DIGITAL PROGRAMMED CONTROL (RUSSIAN), THE.

ACKE 1978 -1 ACKERMAN, L. J.; LUSS, H.; BERKOWITZ, R. S.
IMPLICIT EMUMERATION ALGORITHM FOR SEQUENCING POLICIES APPLIED TO TELEPHONE SWITCHING FACILITIES, AN.

AGUA 1973 -1 AGUADO, I. A.
DISCRETE PROGRAMMING MODEL FOR THE SEQUENCING OF TASKS IN SUGAR PRODUCING INDUSTRIES (SPANISH), A.

AHREA 1978 -1 AHRENS, W.; DEHNERT, G.; GERBER, H. J.
HEURISTISCHE VERFAHREN ZUR TOURENPLANUNG BEI DER HAUSMUELLENTSORGUNG IN LAENDLICHEN REGIONEN.

ALBE 1977 -1 ALBERS, S.
EINSATZPLANUNG VON FLUGZEUGBESATZUNGEN.

ALBE 1979 -1 ALBERS, S.
EXTENDED ALGORITHM FOR OPTIMAL PRODUCT POSITIONING, AN.

ANDRA 1978 -1 ANDREATTA, G.; BENEDETTI, M. A.; MASON, F.
TRANSPORT LINES WITH NONCONSERVATIVE FLOW (ITALIAN).

ARMSC 1979 -1 ARMSTRONG, R. D.; COOK, W. D.; SAIPE, A. L.
OPTIMAL BATCHING IN A SEMI-AUTOMATED ORDER PICKING SYSTEM.

ARNA 1978 -1 ARNAUDOV, D. D.; JANEV, N. I.
METHOD FOR THE APPLICATION OF PARTIAL INTEGER LINEAR PROGRAMMING TO RETRIEVAL OPTIMIZATION IN MULTILEVEL INFORMATION RETRIEVAL SYSTEMS (RUSSIAN), A.

ASHI 1975 -1 ASHIMOV, A.; SAGYNGALIEV, K. S.
SCHEDULING OF BATCH PRODUCTION, THE.

AYLE 1978 -1 AYLES, P. S.; BEALE, E. M. L.; BLUES, R. C.; WILD, S. J.
MATHEMATICAL MODELS FOR THE LOCATION OF GOVERNMENT.

BAIL 1979 -1 BAILEY, F. N.
COMMENTS ON "APPLICATION OF 0-1 INTEGER PROGRAMMING TO MULTITARGET TRACKING PROBLEMS".

BAKEF 1978 -1 BAKER, K. R.; DIXON, P.; MAGAZINE, M. J.; SILVER, E. A.
ALGORITHM FOR THE DYNAMIC LOT-SIZE PROBLEM WITH TIME-VARYING PRODUCTION CAPACITY CONSTRAINTS, AN.

BAKEJ 1977 -1 BAKER, K. R.; SILVER, E. A.; MAGAZINE, M. J.
ALGORITHM FOR THE DYNAMIC LOT-SIZE PROBLEM WITH PRODUCTION CAPACITY CONSTRAINTS, AN.

BALA 1977 -1 BALANDINA, S. V.
FORMULATION OF THE PROBLEM OF THE LOCATION OF THE COMPUTER CENTERS OF A NETWORK, AND POSSIBLE APPROACHES TO ITS SOLUTION (RUSSIAN), A.

BAYB 1980 -2 BAYBARS, I.
OPTIMAL ASSIGNMENT OF BROADCASTING FREQUENCIES.

BENS 1979 -1 BENSEMAN, B.; HALL, K.
SOLVING A PLANT LOCATION PROBLEM WITH INTEGER PROGRAMMING.

BERTO 1980 -1 BERTSEKAS, D. P.; GAFNI, E. M.
PROJECTION METHODS FOR VARIATIONAL INEQUALITIES WITH APPLICATION TO THE TRAFFIC ASSIGNMENT PROBLEM.

BIANA 1978 -1 BIANCO, L.; NICOLETTI, B.; RICCIARDELLI, S.
ALGORITHM FOR OPTIMAL SEQUENCING OF AIRCRAFT IN THE NEAR TERMINAL AREA, AN.

BODIA 1978 -1 BODIN, L. D.; KURSH, S. J.
COMPUTER-ASSISTED SYSTEM FOR THE ROUTING AND SCHEDULING OF STREET SWEEPERS, A.

BODIB 1981 -1 BODIN, L. D.; ROSENFIELD, D. B.; KYDES, A. S.
SCHEDULING AND ESTIMATION TECHNIQUES FOR TRANSPORTATION PLANNING.

BODR 1979 -1 BODRIK, A. G.
SOLUTION OF SOME PRODUCTION PLANNING PROBLEMS (RUSSIAN).

BOFF 1979 -1 BOFFEY, T. B.; EDMOND, E. D.; HINXMAN, A. I.; PURSGLOVE, C. J.
TWO APPROACHES TO SCHEDULING CONTAINER SHIPS WITH AN APPLICATION TO THE NORTH ATLANTIC ROUTE.

BOZY 1979 -1 BOZYIGIT, M.; PAKER, Y.
FIXED ROUTING PROBLEM IN LARGE AND HIGH CONNECTIVITY NETWORKS, A.

BROW 1980 -1 BROWN, G. G.; GEOFFRION, A. M.; BRADLEY, G. H.
PRODUCTION AND SALES PLANNING WITH LIMITED SHARED TOOLING AT THE KEY OPERATION.

BROWA 1981 -1 BROWN, G. G.; GRAVES, G. W.
REAL-TIME DISPATCH OF PETROLEUM TANK TRUCKS.

BUCKA 1979 -1 BUCKLEY, D. J.
TRAFFIC ASSIGNMENT IN A TWO-DIMENSIONAL CONTINUOUS REPRESENTATION OF A TRAFFIC NETWORK WITH FLOW-DEPENDENT SPEEDS.

BURKI 1979 -1 BURKARD, R. E.; NEWGER, E.
OPTIMALE ROHHOLZAUSFORMUNG.

BURM 1976 -1 BURMAN, D.
OPERATOR SCHEDULING SYSTEM, AN.

BURN 1978 -1 BURNESS, G. C.; MILLER, D. M.
LOCATION OF CRASH FIRE FIGHTING FACILITIES AT AIRPORTS.

BURNB 1978 -1 BURNS, R. N.
MANPOWER SCHEDULING WITH VARIABLE DEMANDS AND ALTERNATE WEEKENDS OFF.

CARN 1978 -1 CARNEIRO RIBEIRO, C. DA C.; MACULAN, N.
NETWORK EXPANSION PROBLEM, A.

CHAC 1979 -1 CHACHRA, V.; GHARE, P. M.; MOORE, J. M.
APPLICATIONS OF GRAPH THEORY ALGORITHMS.

CHAI 1978 -1 CHAIKEN, J. M.; DORMONT, P.
PATROL CAR ALLOCATION MODEL: BACKGROUND, A.

CHAI 1978 -2 CHAIKEN, J. M.; DORMONT, P.
PATROL CAR ALLOCATION MODEL: CAPABILITIES AND ALGORITHMS, A.

CHARA 1977 -1 CHARNES, A.; COOPER, W. W.; LEWIS, K. A.; NELSON, A.; NIEHAUS, R. J.
NONLINEAR GOAL-ARC NETWORK EXTENSION OF THE MULTI-LEVEL COHERENCE MODEL FOR EEO, A.

CHENC 1976 -1 CHEN, K.-Y.
NETWORK APPROACH TO THE CAPACITATED LOT-SIZE PROBLEM, A.

CHENE 1978 -1 CHEN, R.; CROWDER, H. P.; JOHNSON, E. L.
SOLVING THE INSTALLATION SCHEDULING PROBLEM USING MIXED INTEGER LINEAR PROGRAMMING.

CHENF 1973 -1 CHEN, Y. H.
MATHEMATICAL MODELING OF WATER AND SEDIMENT ROUTING IN NATURAL CHANNELS.

CHERC 1970 -1 CHERNYSHEV, JU. O.
REDUCTION OF CERTAIN OPTIMAL PROBLEMS OF DISCRETE AUTOMATA DIAGNOSTICS TO THE SOLUTION OF PROBLEMS OF FLOWS IN NETWORKS (RUSSIAN).

CHIE 1964 -1 CHIEN, R. T.; GOMORY, R. E.; HU, T. C.
COMMUNICATION NETWORKS.

CHRID 1979 -1 CHRISTOFIDES, N.; HEWINS, R. D.; SALKIN, G. R.
GRAPH THEORETIC APPROACHES TO FOREIGN EXCHANGE OPERATIONS.

CHRIG 1980 -2 CHRISTOFIDES, N.; MINGOZZI, A.; TOTH, P.
DYNAMIC LOADING AND UNLOADING OF LIQUIDS INTO TANKS.

COHE 1978 -1 COHEN, A. I.
ALGORITHM FOR SCHEDULING SURFACE COAL MINES, AN (REVISED VERSION).

COLLA 1978 -1 COLLINS, M.; COOPER, L.; HELGASON, R. V.; KENNINGTON, J. L.; LEBLANC, L. J.
SOLVING THE PIPE NETWORK ANALYSIS PROBLEM USING OPTIMIZATION TECHNIQUES.

COOPA 1977 -1 COOPER, L.; KENNINGTON, J. L.
STEADY-STATE ANALYSIS OF NONLINEAR RESISTIVE ELECTRICAL NETWORKS USING OPTIMIZATION TECHNIQUES.

COPP 1980 -1 COPPINS, R. J.; PENTICO, D. W.
SCHEDULING THE NATIONAL FOOTBALL LEAGUE.

CORK 1978 -1 CORKINDALE, D.
HOW TO CUT TRANSPORTATION COSTS WHILE MAINTAINING SERVICE LEVELS.

CRAMA 1977 -1 CRAMER, M.; PONSSARD, J.-P.
ORDONNANCEMENT DES MOUVEMENTS DE TRESORERIE.

CRUM 1979 -1 CRUM, R. L.; KLINGMAN, D.; TAVIS, L. A.
STRATEGIC MANAGEMENT OF MULTINATIONAL COMPANIES: NETWORK-BASED PLANNING SYSTEMS.

CUNT 1978 -1 CUNTO, E.
SCHEDULING BOATS TO SAMPLE OIL WELLS IN LAKE MARACAIBO.

DATH 1978 -1 DATHE, M.
ZUR LOESUNG DES ZUORDNUNGSPROBLEMS BEI ZWEI ZIELGROESSEN.

DAVIB 1978 -1 DAVIS, R. P.; MILLER, D. M.
MODEL FOR DETERMINING MACHINE REQUIREMENTS IN A MULTISTAGE MANUFACTURING SYSTEM WITH DISCRETELY DISTRIBUTED DEMAND, A.

DEAK 1981 -1 DEAK, I.; HOFFER, J.; MAYER, J.; NEMETH, A.; POTECZ, B.; PREKOPA, A.; STRAZICKY, B.
OPTIMAL DAILY SCHEDULING OF THE ELECTRICITY PRODUCTION IN HUNGARY.

DEBA 1979 -1 DEBANNE, J. G.
NETWORK BASED REGIONAL ENERGY PLANNING MODELS - AN EVOLUTIONARY EXPOSE.

DECK 1977 -1 DECKRO, R. F.
MULTIPLE OBJECTIVE DISTRICTING: A GENERAL HEURISTIC APPROACH USING MULTIPLE CRITERIA.

DEMBB 1978 -1 DEMBO, R. S.; KLINCEWICZ, J. G.
APPROXIMATE SECOND-ORDER ALGORITHM FOR NETWORK FLOW PROBLEMS WITH CONVEX SEPARABLE COSTS, AN.

DEMBC 1980 -1 DEMBOWSKI, F. L.; SCHWARZ, L.
INTEGER PROGRAMMING APPROACH TO SCHOOL DISTRICT FINANCIAL MANAGEMENT, AN.

DJUK 1977 -1 DJUKANOV, V. G.
LIST REPRESENTATION FOR THE MACHINE SOLUTION OF AN ILL-POSED TRANSPORT PROBLEM (RUSSIAN).

DODU 1975 -1 DODU, J. C.
MODELE D'OPTIMISATION A LONG TERME D'UN RESEAU DE TRANSPORT.

DOMS 1978 -1 DOMSCHKE, W.; ENGELE, E.
MOEGLICHKEITEN DER TRANSFORMATION EINES VERKEHRSNETZES IN EIN DAZU DUALES NETZ ZUM ZWECKE VON KAPAZITAETSUNTERSUCHUNGEN.

DOYL 1978 -1 DOYLE, T. E.; MOORE, T. G.; SACKETT, R. A.
BENDER'S DECOMPOSITION APPROACH TO SCHEDULING SWITCHING SYSTEM REPLACEMENTS AND EQUIPMENT REUSE.

DUBO 1979 -1 DUBOIS, D.; BEL, G.; LLIBRE, M.
SET OF METHODS IN TRANSPORTATION NETWORK SYNTHESIS AND ANALYSIS, A.

DUNC 1979 -1 DUNCAN, I. B.; NOBLE, B. M.
ALLOCATION OF SPECIALTIES TO HOSPITALS IN A HEALTH DISTRICT, THE.

EL-S 1980 -1 EL-SAWY, A. H. A.
MIXED INTEGER SCHEDULING MODEL FOR COMBINED THERMAL AND HYDROELECTRIC-PUMPED STORAGE GENERATOR SYSTEMS, A.

ELMA 1978 -1 ELMAGHRABY, S. E.
ECONOMIC LOT SCHEDULING PROBLEM (ELSP): REVIEW AND EXTENSIONS, THE.

ERLA 1974 -1 ERLANDER, S.; SCHEELE, S.
MATHEMATICAL PROGRAMMING MODEL FOR BUS TRAFFIC IN A NETWORK, A.

ERLE 1978 -2 ERLENKOTTER, D.
SHOULD CALIFORNIA AGRICULTURE RECEIVE PREFERENTIAL WATER RATES.

FALK 1978 -1 FALK, P. G.
EXPERIMENTS IN MIXED INTEGER LINEAR PROGRAMMING CONCURRENT TO A MANUFACTURING HIERARCHY.

FALL 1973 -1 FALLIK, C.
APPLICATIONS ECONOMIQUES DE LA THEORIE DES GRAPHES, EN PARTICULIER AU PROBLEME DES HORAIRES.

FISHA 1978 -1 FISHER, M. L.; HOCHBAUM, D.
DATABASE LOCATION IN COMPUTER NETWORKS.

FISHB 1978 -1 FISHER, M. L.; JAIKUMAR, R.
ALGORITHM FOR THE SPACE-SHUTTLE SCHEDULING PROBLEM, AN.

FISKB 1980 -1 FISK, J. C.; SOLANO, A.
PRODUCTION SCHEDULING FOR HIGH-VOLUME ASSEMBLIES - A CASE STUDY.

FLOR 1975 -1 FLORIAN, M.
TRAFFIC EQUILIBRIUM MODEL OF TRAVEL BY CAR AND PUBLIC TRANSIT MODES, A.

FLORA 1976 -1 FLORIAN, M.; BUSHELL, G.; FERLAND, J. A.; GUERIN, G.; NASTANSKY, L.
ENGINE SCHEDULING PROBLEM IN A RAILWAY NETWORK, THE.

FLORB 1978 -1 FLORIAN, M.; LENSTRA, J. K.; RINNOOY KAN, A. H. G.
DETERMINISTIC PRODUCTION PLANNING: ALGORITHMS AND COMPLEXITY.

FLORC 1976 -1 FLORIAN, M.; NGUYEN, S.
RECENT EXPERIENCE WITH EQUILIBRIUM METHODS FOR THE STUDY OF A CONGESTED URBAN AREA.

FLORD 1977 -1 FLORIAN, M.; NGUYEN, S.; SOUMIS, F.
TWO METHODS FOR ACCELERATING AN EQUILIBRIUM TRAFFIC ASSIGNMENT ALGORITHM.

FRIE 1978 -1 FRIEDMAN, M.
COMBINATORIAL PROBLEMS IN AN ADAPTIVE PUBLIC TRANSPORTATION NETWORK.

GABR 1977 -1 GABRIEL, R.
PROGRAMMSTELLUNG IN SPORTLICHEN MEISTERSCHAFTEN NACH MATHEMATISCHEN MODELLEN.

GARC 1977 -1 GARCIA, R.; HACKBARTH, K.-D.
MATHEMATISCHES PLANUNGSMODELL FUER DIE LANGFRISTIGE KOSTENOPTIMALE GESTALTUNG VON FERNMELDENETZEN.

GATT 1981 -1 GATTASS, E. A.; NEMHAUSER, G. L.
APPLICATION OF VERTEX PACKING ON INTERVAL GRAPHS TO DATA ANALYSIS IN ROAD MAINTENANCE, AN.

GAVIA 1978 -1 GAVISH, B.; SCHWEITZER, P.; SHLIFER, E.
ASSIGNING BUSES TO SCHEDULES IN A METROPOLITAN AREA.

GEOR 1979 -1 GEORGE, J. A.
REPORT ON THE USE OF MIXED INTEGER PROGRAMMING IN AN EVALUATION OF PLANT UPGRADING, A.

GHOS 1978 -1 GHOSH, S.; RAY, S.; BHATTACHARYA, A.
CASE STUDY FOR OPTIMAL PLANT SIZE MIX USING INTEGER LINEAR PROGRAMMING, A.

GIANA 1978 -1 GIANNESSI, F.; JURINA, L.; MAIER, G.
OPTIMAL EXCAVATION PROFILE FOR A PIPELINE FREELY RESTING ON THE SEA FLOOR.

GILEC 1980 -1 GILES, R.; OYAMA, T.; TROTTER, L. E. JR.
RELATED NECESSARY CONDITIONS FOR COMPLETING PARTIAL LATIN SQUARES.
GLOVG 1978 -1 GLOVER, F.; MAC MILLAN, C.; KLINGMAN, D.
MODELING COMBINATORIAL MATHEMATICAL PROGRAMMING PROBLEMS BY NETFORMS: AN ILLUSTRATIVE APPLICATION.
GRAVC 1980 -1 GRAVES, S. C.; LAMAR, B. W.
INTEGER PROGRAMMING PROCEDURE FOR ASSEMBLY SYSTEM DESIGN PROBLEMS, AN.
HALL 1978 -1 HALL, M. A.
PROPERTIES OF THE EQUILIBRIUM STATE IN TRANSPORTATION NETWORKS.
HANN 1979 -1 HANNAN, E. L.
ASSIGNMENT OF PLAYERS TO MATCHES IN A HIGH SCHOOL OR COLLEGE TENNIS MATCH.
HERM 1979 -1 HERMAN, R.; PRIGOGINE, I.
TWO-FLUID APPROACH TO TOWN TRAFFIC, A.
HESS 1977 -1 HESSELBACH, J.; WIJNANDS, J.
DYNAMISCHE PROGRAMMIERUNG - METHODIK, EDV-PROGRAMM, ANWENDUNGSBEISPIEL.
HODG 1981 -1 HODGSON, M. J.
LOCATION OF PUBLIC FACILITIES INTERMEDIATE TO THE JOURNEY TO WORK, THE.
HOLS 1979 -1 HOLST, O.
ACCESSIBILITY AS THE OBJECTIVE OF PUBLIC TRANSPORTATION PLANNING: AN INTEGRATED TRANSPORTATION AND LAND USE MODEL.
HORAB 1978 -1 HORAK, V.
PRACTICAL APPLICATION OF, AND CONSTRUCTION OF ALGORITHMS FOR FINITE LABELLED TREES (CZECHOSLOVAKIAN).
ISHIC 1979 -1 ISHIYAMA, Y.; ISHIZAKI, Y.; SASABE, S.; YOSHIDA, N.
MULTI-COMMODITY FLOW APPROACH TO ASSIGNMENT OF CIRCUITS IN CASE OF FAILURE IN A COMMUNICATION NETWORK.
JARVA 1978 -1 JARVIS, J. J.; RARDIN, R. L.; UNGER, V. E.; MOORE, R. W.; SCHIMPELER, C. C.
OPTIMAL DESIGN OF REGIONAL WASTEWATER SYSTEMS: A FIXED-CHARGE NETWORK FLOW MODEL.
JENK 1980 -3 JENKINS, L.
PARAMETRIC MIXED INTEGER PROGRAMMING: A SOLID WASTE RECYCLING APPLICATION.
JONE 1979 -1 JONES, G. A.; WILSON, J. G.
OPTIMAL SCHEDULING OF JOBS ON A TRANSMISSION NETWORK.
KAZA 1974 -1 KAZAKOVA, M. F.
PROBLEM OF FINDING THE PARETO OPTIMA IN A POLYMATRIX TRAVELLING SALESMAN PROBLEM (RUSSIAN), THE.
KEMP 1979 -1 KEMPER, F. M.
ALGORITHM FOR FORMATION OF THE ESSENTIAL CONSTRAINTS OF A TRANSPORT PROBLEM WITH PROHIBITIONS (RUSSIAN), AN.
KEOW 1978 -1 KEOWN, A. J.; MARTIN, J. D.
CAPITAL BUDGETING IN THE PUBLIC SECTOR: A ZERO-ONE GOAL PROGRAMMING APPROACH.
KIME 1979 -1 KIMEMIA, J.; GERSHWIN, S. B.
NETWORK FLOW OPTIMIZATION IN FLEXIBLE MANUFACTURING SYSTEMS.
KOWA 1977 -1 KOWALCZYK, Z.
TRYING TO APPLY MATHEMATICAL PROGRAMMING TO THE PROBLEM OF CHOOSING AN OPTIMAL PROJECT VARIANT (POLISH).
KRIC 1978 -1 KRICHEL, R.
ANALYSE EINES RECHNERMODELLS DURCH RUECKFUEHRUNG AUF EIN 3-MASCHINEN- FLOW-SHOP-PROBLEM.
LABA 1977 -1 LABADIE, J. W.; MORROW, D. M.; CHEN, Y. H.
HEURISTIC MULTIDIMENSIONAL DYNAMIC PROGRAMMING ALGORITHM FOR URBAN STORMWATER MANAGEMENT.
LAGO 1973 -1 LAGOSHA, B. A.
DETERMINATION OF OPTIMAL ROUTES FOR FREIGHTSHIPS (SPANISH).
LAPOC 1980 -1 LAPORTE, G.; NOBERT, Y.; BIRON, J.
ROTATING SCHEDULES.
LEBL 1979 -2 LEBLANC, L. J.; ABDULAAL, M.
OPTIMIZATION METHODS FOR DESIGN OF MULTIMODEL NETWORKS.
LEBLA 1976 -1 LEBLANC, L. J.; MORLOK, E. K.
ANALYSIS AND COMPARISON OF BEHAVIORAL ASSUMPTIONS IN TRAFFIC ASSIGNMENT, AN.
LEE D 1979 -1 LEE, S. M.; FRANZ, L. S.; WYNNE, A. J.
OPTIMIZING STATE PATROL MANPOWER ALLOCATION.
LINI 1980 -1 LINIS, V. K.; MAKSIM, M. S.
NUMBER OF TRANSPORT FACILITIES NECESSARY FOR FULFILLMENT OF A TRAFFIC SCHEDULE (RUSSIAN), THE.
LODI 1976 -1 LODISH, C. M.
ASSIGNING SALESMEN TO MAXIMIZE PROFIT.
LOVEB 1978 -1 LOVE, R. R. JR; VEMUGANTI, R. R.
SINGLE-PLANT MOLD ALLOCATION PROBLEM WITH CAPACITY AND CHANGEOVER RESTRICTIONS, THE.
MAC K 1978 -1 MAC MASTER, C. L.
ANALYSIS OF ALGORITHMS FOR THE DUTCH NATIONAL FLAG PROBLEM, AN.
MACK 1978 -1 MACK, H. L.; SMITH, L. D.
SCHEDULING WITH LIST PROCESSING AND PROBLEM ORIENTED DATA STRUCTURES; AN ITINERANT TEACHER EXAMPLE.
MAIEA 1975 -1 MAIER, S.
SOLVING THE TRAFFIC ASSIGNMENT AND SUB-AREA FOCUSING PROBLEMS BY GEOGRAPHIC DECOMPOSITION.
MAKS 1980 -1 MAKSIM, M. S.
MINIMIZATION OF THE NUMBER OF TRANSPORT FACILITIES BY CHANGE IN THE DAYS OF FULFILLMENT OF NONDAILY TRIPS (RUSSIAN).
MAND 1978 -1 MANDL, C. E.
ALGORITHMS AND COMPUTER PROGRAMS IN DETERMINISTIC NETWORK OPTIMIZATION APPLIED TO PUBLIC SYSTEMS.
MARL 1979 -1 MARLIN, P. G.
APPLICATION OF THE TRANSPORTATION MODEL TO A LARGE SCALE "DISTRICTING" PROBLEM.
MARSA 1980 -1 MARSTEN, R. E.; MULLER, M. R.
MIXED-INTEGER PROGRAMMING APPROACH TO AIR CARGO FLEET PLANNING, A.
MARSB 1979 -1 MARSTEN, R. E.; MULLER, M. R.; KILLION, C. L.
CREW PLANNING AT FLYING TIGER: A SUCCESSFUL APPLICATION OF INTEGER PROGRAMMING.
MARTC 1978 -2 MARTELLO, S.; TOTH, P.
PROBLEM OF OPTIMAL CHANGE MAKING (ITALIAN), THE.
MATH 1978 -1 MATHAISEL, D. F. X.; MULLER, M. R.
ASSIGNMENT OF CARGO FLOWS TO AN AIRLINE NETWORK.
MEGE 1978 -1 MEGEATH, J. D.
SUCCESSFUL HOSPITAL PERSONNEL SCHEDULING.
MERC 1978 -1 MERCHANT, D. K.; NEMHAUSER, G. L.
MODEL AND AN ALGORITHM FOR THE DYNAMIC TRAFFIC ASSIGNMENT PROBLEM, A.
MERC 1978 -2 MERCHANT, D. K.; NEMHAUSER, G. L.
OPTIMALITY CONDITIONS FOR A DYNAMIC TRAFFIC ASSIGNMENT MODEL.

MILLA 1974 -1 MILLER, H. E.
MATHEMATICAL PROGRAMMING MODELS OF NURSE SCHEDULING AND ALLOCATION.
MITS 1978 -1 MITSUMORI, S.
MINIMUM NUMBER OF VEHICLES TO MEET DYNAMIC TRANSPORTATION DEMAND.
MORIB 1978 -1 MORITZ, A.
MATHEMATISCHES MODELL FUER DIE ERRECHNUNG DER MINIMALEN TRANSPORTKOSTEN IM UNGARISCHEN BINNENHANDEL.
NABE 1977 -1 NABESHIMA, I.
EXTENDED BRANCH AND BOUND ALGORITHM AND ITS APPLICATION TO BIOBJECTIVE PROBLEM.
NACK 1978 -1 NACKEL, J. G.; GOLDMAN, J.; FAIRMAN, W. L.
GROUP DECISION PROCESS FOR RESOURCE ALLOCATION IN THE HEALTH SETTING, A.
NAMBA 1981 -1 NAMBIAR, J. M.; GELDERS, L. F.; WASSENHOVE, L. N. VAN
LARGE SCALE LOCATION-ALLOCATION PROBLEM IN THE NATURAL RUBBER INDUSTRY, A.
NANI 1969 -1 NANIWADA, M.
MULTICOMMODITY FLOWS IN A COMMUNICATION NETWORK.
NAUSA 1981 -1 NAUSS, R. M.; KEELER, B. R.
MINIMIZATION OF LEASE PAYMENTS IN LEVERAGED LEASES: AN APPLICATION OF INTEGER PROGRAMMING.
NGUYB 1973 -1 NGUYEN, S.
MATHEMATICAL PROGRAMMING APPROACH TO EQUILIBRIUM METHODS OF TRAFFIC ASSIGNMENT WITH FIXED DEMANDS, A.
NGUYB 1976 -1 NGUYEN, S.
UNIFIED APPROACH TO EQUILIBRIUM METHODS FOR TRAFFIC ASSIGNMENTS, A.
NIEB 1978 -1 NIEBLAS, M. H.; ESPINOSA, L. P.
ASSIGNMENT OF LOCOMOTIVES TO A RAILWAY TIMETABLE: A PRACTICAL APPLICATION OF THE HUNGARIAN METHOD (SPANISH), THE.
NORT 1979 -1 NORTHUP, W. D.; SHAPIRO, J. F.
LOGS: AN OPTIMIZATION SYSTEM FOR LOGISTICS PLANNING.
NUSS 1978 -1 NUSSINO, R.; PIECZENIK, G.; GRIGGS, J. R.; KLEITMAN, D. J.
ALGORITHMS FOR LOOP MATCHINGS.
ORON 1979 -1 ORON, G.
ALGORITHM FOR OPTIMIZING NON LINEAR CONSTRAINED ZERO-ONE PROBLEMS TO IMPROVE WASTEWASTER TREATMENT, AN.
PAES 1978 -1 PAESSENS, H.
TOURENPLANUNG BEI DER MUELLSAMMLUNG IN STAEDTISCHEN BEREICHEN.
PANA 1979 -1 PANAYIOTOPOULOS, J.-C.
INTEGER PROGRAMMING WITH IRREGULAR DATA SPACE.
PAPAD 1978 -1 PAPAGEORGIOU, J. C.
GOAL PROGRAMMING MODEL FOR RESOURCE ALLOCATION IN THE SCHOOL SYSTEM OF GREECE, A.
PAPEA 1979 -1 PAPE, U.; BOHM, H.-J.; RIEGER, A.
ANWENDUNGSSYSTEM ZUR ERSTELLUNG EINES STAUPLANES FUER CONTAINERSCHIFFE, EIN.
PATE 1979 -1 PATEL, N. R.
LOCATING RURAL SOCIAL SERVICE CENTERS IN INDIA.
PEGE 1975 -1 PEGELS, C. C.
COMPUTER-BASED INTERACTIVE PLANNING SYSTEM FOR SCHEDULING BLOOD COLLECTIONS, A.
PHIL 1977 -1 PHILLIPS, S. JR.; DESSOUKY, M. I.
SOLVING THE PROJECT TIME/COST TRADEOFF PROBLEM USING THE MINIMAL CUT CONCEPT.
PIAN 1979 -1 PIANCA, P.; VOLPENTESTA, A.; ZECCHIN, M.
ON THE SOLUTION OF A CLASS OF EXTREMAL PROBLEMS WITH INTEGER VARIABLES CONNECTED WITH THE PROBLEM OF OPTIMAL ALLOCATION AT A SERVICE CENTER (ITALIAN).
RAMAD 1980 -1 RAMANI, K. V.; RAGHURAM, G.
UTILIZATION OF TRANSPORTATION UNITS: AN OPTIMAL ALLOCATION STUDY.
RATH 1977 -1 RATHMANN, D.
ZUR LOESUNG DISKRETER OPTIMIERUNGSPROBLEME MIT GRUPPENTHEORETISCHEN ANSAETZEN.
REBI 1975 -1 REBIBO, K. K.; YEN, A. M.
AUTOMATED APPROACH TO THE ASSIGNMENT OF DRIVERS IN URBAN TRANSIT, AN.
RIEP 1978 -1 RIEPL, R.-J.
OR-VERFAHREN IM VERKEHRSWESEN.
SAED 1981 -1 SAEDT, A. P. H.
SITING OF GREEN FORAGE DRYING PLANTS FOR USE BY A LARGE NUMBER OF FARMS - A LOCATION-ALLOCATION CASE STUDY, THE.
SAHL 1978 -1 SAHLING, B.-M.
VERKEHRSABLAUF IN NETZEN - EIN GRAPHENTHEORETISCHES OPTIMIERUNGSVERFAHREN.
SAKS 1978 -1 SAKSENA, J. P.
RAKE LINK MINIMISATION PROBLEM.
SAKS 1979 -1 SAKSENA, J. P.
BEAT PATROLLING IN URBAN AREAS. A CASE STUDY.
SALKA 1979 -1 SALKIN, H. M.; LIN, C. H.
AGGREGATIONS OF SUBSIDIARY FIRMS FOR MINIMAL UNEMPLOYMENT COMPENSATION PAYMENTS VIA INTEGER PROGRAMMING.
SCHA 1974 -1 SCHABACK, R.
OPTIMIERUNGSPROBLEM AUS DER KRISTALLOGRAPHIE, EIN.
SCHN 1978 -1 SCHNIEDERJANS, M. J.; KWAK, N. K.
SIMULATED TRANSPORTATION PROBLEM FOR IMPROVED OPERATIONAL PLANNING: AN APPLICATION IN THE TRUCKING INDUSTRY, A.
SCHRC 1980 -1 SCHREUDER, J. A. M.
CONSTRUCTING TIMETABLES FOR SPORT COMPETITIONS.
SCHRC 1981 -1 SCHREUDER, J. A. M.
APPLICATION OF A LOCATION MODEL TO FIRE STATIONS IN ROTTERDAM.
SEN 1972 -1 SEN, S.
MULTICOMMODITY CONCAVE COST MINIMIZATION PROBLEM FOR COMMUNICATION NETWORKS, A.
SEWA 1978 -1 SEWARD, S. M.; PLANE, D. R.; HENDRICK, T. E.
MUNICIPAL RESOURCE ALLOCATION: MINIMIZING THE COST OF FIRE PROTECTION.
SHAH 1981 -1 SHAH, A. R.
OPTIMAL ASSIGNMENT OF MEDICAL GRADUATES TO PRE-REGISTRATION JOBS, AN.
SHEF 1979 -1 SHEFFI, Y.; DAGANZO, C. F.
ALGORITHM FOR NETWORK EQUILIBRATION WITH MULTINOMIAL PROBIT MODELS, AN.
SIMU 1978 -1 SIMUNDICH, T. M.
EFFICIENT ALGORITHM FOR SOLVING A STOCHASTIC, INTEGER PROGRAMMING PROBLEM ARISING IN RADIO NAVIGATION, AN.
SMIT 1980 -1 SMITH, A.; CANI, P. DE
ALGORITHM TO OPTIMIZE THE LAYOUT OF BOXES IN PALLETS, AN.
SMITD 1979 -1 SMITH, J. M.
USE OF QUEUEING NETWORKS AND MIXED INTEGER PROGRAMMING TO OPTIMALLY ALLOCATE RESOURCES WITHIN A LIBRARY.
SMOL 1978 -1 SMOLJAR, L. I.
MODELS OF OPERATIONAL PLANNING IN DISCRETE PRODUCTION (RUSSIAN).

SMOR 1976 -1 SMORODINSKI, JA. A.
TREES AND THE MANY-BODY PROBLEM (RUSSIAN).
STANC 1978 -1 STANICKI, T.
TWO-CRITERION INTEGER OPTIMIZATION OF SUB-ASSEMBLY ASSIGNMENT IN THE DESIGN OF COMPLEX SYSTEMS BY THE METHOD OF VARIABLE CONSTRAINTS AND PARTIAL ENUMERATION (POLISH).
STEI 1978 -1 STEIN, D. M.
ASYMPTOTIC, PROBABILISTIC ANALYSIS OF A ROUTING PROBLEM, AN.
STEI 1978 -2 STEIN, D. M.
SCHEDULING DIAL-A-RIDE TRANSPORTATION SYSTEMS.
SVEN 1978 -1 SVENSSON, A.
EQUILIBRIUM EQUATION FOR ROAD TRAFFIC, AN.
TAYLA 1975 -1 TAYLOR, P. E.
OPTIMUM MANAGEMENT OF AIR TRAFFIC BETWEEN MAJOR AIR TERMINALS, THE.
THOMA 1978 -1 THOMAS, G. S.; JENNINGS, J. C.; ABBOTT, P.
BLENDING PROBLEM USING INTEGER PROGRAMMING ON-LINE, A.
TSUKA 1979 -1 TSUKIYAMA, S.; SHIRAKAWA, I.; ASAHARA, S.
ALGORITHM FOR THE VIA ASSIGNMENT PROBLEM IN MULTILAYER BACKBOARD WIRING, AN.
TURG 1978 -1 TURGEON, A.
OPTIMAL SCHEDULING OF THERMAL GENERATING UNITS.
UZDE 1978 -1 UZDEMIR, A. P.
SOLUTION METHOD FOR A COMBINATORIAL PROBLEM IN THE PLANNING OF NEW ENTERPRISES (RUSSIAN).
VIDA 1978 -1 VIDAL, R. V. V.
DESIGN OF A PIPELINE ROUTE.
VOEL 1978 -1 VOELKL, N.
EINSATZ DER GANZZAHLIGEN OPTIMIERUNG IN DER TEXOGRAPHIE, EIN.
VOIN 1974 -1 VOIN, A. M.
OPTIMAL COMBINATION OF TECHNOLOGICAL OPERATIONS ON A PRODUCTION LINE (RUSSIAN).
WARD 1952 -1 WARDROP, J. G.
SOME THEORETICAL ASPECTS OF ROAD TRAFFIC RESEARCH.
WARR 1978 -1 WARREN, H. S. JR.
STATIC MAIN STORAGE PACKING PROBLEMS.
WEBB 1978 -1 WEBB, W. A.
SCHEDULING OF TRACKING TIMES FOR INTERPLANETARY SPACECRAFT ON THE DEEP SPACE NETWORK.
WEINA 1980 -1 WEINTRAUB, A.; GONZALEZ, J.
ALGORITHM FOR THE TRAFFIC ASSIGNMENT PROBLEM, AN.
WESTA 1979 -1 WESTON, F. C. JR.
SYSTEMS/MATHEMATICAL PROGRAMMING APPROACH TO THE MULTIPLE PRODUCT MAKE-BUY DECISION, A.
WHITF 1970 -1 WHITE, W. W.; WRATHALL, E.
SYSTEM FOR RAILROAD TRAFFIC SCHEDULING, A.
WOLLA 1977 -1 WOLLNER, E.
ANALYSE UND SYNTHESE ZUVERLAESSIGER NETZE.
ZABR 1970 -1 ZABRANSKY, F.
ALUMINUM FOIL SLITTING TRIM LOSS PROBLEM; FORMULATED AS A MIXED INTEGER PROBLEM; SOLVED BY HEURISTIC PROGRAMMING.
ZOLTA 1979 -1 ZOLTNERS, A. A.; SINHA, P.; CHONG, P. S. C.
OPTIMAL ALGORITHM FOR SALES REPRESENTATIVE TIME MANAGEMENT, AN.

****

ALEK 1978 -1 ALEKSEEV, O. G.
APPLICATION OF BRANCH AND BOUND TO THE MINIMAX ASSIGNMENT PROBLEM (RUSSIAN).
AVON 1979 -1 AVONDO-BODINO, G.
GRAPH THEORY AND OPERATIONS RESEARCH.
AYLE 1978 -1 AYLES, P. S.; BEALE, E. M. L.; BLUES, R. C.; WILD, S. J.
MATHEMATICAL MODELS FOR THE LOCATION OF GOVERNMENT.
BAKH 1979 -1 BAKHSHI, H. C.; BHATIA, H. L.; PURI, M. C.
TRADE-OFF RELATIONS IN ASSIGNMENT PROBLEMS.
BARRA 1977 -1 BARR, R. S.; GLOVER, F.; KLINGMAN, D.
ALTERNATING BASIS ALGORITHM FOR ASSIGNMENT PROBLEMS, THE.
BARRA 1978 -2 BARR, R. S.; GLOVER, F.; KLINGMAN, D.
NEW ALTERNATING BASIS ALGORITHM FOR SEMI-ASSIGNMENT NETWORKS, A.
BARRC 1978 -1 BARRER, J. N.
CERTAIN PERMUTATION PROBLEMS AND THEIR RELATION TO THE ASSIGNMENT PROBLEM.
BARRC 1979 -1 BARRER, J. N.
BASES OF THE EXTREME POINTS OF THE ASSIGNMENT POLYTOPE.
BAZAA 1979 -1 BAZARAA, M. S.; ELSHAFEI, A. N.
EXACT BRANCH-AND-BOUND PROCEDURE FOR THE QUADRATIC-ASSIGNMENT PROBLEM, AN.
BAZAC 1979 -1 BAZARAA, M. S.; SHERALI, H. D.
CUTTING PLANE METHODS FOR THE QUADRATIC ASSIGNMENT PROBLEM.
BAZAC 1980 -1 BAZARAA, M. S.; SHERALI, H. D.
BENDERS' PARTITIONING SCHEME APPLIED TO A NEW FORMULATION OF THE QUADRATIC ASSIGNMENT PROBLEM.
BAZAC 1979 -2 BAZARAA, M. S.; SHERALI, H. D.
NEW APPROACHES FOR SOLVING THE QUADRATIC ASSIGNMENT PROBLEM.
BEREA 1978 -1 BERESNEV, V. L.; ZAIKINA, G. M.
PROGRAMME DE L'ALGORITHME DE RESOLUTION DU PROBLEME D'ASSORTIMENT OPTIMAL (RUSSIAN).
BHATA 1979 -1 BHAT, K. V. S.; KINARIWALA, B.
ALGORITHM FOR THE N X N OPTIMUM ASSIGNMENT PROBLEM, AN.
BHATB 1977 -1 BHATIA, H. L.
TIME MINIMIZING ASSIGNMENT PROBLEMS.
BIKO 1978 -1 BIKOV, V. M.
ASSIGNMENT PROBLEM WITH A DISCONTINUOUS TARGET FUNCTION (RUSSIAN), AN.
BREG 1975 -1 BREGMEN, L. M.; ROMANOVSKII, I. V.
ALLOCATION AND OPTIMIZATION IN ASSIGNMENT PROBLEMS (RUSSIAN).
BRON 1979 -1 BRONSTEIN, M. L.; KIM, K. V.
ELIMINATION ON THE POSSIBILITY OF CYCLING IN THE PRIMAL NETWORK METHOD (RUSSIAN).
BRUA 1978 -1 BRUALDI, R. A.
CHROMATIC INDEX OF THE GRAPH OF THE ASSIGNMENT POLYTOPE, THE.
BUHR 1978 -1 BUHR, J.
FOUR METHODS FOR MONTHLY CREW ASSIGNMENT - A COMPARISON OF EFFICIENCY -.
BURK 1978 -2 BURKARD, R. E.
NUMERICAL INVESTIGATIONS ON QUADRATIC ASSIGNMENT PROBLEMS.
BURK 1978 -3 BURKARD, R. E.
QUADRATIC ASSIGNMENT PROBLEMS: SUBOPTIMAL METHODS.
BURK 1979 -3 BURKARD, R. E.
TRAVELLING SALESMAN AND ASSIGNMENT PROBLEMS: A SURVEY.
BURKA 1980 -1 BURKARD, R. E.; DERIGS, U.
ASSIGNMENT AND MATCHING PROBLEMS: SOLUTION METHODS WITH FORTRAN-PROGRAMS.
BURKB 1981 -1 BURKARD, R. E.; FINCKE, U.
ON RANDOM QUADRATIC BOTTLENECK ASSIGNMENT PROBLEMS.
BURKC 1978 -1 BURKARD, R. E.; FROEHLICH, K.
SOME REMARKS ON 3-DIMENSIONAL ASSIGNMENT PROBLEMS (EXTENDED ABSTRACT).
BURKJ 1980 -2 BURKARD, R. E.; ZIMMERMANN, U.
WEAKLY ADMISSIBLE TRANSFORMATIONS FOR SOLVING ALGEBRAIC ASSIGNMENT AND TRANSPORTATION PROBLEMS.
CAIE 1978 -1 CAIE, J.; LINDEN, J.; MAXWELL, W.
SOLUTION OF A MACHINE LOAD PLANNING PROBLEM.
CAIEA 1979 -1 CAIE, J.; LINDEN, J.; OATS, Q.; MAXWELL, W.
HIERARCHICAL MACHINE LOAD PLANNING.
CAMEC 1980 -2 CAMERINI, P. M.; MAFFIOLI, F.
WEIGHTED SATISFIABILITY PROBLEMS AND SOME IMPLICATIONS.
CHALB 1977 -1 CHALMET, L. G.; GELDERS, L. F.
LAGRANGIAN RELAXATIONS FOR A GENERALIZED ASSIGNMENT-TYPE PROBLEM.
CHRIG 1980 -1 CHRISTOFIDES, N.; MINGOZZI, A.; TOTH, P.
CONTRIBUTIONS TO THE QUADRATIC ASSIGNMENT PROBLEM.
CRUS 1979 -1 CRUSE, A. B.
ON REMOVING A VERTEX FROM THE ASSIGNMENT POLYTOPE.
DATH 1978 -1 DATHE, M.
ZUR LOESUNG DES ZUORDNUNGSPROBLEMS BEI ZWEI ZIELGROESSEN.
DERI 1979 -1 DERIGS, U.
DUALITY AND ADMISSIBLE TRANSFORMATIONS IN COMBINATORIAL OPTIMIZATION.
DINI 1976 -1 DINIC, E. A.
SOLUTION OF TWO ASSIGNMENT PROBLEMS (RUSSIAN), THE.
DODO 1977 -1 DODONOV, A. G.; CHERNYSHEV, JU. O.; SADOVOI, N. N.; SHCHETININ, A. M.
SOLUTION OF THE ASSIGNMENT PROBLEM BY REDUCING IT TO THE PROBLEM OF FINDING THE OPTIMAL PATH ON A GRAPH (RUSSIAN).
DORH 1977 -1 DORHOUT, B.
EXPERIMENTS WITH SOME ALGORITHMS FOR THE LINEAR ASSIGNMENT PROBLEM.
DUBE 1979 -1 DUBE, R.; ELSAYED, E. A.
MULTI-MACHINE LABOR ASSIGNMENT FOR VARIABLE OPERATOR SERVICE TIMES, A.
EDWA 1980 -1 EDWARDS, C. S.
BRANCH AND BOUND ALGORITHM FOR THE KOOPMANS-BECKMANN QUADRATIC ASSIGNMENT PROBLEM, A.
ENGQ 1980 -1 ENGQUIST, M.
SUCCESSIVE SHORTEST PATH ALGORITHM FOR THE ASSIGNMENT PROBLEM, A.
FALL 1973 -1 FALLIK, C.
APPLICATIONS ECONOMIQUES DE LA THEORIE DES GRAPHES, EN PARTICULIER AU PROBLEME DES HORAIRES.
FISHB 1978 -2 FISHER, M. L.; JAIKUMAR, R.
DECOMPOSITION ALGORITHM FOR LARGE-SCALE VEHICLE ROUTING, A.
FRIED 1980 -1 FRIEZE, A. M.
ALGORITHM FOR ALGEBRAIC ASSIGNMENT PROBLEMS, AN.
FUJI 1977 -2 FUJISHIGE, S.
PRIMAL APPROACH TO THE INDEPENDENT ASSIGNMENT PROBLEM, A.
GAVIA 1978 -1 GAVISH, B.; SCHWEITZER, P.; SHLIFER, E.
ASSIGNING BUSES TO SCHEDULES IN A METROPOLITAN AREA.

GEND 1977 -1 GENDREAU, M.
ETUDE SUR LA GENERATION DES RESEAUX ALEATOIRES.
GRAN 1979 -1 GRANDON, G. M.
OPTIMIZING HIGH SCHOOL CURRICULUM ASSIGNMENTS.
GROSA 1978 -1 GROSZ, M.
GENERALIZATION OF THE ASSIGNMENT PROBLEM AND ITS SOLUTION (HUNGARIAN), THE.
GUPTF 1979 -1 GUPTA, U. I.; LEE, D. T.; LEUNG, J. Y.-T.
OPTIMAL SOLUTION FOR THE CHANNEL-ASSIGNMENT PROBLEM, AN.
HANN 1979 -1 HANNAN, E. L.
ASSIGNMENT OF PLAYERS TO MATCHES IN A HIGH SCHOOL OR COLLEGE TENNIS MATCH.
HANSC 1978 -1 HANSEN, P.; KAUFMAN, L.; ANTOINE, M.-P.
ASSIGNMENT PROBLEM WITH SOME COMPATIBLE JOBS, THE.
HUNG 1980 -1 HUNG, M. S.; ROM, W. O.
SOLVING THE ASSIGNMENT PROBLEM BY RELAXATION.
HWANA 1978 -1 HWANG, J. S.
COMPLETE UNISEXUAL STABLE MARRIAGES.
HWANB 1977 -1 HWANG, J. S.; SHYR, H. J.
COMPLETE STABLE MARRIAGES.
IBARB 1976 -1 IBARAKI, T.; ISHII, H.; MINE, H.
ASSIGNMENT PROBLEM ON A NETWORK, AN.
IRI 1978 -1 IRI, M.
PRACTICAL ALGORITHM FOR THE MENGER-TYPE GENERALIZATION OF THE INDEPENDENT ASSIGNMENT PROBLEM, A.
IRI C 1976 -1 IRI, M.; TOMIZAWA, N.
ALGORITHM FOR FINDING AN OPTIMAL "INDEPENDENT ASSIGNMENT", AN.
ITOG 1978 -1 ITOGA, S. Y.
UPPER BOUND FOR THE STABLE MARRIAGE PROBLEM, THE.
JONK 1978 -1 JONKER, R.; DELEVE, G.; VANDERVELDE, J. A.; VOLGENANT, A.
SOLVING SYMMETRIC TRAVELING SALESMAN PROBLEMS ASYMMETRICALLY.
JUEN 1979 -1 JUENGER, M.; WESTPHAL, H.
REVISED HUNGARIAN METHOD FOR OPTIMAL INSERTION INTO HASH TABLES, A.
KARN 1978 -1 KARNEY, D.; KLINGMAN, D.
NETGEN REVISITED: A PROGRAM FOR GENERATING LARGE SCALE (UN) CAPACITATED ASSIGNMENT, TRANPORTATION, AND MINIMUM COST FLOW NETWORK PROBLEMS.
KARP 1980 -1 KARP, R. M.
ALGORITHM TO SOLVE THE M X N ASSIGNMENT PROBLEM IN EXPECTED TIME O(MN LOG N), AN.
KAUF 1978 -1 KAUFMAN, L.; BROECKX, F.
ALGORITHM FOR THE QUADRATIC ASSIGNMENT PROBLEM USING BENDERS DECOMPOSITION, AN.
KLAS 1979 -1 KLASTORIN, T. D.
EFFECTIVE SUBGRADIENT ALGORITHM FOR THE GENERALIZED ASSIGNMENT PROBLEM, AN.
KLAS 1979 -2 KLASTORIN, T. D.
ON THE MAXIMAL COVERING LOCATION PROBLEM AND THE GENERALIZED ASSIGNMENT PROBLEM.
KOZU 1977 -1 KOZUHAROV, A. N.; LARICHEV, O. I.
MULTI-TEST ASSIGNMENT PROBLEM.
KOZU 1979 -1 KOZUHAROV, A. N.; LARICHEV, O. I.
MULTIPLE CRITERIA ASSIGNMENT PROBLEM: COMBINING THE COLLECTIVE CRITERION WITH INDIVIDUAL PREFERENCES.
KRAR 1978 -1 KRARUP, J.; PRUZAN, P. M.
COMPUTER-AIDED LAYOUT DESIGN.
KRAVA 1973 -1 KRAVTSOV, M. K.
DIFFERENCE METHOD FOR SOLVING THE ASSIGNMENT PROBLEM (RUSSIAN), A.
LAKS 1979 -1 LAKSHMINARAYAN, S.; LAKSHMANAN, R.; PAPINEAU, R. L.; ROCHETTE, R.
ORDER PRESERVING ALLOCATION OF JOBS TO TWO NON-IDENTICAL PARALLEL MACHINES: A SOLVABLE CASE OF THE MAXIMUM CUT PROBLEM.
LASH 1979 -1 LASHKARI, R. S.; JAISINGH, S. C.
EFFICIENT ALGORITHM FOR QUADRATIC ASSIGNMENT PROBLEM, AN.
LASH 1980 -1 LASHKARI, R. S.; JAISINGH, S. C.
HEURISTIC APPROACH TO QUADRATIC ASSIGNMENT PROBLEM, A.
LEONA 1978 -1 LEONT'EV, V. K.
NUMBER OF OPTIMAL PLANS IN THE PROBLEM OF ASSIGNMENTS (RUSSIAN), THE.
LODI 1976 -1 LODISH, C. M.
ASSIGNING SALESMEN TO MAXIMIZE PROFIT.
LORE 1978 -2 LOREA, M.
MATROIDES SUR LES ENSEMBLES D'ARETES D'HYPERGRAPHES.
LOS A 1981 -1 LOS, M.; NGUYEN, S.
SPATIAL ALLOCATION ON A NETWORK WITH CONGESTION.
LYON 1979 -1 LYON, G.
BATCH SCHEDULING FROM SHORT LISTS.
MAC E 1978 -1 MAC GINNIS, L. F.
IMPLEMENTATION AND TESTING OF A PRIMAL-DUAL ALGORITHM FOR ASSIGNMENT PROBLEM.
MARTC 1980 -1 MARTELLO, S.; TOTH, P.
ALGORITHM FOR THE GENERALIZED ASSIGNMENT PROBLEM, AN.
MECH 1976 -1 MECHTA, A. J.; RIFAI, A. K.
APPLICATION OF LINEAR PROGRAMMING VS. GOAL PROGRAMMING TO ASSIGNMENT PROBLEM.
MIHA 1978 -1 MIHALYFFY, L.
IMPROVED METHOD OF SUCCESSIVE OPTIMA FOR THE ASSIGNMENT PROBLEM, AN.
MIHA 1979 -1 MIHALYFFY, L.
ON THE PROBLEM OF THE SECOND BEST ASSIGNMENT.
MILLC 1975 -1 MILLER, S. D.; PAYNE, H. J.; THOMPSON, W. A.
ALGORITHM FOR TRAFFIC ASSIGNMENT ON CAPACITY CONSTRAINED TRANSPORTATION NETWORKS WITH QUEUES, AN.
MURPC 1979 -1 MURPHY, R. A.; ALLEN, R. E.
PROBLEM OF ASSIGNING SUPPLIERS TO PLANTS, A.
NAKA 1977 -1 NAKAHORI, I.; NAKAZAKI, K.; NISHIKAWA, Y.
GRAPH-THEORETIC CONSIDERATION AND ALGORITHMS FOR A MULTICOMMODITY FLOW ASSIGNMENT PROBLEM, A.
NARUC 1980 -1 NARULA, S. C.; OGBU, U. I.
K-PARTITE ASSIGNMENT PROBLEM, A.
NENG 1980 -1 NENG, B.
ZUR ERSTELLUNG VON OPTIMALEN TRIEBFAHRZEUGLAUFPLAENEN.
NIEB 1978 -1 NIEBLAS, M. H.; ESPINOSA, L. P.
ASSIGNMENT OF LOCOMOTIVES TO A RAILWAY TIMETABLE: A PRACTICAL APPLICATION OF THE HUNGARIAN METHOD (SPANISH), THE.
PANA 1978 -2 PANAYIOTOPOULOS, J.-C.
SOLVING THE ASSIGNMENT PROBLEM IN THREE-DIMENSIONAL SPACE.

PAPO 1977 -1 PAPOULIAS, D. B.
ASSIGNMENT-TO-DAYS PROBLEM IN A SCHOOL TIME-TABLE, A HEURISTIC APPROACH, THE.
PAPO 1980 -1 PAPOULIAS, D. B.
ASSIGNMENT-TO-DAYS PROBLEM IN A SCHOOL TIME-TABLE, A HEURISTIC APPROACH, THE.
PARK 1976 -1 PARKER, C. S.
EXPERIMENTAL INVESTIGATION OF SOME HEURISTIC STRATEGIES FOR COMPONENT PLACEMENT, AN.
PELI 1979 -1 PELIKAN, J.
ON THE SOLUTION OF A SPECIAL ASSIGNMENT PROBLEM (CZECHOSLOVAKIAN).
PILI 1976 -1 PILIPOSJAN, T. E.
CERTAIN ASSIGNMENT PROBLEM (RUSSIAN), A.
PRAK 1978 -1 PRAKASH, S.
ON THE MACHINE-ASSIGNMENT PROBLEM.
QUIN 1976 -1 QUINTART, G.
APPLICATION DE LA THEORIE DES GRAPHES AUX PROBLEMES D'HORAIRE.
RAO 1979 -1 RAO, G. S.; STONE, H. S.; HU, T. C.
ASSIGNMENT OF TASKS IN A DISTRIBUTED PROCESSOR SYSTEM WITH LIMITED MEMORY.
REBI 1975 -1 REBIBO, K. K.; YEN, A. M.
AUTOMATED APPROACH TO THE ASSIGNMENT OF DRIVERS IN URBAN TRANSIT, AN.
ROME 1981 -1 ROMERO, D.
TIC MATRICES. AN EXTENSION OF THE BOTTLENECK ASSIGNMENT PROBLEM.
ROSS 1980 -1 ROSS, G. T.; SOLAND, R. M.
BOUNDED INTERVAL GENERALIZED ASSIGNMENT MODEL, THE.
ROSS 1980 -2 ROSS, G. T.; SOLAND, R. M.
MULTICRITERIA APPROACH TO THE LOCATION OF PUBLIC FACILITIES, A.
ROSSA 1979 -1 ROSS, G. T.; ZOLTNERS, A. A.
WEIGHTED ASSIGNMENT MODELS AND THEIR APPLICATION.
ROUC 1979 -1 ROUCAIROL, C.
REDUCTION METHOD FOR QUADRATIC ASSIGNMENT PROBLEMS, A.
SADY 1979 -1 SADYKOV, R. G.
ON THE SOLUTION OF AN ASSIGNMENT PROBLEM (RUSSIAN).
SAHNB 1975 -1 SAHNI, S.; GONZALEZ, T.
P-COMPLETE APPROXIMATION PROBLEMS.
SCHMA 1978 -1 SCHMID, H. J.
GEOMETRICAL INTERPRETATION OF THE HUNGARIAN METHOD, A.
SCHME 1978 -1 SCHMITZ, P.; SCHOENLEIN, A.
LINEARE UND LINEARISIERBARE OPTIMIERUNGSMODELLE SOWIE IHRE ADV-GESTUETZTE LOESUNG.
SHIL 1979 -2 SHILOACH, Y.
MINIMUM LINEAR ARRANGEMENT ALGORITHM FOR UNDIRECTED TREES, A.
SLOM 1977 -1 SLOMINSKI, L.
EFFICIENT APPROACH TO THE BOTTLENECK ASSIGNMENT PROBLEM, AN.
SLOM 1979 -1 SLOMINSKI, L.
BOTTLENECK ASSIGNMENT PROBLEM: AN EFFICIENT ALGORITHM.
STANC 1978 -1 STANICKI, T.
TWO-CRITERION INTEGER OPTIMIZATION OF SUB-ASSEMBLY ASSIGNMENT IN THE DESIGN OF COMPLEX SYSTEMS BY THE METHOD OF VARIABLE CONSTRAINTS AND PARTIAL ENUMERATION (POLISH).
SUBR 1979 -1 SUBRAHMANYAM, Y. V.
SOME SPECIAL CASES OF ASSIGNMENT PROBLEMS.
SUPR 1974 -1 SUPRUNENKO, D. A.
ON THE ASSIGNMENT PROBLEM (RUSSIAN).
TING 1979 -1 TINGLEY, G. A.
STILL ANOTHER SOLUTION METHOD FOR THE MONTHLY AIRCREW ASSIGNMENT PROBLEM.
TOML 1967 -1 TOMLIN, J. A.
MATHEMATICAL PROGRAMMING MODELS FOR TRAFFIC NETWORK PROBLEMS.
TSUKA 1979 -1 TSUKIYAMA, S.; SHIRAKAWA, I.; ASAHARA, S.
ALGORITHM FOR THE VIA ASSIGNMENT PROBLEM IN MULTILAYER BACKBOARD WIRING, AN.
VASI 1975 -1 VASILEV, L. N.
SPECIAL CASE OF THE ASSIGNMENT PROBLEM (RUSSIAN), A.
WALKB 1979 -1 WALKUP, D. W.
ON THE EXPECTED VALUE OF A RANDOM ASSIGNMENT PROBLEM.
WERR 1977 -1 WERRA, D. DE
ON A MULTIPERIOD ASSIGNMENT PROBLEM.
WERR 1977 -2 WERRA, D. DE
PROGRESSIVE BALANCING IN CHROMATIC SCHEDULING.
WERR 1980 -2 WERRA, D. DE
GEOGRAPHY, GAMES AND GRAPHS.
WONG 1979 -1 WONG, J. K.
NEW IMPLEMENTATION OF AN ALGORITHM FOR THE OPTIMAL ASSIGNMENT PROBLEM: AN IMPROVED VERSION OF MUNKRES' ALGORITHM, A.

ARAOA 1979 -1 ARAOZ, J.
BLOCKING AND ANTI-BLOCKING EXTENSIONS.
ARAOB 1977 -1 ARAOZ, J.; EDMONDS, J.; GRIFFIN, V. J.
POLARITIES GIVEN BY SYSTEMS OF BILINEAR INEQUALITIES.
BAUM 1978 -1 BAUM, S.; TROTTER, L. E. JR.
FINITE CHECKABILITY FOR INTEGER ROUNDING PROPERTIES IN COMBINATORIAL PROBRAMMING PROBLEMS.
BAUM 1978 -2 BAUM, S.; TROTTER, L. E. JR.
INTEGER ROUNDING FOR POLYMATROID AND BRANCHING OPTIMIZATION PROBLEMS.
BLAN 1978 -1 BLAND, R. G.
ELEMENTARY VECTORS AND TWO POLYHEDRAL RELAXATIONS.
HOFF 1978 -1 HOFFMAN, A. J.
ON LATTICE POLYHEDRA III: BLOCKERS AND ANTI-BLOCKERS OF LATTICE CLUTTERS.
HOUCA 1979 -1 HOUCK, D. J.; PITTENGER, A. O.
ANALYTIC PROOFS OF A NETWORK FEASIBILITY THEOREM AND A THEOREM OF FULKERSON.
HUANA 1980 -1 HUANG, H.-C.; TROTTER, L. E. JR.
TECHNIQUE FOR DETERMINING BLOCKING AND ANTIBLOCKING POLYHEDRAL DESCRIPTIONS, A.
JOHND 1980 -1 JOHNSON, E. L.
INTEGER PROGRAMMING, FACETS, SUBADDITIVITY, AND DUALITY FOR GROUP AND SEMI-GROUP PROBLEMS.
JOHND 1978 -2 JOHNSON, E. L.
SUPPORT FUNCTIONS, BLOCKING PAIRS, AND ANTI-BLOCKING PAIRS.
MAC B 1978 -1 MAC DIARMID, C.
BLOCKING, ANTIBLOCKING AND PAIRS OF MATROIDS AND POLYMATROIDS.
MONMC 1979 -1 MONMA, C. L.; TROTTER, L. E. JR.
ON PERFECT GRAPHS AND POLYHEDRA WITH (0,1)-VALUED EXTREME POINTS.
SCHRD 1979 -1 SCHRIJVER, A.
FRACTIONAL PACKING AND COVERING.
TIND 1979 -1 TIND, J.
BLOCKING AND ANTIBLOCKING POLYHEDRA.
TIND 1980 -1 TIND, J.
CERTAIN KINDS OF POLAR SETS AND THEIR RELATION TO MATHEMATICAL PROGRAMMING.
TINDA 1978 -1 TIND, J.; WOLSEY, L. A.
ON THE USE OF PENUMBRAS IN BLOCKING AND ANTIBLOCKING THEORY.
TROT 1978 -1 TROTTER, L. E. JR.; WEINBERGER, D. B.
SYMMETRIC BLOCKING AND ANTI-BLOCKING RELATIONS FOR GENERALIZED CIRCULATIONS.

BOOLEAN METHODS

ASPV	1979 -1	ASPVALL, B.; PLASS, M. F.; TARJAN, R. E. LINEAR-TIME ALGORITHM FOR TESTING THE TRUTH OF CERTAIN QUANTIFIED BOOLEAN FORMULAS, A.
BABAB	1978 -2	BABAEV, DZ. A.; MAMEDOV, K. S. APPROXIMATE METHODS OF SOLUTION OF BOOLEAN PROGRAMMING PROBLEMS OF LARGE DIMENSION (RUSSIAN).
BABAB	1978 -3	BABAEV, DZ. A.; MAMEDOV, K. S. METHOD OF SOLVING A BOOLEAN PROGRAMMING PROBLEM (RUSSIAN), A.
BAER	1978 -1	BAER, G. THEORETISCHE FUNDIERUNG DER DISKRETEN OPTIMIERUNG MIT LOGISCHEN MITTELN, EINE.
BENZ	1980 -1	BENZAKEN, C.; HAMMER, P. L.; SIMEONE, B. GRAPHES DE CONFLIT DES FONCTIONS PSEUDO-BOOLEENNES QUADRATIQUES.
BERMA	1977 -1	BERMAN, G.; COLIJN, A. W. COMPUTER REPRESENTATION OF BOOLEAN AND PSEUDO-BOOLEAN FUNCTIONS, A.
BLAIA	1976 -1	BLAIR, C. E.; JEROSLOW, R. G. CONVERSE FOR DISJUNCTIVE CONSTRAINTS, A.
BORT	1977 -1	BORTOT, P. SOME PROPERTIES OF A SET OF NON LINEAR BOOLEAN INEQUATIONS.
CHANC	1978 -1	CHANDRA, A. K.; MARKOWSKY, G. ON THE NUMBER OF PRIME IMPLICANTS.
CHERC	1977 -1	CHERNYSHEV, JU. O. OPTIMIZATION METHODS FOR COMBINATIONAL DEVICES (RUSSIAN).
COBH	1963 -1	COBHAM, A.; NORTH, J. H. EXTENSION OF THE INTEGER PROGRAMMING APPROACH TO THE MINIMIZATION OF BOOLEAN FUNCTIONS.
COLI	1973 -1	COLIJN, A. W. PSEUDO-BOOLEAN PROGRAMMING.
DESCA	1979 -1	DESCHAMPS, J.; LAPSCHER, F. PRESENTATION ET OPTIMISATION D'UN PROGRAMME DE RECHERCHE DES DECOMPOSITIONS DISJOINTES D'UNE FONCTION BOOLEENNE: EXTENSION AUX FONCTIONS BOOLEENNES GENERALES.
GROP	1978 -2	GROPPEN, V. O. IMPROVING BRANCH-AND-BOUND METHODS FOR DISCRETE PROBLEMS WITH BOOLEAN VARIABLES.
HAMMA	1979 -1	HAMMER, P. L. BOOLEAN ELEMENTS IN COMBINATORIAL OPTIMIZATION.
HAMMB	1981 -1	HAMMER, P. L.; HANSEN, P.; SIMEONE, B. UPPER PLANES OF QUADRATIC 0-1 FUNCTIONS AND STABILITY IN GRAPHS.
HAMMD	1979 -1	HAMMER, P. L.; NGUYEN, S. PARTIAL ORDER IN THE SOLUTION SPACE OF BIVALENT PROGRAMS, A.
HAMME	1979 -1	HAMMER, P. L.; PELED, U. N.; POLLATSCHEK, M. A. ALGORITHM TO DUALIZE A REGULAR SWITCHING FUNCTION, AN.
HARP	1976 -1	HARPER, L. H.; SAVAGE, J. E. COMPLEXITY MADE SIMPLE.
JAIN	1979 -1	JAIN, R. C. ON GLOBALLY MINIMIZING POINTS OF PSEUDO-BOOLEAN QUADRATIC FUNCTIONS.
KARZA	1978 -1	KARZANOV, A. V.; DINIC, E. A. BOOLEAN OPTIMIZATION PROBLEM WITH CONSTRAINTS OF A SPECIAL TYPE (RUSSIAN), A.
KOZEA	1979 -1	KOZERACKAJA, L. N. MODIFICATION OF MC CLUSKEY'S ALGORITHM (RUSSIAN), A.
MAME	1978 -1	MAMEDOV, K. S. TWO-SIDED ESTIMATION OF THE OPTIMAL VALUE OF THE TARGET FUNCTION IN BOOLEAN PROGRAMMING PROBLEMS (RUSSIAN).
NARI	1979 -1	NARIHISA, H. BOOLEAN PROGRAMMING.
PATEA	1976 -1	PATERSON, M. S. INTRODUCTION TO BOOLEAN FUNCTION COMPLEXITY, AN.
PATEA	1976 -2	PATERSON, M. S. NEW BOUNDS ON FORMULA SIZE.
PELEA	1981 -2	PELED, U. N.; SIMEONE, B. POLYNOMIAL-TIME ALGORITHM FOR RECOGNIZING THRESHOLD FUNCTIONS, A.
PIPP	1977 -2	PIPPENGER, N. ON ANOTHER BOOLEAN MATRIX.
PLAI	1976 -1	PLAISTED, D. A. SOME POLYNOMIAL AND INTEGER DIVISIBILITY PROBLEMS ARE NP-HARD.
PROT	1977 -1	PROTASOV, I. V.; TRETJAK, V. P.; CHARIN, V. S. OPTIMIZATION PROBLEM CONNECTED WITH COVERINGS (RUSSIAN), AN.
ROSEC	1963 -1	ROSENBLATT, D. ON THE GRAPHS OF FINITE IDEMPOTENT BOOLEAN RELATION MATRICES.
ROSEC	1967 -1	ROSENBLATT, D. AGGREGATION IN MATRIX MODELS OF RESOURCE FLOWS II. BOOLEAN RELATION MATRIX METHODS.
SCHNA	1976 -1	SCHNORR, C. P. NETWORK COMPLEXITY AND THE BREADTH OF BOOLEAN FUNCTIONS, THE.
SHCH	1976 -1	SHCHERBINA, O. A. OPTIMAL PARTITIONING INTO BLOCKS OF A QUASIBLOCK PROBLEM OF BOOLEAN PROGRAMMING (RUSSIAN).
SIME	1979 -2	SIMEONE, B. QUADRATIC 0-1 PROGRAMMING, BOOLEAN FUNCTIONS AND GRAPHS.
WILS	1977 -1	WILSON, J. M. METHOD FOR REDUCING COEFFICIENTS IN ZERO-ONE LINEAR INEQUALITIES, A.
ZAK	1978 -1	ZAK, JU. A. ALGORITHMS FOR NONLINEAR PSEUDO-BOOLEAN PROGRAMMING.

BHATB 1977 -1 BHATIA, H. L.
TIME MINIMIZING ASSIGNMENT PROBLEMS.
BOYCB 1978 -1 BOYCE, S.; MORTON, T. E.
BOTTLENECK HORIZONS FOR ONE MACHINE SEQUENCING WITH PRECEDENCE CONSTRAINTS (REVISED VERSION).
BURKA 1980 -1 BURKARD, R. E.; DERIGS, U.
ASSIGNMENT AND MATCHING PROBLEMS: SOLUTION METHODS WITH FORTRAN-PROGRAMS.
BURKB 1981 -1 BURKARD, R. E.; FINCKE, U.
ON RANDOM QUADRATIC BOTTLENECK ASSIGNMENT PROBLEMS.
DEAR 1979 -1 DEARING, P. M.; NEWRUCK, F. C.
CAPACITATED BOTTLENECK FACILITY LOCATION PROBLEM, A.
DERI 1980 -4 DERIGS, U.
METHODEN ZUR LOESUNG DES BOTTLENECK-TRANSPORTPROBLEMS.
DERI 1980 -5 DERIGS, U.
ON TWO METHODS FOR SOLVING THE BOTTLENECK MATCHING PROBLEM.
DERIC 1979 -1 DERIGS, U.; ZIMMERMANN, U.
AUGMENTING PATH METHOD FOR SOLVING LINEAR BOTTLENECK TRANSPORTATION PROBLEMS, AN.
FINK 1981 -1 FINKE, G.
BOTTLENECK PROBLEMS WITH OVERSHIPMENTS.
FRANF 1976 -1 FRANKE, B.
QUADRATISCHE BOTTLENECK-ZUORDNUNGS-PROBLEME.
GARFA 1978 -1 GARFINKEL, R. S.; GILBERT, K. C.
BOTTLENECK TRAVELING SALESMAN PROBLEM: ALGORITHMS AND PROBABILISTIC ANALYSIS, THE.
GAULA 1978 -1 GAUL, W.; HARTUNG, J.
ZEIT- UND KOSTENOPTIMIERUNG VON BOTTLENECKWEGEN.
GUPTC 1977 -1 GUPTA, R.
TIME-COST TRANSPORTATION PROBLEM.
NAGE 1980 -2 NAGELHOUT, R. V.; THOMPSON, G. L.
STUDY OF THE BOTTLENECK SINGEL SOURCE TRANSPORTATION PROBLEM, A.
OHSE 1978 -1 OHSE, D.
ZEIT-UMLADE- ODER BOTTLENECK-TRANSSHIPMENTPROBLEM, DAS.
ROME 1981 -1 ROMERO, D.
TIC MATRICES, AN EXTENSION OF THE BOTTLENECK ASSIGNMENT PROBLEM.
SCHME 1978 -1 SCHMITZ, P.; SCHOENLEIN, A.
LINEARE UND LINEARISIERBARE OPTIMIERUNGSMODELLE SOWIE IHRE ADV-GESTUETZTE LOESUNG.
SHARB 1977 -1 SHARMA, J. K.; SWARUP, K.
TIME MINIMIZING TRANSPORTATION PROBLEMS.
SLOM 1977 -1 SLOMINSKI, L.
EFFICIENT APPROACH TO THE BOTTLENECK ASSIGNMENT PROBLEM, AN.
SLOM 1978 -1 SLOMINSKI, L.
BOTTLENECK DISCRETE PROBLEMS.
SLOM 1979 -1 SLOMINSKI, L.
BOTTLENECK ASSIGNMENT PROBLEM: AN EFFICIENT ALGORITHM.
ZEIT 1981 -1 ZEITLIN, Z.
INTEGER ALLOCATION PROBLEMS OF MIN-MAX TYPE WITH QUASICONVEX SEPARABLE FUNCTIONS.
ZIMM 1980 -2 ZIMMERMANN, U.
LINEAR OPTIMIZATION FOR LINEAR AND BOTTLENECK OBJECTIVES WITH ONE NONLINEAR PARAMETER.

ACKE 1978 -1 ACKERMAN, L. J.; LUSS, H.; BERKOWITZ, R. S.
IMPLICIT ENUMERATION ALGORITHM FOR SEQUENCING POLICIES APPLIED TO TELEPHONE SWITCHING FACILITIES, AN.

ADRAB 1977 -1 ADRABINSKI, A.; WODECKI, M.
ALGORITHM FOR SOLVING A MACHINE SEQUENCING PROBLEM WITH PARALLEL MACHINES, AN.

AGRA 1977 -1 AGRAWAL, S. C.
ALTERNATE METHOD ON INTEGER SOLUTIONS TO LINEAR FRACTIONAL FUNCTIONALS BY A BRANCH AND BOUND TECHNIQUE, AN.

AGRAA 1978 -1 AGRAWAL, S. C.; CHAND, M.
ON INTEGER SOLUTIONS TO COMPLEMENTARY PROGRAMMING PROBLEMS WITH LINEAR FRACTIONAL OBJECTIVE FUNCTION BY A BRANCH AND BOUND TECHNIQUE.

ALBE 1980 -1 ALBERS, S.
IMPLICIT ENUMERATION ALGORITHMS FOR THE SET-PARTITIONING PROBLEM.

ALEK 1978 -1 ALEKSEEV, O. G.
APPLICATION OF BRANCH AND BOUND TO THE MINIMAX ASSIGNMENT PROBLEM (RUSSIAN).

ALI B 1980 -2 ALI, A. I.; KENNINGTON, J. L.
M-TRAVELLING SALESMEN PROBLEM: A DUALITY BASED BRANCH-AND-BOUND ALGORITHM, THE.

ANZA 1977 -1 ANZAI, Y.
URBAN ROAD NETWORK MODELING PROBLEM - FORMULATION AND ALGORITHMS.

ARMS 1977 -1 ARMSTRONG, R. D.
EXPERIMENTS IN A MULTIPLE CHOICE MIXED INTEGER PROGRAMMING ALGORITHM.

ARMSB 1979 -1 ARMSTRONG, R. D.; COOK, W. D.; PALACIOS-GOMEZ, F. E.
ALGORITHM FOR A NONLINEAR DISCONTINUOUS KNAPSACK PROBLEM, AN.

AVIS 1980 -1 AVIS, D.
NOTE ON SOME COMPUTATIONALLY DIFFICULT SET COVERING PROBLEMS, A.

BABA 1981 -1 BABAEV, A. A.; DRUGANOV, B. N.
METHOD OF BRANCH AND BOUND IN THE PROBLEM OF COMPOSING WEEKLY SCHEDULE OF STUDIES (RUSSIAN).

BAKEJ 1977 -1 BAKER, K. R.; SILVER, E. A.; MAGAZINE, M. J.
ALGORITHM FOR THE DYNAMIC LOT-SIZE PROBLEM WITH PRODUCTION CAPACITY CONSTRAINTS, AN.

BALAA 1979 -1 BALAS, E.
BIVALENT PROGRAMMING BY IMPLICIT ENUMERATION.

BALAA 1979 -2 BALAS, E.
DISJUNCTIVE PROGRAMMING.

BALAK 1977 -3 BALAS, E.; ZEMEL, E.
SOLVING LARGE ZERO-ONE KNAPSACK PROBLEMS (REVISED VERSION).

BANS 1980 -1 BANSAL, S. P.
SINGLE MACHINE SCHEDULING TO MINIMIZE WEIGHTED SUM OF COMPLETION TIMES WITH SECONDARY CRITERION - A BRANCH AND BOUND APPROACH.

BARAB 1977 -1 BARAUSKAS, R. A.; VALANTINAS, I. I.
OPTIMAL CODING OF THE VERTICES OF AN UNDIRECTED GRAPH (RUSSIAN).

BARC 1978 -1 BARCELO, J.
STATE-OF-THE-ART SURVEY ABOUT ENUMERATIVE METHODS (SPANISH).

BARI 1978 -1 BARI, A.; ARSHAD, M.
BRANCH AND BOUND METHOD FOR INTEGER QUADRATIC PROGRAMMING, A.

BARRA 1979 -2 BARR, R. S.; GLOVER, F.; KLINGMAN, D.
NEW OPTIMIZATION METHOD FOR LARGE-SCALE FIXED CHARGE TRANSPORTATION PROBLEMS, A.

BATY 1979 -1 BATYCKI, T.; KASPRZAK, A.
BRANCH-AND-BOUND ALGORITHM FOR DETERMINATION OF ADAPTIVE ROUTING IN SOME CLASS OF PACKET-SWITCHED COMPUTER COMMUNICATION NETWORKS, THE.

BAZAA 1979 -1 BAZARAA, M. S.; ELSHAFEI, A. N.
EXACT BRANCH-AND-BOUND PROCEDURE FOR THE QUADRATIC-ASSIGNMENT PROBLEM, AN.

BEAL 1979 -1 BEALE, E. M. L.
BRANCH AND BOUND METHODS FOR MATHEMATICAL PROGRAMMING SYSTEMS.

BEST 1979 -1 BESTWICK, P. F.; LOCKYER, K. G.
PRACTICAL APPROACH TO PRODUCTION SCHEDULING, A.

BHAS 1980 -1 BHASKARAN, S.
OVERHAUL SCHEDULING OF NEW ZEALAND POWER GENERATORS.

BOFFA 1979 -1 BOFFEY, T. B.; HINXMAN, A. I.
SOLVING THE OPTIMAL NETWORK PROBLEM.

BONDA 1978 -1 BONDY, J. A.; HEMMINGER, R. L.
RECONSTRUCTION BY ENUMERATION: SOME APPLICATIONS OF A COUNTING THEOREM BY THE GRAPH RECONSTRUCTION PROBLEM.

BROWB 1979 -2 BROWN, J. R.
PREVENTING REDUNDANT SOLUTIONS IN PARTIAL ENUMERATION ALGORITHMS.

BULFB 1979 -1 BULFIN, R. L.; PARKER, R. G.; SHETTY, C. M.
COMPUTATIONAL RESULTS WITH A BRANCH-AND-BOUND ALGORITHM FOR THE GENERAL KNAPSACK PROBLEM.

BURK 1978 -2 BURKARD, R. E.
NUMERICAL INVESTIGATIONS ON QUADRATIC ASSIGNMENT PROBLEMS.

CHAND 1979 -2 CHANDRA, S.; CHANDRAMOHAN, M.
IMPROVED BRANCH AND BOUND METHOD FOR MIXED INTEGER LINEAR FRACTIONAL PROGRAMS, AN.

CHERE 1978 -1 CHERVAK, JU. JU.
RECURRENCE ALGORITHM FOR THE METHOD OF CUTS AND THE METHOD OF BRANCH-AND-BOUND (RUSSIAN), A.

CHRIF 1978 -1 CHRISTOFIDES, N.; MINGOZZI, A.; THOTH, P.
EXACT ALGORITHMS FOR THE VEHICLE ROUTING PROBLEM.

CHRIG 1980 -2 CHRISTOFIDES, N.; MINGOZZI, A.; TOTH, P.
DYNAMIC LOADING AND UNLOADING OF LIQUIDS INTO TANKS.

CIOB 1977 -1 CIOBANU, G.
BRANCH-AND-BOUND ALGORITHM TO SOLVE AN ASSEMBLY LINE BALANCING PROBLEM, A.

CLAR 1980 -1 CLARK, G. M.; RANGANATHAN, A. N.
RESOURCE ALLOCATION ALGORITHM (ALCOT) FOR CONTROLLING MINE DRAINAGE POLLUTION, A.

COHE 1978 -1 COHEN, A. I.
ALGORITHM FOR SCHEDULING SURFACE COAL MINES, AN (REVISED VERSION).

COPP 1980 -1 COPPINS, R. J.; PENTICO, D. W.
SCHEDULING THE NATIONAL FOOTBALL LEAGUE.

CORO 1977 -1 COROMINAS, A.; COMPANYS, R.
GENERALISED BRANCH AND BOUND PROCEDURE (SPANISH), A.

DANI 1978 -1 DANIEL, R. C.
GENERALISATION OF VARIABLE UPPER BOUNDING AND GENERALISED UPPER BOUNDING, A.

DANI 1978 -2 DANIEL, R. C.
REDUCING COMPUTATIONAL EFFORT IN SOLVING A HARD INTEGER PROGRAM.

DANIA 1979 -1 DANIEL, R. C.; JEFFREYS, M.
UNBOUNDEDNESS IN INTEGER AND DISCRETE PROGRAMMING L. P. RELAXATIONS.

DAS B 1978 -1 DAS, S.; PANDIT, S. N. N.
COMPUTATION OF A NEW LOWER BOUND: SEQUENCING N JOBS ON M PARALLEL PROCESSORS.

DECK 1977 -1 DECKRO, R. F.
MULTIPLE OBJECTIVE DISTRICTING: A GENERAL HEURISTIC APPROACH USING MULTIPLE CRITERIA.

DIONA 1979 -1 DIONNE, R.; FLORIAN, M.
EXACT AND APPROXIMATE ALGORITMS FOR OPTIMAL NETWORK DESIGN.
DUMA 1977 -1 DUMAS, M. B.
BRANCH BIAS HEURISTIC SCHEDULING OF THE GENERAL JOB SHOP.
EDWA 1980 -1 EDWARDS, C. S.
BRANCH AND BOUND ALGORITHM FOR THE KOOPMANS-BECKMANN QUADRATIC ASSIGNMENT PROBLEM, A.
ERLE 1978 -1 ERLENKOTTER, D.
DUAL BASED PROCEDURE FOR UNCAPACITATED FACILITY LOCATION, A.
ETCH 1978 -1 ETCHEBERRY, J.; CONCA, C.; STACCHETTI, E.
IMPLICIT ENUMERATION APPROACH FOR INTEGER PROGRAMMING USING SUBGRADIENT OPTIMIZATION, AN.
FIAL 1978 -1 FIALA, F.
VEHICLE ROUTING PROBLEM.
FISH 1978 -2 FISHER, M. L.
LAGRANGIAN RELAXATION METHODS FOR COMBINATORIAL OPTIMZATION (REVISED VERSION).
FOUL 1978 -1 FOULDS, L. R.; GIBBONS, P. B.
BRANCH AND BOUND APPROACH TO THE STEINER PROBLEM IN GRAPHS, A.
FOX 1978 -1 FOX, B. L.; LENSTRA, J. K.; RINNOOY KAN, A. H. G.; SCHRAGE, L. E.
BRANCHING FROM THE LARGEST UPPER BOUND; FOLKLORE AND FACTS.
FREI 1979 -1 FREIDENFELDS, J.; MAC LAUGHLIN, C. D.
HEURISTIC BRANCH-AND-BOUND ALGORITHM FOR TELEPHONE FEEDER CAPACITY EXPANSION, A.
GARF 1979 -1 GARFINKEL, R. S.
BRANCH AND BOUND METHODS FOR INTEGER PROGRAMMING.
GARR 1978 -1 GARROD, N. W.; MOORES, B.
IMPLICIT ENUMERATION ALGORITHM FOR SOLVING ZERO-ONE GOAL PROGRAMMING PROBLEMS, AN.
GEN 1976 -1 GEN, M.; OKUNO, H.; SHINOFUJI, S.
OPTIMIZING METHOD IN SYSTEM RELIABILITY WITH FAILURE-MODES BY IMPLICIT ENUMERATION ALGORITHM, AN.
GERH 1979 -1 GERHARDS, L.; LINDENBERG, W.
CLIQUE DETECTION FOR NONDIRECTED GRAPHS: TWO NEW ALGORITHMS.
GHOS 1978 -1 GHOSH, S.; RAY, S.; BHATTACHARYA, A.
CASE STUDY FOR OPTIMAL PLANT SIZE MIX USING INTEGER LINEAR PROGRAMMING, A.
GLOV 1978 -1 GLOVER, F.
PARAMETRIC BRANCH AND BOUND.
GRANB 1979 -1 GRANOT, D.; GRANOT, F.; KALLBERG, J.
COVERING RELAXATION FOR POSITIVE 0-1 POLYNOMIAL PROGRAMS.
GRIGO 1978 -1 GRIGOREVA, N. S.; ROMANOVSKII, I. V.
PROBLEMS OF CYCLIC SCHEDULING.
GROEB 1981 -1 GROETSCHEL, M.
APPROACHES TO HARD COMBINATORIAL OPTIMIZATION PROBLEMS.
GROP 1978 -2 GROPPEN, V. O.
IMPROVING BRANCH-AND-BOUND METHODS FOR DISCRETE PROBLEMS WITH BOOLEAN VARIABLES.
GROSA 1978 -1 GROSZ, M.
GENERALIZATION OF THE ASSIGNMENT PROBLEM AND ITS SOLUTION (HUNGARIAN), THE.
GUEN 1979 -1 GUENOCHE, A.
ENUMERATION DE CLASSES DE PERMUTATIONS.
GUIGA 1978 -2 GUIGNARD, M.; SPIELBERG, K.
EXPERIMENTAL INTERACTIVE SYSTEM FOR INTEGER PROGRAMMING, AN.
GUPT 1979 -1 GUPTA, J. N. D.
IMPROVED LEXICOGRAPHIC SEARCH ALGORITHM FOR THE FLOWSHOP SCHEDULING PROBLEM, AN.
GUPTB 1980 -1 GUPTA, O. K.
BRANCH AND BOUND EXPERIMENTS IN NONLINEAR INTEGER PROGRAMMING.
GUPTE 1976 -1 GUPTA, S. K.; TURKSON, I. B.
APPLICATION OF BRANCH AND BOUND TECHNIQUE TO PRODUCTION SCHEDULING PROBLEMS.
HABE 1978 -1 HABENICHT, W.
ZUM EINSATZ ENUMERATIVER SCHNITTEBENENVERFAHREN IN B&B-SYSTEMEN.
HARV 1979 -1 HARVEY, R. T.; PATTERSON, J. H.
IMPLICIT ENUMERATION ALGORITHM FOR THE TIME/COST TRADEOFF PROBLEM IN PROJECT NETWORK ANALYSIS, AN.
HINDB 1978 -1 HINDI, K. S.; BRAMELLER, A.; HAMAM, K. M.
SOLUTION OF FIXED COST TRANS-SHIPMENT PROBLEMS BY A BRANCH AND BOUND METHOD.
HOAN 1978 -1 HOANG HAI HOC
SOLVING AN INTEGER PROGRAMMING PROBLEM.
HODZA 1978 -1 HODZINSKII, A. N.
RESULTS OF A COMPUTER EXPERIMENT IN SOLVING A TYPE OF PROBLEM IN SCHEDULING THEORY BY THE BRANCH AND BOUND METHOD AND THE DROP VECTOR METHOD (RUSSIAN).
HUDS 1977 -1 HUDSON, P. D.
IMPROVING THE BRANCH AND BOUND ALGORITHMS FOR THE KNAPSACK PROBLEM.
IBAR 1977 -1 IBARAKI, T.
ON THE COMPUTATIONAL EFFICIENCY OF BRANCH-AND-BOUND ALGORITHMS.
IBAR 1978 -1 IBARAKI, T.
BRANCH-AND-BOUND PROCEDURE AND STATE-SPACE REPRESENTATION OF COMBINATORIAL OPTIMIZATION PROBLEMS.
IBAR 1979 -1 IBARAKI, T.
THEORETICAL AND SIMULATION STUDIES ON COMPUTATIONAL PERFORMANCE OF BRANCH-AND-BOUND ALGORITHMS.
IBAR 1978 -2 IBARAKI, T.
DEPTH-M SEARCH IN BRANCH-AND-BOUND ALGORITHMS.
IMAI 1979 -1 IMAI, M.
PARALLELIZED BRANCH AND BOUND ALGORITHM - IMPLEMENTATION AND EFFICIENCY (JAPANESE), A.
JACQ 1980 -1 JACQMIN, N. E.
BINARY INTEGER LINEAR PROGRAMMING: A HYBRID IMPLICIT ENUMERATION APPROACH.
JAIN 1979 -1 JAIN, R. C.
ON GLOBALLY MINIMIZING POINTS OF PSEUDO-BOOLEAN QUADRATIC FUNCTIONS.
JAMB 1978 -2 JAMBEKAR, A. B.; STEINBERG, D. I.
IMPLICIT ENUMERATION ALGORITHM FOR THE ALL INTEGER PROGRAMMING PROBLEM, AN.
JENKA 1978 -1 JENKYNS, T. A.
EFFICACY OF HEURISTICS COMBINING ENUMERATION AND THE GREEDY ALGORITHM, THE.
JOHNG 1980 -1 JOHNSON, E. L.; SUHL, U.
EXPERIMENTS IN INTEGER PROGRAMMING.
KAAS 1980 -1 KAAS, R.
BRANCH AND BOUND ALGORITHM FOR THE ACYCLIC SUBGRAPH PROBLEM, A.
KAO 1978 -1 KAO, E. P. C.
PREFERENCE ORDER DYNAMIC PROGRAM FOR A STOCHASTIC TRAVELING SALESMAN PROBLEM, A.
KARW 1981 -1 KARWAN, M. H.; RARDIN, R. L.
SURROGATE DUALITY IN A BRANCH-AND-BOUND PROCEDURE.

KARWA 1980 -1 KARWAN, M. H.; VILLARREAL, B.
FATHOMING TOURS IN (MIXED) INTEGER LINEAR PROGRAMMING.

KATK 1977 -1 KATKHANOV, M. N.; BURLAKOV, E. A.; SAFRONOV, V. V.
OPTIMIZATION ALGORITHM OF THE TOLERANCES ON PARAMETERS OF THE ELEMENTS OF A COMPLEX SYSTEM (RUSSIAN).

KHUM 1978 -1 KHUMAWALA, B. M.; NEEBE, A. W.
NOTE ON WARSZAWSKI'S MULTI-COMMODITY LOCATION PROBLEM, A.

KLEIA 1980 -1 KLEIN, D.; HANNAN, E. L.
BRANCH AND BOUND ALGORITHM FOR THE MULTIPLE OBJECTIVE ZERO-ONE LINEAR PROGRAMMING PROBLEM, A.

KOER 1980 -1 KOERNER, F.
EFFEKTIVER BRANCH AND BOUND ALGORITHMUS FUER DAS ISING PROBLEM, EIN.

KOER 1979 -2 KOERNER, F.
SORTIERUNG DER VERZWEIGUNGSREIHENFOLGE, DIE.

KOER 1979 -3 KOERNER, F.
STRUKTURUNTERSUCHUNGEN AM ALGORITHMUS VON KORTE, KRELLE UND OBERHOFER.

KORB 1977 -1 KORBUT, A. A.; SIGAL, I. H.; FINKELSTEIN, JU. JU.
BRANCH AND BOUND METHOD. A SURVEY OF THEORY, ALGORITHMS, PROGRAMS AND APPLICATIONS (RUSSIAN), THE.

KUMAA 1979 -1 KUMAR, S.; SHARMA, J.; RAY, L. M.
NEW TECHNIQUE FOR MULTIDIMENSIONAL CAPACITY EXPANSION PROJECTS, A.

LAGE 1977 -1 LAGEWEG, B. J.; LENSTRA, J. K.; RINNOOY KAN, A. H. G.
JOB-SHOP SCHEDULING BY IMPLICIT ENUMERATION.

LAGE 1978 -1 LAGEWEG, B. J.; LENSTRA, J. K.; RINNOOY KAN, A. H. G.
GENERAL BOUNDING SCHEME FOR THE PERMUTATION FLOW-SHOP PROBLEM, A.

LARSB 1978 -1 LARSON, R. E.; DESSOUKY, M. I.
HEURISTIC PROCEDURES FOR THE SINGLE MACHINE PROBLEM TO MINIMIZE MAXIMUM LATENESS.

LAWI 1979 -1 LAWIS, R. T.; PARKER, R. G.
BIN PACKING, MULTI-PROCESSOR SCHEDULING, AND GRAPH COLORING.

LEE C 1979 -1 LEE, S. M.; FRANZ, L. S.
OPTIMIZING THE LOCATION-ALLOCATION PROBLEM WITH MULTIPLE OBJECTIVES.

LENSA 1976 -1 LENSTRA, J. K.; RINNOOY KAN, A. H. G.
NOTE ON THE EXPECTED PERFORMANCE OF BRANCH-AND-BOUND ALGORITHMS, A.

LENSA 1978 -3 LENSTRA, J. K.; RINNOOY KAN, A. H. G.
ON THE EXPECTED PERFORMANCE OF BRANCH-AND-BOUND ALGORITHMS.

LENSA 1980 -4 LENSTRA, J. K.; RINNOOY KAN, A. H. G.
RECURSIVE APPROACH TO THE IMPLEMENTATION OF ENUMERATION METHODS, A.

LEV 1978 -1 LEV, B.; SOYSTER, A. L.
INTEGER PROGRAMMING WITH BOUNDED VARIABLES VIA CANONICAL SEPARATION.

LJUBA 1977 -1 LJUBOVICKII, L. V.
PROPERTIES OF THE BASIS MATRICES OF A CLASS OF POLYHEDRA (RUSSIAN).

MAC 1980 -2 MAC BRIDE, R. D.; YORMARK, J. S.
IMPLICIT ENUMERATION ALGORITHM FOR QUADRATIC INTEGER PROGRAMMING, AN.

MAKSC 1980 -1 MAKSIMOV, J. B.; KRIVORUCHKO, E. I.
APPLICATION OF THE BRANCH AND BOUND METHOD TO THE SOLUTION OF DISCRETE VOLUME SCHEDULING PROBLEMS (RUSSIAN).

MARS 1975 -1 MARSTEN, R. E.
USE OF THE BOXSTEP METHOD IN DISCRETE OPTIMIZATION, THE.

MARTB 1978 -1 MARTELLO, S.
ALGORITHM FOR FINDING A MINIMAL EQUIVALENT GRAPH OF A STRONGLY CONNECTED DIGRAPH, AN.

MARTC 1977 -1 MARTELLO, S.; TOTH, P.
BRANCH AND BOUND ALGORITHMS FOR THE SOLUTION OF THE GENERAL UNIDIMENSIONAL KNAPSACK PROBLEM.

MARTC 1979 -1 MARTELLO, S.; TOTH, P.
FINDING A MINIMAL EQUIVALENT GRAPH OF A DIGRAPH.

MARTC 1980 -3 MARTELLO, S.; TOTH, P.
OPTIMAL AND CANONICAL SOLUTIONS OF THE CHANGE MAKING PROBLEM.

MEHL 1978 -1 MEHLHORN, K.
EFFIZIENTE ALGORITHMEN: EIN BEISPIEL.

MILI 1978 -1 MILIOTIS, P.
USING CUTTING PLANES TO SOLVE THE SYMMETRIC TRAVELING SALESMAN PROBLEM.

MILLB 1979 -1 MILLER, R. E.; PIPPENGER, N.; ROSENBERG, A. L.; SNYDER, L.
OPTIMAL 2,3-TREES.

MITE 1979 -1 MITEV, J. G.
USE OF A NUMBER OF ADMISSIBLE SOLUTIONS OF EQUATIONS IN ALGORITHMS FOR PURELY INTEGER PROBLEMS OF LINEAR PROGRAMMING (RUSSIAN), THE.

MJEL 1978 -1 MJELDE, K. M.
DISCRETE RESOURCE ALLOCATION BY A BRANCH AND BOUND METHOD.

MORT 1978 -1 MORTON, T. E.; BALA, G. D.
ALGORISTICS FOR SINGLE-MACHINE SEQUENCING WITH PRECEDENCE CONSTRAINTS.

MUEL 1978 -2 MUELLER-MERBACH, H.
KASKADENBAUMVERFAHREN ZUR LOESUNG DES "KNAPSACKPROBLEMS", EIN.

NABE 1977 -1 NABESHIMA, I.
EXTENDED BRANCH AND BOUND ALGORITHM AND ITS APPLICATION TO BIOBJECTIVE PROBLEM.

NABEA 1978 -1 NABESHIMA, I.; MARUYAMA, S.
ON N*M MEAN COMPLETION TIME FLOW SHOP PROBLEM. ANALYTICAL RESULTS, EXTENDED BRANCH AND BOUND ALGORITHM AND COMPUTATIONAL EXPERIENCE.

NARUB 1979 -1 NARULA, S. C.; KINDORF, J. R.
LINEAR 0-1 PROGRAMMING: A COMPARISON OF IMPLICIT ENUMERATION ALGORITHMS.

NAUS 1979 -2 NAUSS, R. M.
SOLVING LOCK BOX LOCATION PROBLEMS.

NAUSA 1981 -1 NAUSS, R. M.; KEELER, B. R.
MINIMIZATION OF LEASE PAYMENTS IN LEVERAGED LEASES: AN APPLICATION OF INTEGER PROGRAMMING.

NEEB 1978 -1 NEEBE, A. W.
BRANCH AND BOUND ALGORITHM FOR THE P-MEDIAN TRANSPORTATION PROBLEM, A.

NEEBA 1981 -1 NEEBE, A. W.; KHUMAWALA, B. M.
IMPROVED ALGORITHM FOR THE MULTICOMMODITY LOCATION PROBLEM, AN.

NEMHB 1978 -1 NEMHAUSER, G. L.; WOLSEY, L. A.
MAXIMIZING SUBMODULAR SET FUNCTIONS: FORMULATIONS AND ANALYSIS OF ALGORITHMS.

OSKO 1975 -1 OSKOLKOV, I. O.
SIMULTANEOUS BRANCHING BY SEVERAL VARIABLES IN THE BRANCH-AND-BOUND METHOD.

PANN 1978 -1 PANNY, W.
VERFAHREN ZUR LOESUNG DES TRAVELLING-SALESMAN-PROBLEMS UNTER BESONDERER BERUECKSICHTIGUNG DER METHODE "BRANCH-AND-BOUND".

PATK 1979 -1 PATKAR, V.; AGGARWAL, S.
BRANCH AND BOUND TECHNIQUE FOR INTEGER GEOMETRIC PROGRAMMING.

PATT 1978 -1 PATTERSON, J. H.
BALASIAN-BASED ENUMERATION PROCEDURES: A STUDY IN COMPUTATION EFFICIENCY.

PEGD 1979 -1 PEGDEN, C. D.; PETERSEN, C. C.
ALGORITHM (GIPC2) FOR SOLVING INTEGER PROGRAMMING PROBLEMS WITH SEPARABLE NONLINEAR OBJECTIVE FUNCTIONS, AN.

PICA 1978 -1 PICARD, J.-C.; QUEYRANNE, M.
TIME-DEPENDENT TRAVELING SALESMAN PROBLEM AND ITS APPLICATION TO THE TARDINESS PROBLEM IN ONE-MACHINE SCHEDULING, THE.

POTR 1979 -1 POTRZEBOWSKI, H.
BRANCH AND BOUND AS A DECOMPOSITION METHOD OF DETERMINING SCHEDULES FOR PARALLEL MACHINES (POLISH).

POTT 1980 -1 POTTS, C. N.
ADAPTIVE BRANCHING RULE FOR THE PERMUTATION FLOW-SHOP PROBLEM, AN.

RARDB 1978 -1 RARDIN, R. L.; LIN, B. W.
WHAT MAKES INTEGER PROGRAMMING PROBLEMS HARD TO SOLVE: AN EMPIRICAL STUDY.

ROHD 1979 -1 ROHDE, M.
ENUMERATIVER ALGORITHMUS ZUR LOESUNG DES SET-PARTITIONING-PROBLEMS MIT RANDBEDINGUNGEN, EIN.

ROTA 1978 -1 ROTARU, S.
DEUX METHODES DE RESOLUTION DE LA PROGRAMMATION ENTIERE (ROMANIAN).

ROUN 1980 -1 ROUNTREE, S. L. K.; GILLETT, B. E.
PARAMETRIC INTEGER LINEAR PROGRAMMING: A SYNTHESIS OF BRANCH AND BOUND WITH CUTTING PLANES.

RUIZA 1979 -1 RUIZDEFCO, F.; LARRANETA, J.
LEXICOGRAPHIC ENUMERATION ALGORITHM FOR THE KNAPSACK PROBLEM, A.

SALC 1973 -1 SALCEDO, E.
METHODS OF PARTIAL ENUMERATION FOR THE SOLUTION OF DISCRETE OPTIMIZATION PROBLEMS (SPANISH), THE.

SALK 1975 -1 SALKIN, H. M.
INTEGER PROGRAMMING.

SANDA 1980 -1 SANDI, C.
0-1 INTEGER PROGRAMMING USING SUBGRADIENT AND ELLIPSOID METHODS.

SAPO 1978 -1 SAPOVALOVSKII, V. I.
ON A PROBLEM OF ENUMERATIVE MATHEMATICAL PROGRAMMING IN NETWORK FORMULATION (UKRAINIAN).

SASAB 1978 -1 SASAKI, R.; TSURUOKA, R.; HARUNA, L.
COMBINATORIAL OPTIMIZATION METHOD OF SYSTEMS WITH FUZZY OBJECTIVES AND UNCERTAIN PARAMETERS AND ITS APPLICATION, A.

SCHRF 1978 -1 SCHROECK, W.
KONSTRUKTION KOSTENOPTIMALER ZERLEGUNGEN VON GRAPHEN.

SEKI 1979 -1 SEKIGUCHI, Y.
SYNTHETICAL ANALYSIS OF ENUMERATIVE ALGORITHMS.

SEKI 1981 -1 SEKIGUCHI, Y.
UNIFYING FRAMEWORK OF COMBINATORIAL OPTIMIZATION ALGORITHMS; TREE PROGRAMMING AND ITS VALIDITY, A.

SESH 1980 -1 SESHAN, C. R.; ACHARY, K. K.
BRANCH AND BOUND ALGORITHM FOR A TRANSPORTATION TYPE PROBLEM WITH PIECEWISE LINEAR CONVEX OBJECTIVE FUNCTION, A.

SHIH 1979 -1 SHIH, WEI
BRANCH AND BOUND METHOD FOR THE MULTICONSTRAINT ZERO-ONE KNAPSACK PROBLEM, A.

SMITH 1980 -1 SMITH, T. H. C.
LIFO IMPLICIT ENUMERATION ALGORITHM FOR THE ASYMMETRIC TRAVELLING SALESMAN PROBLEM USING A ONE-ARBORESCENCE RELAXATION, A.

SOYS 1978 -1 SOYSTER, A. L.; LEV, B.; SLIVKA, W.
ZERO-ONE PROGRAMMING WITH MANY VARIABLES AND FEW CONSTRAINTS.

SPIE 1979 -1 SPIELBERG, K.
ENUMERATIVE METHODS IN INTEGER PROGRAMMING.

SPIEA 1980 -1 SPIELBERG, K.; SUHL, U.
EXPERIMENTAL SOFTWARE SYSTEM FOR LARGE SCALE 0-1 PROBLEMS WITH EFFICIENT DATA STRUCTURES AND ACCESS TO MPSX/370, AN.

STANC 1978 -1 STANICKI, T.
TWO-CRITERION INTEGER OPTIMIZATION OF SUB-ASSEMBLY ASSIGNMENT IN THE DESIGN OF COMPLEX SYSTEMS BY THE METHOD OF VARIABLE CONSTRAINTS AND PARTIAL ENUMERATION (POLISH).

STINB 1978 -1 STINSON, J. P.; DAVIS, E. W.; KHUMAWALA, B. M.
MULTIPLE RESOURCE-CONSTRAINED SCHEDULING USING BRANCH AND BOUND.

SUHL 1978 -1 SUHL, U.
ALGORITHM AND EFFICIENT DATA STRUCTURES FOR THE BINARY KNAPSACK PROBLEM, AN.

SUHL 1978 -2 SUHL, U.
IMPLEMENTATIONSTECHNIKEN FUER EINEN BRANCH-AND-BOUND-ALGORITHMUS ZUR LOESUNG VON (0-1)-PROGRAMMEN.

SUZU 1978 -1 SUZUKI, H.
GENERALIZED KNAPSACK PROBLEM WITH VARIABLE COEFFICIENTS, A.

TABAA 1977 -1 TABATA, K.
BASIS-CONSTRAINED LINEAR PROGRAMMING PROBLEM; ITS FORMULATION AND A BRANCH-AND-BOUND SOLUTION, A.

TCHE 1980 -1 TCHERBINA, O. A.
ON LOCAL ALGORITHM OF INTEGRAL OPTIMIZATION (RUSSIAN).

TCHEA 1978 -1 TCHERVAK, JU. JU.
RETURNING ALGORITHM OF CUTTING-OFF METHOD AND BRANCH-AND-BOUND METHOD (RUSSIAN).

TOYO 1978 -1 TOYODA, Y.
IMPROVEMENT IN IMPLICIT ENUMERATION (JAPANESE), AN.

TRUBA 1981 -1 TRUBIN, V. A.; VOITISHIN, YU. V.
ALGORITHM FOR SOLVING A SET-DIVISION PROBLEM (RUSSIAN), AN.

TRYP 1979 -1 TRYPIA, M. N.
BINARY TREE SEARCH METHOD FOR THE 0-1 LINEAR PROGRAMMING PROBLEM, A.

TYSH 1979 -1 TYSHKEVICH, R. I.
ENUMERATION OF (0,1)-MATRICES DEFINED BY THE NUMBER OF ONES IN ROWS AND COLUMNS (RUSSIAN).

UZDE 1977 -1 UZDEMIR, A. P.
DECOMPOSITION IN SOLUTION OF COMBINATORY PROBLEM OF DETERMINING MOMENTS OF INTRODUCTION OF ENTERPRISES.

UZDE 1978 -1 UZDEMIR, A. P.
SOLUTION METHOD FOR A COMBINATORIAL PROBLEM IN THE PLANNING OF NEW ENTERPRISES (RUSSIAN).

VALI 1979 -2 VALIANT, L. G.
COMPLEXITY OF ENUMERATION AND RELIABILITY PROBLEMS, THE.

VANR 1980 -2 VANROY, T. J.
CROSS DECOMPOSITION FOR INTEGER PROGRAMMING.

VENGA 1975 -1 VENGEROVA, I. V.; FINKELSTEIN, JU. JU.
ON THE QUESTION OF THE EFFICIENCY OF THE BRANCH-AND-BOUND METHOD (RUSSIAN).

BRANCH AND BOUND

****

VERC 1978 -1 VERCELLIS, C.
ENUMERATIVE ALGORITHM FOR COVERING PROBLEMS, AN.

VILLB 1980 -1 VILLARREAL, B.; KARWAN, M. H.; ZIONTS, S.
INTERACTIVE BRANCH AND BOUND PROCEDURE FOR MULTICRITERION INTEGER LINEAR PROGRAMMING, AN.

VIZV 1978 -1 VIZVARI, B.
LAGRANGE MULTIPLIERS IN INTEGER PROGRAMMING.

WDOW 1977 -1 WDOWIAK, J.
DISCRETE LINEAR FRACTIONAL PROGRAMMING PROBLEM (POLISH), A.

WETJ 1977 -1 WETJEN, A.
COMMENTS ON: "A BRANCH AND BOUND CLUSTERING ALGORITHM" (IEEE TRANSACTIONS ON COMPUTERS C-24 (1975), NO. 9, 908-915) BY W. L. G. KOONTZ, P. M. NARENDRA AND K. FUKUNAGA. WITH A REPLY BY KOONTZ.

WOLS 1980 -1 WOLSEY, L. A.
HEURISTIC ANALYSIS, LINEAR PROGRAMMING AND BRANCH AND BOUND.

YORM 1979 -1 YORMARK, J. S.
EFFICIENT FRONTIERS FOR NONLINEAR MULTIDIMENSIONAL KNAPSACK PROBLEMS.

YOUNA 1979 -1 YOUNG, R. D.
BRANCH AND ROUND: AN ENUMERATIVE ALGORITHM FOR INTEGER PROGRAMS.

YUKH 1979 -1 YUKHIMENKO, B. I.
ON CERTAIN SOLUTION ALGORITHMS FOR PROBLEMS OF LINEAR PROGRAMMING WITH BOOLEAN VARIABLES (RUSSIAN).

ZAK 1978 -1 ZAK, JU. A.
ALGORITHMS FOR NONLINEAR PSEUDO-BOOLEAN PROGRAMMING.

ZERN 1976 -1 ZERNAK, A. N.
METHOD OF SOLVING QUASILINEAR INTEGER PROGRAMMING PROBLEMS (RUSSIAN), A.

ZUEV 1979 -1 ZUEV, YU. A.
SET-COVERING PROBLEM: THE COMBINATORIAL-LOCAL APPROACH AND BRANCH AND BOUND METHOD (RUSSIAN).

ABBO 1978 -1 ABBOTT, H. L.; LIU, A. C.
EXISTENCE PROBLEM FOR COLOR CRITICAL LINEAR HYPERGRAPHS, THE.
AKSI 1974 -1 AKSIONOV, V. A.
CONCERNING THE EXTENSION OF THE 3-COLORING OF PLANAR GRAPHS (RUSSIAN).
AKSI 1978 -1 AKSIONOV, V. A.
ON UNIQUELY 3-COLORABLE PLANAR GRAPHS.
ALAV 1971 -1 ALAVI, Y.; BEHZAD, M.
COMPLEMENTARY GRAPHS AND EDGE CHROMATIC NUMBERS.
ALBEA 1977 -1 ALBERTSON, M. O.; BERMAN, D. M.
EVERY PLANAR GRAPH HAS AN ACYCLIC 7-COLORING.
ALBEB 1978 -1 ALBERTSON, M. O.; HUTCHINSON, J. P.
ON THE INDEPENDENCE RATIO OF A GRAPH.
ANDE 1975 -1 ANDERSEN, L. D.
EDGE-COLOURINGS OF SIMPLE AND NON-SIMPLE GRAPHS.
ANDE 1976 -1 ANDERSEN, L. D.
ON EDGE-COLOURINGS OF NON-SIMPLE GRAPHS.
ANDE 1977 -1 ANDERSEN, L. D.
ON EDGE COLORINGS OF GRAPHS.
ANDE 1978 -1 ANDERSEN, L. D.
ON EDGE-COLOURINGS OF GRAPHS.
APPE 1977 -1 APPEL, K.; HAKEN, W.
EVERY PLANAR MAP IS FOUR COLORABLE. I. DISCHARGING.
APPE 1977 -2 APPEL, K.; HAKEN, W.
EVERY PLANAR MAP IS FOUR COLORABLE. II. REDUCIBILITY.
ASRA 1978 -1 ASRATJAN, A. S.
CONSTRUCTION OF AN EDGE COLORING OF A SPECIAL FORM IN A BIPARTITE GRAPH, AND ITS APPLICATION IN PROBLEMS OF SCHEDULING THEORY (RUSSIAN), THE.
AYEL 1979 -1 AYEL, J.
SUR L'EXISTENCE DE DEUX CYCLES SUPPLEMENTAIRES UNICOLORES, DISJOINTS ET DE COULEURS DIFFERENTES DANS UN GRAPHE COMPLET BICOLORE.
BARAA 1978 -1 BARANYAI, Z.
SOME APPLICATIONS OF EQUALIZED MATRICES.
BEHZ 1965 -1 BEHZAD, M.
GRAPHS AND THEIR CHROMATIC NUMBERS.
BEHZA 1967 -1 BEHZAD, M.; CHARTRAND, G.; COOPER, J. K.
COLOUR NUMBERS OF COMPLETE GRAPHS, THE.
BEIN 1976 -1 BEINEKE, L. W.; FIORINI, S.
ON SMALL GRAPHS CRITICAL WITH RESPECT TO EDGE COLOURINGS.
BEINA 1973 -1 BEINEKE, L. W.; WILSON, R. J.
ON THE EDGE-CHROMATIC NUMBER OF A GRAPH.
BERG 1973 -1 BERGE, C.
INTRODUCTION A LA THEORIE DES HYPERGRAPHES.
BERG 1976 -1 BERGE, C.
MULTICOLORINGS OF GRAPHS AND HYPERGRAPHS, THE.
BERG 1978 -1 BERGE, C.
MULTICOLORING OF A GRAPH.
BERG 1979 -1 BERGE, C.
MULTICOLORINGS OF GRAPHS AND HYPERGRAPHS.
BERG 1978 -2 BERGE, C.
MULTICOLORINGS.
BERGA 1978 -1 BERGE, C.; HOFFMAN, A. J.
MULTICOLORATIONS DANS LES HYPERGRAPHES UNIMODULAIRES ET MATRICES DONT LES COEFFICIENTS SONT DES ENSEMBLES.
BERM 1978 -1 BERMAN, D. M.
CRITICAL GRAPHS FOR ACYCLIC COLORINGS.
BIGG 1972 -1 BIGGS, N.
EDGE COLOURING PROBLEM, AN.
BIGG 1977 -1 BIGGS, N.
COLOURING SQUARE LATTICE GRAPHS.
BOLLC 1976 -1 BOLLOBAS, B.; SAUER, N.
UNIQUELY COLOURABLE GRAPHS WITH LARGE GIRTH.
BOSA 1973 -1 BOSAK, J.; FIAMCHIK, I.
CHROMATIC INDEX OF HAMILTONIAN GRAPHS.
BOUW 1980 -1 BOUWSMA, W.; HARARY, F.
ON THE COLOR PARTITIONS OF A GRAPH.
BRADA 1978 -1 BRADLEY, R. C. JR.
REMARK ON NONCOLORABLE CUBIC GRAPHS, A.
BREL 1979 -1 BRELAZ, D.
NEW METHODS TO COLOR THE VERTICES OF A GRAPH.
BROE 1979 -1 BROERE, I.
GRAPHTHEORETIC COLORING PROBLEMS (AFRIKAANS).
BROO 1941 -1 BROOKS, R. L.
ON COLOURING THE NODES OF A NETWORK.
BRUA 1978 -1 BRUALDI, R. A.
CHROMATIC INDEX OF THE GRAPH OF THE ASSIGNMENT POLYTOPE, THE.
BULT 1976 -1 BULTEAU, R.
COLORATION DANS LES GRAPHES, MULTIGRAPHES ET HYPERGRAPHES.
BURR 1976 -1 BURR, S. A.; ERDOES, P.
EXTREMAL RAMSEY THEORY FOR GRAPHS.
BURSA 1976 -1 BURSHTEJN, M. I.
CHROMATIC NUMBER OF PLANAR HYPERGRAPHS (RUSSIAN), THE.
BURSA 1979 -1 BURSHTEJN, M. I.
EVERY 4-VALENT GRAPH HAS AN ACYCLIC 5-COLORING (RUSSIAN).
BURSA 1979 -2 BURSHTEJN, M. I.
NOTE ON EDGE-COLORING OF TRIVALENT GRAPHS (RUSSIAN), A.
BUSO 1978 -1 BUSOLINI, D. T.
ON A PROBLEM OF C. C. CHEN AND D. E. DAYKIN.
BUSO 1978 -2 BUSOLINI, D. T.
2 COLORED TRIANGLES IN EDGE COLORED COMPLETE GRAPHS.
CAMEE 1975 -1 CAMERON, P. J.
ON GROUPS OF DEGREE N AND N-1, AND HIGHLY SYMMETRIC EDGE COLOURINGS.
CAST 1972 -1 CASTAGNA, F.; PRINS, G.
EVERY GENERALISED PETERSEN GRAPH HAS A TAIT COLOURING.
CATL 1978 -1 CATLIN, P. A.
ANOTHER BOUND ON THE CHROMATIC NUMBER OF A GRAPH.

CATL 1978 -2 CATLIN, P. A.
BOUND ON THE CHROMATIC NUMBER OF A GRAPH, A.
CATL 1979 -2 CATLIN, P. A.
HAJOS' GRAPH-COLORING CONJECTURE: VARIATIONS AND COUNTEREXAMPLES.
CATL 1979 -4 CATLIN, P. A.
SURVEY OF EXTENSIONS OF BROOKS' GRAPH COLORING THEOREM.
CHAO 1979 -1 CHAO, C. Y.; WHITEHEAD, E. G. JR.
CHROMATICITY OF SELF-COMPLEMENTARY GRAPHS.
CHARD 1969 -1 CHARTRAND, G.; FRECHEN, J. B.
ON THE CHROMATIC NUMBER OF PERMUTATION GRAPHS.
CHEN 1979 -1 CHEN, C. C.
ON THE STRUCTURE OF COMPLETE GRAPHS WITHOUT ALTERNATING CYCLES.
CVET 1972 -1 CVETKOVIC, D. M.
CHROMATIC NUMBER AND THE SPECTRUM OF A GRAPH.
DELA 1979 -1 DELATTRE, M.; HANSEN, P.
CLUSTER ANALYSIS AND GRAPH COLORING.
DESC 1948 -1 DESCARTES, B.
NETWORK COLOURINGS.
DEWD 1977 -1 DEWDNEY, A. K.; HARARY, F.
ON THE CHROMATIC NUMBERS OF A SIMPLICIAL COMPLEX.
DUCHA 1978 -1 DUCHET, P.
COLORATIONS TRANSITIVES DES GRAPHES.
DUER 1978 -1 DUERRE, K.
APPROXIMATE ALGORITHMS FOR COLORING LARGE GRAPHS.
DUTT 1981 -1 DUTTON, R. D.; BINGHAM, R. C.
NEW GRAPH COLOURING ALGORITHM, A.
EARL 1968 -1 EARLY, S.
EVALUATING A TIME-TABLING ALGORITHM BASED ON GRAPH-RECOLOURING.
EHRE 1976 -1 EHRENFEUCHT, A.; HURSCH, J. L. JR.; MORGENSTERN, C.
GROWTH NUMBER AND COLORABILITY OF GRAPHS II.
FIAM 1978 -1 FIAMCHIK, I.
ACYCLIC CHROMATIC NUMBER OF A GRAPH (RUSSIAN).
FIAMA 1970 -1 FIAMCHIK, I.; JUCOVIC, E.
COLOURING THE EDGES OF A MULTIGRAPH.
FIOR 1974 -1 FIORINI, S.
ON THE CHROMATIC INDEX OF SIMPLE GRAPHS.
FIOR 1975 -1 FIORINI, S.
ON THE CHROMATIC INDEX OF A GRAPH, III: UNIQUELY EDGE COLOURABLE GRAPHS.
FIOR 1976 -1 FIORINI, S.
GRAFO CUBICO, NON-PLANARE, UNICAMENTE TRICOLORABILE, DI VITA 5, UN.
FIOR 1978 -1 FIORINI, S.
BIBLIOGRAPHIC SURVEY OF EDGE COLORINGS, A.
FIOR 1975 -2 FIORINI, S.
ON THE CHROMATIC INDEX OF OUTERPLANAR GRAPHS.
FIOR 1976 -2 FIORINI, S.
ON THE GIRTH OF GRAPHS CRITICAL WITH RESPECT TO EDGE COLOURINGS.
FIORA 1977 -1 FIORINI, S.; WILSON, R. J.
EDGE-COLOURINGS OF GRAPHS.
FIORA 1978 -1 FIORINI, S.; WILSON, R. J.
EDGE-COLORINGS OF GRAPHS.
FOLK 1969 -1 FOLKMAN, J.; FULKERSON, D. R.
EDGE COLORINGS IN BIPARTITE GRAPHS.
FOUR 1977 -1 FOURNIER, J.-C.
METHODE ET THEOREME GENERAL DE COLORATION DES ARETES D'UN MULTIGRAPHE.
FOUR 1978 -3 FOURNIER, J.-C.
THEOREME GENERAL DE COLORATION, UN.
FOURA 1977 -1 FOURNIER, R.
GRAPHS WITH ALMOST NO COLOURING.
FREN 1975 -1 FRENNE, A. DE
PROBLEME DE COLORATION DANS LES GRAPHES ET LES HYPERGRAPHES.
GABOC 1978 -1 GABOW, H. N.; KARIV, O.
ALGORITHMS FOR EDGE COLORING BIPARTITE GRAPHS.
GAREB 1980 -1 GAREY, M. R.; JOHNSON, D. S.; MILLER, G. L.; PAPADIMITRIOU, C. H.
COMPLEXITY OF COLORING CIRCULAR ARCS AND CHORDS, THE.
GELL 1974 -1 GELLER, D. P.; HILTON, A. J. W.
HOW TO COLOR THE LINES OF A BIGRAPH.
GION 1978 -1 GIONFRIDDO, M.
ON L(S) COLORINGS OF FINITE GRAPHS (ITALIAN).
GION 1980 -1 GIONFRIDDO, M.
AUTOMORPHISMES COLORES ET COLORATIONS (R,S) DANS UN GRAPHE (ITALIAN).
GOLDA 1979 -1 GOLDBERG, M. K.
CRITICAL GRAPHS WITH AN EVEN NUMBER OF VERTICES(RUSSIAN).
GOOD 1978 -1 GOODMAN, J. E.; ONISHI, H.
EVEN TRIANGULATIONS OF S**3 AND THE COLORING OF GRAPHS.
GRAV 1977 -1 GRAVER, J. E.; WATKINS, M. E.
COMBINATORICS WITH EMPHASIS ON THE THEORY OF GRAPHS.
GREEB 1973 -1 GREENWELL, D; KRONK, H.
UNIQUELY LINE-COLORABLE GRAPHS.
GRUE 1978 -1 GRUENBAUM, B.; SHEPHARD, G. C.
PERFECT COLORINGS OF TRANSITIVE TILINGS AND PATTERNS IN THE PLANE.
GUNN 1981 -1 GUNN, J. P.
MONOCHROMATIC MAXIMUM INDEPENDENT SETS IN K-COLORED K-GRAPHS.
GUPTD 1966 -1 GUPTA, R. P.
CHROMATIC INDEX AND THE DEGREE OF A GRAPH, THE.
GUPTD 1978 -1 GUPTA, R. P.
EDGE-COLORATION THEOREM FOR BIPARTITE GRAPHS WITH APPLICATIONS, AN.
HAJO 1961 -1 HAJOS, G.
UEBER EINE KONSTRUKTION NICHT N-FAERBBARER GRAPHEN.
HALI 1980 -1 HALIN, R.
GRAPHENTHEORIE I.
HANSD 1978 -1 HANSEN, P.; LOREA, M.
DEUX CONDITIONS DE COLORABILITE DES HYPERGRAPHES.
HAUS 1980 -1 HAUSMANN, D.
ADJACENCY ON POLYTOPES IN COMBINATORIAL OPTIMIZATION.
HAUS 1980 -2 HAUSMANN, D.
FARBKLASSEN UND PSEUDOKNOTEN FUER ADJAZENZCHARAKTERISIERUNGEN.

HAUSC 1978 -1 HAUSMANN, D.; KORTE, B.
COLOURING CRITERIA FOR ADJACENCY ON 0-1-POLYHEDRA.
HEINA 1976 -1 HEINRICH, K.
PROPER 3-COLOURINGS OF K6.
HEINA 1977 -1 HEINRICH, K.
PROPER COLOURINGS OF K(15).
HELL 1981 -2 HELL, P.; KIRKPATRICK, D. G.
SCHEDULING, MATCHING, AND COLORING.
HETY 1974 -1 HETYEI, G.
ON SUBGRAPHS OF J-COLORABLE GRAPHS (HUNGARIAN).
HILT 1975 -1 HILTON, A. J. W.
NOTE ON EDGE-COLOURING MULTIGRAPHS, A.
HILT 1977 -1 HILTON, A. J. W.
DEFINITIONS OF CRITICALITY WITH RESPECT TO EDGE-COLOURING.
HILT 1977 -2 HILTON, A. J. W.
EMBEDDING INCOMPLETE LATIN RECTANGLES AND EXTENDING THE EDGE COLOURINGS OF GRAPHS.
HIME 1974 -1 HIMELWRIGHT, P. E.; WILLIAMSON, J. E.
ON 1-FACTORABILITY AND EDGE-COLORABILITY OF CARTESIAN PRODUCTS OF GRAPHS.
HOFFA 1970 -1 HOFFMAN, A. J.; HOWES, L.
ON EIGENVALUES AND COLORINGS OF GRAPHS, II.
HOME 1977 -1 HOMENKO, N. P.; LYSENKO, N. V.
NECESSARY AND SUFFICIENT CONDITIONS FOR N-COLORINGS OF GRAPHS (RUSSIAN).
HSU A 1979 -1 HSU, W.-L.
HOW TO COLOR CLAW-FREE PERFECT GRAPHS.
IZBI 1962 -1 IZBICKI, H.
ZULAESSIGE KANTENFAERBUNGEN VON PSEUDO-REGULAEREN GRAPHEN 3. GRADES MIT DER KANTENFARBENZAHL 3.
IZBI 1963 -1 IZBICKI, H.
ZULAESSIGE KANTENFAERBUNGEN VON PSEUDO-REGULAEREN GRAPHEN MIT MINIMALER KANTENFARBENZAHL.
IZBI 1964 -1 IZBICKI, H.
EDGE-COLORING PROBLEM, AN.
JAEG 1973 -1 JAEGER, F.
SUR L'INDICE CHROMATIQUE DU GRAPHE REPRESENTATIF DES ARETES D'UN GRAPHE REGULIER.
JAEG 1979 -1 JAEGER, F.
FLOWS AND GENERALIZED COLORING THEOREMS IN GRAPHS.
JAKO 1973 -1 JAKOBSEN, I. T.
SOME REMARKS ON THE CHROMATIC INDEX OF A GRAPH.
JAKO 1975 -1 JAKOBSEN, I. T.
ON GRAPHS CRITICAL WITH RESPECT TO EDGE-COLOURING.
JOHNC 1966 -1 JOHNSON, E. I.
PROOF OF FOUR COLOURING THE EDGES OF A CUBIC GRAPH, A.
KALN 1965 -1 KALNINSH, YA.
NUMBER OF WAYS OF COLOURING THE BRANCHES OF A TREE AND A MULTITREE, THE.
KAREC 1979 -1 KARELIN, V. P.; MIRONOV, B. N.
ALGORITHMUS ZUR OPTIMALEN FAERBUNG DER ECKEN EINES GRAPHEN, DER AUF DER REALISIERUNG IN EINEM ASYNCHRONEN AUTOMATISCHEN MODELL ORIENTIERT IST (RUSSIAN), EIN.
KHAD 1977 -1 KHADZHIIVANOV, N. G.
GRAPH INEQUALITES (RUSSIAN).
KORF 1978 -1 KORFHAGE, R. R.
SIGMA-POLYNOMIALS AND GRAPH COLORING.
KORM 1975 -1 KORMAN, S. M.
GRAPH COLOURING AND RELATED PROBLEMS IN OPERATIONS RESEARCH.
KORM 1979 -1 KORMAN, S. M.
GRAPH-COLOURING PROBLEM, THE.
KOSTA 1977 -1 KOSTOCHKA, A. V.; MAZUROVA, N. P.
ESTIMATION DANS LA THEORIE DU COLORIAGE DES GRAPHES (RUSSIAN), UNE.
KOTZ 1975 -1 KOTZIG, A.
TRANSFORMATIONS OF EDGE-COLOURINGS OF GRAPHS.
KOTZ 1977 -1 KOTZIG, A.
CHANGE GRAPHS OF EDGE-COLOURINGS OF PLANAR CUBIC GRAPHS.
KRON 1974 -1 KRONK, H.; RADLOWSKI, M.; FRANEN, B.
ON THE LINE CHROMATIC NUMBER OF TRIANGLE-FREE GRAPHS.
KUBA 1978 -1 KUBALE, M.; DABROWSKI, J.
EMPIRICAL COMPARISON OF EFFICIENCY OF SOME GRAPH COLOURING ALGORITHMS.
LASK 1971 -1 LASKER, R.; HARE, W.
CHROMATIC NUMBERS OF CERTAIN GRAPHS.
LEIG 1979 -1 LEIGHTON, F. T.
GRAPH COLORING ALGORITHM FOR LARGE SCHEDULING PROBLEMS, A.
LESNA 1977 -1 LESNIAK-FOSTER, L. M.; STRAIGHT, H. J.
COCHROMATIC NUMBER OF A GRAPH, THE.
LICK 1975 -1 LICK, D. R.
ACYCLIC COLOR FUNCTIONS ON GRAPHS.
LIND 1978 -1 LINDSTROEM, B.
ON THE CHROMATIC NUMBER OF REGULAR MATROIDS.
LIPT 1978 -1 LIPTON, R. J.; MILLER, R. E.
BATCHING METHOD FOR COLORING PLANAR GRAPHS, A.
LUKO 1977 -1 LUKO, G.
TRUTH FUNCTIONS AND PROBLEMS IN GRAPH COLORING.
MAC B 1979 -1 MAC DIARMID, C.
DETERMINING THE CHROMATIC NUMBER OF A GRAPH.
MARTG 1977 -1 MARTINOV, N. J.
3-COLORABLE PLANAR GRAPHS (RUSSIAN).
MEDG 1950 -1 MEDGYESSY, P.
SUR LA STRUCTURE DES RESEAUX FINIS, CUBIQUES ET COLORIES.
MEHTA 1980 -1 MEHTA, N. K.
PERFORMANCE OF SELECTED GRAPH COLORING ALGORITHMS - EMPIRICAL RESULTS.
MELNA 1970 -1 MELNIKOV, L. S.
CHROMATIC CLASS AND THE LOCATION OF A GRAPH ON A CLOSED SURFACE, THE.
MERE 1973 -1 MEREDITH, G. H. J.
REGULAR N-VALENT, N-CONNECTED, NON-HAMILTONIAN, NON-N-EDGE-COLOURABLE GRAPHS.
MEYN 1978 -1 MEYNIEL, H.
5-COLORATIONS D'UN GRAPHE PLANAIRE FORMENT UNE CLASSE DE COMMUTATION UNIQUE, LES.
MINT 1967 -1 MINTY, G. J.
THEOREM ON THREE-COLORING THE EDGES OF A TRIVALENT GRAPH, A.
MITCA 1979 -1 MITCHELL, S.; HEDETNIEMI, S. T.
LINEAR ALGORITHMS FOR EDGE-COLORING TREES AND UNICYCLIC GRAPHS.

MULD 1979 -1 MULDER, H. M.
RAMSEY THEORY.
MYCI 1955 -1 MYCIELSKI, J.
SUR LE COLORIAGE DES GRAPHES.
NAKAB 1973 -1 NAKANISHI, N.
QUANTUM FIELD THEORY AND THE COLORING PROBLEM OF GRAPHS.
NENO 1979 -1 NENOV, N. D.; KHADZHIIVANOV, N. G.
SUR LES GRAPHES CONTENANT UN TRIANGLE MONOCHROMATIQUE DANS LE CAS DE COLORATION ARBITRAIRE DES ARETES AVEC DEUX COULEURS (RUSSIAN).
OXLE 1978 -2 OXLEY, J. G.
COLORING, PACKING AND THE CRITICAL PROBLEM.
PARKA 1973 -1 PARKER, E.
EDGE COLORING NUMBERS OF SOME REGULAR GRAPHS.
PLES 1978 -1 PLESNIK, J.
BOUNDS ON CHROMATIC NUMBERS OF MULTIPLE FACTORS OF A COMPLETE GRAPH.
PLES 1980 -1 PLESNIK, J.
COLORING OF GRAPHS BY PARTITIONING.
RADO 1978 -1 RADO, R.
MONOCHROMATIC PATHS IN GRAPHS.
RAMAA 1977 -1 RAMACHANDRAN, S.
NOTE ON COLORING LINE GRAPHS THAT ARE PLANAR, A.
RAMAA 1978 -1 RAMACHANDRAN, S.
PLANAR GRAPHS WITH SQUARE OR CUBE ROOT ARE FOUR-COLOURABLE.
RING 1959 -1 RINGEL, G.
FAERBUNGSPROBLEM AUF FLAECHEN UND GRAPHEN.
ROMA 1978 -1 ROMAN, S.
PROBLEM ON MULTICOLORINGS OF GRAPHS, A.
ROSEE 1970 -1 ROSENFELD, M.
ON TAIT COLORING OF CUBIC GRAPHS.
RYZK 1978 -1 RYZKOV, A. P.
METHODS OF SOLVING A PROBLEM OF WEIGHTED COLORING OF A GRAPH.
SAMP 1977 -1 SAMPATHKUMAR, E.; NEERALAGI, P. S.; VENKATACHALAM, C. V.
GENERALIZATION OF THE CHROMATIC AND LINE CHROMATIC NUMBERS OF A GRAPH, A.
SAND 1974 -1 SANDBERG, V. JU.
HEURISTIC ALGORITHM FOR GRAPH COLORING (RUSSIAN), A.
SANI 1979 -1 SANIKIDZE, D. D.
ALGORITHM FOR FINDING THE SHORTEST COVERING USING THE COLORING OF NONORIENTED GRAPHS IN SOLVING SOME PROBLEMS OF MINIMIZATION (RUSSIAN), AN.
SCHE 1974 -1 SCHEIM, D. E.
NUMBER OF EDGE 3-COLORINGS OF A PLANAR CUBIC GRAPH AS A PERMANENT, THE.
SCHM 1980 -1 SCHMERL, J. H.
RECURSIVE COLORINGS OF GRAPHS.
SCHRD 1978 -3 SCHRIJVER, A.
VERTEX-CRITICAL SUBGRAPHS OF KNESER GRAPHS.
SEYM 1979 -2 SEYMOUR, P. D.
ON MULTI-COLOURINGS OF CUBIC GRAPHS, AND CONJECTURES OF FULKERSON AND TUTTE.
SHAN 1949 -1 SHANNON, C. E.
THEOREM ON COLORING THE LINES OF A NETWORK, A.
SPER 1979 -1 SPERANZA, F.
SUR LES COLORATIONS DES GRAPHES ORIENTES.
SZEK 1975 -1 SZEKERES, G.
NON-COLOURABLE TRIVALENT GRAPHS.
TEMPA 1971 -1 TEMPERLEY, H. N. V.; LIEB, E. H.
RELATIONS BETWEEN THE "PERCOLATION" AND "COLOURING" PROBLEM AND OTHER GRAPH-THEORETICAL PROBLEMS ASSOCIATED WITH REGULAR PLANAR LATTICES: SOME EXACT RESULTS FOR THE "PERCOLATION" PROBLEM.
THEP 1981 -1 THEPOT, J.
CLUSTER ANALYSIS FOR GRAPH COLORING.
THEPA 1980 -1 THEPOT, J.; LECHENAULT, G.
METHODE DE CLASSIFICATION POUR LA COLORATION DES GRAPHES.
THOMB 1978 -1 THOMASON, A. G.
HAMILTONIAN CYCLES AND UNIQUELY EDGE COLOURABLE GRAPHS.
TIET 1978 -1 TIETZE, W.
PROBLEM DER DREIERCLIQUEN. EIN BEITRAG ZUR GRAPHENTHEORIE, DAS.
TOFT 1978 -1 TOFT, B.
INVESTIGATION OF COLOUR-CRITICAL GRAPHS WITH COMPLEMENTS OF LOW CONNECTIVITY, AN.
TOME 1978 -1 TOMESCU, I.
SUR LES CYCLES ELEMENTAIRES DANS LES GRAPHES ET HYPERGRAPHES K-CHROMATIQUES.
TOME 1979 -1 TOMESCU, I.
NOMBRE MAXIMAL DE COLORIAGES DES ARETES D'UN GRAPHE, LE.
TUCK 1980 -1 TUCKER, A. C.
APPLIED COMBINATORICS.
TUTT 1960 -1 TUTTE, W. T.
NON-HAMILTONIAN GRAPH, A.
TUTT 1961 -1 TUTTE, W. T.
ON THE COLORING OF GRAPHS.
TUTT 1966 -1 TUTTE, W. T.
ON THE ALGEBRAIC THEORY OF GRAPH COLORINGS.
TUTT 1978 -1 TUTTE, W. T.
COLOURING PROBLEMS.
TUTTA 1980 -1 TUTTE, W. T.; ADAM, A. T.
PROBLEMES DE COLORATION (HUNGARIAN).
VIGN 1967 -1 VIGNERON, L.
DENOMBREMENT DES COLORATIONS QUE L'ON PEUT TRACER SUR UN GRAPHE G PLANAIRE, CUBIQUE SANS ISTHME, CONNEXE, EN UTILISANT AU PLUS TROIS COULEURS D'ARETES.
VIGN 1978 -1 VIGNERON, L.
A PROPOS DE LA CONJECTURE DE TAIT. DEFINITION DE LA C-PARITE D'UN CYCLE BICOLORE D'ARETES; EFFETS PRODUITS PAR L'ECHANGE DES COULEURS SUR UN CYCLE DANS LE CAS OU IL EST C-PAIR ET DANS LE CAS OU IL EST C-IMPAIR.
VITA 1981 -1 VITANYI, P. M. B.
HOW WELL CAN A GRAPH BE N-COLORED?
VIZI 1964 -1 VIZING, V. G.
ON AN ESTIMATE OF THE CHROMATIC CLASS OF A P-GRAPH (RUSSIAN).
VIZI 1965 -1 VIZING, V. G.
CHROMATIC CLASS OF A MULTIGRAPH, THE.

VIZI 1976 -1 VIZING, V. G.
COLORING THE VERTICES OF A GRAPH IN PRESCRIBED COLORS (RUSSIAN).
VIZI 1964 -2 VIZING, V. G.
ON THE CHROMATIC CLASS OF A MULTIGRAPH (RUSSIAN).
VIZI 1965 -2 VIZING, V. G.
CHROMATIC CLASS OF MULTIGRAPHS (RUSSIAN), THE.
VIZI 1965 -3 VIZING, V. G.
CRITICAL GRAPHS WITH A GIVEN CHROMATIC CLASS (RUSSIAN).
WALLA 1976 -1 WALLIS, W. D.
NUMBER OF MONOCHROMATIC TRIANGLES IN EDGE-COLOURINGS OF A COMPLETE GRAPH, THE.
WALS 1976 -1 WALSH, A. M.
POLYNOMIAL ALGORITHMS FOR CERTAIN GRAPH-THEORETIC PROBLEMS.
WALSA 1975 -1 WALSH, A. M.; BURKHARD, W. A.
POLYNOMIAL ALGORITHMS FOR (3,1) GRAPHS.
WALSA 1977 -1 WALSH, A. M.; BURKHARD, W. A.
EFFICIENT ALGORITHMS FOR (3,1) GRAPHS.
WATK 1969 -1 WATKINS, M. E.
THEOREM ON TAIT COLORINGS WITH AN APPLICATION TO THE GENERALIZED PETERSEN GRAPHS, A.
WELS 1979 -1 WELSH, D. J. A.
COLOURING PROBLEMS AND MATROIDS.
WELS 1980 -1 WELSH, D. J. A.
COLOURINGS, FLOWS AND PRODUCTIVE GEOMETRY.
WERR 1972 -1 WERRA, D. DE
INVESTIGATIONS ON AN EDGE-COLORING PROBLEM.
WERR 1974 -1 WERRA, D. DE
NOTE ON GRAPH COLORING, A.
WERR 1976 -1 WERRA, D. DE
ERRATA TO "ON GOOD AND EQUITABLE EDGE COLORINGS" (CAHIERS DU CENTRE D'ETUDES DE RECHERCHE OPERATIONELLE 17, 1975, 417-426).
WERR 1979 -1 WERRA, D. DE
ON A CLASS OF HYPERGRAPHS OCCURRING IN CHROMATIC SCHEDULING.
WERR 1980 -1 WERRA, D. DE
FANTAISIES CHROMATIQUES SUR DIVERSES PARTITIONS.
WERR 1977 -2 WERRA, D. DE
PROGRESSIVE BALANCING IN CHROMATIC SCHEDULING.
WERR 1979 -2 WERRA, D. DE
ON THE USE OF ALTERNATING CHAINS AND HYPERGRAPHS IN EDGE COLORING.
WERR 1978 -3 WERRA, D. DE
ON LINE PERFECT GRAPHS.
WERR 1979 -3 WERRA, D. DE
OPTIMIZATION IN EDGE CHROMATIC SCHEDULING.
WERR 1980 -3 WERRA, D. DE
OBSTRUCTIONS FOR REGULAR COLORINGS.
WERR 1981 -3 WERRA, D. DE
SOME PARTITIONING PROBLEMS FOR GRAPHS AND HYPERGRAPHS.
WERR 1979 -4 WERRA, D. DE
PARTIAL COMPACTNESS IN EDGE-CHROMATIC SCHEDULING.
WERR 1980 -4 WERRA, D. DE
ORDONNANCEMENT CHROMATIQUE ET PROBLEMES DE COLORATION.
WERR 1979 -5 WERRA, D. DE
REGULAR AND CANONICAL COLORINGS.
WILSA 1975 -1 WILSON, R. J.
SOME CONJECTURES ON EDGE-COLOURINGS OF GRAPHS.
WILSA 1976 -1 WILSON, R. J.
EDGE-COLORINGS OF CRITICAL GRAPHS.
WILSA 1978 -1 WILSON, R. J.
EDGE COLOURINGS OF GRAPHS - A SURVEY.
WOODA 1977 -1 WOODALL, D. R.
ZEROS OF CHROMATIC POLYNOMIALS.
ZELI 1973 -1 ZELINKA, B.
EDGE-COLOURINGS OF PERMUTATION GRAPHS.
ZELI 1978 -2 ZELINKA, B.
ON A PROBLEM OF R. HAEGGKVIST CONCERNING EDGE-COLOURINGS OF GRAPHS.

COMBINATORIAL OPTIMIZATION PROBLEMS (UNLESS SPECIFIED ELSEWHERE)
****

AHO 1973 -1 AHO, A. V.; HOPCROFT, J. E.; ULLMAN, J. D.
ON FINDING LOWEST COMMON ANCESTORS IN TREES.

AHUJ 1979 -1 AHUJA, V.
ALGORITHM TO CHECK NETWORK STATES FOR DEADLOCK.

AKL A 1978 -1 AKL, S. G.; TOUSSAINT, G. T.
FAST CONVEX HULL ALGORITHM, A.

ALBA 1980 -1 ALBANO, A.; ORSINI, R.
HEURISTIC SOLUTION OF THE RECTANGULAR CUTTING STOCK PROBLEM, A.

ALLIA 1980 -1 ALLINEY, S.; BARNABEI, M.; PEZZOLI, L.
W-OPTIMAL ASSIGNABLE SETS AND ALLOCATION PROBLEMS.

AUSI 1981 -1 AUSIELLO, G.; MARCHETTI-SPACCAMELA, A.; PROTASI, M.
PROBABILISTIC ANALYSIS OF THE PERFORMANCE OF GREEDY STRATEGIES OVER DIFFERENT CLASSES OF COMBINATORIAL PROBLEMS.

BAER 1978 -1 BAER, G.
THEORETISCHE FUNDIERUNG DER DISKRETEN OPTIMIERUNG MIT LOGISCHEN MITTELN, EINE.

BAGC 1979 -1 BAGCHI, A.; ROY, J. K.
ON V-OPTIMAL TREES.

BALU 1979 -1 BALUTA, M.; DOBRESCU, V.; PAUN, G.
ALGORITHM FOR SOLVING A COMBINATORIAL PROBLEM OF OPTIMAL SELECTION.

BAUE 1981 -1 BAUER, D.; BOESCH, F.; SUFFEL, C.; TINDELL, R.
CONNECTIVITY EXTREMAL PROBLEMS AND THE DESIGN OF RELIABLE PROBABILISTIC NETWORKS.

BENH 1979 -1 BENHAMAMOUCH, D.
ALGORITHME DE DECOUPE OPTIMALE DANS R**2, UN.

BERTA 1979 -1 BERTONI, A.; MAURI, G.; TORELLI, M.
THREE EFFICIENT ALGORITHMS FOR COUNTING PROBLEMS.

BIES 1977 -1 BIESS, G.; JAENICKE, W.; MEISSLER, H. G.
ALGORITHMUS ZUR BESTIMMUNG ALLER ELEMENTARKREISE EINES GERICHTETEN GRAPHEN, EIN.

BOYC 1980 -1 BOYCE, D. E.; JANSON, B. N.
DISCRETE TRANSPORTATION NETWORK DESIGN PROBLEM WITH COMBINED TRIP DISTRIBUTION AND ASSIGNMENT, A.

BRUC 1978 -1 BRUCKER, P.
APPROXIMATIVE VERFAHREN ZUR LOESUNG VON DISKRETEN OPTIMIERUNGSPROBLEMEN.

BURK 1979 -1 BURKARD, R. E.
ON THE USE OF ALGEBRAIC OBJECTIVE FUNCTIONS IN COMBINATORIAL PROGRAMMING.

BURKJ 1980 -1 BURKARD, R. E.; ZIMMERMANN, U.
COMBINATORIAL OPTIMIZATION IN LINEARLY ORDERED SEMIMODULES: A SURVEY.

BURR 1976 -1 BURR, S. A.; ERDOES, P.
EXTREMAL RAMSEY THEORY FOR GRAPHS.

BUTZ 1982 -1 BUTZ, L.
CONNECTIVITY IN MULTI-FACTOR DESIGNS: A COMBINATORIAL APPROACH.

CAHI 1978 -1 CAHIT, I.; CAHIT, R.
TRANSFORMATIONS ON SPANNING TREES.

CAMEA 1980 -2 CAMERINI, P. M.; FRATTA, L.; MAFFIOLI, F.
RANKING ARBORESCENCES IN O(KM LOG N) TIME.

CAMEC 1980 -2 CAMERINI, P. M.; MAFFIOLI, F.
WEIGHTED SATISFIABILITY PROBLEMS AND SOME IMPLICATIONS.

CAMED 1979 -1 CAMERON, K.; EDMONDS, J.
ALGORITHMS FOR OPTIMUM ANTICHAINS.

CANI 1978 -1 CANI, P. DE
NOTE ON THE TWO-DIMENSIONAL RECTANGULAR CUTTING-STOCK PROBLEM, A.

CHUND 1978 -1 CHUNGPHAISAN, V.
CONSTRUCTION OF HAMILTONIAN GRAPHS AND BIGRAPHS WITH PRESCRIBED DEGREES.

CORN 1978 -1 CORNEIL, D. G.; WOODWARD, M. E.
COMPARISON AND EVALUATION OF GRAPH THEORETICAL CLUSTERING TECHNIQUES, A.

CROI 1979 -1 CROITORU, C.
ON A DISCRETE MAX-MIN PROBLEM.

CROI 1980 -1 CROITORU, C.
ON APPROXIMATE ALGORITHMS FOR COMBINATORIAL LINEAR MAXIMIZATION PROBLEMS.

DEHA 1979 -1 DEHAAN, A.
SOLUTION OF A GENERALIZED CUTTING-STOCK PROBLEM BY MPSX/MIP, THE.

DINIB 1978 -1 DINIC, E. A.; ZAICEV, M. A.
GENERATION OF MARKED TREES AND SEPARABLE NETWORKS (RUSSIAN).

DINIB 1978 -2 DINIC, E. A.; ZAICEV, M. A.
LINEAR ORDERING AND GENERATION OF TREES (RUSSIAN).

DION 1978 -1 DIONNE, R.
ETUDE ET EXTENSION D'UN ALGORITHME DE MURCHLAND.

EBER 1977 -1 EBERT, J.
OPERATOR-ALGORITHMEN AUF MATRIZEN-DARSTELLUNGEN VON GRAPHEN.

ECKS 1977 -1 ECKSTEIN, D. M.; ALTON, D. A.
PARALLEL GRAPH PROCESSING USING DEPTH-FIRST SEARCH.

EHNE 1976 -1 EHNERT, G.
SOME REMARKS ON AN ALGORITHM FOR TESTING PLANAR GRAPHS.

EVENA 1981 -1 EVEN, S.; SHILOACH, Y.
ON-LINE EDGE-DELETION PROBLEM, AN.

EVERA 1977 -1 EVERSHEIM, W.; HEMGESBERG, G.
ENTWICKLUNG EINES SYSTEMS ZUR OPTIMALEN ZWEIDIMENSIONALEN VERSCHNITTOPTIMIERUNG IN DER EINZEL- UND KLEINSERIENFERTIGUNG MIT HILFE DIALOGFAEHIGER RECHENANLAGEN.

FAIG 1979 -1 FAIGLE, U.
GREEDY ALGORITHM FOR PARTIALLY ORDERED SETS, THE.

FARA 1978 -1 FARADZEV, I. A.
GENERATION OF NONISOMORPHIC GRAPHS WITH A GIVEN DISTRIBUTION OF THE DEGREES OF VERTICES (RUSSIAN).

FARA 1978 -3 FARADZEV, I. A.
OBTAINING OF A COMPLETE LIST OF SELFCOMPLEMENTARY GRAPHS UP TO 12 VERTICES (RUSSIAN), THE.

FERN 1977 -1 FERNANDEZ, R. R.
STOPPING RULE FOR A HEURISTIC APPROACH TO THE CUTTING STOCK PROBLEM, A.

FERNA 1977 -1 FERNANDEZ, R. R.; SWART, W. W.
SYSTEM FOR SOLVING CUTTING STOCK PROBLEMS, A.

FLET 1980 -1 FLETCHER, J. G.
MORE GENERAL ALGORITHM FOR COMPUTING CLOSED SEMIRING COSTS BETWEEN VERTICES OF A DIRECTED GRAPH, A.

FORTA 1979 -1 FORTUNE, S.; HOPCROFT, J. E.
NOTE ON RABIN'S NEAREST-NEIGHBOUR ALGORITHM, A.

FRANA 1977 -1 FRANCON, J.
ON THE ANALYSIS OF ALGORITHMS FOR TREES.

FRANB 1980 -5 FRANK, A.
ON CHAIN AND ANTICHAIN FAMILIES OF A PARTIALLY ORDERED SET.

FRANB 1981 -5 FRANK, A.
WEIGHTED MATROID INTERSECTION ALGORITHM, A.

FRANC 1978 -2 FRANK, A.; GYARFAS, A.
HOW TO ORIENT THE EDGES OF A GRAPH.

FRID 1976 -1 FRIDMAN, A. A.; FRUMKIN, M. A.; HMELEVSKII, JU. I.; LEVNER, E. V.
STUDY OF ALGORITHM EFFICIENCY FOR DISCRETE AND COMBINATORIAL PROBLEMS. THEORY OF PROBLEM REDUCIBILITY AND UNIVERSAL PROBLEMS (RUSSIAN).

FRIEC 1981 -1 FRIESZ, T.
MULTIOBJECTIVE OPTIMIZATION IN TRANSPORTATION: THE CASE OF EQUILIBRIUM NETWORK DESIGN.

FUJI 1977 -1 FUJISHIGE, S.
ALGORITHM FOR FINDING AN OPTIMAL INDEPENDENT LINKAGE, AN.

FUSS 1979 -1 FUSSENEGGER, F.; GABOW, H. N.
COUNTING APPROACH TO LOWER BOUNDS FOR SELECTION PROBLEMS, A.

GALIA 1979 -1 GALIL, Z.; MEGIDDO, N.
FAST SELECTION ALGORITHM AND THE PROBLEM OF OPTIMUM DISTRIBUTION OF EFFORT, A.

GALIC 1977 -1 GALIL, Z.; SEIFERAS, J.
SAVING SPACE IN FAST STRING-MATCHING.

GAREC 1978 -1 GAREY, M. R.; JOHNSON, D. S.; PREPARATA, F. P.; TARJAN, R. E.
TRIANGULATING A SIMPLE POLYGON.

GAUD 1979 -1 GAUDIOSO, M.
HEURISTIC APPROACH TO THE CUTTING STOCK PROBLEM, A.

GENS 1979 -1 GENS, G. V.; LEVNER, E. V.
COMPLEXITY OF APPROXIMATION ALGORITHMS FOR COMBINATORIAL PROBLEMS: A SURVEY.

GEORA 1980 -1 GEORGE, J. A.; ROBINSON, D. F.
HEURISTIC FOR PACKING BOXES INTO A CONTAINER, A.

GESS 1979 -1 GESSEL, I.; WANG, D.-L.
DEPTH-FIRST SEARCH AS A COMBINATORIAL CORRESPONDENCE.

GILM 1979 -1 GILMORE, P. C.
CUTTING STOCK, LINEAR PROGRAMMING, KNAPSACKING, DYNAMIC PROGRAMMING AND INTEGER PROGRAMMING, SOME INTERCONNECTIONS.

GOLDB 1978 -1 GOLDEN, B. L.
POINT ESTIMATION OF A GLOBAL OPTIMUM FOR LARGE COMBINATORIAL PROBLEMS.

GOND 1978 -1 GONDRAN, M.
DEUX TRANSFORMATIONS IDEALES POUR REGULARISER LES PROBLEMES COMBINATOIRES.

GOND 1979 -2 GONDRAN, M.
OPTIMISATION COMBINATOIRE.

GORB 1980 -1 GORBUNCOV, V. V.
ALGEBRAIC APPROACH TO THE SOLUTION OF A CLASS OF EXTREMAL COMBINATORIAL PROBLEMS (RUSSIAN), AN.

GROEB 1981 -1 GROETSCHEL, M.
APPROACHES TO HARD COMBINATORIAL OPTIMIZATION PROBLEMS.

GUAN 1978 -1 GUAN, M. G.
METHOD FOR FINDING THE MINIMUM ARBORESCENCE OF THE DIRECTED GRAPHS ARISING IN THE CHANNEL DESIGN PROBLEM (CHINESE), A.

HAESC 1976 -1 HAESSLER, R. W.
SOME MODIFICATIONS TO THE GILMORE-GOMORY CUTTING STOCK ALGORITHM.

HAESC 1980 -1 HAESSLER, R. W.
NOTE ON COMPUTATIONAL MODIFICATIONS TO THE GILMORE-GOMORY CUTTING STOCK ALGORITHM, A.

HAESC 1979 -2 HAESSLER, R. W.
SOLVING A BOXCAR LOADING PROBLEM.

HAESC 1979 -3 HAESSLER, R. W.
SOLVING THE TWO-STAGE CUTTING STOCK PROBLEM.

HAESD 1980 -1 HAESSLER, R. W.; TALBOT, F. B.
0-1 MODEL FOR SOLVING THE CORRUGATOR TRIM PROBLEM, A.

HALP 1979 -2 HALPERN, J.
SIMPLE EDGE ELIMINATION CRITERION IN A SEARCH FOR THE CENTER OF A GRAPH, A.

HARB 1979 -1 HARBORTH, H.; MENGERSEN, I.
EXTREMALPROBLEM FUER MATRIZEN AUS NULLEN UND EINSEN, EIN.

HEIC 1980 -1 HEICKEN, K.; KOENIG, W.
INTEGRATION EINES HEURISTISCH-OPTIMIERENDEN VERFAHRENS ZUR LOESUNG EINES EINDIMENSIONALEN VERSCHNITTPROBLEMS IN EINEM EDV-GESTUETZTEN PRODUKTIONSPLANUNGS- UND -STEUERUNGSSYSTEMS.

HINX 1980 -1 HINXMAN, A. I.
TRIM-LOSS AND ASSORTMENT PROBLEMS: A SURVEY, THE.

HIRS 1978 -1 HIRSCHBERG, D. S.
FAST PARALLEL SORTING ALGORITHMS.

HOLMA 1976 -1 HOLMBERG, G.
EXTENSIONS OF THE METHOD SUGGESTED BY GILMORE AND GOMORY FOR SOLVING CUTTING STOCK PROBLEMS.

HORAB 1978 -1 HORAK, V.
PRACTICAL APPLICATION OF, AND CONSTRUCTION OF ALGORITHMS FOR FINITE LABELLED TREES (CZECHOSLOVAKIAN).

HU 1979 -1 HU, T. C.; KLEITMAN, D. J.; TAMAKI, J. K.
BINARY TREES OPTIMUM UNDER VARIOUS CRITERIA.

HUAN 1976 -1 HUANG, H.-C.
INVESTIGATIONS ON COMBINATORIAL OPTIMIZATION.

IBAR 1978 -1 IBARAKI, T.
BRANCH-AND-BOUND PROCEDURE AND STATE-SPACE REPRESENTATION OF COMBINATORIAL OPTIMIZATION PROBLEMS.

INSTA 1978 -1 INSTITUT FUER OEKONOMETRIE & OPERATIONS RESEARCH
WORKSHOP ON COMBINATORIAL OPTIMIZATION, BONN, SEPTEMBER 11-13, 1978. ABSTRACTS.

INSTA 1980 -1 INSTITUT FUER OEKONOMETRIE & OPERATIONS RESEARCH
IV. WORKSHOP ON COMBINATORIAL OPTIMIZATION, BONN, AUGUST 28-30, 1980. ABSTRACTS.

KANNB 1978 -1 KANNAN, R.; KORTE, B.
APPROXIMATIVE COMBINATORIAL ALGORITHMS.

KARP 1975 -1 KARP, R. M.
COMPUTATIONAL COMPLEXITY OF COMBINATORIAL AND GRAPH-THEORETIC PROBLEMS.

KAUFE 1977 -1 KAUFMANN, A.; PICHAT, E.
METHODES MATHEMATIQUES NON NUMERIQUES ET LEURS ALGORITHMES. TOME 1 ALGORITHMES DE RECHERCHE DES ELEMENTS MAXIMAUX.

KAUFE 1977 -2 KAUFMANN, A.; PICHAT, E.
METHODES MATHEMATIQUES NON NUMERIQUES ET LEURS ALGORITHMES. TOME 2 ALGORITHMES DE RECHERCHE DE CHEMINS ET PROBLEMS ASSOCIES.

KIRK 1976 -1 KIRKPATRICK, D.
DETERMINING GRAPH PROPERTIES FROM MATRIX REPRESENTATIONS.

COMBINATORIAL OPTIMIZATION PROBLEMS (UNLESS SPECIFIED ELSEWHERE)

KLEE 1979 -1 KLEE, V.
COMBINATORIAL OPTIMIZATION: WHAT IS THE STATE OF THE ART?
KLEE 1980 -1 KLEE, V.
COMBINATORIAL OPTIMIZATION: WHAT IS THE STATE OF THE ART?
KLEID 1975 -1 KLEITMAN, D. J.
ALGORITHMS.
KLET 1979 -1 KLETIN, V. A.
ANALYSE DE L'EFFICACITE DES ALGORITHMES COMBINATOIRES DE RECHERCHE DES ARBRES EXTREMAUX SUR LES GRAPHES ORIENTES PONDERES (RUSSIAN).
KOBA 1979 -1 KOBAYASHI, T.
COMBINATORIAL PROBLEMS AND THEIR ALGORITHMS IN OPERATIONS RESEARCH (JAPANESE).
KOCHA 1979 -1 KOCH, R.
ZUR LOESUNG ZWEIDIMENSIONALER ZUSCHNITTPROBLEME DURCH DIE ERZEUGUNG GUENSTIGER ZUSCHNITTVARIANTEN.
KOLC 1976 -1 KOLCOV, V. N.
DECOMPOSITION OF A BIPARTITE GRAPH INTO A MINIMAL NUMBER OF PLANE SUBGRAPHS (RUSSIAN).
KONV 1978 -1 KONVALINA, J.; KOSLOSKI, R. H.
COMBINATORIAL ALGORITHM FOR GENERATING CYCLIC QUASI-HADAMARD MATRICES, A.
KORB 1979 -1 KORBUT, A. A.; SIGAL, I. H.; FINKELSTEIN, JU. JU.
EFFECTIVENESS OF COMBINATORIAL METHODS IN DISCRETE PROGRAMMING (RUSSIAN), THE.
KORN 1978 -1 KORNBLUM, D. F.
"GREEDY" ALGORITHMS FOR SOME LATTICE POLYHEDRA PROBLEMS.
KORN 1978 -2 KORNBLUM, D. F.
GREEDY ALGORITHMS FOR SOME OPTIMIZATION PROBLEMS ON A LATTICE POLYHEDRON.
KORNC 1978 -1 KORNILOVA, L. E.; VOITISHIN, YU. V.
CERTAIN PROPERTIES OF ANTICHAINS OF PARTIALLY ORDERED SETS (RUSSIAN).
KORTA 1979 -1 KORTE, B.
APPROXIMATIVE ALGORITHMS FOR DISCRETE OPTIMIZATION PROBLEMS.
KORTD 1981 -2 KORTE, B.; SCHRADER, R.
SURVEY ON ORACLE TECHNIQUES, A.
KOVAC 1978 -1 KOVALEV, M. M.; ISACHENKO, A. N.; NGUEN NGIA
LINEARISATION DES PROBLEMES COMBINATOIRES D'OPTIMISATION (RUSSIAN).
KRAP 1978 -1 KRAPIVA, A. J.
ON CONSTRUCTING THE MINIMUM CUTTING-OFF SET OF THE GRAPH (RUSSIAN).
KUNDA 1979 -1 KUNDU, S.
INTERMEDIATE-VALUE THEOREM FOR OPTIMUM TREE VALUATION, AN.
LEBL 1979 -1 LEBLANC, L. J.; ABOULAAL, M.
EFFICIENT DUAL APPROACH TO THE URBAN ROAD NETWORK DESIGN PROBLEM, AN.
LEE 1978 -1 LEE, D. T.; PREPARATA, F. P.
ALL NEAREST-NEIGHBOUR PROBLEM FOR CONVEX POLYGONS, THE.
LEONA 1979 -1 LEONT'EV, V. K.
DISCRETE EXTREMAL PROBLEMS (RUSSIAN).
LEVID 1979 -2 LEVIN, V. I.
METHODE STRUCTURELLE ET LOGIQUE D'OPTIMISATION COMBINATOIRE, EN PRESENCE DE CONSTRAINTES (RUSSIAN).
LEVID 1979 -3 LEVIN, V. I.
STRUCTURAL AND LOGICAL METHODS OF COMBINATORIAL OPTIMIZATION.
LEVNA 1978 -1 LEVNER, E. V.; GENS, G. V.
DISCRETE OPTIMIZATION PROBLEMS AND EFFICIENT APPROXIMATION ALGORITHMS (RUSSIAN).
LIKH 1974 -1 LIKHACHEV, V. M.
SEARCH ALGORITHM FOR THE MINIMUM NUMBER OF VERTICES IN AN ORIENTED GRAPH THROUGH WHICH PASS ALL CIRCUITS OF THE GRAPH.
LINT 1976 -1 LINT, J. H. VAN
RECENT DEVELOPMENTS IN COMBINATORICS (DUTCH).
LOVA 1975 -1 LOVASZ, L.
COMBINATORIAL MINIMAX THEOREMS (HUNGARIAN).
LOWEB 1978 -1 LOWE, T. J.; THORNTON, V. D.; FRANCIS, R. L.
LAYOUT OF DIVISIBLE ACTIVITIES ON THE LINE, THE.
LOZA 1978 -1 LOZANO-PEREZ, T.; WESLEY, M. A.
ALGORITHM FOR PLANNING COLLISION-FREE PATHS AMONGST POLYHEDRAL OBSTACLES, AN.
MAGRA 1976 -1 MAGRUPOW, T. M.
NEW APPROACH TO THE CONSTRUCTION OF A MINIMAL TREE (RUSSIAN), A.
MEGI 1978 -1 MEGIDDO, N.
COMBINATORIAL OPTIMIZATION WITH RATIONAL OBJECTIVE FUNCTIONS.
MEGI 1979 -1 MEGIDDO, N.
COMBINATORIAL OPTIMIZATION WITH RATIONAL OBJECTIVE FUNCTIONS.
MILLB 1979 -1 MILLER, R. E.; PIPPENGER, N.; ROSENBERG, A. L.; SNYDER, L.
OPTIMAL 2,3-TREES.
MISR 1979 -1 MISRA, R. B.
ALGORITHM FOR ENUMERATING ALL SIMPLE PATHS IN A COMMUNICATION NETWORK, AN.
MISZ 1979 -1 MISZCZYNSKI, M. T.; STRZELEC, K. R.
OPTIMAL CUTTING ALGORITHM FOR RECTANGLE ELEMENTS.
NIGM 1978 -1 NIGMATULLIN, R. G.
ON APPROXIMATE ALGORITHMS WITH RESTRICTED ABSOLUTE ERROR FOR DISCRETE EXTREMUM PROBLEMS (RUSSIAN).
NIJE 1979 -1 NIJENHUIS, A.
MINIMAL-PATH ALGORITHM FOR THE "MONEY CHANGING PROBLEM", A.
OHTS 1981 -1 OHTSUKI, T.
TWO DISJOINT PATH PROBLEM AND WIRE ROUTING DESIGN, THE.
PAID 1980 -1 PAIDAK, I. N.
METHOD FOR SOLVING SOME MULTICRITERIAL COMBINATORIAL PROBLEMS (RUSSIAN).
POBI 1978 -1 POBISOVA, M.
AUFGABEN UEBER DIE TEILUNG DES STANGENMATERIALS, DIE.
RATH 1977 -1 RATHMANN, D.
ZUR LOESUNG DISKRETER OPTIMIERUNGSPROBLEME MIT GRUPPENTHEORETISCHEN ANSAETZEN.
REIS 1979 -1 REISS, S. P.
RATIONAL SEARCH.
RICHA 1979 -1 RICHTER, K.
DYNAMISCHE AUFGABEN DER DISKRETEN OPTIMIERUNG.
ROHL 1978 -1 ROHL, J. S.
GENERATING PERMUTATIONS BY CHOOSING.
ROY A 1978 -1 ROY, M. K.
EVALUATION OF PERMUTATION ALGORITHMS.
RUSK 1978 -1 RUSKEY, F.
GENERATING T-ARY TREES LEXICOGRAPHICALLY.

SARV 1977 -1 SARVANOV, V. I.
APPROXIMATE SOLUTION OF A LINEAR MINIMISATION PROBLEM OVER THE SET OF CYCLIC PERMUTATIONS (RUSSIAN).

SCHNA 1978 -1 SCHNORR, C. P.
ALGORITHM FOR TRANSITIVE CLOSURE WITH LINEAR EXPECTED TIME, AN.

SCHRF 1978 -1 SCHROECK, W.
KONSTRUKTION KOSTENOPTIMALER ZERLEGUNGEN VON GRAPHEN.

SENO 1977 -1 SENO, A.; FUKUNAGA, K.; KASAI, T.
ALGORITHM FOR GRAPH ISOMORPHISM, AN.

SHEN 1978 -1 SHENDEROV, I. B.
MODIFICATION OF RANDOM SEARCH FOR THE SOLUTION OF DISCRETE OPTIMIZATION PROBLEMS (RUSSIAN).

SHIL 1979 -2 SHILOACH, Y.
MINIMUM LINEAR ARRANGEMENT ALGORITHM FOR UNDIRECTED TREES, A.

SIMOC 1979 -1 SIMOVICI, D. A.; GRIGORAS, G.
EVEN INITIAL FEEDBACK VERTEX SET PROBLEM IS NP-COMPLETE.

STAP 1980 -1 STAPLES, J.
OPTIMAL EVALUATIONS OF GRAPH-LIKE EXPRESSIONS.

STEU 1979 -1 STEUDEL, H. J.
GENERATING PALLET LOADING PATTERNS: A SPECIAL CASE OF THE TWO-DIMENSIONAL CUTTING STOCK PROBLEM.

SYSL 1977 -2 SYSLO, M. M.
LINEAR TIME ALGORITHM FOR CODING OUTERPLANAR GRAPHS.

SYSLA 1976 -1 SYSLO, M. M.; IRI, M.
EFFICIENT OUTERPLANARITY TESTING.

TARJ 1978 -1 TARJAN, R. E.
COMPLEXITY OF COMBINATORIAL ALGORITHMS.

TROJ 1978 -1 TROJANOWSKI, A. E.
RANKING AND LISTING ALGORITHMS FOR K-ARY TREES.

UNTE 1979 -1 UNTERAUER, K.
DYNAMIC WEIGHTED BINARY SEARCH TREES.

URSI 1975 -1 URSIC, S.
DISCRETE OPTIMIZATION ALGORITHM BASED ON BINOMIAL POLYTOPES, A.

VALI 1979 -1 VALIANT, L. G.
COMPLEXITY OF COMPUTING THE PERMANENT, THE.

VASIA 1979 -1 VASILEVA, E. M.; LEVIT, B. JU.; LIVSIC, V. N.
CHOICE OF OPTIMAL TRAJECTORY IN THE DEVELOPMENT OF A TURNPIKE TRANSPORTATION NETWORK (RUSSIAN), THE.

VINC 1978 -1 VINCKE, P.
ORDRES ET PREORDRES TOTAUX A DISTANCE MINIMUM D'UN QUASI-ORDRE.

WADI 1979 -1 WADIA, A. B.
GENERATION OF NODE LISTS USING SEGMENT ANALYSIS.

WANGA 1981 -1 WANG, P. Y.
TWO ALGORITHMS FOR CONSTRAINED TWO-DIMENSIONAL CUTTING STOCK PROBLEMS.

WILF 1979 -1 WILF, H. S.
"WHY DON'T YOU JUST ...?" BARRIER IN DISCRETE ALGORITHMS, THE.

WONGB 1980 -1 WONG, R. T.
WORST-CASE ANALYSIS OF NETWORK DESIGN PROBLEM HEURISTICS.

WONGB 1981 -1 WONG, R. T.
PROBABILISTIC ANALYSIS OF AN OPTIMAL NETWORK PROBLEM HEURISTIC.

WYSK 1980 -1 WYSK, R. A.; DAVIS, R. P.; TANCHOCO, J. M. A.
MACHINING PARAMETER OPTIMIZATION WITH LOT SIZE CONSIDERATIONS.

YOUN 1978 -1 YOUNG, H. P.
ON PERMUTATIONS AND PERMUTATION POLYTOPES.

ZAIC 1978 -1 ZAICENKO, V. A.; IVANOV, A. V.; ROZENFEL'D, M. Z.; FARADZEV, I. A.
ALGORITHM FOR CHECKING THE CANONICITY OF A PARTIALLY AUGMENTED ADJACENCY MATRIX OF A GRAPH (RUSSIAN), AN.

ZAKSA 1979 -1 ZAKS, S.; RICHARDS, D.
GENERATING TREES AND OTHER COMBINATORIAL OBJECTS LEXICOGRAPHICALLY.

ABDE 1978 -1 ABDEL-WAHAB, H. M.; KAMEDA, T.
SCHEDULING TO MINIMIZE MAXIMUM CUMULATIVE COST SUBJECT TO SERIES-PARALLEL PRECEDENCE CONSTRAINTS.

AIEL 1977 -1 AIELLO, A.; BURATTINI, E.; MASSAROTTI, A.
REDUCIBILITY AS A TOOL TO EXTEND THE POWER OF APPROXIMATION ALGORITHMS. THE MINIMIZATION OF BOOLEAN EXPRESSIONS.

AKL A 1978 -1 AKL, S. G.; TOUSSAINT, G. T.
FAST CONVEX HULL ALGORITHM, A.

ALVA 1977 -1 ALVARADO, F. L.
COMPUTATIONAL COMPLEXITY OF OPERATIONS INVOLVING PERFECT ELIMINATION OF SPARSE MATRICES.

ANGL 1978 -1 ANGLUIN, D.
ON THE COMPLEXITY OF MINIMUM INFERENCE OF REGULAR SETS.

ARIY 1979 -1 ARIYOSHI, H.; TSUKIYAMA, S.; SHIRAKAWA, I.; OZAKI, H.
ALGORITHMS FOR ENUMERATING ALL THE S-T CUTSETS IN O(!V!+!E!) PER CUTSET (JAPANESE).

ASANA 1977 -1 ASANO, T.; NISHIZEKI, T.; SAITO, N.
NP-COMPLETE PROBLEMS OF FINDING A MAXIMUM CUTSET AND OF REDUCING GRAPHS TO BIPARTITE GRAPHS.

ATRI 1981 -1 ATRI, G. D'
PROBABILISTIC ANALYSIS OF KNAPSACK-TYPE PROBLEMS.

AUSI 1980 -1 AUSIELLO, G.; MARCHETTI-SPACCAMELA, A.; PROTASI, M.
TOWARD A UNIFIED APPROACH FOR THE CLASSIFICATION OF NP-COMPLETE OPTIMIZATION PROBLEMS.

BABAE 1980 -1 BABAI, L.
ON THE COMPLEXITY OF CANONICAL LABELING OF STRONGLY REGULAR GRAPHS.

BACH 1980 -1 BACHEM, A.
KOMPLEXITAETSTHEORIE IM OPERATIONS RESEARCH.

BACHC 1979 -1 BACHEM, A.; KANNAN, R.
APPLICATIONS OF POLYNOMIAL SMITH NORMAL FORM CALCULATIONS.

BAKEK 1979 -1 BAKER, T. B.
ON "PROVABLE" ANALOGS OF P AND NP.

BALL 1980 -1 BALL, M. O.
COMPLEXITY OF NETWORK RELIABILITY COMPUTATIONS.

BARA 1980 -1 BARAHONA, F.
APPLICATION DE L'OPTIMISATION COMBINATOIRE A CERTAINS MODELES DES VERRES DE SPINS: COMPLEXITE ET SIMULATIONS.

BARA 1980 -2 BARAHONA, F.
ON THE COMPLEXITY OF MAX CUT.

BERTB 1980 -1 BERTOSSI, A. A.
ON THE COMPLEXITY OF SCHEDULING JOBS ON DEDICATED RESOURCES TO MINIMIZE SET-UP COSTS.

BHAT 1980 -1 BHAT, K. V. S.
ON THE COMPLEXITY OF TESTING A GRAPH FOR N-CUBE.

BIRD 1976 -1 BIRD, R.
PROGRAMS AND MACHINES. AN INTRODUCTION TO THE THEORY OF COMPUTING.

BITRD 1981 -1 BITRAN, G. R.; YANASSE, H. H.
COMPUTATIONAL COMPLEXITY OF THE CAPACITATED LOT SIZE PROBLEM.

BLAZ 1978 -1 BLAZEWICZ, J.
COMPLEXITY OF COMPUTER SCHEDULING ALGORITHMS UNDER RESOURCE CONSTRAINTS.

BLAZA 1980 -1 BLAZEWICZ, J.; LENSTRA, J. K.; RINNOOY KAN, A. H. G.
SCHEDULING SUBJECT TO RESOURCE CONSTRAINTS: CLASSIFICATION AND COMPLEXITY.

BLAZB 1978 -1 BLAZEWICZ, J.; WEGLARZ, J.
DETERMINISTIC TASK SCHEDULING PROBLEM ON PROCESSORS OF COMPUTER SYSTEMS WITH ALLOWANCE FOR ADDITIONAL RESOURCES (POLISH).

BLAZB 1978 -2 BLAZEWICZ, J.; WEGLARZ, J.
SCHEDULING TO MEET DEADLINES WITH RESOURCE CONSTRAINTS - COMPLEXITY RESULTS.

BOAS 1977 -1 BOASSON, L.; COURCELLE, B.; NIVAT, M.
NEW COMPLEXITY MEASURE FOR LANGUAGES, A.

BOLL 1978 -1 BOLLOBAS, B.; ELDRIDGE, S. E.
PACKINGS OF GRAPHS AND APPLICATIONS TO COMPUTATIONAL COMPLEXITY.

BONU 1979 -1 BONUCCELLI, M. A.; BOVET, D. P.
MINIMUM NODE DISJOINT PATH COVERING FOR CIRCULAR-ARC GRAPHS.

BOOK 1979 -1 BOOK, R. V.
POLYNOMIAL SPACE AND TRANSITIVE CLOSURE.

BOOT 1978 -1 BOOTH, K. S.
ISOMORPHISM TESTING FOR GRAPHS, SEMIGROUPS, AND FINITE AUTOMATA ARE POLYNOMIALLY EQUIVALENT PROBLEMS.

BOOT 1980 -1 BOOTH, K. S.
DOMINATING SETS IN CHORDAL GRAPHS.

BREI 1979 -1 BREITBARD, Y.; LEWIS, F. D.
COMBINED COMPLEXITY CLASSES FOR FINITE FUNCTIONS.

BROWB 1979 -3 BROWN, J. R.
SHARING PROBLEM, THE.

BRUC 1979 -1 BRUCKER, P.
NP-COMPLETE OPERATIONS RESEARCH PROBLEMS AND APPROXIMATION ALGORITHMS.

BRUNA 1978 -1 BRUNO, J.; DOWNEY, P.
COMPLEXITY OF TASK SEQUENCING WITH DEADLINES, SET-UP TIMES AND CHANGEOVER COSTS.

CAMEA 1980 -2 CAMERINI, P. M.; FRATTA, L.; MAFFIOLI, F.
RANKING ARBORESCENCES IN O(KM LOG N) TIME.

CAMEB 1980 -1 CAMERINI, P. M.; GALBIATI, G.; MAFFIOLI, F.
COMPLEXITY OF SPANNING TREE PROBLEMS: PART I.

CAMEC 1978 -1 CAMERINI, P. M.; MAFFIOLI, F.
EXACT AND HEURISTIC METHODS FOR NP-HARD MATROID PROBLEMS.

CAMEC 1979 -1 CAMERINI, P. M.; MAFFIOLI, F.
POLYNOMIAL BOUNDING FOR NP-HARD PROBLEMS.

CAMEC 1980 -1 CAMERINI, P. M.; MAFFIOLI, F.
POLYNOMIAL BOUNDING FOR NP-HARD PROBLEMS.

CHANB 1978 -1 CHANDRA, A. K.; HIRSCHBERG, D. S.; WONG, C. K.
BIN PACKING WITH GEOMETRIC CONSTRAINTS IN COMPUTER NETWORK DESIGN.

CHANH 1978 -1 CHANDRASEKARAN, R.; TAMIR, A.
POLYNOMIALLY BOUNDED ALGORITHMS FOR LOCATING P-CENTERS ON A TREE.

CHANH 1980 -1 CHANDRASEKARAN, R.; TAMIR, A.
O((N LOG P)**2) ALGORITHM FOR THE CONTINUOUS P-CENTER PROBLEM ON A TREE, AN.

CHERA 1977 -1 CHERKASSKII, B. V.
O((N**2)*(P**0.5)) ALGORITHM FOR CONSTRUCTING THE MAXIMUM FLOW IN A NETWORK (RUSSIAN), AN.

CHUNC 1979 -1 CHUNG, S.-J.
NOTE ON THE COMPLEXITY OF LCP: THE LCP IS NP-COMPLETE, A.

CHUNC 1979 -2 CHUNG, S.-J.
NP-COMPLETE ADJACENCY DECISION PROBLEMS ON SOME 0-1 CONVEX POLYTOPE.

****

COCK 1978 -1 COCKAYNE, E. J.; HARTNELL, B. L.; HEDETNIEMI, S. T.
LINEAR ALGORITHM FOR DISJOINT MATCHINGS IN TREES, A.
COFF 1978 -1 COFFMAN, E. G. JR.
DETERMINISTIC SEQUENCING: COMPLEXITY AND OPTIMAL ALGORITHMS.
COFFA 1977 -1 COFFMAN, E. G. JR.; CODY, R. A.; JOHNSON, D. B.
ANALYSIS OF A BIN-PACKING ALGORITHM FOR REDUCING ACCESS TIMES ON DRUM-LIKE STORAGE DEVICES.
COLB 1979 -1 COLBOURN, C. J.
COMPLEXITY OF SYMMETRIZING MATRICES, THE.
CORN 1978 -1 CORNEIL, D. G.; WOODWARD, M. E.
COMPARISON AND EVALUATION OF GRAPH THEORETICAL CLUSTERING TECHNIQUES, A.
CORNC 1980 -2 CORNUEJOLS, G.; NEMHAUSER, G. L.; WOLSEY, L. A.
WORST-CASE AND PROBABILISTIC ANALYSIS OF ALGORITHMS FOR A LOCATION PROBLEM.
CORND 1980 -1 CORNUEJOLS, G.; PULLEYBLANK, W. R.
MATCHING PROBLEM WITH SIDE CONDITIONS, A.
CORT 1978 -1 CORT, J. D.
COMPLEXITY OF COMBINATORIAL PROBLEMS (SPANISH).
CUNN 1979 -2 CUNNINGHAM, W. H.
THEORETICAL PROPERTIES OF A NETWORK SIMPLEX METHOD.
DAS D 1978 -1 DAS, S. R.; SHENG, C. L.; CHEN, Z.
ALGORITHM FOR FINDING ALL MAXIMAL COMPLETE SUBGRAPHS AND AN ESTIMATE OF THE ORDER OF COMPUTATIONAL COMPLEXITY, AN.
DEWI 1979 -1 DEWITT, H. K.; KRIEGER, M. M.
EXPECTED LENGTH OF SHORTEST PATHS AND ALGORITHM BEHAVIOR.
DOBK 1978 -1 DOBKIN, D. P.; LIPTON, R. J.
LOWER BOUND OF 1/2*N**2 ON LINEAR SEARCH PROGRAMS FOR THE KNAPSACK PROBLEM.
DOBK 1979 -1 DOBKIN, D. P.; LIPTON, R. J.
ON THE COMPLEXITY OF COMPUTATIONS UNDER VARYING SETS OF PRIMITIVES.
DOBKA 1978 -1 DOBKIN, D. P.; LIPTON, R. J.; REISS, S. P.
EXCURSIONS INTO GEOMETRY.
ECKE 1977 -1 ECKER, K.
ORGANISATION VON PARALLELEN PROZESSEN. THEORIE DETERMINISTISCHER SCHEDULES.
EVEN 1979 -1 EVEN, S.
GRAPH ALGORITHMS.
FISHA 1978 -2 FISHER, M. L.; HOCHBAUM, D.
PROBABILISTIC ANALYSIS OF THE EUCLIDEAN K-MEDIAN PROBLEM.
FLORB 1978 -1 FLORIAN, M.; LENSTRA, J. K.; RINNOOY KAN, A. H. G.
DETERMINISTIC PRODUCTION PLANNING: ALGORITHMS AND COMPLEXITY.
FORT 1979 -1 FORTUNE, S.
NOTE ON SPARSE COMPLETE SETS, A.
FORTA 1979 -1 FORTUNE, S.; HOPCROFT, J. E.
NOTE ON RABIN'S NEAREST-NEIGHBOUR ALGORITHM, A.
FORTB 1980 -1 FORTUNE, S.; HOPCROFT, J. E.; WYLLIE, J.
DIRECTED SUBGRAPH HOMEOMORPHISM PROBLEM, THE.
FRAE 1979 -1 FRAENKEL, A. S.; YESHA, Y.
COMPLEXITY OF PROBLEMS IN GAMES, GRAPHS AND ALGEBRAIC EQUATIONS.
FRAE 1980 -1 FRAENKEL, A. S.; YESHA, Y.
COMPLEXITY OF SOLVING ALGEBRAIC EQUATIONS.
FRANA 1977 -1 FRANCON, J.
ON THE ANALYSIS OF ALGORITHMS FOR TREES.
FRED 1977 -1 FREDERICKSON, G. N.
APPROXIMATION ALGORITHMS FOR NP-HARD ROUTING PROBLEMS.
FRED 1979 -1 FREDERICKSON, G. N.
APPROXIMATION ALGORITHMS FOR SOME POSTMAN PROBLEMS.
FRED 1980 -1 FREDERICKSON, G. N.
PROBABILISTIC ANALYSIS FOR SIMPLE ONE- AND TWO-DIMENSIONAL BIN PACKING ALGORITHMS.
FREDA 1976 -1 FREDERICKSON, G. N.; HECHT, M. S.; KIM, C. E.
APPROXIMATION ALGORITHMS FOR SOME ROUTING PROBLEMS.
FRIED 1978 -1 FRIEZE, A. M.
GENERALISATION OF THE GREEDY ALGORITHM FOR INDEPENDENCE SYSTEMS, A.
FRIED 1979 -3 FRIEZE, A. M.
PROBABILISTIC ANALYSIS OF SOME EUCLIDEAN CLUSTERING.
FRUMA 1980 -1 FRUMKIN, M. A.; GENS, G. V.; HMELEVSKII, JU. I.; LEVNER, E. V.
ON COMPUTATIONAL COMPLEXITY OF OPTIMIZATION COMBINATORIAL PROBLEMS.
GABOA 1979 -1 GABOVICH, E. J.; MELAMED, I. J.
COMPUTATIONAL COMPLEXITY OF ROUTING PROBLEMS (RUSSIAN).
GABOB 1978 -1 GABOW, H. N.
GOOD ALGORITHM FOR SMALLEST SPANNING TREES WITH A DEGREE CONSTRAINT, A.
GALI 1975 -1 GALIL, Z.
ON THE COMPLEXITY OF REGULAR RESOLUTION AND THE DAVIS-PUTNAM PROCEDURE.
GALI 1978 -2 GALIL, Z.
ON THE THEORETICAL EFFICIENCY OF VARIOUS NETWORK FLOW ALGORITHMS.
GALIA 1977 -1 GALIL, Z.; MEGIDDO, N.
FAST SELECTION ALGORITHM AND THE PROBLEM OF OPTIMUM DISTRIBUTION OF EFFORT, A.
GALIB 1979 -1 GALIL, Z.; NAAMAD, A.
NETWORK FLOW AND GENERALIZED PATH COMPRESSION.
GALIB 1980 -1 GALIL, Z.; NAAMAD, A.
O(EV(LOG V)**2) ALGORITHM FOR THE MAXIMAL FLOW PROBLEM, AN.
GALIC 1977 -1 GALIL, Z.; SEIFERAS, J.
SAVING SPACE IN FAST STRING-MATCHING.
GAREA 1978 -1 GAREY, M. R.; JOHNSON, D. S.
"STRONG" NP-COMPLETENESS RESULTS: MOTIVATION, EXAMPLES AND IMPLICATIONS.
GAREB 1980 -1 GAREY, M. R.; JOHNSON, D. S.; MILLER, G. L.; PAPADIMITRIOU, C. H.
COMPLEXITY OF COLORING CIRCULAR ARCS AND CHORDS, THE.
GARED 1978 -1 GAREY, M. R.; TARJAN, R. E.
LINEAR-TIME ALGORITHM FOR FINDING ALL FEEDBACK VERTICES, A.
GARFA 1978 -1 GARFINKEL, R. S.; GILBERT, K. C.
BOTTLENECK TRAVELING SALESMAN PROBLEM: ALGORITHMS AND PROBABILISTIC ANALYSIS, THE.
GAVR 1977 -1 GAVRIL, F.
SOME NP-COMPLETE PROBLEMS ON GRAPHS.
GENS 1979 -1 GENS, G. V.; LEVNER, E. V.
COMPLEXITY OF APPROXIMATION ALGORITHMS FOR COMBINATORIAL PROBLEMS: A SURVEY.
GENS 1979 -2 GENS, G. V.; LEVNER, E. V.
COMPUTATIONAL COMPLEXITY OF APPROXIMATION ALGORITHMS FOR COMBINATORIAL PROBLEMS.
GIUL 1977 -1 GIULIANELLI, S.; LUCERTINI, M.
METHOD FOR REDUCING COMPUTATIONAL COMPLEXITY OF ILPC PROBLEMS, A.

GOLU 1980 -1 GOLUMBIC, M. C.
ALGORITHMIC GRAPH THEORY AND PERFECT GRAPHS.

GONZ 1979 -2 GONZALEZ, T.
NP-HARD SHOP PROBLEMS.

GONZB 1978 -1 GONZALEZ, T.; SAHNI, S.
FLOWSHOP AND JOBSHOP SCHEDULES: COMPLEXITY AND APPROXIMATION.

GRAHA 1978 -1 GRAHAM, R. L.; LAWLER, E. L.; LENSTRA, J. K.; RINNOOY KAN, A. H. G.
OPTIMIZATION AND APPROXIMATION IN DETERMINISTIC SEQUENCING AND SCHEDULING: A SURVEY.

GRAHA 1979 -1 GRAHAM, R. L.; LAWLER, E. L.; LENSTRA, J. K.; RINNOOY KAN, A. H. G.
OPTIMIZATION AND APPROXIMATION IN DETERMINISTIC SEQUENCING AND SCHEDULING: A SURVEY.

GRANE 1980 -1 GRANT, P. W.
SOME MORE INDEPENDENCE RESULTS IN COMPLEXITY THEORY.

GRIGB 1979 -1 GRIGORAS, G.
ON THE NP-COMPLETENESS OF A PROBLEM IN FINITE AUTOMATA THEORY.

GROEB 1981 -1 GROETSCHEL, M.
APPROACHES TO HARD COMBINATORIAL OPTIMIZATION PROBLEMS.

GROED 1981 -1 GROETSCHEL, M.; LOVASZ, L.; SCHRIJVER, A.
ELLIPSOID METHOD AND ITS CONSEQUENCES IN COMBINATORIAL OPTIMIZATION, THE.

GROED 1981 -2 GROETSCHEL, M.; LOVASZ, L.; SCHRIJVER, A.
POLYNOMIAL ALGORITHMS FOR PERFECT GRAPHS.

GURA 1978 -1 GURARI, E. M.; IBARRA, O. H.
NP-COMPLETE NUMBER-THEORETIC PROBLEM, AN.

HAJE 1977 -1 HAJEK, P.
ARITHMETICAL COMPLEXITY OF SOME PROBLEMS IN COMPUTER SCIENCE.

HANSB 1980 -2 HANSEN, P.
O(M LOG D) ALGORITHM FOR SHORTEST PATHS, AN.

HARP 1976 -1 HARPER, L. H.; SAVAGE, J. E.
COMPLEXITY MADE SIMPLE.

HAUS 1979 -1 HAUSMANN, D.
COMPLEXITY OF THE TESTING OF ADJACENCY ON THE B-MATCHING POLYHEDRON.

HAUS 1978 -2 HAUSMANN, D.
POLYNOMIALER ALGORITHMUS FUER DIE ADJAZENZUEBERPRUEFUNG AUF DEM BRANCHING-POLYEDER, EIN.

HAUSA 1980 -1 HAUSMANN, D.; JENKYNS, T. A.; KORTE, B.
WORST CASE ANALYSIS OF GREEDY TYPE ALGORITHMS FOR INDEPENDENCE SYSTEMS.

HAUSB 1979 -1 HAUSMANN, D.; KANNAN, R.; KORTE, B.
EXPONENTIELLE UNTERE KOMPLEXITAETSSCHRANKEN FUER EINE KLASSE VON KNAPSACK-PROBLEMEN.

HAUSB 1981 -1 HAUSMANN, D.; KANNAN, R.; KORTE, B.
EXPONENTIAL LOWER BOUNDS ON A CLASS OF KNAPSACK ALGORITHMS.

HAUSB 1979 -2 HAUSMANN, D.; KANNAN, R.; KORTE, B.
EXPONENTIELLE UNTERE KOMPLEXITAETSSCHRANKEN FUER EINE KLASSE VON KNAPSACKPROBLEMEN (EXTENDED ABSTRACT).

HAUSC 1978 -3 HAUSMANN, D.; KORTE, B.
LOWER BOUNDS ON THE WORST-CASE COMPLEXITY OF SOME ORACLE ALGORITHMS.

HAUSC 1978 -4 HAUSMANN, D.; KORTE, B.
WORST-CASE BEHAVIOUR OF POLYNOMIAL BOUNDED ALGORITHMS FOR INDEPENDENCE SYSTEMS.

HERMA 1973 -1 HERMANN, P. P.
ON REDUCIBILITY AMONG COMBINATORIAL PROBLEMS.

HIRA 1979 -1 HIRATA, T.; MAROUOKA, A.; KIMURA, M.
POLYNOMIAL TIME ALGORITHM TO FIND A PATH COVER OF A REDUCIBLE FLOW GRAPH (JAPANESE), A.

HOCH 1979 -1 HOCHBAUM, D.
ESTABLISHING A RELATIONSHIP BETWEEN SOME HARD PROBLEMS.

HOED 1979 -1 HOEDE, C.
ZWIEBELSTRUKTUREN EINIGER KLASSEN VON KOMBINATORISCHEN UND GRAPHENTHEORETISCHEN PROBLEMEN, DIE.

HONG 1979 -1 HONG, J. W.
ON LOWER BOUNDS OF TIME COMPLEXITY OF SOME ALGORITHMS.

HORO 1978 -1 HOROWITZ, E.; SAHNI, S.
FUNDAMENTALS OF COMPUTER ALGORITHMS.

HSU B 1979 -2 HSU, W.-L.; NEMHAUSER, G. L.
EASY AND HARD BOTTLENECK LOCATION PROBLEMS.

HWAN 1979 -1 HWANG, F. K.
O(N LOG N) ALGORITHM FOR RECTILINEAR MINIMAL SPANNING TREES, AN.

IBAR 1977 -1 IBARAKI, T.
ON THE COMPUTATIONAL EFFICIENCY OF BRANCH-AND-BOUND ALGORITHMS.

ITAI 1978 -1 ITAI, A.
TWO-COMMODITY FLOW.

ITAIA 1977 -1 ITAI, A.; RODEH, M.
FINDING A MINIMUM CIRCUIT IN A GRAPH.

ITAIB 1978 -1 ITAI, A.; RODEH, M.; TANIMOTO, S. L.
SOME MATCHING PROBLEMS FOR BIPARTITE GRAPHS.

ITOG 1978 -1 ITOGA, S. Y.
UPPER BOUND FOR THE STABLE MARRIAGE PROBLEM, THE.

JENKA 1979 -2 JENKYNS, T. A.
GREEDY TRAVELLING SALESMAN'S PROBLEM, THE.

JENSB 1978 -1 JENSEN, P. M.; KORTE, B.
COMPLEXITY OF MATROID PROPERTY ALGORITHMS.

JOHNB 1978 -1 JOHNSON, D. S.; LENSTRA, J. K.; RINNOOY KAN, A. H. G.
COMPLEXITY OF THE NETWORK DESIGN PROBLEM, THE.

JOHNI 1977 -1 JOHNSON, L. F.
ALGORITHMS FOR ENUMERATING THE SIMPLE CYCLES OF A DIGRAPH.

KAME 1973 -1 KAMEDA, T.; TOIDA, S.
EFFICIENT ALGORITHMS FOR DETERMINING AN EXTREMAL TREE OF A GRAPH (EXTENDED ABSTRACT).

KANN 1980 -1 KANNAN, R.
POLYNOMIAL ALGORITHM FOR THE TWO-VARIABLE INTEGER PROGRAMMING PROBLEM, A.

KANN 1980 -2 KANNAN, R.
POLYNOMIAL-TIME AGGREGATION OF INTEGER PROGRAMMING PROBLEMS.

KANN 1980 -3 KANNAN, R.
SIZE OF NUMBERS IN THE ANALYSIS OF CERTAIN ALGORITHMS, THE.

KANNA 1979 -1 KANNAN, R.; BACHEM, A.
POLYNOMIAL ALGORITHMS FOR COMPUTING THE SMITH AND HERMITE NORMAL FORMS OF AN INTEGER MATRIX.

KANNB 1978 -1 KANNAN, R.; KORTE, B.
APPROXIMATIVE COMBINATORIAL ALGORITHMS.

KANNC 1980 -1 KANNAN, R.; LIPTON, R. J.
ORBIT PROBLEM IS DECIDABLE, THE.

KARP 1975 -1 KARP, R. M.
COMPUTATIONAL COMPLEXITY OF COMBINATORIAL AND GRAPH-THEORETIC PROBLEMS.

KARPB 1980 -1 KARP, R. M.; PAPADIMITRIOU, C. H.
ON LINEAR CHARACTERIZATIONS OF COMBINATORIAL OPTIMIZATION PROBLEMS.
KATOA 1979 -1 KATOH, N.; IBARAKI, T.; MINE, H.
ALGORITHMS FOR A VARIANT OF THE RESOURCE ALLOCATION PROBLEM.
KEVO 1978 -1 KEVORKIAN, A. K.
GENERAL TOPOLOGICAL RESULTS ON THE CONSTRUCTION OF A MINIMUM ESSENTIAL SET OF A DIGRAPH.
KIKU 1980 -1 KIKUNO, T.; YOSHIDA, N.; KAKUDA, Y.
NP-COMPLETENESS OF SOME TYPE OF P-CENTER PROBLEM.
KIM 1976 -1 KIM, C.
ANALYSIS OF THE EXPECTED PERFORMANCE OF ALGORITHMS FOR THE PARTITION PROBLEM.
KING 1979 -1 KING, J. R.
SCHEDULING AND THE PROBLEM OF COMPUTATIONAL COMPLEXITY.
KIRKA 1978 -1 KIRKPATRICK, D. G.; HELL, P.
ON THE COMPLEXITY OF A GENERALIZED MATCHING PROBLEM.
KISE 1978 -1 KISE, H.; IBARAKI, T.; MINE, H.
SOLVABLE CASE OF THE ONE-MACHINE SCHEDULING PROBLEM WITH READY AND DUE TIMES, A.
KLET 1979 -1 KLETIN, V. A.
ANALYSE DE L'EFFICACITE DES ALGORITHMES COMBINATOIRES DE RECHERCHE DES ARBRES EXTREMAUX SUR LES GRAPHES ORIENTES PONDERES (RUSSIAN).
KNOE 1981 -1 KNOEDEL, W.
BIN PACKING ALGORITHM WITH COMPLEXITY O(N LOG N) AND PERFORMANCE 1 IN THE STOCHASTIC LIMIT, A.
KNUT 1974 -1 KNUTH, D.
POSTSCRIPT ABOUT NP-HARD PROBLEMS.
KOLE 1979 -1 KOLEN, A.
COMPLEXITY OF LOCATION PROBLEMS ON NETWORKS.
KORTA 1979 -1 KORTE, B.
APPROXIMATIVE ALGORITHMS FOR DISCRETE OPTIMIZATION PROBLEMS.
KORTC 1979 -1 KORTE, B.; MONMA, C. L.
SOME REMARKS ON A CLASSIFICATION OF ORACLE-TYPE-ALGORITHMS.
KORTD 1981 -1 KORTE, B.; SCHRADER, R.
ON THE EXISTENCE OF FAST APPROXIMATION SCHEMES.
KORTD 1981 -2 KORTE, B.; SCHRADER, R.
SURVEY ON ORACLE TECHNIQUES, A.
KOSA 1978 -1 KOSARAJU, S. R.
INSERTIONS AND DELETIONS IN ONE-SIDED HEIGHT-BALANCED TREES.
KOSO 1978 -1 KOSOVSKII, N. K.
KOLMOGOROV'S SUBRECURSIVE ALGORITHMIC COMPLEXITY (RUSSIAN).
KOZE 1978 -1 KOZEN, D.
CLIQUE PROBLEM EQUIVALENT TO GRAPH ISOMORPHISM, A.
KRIS 1975 -1 KRISHNAMOORTHY, M. S.
NP-HARD PROBLEM IN BIPARTITE GRAPHS, AN.
KRISA 1979 -1 KRISHNAMOORTHY, M. S.; DEO, N.
COMPLEXITY OF THE MINIMUM-DUMMY-ACTIVITIES PROBLEM IN A PERT NETWORK.
KRISA 1979 -2 KRISHNAMOORTHY, M. S.; DEO, N.
NODE-DELETION NP-COMPLETE PROBLEMS.
LABE 1978 -1 LABETOULLE, J.; LAWLER, E. L.; LENSTRA, J. K.; RINNOOY KAN, A. H. G.
PREEMPTIVE SCHEDULING OF UNIFORM MACHINES (PRELIMINARY DRAFT).
LABE 1979 -1 LABETOULLE, J.; LAWLER, E. L.; LENSTRA, J. K.; RINNOOY KAN, A. H. G.
PREEMPTIVE SCHEDULING OF UNIFORM MACHINES SUBJECT TO RELEASE DATES.
LADE 1979 -1 LADERMAN, J. D.
COMPUTATIONAL COMPLEXITY: ALGORITHMS WITH FEWEST OPERATIONS.
LAGE 1977 -1 LAGEWEG, B. J.; LENSTRA, J. K.; RINNOOY KAN, A. H. G.
JOB-SHOP SCHEDULING BY IMPLICIT ENUMERATION.
LAM 1975 -1 LAM, S.
WORST CASE ANALYSIS OF MULTIPROCESSOR SCHEDULING ALGORITHMS.
LAPA 1978 -1 LAPAUGH, A. S.; RIVEST, R. L.
SUBGRAPH HOMOMORPHISM PROBLEM, THE.
LAWLB 1980 -1 LAWLER, E. L.; LENSTRA, J. K.; RINNOOY KAN, A. H. G.
GENERATING ALL MAXIMAL INDEPENDENT SETS: NP-HARDNESS AND POLYNOMIAL-TIME ALGORITHMS.
LEE 1978 -1 LEE, D. T.; PREPARATA, F. P.
ALL NEAREST-NEIGHBOUR PROBLEM FOR CONVEX POLYGONS, THE.
LEGG 1977 -1 LEGGETT, E. W.
TOOLS AND TECHNIQUES FOR CLASSIFYING NP-HARD PROBLEMS.
LENS 1981 -1 LENSTRA, H. W. JR.
INTEGER PROGRAMMING WITH A FIXED NUMBER OF VARIABLES.
LENSA 1978 -1 LENSTRA, J. K.; RINNOOY KAN, A. H. G.
COMPLEXITY OF SCHEDULING UNDER PRECEDENCE CONSTRAINTS.
LENSA 1980 -1 LENSTRA, J. K.; RINNOOY KAN, A. H. G.
COMPLEXITY RESULTS FOR SCHEDULING CHAINS ON A SINGLE MACHINE.
LENSA 1978 -2 LENSTRA, J. K.; RINNOOY KAN, A. H. G.
COMPUTATIONAL COMPLEXITY OF DISCRETE OPTIMIZATION PROBLEMS.
LENSA 1979 -2 LENSTRA, J. K.; RINNOOY KAN, A. H. G.
COMPLEXITY OF PACKING, COVERING AND PARTITIONING PROBLEMS.
LENSA 1978 -3 LENSTRA, J. K.; RINNOOY KAN, A. H. G.
ON THE EXPECTED PERFORMANCE OF BRANCH-AND-BOUND ALGORITHMS.
LENSA 1979 -3 LENSTRA, J. K.; RINNOOY KAN, A. H. G.
COMPLEXITY OF VEHICLE ROUTING AND SCHEDULING PROBLEMS.
LENSA 1979 -4 LENSTRA, J. K.; RINNOOY KAN, A. H. G.
COMPUTATIONAL COMPLEXITY OF DISCRETE OPTIMIZATION PROBLEMS.
LENSA 1980 -5 LENSTRA, J. K.; RINNOOY KAN, A. H. G.
THEORIE DE LA COMPLEXITE DE CALCUL APPLIQUEE AUX PROBLEMES DE COUPLAGE, RECOUVREMENT ET PARTITIONNEMENT.
LEUN 1977 -1 LEUNG, J. Y.-T.
FAST ALGORITHMS FOR PACKING PROBLEMS.
LEWIA 1978 -1 LEWIS, H. R.; CHRISTOS, H. P.
EFFICIENCY OF ALGORITHMS, THE.
LEWIB 1978 -1 LEWIS, H. R.; PAPADIMITRIOU, C. H.
EFFICACITE DES ALGORITHMES, L'.
LEWIC 1978 -1 LEWIS, J. M.
ON THE COMPLEXITY OF THE MAXIMUM SUBGRAPH PROBLEM.
LEWID 1980 -1 LEWIS, J. M.; YANNAKAKIS, M.
NODE-DELETION PROBLEM FOR HEREDITARY PROPERTIES IS NP-COMPLETE, THE.
LIAN 1980 -1 LIANG, F. M.
LOWER BOUND FOR ON-LINE BIN PACKING, A.

LIEB 1977 -1 LIEBERHERR, K.
INFORMATIONSVERDICHTUNG VON MODELLEN IN DER AUSSAGENLOGIK UND DAS P = NP-PROBLEM.

LIFS 1980 -1 LIFSCHITZ, V.
EFFICIENCY OF AN ALGORITHM OF INTEGER PROGRAMMING: A PROBABILISTIC ANALYSIS, THE.

LIPT 1978 -1 LIPTON, R. J.; MILLER, R. E.
BATCHING METHOD FOR COLORING PLANAR GRAPHS, A.

LIVSA 1972 -1 LIVSHIC, E. M.; RUBLINECKII, V. I.
ON RELATIVE COMPLEXITY OF DISCRETE OPTIMIZATION PROBLEMS (RUSSIAN).

LOIZ 1980 -1 LOIZOU, G.
ON A CYCLE FINDING ALGORITHM.

LOVA 1981 -1 LOVASZ, L.
BOUNDING THE INDEPENDENCE NUMBER OF A GRAPH.

LUEK 1975 -1 LUEKER, G. S.
EFFICIENT ALGORITHMS FOR CHORDAL GRAPHS AND INTERVAL GRAPHS.

MAC B 1979 -1 MAC DIARMID, C.
DETERMINING THE CHROMATIC NUMBER OF A GRAPH.

MAC K 1978 -1 MAC MASTER, C. L.
ANALYSIS OF ALGORITHMS FOR THE DUTCH NATIONAL FLAG PROBLEM, AN.

MACH 1978 -1 MACHTEY, M.; WINKLMANN, K.; YOUNG, P.
SIMPLE GODEL NUMBERINGS, ISOMORPHISMS, AND PROGRAMMING PROPERTIES.

MAFF 1978 -1 MAFFIOLI, F.
DISCREET CHARM OF MATROID PROBLEMS, THE.

MAFF 1979 -1 MAFFIOLI, F.
COMPLEXITY OF COMBINATORIAL OPTIMIZATION ALGORITHMS AND THE CHALLENGE OF HEURISTICS, THE.

MAGA 1979 -1 MAGAZINE, M. J.; OGUZ, O.
FULLY POLYNOMIAL APPROXIMATE ALGORITHM FOR THE 0-1 KNAPSACK PROBLEM, A. (REVISED VERSION).

MAHR 1978 -1 MAHR, B.
STRATEGIES AND ARITHMETIC COMPLEXITY OF PATHALGORITHMS.

MAIE 1977 -1 MAIER, D.; STORER, J. A.
NOTE ON THE COMPLEXITY OF THE SUPERSTRING PROBLEM, A.

MALH 1978 -1 MALHOTRA, V. M.; KUMAR, M. P.; MAHESHWARI, S. N.
O(!V!**3) ALGORITHM FOR FINDING MAXIMUM FLOWS IN NETWORKS, AN.

MARTA 1975 -1 MARTELLI, A.
SOME REMARKS ON THE COMPLEXITY OF HEURISTIC SEARCH ALGORITHMS.

MARTC 1979 -1 MARTELLO, S.; TOTH, P.
FINDING A MINIMAL EQUIVALENT GRAPH OF A DIGRAPH.

MATHA 1979 -1 MATHON, R.
NOTE ON THE GRAPH ISOMORPHISM COUNTING PROBLEM, A.

MAURC 1978 -1 MAURRAS, J. F.
GOOD ALGORITHMS, OLD IDEAS.

MEGI 1979 -1 MEGIDDO, N.
COMBINATORIAL OPTIMIZATION WITH RATIONAL OBJECTIVE FUNCTIONS.

MEGIA 1979 -1 MEGIDDO, N.; GALIL, Z.
ON FULKERSON'S CONJECTURE ABOUT CONSISTENT LABELING PROCESSES.

MEGIB 1978 -1 MEGIDDO, N.; TAMIR, A.
O(N TIMES LOG N) ALGORITHM FOR A CLASS OF MATCHING PROBLEMS, AN.

MEHL 1978 -1 MEHLHORN, K.
EFFIZIENTE ALGORITHMEN: EIN BEISPIEL.

MEYE 1979 -1 MEYER, A. R.; WINKLMANN, K.
FUNDAMENTAL THEOREM OF COMPLEXITY THEORY (PRELIMINARY VERSION), THE.

MEYEA 1981 -1 MEYER, H.
KOMPLEXITAETSPROBLEME IN GERT-NETZPLAENEN.

MONM 1980 -1 MONMA, C. L.
DISSECTION STRATEGIES FOR MULTIGRAM CODES.

MONM 1980 -2 MONMA, C. L.
LINEAR-TIME ALGORITHMS FOR SCHEDULING EQUAL-LENGTH TASKS WITH DUE DATES ON PARALLEL PROCESSORS SUBJECT TO PRECEDENCE CONSTRANINTS.

MORI 1977 -1 MORITA, K.; UMEO, H.; SUGATA, K.
COMPUTATIONAL COMPLEXITY OF L(M,N) TAPE-BOUNDED TWO-DIMENSIONAL TURING MACHINES.

MUELA 1981 -1 MUELLER, H.
ZUR STRUKTUR UND KOMPLEXITAET DISKRETER OPTIMIERUNGSPROBLEME, DIE DURCH ERBLICHE EIGENSCHAFTEN AUF ENDLICHEN MENGENSYSTEMEN GEGEBEN SIND.

NEMHB 1978 -1 NEMHAUSER, G. L.; WOLSEY, L. A.
MAXIMIZING SUBMODULAR SET FUNCTIONS: FORMULATIONS AND ANALYSIS OF ALGORITHMS.

NIGM 1975 -1 NIGMATULLIN, R. G.
COMPLEXITY OF APPROXIMATE SOLUTION OF COMBINATORIAL PROBLEMS (RUSSIAN).

NIGM 1978 -1 NIGMATULLIN, R. G.
ON APPROXIMATE ALGORITHMS WITH RESTRICTED ABSOLUTE ERROR FOR DISCRETE EXTREMUM PROBLEMS (RUSSIAN).

NTAF 1979 -1 NTAFOS, S. C.; HAKIMI, S. L.
ON PATH COVER PROBLEMS IN DIGRAPHS AND APPLICATIONS TO PROGRAM TESTING.

OKAW 1979 -1 OKAWA, S.; NISHITANI, Y.; HONDA, N.
BIPARTITE SUBGRAPH PROBLEMS WITH DEGREE AT MOST THREE (JAPANESE), THE.

OPAT 1979 -1 OPATRNY, J.
TOTAL ORDERING PROBLEM.

PAGE 1978 -1 PAGET, M.
PROPRIETES DE COMPLEXITE POUR UNE FAMILLE D'ALGORITHMES DE MARKOV.

PAPA 1976 -1 PAPADIMITRIOU, C. H.
COMPLEXITY OF COMBINATORIAL OPTIMIZATION PROBLEMS, THE.

PAPA 1978 -1 PAPADIMITRIOU, C. H.
ADJACENCY RELATION ON THE TRAVELLING SALESMAN POLYTOPE IS NP-COMPLETE, THE.

PAPA 1980 -1 PAPADIMITRIOU, C. H.
WORST-CASE AND PROBABILISTIC ANALYSIS OF A GEOMETRIC LOCATION PROBLEM.

PAPA 1978 -2 PAPADIMITRIOU, C. H.
COMPLEXITY OF THE CAPACITATED TREE PROBLEM, THE.

PAPAC 1979 -1 PAPADIMITRIOU, C. H.; YANNAKAKIS, M.
COMPLEXITY OF RESTRICTED SPANNING TREE PROBLEMS, THE.

PATEA 1970 -1 PATERSON, M. S.
UNSOLVABILITY IN 3 X 3 MATRICES.

PATEA 1975 -1 PATERSON, M. S.
COMPLEXITY OF MATRIX ALGORITHMS.

PATEA 1976 -1 PATERSON, M. S.
INTRODUCTION TO BOOLEAN FUNCTION COMPLEXITY, AN.

PAULB 1978 -1 PAUL, W. J.
KOMPLEXITAETSTHEORIE.

PIPP 1977 -2 PIPPENGER, N.
ON ANOTHER BOOLEAN MATRIX.
PIPPA 1979 -1 PIPPENGER, N.; FISCHER, M. J.
RELATIONS AMONG COMPLEXITY MEASURES.
PLAI 1976 -1 PLAISTED, D. A.
SOME POLYNOMIAL AND INTEGER DIVISIBILITY PROBLEMS ARE NP-HARD.
PLAIA 1980 -1 PLAISTED, D. A.; ZAKS, S.
NP-COMPLETE MATCHING PROBLEM, AN.
PLES 1979 -1 PLESNIK, J.
NP-COMPLETENESS OF THE HAMILTONIAN CYCLE PROBLEM IN PLANAR DIGRAPHS WITH DEGREE BOUND TWO, THE.
PLES 1980 -2 PLESNIK, J.
ON THE COMPUTATIONAL COMPLEXITY ON CENTERS LOCATING IN A GRAPH.
PRIE 1979 -1 PRIESE, L.
TOWARDS A PRECISE CHARACTERIZATION OF THE COMPLEXITY OF UNIVERSAL AND NONUNIVERSAL TURING MACHINES.
PULL 1979 -2 PULLEYBLANK, W. R.
NOTE ON GRAPHS SPANNED BY EULERIAN GRAPHS, A.
RADZ 1977 -1 RADZISZOWSKI, S.
PROGRAMMABILITY AND P = NP CONJECTURE.
RADZ 1978 -1 RADZISZOWSKI, S.
PROGRAMMABILITY AND P=NP CONJECTURE.
RIVE 1976 -1 RIVEST, R. L.; VUILLEMIN, J.
ON THE TIME REQUIRED TO RECOGNIZE PROPERTIES OF GRAPHS FROM THEIR ADJACENCY MATRICES.
ROBIC 1980 -1 ROBINSON, G. C.; WELSH, D. J. A.
COMPUTATIONAL COMPLEXITY OF MATROID PROPERTIES, THE.
ROMAA 1980 -1 ROMANI, F.
SHORTEST-PATH PROBLEM IS NOT HARDER THAN MATRIX MULTIPLICATION.
ROSE 1978 -1 ROSE, D. J.; TARJAN, R. E.
ALGORITHMIC ASPECTS OF VERTEX ELIMINATION ON DIRECTED GRAPHS.
SAHNA 1979 -1 SAHNI, S.; CHO, Y.
COMPLEXITY OF SCHEDULING SHOPS WITH NO WAIT IN PROCESS.
SAHNB 1975 -1 SAHNI, S.; GONZALEZ, T.
P-COMPLETE APPROXIMATION PROBLEMS.
SAHNC 1978 -1 SAHNI, S.; HOROWITZ, E.
COMBINATORIAL PROBLEMS: REDUCIBILITY AND APPROXIMATION.
SANGA 1979 -1 SANGIOVANNI-VINCENTELLI, A.; BICKART, T. A.
BIPARTITE GRAPHS AND AN OPTIMAL BORDERED TRIANGULAR FORM OF A MATRIX.
SAVAA 1979 -1 SAVAGE, J. E.
SPACE-TIME TRADEOFFS.
SAVI 1976 -1 SAVITCH, W. J.
THREE HARDEST PROBLEMS.
SBIH 1978 -1 SBIHI, N.
ETUDE DES STABLES DANS LES GRAPHES SANS ETOILE.
SCHEB 1979 -1 SCHENK, G.; THIERS, G.
COMPARISON OF SOME ALGORITHMS AND HEURISTICS FOR SOLVING THE HITCHCOCK-KOOPMANS TRANSPORTATION PROBLEM, A.
SCHNA 1976 -1 SCHNORR, C. P.
NETWORK COMPLEXITY AND THE BREADTH OF BOOLEAN FUNCTIONS, THE.
SCHNA 1978 -1 SCHNORR, C. P.
ALGORITHM FOR TRANSITIVE CLOSURE WITH LINEAR EXPECTED TIME, AN.
SETH 1977 -1 SETHI, R.
ON THE COMPLEXITY OF MEAN FLOW TIME SCHEDULING.
SGUR 1977 -1 SGUREV, V. S.; VASILEV, V. S.
DECOMPOSITION METHOD FOR THE SOLUTION OF A CLASS OF INTEGER PROGRAMMING PROBLEMS (BULGARIAN), A.
SHIL 1979 -2 SHILOACH, Y.
MINIMUM LINEAR ARRANGEMENT ALGORITHM FOR UNDIRECTED TREES, A.
SHIL 1980 -2 SHILOACH, Y.
POLYNOMIAL SOLUTION TO THE UNDIRECTED TWO PATHS PROBLEM, A.
SHIR 1976 -1 SHIRAKAWA, I.
SURVEY OF THE ANALYSIS OF THE COMPLEXITY OF COMBINATORIAL PROBLEMS (JAPANESE), A.
SIMOA 1975 -1 SIMON, J.
ON SOME CENTRAL PROBLEMS IN COMPUTATIONAL COMPLEXITY.
SIMOC 1979 -1 SIMOVICI, D. A.; GRIGORAS, G.
EVEN INITIAL FEEDBACK VERTEX SET PROBLEM IS NP-COMPLETE.
SLOM 1980 -1 SLOMINSKI, L.
ON EFFICIENCY OF ALGORITHMS FOR COMBINATORIAL OPTIMIZATION PROBLEMS.
SLOM 1981 -1 SLOMINSKI, L.
ON STATISTICALLY EFFICIENT ALGORITHMS FOR COMBINATORIAL OPTIMIZATION PROBLEMS.
STEI 1978 -1 STEIN, D. M.
ASYMPTOTIC, PROBABILISTIC ANALYSIS OF A ROUTING PROBLEM, AN.
SURY 1979 -1 SURYGIN, V. A.
ESTIMATES OF THE COMPLEXITY OF NORMAL ALGORITHMS (RUSSIAN).
SYSL 1977 -2 SYSLO, M. M.
LINEAR TIME ALGORITHM FOR CODING OUTERPLANAR GRAPHS.
SYSLA 1976 -1 SYSLO, M. M.; IRI, M.
EFFICIENT OUTERPLANARITY TESTING.
TARJ 1978 -1 TARJAN, R. E.
COMPLEXITY OF COMBINATORIAL ALGORITHMS.
TARJ 1979 -1 TARJAN, R. E.
CLASS OF ALGORITHMS WHICH REQUIRE NONLINEAR TIME TO MAINTAIN DISJOINT SETS, A.
TERA 1979 -1 TERADA, R.
POLYNOMIAL TIME ALGORITHMS FOR NP-HARD PROBLEMS WHICH ARE OPTIMAL OR NEAR-OPTIMAL WITH PROBABILITY ONE.
TISH 1977 -1 TISHYADHIGAMA, S.; POLAK, E.; KLESSIG, R.
COMPARATIVE STUDY OF SEVERAL GENERAL CONVERGENCE CONDITIONS FOR ALGORITHMS MODELED BY POINT-TO-SET MAPS, A.
TRAU 1978 -1 TRAUB, F. J.
RECENT RESULTS AND OPEN PROBLEMS IN ANALYTIC COMPUTATIONAL COMPLEXITY.
TRIG 1978 -1 TRIGT, C. VAN
WORST-CASE ANALYSIS OF ALGORITHMS. A. SOME G. C. D. ALGORITHMS.
TRUB 1978 -1 TRUBIN, V. A.
EFFECTIVE ALGORITHM FOR THE WEBER PROBLEM WITH RECTANGULAR METRIC (RUSSIAN).
TRUE 1979 -2 TRUEMPER, K.
COMPLEXITY OF REPRESENTABILITY TESTS FOR MATROIDS.

UNDE 1978 -1 UNDERGROUND, P.
ON GRAPHS WITH HAMILTONIAN SQUARES.
VALI 1979 -1 VALIANT, L. G.
COMPLEXITY OF COMPUTING THE PERMANENT, THE.
VALI 1979 -2 VALIANT, L. G.
COMPLEXITY OF ENUMERATION AND RELIABILITY PROBLEMS, THE.
VANE 1975 -1 VANEMDEN, M. H.
ANALYSIS OF COMPLEXITY, AN (2ND PRINTING).
VORN 1981 -1 VORNBERGER, O.
ALTERNATING CYCLE COVERS AND PATHS.
VOUT 1980 -1 VOUTILAINEN, R.
ON THE PATTERN SEQUENCING PROBLEM - DEFINITIONS, COMPLEXITY, AND APPLICATIONS.
WALS 1976 -1 WALSH, A. M.
POLYNOMIAL ALGORITHMS FOR CERTAIN GRAPH-THEORETIC PROBLEMS.
WALSA 1975 -1 WALSH, A. M.; BURKHARD, W. A.
POLYNOMIAL ALGORITHMS FOR (3,1) GRAPHS.
WANK 1978 -1 WANKMUELLER, F.
GRAPHENKLASSEN, BEI DENEN DAS CLIQUENPROBLEM IN POLYNOMIALER ZEIT LOESBAR IST.
WATA 1981 -1 WATANABE, T.; AE, T.; NAKAMURA, A.
ON THE REMOVAL OF FORBIDDEN GRAPHS BY EDGE-DELETION OR BY EDGE-CONTRACTION.
WEID 1977 -1 WEIDE, B.
SURVEY OF ANALYSIS TECHNIQUES FOR DISCRETE ALGORITHMS, A.
WINO 1980 -1 WINOGRAD, S.
ARITHMETIC COMPLEXITY OF COMPUTATIONS.
WONG 1979 -1 WONG, J. K.
NEW IMPLEMENTATION OF AN ALGORITHM FOR THE OPTIMAL ASSIGNMENT PROBLEM: AN IMPROVED VERSION OF MUNKRES' ALGORITHM, A.
YANN 1978 -1 YANNAKAKIS, M.
NODE- AND EDGE-DELETION NP-COMPLETE PROBLEMS.
YANN 1979 -1 YANNAKAKIS, M.
EFFECT OF A CONNECTIVITY REQUIREMENT ON THE COMPLEXITY OF MAXIMUM SUBGRAPH PROBLEMS, THE.
YANNA 1980 -1 YANNAKAKIS, M.; GAVRIL, F.
EDGE DOMINATING SETS IN GRAPHS.
YAO 1979 -1 YAO, A. C.-C.
COMPLEXITY OF PATTERN MATCHING FOR A RANDOM STRING, THE.
YAO A 1979 -1 YAO, F. F.
GRAPH 2-ISOMORPHISM IS NP-COMPLETE.
ZIJA 1979 -1 ZIJADULLAEV, N. S.; SERBULOV, A. V.
SOME PROBLEMS OF ESTIMATING THE AMOUNT OF CALCULATION INVOLVED IN PROBLEMS OF SCHEDULING THEORY (RUSSIAN).

ALI A 1980 -1 ALI, A. I.; HELGASON, R. V.; KENNINGTON, J. L.; LALL, H. S.
COMPUTATIONAL COMPARISON AMONG THREE MULTICOMMODITY NETWORK FLOW ALGORITHMS.

ARMS 1977 -1 ARMSTRONG, R. D.
EXPERIMENTS IN A MULTIPLE CHOICE MIXED INTEGER PROGRAMMING ALGORITHM.

ARMSE 1980 -1 ARMSTRONG, R. D.; KLINGMAN, D.; WHITMAN, D.
IMPLEMENTATION AND ANALYSIS OF A VARIANT OF THE DUAL METHOD FOR THE CAPACITATED TRANSSHIPMENT PROBLEM.

AVISA 1978 -1 AVIS, D.; CHVATAL, V.
NOTES ON BLAND'S PIVOTING RULE.

BAKED 1980 -1 BAKER, E.; FISHER, M.
COMPUTATIONAL RESULTS FOR VERY LARGE AIR CREW SCHEDULING PROBLEMS.

BALAD 1980 -1 BALAS, E.; HO, A. C.
SET COVERING ALGORITHMS USING CUTTING PLANES, HEURISTICS, AND SUBGRADIENT OPTIMIZATION: A COMPUTATIONAL STUDY.

BALAF 1980 -1 BALAS, E.; MARTIN, C. H.
PIVOT AND COMPLEMENT - A HEURISTIC FOR 0-1 PROGRAMMING.

BALAK 1977 -3 BALAS, E.; ZEMEL, E.
SOLVING LARGE ZERO-ONE KNAPSACK PROBLEMS (REVISED VERSION).

BARRA 1979 -1 BARR, R. S.; GLOVER, F.; KLINGMAN, D.
ENHANCEMENTS OF SPANNING TREE LABELING PROCEDURES FOR NETWORK OPTIMIZATION.

BITR 1979 -1 BITRAN, G. R.
THEORY AND ALGORITHMS FOR LINEAR MULTIPLE OBJECTIVE PROGRAMS WITH ZERO-ONE VARIABLES.

BODIA 1978 -1 BODIN, L. D.; KURSH, S. J.
COMPUTER-ASSISTED SYSTEM FOR THE ROUTING AND SCHEDULING OF STREET SWEEPERS, A.

BRAD 1975 -1 BRADLEY, G. H.; BROWN, G. G.; GRAVES, G.
COMPARISON OF STORAGE STRUCTURE FOR PRIMAL NETWORK CODES, A.

BURK 1978 -2 BURKARD, R. E.
NUMERICAL INVESTIGATIONS ON QUADRATIC ASSIGNMENT PROBLEMS.

CHEU 1980 -1 CHEUNG, T.-Y.
COMPUTATIONAL COMPARISON OF EIGHT METHODS FOR THE MAXIMUM NETWORK FLOW PROBLEM.

CHRIF 1978 -1 CHRISTOFIDES, N.; MINGOZZI, A.; THOTH, P.
EXACT ALGORITHMS FOR THE VEHICLE ROUTING PROBLEM.

CHRIG 1979 -2 CHRISTOFIDES, N.; MINGOZZI, A.; TOTH, P.
VEHICLE ROUTING PROBLEM, THE.

COLLA 1978 -1 COLLINS, M.; COOPER, L.; HELGASON, R. V.; KENNINGTON, J. L.; LEBLANC, L. J.
SOLVING THE PIPE NETWORK ANALYSIS PROBLEM USING OPTIMIZATION TECHNIQUES.

CONR 1979 -1 CONRADT, D.
VERGLEICH AUSGEWAEHLTER MATCHING-ALGORITHMEN.

CROW 1978 -1 CROWDER, H. P.
CLUSTER ANALYSIS: AN APPLICATION OF LAGRANGIAN RELAXATION.

CROWA 1978 -1 CROWDER, H. P.; DEMBO, R. S.; MULVEY, J. M.
REPORTING COMPUTATIONAL EXPERIMENTS IN MATHEMATICAL PROGRAMMING.

DANI 1978 -2 DANIEL, R. C.
REDUCING COMPUTATIONAL EFFORT IN SOLVING A HARD INTEGER PROGRAM.

DEMBB 1978 -1 DEMBO, R. S.; KLINCEWICZ, J. G.
APPROXIMATE SECOND-ORDER ALGORITHM FOR NETWORK FLOW PROBLEMS WITH CONVEX SEPARABLE COSTS, AN.

DERIA 1980 -1 DERIGS, U.; HESKE, A.
COMPUTATIONAL STUDY ON SOME METHODS FOR SOLVING THE CARDINALITY MATCHING PROBLEM, A.

DORH 1977 -1 DORHOUT, B.
EXPERIMENTS WITH SOME ALGORITHMS FOR THE LINEAR ASSIGNMENT PROBLEM.

EDMOA 1978 -1 EDMONDS, J.; JOHNSON, E. L.; LOCKHART, S. C.
BLOSSOM I: A COMPUTER CODE FOR THE MATCHING PROBLEM.

ELAMA 1977 -1 ELAM, J.; KLINGMAN, D.; MULVEY, J. M.
EVALUATION OF MATHEMATICAL PROGRAMMING AND MINICOMPUTERS, AN.

EVAN 1978 -5 EVANS, J. R.
SOLVING MULTICOMMODITY TRANSPORTATION PROBLEMS THROUGH AGGREGATION.

FISHB 1978 -1 FISHER, M. L.; JAIKUMAR, R.
ALGORITHM FOR THE SPACE-SHUTTLE SCHEDULING PROBLEM, AN.

GABR 1981 -1 GABRIEL, R.
LEISTUNGSVERGLEICH KOMMERZIELLER SOFTWARE ZUR LOESUNG SPEZIELLER MIXED-INTEGER-PROBLEME, EIN.

GARFA 1978 -1 GARFINKEL, R. S.; GILBERT, K. C.
BOTTLENECK TRAVELING SALESMAN PROBLEM: ALGORITHMS AND PROBABILISTIC ANALYSIS, THE.

GAVIA 1978 -1 GAVISH, B.; SCHWEITZER, P.; SHLIFER, E.
ASSIGNING BUSES TO SCHEDULES IN A METROPOLITAN AREA.

GELD 1978 -1 GELDERS, L. F.; SAMBANDAM, N.
FOUR SIMPLE HEURISTICS FOR SCHEDULING A FLOW SHOP.

GEOFA 1978 -1 GEOFFRION, A. M.; MAC BRIDE, R. D.
LAGRANGEAN RELAXATION APPLIED TO CAPACITATED FACILITY LOCATION PROBLEMS.

GLOVA 1977 -1 GLOVER, F.; HULTZ, J.; KLINGMAN, D.
NETWORK VERSUS LINEAR PROGRAMMING ALGORITHMS AND IMPLEMENTATIONS.

GLOVC 1977 -1 GLOVER, F.; KARNEY, D.; KLINGMAN, D.
STUDY OF ALTERNATIVE RELAXATION APPROACHES FOR A MANPOWER PLANNING PROBLEM, A.

GLOVF 1979 -1 GLOVER, F.; KLINGMAN, D.; MOTE, J.; WHITMAN, D.
COMPREHENSIVE COMPUTER EVALUATION AND ENHANCEMENT OF MAXIMUM FLOW ALGORITHMS.

GOLDC 1978 -1 GOLDEN, B. L.; ALT, F. B.
INTERVAL ESTIMATION OF A GLOBAL OPTIMUM FOR LARGE COMBINATORIAL PROBLEMS.

GROEB 1980 -2 GROETSCHEL, M.
ON THE SYMMETRIC TRAVELLING SALESMAN PROBLEM: SOLUTION OF 120-CITY PROBLEM.

GUIGA 1978 -2 GUIGNARD, M.; SPIELBERG, K.
EXPERIMENTAL INTERACTIVE SYSTEM FOR INTEGER PROGRAMMING, AN.

HAMA 1979 -1 HAMACHER, H.
COMPUTATIONAL COMPARISON OF THE ALGORITHM OF KARZANOV AND THE LABELING ALGORITHM FOR THE SOLUTION OF MAXIMUM FLOW PROBLEMS, A.

HANS 1978 -1 HANSEL, K.; JAENICKE, W.; WOLIN, JU. M.
ZUR BESTIMMUNG ALLER ELEMENTARKREISE IN GERICHTETEN GRAPHEN.

HILLA 1977 -1 HILLIER, F. S.
FURTHER INVESTIGATION OF EFFICIENT HEURISTIC PROCEDURES FOR INTEGER LINEAR PROGRAMMING WITH AN INTERIOR, A.

HITC 1968 -1 HITCHNER, L. E.
COMPARATIVE INVESTIGATION OF THE COMPUTATIONAL EFFICIENCY OF SHORTEST PATH ALGORITHMS, A.

HULM 1978 -1 HULME, B.; WISNIEWSKI, J. A.
COMPARISON OF SHORTEST PATH ALGORITHMS APPPLIED TO SPARSE GRAPHS, A.

HULT 1978 -1 HULTZ, J.; KLINGMAN, D.
SOLVING SINGULARLY CONSTRAINED GENERALIZED NETWORK PROBLEMS.

JAMB 1978 -1 JAMBEKAR, A. B.; STEINBERG, D. I.
COMPUTATIONAL EXPERIENCE WITH AN ALGORITHM FOR 0-1 INTEGER PROGRAMMING.
JENK 1980 -1 JENKINS, L.
COMPUTATIONAL RESULTS WITH A TECHNIQUE OF PARAMETRIC MIXED INTEGER LINEAR PROGRAMMING.
JOHND 1972 -1 JOHNSON, E. L.
ON SHORTEST PATHS AND SORTING.
KARN 1978 -1 KARNEY, D.; KLINGMAN, D.
NETGEN REVISITED: A PROGRAM FOR GENERATING LARGE SCALE (UN) CAPACITATED ASSIGNMENT, TRANPORTATION, AND MINIMUM COST FLOW NETWORK PROBLEMS.
KLINA 1978 -1 KLINGMAN, D.; MOTE, J.; WHITMAN, D.
IMPROVING FLOW MANAGEMENT AND CONTROL VIA IMPROVING SHORTEST PATH ANALYSIS.
KRAR 1978 -1 KRARUP, J.; PRUZAN, P. M.
COMPUTER-AIDED LAYOUT DESIGN.
KUBA 1978 -1 KUBALE, M.; DABROWSKI, J.
EMPIRICAL COMPARISON OF EFFICIENCY OF SOME GRAPH COLOURING ALGORITHMS.
LAGE 1977 -1 LAGEWEG, B. J.; LENSTRA, J. K.; RINNOOY KAN, A. H. G.
JOB-SHOP SCHEDULING BY IMPLICIT ENUMERATION.
LAGE 1978 -1 LAGEWEG, B. J.; LENSTRA, J. K.; RINNOOY KAN, A. H. G.
GENERAL BOUNDING SCHEME FOR THE PERMUTATION FLOW-SHOP PROBLEM, A.
LAPOA 1978 -1 LAPORTE, G.; BIRON, J.; NOBERT, Y.
ROTATING SCHEDULES.
LEFK 1978 -1 LEFKOVITCH, L. P.
CLUSTER GENERATION AND GROUPING USING MATHEMATICAL PROGRAMMING.
LIEBA 1977 -1 LIEBMAN, J. S.; CHANARATNA, V.; KHACHATURIAN, N.
DISCRETE OPTIMIZATION IN STRUCTURAL DESIGN.
LUGAA 1979 -1 LUGACHEV, M. I.; SHUBINA, L. Y.
OPERATIVE PLANNING PROBLEM FOR A DISCRETE PRODUCTION PROCESS WITH REGARD TO EQUIPMENT READJUSTMENT (RUSSIAN), AN.
MAC E 1978 -1 MAC GINNIS, L. F.
IMPLEMENTATION AND TESTING OF A PRIMAL-DUAL ALGORITHM FOR ASSIGNMENT PROBLEM.
MAC I 1978 -1 MAC KEOWN, P. G.
SOME COMPUTATIONAL RESULTS OF USING THE AHRENS-FINKE METHOD FOR HANDLING DEGENERACY IN FIXED CHARGE TRANSPORTATION PROBLEMS.
MAIRA 1978 -1 MAIRS, T. G.; WAKEFIELD, G. W.; JOHNSON, E. L.; SPIELBERG, K.
ON A PRODUCTION ALLOCATION AND DISTRIBUTION PROBLEM.
MARTC 1978 -1 MARTELLO, S.; TOTH, P.
ALGORITHM 37. ALGORITHM FOR THE SOLUTION OF THE 0-1 SINGLE KNAPSACK PROBLEM.
MARUA 1977 -1 MARUYAMA, K.; CHANG, S. K.; TANG, D. T.
GENERAL PACKING ALGORITHM FOR MULTIDIMENSIONAL RESOURCE REQUIREMENTS, A.
MATTA 1977 -1 MATTHEISS, T. H.; RUBIN, D. S.
SURVEY AND COMPARISON OF METHODS FOR FINDING ALL VERTICES OF CONVEX POLYHEDRAL SETS, A.
MEHTA 1980 -1 MEHTA, N. K.
PERFORMANCE OF SELECTED GRAPH COLORING ALGORITHMS - EMPIRICAL RESULTS.
MEVE 1976 -1 MEVERT, P.; SUHL, U.
ALGORITHMS AND A COMPUTATIONAL STUDY FOR THE MULTIDIMENSIONAL KNAPSACK PROBLEM.
MILI 1978 -1 MILIOTIS, P.
USING CUTTING PLANES TO SOLVE THE SYMMETRIC TRAVELING SALESMAN PROBLEM.
MORT 1978 -1 MORTON, T. E.; BALA, G. D.
ALGORISTICS FOR SINGLE-MACHINE SEQUENCING WITH PRECEDENCE CONSTRAINTS.
MULV 1978 -2 MULVEY, J. M.
TESTING OF LARGE-SCALE NETWORK OPTIMIZATION PROGRAM.
MURPD 1978 -1 MURPHY, R. A.; SKITT, R. A.; SWEENEY, D. J.
HEURISTIC METHODS FOR THE MULTI-ITEM ACTIVITY SCHEDULING PROBLEM.
NABEA 1978 -1 NABESHIMA, I.; MARUYAMA, S.
ON N*M MEAN COMPLETION TIME FLOW SHOP PROBLEM. ANALYTICAL RESULTS, EXTENDED BRANCH AND BOUND ALGORITHM AND COMPUTATIONAL EXPERIENCE.
NARUB 1979 -1 NARULA, S. C.; KINDORF, J. R.
LINEAR 0-1 PROGRAMMING: A COMPARISON OF IMPLICIT ENUMERATION ALGORITHMS.
NOSH 1978 -1 NOSHITA, K.; MASUDA, E.; MACHIDA, H.
ON THE EXPECTED BEHAVIOURS OF THE DIJKSTRA'S SHORTEST PATH ALGORITHM FOR COMPLETE GRAPHS.
OKAM 1979 -1 OKAMURA, K.; YAMASHINA, H.
HEURISTIC ALGORITHM FOR THE ASSEMBLY LINE MODEL-MIX SEQUENCING PROBLEM TO MINIMIZE THE RISK OF STOPPING THE CONVEYOR, A.
PADBA 1980 -1 PADBERG, M. W.; HONG, S.
ON THE SYMMETRIC TRAVELLING SALESMAN PROBLEM: A COMPUTATIONAL STUDY.
PARK 1976 -1 PARKER, C. S.
EXPERIMENTAL INVESTIGATION OF SOME HEURISTIC STRATEGIES FOR COMPONENT PLACEMENT, AN.
PATT 1978 -1 PATTERSON, J. H.
BALASIAN-BASED ENUMERATION PROCEDURES: A STUDY IN COMPUTATION EFFICIENCY.
PINT 1978 -1 PINTO, P. A.; DANNENBERG, D. G.; KHUMAWALA, B. M.
HEURISTIC NETWORK PROCEDURE FOR THE ASSEMBLY LINE BALANCING PROBLEM, A.
PIRY 1979 -1 PIRYANOVICH, V. A.
COMPUTER EXPERIMENTS ON SOLVING INTEGER LINEAR PROGRAMMING PROBLEMS BY LOCALLY STOCHASTIC ALGORITHMS.
RAO B 1981 -1 RAO, R. C.; SHAFTEL, T. L.
CAPACITATED TRANSPORTATION PRODUCTION PROBLEM: COMPUTATIONAL EXPERIENCE, THE.
RARDB 1978 -1 RARDIN, R. L.; LIN, B. W.
WHAT MAKES INTEGER PROGRAMMING PROBLEMS HARD TO SOLVE: AN EMPIRICAL STUDY.
SHAF 1978 -1 SHAFTEL, T. L.
COMPUTATIONAL EXPERIENCE ON AN ALGORITHM FOR THE TRANSPORTATION PROBLEM WITH NON-LINEAR OBJECTIVE FUNCTIONS.
SMITH 1980 -1 SMITH, T. H. C.
LIFO IMPLICIT ENUMERATION ALGORITHM FOR THE ASYMMETRIC TRAVELLING SALESMAN PROBLEM USING A ONE-ARBORESCENCE RELAXATION, A.
SOYS 1978 -1 SOYSTER, A. L.; LEV, B.; SLIVKA, W.
ZERO-ONE PROGRAMMING WITH MANY VARIABLES AND FEW CONSTRAINTS.
SPAE 1978 -1 SPAETH, H.
EXPLIZITE LOESUNG DES DREIDIMENSIONALEN MINIMAX-STANDORTPROBLEMS IN DER CITY-BLOCK-DISTANZ.
STINA 1977 -1 STINSON, J. P.
HEURISTIC ALGORITHM FOR OBTAINING AN INITIAL SOLUTION FOR THE TRAVELING SALESMAN PROBLEM, A.
SUHL 1978 -1 SUHL, U.
ALGORITHM AND EFFICIENT DATA STRUCTURES FOR THE BINARY KNAPSACK PROBLEM, AN.
SUZU 1978 -1 SUZUKI, H.
GENERALIZED KNAPSACK PROBLEM WITH VARIABLE COEFFICIENTS, A.
VLIE 1978 -1 VLIET, D. VAN
IMPROVED SHORTEST PATH ALGORITHMS FOR TRANSPORT NETWORKS.

WASS 1978 -1 WASSENHOVE, L. N. VAN; GELDERS, L. F.
FOUR SOLUTION TECHNIQUES FOR A GENERAL ONE MACHINE SCHEDULING PROBLEM; A COMPARATIVE STUDY.
WHITC 1977 -1 WHITE, G. P.; WILLIAMS, T. A.
HEURISTIC SOLUTION TECHNIQUES FOR MULTIPLE TRIP TIME-CONSTRAINED TRAVELING SALESMAN PROBLEMS.
ZAK 1977 -1 ZAK, JU. A.
ON A CLASS OF INTEGER LINEAR PROGRAMMING PROBLEMS WITH BOOLEAN VARIABLES (RUSSIAN).
ZOLT 1978 -1 ZOLTNERS, A. A.
DIRECT DESCENT BINARY KNAPSACK ALGORITHM, A.

BARAB 1977 -1 BARAUSKAS, R. A.; VALANTINAS, I. I.
OPTIMAL CODING OF THE VERTICES OF AN UNDIRECTED GRAPH (RUSSIAN).

BARRB 1965 -1 BARRACLOUGH, E. D.
APPLICATION OF A DIGITAL COMPUTER TO THE CONSTRUCTION OF TIME-TABLES, THE.

BARTC 1978 -1 BARTNIK, W. G.
ALGORITHMES DE COUPLAGE DANS LES GRAPHES.

BELO 1977 -1 BELOGLA, G. N.; SKOROBOGATOV, V. A.
AUTOMATION SYSTEM FOR THE SOLUTION OF PROBLEMS ON GRAPHS (RUSSIAN), AN.

BIRD 1976 -1 BIRD, R.
PROGRAMS AND MACHINES. AN INTRODUCTION TO THE THEORY OF COMPUTING.

BRANA 1978 -1 BRANMAN, J.
SHORT COMMUNICATION. A NOTE ON PIVOTING IN TRANSPORTATION CODES.

BURKA 1980 -1 BURKARD, R. E.; DERIGS, U.
ASSIGNMENT AND MATCHING PROBLEMS: SOLUTION METHODS WITH FORTRAN-PROGRAMS.

CHIN 1978 -1 CHIN, F. Y.; HOUCK, D. J.
ALGORITHMS FOR UPDATING MINIMAL SPANNING TREES.

CONR 1978 -1 CONRADT, D.
EFFIZIENTE IMPLEMENTIERUNG DES VERFAHRENS VON EDMONDS ZUR BESTIMMUNG EINES MAXIMALEN MATCHING, EINE.

DENAA 1978 -1 DENARDO, E. V.; FOX, B. L.
BUCKETS, SHORTEST PATHS, AND INTEGER PROGRAMMING.

DERIC 1979 -1 DERIGS, U.; ZIMMERMANN, U.
AUGMENTING PATH METHOD FOR SOLVING LINEAR BOTTLENECK TRANSPORTATION PROBLEMS, AN.

DESR 1978 -1 DESROCHES, S.; LAPORTE, G.; ROUSSEAU, J.-M.
HOREX: A COMPUTER PROGRAM FOR THE CONSTRUCTION OF EXAMINATION SCHEDULES.

DIAL 1980 -1 DIAL, R.; GLOVER, F.; KARNEY, D.; KLINGMAN, D.
SHORTEST PATH FOREST WITH TOPOLOGICAL ORDERING: AN ALGORITHM DESCRIPTION IN SDL.

EBER 1980 -1 EBERT, J.
FINDING SPANNING FORESTS: A PROBLEM OF DATA MANIPULATION.

EDMOA 1978 -1 EDMONDS, J.; JOHNSON, E. L.; LOCKHART, S. C.
BLOSSOM I: A COMPUTER CODE FOR THE MATCHING PROBLEM.

FIDR 1978 -1 FIDRMUC, M.
SIMSCRIPT II SIMULATION OF TRAFFIC NETWORK FLOW.

FINKA 1978 -1 FINKE, G.; AHRENS, J. H.
VARIANT OF THE PRIMAL TRANSPORTATION ALGORITHM, A.

GARS 1980 -1 GARSIDE, G. R.; PINTELAS, P. E.
ALGOL 68 PACKAGE FOR IMPLEMENTING GRAPH ALGORITHMS, AN.

GRIGE 1978 -1 GRIGORIADIS, M. D.
ALGORITHMS FOR THE MINIMUM COST SINGLE AND MULTICOMMODITY NETWORK FLOW PROBLEMS.

HAMA 1979 -2 HAMACHER, H.
NUMERICAL INVESTIGATIONS ON THE MAXIMAL FLOW ALGORITHM OF KARZANOV.

HART 1975 -1 HARTIGAN, J. A.
CLUSTERING ALGORITHMS.

HAUS 1980 -1 HAUSMANN, D.
ADJACENCY ON POLYTOPES IN COMBINATORIAL OPTIMIZATION.

HESS 1977 -1 HESSELBACH, J.; WIJNANDS, J.
DYNAMISCHE PROGRAMMIERUNG - METHODIK, EDV-PROGRAMM, ANWENDUNGSBEISPIEL.

HILL 1978 -1 HILL, E. JR.
COMPARATIVE STUDY OF VERY LARGE DATA BASES, A.

HUET 1978 -1 HUET, G.
ALGORITHM TO GENERATE THE BASIS OF SOLUTIONS TO HOMOGENEOUS LINEAR DIOPHANTINE EQUATIONS, AN.

HULM 1978 -1 HULME, B.; WISNIEWSKI, J. A.
COMPARISON OF SHORTEST PATH ALGORITHMS APPPLIED TO SPARSE GRAPHS, A.

JOHNF 1978 -1 JOHNSON, E. L.; POWELL, S.
INTEGER PROGRAMMING CODES.

KANG 1977 -1 KANG, A. N. C.; LEE, R. C. T.; CHANG, C.-L.; CHANG, S. K.
STORAGE REDUCTION THROUGH MINIMAL SPANNING TREES AND SPANNING FORESTS.

KARN 1978 -1 KARNEY, D.; KLINGMAN, D.
NETGEN REVISITED: A PROGRAM FOR GENERATING LARGE SCALE (UN) CAPACITATED ASSIGNMENT, TRANPORTATION, AND MINIMUM COST FLOW NETWORK PROBLEMS.

KIKUA 1979 -1 KIKUST, P. B.
ORGANIZATION OF SORTING IN THE SEARCH FOR THE MAXIMUM CLIQUE OF A GRAPH (RUSSIAN).

KLINA 1978 -1 KLINGMAN, D.; MOTE, J.; WHITMAN, D.
IMPROVING FLOW MANAGEMENT AND CONTROL VIA IMPROVING SHORTEST PATH ANALYSIS.

KONY 1978 -1 KONYA, I.; SOMOGYI, P.; SZABADOS, T.
METHOD OF TIME-TABLE CONSTRUCTION BY COMPUTER, A.

KOSA 1978 -1 KOSARAJU, S. R.
INSERTIONS AND DELETIONS IN ONE-SIDED HEIGHT-BALANCED TREES.

KUCH 1978 -1 KUCHARCZYK, J.
METHODS OF CLUSTER ANALYSIS AND THEIR ALGORITHMS IN THE PROGRAMMING LANGUAGE ALGOL 60. 1: HIERARCHICAL AGGLOMERATIVE METHODS.

KUCH 1978 -2 KUCHARCZYK, J.
METHODS OF CLUSTER ANALYSIS AND THEIR ALGORITHMS IN THE PROGRAMMING LANGUAGE ALGOL 60. 3: METHODS BASED ON A GIVEN ORDERING OF OBJECTS.

KUCH 1978 -3 KUCHARCZYK, J.
METHODS OF CLUSTER ANALYSIS AND THEIR REALIZATION IN THE PROGRAMMING LANGUAGE ALGOL 60. 2: HIERARCHICAL DIVISIVE METHODS DUE TO HUBERT.

LANDA 1979 -1 LAND, A.; POWELL, S.
COMPUTER CODES FOR PROBLEMS OF INTEGER PROGRAMMING.

LAUR 1978 -1 LAURIERE, J. L.
LANGUAGE AND A PROGRAM FOR STATING AND SOLVING COMBINATORIAL PROBLEMS, A.

LAWRB 1973 -1 LAWRIE, N.; VEITCH, H.
TIME-TABLING IN SECONDARY SCHOOLS - A STUDY OF MANUAL AND COMPUTER METHODS.

LUEK 1975 -1 LUEKER, G. S.
EFFICIENT ALGORITHMS FOR CHORDAL GRAPHS AND INTERVAL GRAPHS.

MAND 1978 -1 MANDL, C. E.
ALGORITHMS AND COMPUTER PROGRAMS IN DETERMINISTIC NETWORK OPTIMIZATION APPLIED TO PUBLIC SYSTEMS.

MARTC 1978 -1 MARTELLO, S.; TOTH, P.
ALGORITHM 37. ALGORITHM FOR THE SOLUTION OF THE 0-1 SINGLE KNAPSACK PROBLEM.

MEHL 1978 -1 MEHLHORN, K.
EFFIZIENTE ALGORITHMEN: EIN BEISPIEL.

MILI 1976 -1 MILIOTIS, P.
ALL-INTEGER ARITHMETIC LP-CUTTING PLANES CODE APPLIED TO THE TRAVELLING SALESMAN PROBLEM, AN.

MUKA 1979 -1 MUKAWA, H.; OKAMOTO, Y.; SORIMACHI, Y.; TAMAI, T.
IMPLEMENTATION OF THE HEURISTIC MIXED INTEGER PROGRAM TO THE MATHEMATICAL PROGRAMMING SYSTEM.

NTAF 1979 -1 NTAFOS, S. C.; HAKIMI, S. L.
ON PATH COVER PROBLEMS IN DIGRAPHS AND APPLICATIONS TO PROGRAM TESTING.

PABS 1978 -1 PABST, R.
VERWENDUNGSMOEGLICHKEITEN DER EXTERNEN SPEICHERMEDIEN VON EDV-ANLAGEN BEI DER LOESUNG BESTIMMTER AUFGABEN DER DISKRETEN OPTIMIERUNG.

PAPEA 1979 -1 PAPE, U.; BOHM, H.-J.; RIEGER, A.
ANWENDUNGSSYSTEM ZUR ERSTELLUNG EINES STAUPLANES FUER CONTAINERSCHIFFE, EIN.

PEET 1979 -1 PEETERS, H.
EMPIRISCHER LEISTUNGSVERGLEICH DER KOMMERZIELLEN SOFTWARESYSTEME APEX III, EMPS UND MPSX-MIP/370 BEI GEMISCH-GANZZAHLIGEN OPTIMIERUNGSPROBLEMEN.

PERI 1980 -1 PERIN, C.
USER'S GUIDE TO MATCOV.

PIPP 1977 -1 PIPPENGER, N.
FAST SIMULATION OF COMBINATIONAL LOGIC NETWORKS BY MACHINES WITHOUT RANDOM-ACCESS STORAGE.

POWEA 1978 -1 POWER, L. R.
INTERNAL SORTING USING A MINIMAL TREE MERGE STRATEGY.

RARDB 1980 -1 RARDIN, R. L.; LIN, B. W.
RIP RANDOM INTEGER PROGRAMMING TEST PROBLEM GENERATOR, THE.

ROHL 1978 -1 ROHL, J. S.
GENERATING PERMUTATIONS BY CHOOSING.

ROSEB 1977 -1 ROSENBERG, A. L.; SNYDER, L.
BOUNDS ON THE COSTS OF DATA ENCODINGS.

ROY A 1978 -1 ROY, M. K.
EVALUATION OF PERMUTATION ALGORITHMS.

SCHEA 1979 -2 SCHEITHAUER, G.; TERNO, J.
TSPE - AN ALGOL PROCEDURE FOR SOLVING THE TRAVELING SALESMAN PROBLEM.

SHEPA 1979 -1 SHEPHERD, R. A.; HIRSHFIELD, D. S.
SOFTWARE SUPPORT FOR COMBINATORIAL OPTIMIZATION.

SLAT 1978 -1 SLATE, L.; SPIELBERG, K.
EXTENDED CONTROL LANGUAGE OF MPSX/370 AND POSSIBLE APPLICATIONS, THE.

SPIEA 1980 -1 SPIELBERG, K.; SUHL, U.
EXPERIMENTAL SOFTWARE SYSTEM FOR LARGE SCALE 0-1 PROBLEMS WITH EFFICIENT DATA STRUCTURES AND ACCESS TO MPSX/370, AN.

SUHL 1978 -1 SUHL, U.
ALGORITHM AND EFFICIENT DATA STRUCTURES FOR THE BINARY KNAPSACK PROBLEM, AN.

SUHL 1978 -2 SUHL, U.
IMPLEMENTATIONSTECHNIKEN FUER EINEN BRANCH-AND-BOUND-ALGORITHMUS ZUR LOESUNG VON (0-1)-PROGRAMMEN.

SYSL 1977 -2 SYSLO, M. M.
LINEAR TIME ALGORITHM FOR CODING OUTERPLANAR GRAPHS.

SYSLA 1976 -1 SYSLO, M. M.; IRI, M.
EFFICIENT OUTERPLANARITY TESTING.

TAI 1979 -1 TAI, K.-C.
TREE-TO-TREE CORRECTION PROBLEM, THE.

TROJ 1978 -1 TROJANOWSKI, A. E.
RANKING AND LISTING ALGORITHMS FOR K-ARY TREES.

COVERING

AKIY 1978 -1 AKIYAMA, J.; ERA, H.; KANEKO, K.; SAITO, T.; SATO, I.
PACKING AND COVERING IN GRAPHS (JAPANESE).

AKIYA 1980 -1 AKIYAMA, J.; EXOO, G.; HARARY, F.
COVERING AND PACKING IN GRAPHS. III: CYCLIC AND ACYCLIC INVARIANTS.

AKOP 1979 -1 AKOPJAN, G. C.; GALSTJAN, D. A.
CLASSES OF GRAPHS THAT ARE CRITICAL WITH RESPECT TO COVERINGS (RUSSIAN).

ARORB 1977 -1 ARORA, S. R.; PURI, M. C.; SWARUP, K.
SET COVERING PROBLEM WITH LINEAR FRACTIONAL FUNCTIONAL, THE.

AVIS 1980 -1 AVIS, D.
NOTE ON SOME COMPUTATIONALLY DIFFICULT SET COVERING PROBLEMS, A.

BAKED 1980 -1 BAKER, E.; FISHER, M.
COMPUTATIONAL RESULTS FOR VERY LARGE AIR CREW SCHEDULING PROBLEMS.

BALAA 1980 -1 BALAS, E.
CUTTING PLANES FROM CONDITIONAL BOUNDS: A NEW APPROACH TO SET COVERING.

BALAA 1979 -4 BALAS, E.
SET COVERING WITH CUTTING PLANES FROM CONDITIONAL BOUNDS.

BALAD 1980 -1 BALAS, E.; HO, A. C.
SET COVERING ALGORITHMS USING CUTTING PLANES, HEURISTICS, AND SUBGRADIENT OPTIMIZATION: A COMPUTATIONAL STUDY.

BALAJ 1974 -1 BALAS, E.; SAMUELSSON, H.
FINDING A MINIMUM NODE COVER IN AN ARBITRARY GRAPH. II: THE WEIGHTED CASE.

BALAK 1978 -1 BALAS, E.; ZEMEL, E.
FACETS OF THE KNAPSACK POLYTOPE FROM MINIMAL COVERS.

BART 1979 -1 BARTHOLDI, J. J. III
GUARANTEED-ACCURACY ROUND-OFF ALGORITHM FOR CYCLIC SCHEDULING AND SET COVERING, A.

BROU 1979 -1 BROUWER, A. E.; SCHRIJVER, A.
UNIFORM HYPERGRAPHS.

CHRIE 1979 -1 CHRISTOFIDES, N.; HEY, A.
GRAPH COVERING RELAXATIONS OF THE SET-COVERING PROBLEM - PART I.

CHUN 1980 -1 CHUNG, F. R. K.
ON THE COVERINGS OF GRAPHS.

CHVA 1979 -1 CHVATAL, V.
GREEDY HEURISTIC FOR THE SET-COVERING PROBLEM, A.

CORNE 1980 -1 CORNUEJOLS, G.; THIZY, J.-M.
LOCATION PROBLEMS, SET COVERING PROBLEMS AND THE GREEDY ALGORITHM.

DRIS 1979 -1 DRISCOLL, W. C.; EMMONS, H.
VEHICLE ROUTING FOR MINIMUM COST.

EDWAA 1980 -1 EDWARDS, G. R.
APPROACH TO THE CREW SCHEDULING PROBLEM, AN.

FANI 1977 -1 FANICA, G.
TESTING FOR EQUALITY BETWEEN MAXIMUM MATCHING AND MINIMUM NODE COVERING.

FRANB 1979 -1 FRANK, A.
COVERING BRANCHINGS.

FRIDB 1977 -1 FRIDMAN, G. S.
TWO PROBLEMS ON THE COVERING GRAPHS (RUSSIAN).

GAVR 1977 -2 GAVRIL, F.
TESTING FOR EQUALITY BETWEEN MAXIMUM MATCHING AND MINIMUM NODE COVERING.

GIANO 1977 -1 GIANNESSI, G.
CONTINUED FRACTIONS AND EXPLICIT SOLUTIONS OF A PARTICULAR DISCRETE OPTIMIZATION PROBLEM.

GIMO 1979 -1 GIMOURGINAS, C.; KARWAN, M. H.
COMPUTATIONAL RESULTS OF THE P-MEDIAN AND SET COVERING PROBLEMS FOR AN AMBULANCE LOCATION STUDY IN THE CITY OF BUFFALO.

GOND 1977 -1 GONDRAN, M.
ALGORITHME DE COUPES EN PROGRAMMATION EN NOMBRES ENTIERS, UN.

GRANA 1980 -1 GRANOT, D.; GRANOT, F.
GENERALIZED COVERING RELAXATION FOR 0-1 PROGRAMS.

GRANA 1980 -2 GRANOT, D.; GRANOT, F.
MINIMAL COVERS, EXTENSIONS OF MINIMAL COVERS AND FACETS OF A POSYNOMIAL INEQUALITY IN 0-1 VARIABLES.

GRANC 1980 -1 GRANOT, D.; GRANOT, F.; VAESSEN, W.
ACCELERATED COVERING RELAXATION ALGORITHM FOR SOLVING 0-1 POSITIVE POLYNOMIAL PROGRAMS, AN.

GRIE 1980 -1 GRIESSHABER, R.
MODEL FOR CREW SCHEDULING FOR A SHORT HAUL FLEET.

GRIN 1977 -1 GRINSTEAD, G. M.
ON COVERINGS AND PACKINGS OF THE COMPLETE GRAPH WITH CYCLES.

GROED 1981 -1 GROETSCHEL, M.; LOVASZ, L.; SCHRIJVER, A.
ELLIPSOID METHOD AND ITS CONSEQUENCES IN COMBINATORIAL OPTIMIZATION, THE.

GROSA 1978 -1 GROSZ, M.
GENERALIZATION OF THE ASSIGNMENT PROBLEM AND ITS SOLUTION (HUNGARIAN), THE.

GUBA 1977 -1 GUBA, W.
MAXIMALER LOKALER ALGORITHMUS FUER KLASSEN UNVERKUERZBARER UEBERDECKUNGEN, EIN.

GUPTD 1966 -2 GUPTA, R. P.
THEOREM ON THE COVER INDEX OF AN S-GRAPH, A.

HAMMH 1978 -1 HAMMOND, P.
Q-COVERINGS AND COMPLETELY REGULAR CODES IN DISTANCE-REGULAR GRAPHS.

HARA 1970 -1 HARARY, F.
COVERING AND PACKING IN GRAPHS, I.

HIRA 1979 -1 HIRATA, T.; MAROUOKA, A.; KIMURA, M.
POLYNOMIAL TIME ALGORITHM TO FIND A PATH COVER OF A REDUCIBLE FLOW GRAPH (JAPANESE), A.

HO 1979 -1 HO, A. C.
WORST CASE ANALYSIS OF A CLASS OF SET COVERING HEURISTICS.

HOCH 1980 -1 HOCHBAUM, D.
APPROXIMATION ALGORITHMS FOR THE WEIGHTED SET COVERING AND NODE COVER PROBLEMS.

HOED 1979 -1 HOEDE, C.
ZWIEBELSTRUKTUREN EINIGER KLASSEN VON KOMBINATORISCHEN UND GRAPHENTHEORETISCHEN PROBLEMEN, DIE.

HSU B 1979 -1 HSU, W.-L.; NEMHAUSER, G. L.
ALGORITHMS FOR MINIMUM COVERINGS BY CLIQUES AND MAXIMUM CLIQUES IN CLAW-FREE PERFECT GRAPHS.

ISHIB 1979 -1 ISHII, H.; NISHIDA, T.; DAINO, A.
FRACTIONAL SET COVERING PROBLEMS.

JOHND 1979 -2 JOHNSON, E. L.
SUBADDITIVE LIFTING METHODS FOR PARTITIONING AND KNAPSACK PROBLEMS.

KINB 1980 -1 KINBER, E. B.
POLYNOMIAL ALGORITHM FOR FINDING MINIMAL VERTEX COVERINGS FOR A CLASS OF PLANAR GRAPHS (RUSSIAN), A.

KLEM 1978 -1 KLEMYSEV, O. F.
SOME COVERING PROBLEMS (ALGORITHMS WITH POWER ESTIMATES).

KOMA 1979 -1 KOMAR, J.; LOS, J.
KOENIG THEOREM IN THE INFINITE CASE (EXTENDED ABSTRACT).

KRAV 1979 -1 KRAVETS, V. L.
CONCERNING THE SOLUTION OF A CLASS OF COVERING PROBLEMS BY DISCRETE OPTIMIZATION METHODS (RUSSIAN).

KRISA 1979 -1 KRISHNAMOORTHY, M. S.; DEO, N.
COMPLEXITY OF THE MINIMUM-DUMMY-ACTIVITIES PROBLEM IN A PERT NETWORK.

KUZJ 1979 -1 KUZJURIN, N. N.
QUELQUES ESTIMATIONS RECURRENTES ET ASYMPTOTIQUES DANS LE PROBLEME DE RECOUVREMENTS (RUSSIAN).

LAVA 1979 -1 LAVALLEE, I.
RECTANGLES MAXIMAUX DANS UNE RELATION BINAIRE QUELCONQUE.

LENSA 1979 -2 LENSTRA, J. K.; RINNOOY KAN, A. H. G.
COMPLEXITY OF PACKING, COVERING AND PARTITIONING PROBLEMS.

LENSA 1980 -5 LENSTRA, J. K.; RINNOOY KAN, A. H. G.
THEORIE DE LA COMPLEXITE DE CALCUL APPLIQUEE AUX PROBLEMES DE COUPLAGE, RECOUVREMENT ET PARTITIONNEMENT.

LIHO 1976 -1 LIHOLAT, N. A.
PROBLEM ON THE COVERING OF A GRAPH BY A MINIMAL POWER SET (RUSSIAN), A.

MEIR 1978 -1 MEIR, A.
ON TOTAL COVERING AND MATCHING OF GRAPHS.

MILLD 1979 -1 MILLS, W. H.
COVERING DESIGNS I: COVERINGS BY A SMALL NUMBER OF SUBSETS.

MINI 1978 -1 MINIEKA, E.
OPTIMIZATION ALGORITHMS FOR NETWORKS AND GRAPHS.

MULD 1979 -1 MULDER, H. M.
RAMSEY THEORY.

MULV 1979 -1 MULVEY, J. M.
TESTING OF A NETWORK RELAXATION METHOD FOR 0-1 SET-PARTITIONING AND SET COVERING.

MURT 1981 -1 MURTY, K. G.; PERIN, C.
EDGE COVERING ALGORITHMS AND THEIR APPLICATIONS.

NATA 1979 -1 NATALI, L.; NICOLETTI, B.; SCALAS, M. R.
MANPOWER STAFFING AT AN AIRPORT: A GENERALIZED SET COVERING PROBLEM.

NTAF 1979 -1 NTAFOS, S. C.; HAKIMI, S. L.
ON PATH COVER PROBLEMS IN DIGRAPHS AND APPLICATIONS TO PROGRAM TESTING.

ORLI 1977 -1 ORLIN, J. B.
CONTENTMENT IN GRAPH THEORY: COVERING GRAPHS WITH CLIQUES.

OXLE 1978 -1 OXLEY, J. G.
COCIRCUIT COVERINGS AND PACKINGS FOR BINARY MATROIDS.

OXLE 1978 -2 OXLEY, J. G.
COLORING, PACKING AND THE CRITICAL PROBLEM.

PADB 1979 -1 PADBERG, M. W.
COVERING, PACKING AND KNAPSACK PROBLEMS.

PAYA 1978 -2 PAYAN, C.
COVERINGS BY MINIMAL TRANSVERSALS.

PERI 1980 -1 PERIN, C.
USER'S GUIDE TO MATCOV.

PERI 1981 -1 PERIN, C.
ON THE POLYTOPE OF THE 1-MATCHING/COVERING PROBLEM.

PERI 1981 -2 PERIN, C.
1-MATCHING/COVERING PROBLEM, THE.

PROT 1977 -1 PROTASOV, I. V.; TRETJAK, V. P.; CHARIN, V. S.
OPTIMIZATION PROBLEM CONNECTED WITH COVERINGS (RUSSIAN), AN.

PROT 1979 -1 PROTASOV, I. V.; TRETJAK, V. P.; CHARIN, V. S.
ON THE COVERING PROBLEM (RUSSIAN).

PULL 1977 -1 PULLEYBLANK, W. R.
LINEAR PROGRAMMING RELAXATION OF THE NODE PACKING PROBLEM OR 2-BICRITICAL GRAPHS AND NODE COVERS, A.

RIVI 1978 -1 RIVIERE, M.
RECOUVREMENT DES SOMMETS D'UN GRAPHE PLANAIRE PAR DES ARETES ET DES STABLES.

SAHNB 1975 -1 SAHNI, S.; GONZALEZ, T.
P-COMPLETE APPROXIMATION PROBLEMS.

SALK 1975 -1 SALKIN, H. M.
INTEGER PROGRAMMING.

SANI 1979 -1 SANIKIDZE, D. O.
ALGORITHM FOR FINDING THE SHORTEST COVERING USING THE COLORING OF NONORIENTED GRAPHS IN SOLVING SOME PROBLEMS OF MINIMIZATION (RUSSIAN), AN.

SAPOA 1977 -1 SAPOZENKO, A. A.; ASRATJAN, A. S.; KUZJURIN, N. N.
SURVEY OF SOME RESULTS IN COVERING PROBLEMS (RUSSIAN), A.

SCHMA 1978 -1 SCHMID, H. J.
GEOMETRICAL INTERPRETATION OF THE HUNGARIAN METHOD, A.

SCHRC 1981 -1 SCHREUDER, J. A. M.
APPLICATION OF A LOCATION MODEL TO FIRE STATIONS IN ROTTERDAM.

SCHRO 1979 -1 SCHRIJVER, A.
FRACTIONAL PACKING AND COVERING.

SERV 1975 -1 SERVIT, M.
HEURISTIC METHOD FOR SOLVING WEIGHTED SET COVERING PROBLEMS, A.

SZAM 1979 -2 SZAMKOLOWICZ, L.
SOME REMARKS ON HYPERGRAPHS OF VERTEX COVERINGS FOR SIMPLE GRAPHS WITHOUT LOOPS.

TERA 1979 -1 TERADA, R.
POLYNOMIAL TIME ALGORITHMS FOR NP-HARD PROBLEMS WHICH ARE OPTIMAL OR NEAR-OPTIMAL WITH PROBABILITY ONE.

TING 1979 -1 TINGLEY, G. A.
STILL ANOTHER SOLUTION METHOD FOR THE MONTHLY AIRCREW ASSIGNMENT PROBLEM.

TOME 1980 -1 TOMESCU, I.
SOME PROPERTIES OF IRREDUCIBLE COVERINGS BY CLIQUES OF COMPLETE MULTIPARTITE GRAPHS.

USTY 1979 -1 USTYUZHANINOV, V. G.
QUELQUES PROPRIETES DES RECOUVREMENTS DE TABLES BINAIRES (RUSSIAN).

VERC 1978 -1 VERCELLIS, C.
ENUMERATIVE ALGORITHM FOR COVERING PROBLEMS, AN.

VIDY 1978 -1 VIDYASANKAR, K.
COVERING THE EDGE SET OF A DIRECTED GRAPH WITH TREES.

VOLP 1980 -1 VOLPENTESTA, A.
EQUI-ASSIGNMENTS AND EXPLICIT SOLUTIONS OF A PARTICULAR DISCRETE OPTIMIZATION PROBLEM.

COVERING
****

WALS 1976 -1 WALSH, A. M.
POLYNOMIAL ALGORITHMS FOR CERTAIN GRAPH-THEORETIC PROBLEMS.
WALSA 1977 -1 WALSH, A. M.; BURKHARD, W. A.
EFFICIENT ALGORITHMS FOR (3,1) GRAPHS.
WERR 1978 -2 WERRA, D. DE
NESTED COVERINGS IN BIPARTITE MULTIGRAPHS.
ZORY 1977 -1 ZORYCHTA, K.
ON CONVERTING THE 0-1 LINEAR PROGRAMMING PROBLEM TO A SET-COVERING PROBLEM.
ZUEV 1979 -1 ZUEV, YU. A.
SET-COVERING PROBLEM: THE COMBINATORIAL-LOCAL APPROACH AND BRANCH AND BOUND METHOD (RUSSIAN).

ARMSA 1979 -1 ARMSTRONG, R. D.; CHARNES, A.; PHILLIPS, F.
PAGE CUTS FOR INTEGER INTERVAL LINEAR PROGRAMMING.
BACHE 1980 -1 BACHEM, A.; SCHRADER, R.
MINIMAL INEQUALITIES AND SUBADDITIVE DUALITY.
BALAA 1976 -1 BALAS, E.
DISJUNCTIVE CUT FOR SET PARTITIONING, A.
BALAA 1980 -1 BALAS, E.
CUTTING PLANES FROM CONDITIONAL BOUNDS: A NEW APPROACH TO SET COVERING.
BALAA 1979 -2 BALAS, E.
DISJUNCTIVE PROGRAMMING.
BALAA 1979 -4 BALAS, E.
SET COVERING WITH CUTTING PLANES FROM CONDITIONAL BOUNDS.
BALAD 1980 -1 BALAS, E.; HO, A. C.
SET COVERING ALGORITHMS USING CUTTING PLANES, HEURISTICS, AND SUBGRADIENT OPTIMIZATION: A COMPUTATIONAL STUDY.
BALAE 1980 -1 BALAS, E.; JEROSLOW, R. G.
STRENGTHENING CUTS FOR MIXED INTEGER PROGRAMS.
BALAJ 1974 -2 BALAS, E.; SAMUELSSON, H.
SYMMETRIC SUBGRADIENT CUTTING PLANE METHOD FOR SET PARTITIONING, A.
BALAK 1977 -3 BALAS, E.; ZEMEL, E.
SOLVING LARGE ZERO-ONE KNAPSACK PROBLEMS (REVISED VERSION).
BAZAC 1979 -1 BAZARAA, M. S.; SHERALI, H. D.
CUTTING PLANE METHODS FOR THE QUADRATIC ASSIGNMENT PROBLEM.
BELL 1979 -1 BELL, D. E.
EFFICIENT GROUP CUTS FOR INTEGER PROGRAMS.
BERS 1973 -2 BERSHCHANSKII, JA. M.
ON THE CONVERGENCE OF A MODIFICATION OF THE CUTTING PLANE METHOD (RUSSIAN).
BLAI 1974 -1 BLAIR, C. E.
EXTENSIONS OF SUBADDITIVE FUNCTIONS USED IN CUTTING PLANE THEORY.
BLAI 1980 -1 BLAIR, C. E.
FACIAL DISJUNCTIVE PROGRAMS AND SEQUENCES OF CUTTING-PLANES.
BLAI 1975 -2 BLAIR, C. E.
TOPICS IN INTEGER PROGRAMMING.
BLAIA 1980 -1 BLAIR, C. E.; JEROSLOW, R. G.
VALUE FUNCTION OF AN INTEGER PROGRAM, THE.
BOLW 1979 -1 BOLWELL, S. G.; KARWAN, M. H.
EFFICIENT USE OF SURROGATE DUALITY IN 0-1 INTEGER PROGRAMMING.
BOLW 1979 -2 BOLWELL, S. G.; KARWAN, M. H.
HYBRID SURROGATE DUAL-CUTTING PLANE APPROACH TO INTEGER PROGRAMMING, A.
BURD 1972 -1 BURDET, C.-A.
ALGEBRA AND GEOMETRY OF INTEGER PROGRAMMING CUTS: A COMBINED APPROACH, THE.
CHAND 1980 -2 CHANDRA, S.; CHANDRAMOHAN, M.
NOTE ON INTEGER LINEAR FRACTIONAL PROGRAMMING, A.
CHERE 1978 -1 CHERVAK, JU. JU.
RECURRENCE ALGORITHM FOR THE METHOD OF CUTS AND THE METHOD OF BRANCH-AND-BOUND (RUSSIAN), A.
CHEU 1978 -1 CHEUNG, T.-Y.
STEPPING-STONE PARALLEL-CUT METHOD FOR INTEGER PROGRAMMING, A.
CHRIH 1978 -1 CHRISTOFIDES, N.; WHITLOCK, C.
GRAPH CONNECTIVITY AND VULNERABILITY, A SURVEY.
DUCA 1980 -1 DUCA, D.
ON THE HIERARCHY OF THE EXTREMAL SOLUTIONS OF A FRACTIONAL PROGRAMMING PROBLEM (ROMANIAN).
FERS 1979 -1 FERSTER, V. B.
EFFECTIVELY DECREASING ALGORITHMS OF THE CUTTING PLANE METHOD FOR THE SOLUTION OF INTEGER PROGRAMMING PROBLEMS (RUSSIAN).
GALLE 1975 -1 GALLO, G.; SIMEONE, B.
NEW CUTS FOR INTEGER PROGRAMMING VIA GROUP OPTIMIZATION.
GOND 1977 -1 GONDRAN, M.
ALGORITHME DE COUPES EN PROGRAMMATION EN NOMBRES ENTIERS, UN.
GRANA 1980 -1 GRANOT, D.; GRANOT, F.
GENERALIZED COVERING RELAXATION FOR 0-1 PROGRAMS.
GRANB 1979 -1 GRANOT, D.; GRANOT, F.; KALLBERG, J.
COVERING RELAXATION FOR POSITIVE 0-1 POLYNOMIAL PROGRAMS.
GRANC 1980 -1 GRANOT, D.; GRANOT, F.; VAESSEN, W.
ACCELERATED COVERING RELAXATION ALGORITHM FOR SOLVING 0-1 POSITIVE POLYNOMIAL PROGRAMS, AN.
GROEB 1981 -1 GROETSCHEL, M.
APPROACHES TO HARD COMBINATORIAL OPTIMIZATION PROBLEMS.
GROEB 1980 -2 GROETSCHEL, M.
ON THE SYMMETRIC TRAVELLING SALESMAN PROBLEM: SOLUTION OF 120-CITY PROBLEM.
GUIGA 1978 -2 GUIGNARD, M.; SPIELBERG, K.
EXPERIMENTAL INTERACTIVE SYSTEM FOR INTEGER PROGRAMMING, AN.
HABE 1978 -1 HABENICHT, W.
ZUM EINSATZ ENUMERATIVER SCHNITTEBENENVERFAHREN IN B&B-SYSTEMEN.
HRAM 1979 -1 HRAMOVA, N. K.
SOME GENERALIZATIONS OF THE CUTTING PLANE METHOD (RUSSIAN).
ISHIA 1976 -1 ISHII, H.; IBARAKI, T.; MINE, H.
PRIMAL CUTTING PLANE ALGORITHM FOR INTEGER FRACTIONAL PROGRAMMING PROBLEMS, A.
JEROB 1978 -1 JEROSLOW, R. G.
CUTTING PLANE THEORY: ALGEBRAIC METHODS.
JEROB 1979 -1 JEROSLOW, R. G.
INTRODUCTION TO THE THEORY OF CUTTING-PLANES, AN.
JEROB 1980 -1 JEROSLOW, R. G.
CUTTING-PLANE GAME FOR FACIAL DISJUNCTIVE PROGRAMS, A.
JEROB 1978 -2 JEROSLOW, R. G.
CUTTING-PLANES FOR COMPLEMENTARITY CONSTRAINTS.
JEROB 1979 -2 JEROSLOW, R. G.
MINIMAL INEQUALITIES.
JEROB 1978 -3 JEROSLOW, R. G.
SOME BASIC THEOREMS FOR INTEGRAL MONOIDS.
JEROB 1979 -3 JEROSLOW, R. G.
THEORY OF CUTTING-PLANES, THE.
JOHND 1980 -1 JOHNSON, E. L.
INTEGER PROGRAMMING, FACETS, SUBADDITIVITY, AND DUALITY FOR GROUP AND SEMI-GROUP PROBLEMS.
JOHNG 1980 -1 JOHNSON, E. L.; SUHL, U.
EXPERIMENTS IN INTEGER PROGRAMMING.
KALI 1979 -1 KALISZEWSKI, I.; WALUKIEWICZ, S.
TIGHTER EQUIVALENT FORMULATIONS OF INTEGER PROGRAMMING PROBLEMS.

KLEIB 1979 -1 KLEIN, D.; HOLM, S.
INTEGER PROGRAMMING POST-OPTIMAL ANALYSIS WITH CUTTING PLANES.
LAPOB 1980 -1 LAPORTE, G.; NOBERT, Y.
CUTTING PLANES ALGORITHM FOR THE M-SALESMEN PROBLEM, A.
LEV 1978 -1 LEV, B.; SOYSTER, A. L.
INTEGER PROGRAMMING WITH BOUNDED VARIABLES VIA CANONICAL SEPARATION.
LINK 1979 -1 LINKS, G.; RUBIN, D. S.
FINITE PRIMAL CUTTING PLANE ALGORITHMS FOR INTEGER PROGRAMS.
MILI 1976 -1 MILIOTIS, P.
ALL-INTEGER ARITHMETIC LP-CUTTING PLANES CODE APPLIED TO THE TRAVELLING SALESMAN PROBLEM, AN.
MILI 1978 -1 MILIOTIS, P.
USING CUTTING PLANES TO SOLVE THE SYMMETRIC TRAVELING SALESMAN PROBLEM.
MOORA 1980 -1 MOORE, T. G.
CENTRAL CUTTING PLANE ALGORITHM FOR INTEGER PROGRAMMING, A.
PADBA 1980 -1 PADBERG, M. W.; HONG, S.
ON THE SYMMETRIC TRAVELLING SALESMAN PROBLEM: A COMPUTATIONAL STUDY.
PADBB 1979 -1 PADBERG, M. W.; RAO, M. R.
ODD MINIMUM CUT-SETS AND B-MATCHINGS.
PICAA 1980 -1 PICARD, J.-C.; RATLIFF, H. D.
CUT APPROACH TO A CLASS OF QUADRATIC INTEGER PROGRAMMING PROBLEMS, A.
PIEH 1978 -2 PIEHLER, J.
ZUR DREHUNG VON GOMORY-SCHNITTEN.
POTE 1981 -1 POTEMKINA, A. V.; SHEVCHENKO, V. N.
CONSTRUCTION OF REGULAR CUTTING-OFF IN CONVEX INTEGER PROGRAMMING (RUSSIAN).
RARDB 1978 -1 RARDIN, R. L.; LIN, B. W.
WHAT MAKES INTEGER PROGRAMMING PROBLEMS HARD TO SOLVE: AN EMPIRICAL STUDY.
ROUN 1980 -1 ROUNTREE, S. L. K.; GILLETT, B. E.
PARAMETRIC INTEGER LINEAR PROGRAMMING: A SYNTHESIS OF BRANCH AND BOUND WITH CUTTING PLANES.
SALK 1975 -1 SALKIN, H. M.
INTEGER PROGRAMMING.
SCHRD 1980 -3 SCHRIJVER, A.
ON CUTTING PLANES.
SEEL 1978 -1 SEELAENDER, J.
EINIGE BEMERKUNGEN ZUR BESTIMMUNG DES SCHNITTRANGS IN DER GANZZAHLIGEN LINEAREN OPTIMIERUNG.
SEKI 1981 -1 SEKIGUCHI, Y.
UNIFYING FRAMEWORK OF COMBINATORIAL OPTIMIZATION ALGORITHMS; TREE PROGRAMMING AND ITS VALIDITY, A.
SHEI 1979 -1 SHEINMAN, O. K.
GROUP-THEORETIC METHODS OF CONSTRUCTING CUTS IN INTEGER PROGRAMMING (RUSSIAN).
SHER 1979 -1 SHERALI, H. D.; SHETTY, C. M.
DISJUNCTIVE PROGRAMMING, POLYHEDRAL ANNEXATION TECHNIQUES AND NONDOMINATED DISJUNCTIVE CUTTING PLANES.
SHER 1980 -2 SHERALI, H. D.; SHETTY, C. M.
ON THE GENERATION OF DEEP DISJUNCTIVE CUTTING PLANES.
SHER 1980 -3 SHERALI, H. D.; SHETTY, C. M.
OPTIMIZATION WITH DISJUNCTIVE CONSTRAINTS.
SOLO 1976 -1 SOLOMONOV, L. A.; ZHGUTOV, G. D.
APPLICATION OF THE GOMORY METHOD FOR THE CALCULATION OF AN OPTIMAL PLAN FOR PRODUCTION SHIPMENT (RUSSIAN), AN.
TCHEA 1978 -1 TCHERVAK, JU. JU.
RETURNING ALGORITHM OF CUTTING-OFF METHOD AND BRANCH-AND-BOUND METHOD (RUSSIAN).
VANDC 1980 -1 VANDERVELDE, J. A.; KAAS, R.; DELEVE, G.
STRONGER GOMORY CUTS BY MULTIDIMENSIONAL KNAPSACK PROBLEMS.
WALL 1976 -1 WALLER, D. A.
REGULAR EIGENVALUES OF GRAPHS AND ENUMERATION OF SPANNING TREES.
WOLS 1979 -1 WOLSEY, L. A.
CUTTING PLANE METHODS.
ZWAR 1972 -1 ZWART, P.
INTERSECTION CUTS FOR SEPARABLE PROGRAMMING.

****

AKUL 1978 -1 AKULIC, F. E.
NET DECOMPOSITION ALGORITHM FOR THE SOLUTION OF THE MAXIMUM FLOW PROBLEM (RUSSIAN), A.

AVRAA 1978 -1 AVRAMITA, G. M.
DECOMPOSITION AND SOLVING OF LARGE-SCALE PROBLEMS IN PRODUCTION SCHEDULING.

CASTB 1979 -1 CASTELLANI, G.; GIANNESSI, F.
DECOMPOSITION OF MATHEMATICAL PROGRAMS BY MEANS OF THEOREMS OF ALTERNATIVE FOR LINEAR AND NONLINEAR SYSTEMS.

FISHB 1978 -2 FISHER, M. L.; JAIKUMAR, R.
DECOMPOSITION ALGORITHM FOR LARGE-SCALE VEHICLE ROUTING, A.

HENR 1979 -1 HENRY-LABORDERE, A.
RESOLUTION D'UN PROGRAMME QUADRATIQUE EN VARIANTES BIVALENTES PAR DECOMPOSITION. APPLICATION AU PLACEMENT DE COMMUTATEURS DANS UN RESEAU.

JARVB 1978 -1 JARVIS, J. J.; TUFEKCI, S.
DECOMPOSITION ALGORITHM FOR FINDING THE SHORTEST PATH BETWEEN A SOURCE AND A SINK NODE, A.

JARVB 1978 -2 JARVIS, J. J.; TUFEKCI, S.
DECOMPOSITION ALGORITHM FOR LOCATING MINIMAL CUTS IN A DIRECTED NETWORK, A.

KLUY 1979 -1 KLUYVER, C. A. DE
SOLVING THE MULTI-INDEX TRANSPORTATION PROBLEM BY DECOMPOSITION.

LEVI 1978 -1 LEVIN, G. M.; TANAEV, V. S.
DECOMPOSITION METHODS OF OPTIMIZATION OF PROJECT SOLUTIONS (RUSSIAN).

MAGN 1979 -1 MAGNANTI, T. L.; WONG, R. T.
ACCELERATING BENDERS DECOMPOSITION: ALGORITHMIC ENHANCEMENTS AND MODEL SELECTION CRITERIA.

MEREB 1978 -1 MERESSOO, T.
DECOMPOSITION METHOD FOR THE RESOURCE ALLOCATION PROBLEM (RUSSIAN), A.

POTR 1979 -1 POTRZEBOWSKI, H.
BRANCH AND BOUND AS A DECOMPOSITION METHOD OF DETERMINING SCHEDULES FOR PARALLEL MACHINES (POLISH).

REAR 1974 -1 REARDON, K. J.
DECOMPOSITION OF DUAL-ANGULAR INTEGER PROGRAMS, WITH APPLICATIONS TO MUTLI-STAGE CAPITAL BUDGETING.

SGUR 1977 -1 SGUREV, V. S.; VASILEV, V. S.
DECOMPOSITION METHOD FOR THE SOLUTION OF A CLASS OF INTEGER PROGRAMMING PROBLEMS (BULGARIAN), A.

SWEE 1979 -1 SWEENEY, D. J.; MURPHY, R. A.
METHOD OF DECOMPOSITION FOR INTEGER PROGRAMS, A.

TUFEA 1981 -1 TUFEKCI, S.; TOLEDO, M.
COMPARISON OF DECOMPOSITION ALGORITHMS FOR SHORTEST PATH PROBLEMS, A.

WOLL 1969 -1 WOLLMER, R. D.
DANTZIG-WOLFE DECOMPOSITION PRINCIPLE AND MINIMUM COST MULTICOMMODITY NETWORK FLOWS, THE.

DIOPHANTINE SYSTEMS AND AGGREGATION

BABAB 1978 -1 BABAEV, DZ. A.; MAMEDOV, K. S.
AGGREGATION OF A CLASS OF SYSTEMS OF INTEGER-VALUED EQUATIONS.

BACHC 1979 -1 BACHEM, A.; KANNAN, R.
APPLICATIONS OF POLYNOMIAL SMITH NORMAL FORM CALCULATIONS.

BACHD 1979 -1 BACHEM, A.; RANDOW, R. VON
INTEGER THEOREMS OF FARKAS LEMMA TYPE.

BATI 1977 -1 BATIGNE, D. R.
INTEGRAL GENERALIZED INVERSES OF INTEGRAL MATRICES.

BLAI 1975 -2 BLAIR, C. E.
TOPICS IN INTEGER PROGRAMMING.

BOEH 1964 -1 BOEHM, C.; SANTOLINI, A.
QUASI-DECISION ALGORITHM FOR THE P-EQUIVALENCE OF TWO MATRICES, A.

CHOU 1979 -1 CHOU, T.-W. J.
ALGORITHMS FOR THE SOLUTION OF SYSTEMS OF LINEAR DIOPHANTINE EQUATIONS.

DANG 1979 -1 DANG VAN UYEN
AGGREGATION OF AN INTEGER PROGRAMMING MODEL (SLOVAK).

DEMB 1974 -1 DEMBO, R. S.
NOTE ON CONSTRAINT PAIRING IN INTEGER LINEAR PROGRAMMING, A.

DONA 1979 -1 DONALDSON, J. L.
MINKOWSKI REDUCTION OF INTEGRAL MATRICES.

DUFF 1978 -1 DUFF, I. S.; REID, J. K.
IMPLEMENTATION OF TARJAN'S ALGORITHM FOR THE BLOCK TRIANGULARIZATION OF A MATRIX, AN.

EVAN 1979 -1 EVANS, J. R.
AGGREGATION IN THE GENERALIZED TRANSPORTATION PROBLEM.

FRUM 1979 -1 FRUMKIN, M. A.
ON THE NUMBER OF NONNEGATIVE INTEGER SOLUTIONS OF A LINEAR DIOPHANTINE EQUATIONS SYSTEM.

GEOF 1977 -1 GEOFFRION, A. M.
AGGREGATION THEORY AND ITS APPLICATION TO MODELING IN MATHEMATICAL PROGRAMMING.

GRAH 1980 -1 GRAHAM, R. L.
ON A DIOPHANTINE EQUATION ARISING IN GRAPH THEORY.

HUET 1978 -1 HUET, G.
ALGORITHM TO GENERATE THE BASIS OF SOLUTIONS TO HOMOGENEOUS LINEAR DIOPHANTINE EQUATIONS, AN.

ISMA 1978 -1 ISMATULLAEV, S. A.
NUMBER OF SOLUTIONS OF A SYSTEM OF DIOPHANTINE EQUATIONS (RUSSIAN), THE.

JACKA 1977 -1 JACKSON, W.
CHARACTERIZATION OF THE REDUCIBILITY OF NON-NEGATIVE MATRICES, A.

KANN 1980 -2 KANNAN, R.
POLYNOMIAL-TIME AGGREGATION OF INTEGER PROGRAMMING PROBLEMS.

KANN 1980 -3 KANNAN, R.
SIZE OF NUMBERS IN THE ANALYSIS OF CERTAIN ALGORITHMS, THE.

KANNA 1979 -1 KANNAN, R.; BACHEM, A.
POLYNOMIAL ALGORITHMS FOR COMPUTING THE SMITH AND HERMITE NORMAL FORMS OF AN INTEGER MATRIX.

KERI 1981 -1 KERI, G.
ON THE REDUCTION OF A BIPARTITE GRAPH TO IRREDUCIBLE COMPONENTS.

MEYEB 1979 -1 MEYER, R. R.
EQUIVALENT CONSTRAINTS FOR DISCRETE SETS.

NGUE 1980 -1 NGUEN, N. C.
ON ONE METHOD FOR FINDING A COMMON FORMULA OF INTEGER SOLUTIONS FOR A SYSTEM OF LINEAR INEQUALITIES (RUSSIAN).

NGUEB 1980 -1 NGUEN, N. T.
SOLVABILITY OF A SYSTEM OF LINEAR INEQUALITIES IN INTEGERS UNDER ANY VECTOR OF THE RIGHT-HAND PART (RUSSIAN), THE.

PROL 1978 -1 PROLL, L. G.
SIMPLE BUT EFFECTIVE TRANSFORMATION FOR A CLASS OF ILPS, A.

RAYW 1979 -1 RAYWARD-SMITH, V. J.
ON COMPUTING THE SMITH NORMAL FORM OF AN INTEGER MATRIX.

ROSEC 1967 -1 ROSENBLATT, D.
AGGREGATION IN MATRIX MODELS OF RESOURCE FLOWS II. BOOLEAN RELATION MATRIX METHODS.

SANGA 1979 -1 SANGIOVANNI-VINCENTELLI, A.; BICKART, T. A.
BIPARTITE GRAPHS AND AN OPTIMAL BORDERED TRIANGULAR FORM OF A MATRIX.

SEEL 1978 -1 SEELAENDER, J.
EINIGE BEMERKUNGEN ZUR BESTIMMUNG DES SCHNITTRANGS IN DER GANZZAHLIGEN LINEAREN OPTIMIERUNG.

WEIN 1979 -1 WEINBERG, F.
NECESSARY AND SUFFICIENT CONDITION FOR THE AGGREGATION OF LINEAR DIOPHANTINE EQUATIONS, A.

WEIN 1979 -2 WEINBERG, F.
SPECTRAL ALGORITHM FOR SEQUENTIAL AGGREGATION OF M LINEAR DIOPHANTINE CONSTRAINTS, A.

ZIPK 1979 -1 ZIPKIN, P. H.
AGGREGATION AND DISAGGREGATION IN CONVEX NETWORK PROBLEMS.

ZIPK 1980 -1 ZIPKIN, P. H.
BOUNDS FOR AGGREGATING NODES IN NETWORK PROBLEMS.

****

BALAA 1979 -2 BALAS, E.
DISJUNCTIVE PROGRAMMING.
BLAI 1980 -1 BLAIR, C. E.
FACIAL DISJUNCTIVE PROGRAMS AND SEQUENCES OF CUTTING-PLANES.
JEROB 1980 -2 JEROSLOW, R. G.
SOME INFLUENCES OF GENERALIZED AND ORDINARY CONVEXITY IN DISJUNCTIVE AND INTEGER PROGRAMMING.
SHER 1979 -1 SHERALI, H. D.; SHETTY, C. M.
DISJUNCTIVE PROGRAMMING, POLYHEDRAL ANNEXATION TECHNIQUES AND NONDOMINATED DISJUNCTIVE CUTTING PLANES.
SHER 1980 -1 SHERALI, H. D.; SHETTY, C. M.
FINITELY CONVERGENT PROCEDURE FOR FACIAL DISJUNCTIVE PROGRAMS, A.
SHER 1980 -2 SHERALI, H. D.; SHETTY, C. M.
ON THE GENERATION OF DEEP DISJUNCTIVE CUTTING PLANES.

DUALITY IN INTEGER PROGRAMMING

ARAOB 1977 -1 ARAOZ, J.; EDMONDS, J.; GRIFFIN, V. J.
POLARITIES GIVEN BY SYSTEMS OF BILINEAR INEQUALITIES.

BACHE 1978 -1 BACHEM, A.; SCHRADER, R.
NOTE ON A THEOREM OF JEROSLOW, A.

BACHE 1979 -1 BACHEM, A.; SCHRADER, R.
DUALITY THEOREM AND MINIMAL INEQUALITIES IN MIXED INTEGER PROGRAMMING, A.

BACHE 1980 -1 BACHEM, A.; SCHRADER, R.
MINIMAL INEQUALITIES AND SUBADDITIVE DUALITY.

BURKE 1981 -1 BURKARD, R. E.; HAMACHER, H.; TIND, J.
ON ABSTRACT DUALITY IN MATHEMATICAL PROGRAMMING.

CUNNC 1978 -1 CUNNINGHAM, W. H.; MARSH, A. B. III
PRIMAL ALGORITHM FOR OPTIMUM MATCHING, A.

DERI 1978 -1 DERIGS, U.
DUALITY AND THE ALGEBRAIC MATCHING PROBLEM.

DERI 1979 -1 DERIGS, U.
DUALITY AND ADMISSIBLE TRANSFORMATIONS IN COMBINATORIAL OPTIMIZATION.

DERIC 1978 -1 DERIGS, U.; ZIMMERMANN, U.
DUALITY PRINCIPLES IN ALGEBRAIC LINEAR PROGRAMMING.

FISHD 1975 -1 FISHER, M. L.; NORTHUP, W. D.; SHAPIRO, J. F.
USING DUALITY TO SOLVE DISCRETE OPTIMIZATION PROBLEMS: THEORY AND COMPUTATIONAL EXPERIENCE.

JEROB 1978 -1 JEROSLOW, R. G.
CUTTING PLANE THEORY: ALGEBRAIC METHODS.

JOHND 1980 -1 JOHNSON, E. L.
INTEGER PROGRAMMING, FACETS, SUBADDITIVITY, AND DUALITY FOR GROUP AND SEMI-GROUP PROBLEMS.

JOHND 1978 -2 JOHNSON, E. L.
SUPPORT FUNCTIONS, BLOCKING PAIRS, AND ANTI-BLOCKING PAIRS.

KARW 1979 -1 KARWAN, M. H.; RARDIN, R. L.
SOME RELATIONSHIPS BETWEEN LAGRANGIAN AND SURROGATE DUALITY IN INTEGER PROGRAMMING.

MAC B 1978 -1 MAC DIARMID, C.
BLOCKING, ANTIBLOCKING AND PAIRS OF MATROIDS AND POLYMATROIDS.

MEYEC 1975 -1 MEYER, R. R.; FLEISHER, J. M.
STRONG DUALITY FOR A CLASS OF INTEGER PROGRAMS.

MEYEF 1978 -1 MEYER, R. R.; WAGE, M. L.
ON THE POLYHEDRALITY OF THE CONVEX HULL OF THE FEASIBLE SET OF AN INTEGER PROGRAM.

SAKA 1978 -1 SAKAROVITCH, M.
QUELQUES THEOREMES DE DUALITE COMBINATOIRE.

SCHIB 1975 -1 SCHIEBEL, W.; UNGER, G.
DUALE ENTARTUNG IN DER LINEAREN OPTIMIERUNG, TRANSPORTPROBLEM MIT ZUSAETZLICHEN NEBENBEDINGUNGEN UND RUNDREISEPROBLEM.

SHEI 1978 -1 SHEINMAN, O. K.
DUALITY IN SOME DISCRETE MINIMIZATION PROBLEMS.

SHEI 1980 -1 SHEINMAN, O. K.
DUALITY AND SUBADDITIVE FUNCTIONS IN INTEGER PROGRAMMING (RUSSIAN).

TIND 1980 -1 TIND, J.
CERTAIN KINDS OF POLAR SETS AND THEIR RELATION TO MATHEMATICAL PROGRAMMING.

TIND 1979 -2 TIND, J.
ON DUALITY IN NON-CONVEX AND INTEGER PROGRAMMING.

TINDA 1978 -2 TIND, J.; WOLSEY, L. A.
UNIFYING FRAMEWORK FOR DUALITY THEORY IN MATHEMATICAL PROGRAMMING, A.

TUTT 1977 -1 TUTTE, W. T.
ON THE SPANNING TREES OF SELF-DUAL MAPS.

WILL 1979 -1 WILLIAMS, H. P.
ECONOMIC INTERPRETATION OF DUALITY FOR PRACTICAL MIXED INTEGER PROGRAMMING PROBLEMS, THE.

WOLS 1981 -1 WOLSEY, L. A.
INTEGER PROGRAMMING DUALITY: PRICE FUNCTIONS AND SENSITIVITY ANALYSIS.

ZIMM 1978 -1 ZIMMERMANN, U.
DUALITY AND THE ALGEBRAIC MATROID INTERSECTION PROBLEM.

ZIMM 1979 -1 ZIMMERMANN, U.
DUALITY PRINCIPLES AND THE ALGEBRAIC TRANSPORTATION PROBLEM.

ZIMM 1980 -1 ZIMMERMANN, U.
DUALITY FOR ALGEBRAIC LINEAR PROGRAMMING.

ALEK 1979 -1 ALEKSEEV, O. G.
PROBLEME MULTIDIMENSIONNEL DE STANDARDISATION (RUSSIAN).
BAKEF 1978 -1 BAKER, K. R.; DIXON, P.; MAGAZINE, M. J.; SILVER, E. A.
ALGORITHM FOR THE DYNAMIC LOT-SIZE PROBLEM WITH TIME-VARYING PRODUCTION CAPACITY CONSTRAINTS, AN.
BAKEI 1978 -1 BAKER, K. R.; SCHRAGE, L. E.
FINDING AN OPTIMAL SEQUENCE BY DYNAMIC PROGRAMMING: AN EXTENSION TO PRECEDENCE-RELATED TASKS.
BANS 1977 -1 BANSAL, S. P.
FINDING ALTERNATING MINIMUM COST PATH IN A DIRECTED NETWORK USING DYNAMIC PROGRAMMING.
BELEA 1978 -1 BELETSKIJ, S. A.
INCREASED EFFECTIVENESS OF THE DYNAMIC PROGRAMMING METHOD IN THE SOLUTION OF A CLASS OF DISCRETE OPTIMIZATION PROBLEMS (RUSSIAN).
CAIEA 1979 -1 CAIE, J.; LINDEN, J.; OATS, Q.; MAXWELL, W.
HIERARCHICAL MACHINE LOAD PLANNING.
CRAMA 1977 -1 CRAMER, M.; PONSSARD, J.-P.
ORDONNANCEMENT DES MOUVEMENTS DE TRESORERIE.
DENAA 1978 -1 DENARDO, E. V.; FOX, B. L.
BUCKETS, SHORTEST PATHS, AND INTEGER PROGRAMMING.
DREY 1977 -1 DREYFUS, S. E.; LAW, A. M.
ART AND THEORY OF DYNAMIC PROGRAMMING, THE.
FLORB 1978 -1 FLORIAN, M.; LENSTRA, J. K.; RINNOOY KAN, A. H. G.
DETERMINISTIC PRODUCTION PLANNING: ALGORITHMS AND COMPLEXITY.
FOCK 1978 -1 FOCKE, J.; KLOTZLER, R.
ZUR GRUNDKONZEPTION DER DISKRETEN DYNAMISCHEN OPTIMIERUNG.
GIER 1979 -1 GIERTH, G.; TERNO, J.
NICHOLSON PRINCIPLE IN DISCRETE DYNAMIC OPTIMIZATION, THE.
GILM 1979 -1 GILMORE, P. C.
CUTTING STOCK, LINEAR PROGRAMMING, KNAPSACKING, DYNAMIC PROGRAMMING AND INTEGER PROGRAMMING, SOME INTERCONNECTIONS.
GOND 1979 -1 GONDRAN, M.
ALGORITHMES LINEAIRES POUR LES PROBLEMES DE PARTITION, DE RECOUVREMENT ET DE COUPLAGE DANS LES HYPERGRAPHES D'INTERVALLES, DES.
HAST 1978 -1 HASTINGS, N. A. J.; MELLO, J. M. C.
DECISION NETWORKS.
HAYE 1979 -1 HAYES, G. M. JR.
DISCRETE VARIABLE APPROACH TO MACHINE PARAMETER OPTIMIZATION, A.
HELG 1979 -1 HELGASON, R. V.; KENNINGTON, J. L.
NEW STORAGE REDUCTION TECHNIQUE FOR THE SOLUTION OF THE GROUP PROBLEM, A.
HESS 1977 -1 HESSELBACH, J.; WIJNANDS, J.
DYNAMISCHE PROGRAMMIERUNG - METHODIK, EDV-PROGRAMM, ANWENDUNGSBEISPIEL.
HIND 1979 -1 HINDELANG, T. J.; MUTH, J. F.
DYNAMIC PROGRAMMING ALGORITHM FOR DECISION CPM NETWORKS, A.
HINDA 1977 -1 HINDERER, K.; HUEBNER, G.
IMPROVEMENT OF J. F. SHAPIRO'S TURNPIKE THEOREM FOR THE HORIZON OF FINITE STAGE DISCRETE DYNAMIC PROGRAMS, AN.
KALI 1979 -1 KALISZEWSKI, I.; WALUKIEWICZ, S.
TIGHTER EQUIVALENT FORMULATIONS OF INTEGER PROGRAMMING PROBLEMS.
KAO 1978 -1 KAO, E. P. C.
PREFERENCE ORDER DYNAMIC PROGRAM FOR A STOCHASTIC TRAVELING SALESMAN PROBLEM, A.
KAO A 1981 -1 KAO, E. P. C.; QUEYRANNE, M.
ON DYNAMIC PROGRAMMING METHODS FOR ASSEMBLY LINE BALANCING.
KLAP 1980 -1 KLAPKA, J.; DVORAK, J.
MORE EFFICIENT COMPUTATION OF OPTIMAL LOT SIZES IN A MULTISTAGE PRODUCTION PROCESS (CZECHOSLOVAKIAN), A.
KRIV 1979 -1 KRIVONOZKO, V. E.; PROPOI, A. I.
METHOD FOR THE SOLUTION OF DYNAMIC TRANSPORTATION PROBLEMS.
KUKS 1978 -1 KUKSA, A. I.; LAPTIN, J. P.
DYNAMIC PROGRAMMING IN THE NETWORK PROBLEM FOR OBTAINING THE SHORTEST SCHEDULE.
LABA 1977 -1 LABADIE, J. W.; MORROW, D. M.; CHEN, Y. H.
HEURISTIC MULTIDIMENSIONAL DYNAMIC PROGRAMMING ALGORITHM FOR URBAN STORMWATER MANAGEMENT.
LAWL 1979 -1 LAWLER, E. L.
EFFICIENT IMPLEMENTATION OF DYNAMIC PROGRAMMING ALGORITHMS FOR SEQUENCING PROBLEMS.
LEDI 1979 -1 LEDIN, M. I.
CLASS OF HOMOGENEOUS RESOURCE-ALLOCATION PROBLEMS (RUSSIAN), A.
MAGA 1979 -1 MAGAZINE, M. J.; OGUZ, O.
FULLY POLYNOMIAL APPROXIMATE ALGORITHM FOR THE 0-1 KNAPSACK PROBLEM, A. (REVISED VERSION).
MAKAA 1975 -1 MAKAROV, I. P.; YAVORSKII, V. V.
ONE GENERALIZATION OF THE TRAVELING SALESMAN PROBLEM.
NAME 1979 -1 NAMEKATA, T.; TABATA, Y.; NISHIDA, T.
SEQUENTIAL ALLOCATION PROBLEM WITH TWO KINDS OF TARGETS, A.
NUSS 1978 -1 NUSSINO, R.; PIECZENIK, G.; GRIGGS, J. R.; KLEITMAN, D. J.
ALGORITHMS FOR LOOP MATCHINGS.
PSAR 1980 -1 PSARAFTIS, H. N.
DYNAMIC PROGRAMMING APPROACH FOR SEQUENCING GROUPS OF IDENTICAL JOBS, A.
PSAR 1980 -2 PSARAFTIS, H. N.
DYNAMIC PROGRAMMING SOLUTION TO THE SINGLE VEHICLE MANY-TO-MANY IMMEDIATE REQUEST DIAL-A-RIDE PROBLEM, A.
RICHA 1979 -1 RICHTER, K.
DYNAMISCHE AUFGABEN DER DISKRETEN OPTIMIERUNG.
SCHRB 1978 -1 SCHRAGE, L. E.; BAKER, K. R.
DYNAMIC PROGRAMMING SOLUTION OF SEQUENCING PROBLEMS WITH PRECEDENCE CONSTRAINTS.
SCHRF 1978 -1 SCHROECK, W.
KONSTRUKTION KOSTENOPTIMALER ZERLEGUNGEN VON GRAPHEN.
SEKI 1981 -1 SEKIGUCHI, Y.
UNIFYING FRAMEWORK OF COMBINATORIAL OPTIMIZATION ALGORITHMS; TREE PROGRAMMING AND ITS VALIDITY, A.
SLAD 1980 -1 SLADKY, K.
BOUNDS ON DISCRETE DYNAMIC PROGRAMMING RECURSION I - MODELS WITH NON-NEGATIVE MATRICES.
SNIE 1979 -1 SNIEDOVICH, M.
PREFERENCE ORDER ASSEMBLY LINE PROBLEM: A COUNTER EXAMPLE.
SNIE 1979 -2 SNIEDOVICH, M.
PREFERENCE ORDER STOCHASTIC TRAVELING SALESPERSON PROBLEMS: A COUNTER EXAMPLE.
SNIE 1979 -3 SNIEDOVICH, M.
SOME COMMENTS ON PREFERENCE ORDER DYNAMIC PROGRAMMING MODELS.

****

SNIEA 1979 -1 SNIEDOVICH, M.; SMART, J. S.
DYNAMIC PROGRAMMING: AN INTERACTIVE APPROACH.
SU 1978 -1 SU, Z.-S.; SEVCIK, K. C.
COMBINATORIAL APPROACH TO DYNAMIC SCHEDULING PROBLEMS, A.
TINH 1980 -1 TINHOFER, G.
GRAPHSACK PROBLEM, THE.
TOTH 1980 -1 TOTH, P.
DYNAMIC PROGRAMMING ALGORITHMS FOR THE ZERO-ONE KNAPSACK PROBLEM.
VIDA 1978 -1 VIDAL, R. V. V.
DESIGN OF A PIPELINE ROUTE.
VILLA 1978 -1 VILLARREAL, B.; KARWAN, M. H.
MULTICRITERION INTEGER LINEAR PROGRAMMING A (HYBRID) DYNAMIC PROGRAMMING RECURSIVE APPROACH.
VILLA 1979 -1 VILLARREAL, B.; KARWAN, M. H.
INTERACTIVE DYNAMIC PROGRAMMING APPROACH TO MULTICRITERIA DISCRETE PROGRAMMING, AN.
VILLA 1978 -2 VILLARREAL, B.; KARWAN, M. H.
MULTICRITERION INTEGER LINEAR PROGRAMMING: SOME EXTENSIONS.
WEED 1978 -1 WEEDA, P. J.
DYNAMIC PROGRAMMING FORMULATION FOR THE ONE MACHINE SEQUENCING PROBLEM, A.
WOOD 1978 -1 WOOD, D. M.
DYNAMIC PROGRAMMING SOLUTION TO A PROBLEM OF LOOM BOX SEQUENCE PLANNING, A.
YEE 1979 -1 YEE, J. R.; GOLDEN, B. L.
DETERMINING OPERATING STRATEGIES FOR PROBABILISTIC VEHICLE ROUTING (REVISED VERSION).

ARAOC 1981 -1 ARAOZ, J.; JOHNSON, E. L.
FACETS AND MAPPINGS FOR NON-ABELIAN GROUP PROBLEMS.
BACHA 1979 -1 BACHEM, A.; GROETSCHEL, M.
NEW ASPECTS OF POLYHEDRAL THEORY.
BALAK 1977 -1 BALAS, E.; ZEMEL, E.
CRITICAL CUTSETS OF GRAPHS AND CANONICAL FACETS OF SET-PACKING POLYTOPES.
BALAK 1978 -1 BALAS, E.; ZEMEL, E.
FACETS OF THE KNAPSACK POLYTOPE FROM MINIMAL COVERS.
BOUL 1978 -1 BOULALA, M.
ETUDE DU POLYTOPE ASSOCIE AUX STABLES D'UN GRAPHE ET CARACTERISATION DANS LE CAS DES GRAPHES SERIE-PARALLELES.
BOULA 1979 -1 BOULALA, M.; UHRY, J.-P.
POLYTOPE DES INDEPENDANTS D'UN GRAPHE SERIE-PARALLELE.
CORND 1980 -1 CORNUEJOLS, G.; PULLEYBLANK, W. R.
MATCHING PROBLEM WITH SIDE CONDITIONS, A.
CORNE 1979 -1 CORNUEJOLS, G.; THIZY, J.-M.
SOME FACETS OF THE SIMPLE PLANT LOCATION POLYTOPE.
EMEL 1978 -1 EMELICHEV, V. A.; KRACKOVSKII, A. P.
ASYMPTOTIC PROPERTIES OF TRANSPORTATION POLYHEDRA (RUSSIAN).
GILE 1978 -1 GILES, R.
FACETS AND OTHER FACES OF BRANCHING POLYHEDRA.
GRANA 1980 -2 GRANOT, D.; GRANOT, F.
MINIMAL COVERS, EXTENSIONS OF MINIMAL COVERS AND FACETS OF A POSYNOMIAL INEQUALITY IN 0-1 VARIABLES.
GROEB 1978 -1 GROETSCHEL, M.
HYPO-HAMILTONIAN FACETS OF THE SYMMETRIC TRAVELLING SALESMAN POLYTOPE.
GROEB 1980 -1 GROETSCHEL, M.
ON THE MONOTONE SYMMETRIC TRAVELLING SALESMAN PROBLEM: HYPOHAMILTONIAN/ HYPOTRACEABLE GRAPHS AND FACETS.
GROEB 1979 -2 GROETSCHEL, M.
STRONG BLOCKS AND THE OPTIMUM BRANCHING PROBLEM.
GROEB 1980 -2 GROETSCHEL, M.
ON THE SYMMETRIC TRAVELLING SALESMAN PROBLEM: SOLUTION OF 120-CITY PROBLEM.
GROEE 1979 -1 GROETSCHEL, M.; PADBERG, M. W.
ON THE SYMMETRIC TRAVELLING SALESMAN PROBLEM I: INEQUALITIES.
GROEE 1979 -2 GROETSCHEL, M.; PADBERG, M. W.
ON THE SYMMETRIC TRAVELLING SALESMAN PROBLEM II: LIFTING THEOREMS AND FACETS.
GROEH 1978 -1 GROETSCHEL, M.; WAKABAYASHI, Y.
HYPOTRACEABLE DIGRAPHS.
GROEH 1980 -1 GROETSCHEL, M.; WAKABAYASHI, Y.
HYPOHAMILTONIAN DIGRAPHS.
GROEH 1981 -1 GROETSCHEL, M.; WAKABAYASHI, Y.
ON THE STRUCTURE OF THE MONOTONE ASYMMETRIC TRAVELLING SALESMAN POLYTOPE I: HYPOHAMILTONIAN FACETS.
GROEH 1981 -2 GROETSCHEL, M.; WAKABAYASHI, Y.
ON THE STRUCTURE OF THE MONOTONE ASYMMETRIC TRAVELLING SALESMAN POLYTOPE II: HYPOTRACEABLE FACETS.
GUIG 1971 -1 GUIGNARD, M.
INEGALITES VALIDES DE GOMORY-JOHNSON.
GUIG 1980 -1 GUIGNARD, M.
FRACTIONAL VERTICES, CUTS AND FACETS OF THE SIMPLE PLANT LOCATION PROBLEM.
JECH 1977 -1 JECHLITSCHKA, K.
UEBER DIE KONSTRUKTION VON STUETZHALBRAEUMEN FUER 0-1-POLYEDER.
JOHNO 1980 -1 JOHNSON, E. L.
INTEGER PROGRAMMING, FACETS, SUBADDITIVITY, AND DUALITY FOR GROUP AND SEMI-GROUP PROBLEMS.
JOHNO 1981 -1 JOHNSON, E. L.
CHARACTERIZATION OF FACETS FOR MULTIPLE RIGHT-HAND CHOICE LINEAR PROGRAMS.
JOHNO 1981 -2 JOHNSON, E. L.
ON THE GENERALITY OF THE SUBADDITIVE CHARACTERIZATION OF FACETS.
KRAVA 1979 -1 KRAVTSOV, M. K.
(D-2)-DIMENSIONAL FACES OF A TRANSPORT POLYHEDRON OF DIMENSION D (RUSSIAN).
MATTA 1977 -1 MATTHEISS, T. H.; RUBIN, D. S.
SURVEY AND COMPARISON OF METHODS FOR FINDING ALL VERTICES OF CONVEX POLYHEDRAL SETS, A.
MOUL 1978 -1 MOULOUD, B.
ETUDE DU POLYTOPE ASSOCIE AUX STABLES D'UN GRAPHE ET CARACTERISATION DANS LE CAS LES GRAPHES SERIE-PARALLELES.
OMAR 1977 -1 OMAR, A.
FINDING ALL EXTREME POINTS AND EXTREME RAYS OF A CONVEX POLYHEDRAL SET.
PADB 1979 -1 PADBERG, M. W.
COVERING, PACKING AND KNAPSACK PROBLEMS.
PADB 1980 -1 PADBERG, M. W.
(1,K)-CONFIGURATIONS AND FACETS FOR PACKING PROBLEMS.
PADBA 1980 -1 PADBERG, M. W.; HONG, S.
ON THE SYMMETRIC TRAVELLING SALESMAN PROBLEM: A COMPUTATIONAL STUDY.
SBIH 1978 -1 SBIHI, N.
ETUDE DES STABLES DANS LES GRAPHES SANS ETOILE.
SHLY 1978 -1 SHLYK, V. A.
ON THE FACES OF MASTER GOMORY POLYHEDRA (RUSSIAN).
SHLY 1980 -1 SHLYK, V. A.
PROPERTY OF FACETS OF MASTER GOMORY POLYHEDRA OF CYCLICAL GROUPS (RUSSIAN), A.
WOLS 1977 -1 WOLSEY, L. A.
VALID INEQUALITIES AND SUPERADDITIVITY OF 0-1 INTEGER PROGRAMS.
ZEME 1978 -2 ZEMEL, E.
LIFTING THE FACETS OF ZERO-ONE POLYTOPES.

FIXED CHARGE
****

BABAF 1978 -1 BABAT, L. G.
FIXED-CHARGE PROBLEM (RUSSIAN), A.
BARRA 1979 -2 BARR, R. S.; GLOVER, F.; KLINGMAN, D.
NEW OPTIMIZATION METHOD FOR LARGE-SCALE FIXED CHARGE TRANSPORTATION PROBLEMS, A.
GUIGA 1979 -1 GUIGNARD, M.; SPIELBERG, K.
DIRECT DUAL APPROACH TO A TRANSSHIPMENT FORMULATION FOR MULTI-LAYER NETWORK PROBLEMS WITH FIXED CHARGES, A.
HINDB 1978 -1 HINDI, K. S.; BRAMELLER, A.; HAMAM, K. M.
SOLUTION OF FIXED COST TRANS-SHIPMENT PROBLEMS BY A BRANCH AND BOUND METHOD.
JARVA 1978 -1 JARVIS, J. J.; RARDIN, R. L.; UNGER, V. E.; MOORE, R. W.; SCHIMPELER, C. C.
OPTIMAL DESIGN OF REGIONAL WASTEWATER SYSTEMS: A FIXED-CHARGE NETWORK FLOW MODEL.
JENK 1980 -2 JENKINS, L.
ONTARIO WASTE MANAGEMENT MODEL: TORONTO EXPERIENCE, THE.
MAC I 1978 -1 MAC KEOWN, P. G.
SOME COMPUTATIONAL RESULTS OF USING THE AHRENS-FINKE METHOD FOR HANDLING DEGENERACY IN FIXED CHARGE TRANSPORTATION PROBLEMS.
MAC J 1980 -1 MAC KEOWN, P. G.; SINHA, P.
EASY SOLUTION FOR A SPECIAL CLASS OF FIXED CHARGE PROBLEMS, AN.
MURPC 1979 -1 MURPHY, R. A.; ALLEN, R. E.
PROBLEM OF ASSIGNING SUPPLIERS TO PLANTS, A.
PURI 1974 -1 PURI, M. C.; SWARUP, K.
SIMPLE ENUMERATIVE METHOD FOR FIXED CHARGE PROBLEM.
RARD 1973 -1 RARDIN, R. L.
GROUP THEORETIC AND RELATED APPROACHES TO FIXED CHARGE PROBLEMS.
ROSSA 1979 -1 ROSS, G. T.; ZOLTNERS, A. A.
WEIGHTED ASSIGNMENT MODELS AND THEIR APPLICATION.
SCHME 1978 -1 SCHMITZ, P.; SCHOENLEIN, A.
LINEARE UND LINEARISIERBARE OPTIMIERUNGSMODELLE SOWIE IHRE ADV-GESTUETZTE LOESUNG.
STEIA 1980 -1 STEINBERG, E.; NAPIER, H. A.
OPTIMAL MULTI-LEVEL LOT SIZING FOR REQUIREMENTS PLANNING SYSTEMS.

ABBO 1979 -1 ABBOTT, H. L.; LIU, A. C.
BOUNDS FOR THE COVERING NUMBER OF A GRAPH.
ABDU 1980 -1 ABDUL-KADER, I.
CERTAINES PROPRIETES DES TOURNOIS AYANT UN CIRCUIT HAMILTONIEN UNIQUE.
ABRH 1980 -1 ABRHAM, J.; KOTZIG, A.
TRANSFORMATION OF EULER TOURS.
ACHA 1979 -1 ACHARYA, B. D.
ON THE CYCLOMATIC NUMBER OF A HYPERGRAPH.
AGAS 1975 -1 AGASHE, S. D.
NEW CHARACTERIZATION OF TREES AND CO-TREES, A.
AHLS 1978 -1 AHLSWEDE, R.; KATONA, G. O. H.
GRAPHS WITH MAXIMAL NUMBER OF ADJACENT PAIRS OF EDGES.
AKIYA 1979 -1 AKIYAMA, J.; EXOO, G.; HARARY, F.
GRAPHS WITH ALL INDUCED SUBGRAPHS ISOMORPHIC, THE.
AKIYB 1979 -1 AKIYAMA, J.; HAMADA, T.
DECOMPOSITIONS OF LINE GRAPHS, MIDDLE GRAPHS AND TOTAL GRAPHS OF COMPLETE GRAPHS INTO FORESTS, THE.
AKIYC 1979 -1 AKIYAMA, J.; HARARY, F.
GRAPH AND ITS COMPLEMENT WITH SPECIFIED PROPERTIES. I. CONNECTIVITY, A.
AKOP 1979 -1 AKOPJAN, G. C.; GALSTJAN, O. A.
CLASSES OF GRAPHS THAT ARE CRITICAL WITH RESPECT TO COVERINGS (RUSSIAN).
ALIP 1978 -1 ALIPOV, N. V.; SHUMEJKO, N. A.
SUR UN ALGORITHME DE RESOLUTION DU PROBLEME DE CONNEXION DES FILS DE MONTAGE SOUS FORME DE CIRCUIT FERME (RUSSIAN).
ALSP 1979 -1 ALSPACH, B.
GRAPHS AND PERMUTATION GROUPS WHOSE TRANSITIVE CONSTITUENTS HAVE PRIME DEGREE.
ALSP 1979 -2 ALSPACH, B.
HAMILTONIAN CYCLES IN VERTEX-TRANSITIVE GRAPHS OF ORDER 2P.
ALSPA 1978 -1 ALSPACH, B.; PARSONS, T. D.
ISOMORPHISM OF CIRCULANT GRAPHS AND DIGRAPHS.
ALSPB 1979 -1 ALSPACH, B.; SUTCLIFFE, R. J.
VERTEX-TRANSITIVE GRAPHS OF ORDER 2P.
ANAS 1977 -1 ANASTASJAN, J. G.
CERTAIN PROPERTIES OF BIPARTITE HYPERGRAPHS (RUSSIAN).
ANDE 1979 -1 ANDERSEN, L. D.
LOWER BOUNDS ON THE COVER-INDEX OF A GRAPH.
ANDR 1977 -1 ANDRASFAI, B.
INTRODUCTORY GRAPH THEORY.
ANEJ 1980 -1 ANEJA, Y. P.
INTEGER LINEAR PROGRAMMING APPROACH TO THE STEINER PROBLEM IN GRAPHS, AN.
ANGLA 1977 -1 ANGLUIN, D.; VALIANT, L. G.
FAST PROBABILISTIC ALGORITHMS FOR HAMILTONIAN CIRCUITS AND MATCHINGS.
ANTO 1980 -1 ANTONA, O. D'; KUNG, J. P. S.
COHERENT ORIENTATIONS AND SERIES-PARALLEL NETWORKS.
APPE 1977 -1 APPEL, K.; HAKEN, W.
EVERY PLANAR MAP IS FOUR COLORABLE. I. DISCHARGING.
APPE 1977 -2 APPEL, K.; HAKEN, W.
EVERY PLANAR MAP IS FOUR COLORABLE. II. REDUCIBILITY.
ARDI 1975 -1 ARDITTI, J.-C.
CHEMINEMENTS DANS LE GRAPHE DE COMPARABILITE D'UN ARBRE. PARTITION DES SOMMETS EN CYCLES.
ARDI 1978 -1 ARDITTI, J.-C.
PARTIALLY ORDERED SETS AND THEIR COMPARABILITY GRAPHS, THEIR DIMENSION AND THEIR ADJACENCY.
ARIY 1979 -1 ARIYOSHI, H.; TSUKIYAMA, S.; SHIRAKAWA, I.; OZAKI, H.
ALGORITHMS FOR ENUMERATING ALL THE S-T CUTSETS IN O(!V!+!E!) PER CUTSET (JAPANESE).
ASAN 1981 -1 ASANO, T.; KIKUCHI, S.; SAITO, N.
EFFICIENT ALGORITHM TO FIND A HAMILTONIAN CIRCUIT IN A 4-CONNECTED MAXIMAL PLANAR GRAPH, AN.
ASANA 1977 -1 ASANO, T.; NISHIZEKI, T.; SAITO, N.
NP-COMPLETE PROBLEMS OF FINDING A MAXIMUM CUTSET AND OF REDUCING GRAPHS TO BIPARTITE GRAPHS.
AVDO 1979 -1 AVDOSHIN, S. M.; BELOV, V. V.
METHODE D'ONDE GENERALISEE POUR LA RESOLUTION DES PROBLEMES EXTREMAUX SUR LES GRAPHES (RUSSIAN).
BABAE 1980 -1 BABAI, L.
ON THE COMPLEXITY OF CANONICAL LABELING OF STRONGLY REGULAR GRAPHS.
BAGC 1979 -1 BAGCHI, A.; ROY, J. K.
ON V-OPTIMAL TREES.
BANN 1978 -1 BANNAI, K.
HAMILTONIAN CYCLES IN GENERALIZED PETERSEN GRAPHS.
BARA 1980 -1 BARAHONA, F.
APPLICATION DE L'OPTIMISATION COMBINATOIRE A CERTAINS MODELES DES VERRES DE SPINS: COMPLEXITE ET SIMULATIONS.
BARA 1980 -2 BARAHONA, F.
ON THE COMPLEXITY OF MAX CUT.
BARAB 1977 -1 BARAUSKAS, R. A.; VALANTINAS, I. I.
OPTIMAL CODING OF THE VERTICES OF AN UNDIRECTED GRAPH (RUSSIAN).
BARE 1980 -1 BAREFOOT, C. A.; ENTRINGER, R. C.
EXTREMAL MAXIMAL UNIQUELY HAMILTONIAN GRAPHS.
BARIA 1979 -1 BARI, R. A.
CHROMATIC POLYNOMIALS AND THE INTERNAL AND EXTERNAL ACTIVITIES OF TUTTE.
BATA 1979 -1 BATAGELJ, V.; PISANSKI, T.
ON PARTIALLY DIRECTED EULERIAN MULTIGRAPHS.
BAUE 1981 -1 BAUER, D.; BOESCH, F.; SUFFEL, C.; TINDELL, R.
CONNECTIVITY EXTREMAL PROBLEMS AND THE DESIGN OF RELIABLE PROBABILISTIC NETWORKS.
BAUM 1978 -2 BAUM, S.; TROTTER, L. E. JR.
INTEGER ROUNDING FOR POLYMATROID AND BRANCHING OPTIMIZATION PROBLEMS.
BAYB 1978 -1 BAYBARS, I.
NEW CHARACTERIZATION OF MAXIMAL PLANAR GRAPHS AND A GRAPH THEORETIC APPROACH TO THE FACILITIES DESIGN PROBLEM, A.
BAYB 1979 -1 BAYBARS, I.
ON K-PATH HAMILTONIAN MAXIMAL PLANAR GRAPHS.
BAYB 1980 -1 BAYBARS, I.
CHARACERIZATION OF HAMILTONIAN MAXIMAL PLANAR GRAPHS.
BENZ 1980 -2 BENZAKEN, C.; HAMMER, P. L.; SIMEONE, B.
SOME REMARKS ON CONFLICT GRAPHS OF QUADRATIC PSEUDO-BOOLEAN FUNCTIONS.
BERA 1979 -1 BERAHA, S.; KAHANE, J.
IS THE FOUR-COLOR CONJECTURE ALMOST FALSE?

GRAPH THEORETIC RESULTS (UNLESS SPECIFIED ELSEWHERE)

BERG 1973 -1 BERGE, C.
INTRODUCTION A LA THEORIE DES HYPERGRAPHES.
BERG 1978 -3 BERGE, C.
RESULTATS RECENTS SUR CERTAINES CLASSES D'HYPERGRAPHES QUI GENERALISENT LES GRAPHES BIPARTIS.
BERG 1979 -4 BERGE, C.
REGULARIZABLE GRAPHS.
BERGB 1978 -1 BERGE, C.; VERGNAS, M. LAS
ON THE EXISTENCE OF SUBGRAPHS WITH DEGREE CONSTRAINTS.
BERK 1978 -1 BERKOWITZ, H. W.
RESTRICTED EULERIAN CIRCUITS IN DIRECTED GRAPHS.
BERMB 1980 -1 BERMAN, K. A.
PROOF OF TUTTE'S TRINITY THEOREM AND A NEW DETERMINANT FORMULA, A.
BERMD 1978 -1 BERMOND, J. C.
HAMILTONIAN GRAPHS.
BERME 1979 -1 BERMOND, J. C.; GERMA, A.; HEYDEMANN, M. C.
HAMILTONIAN CYCLES IN STRONG PRODUCTS OF GRAPHS.
BERMF 1978 -1 BERMOND, J. C.; GERMA, A.; HEYDEMANN, M. C.; SOTTEAU, D.
HYPERGRAPHES HAMILTONIENS.
BERMG 1979 -1 BERMOND, J. C.; SIMOES-PEREIRA, J. M. S.; ZAMFIRESCU, C. M.
ON NONHAMILTONIAN HOMOGENEOUSLY TRACEABLE DIGRAPHS.
BERMH 1981 -1 BERMOND, J. C.; THOMASSEN, C.
CYCLES IN DIGRAPHS - A SURVEY.
BESS 1978 -1 BESSONOV, JU. E.; SKOROBOGATOV, V. A.
APPLICATION OF RELATIVE PARTITIONINGS FOR SEARCHING FOR CLIQUES (RUSSIAN).
BEYE 1979 -1 BEYER, T.; JONES, W.; MITCHELL, S.
LINEAR ALGORITHMS FOR ISOMORPHISM OF MAXIMAL OUTERPLANAR GRAPHS.
BHAT 1980 -1 BHAT, K. V. S.
ON THE COMPLEXITY OF TESTING A GRAPH FOR N-CUBE.
BIES 1977 -1 BIESS, G.; JAENICKE, W.; MEISSLER, H. G.
ALGORITHMUS ZUR BESTIMMUNG ALLER ELEMENTARKREISE EINES GERICHTETEN GRAPHEN, EIN.
BIGAA 1979 -1 BIGALKE, A.; JUNG, H. A.
UEBER HAMILTONSCHE KREISE UND UNABHAENGIGE ECKEN IN GRAPHEN.
BIGAB 1979 -1 BIGALKE, A.; KOEHLER, N.
ANTIGERICHTETE HAMILTONLINIEN IN VOLLSTAENDIG GERICHTETEN GRAPHEN.
BIGG 1979 -1 BIGGS, N.
ON THE ALGEBRA OF GRAPH TYPES.
BIGG 1979 -2 BIGGS, N.
RESONANCE AND RECONSTRUCTION.
BILL 1978 -2 BILLIONNET, A.
TRANSFORMATION DU PROBLEME DE PARTITIONNEMENT EN UN PROBLEME D'ENSEMBLE STABLE DE POIDS MAXIMAL.
BINZ 1978 -1 BINZ, J. C.
HAMILTONWEGE IN RECHTECKIGEN UND QUADERFOERMIGEN GITTERGRAPHEN.
BIXBA 1979 -1 BIXBY, R. E.; CUNNINGHAM, W. H.
MATROIDS, GRAPHS, AND 3-CONNECTIVITY.
BIXBB 1978 -1 BIXBY, R. E.; WANG, D.-L.
ALGORITHM FOR FINDING HAMILTONIAN CIRCUITS IN CERTAIN GRAPHS, AN.
BLANA 1979 -1 BLAND, R. G.; HUANG, H.-C.; TROTTER, L. E. JR.
GRAPHICAL PROPERTIES RELATED TO MINIMAL IMPERFECTION.
BOEH 1964 -1 BOEHM, C.; SANTOLINI, A.
QUASI-DECISION ALGORITHM FOR THE P-EQUIVALENCE OF TWO MATRICES, A.
BOLL 1978 -1 BOLLOBAS, B.; ELDRIDGE, S. E.
PACKINGS OF GRAPHS AND APPLICATIONS TO COMPUTATIONAL COMPLEXITY.
BOLLA 1978 -1 BOLLOBAS, B.; HOBBS, A. M.
HAMILTONIAN CYCLES IN REGULAR GRAPHS.
BOLLB 1979 -1 BOLLOBAS, B.; MANVEL, B.
OPTIMAL VERTEX PARTITIONS.
BOND 1972 -1 BONDY, J. A.
VARIATIONS ON THE HAMILTONIAN THEME.
BOND 1976 -1 BONDY, J. A.
DICONNECTED ORIENTATIONS AND A CONJECTURE OF LAS VERGNAS.
BOND 1977 -1 BONDY, J. A.
CYCLES IN DIGRAPHS.
BOND 1978 -1 BONDY, J. A.
HAMILTON CYCLES IN GRAPHS AND DIGRAPHS.
BOND 1978 -2 BONDY, J. A.
REMARK ON TWO SUFFICIENT CONDITIONS FOR HAMILTONIAN CYCLES, A.
BONDA 1978 -1 BONDY, J. A.; HEMMINGER, R. L.
RECONSTRUCTION BY ENUMERATION: SOME APPLICATIONS OF A COUNTING THEOREM BY THE GRAPH RECONSTRUCTION PROBLEM.
BONDB 1980 -1 BONDY, J. A.; SIMONOVITS, M.
LONGEST CYCLES IN 3-CONNECTED 3-REGULAR GRAPHS.
BONG 1979 -1 BONGIOVANNI, G.
PROPERTY OF STRUCTURAL NUMBERS AND CUT SETS, A.
BONU 1979 -1 BONUCCELLI, M. A.; BOVET, D. P.
MINIMUM NODE DISJOINT PATH COVERING FOR CIRCULAR-ARC GRAPHS.
BOOT 1980 -1 BOOTH, K. S.
DOMINATING SETS IN CHORDAL GRAPHS.
BOUL 1978 -1 BOULALA, M.
ETUDE DU POLYTOPE ASSOCIE AUX STABLES D'UN GRAPHE ET CARACTERISATION DANS LE CAS DES GRAPHES SERIE-PARALLELES.
BOULA 1979 -1 BOULALA, M.; UHRY, J.-P.
POLYTOPE DES INDEPENDANTS D'UN GRAPHE SERIE-PARALLELE.
BRAU 1978 -1 BRAUN, H.
LITERATUR UEBER GRAPHEN-ISOMORPHIE, EINDEUTIGE STRUKTURBENENNUNG UND VERWANDTE THEMEN.
BROEA 1979 -1 BROERE, I.; MYNHARDT, C. M.
REMARKS ON THE CRITICAL GRAPH CONJECTURE.
BROU 1979 -1 BROUWER, A. E.; SCHRIJVER, A.
UNIFORM HYPERGRAPHS.
BROWC 1979 -1 BROWN, M. R.
PARTIAL ANALYSIS OF RANDOM HEIGHT-BALANCED TREES, A.
BROWD 1979 -1 BROWN, M. R.; TARJAN, R. E.
FAST MERGING ALGORITHM, A.
BROWE 1978 -1 BROWN, W. G.; ERDOES, P.; SIMONOVITS, M.
ON MULTIGRAPH EXTREMAL PROBLEMS.

BRUA 1979 -1 BRUALDI, R. A.
DIAGONAL HYPERGRAPH OF A MATRIX (BIPARTITE GRAPH), THE.

BRUAA 1980 -1 BRUALDI, R. A.; HARARY, F.; MILLER, Z.
BIGRAPHS VERSUS DIGRAPHS VIA MATRICES.

BRUC 1981 -1 BRUCKER, P.
CHINESE POSTMAN PROBLEM FOR MIXED GRAPHS, THE.

BUCK 1980 -1 BUCKINGHAM, M. A.
CIRCLE GRAPHS.

BUCKB 1979 -1 BUCKLEY, F.; HOFFMAN, A. J.
ON THE MIXED ACHROMATIC NUMBER AND OTHER FUNCTIONS OF GRAPHS.

BURKF 1980 -1 BURKARD, R. E.; HAMMER, P. L.
NOTE ON HAMILTONIAN SPLIT GRAPHS, A.

BURL 1980 -1 BURLET, M.; UHRY, J.-P.
PARITY GRAPHS.

BURO 1979 -1 BUROSCH, G.; DREWS, K.-D.
UEBER DIE UNABHAENGIGKEITSZAHL UND ZERLEGUNGSZAHL EINES GRAPHEN.

BURR 1976 -1 BURR, S. A.; ERDOES, P.
EXTREMAL RAMSEY THEORY FOR GRAPHS.

BURS 1979 -1 BURSCHEID, H. J.
ZUR VORGABE GERICHTETER KANTEN VON VERGLEICHBARKEITSGRAPHEN.

BURSA 1979 -1 BURSHTEJN, M. I.
EVERY 4-VALENT GRAPH HAS AN ACYCLIC 5-COLORING (RUSSIAN).

BUTZ 1980 -1 BUTZ, L.
CHARACTERIZATIONS OF CONNECTIVITY IN ROW COLUMN DESIGNS.

BUTZ 1981 -1 BUTZ, L.
UEBER DIE ZUSAMMENHANGSEIGENSCHAFT IN VERSUCHSPLAENEN MIT MEHRFACHER BLOCKBILDUNG: EINE KOMBINATORISCHE ANALYSE.

BUTZ 1982 -1 BUTZ, L.
CONNECTIVITY IN MULTI-FACTOR DESIGNS: A COMBINATORIAL APPROACH.

CAMEA 1979 -1 CAMERINI, P. M.; FRATTA, L.; MAFFIOLI, F.
NOTE ON FINDING OPTIMUM BRANCHINGS, A.

CAMEA 1980 -2 CAMERINI, P. M.; FRATTA, L.; MAFFIOLI, F.
RANKING ARBORESCENCES IN O(KM LOG N) TIME.

CAMED 1979 -1 CAMERON, K.; EDMONDS, J.
ALGORITHMS FOR OPTIMUM ANTICHAINS.

CAMI 1975 -1 CAMION, P.
HAMILTONIAN CHAINS IN SELF COMPLEMENTARY GRAPHS.

CARR 1979 -1 CARRE, B.
GRAPHS AND NETWORKS.

CART 1979 -1 CARTER, M. W.
FINAL EXAMINATION SCHEDULING FOR CORRESPONDENCE STUDENTS.

CATL 1979 -1 CATLIN, P. A.
BROOKS' GRAPH-COLORING THEOREM AND THE INDEPENDENCE NUMBER.

CATL 1979 -2 CATLIN, P. A.
HAJOS' GRAPH-COLORING CONJECTURE: VARIATIONS AND COUNTEREXAMPLES.

CATL 1979 -3 CATLIN, P. A.
SUBGRAPHS WITH TRIANGULAR COMPONENTS.

CAZA 1978 -1 CAZANESCU, V.-E.; RUDEANU, S.
INDEPENDENT SETS AND KERNELS IN GRAPHS AND HYPERGRAPHS.

CHAC 1979 -1 CHACHRA, V.; GHARE, P. M.; MOORE, J. M.
APPLICATIONS OF GRAPH THEORY ALGORITHMS.

CHARC 1977 -1 CHARTRAND, G.
GRAPHS AS MATHEMATICAL MODELS.

CHARE 1979 -1 CHARTRAND, G.; GOULD, R. J.; KAPOOR, S. F.
ON HOMOGENEOUSLY TRACEABLE NONHAMILTONIAN GRAPHS.

CHARF 1979 -1 CHARTRAND, G.; GOULD, R. J.; POLIMENI, A. D.
NOTE ON LOCALLY CONNECTED AND HAMILTONIAN-CONNECTED GRAPHS, A.

CHEL 1976 -1 CHELNOKOV, V. M.
GRAPHS WITH AN EXTREMAL NUMBER OF TREES, HAMILTONIAN CYCLES AND CIRCUITS (RUSSIAN).

CHERC 1977 -1 CHERNYSHEV, JU. O.
OPTIMIZATION METHODS FOR COMBINATIONAL DEVICES (RUSSIAN).

CHRI 1979 -1 CHRISTEN, C. A.; SELKOW, S. M.
SOME PERFECT COLORING PROPERTIES OF GRAPHS.

CHRIC 1979 -1 CHRISTOFIDES, N.; AINOUCHE, A.
BOUNDS ON THE CONNECTIVITY AND THE INDEPENDENCE NUMBER OF A GRAPH.

CHUNA 1978 -1 CHUNG, F. R. K.; GRAHAM, R. L.
ON UNIVERSAL GRAPHS.

CHUND 1978 -1 CHUNGPHAISAN, V.
CONSTRUCTION OF HAMILTONIAN GRAPHS AND BIGRAPHS WITH PRESCRIBED DEGREES.

CHVAA 1979 -1 CHVATAL, V.; GRAHAM, R. L.; PEROLD, A. F.; WHITESIDES, S. H.
COMBINATORIAL DESIGNS RELATED TO THE STRONG PERFECT GRAPH CONJECTURE.

CIOBA 1978 -1 CIOBOTARU, S.
ON THE ENUMERATION OF HAMILTONIAN ROADS AND CIRCUITS IN CERTAIN PARTIAL GRAPHS OF K(N).

CLARA 1980 -1 CLARK, L.; ENTRINGER, R. C.; JACKSON, D. E.
MINIMUM GRAPHS WITH COMPLETE K-CLOSURE.

COCKA 1978 -1 COCKAYNE, E. J.; HEDETNIEMI, S. T.
DISJOINT CLIQUES IN REGULAR GRAPHS OF DEGREE SEVEN AND EIGHT.

COGI 1979 -1 COGIS, O.; HABIB, M.
NOMBRE DE SAUTS ET GRAPHES SERIE-PARALLELES.

COLB 1978 -1 COLBOURN, C. J.
BIBLIOGRAPHY OF THE GRAPH ISOMORPHISM PROBLEM, A.

COLBA 1979 -1 COLBOURN, C. J.; READ, R. C.
ORDERLY ALGORITHMS FOR GENERATING RESTRICTED CLASSES OF GRAPHS.

COLBB 1978 -1 COLBOURN, M. J.; COLBOURN, C. J.
GRAPH ISOMORPHISM AND SELF-COMPLEMENTARY GRAPHS.

COLL 1978 -1 COLLIER, J. B.; SCHMEICHEL, E. F.
SYSTEMATIC SEARCHES FOR HYPOHAMILTONIAN GRAPHS.

COLLB 1977 -1 COLLOMB, P.; GONDRAN, M.
ALGORITHME EFFICACE POUR UN ARBRE DE CLASSIFICATIONS, UN.

CONR 1978 -1 CONRADT, D.
EFFIZIENTE IMPLEMENTIERUNG DES VERFAHRENS VON EDMONDS ZUR BESTIMMUNG EINES MAXIMALEN MATCHING, EINE.

CORL 1980 -1 CORLEY, H. W.; GOLNABI, H.
MINIMAX TREES, PATHS, AND CUT SETS.

CORNA 1979 -1 CORNUEJOLS, G.
DEGREE SEQUENCES OF RANDOM GRAPHS.

GRAPH THEORETIC RESULTS (UNLESS SPECIFIED ELSEWHERE)

CORND 1981 -1 CORNUEJOLS, G.; PULLEYBLANK, W. R.
CRITICAL GRAPHS, MATCHINGS AND TOURS - A HIERARCHY OF RELAXATIONS FOR THE TRAVELLING SALESMAN PROBLEM.

CULL 1980 -1 CULL, P.
TOURS OF GRAPHS, DIGRAPHS, AND SEQUENTIAL MACHINES.

CUNN 1982 -1 CUNNINGHAM, W. H.
DECOMPOSITION OF SUBMODULAR FUNCTIONS.

CUNNA 1980 -1 CUNNINGHAM, W. H.; EDMONDS, J.
COMBINATORIAL DECOMPOSITION THEORY, A.

CVETA 1979 -1 CVETKOVIC, D. M.; DOOB, M.; SACHS, H.
SPECTRA OF GRAPHS. THEORY AND APPLICATION.

DAS C 1978 -1 DAS, S. R.; SHENG, C. L.
STRONG CONNECTIVITY IN SYMMETRIC GRAPHS AND GENERATION OF MAXIMAL MINIMALLY STRONGLY CONNECTED SUBGRAPHS.

DAS D 1978 -1 DAS, S. R.; SHENG, C. L.; CHEN, Z.
ALGORITHM FOR FINDING ALL MAXIMAL COMPLETE SUBGRAPHS AND AN ESTIMATE OF THE ORDER OF COMPUTATIONAL COMPLEXITY, AN.

DAS E 1979 -1 DAS, S. R.; SHENG, C. L.; CHEN, Z.; LIN, T.
MAGNITUDE ORDERING OF DEGREE COMPLEMENTS OF CERTAIN NODE PAIRS IN AN UNDIRECTED GRAPH AND AN ALGORITHM TO FIND A CLASS OF MAXIMAL SUBGRAPHS.

DEBO 1977 -1 DEBOWY, J.
ALGORITHM FOR OPTIMAL PARTITIONING OF A GRAPH, AN.

DEMIA 1979 -1 DEMING, R. W.
INDEPENDENCE NUMBERS OF GRAPHS - AN EXTENSION OF THE KOENIG-EGERVARY THEOREM.

DEO 1979 -1 DEO, N.
MINIMUM-LENGTH FUNDAMENTAL CYCLE SET.

DIEN 1979 -1 DIENES, I.; KOVACS, L. B.
MAXIMUM TRANSITIVE PATHS AND THEIR APPLICATION TO A GEOLOGICAL PROBLEM SETTING UP STRATIGRAPHIC UNITS.

DINE 1976 -1 DINESCU, C.
OPTIMAL ELEMENTARY PATHS IN NETWORKS WITH CIRCUITS.

DINIA 1976 -1 DINIC, E. A.; KARZANOV, A. V.; LOMONOSOV, M. V.
STRUCTURE OF A SYSTEM OF MINIMAL EDGE CUTS OF A GRAPH (RUSSIAN), THE.

DIRA 1973 -1 DIRAC, G. A.
NOTE ON HAMILTON CIRCUITS AND HAMILTON PATHS.

DIRA 1978 -1 DIRAC, G. A.
HAMILTON CIRCUITS AND LONG CIRCUITS.

DJOK 1970 -1 DJOKOVIC, D. Z.
ISOMCRPHISM PROBLEM FOR A SPECIAL CLASS OF GRAPHS.

DOMB 1977 -1 DOMB, C.
GENERALIZATION OF THE KOENIGSBERG BRIDGES PROBLEM, A.

DOYE 1975 -1 DOYEN, J.; VANDIEST, V.
GRAPHES HYPOHAMILTONIENS.

DROEA 1978 -1 DROESBEKE, F.; FRENNE, A. DE
ETUDE DES BORNES DU NOMBRE CHROMATIQUE D'UN GRAPHE. II.

DUFF 1978 -1 DUFF, I. S.; REID, J. K.
IMPLEMENTATION OF TARJAN'S ALGORITHM FOR THE BLOCK TRIANGULARIZATION OF A MATRIX, AN.

ECKS 1977 -1 ECKSTEIN, D. M.; ALTON, D. A.
PARALLEL GRAPH PROCESSING USING DEPTH-FIRST SEARCH.

ENTR 1977 -1 ENTRINGER, R. C.; SLATER, P. J.
NOTE ON K-CRITICALLY N-CONNECTED GRAPHS, A.

ERUS 1980 -1 ERUSALIMSKY, YA. M.; SVETLOV, G. G.
BICOUPLING POINTS, BIBRIDGES AND BIUNITS OF FLOW GRAPHS (RUSSIAN).

ESSE 1980 -1 ESSER, F.; HARARY, F.
ON THE SPECTRUM OF A COMPLETE MULTIPARTITE GRAPH.

EVEN 1979 -1 EVEN, S.
GRAPH ALGORITHMS.

EVENA 1981 -1 EVEN, S.; SHILOACH, Y.
ON-LINE EDGE-DELETION PROBLEM, AN.

EVST 1978 -1 EVSTIGNEEV, V. A.
LOCAL ALGORITHM FOR FINDING THE STRONGLY CONNECTED SUBGRAPHS OF DIRECTED GRAPHS (RUSSIAN), THE.

EVST 1979 -1 EVSTIGNEEV, V. A.
LOCAL ALGORITHM FOR FINDING THE BICOMPONENTS IN A FLOW GRAPH, A.

FARA 1978 -2 FARADZEV, I. A.
GENERATION OF THREE-CONNECTED GRAPHS AND THE ENUMERATION OF INSEPARABLE NETWORKS (RUSSIAN), THE.

FARL 1979 -1 FARLEY, A.; HEDETNIEMI, S. T.; MITCHELL, S.; PROSKUROWSKI, A.
MINIMUM BROADCAST GRAPHS.

FARR 1980 -1 FARRELL, E. J.
MATCHING POLYNOMIAL AND ITS RELATION TO THE ACYCLIC POLYNOMIAL OF A GRAPH, THE.

FARR 1979 -3 FARRELL, E. J.
ON A CLASS OF POLYNOMIALS OBTAINED FROM THE CIRCUITS IN A GRAPH AND ITS APPLICATION TO CHARACTERISTIC POLYNOMIALS OF GRAPHS.

FICK 1979 -1 FICKETT, J. W.
HIGH VALENCY SUBGRAPHS OF CUBES.

FIED 1979 -1 FIEDLER, M.
OPTIMIERUNG UND GRAPHENTHEORIE.

FISHC 1979 -1 FISHER, M. L.; NEMHAUSER, G. L.; WOLSEY, L. A.
ANALYSIS OF APPROXIMATIONS FOR FINDING A MAXIMUM WEIGHT HAMILTONIAN CIRCUIT, AN.

FLEI 1976 -1 FLEISCHNER, H.; HOBBS, A. M.
HAMILTONIAN CYCLES IN SQUARES OF VERTEX-UNICYCLIC GRAPHS.

FLET 1980 -1 FLETCHER, J. G.
MORE GENERAL ALGORITHM FOR COMPUTING CLOSED SEMIRING COSTS BETWEEN VERTICES OF A DIRECTED GRAPH, A.

FOLD 1977 -1 FOLDES, S.; HAMMER, P. L.
SPLIT GRAPHS.

FOLD 1978 -1 FOLDES, S.; HAMMER, P. L.
ON A CLASS OF MATROID-PRODUCING GRAPHS.

FOLD 1978 -2 FOLDES, S.; HAMMER, P. L.
ON SPLIT GRAPHS AND SOME RELATED QUESTIONS.

FONTA 1975 -1 FONTET, M.
TEST D'ISOMORPHIE DE DEUX GRAPHES PLANAIRES.

FONTA 1976 -1 FONTET, M.
LINEAR ALGORITHM FOR TESTING ISOMORPHISM OF PLANAR GRAPHS, A.

FONTA 1978 -1 FONTET, M.
ON AN ALGORITHM OF HOPCROFT AND TARJAN: A NEW TRICONNECTIVITY ALGORITHM.
FONTA 1979 -1 FONTET, M.
CONNECTIVITE DES GRAPHES ET AUTOMORPHISMES DES CARTES: PROPRIETES ET ALGORITHMES.
FORTA 1979 -1 FORTUNE, S.; HOPCROFT, J. E.
NOTE ON RABIN'S NEAREST-NEIGHBOUR ALGORITHM, A.
FORTB 1980 -1 FORTUNE, S.; HOPCROFT, J. E.; WYLLIE, J.
DIRECTED SUBGRAPH HOMEOMORPHISM PROBLEM, THE.
FOUL 1978 -1 FOULDS, L. R.; GIBBONS, P. B.
BRANCH AND BOUND APPROACH TO THE STEINER PROBLEM IN GRAPHS, A.
FOULA 1978 -1 FOULDS, L. R.; ROBINSON, D. F.
GRAPH THEORETIC HEURISTICS FOR THE PLANT LAYOUT PROBLEM.
FOUQ 1978 -1 FOUQUET, J.-L.
PROBLEMES HAMILTONIENS DANS LES PUISSANCES DE GRAPHES ORIENTES.
FOUQA 1978 -1 FOUQUET, J.-L.; JOLIVET, J.-L.
GRAPHES HYPOHAMILTONIENS ORIENTES.
FOUR 1978 -1 FOURNIER, J.-C.
CARACTERISATION DES GRAPHES DE CORDES, UNE.
FOUR 1978 -2 FOURNIER, J.-C.
GRAPHES DE CORDES, HYPERGRAPHES DE CHAINES D'UN ARBRE ET MATROIDES GRAPHIQUES.
FRANB 1979 -1 FRANK, A.
COVERING BRANCHINGS.
FRANB 1979 -2 FRANK, A.
KERNEL SYSTEMS OF DIRECTED GRAPHS.
FRANB 1980 -2 FRANK, A.
DISJOINT PATHS IN THE PLANE.
FRANB 1980 -3 FRANK, A.
HOW TO MAKE A DIGRAPH STRONGLY CONNECTED.
FRANB 1981 -3 FRANK, A.
HOW TO MAKE A DIRECTED GRAPH STRONGLY CONNECTED.
FRANB 1980 -4 FRANK, A.
NOTE ON K-STRONGLY CONNECTED ORIENTATIONS OF AN UNDIRECTED GRAPH, A.
FRANB 1981 -4 FRANK, A.
ON DISJOINT TREES AND ARBORESCENCES.
FRANB 1980 -6 FRANK, A.
ON THE ORIENTATION OF GRAPHS.
FRANC 1978 -1 FRANK, A.; GYARFAS, A.
DIRECTED GRAPHS AND COMPUTER PROGRAMS.
FRANC 1978 -2 FRANK, A.; GYARFAS, A.
HOW TO ORIENT THE EDGES OF A GRAPH.
FRANE 1978 -1 FRANK, O.
ESTIMATION OF THE NUMBER OF CONNECTED COMPONENTS IN A GRAPH BY USING A SAMPLED SUBGRAPH.
GABOB 1979 -1 GABOW, H. N.
ALGORITHMIC PROOFS OF TWO RELATIONS BETWEEN CONNECTIVITY AND THE 1-FACTORS OF A GRAPH.
GALI 1980 -1 GALIL, Z.
FINDING THE VERTEX CONNECTIVITY OF GRAPHS.
GALLA 1958 -1 GALLAI, T.
MAXIMUM-MINIMUM SAETZE UEBER GRAPHEN.
GALLA 1961 -1 GALLAI, T.
MAXIMUM-MINIMUM SAETZE UND VERALLGEMEINERTE FAKTOREN VON GRAPHEN.
GARED 1978 -1 GAREY, M. R.; TARJAN, R. E.
LINEAR-TIME ALGORITHM FOR FINDING ALL FEEDBACK VERTICES, A.
GARK 1979 -1 GARKAVENKO, S. I.; BERDNIKOVA, L. S.
DETERMINATION OF THE PATHS IN AN ORIENTED ACYCLICAL GRAPH.
GATI 1979 -1 GATI, G.
FURTHER ANNOTATED BIBLIOGRAPHY ON THE ISOMORPHISM DISEASE.
GATTA 1981 -1 GATTINGER, M.; WENZEL, G.
VERALLGEMEINERTE GERUESTE, KOZYKLEN UND ZYKLEN IN GRAPHEN.
GAUL 1978 -1 GAUL, W.
SOME STRUCTURAL PROPERTIES OF PROJECT DIGRAPHS.
GAVR 1977 -1 GAVRIL, F.
SOME NP-COMPLETE PROBLEMS ON GRAPHS.
GEORB 1976 -1 GEORGIEVA, N. C.
ALGORITHM FOR THE EXACT PARTITIONING OF A GRAPH WITH N VERTICES INTO TWO SUBGRAPHS (BULGARIAN), AN.
GERH 1979 -1 GERHARDS, L.; LINDENBERG, W.
CLIQUE DETECTION FOR NONDIRECTED GRAPHS: TWO NEW ALGORITHMS.
GESS 1979 -1 GESSEL, I.; WANG, D.-L.
DEPTH-FIRST SEARCH AS A COMBINATORIAL CORRESPONDENCE.
GHIU 1977 -1 GHIUS, V.
FLOWS IN ARBITRARILY TRACED, GENERALIZED GRAPHS (ROMANIAN).
GILE 1979 -1 GILES, R.
ADJACENCY ON THE POSTMAN POLYHEDRON.
GILEE 1979 -1 GILES, R.; TROTTER, L. E. JR.
ON STABLE SET POLYHEDRA FOR K1,3-FREE GRAPHS.
GOLDA 1979 -1 GOLDBERG, M. K.
CRITICAL GRAPHS WITH AN EVEN NUMBER OF VERTICES(RUSSIAN).
GOLU 1976 -1 GOLUMBIC, M. C.
COMBINATORIAL MERGING.
GOLU 1980 -1 GOLUMBIC, M. C.
ALGORITHMIC GRAPH THEORY AND PERFECT GRAPHS.
GOND 1979 -1 GONDRAN, M.
ALGORITHMES LINEAIRES POUR LES PROBLEMES DE PARTITION, DE RECOUVREMENT ET DE COUPLAGE DANS LES HYPERGRAPHES D'INTERVALLES, DES.
GOND 1980 -1 GONDRAN, M.
CHEMINS ET CONNEXITE.
GONDA 1979 -1 GONDRAN, M.; MINOUX, M.
GRAPHES ET ALGORITHMES.
GORA 1979 -1 GORALCIKOVA, A.; KOUBEK, V.
REDUCT-AND-CLOSURE ALGORITHM FOR GRAPHS, A.
GORD 1980 -1 GORDON, M.; TORKINGTON, J. A.
ENUMERATION OF COLOURED PLANE TREES WITH A GIVEN TYPE PARTITION.
GOROB 1978 -1 GORDON, V. S.; SAFRANSKII, JA. M.
OPTIMAL ORDERING UNDER SERIAL-PARALLEL PRECEDENCE CONSTRAINTS (RUSSIAN).

GOTO 1974 -1 GOTO, S.; OHTSUKI, T.
SIMPLEX ALGORITHM ON A LINEAR GRAPH - A UNIFIED VIEW OF THE EXTREMAL PATH AND CUTSET PROBLEMS ON A GRAPH, THE.

GOUL 1981 -1 GOULD, R. J.
ON LINE GRAPHS AND THE HAMILTONIAN INDEX.

GOUY 1978 -1 GOUYOU-BEAUCHAMPS, D.
ALGORITHME DE RECHERCHE DE CIRCUIT HAMILTONIEN DANS LES GRAPHES 4-CONNEXES PLANAIRES, UN.

GRAH 1970 -1 GRAHAM, R. L.
ON PRIMITIVE GRAPHS AND OPTIMAL VERTEX ASSIGNMENTS.

GRAH 1980 -1 GRAHAM, R. L.
ON A DIOPHANTINE EQUATION ARISING IN GRAPH THEORY.

GRAHB 1978 -1 GRAHAM, R. L.; LOVASZ, L.
DISTANCE MATRIX POLYNOMIALS OF TREES.

GRAV 1977 -1 GRAVER, J. E.; WATKINS, M. E.
COMBINATORICS WITH EMPHASIS ON THE THEORY OF GRAPHS.

GRIG 1979 -1 GRIGGS, J. R.
EXTREMAL VALUES OF THE INTERVAL NUMBER OF A GRAPH, II.

GRIGA 1980 -1 GRIGGS, J. R.; WEST, D. B.
EXTREMAL VALUES OF THE INTERVAL NUMBER OF A GRAPH.

GROE 1979 -1 GROEFLIN, H.; LIEBLING, T. M.
CONNECTED AND ALTERNATING VECTORS POLYHEDRA AND ALGORITHMS.

GROEA 1981 -1 GROEFLIN, H.; LIEBLING, T. M.; PRODON, A.
OPTIMAL SUBTREES AND EXTENSIONS.

GROEB 1979 -1 GROETSCHEL, M.
ON MINIMAL STRONG BLOCKS.

GROEB 1980 -1 GROETSCHEL, M.
ON THE MONOTONE SYMMETRIC TRAVELLING SALESMAN PROBLEM: HYPOHAMILTONIAN/ HYPOTRACEABLE GRAPHS AND FACETS.

GROEB 1979 -2 GROETSCHEL, M.
STRONG BLOCKS AND THE OPTIMUM BRANCHING PROBLEM.

GROEC 1979 -1 GROETSCHEL, M.; HARARY, F.
GRAPHS FOR WHICH ALL STRONG ORIENTATIONS ARE HAMILTONIAN, THE.

GROED 1981 -1 GROETSCHEL, M.; LOVASZ, L.; SCHRIJVER, A.
ELLIPSOID METHOD AND ITS CONSEQUENCES IN COMBINATORIAL OPTIMIZATION, THE.

GROEF 1981 -1 GROETSCHEL, M.; PULLEYBLANK, W. R.
CLIQUE TREES AND THE TRAVELLING SALESMAN PROBLEM.

GROEF 1981 -2 GROETSCHEL, M.; PULLEYBLANK, W. R.
WEAKLY BIPARTITE GRAPHS AND THE MAX-CUT PROBLEM.

GROEG 1980 -1 GROETSCHEL, M.; THOMASSEN, C.; WAKABAYASHI, Y.
HYPOTRACEABLE DIGRAPHS.

GROEH 1978 -1 GROETSCHEL, M.; WAKABAYASHI, Y.
HYPOTRACEABLE DIGRAPHS.

GROEH 1980 -1 GROETSCHEL, M.; WAKABAYASHI, Y.
HYPOHAMILTONIAN DIGRAPHS.

GROEH 1981 -1 GROETSCHEL, M.; WAKABAYASHI, Y.
ON THE STRUCTURE OF THE MONOTONE ASYMMETRIC TRAVELLING SALESMAN POLYTOPE I: HYPOHAMILTONIAN FACETS.

GROEH 1981 -2 GROETSCHEL, M.; WAKABAYASHI, Y.
ON THE STRUCTURE OF THE MONOTONE ASYMMETRIC TRAVELLING SALESMAN POLYTOPE II: HYPOTRACEABLE FACETS.

GROP 1977 -1 GROPPEN, V. O.
EXTREMAL PROBLEMS OF GRAPHS WITH A MINIMAX GOAL FUNCTIONAL.

GROS 1979 -1 GROSS, J. L.; ROSEN, R. H.
LINEAR TIME PLANARITY ALGORITHM FOR 2-COMPLEXES, A.

GUAN 1978 -1 GUAN, M. G.
METHOD FOR FINDING THE MINIMUM ARBORESCENCE OF THE DIRECTED GRAPHS ARISING IN THE CHANNEL DESIGN PROBLEM (CHINESE), A.

GUSA 1976 -1 GUSAKOV, V. J.; JAKUBOVIC, S. M.
CLASSIFICATION ALGORITHMS (RUSSIAN).

GUTT 1977 -1 GUTT, S.
INFINITE FAMILIES OF HYPOHAMILTONIAN GRAPHS.

GYAR 1978 -1 GYARFAS, A.; LEHEL, J.
PACKING TREES OF DIFFERENT ORDER INTO K(N).

HACK 1979 -2 HACKBARTH, K.-D.
BERECHNUNG KANTENDISJUNKTER WEGE ZWISCHEN ZWEI KNOTEN IN EINEM GRAPHEN.

HADZ 1979 -1 HADZIIVANOV, N. G.; NIKIFOROV, V. S.
ESTIMATES FOR THE NUMBER OF CLIQUES OF A GRAPH WITH A GIVEN VERTEX NUMBER OF INDEPENDENCE (RUSSIAN).

HAEG 1979 -1 HAEGGKVIST, R.
ON F-HAMILTONIAN GRAPHS.

HAEGA 1981 -1 HAEGGKVIST, R.; NICOGHOSSIAN, G. G.
REMARK ON HAMILTONIAN CYCLES, A.

HAEM 1980 -1 HAEMERS, W. H.
EIGENVALUE TECHNIQUES IN DESIGN AND GRAPH THEORY.

HALI 1980 -1 HALIN, R.
GRAPHENTHEORIE I.

HALP 1979 -2 HALPERN, J.
SIMPLE EDGE ELIMINATION CRITERION IN A SEARCH FOR THE CENTER OF A GRAPH, A.

HAMA 1980 -5 HAMACHER, H.
OPTIMAL CUTS.

HAMI 1978 -1 HAMIDOUNE, Y. O.
SUR LES SOMMETS DE DEMI-DEGRE H D'UN GRAPHE FORTEMENT H-CONNEXE MINIMAL.

HAMMB 1981 -1 HAMMER, P. L.; HANSEN, P.; SIMEONE, B.
UPPER PLANES OF QUADRATIC 0-1 FUNCTIONS AND STABILITY IN GRAPHS.

HAMMC 1978 -1 HAMMER, P. L.; IBARAKI, T.; SIMEONE, B.
DEGREE SEQUENCES OF THRESHOLD GRAPHS.

HAMMF 1977 -1 HAMMER, P. L.; SIMEONE, B.
SPLITTANCE OF A GRAPH, THE.

HANS 1978 -1 HANSEL, K.; JAENICKE, W.; WOLIN, JU. M.
ZUR BESTIMMUNG ALLER ELEMENTARKREISE IN GERICHTETEN GRAPHEN.

HANSB 1980 -1 HANSEN, P.
BORNES ET ALGORITHMES POUR LES STABLES D'UN GRAPHE.

HANSB 1979 -2 HANSEN, P.
UPPER BOUNDS FOR THE STABILITY NUMBER OF A GRAPH.

HARA 1970 -1 HARARY, F.
COVERING AND PACKING IN GRAPHS, I.

HARA 1979 -1 HARARY, F.
STRUCTURE OF THRESHOLD GRAPHS, THE.
HARAA 1978 -1 HARARY, F.; KABELL, J. A.
GRAPHICAL CONFLICT I: A NEW CLASS OF EXTREMAL PROBLEMS.
HARAA 1980 -1 HARARY, F.; KABELL, J. A.
INTUITIVE APPROACH TO INTERVAL NUMBERS OF GRAPHS, AN.
HARAB 1979 -1 HARARY, F.; KOMMEL, H. J.
GRAPHS WITH ONLY SELF-DUAL SIGNINGS, THE.
HARAC 1980 -1 HARARY, F.; KOVACS, P.
REGULAR GRAPHS WITH GIVEN GIRTH PAIR.
HARAD 1978 -1 HARARY, F.; MARCH, L.; ROBINSON, R. W.
ON ENUMERATING CERTAIN DESIGN PROBLEMS IN TERMS OF BICOLOURED GRAPHS WITH NO ISOLATES.
HARAE 1979 -1 HARARY, F.; ROBINSON, R. W.
LABELED BIPARTITE BLOCKS.
HARTO 1975 -1 HARTNELL, B. L.; MILGRAM, M.
DECOMPOSITION OF K*(P), FOR P A PRIME, INTO K-CIRCUITS.
HAUS 1980 -2 HAUSMANN, D.
FARBKLASSEN UND PSEUDOKNOTEN FUER ADJAZENZCHARAKTERISIERUNGEN.
HEINB 1978 -1 HEINRICH, K.; WALLIS, W. D.
HAMILTONIAN CYCLES IN CERTAIN GRAPHS.
HEINC 1979 -1 HEINRICH, P.
BEZIEHUNG ZWISCHEN DEN WEG-KREIS-SYSTEMEN IN EINEM GERICHTETEN GRAPHEN UND DEN UNTERDETERMINANTEN SEINER CHARAKTERISTISCHEN MATRIX, EINE.
HEIND 1979 -1 HEINRICH, P.; SCHAAR, G.
UEBER ZUSAMMENHAENGENDE GRAPHEN MIT P-HAMILTONSCHER (P+1)-TER POTENZ (P >= 4).
HETY 1974 -1 HETYEI, G.
ON SUBGRAPHS OF J-COLORABLE GRAPHS (HUNGARIAN).
HETY 1975 -1 HETYEI, G.
ON THE 1-FACTORS AND THE HAMILTONIAN CIRCUITS OF COMPLETE N-COLORABLE GRAPHS (HUNGARIAN).
HEYD 1980 -1 HEYDEMANN, M. C.
ON CYCLES AND PATHS IN DIGRAPHS.
HINT 1976 -1 HINTEREGGER, J.
VERBESSERTES VERFAHREN ZUR FESTSTELLUNG DER ISOMORPHIE ENDLICHER GRAPHEN, EIN.
HIRA 1979 -1 HIRATA, T.; MAROUOKA, A.; KIMURA, M.
POLYNOMIAL TIME ALGORITHM TO FIND A PATH COVER OF A REDUCIBLE FLOW GRAPH (JAPANESE), A.
HIRSA 1979 -1 HIRSCHBERG, D. S.; WONG, C. K.
UPPER AND LOWER BOUNDS FOR GRAPH-DIAMETER PROBLEMS WITH APPLICATION TO RECORD ALLOCATION.
HOBB 1979 -1 HOBBS, A. M.
HAMILTONIAN SQUARES OF CACTI.
HOBB 1979 -2 HOBBS, A. M.
J-COMPONENTS, BRIDGES, AND J-FRAGMENTS.
HOBB 1979 -3 HOBBS, A. M.
MAXIMAL HAMILTONIAN CYCLES IN SQUARES OF GRAPHS.
HOED 1978 -1 HOEDE, C.
ON CHARACTERIZATION OF HAMILTONIAN GRAPHS.
HOED 1979 -1 HOEDE, C.
ZWIEBELSTRUKTUREN EINIGER KLASSEN VON KOMBINATORISCHEN UND GRAPHENTHEORETISCHEN PROBLEMEN, DIE.
HOEDA 1981 -1 HOEDE, C.; VELDMAN, H. J.
CONTRACTION THEOREMS IN HAMILTONIAN GRAPH THEORY.
HOFFA 1970 -1 HOFFMAN, A. J.; HOWES, L.
ON EIGENVALUES AND COLORINGS OF GRAPHS, II.
HOLY 1979 -1 HOLYER, I. J.; COCKAYNE, E. J.
ON THE SUM OF CARDINALITIES OF EXTREMUM MAXIMAL INDEPENDENT SETS.
HOMEA 1976 -1 HOMENKO, N. P.; VIVROT, T. M.
(0,1)-MATRICES (RUSSIAN).
HOMEB 1977 -1 HOMENKO, N. P.; VYVROT, T. M.
PROPERTIES OF THE MATRIX OF INDEPENDENT CYCLES OF A GRAPH (RUSSIAN).
HORA 1979 -1 HORAK, P.
DIGRAPHS MAXIMAL WITH RESPECT TO CONNECTIVITY.
HORAA 1979 -1 HORAK, P.; TOVAREK, L.
ON HAMILTONIAN CYCLES OF COMPLETE N-PARTITE GRAPHS.
HOWO 1979 -1 HOWORKA, E.
ON METRIC PROPERTIES OF CERTAIN CLIQUE GRAPHS.
HSU B 1979 -1 HSU, W.-L.; NEMHAUSER, G. L.
ALGORITHMS FOR MINIMUM COVERINGS BY CLIQUES AND MAXIMUM CLIQUES IN CLAW-FREE PERFECT GRAPHS.
IBARC 1978 -1 IBARAKI, T.; PELED, U. N.
SUFFICIENT CONDITIONS FOR GRAPHS WITH THRESHOLD NUMBER 2.
IRI 1978 -1 IRI, M.
PRACTICAL ALGORITHM FOR THE MENGER-TYPE GENERALIZATION OF THE INDEPENDENT ASSIGNMENT PROBLEM, A.
ISHI 1978 -1 ISHII, H.
NEW METHOD FINDING THE K-TH BEST PATH IN A GRAPH, A.
ITAIA 1977 -1 ITAI, A.; RODEH, M.
FINDING A MINIMUM CIRCUIT IN A GRAPH.
JACK 1979 -1 JACKSON, B.
EDGE-DISJOINT HAMILTON CYCLES IN REGULAR GRAPHS OF LARGE DEGREE.
JACK 1980 -1 JACKSON, B.
HAMILTON CYCLES IN REGULAR 2-CONNECTED GRAPHS.
JACK 1979 -2 JACKSON, B.
HAMILTON CYCLES IN REGULAR TWO-CONNECTED GRAPHS.
JACKA 1978 -1 JACKSON, W.
CYCLES IN BIPARTITE GRAPHS.
JAEG 1978 -1 JAEGER, F.
ON INTERVAL HYPERGRAPHS AND NOWHERE-ZERO FLOWS IN GRAPHS.
JAVD 1979 -1 JAVDEKAR, M. M.
MINIMALLY (P-7)-HAMILTONIAN GRAPHS.
JOHND 1965 -1 JOHNSON, E. L.
PROGRAMMING IN NETWORKS AND GRAPHS.
JOHNE 1980 -1 JOHNSON, E. L.; PADBERG, M. W.
DEGREE-TWO INEQUALITIES, CLIQUE FACETS, AND BIPEFECT GRAPHS.
JOHNI 1977 -1 JOHNSON, L. F.
ALGORITHMS FOR ENUMERATING THE SIMPLE CYCLES OF A DIGRAPH.
JOVA 1973 -1 JOVANOVICH, A. D.; CHOBELJICH, S. N.
FAST ALGORITHM FOR FINDING A FOREST OF A LINEAR GRAPH.

JUNG 1978 -1 JUNG, H. A.
ON MAXIMAL CIRCUITS IN FINITE GRAPHS.

KAAS 1980 -1 KAAS, R.
BRANCH AND BOUND ALGORITHM FOR THE ACYCLIC SUBGRAPH PROBLEM, A.

KAEM 1979 -1 KAEMPFE, H.
RATIONELLE LOESUNG DES GOZINTOPROBLEMS IM KREISFREIEN BEWERTETEN GERICHTETEN GRAPHEN UND WEITERE OEKONOMISCHE INTERPRETATIONEN, EINE.

KAJI 1979 -1 KAJITANI, Y.; UENO, S.
ON THE RANK OF CERTAIN CLASSES OF CUT-SETS AND TIE-SETS OF A GRAPH.

KAPP 1979 -1 KAPPAUF, C. H.; KOEHLER, G. J.
MIXED POSTMAN PROBLEM, THE.

KARE 1980 -1 KAREJAN, Z. A.; MOSESJAN, K. M.
HAMILTONIAN COMPLETION NUMBER OF A DIGRAPH (RUSSIAN), THE.

KARP 1975 -1 KARP, R. M.
COMPUTATIONAL COMPLEXITY OF COMBINATORIAL AND GRAPH-THEORETIC PROBLEMS.

KARP 1978 -1 KARP, R. M.
CHARACTERIZATION OF THE MINIMUM CYCLE MEAN IN A DIGRAPH, A.

KERG 1980 -1 KERGALL, Y.
CHAINES DE LONGUEUR MAXIMUM D'UN ARBRE.

KERI 1981 -1 KERI, G.
ON THE REDUCTION OF A BIPARTITE GRAPH TO IRREDUCIBLE COMPONENTS.

KEVO 1978 -1 KEVORKIAN, A. K.
GENERAL TOPOLOGICAL RESULTS ON THE CONSTRUCTION OF A MINIMUM ESSENTIAL SET OF A DIGRAPH.

KEVO 1979 -1 KEVORKIAN, A. K.
GRAPH-THEORETIC CHARACTERIZATION OF THE MATRIX PROPERTY OF FULL IRREDUCIBILITY WITHOUT USING A TRANSVERSAL.

KHAD 1977 -1 KHADZHIIVANOV, N. G.
GRAPH INEQUALITES (RUSSIAN).

KHADA 1978 -1 KHADZHIIVANOV, N. G.; NIKIFOROV, V. S.
INEGALITE DE NORDHAUS-STEWART-MOON-MOSER (RUSSIAN).

KIKUA 1979 -1 KIKUST, P. B.
ORGANIZATION OF SORTING IN THE SEARCH FOR THE MAXIMUM CLIQUE OF A GRAPH (RUSSIAN).

KINB 1980 -1 KINBER, E. B.
POLYNOMIAL ALGORITHM FOR FINDING MINIMAL VERTEX COVERINGS FOR A CLASS OF PLANAR GRAPHS (RUSSIAN), A.

KINN 1977 -1 KINNEY, J. M.
ALMOST TRACEABLE GRAPHS AND TRACEABILITY.

KIRK 1976 -1 KIRKPATRICK, D.
DETERMINING GRAPH PROPERTIES FROM MATRIX REPRESENTATIONS.

KLET 1979 -1 KLETIN, V. A.
ANALYSE DE L'EFFICACITE DES ALGORITHMES COMBINATOIRES DE RECHERCHE DES ARBRES EXTREMAUX SUR LES GRAPHES ORIENTES PONDERES (RUSSIAN).

KOEHA 1978 -1 KOEHLER, N.
BEWERTETE BAEUME.

KOH A 1979 -1 KOH, K. M.; TAN, T.; ROGERS, D. G.
TWO THEOREMS ON GRACEFUL TREES.

KOKH 1977 -1 KOKHOV, V. O.; LAZARJEV, V. O.; SHAMAJEVA, O. YU.
EFFECTIVE ALGORITHM FOR THE RECOGNITION OF THE ISOMORPHISM OF DIRECTED GRAPHS (UKRAINIAN).

KOLA 1980 -1 KOLASINSKA, E.
ON A MINIMUM CYCLE BASIS OF A GRAPH.

KOLC 1976 -1 KOLCOV, V. N.
DECOMPOSITION OF A BIPARTITE GRAPH INTO A MINIMAL NUMBER OF PLANE SUBGRAPHS (RUSSIAN).

KONOA 1978 -1 KONONENKO, A. M.; TRUKHANOVSKIJ, N. N.
ENUMERATION DES ARBRES MAXIMAUX D'UNE CLASSE DE GRAPHES BIPARTIS (RUSSIAN).

KORS 1977 -1 KORSHUNOV, A. D.
SOLUTION OF A PROBLEM OF P. ERDOES AND A. RENYI ON HAMILTONIAN CYCLES IN NON-ORIENTED GRAPHS (RUSSIAN).

KORZ 1978 -1 KORZAN, B.
ELEMENTS OF THE THEORY OF GRAPHS AND NETWORKS. METHODS AND APPLICATIONS (POLISH).

KOTZA 1978 -1 KOTZIG, A.; LABELLE, J.
STRONGLY HAMILTONIAN GRAPHS.

KOTZA 1979 -1 KOTZIG, A.; LABELLE, J.
QUELQUES PROBLEMES OUVERTS CONCERNANT LES GRAPHES FORTEMENT HAMILTONIENS.

KOZE 1978 -1 KOZEN, D.
CLIQUE PROBLEM EQUIVALENT TO GRAPH ISOMORPHISM, A.

KRAP 1978 -1 KRAPIVA, A. J.
ON CONSTRUCTING THE MINIMUM CUTTING-OFF SET OF THE GRAPH (RUSSIAN).

KRIS 1975 -1 KRISHNAMOORTHY, M. S.
NP-HARD PROBLEM IN BIPARTITE GRAPHS, AN.

KRISA 1979 -2 KRISHNAMOORTHY, M. S.; DEO, N.
NODE-DELETION NP-COMPLETE PROBLEMS.

KUBOA 1977 -1 KUBO, N.; TSUKIYAMA, S.; SHIRAKAWA, I.; ARIYOSHI, H.
ALGORITHM FOR FINDING A MAXIMAL CUT, AN.

KULK 1978 -1 KULKARNI, K. H.
MINIMALLY LOCALLY 1-CONNECTED GRAPHS.

KURE 1979 -1 KUREJCHIK, V. M.
ALGORITHME POUR DETERMINER LES SOUS-ENSEMBLES EXTERIEUREMENT STABLES EN SE BASANT SUR LES NOMBRES STRUCTURAUX (RUSSIAN).

KUREA 1979 -1 KUREJCHIK, V. M.; LITVINENKO, V. A.
DETERMINATION OF THE CLIQUES OF A SYMMETRIC GRAPH (RUSSIAN).

LAKS 1979 -1 LAKSHMINARAYAN, S.; LAKSHMANAN, R.; PAPINEAU, R. L.; ROCHETTE, R.
ORDER PRESERVING ALLOCATION OF JOBS TO TWO NON-IDENTICAL PARALLEL MACHINES: A SOLVABLE CASE OF THE MAXIMUM CUT PROBLEM.

LAPA 1978 -1 LAPAUGH, A. S.; RIVEST, R. L.
SUBGRAPH HOMOMORPHISM PROBLEM, THE.

LATU 1973 -1 LATUSKIEWICZ, J.
ALGORITHM FOR EXAMINING WHETHER A GRAPH IS A HAMILTONIAN GRAPH. II (POLISH), AN.

LAUF 1980 -1 LAUFER, P. J.
ON STRONGLY HAMILTONIAN COMPLETE BIPARTITE GRAPHS.

LAWI 1979 -1 LAWIS, R. T.; PARKER, R. G.
BIN PACKING, MULTI-PROCESSOR SCHEDULING, AND GRAPH COLORING.

LERO 1977 -1 LEROUX, A.
GRAPHES DE TRANSFERT ET LA NOTION DE GRAPHE INVERSE, LES.

LESC 1980 -1 LESCH, J.; LESCH, M.; SCHMEICHEL, I.
VERFAHREN ZUR ERMITTLUNG DER MAXIMALEN STABILEN MENGEN IN EINEM UNGERICHTETEN GRAPHEN, EIN.

LESN 1977 -1 LESNIAK-FOSTER, L. M.
ON CRITICALLY HAMILTONIAN GRAPHS.
LESN 1978 -1 LESNIAK-FOSTER, L. M.
ON N-DISTANT HAMILTONIAN LINE GRAPHS.
LEWIC 1978 -1 LEWIS, J. M.
ON THE COMPLEXITY OF THE MAXIMUM SUBGRAPH PROBLEM.
LEWID 1980 -1 LEWIS, J. M.; YANNAKAKIS, M.
NODE-DELETION PROBLEM FOR HEREDITARY PROPERTIES IS NP-COMPLETE, THE.
LI A 1977 -1 LI, W.-X.
CONNECTIVITY OF COMPLEMENTARY GRAPHS (CHINESE), THE.
LIHO 1976 -1 LIHOLAT, N. A.
PROBLEM ON THE COVERING OF A GRAPH BY A MINIMAL POWER SET (RUSSIAN), A.
LIKH 1974 -1 LIKHACHEV, V. M.
SEARCH ALGORITHM FOR THE MINIMUM NUMBER OF VERTICES IN AN ORIENTED GRAPH THROUGH WHICH PASS ALL CIRCUITS OF THE GRAPH.
LIPTA 1979 -1 LIPTON, R. J.; TARJAN, R. E.
SEPARATOR THEOREM FOR PLANAR GRAPHS, A.
LIU C 1980 -1 LIU, Z. H.; MA, Z. F.; ZHU, Y. J.; CAI, M. C.
MINIMUM SPANNING TREES WITH DEGREE CONSTRAINTS (CHINESE).
LJUB 1978 -1 LJUBCHENKO, G. G.
NUMERICAL GRAPHS (RUSSIAN).
LOIZ 1980 -1 LOIZOU, G.
ON A CYCLE FINDING ALGORITHM.
LOVA 1976 -1 LOVASZ, L.
CHROMATIC NUMBER OF HYPERGRAPHS AND LINEAR ALGEBRA.
LOVA 1977 -1 LOVASZ, L.
FLATS IN MATROIDS AND GEOMETRIC GRAPHS.
LOVA 1978 -1 LOVASZ, L.
SOME FINITE BASIS THEOREMS ON GRAPH THEORY.
LOVA 1979 -1 LOVASZ, L.
GRAPH THEORY AND INTEGER PROGRAMMING.
LOVA 1981 -1 LOVASZ, L.
BOUNDING THE INDEPENDENCE NUMBER OF A GRAPH.
LOVA 1976 -2 LOVASZ, L.
GRAPH THEORY AND INTEGER PROGRAMMING (HUNGARIAN).
LOVA 1979 -4 LOVASZ, L.
TOPOLOGICAL AND ALGEBRAIC METHODS IN GRAPH THEORY.
LOZO 1979 -1 LOZOVANU, D. D.
OPTIMAL OUTGOING TREES IN DIGRAPHS (RUSSIAN).
LOZO 1981 -1 LOZOVANU, D. D.
OPTIMUM SUBGRAPHS IN A WEIGHTED DIGRAPH (RUSSIAN).
LUCC 1976 -1 LUCCHESI, C.
MINIMAX EQUALITY FOR DIRECTED GRAPHS, A.
LUCCA 1978 -1 LUCCHESI, C.; YOUNGER, D. H.
MINIMAX THEOREM FOR DIRECTED GRAPHS, A.
LUEK 1975 -1 LUEKER, G. S.
EFFICIENT ALGORITHMS FOR CHORDAL GRAPHS AND INTERVAL GRAPHS.
LUEK 1978 -1 LUEKER, G. S.
MAXIMIZATION PROBLEMS ON GRAPHS WITH EDGE WEIGHTS CHOSEN FROM A NORMAL DISTRIBUTION.
LUEK 1979 -1 LUEKER, G. S.
OPTIMIZATION PROBLEMS ON GRAPHS WITH INDEPENDENT RANDOM EDGE WEIGHTS.
LUEKA 1979 -1 LUEKER, G. S.; BOOTH, K. S.
LINEAR TIME ALGORITHM FOR DECIDING INTERVAL GRAPH ISOMORPHISM, A.
MAAM 1981 -1 MAAMOUN, M.
PARITE DES CYCLES CONTENANT DES SOMMETS SPECIFIES D'UN GRAPHE.
MAC B 1979 -1 MAC DIARMID, C.
DETERMINING THE CHROMATIC NUMBER OF A GRAPH.
MAC D 1978 -1 MAC ELIECE, R. J.; RODEMICH, E. R.; RUMSEY, H. C. JR.
LOVASZ BOUND AND SOME GENERALIZATIONS, THE.
MAC H 1979 -1 MAC GREGOR, J. J.
RELATIONAL CONSISTENCY ALGORITHMS AND THEIR APPLICATION IN FINDING SUBGRAPH AND GRAPH ISOMORPHISMS.
MADE 1979 -1 MADER, W.
CONNECTIVITY AND EDGE-CONNECTIVITY IN FINITE GRAPHS.
MADE 1979 -2 MADER, W.
REDUKTIONSMETHODE FUER DEN KANTENZUSAMMENHANG IN GRAPHEN, EINE.
MADE 1979 -3 MADER, W.
ZUR STRUKTUR MINIMAL N-FACH ZUSAMMENHAENGENDER GRAPHEN.
MAGRA 1976 -1 MAGRUPOW, T. M.
NEW APPROACH TO THE CONSTRUCTION OF A MINIMAL TREE (RUSSIAN), A.
MAKA 1978 -1 MAKAROV, G. D.; LIHOLAT, N. A.
EXTREMAL PROBLEM ON GRAPHS (RUSSIAN), AN.
MALO 1978 -1 MALOJI, M. W.; UHRY, J.-P.
PRIMAL, ONE-PASS ALGORITHM FOR CONSTRUCTING A MINIMUM-WEIGHT ROOTED SPANNING ARBORESCENCE, A.
MALY 1977 -1 MALYSHKO, V. V.
SOME PROPERTIES OF ARC GRAPHS (RUSSIAN).
MANC 1979 -1 MANCA, P.
ON A SIMPLE CHARACTERIZATION OF THRESHOLD GRAPHS.
MARC 1976 -1 MARCU, D.
APPLICATION OF VECTOR SPACES TO THE CALCULATION OF THE NUMBER OF CONNECTED COMPONENTS OF A FINITE DIRECTED GRAPH (ROMANIAN), AN.
MARC 1978 -1 MARCU, D.
SUR LA CONNEXITE SEMI-FORTE D'UN DIGRAPHE.
MARC 1979 -1 MARCU, D.
METHOD FOR FINDING THE STRONG COMPONENTS OF A DIGRAPH, A.
MARC 1979 -2 MARCU, D.
METHOD FOR FINDING THE STRONGLY CONNECTED COMPONENTS OF A DIGRAPH, A.
MARC 1979 -3 MARCU, D.
ON CERTAIN VECTOR SPACES ASSOCIATED TO THE ORIENTED FINITE GRAPHS.
MARK 1977 -1 MARKOSJAN, A. G.; MARKOSJAN, S. E.
ALGORITHM FOR THE DECOMPOSITION OF A DIGRAPH INTO A DIFOREST (RUSSIAN).
MARTB 1978 -1 MARTELLO, S.
ALGORITHM FOR FINDING A MINIMAL EQUIVALENT GRAPH OF A STRONGLY CONNECTED DIGRAPH, AN.
MARTC 1979 -1 MARTELLO, S.; TOTH, P.
FINDING A MINIMAL EQUIVALENT GRAPH OF A DIGRAPH.

MATHA 1979 -1 MATHON, R.
NOTE ON THE GRAPH ISOMORPHISM COUNTING PROBLEM, A.
MAURA 1979 -1 MAURER, S. B.
VERTEX COLORINGS WITHOUT ISOLATES.
MAURB 1978 -1 MAURER, S. B.; SLATER, P. J.
ON K-CRITICAL N-CONNECTED GRAPHS.
MAURB 1979 -1 MAURER, S. B.; SLATER, P. J.
MINIMALLY 2-EDGE-CONNECTED GRAPHS.
MEEU 1980 -1 MEEUSEN, W.
ON THE MAXIMAL NUMBER OF K-CLIQUES IN A GRAPH WITH N VERTICES (TOWARDS AN APPLICATION ON THE MEASUREMENT OF FINANCIAL CONCENTRATION).
MEHTA 1980 -1 MEHTA, N. K.
PERFORMANCE OF SELECTED GRAPH COLORING ALGORITHMS - EMPIRICAL RESULTS.
MEND 1970 -1 MENDELSOHN, N. S.
LINEAR DIOPHANTINE EQUATION WITH APPLICATIONS TO NON-NEGATIVE MATRICES, A.
MEREA 1972 -1 MEREDITH, G. H. J.; LLOYD, E. K.
HAMILTONIAN GRAPHS 04 TO 07, THE.
MILG 1977 -1 MILGRAM, M.; DUBUISSON, B.
ALGORITHME HEURISTIQUE DE DECOMPOSITION D'UN GRAPHE, UN.
MILL 1978 -1 MILLER, G. L.
ON THE N**(LOG(2)N) ISOMORPHISM TECHNIQUE.
MILL 1979 -1 MILLER, G. L.
GRAPH ISOMORPHISM, GENERAL REMARKS.
MINI 1977 -1 MINIEKA, E.
OPTIMUM BRANCHINGS WITH A SPECIFIED NUMBER OF ARCS.
MINI 1979 -1 MINIEKA, E.
CHINESE POSTMAN PROBLEM FOR MIXED NETWORKS, THE.
MINT 1980 -1 MINTY, G. J.
ON MAXIMAL INDEPENDENT SETS OF VERTICES IN CLAW-FREE GRAPHS.
MISR 1979 -1 MISRA, R. B.
ALGORITHM FOR ENUMERATING ALL SIMPLE PATHS IN A COMMUNICATION NETWORK, AN.
MITC 1979 -1 MITCHELL, S.; COCKAYNE, E. J.; HEDETNIEMI, S. T.
LINEAR ALGORITHMS ON RECURSIVE REPRESENTATIONS OF TREES.
MOHA 1979 -1 MOHANTY, S. P.; RAO, D.
CHARACTERIZATION AND ENUMERATION OF HYPOTRAVERSABLE GRAPHS.
MOLL 1979 -1 MOLLUZZO, J. C.
SOME HAMILTONIAN COUNTEREXAMPLES.
MOLL 1979 -2 MOLLUZZO, J. C.
TOUGHNESS, HAMILTONIAN-CONNECTEDNESS, AND N-HAMILTONICITY.
MOUS 1980 -1 MOUSTAKIDES, G.; BEDROSIAN, S. D.
FINDING THE GRAPH WITH THE MAXIMUM NUMBER OF SPANNING TREES.
MUEH 1979 -1 MUEHLBACHER, J.
F-FACTORS OF GRAPHS: A GENERALIZED MATCHING PROBLEM.
MUELA 1981 -1 MUELLER, H.
ZUR STRUKTUR UND KOMPLEXITAET DISKRETER OPTIMIERUNGSPROBLEME, DIE DURCH ERBLICHE EIGENSCHAFTEN AUF ENDLICHEN MENGENSYSTEMEN GEGEBEN SIND.
MUELB 1979 -1 MUELLER, V.
ON COLORINGS OF GRAPHS WITHOUT SHORT CYCLES.
MUELC 1978 -1 MUELLER, V.; PELANT, J.
NUMBER OF HAMILTONIAN CIRCUITS, THE.
MULD 1979 -1 MULDER, H. M.
RAMSEY THEORY.
NADDA 1980 -1 NADDEF, D.; PULLEYBLANK, W. R.
EAR DECOMPOSITIONS OF ELEMENTARY GRAPHS AND GF(2)-RANK OF PERFECT MATCHINGS.
NADDA 1980 -2 NADDEF, D.; PULLEYBLANK, W. R.
HAMILTONICITY AND COMBINATORIAL POLYHEDRA.
NAKAA 1977 -1 NAKAMURA, T.; YAMASAKI, M.
EXTREMAL LENGTH OF AN INFINITE NETWORK WHICH IS NOT NECESSARILY LOCALLY FINITE.
NAKAC 1979 -1 NAKASHIMA, K.; HATTORI, Y.
EFFICIENT BOTTOM-UP ALGORITHM FOR ENUMERATING MINIMAL CUT SETS OF FAULT TREES, AN.
NATAA 1978 -1 NATARAJAN, K. S.; WHITE, L. J.
OPTIMUM DOMINATION IN WEIGHTED TREES.
NEBE 1976 -1 NEBESKY, L.
GENERALIZATION OF HAMILTONIAN CYCLES FOR TREES, A.
NEBE 1978 -1 NEBESKY, L.
ON PANCYCLIC LINE GRAPHS.
NEBE 1979 -1 NEBESKY, L.
ON EULERIAN SUBGRAPHS OF COMPLEMENTARY GRAPHS.
NEME 1977 -1 NEMETH, E.
NOTE ON A MINI-MAX PROBLEM IN SCHEDULING, A.
NESE 1979 -1 NESETRIL, J.; ROEDL, V.
SHORT PROOF OF THE EXISTENCE OF HIGHLY CHROMATIC HYPERGRAPHS WITHOUT SHORT CYCLES, A.
NEUM 1980 -1 NEUMAIER, A.
CLIQUES AND CLAWS IN EDGE-TRANSITIVE STRONGLY REGULAR GRAPHS.
NICU 1979 -1 NICULESCU, S.
ALGORITHM FOR FINDING THE PATHS BETWEEN TWO VERTICES OF A GRAPH (ROMANIAN), AN.
NICU 1979 -2 NICULESCU, S.
ALGORITHM FOR FINDING THE PATHS BETWEEN TWO VERTICES OF A GRAPH, AN.
NICU 1979 -3 NICULESCU, S.
ALGORITHM TO FIND HAMILTONIAN PATHS IN GRAPHS, AN.
NIKO 1976 -1 NIKOGOSJAN, Z. G.
THEOREMS ON HAMILTONIAN CYCLES AND SKELETONS (RUSSIAN).
NIRM 1979 -1 NIRMALA, K.
COMPLEMENTARY GRAPHS AND TOTAL CHROMATIC NUMBERS.
NORB 1979 -1 NORBACK, J. P.; LOVE, R. F.
HEURISTIC FOR THE HAMILTONIAN PATH PROBLEM IN EUCLIDEAN TWO-SPACE.
NTAF 1979 -1 NTAFOS, S. C.; HAKIMI, S. L.
ON PATH COVER PROBLEMS IN DIGRAPHS AND APPLICATIONS TO PROGRAM TESTING.
NUFF 1978 -1 NUFFELEN, C. VAN
ON THE RANK OF THE ADJACENCY MATRIX.
NUFF 1980 -1 NUFFELEN, C. VAN
REMARKS ON THE ADJACENCY MATRIX OF A GRAPH.
OBER 1979 -1 OBERLY, D. J.; SUMNER, D. P.
EVERY CONNECTED, LOCALLY CONNECTED NONTRIVIAL GRAPH WITH NO INDUCED CLAW IS HAMILTONIAN.
OHTS 1981 -1 OHTSUKI, T.
TWO DISJOINT PATH PROBLEM AND WIRE ROUTING DESIGN, THE.

OKAW 1979 -1 OKAWA, S.; NISHITANI, Y.; HONDA, N.
BIPARTITE SUBGRAPH PROBLEMS WITH DEGREE AT MOST THREE (JAPANESE), THE.
OLAR 1979 -1 OLARU, E.; SUCIU, G.
DAUERSTABILE UND KRITISCH IMPERFEKTE GRAPHEN.
OVER 1975 -1 OVERBECK-LARISCH, M.
HAMILTONISCHE LINIEN IN DIGRAPHEN.
OVERA 1979 -1 OVERTON, M. L.; PROSKUROWSKI, A.
CANONICAL INCIDENCE MATRICES OF GRAPHS.
PALL 1978 -1 PALLOTTINO, S.; STORCHI, G.
ALGORITHM FOR DETERMINING THE FUNDAMENTAL CYCLES AND THE MAXIMAL FORESTS OF K-CONNECTED GRAPHS (ITALIAN), AN.
PART 1975 -1 PARTHASARATHY, K. R.; CHOUDUM, S. A.
INTERSECTION NUMBER OF K(4)-FREE GRAPHS, THE.
PARTA 1979 -1 PARTHASARATHY, K. R.; RAVINDRA, G.
VALIDITY OF THE STRONG PERFECT-GRAPH CONJECTURE FOR (K4 - E)-FREE GRAPHS, THE.
PAYA 1979 -1 PAYAN, C.
REMARKS ON CLIQUES AND DOMINATING SETS IN GRAPHS.
PAYA 1980 -1 PAYAN, C.
CLASS OF THRESHOLD AND DOMISHOLD GRAPHS: EQUISTABLE AND EQUIDOMINATING GRAPHS, A.
PECK 1980 -1 PECK, G. W.
HAMILTONIAN CYCLES OF ADJACENT TRIPLES.
PELEA 1981 -1 PELED, U. N.; SIMEONE, B.
BOX-THRESHOLD GRAPHS.
PERLB 1981 -1 PERL, Y.; ZAKS, S.
DEFICIENT GENERALIZED FIBONACCI MAXIMUM PATH GRAPHS.
PHIL 1977 -1 PHILLIPS, S. JR.; DESSOUKY, M. I.
SOLVING THE PROJECT TIME/COST TRADEOFF PROBLEM USING THE MINIMAL CUT CONCEPT.
PIER 1980 -1 PIERONI, P.
DUAL DECOMPOSITION APPROACH FOR ORIENTING ONE-WAY STREETS AND LANES IN A CITY NETWORK, A.
PIOT 1976 -1 PIOTROVSKI, M.
CLASS OF HAMILTONIAN GRAPHS (RUSSIAN), A.
PIOT 1977 -1 PIOTROVSKI, M.
ON A THEOREM OF L. POSA TYPE FOR HAMILTONIAN GRAPHS (RUSSIAN).
PIOT 1976 -2 PIOTROVSKI, M.
SOME PROPERTIES OF HAMILTONIAN GRAPHS (RUSSIAN).
PLES 1979 -1 PLESNIK, J.
NP-COMPLETENESS OF THE HAMILTONIAN CYCLE PROBLEM IN PLANAR DIGRAPHS WITH DEGREE BOUND TWO, THE.
PLUM 1981 -1 PLUMMER, M. D.
SOME RECENT RESULTS ON CYCLE TRAVERSABILITY IN GRAPHS.
POLA 1979 -1 POLANSKY, O. E.; GUTMAN, I.
ZUR WEGEMATRIX SCHLICHTER GRAPHEN.
POPE 1979 -1 POPESCU, D.
PROPRIETES DES GRAPHES SIGNES (ROMANIAN).
POPE 1979 -2 POPESCU, D.
SOME HAMILTONIAN PROPERTIES OF SOME CLASSES OF GRAPHS WHICH EXTEND PETERSEN'S GRAPH (ROMANIAN).
POUZ 1979 -1 POUZET, M.
NOTE SUR LE PROBLEME DE ULAM.
PRIC 1978 -1 PRICE, W. L.
ALGORITHM WHICH GENERATES THE HAMILTONIAN CIRCUITS OF A CUBIC PLANAR MAP, AN.
PROS 1979 -1 PROSKUROWSKI, A.
MINIMUM DOMINATING CYCLES IN 2-TREES.
PULL 1977 -1 PULLEYBLANK, W. R.
LINEAR PROGRAMMING RELAXATION OF THE NODE PACKING PROBLEM OR 2-BICRITICAL GRAPHS AND NODE COVERS, A.
PULL 1979 -1 PULLEYBLANK, W. R.
MINIMUM NODE COVERS AND 2-BICRITICAL GRAPHS.
PULL 1979 -2 PULLEYBLANK, W. R.
NOTE ON GRAPHS SPANNED BY EULERIAN GRAPHS, A.
RAI 1980 -1 RAI, S.; AGGARWAL, K. K.
ON COMPLEMENTATION OF PATHSETS AND CUTSETS.
RAO C 1979 -1 RAO, S. B.
SOLUTION OF THE HAMILTONIAN PROBLEM FOR SELF-COMPLEMENTARY GRAPHS.
RAO D 1977 -1 RAO, S. B.; RAVINDRA, G.
CHARACTERIZATION OF PERFECT TOTAL GRAPHS, A.
RAVI 1979 -1 RAVINDRA, G.
B-GRAPHS.
READ 1979 -1 READ, R. C.
ALGORITHMS IN GRAPH THEORY.
ROBIA 1980 -1 ROBINSON, D. F.; FOULDS, L. R.
DIGRAPHS: THEORY AND TECHNIQUES.
ROBID 1977 -1 ROBINSON, J. M.
DETERMINING THE K-TH SHORTEST PATH BY MATRIX METHOD (HUNGARIAN).
ROSE 1978 -1 ROSE, D. J.; TARJAN, R. E.
ALGORITHMIC ASPECTS OF VERTEX ELIMINATION ON DIRECTED GRAPHS.
ROSEA 1978 -1 ROSENBERG, A. L.
NOTE ON PATHS EMBEDDED IN TREES, A.
ROSEB 1978 -1 ROSENBERG, A. L.; SNYDER, L.
COMPACT B-TREES.
ROSEC 1963 -1 ROSENBLATT, D.
ON THE GRAPHS OF FINITE IDEMPOTENT BOOLEAN RELATION MATRICES.
ROUX 1975 -1 ROUX, M.
NOTES SUR L'ARBRE DE LONGUEUR MINIMA.
RUBI 1978 -1 RUBIN, F.
ENUMERATING ALL SIMPLE PATHS IN A GRAPH.
RUES 1981 -1 RUESCHENDORF, L.
EQUIVALENCE OF TWO NODE CONDITIONS IN BIPARTITE GRAPHS, THE.
RYANA 1979 -1 RYANG, S. Y.; RYU, H. D.
NEW METHOD OF DECIDING HAMILTONIAN CIRCLES AND SPANNING PARTIAL GRAPHS, (KOREAN), A.
RYU 1978 -1 RYU, H. D.
FORMULA DECIDING THE WHOLE OF THE HAMILTONIAN CIRCLE OF A GRAPH (KOREAN), A.
RYU 1978 -2 RYU, H. D.
FORMULA FOR COMPLETELY DETERMINING AN EULERIAN SPANNING PATH OF A GRAPH (KOREAN), A.
SAMP 1977 -1 SAMPATHKUMAR, E.; NEERALAGI, P. S.; VENKATACHALAM, C. V.
GENERALIZATION OF THE CHROMATIC AND LINE CHROMATIC NUMBERS OF A GRAPH, A.

GRAPH THEORETIC RESULTS (UNLESS SPECIFIED ELSEWHERE)

SAND 1974 -1 SANDBERG, V. JU.
HEURISTIC ALGORITHM FOR GRAPH COLORING (RUSSIAN), A.
SANGA 1979 -1 SANGIOVANNI-VINCENTELLI, A.; BICKART, T. A.
BIPARTITE GRAPHS AND AN OPTIMAL BORDERED TRIANGULAR FORM OF A MATRIX.
SAPA 1977 -1 SAPAK, O.
REPRESENTATION OF THE FINITE DIRECTED ACYCLIC GRAPH.
SATOA 1978 -1 SATO, I.
ON A FEW CLIQUE-GRAPH EQUATIONS.
SBIH 1978 -1 SBIHI, N.
ETUDE DES STABLES DANS LES GRAPHES SANS ETOILE.
SBIH 1980 -1 SBIHI, N.
ALGORITHME DE RECHERCHE D'UN STABLE DE CARDINALITE MAXIMUM DANS UN GRAPHE SANS ETOILE.
SCHMB 1976 -1 SCHMIDT, D. C.; DRUFFEL, L. E.
FAST BACKTRACKING ALGORITHM TO TEST DIRECTED GRAPHS FOR ISOMORPHISM USING DISTANCE MATRICES, A.
SCHMD 1979 -2 SCHMIDT, R.
ZYKLISCHE ORIENTIERUNGEN ENDLICHER BEWERTETER GRAPHEN.
SCHR 1981 -1 SCHRADER, R.
APPROXIMATIONS TO CLUSTERING AND SUBGRAPH PROBLEMS ON TREES.
SCHR 1981 -2 SCHRADER, R.
NOTE ON APPROXIMATION ALGORITHMS FOR GRAPH PARTITIONING PROBLEMS, A.
SCHRD 1979 -1 SCHRIJVER, A.
FRACTIONAL PACKING AND COVERING.
SCHRD 1980 -1 SCHRIJVER, A.
COUNTEREXAMPLE TO A CONJECTURE OF EDMONDS AND GILES, A.
SCHRD 1980 -2 SCHRIJVER, A.
MIN-MAX RELATIONS FOR DIRECTED GRAPHS.
SCHRD 1978 -3 SCHRIJVER, A.
VERTEX-CRITICAL SUBGRAPHS OF KNESER GRAPHS.
SCHRE 1979 -1 SCHRIJVER, A.; SEYMOUR, P. D.
SOLUTION OF TWO FRACTIONAL PACKING PROBLEMS OF LOVASZ.
SCHRF 1978 -1 SCHROECK, W.
KONSTRUKTION KOSTENOPTIMALER ZERLEGUNGEN VON GRAPHEN.
SEID 1978 -1 SEIDMAN, S. B.; FOSTER, B. L.
GRAPH-THEORETIC GENERALIZATION OF THE CLIQUE CONCEPT, A.
SENG 1979 -1 SENGUPTA, A.; PALIT, A.
ON CLIQUE GENERATION USING BOOLEAN EQUATIONS.
SENO 1977 -1 SENO, A.; FUKUNAGA, K.; KASAI, T.
ALGORITHM FOR GRAPH ISOMORPHISM, AN.
SEYM 1979 -2 SEYMOUR, P. D.
ON MULTI-COLOURINGS OF CUBIC GRAPHS, AND CONJECTURES OF FULKERSON AND TUTTE.
SEYM 1980 -2 SEYMOUR, P. D.
DISJOINT PATHS IN GRAPHS.
SEYM 1979 -3 SEYMOUR, P. D.
ON ODD CUTS AND PLANE MULTICOMMODITY FLOWS.
SEYM 1979 -5 SEYMOUR, P. D.
SUMS OF CIRCUITS.
SHAM 1979 -1 SHAMIR, A.
LINEAR TIME ALGORITHM FOR FINDING MINIMUM CUTSETS IN REDUCIBLE GRAPHS, A.
SHIL 1979 -1 SHILOACH, Y.
EDGE-DISJOINT BRANCHING IN DIRECTED MULTIGRAPHS.
SHIL 1980 -1 SHILOACH, Y.
MULTI-TERMINAL MINIMUM CUT ALGORITHM FOR PLANAR GRAPHS, A.
SHIL 1980 -2 SHILOACH, Y.
POLYNOMIAL SOLUTION TO THE UNDIRECTED TWO PATHS PROBLEM, A.
SHIM 1978 -1 SHIMAMOTO, Y.
ON AN EXTENSION OF THE GRINBERG THEOREM.
SIME 1979 -2 SIMEONE, B.
QUADRATIC 0-1 PROGRAMMING, BOOLEAN FUNCTIONS AND GRAPHS.
SIMM 1979 -1 SIMMONS, G. J.; SLATER, P. J.
GENERALIZED PETERSEN GRAPHS G(N,4) ARE HAMILTONIAN FOR ALL N NOT = 8, THE.
SIMOC 1979 -1 SIMOVICI, D. A.; GRIGORAS, G.
EVEN INITIAL FEEDBACK VERTEX SET PROBLEM IS NP-COMPLETE.
SKUP 1974 -1 SKUPIEN, Z.
HAMILTONIAN CIRCUITS AND PATH COVERINGS OF VERTICES IN GRAPHS.
SKUP 1977 -1 SKUPIEN, Z.
ON EXTENDING PATH SYSTEMS AND (Q, R)-EDGE HAMILTONIAN GRAPHS.
SKUP 1978 -1 SKUPIEN, Z.
FINDING ALL MAXIMAL PATH FACTORS OF A TREE AND RELATED PROBLEMS.
SKUP 1979 -1 SKUPIEN, Z.
ON MAXIMAL NON-HAMILTONIAN GRAPHS.
SKUPA 1974 -1 SKUPIEN, Z.; WOJDA, A. P.
ON HIGHLY HAMILTONIAN GRAPHS.
SKUPA 1975 -1 SKUPIEN, Z.; WOJDA, A. P.
EXTREMAL NON-(P, Q)-HAMILTONIAN GRAPHS.
SLATA 1978 -1 SLATER, P. J.
CENTRAL PATHS IN A GRAPH.
SMITA 1978 -1 SMITH, C. A. B.
ON TUTTE'S DICHROMATE POLYNOMIAL.
SRIM 1979 -1 SRIMANI, P. K.; SENGUPTA, A.
ALGEBRAIC DETERMINATION OF CIRCUITS IN A DIRECTED GRAPH.
STAP 1979 -1 STAPLES, J.
ON SOME SUBCLASSES OF WELL-COVERED GRAPHS.
STAP 1980 -1 STAPLES, J.
OPTIMAL EVALUATIONS OF GRAPH-LIKE EXPRESSIONS.
STER 1979 -1 STERBOUL, F.
CHARACTERIZATION OF THE GRAPHS IN WHICH THE TRANSVERSAL NUMBER EQUALS THE MATCHING NUMBER, A.
STERA 1981 -1 STERBOUL, F.; WERTHEIMER, D.
COMMENT CONSTRUIRE UN GRAPHE PERT MINIMAL.
STRA 1979 -1 STRAIGHT, H. J.
PACKING TREES OF DIFFERENT SIZE INTO THE COMPLETE GRAPH.
STRO 1979 -1 STROEHLEIN, T.
TIGHTNESS AND FLEXIBILITY IN TIMETABLE PROBLEMS.
SUFF 1979 -1 SUFFEL, C.
SPANNING SUBGRAPHS OF EULERIAN GRAPHS, THE.

SUMN 1979 -1 SUMNER, D. P.
RANDOMLY MATCHABLE GRAPHS.
SURA 1975 -1 SURANYI, L.
LARGE ALPHA-CRITICAL GRAPHS WITH SMALL DEFICIENCY. ON LINE-CRITICAL GRAPHS. II.
SYSL 1978 -1 SYSLO, M. M.
ON CHARACTERIZATIONS OF CYCLE GRAPHS AND ON OTHER FAMILIES OF INTERSECTION GRAPHS.
SYSL 1979 -1 SYSLO, M. M.
CHARACTERIZATION OF HYPERGRAPHS GENERATED BY ARBORESCENCES, A.
SYSL 1981 -1 SYSLO, M. M.
EFFICIENT CYCLE VECTOR SPACE ALGORITHM FOR LISTING ALL CYCLES OF A PLANAR GRAPH, AN.
SYSL 1979 -2 SYSLO, M. M.
ON CYCLE BASES OF A GRAPH.
SYSL 1981 -2 SYSLO, M. M.
ON THE FAMILY OF ALL FUNDAMENTAL CYCLE SETS OF A GRAPH.
SYSL 1977 -3 SYSLO, M. M.
ON SOME PROBLEMS RELATED TO FUNDAMENTAL CYCLE SETS OF A GRAPH.
SYSL 1979 -3 SYSLO, M. M.
ON THE CYCLE SPACE METHODS (EXTENDED ABSTARCT).
SYSL 1979 -4 SYSLO, M. M.
ON THE STRUCTURE OF CYCLES IN A GRAPH.
SYSL 1979 -5 SYSLO, M. M.
ON TWO CYCLE SPACE METHODS FOR LISTING CYCLES OF A GRAPH.
SYSLA 1976 -1 SYSLO, M. M.; IRI, M.
EFFICIENT OUTERPLANARITY TESTING.
SYSLB 1977 -1 SYSLO, M. M.; SKUPIEN, Z.
APPLIED GRAPH THEORY. III. EULER AND HAMILTONIAN GRAPHS. THE TRAVELING SALESMAN PROBLEM (POLISH).
SZAM 1979 -1 SZAMKOLOWICZ, L.
ON PROBLEMS RELATED TO CHARACTERISTIC VERTICES OF GRAPHS.
TAKA 1979 -1 TAKAHASHI, H.; MATSUYAMA, A.
APPROXIMATE SOLUTION FOR THE STEINER PROBLEM IN GRAPHS, AN.
TAKAA 1980 -1 TAKAMIZAWA, K.; NISHIZEKI, T.; SAITO, N.
ALGORITHM FOR FINDING A SHORT CLOSED SPANNING WALK IN A GRAPH, AN.
TAKAA 1981 -1 TAKAMIZAWA, K.; NISHIZEKI, T.; SAITO, N.
COMBINATORIAL PROBLEMS ON SERIES-PARALLEL GRAPHS.
TAKAA 1980 -2 TAKAMIZAWA, K.; NISHIZEKI, T.; SAITO, N.
LINEAR TIME COMPUTABILITY OF COMBINATORIAL PROBLEMS ON SERIES-PARALLEL GRAPHS.
TAKAA 1981 -2 TAKAMIZAWA, K.; NISHIZEKI, T.; SAITO, N.
COMBINATORIAL PROBLEMS ON SERIES-PARALLEL GRAPHS.
TARJ 1974 -1 TARJAN, R. E.
TESTING GRAPH CONNECTIVITY.
TAZA 1979 -1 TAZAWA, S.
CLAW-DECOMPOSITION AND EVENLY-PARTITE-CLAW-DECOMPOSITION OF COMPLETE MULTI-PARTITE GRAPHS.
TELE 1978 -1 TELEMTAEV, M. M.
OPTIMALITY CONDITION FOR A HAMILTONIAN CYCLE (RUSSIAN).
TERA 1979 -1 TERADA, R.
POLYNOMIAL TIME ALGORITHMS FOR NP-HARD PROBLEMS WHICH ARE OPTIMAL OR NEAR-OPTIMAL WITH PROBABILITY ONE.
THOMB 1978 -1 THOMASON, A. G.
HAMILTONIAN CYCLES AND UNIQUELY EDGE COLOURABLE GRAPHS.
THOMC 1974 -1 THOMASSEN, C.
GRAPHS IN WHICH EVERY PATH IS CONTAINED IN A HAMILTONIAN PATH.
THOMC 1976 -1 THOMASSEN, C.
PATHS AND CYCLES IN GRAPHS.
THOMC 1978 -1 THOMASSEN, C.
HYPOHAMILTONIAN GRAPHS AND DIGRAPHS.
THOMC 1979 -1 THOMASSEN, C.
LONG CYCLES IN DIGRAPHS WITH CONSTRAINTS ON THE DEGREES.
THOMC 1980 -1 THOMASSEN, C.
HAMILTONIAN-CONNECTED TOURNAMENTS.
THOMC 1981 -1 THOMASSEN, C.
PLANAR CUBIC HYPOHAMILTONIAN AND HYPOTRACEABLE GRAPHS.
THOMC 1979 -2 THOMASSEN, C.
NONSEPARATING CYCLES IN K-CONNECTED GRAPHS.
THOMC 1980 -2 THOMASSEN, C.
2-LINKED GRAPHS.
TIMO 1977 -1 TIMOFEEV, E. A.
ON THE CONSTRUCTION OF AN EDGEWISE M-CONNECTED SKELETAL SUBGRAPH WITH MINIMUM LENGTH OF A MAXIMAL EDGE.
TINH 1977 -1 TINHOFER, G.
ON THE ISOMORPHISMS OF STRUCTURES.
TOFT 1978 -1 TOFT, B.
INVESTIGATION OF COLOUR-CRITICAL GRAPHS WITH COMPLEMENTS OF LOW CONNECTIVITY, AN.
TOME 1977 -1 TOMESCU, I.
SUR LES PLUS LONGUES CYCLES DANS LES GRAPHES CHROMATIQUES.
TOME 1978 -1 TOMESCU, I.
SUR LES CYCLES ELEMENTAIRES DANS LES GRAPHES ET HYPERGRAPHES K-CHROMATIQUES.
TOME 1980 -1 TOMESCU, I.
SOME PROPERTIES OF IRREDUCIBLE COVERINGS BY CLIQUES OF COMPLETE MULTIPARTITE GRAPHS.
TOME 1979 -2 TOMESCU, I.
NOMBRE MINIMAL DE COLORATIONS D'UN HYPERGRAPHE K-CHROMATIQUE, LE.
TOUS 1979 -1 TOUSSAINT, G. T.
RELATIVE NEIGHBOURHOOD GRAPH OF A FINITE PLANAR SET, THE.
TOUS 1980 -1 TOUSSAINT, G. T.
COMMENT:"ALGORITHMS FOR COMPUTING RELATIVE NEIGHBORHOOD GRAPH" BY R. B. URQUHART. WITH A REPLY BY URQUHART.
TOUSA 1981 -1 TOUSSAINT, G. T.; MENARD, R.
FAST ALGORITHMS FOR COMPUTING THE PLANAR RELATIVE NEIGHBORHOOD GRAPH.
TROTA 1978 -1 TROTTER, W. T. JR.; ERDOES, P.
WHEN THE CARTESIAN PRODUCT OF DIRECTED CYCLES IS HAMILTONIAN.
TROTB 1979 -1 TROTTER, W. T. JR.; HARARY, F.
ON DOUBLE AND MULTIPLE INTERVAL GRAPHS.
TRUD 1976 -1 TRUDEAU, R. J.
DOTS AND LINES.
TRUEA 1979 -1 TRUEMPER, K.; SOUN, Y.
MINIMAL FORBIDDEN SUBGRAPHS OF UNIMODULAR MULTICOMMODITY NETWORKS.

GRAPH THEORETIC RESULTS (UNLESS SPECIFIED ELSEWHERE)

TSIM 1979 -1 TSIMBALIST, E. I.; RUZAEV, E. N.; KANUNOV, A. I.
ALGORITHME DE RECHERCHE DES ISTHMES D'UN GRAPHE (RUSSIAN).
TSUK 1980 -1 TSUKIYAMA, S.; ARIYOSHI, H.; SHIRAKAWA, I.; OZAKI, H.
ALGORITHM TO ENUMERATE ALL CUTSETS OF A GRAPH IN LINEAR TIME PER CUTSET, AN.
TUCK 1980 -1 TUCKER, A. C.
APPLIED COMBINATORICS.
TUTT 1979 -1 TUTTE, W. T.
ALL THE KING'S HORSES (A GUIDE TO RECONSTRUCTION).
TUTT 1980 -1 TUTTE, W. T.
1-FACTORS AND POLYNOMIALS.
TYSHA 1979 -1 TYSHKEVICH, R. I.; CHERNJAK, A. A.
CANONICAL DECOMPOSITION OF A GRAPH DEFINED BY THE POWERS OF ITS VERTICES (RUSSIAN).
UNDE 1978 -1 UNDERGROUND, P.
ON GRAPHS WITH HAMILTONIAN SQUARES.
UNTE 1979 -1 UNTERAUER, K.
DYNAMIC WEIGHTED BINARY SEARCH TREES.
URQU 1980 -1 URQUHART, R. B.
ALGORITHMS FOR COMPUTATION OF RELATIVE NEIGHBOURHOOD GRAPH.
VAJN 1980 -1 VAJNSHTEJN, A. D.
METHODE DE DICHOTOMIE DANS QUELQUES PROBLEMES MINIMAX SUR LES GRAPHES (RUSSIAN).
VANDA 1975 -1 VANDERJAGT, D. W.
EDGE-CONNECTIVITY AND LOCAL EDGE-CONNECTIVITY OF GRAPHS.
VENG 1979 -1 VENGEROV, V. N.; NIKITIN, A. S.
HEURISTIC ALGORITHM FOR CUTTING WEIGHTED GRAPHS (RUSSIAN).
VERGA 1971 -1 VERGNAS, M. LAS
SUR UNE PROPRIETE DES ARBRES MAXIMAUX DANS UN GRAPHE.
VIDY 1978 -1 VIDYASANKAR, K.
COVERING THE EDGE SET OF A DIRECTED GRAPH WITH TREES.
VIDY 1980 -1 VIDYASANKAR, K.
COVERS AND STRONG COVERS IN DIRECTED BIPARTITE GRAPHS.
VIDY 1978 -2 VIDYASANKAR, K.
MINIMUM STRONG COVER IN CIRCUIT-BALANCED GRAPHS.
VINN 1975 -1 VINNICHENKO, N. G.
NUMBER OF EDGES OF AN N-VERTEX K-CONNECTED GRAPH WITH GIVEN STABILITY NUMBER (RUSSIAN), THE.
VOIN 1974 -1 VOIN, A. M.
OPTIMAL COMBINATION OF TECHNOLOGICAL OPERATIONS ON A PRODUCTION LINE (RUSSIAN).
VORN 1981 -1 VORNBERGER, O.
ALTERNATING CYCLE COVERS AND PATHS.
VOSS 1980 -1 VOSS, H.-J.
GRAPHS HAVING ODD CIRCUITS WITH AT LEAST K CHORDS.
VOSSA 1977 -1 VOSS, H.-J.; ZULUAGA, C.
MAXIMALE GERADE UND UNGERADE KREISE IN GRAPHEN. I.
WADI 1979 -1 WADIA, A. B.
GENERATION OF NODE LISTS USING SEGMENT ANALYSIS.
WALLA 1976 -1 WALLIS, W. D.
NUMBER OF MONOCHROMATIC TRIANGLES IN EDGE-COLOURINGS OF A COMPLETE GRAPH, THE.
WALS 1976 -1 WALSH, A. M.
POLYNOMIAL ALGORITHMS FOR CERTAIN GRAPH-THEORETIC PROBLEMS.
WALSA 1975 -1 WALSH, A. M.; BURKHARD, W. A.
POLYNOMIAL ALGORITHMS FOR (3,1) GRAPHS.
WALSA 1977 -1 WALSH, A. M.; BURKHARD, W. A.
EFFICIENT ALGORITHMS FOR (3,1) GRAPHS.
WALSB 1978 -1 WALSH, T. R. S.; WRIGHT, E. M.
K-CONNECTEDNESS OF UNLABELLED GRAPHS, THE.
WANT 1979 -1 WANTULA, B. P.
ON A CERTAIN CHARACTERIZATION OF K-CONNECTED GRAPHS (POLISH).
WATA 1981 -1 WATANABE, T.; AE, T.; NAKAMURA, A.
ON THE REMOVAL OF FORBIDDEN GRAPHS BY EDGE-DELETION OR BY EDGE-CONTRACTION.
WATAA 1979 -1 WATANABE, T.; ASANO, T.; SAITO, N.
UPPER BOUNDS ON THE LENGTHS OF CHINESE POSTMAN WALKS IN UNDIRECTED GRAPHS (JAPANESE).
WERR 1978 -1 WERRA, D. DE
GRAPHS, HYPERGRAPHS AND TIMETABLING.
WERR 1979 -2 WERRA, D. DE
ON THE USE OF ALTERNATING CHAINS AND HYPERGRAPHS IN EDGE COLORING.
WERR 1981 -2 WERRA, D. DE
REMARKS ON THE REQUIREMENT MATRIX OF SCHOOL TIMETABLE PROBLEMS AND REGULAR EMBEDDINGS OF GRAPHS.
WERR 1978 -3 WERRA, D. DE
ON LINE PERFECT GRAPHS.
WHITH 1981 -1 WHITESIDES, S. H.
ALGORITHM FOR FINDING CLIQUE CUT-SETS, AN.
WILLA 1968 -1 WILLIAMS, M. R.
GRAPH THEORY MODEL FOR THE SOLUTION OF TIMETABLES, A.
WILSA 1976 -1 WILSON, R. J.
EDGE-COLORINGS OF CRITICAL GRAPHS.
WIN 1979 -1 WIN, S.
ON A CONJECTURE OF LAS VERGNAS CONCERNING CERTAIN SPANNING TREES IN GRAPHS.
WOJD 1978 -1 WOJDA, A. P.
ON A CLASS OF HAMILTONIAN-TYPE NOTIONS.
WOJD 1978 -2 WOJDA, A. P.
STRONGLY (P,Q)-HAMILTONIAN GRAPHS (SOME RESULTS).
WOODA 1974 -1 WOODALL, D. R.
APPLICATIONS OF POLYMATROIDS AND LINEAR PROGRAMMING TO TRANSVERSALS AND GRAPHS.
WOODA 1977 -1 WOODALL, D. R.
ZEROS OF CHROMATIC POLYNOMIALS.
WOODA 1978 -1 WOODALL, D. R.
MINIMAX THEOREMS IN GRAPH THEORY.
YAKA 1979 -1 YAKAJITANI, Y.; UENO, S.
ON THE RANK OF CERTAIN CLASSES OF CUT-SETS AND TIE-SETS OF A GRAPH.
YAMA 1978 -1 YAMAMOTO, Y.
HELD-KARP ALGORITHM AND DEGREE-CONSTRAINED MINIMUM 1-TREES, THE.
YANN 1978 -1 YANNAKAKIS, M.
NODE- AND EDGE-DELETION NP-COMPLETE PROBLEMS.
YANN 1979 -1 YANNAKAKIS, M.
EFFECT OF A CONNECTIVITY REQUIREMENT ON THE COMPLEXITY OF MAXIMUM SUBGRAPH PROBLEMS, THE.

YANNA 1980 -1 YANNAKAKIS, M.; GAVRIL, F.
EDGE DOMINATING SETS IN GRAPHS.
YAO A 1979 -1 YAO, F. F.
GRAPH 2-ISOMORPHISM IS NP-COMPLETE.
YOUNB 1979 -1 YOUNGER, D. H.
FROM SHORTEST PATHS TO DIRECTED CUT TRANSVERSALS.
ZABE 1978 -1 ZABELLO, L. E.; FEDULOV, L. V.
METHOD FOR THE IMPROVEMENT OF ADMISSIBLE VARIANTS OF JOBS DEFINED BY A NETLIKE GRAPH (RUSSIAN), A.
ZAKS 1978 -1 ZAKS, J.
SOME HAMILTONIAN RESULTS IN POLYTOPAL GRAPHS.
ZAMB 1978 -1 ZAMBICKII, D. K.; LOZOVANU, D. D.
ALGORITHM FOR FINDING THE S-, P- AND R-CENTERS OF A TREE (RUSSIAN), AN.
ZAMF 1980 -1 ZAMFIRESCU, T.
THREE SMALL CUBIC GRAPHS WITH INTERESTING HAMILTONIAN PROPERTIES.
ZELI 1979 -1 ZELINKA, B.
EMBEDDING TREES INTO CLIQUE-BRIDGE-CLIQUE GRAPHS.
ZELI 1979 -2 ZELINKA, B.
SOME REMARKS ON EULERIAN GRAPHS.
ZELI 1979 -3 ZELINKA, B.
STRONGLY CONNECTED DIGRAPHS IN WHICH EACH EDGE IS CONTAINED IN EXACTLY TWO CYCLES.
ZEPS 1980 -1 ZEPS, D. A.
EXHAUSTIVE SEARCH ALGORITHM FOR FINDING HAMILTONIAN CYCLES (RUSSIAN), AN.

ARAOC 1981 -1 ARAOZ, J.; JOHNSON, E. L.
FACETS AND MAPPINGS FOR NON-ABELIAN GROUP PROBLEMS.
ARAOC 1981 -2 ARAOZ, J.; JOHNSON, E. L.
POLYHEDRA OF ADDITIVE SYSTEM PROBLEMS.
BACHB 1981 -1 BACHEM, A.; JOHNSON, E. L.; SCHRADER, R.
CHARACTERIZATION OF MINIMAL INEQUALITIES FOR MIXED INTEGER PROGRAMS, A.
BACHE 1978 -1 BACHEM, A.; SCHRADER, R.
NOTE ON A THEOREM OF JEROSLOW, A.
BELL 1974 -1 BELL, D. E.
CONSTRUCTIVE GROUP RELAXATIONS FOR INTEGER PROGRAMS.
BELL 1979 -1 BELL, D. E.
EFFICIENT GROUP CUTS FOR INTEGER PROGRAMS.
BELL 1980 -1 BELL, D. E.
GROUP APPROACH TO INTEGER PROGRAMMING: AN OUTLINE OF RECENT PROGRESS, THE.
BERT 1980 -1 BERTOLAZZI, P.; LEPORELLI, C.; LUCERTINI, M.
ALTERNATIVE GROUP RELAXATION OF INTEGER PROGRAMMING PROBLEMS.
BLAI 1975 -2 BLAIR, C. E.
TOPICS IN INTEGER PROGRAMMING.
BLAIA 1980 -1 BLAIR, C. E.; JEROSLOW, R. G.
VALUE FUNCTION OF AN INTEGER PROGRAM, THE.
BURDA 1974 -1 BURDET, C.-A.; JOHNSON, E. L.
LINEARLY CONSTRAINED GROUP MINIMIZATION.
FANE 1978 -1 FANELLI, S.
EXTENSION OF HU'S GROUP MINIMIZATION ALGORITHM, AN.
FANE 1979 -1 FANELLI, S.
ON THE USE OF THE ASYMPTOTIC ALGORITHM IN APPLIED PROBLEMS OF INTEGER LINEAR PROGRAMMING (ITALIAN).
GALLE 1975 -1 GALLO, G.; SIMEONE, B.
NEW CUTS FOR INTEGER PROGRAMMING VIA GROUP OPTIMIZATION.
GIUL 1979 -1 GIULIANELLI, S.; LUCERTINI, M.
GROUP THEORETIC METHOD FOR THE SOLUTION OF INTEGER PROGRAMMING PROBLEMS (ITALIAN).
HASA 1980 -1 HASANUDDIN AHMAD, S.
GROUP THEORETIC APPROACH OF INTEGER PROGRAMMING - A SURVEY.
HELG 1979 -1 HELGASON, R. V.; KENNINGTON, J. L.
NEW STORAGE REDUCTION TECHNIQUE FOR THE SOLUTION OF THE GROUP PROBLEM, A.
JEROB 1975 -1 JEROSLOW, R. G.
SOME STRUCTURE AND BASIS THEOREMS FOR INTEGRAL MONOIDS.
JEROB 1978 -1 JEROSLOW, R. G.
CUTTING PLANE THEORY: ALGEBRAIC METHODS.
JEROB 1979 -2 JEROSLOW, R. G.
MINIMAL INEQUALITIES.
JEROB 1978 -3 JEROSLOW, R. G.
SOME BASIC THEOREMS FOR INTEGRAL MONOIDS.
JOHND 1979 -1 JOHNSON, E. L.
ON THE GROUP PROBLEM AND A SUBADDITIVE APPROACH TO INTEGER PROGRAMMING.
JOHND 1980 -1 JOHNSON, E. L.
INTEGER PROGRAMMING, FACETS, SUBADDITIVITY, AND DUALITY FOR GROUP AND SEMI-GROUP PROBLEMS.
JOHND 1981 -2 JOHNSON, E. L.
ON THE GENERALITY OF THE SUBADDITIVE CHARACTERIZATION OF FACETS.
RATH 1977 -1 RATHMANN, D.
ZUR LOESUNG DISKRETER OPTIMIERUNGSPROBLEME MIT GRUPPENTHEORETISCHEN ANSAETZEN.
SALK 1975 -1 SALKIN, H. M.
INTEGER PROGRAMMING.
SEEL 1978 -1 SEELAENDER, J.
EINIGE BEMERKUNGEN ZUR BESTIMMUNG DES SCHNITTRANGS IN DER GANZZAHLIGEN LINEAREN OPTIMIERUNG.
SHEI 1979 -1 SHEINMAN, O. K.
GROUP-THEORETIC METHODS OF CONSTRUCTING CUTS IN INTEGER PROGRAMMING (RUSSIAN).
SHEV 1981 -1 SHEVCHENKO, V. N.
ON THE NUMBER OF EXTREME POINTS IN INTEGRAL PROGRAMMING (RUSSIAN).
SHLY 1978 -1 SHLYK, V. A.
ON THE FACES OF MASTER GOMORY POLYHEDRA (RUSSIAN).
SHLY 1980 -1 SHLYK, V. A.
PROPERTY OF FACETS OF MASTER GOMORY POLYHEDRA OF CYCLICAL GROUPS (RUSSIAN), A.
SIME 1979 -1 SIMEONE, B.
CONIC ALGORITHM FOR THE GROUP MINIMIZATION PROBLEM, A.
YAMA 1980 -1 YAMAMOTO, Y.
GROUP THEORETIC DUAL PROBLEM WITHOUT DUALITY GAPS FOR BOUNDED INTEGER PROGRAMS, A.

AHREA 1978 -1 AHRENS, W.; DEHNERT, G.; GERBER, H. J.
HEURISTISCHE VERFAHREN ZUR TOURENPLANUNG BEI DER HAUSMUELLENTSORGUNG IN LAENDLICHEN REGIONEN.

AIEL 1977 -1 AIELLO, A.; BURATTINI, E.; MASSAROTTI, A.
REDUCIBILITY AS A TOOL TO EXTEND THE POWER OF APPROXIMATION ALGORITHMS. THE MINIMIZATION OF BOOLEAN EXPRESSIONS.

AIELA 1980 -1 AIELLO, A.; BURATTINI, E.; MASSAROTTI, A.; VENTRIGLIA, F.
'A POSTERIORI' EVALUATION OF BIN PACKING APPROXIMATION ALGORITHMS.

APPEA 1978 -1 APPELBE, W. F.; ITO, M. R.
SCHEDULING HEURISTICS IN A MULTIPROGRAMMING ENVIRONMENT.

ARTE 1981 -1 ARTEMENKO, V. I.
ON ONE METHOD OF SEARCH FOR APPROXIMATE SOLUTIONS OF MIXED INTEGER LINEAR PROGRAMMING PROBLEMS (RUSSIAN).

ATRI 1980 -1 ATRI, G. D'
NOTE ON HEURISTICS FOR THE TRAVELING SALESMAN PROBLEM, A.

ATRI 1978 -3 ATRI, G. D'
PROBABILISTIC ANALYSIS OF THE KNAPSACK PROBLEM.

AUSI 1981 -1 AUSIELLO, G.; MARCHETTI-SPACCAMELA, A.; PROTASI, M.
PROBABILISTIC ANALYSIS OF THE PERFORMANCE OF GREEDY STRATEGIES OVER DIFFERENT CLASSES OF COMBINATORIAL PROBLEMS.

AVIS 1978 -1 AVIS, D.
TWO GREEDY HEURISTICS FOR THE WEIGHTED MATCHING PROBLEM.

BABAA 1968 -1 BABAEV, DZ. A.; BABAJEVA, D. C.; ASKEROVA, L. M.
APPROXIMATIVE ALGORITHM FOR THE SOLUTION OF CONVEX INTEGER PROGRAMS (RUSSIAN), AN.

BABAB 1978 -2 BABAEV, DZ. A.; MAMEDOV, K. S.
APPROXIMATE METHODS OF SOLUTION OF BOOLEAN PROGRAMMING PROBLEMS OF LARGE DIMENSION (RUSSIAN).

BAKED 1980 -1 BAKER, E.; FISHER, M.
COMPUTATIONAL RESULTS FOR VERY LARGE AIR CREW SCHEDULING PROBLEMS.

BALAD 1980 -1 BALAS, E.; HO, A. C.
SET COVERING ALGORITHMS USING CUTTING PLANES, HEURISTICS, AND SUBGRADIENT OPTIMIZATION: A COMPUTATIONAL STUDY.

BALAF 1980 -1 BALAS, E.; MARTIN, C. H.
PIVOT AND COMPLEMENT - A HEURISTIC FOR 0-1 PROGRAMMING.

BALAK 1977 -3 BALAS, E.; ZEMEL, E.
SOLVING LARGE ZERO-ONE KNAPSACK PROBLEMS (REVISED VERSION).

BALLA 1979 -1 BALL, M. O.; BODIN, L. D.; GOLDEN, B. L.; ASSAD, A.; STATHES, C.
TRUCK FLEET ACQUISITION/ROUTING PROBLEM, A.

BARNA 1981 -1 BARNES, E. R.
ALGORITHM FOR PARTITIONING THE NODES OF A GRAPH, AN.

BART 1979 -1 BARTHOLDI, J. J. III
GUARANTEED-ACCURACY ROUND-OFF ALGORITHM FOR CYCLIC SCHEDULING AND SET COVERING, A.

BERL 1974 -1 BERLIN, V. G.
APPROXIMATE METHOD FOR SOLVING THE SIMPLEST PROBLEM OF SCHEDULING THEORY (RUSSIAN), AN.

BESH 1979 -1 BESHARA, S. B.; MAGAZINE, M. J.
MYOPIC HEURISTICS FOR SINGLE MACHINE SCHEDULING PROBLEMS.

BIKOA 1978 -1 BIKOV, V. M.; SERGIENKO, I. V.
METHOD OF SOLVING PROBLEMS OF DISCRETE PROGRAMMING APPROXIMATELY (RUSSIAN), A.

BIXBB 1978 -1 BIXBY, R. E.; WANG, D.-L.
ALGORITHM FOR FINDING HAMILTONIAN CIRCUITS IN CERTAIN GRAPHS, AN.

BOEN 1979 -1 BOENCHENDORF, K.
HEURISTIKEN FUER DAS N !1! PREC ! SUM(WI*CI) REIHENFOLGEPROBLEM.

BOEN 1981 -1 BOENCHENDORF, K.
SUBGRADIENT-LIKE HEURISTIC METHODS.

BOFFA 1979 -1 BOFFEY, T. B.; HINXMAN, A. I.
SOLVING THE OPTIMAL NETWORK PROBLEM.

BREE 1978 -1 BREE, D. S.; LAGEWEG, B. J.; LENSTRA, J. K.; RINNOOY KAN, A. H. G.; VANBEZOUWEN, G.
HIERARCHICAL CLUSTERING SCHEME FOR ASYMMETRIC MATRICES, A.

BREL 1979 -1 BRELAZ, D.
NEW METHODS TO COLOR THE VERTICES OF A GRAPH.

BRUC 1978 -1 BRUCKER, P.
APPROXIMATIVE VERFAHREN ZUR LOESUNG VON DISKRETEN OPTIMIERUNGSPROBLEMEN.

BUTA 1975 -1 BUTAN, E. I.; NECVAL, N. A.
ALGORITHMS FOR THE OPERATIONAL CONTROL OF ARRIVAL FLOWS IN A TRANSPORTATION NETWORK (RUSSIAN).

CAMEA 1975 -1 CAMERINI, P. M.; FRATTA, L.; MAFFIOLI, F.
TRAVELLING SALESMAN PROBLEM: HEURISTICALLY GUIDED SEARCH AND MODIFIED GRADIENT TECHNIQUES.

CAMEC 1978 -1 CAMERINI, P. M.; MAFFIOLI, F.
EXACT AND HEURISTIC METHODS FOR NP-HARD MATROID PROBLEMS.

CAMEC 1978 -2 CAMERINI, P. M.; MAFFIOLI, F.
HEURISTICALLY GUIDED ALGORITHM FOR K-PARITY MATROID PROBLEMS.

CART 1979 -1 CARTER, M. W.
FINAL EXAMINATION SCHEDULING FOR CORRESPONDENCE STUDENTS.

CHAL 1977 -1 CHALKOV, V. D.
EFFECTIVE APPROXIMATE ALGORITHM FOR THE SOLUTION OF THE TRAVELLING SALESMAN PROBLEM (BULGARIAN), AN.

CHOUA 1978 -1 CHOUKHMANE, E.-A.
HEURISTIQUE POUR LE PROBLEME DE L'ARBRE DE STEINER, UNE.

CHVA 1979 -1 CHVATAL, V.
GREEDY HEURISTIC FOR THE SET-COVERING PROBLEM, A.

COFFB 1978 -1 COFFMAN, E. G. JR.; GAREY, M. R.; JOHNSON, D. S.
APPLICATION OF BIN-PACKING TO MULTIPROCESSOR SCHEDULING, AN.

COFFF 1978 -1 COFFMAN, E. G. JR.; LEUNG, J. Y.-T.; SLUTZ, D.
ON THE OPTIMALITY OF FAST HEURISTICS FOR SCHEDULING AND STORAGE ALLOCATION PROBLEMS.

COFFH 1976 -1 COFFMAN, E. G. JR.; SETHI, R.
GENERALIZED BOUND ON LPT SEQUENCING, A.

CONN 1971 -1 CONNER, J. L.
SEQUENCE PROGRAMMING: A HEURISTIC ALGORITHM FOR THE SOLUTION OF LARGE GENERAL JOB SHOP SCHEDULING PROBLEMS.

CONN 1972 -1 CONNER, J. L.
HEURISTIC METHOD FOR SOLVING JOBSHOP SEQUENCING PROBLEMS, A.

COOKA 1979 -1 COOK, W. D.; SHIELDS, W. S.
ASSIGNMENT OF MILITARY OFFICERS TO GROUPS: A MULTI-ATTRIBUTE TEAM BALANCING PROBLEM.

COPP 1980 -1 COPPINS, R. J.; PENTICO, D. W.
SCHEDULING THE NATIONAL FOOTBALL LEAGUE.

CORNC 1980 -2 CORNUEJOLS, G.; NEMHAUSER, G. L.; WOLSEY, L. A.
WORST-CASE AND PROBABILISTIC ANALYSIS OF ALGORITHMS FOR A LOCATION PROBLEM.
CROI 1980 -1 CROITORU, C.
ON APPROXIMATE ALGORITHMS FOR COMBINATORIAL LINEAR MAXIMIZATION PROBLEMS.
CRUY 1978 -1 CRUYSSEN, P. VAN DER; RIJCKAERT, M. J.
HEURISTIC FOR THE ASYMMETRIC TRAVELLING SALESMAN PROBLEM.
CULLA 1980 -1 CULLEN, F. H.; JARVIS, J. J.; RATLIFF, H. D.
SET PARTITIONING BASED HEURISTICS FOR INTERACTIVE ROUTING.
DAMM 1978 -1 DAMM, E.
SHORTEST PATH IN A RECTANGULAR GRID, THE.
DE 1977 -1 DE, P.; MORTON, T. E.
MAKESPAN SCHEDULING FOR UNEQUAL PARALLEL PROCESSORS (REVISED VERSION).
DHAL 1978 -1 DHALL, S. K.; LIU, C. L.
ON A REAL-TIME SCHEDULING PROBLEM.
DIONA 1979 -1 DIONNE, R.; FLORIAN, M.
EXACT AND APPROXIMATE ALGORITMS FOR OPTIMAL NETWORK DESIGN.
DOGR 1979 -1 DOGRAMACI, A.; SURKIS, J.
EVALUATION OF A HEURISTIC FOR SCHEDULING INDEPENDENT JOBS ON PARALLEL IDENTICAL PROCESSORS.
DREZ 1978 -1 DREZNER, Z.; WESOLOWSKY, G. O.
FACILITY LOCATION ON A SPHERE.
DRIS 1979 -1 DRISCOLL, W. C.; EMMONS, H.
VEHICLE ROUTING FOR MINIMUM COST.
DUER 1978 -1 DUERRE, K.
APPROXIMATE ALGORITHMS FOR COLORING LARGE GRAPHS.
DUMA 1977 -1 DUMAS, M. B.
BRANCH BIAS HEURISTIC SCHEDULING OF THE GENERAL JOB SHOP.
DUMA 1978 -1 DUMAS, M. B.
BOUND CUTOFF HEURISTIC SCHEDULING OF THE GENERAL JOB SHOP.
ECKE 1977 -1 ECKER, K.
ORGANISATION VON PARALLELEN PROZESSEN. THEORIE DETERMINISTISCHER SCHEDULES.
EILO 1978 -1 EILON, S.; GALVAO, R. D.
SINGLE AND DOUBLE VERTEX SUBSTITUTION IN HEURISTIC PROCEDURES FOR THE P-MEDIAN PROBLEM.
ELMAA 1980 -1 ELMAGHRABY, S. E.; ELIMAM, A. A.
KNAPSACK-BASED APPROACHES TO THE MAKESPAN PROBLEM ON MULTIPLE PROCESSORS.
FAAL 1979 -1 FAALAND, B. H.; HILLIER, F. S.
INTERIOR PATH METHODS FOR HEURISTIC INTEGER PROGRAMMING PROCEDURES.
FEIN 1979 -1 FEINBERG, I.
HEURISTIC WAREHOUSE LOCATION MODEL CONSIDERING TRANSPORTATION AND OTHER COSTS AND CAPACITY CONSTRAINTS, A.
FERNA 1977 -1 FERNANDEZ, R. R.; SWART, W. W.
SYSTEM FOR SOLVING CUTTING STOCK PROBLEMS, A.
FIAL 1978 -1 FIALA, F.
VEHICLE ROUTING PROBLEM.
FILO 1979 -1 FILONENKO, N. V.
APPROXIMATE SOLUTION OF PARAMETRIC INTEGER PROGRAMMING PROBLEMS.
FINKB 1980 -1 FINKELSTEIN, JU. JU.
ABOUT THE POLYNOMIAL ALGORITHM OF EPSILON-OPTIMIZATION IN THE MULTIDIMENSIONAL KNAPSACK PROBLEM (RUSSIAN).
FISH 1980 -1 FISHER, M. L.
WORST-CASE ANALYSIS OF HEURISTIC ALGORITHMS.
FISH 1978 -3 FISHER, M. L.
WORST-CASE ANALYSIS OF HEURISTICS.
FISHA 1978 -2 FISHER, M. L.; HOCHBAUM, D.
PROBABILISTIC ANALYSIS OF THE EUCLIDEAN K-MEDIAN PROBLEM.
FISHC 1978 -1 FISHER, M. L.; NEMHAUSER, G. L.; WOLSEY, L. A.
ANALYSIS OF APPROXIMATIONS FOR MAXIMIZING SUBMODULAR SET FUNCTIONS - II, AN.
FISHC 1979 -1 FISHER, M. L.; NEMHAUSER, G. L.; WOLSEY, L. A.
ANALYSIS OF APPROXIMATIONS FOR FINDING A MAXIMUM WEIGHT HAMILTONIAN CIRCUIT, AN.
FISK 1979 -1 FISK, J. C.; HUNG, M. S.
HEURISTIC ROUTINE FOR SOLVING LARGE LOADING PROBLEMS, A.
FOULA 1978 -1 FOULDS, L. R.; ROBINSON, D. F.
GRAPH THEORETIC HEURISTICS FOR THE PLANT LAYOUT PROBLEM.
FRED 1977 -1 FREDERICKSON, G. N.
APPROXIMATION ALGORITHMS FOR NP-HARD ROUTING PROBLEMS.
FRED 1979 -1 FREDERICKSON, G. N.
APPROXIMATION ALGORITHMS FOR SOME POSTMAN PROBLEMS.
FRED 1980 -1 FREDERICKSON, G. N.
PROBABILISTIC ANALYSIS FOR SIMPLE ONE- AND TWO-DIMENSIONAL BIN PACKING ALGORITHMS.
FREDA 1976 -1 FREDERICKSON, G. N.; HECHT, M. S.; KIM, C. E.
APPROXIMATION ALGORITHMS FOR SOME ROUTING PROBLEMS.
FRIED 1978 -1 FRIEZE, A. M.
GENERALISATION OF THE GREEDY ALGORITHM FOR INDEPENDENCE SYSTEMS, A.
FRIED 1979 -1 FRIEZE, A. M.
APPROXIMATE ALGORITHM FOR THE M-DIMENSIONAL 0-1 KNAPSACK PROBLEM, AN.
FRIED 1979 -2 FRIEZE, A. M.
ON THE WORST-CASE PERFORMANCE OF SOME ALGORITHMS FOR THE ASYMMETRIC TRAVELLING SALESMAN PROBLEM.
FRIED 1979 -3 FRIEZE, A. M.
PROBABILISTIC ANALYSIS OF SOME EUCLIDEAN CLUSTERING.
FRIED 1979 -4 FRIEZE, A. M.
WORST-CASE ANALYSIS OF ALGORITHMS FOR TRAVELLING SALESMAN PROBLEMS.
FULL 1978 -1 FULLER, J. A.
OPTIMAL SOLUTIONS VERSUS "GOOD" SOLUTIONS. AN ANALYSIS OF HEURISTIC DECISION MAKING.
GARE 1978 -1 GAREY, M. R.; GRAHAM, R. L.; JOHNSON, D. S.
PERFORMANCE GUARANTEES FOR SCHEDULING ALGORITHMS.
GAREA 1978 -1 GAREY, M. R.; JOHNSON, D. S.
"STRONG" NP-COMPLETENESS RESULTS: MOTIVATION, EXAMPLES AND IMPLICATIONS.
GARFA 1978 -1 GARFINKEL, R. S.; GILBERT, K. C.
BOTTLENECK TRAVELING SALESMAN PROBLEM: ALGORITHMS AND PROBABILISTIC ANALYSIS, THE.
GAUD 1979 -1 GAUDIOSO, M.
HEURISTIC APPROACH TO THE CUTTING STOCK PROBLEM, A.
GELD 1978 -1 GELDERS, L. F.; SAMBANDAM, N.
FOUR SIMPLE HEURISTICS FOR SCHEDULING A FLOW SHOP.
GENS 1977 -1 GENS, G. V.; LEVNER, E. V.
ON E-ALGORITHMS FOR UNIVERSAL DISCRETE PROBLEMS (RUSSIAN).

GENS 1978 -1 GENS, G. V.; LEVNER, E. V.
APPROXIMATE ALGORITHMS FOR CERTAIN UNIVERSAL PROBLEMS IN SCHEDULING THEORY.
GENS 1979 -1 GENS, G. V.; LEVNER, E. V.
COMPLEXITY OF APPROXIMATION ALGORITHMS FOR COMBINATORIAL PROBLEMS: A SURVEY.
GENS 1979 -2 GENS, G. V.; LEVNER, E. V.
COMPUTATIONAL COMPLEXITY OF APPROXIMATION ALGORITHMS FOR COMBINATORIAL PROBLEMS.
GENS 1979 -3 GENS, G. V.; LEVNER, E. V.
EFFICIENT APPROXIMATION ALGORITHMS FOR THE INTEGER PROGRAMMING PROBLEMS OF KNAPSACK TYPE.
GENS 1979 -4 GENS, G. V.; LEVNER, E. V.
PROBLEMES D'OPTIMISATION DISCRETE ET ALGORITHMES APPROCHES EFFECTIFS (REVUE) (RUSSIAN).
GEORA 1980 -1 GEORGE, J. A.; ROBINSON, D. F.
HEURISTIC FOR PACKING BOXES INTO A CONTAINER, A.
GIOR 1975 -1 GIORDANO, F. R.
HEURISTIC FOR THE CONSTRUCTION OF SURROGATE CONSTRAINTS FOR THE SOLUTION OF THE LINEAR ZERO-ONE INTEGER PROBLEM, A.
GLOV 1977 -1 GLOVER, F.
FRESH LOOK AT HEURISTIC PRINCIPLES FOR INTEGER PROGRAMMING, A.
GOLDB 1978 -2 GOLDEN, B. L.
STATISTICAL ESTIMATION IN COMBINATORIAL DECISION PROBLEMS.
GOLDC 1978 -1 GOLDEN, B. L.; ALT, F. B.
INTERVAL ESTIMATION OF A GLOBAL OPTIMUM FOR LARGE COMBINATORIAL PROBLEMS.
GONZB 1978 -1 GONZALEZ, T.; SAHNI, S.
FLOWSHOP AND JOBSHOP SCHEDULES: COMPLEXITY AND APPROXIMATION.
GRAND 1978 -1 GRANOT, F.
EFFICIENT HEURISTIC ALGORITHMS FOR POSITIVE 0-1 POLYNOMIAL PROGRAMMING PROBLEMS.
GRAT 1972 -1 GRATZER, F. J.; STEIGLITZ, K.
HEURISTIC APPROACH TO LARGE MULTICOMMODITY FLOW PROBLEMS, A.
GRAVB 1978 -1 GRAVES, S. C.; HAESSLER, R. W.
ON "PRODUCTION RUNS FOR MULTIPLE PRODUCTS: THE TWO-PRODUCT HEURISTIC".
GROEB 1981 -1 GROETSCHEL, M.
APPROACHES TO HARD COMBINATORIAL OPTIMIZATION PROBLEMS.
GUIGA 1978 -1 GUIGNARD, M.; SPIELBERG, K.
DUAL METHOD FOR THE MIXED PLANT LOCATION PROBLEM, A. (REVISED VERSION).
HAESC 1973 -1 HAESSLER, R. W.
DEVELOPMENT OF A HEURISTIC PROCEDURE TO SOLVE A PRODUCTION SCHEDULING PROBLEM, THE.
HAMM 1979 -1 HAMMER, G.
RANDOMISIERTE HEURISTIKEN.
HAUSA 1980 -1 HAUSMANN, D.; JENKYNS, T. A.; KORTE, B.
WORST CASE ANALYSIS OF GREEDY TYPE ALGORITHMS FOR INDEPENDENCE SYSTEMS.
HAUSC 1978 -2 HAUSMANN, D.; KORTE, B.
K-GREEDY ALGORITHMS FOR INDEPENDENCE SYSTEMS.
HAUSC 1978 -3 HAUSMANN, D.; KORTE, B.
LOWER BOUNDS ON THE WORST-CASE COMPLEXITY OF SOME ORACLE ALGORITHMS.
HEND 1975 -1 HENDERSON, P. B.
HEURISTIC SCHEDULING POLICIES FOR SERVICE SYSTEMS WITH QUADRATIC WAITING COSTS.
HILLA 1977 -1 HILLIER, F. S.
FURTHER INVESTIGATION OF EFFICIENT HEURISTIC PROCEDURES FOR INTEGER LINEAR PROGRAMMING WITH AN INTERIOR, A.
HO 1979 -1 HO, A. C.
WORST CASE ANALYSIS OF A CLASS OF SET COVERING HEURISTICS.
HOCH 1980 -1 HOCHBAUM, D.
APPROXIMATION ALGORITHMS FOR THE WEIGHTED SET COVERING AND NODE COVER PROBLEMS.
HOCH 1979 -2 HOCHBAUM, D.
HEURISTICS FOR THE FIXED COST MEDIAN PROBLEM.
HOCH 1980 -2 HOCHBAUM, D.
FAST APPROXIMATION ALGORITHMS FOR SOME INTEGER PROGRAMMING PROBLEMS.
IBAR 1978 -1 IBARAKI, T.
BRANCH-AND-BOUND PROCEDURE AND STATE-SPACE REPRESENTATION OF COMBINATORIAL OPTIMIZATION PROBLEMS.
IBAR 1980 -1 IBARAKI, T.
APPROXIMATE ALGORITHMS FOR THE MULTIPLE-CHOICE CONTINUOUS KNAPSACK PROBLEMS.
ISKA 1978 -1 ISKANDER, W.
NEAR - OPTIMAL SOLUTION TO THE DYNAMIC JOB SHOP SEQUENCING PROBLEM, A.
JACOA 1977 -2 JACOBSEN, S. K.
HEURISTIC SOLUTIONS TO DYNAMIC PLANT LOCATION PROBLEMS.
JANK 1978 -1 JANKO, W.
COMBINATORIAL CONSIDERATIONS ON THE OPTIMALITY OF HEURISTIC SOLUTIONS OF PROBLEMS.
JENKA 1978 -1 JENKYNS, T. A.
EFFICACY OF HEURISTICS COMBINING ENUMERATION AND THE GREEDY ALGORITHM, THE.
JENKA 1979 -1 JENKYNS, T. A.
GREEDY BUT NOT-SO-STUPID ALGORITHMS.
KANEA 1980 -1 KANELLAKIS, P. C.; PAPADIMITRIOU, C. H.
LOCAL SEARCH FOR THE ASYMMETRIC TRAVELING SALESMAN PROBLEM.
KANNB 1978 -1 KANNAN, R.; KORTE, B.
APPROXIMATIVE COMBINATORIAL ALGORITHMS.
KAPL 1973 -1 KAPLINSKII, A. I.; CERNYSOVA, G. D.
CONSTRUCTION OF PROBABILISTIC ITERATIVE ALGORITHMS FOR THE SOLUTION OF INTEGER PROGRAMMING PROBLEMS (RUSSIAN).
KARP 1978 -2 KARP, R. M.
PROBABILISTIC ANALYSIS OF PARTITIONING ALGORITHMS FOR THE TRAVELING-SALESMAN PROBLEM IN THE PLANE.
KEVO 1978 -1 KEVORKIAN, A. K.
GENERAL TOPOLOGICAL RESULTS ON THE CONSTRUCTION OF A MINIMUM ESSENTIAL SET OF A DIGRAPH.
KISE 1979 -1 KISE, H.; IBARAKI, T.; MINE, H.
PERFORMANCE ANALYSIS OF SIX APPROXIMATION ALGORITHMS FOR THE ONE-MACHINE MAXIMUM LATENESS SCHEDULING PROBLEM WITH READY TIMES.
KISEA 1979 -1 KISE, H.; KABATA, M.; UNO, M.; IBARAKI, T.; MINE, H.
APPROXIMATION ALGORITHM FOR THE PARALLEL-MACHINE MAXIMUM LATENESS SCHEDULING PROBLEM WITH READY TIME CONSTRAINT.
KORTA 1979 -1 KORTE, B.
APPROXIMATIVE ALGORITHMS FOR DISCRETE OPTIMIZATION PROBLEMS.
KORTD 1981 -1 KORTE, B.; SCHRADER, R.
ON THE EXISTENCE OF FAST APPROXIMATION SCHEMES.
KOU 1978 -1 KOU, L.; MARKOWSKY, G.; BERMAN, L.
FAST ALGORITHM FOR STEINER TREES, A.

KOVA 1980 -1 KOVALEV, M. M.
ANALYSIS OF THE GREEDY ALGORITHM FOR CONVEX INTEGER PROGRAMMING (RUSSIAN).
KRAR 1978 -1 KRARUP, J.; PRUZAN, P. M.
COMPUTER-AIDED LAYOUT DESIGN.
LABA 1977 -1 LABADIE, J. W.; MORROW, D. M.; CHEN, Y. H.
HEURISTIC MULTIDIMENSIONAL DYNAMIC PROGRAMMING ALGORITHM FOR URBAN STORMWATER MANAGEMENT.
LAM 1975 -1 LAM, S.
WORST CASE ANALYSIS OF MULTIPROCESSOR SCHEDULING ALGORITHMS.
LAM A 1975 -1 LAM, S.; SETHI, R.
WORST CASE ANALYSIS OF THE COFFMAN-GRAHAM SCHEDULING ALGORITHM.
LARSB 1978 -1 LARSON, R. E.; DESSOUKY, M. I.
HEURISTIC PROCEDURES FOR THE SINGLE MACHINE PROBLEM TO MINIMIZE MAXIMUM LATENESS.
LAWL 1977 -1 LAWLER, E. L.
FAST APPROXIMATION ALGORITHMS FOR KNAPSACK PROBLEMS.
LAWL 1978 -1 LAWLER, E. L.
FAST APPROXIMATION ALGORITHMS FOR KNAPSACK PROBLEMS.
LAWL 1979 -2 LAWLER, E. L.
FAST APPROXIMATION ALGORITHMS FOR KNAPSACK PROBLEMS.
LENSA 1979 -3 LENSTRA, J. K.; RINNOOY KAN, A. H. G.
COMPLEXITY OF VEHICLE ROUTING AND SCHEDULING PROBLEMS.
LEUN 1977 -1 LEUNG, J. Y.-T.
FAST ALGORITHMS FOR PACKING PROBLEMS.
LEVNA 1978 -1 LEVNER, E. V.; GENS, G. V.
DISCRETE OPTIMIZATION PROBLEMS AND EFFICIENT APPROXIMATION ALGORITHMS (RUSSIAN).
LEWIB 1978 -1 LEWIS, H. R.; PAPADIMITRIOU, C. H.
EFFICACITE DES ALGORITHMES, L'.
LIEB 1980 -1 LIEBERHERR, K.
P-OPTIMAL HEURISTICS.
LING 1978 -1 LINGURAJ, B. P.; WOLFE, H.
HEURISTIC METHOD FOR OBTAINING AN INTEGER SOLUTION TO A FACILITY DESIGN OPTIMIZATION PROBLEM, A.
LIVS 1969 -1 LIVSHIC, E. M.
PERFORMANCE BOUNDS FOR APPROXIMATE SOLUTIONS OF OPTIMIZATION NETWORK PROBLEMS (RUSSIAN).
LOUL 1979 -1 LOULOU, R.; MICHAELIDES, E.
NEW GREEDY-LIKE HEURISTICS FOR THE MULTIDIMENSIONAL 0-1 KNAPSACK PROBLEM.
LUCE 1979 -1 LUCERTINI, M.; MARCHETTI-SPACCAMELA, A.
APPROXIMATE SOLUTIONS OF AN INTEGER LINEAR PROGRAMMING PROBLEM WITH RESOURCE VARIATIONS.
MAC F 1978 -1 MAC GINNIS, L. F.; CULVER, W. D.; DEANE, R. H.
ONE- AND TWO-PHASE HEURISTICS FOR WORKFORCE SCHEDULING.
MACK 1978 -1 MACK, H. L.; SMITH, L. D.
SCHEDULING WITH LIST PROCESSING AND PROBLEM ORIENTED DATA STRUCTURES; AN ITINERANT TEACHER EXAMPLE.
MAFF 1979 -1 MAFFIOLI, F.
COMPLEXITY OF COMBINATORIAL OPTIMIZATION ALGORITHMS AND THE CHALLENGE OF HEURISTICS, THE.
MAGA 1979 -1 MAGAZINE, M. J.; OGUZ, O.
FULLY POLYNOMIAL APPROXIMATE ALGORITHM FOR THE 0-1 KNAPSACK PROBLEM, A. (REVISED VERSION).
MAGAA 1979 -1 MAGAZINE, M. J.; WEE, T. S.
GENERALIZATION OF BIN-PACKING HEURISTICS TO THE LINE BALANCING PROBLEM, THE.
MAND 1978 -1 MANDL, C. E.
ALGORITHMS AND COMPUTER PROGRAMS IN DETERMINISTIC NETWORK OPTIMIZATION APPLIED TO PUBLIC SYSTEMS.
MARTC 1979 -2 MARTELLO, S.; TOTH, P.
HEURISTIC ALGORITHMS FOR THE MULTIPLE KNAPSACK PROBLEM.
MARUA 1977 -1 MARUYAMA, K.; CHANG, S. K.; TANG, D. T.
GENERAL PACKING ALGORITHM FOR MULTIDIMENSIONAL RESOURCE REQUIREMENTS, A.
MAURC 1978 -1 MAURRAS, J. F.
GOOD ALGORITHMS, OLD IDEAS.
MAYB 1978 -1 MAYBERRY, J. P.; SAIPE, A. L.
REPLY TO GRAVES AND HAESSLER'S NOTE ON THE PAPER "PRODUCTION RUNS FOR MULTIPLE PRODUCTS: THE TWO-PRODUCT HEURISTIC".
MEIS 1978 -1 MEISSNER, J.-D.
HEURISTISCHE PROGRAMMIERUNG.
MELA 1979 -1 MELAMED, I. J.; PLOTINSKIJ, Y. M.
ALGORITHME HEURISTIQUE DE RESOLUTION DU PROBLEME DE LIVRAISON GENERALISE (RUSSIAN).
MILG 1977 -1 MILGRAM, M.; DUBUISSON, B.
ALGORITHME HEURISTIQUE DE DECOMPOSITION D'UN GRAPHE, UN.
MINA 1980 -1 MINAEV, YU. N.
UNIFIED FORMAL-HEURISTIC ALGORITHM FOR SOLVING INTEGRAL LINEAR PROGRAMMING PROBLEM (RUSSIAN), A.
MINIA 1975 -1 MININA, T. R.; PEREKREST, V. T.
CERTAIN WAY OF APPROXIMATING THE SOLUTIONS OF THE TRAVELING SALESMAN PROBLEM (RUSSIAN), A.
MINO 1978 -1 MINOUX, M.
ACCELERATED GREEDY ALGORITHMS FOR MAXIMIZING SUBMODULAR SET FUNCTIONS.
MONT 1979 -1 MONTEROSSO, C. D. B.; BORNSTEIN, C. T.
HEURISTIC ALGORITHM FOR THE LOCATION AND DIMENSIONING OF WAREHOUSES, A.
MORT 1978 -1 MORTON, T. E.; BALA, G. D.
ALGORISTICS FOR SINGLE-MACHINE SEQUENCING WITH PRECEDENCE CONSTRAINTS.
MUEL 1978 -2 MUELLER-MERBACH, H.
KASKADENBAUMVERFAHREN ZUR LOESUNG DES "KNAPSACKPROBLEMS", EIN.
NEMHB 1978 -1 NEMHAUSER, G. L.; WOLSEY, L. A.
MAXIMIZING SUBMODULAR SET FUNCTIONS: FORMULATIONS AND ANALYSIS OF ALGORITHMS.
NEMHC 1978 -1 NEMHAUSER, G. L.; WOLSEY, L. A.; FISHER, M. L.
ANALYSIS OF APPROXIMATIONS FOR MAXIMIZING SUBMODULAR SET FUNCTIONS-1, AN.
NIGM 1975 -1 NIGMATULLIN, R. G.
COMPLEXITY OF APPROXIMATE SOLUTION OF COMBINATORIAL PROBLEMS (RUSSIAN).
NIGM 1978 -1 NIGMATULLIN, R. G.
ON APPROXIMATE ALGORITHMS WITH RESTRICTED ABSOLUTE ERROR FOR DISCRETE EXTREMUM PROBLEMS (RUSSIAN).
NORB 1979 -1 NORBACK, J. P.; LOVE, R. F.
HEURISTIC FOR THE HAMILTONIAN PATH PROBLEM IN EUCLIDEAN TWO-SPACE.
OGUZ 1979 -1 OGUZ, O.; MAGAZINE, M. J.
POLYNOMIAL TIME APPROXIMATION ALGORITHM FOR THE MULTIDIMENSIONAL 0/1 KNAPSACK PROBLEM, A.
OKAM 1979 -1 OKAMURA, K.; YAMASHINA, H.
HEURISTIC ALGORITHM FOR THE ASSEMBLY LINE MODEL-MIX SEQUENCING PROBLEM TO MINIMIZE THE RISK OF STOPPING THE CONVEYOR, A.

OSKOA 1968 -1 OSKOLKOVA, S. E.; OSKOLKOV, I. O.
APPLICATION OF CERTAIN HEURISTIC METHODS TO THE SOLUTION OF SCHEDULING PROBLEMS (SURVEY).
PAPE 1980 -1 PAPE, U.
HEURISTISCHES VERFAHREN ZUR ERMITTLUNG VON FAHRPLAENEN IN DER CONTAINER-SCHIFFAHRT, EIN.
PAPO 1977 -1 PAPOULIAS, D. B.
ASSIGNMENT-TO-DAYS PROBLEM IN A SCHOOL TIME-TABLE, A HEURISTIC APPROACH, THE.
PAPO 1980 -1 PAPOULIAS, D. B.
ASSIGNMENT-TO-DAYS PROBLEM IN A SCHOOL TIME-TABLE, A HEURISTIC APPROACH, THE.
PARK 1976 -1 PARKER, C. S.
EXPERIMENTAL INVESTIGATION OF SOME HEURISTIC STRATEGIES FOR COMPONENT PLACEMENT, AN.
PETEA 1979 -1 PETERSOHN, U.; STAHN, H.
NAEHERUNGSVERFAHREN ZUR POLYOPTIMALEN LOESUNG DES MASCHINENBELEGUNGSPROBLEMS.
PINT 1978 -1 PINTO, P. A.; DANNENBERG, D. G.; KHUMAWALA, B. M.
HEURISTIC NETWORK PROCEDURE FOR THE ASSEMBLY LINE BALANCING PROBLEM, A.
POTT 1980 -3 POTTS, C. N.
ANALYSIS OF A HEURISTIC FOR ONE MACHINE SEQUENCING WITH RELEASE DATES AND DELIVERY TIMES.
ROSED 1979 -1 ROSENBLATT, M. J.
FACILITIES LAYOUT PROBLEM: A MULTI-GOAL APPROACH, THE.
ROSEF 1979 -1 ROSENFELD, P.
TESTING THE PERFORMANCE OF A HEURISTIC FOR A SCHEDULING PROBLEM WHICH HAS NO KNOWN SOLUTION TECHNIQUE.
ROSI 1979 -1 ROSING, K. E.; HILLSMAN, E. L.; ROSING-VOGELAAR, H.
NOTE COMPARING OPTIMAL AND HEURISTIC SOLUTIONS TO THE P-MEDIAN PROBLEM, A.
RUSS 1979 -1 RUSSELL, R.; IGO, W.
ASSIGNMENT ROUTING PROBLEM, AN.
SADO 1978 -1 SADOWSKI, R. P.; JACOBSON, R. E.
SCHEDULING ALGORITHMS FOR THE UNBALANCED PRODUCTION LINE: AN ANALYSIS AND COMPARISON.
SAHNB 1975 -1 SAHNI, S.; GONZALEZ, T.
P-COMPLETE APPROXIMATION PROBLEMS.
SAHNC 1978 -1 SAHNI, S.; HOROWITZ, E.
COMBINATORIAL PROBLEMS: REDUCIBILITY AND APPROXIMATION.
SAND 1974 -1 SANDBERG, V. JU.
HEURISTIC ALGORITHM FOR GRAPH COLORING (RUSSIAN), A.
SARV 1977 -1 SARVANOV, V. I.
APPROXIMATE SOLUTION OF A LINEAR MINIMISATION PROBLEM OVER THE SET OF CYCLIC PERMUTATIONS (RUSSIAN).
SCHEB 1979 -1 SCHENK, G.; THIERS, G.
COMPARISON OF SOME ALGORITHMS AND HEURISTICS FOR SOLVING THE HITCHCOCK-KOOPMANS TRANSPORTATION PROBLEM, A.
SCHR 1981 -1 SCHRADER, R.
APPROXIMATIONS TO CLUSTERING AND SUBGRAPH PROBLEMS ON TREES.
SCHR 1981 -2 SCHRADER, R.
NOTE ON APPROXIMATION ALGORITHMS FOR GRAPH PARTITIONING PROBLEMS, A.
SCOTA 1980 -1 SCOTT, J. L.
HEURISTIC ALGORITHM FOR EXAMINATION TIMETABLING, A.
SERV 1975 -1 SERVIT, M.
HEURISTIC METHOD FOR SOLVING WEIGHTED SET COVERING PROBLEMS, A.
SEVA 1978 -1 SEVASTYANOV, S. V.
ON APPROXIMATE SOLUTION OF SCHEDULING PROBLEMS (RUSSIAN).
SEXT 1978 -1 SEXTON, T. R.
MULTI-VEHICLE SUBSCRIPTION PROBLEM: A HEURISTIC ALGORITHM, THE.
SHERA 1978 -1 SHERMAN, A. I.
ALGORITHM FOR THE APPROXIMATE SOLUTION OF INTEGER LINEAR PROGRAMMING PROBLEMS (RUSSIAN), AN.
SHIMA 1978 -1 SHIMSHAK, D. G.; KASLIK, J. A.; BARCLAY, T. D.
EFFECTIVE HEURISTIC FOR VOGELS'S APPROXIMATION METHOD.
SIME 1978 -1 SIMEONE, B.
ASYMPTOTICALLY EXACT POLYNOMIAL ALGORITHM FOR EQUIPARTITION PROBLEMS, AN.
SLOW 1978 -1 SLOWINSKI, R.
NODE ORDERING HEURISTIC FOR NETWORK SCHEDULING UNDER MULTIPLE RESOURCE CONSTRAINTS, A.
SMITE 1980 -1 SMITH, J. M.; LIEBMAN, J. S.
O(N**2) HEURISTIC ALGORITHM FOR THE DIRECTED STEINER MINIMAL TREE PROBLEM, AN.
SMITF 1979 -1 SMITH, R. L.
DEFERRAL STRATEGIES FOR A DYNAMIC COMMUNICATIONS NETWORK.
SONN 1979 -1 SONNTAG, H.
HEURISTISCHES VERFAHREN ZUM ENTWURF NACHFRAGEORIENTIERTER LINIENFUEHRUNG IM OEFFENTLICHEN PERSONENNAHVERKEHR, EIN.
SPAC 1979 -1 SPACHIS, A. S.; KING, J. R.
JOB-SHOP SCHEDULING HEURISTICS WITH LOCAL NEIGHBOURHOOD SEARCH.
STEI 1978 -1 STEIN, D. M.
ASYMPTOTIC, PROBABILISTIC ANALYSIS OF A ROUTING PROBLEM, AN.
STEWA 1979 -1 STEWART, W. R.; GOLDEN, B. L.
VEHICLE ROUTING ALGORITHM BASED ON GENERALIZED LAGRANGE MULTIPLIERS (ROUGH DRAFT).
STINA 1977 -1 STINSON, J. P.
HEURISTIC ALGORITHM FOR OBTAINING AN INITIAL SOLUTION FOR THE TRAVELING SALESMAN PROBLEM, A.
TAKA 1979 -1 TAKAHASHI, H.; MATSUYAMA, A.
APPROXIMATE SOLUTION FOR THE STEINER PROBLEM IN GRAPHS, AN.
TERA 1979 -1 TERADA, R.
POLYNOMIAL TIME ALGORITHMS FOR NP-HARD PROBLEMS WHICH ARE OPTIMAL OR NEAR-OPTIMAL WITH PROBABILITY ONE.
VENG 1979 -1 VENGEROV, V. N.; NIKITIN, A. S.
HEURISTIC ALGORITHM FOR CUTTING WEIGHTED GRAPHS (RUSSIAN).
WALS 1976 -1 WALSH, A. M.
POLYNOMIAL ALGORITHMS FOR CERTAIN GRAPH-THEORETIC PROBLEMS.
WHITC 1977 -1 WHITE, G. P.; WILLIAMS, T. A.
HEURISTIC SOLUTION TECHNIQUES FOR MULTIPLE TRIP TIME-CONSTRAINED TRAVELING SALESMAN PROBLEMS.
WOLS 1980 -1 WOLSEY, L. A.
HEURISTIC ANALYSIS, LINEAR PROGRAMMING AND BRANCH AND BOUND.
WOLS 1980 -2 WOLSEY, L. A.
MAXIMIZING REAL-VALUED SUBMODULAR FUNCTIONS: PRIMAL AND DUAL HEURISTICS FOR LOCATION PROBLEMS.
WONGB 1980 -1 WONG, R. T.
WORST-CASE ANALYSIS OF NETWORK DESIGN PROBLEM HEURISTICS.
WONGB 1981 -1 WONG, R. T.
PROBABILISTIC ANALYSIS OF AN OPTIMAL NETWORK PROBLEM HEURISTIC.

ZABR 1970 -1 ZABRANSKY, F.
ALUMINUM FOIL SLITTING TRIM LOSS PROBLEM; FORMULATED AS A MIXED INTEGER PROBLEM; SOLVED BY HEURISTIC PROGRAMMING.

ZAJT 1979 -1 ZAJTSEV, I. D.; SALYGA, V. I.; VAJNER, V. G.
SUR UN PROBLEME DE LA THEORIE DES RESEAUX DE COMMUNICATION (RUSSIAN).

ZEME 1978 -1 ZEMEL, E.
FUNCTIONS FOR MEASURING THE QUALITY OF PROXIMATE SOLUTIONS TO ZERO-ONE PROGRAMMING PROBLEMS.

ZUEN 1979 -1 ZUENKOV, M. A.; IGNATUSHCHENKO, V. V.
APPROXIMATE METHOD OF SOLUTION OF ONE-DIMENSIONAL KNAPSACK PROBLEM.

ARAO 1973 -1 ARAOZ, A. A.
POLYHEDRAL NEOPOLARITIES.

BACHA 1979 -1 BACHEM, A.; GROETSCHEL, M.
NEW ASPECTS OF POLYHEDRAL THEORY.

BACHA 1981 -2 BACHEM, A.; GROETSCHEL, M.
HOMOGENIZATION OF POLYHEDRA.

BALAG 1980 -2 BALAS, E.; MAZZOLA, J. B.
VALID INEQUALITIES FOR 0-1 PROGRAMMING POLYTOPES.

BALAI 1981 -1 BALAS, E.; PULLEYBLANK, W. R.
LINEAR CHARACTERIZATION OF THE PERFECTLY MATCHABLE SUBGRAPH POLYHEDRON, A.

BALAK 1978 -1 BALAS, E.; ZEMEL, E.
FACETS OF THE KNAPSACK POLYTOPE FROM MINIMAL COVERS.

BARA 1980 -2 BARAHONA, F.
ON THE COMPLEXITY OF MAX CUT.

BARRC 1979 -1 BARRER, J. N.
BASES OF THE EXTREME POINTS OF THE ASSIGNMENT POLYTOPE.

BLAN 1978 -1 BLAND, R. G.
ELEMENTARY VECTORS AND TWO POLYHEDRAL RELAXATIONS.

CALV 1980 -1 CALVILLO, G.
CONCAVITY AND INTERSECTION PROPERTIES FOR INTEGRAL POLYHEDRA, THE.

CUNN 1981 -3 CUNNINGHAM, W. H.
POLYHEDRA FOR COMPOSED INDEPENDENCE SYSTEMS.

CUNN 1981 -4 CUNNINGHAM, W. H.
TESTING MEMBERSHIP IN MATROID POLYHEDRA.

DORF 1979 -1 DORFMAN, V. A.
POLYHEDRON FOR A PROBLEM OF ORDERING TASKS AT A MACHINE (RUSSIAN).

EMELA 1977 -1 EMELICHEV, V. A.; KRAVTSOV, M. K.; KRACKOVSKII, A. P.
BEWEIS EINER HYPOTHESE VON BOLKER (RUSSIAN).

EMELB 1977 -1 EMELICHEV, V. A.; TRUKHANOVSKIJ, N. N.
SPECTRUM OF TRANSPORTATION POLYHEDRA (RUSSIAN), THE.

EMELC 1977 -1 EMELICHEVA, V. S.; KRAVTSOV, M. K.
FACES OF A DEGENERATE TRANSPORTATION POLYHEDRON (RUSSIAN), THE.

FEDE 1977 -1 FEDENJA, O. A.
POLYHEDRA OF A MULTI-INDEX PLANAR TRANSPORT PROBLEM WITH A MINIMAL NUMBER OF VERTICES I (RUSSIAN), THE.

FEDE 1977 -2 FEDENJA, O. A.
POLYHEDRA OF A MULTI-INDEX PLANAR TRANSPORT PROBLEM WITH A MINIMAL NUMBER OF VERTICES II (RUSSIAN), THE.

FELZ 1979 -1 FELZENBAUM, A.; TAMIR, A.
CYCLIC PERMUTATIONS AND NEARLY SYMMETRIC INTEGER VECTORS.

FRANB 1981 -1 FRANK, A.
FINDING FEASIBLE VECTORS OF EDMONDS-GILES POLYHEDRA.

FRANB 1981 -2 FRANK, A.
GENERALIZED POLYMATROIDS.

GALLF 1979 -3 GALLO, G.; SODINI, C.
EXTREME POINTS AND ADJACENCY RELATIONSHIP IN THE FLOW POLYTOPE.

GILED 1979 -1 GILES, R.; PULLEYBLANK, W. R.
TOTAL DUAL INTEGRALITY AND INTEGER POLYHEDRA.

GILEE 1979 -1 GILES, R.; TROTTER, L. E. JR.
ON STABLE SET POLYHEDRA FOR K1,3-FREE GRAPHS.

GREE 1980 -1 GREEN-KROTKI, J. J.
MATCHING POLYHEDRA.

GROE 1979 -1 GROEFLIN, H.; LIEBLING, T. M.
CONNECTED AND ALTERNATING VECTORS POLYHEDRA AND ALGORITHMS.

HANSA 1977 -1 HANSEN, A. B.
ON A CERTAIN CLASS OF POLYTOPES ASSOCIATED WITH INDEPENDENCE SYSTEMS.

HAUS 1978 -2 HAUSMANN, D.
POLYNOMIALER ALGORITHMUS FUER DIE ADJAZENZUEBERPRUEFUNG AUF DEM BRANCHING-POLYEDER, EIN.

HAUSC 1978 -1 HAUSMANN, D.; KORTE, B.
COLOURING CRITERIA FOR ADJACENCY ON 0-1-POLYHEDRA.

HOFF 1978 -1 HOFFMAN, A. J.
ON LATTICE POLYHEDRA III: BLOCKERS AND ANTI-BLOCKERS OF LATTICE CLUTTERS.

HOUCA 1979 -1 HOUCK, D. J.; PITTENGER, A. O.
ANALYTIC PROOFS OF A NETWORK FEASIBILITY THEOREM AND A THEOREM OF FULKERSON.

KARPB 1980 -1 KARP, R. M.; PAPADIMITRIOU, C. H.
ON LINEAR CHARACTERIZATIONS OF COMBINATORIAL OPTIMIZATION PROBLEMS.

KONO 1971 -1 KONONENKO, A. M.
TRANSPORTATION POLYTOPES OF ORDER 2 X N (RUSSIAN).

KONOA 1979 -1 KONONENKO, A. M.; TRUKHANOVSKIJ, N. N.
CLASSES DE POLYEDRES DE TRANSPORT AVEC UN NOMBRE MAXIMAL DE SOMMETS (RUSSIAN).

KONOA 1978 -2 KONONENKO, A. M.; TRUKHANOVSKIJ, N. N.
POLYEDRES DE TRANSPORT AVEC UN NOMBRE MAXIMAL DE SOMMETS (RUSSIAN).

KORN 1978 -1 KORNBLUM, D. F.
"GREEDY" ALGORITHMS FOR SOME LATTICE POLYHEDRA PROBLEMS.

KORN 1978 -2 KORNBLUM, D. F.
GREEDY ALGORITHMS FOR SOME OPTIMIZATION PROBLEMS ON A LATTICE POLYHEDRON.

KOVAA 1978 -1 KOVALEV, M. M.; GIRLICH, E.
EXACT NUMBER OF VERTICES OF POLYHEDRA IN THE CONDITIONS OF THE STANDARDIZATION PROBLEM (RUSSIAN), THE.

KOVAB 1979 -1 KOVALEV, M. M.; ISACHENKO, A. N.
SEMIMATROIDE.

KOVAC 1978 -1 KOVALEV, M. M.; ISACHENKO, A. N.; NGUEN NGIA
LINEARISATION DES PROBLEMES COMBINATOIRES D'OPTIMISATION (RUSSIAN).

KRACA 1979 -1 KRACKOVSKII, A. P.; EMELICHEV, V. A.
ESTIMATION OF THE UPPER LIMIT FOR THE TRANSPORT POLYTOPE DIAMETER (RUSSIAN).

KRAVB 1979 -1 KRAVTSOV, M. K.; EMELICHEV, V. A.
ESTIMATION PAR EXCES DU DIAMETRE D'UN POLYEDRE DE TRANSPORT (RUSSIAN).

KRAVC 1979 -1 KRAVTSOV, M. K.; KORZNIKOV, A. D.
ENUMERATION PROBLEMS ON TRUNCATED TRANSPORT POLYTOPES (RUSSIAN).

MATTA 1977 -1 MATTHEISS, T. H.; RUBIN, D. S.
SURVEY AND COMPARISON OF METHODS FOR FINDING ALL VERTICES OF CONVEX POLYHEDRAL SETS, A.

MAZZ 1980 -1 MAZZOLA, J. B.
PROCEDURE FOR GENERATING THE CONVEX HULL OF A 0-1 PROGRAMMING POLYTOPE WITH POSITIVE COEFFICIENTS, A.

MEYEF 1978 -1 MEYER, R. R.; WAGE, M. L.
ON THE POLYHEDRALITY OF THE CONVEX HULL OF THE FEASIBLE SET OF AN INTEGER PROGRAM.

INTEGER POLYHEDRA (UNLESS SPECIFIED ELSEWHERE)

MONMC 1979 -1 MONMA, C. L.; TROTTER, L. E. JR.
ON PERFECT GRAPHS AND POLYHEDRA WITH (0,1)-VALUED EXTREME POINTS.

NADDA 1980 -2 NADDEF, D.; PULLEYBLANK, W. R.
HAMILTONICITY AND COMBINATORIAL POLYHEDRA.

OMAR 1977 -1 OMAR, A.
FINDING ALL EXTREME POINTS AND EXTREME RAYS OF A CONVEX POLYHEDRAL SET.

PIEH 1980 -1 PIEHLER, J.
UEBER GITTERPUNKTE IN KEGELN.

RIIV 1979 -1 RIIVES, K.
DETERMINATION OF THE VERTICES OF TRANSPORT POLYTOPES (RUSSIAN). A.

SCHMA 1978 -1 SCHMID, H. J.
GEOMETRICAL INTERPRETATION OF THE HUNGARIAN METHOD. A.

SCHRD 1979 -1 SCHRIJVER, A.
FRACTIONAL PACKING AND COVERING.

SEEL 1980 -3 SEELAENDER, J.
ZUR EXISTENZ VON GITTER- UND HALBGITTERPUNKTEN IN BESTIMMTEN POLYEDRISCHEN MENGEN.

SHLY 1978 -1 SHLYK, V. A.
ON THE FACES OF MASTER GOMORY POLYHEDRA (RUSSIAN).

TIND 1980 -1 TIND, J.
CERTAIN KINDS OF POLAR SETS AND THEIR RELATION TO MATHEMATICAL PROGRAMMING.

WOLS 1977 -1 WOLSEY, L. A.
VALID INEQUALITIES AND SUPERADDITIVITY OF 0-1 INTEGER PROGRAMS.

YOUN 1978 -1 YOUNG, H. P.
ON PERMUTATIONS AND PERMUTATION POLYTOPES.

ZEME 1976 -1 ZEMEL, E.
ON THE FACIAL STRUCTURE OF 0-1 POLYTOPES.

AFAN 1976 -1 AFANAS'EV, JU. A.; POMANSKII, A. B.
NEW APPROACH TO THE CONSTRUCTION OF ALGORITHMS FOR THE SOLUTION OF PROBLEMS WITH DISCRETE VARIABLES (RUSSIAN), A.

AKHM 1979 -1 AKHMEDOV, A.; MAJZLIN, M.; CHARYEV, G.
SOLUTION OF SOME MULTIPLE-PRODUCT PROBLEM OF INTEGER PROGRAMMING (RUSSIAN).

ALT 1976 -1 ALT, A. M.
CLASS OF INTEGER OPTIMIZATION PROBLEMS (RUSSIAN), A.

ARMSE 1980 -1 ARMSTRONG, R. D.; KLINGMAN, D.; WHITMAN, D.
IMPLEMENTATION AND ANALYSIS OF A VARIANT OF THE DUAL METHOD FOR THE CAPACITATED TRANSSHIPMENT PROBLEM.

BABAD 1979 -1 BABAEV, DZ. A.; VELIEV, G. P.; MAMEDOV, K. S.
A PRIORI DETERMINATION OF OPTIMAL VARIABLE VALUES IN DISCRETE PROGRAMMING PROBLEMS, THE.

BABAF 1979 -1 BABAT, L. G.
GROWTH OF COEFFICIENTS IN INTEGRAL LINEAR PROGRAMMING (RUSSIAN).

BAER 1977 -1 BAER, G.
BEITRAG ZUR TRANSFORMATION GANZZAHLIGER OPTIMIERUNGSPROBLEME, EIN.

BAER 1978 -1 BAER, G.
THEORETISCHE FUNDIERUNG DER DISKRETEN OPTIMIERUNG MIT LOGISCHEN MITTELN, EINE.

BIKO 1978 -2 BIKOV, V. M.
IMPROVING THE EFFICIENCY OF THE LOCAL OPTIMIZATION METHODS FOR SOME CLASSES OF INTEGER PROGRAMMING PROBLEMS (RUSSIAN).

BLAIA 1980 -1 BLAIR, C. E.; JEROSLOW, R. G.
VALUE FUNCTION OF AN INTEGER PROGRAM, THE.

CHERB 1978 -1 CHERNIKOVA, N. V.
NON-NEGATIVE INTEGER SOLUTIONS OF A SYSTEM OF LINEAR EQUATIONS AND SOME QUESTIONS OF LINEAR INTEGER PROGRAMMING (RUSSIAN).

CHERD 1977 -1 CHERNYSHEV, JU. O.; OSTROUH, E. N.
POSSIBILITY OF REDUCING A CERTAIN CLASS OF LINEAR PROGRAMMING PROBLEMS TO PROBLEMS OF TRANSPORT TYPE (RUSSIAN), THE.

CONL 1978 -1 CONLEY, W.
SIMPLIFYING THE TEACHING OF INTEGER PROGRAMMING.

CONLA 1977 -1 CONLEY, W.; TRACY, D. S.
INTEGER PROGRAMMING WITH A COMPUTER: A STATISTICAL APPROACH.

COUR 1965 -1 COURTILLOT, M.
SUR LA RESOLUTION DES PROGRAMMES A SOLUTIONS ENTIERES.

CUNI 1981 -1 CUNINGHAME-GREEN, R. A.
INTEGER PROGRAMMING BY LONG DIVISION.

DANI 1978 -1 DANIEL, R. C.
GENERALISATION OF VARIABLE UPPER BOUNDING AND GENERALISED UPPER BOUNDING, A.

EROK 1981 -1 EROKHIN, I. L.; KAPLAN, S. G.
PARTIAL SEARCH ALGORITHM FOR INTEGER PROBLEMS SOLUTION (RUSSIAN).

ETCH 1978 -1 ETCHEBERRY, J.; CONCA, C.; STACCHETTI, E.
IMPLICIT ENUMERATION APPROACH FOR INTEGER PROGRAMMING USING SUBGRADIENT OPTIMIZATION, AN.

FAYA 1979 -1 FAYARD, D.; PLATEAU, G.
CONTRIBUTION A LA RESOLUTION DES PROGRAMMES MATHEMATIQUES EN NOMBRES ENTIERS.

FISH 1978 -1 FISHER, M. L.
LAGRANGIAN RELAXATION METHODS FOR COMBINATORIAL OPTIMIZATION.

FLEIA 1978 -1 FLEISHER, J. M.; MEYER, R. R.
NEW SUFFICIENT OPTIMALITY CONDITIONS FOR INTEGER PROGRAMMING AND THEIR APPLICATION.

FRID 1976 -1 FRIDMAN, A. A.; FRUMKIN, M. A.; HMELEVSKII, JU. I.; LEVNER, E. V.
STUDY OF ALGORITHM EFFICIENCY FOR DISCRETE AND COMBINATORIAL PROBLEMS. THEORY OF PROBLEM REDUCIBILITY AND UNIVERSAL PROBLEMS (RUSSIAN).

GENS 1977 -1 GENS, G. V.; LEVNER, E. V.
ON E-ALGORITHMS FOR UNIVERSAL DISCRETE PROBLEMS (RUSSIAN).

GIANB 1976 -1 GIANNESSI, F.; NICCOLUCCI, F.
CONNECTIONS BETWEEN NONLINEAR AND INTEGER PROGRAMMING PROBLEMS.

GIAND 1977 -1 GIANNESSI, G.
CONTINUED FRACTIONS AND EXPLICIT SOLUTIONS OF A PARTICULAR DISCRETE OPTIMIZATION PROBLEM.

GILED 1979 -1 GILES, R.; PULLEYBLANK, W. R.
TOTAL DUAL INTEGRALITY AND INTEGER POLYHEDRA.

GLUS 1980 -1 GLUSHKOV, V. M.; KASPSHITCKAYA, M. F.; SERGIENKO, I. V.
FORMALIZATION QUESTIONS AND SOLUTIONS OF ONE CLASS OF PROBLEMS OF DISCRETE OPTIMIZATION (RUSSIAN), THE.

GOLDC 1978 -1 GOLDEN, B. L.; ALT, F. B.
INTERVAL ESTIMATION OF A GLOBAL OPTIMUM FOR LARGE COMBINATORIAL PROBLEMS.

GOND 1977 -1 GONDRAN, M.
ALGORITHME DE COUPES EN PROGRAMMATION EN NOMBRES ENTIERS, UN.

GOND 1978 -1 GONDRAN, M.
DEUX TRANSFORMATIONS IDEALES POUR REGULARISER LES PROBLEMES COMBINATOIRES.

GUIGA 1978 -2 GUIGNARD, M.; SPIELBERG, K.
EXPERIMENTAL INTERACTIVE SYSTEM FOR INTEGER PROGRAMMING, AN.

HOCH 1980 -2 HOCHBAUM, D.
FAST APPROXIMATION ALGORITHMS FOR SOME INTEGER PROGRAMMING PROBLEMS.

IBAR 1980 -2 IBARAKI, T.
NUMBER OF ADDITIONAL VARIABLES REQUIRED FOR THE INTEGER PROGRAMMING FORMULATION, THE.

JAMB 1978 -2 JAMBEKAR, A. B.; STEINBERG, D. I.
IMPLICIT ENUMERATION ALGORITHM FOR THE ALL INTEGER PROGRAMMING PROBLEM, AN.

JEROB 1980 -2 JEROSLOW, R. G.
SOME INFLUENCES OF GENERALIZED AND ORDINARY CONVEXITY IN DISJUNCTIVE AND INTEGER PROGRAMMING.

JOHNF 1978 -1 JOHNSON, E. L.; POWELL, S.
INTEGER PROGRAMMING CODES.

KALI 1979 -1 KALISZEWSKI, I.; WALUKIEWICZ, S.
TIGHTER EQUIVALENT FORMULATIONS OF INTEGER PROGRAMMING PROBLEMS.

KANN 1980 -1 KANNAN, R.
POLYNOMIAL ALGORITHM FOR THE TWO-VARIABLE INTEGER PROGRAMMING PROBLEM, A.

KAPL 1973 -1 KAPLINSKII, A. I.; CERNYSOVA, G. D.
CONSTRUCTION OF PROBABILISTIC ITERATIVE ALGORITHMS FOR THE SOLUTION OF INTEGER PROGRAMMING PROBLEMS (RUSSIAN).

KATK 1977 -1 KATKHANOV, M. N.; BURLAKOV, E. A.; SAFRONOV, V. V.
OPTIMIZATION ALGORITHM OF THE TOLERANCES ON PARAMETERS OF THE ELEMENTS OF A COMPLEX SYSTEM (RUSSIAN).

KAUFO 1977 -1 KAUFMANN, A.; HENRY-LABORDERE, A.
INTEGER AND MIXED PROGRAMMING. THEORY AND APPLICATIONS.

KELA 1978 -1 KELAHAN, R. C.; GADDY, J. L.
APPLICATION OF THE ADAPTIVE RANDOM SEARCH TO DISCRETE AND MIXED INTEGER OPTIMIZATION.

INTEGER PROGRAMMING (GENERAL)

KIVI 1979 -1 KIVISTIK, L. A.
SOLUTION OF INTEGER PROGRAMMING PROBLEMS WITH ADDITIONAL ALTERNATIVE CONDITIONS (RUSSIAN), THE.
KIVI 1980 -1 KIVISTIK, L. A.
DISCRETE MATHEMATICAL PROGRAMMING PROBLEMS WITH SEPARABLE FUNCTIONS (RUSSIAN).
KLEIB 1979 -1 KLEIN, D.; HOLM, S.
INTEGER PROGRAMMING POST-OPTIMAL ANALYSIS WITH CUTTING PLANES.
KORB 1979 -1 KORBUT, A. A.; SIGAL, I. H.; FINKELSTEIN, JU. JU.
EFFECTIVENESS OF COMBINATORIAL METHODS IN DISCRETE PROGRAMMING (RUSSIAN), THE.
KORNA 1978 -1 KORNIENKO, N. M.; METELSKIJ, N. N.
DESCRIPTION OF PARTIAL ORDERINGS OF FEASIBLE SOLUTIONS OF INTEGER LINEAR PROGRAMMING PROBLEMS (RUSSIAN).
KORTA 1979 -2 KORTE, B.
GANZZAHLIGE PROGRAMMIERUNG.
KRARB 1980 -1 KRARUP, J.; WALUKIEWICZ, S.
RELATIONS AMONG INTEGER PROGRAMS.
KRAU 1979 -1 KRAUS, V.
USE OF MARKOV CHAINS IN SOLVING INTEGER OPTIMIZATION PROBLEMS (CZECHOSLOVAKIAN), THE.
KUPC 1976 -1 KUPCOV, L. P.; SEROV, S. S.
SEARCH FOR THE COMPLETE OPTIMAL SOLUTION IN AN INTEGER LINEAR PROGRAMMING PROBLEM (RUSSIAN), THE.
LEE F 1977 -1 LEE, S. M.; MORRIS, R. L.
INTEGER GOAL PROGRAMMING METHODS.
LENS 1981 -1 LENSTRA, H. W. JR.
INTEGER PROGRAMMING WITH A FIXED NUMBER OF VARIABLES.
LEV 1978 -1 LEV, B.; SOYSTER, A. L.
INTEGER PROGRAMMING WITH BOUNDED VARIABLES VIA CANONICAL SEPARATION.
LIEBA 1977 -1 LIEBMAN, J. S.; CHANARATNA, V.; KHACHATURIAN, N.
DISCRETE OPTIMIZATION IN STRUCTURAL DESIGN.
LOVA 1976 -2 LOVASZ, L.
GRAPH THEORY AND INTEGER PROGRAMMING (HUNGARIAN).
MALA 1980 -1 MALASHENKO, YU. E.; STANEVICHUS, A.-J. A.
ON THE SOLUTION OF AN INTEGER PROGRAMMING PROBLEM (RUSSIAN).
METE 1977 -1 METELSKIJ, N. N.; SLYK, V. A.
CONDITIONS FOR THE SOLVABILITY OF THE INTEGER LINEAR PROGRAMMING PROBLEM (RUSSIAN).
MEYEC 1975 -1 MEYER, R. R.; FLEISHER, J. M.
STRONG DUALITY FOR A CLASS OF INTEGER PROGRAMS.
MIKH 1980 -1 MIKHALEVICH, V. S.; VOLKOVICH, V. L.; VOLOSHIN, A. F.; POSDNYAKOV, YU. M.
ALGORITHMS OF SEQUENTIAL ANALYSIS AND "SCREENING" OF VARIANTS IN DISCRETE OPTIMIZATION PROBLEMS (RUSSIAN).
MITE 1979 -1 MITEV, J. G.
USE OF A NUMBER OF ADMISSIBLE SOLUTIONS OF EQUATIONS IN ALGORITHMS FOR PURELY INTEGER PROBLEMS OF LINEAR PROGRAMMING (RUSSIAN), THE.
MITE 1981 -1 MITEV, J. G.
SUCCESSIVE SOLUTIONS METHOD FOR AN INTEGER OPTIMIZATIONAL PROBLEM (RUSSIAN).
NASE 1979 -1 NASEKIN, V. J.
METHOD FOR THE SOLUTION OF MONOTONIC INTEGER LINEAR PROGRAMMING PROBLEMS, A.
NGUE 1980 -1 NGUEN, N. C.
ON ONE METHOD FOR FINDING A COMMON FORMULA OF INTEGER SOLUTIONS FOR A SYSTEM OF LINEAR INEQUALITIES (RUSSIAN).
NGUEA 1981 -1 NGUEN, N. C.; CHERNIKOVA, N. V.
NEW ALGORITHM OF SOLUTION OF DISCRETE PROGRAMMING PROBLEM (RUSSIAN), A.
NIEP 1977 -1 NIEPAGE, H.-D.
GANZZAHLIGE ZENTRENMETHODE, DIE.
NIEP 1977 -2 NIEPAGE, H.-D.
UEBERDECKUNGSPRINZIP ZUR LOESUNG FREIER GANZZAHLIGER MINIMUMPROBLEME, EIN.
NJAR 1980 -1 NJARIPJA, H.
SOME NEW ESTIMATION PROBLEMS FOR PROBLEMS OF INTEGER LINEAR PROGRAMMING (RUSSIAN).
PANA 1979 -1 PANAYIOTOPOULOS, J.-C.
INTEGER PROGRAMMING WITH IRREGULAR DATA SPACE.
PATK 1979 -1 PATKAR, V.; AGGARWAL, S.
BRANCH AND BOUND TECHNIQUE FOR INTEGER GEOMETRIC PROGRAMMING.
PEGD 1979 -1 PEGDEN, C. D.; PETERSEN, C. C.
ALGORITHM (GIPC2) FOR SOLVING INTEGER PROGRAMMING PROBLEMS WITH SEPARABLE NONLINEAR OBJECTIVE FUNCTIONS, AN.
PIEH 1979 -1 PIEHLER, J.
DIOPHANTISCHE GLEICHUNGEN IN DER GANZZAHLIGEN OPTIMIERUNG.
RARDB 1978 -1 RARDIN, R. L.; LIN, B. W.
WHAT MAKES INTEGER PROGRAMMING PROBLEMS HARD TO SOLVE: AN EMPIRICAL STUDY.
RARDB 1980 -1 RARDIN, R. L.; LIN, B. W.
RIP RANDOM INTEGER PROGRAMMING TEST PROBLEM GENERATOR, THE.
RATH 1977 -1 RATHMANN, D.
ZUR LOESUNG DISKRETER OPTIMIERUNGSPROBLEME MIT GRUPPENTHEORETISCHEN ANSAETZEN.
ROTA 1978 -1 ROTARU, S.
DEUX METHODES DE RESOLUTION DE LA PROGRAMMATION ENTIERE (ROMANIAN).
SAHNB 1975 -1 SAHNI, S.; GONZALEZ, T.
P-COMPLETE APPROXIMATION PROBLEMS.
SALC 1973 -1 SALCEDO, E.
METHODS OF PARTIAL ENUMERATION FOR THE SOLUTION OF DISCRETE OPTIMIZATION PROBLEMS (SPANISH), THE.
SALK 1975 -1 SALKIN, H. M.
INTEGER PROGRAMMING.
SAXE 1979 -1 SAXENA, P. C.; PATKAR, V.; PARKASH, O.
NOTE ON AN ALGORITHM FOR INTEGER SOLUTION TO LINEAR AND PIECEWISE LINEAR PROGRAMS, A.
SCHO 1979 -1 SCHOCH, M.
NEUERE ERGEBNISSE IN DER DISKRETEN OPTIMIERUNG.
SEKI 1981 -1 SEKIGUCHI, Y.
UNIFYING FRAMEWORK OF COMBINATORIAL OPTIMIZATION ALGORITHMS; TREE PROGRAMMING AND ITS VALIDITY, A.
SEN A 1980 -1 SEN, S. K.
NONNEGATIVE INTEGRAL SOLUTION OF LINEAR EQUATIONS.
SEND 1978 -1 SENDEROV, I. B.
MODIFIZIERUNG EINES ZUFAELLIGEN SUCHALGORITHMUS FUER DIE LOESUNG VON PROBLEMEN DER DISKRETEN PROGRAMMIERUNG (RUSSIAN), EINE.

SERE 1975 -1 SEREK, M.; ZAVIACIC, V.
USE OF DISCRETE LINEAR PROGRAMMING IN THE SOLUTION OF THE PROBLEM OF PURITY OF SURFACE WATERS, THE.

SERGA 1980 -1 SERGIENKO, I. V.; LEBEDEVA, T. T.; ROSHCHIN, V. A.
APPROXIMATE METHODS FOR THE SOLUTION OF DISCRETE OPTIMIZATION PROBLEMS (RUSSIAN).

SEVC 1975 -1 SEVCENKO, V. N.
SOLUTION OF THE ELEMENTARY INTEGER LINEAR PROGRAMMING PROBLEM (RUSSIAN), THE.

SGUR 1977 -1 SGUREV, V. S.; VASILEV, V. S.
DECOMPOSITION METHOD FOR THE SOLUTION OF A CLASS OF INTEGER PROGRAMMING PROBLEMS (BULGARIAN), A.

SHCH 1980 -1 SHCHERBINA, O. A.
SUR UN ALGORITHME LOCAL POUR LES PROBLEMES D'OPTIMISATION A VALEURS ENTIERES (RUSSIAN).

SHEN 1978 -1 SHENDEROV, I. B.
MODIFICATION OF RANDOM SEARCH FOR THE SOLUTION OF DISCRETE OPTIMIZATION PROBLEMS (RUSSIAN).

SHEV 1981 -1 SHEVCHENKO, V. N.
ON THE NUMBER OF EXTREME POINTS IN INTEGRAL PROGRAMMING (RUSSIAN).

SHME 1978 -1 SHMELEV, V. V.
SOLVING INTEGER LINEAR PROGRAMMING PROBLEMS BY THE PENALTY FUNCTION METHOD.

SMIR 1980 -1 SMIRNOV, A. N.; SHEVCHENKO, V. N.
MARTIN'S ALGORITHM AND REGULAR CUT-OFFS FOR INTEGER LINEAR PROGRAMMING (RUSSIAN).

TERN 1978 -1 TERNO, J.
GRUNDPRINZIPIEN DER DISKRETEN OPTIMIERUNG.

TERZ 1980 -1 TERZI, D. G.
INVESTIGATION OF DISCRETE PROGRAMMING ALGORITHMS (RUSSIAN).

TRYP 1975 -1 TRYPIA, M. N.
METHODS FOR INTEGER PROGRAMMING.

VILLA 1978 -1 VILLARREAL, B.; KARWAN, M. H.
MULTICRITERION INTEGER LINEAR PROGRAMMING A (HYBRID) DYNAMIC PROGRAMMING RECURSIVE APPROACH.

VIZV 1977 -1 VIZVARI, B.
ON THE OPTIMAL SOLUTIONS OF DISCRETE PROGRAMMING PROBLEMS (HUNGARIAN).

VOLP 1977 -1 VOLPENTESTA, A.
EQUI-ASSIGNED BINARY VECTORS AND EXPLICIT SOLUTIONS OF A PARTICULAR DISCRETE OPTIMIZATION PROBLEM.

VOLP 1978 -2 VOLPENTESTA, A.
ON THE PROBLEM OF CHARACTERIZING THE OPTIMAL SET OF A PARTICULAR DISCRETE OPTIMIZATION PROBLEM.

VRAC 1975 -1 VRACIU, G.; LUPSOIU, C.
ALGORITHM FOR DISCRETE PROGRAMMING WITH APPLICATIONS FOR PRODUCTION PROGRAMMING (ROMANIAN).

WDOW 1978 -1 WDOWIAK, J.
DISCRETE LINEAR FRACTIONAL PROGRAMMING PROBLEM II (POLISH), A.

ZIMM 1981 -1 ZIMMERMANN, U.
LINEAR AND COMBINATORIAL OPTIMIZATION IN ORDERED ALGEBRAIC STRUCTURES.

ALBA 1980 -2 ALBANO, A.; ORSINI, R.
TREE SEARCH APPROACH TO THE M-PARTITION AND KNAPSACK PROBLEMS, A.
ARMSB 1979 -1 ARMSTRONG, R. D.; COOK, W. D.; PALACIOS-GOMEZ, F. E.
ALGORITHM FOR A NONLINEAR DISCONTINUOUS KNAPSACK PROBLEM, AN.
ATRI 1979 -1 ATRI, G. D'
ANALYSE PROBABILISTE DU PROBLEME DU SAC-A-DOS.
ATRI 1981 -1 ATRI, G. D'
PROBABILISTIC ANALYSIS OF KNAPSACK-TYPE PROBLEMS.
ATRI 1978 -3 ATRI, G. D'
PROBABILISTIC ANALYSIS OF THE KNAPSACK PROBLEM.
BABAC 1978 -1 BABAEV, DZ. A.; MAMEDOV, K. S.; MEKHTIEV, M. G.
METHODS OF CONSTRUCTING SUBOPTIMAL SOLUTIONS OF THE MULTIDIMENSIONAL RUCKSACK PROBLEM.
BALAK 1978 -1 BALAS, E.; ZEMEL, E.
FACETS OF THE KNAPSACK POLYTOPE FROM MINIMAL COVERS.
BALAK 1980 -1 BALAS, E.; ZEMEL, E.
ALGORITHM FOR LARGE ZERO-ONE KNAPSACK PROBLEMS, AN.
BALAK 1977 -2 BALAS, E.; ZEMEL, E.
SOLVING LARGE KNAPSACK PROBLEMS.
BALAK 1977 -3 BALAS, E.; ZEMEL, E.
SOLVING LARGE ZERO-ONE KNAPSACK PROBLEMS (REVISED VERSION).
BIRO 1980 -1 BIRO, M.
EFFICIENT METHOD APPLYING INCOMPLETE ORDERING FOR SOLVING THE BINARY KNAPSACK PROBLEM.
BITRA 1977 -1 BITRAN, G. R.; HAX, A. C.
ON THE SOLUTION OF CONVEX KNAPSACK PROBLEMS WITH BOUNDED VARIABLES.
BROWB 1979 -1 BROWN, J. R.
KNAPSACK SHARING PROBLEM, THE.
BULFB 1979 -1 BULFIN, R. L.; PARKER, R. G.; SHETTY, C. M.
COMPUTATIONAL RESULTS WITH A BRANCH-AND-BOUND ALGORITHM FOR THE GENERAL KNAPSACK PROBLEM.
CHRIG 1979 -1 CHRISTOFIDES, N.; MINGOZZI, A.; TOTH, P.
LOADING PROBLEMS.
CHUNC 1979 -1 CHUNG, S.-J.
NOTE ON THE COMPLEXITY OF LCP: THE LCP IS NP-COMPLETE, A.
CHUNC 1979 -2 CHUNG, S.-J.
NP-COMPLETE ADJACENCY DECISION PROBLEMS ON SOME 0-1 CONVEX POLYTOPE.
CHVA 1980 -1 CHVATAL, V.
HARD KNAPSACK PROBLEMS.
DEMBA 1980 -1 DEMBO, R. S.; HAMMER, P. L.
REDUCTION ALGORITHM FOR KNAPSACK PROBLEMS, A.
DOBK 1978 -1 DOBKIN, D. P.; LIPTON, R. J.
LOWER BOUND OF 1/2*N**2 ON LINEAR SEARCH PROGRAMS FOR THE KNAPSACK PROBLEM.
DOBKA 1978 -1 DOBKIN, D. P.; LIPTON, R. J.; REISS, S. P.
EXCURSIONS INTO GEOMETRY.
ELMAA 1980 -1 ELMAGHRABY, S. E.; ELIMAM, A. A.
KNAPSACK-BASED APPROACHES TO THE MAKESPAN PROBLEM ON MULTIPLE PROCESSORS.
FAYA 1979 -1 FAYARD, D.; PLATEAU, G.
CONTRIBUTION A LA RESOLUTION DES PROGRAMMES MATHEMATIQUES EN NOMBRES ENTIERS.
FAYA 1979 -2 FAYARD, D.; PLATEAU, G.
LE PROBLEME DU KNAPSACK "BAUDRUCHE" EN VARIABLES 0-1.
FAYA 1979 -3 FAYARD, D.; PLATEAU, G.
PROBLEME DU KNAPSACK NON LINEAIRE EN VARIABLES 0-1, UN.
FINKB 1980 -1 FINKELSTEIN, JU. JU.
ABOUT THE POLYNOMIAL ALGORITHM OF EPSILON-OPTIMIZATION IN THE MULTIDIMENSIONAL KNAPSACK PROBLEM (RUSSIAN).
FISH 1978 -3 FISHER, M. L.
WORST-CASE ANALYSIS OF HEURISTICS.
FISK 1979 -1 FISK, J. C.; HUNG, M. S.
HEURISTIC ROUTINE FOR SOLVING LARGE LOADING PROBLEMS, A.
FREI 1979 -1 FREIDENFELDS, J.; MAC LAUGHLIN, C. D.
HEURISTIC BRANCH-AND-BOUND ALGORITHM FOR TELEPHONE FEEDER CAPACITY EXPANSION, A.
FRIDA 1975 -1 FRIDMAN, F. A.
SOLUTION OF THE KNAPSACK PROBLEM WITH SPECIAL SUPPLEMENTARY CONSTRAINTS (RUSSIAN).
FRIED 1979 -1 FRIEZE, A. M.
APPROXIMATE ALGORITHM FOR THE M-DIMENSIONAL 0-1 KNAPSACK PROBLEM, AN.
GALLC 1980 -1 GALLO, G.; HAMMER, P. L.; SIMEONE, B.
QUADRATIC KNAPSACK PROBLEMS.
GAUD 1979 -1 GAUDIOSO, M.
HEURISTIC APPROACH TO THE CUTTING STOCK PROBLEM, A.
GENS 1980 -1 GENS, G. V.; LEVNER, E. V.
FAST APPROXIMATION ALGORITHMS FOR KNAPSACK TYPE PROBLEMS.
GENS 1979 -2 GENS, G. V.; LEVNER, E. V.
COMPUTATIONAL COMPLEXITY OF APPROXIMATION ALGORITHMS FOR COMBINATORIAL PROBLEMS.
GENS 1979 -3 GENS, G. V.; LEVNER, E. V.
EFFICIENT APPROXIMATION ALGORITHMS FOR THE INTEGER PROGRAMMING PROBLEMS OF KNAPSACK TYPE.
GILM 1979 -1 GILMORE, P. C.
CUTTING STOCK, LINEAR PROGRAMMING, KNAPSACKING, DYNAMIC PROGRAMMING AND INTEGER PROGRAMMING, SOME INTERCONNECTIONS.
GLOVE 1979 -1 GLOVER, F.; KLINGMAN, D.
O(N LOG N) ALGORITHM FOR LP KNAPSACKS WITH GUB CONSTRAINTS, A.
GREEA 1980 -1 GREENBERG, H.; FELDMAN, I.
BETTER STEP-OFF ALGORITHM FOR THE KNAPSACK PROBLEM, A.
HAUSB 1979 -1 HAUSMANN, D.; KANNAN, R.; KORTE, B.
EXPONENTIELLE UNTERE KOMPLEXITAETSSCHRANKEN FUER EINE KLASSE VON KNAPSACK-PROBLEMEN.
HAUSB 1981 -1 HAUSMANN, D.; KANNAN, R.; KORTE, B.
EXPONENTIAL LOWER BOUNDS ON A CLASS OF KNAPSACK ALGORITHMS.
HAUSB 1979 -2 HAUSMANN, D.; KANNAN, R.; KORTE, B.
EXPONENTIELLE UNTERE KOMPLEXITAETSSCHRANKEN FUER EINE KLASSE VON KNAPSACKPROBLEMEN (EXTENDED ABSTRACT).
HUDS 1977 -1 HUDSON, P. D.
IMPROVING THE BRANCH AND BOUND ALGORITHMS FOR THE KNAPSACK PROBLEM.
IBAR 1980 -1 IBARAKI, T.
APPROXIMATE ALGORITHMS FOR THE MULTIPLE-CHOICE CONTINUOUS KNAPSACK PROBLEMS.
IBARA 1978 -1 IBARAKI, T.; HASEGAWA, T.; TERANAKA, K.; IWASE, J.
MULTIPLE-CHOICE KNAPSACK PROBLEM, THE.
IOSL 1978 -1 IOSLOVIC, I. V.; ROZNOVA, O. V.
MATHEMATICAL MODELS FOR THE CHOICE OF SHIPLOAD IN AVIATION TRANSPORT (RUSSIAN).

JOHND 1979 -2 JOHNSON, E. L.
SUBADDITIVE LIFTING METHODS FOR PARTITIONING AND KNAPSACK PROBLEMS.
KANN 1980 -2 KANNAN, R.
POLYNOMIAL-TIME AGGREGATION OF INTEGER PROGRAMMING PROBLEMS.
KAREB 1980 -1 KARELIN, V. P.; KOVALEV, S. M.
PROBLEM OF THE PACKING OF SEVERAL KNAPSACKS (RUSSIAN), A.
KOER 1979 -1 KOERNER, F.
BEMERKUNGEN ZUM RUCKSACKPROBLEM.
LAWL 1977 -1 LAWLER, E. L.
FAST APPROXIMATION ALGORITHMS FOR KNAPSACK PROBLEMS.
LAWL 1978 -1 LAWLER, E. L.
FAST APPROXIMATION ALGORITHMS FOR KNAPSACK PROBLEMS.
LAWL 1979 -2 LAWLER, E. L.
FAST APPROXIMATION ALGORITHMS FOR KNAPSACK PROBLEMS.
LIBU 1977 -1 LIBURA, M.
SENSITIVITY ANALYSIS OF SOLUTIONS OF THE INTEGER KNAPSACK PROBLEM (POLISH).
LOUL 1979 -1 LOULOU, R.; MICHAELIDES, E.
NEW GREEDY-LIKE HEURISTICS FOR THE MULTIDIMENSIONAL 0-1 KNAPSACK PROBLEM.
MAGA 1979 -1 MAGAZINE, M. J.; OGUZ, O.
FULLY POLYNOMIAL APPROXIMATE ALGORITHM FOR THE 0-1 KNAPSACK PROBLEM, A. (REVISED VERSION).
MARTC 1977 -1 MARTELLO, S.; TOTH, P.
BRANCH AND BOUND ALGORITHMS FOR THE SOLUTION OF THE GENERAL UNIDIMENSIONAL KNAPSACK PROBLEM.
MARTC 1978 -1 MARTELLO, S.; TOTH, P.
ALGORITHM 37. ALGORITHM FOR THE SOLUTION OF THE 0-1 SINGLE KNAPSACK PROBLEM.
MARTC 1978 -2 MARTELLO, S.; TOTH, P.
PROBLEM OF OPTIMAL CHANGE MAKING (ITALIAN), THE.
MARTC 1979 -2 MARTELLO, S.; TOTH, P.
HEURISTIC ALGORITHMS FOR THE MULTIPLE KNAPSACK PROBLEM.
MARTC 1980 -2 MARTELLO, S.; TOTH, P.
NOTE ON THE INGARGIOLA-KORSH ALGORITHM FOR ONE-DIMENSIONAL KNAPSACK PROBLEMS, A.
MARTC 1979 -3 MARTELLO, S.; TOTH, P.
0-1 KNAPSACK PROBLEM, THE.
MARTC 1980 -4 MARTELLO, S.; TOTH, P.
SOLUTION OF THE ZERO-ONE MULTIPLE KNAPSACK PROBLEM.
MEVE 1976 -1 MEVERT, P.; SUHL, U.
ALGORITHMS AND A COMPUTATIONAL STUDY FOR THE MULTIDIMENSIONAL KNAPSACK PROBLEM.
MUEL 1978 -1 MUELLER-MERBACH, H.
IMPROVED UPPER BOUND FOR THE ZERO-ONE KNAPSACK PROBLEM; A NOTE ON THE PAPER BY MARTELLO AND TOTH, AN.
MUEL 1978 -2 MUELLER-MERBACH, H.
KASKADENBAUMVERFAHREN ZUR LOESUNG DES "KNAPSACKPROBLEMS", EIN.
NAUS 1978 -2 NAUSS, R. M.
0-1 KNAPSACK PROBLEM WITH MULTIPLE CHOICE CONSTRAINTS, THE.
OGUZ 1979 -1 OGUZ, O.; MAGAZINE, M. J.
POLYNOMIAL TIME APPROXIMATION ALGORITHM FOR THE MULTIDIMENSIONAL 0/1 KNAPSACK PROBLEM, A.
PADB 1979 -1 PADBERG, M. W.
COVERING, PACKING AND KNAPSACK PROBLEMS.
PADB 1980 -1 PADBERG, M. W.
(1,K)-CONFIGURATIONS AND FACETS FOR PACKING PROBLEMS.
PIEH 1978 -1 PIEHLER, J.
BEMERKUNGEN ZU EINER ARBEIT VON ACHOU UEBER DIE ANZAHL ZULAESSIGER LOESUNGEN EINES KNAPSACK PROBLEMS.
POSN 1980 -1 POSNER, M. E.
CONTINUOUS COLLAPSING KNAPSACK PROBLEM, THE.
POSNA 1978 -1 POSNER, M. E.; GUIGNARD, M.
COLLAPSING 0-1 KNAPSACK PROBLEM, THE.
PRZY 1979 -1 PRZYBYLAK, F.
CALCULATION OF A ONE-DIMENSIONAL KNAPSACK FUNCTION (POLISH).
PRZY 1979 -2 PRZYBYLAK, F.
GENERALIZED ONE-DIMENSIONAL KNAPSACK FUNCTION (POLISH).
RAGH 1978 -1 RAGHAVACHARI, M.; SABHARWAL, Y. P.
ON THE NUMBER OF NON-NEGATIVE INTEGRAL SOLUTIONS TO THE KNAPSACK PROBLEM.
ROSSA 1979 -1 ROSS, G. T.; ZOLTNERS, A. A.
WEIGHTED ASSIGNMENT MODELS AND THEIR APPLICATION.
RUIZA 1979 -1 RUIZDEFCO, F.; LARRANETA, J.
LEXICOGRAPHIC ENUMERATION ALGORITHM FOR THE KNAPSACK PROBLEM, A.
SAHNC 1978 -1 SAHNI, S.; HOROWITZ, E.
COMBINATORIAL PROBLEMS: REDUCIBILITY AND APPROXIMATION.
SALK 1975 -1 SALKIN, H. M.
INTEGER PROGRAMMING.
SERG 1980 -1 SERGIENKO, I. V.; BIKOV, V. M.
METHOD FOR SOLVING A GENERALIZED KNAPSACK PROBLEM USING PARALLEL COMPUTATIONS (RUSSIAN), A.
SHEV 1981 -1 SHEVCHENKO, V. N.
ON THE NUMBER OF EXTREME POINTS IN INTEGRAL PROGRAMMING (RUSSIAN).
SHIH 1979 -1 SHIH, WEI
BRANCH AND BOUND METHOD FOR THE MULTICONSTRAINT ZERO-ONE KNAPSACK PROBLEM, A.
SINH 1979 -1 SINHA, P.; ZOLTNERS, A. A.
MULTIPLE-CHOICE KNAPSACK PROBLEM, THE.
SNIE 1980 -1 SNIEDOVICH, M.
PREFERENCE ORDER STOCHASTIC KNAPSACK PROBLEMS: METHODOLOGICAL ISSUES.
SUHL 1978 -1 SUHL, U.
ALGORITHM AND EFFICIENT DATA STRUCTURES FOR THE BINARY KNAPSACK PROBLEM, AN.
SUZU 1978 -1 SUZUKI, H.
GENERALIZED KNAPSACK PROBLEM WITH VARIABLE COEFFICIENTS, A.
TENG 1978 -1 TENG, J. T.; HWANG, F. K.
MATRIX ALGORITHM FOR LARGER KNAPSACK PROBLEMS, A.
TINH 1980 -1 TINHOFER, G.
GRAPHSACK PROBLEM, THE.
TOTH 1976 -1 TOTH, P.
NEW REDUCTION ALGORITHM FOR 0-1 KNAPSACK PROBLEMS, A.
TOTH 1980 -1 TOTH, P.
DYNAMIC PROGRAMMING ALGORITHMS FOR THE ZERO-ONE KNAPSACK PROBLEM.
VANDC 1980 -1 VANDERVELDE, J. A.; KAAS, R.; DELEVE, G.
STRONGER GOMORY CUTS BY MULTIDIMENSIONAL KNAPSACK PROBLEMS.
YORM 1979 -1 YORMARK, J. S.
EFFICIENT FRONTIERS FOR NONLINEAR MULTIDIMENSIONAL KNAPSACK PROBLEMS.

****

ZEME 1980 -1 ZEMEL, E.
LINEAR MULTIPLE CHOICE KNAPSACK, THE.
ZOLT 1978 -1 ZOLTNERS, A. A.
DIRECT DESCENT BINARY KNAPSACK ALGORITHM, A.
ZUEN 1979 -1 ZUENKOV, M. A.; IGNATUSHCHENKO, V. V.
APPROXIMATE METHOD OF SOLUTION OF ONE-DIMENSIONAL KNAPSACK PROBLEM.

ALLIA 1980 -1 ALLINEY, S.; BARNABEI, M.; PEZZOLI, L.
W-OPTIMAL ASSIGNABLE SETS AND ALLOCATION PROBLEMS.

ALVAA 1977 -1 ALVAREZ, C.; DOMINGUEZ, H.; FRIEDMAN, P.
USE OF LINEAR PROGRAMMING FOR THE MACROLOCATION OF INDUSTRIAL PLANTS (SPANISH), THE.

ALY 1979 -1 ALY, A. A.; LITWHILER, D. W. JR.
POLICE BRIEFING STATIONS: A LOCATION PROBLEM.

ARMS 1977 -2 ARMSTRONG, R. D.
PRIMAL SIMPLEX ALGORITHM TO SOLVE A RECTILINEAR DISTANCE FACILITY LOCATION PROBLEM, A.

ARYA 1979 -1 ARYANIN, A. N.; YAKOBSON, M. V.
SUR LA METHODE DE PARTITION DANS LES PROBLEMES D'ALLOCATION (RUSSIAN).

BABI 1978 -1 BABICH, G.
EFFICIENT ALGORITHM FOR SOLVING THE RECTILINEAR LOCATION-ALLOCATION PROBLEM, AN.

BABIA 1979 -1 BABINA, N. B.
RESOURCE ALLOCATION PROBLEM WITH NONCONTRADICTORY INTERESTS (RUSSIAN), A.

BALA 1977 -1 BALANDINA, S. V.
FORMULATION OF THE PROBLEM OF THE LOCATION OF THE COMPUTER CENTERS OF A NETWORK, AND POSSIBLE APPROACHES TO ITS SOLUTION (RUSSIAN), A.

BAYB 1978 -1 BAYBARS, I.
NEW CHARACTERIZATION OF MAXIMAL PLANAR GRAPHS AND A GRAPH THEORETIC APPROACH TO THE FACILITIES DESIGN PROBLEM, A.

BEDN 1979 -1 BEDNAR, L.; STROHMEIER, E.
LAGERSTANDORTOPTIMIERUNG UND FUHRPARKEINSATZPLANUNG IN DER KONSUMGUETER-INDUSTRIE.

BENI 1981 -1 BENITO-ALONSO, M. A.; DEVAUX, P.
LOCATION AND SIZE OF DAY NURSERIES - A MULTIPLE GOAL APPROACH.

BENS 1979 -1 BENSEMAN, B.; HALL, K.
SOLVING A PLANT LOCATION PROBLEM WITH INTEGER PROGRAMMING.

BEREA 1978 -1 BERESNEV, V. L.; ZAIKINA, G. M.
PROGRAMME DE L'ALGORITHME DE RESOLUTION DU PROBLEME D'ASSORTIMENT OPTIMAL (RUSSIAN).

BERMC 1981 -1 BERMAN, O.; LARSON, R. C.; ODONI, A. R.
DEVELOPMENTS IN NETWORK LOCATION WITH MOBILE AND CONGESTED FACILITIES.

BITRB 1980 -1 BITRAN, G. R.; LAWRENCE, K. D.
LOCATING SERVICE OFFICES : A MULTICRITERIA APPROACH.

BITRC 1979 -1 BITRAN, G. R.; SEMPOLINSKI, D. E.; SHAPIRO, J. F.
INVERSE OPTIMIZATION: AN APPLICATION TO THE CAPACITATED PLANT LOCATION PROBLEM.

BOUR 1978 -1 BOURI, V. K.
SOLUTION TECHNIQUE FOR THE TOTAL COST RECTILINEAR DISTANCE SINGLE FACILITY LOCATION PROBLEM, A.

BREG 1975 -1 BREGMEN, L. M.; ROMANOVSKII, I. V.
ALLOCATION AND OPTIMIZATION IN ASSIGNMENT PROBLEMS (RUSSIAN).

BRIC 1978 -1 BRICKER, D. L.; CHANG, T.-S.
SURROGATE DUAL FOR THE SIMPLE PLANT LOCATION PROBLEMS, A.

BUCC 1977 -1 BUCCI, G.; GOLINELLI, S.
DISTRIBUTED STRATEGY FOR RESOURCE ALLOCATION IN INFORMATION NETWORKS, A.

BURN 1978 -1 BURNESS, G. C.; MILLER, D. M.
LOCATION OF CRASH FIRE FIGHTING FACILITIES AT AIRPORTS.

CAIE 1978 -1 CAIE, J.; LINDEN, J.; MAXWELL, W.
SOLUTION OF A MACHINE LOAD PLANNING PROBLEM.

CAIEA 1979 -1 CAIE, J.; LINDEN, J.; OATS, Q.; MAXWELL, W.
HIERARCHICAL MACHINE LOAD PLANNING.

CALA 1980 -1 CALAMAI, P.; CHARALAMBOUS, C.
SOLVING MULTIFACILITY LOCATION PROBLEMS INVOLVING EUCLIDEAN DISTANCES.

CASTA 1975 -1 CASTELLANI, G.
EXPLICIT SOLUTION FOR A CLASS OF ALLOCATION PROBLEMS.

CHAI 1978 -1 CHAIKEN, J. M.; DORMONT, P.
PATROL CAR ALLOCATION MODEL: BACKGROUND, A.

CHAI 1978 -2 CHAIKEN, J. M.; DORMONT, P.
PATROL CAR ALLOCATION MODEL: CAPABILITIES AND ALGORITHMS, A.

CHALA 1981 -1 CHALMET, L. G.; FRANCIS, R. L.; KOLEN, A.
FINDING EFFICIENT SOLUTIONS FOR RECTILINEAR DISTANCE LOCATION PROBLEMS EFFICIENTLY.

CHALC 1981 -1 CHALMET, L. G.; LAWPHONGPANICH, S.
EFFICIENT SOLUTIONS FOR POINT-OBJECTIVE DISCRETE FACILITY LOCATION PROBLEMS.

CHAN 1979 -1 CHAN, A. W.; FRANCIS, R. L.
SOME LAYOUT PROBLEMS ON THE LINE WITH INTERDISTANCE CONSTRAINTS AND COSTS.

CHANA 1979 -1 CHANDRA, A.; VRAT, P.
INVESTIGATIONS ON SINGLE FACILITY LOCATION PROBLEM WITH MIXED MODE OF TRAVEL.

CHANF 1978 -1 CHANDRASEKARAN, R.; DAUGHETY, A.
PROBLEMS OF LOCATION ON TREES.

CHANF 1981 -1 CHANDRASEKARAN, R.; DAUGHETY, A.
LOCATION ON TREE NETWORKS: P-CENTRE AND N-DISPERSION PROBLEMS.

CHANG 1980 -1 CHANDRASEKARAN, R.; PACCA, M. J. A. P.
WEIGHTED MIN-MAX LOCATION PROBLEMS: POLYNOMIALLY BOUNDED ALGORITHMS.

CHANH 1978 -1 CHANDRASEKARAN, R.; TAMIR, A.
POLYNOMIALLY BOUNDED ALGORITHMS FOR LOCATING P-CENTERS ON A TREE.

CHANH 1980 -1 CHANDRASEKARAN, R.; TAMIR, A.
O((N LOG P)**2) ALGORITHM FOR THE CONTINUOUS P-CENTER PROBLEM ON A TREE, AN.

CHER 1979 -1 CHERENKOV, A. P.
INTEGRAL RESOURCE ALLOCATION PROBLEM (RUSSIAN), AN.

CHEU 1980 -2 CHEUNG, T.-Y.
MULTIFACILITY LOCATION PROBLEM WITH RECTILINEAR DISTANCE BY THE MINIMUM-CUT APPROACH.

CHUR 1978 -1 CHURCH, R. L.; GARFINKEL, R. S.
LOCATING AN OBNOXIOUS FACILITY ON A NETWORK.

COEL 1981 -1 COELHO, J. D.
LOCATIONAL SURPLUS MAXIMIZATION APPROACH TO PUBLIC FACILITY LOCATION, A.

COFFD 1979 -1 COFFMAN, E. G. JR.; JOHNSON, D. B.; LEUNG, J. Y.-T.
EFFICIENT ALGORITHM FOR ALLOCATING PAGED, DRUM-LIKE STORAGE, AN.

COFFF 1978 -1 COFFMAN, E. G. JR.; LEUNG, J. Y.-T.; SLUTZ, D.
ON THE OPTIMALITY OF FAST HEURISTICS FOR SCHEDULING AND STORAGE ALLOCATION PROBLEMS.

COMB 1979 -1 COMBOT, J.-P.; MASON, L. G.
OPTIMAL SWITCH-CONCENTRATOR LOCATION FOR A TELEPHONE NETWORK.

COOKA 1979 -1 COOK, W. D.; SHIELDS, W. S.
ASSIGNMENT OF MILITARY OFFICERS TO GROUPS: A MULTI-ATTRIBUTE TEAM BALANCING PROBLEM.

CORNA 1978 -1 CORNUEJOLS, G.
ANALYSIS OF ALGORITHMS FOR A CLASS OF LOCATION PROBLEMS.

CORNB 1979 -1 CORNUEJOLS, G.; FISHER, M. L.; NEMHAUSER, G. L.
ON "LOCATION OF BANK ACCOUNTS TO OPTIMIZE FLOAT: AN ANALYTIC STUDY OF EXACT AND APPROXIMATE ALGORITHMS".

LOCATION AND ALLOCATION

CORNC 1980 -1 CORNUEJOLS, G.; NEMHAUSER, G. L.; WOLSEY, L. A.
CANONICAL REPRESENTATION OF SIMPLE PLANT LOCATION PROBLEMS AND ITS APPLICATIONS, A.

CORNC 1980 -2 CORNUEJOLS, G.; NEMHAUSER, G. L.; WOLSEY, L. A.
WORST-CASE AND PROBABILISTIC ANALYSIS OF ALGORITHMS FOR A LOCATION PROBLEM.

CORNE 1979 -1 CORNUEJOLS, G.; THIZY, J.-M.
SOME FACETS OF THE SIMPLE PLANT LOCATION POLYTOPE.

CORNE 1980 -1 CORNUEJOLS, G.; THIZY, J.-M.
LOCATION PROBLEMS, SET COVERING PROBLEMS AND THE GREEDY ALGORITHM.

CRAM 1979 -1 CRAMER, J.; POLLATSCHEK, M. A.
CANDIDATE TO JOB ALLOCATION PROBLEM WITH A LEXICOGRAPHIC OBJECTIVE.

CROW 1978 -1 CROWDER, H. P.
CLUSTER ANALYSIS: AN APPLICATION OF LAGRANGIAN RELAXATION.

CUTLA 1978 -1 CUTLER, M.; SHILOACH, Y.
PERMUTATION LAYOUT.

CZAP 1977 -1 CZAPNIK, J.
ALGORITHM FOR RESOURCE ALLOCATION IN MULTIPROGRAMMING SYSTEMS (POLISH), AN.

DALB 1980 -1 DALBERTO, L. M.
PRACTICAL SOLUTION APPROACHES TO THE CAPACITATED PLANT LOCATION PROBLEM.

DASA 1980 -1 DASARATHY, B.; WHITE, L. J.
MAXMIN LOCATION PROBLEM, A.

DEAR 1979 -1 DEARING, P. M.; NEWRUCK, F. C.
CAPACITATED BOTTLENECK FACILITY LOCATION PROBLEM, A.

DREY 1977 -1 DREYFUS, S. E.; LAW, A. M.
ART AND THEORY OF DYNAMIC PROGRAMMING, THE.

DREZ 1978 -1 DREZNER, Z.; WESOLOWSKY, G. O.
FACILITY LOCATION ON A SPHERE.

DREZ 1980 -1 DREZNER, Z.; WESOLOWSKY, G. O.
OPTIMAL LOCATION OF A FACILITY RELATIVE TO AREA DEMANDS.

DREZ 1978 -2 DREZNER, Z.; WESOLOWSKY, G. O.
NEW METHOD FOR THE MULTIFACILITY MINIMAX LOCATION PROBLEM, A.

DREZ 1980 -2 DREZNER, Z.; WESOLOWSKY, G. O.
SINGLE FACILITY L(P)-DISTANCE MINIMAX LOCATION.

DREZ 1978 -3 DREZNER, Z.; WESOLOWSKY, G. O.
TRAJECTORY METHOD FOR THE OPTIMIZATION OF THE MULTI-FACILITY LOCATION PROBLEM WITH LP DISTANCES, A.

DUNS 1978 -1 DUNSMUIR, A. M.
SIMPLE ALLOCATION ALGORITHM IN PRODUCTION PLANNING, A.

EILO 1978 -1 EILON, S.; GALVAO, R. D.
SINGLE AND DOUBLE VERTEX SUBSTITUTION IN HEURISTIC PROCEDURES FOR THE P-MEDIAN PROBLEM.

ELKE 1979 -1 ELKEN, T. R.; FREEDMAN, H. T.; GIBSON, A. E.
POLYNOMIAL BOUND ALGORITHM FOR A NONLINEAR NETWORK ALLOCATION PROBLEM,A.

ENGE 1981 -1 ENGELE, G.
SIMULTANE STANDORT- UND TOURENPLANUNG.

ERLE 1977 -1 ERLENKOTTER, D.
FACILITY LOCATION WITH PRICE-SENSITIVE DEMANDS: PRIVATE, PUBLIC AND QUASI-PUBLIC.

ERLE 1978 -1 ERLENKOTTER, D.
DUAL BASED PROCEDURE FOR UNCAPACITATED FACILITY LOCATION, A.

ERLE 1981 -1 ERLENKOTTER, D.
COMPARATIVE STUDY OF APPROACHES TO DYNAMIC LOCATION PROBLEMS, A.

ERLE 1978 -2 ERLENKOTTER, D.
SHOULD CALIFORNIA AGRICULTURE RECEIVE PREFERENTIAL WATER RATES.

FEDEA 1980 -1 FEDERGRUEN, A.; LAGEWEG, B. J.
HIERARCHICAL DISTRIBUTION MODELLING WITH ROUTING COSTS.

FEDEB 1980 -1 FEDERGRUEN, A.; ZIPKIN, P. H.
COMBINED VEHICLE ROUTING AND INVENTORY ALLOCATION PROBLEM, A.

FEIN 1979 -1 FEINBERG, I.
HEURISTIC WAREHOUSE LOCATION MODEL CONSIDERING TRANSPORTATION AND OTHER COSTS AND CAPACITY CONSTRAINTS, A.

FISHA 1978 -1 FISHER, M. L.; HOCHBAUM, D.
DATABASE LOCATION IN COMPUTER NETWORKS.

FISHA 1978 -2 FISHER, M. L.; HOCHBAUM, D.
PROBABILISTIC ANALYSIS OF THE EUCLIDEAN K-MEDIAN PROBLEM.

FISK 1979 -1 FISK, J. C.; HUNG, M. S.
HEURISTIC ROUTINE FOR SOLVING LARGE LOADING PROBLEMS, A.

FONG 1978 -1 FONG, C. O.; SRINIVASAN, V.
MULTI-REGION DYNAMIC CAPACITY EXPANSION PROBLEM - II, THE.

FOULA 1978 -1 FOULDS, L. R.; ROBINSON, D. F.
GRAPH THEORETIC HEURISTICS FOR THE PLANT LAYOUT PROBLEM.

FRAN 1978 -1 FRANCIS, R. L.; LOWE, T. J.; RATLIFF, H. D.
DISTANCE CONSTRAINTS FOR TREE NETWORK MULTIFACILITY LOCATION PROBLEMS.

GALIA 1977 -1 GALIL, Z.; MEGIDDO, N.
FAST SELECTION ALGORITHM AND THE PROBLEM OF OPTIMUM DISTRIBUTION OF EFFORT, A.

GALV 1980 -1 GALVAO, R. D.
DUAL-BOUNDED ALGORITHM FOR THE P-MEDIAN PROBLEM, A.

GALV 1981 -1 GALVAO, R. D.
GRAPH THEORETICAL BOUND FOR THE P-MEDIAN PROBLEM, A.

GARD 1977 -1 GARDARIN, G.
ALLOCATION DE RESSOURCES SIMULTANEMENT PARTAGEABLES AVEC RESOLUTION DU VERROU MORTEL.

GEN 1976 -1 GEN, M.; OKUNO, H.; SHINOFUJI, S.
OPTIMIZING METHOD IN SYSTEM RELIABILITY WITH FAILURE-MODES BY IMPLICIT ENUMERATION ALGORITHM, AN.

GENS 1979 -2 GENS, G. V.; LEVNER, E. V.
COMPUTATIONAL COMPLEXITY OF APPROXIMATION ALGORITHMS FOR COMBINATORIAL PROBLEMS.

GEOFA 1978 -1 GEOFFRION, A. M.; MAC BRIDE, R. D.
LAGRANGEAN RELAXATION APPLIED TO CAPACITATED FACILITY LOCATION PROBLEMS.

GIMO 1979 -1 GIMOURGINAS, C.; KARWAN, M. H.
COMPUTATIONAL RESULTS OF THE P-MEDIAN AND SET COVERING PROBLEMS FOR AN AMBULANCE LOCATION STUDY IN THE CITY OF BUFFALO.

GIZE 1980 -1 GIZELIS, A. G.; SAMOUILIDIS, J. E.
SIMPLIFIED ALGORITHM FOR THE DEPOT LOCATION PROBLEM, A.

GOLDB 1978 -2 GOLDEN, B. L.
STATISTICAL ESTIMATION IN COMBINATORIAL DECISION PROBLEMS.

GUIG 1980 -1 GUIGNARD, M.
FRACTIONAL VERTICES, CUTS AND FACETS OF THE SIMPLE PLANT LOCATION PROBLEM.

GUIGA 1978 -1 GUIGNARD, M.; SPIELBERG, K.
DUAL METHOD FOR THE MIXED PLANT LOCATION PROBLEM, A. (REVISED VERSION).

GUIGA 1979 -2 GUIGNARD, M.; SPIELBERG, K.
DIRECT DUAL METHOD FOR THE MIXED PLANT LOCATION PROBLEM WITH SOME SIDE CONSTRAINTS, A.

HAKIA 1978 -1 HAKIMI, S. L.; SCHMEICHEL, E. F.; PIERCE, J. G.
ON P-CENTERS IN NETWORKS.

HAND 1978 -1 HANDLER, G. Y.
FINDING TWO CENTERS OF A TREE: THE CONTINUOUS CASE.

HAND 1979 -1 HANDLER, G. Y.
COMPLEXITY AND EFFICIENCY IN MINIMAX NETWORK LOCATION.

HANDA 1979 -1 HANDLER, G. Y.; MIRCHANDANI, P. B.
LOCATION ON NETWORKS - THEORY AND ALGORITHMS.

HANJ 1980 -1 HANJOUL, P.; THISSE, J.-F.
LOCALISATION SUR UN RESEAU.

HANSE 1980 -1 HANSEN, P.; PERREUR, J.; THISSE, J.-F.
LOCATION THEORY, DOMINANCE, AND CONVEXITY: SOME FURTHER RESULTS.

HANSF 1981 -1 HANSEN, P.; THISSE, J.-F.; HANJOUL, P.
SIMPLE PLANT LOCATION UNDER UNIFORM DELIVERED PRICING.

HEIN 1978 -1 HEINHOLD, M.
OPERATIONAL RESEARCH APPROACH TO ALLOCATION OF CLIENTS TO A CERTAIN CLASS OF SERVICE INSTITUTIONS, AN.

HIRSA 1979 -1 HIRSCHBERG, D. S.; WONG, C. K.
UPPER AND LOWER BOUNDS FOR GRAPH-DIAMETER PROBLEMS WITH APPLICATION TO RECORD ALLOCATION.

HO A 1980 -1 HO, Y. C.; SERVI, L.; SURI, R.
CLASS OF CENTER-FREE RESOURCE ALLOCATION ALGORITHMS, A.

HOCH 1979 -2 HOCHBAUM, D.
HEURISTICS FOR THE FIXED COST MEDIAN PROBLEM.

HOCH 1979 -3 HOCHBAUM, D.
PROBABILISTIC ASYMPTOTIC PROPERTIES OF SOME COMBINATORIAL GEOMETRIC PROBLEMS, THE.

HODG 1978 -1 HODGSON, M. J.
TOWARD MORE REALISTIC ALLOCATION IN LOCATION-ALLOCATION MODELS: AN INTERACTION APPROACH.

HODG 1981 -1 HODGSON, M. J.
LOCATION OF PUBLIC FACILITIES INTERMEDIATE TO THE JOURNEY TO WORK, THE.

HSU B 1979 -2 HSU, W.-L.; NEMHAUSER, G. L.
EASY AND HARD BOTTLENECK LOCATION PROBLEMS.

JACOA 1977 -1 JACOBSEN, S. K.
HEURISTIC PROCEDURES FOR DYNAMIC PLANT LOCATION.

JACOA 1977 -2 JACOBSEN, S. K.
HEURISTIC SOLUTIONS TO DYNAMIC PLANT LOCATION PROBLEMS.

JACOB 1980 -1 JACOBSEN, S. K.; MADSEN, O. B. G.
COMPARATIVE STUDY OF HEURISTICS FOR A TWO-LEVEL ROUTING-LOCATION PROBLEM, A.

JAINA 1979 -1 JAIN, R. C.; PANNE, C. VAN DE
TRANSPORTATION-TYPE METHODS FOR THE PLANT LOCATION PROBLEM.

JAKU 1978 -1 JAKUBOWSKI, A.
STOCHASTIC MODEL OF RESOURCE ALLOCATION TO R & D ACTIVITIES UNDER COST VALUE UNCERTAINTY.

JENK 1979 -1 JENKINS, L.
PARAMETRIC ANALYSIS ON A LOCATION MODEL OF MUNICIPAL RESOURCE RECOVERY.

JOHNJ 1979 -1 JOHNSON, M.; ZOLTNERS, A. A.; SINHA, P.
ALLOCATION MODEL FOR CATALOG SPACE PLANNING, AN.

JUEL 1980 -1 JUEL, H.; LOVE, R. F.
SUFFICIENT CONDITIONS FOR OPTIMAL FACILITY LOCATIONS TO COINCIDE.

KABE 1980 -1 KABE, D. G.
DIRECT SOLUTIONS TO THE M-MEDIAN AND FRACTIONAL TRANSPORTATION PROBLEMS.

KACPA 1980 -1 KACPRZYK, J.; STANCZAK, W.
OPTIMAL LOCATION OF A CENTRAL SUPPLY POINT IN URBAN REGIONS (POLISH).

KARI 1979 -1 KARIV, O.; HAKIMI, S. L.
ALGORITHMIC APPROACH TO NETWORK LOCATION PROBLEMS. I: THE P-CENTERS, AN.

KARI 1979 -2 KARIV, O.; HAKIMI, S. L.
ALGORITHMIC APPROACH TO NETWORK LOCATION PROBLEMS. II: THE P-MEDIANS, AN.

KATOA 1979 -1 KATOH, N.; IBARAKI, T.; MINE, H.
ALGORITHMS FOR A VARIANT OF THE RESOURCE ALLOCATION PROBLEM.

KATOA 1980 -1 KATOH, N.; IBARAKI, T.; MINE, H.
NOTES ON THE PROBLEM OF THE ALLOCATION OF RESOURCES TO ACTIVITIES IN DISCRETE QUANTITIES.

KATOA 1979 -2 KATOH, N.; IBARAKI, T.; MINE, H.
POLYNOMIAL TIME ALGORITHM FOR THE RESOURCE ALLOCATION PROBLEM WITH A CONVEX OBJECTIVE FUNCTION, A.

KATZ 1979 -1 KATZ, I. N.; COOPER, L.
FACILITY LOCATION IN THE PRESENCE OF FORBIDDEN REGIONS, I: FORMULATION, AND THE CASE OF EUCLIDEAN DISTANCE WITH ONE FORBIDDEN CIRCLE.

KAUF 1981 -1 KAUFMAN, L.; BROECKX, F.
CENTER LOCATION PROBLEM WITH AN INVESTMENT CONSTRAINT, A.

KAUFA 1977 -1 KAUFMAN, L.; EEDE, M. VANDEN; HANSEN, P.
PLANT AND WAREHOUSE LOCATION PROBLEM, A.

KAUFB 1980 -1 KAUFMAN, L.; PLASTRIA, F.
GENERALISATION OF THE WEBER LOCATION PROBLEM, A.

KHUM 1978 -1 KHUMAWALA, B. M.; NEEBE, A. W.
NOTE ON WARSZAWSKI'S MULTI-COMMODITY LOCATION PROBLEM, A.

KHUMA 1979 -1 KHUMAWALA, B. M.; STEINBERG, E.
EFFICIENT HEURISTIC FOR THE SINGLE SOURCE USER CAPACITATED WAREHOUSE LOCATION PROBLEM, AN.

KIKU 1980 -1 KIKUNO, T.; YOSHIDA, N.; KAKUDA, Y.
NP-COMPLETENESS OF SOME TYPE OF P-CENTER PROBLEM.

KLAS 1979 -2 KLASTORIN, T. D.
ON THE MAXIMAL COVERING LOCATION PROBLEM AND THE GENERALIZED ASSIGNMENT PROBLEM.

KLEI 1973 -1 KLEIMANN, P.
INHOMOGENEOUS MODELS OF ALLOCATION WITH FIXED SURCHARGES OF TWO CLASSES (RUSSIAN).

KNUTA 1977 -1 KNUTH, E.
ON THE SOLVABILITY OF RESOURCE ALLOCATION PROBLEMS (HUNGARIAN).

KOCHB 1981 -1 KOCHMAN, G. A.; MAC CALLUM, C. J. JR.
FACILITY LOCATION MODELS FOR PLANNING A TRANSATLANTIC COMMUNICATIONS NETWORK.

KOLE 1979 -1 KOLEN, A.
COMPLEXITY OF LOCATION PROBLEMS ON NETWORKS.

KOLE 1980 -1 KOLEN, A.
DUALITY AND THE NONLINEAR ROUND-TRIP L-CENTER AND COVERING PROBLEMS ON A TREE.

KOLE 1979 -2 KOLEN, A.
ON "A CUT APPROACH TO THE RECTILINEAR DISTANCE FACILITY LOCATION PROBLEM" BY J.-C. PICARD AND H.D. RATLIFF.

KOLE 1979 -3 KOLEN, A.
P-MEDIAN PROBLEM WITH MUTUAL COMMUNICATION ON A TREE, THE.

KRAR 1978 -1 KRARUP, J.; PRUZAN, P. M.
COMPUTER-AIDED LAYOUT DESIGN.
KRAR 1979 -1 KRARUP, J.; PRUZAN, P. M.
SELECTED FAMILIES OF LOCATION PROBLEMS.
KRAR 1980 -1 KRARUP, J.; PRUZAN, P. M.
IMPACT OF DISTANCE ON LOCATION PROBLEMS, THE.
KRAR 1981 -1 KRARUP, J.; PRUZAN, P. M.
REDUCIBILITY OF MINIMAX TO MINISUM 0-1 PROGRAMMING PROBLEMS.
KUZNA 1978 -1 KUZNETSOV, V. F.
SOLUTION OF AN INTEGER-VALUED PROBLEM OF DISTRIBUTION OF RESOURCES IN THE CASE OF RENEWAL OPERATIONS.
LAPOB 1979 -1 LAPORTE, G.; NOBERT, Y.
EXACT ALGORITHM FOR MINIMIZING DELIVERY AND OPERATING COSTS IN DEPOT LOCATION, AN.
LAPOB 1981 -1 LAPORTE, G.; NOBERT, Y.
EXACT ALGORITHM FOR MINIMIZING ROUTING AND OPERATING COSTS IN DEPOT LOCATION, AN.
LARSA 1980 -1 LARSON, R. C.; SADIQ, G.
FACILITY LOCATIONS WITH THE L(1) METRIC IN THE PRESENCE OF BARRIERS TO TRAVEL.
LAWRA 1981 -1 LAWRENCE, S.; LAWRENCE, K.; REEVES, G.
MULTIPLE GOAL MODEL FOR ALLOCATION OF TEACHING PERSONNEL, A.
LEDI 1979 -1 LEDIN, M. I.
CLASS OF HOMOGENEOUS RESOURCE-ALLOCATION PROBLEMS (RUSSIAN), A.
LEE C 1979 -1 LEE, S. M.; FRANZ, L. S.
OPTIMIZING THE LOCATION-ALLOCATION PROBLEM WITH MULTIPLE OBJECTIVES.
LEE E 1981 -1 LEE, S. M.; GREEN, G. I.; KIM, C. S.
MULTIPLE CRITERIA MODEL FOR THE LOCATION-ALLOCATION PROBLEM, A.
LEON 1978 -1 LEONARDI, G.
OPTIMUM FACILITY LOCATION BY ACCESSIBILITY MAXIMIZING.
LI A 1979 -1 LI, W.-X.
OPTIMAL ALLOCATION OF EXPERIMENTS WITH TIME DELAY OF FOUR PERIODS (CHINESE).
LING 1978 -1 LINGURAJ, B. P.; WOLFE, H.
HEURISTIC METHOD FOR OBTAINING AN INTEGER SOLUTION TO A FACILITY DESIGN OPTIMIZATION PROBLEM, A.
LITVA 1977 -1 LITVINOV, V. N.
APPROACH TO THE SOLUTION OF THE PROBLEM OF THE MINIMIZATION OF THE LENGTH OF A CONNNECTING NET IN THE PLACING OF GEOMETRIC OBJECTS (RUSSIAN), AN.
LITW 1979 -1 LITWHILER, D. W. JR.; ALY, A. A.
LARGE REGION LOCATION PROBLEMS.
LITW 1980 -1 LITWHILER, D. W. JR.; ALY, A. A.
STEINER'S PROBLEM AND FAGNANO'S RESULT ON THE SPHERE.
LOVE 1976 -1 LOVE, R. F.; JUEL, H.
PROPERTIES AND SOLUTION METHODS FOR LARGE LOCATION-ALLOCATION PROBLEMS.
LOVEA 1978 -1 LOVE, R. F.; MORRIS, J. G.
ON CONVEXITY PROOFS IN LOCATION THEORY.
LOVEB 1978 -1 LOVE, R. R. JR; VEMUGANTI, R. R.
SINGLE-PLANT MOLD ALLOCATION PROBLEM WITH CAPACITY AND CHANGEOVER RESTRICTIONS, THE.
LOWE 1978 -1 LOWE, T. J.
EFFICIENT SOLUTIONS IN MULTIOBJECTIVE TREE NETWORK LOCATION PROBLEMS.
LOWEB 1978 -1 LOWE, T. J.; THORNTON, V. D.; FRANCIS, R. L.
LAYOUT OF DIVISIBLE ACTIVITIES ON THE LINE, THE.
LOZOA 1980 -1 LOZOVANU, D. D.; ZAMBICKII, D. K.
PROBLEM OF OPTIMAL PLACEMENT OF A NETWORK SOURCE ENSURING A FLOW OF MINIMAL COST (RUSSIAN), THE.
LUDW 1979 -1 LUDWIG, R.
ZUR LOESUNG GROSSER STANDORTPROBLEME.
MAC E 1975 -1 MAC GINNIS, L. F.
APPROXIMATE AND EXACT SOLUTION PROCEDURES FOR A CLASS OF FACILITIES LOCATION PROBLEMS.
MAC G 1978 -1 MAC GINNIS, L. F.; WHITE, J. A.
SINGLE FACILITY RECTILINEAR LOCATION PROBLEM WITH MULTIPLE CRITERIA, A.
MAIR 1979 -1 MAIRS, T. G.
ON A PRODUCTION ALLOCATION AND DISTRIBUTION PROBLEM.
MAIRA 1978 -1 MAIRS, T. G.; WAKEFIELD, G. W.; JOHNSON, E. L.; SPIELBERG, K.
ON A PRODUCTION ALLOCATION AND DISTRIBUTION PROBLEM.
MAND 1978 -1 MANDL, C. E.
ALGORITHMS AND COMPUTER PROGRAMS IN DETERMINISTIC NETWORK OPTIMIZATION APPLIED TO PUBLIC SYSTEMS.
MARS 1975 -1 MARSTEN, R. E.
USE OF THE BOXSTEP METHOD IN DISCRETE OPTIMIZATION, THE.
MARU 1979 -1 MARUCHECK, A. S.; ALY, A. A.
EFFICIENT ALGORITHM FOR THE LOCATION-ALLOCATION PROBLEM WITH RECTANGULAR REGIONS, AN.
MAUR 1981 -1 MAURER, H.
POST-OFFICE PROBLEM AND RELATED QUESTIONS, THE.
MAVR 1979 -1 MAVRIDES, L. P.
INDIRECT METHOD FOR THE GENERALIZED K-MEDIAN PROBLEM APPLIED TO LOCK-BOX LOCATION, AN.
MEGIC 1979 -1 MEGIDDO, N.; TAMIR, A.; ZEMEL, E.; CHANDRASEKARAN, R.
O(N(LOG N)(LOG N)) ALGORITHM FOR THE KTH LONGEST PATH IN A TREE WITH APPLICATIONS TO LOCATION PROBLEMS, AN.
MEREB 1978 -1 MERESSOO, T.
DECOMPOSITION METHOD FOR THE RESOURCE ALLOCATION PROBLEM (RUSSIAN), A.
MILA 1979 -1 MILANOV, P. B.
ALGORITHME EFFECTIF DE RESOLUTION D'UN PROBLEME D'ALLOCATION DE RESSOURCES AVEC UNE FONCTION D'OBJECTIF CONVEXE (RUSSIAN).
MILLA 1974 -1 MILLER, H. E.
MATHEMATICAL PROGRAMMING MODELS OF NURSE SCHEDULING AND ALLOCATION.
MINI 1978 -1 MINIEKA, E.
OPTIMIZATION ALGORITHMS FOR NETWORKS AND GRAPHS.
MINI 1980 -1 MINIEKA, E.
CONDITIONAL CENTERS AND MEDIANS OF A GRAPH.
MIRC 1979 -1 MIRCHANDANI, P. B.; ODONI, A. R.
LOCATING NEW PASSENGER FACILITIES ON A TRANSPORTATION NETWORK.
MIRC 1979 -2 MIRCHANDANI, P. B.; ODONI, A. R.
LOCATIONS OF MEDIANS ON STOCHASTIC NETWORKS.
MIRCA 1980 -1 MIRCHANDANI, P. B.; OUDJIT, A.
LOCALIZING 2-MEDIANS ON PROBABILISTIC AND DETERMINISTIC TREE NETWORKS.
MJEL 1978 -1 MJELDE, K. M.
DISCRETE RESOURCE ALLOCATION BY A BRANCH AND BOUND METHOD.

MJEL 1980 -1 MJELDE, K. M.
BOUNDED ALLOCATIONS OF DISCRETE AND BINARY RESOURCES.
MOLN 1979 -1 MOLNAR, A.
PRACTICAL SOLUTION OF THE PLANT LOCATION PROBLEM (HUNGARIAN).
MONT 1979 -1 MONTEROSSO, C. D. B.; BORNSTEIN, C. T.
HEURISTIC ALGORITHM FOR THE LOCATION AND DIMENSIONING OF WAREHOUSES, A.
MOON 1979 -1 MOON, I. D.
DISTANCE CONSTRAINTS WITH LOWER BOUNDS FOR TREE NETWORK LOCATION PROBLEMS.
MOON 1980 -1 MOON, I. D.
TREE NETWORK LOCATION PROBLEMS WITH MAXIMUM SEPARATIONS.
MORRA 1979 -1 MORRIS, J. G.; NORBACK, J. P.
SIMPLE APPROACH TO LINEAR FACILITY LOCATION, A (REVISED VERSION).
NACK 1978 -1 NACKEL, J. G.; GOLDMAN, J.; FAIRMAN, W. L.
GROUP DECISION PROCESS FOR RESOURCE ALLOCATION IN THE HEALTH SETTING, A.
NAGE 1981 -1 NAGELHOUT, R. V.; THOMPSON, G. L.
COST OPERATOR APPROACH TO MULTISTAGE LOCATION-ALLOCATION, A.
NAMB 1979 -1 NAMBIAR, J. M.; CHALMET, L. G.
LOCATION AND VEHICLE SCHEDULING PROBLEM IN COLLECTING AND PROCESSING RUBBER, A.
NAMBA 1981 -1 NAMBIAR, J. M.; GELDERS, L. F.; WASSENHOVE, L. N. VAN
LARGE SCALE LOCATION-ALLOCATION PROBLEM IN THE NATURAL RUBBER INDUSTRY, A.
NARU 1981 -1 NARULA, S. C.
LAGRANGEAN RELAXATION IN AN HIERARCHICAL LOCATION-ALLOCATION PROBLEM.
NARUC 1979 -1 NARULA, S. C.; OGBU, U. I.
HIERARCHICAL LOCATION ALLOCATION PROBLEM, AN.
NASH 1979 -1 NASH, B. W.
SIMPLIFIED ALTERNATIVE TO CURRENT AIRLINE FUEL ALLOCATION MODELS, A.
NAUS 1978 -1 NAUSS, R. M.
IMPROVED ALGORITHM FOR THE CAPACITATED FACILITY LOCATION PROBLEM, AN.
NAUS 1979 -2 NAUSS, R. M.
SOLVING LOCK BOX LOCATION PROBLEMS.
NEEB 1978 -1 NEEBE, A. W.
BRANCH AND BOUND ALGORITHM FOR THE P-MEDIAN TRANSPORTATION PROBLEM, A.
NEEBA 1981 -1 NEEBE, A. W.; KHUMAWALA, B. M.
IMPROVED ALGORITHM FOR THE MULTICOMMODITY LOCATION PROBLEM, AN.
NEMH 1978 -1 NEMHAUSER, G. L.; SHEU, W.-L.
EASY AND HARD BOTTLENECK LOCATION PROBLEMS.
NIJK 1981 -1 NIJKAMP, P.; SPRONK, J.
MULTIDIMENSIONAL LOCATIONAL DECISIONS AND INTERACTIVE PROGRAMMING.
OHUC 1979 -1 OHUCKI, A.; KAJI, I.
ALGORITHMS AND SENSITIVITY ANALYSIS FOR OPTIMAL ALLOCATION PROBLEMS HAVING QUADRATIC OBJECTIVE FUNCTIONS.
OI 1978 -1 OI, K.; SAYAMA, H.; TAKAMATSU, T.
MULTIMODALITY ANALYSIS OF A CLASS OF MULTISTAGE ALLOCATION PROBLEMS.
OR 1979 -1 OR, I.; PIERSKALLA, W. P.
TRANSPORTATION LOCATION-ALLOCATION MODEL FOR REGIONAL BLOOD BANKING, A.
OSTR 1978 -1 OSTRESH, L. M. JR.
CONVERGENCE AND DESCENT IN THE FERMAT LOCATION PROBLEM.
OSTR 1978 -2 OSTRESH, L. M. JR.
ON THE CONVERGENCE OF A CLASS OF ITERATIVE METHODS FOR SOLVING THE WEBER LOCATION PROBLEM.
OSTR 1978 -3 OSTRESH, L. M. JR.
STEPWISE LOCATION-ALLOCATION PROBLEM: EXACT SOLUTIONS IN CONTINUOUS AND DISCRETE SPACES, THE.
OUDH 1980 -1 OUDHEUSDEN, D. VAN; PLASTRIA, F.
MODELE DE LOCALISATION COMME APPLICATION DE LA THEORIE DES JEUX, UN.
PANA 1978 -1 PANAYIOTOPOULOS, J.-C.
NEW APPROACH TO PLANT LOCATION ANALYSIS, A.
PANAA 1979 -1 PANAYIOTOPOULOS, J.-C.; PAPOULIAS, D. B.
GENERAL PROBLEM OF M PERSONS AND N POSITIONS FOR SHORT- AND LONG-TERM DECISION-MAKING, THE.
PAPA 1980 -1 PAPADIMITRIOU, C. H.
WORST-CASE AND PROBABILISTIC ANALYSIS OF A GEOMETRIC LOCATION PROBLEM.
PERS 1973 -1 PERSHIN, O. JU.
ALGORITHM FOR SOLVING THE PROBLEM OF M CENTERS (RUSSIAN), AN.
PERSA 1973 -1 PERSHIN, O. JU.; ZELCER, M. A.
SOME APPLICATIVE ASPECTS OF THE PROBLEM OF M CENTERS (RUSSIAN).
PETR 1978 -1 PETROVIC, R.
RESOURCE ALLOCATION IN A SET OF NETWORKS UNDER MULTIPLE OBJECTIVES.
PICAA 1978 -1 PICARD, J.-C.; RATLIFF, H. D.
CUT APPROACH TO THE RECTILINEAR DISTANCE FACILITY LOCATION PROBLEM, A.
PLES 1980 -2 PLESNIK, J.
ON THE COMPUTATIONAL COMPLEXITY ON CENTERS LOCATING IN A GRAPH.
PRAS 1981 -1 PRASTACOS, G. P.
ALLOCATION OF A PERISHABLE PRODUCT INVENTORY.
RAMAD 1980 -1 RAMANI, K. V.; RAGHURAM, G.
UTILIZATION OF TRANSPORTATION UNITS: AN OPTIMAL ALLOCATION STUDY.
RAMAE 1976 -1 RAMANKULOV, S.; KUPUEV, P.
MATHEMATICAL MODEL FOR RESOURCE ALLOCATION (RUSSIAN), A.
RAVIA 1980 -1 RAVINDRAN, A.; HANLINE, D. L.
OPTIMAL LOCATION OF COAL BLENDING PLANTS BY MIXED-INTEGER PROGRAMMING.
REES 1980 -1 REESE, J.
STANDORT- UND BELEGUNGSPLANUNG FUER MASCHINEN IN MEHRSTUFIGEN PRODUKTIONSPROZESSEN.
REVE 1981 -1 REVELLE, C.; COHON, J.; SHOBRYS, D.
MULTIPLE OBJECTIVES IN FACILITY LOCATION: A REVIEW.
ROSED 1979 -1 ROSENBLATT, M. J.
FACILITIES LAYOUT PROBLEM: A MULTI-GOAL APPROACH, THE.
ROSI 1979 -1 ROSING, K. E.; HILLSMAN, E. L.; ROSING-VOGELAAR, H.
NOTE COMPARING OPTIMAL AND HEURISTIC SOLUTIONS TO THE P-MEDIAN PROBLEM, A.
ROSS 1980 -2 ROSS, G. T.; SOLAND, R. M.
MULTICRITERIA APPROACH TO THE LOCATION OF PUBLIC FACILITIES, A.
ROSSA 1979 -1 ROSS, G. T.; ZOLTNERS, A. A.
WEIGHTED ASSIGNMENT MODELS AND THEIR APPLICATION.
ROY 1978 -1 ROY, J. R.; KARLQVIST, A.
SOME NUMERICAL CONSIDERATIONS OF OPTIMAL ALLOCATION WITH GRAVITY FLOW COSTS.
ROY B 1977 -1 ROY, S.
APPLICATION OF NON-LINEAR PROGRAMMING IN POWER PLANT LOCATION PROBLEM, AN.
RUBIB 1980 -1 RUBINSHTEIN, M. I.; CHERKASHIN, A. M.
DISCRETE PROBLEM OF OPTIMAL RESOURCE ALLOCATION IN ACTIVITY NETWORKS.

RUBIB 1980 -2 RUBINSHTEIN, M. I.; CHERKASHIN, A. M.
PROBLEME DISCRET D'ALLOCATION OPTIMALE DES RESSOURCES DANS UN COMPLEXE D'OPERATIONS EN RESEAU (RUSSIAN).

RUSN 1978 -1 RUSNAK, Z.
ATTEMPT TO SOLVE THE LOCATION PROBLEM WITH WEIGHTS ON THE PLANE (POLISH), AN.

RUTK 1978 -1 RUTKAUSKAS, P.
APPROXIMATION D'UN PROCESSUS DISCRET D'ALLOCATION DE RESSOURCES PAR UN ANALOGUE CONTINU OPTIMAL (RUSSIAN).

SAED 1981 -1 SAEDT, A. P. H.
SITING OF GREEN FORAGE DRYING PLANTS FOR USE BY A LARGE NUMBER OF FARMS - A LOCATION-ALLOCATION CASE STUDY, THE.

SAHU 1977 -1 SAHU, S.
ANALYSIS STUDIES ON SOME ASPECTS OF PLANT LAYOUT AND DESIGN.

SCHI 1980 -1 SCHICK, G. J.; STROUP, J. W.
EXPERIENCE WITH A MULTI-YEAR PLANNING MODEL.

SCHIC 1979 -1 SCHILLING, D.; ELZINGA, D. J.; COHON, J.; CHURCH, R. L.; REVELLE, C.
TEAM/FLEET MODELS FOR SIMULTANEOUS FACILITY AND EQUIPMENT SITING, THE.

SCHRC 1981 -1 SCHREUDER, J. A. M.
APPLICATION OF A LOCATION MODEL TO FIRE STATIONS IN ROTTERDAM.

SCHRG 1979 -1 SCHRUBEN, L. W.
ASSIGNMENT OF PRIMARY RESPONSE ZONES TO EMERGENCY MEDICAL UNITS.

SCHUA 1979 -1 SCHUTT, J. H.
MIXED INTEGER LINEAR PROGRAMMING FORMULATIONS FOR DISTRIBUTION NETWORKS.

SCOT 1979 -1 SCOTT, C. H.; JEFFERSON, T. R.; KERDVONBUNDIT, P.
GEOMETRIC PROGRAMMING DUALITY APPLIED TO THE RESOURCE ALLOCATION PROBLEM.

SHAP 1979 -1 SHAPIRO, B. I.
PROBLEME D'ALLOCATION DES RESSOURCES DANS LES CONDITIONS D'ORGANISATION DE PROJETS ET SA METHODE DE RESOLUTION NUMERIQUE (RUSSIAN).

SHER 1978 -1 SHERALI, H. D.; SHETTY, C. M.
PRIMAL SIMPLEX BASED SOLUTION PROCEDURE FOR THE RECTILINEAR DISTANCE MULTIFACILITY LOCATION PROBLEM, A.

SHET 1980 -1 SHETTY, C. M.; SHERALI, H. D.
RECTILINEAR DISTANCE LOCATION-ALLOCATION PROBLEM: A SIMPLEX BASED ALGORITHM.

SHIRA 1979 -1 SHIRLAND, L. E.; ELLIS, P. M.
OPTIMUM LOCATION OF TRAINING CENTERS.

SMITD 1979 -1 SMITH, J. M.
USE OF QUEUEING NETWORKS AND MIXED INTEGER PROGRAMMING TO OPTIMALLY ALLOCATE RESOURCES WITHIN A LIBRARY.

SPAE 1978 -1 SPAETH, H.
EXPLIZITE LOESUNG DES DREIDIMENSIONALEN MINIMAX-STANDORTPROBLEMS IN DER CITY-BLOCK-DISTANZ.

SPAE 1979 -1 SPAETH, H.
LOESUNG MULTIPLER STANDORTPROBLEME BEI GEMISCHT GERADLINIGEN UND RECHTWINKELIGEN ENTFERNUNGEN, DIE.

STAH 1979 -1 STAHL, W.; DOMSCHKE, W.
VERFAHREN ZUR BESTIMMUNG OPTIMALER MASCHINENSTANDORTE BEI RECHTWINKLIGER ENTFERNUNGSMESSUNG, EIN.

STEF 1979 -1 STEFFEN, A. E.; ALY, A. A.
SINGLE FACILITY LOCATION PROBLEM AMONG RECTANGULAR REGIONS, A.

STIE 1975 -1 STIERLIN, C.
ALGORITHM FOR THE SIMULTANEOUS LOCATION OF EMERGENCY ROOMS AND OF AMBULANCE CENTERS, AN.

SULL 1980 -1 SULLIVAN, P. J.; PETERS, N.
FLEXIBLE USER-ORIENTED LOCATION-ALLOCATION ALGORITHM, A.

TAMIA 1979 -1 TAMIR, A.; ZEMEL, E.
LOCATING CENTERS ON A TREE WITH DISCONTINUOUS SUPPLY AND DEMAND REGIONS.

TANS 1980 -1 TANSEL, B. C.; FRANCIS, R. L.; LOWE, T. J.
BINDING INEQUALITIES FOR TREE NETWORK LOCATION PROBLEMS WITH DISTANCE CONSTRAINTS.

TAYL 1978 -1 TAYLOR, B. W. III; KEOWN, A. J.
PLANNING URBAN RECREATIONAL FACILITIES WITH INTEGER GOAL PROGRAMMING.

TEMP 1980 -1 TEMPELMEIER, H.
BESTIMMUNG DES OPTIMALEN STANDORTS EINES AUSLIEFERUNGSLAGERS BEI ENTFERNUNGSABHAENGIGER NACHFRAGE UND NICHTLINEAREN TRANSPORTKOSTEN, DIE.

THOM 1977 -1 THOMAS, A.
MODELS FOR OPTIMAL CAPACITY EXPANSION.

TRUB 1977 -1 TRUBIN, V. A.
ONE-PARAMETER ALLOCATION AND UNIFICATION PROBLEMS (RUSSIAN).

TRUB 1978 -1 TRUBIN, V. A.
EFFECTIVE ALGORITHM FOR THE WEBER PROBLEM WITH RECTANGULAR METRIC (RUSSIAN).

USHA 1979 -1 USHAKOV, I. A.
METHODE APPROCHEE D'OPTIMISATION DES SYSTEMES A OBJETS REPARTIS (RUSSIAN).

UZDE 1979 -1 UZDEMIR, A. P.
DYNAMIC LOCATION OF INDUSTRIAL PLANTS I.

UZDE 1977 -2 UZDEMIR, A. P.
ESTIMATION PROBLEMS IN A NUMERICAL METHOD OF SOLUTION OF DYNAMIC INDUSTRIAL PLANT LOCATION PROBLEM.

UZDE 1979 -2 UZDEMIR, A. P.
DYNAMIC LOCATION OF INDUSTRIAL PLANTS II.

VANR 1980 -1 VANROY, T. J.
CROSS DECOMPOSITION ALGORITHM FOR CAPACITATED FACILITY LOCATION, A.

VLAC 1978 -1 VLACH, M.
MULTICOMMODITY LOCATION PROBLEMS.

WOLS 1980 -2 WOLSEY, L. A.
MAXIMIZING REAL-VALUED SUBMODULAR FUNCTIONS: PRIMAL AND DUAL HEURISTICS FOR LOCATION PROBLEMS.

ZANA 1981 -1 ZANAKIS, S.
METHOD FOR LARGE-SCALE INTEGER GOAL PROGRAMMING WITH AN APPLICATION TO A FACILITY LOCATION/ ALLOCATION PROBLEM, A.

ZANAA 1977 -1 ZANAKIS, S.; LAWRENCE, K. D.
EFFECTIVE SHIFT ALLOCATION IN MULTIPRODUCT LINES: A MIXED INTEGER PROGRAMMING APPROACH.

ZEIT 1981 -1 ZEITLIN, Z.
INTEGER ALLOCATION PROBLEMS OF MIN-MAX TYPE WITH QUASICONVEX SEPARABLE FUNCTIONS.

ZUSU 1974 -1 ZUSUPBAEV, A.
PRODUCTION ALLOCATION PROBLEM WITH A CONVEX SEPARABLE FUNCTIONAL (RUSSIAN), THE.

ANGLA 1977 -1 ANGLUIN, D.; VALIANT, L. G.
FAST PROBABILISTIC ALGORITHMS FOR HAMILTONIAN CIRCUITS AND MATCHINGS.

AVIS 1978 -1 AVIS, D.
TWO GREEDY HEURISTICS FOR THE WEIGHTED MATCHING PROBLEM.

BALAA 1979 -3 BALAS, E.
INTEGER AND FRACTIONAL MATCHINGS.

BALAH 1979 -2 BALAS, E.; PADBERG, M. W.
SET PARTITIONING - A SURVEY.

BALAI 1981 -1 BALAS, E.; PULLEYBLANK, W. R.
LINEAR CHARACTERIZATION OF THE PERFECTLY MATCHABLE SUBGRAPH POLYHEDRON, A.

BARTB 1978 -1 BARTHOLDI, J. J. III; RATLIFF, H. D.
UNNETWORKS WITH APPLICATIONS TO IDLE TIME SCHEDULING.

BARTC 1978 -1 BARTNIK, W. G.
ALGORITHMES DE COUPLAGE DANS LES GRAPHES.

BRAC 1974 -1 BRACE, A.; DAYKIN, D. E.
PSEUDO-MATCHINGS OF A BIPARTITE GRAPH.

BURKA 1980 -1 BURKARD, R. E.; DERIGS, U.
ASSIGNMENT AND MATCHING PROBLEMS: SOLUTION METHODS WITH FORTRAN-PROGRAMS.

CHAT 1979 -1 CHATY, G.; CHEIN, M.
ORDERED MATCHING AND MATCHINGS WITHOUT ALTERNATING CYCLES IN BIPARTITE GRAPHS.

COCK 1978 -1 COCKAYNE, E. J.; HARTNELL, B. L.; HEDETNIEMI, S. T.
LINEAR ALGORITHM FOR DISJOINT MATCHINGS IN TREES, A.

CONR 1978 -1 CONRADT, D.
EFFIZIENTE IMPLEMENTIERUNG DES VERFAHRENS VON EDMONDS ZUR BESTIMMUNG EINES MAXIMALEN MATCHING, EINE.

CONR 1979 -1 CONRADT, D.
VERGLEICH AUSGEWAEHLTER MATCHING-ALGORITHMEN.

CORND 1980 -1 CORNUEJOLS, G.; PULLEYBLANK, W. R.
MATCHING PROBLEM WITH SIDE CONDITIONS, A.

CORND 1981 -1 CORNUEJOLS, G.; PULLEYBLANK, W. R.
CRITICAL GRAPHS, MATCHINGS AND TOURS - A HIERARCHY OF RELAXATIONS FOR THE TRAVELLING SALESMAN PROBLEM.

CORND 1980 -2 CORNUEJOLS, G.; PULLEYBLANK, W. R.
PERFECT TRIANGLE-FREE 2-MATCHINGS.

CORND 1980 -3 CORNUEJOLS, G.; PULLEYBLANK, W. R.
TRAVELLING SALESMAN POLYTOPE AND (0,2)-MATCHINGS, THE.

CUMM 1977 -1 CUMMINGS, L. J.; WALLIS, W. D.
TRANSVERSAL ALGORITHM FOR REGULAR SQUARE INCIDENCE MATRICES, A.

CUNNC 1978 -1 CUNNINGHAM, W. H.; MARSH, A. B. III
PRIMAL ALGORITHM FOR OPTIMUM MATCHING, A.

DERI 1978 -1 DERIGS, U.
DUALITY AND THE ALGEBRAIC MATCHING PROBLEM.

DERI 1979 -1 DERIGS, U.
DUALITY AND ADMISSIBLE TRANSFORMATIONS IN COMBINATORIAL OPTIMIZATION.

DERI 1980 -1 DERIGS, U.
CARDINALITY MATCHING PROBLEM - METHODS AND COMPUTATION, THE.

DERI 1981 -1 DERIGS, U.
F-FACTORS, PERFECT MATCHINGS AND RELATED CONCEPTS.

DERI 1979 -2 DERIGS, U.
GENERALIZED HUNGARIAN METHOD FOR SOLVING MINIMUM WEIGHT PERFECT MATCHING PROBLEMS WITH ALGEBRAIC OBJECTIVE, A.

DERI 1979 -3 DERIGS, U.
SHORTEST AUGMENTING PATH METHOD FOR SOLVING MINIMAL PERFECT MATCHING PROBLEMS, A.

DERI 1980 -3 DERIGS, U.
LOESUNG MINIMALER PERFEKTER MATCHINGPROBLEME MITTELS KUERZESTER ERWEITERNDER PFADE, DIE.

DERI 1980 -5 DERIGS, U.
ON TWO METHODS FOR SOLVING THE BOTTLENECK MATCHING PROBLEM.

DERIA 1980 -1 DERIGS, U.; HESKE, A.
COMPUTATIONAL STUDY ON SOME METHODS FOR SOLVING THE CARDINALITY MATCHING PROBLEM, A.

DERIB 1979 -1 DERIGS, U.; KAZAKIDIS, G.
ON TWO METHODS FOR SOLVING MINIMAL PERFECT MATCHING PROBLEMS.

EDMOA 1978 -1 EDMONDS, J.; JOHNSON, E. L.; LOCKHART, S. C.
BLOSSOM I: A COMPUTER CODE FOR THE MATCHING PROBLEM.

FANI 1977 -1 FANICA, G.
TESTING FOR EQUALITY BETWEEN MAXIMUM MATCHING AND MINIMUM NODE COVERING.

FARR 1978 -1 FARRELL, E. J.
MATCHINGS IN LADDERS.

FARR 1979 -1 FARRELL, E. J.
INTRODUCTION TO MATCHING POLYNOMIALS, AN.

FARR 1981 -1 FARRELL, E. J.
DEFECT-D MATCHINGS IN GRAPHS WITH CYCLOMATIC NUMBERS 0, 1 AND 2.

FARR 1979 -2 FARRELL, E. J.
MATCHING IN WHEELS.

FARR 1980 -2 FARRELL, E. J.
MATCHINGS IN COMPLETE GRAPHS AND COMPLETE BIPARTITE GRAPHS.

GABOB 1979 -1 GABOW, H. N.
ALGORITHMIC PROOFS OF TWO RELATIONS BETWEEN CONNECTIVITY AND THE 1-FACTORS OF A GRAPH.

GAVR 1977 -2 GAVRIL, F.
TESTING FOR EQUALITY BETWEEN MAXIMUM MATCHING AND MINIMUM NODE COVERING.

GILE 1979 -2 GILES, R.
OPTIMUM MATCHING FORESTS (EXTENDED ABSTRACT).

GILEC 1980 -1 GILES, R.; OYAMA, T.; TROTTER, L. E. JR.
RELATED NECESSARY CONDITIONS FOR COMPLETING PARTIAL LATIN SQUARES.

GODS 1981 -1 GODSIL, C. D.; GUTMAN, I.
ON THE MATCHING POLYNOMIAL OF A GRAPH.

GONDA 1979 -1 GONDRAN, M.; MINOUX, M.
GRAPHES ET ALGORITHMES.

GRAV 1977 -1 GRAVER, J. E.; WATKINS, M. E.
COMBINATORICS WITH EMPHASIS ON THE THEORY OF GRAPHS.

GREE 1980 -1 GREEN-KROTKI, J. J.
MATCHING POLYHEDRA.

GROED 1981 -1 GROETSCHEL, M.; LOVASZ, L.; SCHRIJVER, A.
ELLIPSOID METHOD AND ITS CONSEQUENCES IN COMBINATORIAL OPTIMIZATION, THE.

GUTM 1979 -1 GUTMAN, I.
MATCHING POLYNOMIAL, THE.

HARTC 1977 -1 HARTNELL, B. L.
CHARACTERIZATION OF UNICYCLIC GRAPHS WHICH DO NOT HAVE TWO DISJOINT MAXIMAL MATCHINGS, A.
HAUS 1979 -1 HAUSMANN, D.
COMPLEXITY OF THE TESTING OF ADJACENCY ON THE B-MATCHING POLYHEDRON.
HAUS 1981 -1 HAUSMANN, D.
ADJACENT VERTICES ON THE B-MATCHING POLYHEDRON.
HELL 1981 -1 HELL, P.; KIRKPATRICK, D. G.
ON GENERALIZED MATCHING PROBLEMS.
HELL 1981 -2 HELL, P.; KIRKPATRICK, D. G.
SCHEDULING, MATCHING, AND COLORING.
ITAIB 1978 -1 ITAI, A.; RODEH, M.; TANIMOTO, S. L.
SOME MATCHING PROBLEMS FOR BIPARTITE GRAPHS.
JOHND 1978 -1 JOHNSON, E. L.
MATCHINGS AND BIDIRECTED GRAPHS.
KARZ 1976 -1 KARZANOV, A. V.
ECONOMICAL REALIZATION OF THE EDMONDS ALGORITHMS FOR MATCHING MAXIMAL POWER AND MAXIMAL WEIGHT (RUSSIAN).
KIRKA 1978 -1 KIRKPATRICK, D. G.; HELL, P.
ON THE COMPLEXITY OF A GENERALIZED MATCHING PROBLEM.
KNAU 1979 -1 KNAUER, B.
SIMPLE ALGORITHM FOR MAXIMUM MATCHING OF GRAPHS, A.
KOCH 1979 -1 KOCH, E.
RAMIFICATIONS OF MATCHING THEORY.
LENSA 1980 -5 LENSTRA, J. K.; RINNOOY KAN, A. H. G.
THEORIE DE LA COMPLEXITE DE CALCUL APPLIQUEE AUX PROBLEMES DE COUPLAGE, RECOUVREMENT ET PARTITIONNEMENT.
LOVA 1979 -2 LOVASZ, L.
ON DETERMINANTS, MATCHINGS, AND RANDOM ALGORITHMS.
MAC A 1978 -1 MAC CARTHY, P. J.
MATCHINGS IN GRAPHS III: INFINITE GRAPHS.
MAC A 1978 -2 MAC CARTHY, P. J.
MATCHINGS IN INFINITE GRAPHS.
MAFF 1980 -1 MAFFIOLI, F.
COUPLAGES ET MATROIDES.
MAURC 1978 -1 MAURRAS, J. F.
GOOD ALGORITHMS, OLD IDEAS.
MEGIB 1978 -1 MEGIDDO, N.; TAMIR, A.
O(N TIMES LOG N) ALGORITHM FOR A CLASS OF MATCHING PROBLEMS, AN.
MEIR 1978 -1 MEIR, A.
ON TOTAL COVERING AND MATCHING OF GRAPHS.
MINI 1978 -1 MINIEKA, E.
OPTIMIZATION ALGORITHMS FOR NETWORKS AND GRAPHS.
MINO 1980 -1 MINOUX, M.
SOLUTIONS ENTIERES ET SOLUTIONS CONTINUES DES PROBLEMES DE COUPLAGES DANS LES GRAPHES PONDERES FINIS.
MUEH 1979 -1 MUEHLBACHER, J.
F-FACTORS OF GRAPHS: A GENERALIZED MATCHING PROBLEM.
MURTA 1978 -1 MURTY, U. S. R.
APPLICATION OF RADO'S THEOREM TO DISJOINT MATCHINGS IN BIPARTITE GRAPHS, AN.
NADD 1978 -1 NADDEF, D.
RANG DES COUPLAGES MAXIMUMS D'UN GRAPHE.
NADDA 1980 -1 NADDEF, D.; PULLEYBLANK, W. R.
EAR DECOMPOSITIONS OF ELEMENTARY GRAPHS AND GF(2)-RANK OF PERFECT MATCHINGS.
NEMHA 1979 -1 NEMHAUSER, G. L.; WEBER, G. M.
OPTIMAL SET PARTITIONING, MATCHINGS AND LAGRANGIAN DUALITY.
NIGM 1980 -1 NIGMATULLIN, R. G.
O(M+N)-ALGORITHM FOR MATCHING MAXIMALITY RECOGNITION (RUSSIAN), AN.
NISH 1978 -1 NISHIZEKI, T.
LOWER BOUNDS ON THE CARDINALITY OF THE MAXIMUM MATCHINGS OF GRAPHS.
NISH 1979 -1 NISHIZEKI, T.
ON THE RELATIONSHIP BETWEEN THE GENUS AND THE CARDINALITY OF THE MAXIMUM MATCHINGS OF A GRAPH.
NUSS 1978 -1 NUSSINO, R.; PIECZENIK, G., GRIGGS, J. R.; KLEITMAN, D. J.
ALGORITHMS FOR LOOP MATCHINGS.
OBERA 1981 -1 OBERSCHELP, W.
MATCHING POLYNOMIALS AND ROOK THEORY.
PADBB 1979 -1 PADBERG, M. W.; RAO, M. R.
ODD MINIMUM CUT-SETS AND B-MATCHINGS.
PAPEB 1979 -1 PAPE, U.; CONRADT, D.
MAXIMALES MATCHING IN GRAPHEN.
PAYA 1978 -1 PAYAN, C.
COUPLAGES MAXIMAUX DISJOINTS.
PERI 1980 -1 PERIN, C.
USER'S GUIDE TO MATCOV.
PERI 1981 -1 PERIN, C.
ON THE POLYTOPE OF THE 1-MATCHING/COVERING PROBLEM.
PERI 1981 -2 PERIN, C.
1-MATCHING/COVERING PROBLEM, THE.
PLAIA 1980 -1 PLAISTED, D. A.; ZAKS, S.
NP-COMPLETE MATCHING PROBLEM, AN.
PLES 1975 -1 PLESNIK, J.
SIMPLE PROOF OF THE PERFECT MATCHING THEOREM, A.
PLES 1979 -2 PLESNIK, J.
REMARK ON MATCHINGS IN REGULAR GRAPHS.
PULL 1980 -1 PULLEYBLANK, W. R.
MATCHING RANK OF HALIN GRAPHS, THE.
PULL 1980 -1 PULLEYBLANK, W. R.
DUAL INTEGRALITY IN B-MATCHING PROBLEMS.
PULL 1981 -1 PULLEYBLANK, W. R.
MATCHING RANK OF HALIN GRAPHS, THE.
PULL 1981 -3 PULLEYBLANK, W. R.
TOTAL DUAL INTEGRALITY AND B-MATCHINGS.
SAVA 1980 -1 SAVAGE, C.
MAXIMUM MATCHINGS AND TREES.
SBIH 1978 -1 SBIHI, N.
ETUDE DES STABLES DANS LES GRAPHES SANS ETOILE.

SLATA 1978 -2 SLATER, P. J.
CONSTRUCTIVE CHARACTERIZATION OF TREES WITH AT LEAST K DISJOINT MAXIMUM MATCHINGS. A.
STER 1978 -1 STERBOUL, F.
HYPERGRAPHES TRANSVERSAUX DES COUPLAGES.
STER 1978 -2 STERBOUL, F.
SUR LE NOMBRE TRANSVERSAL DES HYPERGRAPHES UNIFORMES.
SUMN 1979 -1 SUMNER, D. P.
RANDOMLY MATCHABLE GRAPHS.
SUSH 1975 -1 SUSHKOV, Y. A.
(1,Q)-MATCHINGS.
SZWAB 1979 -1 SZWARCFITER, J. L.
SYSTEMS OF DISTINCT REPRESENTATIVES FOR K FAMILIES OF SETS.
TARJ 1974 -1 TARJAN, R. E.
TESTING GRAPH CONNECTIVITY.
TERA 1979 -1 TERADA, R.
POLYNOMIAL TIME ALGORITHMS FOR NP-HARD PROBLEMS WHICH ARE OPTIMAL OR NEAR-OPTIMAL WITH PROBABILITY ONE.
TOKU 1979 -1 TOKUMASU, S.; MOTOI, N.; ODAMURA, M.
SPECIAL MATCHING PROBLEM AND AN ALGORITHM FOR IT (JAPANESE). A.
TORR 1975 -1 TORRIGIANI, M.
ON A MORE GENERAL DEFINITION OF DISTINCT MATCHINGS (ITALIAN).
TREH 1978 -1 TREHEL, M.
NOTES SUR LE COUPLAGE DIRECT - COUPLAGE DANS LES COMBINAISONS.
VERGA 1975 -1 VERGNAS, M. LAS
DEGREE-CONSTRAINED SUBGRAPHS AND MATROID THEORY.
WALKB 1977 -1 WALKUP, D. W.
MATCHINGS IN RANDOM REGULAR BIPARTITE DIGRAPHS.
WALKB 1977 -2 WALKUP, D. W.
MATCHINGS IN RANDOM REGULAR BIPARTITE GRAPHS.
WERR 1981 -2 WERRA, D. DE
REMARKS ON THE REQUIREMENT MATRIX OF SCHOOL TIMETABLE PROBLEMS AND REGULAR EMBEDDINGS OF GRAPHS.
WOODA 1978 -1 WOODALL, D. R.
MINIMAX THEOREMS IN GRAPH THEORY.

ACKEA 1978 -1 ACKETA, D. M.
ON THE ENUMERATION OF MATROIDS OF RANK 2.

ANTO 1980 -1 ANTONA, O. D'; KUNG, J. P. S.
COHERENT ORIENTATIONS AND SERIES-PARALLEL NETWORKS.

ASANB 1978 -1 ASANO, T.; NISHIZEKI, T.; SAITO, S.
ON THE MAXIMAL BIPARTITE MATROIDS (JAPANESE).

ASTI 1978 -1 ASTIE-VIDAL, A.
AUTOMORPHISMES D'ARETES DES HYPERGRAPHES DES BASES D'UN MATROIDE.

ASTI 1980 -1 ASTIE-VIDAL, A.
AUTOMORPHISM GROUP OF A MATROID, THE.

ASTI 1978 -2 ASTIE-VIDAL, A.
GROUPES D'AUTOMORPHISMES DES GRAPHES D'INTERSECTION AUX BASES D'UN MATROIDE.

ASTI 1980 -2 ASTIE-VIDAL, A.
FACTOR GROUP OF THE AUTOMORPHISM GROUP OF A MATROID BASIS GRAPH WITH RESPECT TO THE AUTOMORPHISM GROUP OF THE MATROID.

AUSI 1981 -1 AUSIELLO, G.; MARCHETTI-SPACCAMELA, A.; PROTASI, M.
PROBABILISTIC ANALYSIS OF THE PERFORMANCE OF GREEDY STRATEGIES OVER DIFFERENT CLASSES OF COMBINATORIAL PROBLEMS.

AVIS 1978 -1 AVIS, D.
TWO GREEDY HEURISTICS FOR THE WEIGHTED MATCHING PROBLEM.

BACH 1980 -2 BACHEM, A.
THEOREMS OF THE ALTERNATIVE IN COMBINATORIAL PROGRAMMING.

BACL 1979 -1 BACLAWSKI, K.; WHITE, N. L.
HIGHER ORDER INDEPENDENCE IN MATROIDS.

BALLB 1979 -1 BALL, M. O.; NEMHAUSER, G. L.
MATROIDS AND A RELIABILITY ANALYSIS PROBLEM.

BALLC 1980 -1 BALL, M. O.; PROVAN, J. S.
BOUNDS ON THE RELIABILITY POLYNOMIAL FOR SHELLABLE INDEPENDENCE SYSTEMS.

BARN 1980 -1 BARNABEI, M.; NICOLETTI, G.
AXIOMATIZING MATROIDS BY MEANS OF THE SET OF NONGENERATORS.

BAUM 1978 -2 BAUM, S.; TROTTER, L. E. JR.
INTEGER ROUNDING FOR POLYMATROID AND BRANCHING OPTIMIZATION PROBLEMS.

BENE 1980 -1 BENETEAU, L.
CLASSE PARTICULIERE DE MATROIDES PARFAITS, UNE.

BIXB 1979 -1 BIXBY, R. E.
ON REID'S CHARACTERIZATION OF THE TERNARY MATROIDS.

BIXBA 1979 -1 BIXBY, R. E.; CUNNINGHAM, W. H.
MATROIDS, GRAPHS, AND 3-CONNECTIVITY.

BIXBA 1980 -1 BIXBY, R. E.; CUNNINGHAM, W. H.
CONVERTING LINEAR PROGRAMS TO NETWORK PROBLEMS.

BJOE 1980 -1 BJOERNER, A.
SOME MATROID INEQUALITIES.

BLAN 1978 -2 BLAND, R. G.
PIVOTING IN ORIENTED MATROIDS.

BLANB 1979 -1 BLAND, R. G.; VERGNAS, M. LAS
MINTY COLORINGS AND ORIENTATIONS OF MATROIDS.

BRIN 1980 -1 BRINI, A.
CLASS OF RANK-INVARIANTS FOR PERFECT MATROID DESIGNS, A.

BRUNF 1970 -1 BRUNO, J.; WEINBERG, L.
PRINCIPAL PARTITION AND PRINCIPAL MINORS OF A MATROID, WITH APPLICATIONS.

BRUT 1969 -1 BRUTER, C.
SUR DIFFERENTS PROBLEMES POSES EN THEORIE DES MATROIDES.

BRYA 1978 -1 BRYANT, V.; DAWSON, J. E.
DESIGNS AND CIRCUIT BASES.

BRYAA 1980 -1 BRYANT, V.; PERFECT, H.
INDEPENDENCE THEORY IN COMBINATORICS. AN INTRODUCTORY ACCOUNT WITH APPLICATIONS TO GRAPHS AND TRANSVERSALS.

BRYL 1975 -1 BRYLAWSKI, T.
AFFINE REPRESENTATION FOR TRANSVERSAL GEOMETRIES, AN.

BRYL 1977 -1 BRYLAWSKI, T.
THE BROKEN-CIRCUIT COMPLEX.

BRYL 1979 -1 BRYLAWSKI, T.
INTERSECTION THEORY FOR EMBEDDINGS OF MATROIDS INTO UNIFORM GEOMETRIES.

BRYLA 1978 -1 BRYLAWSKI, T.; KELLY, D. G.
MATROIDS AND COMBINATORIAL GEOMETRIES.

BRYLA 1980 -1 BRYLAWSKI, T.; KELLY, D. G.
MATROIDS AND COMBINATORIAL GEOMETRIES.

BRYLB 1976 -1 BRYLAWSKI, T.; LUCAS, D.
UNIQUELY REPRESENTABLE COMBINATORIAL GEOMETRIES.

BRYLC 1980 -1 BRYLAWSKI, T.; OXLEY, J. G.
SEVERAL IDENTITIES FOR THE CHARACTERISTIC POLYNOMIAL OF A COMBINATORIAL GEOMETRY.

BURKD 1981 -1 BURKARD, R. E.; HAMACHER, H.
MINIMAL COST FLOWS IN REGULAR MATROIDS.

CALV 1980 -1 CALVILLO, G.
CONCAVITY AND INTERSECTION PROPERTIES FOR INTEGRAL POLYHEDRA, THE.

CAMEC 1978 -1 CAMERINI, P. M.; MAFFIOLI, F.
EXACT AND HEURISTIC METHODS FOR NP-HARD MATROID PROBLEMS.

CAMEC 1978 -2 CAMERINI, P. M.; MAFFIOLI, F.
HEURISTICALLY GUIDED ALGORITHM FOR K-PARITY MATROID PROBLEMS.

CAMEC 1980 -2 CAMERINI, P. M.; MAFFIOLI, F.
WEIGHTED SATISFIABILITY PROBLEMS AND SOME IMPLICATIONS.

CAZA 1978 -1 CAZANESCU, V.-E.; RUDEANU, S.
INDEPENDENT SETS AND KERNELS IN GRAPHS AND HYPERGRAPHS.

CHVA 1979 -1 CHVATAL, V.
GREEDY HEURISTIC FOR THE SET-COVERING PROBLEM, A.

CLAUB 1980 -1 CLAUSEN, J.; HANSEN, L. A.
FINDING K EDGE-DISJOINT SPANNING TREES OF MINIMUM TOTAL WEIGHT IN A NETWORK: AN APPLICATION OF MATROID THEORY.

CLOC 1976 -1 CLOCOTICI, V.
SOME RELATIONS BETWEEN BASES AND CIRCUITS OF A MATROID.

CORD 1979 -1 CORDOVIL, R.
CONTRIBUTIONS A LA THEORIE DES GEOMETRIES COMBINATOIRES: GEOMETRIES SIMPLICIALES, COMPATIBILITE DES EXTENSIONS.

CORD 1980 -1 CORDOVIL, R.
REPRESENTATION OVER A FIELD OF FULL SIMPLICIAL MATROIDS.

CORD 1980 -2 CORDOVIL, R.
SUR L'EVALUATION T(M;2,0) DU POLYNOME DE TUTTE D'UN MATROIDE ET UNE CONJECTURE DE B. GRUENBAUM RELATIVE AUX ARRANGEMENTS DE DROITES DU PLAN.

CORDA 1979 -1 CORDOVIL, R.; VERGNAS, M. LAS
GEOMETRIES SIMPLICIALES UNIMODULAIRES.

CORNE 1980 -1 CORNUEJOLS, G.; THIZY, J.-M.
LOCATION PROBLEMS, SET COVERING PROBLEMS AND THE GREEDY ALGORITHM.

CRAP 1970 -1 CRAPO, H. H.
ERECTING GEOMETRIES.

CUNN 1979 -1 CUNNINGHAM, W. H.
BINARY MATROID SUMS.

CUNN 1982 -1 CUNNINGHAM, W. H.
DECOMPOSITION OF SUBMODULAR FUNCTIONS.

CUNN 1981 -2 CUNNINGHAM, W. H.
ON MATROID CONNECTIVITY.

CUNN 1981 -3 CUNNINGHAM, W. H.
POLYHEDRA FOR COMPOSED INDEPENDENCE SYSTEMS.

CUNN 1981 -4 CUNNINGHAM, W. H.
TESTING MEMBERSHIP IN MATROID POLYHEDRA.

DAWS 1980 -1 DAWSON, J. E.
NOTE ON SOME ALGORITHMS FOR MATROIDS, A.

DAWS 1980 -2 DAWSON, J. E.
OPTIMAL MATROID BASES: AN ALGORITHM BASED ON COCIRCUITS.

DOWL 1980 -1 DOWLING, T. A.
ON THE INDEPENDENT SET NUMBERS OF A FINITE MATROID.

DOWLA 1976 -1 DOWLING, T. A.; KELLY, D. G.
ELEMENTARY STRONG MAPS BETWEEN COMBINATORIAL GEOMETRIES.

DUCH 1973 -1 DUCHAMP, A.
SUR LA STRUCTURE DES REPRESENTATIONS D'UN MATROIDE TRANSVERSAL.

DUCH 1980 -1 DUCHAMP, A.
FORMES BILINEAIRES SYMETRIQUES SUR UN ESPACE VECTORIEL DE DIMENSION FINIE SUR LE CORPS A DEUX ELEMENTS, APPLICATIONS AUX MATROIDES BINAIRES.

DUNSA 1976 -1 DUNSTAN, F. D. J.
MATROIDS AND SUBMODULAR FUNCTIONS.

EBER 1980 -1 EBERT, J.
FINDING SPANNING FORESTS: A PROBLEM OF DATA MANIPULATION.

EDMO 1979 -1 EDMONDS, J.
MATROID INTERSECTION.

EULE 1979 -1 EULER, R.
ON RANK FUNCTIONS OF GENERAL INDEPENDENCE SYSTEMS (EXTENDED ABSTRACT).

EULE 1980 -1 EULER, R.
AUGMENTING PATHS AND A CLASS OF INDEPENDENCE SYSTEMS.

EULE 1981 -1 EULER, R.
ON A CLASSIFICATION OF INDEPENDENCE SYSTEMS.

EULE 1980 -2 EULER, R.
ON A CLASSIFICATION OF INDEPENDENCE SYSTEMS.

EULE 1981 -2 EULER, R.
REGULAR (2,2)-SYSTEMS.

EULE 1980 -3 EULER, R.
RANK-AXIOMATIC CHARACTERIZATIONS OF INDEPENDENCE SYSTEMS.

EVANB 1977 -1 EVANS, J. R.; JARVIS, J. J.; DUKE, R. A.
GRAPHIC MATROIDS AND THE MULTICOMMODITY TRANSPORTATION PROBLEM.

FAIG 1979 -1 FAIGLE, U.
GREEDY ALGORITHM FOR PARTIALLY ORDERED SETS, THE.

FAIG 1980 -1 FAIGLE, U.
GEOMETRIES ON PARTIALLY ORDERED SETS.

FAIG 1981 -1 FAIGLE, U.
ON SUPERMATROIDS WITH SUBMODULAR RANK FUNCTION.

FISHC 1978 -1 FISHER, M. L.; NEMHAUSER, G. L.; WOLSEY, L. A.
ANALYSIS OF APPROXIMATIONS FOR MAXIMIZING SUBMODULAR SET FUNCTIONS - II, AN.

FOLD 1978 -1 FOLDES, S.; HAMMER, P. L.
ON A CLASS OF MATROID-PRODUCING GRAPHS.

FOLD 1978 -2 FOLDES, S.; HAMMER, P. L.
ON SPLIT GRAPHS AND SOME RELATED QUESTIONS.

FOLKA 1978 -1 FOLKMAN, J.; LAWRENCE, J.
ORIENTED MATROIDS.

FONL 1979 -1 FONLUPT, J.
ON THE NUMBER OF COMPLEMENTARY BASES IN A MATROID.

FOUR 1973 -1 FOURNIER, J.-C.
INTRODUCTION A LA NOTION DE MATROIDE (GEOMETRIE COMBINATOIRE).

FOUR 1978 -2 FOURNIER, J.-C.
GRAPHES DE CORDES, HYPERGRAPHES DE CHAINES D'UN ARBRE ET MATROIDES GRAPHIQUES.

FRANB 1980 -1 FRANK, A.
ALGORITHM FOR SUBMODULAR FUNCTIONS ON GRAPHS, AN.

FRANB 1981 -1 FRANK, A.
FINDING FEASIBLE VECTORS OF EDMONDS-GILES POLYHEDRA.

FRANB 1981 -2 FRANK, A.
GENERALIZED POLYMATROIDS.

FRANB 1981 -5 FRANK, A.
WEIGHTED MATROID INTERSECTION ALGORITHM, A.

FRANB 1980 -7 FRANK, A.
WEIGHTED MATROID INTERSECTION ALGORITHM, A.

FRAND 1982 -1 FRANK, A.; TARDOS, E.
MATROIDS FROM CROSSING FAMILIES.

FRAY 1978 -1 FRAYSSEIX, H. DE
PROPRIETES DE PARITE DES BASES D'UN MATROIDE BINAIRE.

FRIED 1977 -1 FRIEZE, A. M.
ALGORITHMS FOR GENERALISATIONS OF MATROIDS.

FRIED 1978 -1 FRIEZE, A. M.
GENERALISATION OF THE GREEDY ALGORITHM FOR INDEPENDENCE SYSTEMS, A.

FUJI 1979 -1 FUJISHIGE, S.
MATROID THEORY AND ITS APPLICATION TO SYSTEMS ENGINEERING PROBLEMS (JAPANESE).

FUJI 1980 -1 FUJISHIGE, S.
LEXICOGRAPHICALLY OPTIMAL BASE OF A POLYMATROID WITH RESPECT TO A WEIGHT VECTOR.

FUJI 1981 -1 FUJISHIGE, S.
CANONICAL DECOMPOSITIONS OF SYMMETRIC SUBMODULAR SYSTEMS.

FUJI 1980 -2 FUJISHIGE, S.
PRINCIPAL STRUCTURES OF SUBMODULAR SYSTEMS.
GABOE 1979 -1 GABOW, H. N.; TARJAN, R. E.
EFFICIENT ALGORITHMS FOR SIMPLE MATROID INTERSECTION PROBLEMS.
GATTA 1981 -1 GATTINGER, M.; WENZEL, G.
VERALLGEMEINERTE GERUESTE, KOZYKLEN UND ZYKLEN IN GRAPHEN.
GILEB 1979 -1 GILES, R.; KANNAN, R.
CHARACTERIZATION OF THRESHOLD MATROIDS (EXTENDED ABSTRACT), A.
GILEB 1980 -1 GILES, R.; KANNAN, R.
CHARACTERIZATION OF THRESHOLD MATROIDS, A.
GOND 1979 -2 GONDRAN, M.
OPTIMISATION COMBINATOIRE.
GONDA 1979 -1 GONDRAN, M.; MINOUX, M.
GRAPHES ET ALGORITHMES.
GRAV 1977 -1 GRAVER, J. E.; WATKINS, M. E.
COMBINATORICS WITH EMPHASIS ON THE THEORY OF GRAPHS.
GROED 1981 -1 GROETSCHEL, M.; LOVASZ, L.; SCHRIJVER, A.
ELLIPSOID METHOD AND ITS CONSEQUENCES IN COMBINATORIAL OPTIMIZATION, THE.
GUSF 1979 -1 GUSFIELD, D.
MATROID OPTIMIZATION WITH THE INTERLEAVING OF TWO ORDERED SETS.
GYOR 1975 -1 GYORI, E.
COMPARISON OF INFINITE MATROIDS (HUNGARIAN).
HAMA 1980 -1 HAMACHER, H.
ALGEBRAIC FLOWS IN REGULAR MATROIDS.
HAMA 1981 -1 HAMACHER, H.
FLOWS IN REGULAR MATROIDS.
HAMA 1980 -2 HAMACHER, H.
ALGEBRAISCHE FLUSSPROBLEME IN REGULAEREN MATROIDEN.
HAMA 1980 -4 HAMACHER, H.
ON A CLASS OF EASILY SOLVABLE OPTIMAL COCIRCUIT PROBLEMS IN REGULAR MATROIDS.
HANSA 1977 -1 HANSEN, A. B.
ON A CERTAIN CLASS OF POLYTOPES ASSOCIATED WITH INDEPENDENCE SYSTEMS.
HAUSA 1980 -1 HAUSMANN, D.; JENKYNS, T. A.; KORTE, B.
WORST CASE ANALYSIS OF GREEDY TYPE ALGORITHMS FOR INDEPENDENCE SYSTEMS.
HAUSC 1980 -1 HAUSMANN, D.; KORTE, B.
COMPUTATIONAL RELATIONS BETWEEN VARIOUS DEFINITIONS OF MATROIDS AND INDEPENDENCE SYSTEMS.
HAUSC 1981 -1 HAUSMANN, D.; KORTE, B.
ALGORITHMIC VERSUS AXIOMATIC DEFINITIONS OF MATROIDS.
HAUSC 1978 -2 HAUSMANN, D.; KORTE, B.
K-GREEDY ALGORITHMS FOR INDEPENDENCE SYSTEMS.
HAUSC 1980 -2 HAUSMANN, D.; KORTE, B.
RELATIVE STRENGTH OF ORACLES FOR INDEPENDENCE SYSTEMS, THE.
HAUSC 1978 -3 HAUSMANN, D.; KORTE, B.
LOWER BOUNDS ON THE WORST-CASE COMPLEXITY OF SOME ORACLE ALGORITHMS.
HAUSC 1978 -4 HAUSMANN, D.; KORTE, B.
WORST-CASE BEHAVIOUR OF POLYNOMIAL BOUNDED ALGORITHMS FOR INDEPENDENCE SYSTEMS.
HILT 1978 -1 HILTON, A. J. W.
DIMENSION IN LINEAR SPACES.
INUK 1979 -1 INUKAI, T.; WEINBERG, L.
GRAPH-REALIZABILITY OF MATROIDS.
IRI 1978 -1 IRI, M.
PRACTICAL ALGORITHM FOR THE MENGER-TYPE GENERALIZATION OF THE INDEPENDENT ASSIGNMENT PROBLEM, A.
IRI 1979 -1 IRI, M.
REVIEW OF RECENT WORK IN JAPAN ON PRINCIPAL PARTITIONS OF MATROIDS AND THEIR APPLICATIONS, A.
IRI A 1981 -1 IRI, M.; FUJISHIGE, S.
USE OF MATROID THEORY IN OPERATIONS RESEARCH, CIRCUITS AND SYSTEMS THEORY.
JAEG 1979 -2 JAEGER, F.
INTERVAL MATROIDS AND GRAPHS.
JAEG 1979 -3 JAEGER, F.
TWO CHARACTERIZATIONS OF COGRAPHIC MATROIDS.
JENKA 1977 -1 JENKYNS, T. A.
P-SYSTEMS AS INTERSECTIONS OF MATROIDS.
JENKA 1978 -1 JENKYNS, T. A.
EFFICACY OF HEURISTICS COMBINING ENUMERATION AND THE GREEDY ALGORITHM, THE.
JENKA 1979 -1 JENKYNS, T. A.
GREEDY BUT NOT-SO-STUPID ALGORITHMS.
JENKA 1979 -2 JENKYNS, T. A.
GREEDY TRAVELLING SALESMAN'S PROBLEM, THE.
JENSA 1981 -1 JENSEN, P. M.
BINARY FUNDAMENTAL MATROIDS.
JENSB 1978 -1 JENSEN, P. M.; KORTE, B.
COMPLEXITY OF MATROID PROPERTY ALGORITHMS.
KAHN 1980 -1 KAHN, J.
SOME NON-SPERNER PAVING MATROIDS.
KAHNA 1980 -1 KAHN, J.; KUNG, J. P. S.
VARIETIES AND UNIVERSAL MODELS IN THE THEORY OF COMBINATORIAL GEOMETRIES.
KELM 1980 -1 KELMANS, A. K.
CONCEPT OF A VERTEX IN A MATROID AND 3-CONNECTED GRAPHS.
KELM 1981 -1 KELMANS, A. K.
CONCEPT OF A VERTEX IN A MATROID, THE NON-SEPARATING CYCLES OF A GRAPH AND A NEW CRITERION FOR GRAPH PLANARITY, THE.
KESTA 1978 -1 KESTENBAND, B. C.; YOUNG, H. P.
MATROID DESIGNS OF PRIME POWER INDEX.
KORN 1978 -1 KORNBLUM, D. F.
"GREEDY" ALGORITHMS FOR SOME LATTICE POLYHEDRA PROBLEMS.
KORN 1978 -2 KORNBLUM, D. F.
GREEDY ALGORITHMS FOR SOME OPTIMIZATION PROBLEMS ON A LATTICE POLYHEDRON.
KORTA 1981 -1 KORTE, B.
MATROID PROPERTIES AND MATROID ORACLES.
KORTA 1981 -2 KORTE, B.
MATROIDS AND INDEPENDENCE SYSTEMS.
KORTB 1981 -1 KORTE, B.; LOVASZ, L.
MATHEMATICAL STRUCTURES UNDERLYING GREEDY ALGORITHMS.

KORTC 1979 -1 KORTE, B.; MONMA, C. L.
SOME REMARKS ON A CLASSIFICATION OF ORACLE-TYPE-ALGORITHMS.
KOVA 1979 -1 KOVALEV, M. M.
POLYHEDRAL SEMIMATROIDS (RUSSIAN).
KOVA 1980 -1 KOVALEV, M. M.
ANALYSIS OF THE GREEDY ALGORITHM FOR CONVEX INTEGER PROGRAMMING (RUSSIAN).
KOVAB 1979 -1 KOVALEV, M. M.; ISACHENKO, A. N.
SEMIMATROIDE.
KUNG 1978 -1 KUNG, J. P. S.
ALPHA FUNCTION OF A MATROID. I. TRANSVERSAL MATROIDS, THE.
KUNG 1980 -1 KUNG, J. P. S.
ON SPECIALIZATIONS OF MATROIDS.
KUNG 1978 -2 KUNG, J. P. S.
ALTERNATING BASIS EXCHANGES IN MATROIDS.
KUNG 1978 -3 KUNG, J. P. S.
BIMATROIDS AND INVARIANTS.
LANDB 1979 -1 LANDAUER, C.
REPRESENTATIONS OF MATROIDS.
LAWL 1980 -1 LAWLER, E. L.
INTRODUCTION TO POLYMATROIDAL NETWORK FLOWS, AN.
LAWLB 1980 -1 LAWLER, E. L.; LENSTRA, J. K.; RINNOOY KAN, A. H. G.
GENERATING ALL MAXIMAL INDEPENDENT SETS: NP-HARDNESS AND POLYNOMIAL-TIME ALGORITHMS.
LAWLC 1980 -1 LAWLER, E. L.; MARTEL, C. U.
COMPUTING MAXIMAL "POLYMATROIDAL" NETWORK FLOWS.
LAWR 1980 -1 LAWRENCE, J.; WEINBERG, L.
UNIONS OF ORIENTED MATROIDS.
LECL 1978 -1 LECLERC, B.
MATROIDES SUR UN ENSEMBLE PREORDONNE, BASES MINIMALES, CIRCUITS ET COCIRCUITS, PARTIES COMMENCANTES.
LIND 1978 -1 LINDSTROEM, B.
ON THE CHROMATIC NUMBER OF REGULAR MATROIDS.
LIND 1979 -1 LINDSTROEM, B.
NON-REGULAR SIMPLICIAL MATROIDS.
LONG 1980 -1 LONGYEAR, J. Q.
CIRCUIT BASIS IN BINARY MATROIDS, THE.
LORE 1978 -1 LOREA, M.
HYPERGRAPHES ET MATROIDES.
LORE 1979 -1 LOREA, M.
ON MATROIDAL FAMILIES.
LORE 1978 -2 LOREA, M.
MATROIDES SUR LES ENSEMBLES D'ARETES D'HYPERGRAPHES.
LOUL 1979 -1 LOULOU, R.; MICHAELIDES, E.
NEW GREEDY-LIKE HEURISTICS FOR THE MULTIDIMENSIONAL 0-1 KNAPSACK PROBLEM.
LOVA 1977 -1 LOVASZ, L.
FLATS IN MATROIDS AND GEOMETRIC GRAPHS.
LOVA 1980 -1 LOVASZ, L.
MATROID MATCHING AND SOME APPLICATIONS.
LOVA 1980 -2 LOVASZ, L.
MATROIDS AND SPERNER'S LEMMA.
LOVA 1981 -2 LOVASZ, L.
MATROID MATCHING PROBLEM, THE.
LOVA 1979 -3 LOVASZ, L.
SELECTING INDEPENDENT LINES FROM A FAMILY OF LINES IN A SPACE.
LOWEA 1979 -1 LOWE, T. J.; FRANCIS, R. L.; REINHARDT, E. W.
GREEDY NETWORK FLOW ALGORITHM FOR A WAREHOUSE LEASING PROBLEM, A.
MA 1980 -1 MA, Z. F.; LIU, Z. H.; CAI, M. C.
OPTIMUM RESTRICTED BASE OF A MATROID.
MAC A 1979 -1 MAC CARTHY, P. J.
CHARACTERIZATION OF STRICT MATCHING MATROIDS, A.
MAC B 1978 -1 MAC DIARMID, C.
BLOCKING, ANTIBLOCKING AND PAIRS OF MATROIDS AND POLYMATROIDS.
MAFF 1978 -1 MAFFIOLI, F.
DISCREET CHARM OF MATROID PROBLEMS, THE.
MAFF 1980 -1 MAFFIOLI, F.
COUPLAGES ET MATROIDES.
MASO 1981 -1 MASON, J. H.
GLUEING MATROIDS TOGETHER: A STUDY OF DILWORTH TRUNCATIONS AND MATROID ANALOGUES OF EXTERIOR AND SYMMETRIC POWERS.
MASOA 1980 -1 MASON, J. H.; OXLEY, J. G.
CIRCUIT COVERING RESULT FOR MATROIDS, A.
MATTB 1977 -1 MATTHEWS, L. R.
MATROIDS FROM GRAPHS AND DIRECTED GRAPHS.
MATTB 1978 -1 MATTHEWS, L. R.
MATROIDS FROM DIRECTED GRAPHS.
MATTB 1979 -1 MATTHEWS, L. R.
DUALITY IN INDEPENDENCE SYSTEMS.
MATTB 1978 -2 MATTHEWS, L. R.
NOTE ON THE MUTUAL INDEPENDENCE OF EVENTS, A.
MATTB 1979 -2 MATTHEWS, L. R.
INFINITE SUBGRAPHS AS MATROID CIRCUITS.
MATTB 1978 -3 MATTHEWS, L. R.
PROPERTIES OF BICIRCULAR MATROIDS.
MINO 1978 -1 MINOUX, M.
ACCELERATED GREEDY ALGORITHMS FOR MAXIMIZING SUBMODULAR SET FUNCTIONS.
MUELA 1981 -1 MUELLER, H.
ZUR STRUKTUR UND KOMPLEXITAET DISKRETER OPTIMIERUNGSPROBLEME, DIE DURCH ERBLICHE EIGENSCHAFTEN AUF ENDLICHEN MENGENSYSTEMEN GEGEBEN SIND.
MURTB 1978 -1 MURTY, U. S. R.; SIMON, I.
BETA-FUNCTION THAT IS NOT A SUM OF RANK FUNCTIONS OF MATROIDS, A.
NADDB 1980 -1 NADDEF, D.; SBIHI, N.; TCHUENTE, M.
INDEPENDENCE SYSTEMS WITH CONTINUOUS CARDINALITY OF BASES.
NEMHB 1978 -1 NEMHAUSER, G. L.; WOLSEY, L. A.
MAXIMIZING SUBMODULAR SET FUNCTIONS: FORMULATIONS AND ANALYSIS OF ALGORITHMS.
NEMHC 1978 -1 NEMHAUSER, G. L.; WOLSEY, L. A.; FISHER, M. L.
ANALYSIS OF APPROXIMATIONS FOR MAXIMIZING SUBMODULAR SET FUNCTIONS-I, AN.

MATROIDS AND INDEPENDENCE SYSTEMS

NGUYA 1978 -1 NGUYEN, H. Q.
SEMIMODULAR FUNCTIONS AND COMBINATORIAL GEOMETRIES.
NGUYA 1979 -1 NGUYEN, H. Q.
WEAK CUTS OF COMBINATORIAL GEOMETRIES.
NICOA 1980 -1 NICOLETTI, G.
GENERATING CRYPTOMORPHIC AXIOMATIZATIONS OF MATROIDS.
NISHA 1977 -1 NISHIZEKI, T.; ASANO, T.; SAITO, N.
ON THE MAXIMAL EVEN MATROIDS.
OUBI 1978 -1 OUBINA, L.
LOCALISATION D'UNE PROPRIETE DU GRAPHE DES BASES D'UN MATROIDE BINAIRE.
OXLE 1978 -1 OXLEY, J. G.
COCIRCUIT COVERINGS AND PACKINGS FOR BINARY MATROIDS.
OXLE 1979 -1 OXLEY, J. G.
GENERALIZATION OF A COVERING PROBLEM OF MULLIN AND STANTON FOR MATROIDS, A.
OXLE 1980 -1 OXLEY, J. G.
ON A COVERING PROBLEM OF MULLIN AND STANTON FOR BINARY MATROIDS.
OXLE 1980 -2 OXLEY, J. G.
ON HARTFIEL AND MAXSON'S DEFINITION OF CONNECTED SETS OF A MATROID.
OXLE 1978 -3 OXLEY, J. G.
INFINITE MATROIDS AND DUALITY.
OXLE 1978 -4 OXLEY, J. G.
INFINITE MATROIDS.
OXLEA 1979 -2 OXLEY, J. G.; WELSH, D. J. A.
TUTTE POLYNOMIAL AND PERCOLATION, THE.
PELE 1978 -1 PELED, U. N.
MATROIDAL GRAPHS.
POLE 1976 -1 POLESSKII, V. P.
LATTICE OF ISTHMUSES OF A SUMMED MATROID (RUSSIAN), THE.
RAMA 1975 -1 RAMACHANDRA RAO, A.; BHASKARA RAO, K. P. S.
MODULARITY IN COMBINATORIAL GEOMETRIES.
RECS 1975 -1 RECSKI, A.
APPLICATION OF MATROIDS IN THE ANALYSIS OF ELECTRICAL NETWORKS. II. (HUNGARIAN).
RECS 1978 -1 RECSKI, A.
CONTRIBUTIONS TO THE N-PORT INTERCONNECTION PROBLEM BY MEANS OF MATROIDS.
RECS 1981 -1 RECSKI, A.
ALGORITHM TO DETERMINE WHETHER THE SUM OF SOME GRAPHIC MATROIDS IS GRAPHIC, AN.
RECS 1978 -2 RECSKI, A.
DECOMPOSITIONS OF A GRAPHIC MATROID.
RECS 1978 -3 RECSKI, A.
MATROIDAL STRUCTURE OF N-PORTS.
RECSA 1980 -1 RECSKI, A.; IRI, M.
NETWORK THEORY AND TRANSVERSAL MATROIDS.
RETK 1978 -1 RETKIN, H.; MOGI, S.
SOME COMBINATORIAL IDENTITIES ON MATROIDS.
REVJ 1976 -1 REVJAKIN, A. M.
DESCRIPTION OF THE FACTORS OF COMBINATORIAL GEOMETRIES (RUSSIAN), A.
REVJ 1976 -2 REVJAKIN, A. M.
ONE-POINT EXTENSIONS OF COMBINATORIAL GEOMETRIES (RUSSIAN).
ROBIC 1980 -1 ROBINSON, G. C.; WELSH, D. J. A.
COMPUTATIONAL COMPLEXITY OF MATROID PROPERTIES, THE.
SATO 1978 -1 SATO, H.; KOBAYASHI, K.; HOSHI, M.
ON MAPS BETWEEN MATROIDS (JAPANESE).
SCHMD 1979 -1 SCHMIDT, R.
ON THE EXISTENCE OF UNCOUNTABLY MANY MATROIDAL FAMILIES.
SCHRD 1978 -1 SCHRIJVER, A.
LINKING OF MATROIDS BY LINKING SYSTEMS, THE.
SCHRD 1979 -1 SCHRIJVER, A.
FRACTIONAL PACKING AND COVERING.
SCHRD 1978 -2 SCHRIJVER, A.
ON THE STRUCTURE OF DELTOIDS.
SCHRD 1979 -2 SCHRIJVER, A.
MATROIDS AND LINKING SYSTEMS.
SCHRD 1980 -2 SCHRIJVER, A.
MIN-MAX RELATIONS FOR DIRECTED GRAPHS.
SEYM 1978 -1 SEYMOUR, P. D.
MATROIDS REPRESENTABLE OVER GF(3), THE.
SEYM 1979 -1 SEYMOUR, P. D.
MATROID REPRESENTATION OVER GF(3).
SEYM 1980 -1 SEYMOUR, P. D.
DECOMPOSITION OF REGULAR MATROIDS.
SEYM 1981 -1 SEYMOUR, P. D.
SOME APPLICATIONS OF MATROID DECOMPOSITION.
SEYM 1980 -4 SEYMOUR, P. D.
ON TUTTE'S CHARACTERIZATION OF GRAPHIC MATROIDS.
SEYM 1980 -5 SEYMOUR, P. D.
PACKING AND COVERING WITH MATROID CIRCUITS.
SIMO 1978 -1 SIMOES-PEREIRA, J. M. S.
COMMENT ON MATROIDAL FAMILIES, A.
SIMS 1977 -1 SIMS, J. A.
COMPLETE CLASS OF MATROIDS, A.
SMITA 1978 -1 SMITH, C. A. B.
ON TUTTE'S DICHROMATE POLYNOMIAL.
STERD 1981 -1 STERN, M.
GENERALIZED MATROID LATTICES.
SZAM 1976 -1 SZAMKOLOWICZ, L.
SOME REMARKS ON GRAPHICITY OF SIMPLE MATROIDS.
TOMI 1976 -1 TOMIZAWA, N.
STRONGLY IRREDUCIBLE MATROIDS AND PRINCIPAL PARTITION OF A MATROID INTO STRONGLY IRREDUCIBLE MINORS.
TRUE 1979 -1 TRUEMPER, K.
ALPHA-BALANCED MATRICES AND GF(3)-REPRESENTABILITY OF MATROIDS.
TRUE 1980 -1 TRUEMPER, K.
EFFICIENT TEST FOR REGULARITY OF MATROIDS, AN.
TRUE 1979 -2 TRUEMPER, K.
COMPLEXITY OF REPRESENTABILITY TESTS FOR MATROIDS.

VAMO 1978 -1 VAMOS, P.
MISSING AXIOM OF MATROID THEORY IS LOST FOREVER, THE.
VERGA 1975 -1 VERGNAS, M. LAS
DEGREE-CONSTRAINED SUBGRAPHS AND MATROID THEORY.
VERGA 1978 -1 VERGNAS, M. LAS
BASES IN ORIENTED MATROIDS.
VERGA 1980 -1 VERGNAS, M. LAS
CONVEXITY IN ORIENTED MATROIDS.
VERGA 1978 -2 VERGNAS, M. LAS
EXTENSIONS PONCTUELLES COMPATIBLES D'UNE GEOMETRIE COMBINATOIRE.
VERGA 1980 -2 VERGNAS, M. LAS
FUNDAMENTAL CIRCUITS AND A CHARACTERIZATION OF BINARY MATROIDS.
VERGA 1978 -3 VERGNAS, M. LAS
EXTENSIONS PONCTUELLES D'UNE GEOMETRIE COMBINATOIRE ORIENTEE.
VERGA 1980 -3 VERGNAS, M. LAS
ON THE TUTTE POLYNOMIAL OF A MORPHISM OF MATROIDS.
VERGA 1978 -4 VERGNAS, M. LAS
SUR LES ACTIVITES DES ORIENTATIONS D'UNE GEOMETRIE COMBINATOIRE.
WALTA 1980 -1 WALTON, P. N.; WELSH, D. J. A.
ON THE CHROMATIC NUMBER OF BINARY MATROIDS.
WANG 1978 -1 WANG, D.-L.; WANG, P.
SOME RESULTS ABOUT THE CHVATAL CONJECTURE.
WELS 1971 -1 WELSH, D. J. A.
COMBINATORIAL PROBLEMS IN MATROID THEORY.
WELS 1979 -1 WELSH, D. J. A.
COLOURING PROBLEMS AND MATROIDS.
WHITD 1980 -1 WHITE, N. L.
UNIQUE EXCHANGE PROPERTY FOR BASES, A.
WOLS 1980 -2 WOLSEY, L. A.
MAXIMIZING REAL-VALUED SUBMODULAR FUNCTIONS: PRIMAL AND DUAL HEURISTICS FOR LOCATION PROBLEMS.
WONGA 1978 -1 WONG, P.-K.
ON CERTAIN N-CONNECTED MATROIDS.
WOODA 1974 -1 WOODALL, D. R.
APPLICATIONS OF POLYMATROIDS AND LINEAR PROGRAMMING TO TRANSVERSALS AND GRAPHS.
YAMA 1976 -1 YAMAMOTO, Y.
ALGORITHM FOR FINDING A COMMON BASIS OF TWO MATROIDS, AN.
YAMA 1978 -1 YAMAMOTO, Y.
HELD-KARP ALGORITHM AND DEGREE-CONSTRAINED MINIMUM 1-TREES, THE.
ZAME 1977 -1 ZAME, A.
TRANSVERSAL THEORY AND RANK FUNCTIONS.
ZELI 1980 -1 ZELINKA, B.
BASES OF CLASSES OF TREES CLOSED UNDER SUBDIVISIONS.
ZIMM 1978 -1 ZIMMERMANN, U.
DUALITY AND THE ALGEBRAIC MATROID INTERSECTION PROBLEM.
ZIMM 1981 -1 ZIMMERMANN, U.
LINEAR AND COMBINATORIAL OPTIMIZATION IN ORDERED ALGEBRAIC STRUCTURES.
ZIMM 1978 -2 ZIMMERMANN, U.
THRESHOLD METHODS FOR BOOLEAN OPTIMIZATION PROBLEMS WITH SEPARABLE OBJECTIVES.
ZIMM 1979 -2 ZIMMERMANN, U.
MATROID INTERSECTION PROBLEMS WITH GENERALIZED OBJECTIVES.
ZIMM 1981 -2 ZIMMERMANN, U.
MINIMIZATION OF SOME NONLINEAR FUNCTIONS OVER POLYMATROIDAL FLOWS.

ALBE 1979 -1 ALBERS, S.
EXTENDED ALGORITHM FOR OPTIMAL PRODUCT POSITIONING, AN.
AMMO 1979 -1 AMMON, P.; PEEMOELLER, W.
LOESUNG GEMISCHT-GANZZAHLIGER PROBLEME MIT NETZWERKSTRUKTUR.
ARMS 1977 -1 ARMSTRONG, R. D.
EXPERIMENTS IN A MULTIPLE CHOICE MIXED INTEGER PROGRAMMING ALGORITHM.
ARMSC 1979 -1 ARMSTRONG, R. D.; COOK, W. D.; SAIPE, A. L.
OPTIMAL BATCHING IN A SEMI-AUTOMATED ORDER PICKING SYSTEM.
ARTE 1981 -1 ARTEMENKO, V. I.
ON ONE METHOD OF SEARCH FOR APPROXIMATE SOLUTIONS OF MIXED INTEGER LINEAR PROGRAMMING PROBLEMS (RUSSIAN).
BACHB 1981 -1 BACHEM, A.; JOHNSON, E. L.; SCHRADER, R.
CHARACTERIZATION OF MINIMAL INEQUALITIES FOR MIXED INTEGER PROGRAMS, A.
BACHE 1978 -1 BACHEM, A.; SCHRADER, R.
NOTE ON A THEOREM OF JEROSLOW, A.
BACHE 1979 -1 BACHEM, A.; SCHRADER, R.
DUALITY THEOREM AND MINIMAL INEQUALITIES IN MIXED INTEGER PROGRAMMING, A.
BACHE 1980 -1 BACHEM, A.; SCHRADER, R.
MINIMAL INEQUALITIES AND SUBADDITIVE DUALITY.
BALAB 1977 -1 BALAS, E.; BERGTHALLER, C.
BENDERS'S METHOD REVISITED.
BALAE 1980 -1 BALAS, E.; JEROSLOW, R. G.
STRENGTHENING CUTS FOR MIXED INTEGER PROGRAMS.
BAYBA 1979 -1 BAYBARS, I.; KORTANEK, K. O.; MIZUNO, N.
MIXED INTEGER PROGRAMMING MODEL FOR TRANSMISSION SYSTEM PLANNING IN TELECOMMUNICATIONS NETWORKS WITH GENERAL CIRCUIT REQUIREMENTS, A.
BENS 1979 -1 BENSEMAN, B.; HALL, K.
SOLVING A PLANT LOCATION PROBLEM WITH INTEGER PROGRAMMING.
BLAI 1975 -1 BLAIR, C. E.
MINIMAL INEQUALITIES FOR MIXED-INTEGER PROGRAMS.
BLAI 1975 -2 BLAIR, C. E.
TOPICS IN INTEGER PROGRAMMING.
BLAIA 1981 -1 BLAIR, C. E.; JEROSLOW, R. G.
EXACT PENALTY METHOD FOR MIXED-INTEGER PROGRAMS, AN.
BROW 1980 -1 BROWN, G. G.; GEOFFRION, A. M.; BRADLEY, G. H.
PRODUCTION AND SALES PLANNING WITH LIMITED SHARED TOOLING AT THE KEY OPERATION.
CHAND 1979 -1 CHANDRA, S.; CHANDRAMOHAN, M.
DUALITY IN MIXED INTEGER NONCONVEX AND NONDIFFERENTIABLE PROGRAMMING.
CHENE 1978 -1 CHEN, R.; CROWDER, H. P.; JOHNSON, E. L.
SOLVING THE INSTALLATION SCHEDULING PROBLEM USING MIXED INTEGER LINEAR PROGRAMMING.
CLAUA 1981 -1 CLAUS, A.; KRAETZIG, S.
OPTIMAL PLANNING OF NETWORK STRUCTURES WITHIN AN EXCHANGE AREA.
COBI 1981 -1 COBIAN, J. M.; RUIZ C., M.
OPTIMIZATION MODEL FOR THE PLANNING OF ELECTRICAL DISTRIBUTION NETWORKS, AN.
DANG 1979 -1 DANG VAN UYEN
AGGREGATION OF AN INTEGER PROGRAMMING MODEL (SLOVAK).
DANG 1979 -2 DANG VAN UYEN
SOLUTION TO A CLASS OF MIXED INTEGER PROGRAMMING PROBLEMS WITH 0-1 AND AND CONTINUOUS VARIABLES (CZECHOSLOVAKIAN), A.
DANIA 1979 -1 DANIEL, R. C.; JEFFREYS, M.
UNBOUNDEDNESS IN INTEGER AND DISCRETE PROGRAMMING L. P. RELAXATIONS.
DEAK 1981 -1 DEAK, I.; HOFFER, J.; MAYER, J.; NEMETH, A.; POTECZ, B.; PREKOPA, A.; STRAZICKY, B.
OPTIMAL DAILY SCHEDULING OF THE ELECTRICITY PRODUCTION IN HUNGARY.
DOYL 1978 -1 DOYLE, T. E.; MOORE, T. G.; SACKETT, R. A.
BENDER'S DECOMPOSITION APPROACH TO SCHEDULING SWITCHING SYSTEM REPLACEMENTS AND EQUIPMENT REUSE.
DUMIA 1979 -1 DUMITRU, V.; LUBAN, F.
MEMBERSHIP FUNCTIONS, SOME MATHEMATICAL PROGRAMMING MODELS AND PRODUCTION SCHEDULING.
DUMIA 1980 -1 DUMITRU, V.; LUBAN, F.
MATHEMATICAL PROGRAMMING REAL VARIABLE MODELS FOR INTEGER AND MIXED-INTEGER PROBLEMS.
FAAL 1979 -1 FAALAND, B. H.; HILLIER, F. S.
INTERIOR PATH METHODS FOR HEURISTIC INTEGER PROGRAMMING PROCEDURES.
FABI 1981 -1 FABIAN, C.
CONVEX MIXED-INTEGER NONSEPARABLE PROGRAMMING.
FALK 1978 -1 FALK, P. G.
EXPERIMENTS IN MIXED INTEGER LINEAR PROGRAMMING CONCURRENT TO A MANUFACTURING HIERARCHY.
FALK 1980 -1 FALK, P. G.
EXPERIMENTS IN MIXED INTEGER LINEAR PROGRAMMING IN A MANUFACTURING SYSTEM.
FOX A 1980 -1 FOX, D. B.
OPTIMIZATION IN ENGINEERING DESIGN.
GABR 1981 -1 GABRIEL, R.
LEISTUNGSVERGLEICH KOMMERZIELLER SOFTWARE ZUR LOESUNG SPEZIELLER MIXED-INTEGER-PROBLEME, EIN.
GEOR 1979 -1 GEORGE, J. A.
REPORT ON THE USE OF MIXED INTEGER PROGRAMMING IN AN EVALUATION OF PLANT UPGRADING, A.
GISV 1971 -1 GISVOLD, K. M.; MOE, J.
METHOD FOR NONLINEAR MIXED-INTEGER PROGRAMMING AND ITS APPLICATION TO DESIGN PROBLEMS, A.
GUIGA 1978 -1 GUIGNARD, M.; SPIELBERG, K.
DUAL METHOD FOR THE MIXED PLANT LOCATION PROBLEM, A. (REVISED VERSION).
HABE 1978 -1 HABENICHT, W.
ZUM EINSATZ ENUMERATIVER SCHNITTEBENENVERFAHREN IN B&B-SYSTEMEN.
HOAN 1978 -1 HOANG HAI HOC
SOLVING AN INTEGER PROGRAMMING PROBLEM.
HUCKA 1980 -1 HUCKERT, K.; RHODE, R.; ROGLIN, O.; WEBER, R.
ON THE INTERACTIVE SOLUTION TO A MULTICRITERIA SCHEDULING PROBLEM.
JENK 1980 -1 JENKINS, L.
COMPUTATIONAL RESULTS WITH A TECHNIQUE OF PARAMETRIC MIXED INTEGER LINEAR PROGRAMMING.
JENK 1980 -2 JENKINS, L.
ONTARIO WASTE MANAGEMENT MODEL: TORONTO EXPERIENCE, THE.
JENK 1980 -3 JENKINS, L.
PARAMETRIC MIXED INTEGER PROGRAMMING: A SOLID WASTE RECYCLING APPLICATION.
JEROB 1977 -1 JEROSLOW, R. G.
REPRESENTATIONS OF UNBOUNDED OPTIMIZATIONS AS INTEGER PROGRAMS.
JEROB 1978 -1 JEROSLOW, R. G.
CUTTING PLANE THEORY: ALGEBRAIC METHODS.

JEROB 1979 -2 JEROSLOW, R. G.
MINIMAL INEQUALITIES.
JEROB 1978 -3 JEROSLOW, R. G.
SOME BASIC THEOREMS FOR INTEGRAL MONOIDS.
JOHND 1981 -1 JOHNSON, E. L.
CHARACTERIZATION OF FACETS FOR MULTIPLE RIGHT-HAND CHOICE LINEAR PROGRAMS.
JOHNF 1978 -1 JOHNSON, E. L.; POWELL, S.
INTEGER PROGRAMMING CODES.
KAUF 1978 -1 KAUFMAN, L.; BROECKX, F.
ALGORITHM FOR THE QUADRATIC ASSIGNMENT PROBLEM USING BENDERS DECOMPOSITION, AN.
KAUFD 1977 -1 KAUFMANN, A.; HENRY-LABORDERE, A.
INTEGER AND MIXED PROGRAMMING. THEORY AND APPLICATIONS.
KELA 1978 -1 KELAHAN, R. C.; GADDY, J. L.
APPLICATION OF THE ADAPTIVE RANDOM SEARCH TO DISCRETE AND MIXED INTEGER OPTIMIZATION.
KELL 1979 -1 KELLER, H.; MUELLER, W.
OPTIMIERUNG DES SCHUELERNAHVERKEHRS DURCH GEMISCHT GANZZAHLIGE PROGRAMMIERUNG.
LEBE 1977 -1 LEBEDEV, V. YU.
SCHEME FOR SOLVING A PARTIALLY INTEGER-VALUED PROBLEM OF MATHEMATICAL PROGRAMMING, A.
LEBEA 1978 -1 LEBEDEVA, T. T.
APPLICATION OF THE DIRECTING VICINITY METHOD FOR SOLVING PARTIALLY INTEGRAL PROBLEMS OF LINEAR PROGRAMMING (RUSSIAN).
LIIT 1978 -1 LIITTSCHWAGER, J. M.; WANG, C.
INTEGER PROGRAMMING SOLUTION OF A CLASSIFICATION PROBLEM.
LJUBA 1977 -1 LJUBOVICKII, L. V.
PROPERTIES OF THE BASIS MATRICES OF A CLASS OF POLYHEDRA (RUSSIAN).
MAGN 1979 -1 MAGNANTI, T. L.; WONG, R. T.
ACCELERATING BENDERS DECOMPOSITION: ALGORITHMIC ENHANCEMENTS AND MODEL SELECTION CRITERIA.
MARSA 1980 -1 MARSTEN, R. E.; MULLER, M. R.
MIXED-INTEGER PROGRAMMING APPROACH TO AIR CARGO FLEET PLANNING, A.
MEYEB 1981 -1 MEYER, R. R.
THEORETICAL AND COMPUTATIONAL COMPARISON OF "EQUIVALENT" MIXED-INTEGER FORMULATIONS, A.
MEYEE 1980 -1 MEYER, R. R.; THAKKAR, M. V.; HALLMAN, W. P.
RATIONAL MIXED-INTEGER AND POLYHEDRAL UNION MINIMIZATION MODELS.
MOORA 1980 -1 MOORE, T. G.
CENTRAL CUTTING PLANE ALGORITHM FOR INTEGER PROGRAMMING, A.
MORR 1978 -1 MORRIS, J. G.
ON THE EXTENT TO WHICH CERTAIN FIXED-CHARGE DEPOT LOCATION PROBLEMS CAN BE SOLVED BY LP.
NEMHB 1978 -1 NEMHAUSER, G. L.; WOLSEY, L. A.
MAXIMIZING SUBMODULAR SET FUNCTIONS: FORMULATIONS AND ANALYSIS OF ALGORITHMS.
NORT 1979 -1 NORTHUP, W. D.; SHAPIRO, J. F.
LOGS: AN OPTIMIZATION SYSTEM FOR LOGISTICS PLANNING.
PAST 1977 -1 PASTIJN, H. J. A. M.
HYBRID ALGORITHM FOR THE GENERAL MIP-PROBLEM, A.
PETE 1975 -1 PETERS, R. J.
MIXED INTEGER LINEAR PROGRAMMING IN PRODUCTION PLANNING (DUTCH).
PLAN 1979 -1 PLANKE, W.
UEBER EINIGE VERBESSERUNGEN DES VERZWEIGUNGSVERFAHRENS VON DRIEBEEK IN DER GEMISCHT GANZZAHLIGEN LINEAREN OPTIMIERUNG.
RESI 1977 -1 RESINA, C.
PROPOSED SOLUTION METHOD FOR A CLASS OF MIXED INTEGER PROGRAMMING PROBLEMS (ITALIAN).
ROSHA 1978 -1 ROSHCHIN, V. A.
APPROACH TO THE SOLUTION OF PARTIALLY INTEGRAL PROBLEMS OF LINEAR PROGRAMMING (RUSSIAN), AN.
SANN 1979 -1 SANNOMIYA, N.
METHOD FOR SOLVING MIXED-INTEGER LINEAR PROGRAMMING PROBLEMS WITH ANGULAR STRUCTURE, A.
SCHA 1974 -1 SCHABACK, R.
OPTIMIERUNGSPROBLEM AUS DER KRISTALLOGRAPHIE, EIN.
SCHME 1978 -1 SCHMITZ, P.; SCHOENLEIN, A.
LINEARE UND LINEARISIERBARE OPTIMIERUNGSMODELLE SOWIE IHRE ADV-GESTUETZTE LOESUNG.
SCHUA 1979 -1 SCHUTT, J. H.
MIXED INTEGER LINEAR PROGRAMMING FORMULATIONS FOR DISTRIBUTION NETWORKS.
SEEL 1980 -2 SEELAENDER, J.
UEBER DIE BESTIMMUNG VON STABILITAETSBEREICHEN BEI SPEZIELLEN GEMISCHT-GANZZAHLIGEN LINEAREN OPTIMIERUNGSPROBLEMEN.
SERGA 1980 -1 SERGIENKO, I. V.; LEBEDEVA, T. T.; ROSHCHIN, V. A.
APPROXIMATE METHODS FOR THE SOLUTION OF DISCRETE OPTIMIZATION PROBLEMS (RUSSIAN).
SHAPA 1978 -1 SHAPIRO, J. F.
FUTURE DIRECTIONS OF LARGE SCALE MIXED INTEGER PROGRAMMING.
SHARA 1980 -1 SHARMA, J. K.; SHARMA, M. M.
ON MIXED INTEGER SOLUTIONS TO GOAL PROGRAMMING PROBLEMS.
SINC 1979 -1 SINCLAIR, M.
AUGMENTED LAGRANGEAN RELAXATIONS IN GENERAL MIXED INTEGER PROGRAMMING.
SUZU 1978 -1 SUZUKI, H.
GENERALIZED KNAPSACK PROBLEM WITH VARIABLE COEFFICIENTS, A.
TSAR 1977 -1 TSAROUCHIS, N.
SIMPLEX-TYPE ALGORITHM FOR A HYBRID ZERO-ONE PROGRAMMING PROBLEM, A.
TURG 1978 -1 TURGEON, A.
OPTIMAL SCHEDULING OF THERMAL GENERATING UNITS.
VAND 1976 -1 VANDENMEERENDONK, H. W.
SINGLE MACHINE MULTI-PRODUCT PLANNING PROBLEMS.
VILLA 1979 -1 VILLARREAL, B.; KARWAN, M. H.
INTERACTIVE DYNAMIC PROGRAMMING APPROACH TO MULTICRITERIA DISCRETE PROGRAMMING, AN.
WALL 1976 -1 WALLER, D. A.
REGULAR EIGENVALUES OF GRAPHS AND ENUMERATION OF SPANNING TREES.
WALU 1978 -1 WALUKIEWICZ, S.
USING PSEUDOBOOLEAN PROGRAMMING IN DECOMPOSITION METHOD.
WILL 1978 -1 WILLIAMS, H. P.
REFORMULATION OF TWO MIXED INTEGER PROGRAMMING PROBLEMS, THE.
WILL 1979 -1 WILLIAMS, H. P.
ECONOMIC INTERPRETATION OF DUALITY FOR PRACTICAL MIXED INTEGER PROGRAMMING PROBLEMS, THE.
WOLT 1979 -1 WOLTERS, J. A. M.
MINIMISING THE NUMBER OF AIRCRAFT FOR A TRANSPORTATION NETWORK.
WONGB 1981 -1 WONG, R. T.
PROBABILISTIC ANALYSIS OF AN OPTIMAL NETWORK PROBLEM HEURISTIC.
ZABR 1970 -1 ZABRANSKY, F.
ALUMINUM FOIL SLITTING TRIM LOSS PROBLEM; FORMULATED AS A MIXED INTEGER PROBLEM; SOLVED BY HEURISTIC PROGRAMMING.

ZANAA 1977 -1 ZANAKIS, S.; LAWRENCE, K. D.
EFFECTIVE SHIFT ALLOCATION IN MULTIPRODUCT LINES: A MIXED INTEGER PROGRAMMING APPROACH.

ALI A 1980 -1 ALI, A. I.; HELGASON, R. V.; KENNINGTON, J. L.; LALL, H. S.
COMPUTATIONAL COMPARISON AMONG THREE MULTICOMMODITY NETWORK FLOW ALGORITHMS.
ANEJA 1979 -1 ANEJA, Y. P.; AGGARWAL, V.; NAIR, K. P. K.
MAXIMIZATION OF THE VECTOR-FLOW IN MULTICOMMODITY NETWORKS.
ANEJB 1979 -2 ANEJA, Y. P.; NAIR, K. P. K.
TWO PROBLEMS IN MULTICOMMODITY NETWORKS.
ASSA 1978 -1 ASSAD, A.
MULTICOMMODITY NETWORK FLOWS - A SURVEY.
BARTD 1979 -1 BARTON, R. R.; HEARN, D. W.
DECOMPOSITION TECHNIQUES FOR NONLINEAR COST MULTICOMMODITY FLOW PROBLEMS.
BAZA 1978 -1 BAZARAA, M. S.
INFEASIBILITY PRICING ALGORITHM FOR THE MULTICOMMODITY MINIMUM COST FLOW PROBLEM, AN.
BERTC 1979 -1 BERTSEKAS, D. P.
ALGORITHMS FOR NONLINEAR MULTICOMMODITY NETWORK FLOW PROBLEMS.
BERTE 1979 -1 BERTSEKAS, D. P.; GAFNI, E. M.; VASTOLA, K. S.
VALIDATION OF ALGORITHMS FOR OPTIMAL ROUTING OF FLOW IN NETWORKS.
BOYE 1968 -1 BOYER, D. D.; HUNT, D. J.
MODIFIED SIMPLEX ALGORITHM FOR SOLVING THE MULTICOMMODITY FLOW PROBLEM, A.
CHAR 1961 -1 CHARNES, A.; COOPER, W. W.
MULTICOPY TRAFFIC NETWORK MODELS.
CHU 1974 -1 CHU, Y. C.; TIEN, F.; MA, Z. F.; CAI, M. C.
ON THE CHARACTERIZATION OF AN EXTREME FLOW IN A TWO-COMMODITY NETWORK FLOW PROBLEM.
DEMM 1969 -1 DEMMY, W. S.
MULTI-COMMODITY FLOWS IN GENERALIZED NETWORKS.
EISE 1978 -1 EISELT, H.
INHOMOGENE FLUSSPROBLEME: DAS MIN-MAX THEOREM.
EVAN 1975 -1 EVANS, J. R.
THEORETICAL AND COMPUTATIONAL ASPECTS OF INTEGER MULTICOMMODITY NETWORK FLOW PROBLEMS.
EVAN 1980 -1 EVANS, J. R.
REDUCING COMPUTATIONAL EFFORT IN DETECTING INTEGRAL MULTICOMMODITY NETWORKS.
EVAN 1978 -2 EVANS, J. R.
ON EQUIVALENT REPRESENTATIONS OF CERTAIN MULTICOMMODITY NETWORKS AS SINGLE COMMODITY FLOW PROBLEMS.
EVAN 1978 -3 EVANS, J. R.
SIMPLEX METHOD FOR INTEGRAL MULTICOMMODITY NETWORKS, THE.
EVAN 1978 -4 EVANS, J. R.
SINGLE-COMMODITY TRANSFORMATION FOR CERTAIN MULTICOMMODITY NETWORKS, A.
EVAN 1978 -5 EVANS, J. R.
SOLVING MULTICOMMODITY TRANSPORTATION PROBLEMS THROUGH AGGREGATION.
EVANA 1978 -1 EVANS, J. R.; JARVIS, J. J.
NETWORK TOPOLOGY AND INTEGRAL MULTICOMMODITY FLOW PROBLEMS.
EVANC 1978 -1 EVANS, J. R.; MARTIN, K.
NOTE ON FEASIBLE FLOWS IN LOWER-BOUNDED MULTICOMMODITY NETWORKS, A.
FERLA 1978 -1 FERLAND, J. A.; GIRARD, A.; LAFOND, L.
MULTICOMMODITY FLOW PROBLEM WITH VARIABLE ARCS CAPACITIES.
FLOR 1975 -1 FLORIAN, M.
TRAFFIC EQUILIBRIUM MODEL OF TRAVEL BY CAR AND PUBLIC TRANSIT MODES, A.
FRANB 1982 -1 FRANK, A.
DISJOINT PATHS IN A RECTILINEAR GRID.
GALL 1977 -1 GALLAGHER, R. G.
LOOPS IN MULTICOMMODITY FLOWS.
GALLF 1979 -2 GALLO, G.; SODINI, C.
CONCAVE COST MINIMIZATION ON NETWORKS.
GLOVE 1979 -2 GLOVER, F.; KLINGMAN, D.
SIMPLEX SON ALGORITHM FOR LP-EMBEDDED NETWORK PROBLEMS (REVISED VERSION), THE.
GRAT 1972 -1 GRATZER, F. J.; STEIGLITZ, K.
HEURISTIC APPROACH TO LARGE MULTICOMMODITY FLOW PROBLEMS, A.
GRIGE 1978 -1 GRIGORIADIS, M. D.
ALGORITHMS FOR THE MINIMUM COST SINGLE AND MULTICOMMODITY NETWORK FLOW PROBLEMS.
HAKI 1962 -1 HAKIMI, S. L.
SIMULTANEOUS FLOWS THROUGH A COMMUNICATION NETWORK.
ISHIC 1979 -1 ISHIYAMA, Y.; ISHIZAKI, Y.; SASABE, S.; YOSHIDA, N.
MULTI-COMMODITY FLOW APPROACH TO ASSIGNMENT OF CIRCUITS IN CASE OF FAILURE IN A COMMUNICATION NETWORK.
ITAI 1978 -1 ITAI, A.
TWO-COMMODITY FLOW.
JARV 1977 -1 JARVIS, J. J.; MARTINEZ, O. M.
SENSITIVITY ANALYSIS OF MULTICOMMODITY NETWORK FLOWS, A.
KARK 1981 -1 KARKAZIS, J.; BOFFEY, T. B.
SUBGRADIENT-BASED OPTIMAL SOLUTION METHOD FOR THE MULTICOMMODITY PROBLEM, A.
KASA 1978 -1 KASAI, T.; KURODA, K.
GRAPH THEORETICAL CONSIDERATION ON INTERFERENCE BETWEEN SIMULTANEOUS TWO-COMMODITY FLOWS IN A DIRECTED NETWORK.
KENN 1978 -1 KENNINGTON, J. L.
SURVEY OF LINEAR COST MULTICOMMODITY NETWORK FLOWS, A.
KENNA 1976 -1 KENNINGTON, J. L.; SHALABY, M.
EFFECTIVE SUBGRADIENT PROCEDURE FOR MINIMAL COST MULTICOMMODITY FLOW PROBLEMS, AN.
KLEIF 1972 -1 KLEITMAN, D. J.; CLAUS, A.
LARGE SCALE MULTICOMMODITY FLOW PROBLEM: TELPAK, A.
KUHN 1977 -1 KUHN, H. W.
PATHFIX: AN ALGORITHM FOR COMPUTING TRAFFIC EQUILIBRIA.
LEBLA 1976 -1 LEBLANC, L. J.; MORLOK, E. K.
ANALYSIS AND COMPARISON OF BEHAVIORAL ASSUMPTIONS IN TRAFFIC ASSIGNMENT, AN.
MAIEA 1969 -1 MAIER, S.
MULTI-ITEM NETWORK FLOW MODEL WITH CAPACITY CONSTRAINTS, A.
MAIEA 1975 -1 MAIER, S.
SOLVING THE TRAFFIC ASSIGNMENT AND SUB-AREA FOCUSING PROBLEMS BY GEOGRAPHIC DECOMPOSITION.
MAND 1978 -1 MANDL, C. E.
ALGORITHMS AND COMPUTER PROGRAMS IN DETERMINISTIC NETWORK OPTIMIZATION APPLIED TO PUBLIC SYSTEMS.
MATS 1977 -2 MATSUI, K.
SUFFICIENT CONDITION FOR SYNTHESIS OF DIRECTED NETWORKS WITH TWO-COMMODITY FLOWS, A.
MOLI 1979 -1 MOLISZ, W.
OPTIMIZATION OF MULTICOMMODITY FLOWS IN A COMPUTER NETWORK (POLISH).
MUSA 1980 -1 MUSALEM, J. S.
CONVERTING LINEAR MODELS TO NETWORK MODELS.

MULTICOMMODITY FLOW PROBLEMS

NAKA 1977 -1 NAKAHORI, I.; NAKAZAKI, K.; NISHIKAWA, Y.
GRAPH-THEORETIC CONSIDERATION AND ALGORITHMS FOR A MULTICOMMODITY FLOW ASSIGNMENT PROBLEM, A.

NANI 1969 -1 NANIWADA, M.
MULTICOMMODITY FLOWS IN A COMMUNICATION NETWORK.

NGUYB 1976 -1 NGUYEN, S.
UNIFIED APPROACH TO EQUILIBRIUM METHODS FOR TRAFFIC ASSIGNMENTS, A.

PAPEC 1976 -1 PAPERNOV, B. A.
FEASIBILITY OF MULTICOMMODITY FLOWS (RUSSIAN).

PINO 1976 -1 PINOCHET, M. R.
CENTRALIZATION AND DECENTRALIZATION OF DECISION-MAKING IN TRANSPORTATION NETWORKS.

RAMAB 1980 -1 RAMAKRISHNAN, K. G.
SOLVING TWO-COMMODITY TRANSPORTATION PROBLEMS WITH COUPLING CONSTRAINTS.

RARDA 1979 -1 RARDIN, R. L.; CHOE, U.
TIGHTER RELAXATIONS OF FIXED CHARGE NETWORK FLOW PROBLEMS.

ROBA 1956 -1 ROBACKER, J. T.
NOTES ON LINEAR PROGRAMMING: PART XXXVII CONCERNING MULTICOMMODITY NETWORKS.

ROTHA 1970 -1 ROTHFARB, B.; FRISCH, I. T.
COMMON TERMINAL MULTICOMMODITY FLOW WITH A CONCAVE COST FUNCTION.

ROTHB 1969 -1 ROTHSCHILD, B.; WHINSTON, A.
MULTICOMMODITY NETWORK FLOWS.

SAHNB 1975 -1 SAHNI, S.; GONZALEZ, T.
P-COMPLETE APPROXIMATION PROBLEMS.

SASA 1976 -1 SASAKI, M.; SAKAKIBARA, T.; MATSUI, K.
NEW CONDITION OF THE FEASIBILITY OF TWO-COMMODITY FLOWS IN A COMMUNICATION NETWORK, A.

SEN 1972 -1 SEN, S.
MULTICOMMODITY CONCAVE COST MINIMIZATION PROBLEM FOR COMMUNICATION NETWORKS, A.

SEYM 1978 -2 SEYMOUR, P. D.
TWO-COMMODITY CUT THEOREM, A.

SEYM 1979 -3 SEYMOUR, P. D.
ON ODD CUTS AND PLANE MULTICOMMODITY FLOWS.

SEYM 1980 -3 SEYMOUR, P. D.
FOUR-TERMINUS FLOWS.

SOUN 1980 -1 SOUN, Y.; TRUEMPER, K.
SINGLE COMMODITY REPRESENTATION OF MULTICOMMODITY NETWORKS.

TANG 1964 -1 TANG, D. T.
BIPATH NETWORKS AND MULTICOMMODITY FLOWS.

TANG 1965 -1 TANG, D. T.
COMMENTS ON FEASIBILITY CONDITIONS OF SIMULTANEOUS FLOWS IN A NETWORK.

TINDB 1972 -1 TINDALL, J. B.
MINIMAL DISCONNECTING SETS IN DIRECTED MULTI-COMMODITY NETWORKS.

TOML 1967 -1 TOMLIN, J. A.
MATHEMATICAL PROGRAMMING MODELS FOR TRAFFIC NETWORK PROBLEMS.

TRUEA 1979 -1 TRUEMPER, K.; SOUN, Y.
MINIMAL FORBIDDEN SUBGRAPHS OF UNIMODULAR MULTICOMMODITY NETWORKS.

WARD 1952 -1 WARDROP, J. G.
SOME THEORETICAL ASPECTS OF ROAD TRAFFIC RESEARCH.

WHITE 1972 -1 WHITE, W. W.
MATHEMATICAL PROGRAMMING, MULTICOMMODITY FLOWS, AND COMMUNICATION NETS.

WOLL 1969 -1 WOLLMER, R. D.
DANTZIG-WOLFE DECOMPOSITION PRINCIPLE AND MINIMUM COST MULTICOMMODITY NETWORK FLOWS, THE.

WOLL 1980 -1 WOLLMER, R. D.
INVESTMENT IN STOCHASTIC MINIMUM COST GENERALIZED MULTICOMMODITY NETWORKS WITH APPLICATION TO COAL TRANSPORT.

YATS 1972 -1 YATSUBOSHI, R.; HIRAYAMA, H.
ALGORITHM FOR FINDING FEASIBILITY CONDITIONS OF MULTICOMMODITY FLOWS IN A NETWORK, AN.

ABDUA 1977 -1 ABDULAAL, M.; LEBLANC, L. J.
MULTIMODAL NETWORK EQUILIBRIUM.
ABDUA 1979 -1 ABDULAAL, M.; LEBLANC, L. J.
CONTINUOUS EQUILIBRIUM NETWORK DESIGN MODELS.
ABEL 1979 -1 ABEL, U.; CARSTENS, H. G.; DEUBER, W.; PROEMEL, H. J.
ON HYPERGRAPHIC NETWORKS.
AKUL 1978 -1 AKULIC, F. E.
NET DECOMPOSITION ALGORITHM FOR THE SOLUTION OF THE MAXIMUM FLOW PROBLEM (RUSSIAN), A.
ALI 1978 -1 ALI, A. I.; HELGASON, R. V.; KENNINGTON, J. L.
CONVEX COST NETWORK FLOW PROBLEM: A SURVEY OF ALGORITHMS, THE.
ALI A 1978 -1 ALI, A. I.; HELGASON, R. V.; KENNINGTON, J. L.; LALL, H. S.
PRIMAL SIMPLEX NETWORK CODES: STATE-OF-THE-ART IMPLEMENTATION TECHNOLOGY.
ALTR 1979 -1 ALTROGGE, G.
BEDINGUNGEN EINER ALLGEMEINEN NETZPLANSTRUKTUR.
AMMO 1979 -1 AMMON, P.; PEEMOELLER, W.
LOESUNG GEMISCHT-GANZZAHLIGER PROBLEME MIT NETZWERKSTRUKTUR.
ANDRA 1978 -1 ANDREATTA, G.; BENEDETTI, M. A.; MASON, F.
TRANSPORT LINES WITH NONCONSERVATIVE FLOW (ITALIAN).
ANEJB 1980 -1 ANEJA, Y. P.; NAIR, K. P. K.
MAXIMAL EXPECTED FLOW IN A NETWORK SUBJECT TO ARC FAILURES.
ANZA 1977 -1 ANZAI, Y.
URBAN ROAD NETWORK MODELING PROBLEM - FORMULATION AND ALGORITHMS.
ARROA 1977 -1 ARROWSMITH, D. K.; ESSAM, J. W.
PERCOLATION THEORY ON DIRECTED GRAPHS.
ARTZ 1979 -1 ARTZNER, P.; RADO, R.
THEOREM ON FLOW IN DIRECTED GRAPHS, A.
AVON 1979 -1 AVONDO-BODINO, G.
GRAPH THEORY AND OPERATIONS RESEARCH.
AVRA 1977 -1 AVRAMESCO, A.
QUELQUES ABOUTISSEMENTS EN THEORIE DES RESEAUX.
BAKO 1975 -1 BAKO, A.
SUB-CRITICAL PATHS IN ACTIVITY NETWORK (HUNGARIAN).
BALAK 1977 -1 BALAS, E.; ZEMEL, E.
CRITICAL CUTSETS OF GRAPHS AND CANONICAL FACETS OF SET-PACKING POLYTOPES.
BALL 1980 -1 BALL, M. O.
COMPLEXITY OF NETWORK RELIABILITY COMPUTATIONS.
BALLA 1979 -1 BALL, M. O.; BODIN, L. D.; GOLDEN, B. L.; ASSAD, A.; STATHES, C.
TRUCK FLEET ACQUISITION/ROUTING PROBLEM, A.
BARRA 1977 -1 BARR, R. S.; GLOVER, F.; KLINGMAN, D.
ALTERNATING BASIS ALGORITHM FOR ASSIGNMENT PROBLEMS, THE.
BARRA 1979 -1 BARR, R. S.; GLOVER, F.; KLINGMAN, D.
ENHANCEMENTS OF SPANNING TREE LABELING PROCEDURES FOR NETWORK OPTIMIZATION.
BARRA 1978 -2 BARR, R. S.; GLOVER, F.; KLINGMAN, D.
NEW ALTERNATING BASIS ALGORITHM FOR SEMI-ASSIGNMENT NETWORKS, A.
BARTB 1978 -1 BARTHOLDI, J. J. III; RATLIFF, H. D.
UNNETWORKS WITH APPLICATIONS TO IDLE TIME SCHEDULING.
BAZAB 1977 -1 BAZARAA, M. S.; JARVIS, J. J.
LINEAR PROGRAMMING AND NETWORK FLOWS.
BELE 1979 -1 BELENOVA, N. K.
FLOW PROBLEM IN A CAPACITATED NETWORK.
BERS 1973 -1 BERSHCHANSKII, JA. M.
METHOD FOR THE MINIMIZATION OF THE RESOURCE LEVEL IN A PROBLEM OF NETWORK PLANNING (RUSSIAN), A.
BERTD 1980 -1 BERTSEKAS, D. P.; GAFNI, E. M.
PROJECTION METHODS FOR VARIATIONAL INEQUALITIES WITH APPLICATION TO THE TRAFFIC ASSIGNMENT PROBLEM.
BIGA 1978 -1 BIGALKE, A.
KOMBINATORISCHER BEWEIS DES SATZES VON R. L. FORD UND D. R. FULKERSON, EIN.
BILL 1978 -1 BILLIONNET, A.
MODELE ADAPTANT LES POLITIQUES DE PERSONNEL AUX BESOINS PREVISIONNELS.
BILLA 1977 -1 BILLSTEIN, N.; RADERMACHER, F. J.
TIME-COST OPTIMIZATION.
BIXBA 1980 -1 BIXBY, R. E.; CUNNINGHAM, W. H.
CONVERTING LINEAR PROGRAMS TO NETWORK PROBLEMS.
BLAZ 1981 -1 BLAZEWICZ, J.
SOLVING THE RESOURCE CONSTRAINED DEADLINE SCHEDULING PROBLEM VIA REDUCTION TO THE NETWORK FLOW PROBLEM.
BOFFA 1979 -1 BOFFEY, T. B.; HINXMAN, A. I.
SOLVING THE OPTIMAL NETWORK PROBLEM.
BOOKA 1980 -1 BOOKBINDER, J. H.; SETHI, S. P.
DYNAMIC TRANSPORTATION PROBLEM: A SURVEY, THE.
BOYCA 1979 -1 BOYCE, D. E.; SOBERANES, J. L.
SOLUTIONS TO THE OPTIMAL NETWORK DESIGN PROBLEM WITH SHIPMENTS RELATED TO TRANSPORTATION COST.
BOZY 1979 -1 BOZYIGIT, M.; PAKER, Y.
FIXED ROUTING PROBLEM IN LARGE AND HIGH CONNECTIVITY NETWORKS, A.
BRAD 1975 -1 BRADLEY, G. H.; BROWN, G. G.; GRAVES, G.
COMPARISON OF STORAGE STRUCTURE FOR PRIMAL NETWORK CODES, A.
BRAE 1979 -1 BRAESS, D.; KOCH, G.
ON THE EXISTENCE OF EQUILIBRIA IN ASYMMETRICAL MULTICLASS-USER TRANSPORTATION NETWORKS.
BRES 1980 -1 BRESKO, D.; CAREY, M.; HENDRICKSON, C.; OPPENHEIM, I.
BOUNDS ON EXPECTED NETWORKS PERFORMANCE WITH UNRELIABLE LINKS.
BRON 1979 -1 BRONSTEIN, M. L.; KIM, K. V.
ELIMINATION ON THE POSSIBILITY OF CYCLING IN THE PRIMAL NETWORK METHOD (RUSSIAN).
BROWB 1979 -3 BROWN, J. R.
SHARING PROBLEM, THE.
BRUC 1973 -1 BRUCKER, P.
ERSTELLUNG VON CPM-NETZPLAENEN, DIE.
BUCKA 1974 -1 BUCKLEY, D. J.
TRANSPORTATION AND TRAFFIC THEORY.
BUCKA 1979 -1 BUCKLEY, D. J.
TRAFFIC ASSIGNMENT IN A TWO-DIMENSIONAL CONTINUOUS REPRESENTATION OF A TRAFFIC NETWORK WITH FLOW-DEPENDENT SPEEDS.
BUHR 1978 -1 BUHR, J.
FOUR METHODS FOR MONTHLY CREW ASSIGNMENT - A COMPARISON OF EFFICIENCY -.

BURJ 1977 -1 BURJAN, S. B.; SEROV, S. S.; UZDEMIR, A. P.
METHOD FOR SOLVING THE PARAMETRIC PROBLEM OF FINDING CIRCULATION OF MINIMAL COST IN A NETWORK.
BUTA 1975 -1 BUTAN, E. I.; NECVAL, N. A.
ALGORITHMS FOR THE OPERATIONAL CONTROL OF ARRIVAL FLOWS IN A TRANSPORTATION NETWORK (RUSSIAN).
CARN 1978 -1 CARNEIRO RIBEIRO, C. DA C.; MACULAN, N.
NETWORK EXPANSION PROBLEM, A.
CARR 1979 -1 CARRE, B.
GRAPHS AND NETWORKS.
CHAC 1979 -1 CHACHRA, V.; GHARE, P. M.; MOORE, J. M.
APPLICATIONS OF GRAPH THEORY ALGORITHMS.
CHAM 1979 -1 CHAMBER, M. T.
MINIMAL CUTSETS FROM UNDIRECTED NETWORK DUALS.
CHANE 1981 -1 CHANDRASEKARAN, R.; ANEJA, Y. P.; NAIR, K. P. K.
MINIMAL COST-RELIABILITY RATIO SPANNING TREE.
CHAR 1961 -1 CHARNES, A.; COOPER, W. W.
MULTICOPY TRAFFIC NETWORK MODELS.
CHENB 1979 -1 CHEN, I.-N.; CHEN, P. Y.; FENG, T.
ASSOCIATIVE PROCESSING OF NETWORK FLOW PROBLEMS.
CHENC 1976 -1 CHEN, K.-Y.
NETWORK APPROACH TO THE CAPACITATED LOT-SIZE PROBLEM, A.
CHERA 1977 -1 CHERKASSKII, B. V.
O((N**2)*(P**0.5)) ALGORITHM FOR CONSTRUCTING THE MAXIMUM FLOW IN A NETWORK (RUSSIAN), AN.
CHERA 1977 -2 CHERKASSKII, B. V.
SOLUTION OF A PROBLEM OF MULTIPRODUCT FLOWS IN A NETWORK (RUSSIAN).
CHERC 1970 -1 CHERNYSHEV, JU. O.
REDUCTION OF CERTAIN OPTIMAL PROBLEMS OF DISCRETE AUTOMATA DIAGNOSTICS TO THE SOLUTION OF PROBLEMS OF FLOWS IN NETWORKS (RUSSIAN).
CHEU 1980 -1 CHEUNG, T.-Y.
COMPUTATIONAL COMPARISON OF EIGHT METHODS FOR THE MAXIMUM NETWORK FLOW PROBLEM.
CHIE 1964 -1 CHIEN, R. T.; GOMORY, R. E.; HU, T. C.
COMMUNICATION NETWORKS.
CHRID 1979 -1 CHRISTOFIDES, N.; HEWINS, R. D.; SALKIN, G. R.
GRAPH THEORETIC APPROACHES TO FOREIGN EXCHANGE OPERATIONS.
CHRIH 1978 -1 CHRISTOFIDES, N.; WHITLOCK, C.
GRAPH CONNECTIVITY AND VULNERABILITY. A SURVEY.
CIUR 1979 -1 CIUREA, E.
DEUX REMARQUES SUR LE FLOT DYNAMIQUE MAXIMAL DE COUT MINIMAL.
CIUR 1979 -2 CIUREA, E.
SUR LES FLOTS DYNAMIQUES.
CLAUA 1981 -1 CLAUS, A.; KRAETZIG, S.
OPTIMAL PLANNING OF NETWORK STRUCTURES WITHIN AN EXCHANGE AREA.
CLEE 1979 -1 CLEEF, H. J.; GAUL, W.
STOCHASTIC FLOW PROBLEM.
CLEE 1981 -1 CLEEF, H. J.; GAUL, W.
FLOWS IN GRAPHS AND STOCHASTIC PROGRAMMING.
CLIM 1981 -1 CLIMACO, J. C. N.; MARTINS, E. Q. V.
ON THE DETERMINATION OF THE NONDOMINATED PATHS IN A MULTIOBJECTIVE NETWORK PROBLEM.
COLLA 1978 -1 COLLINS, M.; COOPER, L.; HELGASON, R. V.; KENNINGTON, J. L.; LEBLANC, L. J.
SOLVING THE PIPE NETWORK ANALYSIS PROBLEM USING OPTIMIZATION TECHNIQUES.
CRAM 1979 -1 CRAMER, J.; POLLATSCHEK, M. A.
CANDIDATE TO JOB ALLOCATION PROBLEM WITH A LEXICOGRAPHIC OBJECTIVE.
CRUM 1979 -1 CRUM, R. L.; KLINGMAN, D.; TAVIS, L. A.
STRATEGIC MANAGEMENT OF MULTINATIONAL COMPANIES: NETWORK-BASED PLANNING SYSTEMS.
CUNN 1981 -1 CUNNINGHAM, W. H.
CLASS OF LINEAR PROGRAMS CONVERTIBLE TO NETWORK PROBLEMS, A.
CUNN 1982 -1 CUNNINGHAM, W. H.
DECOMPOSITION OF SUBMODULAR FUNCTIONS.
CUNN 1979 -2 CUNNINGHAM, W. H.
THEORETICAL PROPERTIES OF A NETWORK SIMPLEX METHOD.
CUNN 1981 -4 CUNNINGHAM, W. H.
TESTING MEMBERSHIP IN MATROID POLYHEDRA.
CUNNB 1981 -1 CUNNINGHAM, W. H.; KLINCEWICZ, J. G.
ON CYCLING IN THE NETWORK SIMPLEX METHOD.
DANT 1979 -1 DANTZIG, G. B.; HARVEY, R. P.; LANSDOWNE, Z. F.; ROBINSON, D. W.; MAIER, S. F.
FORMULATING AND SOLVING THE NETWORK DESIGN PROBLEM BY DECOMPOSITION.
DEBA 1979 -1 DEBANNE, J. G.
NETWORK BASED REGIONAL ENERGY PLANNING MODELS - AN EVOLUTIONARY EXPOSE.
DEJO 1978 -1 DEJON, B.
SPATIAL INTERACTION NETWORK FLOW MODELS.
DELF 1975 -1 DELFINO, W. C. D.
OPTIMAL DESIGN OF WATER DISTRIBUTION PIPELINE NETWORKS.
DEMBB 1978 -1 DEMBO, R. S.; KLINCEWICZ, J. G.
APPROXIMATE SECOND-ORDER ALGORITHM FOR NETWORK FLOW PROBLEMS WITH CONVEX SEPARABLE COSTS, AN.
DEMBB 1979 -1 DEMBO, R. S.; KLINCEWICZ, J. G.
SCALED REDUCED GRADIENT ALGORITHM FOR NETWORK FLOW PROBLEMS WITH CONVEX SEPARABLE COSTS, A (REVISED VERSION).
DENA 1977 -1 DENARDO, E. V.
PERIODS OF CONNECTED NETWORKS AND POWER OF NONNEGATIVE MATRICES.
DENAA 1979 -1 DENARDO, E. V.; FOX, B. L.
SHORTEST-ROUTE METHODS: 1. REACHING, PRUNING, AND BUCKETS.
DENAA 1980 -1 DENARDO, E. V.; FOX, B. L.
ENFORCING CONSTRAINTS ON EXPANDED NETWORKS.
DESSB 1975 -1 DESSOUKY, M. I.; LIEBMAN, J. S.; PHILLIPS, S. JR.; HOGG, G. L.
CUT-SEARCH TO THE MAXIMAL-FLOW MINIMAL-CUT PROBLEM.
DINE 1976 -1 DINESCU, C.
OPTIMAL ELEMENTARY PATHS IN NETWORKS WITH CIRCUITS.
DINEA 1978 -1 DINESCU, C.; SAVULESCU, B.
NEW RESULTS IN THE FLOW TRANSPORT PROBLEM.
DINEA 1979 -1 DINESCU, C.; SAVULESCU, B.
ABOUT THE DETERMINATION OF MAXIMUM FLOW IN A NETWORK.
DINIB 1978 -1 DINIC, E. A.; ZAICEV, M. A.
GENERATION OF MARKED TREES AND SEPARABLE NETWORKS (RUSSIAN).

DIONA 1979 -1 DIONNE, R.; FLORIAN, M.
EXACT AND APPROXIMATE ALGORITMS FOR OPTIMAL NETWORK DESIGN.
DODU 1975 -1 DODU, J. C.
MODELE D'OPTIMISATION A LONG TERME D'UN RESEAU DE TRANSPORT.
DODU 1978 -1 DODU, J. C.
MODELE DYNAMIQUE D'OPTIMISATION A LONG TERME D'UN RESEAU DE TRANSPORT D'ENERGIE ELECTRIQUE.
DOKU 1979 -1 DOKUCAEV, V. N.
ANALYSIS OF A NETWORK MODEL OF DELIVERY CONTROL (RUSSIAN).
DRAG 1976 -1 DRAGAN, I.
NETWORK FLOW MODEL FOR SOLVING A COOPERATIVE GAME, A.
EISE 1978 -1 EISELT, H.
INHOMOGENE FLUSSPROBLEME: DAS MIN-MAX THEOREM.
ELAM 1979 -1 ELAM, J.; GLOVER, F.; KLINGMAN, D.
STRONGLY CONVERGENT PRIMAL SIMPLEX ALGORITHM FOR GENERALIZED NETWORKS, A.
ELKE 1979 -1 ELKEN, T. R.; FREEDMAN, H. T.; GIBSON, A. E.
POLYNOMIAL BOUND ALGORITHM FOR A NONLINEAR NETWORK ALLOCATION PROBLEM,A.
ERUS 1980 -1 ERUSALIMSKY, YA. M.; SVETLOV, G. G.
BICOUPLING POINTS, BIBRIDGES AND BIUNITS OF FLOW GRAPHS (RUSSIAN).
EVEN 1976 -1 EVEN, S.
MAX FLOW ALGORITHM OF DINIC AND KARZANOV: AN EXPOSITION, THE.
EVEN 1979 -1 EVEN, S.
GRAPH ALGORITHMS.
EVST 1979 -1 EVSTIGNEEV, V. A.
LOCAL ALGORITHM FOR FINDING THE BICOMPONENTS IN A FLOW GRAPH, A.
FARA 1978 -2 FARADZEV, I. A.
GENERATION OF THREE-CONNECTED GRAPHS AND THE ENUMERATION OF INSEPARABLE NETWORKS (RUSSIAN), THE.
FIDR 1978 -1 FIDRMUC, M.
SIMSCRIPT II SIMULATION OF TRAFFIC NETWORK FLOW.
FIED 1979 -1 FIEDLER, M.
OPTIMIERUNG UND GRAPHENTHEORIE.
FLOR 1977 -1 FLORIAN, M.
IMPROVED LINEAR APPROXIMATION ALGORITHM FOR THE NETWORK EQUILIBRIUM (PACKET SWITCHING) PROBLEM, AN.
FRANB 1981 -1 FRANK, A.
FINDING FEASIBLE VECTORS OF EDMONDS-GILES POLYHEDRA.
FRANB 1981 -3 FRANK, A.
HOW TO MAKE A DIRECTED GRAPH STRONGLY CONNECTED.
FRANB 1980 -5 FRANK, A.
ON CHAIN AND ANTICHAIN FAMILIES OF A PARTIALLY ORDERED SET.
FRANC 1978 -1 FRANK, A.; GYARFAS, A.
DIRECTED GRAPHS AND COMPUTER PROGRAMS.
FREI 1979 -1 FREIDENFELDS, J.; MAC LAUGHLIN, C. D.
HEURISTIC BRANCH-AND-BOUND ALGORITHM FOR TELEPHONE FEEDER CAPACITY EXPANSION, A.
FRIEA 1980 -1 FRIESDORF, H.
FLUSSPROBLME MIT GEWICHTETEN KOSTEN.
FUJI 1978 -1 FUJISHIGE, S.
ALGORITHMS FOR SOLVING THE INDEPENDENT FLOW PROBLEMS.
FULK 1977 -1 FULKERSON, D. R.; HARDING, G. C.
MAXIMIZING THE MINIMUM SOURCE-SINK PATH SUBJECT TO A BUDGET CONSTRAINT.
GABA 1979 -1 GABASOV, R. F.; KOSTJUKOVA, O. I.
ON AN ALGORITHM FOR SOLVING A NETWORK DISTRIBUTOR PROBLEM.
GALI 1978 -1 GALIL, Z.
NEW ALGORITHM FOR THE MAXIMAL FLOW PROBLEM, A.
GALI 1978 -2 GALIL, Z.
ON THE THEORETICAL EFFICIENCY OF VARIOUS NETWORK FLOW ALGORITHMS.
GALI 1980 -2 GALIL, Z.
O(V**(5/3)E**(2/3)) ALGORITHM FOR THE MAXIMAL FLOW PROBLEM, AN.
GALIB 1979 -1 GALIL, Z.; NAAMAD, A.
NETWORK FLOW AND GENERALIZED PATH COMPRESSION.
GALIB 1980 -1 GALIL, Z.; NAAMAD, A.
O(EV(LOG V)**2) ALGORITHM FOR THE MAXIMAL FLOW PROBLEM, AN.
GALLD 1980 -1 GALLO, G.; SANDI, C.; SODINI, C.
ALGORITHM FOR THE MIN CONCAVE COST FLOW PROBLEM, AN.
GALLF 1979 -1 GALLO, G.; SODINI, C.
ADJACENT EXTREME FLOWS AND APPLICATION TO MIN CONCAVE COST FLOW PROBLEMS.
GALLF 1979 -3 GALLO, G.; SODINI, C.
EXTREME POINTS AND ADJACENCY RELATIONSHIP IN THE FLOW POLYTOPE.
GANS 1979 -1 GANSHIN, G. S.
OPTIMISATION D'ALGORITHMES DANS LES CLASSES DE RESEAUX (RUSSIAN).
GEND 1977 -1 GENDREAU, M.
ETUDE SUR LA GENERATION DES RESEAUX ALEATOIRES.
GERL 1978 -1 GERLOVIN, E. L.; SROGOVICH, E. B.
METHODS FOR SOLVING NONLINEAR NETWORK TRANSPORTATION PROBLEMS (RUSSIAN).
GHIU 1977 -1 GHIUS, V.
FLOWS IN ARBITRARILY TRACED, GENERALIZED GRAPHS (ROMANIAN).
GIK 1977 -1 GIK, E. JA.; LEVNER, E. V.
PROBLEM ON THE ANALYSIS OF CIRCULATIONS IN NETWORKS (RUSSIAN), A.
GIK A 1978 -1 GIK, Y. Y.; ZHORNITSKIY, A. B.
PROPERTIES OF CYCLIC EXTENSIONS OF FLOWS IN A NETWORK.
GILEC 1980 -1 GILES, R.; OYAMA, T.; TROTTER, L. E. JR.
RELATED NECESSARY CONDITIONS FOR COMPLETING PARTIAL LATIN SQUARES.
GLIN 1977 -1 GLINZ, M.; MOEHRING, R. H.
REDUCTION THEOREMS FOR NETWORKS WITH GENERAL SEQUENCING RELATIONS.
GLOVA 1977 -1 GLOVER, F.; HULTZ, J.; KLINGMAN, D.
NETWORK VERSUS LINEAR PROGRAMMING ALGORITHMS AND IMPLEMENTATIONS.
GLOVB 1978 -1 GLOVER, F.; HULTZ, J.; KLINGMAN, D.; STUTZ, J.
GENERALIZED NETWORKS: A FUNDAMENTAL COMPUTER-BASED PLANNING TOOL.
GLOVE 1977 -1 GLOVER, F.; KLINGMAN, D.
NETWORK APPLICATION IN INDUSTRY AND GOVERNMENT.
GLOVE 1980 -1 GLOVER, F.; KLINGMAN, D.
RECENT DEVELOPMENTS IN COMPUTER IMPLEMENTATION TECHNOLOGY FOR NETWORK FLOW ALGORITHMS.
GLOVE 1979 -2 GLOVER, F.; KLINGMAN, D.
SIMPLEX SON ALGORITHM FOR LP-EMBEDDED NETWORK PROBLEMS (REVISED VERSION), THE.
GLOVF 1979 -1 GLOVER, F.; KLINGMAN, D.; MOTE, J.; WHITMAN, D.
COMPREHENSIVE COMPUTER EVALUATION AND ENHANCEMENT OF MAXIMUM FLOW ALGORITHMS.

GLOVF 1980 -1 GLOVER, F.; KLINGMAN, D.; MOTE, J.; WHITMAN, D.
EXTENDED ABSTRACT OF AN INDEPTH ALGORITHMIC AND COMPUTATIONAL STUDY FOR MAXIMUM FLOW PROBLEMS, AN.

GLOVF 1979 -2 GLOVER, F.; KLINGMAN, D.; MOTE, J.; WHITMAN, D.
PRIMAL SIMPLEX VARIANT FOR THE MAXIMUM FLOW PROBLEM, A.

GLOVG 1978 -1 GLOVER, F.; MAC MILLAN, C.; KLINGMAN, D.
MODELING COMBINATORIAL MATHEMATICAL PROGRAMMING PROBLEMS BY NETFORMS: AN ILLUSTRATIVE APPLICATION.

GLOVH 1980 -1 GLOVER, F.; MULVEY, J. M.
EQUIVALENCE OF THE 0-1 INTEGER PROGRAMMING PROBLEM TO DISCRETE GENERALIZED AND PURE NETWORKS.

GOLDG 1977 -1 GOLDFARB, D.
STEEPEST EDGE SIMPLEX ALGORITHMS FOR NETWORK FLOW PROBLEMS.

GOND 1979 -2 GONDRAN, M.
OPTIMISATION COMBINATOIRE.

GOND 1980 -2 GONDRAN, M.
CLASSIFICATION HIERARCHIQUE ET FLOTS DANS UN GRAPHE.

GONDA 1979 -1 GONDRAN, M.; MINOUX, M.
GRAPHES ET ALGORITHMES.

GRABA 1979 -1 GRABOWSKI, J.; SKUBALSKA, E.
MAXIMAL FLOW PROBLEM IN A NETWORK WITH A VARIABLE STRUCTURE, THE.

GRABA 1981 -1 GRABOWSKI, J.; SKUBALSKA, E.
MAXIMAL FLOW PROBLEM IN A NETWORK WITH A VARIABLE STRUCTURE, THE.

GRAV 1977 -1 GRAVER, J. E.; WATKINS, M. E.
COMBINATORICS WITH EMPHASIS ON THE THEORY OF GRAPHS.

GRIGE 1978 -1 GRIGORIADIS, M. D.
ALGORITHMS FOR THE MINIMUM COST SINGLE AND MULTICOMMODITY NETWORK FLOW PROBLEMS.

GUAN 1979 -1 GUAN, M. G.
BRIEF SURVEY OF RESEARCH WORKS ON NETWORK THEORY BY CHINESE MATHEMATICIANS, A.

GUIGA 1979 -1 GUIGNARD, M.; SPIELBERG, K.
DIRECT DUAL APPROACH TO A TRANSSHIPMENT FORMULATION FOR MULTI-LAYER NETWORK PROBLEMS WITH FIXED CHARGES, A.

HACKA 1980 -1 HACKSTEIN, R.; KOCH, F.
VORTEILE EINER TERMINIERUNG VON NETZPLAENEN MITTELS MINIMALER VORGANGSDAUERN.

HADL 1979 -2 HADLOCK, F.
TREE SYSTEMS FOR NETWORK FLOW CONTROL AND ROUTING.

HAES 1979 -1 HAESSIG, K.
GRAPHENTHEORETISCHE METHODEN IN DER LOGISTIK.

HAESA 1978 -1 HAESSIG, K.; REISER, P.; STIERLIN, C.
NOTE ON PRIMAL NETWORK FLOW ALGORITHMS, A.

HAESB 1979 -1 HAESSIG, K.; SENN, W.
ENGPAESSE, STAUSTELLEN UND GLATTE HOMOGENE STROEME IN NETZEN - EINE ALTERNATIVE ZU STECKHAN'S KONZEPT.

HALP 1979 -1 HALPERN, J.
GENERALIZED DYNAMIC FLOWS PROBLEM, A.

HAMA 1979 -1 HAMACHER, H.
COMPUTATIONAL COMPARISON OF THE ALGORITHM OF KARZANOV AND THE LABELING ALGORITHM FOR THE SOLUTION OF MAXIMUM FLOW PROBLEMS, A.

HAMA 1980 -1 HAMACHER, H.
ALGEBRAIC FLOWS IN REGULAR MATROIDS.

HAMA 1981 -1 HAMACHER, H.
FLOWS IN REGULAR MATROIDS.

HAMA 1979 -2 HAMACHER, H.
NUMERICAL INVESTIGATIONS ON THE MAXIMAL FLOW ALGORITHM OF KARZANOV.

HAMA 1980 -2 HAMACHER, H.
ALGEBRAISCHE FLUSSPROBLEME IN REGULAEREN MATROIDEN.

HAMA 1981 -2 HAMACHER, H.
OPTIMAL (S,T)-CUTS.

HAMA 1980 -3 HAMACHER, H.
MAXIMAL ALGEBRAIC FLOWS: ALGORITHMS AND EXAMPLES.

HAMA 1980 -5 HAMACHER, H.
OPTIMAL CUTS.

HANN 1978 -1 HANNAN, E. L.
APPLICATION OF GOAL PROGRAMMING TECHNIQUES TO THE CPM PROBLEM, THE.

HAST 1978 -1 HASTINGS, N. A. J.; MELLO, J. M. C.
DECISION NETWORKS.

HELG 1976 -1 HELGASON, R. V.; KENNINGTON, J. L.
NETFLO PROGRAM DOCUMENTATION.

HELG 1978 -1 HELGASON, R. V.; KENNINGTON, J. L.
EFFICIENT SPECIALIZATION OF THE CONVEX SIMPLEX METHOD FOR NONLINEAR NETWORK FLOW PROBLEMS, AN.

HIND 1979 -1 HINDELANG, T. J.; MUTH, J. F.
DYNAMIC PROGRAMMING ALGORITHM FOR DECISION CPM NETWORKS, A.

HIRA 1979 -1 HIRATA, T.; MAROUOKA, A.; KIMURA, M.
POLYNOMIAL TIME ALGORITHM TO FIND A PATH COVER OF A REDUCIBLE FLOW GRAPH (JAPANESE), A.

HOAN 1979 -1 HOANG HAI HOC
NETWORK IMPROVEMENTS VIA MATHEMATICAL PROGRAMMING.

HORS 1980 -1 HORST, R.
MAXIMALE FLUESSE IN NETZWERKEN MIT KANTENGEWINNEN: VERGLEICH DREIER ALGORITHMEN.

HOUCA 1979 -1 HOUCK, D. J.; PITTENGER, A. O.
ANALYTIC PROOFS OF A NETWORK FEASIBILITY THEOREM AND A THEOREM OF FULKERSON.

HU A 1980 -1 HU, T. C.; RUSKEY, F.
CIRCULAR CUTS IN A NETWORK.

HULT 1978 -1 HULTZ, J.; KLINGMAN, D.
SOLVING SINGULARLY CONSTRAINED GENERALIZED NETWORK PROBLEMS.

ICHI 1979 -1 ICHIMORI, T.; ISHII, H.; NISHIDA, T.
MINIMAX FLOW PROBLEM, A.

ICHI 1980 -1 ICHIMORI, T.; ISHII, H.; NISHIDA, T.
FINDING THE WEIGHTED MINIMAX FLOW IN A POLYNOMIAL TIME.

ICHI 1981 -1 ICHIMORI, T.; ISHII, H.; NISHIDA, T.
WEIGHTED MINIMAX REAL-VALUED FLOWS.

ICHI 1980 -2 ICHIMORI, T.; ISHII, H.; NISHIDA, T.
FLOW IN A NETWORK WITH A CHECK NODE.

IGEL 1979 -1 IGELMUND, G.; RADERMACHER, F. J.
PRESELECTIVE STRATEGIES FOR THE OPTIMIZATION OF STOCHASTIC PROJECT NETWORKS UNDER RESOURCE CONSTRAINTS (ABSTRACT).

INFAA 1979 -1 INFANTE MACIAS, R.; VARGAS GONZALEZ, L.
ESTIMATES OF THE RESOURCE REQUIREMENTS IN NETWORK OPTIMIZATION PROBLEMS.
IRI 1978 -1 IRI, M.
PRACTICAL ALGORITHM FOR THE MENGER-TYPE GENERALIZATION OF THE INDEPENDENT ASSIGNMENT PROBLEM, A.
IRI 1979 -2 IRI, M.
THEORY OF FLOWS IN CONTINUA AS APPROXIMATION TO FLOWS IN NETWORKS.
IRI B 1979 -1 IRI, M.; RECSKI, A.
REFLECTION ON THE CONCEPTS OF DUAL, INVERSE AND ADJOINT NETWORKS.
IRI B 1980 -1 IRI, M.; RECSKI, A.
REFLECTION ON THE CONCEPTS OF DUAL, INVERSE AND ADJOINT NETWORKS, II: TOWARDS A QUALITATIVE THEORY.
ITAI 1978 -1 ITAI, A.
TWO-COMMODITY FLOW.
ITAIB 1978 -1 ITAI, A.; RODEH, M.; TANIMOTO, S. L.
SOME MATCHING PROBLEMS FOR BIPARTITE GRAPHS.
ITAIC 1979 -1 ITAI, A.; SHILOACH, Y.
MAXIMUM FLOW IN PLANAR NETWORKS.
JACO 1979 -1 JACOBS, K.
CONTINUOUS MAX-FLOW PROBLEM, A.
JAEG 1978 -1 JAEGER, F.
ON INTERVAL HYPERGRAPHS AND NOWHERE-ZERO FLOWS IN GRAPHS.
JAEG 1979 -1 JAEGER, F.
FLOWS AND GENERALIZED COLORING THEOREMS IN GRAPHS.
JARVA 1978 -1 JARVIS, J. J.; RARDIN, R. L.; UNGER, V. E.; MOORE, R. W.; SCHIMPELER, C. C.
OPTIMAL DESIGN OF REGIONAL WASTEWATER SYSTEMS: A FIXED-CHARGE NETWORK FLOW MODEL.
JARVB 1978 -2 JARVIS, J. J.; TUFEKCI, S.
DECOMPOSITION ALGORITHM FOR LOCATING MINIMAL CUTS IN A DIRECTED NETWORK, A.
JENS 1980 -1 JENSEN, P. A.; BARNES, J. W.
NETWORK FLOW PROGRAMMING.
JOHNB 1978 -1 JOHNSON, D. S.; LENSTRA, J. K.; RINNOOY KAN, A. H. G.
COMPLEXITY OF THE NETWORK DESIGN PROBLEM, THE.
JOHND 1965 -1 JOHNSON, E. L.
PROGRAMMING IN NETWORKS AND GRAPHS.
KAEM 1979 -1 KAEMPFE, H.
RATIONELLE LOESUNG DES GOZINTOPROBLEMS IM KREISFREIEN BEWERTETEN GERICHTETEN GRAPHEN UND WEITERE OEKONOMISCHE INTERPRETATIONEN, EINE.
KAER 1977 -1 KAERKES, R.
NETZPLAN THEORY.
KAER 1979 -1 KAERKES, R.
OPTIMIZATION OF (STOCHASTIC) NETWORKS UNDER RESOURCE CONSTRAINTS (ABSTRACT).
KAERA 1977 -1 KAERKES, R.; LEIPHOLZ, B.
GENERALIZED NETWORK FUNCTIONS IN FLOW NETWORKS.
KAERB 1977 -1 KAERKES, R.; RADERMACHER, F. J.
PROFILES, NETWORK FUNCTIONS AND FACTORIZATION.
KAMEA 1973 -1 KAMENAROV, S.
CERTAIN OPTIMIZATION METHODS FOR FLOWS IN NETWORKS (BULGARIAN).
KARN 1978 -1 KARNEY, D.; KLINGMAN, D.
NETGEN REVISITED: A PROGRAM FOR GENERATING LARGE SCALE (UN) CAPACITATED ASSIGNMENT, TRANPORTATION, AND MINIMUM COST FLOW NETWORK PROBLEMS.
KAS 1977 -1 KAS, P.
ON PROBLEMS OF PREEMPTIVE SCHEDULING INTERPRETED BY NETWORK FLOW PROBLEMS (HUNGARIAN).
KATSA 1979 -1 KATSNEL'SON, M. B.; KHRANOVICH, I. L.
TRANSPORT PROBLEM ON A NETWORK WITH AMPLIFICATION IN THE ARCS. I. THE SOLUTION METHOD.
KIME 1979 -1 KIMEMIA, J.; GERSHWIN, S. B.
NETWORK FLOW OPTIMIZATION IN FLEXIBLE MANUFACTURING SYSTEMS.
KLIN 1979 -2 KLINGMAN, D.; MOTE, J.
SOLUTION APPROACHES FOR NETWORK FLOW PROBLEMS WITH MULTIPLE CRITERIA.
KNOE 1980 -1 KNOEDEL, W.
O(N**3) ALGORITHM FOR THE DECOMPOSITION OF A DIGRAPH, AN.
KOEH 1979 -1 KOEHLER, A. B.; MAC CLURE, R. H.
USE OF ARCS AND NODES FOR THE DETERMINATION OF CRITICAL PATHS IN PERT/CPM NETWORKS, THE.
KOEN 1981 -1 KOENE, J.
MAXIMAL FLOW THROUGH A PROCESSING NETWORK WITH THE SOURCE AS THE ONLY PROCESSING NODE.
KORC 1977 -1 KORCHEMKIN, M. B.
DECOMPOSITION OF NETWORK PROBLEMS BY THE METHOD OF SEPARATING AND GROUPING SIMPLE CIRCUITS (RUSSIAN).
KORNB 1977 -3 KORNILOVA, L. E.; NGUYEN VAN VI
TWO NONSTATIONARY NETWORK PROBLEMS (RUSSIAN).
KORZ 1978 -1 KORZAN, B.
ELEMENTS OF THE THEORY OF GRAPHS AND NETWORKS. METHODS AND APPLICATIONS (POLISH).
KOST 1979 -1 KOSTJUKOVA, O. I.
DUAL SUPPORT METHOD FOR SOLVING A MINIMAL COST FLOW PROBLEM ON A GENERALIZED NETWORK.
KOUB 1981 -1 KOUBEK, V.; RIHA, A.
MAXIMUM K-FLOW IN A NETWORK, THE.
KOVAA 1978 -1 KOVALEV, M. M.; GIRLICH, E.
EXACT NUMBER OF VERTICES OF POLYHEDRA IN THE CONDITIONS OF THE STANDARDIZATION PROBLEM (RUSSIAN), THE.
KOVAB 1979 -1 KOVALEV, M. M.; ISACHENKO, A. N.
SEMIMATROIDE.
KRISA 1979 -1 KRISHNAMOORTHY, M. S.; DEO, N.
COMPLEXITY OF THE MINIMUM-DUMMY-ACTIVITIES PROBLEM IN A PERT NETWORK.
KRISB 1979 -1 KRISHNAMOORTHY, M. S.; SAKSENA, J. P.
ALGEBRA OF PROJECT NETWORKS.
KUBOA 1977 -1 KUBO, N.; TSUKIYAMA, S.; SHIRAKAWA, I.; ARIYOSHI, H.
ALGORITHM FOR FINDING A MAXIMAL CUT, AN.
KUCE 1981 -1 KUCERA, L.
MAXIMUM FLOW IN PLANAR NETWORKS.
KUMA 1979 -1 KUMAR, S.
MAXIMUM RELIABILITY ROUTE SUBJECT TO M IMPROVEMENTS IN A NONDIRECTED NETWORK.
LARS 1980 -1 LARSON, R. C.; LI, V. O. K.
FINDING MINIMUM RECTILINEAR DISTANCE PATHS IN THE PRESENCE OF BARRIERS.
LAWL 1980 -1 LAWLER, E. L.
INTRODUCTION TO POLYMATROIDAL NETWORK FLOWS, AN.
LAWL 1979 -4 LAWLER, E. L.
SHORTEST PATH AND NETWORK FLOW ALGORITHMS.

LAWLC 1980 -1 LAWLER, E. L.; MARTEL, C. U.
COMPUTING MAXIMAL "POLYMATROIDAL" NETWORK FLOWS.
LEBL 1979 -2 LEBLANC, L. J.; ABOULAAL, M.
OPTIMIZATION METHODS FOR DESIGN OF MULTIMODEL NETWORKS.
LEHM 1979 -1 LEHMAN, A.
ON THE WIDTH-LENGTH INEQUALITY.
LEVIA 1975 -1 LEVIN, M. I.
NETWORKS WITH A COMPLEX TECHNOLOGICAL CHARACTERISTICS (RUSSIAN).
LEVIB 1980 -1 LEVIN, M. S.
ON EFFICIENT SOLUTION OF SOME PROBLEMS OF THE NETWORK SCHEDULE THEORY (RUSSIAN).
LEVIE 1977 -1 LEVITIN, E. S.; HRANOVIC, I. L.
ESTIMATE OF THE INFLUENCE OF ERRORS IN THE ORIGINAL DATA ON THE ACCURACY OF THE SOLUTION OF THE PROBLEM OF THE OPTIMAL DISTRIBUTION OF FLOWS ON A NETWORK (RUSSIAN), AN.
LEVN 1976 -1 LEVNER, E. V.
PARAMETRIC MODEL OF NETWORK PLANNING (RUSSIAN), A.
LIVS 1968 -1 LIVSHIC, E. M.
ANALYSIS OF ALGORITHMS FOR NETWORK MODEL OPTIMIZATION (RUSSIAN).
LIVS 1969 -1 LIVSHIC, E. M.
PERFORMANCE BOUNDS FOR APPROXIMATE SOLUTIONS OF OPTIMIZATION NETWORK PROBLEMS (RUSSIAN).
LOMO 1978 -1 LOMONOSOV, M. V.
ON THE SYSTEM OF FLOWS IN A NETWORK.
LOS 1979 -1 LOS, M.
DISCRETE-CONVEX PROGRAMMING APPROACH TO THE SIMULTANEOUS OPTIMIZATION OF LAND USE AND TRANSPORTATION, A.
LOVEB 1978 -1 LOVE, R. R. JR; VEMUGANTI, R. R.
SINGLE-PLANT MOLD ALLOCATION PROBLEM WITH CAPACITY AND CHANGEOVER RESTRICTIONS, THE.
LOWE 1978 -1 LOWE, T. J.
EFFICIENT SOLUTIONS IN MULTIOBJECTIVE TREE NETWORK LOCATION PROBLEMS.
LOWEA 1979 -1 LOWE, T. J.; FRANCIS, R. L.; REINHARDT, E. W.
GREEDY NETWORK FLOW ALGORITHM FOR A WAREHOUSE LEASING PROBLEM, A.
LOZOA 1980 -1 LOZOVANU, D. D.; ZAMBICKII, D. K.
PROBLEM OF OPTIMAL PLACEMENT OF A NETWORK SOURCE ENSURING A FLOW OF MINIMAL COST (RUSSIAN), THE.
MALH 1978 -1 MALHOTRA, V. M.; KUMAR, M. P.; MAHESHWARI, S. N.
O(!V!**3) ALGORITHM FOR FINDING MAXIMUM FLOWS IN NETWORKS, AN.
MAND 1978 -1 MANDL, C. E.
ALGORITHMS AND COMPUTER PROGRAMS IN DETERMINISTIC NETWORK OPTIMIZATION APPLIED TO PUBLIC SYSTEMS.
MAND 1979 -1 MANDL, C. E.
APPLIED NETWORK OPTIMIZATION.
MARQ 1979 -1 MARQUEZ DIEZ CANEDO, J.; MEDINA-MORA ESCALANTE, O.
NETWORK SOLUTION TO A GENERAL VEHICLE SCHEDULING PROBLEM, A.
MATH 1978 -1 MATHAISEL, D. F. X.; MULLER, M. R.
ASSIGNMENT OF CARGO FLOWS TO AN AIRLINE NETWORK.
MATS 1977 -1 MATSUI, K.
SOME PROPERTIES FOR EQUIVALENCE CLASSES OF FLOW NETWORKS.
MAXE 1975 -1 MAXEMCHUK, N. F.
DISPERSITY ROUTING IN STORE-AND-FORWARD NETWORKS.
MEGIA 1979 -1 MEGIDDO, N.; GALIL, Z.
ON FULKERSON'S CONJECTURE ABOUT CONSISTENT LABELING PROCESSES.
MELN 1978 -1 MELNIK, I. M.
INHOMOGENEOUS NETWORK TRANSPORT PROBLEM (RUSSIAN).
MEYEA 1981 -1 MEYER, H.
KOMPLEXITAETSPROBLEME IN GERT-NETZPLAENEN.
MINI 1978 -1 MINIEKA, E.
OPTIMIZATION ALGORITHMS FOR NETWORKS AND GRAPHS.
MINI 1979 -1 MINIEKA, E.
CHINESE POSTMAN PROBLEM FOR MIXED NETWORKS, THE.
MISH 1978 -1 MISHCHENKO, A. E.; SHAFRANSKIJ, V. V.
USE OF NETWORK MODELS WITH "INTERMEDIATE" RESOURCES FOR CALENDAR-SIZE SCHEDULING OF COMPLEX JOBS (RUSSIAN), THE.
MITS 1978 -1 MITSUMORI, S.
MINIMUM NUMBER OF VEHICLES TO MEET DYNAMIC TRANSPORTATION DEMAND.
MOEH 1979 -1 MOEHRING, R. H.
MINIMIZING COSTS OF RESOURCE REQUIREMENTS SUBJECT TO A FIXED COMPLETION TIME (ABSTRACT).
MORL 1980 -1 MORLOCK, M.
ZEITPLANUNG MIT EINER ERWEITERUNG VON CPM.
MULV 1978 -1 MULVEY, J. M.
PIVOT STRATEGIES FOR PRIMAL-SIMPLEX NETWORK CODES.
MULV 1978 -2 MULVEY, J. M.
TESTING OF LARGE-SCALE NETWORK OPTIMIZATION PROGRAM.
MUSA 1980 -1 MUSALEM, J. S.
CONVERTING LINEAR MODELS TO NETWORK MODELS.
NAKAA 1977 -1 NAKAMURA, T.; YAMASAKI, M.
EXTREMAL LENGTH OF AN INFINITE NETWORK WHICH IS NOT NECESSARILY LOCALLY FINITE.
NAKAA 1977 -2 NAKAMURA, T.; YAMASAKI, M.
MINIMAL CUT PROBLEMS ON AN INFINITE NETWORK.
NGUY 1979 -1 NGUYEN VAN VI
SOME CLASSES OF PROBLEMS ON ADMISSIBLE DYNAMICAL FLOW WITH MINIMUM TIME (RUSSIAN).
NICO 1979 -1 NICOLAI, W.
OPTIMIERUNG SPEZIELLER GERT-NETZPLAENE.
NICO 1981 -1 NICOLAI, W.
TIME-ORIENTED ANALYSIS OF PROJECTS USING STOCHASTIC NETWORK TECHNIQUES.
NIEM 1980 -1 NIEMINEN, J.
ON MINIMALLY INTERCONNECTED SUBNETWORKS OF A NETWORK.
OECH 1981 -1 OECHSLEIN, H.
PRIMAL-DUALE VERFAHREN FUER NICHTLINEARE, INSBESONDERE FUER SCHLECHT KONDITIONIERTE NETZWERKPROBLEME.
OGAW 1978 -1 OGAWA, H.; NISHIZEKI, T.; SAITO, S.
METHOD FOR APPROXIMATE CALCULATION OF MAXIMUM CUTS (JAPANESE), A.
ONAG 1979 -1 ONAGA, K.; MAYEDA, W.
BOOLEAN THEORY OF NETWORK FLOWS AND METRICS AND ITS APPLICATIONS TO PARTICLE TRANSMISSION AND CLUSTERING, A.
ONAGA 1978 -1 ONAGA, K.; MURATA, T.
DT-POLYNOMIAL APPROACH TO DISCRETE TIME-VARYING NETWORK FLOW PROBLEMS, THE.

****

ORLI 1980 -1 ORLIN, J. B.
MAXIMUM DYNAMIC NETWORK FLOWS.
ORLI 1980 -2 ORLIN, J. B.
MINIMUM CONVEX COST DYNAMIC NETWORK FLOWS.
OSYC 1980 -1 OSYCZKA, A.
MULTICRITERION NETWORK OPTIMIZATION PROBLEM.
OXLEA 1979 -1 OXLEY, J. G.; WELSH, D. J. A.
ON SOME PERCOLATION RESULTS OF J. M. HAMMERSLEY.
OXLEA 1979 -2 OXLEY, J. G.; WELSH, D. J. A.
TUTTE POLYNOMIAL AND PERCOLATION, THE.
PADBB 1979 -1 PADBERG, M. W.; RAO, M. R.
ODD MINIMUM CUT-SETS AND B-MATCHINGS.
PEAR 1979 -1 PEARMAN, A. D.
STRUCTURE OF THE SOLUTION SET TO NETWORK OPTIMISATION PROBLEMS, THE.
PHIL 1977 -1 PHILLIPS, S. JR.; DESSOUKY, M. I.
SOLVING THE PROJECT TIME/COST TRADEOFF PROBLEM USING THE MINIMAL CUT CONCEPT.
PHIL 1979 -1 PHILLIPS, S. JR.; DESSOUKY, M. I.
CUT SEARCH ALGORITHM WITH ARC CAPACITIES AND LOWER BOUNDS, THE.
PICA 1980 -1 PICARD, J.-C.; QUEYRANNE, M.
ON THE STRUCTURE OF ALL MINIMUM CUTS IN A NETWORK AND APPLICATIONS.
PRIT 1979 -1 PRITSKER, A. A. B.
MODELING AND ANALYSIS USING Q-GERT NETWORKS.
RADE 1977 -1 RADERMACHER, F. J.
FLOATS IN PROJECT NETWORKS.
RADO 1981 -1 RADO, R.
SATZ UEBER STROEMUNGEN IN GERICHTETEN GRAPHEN, EIN.
RARDA 1979 -1 RARDIN, R. L.; CHOE, U.
TIGHTER RELAXATIONS OF FIXED CHARGE NETWORK FLOW PROBLEMS.
RARDC 1979 -1 RARDIN, R. L.; ROSENTHAL, R. E.
GRAPH STRUCTURES UNDERLYING SUBMATRICES OF NETWORK FLOW TABLEAUX.
RAUS 1975 -1 RAUSCHER, C.
EINFUEHRUNG IN DIE OPTIMIERUNG VON NETZWERKEN.
RECS 1978 -1 RECSKI, A.
CONTRIBUTIONS TO THE N-PORT INTERCONNECTION PROBLEM BY MEANS OF MATROIDS.
RECS 1978 -3 RECSKI, A.
MATROIDAL STRUCTURE OF N-PORTS.
RECSA 1980 -1 RECSKI, A.; IRI, M.
NETWORK THEORY AND TRANSVERSAL MATROIDS.
REIB 1979 -1 REIBIGER, A.; STRAUBE, B.
UEBER DIE AXIOMATISCHE BEGRUENDUNG EINER ALLGEMEINEN NETZWERKTHEORIE.
REIF 1981 -1 REIF, J. H.
MINIMUM S-T CUT OF A PLANAR UNDIRECTED NETWORK IN O(N LOG**2 N) TIME.
REVA 1980 -1 REVA, V. N.
OPTIMAL ORDERING OF THE FLOW GRAPH VERTICES (RUSSIAN).
ROBIA 1980 -1 ROBINSON, D. F.; FOULDS, L. R.
DIGRAPHS: THEORY AND TECHNIQUES.
ROEC 1980 -1 ROECK, H.
SCALING TECHNIQUES FOR MINIMAL COST NETWORK FLOWS.
ROSA 1979 -1 ROSA, M. S.
FINDING THE PATH WITH SMALLEST AVERAGE SPEED FROM A GIVEN SOURCE TO A GIVEN DESTINATION IN A DIRECTED NETWORK WITHOUT CYCLES.
ROSEG 1977 -1 ROSENTHAL, R. E.
SCHEDULING RESERVOIR RELEASES FOR MAXIMUM HYDROPOWER BENEFIT BY NONLINEAR PROGRAMMING ON A NETWORK.
ROTH 1979 -1 ROTHENGATTER, W.
APPLICATION OF OPTIMAL SUBSET SELECTION TO PROBLEMS OF DESIGN AND SCHEDULING IN URBAN TRANSPORTATION NETWORKS.
RUHE 1979 -1 RUHE, G.
TERMINRECHNUNG DES LEINET ALS POTENTIALPROBLEM AUF EINEM GRAPH MIT PAAREN GEKOPPELTER BOEGEN, DIE.
SAHA 1975 -1 SAHA, J. L.
ON SOME PROBLEMS IN RAILWAY NETWORKS.
SAHL 1978 -1 SAHLING, B.-M.
VERKEHRSABLAUF IN NETZEN - EIN GRAPHENTHEORETISCHES OPTIMIERUNGSVERFAHREN.
SAPO 1978 -1 SAPOVALOVSKII, V. I.
ON A PROBLEM OF ENUMERATIVE MATHEMATICAL PROGRAMMING IN NETWORK FORMULATION (UKRAINIAN).
SAUN 1978 -1 SAUNDERS, B. D.; SCHNEIDER, H.
FLOWS ON GRAPHS APPLIED TO DIAGONAL SIMILARITY AND DIAGONAL EQUIVALENCE FOR MATRICES.
SCHAA 1978 -1 SCHAEFER, A.
NETZE MIT VERTEILUNGSFAKTOREN.
SCHME 1978 -1 SCHMITZ, P.; SCHOENLEIN, A.
LINEARE UND LINEARISIERBARE OPTIMIERUNGSMODELLE SOWIE IHRE ADV-GESTUETZTE LOESUNG.
SCHNA 1976 -1 SCHNORR, C. P.
NETWORK COMPLEXITY AND THE BREADTH OF BOOLEAN FUNCTIONS, THE.
SCHNA 1979 -1 SCHNORR, C. P.
BOTTLENECKS AND EDGE CONNECTIVITY IN UNSYMMETRICAL NETWORKS.
SCHNA 1978 -2 SCHNORR, C. P.
MULTITERMINAL NETWORK FLOW AND CONNECTIVITY IN UNSYMMETRICAL NETWORKS.
SEELA 1979 -1 SEELING, R.
ZEIT-KOSTEN-OPTIMIERUNG VON NETZPLAENEN.
SERO 1978 -1 SEROV, S. S.
DECOMPOSITION METHOD FOR NETWORK FLOW PROBLEMS.
SEYM 1979 -4 SEYMOUR, P. D.
SHORT PROOF OF THE TWO-COMMODITY FLOW THEOREM, A.
SEYM 1979 -5 SEYMOUR, P. D.
SUMS OF CIRCUITS.
SHIEA 1980 -1 SHIER, D. R.; WITZGALL, C.
ARC TOLERANCES IN SHORTEST PATH AND NETWORK FLOW PROBLEMS.
SHIL 1979 -3 SHILOACH, Y.
MULTI-TERMINAL 0-1 FLOW.
SHIL 1979 -4 SHILOACH, Y.
STRONG LINEAR ORDERINGS OF A DIRECTED NETWORK.
SIEB 1979 -1 SIEBER, N.
PROBLEMS OF OPTIMIZATION IN A NETWORK MODEL.
SIED 1981 -1 SIEDERSLEBEN, J.
COMBINATORIAL PROBLEMS WITH GERT NETWORKS.

SILV 1975 -1 SILVERI, G.
INPUT GENERATOR FOR A MAXIMAL NETWORK FLOW ALGORITHM AND AN APPLICATION TO WATER RESOURCE MANAGEMENT (ITALIAN), AN.
SING 1979 -1 SINGHAL, K.; NAIR, K. P. K.
NETWORK PLANNING IN PROJECTS SUBJECT TO TECHNOLOGICAL INTERACTIONS AMONG ACTIVITY ALTERNATIVES.
SLOM 1980 -2 SLOMINSKI, L.
SYSTEMS OF REPRESENTATIVE PROBLEMS AND COMBINATORIAL FLOW NETWORKS.
SMITF 1979 -1 SMITH, R. L.
DEFERRAL STRATEGIES FOR A DYNAMIC COMMUNICATIONS NETWORK.
SMYT 1978 -1 SMYTHE, R. T.; WIERMAN, J. C.
FIRST-PASSAGE PERCOLATION ON THE SQUARE LATTICE.
SOME 1980 -1 SOMERS, J.; ADLER, I.
MAX-FLOW PROBLEM WITH PARAMETRIC CAPACITIES, THE.
SONN 1979 -1 SONNTAG, H.
HEURISTISCHES VERFAHREN ZUM ENTWURF NACHFRAGEORIENTIERTER LINIENFUEHRUNG IM OEFFENTLICHEN PERSONENNAHVERKEHR, EIN.
SPEL 1977 -1 SPELDE, H. G.
BOUNDS FOR THE DISTRIBUTION FUNCTION OF NETWORK VARIABLES.
STAN 1979 -1 STANAT, D. F.; MAGO, G. A.
MINIMIZING MAXIMUM FLOWS IN LINEAR GRAPHS.
STEC 1978 -1 STECKHAN, H.
ENGPAESSE, STAUSTELLEN UND GLATTE HOMOGENE STROEME IN NETZEN.
STEC 1979 -1 STECKHAN, H.
KONSISTENZTEST FUER BASISDATEN VON PROJEKTNETZEN.
STEC 1979 -2 STECKHAN, H.
NETZFLUSS-ANALYSE.
STEIA 1980 -1 STEINBERG, E.; NAPIER, H. A.
OPTIMAL MULTI-LEVEL LOT SIZING FOR REQUIREMENTS PLANNING SYSTEMS.
STON 1977 -1 STONE, H. S.
MULTIPROCESSOR SCHEDULING WITH THE AID OF NETWORK FLOW ALGORITHMS.
SZWA 1979 -1 SZWARC, W.
CRITICAL PATH APPROACH IN THE FLOW-SHOP PROBLEM, THE.
SZWAB 1979 -1 SZWARCFITER, J. L.
SYSTEMS OF DISTINCT REPRESENTATIVES FOR K FAMILIES OF SETS.
TAGU 1978 -1 TAGUCHI, A.
MAXIMUM-FLOW PROBLEM IN DISCRETE CONTINUOUS COMPOUND SYSTEM AND ITS NUMERICAL APPROACH.
TARJ 1974 -1 TARJAN, R. E.
TESTING GRAPH CONNECTIVITY.
TEMPA 1971 -1 TEMPERLEY, H. N. V.; LIEB, E. H.
RELATIONS BETWEEN THE "PERCOLATION" AND "COLOURING" PROBLEM AND OTHER GRAPH-THEORETICAL PROBLEMS ASSOCIATED WITH REGULAR PLANAR LATTICES: SOME EXACT RESULTS FOR THE "PERCOLATION" PROBLEM.
THUE 1979 -1 THUENTE, D. J.
TWO ALGORITHMS FOR SHORTEST PATHS THROUGH MULTIPLE CRITERIA NETWORKS.
TONE 1977 -1 TONE, K.
ON OPTIMAL PATTERN FLOWS.
TONE 1979 -1 TONE, K.
ON OPTIMAL PATTERN FLOWS.
TROJA 1981 -1 TROJANOWSKI, M.
GRAPH THEORY AND ALGEBRAIC APPROACH TO SOLVING NETWORK CONCAVE PROBLEMS, A.
TROT 1978 -1 TROTTER, L. E. JR.; WEINBERGER, D. B.
SYMMETRIC BLOCKING AND ANTI-BLOCKING RELATIONS FOR GENERALIZED CIRCULATIONS.
TRUE 1978 -2 TRUEMPER, K.
OPTIMAL FLOWS IN NONLINEAR GAIN NETWORKS.
TUCK 1980 -1 TUCKER, A. C.
APPLIED COMBINATORICS.
TUFE 1980 -1 TUFEKCI, S.
SOLVING THE PROJECT TIME/COST TRADEOFF PROBLEM USING THE FIRST-LABELED FIRST-SCANNED MAXIMAL FLOW ALGORITHM.
USHAA 1977 -1 USHAKOV, I. A.; LITVAK, YE. I.
UPPER AND LOWER ESTIMATES OF PARAMETERS OF TWO-POLE NETWORKS.
UZDEA 1978 -1 UZDEMIR, A. P.; SHMELEV, V. V.
INTEGER DYNAMIC PROBLEMS OF ECONOMIC PLANNING WITH NETWORK CONSTRAINTS. I.
VASIA 1979 -1 VASILEVA, E. M.; LEVIT, B. JU.; LIVSIC, V. N.
CHOICE OF OPTIMAL TRAJECTORY IN THE DEVELOPMENT OF A TURNPIKE TRANSPORTATION NETWORK (RUSSIAN), THE.
VOIT 1980 -2 VOITISHIN, YU. V.
PROBLEM ON THE MINIMAL FLOW IN THE NETWORK AND ALGORITHMS OF ITS SOLUTION (RUSSIAN), THE.
WALK 1980 -1 WALK, M.
DUALITAET EINES VERALLGEMEINERTEN TRANSPORT- UND POTENTIALPROBLEMS.
WALK 1980 -2 WALK, M.
OPTIMALE PROGRAMME FUER MULTISTROEME AUF ENDLICHEN GERICHTETEN GRAPHEN.
WALKA 1976 -1 WALK, M.; VERBESEK, W.
VERALLGEMEINERTE STROEME UND SPANNUNGEN UEBER ENDLICHEN GERICHTETEN GRAPHEN.
WALT 1979 -1 WALTHER, H.
ANWENDUNGEN DER GRAPHENTHEORIE.
WELS 1978 -1 WELSH, D. J. A.
COMBINATORIAL PROBLEMS IN PERCOLATION THEORY.
WELS 1979 -1 WELSH, D. J. A.
COLOURING PROBLEMS AND MATROIDS.
WELS 1980 -1 WELSH, D. J. A.
COLOURINGS, FLOWS AND PRODUCTIVE GEOMETRY.
WELS 1979 -2 WELSH, D. J. A.
STOCHASTIC OPTIMIZATION ON NETWORKS.
WILLC 1980 -1 WILLIE, R. R.
DETERMINING RELIABILITY CUT AND PATH SET FAMILIES FOR A CAPACITATED FLOW NETWORK.
WOEH 1979 -1 WOEHNER, W.
METHODE ZUR OPTIMALEN PLANUNG GEWISSER TRANSPORTPROZESSE IN NETZEN, EINE.
WOLLA 1977 -1 WOLLNER, E.
ANALYSE UND SYNTHESE ZUVERLAESSIGER NETZE.
WOODA 1978 -1 WOODALL, D. R.
MINIMAX THEOREMS IN GRAPH THEORY.
ZAJT 1979 -1 ZAJTSEV, I. D.; SALYGA, V. I.; VAJNER, V. G.
SUR UN PROBLEME DE LA THEORIE DES RESEAUX DE COMMUNICATION (RUSSIAN).

ZIMM 1981 -1 ZIMMERMANN, U.
LINEAR AND COMBINATORIAL OPTIMIZATION IN ORDERED ALGEBRAIC STRUCTURES.

ZIMM 1981 -2 ZIMMERMANN, U.
MINIMIZATION OF SOME NONLINEAR FUNCTIONS OVER POLYMATROIDAL FLOWS.

ZIMMA 1975 -1 ZIMMERMANN, W. J.
TOPICS IN NETWORK SCHEDULING.

ZIPK 1979 -1 ZIPKIN, P. H.
AGGREGATION AND DISAGGREGATION IN CONVEX NETWORK PROBLEMS.

ZIPK 1980 -1 ZIPKIN, P. H.
BOUNDS FOR AGGREGATING NODES IN NETWORK PROBLEMS.

ZJUZ 1979 -1 ZJUZIN-ZINCHENKO, A. A.
MEASURES OF CRITICALITY IN A NETWORK MODEL IN THE CASE OF LIMITED RESOURCES (RUSSIAN).

ZLOT 1978 -1 ZLOTOV, A. V.
COMBINATORIAL ALGORITHM FOR THE CONSTRUCTION OF A NETWORK WITH A DISCONTINUOUS COST FUNCTION (RUSSIAN), A.

NONLINEAR INTEGER PROGRAMMING

AGRA 1975 -1 AGRAWAL, S. C.
ON INTEGER SOLUTIONS TO LINEAR FRACTIONAL FUNCTIONAL PROGRAMMING PROBLEMS.
AGRA 1977 -1 AGRAWAL, S. C.
ALTERNATE METHOD ON INTEGER SOLUTIONS TO LINEAR FRACTIONAL FUNCTIONALS BY A BRANCH AND BOUND TECHNIQUE, AN.
AGRAA 1978 -1 AGRAWAL, S. C.; CHAND, M.
ON INTEGER SOLUTIONS TO COMPLEMENTARY PROGRAMMING PROBLEMS WITH LINEAR FRACTIONAL OBJECTIVE FUNCTION BY A BRANCH AND BOUND TECHNIQUE.
AGRAA 1979 -1 AGRAWAL, S. C.; CHAND, M.
ON INTERSECTION CUTS IN FRACTIONAL INTERVAL INTEGER PROGRAMMING.
AGRAA 1980 -1 AGRAWAL, S. C.; CHAND, M.
ON INTEGER SOLUTIONS TO COMPLEMENTARY PROGRAMMING PROBLEMS WITH LINEAR FRACTIONAL OBJECTIVE FUNCTIONS.
AGRAB 1974 -1 AGRAWAL, S. C.; SWARUP, K.
ON INTEGER SOLUTIONS TO QUADRATIC PROGRAMS.
ALI 1978 -1 ALI, A. I.; HELGASON, R. V.; KENNINGTON, J. L.
CONVEX COST NETWORK FLOW PROBLEM: A SURVEY OF ALGORITHMS, THE.
ARORB 1977 -1 ARORA, S. R.; PURI, M. C.; SWARUP, K.
SET COVERING PROBLEM WITH LINEAR FRACTIONAL FUNCTIONAL, THE.
ARTH 1980 -1 ARTHUR, J. L.; RAVINDRAN, A.
BRANCH AND BOUND ALGORITHM WITH CONSTRAINT PARTITIONING FOR INTEGER GOAL PROGRAMMING PROBLEMS, A.
BABAA 1968 -1 BABAEV, DZ. A.; BABAJEVA, D. C.; ASKEROVA, L. M.
APPROXIMATIVE ALGORITHM FOR THE SOLUTION OF CONVEX INTEGER PROGRAMS (RUSSIAN), AN.
BALAG 1980 -1 BALAS, E.; MAZZOLA, J. B.
LINEARIZING NONLINEAR 0-1 PROGRAMS.
BANKA 1974 -1 BANK, B.; KLEINMAN, P.; ALONSO, A.
ON A METHOD FOR THE SOLUTION OF A SPECIAL TYPE OF INTEGER PROGRAMS WITH LINEAR CONSTRAINTS (SPANISH).
BAREA 1969 -1 BARENBAUM, F. B.
CERTAIN TRANSPORT PROBLEM WITH A CONCAVE TARGET FUNCTION (RUSSIAN), A.
BARI 1978 -1 BARI, A.; ARSHAD, M.
BRANCH AND BOUND METHOD FOR INTEGER QUADRATIC PROGRAMMING, A.
BEAL 1980 -1 BEALE, E. M. L.
FRACTIONAL PROGRAMMING WITH ZERO-ONE VARIABLES.
BECT 1978 -1 BECTOR, C. R.; JOLLY, P. L.
PSEUDO-MONOTONIC INTEGER PROGRAMMING.
BELJ 1976 -1 BELJAEVA, L. V.; ZURBENKO, N. G.; SOR, N. Z.
NONLINEAR TRANSPORTATION PROBLEM (RUSSIAN), A.
BENI 1981 -1 BENITO-ALONSO, M. A.; DEVAUX, P.
LOCATION AND SIZE OF DAY NURSERIES - A MULTIPLE GOAL APPROACH.
BHATB 1978 -1 BHATIA, H. L.
SOLID TRANSPORTATION PROBLEM IN LINEAR FRACTIONAL PROGRAMMING.
BODI 1979 -1 BODIN, L. D.; BERMAN, L.
MODEL FOR THE CLASSIFICATION OF RAIL FREIGHT CARS, A.
BOLS 1972 -1 BOLSHAKOV, I. A.; BRIKKER, B. I.
"QUASIDIAGONALISATION" FOR INTEGER QUADRATIC PROGRAMS (RUSSIAN).
BOUR 1978 -1 BOURI, V. K.
SOLUTION TECHNIQUE FOR THE TOTAL COST RECTILINEAR DISTANCE SINGLE FACILITY LOCATION PROBLEM, A.
BURKG 1980 -1 BURKARD, R. E.; KEIDING, H.; KRARUP, J.; PRUZAN, P. M.
RELATIONSHIP BETWEEN OPTIMALITY AND EFFICIENCY IN MULTICRITERIA 0-1 PROGRAMMING PROBLEMS, A.
BURKH 1980 -1 BURKARD, R. E.; KRARUP, J.; PRUZAN, P. M.
EFFICIENCY AND OPTIMALITY IN MINISUM, MINIMAX 0-1 PROGRAMMING PROBLEMS.
BUTA 1975 -1 BUTAN, E. I.; NECVAL, N. A.
ALGORITHMS FOR THE OPERATIONAL CONTROL OF ARRIVAL FLOWS IN A TRANSPORTATION NETWORK (RUSSIAN).
CARLB 1979 -1 CARLSON, R. C.; SHUKLA, P. R.
ROBUSTNESS OF THE INTERACTIVE ALGORITHM FOR MULTICRITERION ZERO-ONE VARIABLE PROBLEMS UNDER PROBABILISTIC TRADEOFFS.
CARLC 1979 -1 CARLSON, R. C.; SHUKLA, P. R.; BAUM, S.
INTERACTIVE SOLUTION OF DISCRETE MULTICRITERION PROBLEMS: AN ALGORITHM AND COMPUTATIONAL RESULTS FOR THE BINARY VARIABLE CASE.
CART 1980 -1 CARTER, M. W.
INDEFINITE ZERO-ONE QUADRATIC PROBLEM, THE.
CHAND 1980 -1 CHANDRA, S.; CHANDRAMOHAN, M.
ALL INTEGER METHOD FOR INTEGER CONVEX PROGRAMS, AN.
CHAND 1979 -2 CHANDRA, S.; CHANDRAMOHAN, M.
IMPROVED BRANCH AND BOUND METHOD FOR MIXED INTEGER LINEAR FRACTIONAL PROGRAMS, AN.
CIOF 1979 -1 CIOFFI, G.; JULIO, S. DE; LUCERTINI, M.
OPTIMAL DECOMPOSITION OF SEQUENTIAL MACHINES VIA INTEGER NON-LINEAR PROGRAMMING: A COMPUTATIONAL ALGORITHM.
CLAR 1980 -1 CLARK, G. M.; RANGANATHAN, A. N.
RESOURCE ALLOCATION ALGORITHM (ALCOT) FOR CONTROLLING MINE DRAINAGE POLLUTION, A.
COLLA 1978 -1 COLLINS, M.; COOPER, L.; HELGASON, R. V.; KENNINGTON, J. L.; LEBLANC, L. J.
SOLVING THE PIPE NETWORK ANALYSIS PROBLEM USING OPTIMIZATION TECHNIQUES.
COOPB 1979 -1 COOPER, M. W.
IMPROVED ALGORITHM FOR NON-LINEAR INTEGER PROGRAMMING, AN.
COOPB 1979 -2 COOPER, M. W.
SURVEY OF METHODS FOR PURE NONLINEAR INTEGER PROGRAMMING, A.
DEMJ 1965 -1 DEMJANOV, B. F.; KHUDJAKOV, L. JU.
SOLUTION OF INTEGER QUADRATIC PROGRAMS (RUSSIAN), THE.
DESP 1974 -1 DESPONTIN, M.; OUDHEUSDEN, D. VAN; HANSEN, P.
CHOIX DE MEDIAS PAR PROGRAMMATION QUADRATIQUE EN VARIABLES 0-1.
DUMI 1979 -1 DUMITRU, V.
INTEGER NONLINEAR PROGRAMMING VIA SUMT TECHNIQUES.
FABI 1979 -1 FABIAN, C.
ALGORITHM FOR INTEGER CONVEX PROGRAMMING, AN.
FRIEC 1981 -1 FRIESZ, T.
MULTIOBJECTIVE OPTIMIZATION IN TRANSPORTATION: THE CASE OF EQUILIBRIUM NETWORK DESIGN.
GIRL 1980 -1 GIRLICH, E.; KOVALEV, M. M.
PROBLEMKLASSE DER NICHTLINEAREN DISKRETEN OPTIMIERUNG, EINE.
GISV 1971 -1 GISVOLD, K. M.; MOE, J.
METHOD FOR NONLINEAR MIXED-INTEGER PROGRAMMING AND ITS APPLICATION TO DESIGN PROBLEMS, A.
GLAN 1978 -1 GLANKWAHMDEE, A.; LIEBMAN, J. S.; HOGG, G. L.
UNCONSTRAINED DISCRETE NONLINEAR PROGRAMMING.

GLEB 1978 -1 GLEBOV, N. I.
APPLICABILITY OF THE COORDINATE-WISE SLOPE METHOD TO SOME PROBLEMS OF CONVEX INTEGER PROGRAMMING (RUSSIAN).
GRUNA 1981 -1 GRUNEWALD, F. J.; SEGAL, D.
HOW TO SOLVE A QUADRATIC EQUATION IN INTEGERS.
GUPTB 1980 -1 GUPTA, O. K.
BRANCH AND BOUND EXPERIMENTS IN NONLINEAR INTEGER PROGRAMMING.
GUPTB 1980 -2 GUPTA, O. K.
NONLINEAR INTEGER PROGRAMMING ALGORITHMS: A SURVEY.
GURA 1978 -1 GURARI, E. M.; IBARRA, O. H.
NP-COMPLETE NUMBER-THEORETIC PROBLEM, AN.
HARTB 1977 -1 HARTMANN, K.
VERFAHREN ZUR LOESUNG GANZZAHLIGER NICHTLINEARER OPTIMIERUNGSPROBLEME.
HELG 1978 -1 HELGASON, R. V.; KENNINGTON, J. L.
EFFICIENT SPECIALIZATION OF THE CONVEX SIMPLEX METHOD FOR NONLINEAR NETWORK FLOW PROBLEMS, AN.
HENR 1979 -1 HENRY-LABORDERE, A.
RESOLUTION D'UN PROGRAMME QUADRATIQUE EN VARIANTES BIVALENTES PAR DECOMPOSITION. APPLICATION AU PLACEMENT DE COMMUTATEURS DANS UN RESEAU.
ISHIA 1976 -1 ISHII, H.; IBARAKI, T.; MINE, H.
PRIMAL CUTTING PLANE ALGORITHM FOR INTEGER FRACTIONAL PROGRAMMING PROBLEMS, A.
ISHIB 1979 -1 ISHII, H.; NISHIDA, T.; DAINO, A.
FRACTIONAL SET COVERING PROBLEMS.
KATK 1977 -1 KATKHANOV, M. N.; BURLAKOV, E. A.; SAFRONOV, V. V.
OPTIMIZATION ALGORITHM OF THE TOLERANCES ON PARAMETERS OF THE ELEMENTS OF A COMPLEX SYSTEM (RUSSIAN).
KEOWA 1980 -1 KEOWN, A. J.; TAYLOR, B. W. III
CHANCE-CONSTRAINED INTEGER GOAL PROGRAMMING MODEL FOR CAPITAL BUDGETING IN THE PRODUCTION AREA, A.
KOER 1979 -2 KOERNER, F.
SORTIERUNG DER VERZWEIGUNGSREIHENFOLGE, DIE.
KOER 1980 -2 KOERNER, F.
UEBER DAS DISKRETE QUADRATISCHE OPTIMIERUNGSPROBLEM.
KOER 1979 -3 KOERNER, F.
STRUKTURUNTERSUCHUNGEN AM ALGORITHMUS VON KORTE, KRELLE UND OBERHOFER.
KOVA 1980 -1 KOVALEV, M. M.
ANALYSIS OF THE GREEDY ALGORITHM FOR CONVEX INTEGER PROGRAMMING (RUSSIAN).
KOVA 1980 -2 KOVALEV, M. M.
PARTIAL ORDER METHOD (RUSSIAN).
LANG 1980 -1 LANGE, E.
INTERAKTIVES SYSTEM ZUR LINEAREN PROGRAMMIERUNG BEI MEHRFACHEN ZIELEN UND GANZZAHLIGKEITSBEDINGUNGEN, EIN.
LASH 1979 -1 LASHKARI, R. S.; JAISINGH, S. C.
EFFICIENT ALGORITHM FOR QUADRATIC ASSIGNMENT PROBLEM, AN.
LAWRA 1981 -1 LAWRENCE, S.; LAWRENCE, K.; REEVES, G.
MULTIPLE GOAL MODEL FOR ALLOCATION OF TEACHING PERSONNEL, A.
LEBEB 1978 -1 LEBEDEVA, T. T.; SERGIENKO, I. V.
METHOD OF DIRECTED VICINITIES (RUSSIAN), THE.
LEE A 1979 -1 LEE, S. M.
GOAL PROGRAMMING METHODS FOR MULTIPLE OBJECTIVE INTEGER PROGRAMS.
LIBU 1981 -1 LIBURA, M.
INTEGER PROGRAMMING PROBLEMS WITH INEXACT OBJECTIVE FUNCTION.
LOS A 1981 -1 LOS, M.; NGUYEN, S.
SPATIAL ALLOCATION ON A NETWORK WITH CONGESTION.
MAC 1978 -1 MAC BRIDE, R. D.; YORMARK, J. S.
PARAMETRIC QUADRATIC INTEGER PROGRAMMING AGAINST ONE CONSTRAINT.
MAC 1980 -1 MAC BRIDE, R. D.; YORMARK, J. S.
FINDING ALL SOLUTIONS FOR A CLASS OF PARAMETRIC QUADRATIC INTEGER PROGRAMMING PROBLEMS.
MAC 1980 -2 MAC BRIDE, R. D.; YORMARK, J. S.
IMPLICIT ENUMERATION ALGORITHM FOR QUADRATIC INTEGER PROGRAMMING, AN.
MAJE 1980 -1 MAJER, A. B.
METHODE DE DESCENTE PAR COORDONNEES POUR UNE CLASSE DE PROBLEMES DE PROGRAMMATION ENTIERE ET NON LINEAIRE (RUSSIAN).
MEYED 1978 -1 MEYER, R. R.; SMITH, M. L.
ALGORITHMS FOR A CLASS OF "CONVEX" NONLINEAR INTEGER PROGRAMS.
MISHA 1980 -1 MISHRA, B. K.; DAS, C.
MINIMAX AND SYMMETRIC DUALITY FOR A NONLINEAR MIXED-INTEGER PROGRAMMING PROBLEM.
MOORA 1980 -1 MOORE, T. G.
CENTRAL CUTTING PLANE ALGORITHM FOR INTEGER PROGRAMMING, A.
NIEP 1980 -1 NIEPAGE, H.-D.
LINEARISIERTE GANZZAHLIGE ZENTRENVERFAHREN.
NIJK 1981 -1 NIJKAMP, P.; SPRONK, J.
MULTIDIMENSIONAL LOCATIONAL DECISIONS AND INTERACTIVE PROGRAMMING.
PICAA 1980 -1 PICARD, J.-C.; RATLIFF, H. D.
CUT APPROACH TO A CLASS OF QUADRATIC INTEGER PROGRAMMING PROBLEMS, A.
POSNA 1978 -1 POSNER, M. E.; GUIGNARD, M.
COLLAPSING 0-1 KNAPSACK PROBLEM, THE.
POTE 1981 -1 POTEMKINA, A. V.; SHEVCHENKO, V. N.
CONSTRUCTION OF REGULAR CUTTING-OFF IN CONVEX INTEGER PROGRAMMING (RUSSIAN).
REVE 1981 -1 REVELLE, C.; COHON, J.; SHOBRYS, D.
MULTIPLE OBJECTIVES IN FACILITY LOCATION: A REVIEW.
RICH 1975 -1 RICHTER, D.
UEBER DIE LOESUNG DISKRETER, NICHTLINEARER OPTIMIERUNGSAUFGABEN.
ROBI 1980 -1 ROBIN, G.
SUR UN PROBLEME D'OPTIMISATION EN NOMBRES ENTIERS.
ROSEG 1977 -1 ROSENTHAL, R. E.
SCHEDULING RESERVOIR RELEASES FOR MAXIMUM HYDROPOWER BENEFIT BY NONLINEAR PROGRAMMING ON A NETWORK.
ROY B 1977 -1 ROY, S.
APPLICATION OF NON-LINEAR PROGRAMMING IN POWER PLANT LOCATION PROBLEM, AN.
SAMY 1978 -1 SAMYLOVSKII, A. I.; SUSKOV, B. G.
CONSTRUCTION OF THE CHARACTERISTIC FUNCTION OF A NON-CONVEX SET AND THE RELATED PROBLEM OF QUADRATIC INTEGER-VALUED PROGRAMMING.
SAMY 1978 -2 SAMYLOVSKII, A. I.; SUSKOV, B. G.
NON-CONVEX SET CHARACTERISTIC FUNCTION CONSTRUCTION AND CONNECTED INTEGER QUADRATIC PROGRAMMING PROBLEM.

NONLINEAR INTEGER PROGRAMMING

SARC 1979 -1 SARCHIMELIYA, R. A.
ON THE REPRESENTATION OF INTEGRAL SOLUTIONS IN A DISCRETE PROGRAMMING PROBLEM (RUSSIAN).

SASAA 1979 -1 SASAKI, R.; SHINGAI, S.; TAKARAKI, K.
EXTENDED MAO & WALLINGFORD'S METHOD FOR SOLVING NONLINEAR INTEGER PROGRAMMING PROBLEMS AND ITS APPLICATION, AN.

SASAB 1978 -1 SASAKI, R.; TSURUOKA, R.; HARUNA, L.
COMBINATORIAL OPTIMIZATION METHOD OF SYSTEMS WITH FUZZY OBJECTIVES AND UNCERTAIN PARAMETERS AND ITS APPLICATION, A.

SCHA 1974 -1 SCHABACK, R.
OPTIMIERUNGSPROBLEM AUS DER KRISTALLOGRAPHIE, EIN.

SCHOA 1978 -1 SCHOCH, M.; LYSKA, W.
KOMBINATORISCHE ALGORITHMEN ZUR LOESUNG SPEZIELLER NICHTLINEARER 0-1 OPTIMIERUNGSAUFGABEN.

SEDI 1970 -1 SEDIKH, L. G.
ALGORITHM FOR THE SOLUTION OF QUADRATIC INTEGER PROGRAMS (RUSSIAN), AN.

SESHA 1980 -1 SESHAN, C. R.; TIKEKAR, V. G.
ALGORITHMS FOR INTEGER FRACTIONAL PROGRAMMING.

SGUR 1978 -1 SGUREV, V. S.; VASILEV, V. S.
OPTIMIZATION OF A CLOSED TRANSPORT SYSTEM (BULGARIAN).

SHAF 1978 -1 SHAFTEL, T. L.
COMPUTATIONAL EXPERIENCE ON AN ALGORITHM FOR THE TRANSPORTATION PROBLEM WITH NON-LINEAR OBJECTIVE FUNCTIONS.

SHARA 1980 -1 SHARMA, J. K.; SHARMA, M. M.
ON MIXED INTEGER SOLUTIONS TO GOAL PROGRAMMING PROBLEMS.

SHARC 1970 -1 SHARP, J. F.; SNYDER, J. C.; GREENE, J. H.
DECOMPOSITION ALGORITHM FOR SOLVING THE MULTIFACILITY PRODUCTION-TRANSPORTATION PROBLEM WITH NONLINEAR PRODUCTION COSTS, A.

SHUK 1979 -1 SHUKLA, P. R.; CARLSON, R. C.
ANALYSIS AND SOLUTION OF DISCRETE MULTICRITERION PROBLEMS WITH RANGED TRADEOFFS.

SIME 1979 -2 SIMEONE, B.
QUADRATIC 0-1 PROGRAMMING, BOOLEAN FUNCTIONS AND GRAPHS.

SOLO 1976 -1 SOLOMONOV, L. A.; ZHGUTOV, G. O.
APPLICATION OF THE GOMORY METHOD FOR THE CALCULATION OF AN OPTIMAL PLAN FOR PRODUCTION SHIPMENT (RUSSIAN), AN.

SWAR 1966 -1 SWARUP, K.
TRANSPORTATION TECHNIQUE IN LINEAR FRACTIONAL FUNCTIONAL PROGRAMMING.

TAYL 1978 -1 TAYLOR, B. W. III; KEOWN, A. J.
PLANNING URBAN RECREATIONAL FACILITIES WITH INTEGER GOAL PROGRAMMING.

THUE 1979 -1 THUENTE, D. J.
TWO ALGORITHMS FOR SHORTEST PATHS THROUGH MULTIPLE CRITERIA NETWORKS.

TSAR 1977 -1 TSAROUCHIS, N.
SIMPLEX-TYPE ALGORITHM FOR A HYBRID ZERO-ONE PROGRAMMING PROBLEM, A.

TURG 1978 -1 TURGEON, A.
OPTIMAL SCHEDULING OF THERMAL GENERATING UNITS.

VAND 1976 -1 VANDENMEERENDONK, H. W.
SINGLE MACHINE MULTI-PRODUCT PLANNING PROBLEMS.

VILLB 1980 -1 VILLARREAL, B.; KARWAN, M. H.; ZIONTS, S.
INTERACTIVE BRANCH AND BOUND PROCEDURE FOR MULTICRITERION INTEGER LINEAR PROGRAMMING, AN.

WOOW 1977 -1 WOOWIAK, J.
DISCRETE LINEAR FRACTIONAL PROGRAMMING PROBLEM (POLISH), A.

WOOW 1978 -1 WOOWIAK, J.
DISCRETE LINEAR FRACTIONAL PROGRAMMING PROBLEM II (POLISH), A.

WEI- 1979 -1 WEI-XUAN, L.; ZHU-YIN, W.
ON THE FINDING OF ALL SOLUTIONS FOR THE OPTIMAL BLOCK SEARCH (CHINESE).

ZAK 1978 -1 ZAK, JU. A.
ALGORITHMS FOR NONLINEAR PSEUDO-BOOLEAN PROGRAMMING.

ZANA 1981 -1 ZANAKIS, S.
METHOD FOR LARGE-SCALE INTEGER GOAL PROGRAMMING WITH AN APPLICATION TO A FACILITY LOCATION/ ALLOCATION PROBLEM, A.

ZION 1978 -1 ZIONTS, S.
INTEGER LINEAR PROGRAMMING WITH MULTIPLE OBJECTIVES.

ZION 1979 -1 ZIONTS, S.
SURVEY OF MULTIPLE CRITERIA INTEGER PROGRAMMING METHODS, A.

****

AIELA 1980 -1 AIELLO, A.; BURATTINI, E.; MASSAROTTI, A.; VENTRIGLIA, F.
'A POSTERIORI' EVALUATION OF BIN PACKING APPROXIMATION ALGORITHMS.
AKIY 1978 -1 AKIYAMA, J.; ERA, H.; KANEKO, K.; SAITO, T.; SATO, I.
PACKING AND COVERING IN GRAPHS (JAPANESE).
AKIYA 1980 -1 AKIYAMA, J.; EXOO, G.; HARARY, F.
COVERING AND PACKING IN GRAPHS. III: CYCLIC AND ACYCLIC INVARIANTS.
ALBEB 1978 -1 ALBERTSON, M. O.; HUTCHINSON, J. P.
ON THE INDEPENDENCE RATIO OF A GRAPH.
BAKE 1979 -1 BAKER, B. S.; BROWN, D. J.; KATSEFF, H. P.
LOWER BOUNDS FOR ON-LINE TWO-DIMENSIONAL PACKING ALGORITHMS.
BAKEA 1980 -1 BAKER, B. S.; COFFMAN, E. G. JR.; RIVEST, R. L.
ORTHOGONAL PACKINGS IN TWO DIMENSIONS.
BAKEB 1979 -1 BAKER, B. S.; SCHWARZ, J. S.
SHELF ALGORITHMS FOR TWO-DIMENSIONAL PACKING PROBLEMS.
BALAH 1979 -2 BALAS, E.; PADBERG, M. W.
SET PARTITIONING - A SURVEY.
BALAK 1977 -1 BALAS, E.; ZEMEL, E.
CRITICAL CUTSETS OF GRAPHS AND CANONICAL FACETS OF SET-PACKING POLYTOPES.
BARNB 1979 -1 BARNES, F. W.
PACKING THE MAXIMUM NUMBER OF M X N TILES IN A LARGE P X Q RECTANGLE.
BERG 1979 -2 BERGE, C.
PACKING PROBLEMS AND HYPERGRAPH THEORY: A SURVEY.
BERG 1979 -3 BERGE, C.
PACKING PROBLEMS.
BOLL 1978 -1 BOLLOBAS, B.; ELDRIDGE, S. E.
PACKINGS OF GRAPHS AND APPLICATIONS TO COMPUTATIONAL COMPLEXITY.
BROU 1979 -1 BROUWER, A. E.; SCHRIJVER, A.
UNIFORM HYPERGRAPHS.
BULI 1978 -1 BULICHEV, S. F.; VOLCHENKOV, S. G.
OPTIMAL PLANE PACKINGS OF TREES (RUSSIAN).
CHANB 1978 -1 CHANDRA, A. K.; HIRSCHBERG, D. S.; WONG, C. K.
BIN PACKING WITH GEOMETRIC CONSTRAINTS IN COMPUTER NETWORK DESIGN.
CHRIG 1979 -1 CHRISTOFIDES, N.; MINGOZZI, A.; TOTH, P.
LOADING PROBLEMS.
COFFA 1977 -1 COFFMAN, E. G. JR.; CODY, R. A.; JOHNSON, D. B.
ANALYSIS OF A BIN-PACKING ALGORITHM FOR REDUCING ACCESS TIMES ON DRUM-LIKE STORAGE DEVICES.
COFFB 1978 -1 COFFMAN, E. G. JR.; GAREY, M. R.; JOHNSON, D. S.
APPLICATION OF BIN-PACKING TO MULTIPROCESSOR SCHEDULING, AN.
COFFC 1980 -1 COFFMAN, E. G. JR.; GAREY, M. R.; JOHNSON, D. S.; TARJAN, R. E.
PERFORMANCE BOUNDS FOR LEVEL-ORIENTATED TWO-DIMENSIONAL PACKING ALGORITHMS.
COFFG 1977 -1 COFFMAN, E. G. JR.; LEUNG, J. Y.-T.; TING, D. W.
BIN-PACKING PROBLEMS AND THEIR APPLICATIONS IN STORAGE AND PROCESSOR ALLOCATION.
COFFG 1978 -1 COFFMAN, E. G. JR.; LEUNG, J. Y.-T.; TING, D. W.
BIN-PACKING: MAXIMIZING THE NUMBER OF PIECES PACKED.
ECKE 1977 -1 ECKER, K.
ORGANISATION VON PARALLELEN PROZESSEN. THEORIE DETERMINISTISCHER SCHEDULES.
ERDO 1977 -1 ERDOES, P.; ROTHSCHILD, B. L.; SINGHI, N. M.
CHARACTERIZING CLIQUES IN HYPERGRAPHS.
FRANB 1979 -1 FRANK, A.
COVERING BRANCHINGS.
FRED 1980 -1 FREDERICKSON, G. N.
PROBABILISTIC ANALYSIS FOR SIMPLE ONE- AND TWO-DIMENSIONAL BIN PACKING ALGORITHMS.
GATT 1981 -1 GATTASS, E. A.; NEMHAUSER, G. L.
APPLICATION OF VERTEX PACKING ON INTERVAL GRAPHS TO DATA ANALYSIS IN ROAD MAINTENANCE, AN.
GEOFB 1978 -1 GEOFFROY, D. P.; SUMNER, D. P.
UPPER BOUND ON THE SIZE OF A LARGEST CLIQUE IN A GRAPH, AN.
GEORA 1980 -1 GEORGE, J. A.; ROBINSON, D. F.
HEURISTIC FOR PACKING BOXES INTO A CONTAINER, A.
GOLU 1978 -1 GOLUMBIC, M. C.
TRIVIALLY PERFECT GRAPHS.
GRES 1976 -1 GRESNEV, S. N.
THEOREMS ON THE REDUCTION OF THE PACKING OF DIGRAPH VERTICES (RUSSIAN).
GRIN 1977 -1 GRINSTEAD, G. M.
ON COVERINGS AND PACKINGS OF THE COMPLETE GRAPH WITH CYCLES.
GROED 1981 -1 GROETSCHEL, M.; LOVASZ, L.; SCHRIJVER, A.
ELLIPSOID METHOD AND ITS CONSEQUENCES IN COMBINATORIAL OPTIMIZATION, THE.
GYAR 1978 -1 GYARFAS, A.; LEHEL, J.
PACKING TREES OF DIFFERENT ORDER INTO K(N).
HARA 1970 -1 HARARY, F.
COVERING AND PACKING IN GRAPHS, I.
HOFR 1980 -1 HOFRI, M.
TWO-DIMENSIONAL PACKING: EXPECTED PERFORMANCE OF SIMPLE LEVEL ALGORITHMS.
JOHN 1973 -1 JOHNSON, D. S.
NEAR-OPTIMAL BIN PACKING ALGORITHMS.
JOHN 1974 -1 JOHNSON, D. S.
FAST ALGORITHMS FOR BIN PACKING.
JOHNA 1974 -1 JOHNSON, D. S.; DEMERS, A.; ULLMAN, J. D.; GAREY, M. R.; GRAHAM, R. L.
WORST-CASE PERFORMANCE BOUNDS FOR SIMPLE ONE-DIMENSIONAL PACKING ALGORITHMS.
JOHND 1979 -2 JOHNSON, E. L.
SUBADDITIVE LIFTING METHODS FOR PARTITIONING AND KNAPSACK PROBLEMS.
KAUFC 1972 -1 KAUFMAN, M. T.
ANOMALIES IN SCHEDULING UNIT-TIME TASKS.
KEVO 1978 -1 KEVORKIAN, A. K.
GENERAL TOPOLOGICAL RESULTS ON THE CONSTRUCTION OF A MINIMUM ESSENTIAL SET OF A DIGRAPH.
KNOE 1981 -1 KNOEDEL, W.
BIN PACKING ALGORITHM WITH COMPLEXITY O(N LOG N) AND PERFORMANCE 1 IN THE STOCHASTIC LIMIT, A.
KOH 1977 -1 KOH, K. M.
ON THE STABILITY NUMBER OF A GRAPH.
KURE 1977 -1 KUREJCHIK, V. M.
APPLICATION OF STRUCTURAL NUMBERS TO THE CONSTRUCTION OF INDEPENDENT SUBSETS OF THE SET OF VERTICES OF A GRAPH (RUSSIAN).
LAWI 1979 -1 LAWIS, R. T.; PARKER, R. G.
BIN PACKING, MULTI-PROCESSOR SCHEDULING, AND GRAPH COLORING.
LENSA 1979 -2 LENSTRA, J. K.; RINNOOY KAN, A. H. G.
COMPLEXITY OF PACKING, COVERING AND PARTITIONING PROBLEMS.

****

LEUN 1977 -1 LEUNG, J. Y.-T.
FAST ALGORITHMS FOR PACKING PROBLEMS.
LIAN 1980 -1 LIANG, F. M.
LOWER BOUND FOR ON-LINE BIN PACKING, A.
MAGAA 1979 -1 MAGAZINE, M. J.; WEE, T. S.
GENERALIZATION OF BIN-PACKING HEURISTICS TO THE LINE BALANCING PROBLEM, THE.
MARUA 1977 -1 MARUYAMA, K.; CHANG, S. K.; TANG, D. T.
GENERAL PACKING ALGORITHM FOR MULTIDIMENSIONAL RESOURCE REQUIREMENTS, A.
MOUL 1978 -1 MOULOUD, B.
ETUDE DU POLYTOPE ASSOCIE AUX STABLES D'UN GRAPHE ET CARACTERISATION DANS LE CAS LES GRAPHES SERIE-PARALLELES.
ORLI 1977 -1 ORLIN, J. B.
CONTENTMENT IN GRAPH THEORY: COVERING GRAPHS WITH CLIQUES.
OXLE 1978 -1 OXLEY, J. G.
COCIRCUIT COVERINGS AND PACKINGS FOR BINARY MATROIDS.
OXLE 1978 -2 OXLEY, J. G.
COLORING, PACKING AND THE CRITICAL PROBLEM.
PADB 1979 -1 PADBERG, M. W.
COVERING, PACKING AND KNAPSACK PROBLEMS.
PADB 1980 -1 PADBERG, M. W.
(1,K)-CONFIGURATIONS AND FACETS FOR PACKING PROBLEMS.
PELE 1978 -1 PELED, U. N.
MATROIDAL GRAPHS.
PEVZ 1979 -1 PEVZNER, P. A.
ON THE PROBLEM OF TWO-PRODUCT PACKING OF CUTS (RUSSIAN).
PULL 1977 -1 PULLEYBLANK, W. R.
LINEAR PROGRAMMING RELAXATION OF THE NODE PACKING PROBLEM OR 2-BICRITICAL GRAPHS AND NODE COVERS, A.
SBIH 1978 -1 SBIHI, N.
ETUDE DES STABLES DANS LES GRAPHES SANS ETOILE.
SCHRD 1979 -1 SCHRIJVER, A.
FRACTIONAL PACKING AND COVERING.
SEID 1978 -1 SEIDMAN, S. B.; FOSTER, B. L.
GRAPH-THEORETIC GENERALIZATION OF THE CLIQUE CONCEPT, A.
SELK 1978 -1 SELKOW, S. M.
NEW BOUNDS FOR THE CLIQUE NUMBER OF A GRAPH.
SLEA 1980 -1 SLEATOR, D. D. K. D. B.
2.5 TIMES OPTIMAL ALGORITHM FOR PACKING IN TWO DIMENSIONS, A.
SMIT 1980 -1 SMITH, A.; CANI, P. DE
ALGORITHM TO OPTIMIZE THE LAYOUT OF BOXES IN PALLETS, AN.
STIN 1977 -1 STINSON, D.
DETERMINATION OF A PACKING NUMBER.
STRA 1979 -1 STRAIGHT, H. J.
PACKING TREES OF DIFFERENT SIZE INTO THE COMPLETE GRAPH.
SZAM 1977 -1 SZAMKOLOWICZ, L.
SOME REMARKS ON STABLE SETS OF A HYPERGRAPH.
TERA 1979 -1 TERADA, R.
POLYNOMIAL TIME ALGORITHMS FOR NP-HARD PROBLEMS WHICH ARE OPTIMAL OR NEAR-OPTIMAL WITH PROBABILITY ONE.
WALS 1976 -1 WALSH, A. M.
POLYNOMIAL ALGORITHMS FOR CERTAIN GRAPH-THEORETIC PROBLEMS.
WALSA 1975 -1 WALSH, A. M.; BURKHARD, W. A.
POLYNOMIAL ALGORITHMS FOR (3,1) GRAPHS.
WALSA 1977 -1 WALSH, A. M.; BURKHARD, W. A.
EFFICIENT ALGORITHMS FOR (3,1) GRAPHS.
WANK 1978 -1 WANKMUELLER, F.
GRAPHENKLASSEN, BEI DENEN DAS CLIQUENPROBLEM IN POLYNOMIALER ZEIT LOESBAR IST.
YAO 1980 -1 YAO, A. C.-C.
NEW ALGORITHMS FOR BIN PACKING.
ZELI 1977 -1 ZELINKA, B.
REMARK ON SYSTEMS OF MAXIMAL CLIQUES OF A GRAPH, A.

BAILA 1980 -1 BAILEY, M. G.; GILLETT, B. E.
PARAMETRIC INTEGER PROGRAMMING ANALYSIS: A CONTRACTION APPROACH.
BANK 1978 -1 BANK, B.
QUALITATIVE STABILITAETSUNTERSUCHUNGEN REIN- UND GEMISCHT-GANZZAHLIGER LINEARER PARAMETRISCHER OPTIMIERUNGSPROBLEME.
BANK 1980 -1 BANK, B.
STABILITY ANALYSIS IN PURE AND MIXED-INTEGER LINEAR PROGRAMMING.
BOFI 1976 -1 BOFILL, A.; DIAZ, A.
SENSITIVITY ANALYSIS FOR THE TRANSPORTATION PROBLEM IN LINEAR PROGRAMMING (SPANISH).
BURJ 1977 -1 BURJAN, S. B.; SEROV, S. S.; UZDEMIR, A. P.
METHOD FOR SOLVING THE PARAMETRIC PROBLEM OF FINDING CIRCULATION OF MINIMAL COST IN A NETWORK.
FILO 1979 -1 FILONENKO, N. V.
APPROXIMATE SOLUTION OF PARAMETRIC INTEGER PROGRAMMING PROBLEMS.
FINKA 1978 -1 FINKE, G.; AHRENS, J. H.
VARIANT OF THE PRIMAL TRANSPORTATION ALGORITHM, A.
HOLM 1978 -1 HOLM, S.; KLEIN, D.
NONTRIVIAL METHODS FOR POSTOPTIMAL ANALYSIS IN INTEGER LINEAR PROGRAMMING.
INTRA 1980 -1 INTRATOR, J.; ENGELBERG, A.
SENSITIVITY ANALYSIS AS A MEANS OF REDUCING THE DIMENSIONALITY OF A CERTAIN CLASS OF TRANSPORTATION PROBLEMS.
JARV 1977 -1 JARVIS, J. J.; MARTINEZ, O. M.
SENSITIVITY ANALYSIS OF MULTICOMMODITY NETWORK FLOWS, A.
JENK 1979 -1 JENKINS, L.
PARAMETRIC ANALYSIS ON A LOCATION MODEL OF MUNICIPAL RESOURCE RECOVERY.
JENK 1980 -1 JENKINS, L.
COMPUTATIONAL RESULTS WITH A TECHNIQUE OF PARAMETRIC MIXED INTEGER LINEAR PROGRAMMING.
JENK 1980 -2 JENKINS, L.
ONTARIO WASTE MANAGEMENT MODEL: TORONTO EXPERIENCE, THE.
JENK 1980 -3 JENKINS, L.
PARAMETRIC MIXED INTEGER PROGRAMMING: A SOLID WASTE RECYCLING APPLICATION.
KASS 1978 -1 KASSAY, F.
SENSITIVITY ANALYSIS OF A TRANSPORTATION PROBLEM. A CHANGE OF OBJECTIVE FUNCTION COEFFICIENTS-C(IJ) (CZECHOSLOVAKIAN).
LIBU 1977 -1 LIBURA, M.
SENSITIVITY ANALYSIS OF SOLUTIONS OF THE INTEGER KNAPSACK PROBLEM (POLISH).
LIBU 1977 -2 LIBURA, M.
SENSITIVITY PROBLEMS OF INTEGER PROGRAMMING SOLUTIONS.
MAC 1978 -1 MAC BRIDE, R. D.; YORMARK, J. S.
PARAMETRIC QUADRATIC INTEGER PROGRAMMING AGAINST ONE CONSTRAINT.
MAC 1980 -1 MAC BRIDE, R. D.; YORMARK, J. S.
FINDING ALL SOLUTIONS FOR A CLASS OF PARAMETRIC QUADRATIC INTEGER PROGRAMMING PROBLEMS.
MEYEF 1978 -1 MEYER, R. R.; WAGE, M. L.
ON THE POLYHEDRALITY OF THE CONVEX HULL OF THE FEASIBLE SET OF AN INTEGER PROGRAM.
MURP 1979 -2 MURPHY, F. H.; SOYSTER, A. L.
SENSITIVITY ANALYSIS OF THE COSTS IN THE DYNAMIC LOT SIZE MODEL.
NAUS 1979 -1 NAUSS, R. M.
PARAMETRIC INTEGER PROGRAMMING.
ROUN 1980 -1 ROUNTREE, S. L. K.; GILLETT, B. E.
PARAMETRIC INTEGER LINEAR PROGRAMMING: A SYNTHESIS OF BRANCH AND BOUND WITH CUTTING PLANES.
SEEL 1980 -1 SEELAENDER, J.
EINIGE BEMERKUNGEN ZUR BESTIMMUNG VON STABILITAETSBEREICHEN IN DER REIN GANZZAHLIGEN LINEAREN OPTIMIERUNG.
VILLA 1978 -2 VILLARREAL, B.; KARWAN, M. H.
MULTICRITERION INTEGER LINEAR PROGRAMMING: SOME EXTENSIONS.
WUESA 1980 -1 WUESTEFELD, A.; ZIMMERMANN, U.
NONLINEAR ONE-PARAMETRIC LINEAR PROGRAMMING AND T-NORM TRANSPORTATION PROBLEMS.
ZIMM 1980 -2 ZIMMERMANN, U.
LINEAR OPTIMIZATION FOR LINEAR AND BOTTLENECK OBJECTIVES WITH ONE NONLINEAR PARAMETER.

ALBA 1980 -2 ALBANO, A.; ORSINI, R.
TREE SEARCH APPROACH TO THE M-PARTITION AND KNAPSACK PROBLEMS, A.
ALBE 1978 -1 ALBERS, S.
ZUR LOESUNG DES QUADRATISCHEN SET-PARTITIONING-PROBLEMS.
ALBE 1980 -1 ALBERS, S.
IMPLICIT ENUMERATION ALGORITHMS FOR THE SET-PARTITIONING PROBLEM.
ARDI 1975 -1 ARDITTI, J.-C.
CHEMINEMENTS DANS LE GRAPHE DE COMPARABILITE D'UN ARBRE. PARTITION DES SOMMETS EN CYCLES.
ARORA 1977 -1 ARORA, S. R.
SET PARTITIONING PROBLEM WITH LINEAR FRACTIONAL OBJECTIVE FUNCTION, A.
ARYA 1979 -1 ARYANIN, A. N.; YAKOBSON, M. V.
SUR LA METHODE DE PARTITION DANS LES PROBLEMES D'ALLOCATION (RUSSIAN).
BALAA 1976 -1 BALAS, E.
DISJUNCTIVE CUT FOR SET PARTITIONING, A.
BALAH 1979 -2 BALAS, E.; PADBERG, M. W.
SET PARTITIONING - A SURVEY.
BALAJ 1974 -2 BALAS, E.; SAMUELSSON, H.
SYMMETRIC SUBGRADIENT CUTTING PLANE METHOD FOR SET PARTITIONING, A.
BARNA 1981 -1 BARNES, E. R.
ALGORITHM FOR PARTITIONING THE NODES OF A GRAPH, AN.
BAZAC 1980 -1 BAZARAA, M. S.; SHERALI, H. D.
BENDERS' PARTITIONING SCHEME APPLIED TO A NEW FORMULATION OF THE QUADRATIC ASSIGNMENT PROBLEM.
BILL 1978 -2 BILLIONNET, A.
TRANSFORMATION DU PROBLEME DE PARTITIONNEMENT EN UN PROBLEME D'ENSEMBLE STABLE DE POIDS MAXIMAL.
BLAS 1978 -1 BLASS, A.
GRAPHS WITH UNIQUE MAXIMAL CLUMPINGS.
BOLLB 1979 -1 BOLLOBAS, B.; MANVEL, B.
OPTIMAL VERTEX PARTITIONS.
BREE 1978 -1 BREE, D. S.; LAGEWEG, B. J.; LENSTRA, J. K.; RINNOOY KAN, A. H. G.; VANBEZOUWEN, G.
HIERARCHICAL CLUSTERING SCHEME FOR ASYMMETRIC MATRICES, A.
CARL 1976 -1 CARLITZ, L.
SET PARTITIONS.
CIOB 1977 -1 CIOBANU, G.
BRANCH-AND-BOUND ALGORITHM TO SOLVE AN ASSEMBLY LINE BALANCING PROBLEM, A.
COLLB 1977 -1 COLLOMB, P.; GONDRAN, M.
ALGORITHME EFFICACE POUR UN ARBRE DE CLASSIFICATIONS, UN.
CORN 1978 -1 CORNEIL, D. G.; WOODWARD, M. E.
COMPARISON AND EVALUATION OF GRAPH THEORETICAL CLUSTERING TECHNIQUES, A.
CROW 1978 -1 CROWDER, H. P.
CLUSTER ANALYSIS: AN APPLICATION OF LAGRANGIAN RELAXATION.
DEBO 1977 -1 DEBOWY, J.
ALGORITHM FOR OPTIMAL PARTITIONING OF A GRAPH, AN.
DECK 1977 -1 DECKRO, R. F.
MULTIPLE OBJECTIVE DISTRICTING: A GENERAL HEURISTIC APPROACH USING MULTIPLE CRITERIA.
FIAL 1978 -1 FIALA, F.
VEHICLE ROUTING PROBLEM.
FRIED 1979 -3 FRIEZE, A. M.
PROBABILISTIC ANALYSIS OF SOME EUCLIDEAN CLUSTERING.
FUES 1977 -1 FUESTOES, L.; MESZENA, G.; SIMONNE MOSOLYGO, N.
CLUSTER ANALYSIS (HUNGARIAN).
FUTO 1977 -1 FUTO, P.
NEW MODEL AND ALGORITHM FOR CLUSTER ANALYSIS (HUNGARIAN), A.
GEORB 1976 -1 GEORGIEVA, N. C.
ALGORITHM FOR THE EXACT PARTITIONING OF A GRAPH WITH N VERTICES INTO TWO SUBGRAPHS (BULGARIAN), AN.
GOND 1977 -1 GONDRAN, M.
ALGORITHME DE COUPES EN PROGRAMMATION EN NOMBRES ENTIERS, UN.
GUPTF 1979 -1 GUPTA, U. I.; LEE, D. T.; LEUNG, J. Y.-T.
OPTIMAL SOLUTION FOR THE CHANNEL-ASSIGNMENT PROBLEM, AN.
HART 1975 -1 HARTIGAN, J. A.
CLUSTERING ALGORITHMS.
HENDA 1980 -1 HENDY, M. D.; FOULDS, L. R.; PENNY, D.
PROVING PHYLOGENETIC TREES MINIMAL WITH L-CLUSTERING AND SET PARTITIONING.
HEPP 1976 -1 HEPPES, A.; MALYUSZ, K.; STAHL, J.
ON THE SOLUTION OF A SORTING PROBLEM (HUNGARIAN).
JOHND 1979 -2 JOHNSON, E. L.
SUBADDITIVE LIFTING METHODS FOR PARTITIONING AND KNAPSACK PROBLEMS.
KARP 1978 -2 KARP, R. M.
PROBABILISTIC ANALYSIS OF PARTITIONING ALGORITHMS FOR THE TRAVELING-SALESMAN PROBLEM IN THE PLANE.
KAST 1977 -1 KASTEV, S. B.
SOLUTION OF A GENERALIZED PROBLEM OF SET PARTITIONING (RUSSIAN).
KIM 1976 -1 KIM, C.
ANALYSIS OF THE EXPECTED PERFORMANCE OF ALGORITHMS FOR THE PARTITION PROBLEM.
KUCH 1978 -1 KUCHARCZYK, J.
METHODS OF CLUSTER ANALYSIS AND THEIR ALGORITHMS IN THE PROGRAMMING LANGUAGE ALGOL 60. 1: HIERARCHICAL AGGLOMERATIVE METHODS.
KUCH 1978 -2 KUCHARCZYK, J.
METHODS OF CLUSTER ANALYSIS AND THEIR ALGORITHMS IN THE PROGRAMMING LANGUAGE ALGOL 60. 3: METHODS BASED ON A GIVEN ORDERING OF OBJECTS.
KUCH 1978 -3 KUCHARCZYK, J.
METHODS OF CLUSTER ANALYSIS AND THEIR REALIZATION IN THE PROGRAMMING LANGUAGE ALGOL 60. 2: HIERARCHICAL DIVISIVE METHODS DUE TO HUBERT.
LEFK 1978 -1 LEFKOVITCH, L. P.
CLUSTER GENERATION AND GROUPING USING MATHEMATICAL PROGRAMMING.
LENSA 1979 -2 LENSTRA, J. K.; RINNOOY KAN, A. H. G.
COMPLEXITY OF PACKING, COVERING AND PARTITIONING PROBLEMS.
LENSA 1980 -5 LENSTRA, J. K.; RINNOOY KAN, A. H. G.
THEORIE DE LA COMPLEXITE DE CALCUL APPLIQUEE AUX PROBLEMES DE COUPLAGE, RECOUVREMENT ET PARTITIONNEMENT.
MITE 1979 -1 MITEV, J. G.
USE OF A NUMBER OF ADMISSIBLE SOLUTIONS OF EQUATIONS IN ALGORITHMS FOR PURELY INTEGER PROBLEMS OF LINEAR PROGRAMMING (RUSSIAN), THE.

MULV 1979 -1 MULVEY, J. M.
TESTING OF A NETWORK RELAXATION METHOD FOR 0-1 SET-PARTITIONING AND SET COVERING.
NEMHA 1979 -1 NEMHAUSER, G. L.; WEBER, G. M.
OPTIMAL SET PARTITIONING, MATCHINGS AND LAGRANGIAN DUALITY.
PERL 1976 -1 PERL, J.
ON FINDING ALL SOLUTIONS OF THE PARTITIONING PROBLEM.
PERLA 1981 -1 PERL, Y.; SCHACH, S. R.
MAX-MIN TREE PARTITIONING.
POHL 1970 -1 POHL, I.
SORTING PROBLEM AND ITS COMPLEXITY, A.
ROHD 1978 -1 ROHDE, M.
SET-PARTITIONING-PROBLEM - WIRTSCHAFTLICHE ANWENDUNGEN UND ALGORITHMEN -,DAS.
ROHD 1979 -1 ROHDE, M.
ENUMERATIVER ALGORITHMUS ZUR LOESUNG DES SET-PARTITIONING-PROBLEMS MIT RANDBEDINGUNGEN, EIN.
ROHD 1979 -2 ROHDE, M.
SET PARTITIONING MIT LINEAREN RANDBEDINGUNGEN.
SAHNB 1975 -1 SAHNI, S.; GONZALEZ, T.
P-COMPLETE APPROXIMATION PROBLEMS.
SALK 1975 -1 SALKIN, H. M.
INTEGER PROGRAMMING.
SCHR 1981 -1 SCHRADER, R.
APPROXIMATIONS TO CLUSTERING AND SUBGRAPH PROBLEMS ON TREES.
SCHR 1981 -2 SCHRADER, R.
NOTE ON APPROXIMATION ALGORITHMS FOR GRAPH PARTITIONING PROBLEMS, A.
SIME 1978 -1 SIMEONE, B.
ASYMPTOTICALLY EXACT POLYNOMIAL ALGORITHM FOR EQUIPARTITION PROBLEMS, AN.
VANR 1980 -2 VANROY, T. J.
CROSS DECOMPOSITION FOR INTEGER PROGRAMMING.
VOIT 1980 -1 VOITISHIN, YU. V.
ON ONE METHOD FOR ESTIMATE CALCULATION IN THE PROBLEM OF SET PARTITIONING (RUSSIAN).
WERR 1981 -3 WERRA, D. DE
SOME PARTITIONING PROBLEMS FOR GRAPHS AND HYPERGRAPHS.

RELAXATIONS

ATRI 1978 -2 ATRI, G. D'
IMPROVED LOWER BOUNDS TO 0/1 PROBLEMS VIA LAGRANGEAN RELAXATION.

AVRU 1976 -1 AVRUTIK, S. V.
SUPPLEMENTARY-STEP METHOD FOR THE INVESTIGATION OF THE NEIGHBORHOOD OF A DISCRETE OPTIMUM (RUSSIAN), THE.

BALAC 1979 -1 BALAS, E.; CHRISTOFIDES, N.
RESTRICTED LAGRANGEAN APPROACH TO THE TRAVELING SALESMAN PROBLEM, A.

BALAD 1980 -1 BALAS, E.; HO, A. C.
SET COVERING ALGORITHMS USING CUTTING PLANES, HEURISTICS, AND SUBGRADIENT OPTIMIZATION: A COMPUTATIONAL STUDY.

BITRC 1979 -1 BITRAN, G. R.; SEMPOLINSKI, D. E.; SHAPIRO, J. F.
INVERSE OPTIMIZATION: AN APPLICATION TO THE CAPACITATED PLANT LOCATION PROBLEM.

BLAN 1978 -1 BLAND, R. G.
ELEMENTARY VECTORS AND TWO POLYHEDRAL RELAXATIONS.

BOLW 1979 -1 BOLWELL, S. G.; KARWAN, M. H.
EFFICIENT USE OF SURROGATE DUALITY IN 0-1 INTEGER PROGRAMMING.

BOLW 1979 -2 BOLWELL, S. G.; KARWAN, M. H.
HYBRID SURROGATE DUAL-CUTTING PLANE APPROACH TO INTEGER PROGRAMMING, A.

BOUR 1978 -1 BOURI, V. K.
SOLUTION TECHNIQUE FOR THE TOTAL COST RECTILINEAR DISTANCE SINGLE FACILITY LOCATION PROBLEM, A.

BROW 1980 -1 BROWN, G. G.; GEOFFRION, A. M.; BRADLEY, G. H.
PRODUCTION AND SALES PLANNING WITH LIMITED SHARED TOOLING AT THE KEY OPERATION.

BURK 1980 -1 BURKARD, R. E.
SUBGRADIENT METHODS IN COMBINATORIAL OPTIMIZATION.

CAIE 1978 -1 CAIE, J.; LINDEN, J.; MAXWELL, W.
SOLUTION OF A MACHINE LOAD PLANNING PROBLEM.

CAIEA 1979 -1 CAIE, J.; LINDEN, J.; OATS, O.; MAXWELL, W.
HIERARCHICAL MACHINE LOAD PLANNING.

CHALB 1977 -1 CHALMET, L. G.; GELDERS, L. F.
LAGRANGIAN RELAXATIONS FOR A GENERALIZED ASSIGNMENT-TYPE PROBLEM.

CHRIE 1979 -1 CHRISTOFIDES, N.; HEY, A.
GRAPH COVERING RELAXATIONS OF THE SET-COVERING PROBLEM - PART 1.

CROW 1978 -1 CROWDER, H. P.
CLUSTER ANALYSIS: AN APPLICATION OF LAGRANGIAN RELAXATION.

DANIA 1979 -1 DANIEL, R. C.; JEFFREYS, M.
UNBOUNDEDNESS IN INTEGER AND DISCRETE PROGRAMMING L. P. RELAXATIONS.

ETCH 1978 -1 ETCHEBERRY, J.; CONCA, C.; STACCHETTI, E.
IMPLICIT ENUMERATION APPROACH FOR INTEGER PROGRAMMING USING SUBGRADIENT OPTIMIZATION, AN.

FISH 1978 -1 FISHER, M. L.
LAGRANGIAN RELAXATION METHODS FOR COMBINATORIAL OPTIMIZATION.

FISH 1981 -1 FISHER, M. L.
LAGRANGIAN RELAXATION METHOD FOR SOLVING INTEGER PROGRAMMING PROBLEMS, THE.

FISH 1978 -2 FISHER, M. L.
LAGRANGIAN RELAXATION METHODS FOR COMBINATORIAL OPTIMZATION (REVISED VERSION).

FLEIA 1979 -1 FLEISHER, J. M.; MEYER, R. R.
DOUBLE-RELAXATION OPTIMALITY CONDITIONS FOR INTEGER PROGRAMMING.

GAVI 1978 -1 GAVISH, B.
ON OBTAINING THE 'BEST' MULTIPLIERS FOR A LAGRANGEAN RELAXATION FOR INTEGER PROGRAMMING.

GEOFA 1978 -1 GEOFFRION, A. M.; MAC BRIDE, R. D.
LAGRANGEAN RELAXATION APPLIED TO CAPACITATED FACILITY LOCATION PROBLEMS.

GLAN 1978 -1 GLANKWAHMDEE, A.; LIEBMAN, J. S.; HOGG, G. L.
UNCONSTRAINED DISCRETE NONLINEAR PROGRAMMING.

GLOVC 1977 -1 GLOVER, F.; KARNEY, D.; KLINGMAN, D.
STUDY OF ALTERNATIVE RELAXATION APPROACHES FOR A MANPOWER PLANNING PROBLEM, A.

GROEB 1981 -1 GROETSCHEL, M.
APPROACHES TO HARD COMBINATORIAL OPTIMIZATION PROBLEMS.

HUNG 1980 -1 HUNG, M. S.; ROM, W. O.
SOLVING THE ASSIGNMENT PROBLEM BY RELAXATION.

JERO 1980 -1 JEROMIN, B.
BEMERKUNGEN ZUR LAGRANGE-RELAXATION.

KLAS 1979 -1 KLASTORIN, T. D.
EFFECTIVE SUBGRADIENT ALGORITHM FOR THE GENERALIZED ASSIGNMENT PROBLEM, AN.

MARS 1975 -1 MARSTEN, R. E.
USE OF THE BOXSTEP METHOD IN DISCRETE OPTIMIZATION, THE.

MURPD 1978 -1 MURPHY, R. A.; SKITT, R. A.; SWEENEY, D. J.
HEURISTIC METHODS FOR THE MULTI-ITEM ACTIVITY SCHEDULING PROBLEM.

NEMHA 1979 -1 NEMHAUSER, G. L.; WEBER, G. M.
OPTIMAL SET PARTITIONING, MATCHINGS AND LAGRANGIAN DUALITY.

NEMHC 1978 -1 NEMHAUSER, G. L.; WOLSEY, L. A.; FISHER, M. L.
ANALYSIS OF APPROXIMATIONS FOR MAXIMIZING SUBMODULAR SET FUNCTIONS-1, AN.

POLJ 1967 -1 POLJAK, B. T.
GENERAL METHOD FOR SOLVING EXTREMUM PROBLEMS, A.

POWE 1980 -1 POWELL, S.
ROW GENERATION METHODS.

PULL 1977 -1 PULLEYBLANK, W. R.
LINEAR PROGRAMMING RELAXATION OF THE NODE PACKING PROBLEM OR 2-BICRITICAL GRAPHS AND NODE COVERS, A.

SANDA 1979 -1 SANDI, C.
SUBGRADIENT OPTIMIZATION.

SHAPA 1979 -1 SHAPIRO, J. F.
SURVEY OF LAGRANGIAN TECHNIQUES FOR DISCRETE OPTIMIZATION, A.

SHEP 1980 -1 SHEPARDSON, F.; MARSTEN, R. E.
LAGRANGEAN RELAXATION ALGORITHM FOR THE TWO DUTY PERIOD SCHEDULING PROBLEM, A.

SINC 1979 -1 SINCLAIR, M.
AUGMENTED LAGRANGEAN RELAXATIONS IN GENERAL MIXED INTEGER PROGRAMMING.

SMITI 1975 -1 SMITH, T. H. C.; THOMPSON, G. L.
COMPARISON OF TWO DIFFERENT LAGRANGEAN RELAXATIONS OF THE TSP, A.

SWEE 1979 -1 SWEENEY, D. J.; MURPHY, R. A.
METHOD OF DECOMPOSITION FOR INTEGER PROGRAMS, A.

TRIP 1980 -1 TRIPATHY, A.
LAGRANGEAN RELAXATION APPROACH TO COURSE TIMETABLING, A.

VANR 1980 -2 VANROY, T. J.
CROSS DECOMPOSITION FOR INTEGER PROGRAMMING.

VIZV 1976 -1 VIZVARI, B.
USE OF LAGRANGIAN MULTIPLIERS IN INTEGER PROGRAMMING ALGORITHMS (HUNGARIAN), THE.

VIZV 1978 -1 VIZVARI, B.
LAGRANGE MULTIPLIERS IN INTEGER PROGRAMMING.

ZARY 1977 -1 ZARYAN, L. L.; LEBEDEV, S. S.; MESTETSKIJ, L. M.
SOLUTION OF INTEGER TRANSPORTATION PROBLEMS BY GENERALIZED LAGRANGE MULTIPLIERS (RUSSIAN).

****

AHREA 1978 -1 AHRENS, W.; DEHNERT, G.; GERBER, H. J.
HEURISTISCHE VERFAHREN ZUR TOURENPLANUNG BEI DER HAUSMUELLENTSORGUNG IN LAENDLICHEN REGIONEN.

ALLI 1981 -1 ALLINEY, S.
ALGORITHM FOR A ROUTING PROBLEM, AN.

BALLA 1979 -1 BALL, M. O.; BODIN, L. D.; GOLDEN, B. L.; ASSAD, A.; STATHES, C.
TRUCK FLEET ACQUISITION/ROUTING PROBLEM, A.

BATY 1979 -1 BATYCKI, T.; KASPRZAK, A.
BRANCH-AND-BOUND ALGORITHM FOR DETERMINATION OF ADAPTIVE ROUTING IN SOME CLASS OF PACKET-SWITCHED COMPUTER COMMUNICATION NETWORKS, THE.

BERTC 1980 -1 BERTSEKAS, D. P.
CLASS OF OPTIMAL ROUTING ALGORITHMS FOR COMMUNICATION NETWORKS, A.

BERTE 1979 -1 BERTSEKAS, D. P.; GAFNI, E. M.; VASTOLA, K. S.
VALIDATION OF ALGORITHMS FOR OPTIMAL ROUTING OF FLOW IN NETWORKS.

BIJL 1975 -1 BIJLSMA, S. J.
ON MINIMAL-TIME SHIP ROUTING.

BODI 1979 -2 BODIN, L. D.; BERMAN, L.
ROUTING AND SCHEDULING OF SCHOOL BUSES BY COMPUTER.

BODIA 1978 -1 BODIN, L. D.; KURSH, S. J.
COMPUTER-ASSISTED SYSTEM FOR THE ROUTING AND SCHEDULING OF STREET SWEEPERS, A.

BODIA 1979 -1 BODIN, L. D.; KURSH, S. J.
DETAILED DESCRIPTION OF A COMPUTER SYSTEM FOR THE ROUTING AND SCHEDULING OF STREET SWEEPERS, A.

BODIC 1979 -1 BODIN, L. D.; SEXTON, T. R.
SUBSCRIBER DIAL-A-RIDE PROBLEM, THE.

BRUC 1981 -1 BRUCKER, P.
CHINESE POSTMAN PROBLEM FOR MIXED GRAPHS, THE.

CHAC 1979 -1 CHACHRA, V.; GHARE, P. M.; MOORE, J. M.
APPLICATIONS OF GRAPH THEORY ALGORITHMS.

CHENF 1973 -1 CHEN, Y. H.
MATHEMATICAL MODELING OF WATER AND SEDIMENT ROUTING IN NATURAL CHANNELS.

CHRIB 1971 -1 CHRISTOFIDES, N.
OPTIMUM TRAVERSAL OF A GRAPH, THE.

CHRIF 1978 -1 CHRISTOFIDES, N.; MINGOZZI, A.; THOTH, P.
EXACT ALGORITHMS FOR THE VEHICLE ROUTING PROBLEM.

CHRIG 1979 -2 CHRISTOFIDES, N.; MINGOZZI, A.; TOTH, P.
VEHICLE ROUTING PROBLEM, THE.

CULLA 1980 -1 CULLEN, F. H.; JARVIS, J. J.; RATLIFF, H. D.
SET PARTITIONING BASED HEURISTICS FOR INTERACTIVE ROUTING.

DAVIA 1968 -1 DAVIS, R. D.
ON THE DELIVERY PROBLEM AND SOME RELATED TOPICS.

DENAA 1979 -1 DENARDO, E. V.; FOX, B. L.
SHORTEST-ROUTE METHODS: 1. REACHING, PRUNING, AND BUCKETS.

DOLL 1980 -1 DOLL, C. L.
QUICK AND DIRTY VEHICLE ROUTING PROCEDURE.

DRIS 1979 -1 DRISCOLL, W. C.; EMMONS, H.
VEHICLE ROUTING FOR MINIMUM COST.

DUBO 1979 -1 DUBOIS, D.; BEL, G.; LLIBRE, M.
SET OF METHODS IN TRANSPORTATION NETWORK SYNTHESIS AND ANALYSIS, A.

DULA 1980 -1 DULAC, G.; FERLAND, J. A.; FORGUES, P. A.
SCHOOL BUS ROUTES GENERATOR IN URBAN SURROUNDINGS.

FEDEB 1980 -1 FEDERGRUEN, A.; ZIPKIN, P. H.
COMBINED VEHICLE ROUTING AND INVENTORY ALLOCATION PROBLEM, A.

FIAL 1978 -1 FIALA, F.
VEHICLE ROUTING PROBLEM.

FISHB 1978 -2 FISHER, M. L.; JAIKUMAR, R.
DECOMPOSITION ALGORITHM FOR LARGE-SCALE VEHICLE ROUTING, A.

FRED 1977 -1 FREDERICKSON, G. N.
APPROXIMATION ALGORITHMS FOR NP-HARD ROUTING PROBLEMS.

FRED 1979 -1 FREDERICKSON, G. N.
APPROXIMATION ALGORITHMS FOR SOME POSTMAN PROBLEMS.

FREDA 1976 -1 FREDERICKSON, G. N.; HECHT, M. S.; KIM, C. E.
APPROXIMATION ALGORITHMS FOR SOME ROUTING PROBLEMS.

GABOA 1979 -1 GABOVICH, E. J.; MELAMED, I. J.
COMPUTATIONAL COMPLEXITY OF ROUTING PROBLEMS (RUSSIAN).

GAVIB 1979 -1 GAVISH, B.; SHLIFER, E.
APPROACH FOR SOLVING A CLASS OF TRANSPORTATION SCHEDULING PROBLEMS, AN.

GILE 1979 -1 GILES, R.
ADJACENCY ON THE POSTMAN POLYHEDRON.

GILL 1976 -1 GILLETT, B. E.
VEHICLE DISPATCHING: SWEEP ALGORITHM AND EXTENSIONS.

GOLDB 1976 -1 GOLDEN, B. L.
LARGE-VEHICLE ROUTING AND RELATED COMBINATORIAL PROBLEMS.

GOLDB 1978 -2 GOLDEN, B. L.
STATISTICAL ESTIMATION IN COMBINATORIAL DECISION PROBLEMS.

GOLDF 1979 -1 GOLDEN, B. L.; WONG, R. T.
CAPACITATED ARC ROUTING PROBLEMS.

GRIGC 1977 -1 GRIGOREV, D. JU.
PROBLEM OF PATH CONNECTIONS ON GRAPHS (RUSSIAN), THE.

HADL 1979 -2 HADLOCK, F.
TREE SYSTEMS FOR NETWORK FLOW CONTROL AND ROUTING.

HADLA 1979 -1 HADLOCK, F.; HOFFMAN, F.
MINIMUM FLEET SIZE ROUTING PROBLEM, A.

HAYS 1967 -1 HAYS, R.
DELIVERY PROBLEM, THE.

JACOB 1980 -1 JACOBSEN, S. K.; MADSEN, O. B. G.
COMPARATIVE STUDY OF HEURISTICS FOR A TWO-LEVEL ROUTING-LOCATION PROBLEM, A.

JOHNH 1975 -1 JOHNSON, J. G.
HEURISTIC ALGORITHM FOR THE MULTI-TERMINAL VEHICLE DISPATCH PROBLEM USING THE MODIFIED SWEEP ALGORITHM, A.

KAPP 1979 -1 KAPPAUF, C. H.; KOEHLER, G. J.
MIXED POSTMAN PROBLEM, THE.

KOMAA 1977 -1 KOMATSU, M.; OUCHI, Y.; NAKANISHI, H.; SANADA, H.; TEZUKA, Y.
OPTIMUM ROUTE ASSIGNMENT THEOREM AND ITS APPLICATION TO ADAPTIVE ROUTING PROCEDURE IN MESSAGE SWITCHING NETWORKS.

LANS 1981 -1 LANSDOWNE, Z. F.
RAIL FREIGHT TRAFFIC ASSIGNMENT.
LAPOB 1981 -1 LAPORTE, G.; NOBERT, Y.
EXACT ALGORITHM FOR MINIMIZING ROUTING AND OPERATING COSTS IN DEPOT LOCATION, AN.
LENSA 1979 -3 LENSTRA, J. K.; RINNOOY KAN, A. H. G.
COMPLEXITY OF VEHICLE ROUTING AND SCHEDULING PROBLEMS.
LEVY 1980 -1 LEVY, L.; GOLDEN, B. L.; ASSAD, A.
FLEET SIZE AND MIX VEHICLE ROUTING PROBLEM, THE.
MAND 1978 -1 MANDL, C. E.
ALGORITHMS AND COMPUTER PROGRAMS IN DETERMINISTIC NETWORK OPTIMIZATION APPLIED TO PUBLIC SYSTEMS.
MAND 1979 -1 MANDL, C. E.
APPLIED NETWORK OPTIMIZATION.
MAND 1980 -1 MANDL, C. E.
EVALUATION AND OPTIMIZATION OF URBAN PUBLIC TRANSPORTATION NETWORKS.
MARTH 1978 -1 MARTYNA, J.
STUDY OF JOB ROUTING BEHAVIOR IN AN OPERATING SYSTEM (POLISH), A.
MATT 1978 -1 MATTHAEUS, F.
TOURENPLANUNG - VERFAHREN ZUR EINSATZDISPOSITION VON FUHRPARKS.
MAXE 1975 -1 MAXEMCHUK, N. F.
DISPERSITY ROUTING IN STORE-AND-FORWARD NETWORKS.
MINI 1978 -1 MINIEKA, E.
OPTIMIZATION ALGORITHMS FOR NETWORKS AND GRAPHS.
MINI 1979 -1 MINIEKA, E.
CHINESE POSTMAN PROBLEM FOR MIXED NETWORKS, THE.
MOLE 1979 -1 MOLE, R. H.
SURVEY OF LOCAL DELIVERY VEHICLE ROUTING METHODOLOGY, A.
NAMB 1979 -1 NAMBIAR, J. M.; CHALMET, L. G.
LOCATION AND VEHICLE SCHEDULING PROBLEM IN COLLECTING AND PROCESSING RUBBER, A.
NEIT 1977 -1 NEITZEL, W.
TOURENPLANUNG. PROBLEMDARSTELLUNG UND LOESUNSVERFAHREN FUER EIN-DEPOT-PROBLEME.
NEWE 1979 -1 NEWELL, G. F.
SOME ISSUES RELATING TO THE OPTIMAL DESIGN OF BUS ROUTES.
OHTS 1981 -1 OHTSUKI, T.
TWO DISJOINT PATH PROBLEM AND WIRE ROUTING DESIGN, THE.
PAES 1978 -1 PAESSENS, H.
TOURENPLANUNG BEI DER MUELLSAMMLUNG IN STAEDTISCHEN BEREICHEN.
PAPA 1976 -1 PAPADIMITRIOU, C. H.
COMPLEXITY OF COMBINATORIAL OPTIMIZATION PROBLEMS, THE.
PSAR 1978 -1 PSARAFTIS, H. N.
REAL-TIME FLEXIBLE-ROUTE SCHEDULING ALGORITHM, A.
ROBB 1976 -1 ROBBINS, J.
PROGRAM FOR SOLUTION OF LARGE SCALE VEHICLE ROUTING PROBLEMS, A.
RUSS 1979 -1 RUSSELL, R.; IGO, W.
ASSIGNMENT ROUTING PROBLEM, AN.
SCHU 1979 -1 SCHULTZ, H. K.
PRACTICAL METHOD FOR VEHICLE SCHEDULING, A.
SEXT 1978 -1 SEXTON, T. R.
MULTI-VEHICLE SUBSCRIPTION PROBLEM: A HEURISTIC ALGORITHM, THE.
SONN 1978 -1 SONNTAG, H.
LINIENPLANUNG IM OEFFENTLICHEN PERSONENNAHVERKEHR.
SONN 1979 -2 SONNTAG, H.
VERFAHREN ZUR ALTERNATIVROUTENSUCHE IN VERKEHRSNETZEN, EIN.
SOUM 1980 -1 SOUMIS, F.; FERLAND, J. A.; ROUSSEAU, J.-M.
MODEL FOR LARGE-SCALE AIRCRAFT ROUTING AND SCHEDULING PROBLEMS, A.
STEI 1978 -1 STEIN, D. M.
ASYMPTOTIC, PROBABILISTIC ANALYSIS OF A ROUTING PROBLEM, AN.
STERC 1979 -1 STERN, H. I.; DROR, M.
ROUTING ELECTRIC METER READERS.
STEWA 1979 -1 STEWART, W. R.; GOLDEN, B. L.
VEHICLE ROUTING ALGORITHM BASED ON GENERALIZED LAGRANGE MULTIPLIERS (ROUGH DRAFT).
STEWA 1980 -1 STEWART, W. R.; GOLDEN, B. L.
CHANCE-CONSTRAINED APPROACH TO THE STOCHASTIC VEHICLE ROUTING PROBLEM, A.
STEWA 1980 -2 STEWART, W. R.; GOLDEN, B. L.
SUBSCRIBER BUS ROUTING PROBLEM, THE
TURC 1981 -1 TURCHANYI, P. S.
DISTRIBUTED ROUTING ALGORITHM IN A NETWORK WITH PRIORITY CLASSES, A.
WATAA 1979 -1 WATANABE, T.; ASANO, T.; SAITO, N.
UPPER BOUNDS ON THE LENGTHS OF CHINESE POSTMAN WALKS IN UNDIRECTED GRAPHS (JAPANESE).
WHITA 1980 -1 WHITE, G. P.
EASY LOWER BOUND ON THE NUMBER OF TRUCKS NEEDED TO SERVICE A SET OF DESTINATIONS, AN.
YEE 1979 -1 YEE, J. R.; GOLDEN, B. L.
DETERMINING OPERATING STRATEGIES FOR PROBABILISTIC VEHICLE ROUTING (REVISED VERSION).
ZARE 1979 -1 ZARETZKY, L. S.
TRAVELLING SALESMAN AND DELIVERY PROBLEMS SOLVING BY METHOD OF STATE FUNCTIONS CORRECTION (RUSSIAN).

ABAE 1975 -1 ABAEV, T. G.
PROBLEM OF COMPILING AN OPTIMAL SCHEDULE FOR THE WORK OF A GROUP OF AUTOMATA STATIONS WITH DIGITAL PROGRAMMED CONTROL (RUSSIAN), THE.

ABDE 1978 -1 ABDEL-WAHAB, H. M.; KAMEDA, T.
SCHEDULING TO MINIMIZE MAXIMUM CUMULATIVE COST SUBJECT TO SERIES-PARALLEL PRECEDENCE CONSTRAINTS.

ABDE 1980 -1 ABDEL-WAHAB, H. M.; KAMEDA, T.
ON STRICTLY OPTIMAL SCHEDULES FOR THE CUMULATIVE COST-OPTIMAL SCHEDULING PROBLEM.

ACHU 1981 -1 ACHUGBUE, J. O.; CHIN, F. Y.
BOUNDS ON SCHEDULES FOR INDEPENDENT TASKS WITH SIMILAR EXECUTION TIMES.

ACKE 1978 -1 ACKERMAN, L. J.; LUSS, H.; BERKOWITZ, R. S.
IMPLICIT ENUMERATION ALGORITHM FOR SEQUENCING POLICIES APPLIED TO TELEPHONE SWITCHING FACILITIES, AN.

ADAM 1980 -1 ADAM, N. R.; SURKIS, J.
PRIORITY UPDATE INTERVALS AND ANOMALIES IN DYNAMIC RATIO TYPE JOB SHOP SCHEDULING RULES.

ADAMA 1980 -1 ADAMSKI, A.
OPTIMAL DISPATCHING CONTROL OF BUS LINES.

ADRA 1977 -1 ADRABINSKI, A.; GRABOWSKI, J.
ALGORITHM FOR SOLVING THE MACHINE SEQUENCING PROBLEM, AN.

ADRAA 1980 -1 ADRABINSKI, A.; GRABOWSKI, J.; WODECKI, M.
ALGORITHM FOR SOLVING THE GENERAL SEQUENCING PROBLEM (POLISH), AN.

ADRAB 1977 -1 ADRABINSKI, A.; WODECKI, M.
ALGORITHM FOR SOLVING A MACHINE SEQUENCING PROBLEM WITH PARALLEL MACHINES, AN.

ALBE 1977 -1 ALBERS, S.
EINSATZPLANUNG VON FLUGZEUGBESATZUNGEN.

ALEK 1978 -2 ALEKSEEV, O. G.
MINIMAX SCHEDULING PROBLEM, A.

APPEA 1978 -1 APPELBE, W. F.; ITO, M. R.
SCHEDULING HEURISTICS IN A MULTIPROGRAMMING ENVIRONMENT.

ARAB 1966 -1 ARABEYRE, J. P.
METHODS OF CREW SCHEDULING.

ARMSF 1977 -1 ARMSTRONG, R. D.; SINHA, P.
CYCLIC SEPARATION SCHEDULING PROBLEM, THE.

AROR 1980 -1 ARORA, R. K.; RANA, S. P.
SCHEDULING IN A SEMI-ORDERED FLOW-SHOP WITHOUT INTERMEDIATE QUEUES.

ARTA 1980 -1 ARTAMONOV, I. M.
SCHEDULING ALGORITHM FOR A PRODUCTION UNIT AND ESTIMATION OF SCHEDULE LENGTHS (RUSSIAN), A.

ARUM 1980 -1 ARUMUGAM, V.; RAMANI, S.
EVALUATION OF VALUE TIME SEQUENCING RULES IN A REAL WORLD JOB SHOP.

ASHI 1975 -1 ASHIMOV, A.; SAGYNGALIEV, K. S.
SCHEDULING OF BATCH PRODUCTION, THE.

ASRA 1978 -1 ASRATJAN, A. S.
CONSTRUCTION OF AN EDGE COLORING OF A SPECIAL FORM IN A BIPARTITE GRAPH, AND ITS APPLICATION IN PROBLEMS OF SCHEDULING THEORY (RUSSIAN), THE.

ASSC 1979 -1 ASSCHE, A. VAN; HERROELEN, W. S.
OPTIMAL PROCEDURE FOR THE SINGLE-MODEL DETERMINISTIC ASSEMBLY LINE BALANCING PROBLEM, AN.

AVON 1979 -1 AVONDO-BODINO, G.
GRAPH THEORY AND OPERATIONS RESEARCH.

AVRAA 1978 -1 AVRAMITA, G. M.
DECOMPOSITION AND SOLVING OF LARGE-SCALE PROBLEMS IN PRODUCTION SCHEDULING.

AXSA 1980 -1 AXSAETER, S.
ECONOMIC LOT SIZES AND VEHICLE SCHEDULING.

AXSAA 1980 -1 AXSAETER, S.; LUNDELL, P.
MULTI-STAGE LOT SIZING IN A CASE WITH INITIAL INVENTORIES.

BABU 1977 -1 BABUSHKIN, A. I.; BASHTA, A. L.; BELOV, I. S.; DUSHIN, B. I.
OPTIMIZING THE SEQUENCE OF PRODUCT ASSEMBLY.

BAGG 1978 -1 BAGGA, P. C.
NOTE ON EQUIVALENT JOBS FOR JOB BLOCKS IN JOB SEQUENCING PROBLEM, A.

BAGGA 1979 -1 BAGGA, P. C.; KALRA, K. R.; BANSAL, S. P.
SEQUENCING UNDER REQUIRED PRECEDENCE AMONG JOBS.

BAKEC 1979 -1 BAKER, E.; BODIN, L. D.; FINNEGAN, W. F.; PONDER, R. J.
EFFICIENT HEURISTIC SOLUTIONS TO AN AIRLINE CREW SCHEDULING PROBLEM.

BAKED 1980 -1 BAKER, E.; FISHER, M.
COMPUTATIONAL RESULTS FOR VERY LARGE AIR CREW SCHEDULING PROBLEMS.

BAKEE 1979 -1 BAKER, K. R.; BURNS, R. N.; CARTER, M. W.
STAFF SCHEDULING WITH DAY-OFF AND WORKSTRETCH CONSTRAINTS.

BAKEF 1978 -1 BAKER, K. R.; DIXON, P.; MAGAZINE, M. J.; SILVER, E. A.
ALGORITHM FOR THE DYNAMIC LOT-SIZE PROBLEM WITH TIME-VARYING PRODUCTION CAPACITY CONSTRAINTS, AN.

BAKEG 1980 -1 BAKER, K. R.; LAWLER, E. L.; LENSTRA, J. K.; RINNOOY KAN, A. H. G.
PREEMPTIVE SCHEDULING OF A SINGLE MACHINE TO MINIMIZE MAXIMUM COST SUBJECT TO RELEASE DATES AND PRECEDENCE CONSTRAINTS.

BAKEH 1980 -1 BAKER, K. R.; NUTTLE, H. L. W.
SEQUENCING INDEPENDENT JOBS WITH A SINGLE RESOURCE.

BAKEI 1978 -1 BAKER, K. R.; SCHRAGE, L. E.
FINDING AN OPTIMAL SEQUENCE BY DYNAMIC PROGRAMMING: AN EXTENSION TO PRECEDENCE-RELATED TASKS.

BANS 1979 -1 BANSAL, S. P.
ON LOWER BOUNDS IN PERMUTATION FLOWSHOP PROBLEMS.

BANS 1980 -1 BANSAL, S. P.
SINGLE MACHINE SCHEDULING TO MINIMIZE WEIGHTED SUM OF COMPLETION TIMES WITH SECONDARY CRITERION - A BRANCH AND BOUND APPROACH.

BANSA 1977 -1 BANSAL, S. P.; BAGGA, P. C.
MINIMIZING WAITING COSTS OF A NX2 FLOWSHOP PROBLEM.

BARD 1981 -1 BARDSWITCH, E.; HUNDERT, M.
COMBINATORIAL OPTIMIZATION APPROACH TO CYCLIC SCHEDULING OF PERSONNEL, THE.

BARH 1978 -1 BARHAM, A. M.; WESTWOOD, J. B.
SIMPLE HEURISTIC TO FALICITATE COURSE TIMETABLING, A.

BARNC 1981 -1 BARNES, J. W.; VANSTON, L. K.
SCHEDULING JOBS WITH LINEAR DELAY PENALTIES AND SEQUENCE DEPENDENT SETUP COSTS.

BARRC 1978 -1 BARRER, J. N.
CERTAIN PERMUTATION PROBLEMS AND THEIR RELATION TO THE ASSIGNMENT PROBLEM.

BART 1979 -1 BARTHOLDI, J. J. III
GUARANTEED-ACCURACY ROUND-OFF ALGORITHM FOR CYCLIC SCHEDULING AND SET COVERING, A.

BARTA 1980 -1 BARTHOLDI, J. J. III; ORLIN, J. B.; RATLIFF, H. D.
CYCLIC SCHEDULING VIA INTEGER PROGRAMS WITH CIRCULAR ONES.

BARTB 1978 -1 BARTHOLDI, J. J. III; RATLIFF, H. D.
UNNETWORKS WITH APPLICATIONS TO IDLE TIME SCHEDULING.
BECH 1979 -1 BECHTOLD, S. E.
QUANTITATIVE MODELS FOR OPTIMAL REST PERIOD SCHEDULING: A NOTE.
BEEC 1979 -1 BEECHAM, A. F.; HURLEY, A. C.
SCHEDULING PROBLEM WITH A SIMPLE GRAPHICAL SOLUTION, A.
BELLA 1968 -1 BELL, T. E.
GRAPHICAL ANALYSIS PROCEDURES FOR SIMULATION AND SCHEDULING.
BELOA 1974 -1 BELOV, I. S.; STOLIN, JA. I.
ALGORITHM FOR A FLOW-SHOP SCHEDULING PROBLEM (RUSSIAN), AN.
BERL 1974 -1 BERLIN, V. G.
APPROXIMATE METHOD FOR SOLVING THE SIMPLEST PROBLEM OF SCHEDULING THEORY (RUSSIAN), AN.
BERTB 1980 -1 BERTOSSI, A. A.
ON THE COMPLEXITY OF SCHEDULING JOBS ON DEDICATED RESOURCES TO MINIMIZE SET-UP COSTS.
BESH 1979 -1 BESHARA, S. B.; MAGAZINE, M. J.
MYOPIC HEURISTICS FOR SINGLE MACHINE SCHEDULING PROBLEMS.
BEST 1979 -1 BESTWICK, P. F.; LOCKYER, K. G.
PRACTICAL APPROACH TO PRODUCTION SCHEDULING, A.
BHATD 1979 -1 BHATNAGAR, V. L.; DAS, G.; MEHTA, O. P.
N-JOB, 2-MACHINE FLOW JOB SHOP SCHEDULING PROBLEM HAVING MINIMUM TOTAL WAITING TIME FOR ALL JOBS.
BIAN 1980 -1 BIANCO, L.; CINI, M.; GRIPPO, L.
STRATEGIC APPROACH TO AIR TRAFFIC CONTROL, A.
BIANA 1978 -1 BIANCO, L.; NICOLETTI, B.; RICCIARDELLI, S.
ALGORITHM FOR OPTIMAL SEQUENCING OF AIRCRAFT IN THE NEAR TERMINAL AREA, AN.
BIANB 1981 -1 BIANCO, L.; RICCIARDELLI, S.
MINIMIZING MEAN WEIGHTED COMPLETION TIME IN ONE MACHINE SCHEDULING PROBLEM.
BIGH 1979 -1 BIGHAM, P. E.; MOGG, J. M.
CONVERGING BRANCH MULTI-STAGE PRODUCTION SCHEDULES WITH FINITE PRODUCTION RATES AND START-UP DELAYS.
BIGH 1979 -2 BIGHAM, P. E.; MOGG, J. M.
LOWER BOUND SOLUTIONS TO MULTI-STAGE PRODUCTION SCHEDULING PROBLEMS WITH STARTUP DELAYS.
BITRD 1981 -1 BITRAN, G. R.; YANASSE, H. H.
COMPUTATIONAL COMPLEXITY OF THE CAPACITATED LOT SIZE PROBLEM.
BLAZ 1978 -1 BLAZEWICZ, J.
COMPLEXITY OF COMPUTER SCHEDULING ALGORITHMS UNDER RESOURCE CONSTRAINTS.
BLAZ 1979 -1 BLAZEWICZ, J.
DEADLINE SCHEDULING OF TASKS WITH READY TIMES AND RESOURCE CONSTRAINTS.
BLAZ 1980 -1 BLAZEWICZ, J.
SCHEDULING TO MINIMIZE MEAN WEIGHTED INFORMATION LOSS.
BLAZ 1981 -1 BLAZEWICZ, J.
SOLVING THE RESOURCE CONSTRAINED DEADLINE SCHEDULING PROBLEM VIA REDUCTION TO THE NETWORK FLOW PROBLEM.
BLAZ 1978 -2 BLAZEWICZ, J.
SCHEDULING WITH DEADLINES IN MULTIPROCESSOR SYSTEMS.
BLAZ 1979 -2 BLAZEWICZ, J.
SCHEDULING TASKS ON PARALLEL PROCESSORS UNDER RESOURCE CONSTRAINTS TO MINIMIZE MEAN FINISHING TIME.
BLAZA 1980 -1 BLAZEWICZ, J.; LENSTRA, J. K.; RINNOOY KAN, A. H. G.
SCHEDULING SUBJECT TO RESOURCE CONSTRAINTS: CLASSIFICATION AND COMPLEXITY.
BLAZB 1978 -1 BLAZEWICZ, J.; WEGLARZ, J.
DETERMINISTIC TASK SCHEDULING PROBLEM ON PROCESSORS OF COMPUTER SYSTEMS WITH ALLOWANCE FOR ADDITIONAL RESOURCES (POLISH).
BLAZB 1979 -1 BLAZEWICZ, J.; WEGLARZ, J.
SCHEDULING UNDER RESOURCE CONSTRAINTS - ACHIEVEMENTS AND PROSPECTS.
BLAZB 1978 -2 BLAZEWICZ, J.; WEGLARZ, J.
SCHEDULING TO MEET DEADLINES WITH RESOURCE CONSTRAINTS - COMPLEXITY RESULTS.
BODIA 1979 -1 BODIN, L. D.; KURSH, S. J.
DETAILED DESCRIPTION OF A COMPUTER SYSTEM FOR THE ROUTING AND SCHEDULING OF STREET SWEEPERS, A.
BODIB 1981 -1 BODIN, L. D.; ROSENFIELD, D. B.; KYDES, A. S.
SCHEDULING AND ESTIMATION TECHNIQUES FOR TRANSPORTATION PLANNING.
BODIC 1979 -1 BODIN, L. D.; SEXTON, T. R.
SUBSCRIBER DIAL-A-RIDE PROBLEM, THE.
BOEB 1978 -1 BOEBION, J.; ALMAR, A.; PUN, L.
SCHEDULING METHOD SYNCHRONIZING TWO LINES OF ACTIVITIES AND MINIMIZING WAITING AND PASS-TIME.
BOEN 1979 -1 BOENCHENDORF, K.
HEURISTIKEN FUER DAS N !1! PREC ! SUM(WI*CI) REIHENFOLGEPROBLEM.
BOFF 1979 -1 BOFFEY, T. B.; EDMOND, E. D.; HINXMAN, A. I.; PURSGLOVE, C. J.
TWO APPROACHES TO SCHEDULING CONTAINER SHIPS WITH AN APPLICATION TO THE NORTH ATLANTIC ROUTE.
BOKI 1980 -1 BOKINGE, U.; HASSELSTROEM, D.
IMPROVED VEHICLE SCHEDULING IN PUBLIC TRANSPORT THROUGH SYSTEMATIC CHANGES IN THE TIME-TABLE.
BOOL 1980 -1 BOOLER, J. M. P.
SOLUTION OF A RAILWAY LOCOMOTIVE SCHEDULING PROBLEM, THE.
BORO 1977 -1 BOROHOVIC, R. E.; ZENIN, F. B.; ZENINA, JA. A.
ALGORITHM FOR THE COMPILATION OF A SCHEDULE UNDER THE CONDITIONS OF AN AUTOMATIC CONTROL SYSTEM (RUSSIAN), AN.
BOVE 1980 -1 BOVET, D. P.; PETRINI, M.
EVALUATION OF SCHEDULING ALGORITHMS FOR RESOURCES WITH HIGH SET-UP TIME.
BOYCB 1978 -1 BOYCE, S.; MORTON, T. E.
BOTTLENECK HORIZONS FOR ONE MACHINE SEQUENCING WITH PRECEDENCE CONSTRAINTS (REVISED VERSION).
BROWF 1978 -1 BROWNE, J.; PROPP, J. G.; TIBREWALA, R.
CONDITIONS FOR OPTIMAL SCHEDULING CONSECUTIVE WORK PERIODS.
BRUC 1973 -2 BRUCKER, P.
ON HU'S "CUTTING THE LONGEST QUEUE"-ALGORITHM.
BRUC 1981 -2 BRUCKER, P.
ON JOB-SHOP SCHEDULING WITH UNIT-TIME TASKS.
BRUN 1975 -1 BRUNO, J.
ON TASK SCHEDULING WITH A (USUALLY) FINITE PLANNING HORIZON.
BRUNA 1978 -1 BRUNO, J.; DOWNEY, P.
COMPLEXITY OF TASK SEQUENCING WITH DEADLINES, SET-UP TIMES AND CHANGEOVER COSTS.

BRUNB 1981 -1 BRUNO, J.; DOWNEY, P.; FREDERICKSON, G. N.
SEQUENCING TASKS WITH EXPONENTIAL SERVICE TIMES TO MINIMIZE THE EXPECTED FLOW TIME OR MAKESPAN.
BRUNC 1976 -1 BRUNO, J.; GONZALEZ, T.
SCHEDULING INDEPENDENT TASKS WITH RELEASE DATES AND DUE DATES ON PARALLEL MACHINES.
BRUND 1980 -1 BRUNO, J.; JONES, J. W., III; SO, K.
DETERMINISTIC SCHEDULING WITH PIPELINED PROCESSORS.
BRUNE 1978 -1 BRUNO, J.; SETHI, R.
TASK SEQUENCING IN A BATCH ENVIRONMENT WITH SETUP TIMES.
BRZE 1980 -1 BRZEZINSKI, J.
PREEMPTIVE SCHEDULING OF PROCESSORS WITH PRIVATE MEMORIES.
BULF 1975 -1 BULFIN, R. L.
MAN-MACHINE TASK ALLOCATION PROBLEM WITH SEQUENCING CONSIDERATIONS, THE.
BULFA 1980 -1 BULFIN, R. L.; PARKER, R. G.
SCHEDULING JOBS ON TWO FACILITIES TO MINIMIZE MAKESPAN.
BURK 1979 -2 BURKARD, R. E.
REMARKS ON SOME SCHEDULING PROBLEMS WITH ALGEBRAIC OBJECTIVE FUNCTIONS.
BURK 1979 -4 BURKARD, R. E.
UEBER EINE ANWENDUNG ALGEBRAISCHER TRANSPORTPROBLEME BEI REIHENFOLGEPROBLEMEN.
BURM 1976 -1 BURMAN, D.
OPERATOR SCHEDULING SYSTEM, AN.
BURNA 1978 -1 BURNS, F.; ROOKER, J.
THREE-STAGE FLOW-SHOPS WITH RECESSIVE SECOND STAGE.
BURNB 1978 -1 BURNS, R. N.
MANPOWER SCHEDULING WITH VARIABLE DEMANDS AND ALTERNATE WEEKENDS OFF.
CAIE 1980 -1 CAIE, J.; LINDEN, J.; MAXWELL, W.
SOLUTION OF A SINGLE STAGE MACHINE LOAD PLANNING PROBLEM.
CAIEA 1979 -1 CAIE, J.; LINDEN, J.; OATS, Q.; MAXWELL, W.
HIERARCHICAL MACHINE LOAD PLANNING.
CARLA 1979 -1 CARLSON, R. C.; JUCKER, J. V.; KROPP, D. H.
LESS NERVOUS MRP SYSTEMS: A DYNAMIC ECONOMIC LOT-SIZING APPROACH.
CART 1979 -1 CARTER, M. W.
FINAL EXAMINATION SCHEDULING FOR CORRESPONDENCE STUDENTS.
CARTA 1978 -1 CARTER, P. L.; REMUS, W. E.; JENICKE, L. O.
PRODUCTION SCHEDULING DECISION RULES IN CHANGING AND NON-LINEAR ENVIRONMENTS.
CASTB 1979 -1 CASTELLANI, G.; GIANNESSI, F.
DECOMPOSITION OF MATHEMATICAL PROGRAMS BY MEANS OF THEOREMS OF ALTERNATIVE FOR LINEAR AND NONLINEAR SYSTEMS.
CAVA 1975 -1 CAVANAGH, R. A.
AIRLINE CREW SCHEDULING.
CHAC 1979 -1 CHACHRA, V.; GHARE, P. M.; MOORE, J. M.
APPLICATIONS OF GRAPH THEORY ALGORITHMS.
CHANI 1978 -1 CHANG, Q. L.
PROBLEM OF SCHEDULING PRODUCTION SO AS TO MINIMIZE LATE DELIVERIES (CHINESE), THE.
CHEB 1976 -1 CHEBOTAREV, A. S.; SAFRANSKII, V. V.
PROBLEM OF SCHEDULING A COMPLEX OF PERFORMANCES THAT IS REPRESENTED BY A RESOURCE NETWORK MODEL OF SPECIAL FORM (RUSSIAN), THE.
CHENA 1978 -1 CHEN, D.-S.
SIMPLE ALGORITHM FOR A WORKFORCE SCHEDULING MODEL, A.
CHEND 1975 -1 CHEN, N.-F.
ANALYSIS OF SCHEDULING ALGORITHMS IN MULTIPROCESSOR COMPUTING SYSTEMS, AN.
CHENE 1978 -1 CHEN, R.; CROWDER, H. P.; JOHNSON, E. L.
SOLVING THE INSTALLATION SCHEDULING PROBLEM USING MIXED INTEGER LINEAR PROGRAMMING.
CHRIA 1971 -1 CHRISTIE, A.
MULTI-DIMENSIONAL SCHEDULING ALGORITHMS.
CIOB 1977 -1 CIOBANU, G.
BRANCH-AND-BOUND ALGORITHM TO SOLVE AN ASSEMBLY LINE BALANCING PROBLEM, A.
CIOB 1981 -1 CIOBANU, G.
ON FEASIBLE SOLUTIONS FOR PROJECT SCHEDULING PROBLEM.
COFF 1978 -1 COFFMAN, E. G. JR.
DETERMINISTIC SEQUENCING: COMPLEXITY AND OPTIMAL ALGORITHMS.
COFFB 1978 -1 COFFMAN, E. G. JR.; GAREY, M. R.; JOHNSON, D. S.
APPLICATION OF BIN-PACKING TO MULTIPROCESSOR SCHEDULING, AN.
COFFE 1976 -1 COFFMAN, E. G. JR.; LABETOULLE, J.
SCHEDULING TO MINIMIZE MEAN NUMBER IN SYSTEM.
COFFF 1977 -1 COFFMAN, E. G. JR.; LEUNG, J. Y.-T.; SLUTZ, D.
ON THE OPTIMALITY OF FIRST-FIT AND LEVEL ALGORITHMS FOR PARALLEL MACHINE ASSIGNMENT AND SEQUENCING.
COFFF 1978 -1 COFFMAN, E. G. JR.; LEUNG, J. Y.-T.; SLUTZ, D.
ON THE OPTIMALITY OF FAST HEURISTICS FOR SCHEDULING AND STORAGE ALLOCATION PROBLEMS.
COFFH 1976 -1 COFFMAN, E. G. JR.; SETHI, R.
GENERALIZED BOUND ON LPT SEQUENCING, A.
COMP 1975 -1 COMPANYS, R.
COMBINATORIAL PROGRAMMING: APPLICATION TO JOB SCHEDULING IN AN ORDINATOR WITH DISC OPERATIVE SYSTEM (SPANISH).
CONN 1971 -1 CONNER, J. L.
SEQUENCE PROGRAMMING: A HEURISTIC ALGORITHM FOR THE SOLUTION OF LARGE GENERAL JOB SHOP SCHEDULING PROBLEMS.
CONN 1972 -1 CONNER, J. L.
HEURISTIC METHOD FOR SOLVING JOBSHOP SEQUENCING PROBLEMS, A.
CONN 1973 -1 CONNER, J. L.
INTERACTIVE MANUFACTURING SCHEDULING AND CONTROL SYSTEM.
CONN 1973 -2 CONNER, J. L.
INTERACTIVE PRODUCTION CONTROL IN CAPACITY LIMITED SHOP.
COOK 1980 -1 COOK, W. D.; SAIPE, A. L.; SEIFORD, L. M.
PRODUCTION RUNS FOR MULTIPLE PRODUCTS: THE FULL-CAPACITY HEURISTIC.
CORK 1978 -1 CORKINDALE, D.
HOW TO CUT TRANSPORTATION COSTS WHILE MAINTAINING SERVICE LEVELS.
CUNT 1978 -1 CUNTO, E.
SCHEDULING BOATS TO SAMPLE OIL WELLS IN LAKE MARACAIBO.
DAR- 1978 -1 DAR-EL, E. M.
MIXED-MODEL ASSEMBLY LINE SEQUENCING PROBLEMS.
DAR-A 1980 -1 DAR-EL, E. M.; KARNI, R.
HYBRID ALGORITHM FOR INDEPENDENT TASK PARALLEL MACHINE SCHEDULING, A.
DAR-B 1979 -1 DAR-EL, E. M.; RUBINOVITCH, Y.
MUST - A MULTIPLE SOLUTIONS TECHNIQUE FOR BALANCING SINGLE MODEL ASSEMBLY LINES.

DAS 1978 -1 DAS, G.
EQUIVALENT-JOBS FOR JOB-BLOCKS FOR 'N-JOB, 3-MACHINE' SEQUENCING PROBLEMS.
DAS A 1978 -1 DAS, K. S.; TEOREY, T. J.
EFFICIENT JOB SCHEDULING ALGORITHM FOR MIXED TURNAROUND AND DEADLINE APPLICATIONS, AN.
DAS B 1978 -1 DAS, S.; PANDIT, S. N. N.
COMPUTATION OF A NEW LOWER BOUND: SEQUENCING N JOBS ON M PARALLEL PROCESSORS.
DAVI 1979 -1 DAVIO, M.; THAYSE, A.
ALGORITHMS FOR MINIMAL-LENGTH SCHEDULES.
DAVIB 1978 -1 DAVIS, R. P.; MILLER, D. M.
MODEL FOR DETERMINING MACHINE REQUIREMENTS IN A MULTISTAGE MANUFACTURING SYSTEM WITH DISCRETELY DISTRIBUTED DEMAND, A.
DAVIC 1979 -1 DAVIS, R. P.; WYSK, R. A.; KIMBLER, D. L.
TOOL-CHANGE SCHEDULING MODEL FOR MACHINING CENTRES, A.
DE 1977 -1 DE, P.; MORTON, T. E.
MAKESPAN SCHEDULING FOR UNEQUAL PARALLEL PROCESSORS (REVISED VERSION).
DELP 1976 -1 DELPORTE, C. M.; THOMAS, L. J.
LOT SIZE AND SEQUENCING FOR N PRODUCTS ON ONE FACILITY.
DESRA 1980 -1 DESROSIERS, J.; FERLAND, J. A.; ROUSSEAU, J.-M.; LAPALME, G.; CHAPLEAU, L.
SCHOOL BUSING SYSTEM, A.
DESS 1981 -1 DESSOUKY, M. I.; DEOGUN, J. S.
SEQUENCING JOBS WITH UNEQUAL READY TIMES TO MINIMIZE MEAN FLOW TIME.
DESSA 1978 -1 DESSOUKY, M. I.; LARSON, R. E.
SYMMETRY AND OPTIMALITY PROPERTIES OF THE SINGLE MACHINE PROBLEM.
DEWE 1977 -1 DEWESS, G.
LOESUNG EINES MASCHINENBELEGUNGSPROBLEMS DURCH NETZPLANUNG MIT RESSOURCENBESCHRAENKUNG.
DHAL 1978 -1 DHALL, S. K.; LIU, C. L.
ON A REAL-TIME SCHEDULING PROBLEM.
DHAV 1978 -1 DHAVALE, D.; AGGARWAL, S.
INVESTIGATION OF MULTIPRODUCT, MULTIMACHINE PRODUCTION SCHEDULING AND INVENTORY CONTROL OF FLOW-SHOP SYSTEM, AN.
DIRU 1980 -1 DIRUF, G.
KUNDENZEITSCHRANKEN IN DER COMPUTERGESTUETZTEN TOURENPLANUNG.
DOGR 1978 -1 DOGRAMACI, A.; SURKIS, J.
LIMITATIONS OF A PARALLEL PROCESSOR SCHEDULING ALGORITHM.
DOGR 1979 -1 DOGRAMACI, A.; SURKIS, J.
EVALUATION OF A HEURISTIC FOR SCHEDULING INDEPENDENT JOBS ON PARALLEL IDENTICAL PROCESSORS.
DORF 1979 -1 DORFMAN, V. A.
POLYHEDRON FOR A PROBLEM OF ORDERING TASKS AT A MACHINE (RUSSIAN).
DOUM 1978 -1 DOUMEINGTS, G.; PUN, L.; MONDAIN, M.; BREUIL, D.
DECISION-MAKING SYSTEMS FOR PRODUCTION CONTROL PLANNING AND SCHEDULING.
DRIS 1977 -1 DRISCOLL, W. C.; EMMONS, H.
SCHEDULING PRODUCTION ON ONE MACHINE WITH CHANGEOVER COSTS.
DUMA 1977 -1 DUMAS, M. B.
BRANCH BIAS HEURISTIC SCHEDULING OF THE GENERAL JOB SHOP.
DUMA 1978 -1 DUMAS, M. B.
BOUND CUTOFF HEURISTIC SCHEDULING OF THE GENERAL JOB SHOP.
DUMIA 1979 -1 DUMITRU, V.; LUBAN, F.
MEMBERSHIP FUNCTIONS, SOME MATHEMATICAL PROGRAMMING MODELS AND PRODUCTION SCHEDULING.
DUPR 1979 -1 DUPRE, R.; HUCKERT, K.
NAEHERUNGSVERFAHREN FUER MASCHINENBELEGUNGSPROBLEME, EIN.
DUUR 1970 -1 DUUREN, A. VAN; VERANTVOORT, J.
JOB-SHOP SCHEDULING.
ECKE 1977 -1 ECKER, K.
ORGANISATION VON PARALLELEN PROZESSEN. THEORIE DETERMINISTISCHER SCHEDULES.
EDWAA 1980 -1 EDWARDS, G. R.
APPROACH TO THE CREW SCHEDULING PROBLEM, AN.
EL-S 1980 -1 EL-SAWY, A. H. A.
MIXED INTEGER SCHEDULING MODEL FOR COMBINED THERMAL AND HYDROELECTRIC-PUMPED STORAGE GENERATOR SYSTEMS, A.
ELMA 1978 -1 ELMAGHRABY, S. E.
ECONOMIC LOT SCHEDULING PROBLEM (ELSP): REVIEW AND EXTENSIONS, THE.
ELMAA 1980 -1 ELMAGHRABY, S. E.; ELIMAM, A. A.
KNAPSACK-BASED APPROACHES TO THE MAKESPAN PROBLEM ON MULTIPLE PROCESSORS.
ELMAB 1980 -1 ELMAGHRABY, S. E.; HERROELEN, W. S.
ON THE MEASUREMENT OF COMPLEXITY IN ACTIVITY NETWORKS.
EMMO 1978 -1 EMMONS, H.
SURVEY OF STATIC JOB SHOP SCHEDULING THEORY, A. (REVISED VERSION).
ENGE 1981 -1 ENGELE, G.
SIMULTANE STANDORT- UND TOURENPLANUNG.
ERSC 1979 -1 ERSCHLER, J.; FONTAN, G.; ROUBELLAT, F.
POTENTIELS SUR UN GRAPHE NON CONJONCTIF ET ANALYSE D'UN PROBLEME D'ORDONNANCEMENT A MOYENS LIMITES.
ERSC 1980 -1 ERSCHLER, J.; FONTAN, G.; ROUBELLAT, F.
GRAPHES POTENTIELS-TACHES NON CONJONCTIFS ET PROBLEMES D'ORDONNANCEMENT.
ERSCA 1977 -1 ERSCHLER, J.; ROUBELLAT, F.
LIMITED RESOURCE SCHEDULING WITH EXECUTION TIME CONSTRAINTS.
ERSCB 1980 -1 ERSCHLER, J.; ROUBELLAT, F.; VERNHES, J. P.
CHARACTERIZING THE SET OF FEASIBLE SEQUENCES FOR N JOBS TO BE CARRIED OUT ON A SINGLE MACHINE.
EVER 1965 -1 EVERS, G. H. E.
RELEVANT FACTORS AROUND CREW-UTILIZATION.
FARN 1979 -1 FARN, C.-K.; MUHLEMANN, A. P.
DYNAMIC ASPECTS OF A PRODUCTION SCHEDULING PROBLEM, THE.
FAYO 1978 -1 FAYOLLE, G.; IASNOGORODSKY, R.; MITRANI, I.
ON THE SHARING OF A PROCESSOR AMONG MANY JOB CLASSES.
FEIG 1979 -1 FEIGIN, L. I.
ON THE DISTINGUISHABILITY OF OPERATIONS IN SCHEDULING.
FEIG 1979 -2 FEIGIN, L. I.
SEPARABILITE DES OPERATIONS D'ORNANNCEMENT (RUSSIAN).
FIALA 1977 -1 FIALA, T.
NEAR OPTIMAL ALGORITHM FOR THE THREE MACHINE PROBLEM (HUNGARIAN).
FINN 1979 -1 FINN, G.; HOROWITZ, E.
LINEAR TIME APPROXIMATION ALGORITHM FOR MULTIPROCESSOR SCHEDULING, A.
FISHB 1978 -1 FISHER, M. L.; JAIKUMAR, R.
ALGORITHM FOR THE SPACE-SHUTTLE SCHEDULING PROBLEM, AN.

FISKB 1980 -1 FISK, J. C.; SOLANO, A.
PRODUCTION SCHEDULING FOR HIGH-VOLUME ASSEMBLIES - A CASE STUDY.
FLOW 1977 -1 FLOWERS, A. D.; PRESTON, S. E.
WORK FORCE SCHEDULING WITH THE SEARCH DECISION RULE.
FONT 1980 -1 FONTAN, G.
NOTION DE DOMINANCE ET SON APPLICATION A L'ETUDE DE CERTAINS PROBLEMES D'ORDONNANCEMENT.
FRIEB 1981 -1 FRIESEN, D. K.; DEUERMEYER, B. L.
ANALYSIS OF GREEDY SOLUTIONS FOR A REPLACEMENT PART SEQUENCING PROBLEM.
FUJIA 1978 -1 FUJITA, S.
APPLICATION OF MARGINAL ANALYSIS TO THE ECONOMIC LOT SCHEDULING PROBLEM, THE.
FUNG 1978 -1 FUNG, K. T.
ON A RESTRICTIVE SCHEDULING SCHEME.
GAAL 1978 -1 GAALMAN, G. J.
OPTIMAL AGGREGATION OF MULTI-ITEM PRODUCTION SMOOTHING MODELS.
GAIT 1980 -1 GAITANIDES, M.
AUFGABENSTRUKTURPLANUNG UND FLEXIBILITAET VON PRODUKTIONSPROZESSEN.
GARE 1978 -1 GAREY, M. R.; GRAHAM, R. L.; JOHNSON, D. S.
PERFORMANCE GUARANTEES FOR SCHEDULING ALGORITHMS.
GARFB 1980 -1 GARFINKEL, R. S.; PLOTNICKI, W. J.
SOLVABLE CYCLIC SCHEDULING PROBLEM WITH SERIAL PRECEDENCE STRUCTURE, A.
GARY 1975 -1 GARY, D.
SCHEDULING TO MINIMIZE INTERACTION COSTS WITH FACILITY CONSTRAINTS.
GATI 1978 -1 GATI, G.
LEVEL-SCHEDULING FOR SPECIAL AND GENERAL PRECEDENCE GRAPHS.
GAVIB 1979 -1 GAVISH, B.; SHLIFER, E.
APPROACH FOR SOLVING A CLASS OF TRANSPORTATION SCHEDULING PROBLEMS, AN.
GELD 1978 -1 GELDERS, L. F.; SAMBANDAM, N.
FOUR SIMPLE HEURISTICS FOR SCHEDULING A FLOW SHOP.
GENS 1978 -1 GENS, G. V.; LEVNER, E. V.
APPROXIMATE ALGORITHMS FOR CERTAIN UNIVERSAL PROBLEMS IN SCHEDULING THEORY.
GERT 1978 -1 GERTSBACH, I.; STERN, H. I.
MINIMAL RESOURCES FOR FIXED AND VARIABLE JOB SCHEDULES.
GIAN 1980 -1 GIANNESSI, F.
CONTINUED FRACTIONS AND EXPLICIT SOLUTIONS OF A PARTICULAR DISCRETE OPTIMIZATION PROBLEM.
GIANC 1979 -1 GIANNESSI, F.; NICOLETTI, B.
CREW SCHEDULING PROBLEM: A TRAVELLING SALESMAN APPROACH, THE.
GLAZ 1980 -1 GLAZEBROOK, K. D.
ON SINGLE-MACHINE SEQUENCING WITH ORDER CONSTRAINTS.
GLAZA 1981 -1 GLAZEBROOK, K. D.; GITTINS, J. C.
ON SINGLE-MACHINE SCHEDULING WITH PRECEDENCE RELATIONS AND LINEAR OR DISCOUNTED COSTS.
GLEB 1978 -2 GLEBOV, N. I.
SOME CASES OF REDUCIBILITY OF JOHNSON'S M-MACHINE PROBLEM TO A PROBLEM OF TWO MACHINES (RUSSIAN).
GLIC 1978 -1 GLICKMAN, T. S.
NOTE ON MULTIPROJECT SCHEDULING TO MINIMIZE THE COST OF SUPPLEMENTAL EXTERNAL RESOURCES, A.
GLOVH 1976 -1 GLOVER, F.; MULVEY, J. M.
NETWORK-RELATED SCHEDULING MODELS FOR PROBLEMS WITH QUASI-ADJACENCY AND BLOCK ADJACENCY STRUCTURE.
GODA 1975 -1 GODAMBE, S. B.
MIXED-MODEL PRODUCTION SCHEDULING.
GODI 1969 -1 GODIN, V. B.
INTERACTIVE COMPUTER SYSTEM FOR PRODUCTION SCHEDULING, AN.
GODI 1978 -1 GODIN, V. B.
INTERACTIVE SCHEDULING: HISTORICAL SURVEY AND STATE OF THE ART.
GOLD 1980 -1 GOLDBERG, H. M.
JACKSON'S CONJECTURE ON EARLIEST DUE DATE SCHEDULING.
GONZ 1977 -1 GONZALEZ, T.
OPTIMAL MEAN FINISH TIME PREEMPTIVE SCHEDULES.
GONZ 1979 -1 GONZALEZ, T.
NOTE ON OPEN SHOP PREEMPTIVE SCHEDULES, A.
GONZ 1979 -2 GONZALEZ, T.
NP-HARD SHOP PROBLEMS.
GONZA 1980 -1 GONZALEZ, T.; JOHNSON, D. B.
NEW ALGORITM FOR PREEMPTIVE SCHEDULING OF TREES, A.
GONZB 1978 -1 GONZALEZ, T.; SAHNI, S.
FLOWSHOP AND JOBSHOP SCHEDULES: COMPLEXITY AND APPROXIMATION.
GORDA 1977 -1 GORDON, V. S.; CEGOLINA, E. P.
SINGLE-STAGE PROBLEM OF THE SCHEDULING THEORY WITH A TREE-ORDERED SET OF DEMANDS (RUSSIAN), THE.
GORDB 1978 -1 GORDON, V. S.; SAFRANSKII, JA. M.
OPTIMAL ORDERING UNDER SERIAL-PARALLEL PRECEDENCE CONSTRAINTS (RUSSIAN).
GOSP 1978 -1 GOSPODAROWICZ, A.
ON SOME PROBLEMS OF SCHEDULING THEORY (POLISH).
GOUR 1979 -1 GOURLAY, A. R.
HEURISTIC ALGORITHM FOR THE SOLUTION OF SERIATION PROBLEMS, A.
GOYA 1977 -1 GOYAL, D. K.
NON-PREEMPTIVE SCHEDULING OF UNEQUAL EXECUTION TIME TASKS ON TWO IDENTICAL PROCESSORS.
GOYAA 1978 -1 GOYAL, S. K.
NOTE ON AN EXTENSION OF JOHNSON'S RESULT ON TWO-STATE PRODUCTION SCHEDULES.
GRAB 1977 -1 GRABOWSKI, J.
NEW FORMULATION AND SOLUTION OF THE SEQUENCING PROBLEM: ALGORITHM, A.
GRAB 1979 -1 GRABOWSKI, J.
GENERALIZED PROBLEMS OF OPTIMIZATION OF SEQUENCING OPERATIONS IN DISCRETE PRODUCTION SYSTEMS (POLISH).
GRAB 1980 -1 GRABOWSKI, J.
ON TWO-MACHINE SCHEDULING WITH RELEASE AND DUE DATES TO MINIMIZE MAXIMUM LATENESS.
GRAB 1981 -1 GRABOWSKI, J.
ON FLOW-SHOP PROBLEM WITH RELEASE AND DUE DATES TO MINIMIZE MAXIMUM LATENESS.
GRAB 1978 -2 GRABOWSKI, J.
FORMULATION AND SOLUTION OF THE SEQUENCING PROBLEM WITH PARALLEL MACHINES (POLISH).
GRAB 1978 -3 GRABOWSKI, J.
FORMULATION AND SOLUTION OF THE SEQUENCING PROBLEM WITH PARALLEL MACHINES.
GRAB 1978 -4 GRABOWSKI, J.
FORMULATION AND SOLUTION OF THE SEQUENCING PROBLEM WITH PARALLEL MACHINES.
GRAH 1978 -1 GRAHAM, R. L.
COMBINATORIAL MATHEMATICS OF SCHEDULING, THE.

GRAH 1978 -2 GRAHAM, R. L.
COMBINATORIAL SCHEDULING THEORY.
GRAHA 1978 -1 GRAHAM, R. L.; LAWLER, E. L.; LENSTRA, J. K.; RINNOOY KAN, A. H. G.
OPTIMIZATION AND APPROXIMATION IN DETERMINISTIC SEQUENCING AND SCHEDULING: A SURVEY.
GRAHA 1979 -1 GRAHAM, R. L.; LAWLER, E. L.; LENSTRA, J. K.; RINNOOY KAN, A. H. G.
OPTIMIZATION AND APPROXIMATION IN DETERMINISTIC SEQUENCING AND SCHEDULING: A SURVEY.
GRAVA 1979 -1 GRAVES, S. C.
ON THE DETERMINISTIC DEMAND MULTI-PRODUCT SINGLE-MACHINE LOT SCHEDULING PROBLEM.
GRAVB 1978 -1 GRAVES, S. C.; HAESSLER, R. W.
ON "PRODUCTION RUNS FOR MULTIPLE PRODUCTS: THE TWO-PRODUCT HEURISTIC".
GRIE 1980 -1 GRIESSHABER, R.
MODEL FOR CREW SCHEDULING FOR A SHORT HAUL FLEET.
GRIGD 1978 -1 GRIGOREVA, N. S.; ROMANOVSKII, I. V.
PROBLEMS OF CYCLIC SCHEDULING.
GUIGA 1979 -3 GUIGNARD, M.; SPIELBERG, K.
MAINTENANCE SCHEDULING.
GUPT 1979 -1 GUPTA, J. N. D.
IMPROVED LEXICOGRAPHIC SEARCH ALGORITHM FOR THE FLOWSHOP SCHEDULING PROBLEM, AN.
GUPTA 1978 -1 GUPTA, J. N. D.; REDDI, S. S.
IMPROVED DOMINANCE CONDITIONS FOR THE THREE-MACHINE FLOWSHOP SCHEDULING PROBLEM.
GUPTE 1976 -1 GUPTA, S. K.; TURKSON, I. B.
APPLICATION OF BRANCH AND BOUND TECHNIQUE TO PRODUCTION SCHEDULING PROBLEMS.
GUST 1973 -1 GUSTAFSON, C. E.
COMPUTER ASSISTED INTERACTIVE RESOURCE SCHEDULING SYSTEM.
HAESC 1973 -1 HAESSLER, R. W.
DEVELOPMENT OF A HEURISTIC PROCEDURE TO SOLVE A PRODUCTION SCHEDULING PROBLEM, THE.
HAESC 1979 -1 HAESSLER, R. W.
IMPROVED EXTENDED BASIC PERIOD PROCEDURE FOR SOLVING THE ECONOMIC LOT SCHEDULING PROBLEM, AN.
HAID 1972 -1 HAIDER, S. W.
INVESTIGATION OF THE USE OF AN INTERACTIVE COMPUTER MODE FOR BALANCING PACED ASSEMBLY LINES, AN.
HAID 1976 -1 HAIDER, S. W.
INVESTIGATION OF THE ADVANTAGES OF USING A MAN-COMPUTER INTERACTIVE MODE FOR SCHEDULING JOB SHOPS, AN.
HARTE 1975 -1 HARTWIG, A.
ANWENDUNG DES ERWEITERUNGSPRINZIPS AUF SPEZIELLE REIHENFOLGEPROBLEME.
HARTF 1978 -1 HARTWIG, A.; TERNO, J.
TRANSFORMATION VON REIHENFOLGEPROBLEMEN AUF RUNDREISEPROBLEME.
HELL 1981 -2 HELL, P.; KIRKPATRICK, D. G.
SCHEDULING, MATCHING, AND COLORING.
HEND 1975 -1 HENDERSON, P. B.
HEURISTIC SCHEDULING POLICIES FOR SERVICE SYSTEMS WITH QUADRATIC WAITING COSTS.
HILLB 1979 -1 HILLIER, F. S.; BOLING, R. W.
ON THE OPTIMAL ALLOCATION OF WORK IN SYMMETRICALLY UNBALANCED PRODUCTION LINE SYSTEMS WITH VARIABLE OPERATING TIMES.
HINE 1978 -1 HINE, J. H.
SCHEDULING SEVERAL CLASSES OF JOBS IN A NETWORK OF SERVERS.
HODZ 1978 -1 HODZAEV, F. Z.
PROBLEM OF SPECIFYING ASSEMBLY PROCEDURES IN A MACHINE SHOP (RUSSIAN), THE.
HODZA 1978 -1 HODZINSKII, A. N.
RESULTS OF A COMPUTER EXPERIMENT IN SOLVING A TYPE OF PROBLEM IN SCHEDULING THEORY BY THE BRANCH AND BOUND METHOD AND THE DROP VECTOR METHOD (RUSSIAN).
HOEN 1979 -1 HOENEMANN, F.
STRUKTURIERUNG DISKONTINUIERLICH DISKRETER PROZESSE.
HOENA 1979 -1 HOENERLOH, H.
LOESUNG DES EINFACHEN MASCHINENBELEGUNGSPROBLEMS (FLOW SHOP SCHEDULING PROBLEM) MIT EINEM SPEZIELLEN RECHNER, DIE.
HOLL 1972 -1 HOLLOWAY, C. A.; NELSON, R. T.
INTERACTIVE PROGRAM FOR THE JOB SHOP SCHEDULING PROBLEM WITH DUE DATES, AN.
HOSI 1980 -1 HOSIOS, A. J.; ROUSSEAU, J.-M.
HEURISTIC SCHEDULING ALGORITHM, A.
HSU 1980 -1 HSU, C.; WILHELM, W. E.
FLOW SHOP SEQUENCING WITH PROBABILISTIC PROCESSING TIMES.
HSU A 1980 -1 HSU, W.-L.
ON THE GENERAL FEASIBILITY TEST OF SCHEDULING LOT SIZES FOR SEVERAL PRODUCTS ON ONE MACHINE.
HUCK 1980 -1 HUCKERT, K.
ZUR ANWENDUNG DER BENDERSSCHEN PARTITIONSMETHODE AUF JOB-SHOP-PROBLEME.
HUCKA 1980 -1 HUCKERT, K.; RHODE, R.; ROGLIN, O.; WEBER, R.
ON THE INTERACTIVE SOLUTION TO A MULTICRITERIA SCHEDULING PROBLEM.
IBARD 1975 -1 IBARRA, O. H.; KIM, C. E.
SCHEDULING FOR MAXIMUM PROFIT.
IGNI 1978 -1 IGNIZIO, J. P.
SOLVING LARGE SCHEDULING PROBLEMS BY MINIMIZING CONFLICT.
IKRA 1975 -1 IKRAM, M.
ON CERTAIN NEW TERMS IN SEQUENCING THEORY AND ON ALTERNATIVE OPTIMAL SEQUENCES.
ILNI 1979 -1 ILNITSKIJ, A. I.
ESTIMATION OF THE TARGET FUNCTION OF A DISCRETE PROBLEM OF SCHEDULING THEORY (RUSSIAN).
INFA 1978 -1 INFANTE MACIAS, R.; PASCUAL ACOSTA, A.
SOME VARIATIONS OF THE VARIABLE DURATION PROBLEM (SPANISH).
INST 1976 -1 INST. PROBL. UPR. (ED.).
SCHEDULING PROBLEMS IN DISCRETE PRODUCTION AND NUMERICAL SOLUTION METHODS (RUSSIAN).
ISKA 1978 -1 ISKANDER, W.
NEAR - OPTIMAL SOLUTION TO THE DYNAMIC JOB SHOP SEQUENCING PROBLEM, A.
JAFF 1980 -1 JAFFE, J. M.
ANALYSIS OF PREEMPTIVE MULTIPROCESSOR JOB SCHEDULING, AN.
JAFF 1980 -2 JAFFE, J. M.
BOUNDS ON THE SCHEDULING OF TYPED TASK SYSTEMS.
JAFF 1980 -3 JAFFE, J. M.
EFFICIENT SCHEDULING OF TASKS WITHOUT FULL USE OF PROCESSOR RESOURCES.
JANB 1977 -1 JANBYH, G. F.; STOLJAROV, B. A.
OPTIMIZATION OF THE STRUCTURE OF MULTIPROGRAMMED COMPUTER SYSTEMS FOR SOLVING SETS OF DEPENDENT TASKS (RUSSIAN).
JOZS 1978 -1 JOZSEF, T.
SCHEDULING OF REGULAR PAIRS OF JOB-FLOWS. I. (HUNGARIAN).

JOZS 1978 -2 JOZSEF, T.
SCHEDULING OF REGULAR PAIRS OF JOB-FLOWS. II. (HUNGARIAN).
KALR 1979 -1 KALRA, K. R.; BANSAL, S. P.
ALTERNATIVE OPTIMALS OF MAKE-SPAN IN TWO MACHINE FLOW SHOP PROBLEMS.
KALRA 1979 -1 KALRA, K. R.; BANSAL, S. P.; BAGGA, P. C.
MINIMIZATION OF WEIGHTED SUM OF COMPLETION TIMES WITH DUE DATES IN PERMUTATION FLOWSHOP PROBLEMS.
KANC 1978 -1 KANCEDAL, S. A.; MAKSIMOV, J. B.
COMPLEX OF LOT SIZE AND SCHEDULING MODELS FOR A SMALL LOT PRODUCTION. (RUSSIAN). A.
KANE 1978 -1 KANELLAKIS, P. C.
ALGORITHMS FOR A SCHEDULING APPLICATION OF THE ASYMMETRIC TRAVELING SALESMAN PROBLEM.
KAO 1979 -1 KAO, E. P. C.
MULTI-PRODUCT DYNAMIC LOT-SIZE MODEL WITH INDIVIDUAL AND JOINT SET-UP COSTS. A.
KAO 1980 -1 KAO, E. P. C.
MULTIPLE OBJECTIVE DECISION THEORETIC APPROACH TO ONE-MACHINE SCHEDULING PROBLEMS. A.
KAO A 1981 -1 KAO, E. P. C.; QUEYRANNE, M.
ON DYNAMIC PROGRAMMING METHODS FOR ASSEMBLY LINE BALANCING.
KAPA 1978 -1 KAPADIA, A. S.; HSI, B. P.
STEADY STATE WAITING TIME IN A MULTICENTER JOB SHOP.
KAS 1977 -1 KAS, P.
ON PROBLEMS OF PREEMPTIVE SCHEDULING INTERPRETED BY NETWORK FLOW PROBLEMS (HUNGARIAN).
KAS 1979 -1 KAS, P.
ON A SPECIAL TYPE OF JOB SEQUENCING PROBLEM.
KATS 1980 -1 KATS, V. B.; MIKHAJLETSKIJ, Z. N.
SOLUTION EXACTE D'UN PROBLEME D'ORDONNANCEMENT OPTIMAL D'UN PROCESSUS CYCLIQUE (RUSSIAN).
KEIT 1979 -1 KEITH, E. G.
OPERATOR SCHEDULING.
KHAN 1974 -1 KHAN, A. W.
ON SEQUENCING ORDERED MATRIX FLOWSHOP PROBLEMS.
KHAT 1979 -1 KHATOR, S.; MOODIE, C.
MACHINE LOADING PROCEDURE WHICH CONSIDERS PART COMPLEXITY AND MACHINE CAPABILITY. A.
KIM A 1975 -1 KIM, C. E.
APPROXIMATION ALGORITHMS FOR SOME P-COMPLETE SCHEDULING PROBLEMS.
KING 1979 -1 KING, J. R.
SCHEDULING AND THE PROBLEM OF COMPUTATIONAL COMPLEXITY.
KINGA 1980 -1 KING, J. R.; SPACHIS, A. S.
HEURISTICS FOR FLOW-SHOP SCHEDULING.
KINGA 1980 -2 KING, J. R.; SPACHIS, A. S.
SCHEDULING: BIBLIOGRAPHY AND REVIEW.
KISE 1978 -1 KISE, H.; IBARAKI, T.; MINE, H.
SOLVABLE CASE OF THE ONE-MACHINE SCHEDULING PROBLEM WITH READY AND DUE TIMES. A.
KISE 1979 -1 KISE, H.; IBARAKI, T.; MINE, H.
PERFORMANCE ANALYSIS OF SIX APPROXIMATION ALGORITHMS FOR THE ONE-MACHINE MAXIMUM LATENESS SCHEDULING PROBLEM WITH READY TIMES.
KISEA 1979 -1 KISE, H.; KABATA, M.; UNO, M.; IBARAKI, T.; MINE, H.
APPROXIMATION ALGORITHM FOR THE PARALLEL-MACHINE MAXIMUM LATENESS SCHEDULING PROBLEM WITH READY TIME CONSTRAINT.
KISEB 1978 -1 KISE, H.; UNO, M.
ONE-MACHINE SCHEDULING PROBLEMS WITH EARLIEST START AND DUE TIME CONSTRAINTS.
KISEC 1979 -1 KISE, H.; UNO, M.; KABATA, M.
APPROXIMATION ALGORITHMS FOR IDENTICAL PARALLEL-MACHINE SCHEDULING PROBLEMS WITH READY TIMES AND PRECEDENCE CONSTRAINTS.
KLAP 1980 -1 KLAPKA, J.; DVORAK, J.
MORE EFFICIENT COMPUTATION OF OPTIMAL LOT SIZES IN A MULTISTAGE PRODUCTION PROCESS (CZECHOSLOVAKIAN). A.
KLEIC 1980 -1 KLEINDORFER, P. R.; LIEBER, Z.
EXISTENCE CONDITIONS FOR THE PRODUCTION SCHEDULING AND EMPLOYMENT SMOOTHING PROBLEM.
KLUYA 1980 -1 KLUYVER, C. A. DE; WHYTE, A. G. D.
FOREST HARVEST SCHEDULING IN FIJI: A COMPARATIVE CASE STUDY OF LINEAR PROGRAMMING, HEURISTIC AND DECOMPOSITION TECHNIQUES.
KOLEA 1981 -1 KOLESNIKOV, V. V.
ON A PROBLEM SOLUTION OF MACHINE PROCESSING SCHEDULE UNDER ORDINARY GRAPH (RUSSIAN).
KOZL 1977 -1 KOZLOV, M. K.; SHAFRANSKIJ, V. V.
TIME SCHEDULING OF OPERATION COMPLEXES WITH LIMITED INTENSITIES OF EXECUTION OF COMPONENT OPERATIONS.
KREI 1979 -1 KREININ, M. I.; NIKONOV, V. A.; SAVICKAJA, T. I.
SOLUTION OF A PROBLEM OF JOB-SHOP LOADING (RUSSIAN).
KRIC 1978 -1 KRICHEL, R.
ANALYSE EINES RECHNERMODELLS DURCH RUECKFUEHRUNG AUF EIN 3-MASCHINEN- FLOW-SHOP-PROBLEM.
KROU 1980 -1 KROUZEK, J.
ON THE DEVELOPMENT OF EFFICIENT PRODUCTION SCHEDULING AND CONTROL MODELS.
KUBOB 1980 -1 KUBOKAWA, S.; SOSHIRODA, M.
SCHEDULING PROCEDURES FOR SPECIAL ORDER ITEMS IN A TWO-STAGE LOT PRODUCTION SYSTEM.
KUKS 1978 -1 KUKSA, A. I.; LAPTIN, J. P.
DYNAMIC PROGRAMMING IN THE NETWORK PROBLEM FOR OBTAINING THE SHORTEST SCHEDULE.
KUND 1981 -1 KUNDE, M.
NONPREEMPTIVE LP-SCHEDULING ON HOMOGENEOUS MULTIPROCESSOR SYSTEMS.
KURB 1980 -1 KURBEL, K.
PRINCIPLES OF SOFTWARE DESIGN FOR QUANTITATIVE METHODS: AN APPLICATION TO LOT SIZE PLANNING, SEQUENCING, AND SCHEDULING.
KURI 1976 -1 KURISU, T.
TWO-MACHINE SCHEDULING UNDER REQUIRED PRECEDENCE AMONG JOBS.
KURI 1977 -1 KURISU, T.
THREE-MACHINE SCHEDULING PROBLEM WITH PRECEDENCE CONSTRAINTS.
KURI 1979 -1 KURISU, T.
SINGLE-MACHINE SEQUENCING WITH PRECEDENCE CONSTRAINTS AND DEFERRAL COSTS.
KURI 1977 -2 KURISU, T.
TWO-MACHINE SCHEDULING UNDER ARBITRARY PRECEDENCE CONSTRAINTS.
KUSH 1981 -1 KUSHNER, D. D.; DAVIS, K. R.
COST ANALYSIS OF FOUR ASSIGNMENT HEURISTICS IN DYNAMIC LINE BALANCING.
KUZD 1979 -1 KUZDRALL, P. J.; MELNYK, S. A.; PIPER, C. J.
COMPARATIVE ANALYSIS OF LOT-SIZING ALGORITHM PERFORMANCE. A.
LABE 1978 -1 LABETOULLE, J.; LAWLER, E. L.; LENSTRA, J. K.; RINNOOY KAN, A. H. G.
PREEMPTIVE SCHEDULING OF UNIFORM MACHINES (PRELIMINARY DRAFT).
LABE 1979 -1 LABETOULLE, J.; LAWLER, E. L.; LENSTRA, J. K.; RINNOOY KAN, A. H. G.
PREEMPTIVE SCHEDULING OF UNIFORM MACHINES SUBJECT TO RELEASE DATES.

LAGE 1977 -1 LAGEWEG, B. J.; LENSTRA, J. K.; RINNOOY KAN, A. H. G.
JOB-SHOP SCHEDULING BY IMPLICIT ENUMERATION.

LAGE 1978 -1 LAGEWEG, B. J.; LENSTRA, J. K.; RINNOOY KAN, A. H. G.
GENERAL BOUNDING SCHEME FOR THE PERMUTATION FLOW-SHOP PROBLEM, A.

LAGE 1979 -1 LAGEWEG, B. J.; LENSTRA, J. K.; RINNOOY KAN, A. H. G.
MINIMIZING MAXIMUM LATENESS ON ONE MACHINE: ALGORITHMS AND APPLICATIONS.

LAHR 1979 -2 LAHRICHI, A.
ORDONNANCEMENTS; LA NOTION DE PARTIE OBLIGATOIRE ET SON APPLICATION AUX PROBLEMES CUMULATIFS.

LAKS 1978 -1 LAKSHMINARAYAN, S.; LAKSHMANAN, R.; PAPINEAU, R. L.; ROCHETTE, R.
OPTIMAL SINGLE MACHINE SCHEDULING WITH EARLINESS AND TARDINESS PENALTIES.

LAKS 1979 -1 LAKSHMINARAYAN, S.; LAKSHMANAN, R.; PAPINEAU, R. L.; ROCHETTE, R.
ORDER PRESERVING ALLOCATION OF JOBS TO TWO NON-IDENTICAL PARALLEL MACHINES: A SOLVABLE CASE OF THE MAXIMUM CUT PROBLEM.

LAM 1975 -1 LAM, S.
WORST CASE ANALYSIS OF MULTIPROCESSOR SCHEDULING ALGORITHMS.

LAM A 1975 -1 LAM, S.; SETHI, R.
WORST CASE ANALYSIS OF THE COFFMAN-GRAHAM SCHEDULING ALGORITHM.

LAMB 1979 -1 LAMBRECHT, M. R.; VANDERVEKEN, H.
HEURISTIC PROCEDURES FOR THE SINGLE OPERATION, MULTI-ITEM LOADING PROBLEM.

LAMB 1979 -2 LAMBRECHT, M. R.; VANDERVEKEN, H.
PRODUCTION SCHEDULING AND SEQUENCING FOR MULTI-STAGE PRODUCTION SYSTEMS.

LAPO 1978 -1 LAPORTE, G.
SERIATION PROBLEM AND THE TRAVELLING SALESMAN PROBLEM, THE.

LAPOA 1978 -1 LAPORTE, G.; BIRON, J.; NOBERT, Y.
ROTATING SCHEDULES.

LAPS 1978 -1 LAPSHIN, S. V.
DYNAMIC FORECASTING OF JOB SEQUENCING AND SIZE IN SERIAL PRODUCTION.

LAPT 1978 -1 LAPTIN, J. P.
COMPARISON OF CERTAIN METHODS OF COMPUTING THE LOWER BOUNDS OF SHORTEST SCHEDULES.

LARSB 1978 -1 LARSON, R. E.; DESSOUKY, M. I.
HEURISTIC PROCEDURES FOR THE SINGLE MACHINE PROBLEM TO MINIMIZE MAXIMUM LATENESS.

LAWI 1979 -1 LAWIS, R. T.; PARKER, R. G.
BIN PACKING, MULTI-PROCESSOR SCHEDULING, AND GRAPH COLORING.

LAWL 1979 -1 LAWLER, E. L.
EFFICIENT IMPLEMENTATION OF DYNAMIC PROGRAMMING ALGORITHMS FOR SEQUENCING PROBLEMS.

LAWL 1979 -3 LAWLER, E. L.
PREEMPTIVE SCHEDULING OF UNIFORM PARALLEL MACHINES TO MINIMIZE THE WEIGHTED NUMBER OF LATE JOBS.

LAWLA 1978 -1 LAWLER, E. L.; LABETOULLE, J.
ON PREEMPTIVE SCHEDULING OF UNRELATED PARALLEL PROCESSORS BY LINEAR PROGRAMMING.

LAWLB 1981 -1 LAWLER, E. L.; LENSTRA, J. K.; RINNOOY KAN, A. H. G.
MINIMIZING MAXIMUM LATENESS IN A TWO-MACHINE OPEN SHOP.

LAWLC 1981 -1 LAWLER, E. L.; MARTEL, C. U.
SCHEDULING PERIODICALLY OCCURRING TASKS ON MULTIPLE PROCESSORS.

LAWLD 1978 -1 LAWLER, E. L.; SIVAZLIAN, B. D.
MINIMIZATION OF TIME-VARYING COSTS IN SINGLE-MACHINE SCHEDULING.

LEBEC 1978 -1 LEBEDINSKAJA, N. B.
MINIMIZATION OF MAXIMUM PENALTY IN THE CASE OF PREEMPTION OF JOBS (RUSSIAN).

LEE B 1978 -1 LEE, S. M.; CLAYTON, R. E.; TAYLOR, B. W. III
GOAL PROGRAMMING APPROACH TO MULTI-PERIOD PRODUCTION LINE SCHEDULING, A.

LEIG 1979 -1 LEIGHTON, F. T.
GRAPH COLORING ALGORITHM FOR LARGE SCHEDULING PROBLEMS, A.

LENSA 1973 -1 LENSTRA, J. K.; RINNOOY KAN, A. H. G.
TOWARDS A BETTER ALGORITHM FOR THE JOB-SHOP SCHEDULING PROBLEM - I.

LENSA 1978 -1 LENSTRA, J. K.; RINNOOY KAN, A. H. G.
COMPLEXITY OF SCHEDULING UNDER PRECEDENCE CONSTRAINTS.

LENSA 1980 -1 LENSTRA, J. K.; RINNOOY KAN, A. H. G.
COMPLEXITY RESULTS FOR SCHEDULING CHAINS ON A SINGLE MACHINE.

LENSA 1980 -2 LENSTRA, J. K.; RINNOOY KAN, A. H. G.
INTRODUCTION A L'ORDONNANCEMENT DE PLUSIEURS MACHINES.

LENSA 1979 -3 LENSTRA, J. K.; RINNOOY KAN, A. H. G.
COMPLEXITY OF VEHICLE ROUTING AND SCHEDULING PROBLEMS.

LENSA 1980 -3 LENSTRA, J. K.; RINNOOY KAN, A. H. G.
INTRODUCTION TO MULTIPROCESSOR SCHEDULING, AN.

LEUNA 1980 -1 LEUNG, J. Y.-T.; MERRILL, M. L.
NOTE ON PREEMPTIVE SCHEDULING OF PERIODIC, REAL-TIME TASKS, A.

LEVIB 1980 -1 LEVIN, M. S.
ON EFFICIENT SOLUTION OF SOME PROBLEMS OF THE NETWORK SCHEDULE THEORY (RUSSIAN).

LEVIC 1978 -1 LEVIN, M. S.; LEVNER, E. V.
EFFECTIVE SOLUTION OF THE BELLMAN-JOHNSON PROBLEM ON A TREE-LIKE NETWORK, AN.

LEVID 1979 -1 LEVIN, V. I.
BLOCK LOGICAL CONSTRUCTIONS IN SOME PROBLEMS OF DISCRETE OPTIMIZATION.

LEVID 1979 -3 LEVIN, V. I.
STRUCTURAL AND LOGICAL METHODS OF COMBINATORIAL OPTIMIZATION.

LEVN 1971 -1 LEVNER, E. V.
SCHEDULING PROBLEM THAT CAN BE REDUCED TO A SHORTEST PATH PROBLEM (RUSSIAN), A.

LI 1977 -1 LI, H. F.
SCHEDULING TREES IN PARALLEL/PIPELINED PROCESSING ENVIRONMENTS.

LIN 1980 -1 LIN, K.-S.
SCHEDULING WITH PARALLEL MACHINES TO MINIMIZE TOTAL JOB TARDINESS.

LIU 1977 -1 LIU, C. L.
DETERMINISTIC JOB SCHEDULING IN COMPUTING SYSTEMS.

LIU A 1974 -1 LIU, J. W. S.; LIU, C. L.
BOUNDS ON SCHEDULING ALGORITHMS FOR HETEROGENEOUS COMPUTING SYSTEMS.

LLOY 1981 -1 LLOYD, E. L.
COFFMAN-GRAHAM SCHEDULING OF UET TASK SYSTEMS WITH 0-1 RESOURCES.

LOCK 1978 -1 LOCKETT, A. G.; MUHLEMANN, A. P.
PROBLEM OF AGGREGATE SCHEDULING, AN APPLICATION OF GOAL PROGRAMMING, A.

LOVEB 1978 -1 LOVE, R. R. JR; VEMUGANTI, R. R.
SINGLE-PLANT MOLD ALLOCATION PROBLEM WITH CAPACITY AND CHANGEOVER RESTRICTIONS, THE.

LU 1970 -1 LU, M. T.
COMPUTERIZED AIRLINE CREW SCHEDULING SYSTEM, A.

LUBA 1979 -1 LUBAN, F.; DUMITRU, V.
ON THE JOB SHOP SCHEDULING BY MATHEMATICAL PROGRAMMING.

LUGA 1979 -1 LUGACHEV, M. I.
PROBLEM OF DISTRIBUTION AND ORDERING IN PRODUCTION SCHEDULING (RUSSIAN), A.

LUSS 1980 -1 LUSS, H.
NETWORK FLOW APPROACH FOR CAPACITY EXPANSION PROBLEMS WITH TWO FACILITY TYPES, A.

LYON 1979 -1 LYON, G.
BATCH SCHEDULING FROM SHORT LISTS.

MAC C 1980 -1 MAC DONALD, G. W.; HODGSON, T. J.
INTERACTIVE SCHEDULING OF A GENERALIZED FLOWSHOP.

MAC F 1978 -1 MAC GINNIS, L. F.; CULVER, W. D.; DEANE, R. H.
ONE- AND TWO-PHASE HEURISTICS FOR WORKFORCE SCHEDULING.

MACK 1978 -1 MACK, H. L.; SMITH, L. D.
SCHEDULING WITH LIST PROCESSING AND PROBLEM ORIENTED DATA STRUCTURES; AN ITINERANT TEACHER EXAMPLE.

MADS 1980 -1 MADSEN, O. B. G.
CUTTING SEQUENCING ALGORITHM, A.

MAGAA 1979 -1 MAGAZINE, M. J.; WEE, T. S.
GENERALIZATION OF BIN-PACKING HEURISTICS TO THE LINE BALANCING PROBLEM, THE.

MAGG 1974 -1 MAGGU, P. L.; ALAM, M. S.; IKRAM, M.
ON CERTAIN TYPE OF SEQUENCING PROBLEM WITH N JOBS AND M MACHINES.

MAGGA 1977 -1 MAGGU, P. L.; DAS, G.
EQUIVALENT JOBS FOR JOB BLOCKS IN JOB SEQUENCING.

MAGGA 1979 -1 MAGGU, P. L.; DAS, G.
ON THE CONCEPT OF DUALITY IN SEQUENCING THEORY.

MAGGA 1979 -2 MAGGU, P. L.; DAS, G.
SHORT NOTE ON THE PAPER: "EQUIVALENT JOBS FOR JOB-BLOCKS IN JOB SEQUENCING" (OPSEARCH 14, 1977, 277-281).

MAGGB 1974 -1 MAGGU, P. L.; IKRAM, M.; ALAM, M. S.
ON CERTAIN THEOREMS IN SEQUENCING THEORY.

MAKSA 1978 -1 MAKSIMENKOV, A. V.
COMPUTER RESOURCE SCHEDULING WITH MINIMUM DISPROPORTIONS (RUSSIAN).

MAKSA 1979 -1 MAKSIMENKOV, A. V.
SCHEDULING WITH RESTRICTION ON RESOURCE USE RATE.

MAKSB 1978 -1 MAKSIMENKOV, A. V.; SHCHERS, A. L.
SCHEDULING THE FILLING OF STANDING ORDER ASSIGNMENTS (RUSSIAN).

MAKSC 1980 -1 MAKSIMOV, J. B.; KRIVORUCHKO, E. I.
APPLICATION OF THE BRANCH AND BOUND METHOD TO THE SOLUTION OF DISCRETE VOLUME SCHEDULING PROBLEMS (RUSSIAN).

MARQ 1979 -1 MARQUEZ DIEZ CANEDO, J.; MEDINA-MORA ESCALANTE, O.
NETWORK SOLUTION TO A GENERAL VEHICLE SCHEDULING PROBLEM, A.

MARS 1975 -1 MARSTEN, R. E.
USE OF THE BOXSTEP METHOD IN DISCRETE OPTIMIZATION, THE.

MARTD 1975 -1 MARTIN-VEGA, L. A.
OPTIMAL RULES AND ALGORITHMS FOR SOME PARALLEL PROCESSOR SCHEDULING PROBLEMS.

MARTE 1977 -1 MARTIN-VEGA, L. A.; RATLIFF, H. D.
SCHEDULING RULES FOR PARALLEL PROCESSORS.

MAYB 1978 -1 MAYBERRY, J. P.; SAIPE, A. L.
REPLY TO GRAVES AND HAESSLER'S NOTE ON THE PAPER "PRODUCTION RUNS FOR MULTIPLE PRODUCTS: THE TWO-PRODUCT HEURISTIC".

MEHT 1975 -1 MEHTA, J. M.
STUDY OF PASSING IN FLOW SHOP SCHEDULING PROBLEMS, THE.

MELNB 1976 -1 MELNIKOV, O. I.
SOLUTION OF CERTAIN BELLMAN-JOHNSON PROBLEMS WITH A (0,1)-MATRIX (RUSSIAN).

MELNC 1979 -1 MELNIKOV, O. I.; SHAFRANSKII, Y. M.
PARAMETRIC PROBLEM IN SCHEDULING THEORY.

MICH 1970 -1 MICHALSEN, H.
WORKING STRATEGY FOR GENERAL SCHOOL SCHEDULING, A.

MILLA 1974 -1 MILLER, H. E.
MATHEMATICAL PROGRAMMING MODELS OF NURSE SCHEDULING AND ALLOCATION.

MITS 1972 -1 MITSUMORI, S.
OPTIMUM PRODUCTION SCHEDULING OF MULTICOMMODITY IN FLOW LINE.

MITT 1979 -1 MITTAL, B. S.; BAGGA, P. C.
FLOW SHOP SCHEDULING WITH PARALLEL MACHINES.

MIYA 1981 -1 MIYAZAKI, S.
ONE MACHINE SCHEDULING PROBLEM WITH DUAL CRITERIA.

MIYAA 1980 -1 MIYAZAKI, S.; NISHIYAMA, N.
ANALYSIS FOR MINIMIZING WEIGHTED MEAN FLOW-TIME IN FLOW-SHOP SCHEDULING.

MIYAB 1978 -1 MIYAZAKI, S.; NISHIYAMA, N.; HASHIMOTO, F.
ADJACENT PAIRWISE APPROACH TO THE MEAN FLOW-TIME SCHEDULING PROBEM, AN.

MOEH 1980 -1 MOEHRING, R. H.
SCHEDULING PROBLEMS WITH A SINGULAR SOLUTION.

MOEH 1981 -1 MOEHRING, R. H.
SCHEDULING PROBLEMS WITH GENERAL PRECEDENCE AND RESOURCE CONSTRAINTS: AN ORDER-THEORETICAL APPROACH.

MONM 1978 -1 MONMA, C. L.
PROPERTIES AND EFFICIENT ALGORITHMS FOR CERTAIN CLASSES OF SEQUENCING PROBLEMS.

MONM 1979 -1 MONMA, C. L.
TWO-MACHINE MAXIMUM FLOW TIME PROBLEM WITH SERIES-PARALLEL PRECEDENCE CONSTRAINTS: AN ALGORITHM AND EXTENSIONS, THE.

MONM 1981 -1 MONMA, C. L.
SEQUENCING WITH GENERAL PRECEDENCE CONSTRAINTS.

MONM 1980 -2 MONMA, C. L.
LINEAR-TIME ALGORITHMS FOR SCHEDULING EQUAL-LENGTH TASKS WITH DUE DATES ON PARALLEL PROCESSORS SUBJECT TO PRECEDENCE CONSTRANINTS.

MONM 1980 -3 MONMA, C. L.
SEQUENCING TO MINIMIZE THE MAXIMUM JOB COST.

MONMA 1981 -1 MONMA, C. L.; RINNOOY KAN, A. H. G.
EFFICIENTLY SOLVABLE SPECIAL CASES OF THE PERMUTATION FLOW-SHOP PROBLEM.

MONMB 1977 -1 MONMA, C. L.; SIDNEY, J. B.
GENERAL ALGORITHM FOR OPTIMAL JOB SEQUENCING WITH SERIES-PARALLEL PRECEDENCE CONSTRAINTS, A.

MORE 1966 -1 MORELAND, J. A.
SCHEDULING OF AIRLINE FLIGHT CREWS.

MORIA 1978 -1 MORITO, S; SALKIN, H. M.
SEARCH ENUMERATION ALGORITHM FOR A MULTIPLANT, MULTIPRODUCT SCHEDULING PROBLEM, A.

MORT 1978 -1 MORTON, T. E.; BALA, G. D.
ALGORISTICS FOR SINGLE-MACHINE SEQUENCING WITH PRECEDENCE CONSTRAINTS.

MUKH 1975 -1 MUKHOPADHYAY, A.
TWO-PROCESSOR SCHEDULES FOR INDEPENDENT TASK SYSTEMS WITH BOUNDED EXECUTION TIMES.
MURP 1979 -1 MURPHY, F. H.; SOYSTER, A. L.
MULTIPRODUCT LOT-SIZE SCHEDULING WITH PROPORTIONAL PRODUCT DEMANDS.
MURP 1979 -2 MURPHY, F. H.; SOYSTER, A. L.
SENSITIVITY ANALYSIS OF THE COSTS IN THE DYNAMIC LOT SIZE MODEL.
MURPA 1978 -1 MURPHY, F. H.; STOHR, E. A.
MATHEMATICAL PROGRAMMING APPROACH TO THE SCHEDULING OF SORTING OPERATIONS, A.
MURPB 1975 -1 MURPHY, J.
CRITICAL PATH SCHEDULING OF FULLY PROFESSIONAL ENGINEERING CURRICULA.
MURPD 1978 -1 MURPHY, R. A.; SKITT, R. A.; SWEENEY, D. J.
HEURISTIC METHODS FOR THE MULTI-ITEM ACTIVITY SCHEDULING PROBLEM.
NABE 1975 -1 NABESHIMA, I.
BRANCH AND BOUND ALGORITHM FOR MULTIPROJECT SCHEDULING WITH RESOURCE CONSTRAINTS WHERE EXPLICIT SET-UP TIME EXISTS.
NABE 1976 -1 NABESHIMA, I.
NOTES ON THE ANALYTICAL RESULTS IN FLOW SHOP SCHEDULING 1.
NABE 1978 -1 NABESHIMA, I.
NOTES ON THE ANALYTICAL RESULTS IN FLOW SHOP SCHEDULING 6.
NABE 1979 -1 NABESHIMA, I.
NOTES ON THE ANALYTICAL RESULTS IN FLOW SHOP SCHEDULING 10.
NABE 1976 -2 NABESHIMA, I.
NOTES ON THE ANALYTICAL RESULTS IN FLOW SHOP SCHEDULING 2.
NABE 1977 -2 NABESHIMA, I.
NOTES ON THE ANALYTICAL RESULTS IN FLOW SHOP SCHEDULING 3.
NABE 1978 -2 NABESHIMA, I.
NOTES ON THE ANALYTICAL RESULTS IN FLOW SHOP SCHEDULING 7.
NABE 1979 -2 NABESHIMA, I.
NOTES ON THE ANALYTICAL RESULTS IN FLOW SHOP SCHEDULING 9.
NABE 1977 -3 NABESHIMA, I.
NOTES ON THE ANALYTICAL RESULTS IN FLOW SHOP SCHEDULING 4.
NABE 1978 -3 NABESHIMA, I.
NOTES ON THE ANALYTICAL RESULTS IN FLOW SHOP SCHEDULING 8.
NABE 1977 -4 NABESHIMA, I.
NOTES ON THE ANALYTICAL RESULTS IN FLOW SHOP SCHEDULING 5.
NABEA 1978 -1 NABESHIMA, I.; MARUYAMA, S.
ON N*M MEAN COMPLETION TIME FLOW SHOP PROBLEM. ANALYTICAL RESULTS, EXTENDED BRANCH AND BOUND ALGORITHM AND COMPUTATIONAL EXPERIENCE.
NAEG 1977 -1 NAEGLER, G.; SIEBER, N.
ANWENDUNG DER GRAPHENTHEORIE IN DER ABLAUFPLANUNG, DIE.
NAND 1978 -1 NANDA, R.
SCHEDULING CREWS FOR CONTINUOUS SHIFT WORK.
NEME 1977 -1 NEMETH, E.
NOTE ON A MINI-MAX PROBLEM IN SCHEDULING, A.
NENG 1980 -1 NENG, B.
ZUR ERSTELLUNG VON OPTIMALEN TRIEBFAHRZEUGLAUFPLAENEN.
NEPO 1978 -1 NEPOMIASTCHY, P.
RESOLUTION D'UN PROBLEME D'ORDONNANCEMENT A RESSOURCES VARIABLES.
NETT 1977 -1 NETT, E.
ON SCHEDULING ALGORITHMS FOR N-FREE TASK DEPENDENCY STRUCTURES.
NETT 1979 -1 NETT, E.
DETERMINISTISCHE STRATEGIEN ZUM SCHEDULING VON TASKABHAENGIGKEITSSTRUKTUREN FUER MEHRPROZESSORSYSTEME.
NICH 1978 -1 NICHOLS, R. A.; BULFIN, R. L.; PARKER, R. G.
INTERACTIVE PROCEDURE FOR MINIMIZING MAKESPAN ON PARALLEL PROCESSORS, AN.
NICHA 1972 -1 NICHOLSON, T. A. J.; PULLEN, R. D.
COMPUTER TERMINAL SYSTEM FOR MANAGING SCHEDULES ORDERS THROUGH PLANTS, A.
NIED 1979 -1 NIEDRINGHAUS, W. P.
SCHEDULING WITHOUT QUEUEING: THE SPACE FACTORY PROBLEM.
OAKF 1966 -1 OAKFORD, A. C.
SCHOOL SCHEDULING - PRACTICE AND THEORY.
OKAM 1979 -1 OKAMURA, K.; YAMASHINA, H.
HEURISTIC ALGORITHM FOR THE ASSEMBLY LINE MODEL-MIX SEQUENCING PROBLEM TO MINIMIZE THE RISK OF STOPPING THE CONVEYOR, A.
ORLI 1981 -1 ORLIN, J. B.
COMPLEXITY OF DYNAMIC LANGUAGES AND DYNAMIC OPTIMIZATION PROBLEMS (EXTENDED ABSTRACT), THE.
OSKOA 1968 -1 OSKOLKOVA, S. E.; OSKOLKOV, I. O.
APPLICATION OF CERTAIN HEURISTIC METHODS TO THE SOLUTION OF SCHEDULING PROBLEMS (SURVEY).
PANW 1978 -1 PANWALKAR, S. S.; CHARLES, O.
STATISTICAL ASPECTS OF FLOW SHOP SEQUENCING.
PANWA 1979 -1 PANWALKAR, S. S.; KHAN, A. W.
ORDERED FLOW SHOP SEQUENCING PROBLEM WITH TWK TYPE DUE DATES AND TOTAL TARDINESS CRITERION, AN.
PANWB 1979 -1 PANWALKAR, S. S.; WOOLLAM, C. R.
FLOW SHOP SCHEDULING PROBLEMS WITH NO IN-PROCESS WAITING: A SPECIAL CASE.
PANWB 1980 -1 PANWALKAR, S. S.; WOOLLAM, C. R.
ORDERED FLOW SHOP PROBLEMS WITH NO IN-PROCESS WAITING: FURTHER RESULTS.
PAPAA 1980 -1 PAPADIMITRIOU, C. H.; KANELLAKIS, P. C.
FLOWSHOP SCHEDULING WITH LIMITED TEMPORARY STORAGE.
PAPAC 1979 -2 PAPADIMITRIOU, C. H.; YANNAKAKIS, M.
SCHEDULING INTERVAL-ORDERED TASKS.
PAPE 1980 -1 PAPE, U.
HEURISTISCHES VERFAHREN ZUR ERMITTLUNG VON FAHRPLAENEN IN DER CONTAINER-SCHIFFAHRT, EIN.
PAPOA 1979 -1 PAPOULIAS, D. B.; PANAYIOTOPOULOS, J.-C.
CONSIDERATIONS ON THE REQUIREMENTS MATRIX OF A NON-REGULAR SCHOOL TIME-TABLE PROBLEM.
PAUL 1980 -1 PAUL, H.; LAW, S. S.; LEONG, H. K.
METHOD FOR SINGLE FACILITY MULTIPLE PRODUCTS SCHEDULING, A.
PAULA 1979 -1 PAUL, R. J.
PRODUCTION SCHEDULING PROBLEM IN THE GLASS-CONTAINER INDUSTRY, A.
PEGE 1975 -1 PEGELS, C. C.
COMPUTER-BASED INTERACTIVE PLANNING SYSTEM FOR SCHEDULING BLOOD COLLECTIONS, A.
PELI 1980 -1 PELIKAN, J.
SCHEDULING WITH MINIMIZATION OF HIGH CONSUMPTION RATE OF A RESOURCE (CZECHOSLOVAKIAN).
PERE 1976 -1 PEREPELITSA, V. A.; SEVASTYANOV, S. V.
ON A PROBLEM OF SCHEDULING THEORY ON A NETWORK (RUSSIAN).

PETEA 1979 -1 PETERSOHN, U.; STAHN, H.
NAEHERUNGSVERFAHREN ZUR POLYOPTIMALEN LOESUNG DES MASCHINENBELEGUNGSPROBLEMS.

PFEI 1974 -1 PFEIFFER, F. K. JR.
SYSTEMATIC HEURISTIC APPROACH TO SCHEDULING IN THE SMALL JOB SHOP, A.

PHEL 1981 -1 PHELPS, R. I.
OPTIMAL BATCH SIZES FOR A TWO-STAGE PRODUCTION SYSTEM.

PICA 1978 -1 PICARD, J.-C.; QUEYRANNE, M.
TIME-DEPENDENT TRAVELING SALESMAN PROBLEM AND ITS APPLICATION TO THE TARDINESS PROBLEM IN ONE-MACHINE SCHEDULING, THE.

PINT 1978 -1 PINTO, P. A.; DANNENBERG, D. G.; KHUMAWALA, B. M.
HEURISTIC NETWORK PROCEDURE FOR THE ASSEMBLY LINE BALANCING PROBLEM, A.

PLAK 1980 -1 PLAKHOTISHIN, A. M.
PROBLEM OF CONSTRUCTION SCHEDULING OF OBJECTS (RUSSIAN), A.

POP 1974 -1 POP, P.
ON L. NEMETI'S MODEL FOR SHOP SCHEDULING (ROMANIAN).

POTR 1979 -1 POTRZEBOWSKI, H.
BRANCH AND BOUND AS A DECOMPOSITION METHOD OF DETERMINING SCHEDULES FOR PARALLEL MACHINES (POLISH).

POTT 1980 -1 POTTS, C. N.
ADAPTIVE BRANCHING RULE FOR THE PERMUTATION FLOW-SHOP PROBLEM, AN.

POTT 1980 -2 POTTS, C. N.
ALGORITHM FOR THE SINGLE MACHINE SEQUENCING PROBLEM WITH PRECEDENCE CONSTRAINTS, AN.

POTT 1980 -3 POTTS, C. N.
ANALYSIS OF A HEURISTIC FOR ONE MACHINE SEQUENCING WITH RELEASE DATES AND DELIVERY TIMES.

PRAK 1978 -1 PRAKASH, S.
ON THE MACHINE-ASSIGNMENT PROBLEM.

PSAR 1978 -1 PSARAFTIS, H. N.
REAL-TIME FLEXIBLE-ROUTE SCHEDULING ALGORITHM, A.

PSAR 1980 -1 PSARAFTIS, H. N.
DYNAMIC PROGRAMMING APPROACH FOR SEQUENCING GROUPS OF IDENTICAL JOBS, A.

PSAR 1980 -2 PSARAFTIS, H. N.
DYNAMIC PROGRAMMING SOLUTION TO THE SINGLE VEHICLE MANY-TO-MANY IMMEDIATE REQUEST DIAL-A-RIDE PROBLEM, A.

PULL 1981 -2 PULLEYBLANK, W. R.
ON MINIMIZING SETUPS IN PRECEDENCE CONSTRAINED SCHEDULING.

QUEY 1977 -1 QUEYRANNE, M.
PROBLEME DU VOYAGEUR DE COMMERCE A COUTS VARIABLES ET QUELQUES APPLICATIONS, LE.

RADE 1981 -1 RADERMACHER, F. J.
COST-DEPENDENT ESSENTIAL SYSTEMS OF ES-STRATEGIES FOR STOCHASTIC SCHEDULING PROBLEMS.

RAMAC 1978 -1 RAMAMOORTHY, C. V.; LI, H. F.
CORRECTIONS TO: "SCHEDULING PARALLEL PROCESSABLE TASKS FOR A UNIPROCESSOR" (IEEE TRANSACTIONS ON COMPUTERS 25 (1976) NO. 5, 485-495) BY C. V. RAMAMOORTHY, T. F. FOX AND H. F. LI.

REES 1980 -1 REESE, J.
STANDORT- UND BELEGUNGSPLANUNG FUER MASCHINEN IN MEHRSTUFIGEN PRODUKTIONSPROZESSEN.

RINN 1976 -1 RINNOOY KAN, A. H. G.
MACHINE SCHEDULING PROBLEMS: CLASSIFICATION, COMPLEXITY AND COMPUTATIONS.

ROGL 1980 -1 ROGLIN, O.
SOME REMARKS ON SCHEDULING NURSING PERSONNEL.

ROLL 1979 -1 ROLLO, J.
GROUPEMENT DES TACHES DE PRODUCTION DANS L'ORDONNANCEMENT DE LA PRODUCTION (CZECHOSLOVAKIAN).

ROSEF 1979 -1 ROSENFELD, P.
TESTING THE PERFORMANCE OF A HEURISTIC FOR A SCHEDULING PROBLEM WHICH HAS NO KNOWN SOLUTION TECHNIQUE.

ROWI 1977 -1 ROWICKI, A.
NOTE ON OPTIMAL PREEMPTIVE SCHEDULING OF TWO-PROCESSOR SYSTEMS, A.

ROWI 1978 -1 ROWICKI, A.
ON OPTIMAL PREEMPTIVE SCHEDULING OF INDEPENDENT TASKS FOR MULTIPROCESSOR SYSTEMS.

ROWI 1977 -2 ROWICKI, A.
ON OPTIMAL PREEMPTIVE SCHEDULING FOR TWO-PROCESSOR SYSTEMS.

ROWI 1978 -2 ROWICKI, A.
ON THE OPTIMAL PREEMPTIVE SCHEDULING FOR MULTIPROCESSOR SYSTEM.

RUBIA 1974 -1 RUBIN, J.
SCHEDULING OF AIRLINE CREWS FOR AIRCRAFT SCHEDULES WITH FREQUENCY EXCEPTIONS.

RUIZ 1977 -1 RUIZ, J. P.; LARA, R. A.
IMPLEMENTATION ON A SMALL COMPUTER OF A SEQUENCING ALGORITHM (SPANISH), THE.

RUSC 1978 -1 RUSCHITZKA, M.
ANALYTICAL TREATMENT OF POLICY FUNCTION SCHEDULERS, AN.

SADO 1978 -1 SADOWSKI, R. P.; JACOBSON, R. E.
SCHEDULING ALGORITHMS FOR THE UNBALANCED PRODUCTION LINE: AN ANALYSIS AND COMPARISON.

SADOA 1979 -1 SADOWSKI, R. P.; MEDEIROS, D. J.
EFFECT OF VARIABILITY ON THE UNBALANCED PRODUCTION LINE, THE.

SADY 1978 -1 SADYKOV, R. G.
OPTIMIZATION OF AN ALGORITHM FOR DEVISING A SCHEDULE OF EDUCATIONAL ACTIVITIES (RUSSIAN).

SAFO 1979 -1 SAFONOVA, T. E.
REALIZATION OF AN ALGORITHM FOR CONSTRUCTING AN OPTIMAL SCHEDULE WITH A STARTING POINT IN A GIVEN INTERVAL (RUSSIAN).

SAFR 1972 -1 SAFRONENKO, V. A.
MATHEMATICAL AND ELECTRONIC SIMULATION OF THE PROBLEM OF OPTIMAL SCHEDULING (RUSSIAN).

SAHN 1979 -1 SAHNI, S.
PREEMPTIVE SCHEDULING WITH DUE DATES.

SAHNA 1979 -1 SAHNI, S.; CHO, Y.
COMPLEXITY OF SCHEDULING SHOPS WITH NO WAIT IN PROCESS.

SAHNA 1980 -1 SAHNI, S.; CHO, Y.
SCHEDULING INDEPENDENT TASKS WITH DUE TIMES ON A UNIFORM PROCESSOR SYSTEM.

SAHNA 1979 -2 SAHNI, S.; CHO, Y.
NEARLY ON LINE SCHEDULING OF A UNIFORM PROCESSOR SYSTEM WITH RELEASE TIMES.

SAHNC 1978 -1 SAHNI, S.; HOROWITZ, E.
COMBINATORIAL PROBLEMS: REDUCIBILITY AND APPROXIMATION.

SALZ 1979 -1 SALZBORN, F. J. M.
SCHEDULING BUS SYSTEMS WITH INTERCHANGES.

SANG 1970 -1 SANG, N.; FLORIAN, M.
NOTE ON LOWER BOUNDS FOR THE MACHINE SCHEDULING PROBLEM, A.

SAPI 1975 -1 SAPIRO, A. D.
SOME ASYMPTOTIC PROPERTIES OF A CERTAIN PROBLEM IN SCHEDULING THEORY (RUSSIAN).

SAWI 1976 -1 SAWIK, T.
MINIMAL-TIME PROGRAMMING FOR MULTI-ASSORTMENT PRODUCTION (POLISH).
SAWI 1978 -1 SAWIK, T.
OPERATIONS SCHEDULING AS A CONTROL PROBLEM WITH BOOLEAN VARIABLES.
SAWI 1976 -2 SAWIK, T.
TIME-OPTIMAL PRODUCTION SCHEDULING IN THE CASE OF A TIME-VARYING SET OF AVAILABLE PRODUCTION EQUIPMENT (POLISH).
SCER 1974 -1 SCERBAK, A. F.; LEVIN, G. L.; VOLCEK, B. A.
CERTAIN CLASS OF OPTIMAL WORK SCHEDULING PROBLEMS (RUSSIAN), A.
SCHID 1976 -1 SCHINDLER, S.
SCHEDULING GENERAL MONITOR SYSTEMS.
SCHL 1979 -1 SCHLUETER, E.
REIHENFOLGEMODELLE MIT PARALLELITAET ZWISCHEN BEARBEITUNGSSTYLEN UND AUFTRAEGEN.
SCHOB 1977 -1 SCHOLZ, K.
ON SCHEDULING MULTI-PROCESSOR SYSTEMS WITH ALGEBRAICAL OBJECTIVES.
SCHRA 1970 -1 SCHRAGE, L. E.
BOUND BASED ON THE EQUIVALENCE OF MIN-MAX-COMPLETION TIME AND MIN-MAX-LATENESS SCHEDULING OBJECTIVES, A.
SCHRB 1978 -1 SCHRAGE, L. E.; BAKER, K. R.
DYNAMIC PROGRAMMING SOLUTION OF SEQUENCING PROBLEMS WITH PRECEDENCE CONSTRAINTS.
SCUL 1979 -1 SCULLI, D.
DYNAMIC ASPECTS OF LINE BALANCING.
SETH 1977 -1 SETHI, R.
ON THE COMPLEXITY OF MEAN FLOW TIME SCHEDULING.
SEVA 1978 -1 SEVASTYANOV, S. V.
ON APPROXIMATE SOLUTION OF SCHEDULING PROBLEMS (RUSSIAN).
SEXT 1978 -1 SEXTON, T. R.
MULTI-VEHICLE SUBSCRIPTION PROBLEM: A HEURISTIC ALGORITHM, THE.
SEXTA 1979 -1 SEXTON, T. R.; BODIN, L. D.
SINGLE VEHICLE MANY TO MANY ROUTING AND SCHEDULING PROBLEM WITH DESIRED DELIVERY TIMES, THE.
SHAK 1978 -1 SHAKHBASJAN, K. V.
STRUCTURAL SOLUTIONS IN PROBLEMS OF SCHEDULING THEORY (RUSSIAN).
SHAK 1979 -1 SHAKHBASJAN, K. V.
ORDERING OF A STRUCTURAL SET OF TASKS MINIMIZING THE TOTAL PENALTY (RUSSIAN), THE.
SHAKA 1977 -1 SHAKHBASJAN, K. V.; LEBEDINSKAJA, N. B.
MINIMIZATION OF THE TOTAL PENALTY IN THE PROBLEM OF THE PARALLEL ORDERING OF N INDEPENDENT TASKS (RUSSIAN).
SHAKA 1977 -2 SHAKHBASJAN, K. V.; LEBEDINSKAJA, N. B.
OPTIMAL SCHEDULINGS WITH GAPS FOR INDEPENDENT TASKS IN A QUEUEING SYSTEM WITH N SERVERS (RUSSIAN).
SHAPB 1980 -1 SHAPIRO, R. D.
SCHEDULING COUPLED TASKS.
SHEP 1980 -1 SHEPARDSON, F.; MARSTEN, R. E.
LAGRANGEAN RELAXATION ALGORITHM FOR THE TWO DUTY PERIOD SCHEDULING PROBLEM, A.
SHTU 1979 -1 SHTUIKYS, V.
ALGORITHM FOR SOLVING A PARALLEL SEQUENCING PROBLEM (RUSSIAN), AN.
SIDN 1978 -1 SIDNEY, J. B.
OPTIMAL JOB-SHOP SCHEDULING WITH EARLINESS AND TARDINESS PENALTIES.
SIDN 1979 -1 SIDNEY, J. B.
TWO-MACHINE MAXIMUM FLOW TIME PROBLEM WITH SERIES PARALLEL PRECEDENCE RELATIONS, THE.
SIME 1978 -1 SIMEONE, B.
ASYMPTOTICALLY EXACT POLYNOMIAL ALGORITHM FOR EQUIPARTITION PROBLEMS, AN.
SIMOB 1978 -1 SIMONS, B.
FAST ALGORITHM FOR SINGLE PROCESSOR SCHEDULING, A.
SIU 1976 -1 SIU, C. L.
DETERMINISTIC JOB SCHEDULING IN COMPUTING SYSTEMS.
SKUR 1977 -1 SKURBA, V. V.; BELETSKIJ, S. A.
NUMERICAL METHODS IN THE SOLUTION OF THE ASSEMBLY LINE BALANCING PROBLEM. A SURVEY.
SLOW 1977 -1 SLOWINSKI, R.
OPTIMAL AND HEURISTIC PROCEDURES FOR PROJECT SCHEDULING WITH MULTIPLE CONSTRAINED RESOURCES - A SURVEY.
SLOW 1978 -1 SLOWINSKI, R.
NODE ORDERING HEURISTIC FOR NETWORK SCHEDULING UNDER MULTIPLE RESOURCE CONSTRAINTS, A.
SLOW 1979 -1 SLOWINSKI, R.
COST-MINIMAL PREEMPTIVE SCHEDULING OF INDEPENDENT JOBS WITH RELEASE AND DUE DATES ON OPEN SHOP UNDER RESOURCE CONSTRAINTS.
SLOWA 1978 -1 SLOWINSKI, R.; WEGLARZ, J.
SOLVING THE GENERAL PROJECT SCHEDULING PROBLEM WITH MULTIPLE CONSTRAINED RESOURCES BY MATHEMATICAL PROGRAMMING.
SMITB 1978 -1 SMITH, D. R.
NEW PROOF OF THE OPTIMALITY OF THE SHORTEST REMAINING PROCESSING TIME DISCIPLINE, A.
SMITC 1979 -1 SMITH, J. A.
APPLICATION OF SCHEDULING THEORY TO ICEBREAKING OPERATIONS, AN.
SMITG 1975 -1 SMITH, R. S.
TWO PHASE EMPLOYEE SCHEDULING ALGORITHM FOR OPERATIONS HAVING VARIABLE MANPOWER REQUIREMENTS WITH APPLICATIONS INVOLVING SINGLE AND COMPOSITE PLANNING CYCLES, A.
SNIE 1979 -1 SNIEDOVICH, M.
PREFERENCE ORDER ASSEMBLY LINE PROBLEM: A COUNTER EXAMPLE.
SOUM 1980 -1 SOUMIS, F.; FERLAND, J. A.; ROUSSEAU, J.-M.
MODEL FOR LARGE-SCALE AIRCRAFT ROUTING AND SCHEDULING PROBLEMS, A.
SPAC 1979 -1 SPACHIS, A. S.; KING, J. R.
JOB-SHOP SCHEDULING HEURISTICS WITH LOCAL NEIGHBOURHOOD SEARCH.
STANB 1978 -1 STANEK, W.
LOESUNG EINES SPEZIELLEN REIHENFOLGEPROBLEMS AUF DEM GEBIET DER FERTIGUNGSSTEUERUNG.
STEI 1978 -2 STEIN, D. M.
SCHEDULING DIAL-A-RIDE TRANSPORTATION SYSTEMS.
STEIA 1980 -1 STEINBERG, E.; NAPIER, H. A.
OPTIMAL MULTI-LEVEL LOT SIZING FOR REQUIREMENTS PLANNING SYSTEMS.
STERA 1981 -1 STERBOUL, F.; WERTHEIMER, D.
COMMENT CONSTRUIRE UN GRAPHE PERT MINIMAL.
STERB 1976 -1 STERN, H. I.
MINIMIZING MAKESPAN FOR INDEPENDENT JOBS ON NONIDENTICAL PARALLEL MACHINES - AN OPTIMAL PROCEDURE.
STINB 1978 -1 STINSON, J. P.; DAVIS, E. W.; KHUMAWALA, B. M.
MULTIPLE RESOURCE-CONSTRAINED SCHEDULING USING BRANCH AND BOUND.

STON 1977 -1 STONE, H. S.
MULTIPROCESSOR SCHEDULING WITH THE AID OF NETWORK FLOW ALGORITHMS.
STRO 1979 -1 STROEHLEIN, T.
TIGHTNESS AND FLEXIBILITY IN TIMETABLE PROBLEMS.
SU 1978 -1 SU, Z.-S.; SEVCIK, K. C.
COMBINATORIAL APPROACH TO DYNAMIC SCHEDULING PROBLEMS, A.
SULE 1979 -1 SULE, D. R.; HARMON, B.
DETERMINATION OF COORDINATED MAINTENANCE SCHEDULING FREQUENCIES FOR A GROUP OF MACHINES.
SZWA 1978 -1 SZWARC, W.
DOMINANCE CONDITIONS FOR THE THREE-MACHINE FLOW-SHOP PROBLEM.
SZWA 1979 -1 SZWARC, W.
CRITICAL PATH APPROACH IN THE FLOW-SHOP PROBLEM, THE.
SZWA 1981 -1 SZWARC, W.
EXTREME SOLUTIONS OF THE TWO MACHINE FLOW-SHOP PROBLEM.
SZYM 1979 -1 SZYMURA, J.
OPTIMIZATION OF THE PRODUCTION LINE SCHEDULE (POLISH).
TALB 1978 -1 TALBOT, F. B.; PATTERSON, J. H.
EFFICIENT INTEGER PROGRAMMING ALGORITHM WITH NETWORK CUTS FOR SOLVING RESOURCE-CONSTRAINED SCHEDULING PROBLEMS, AN.
TAMI 1979 -1 TAMIR, A.
SCHEDULING JOBS TO TWO MACHINES SUBJECT TO BATCH ARRIVAL ORDERING.
TANK 1978 -1 TANKO, J.
DOMINATING SCHEDULES OF STEADY JOB-FLOW PAIRS (HUNGARIAN).
TING 1979 -1 TINGLEY, G. A.
STILL ANOTHER SOLUTION METHOD FOR THE MONTHLY AIRCREW ASSIGNMENT PROBLEM.
TJUT 1976 -1 TJUTJUKIN, V. K.
OPTIMAL TWO-OPERATION SCHEDULING IN THE CASE OF PARALLEL-SERIAL PRODUCTION MOTION (RUSSIAN).
TOWN 1977 -1 TOWNSEND, W.
MINIMISING THE MAXIMUM PENALTY IN THE M-MACHINE SEQUENCING PROBLEM.
TREM 1978 -1 TREMOLIERES, R.
SCHEDULING JOBS OF EQUAL DURATIONS WITH TARDINESS COSTS AND RESOURCE LIMITATIONS.
TREMA 1977 -1 TREMOLIERES, R.; AUBERT, J.-C.
DETERMINATION D'UNE FLOTTE MINIMALE ET ORDONNANCEMENT DES TACHES DANS LA LIVRAISON DU BETON PRET A L'EMPLOI.
TROC 1980 -1 TROCHELMANN, J.
TOURENPLANUNG FUER DAS DETERMINISTISCHE EIN-DEPOT-PROBLEM.
TURG 1978 -1 TURGEON, A.
OPTIMAL SCHEDULING OF THERMAL GENERATING UNITS.
ULLR 1973 -1 ULLRICH, M.
STRUKTURUNTERSUCHUNGEN BEI SPEZIELLEN REIHENFOLGEPROBLEMEN.
UZDEA 1978 -1 UZDEMIR, A. P.; SHMELEV, V. V.
INTEGER DYNAMIC PROBLEMS OF ECONOMIC PLANNING WITH NETWORK CONSTRAINTS. I.
VAIR 1978 -1 VAIRAVAN, K.
IMPROVED SCHEDULING ALGORITHM FOR THE PARALLEL EXECUTION OF TASK SYSTEMS, AN.
VAND 1976 -1 VANDENMEERENDONK, H. W.
SINGLE MACHINE MULTI-PRODUCT PLANNING PROBLEMS.
VEMU 1976 -1 VEMUGANTI, R. R.
ON THE FEASIBILITY OF SCHEDULING LOT SIZES FOR SEVERAL PRODUCTS ON ONE MACHINE.
VEMU 1978 -1 VEMUGANTI, R. R.
ON THE FEASIBILITY OF SCHEDULING LOT SIZES FOR TWO PRODUCTS ON ONE MACHINE.
VERG 1978 -1 VERGIN, R. C.; LEE, T. N.
SCHEDULING RULES FOR THE MULTIPLE PRODUCT SINGLE MACHINE SYSTEM WITH STOCHASTIC DEMAND.
VICK 1980 -1 VICKSON, R. G.
CHOOSING THE JOB SEQUENCE AND PROCESSING TIMES TO MINIMIZE TOTAL PROCESSING PLUS FLOW COST ON A SINGLE MACHINE.
VICK 1980 -2 VICKSON, R. G.
TWO SINGLE MACHINE SEQUENCING PROBLEMS INVOLVING CONTROLLABLE JOB PROCESSING TIMES.
VIDO 1980 -1 VIDOMENKO, V. P.
ASYMMETRY OF THE SCHEDULE PROBLEMS AND ITS EFFECT ON THE SOLUTION ACCURACY (RUSSIAN).
VILL 1975 -1 VILLANUEVA, J. E.
SOME EXECUTION-TIME PROPERTIES OF OPTIMAL SCHEDULES IN MULTIPROCESSOR SYSTEMS.
VIZI 1973 -1 VIZING, V. G.
OBJECT FUNCTION VALUES IN SEQUENCING PROBLEMS DOMINATED BY AN AVERAGE VALUE (RUSSIAN), THE.
VLAC 1979 -1 VLACH, M.
ONE-PROCESSOR SCHEDULING WITH NONUNIFORM READY TIMES.
VOLP 1977 -1 VOLPENTESTA, A.
EQUI-ASSIGNED BINARY VECTORS AND EXPLICIT SOLUTIONS OF A PARTICULAR DISCRETE OPTIMIZATION PROBLEM.
VOLP 1978 -1 VOLPENTESTA, A.
ON THE INTEGER MULTICOMMODITY TRANSPORTATION PROBLEM. AN APPLICATION TO CREW SCHEDULING PROBLEMS.
VOLP 1978 -2 VOLPENTESTA, A.
ON THE PROBLEM OF CHARACTERIZING THE OPTIMAL SET OF A PARTICULAR DISCRETE OPTIMIZATION PROBLEM.
VOUT 1980 -1 VOUTILAINEN, R.
ON THE PATTERN SEQUENCING PROBLEM - DEFINITIONS, COMPLEXITY, AND APPLICATIONS.
WALD 1975 -1 WALDMANN, O.
INTEGRATED OPERATIONAL PLANNING OF FLOW-SHOP-TYPE PRODUCTION LINES WITH REFERENCE TO A PRACTICAL APPLICATION.
WASS 1978 -1 WASSENHOVE, L. N. VAN; GELDERS, L. F.
FOUR SOLUTION TECHNIQUES FOR A GENERAL ONE MACHINE SCHEDULING PROBLEM; A COMPARATIVE STUDY.
WASS 1980 -1 WASSENHOVE, L. N. VAN; GELDERS, L. F.
SOLVING A BICRITERION SCHEDULING PROBLEM.
WEED 1978 -1 WEEDA, P. J.
DYNAMIC PROGRAMMING FORMULATION FOR THE ONE MACHINE SEQUENCING PROBLEM, A.
WEGL 1979 -1 WEGLARZ, J.
PROJECT SCHEDULING WITH DISCRETE AND CONTINUOUS RESOURCES.
WEGL 1980 -1 WEGLARZ, J.
MULTIPROCESSOR SCHEDULING WITH MEMORY ALLOCATION - A DETERMINISTIC APPROACH.
WERR 1979 -3 WERRA, D. DE
OPTIMIZATION IN EDGE CHROMATIC SCHEDULING.
WERR 1978 -4 WERRA, D. DE
SOME COMMENTS ON A NOTE ABOUT TIMETABLING.
WERR 1979 -4 WERRA, D. DE
PARTIAL COMPACTNESS IN EDGE-CHROMATIC SCHEDULING.

****

WERR 1980 -4 WERRA, D. DE
ORDONNANCEMENT CHROMATIQUE ET PROBLEMES DE COLORATION.
WHIT 1979 -1 WHITE, G. M.; CHAN, P.-W.
TOWARDS THE CONSTRUCTION OF OPTIMAL EXAMINATION SCHEDULES.
WHITA 1980 -1 WHITE, G. P.
EASY LOWER BOUND ON THE NUMBER OF TRUCKS NEEDED TO SERVICE A SET OF DESTINATIONS, AN.
WHITB 1980 -1 WHITE, G. P.; SWEENEY, D. J.
USING MULTIDIMENSIONAL SCALING TO SOLVE TRAVELING SALESMAN AND MACHINE SCHEDULING PROBLEMS.
WHITG 1979 -1 WHITEHOUSE, G. E.; BROWN, J. R.
GENRES: AN EXTENSION OF BROOKS ALGORITHM FOR PROJECT SCHEDULING WITH RESOURCE CONSTRAINTS.
WOOD 1978 -1 WOOD, D. M.
DYNAMIC PROGRAMMING SOLUTION TO A PROBLEM OF LOOM BOX SEQUENCE PLANNING, A.
WUND 1979 -1 WUNDERATSCH, H.
DETERMINISTISCHES ZUORDNEN IN HETEROGENEN PROZESSORSYSTEMEN MIT PSEUDO-BOOLE METHODEN.
YELL 1970 -1 YELLOW, P. C.
COMPUTATIONAL MODIFICATION OF THE SAVINGS METHOD OF VEHICLE SCHEDULING, A.
YOSH 1978 -1 YOSHIDA, T.; HITOMI, K.
OPTIMAL GROUP SCHEDULING ON MULTIPLE PRODUCTION STAGES. THEORETICAL ANALYSIS.
YOSH 1979 -1 YOSHIDA, T.; HITOMI, K.
OPTIMAL TWO-STAGE PRODUCTION SCHEDULING WITH SETUP TIMES SEPARATED.
YOSHA 1978 -1 YOSHIDA, T.; NAKAMURA, N.; HITOMI, K.
GROUP PRODUCTION SCHEDULING FOR MINIMUM TOTAL TARDINESS - PART (I).
YUE 1976 -1 YUE, M. Y.
ON THE N JOB, M MACHINE SEQUENCING PROBLEM OF FLOW-SHOP.
YUE A 1979 -1 YUE, M. Y.; HAN, J. Y.
NEW METHOD FOR THE MXN FLOW-SHOP SEQUENCING PROBLEM (CHINESE), A.
ZAHO 1974 -1 ZAHORJAN, J.
PRODUCTION SCHEDULING MODEL TO DETERMINE THE MINIMAL COST TO MEET SEASONAL PRODUCT DEMAND, A.
ZAK 1978 -2 ZAK, JU. A.
CERTAIN PROPERTIES OF SCHEDULING PROBLEMS.
ZIJA 1979 -1 ZIJADULLAEV, N. S.; SERBULOV, A. V.
SOME PROBLEMS OF ESTIMATING THE AMOUNT OF CALCULATION INVOLVED IN PROBLEMS OF SCHEDULING THEORY (RUSSIAN).
ZIMMA 1975 -1 ZIMMERMANN, W. J.
TOPICS IN NETWORK SCHEDULING.

BAKOA 1977 -1 BAKO, A.; KAS, P.
DETERMINING THE KTH SHORTEST PATH BY THE MATRIX METHOD (HUNGARIAN).
BANA 1977 -1 BANASZAK, Z.
CODING OF ROOTED TREES BY THE MAXIMAL PATH METHOD (POLISH).
BANS 1977 -1 BANSAL, S. P.
FINDING ALTERNATING MINIMUM COST PATH IN A DIRECTED NETWORK USING DYNAMIC PROGRAMMING.
BAPT 1979 -1 BAPTIST, P.
OPTIMALE WEGE IN ENDLICHEN GERICHTETEN GRAPHEN.
CHAC 1979 -1 CHACHRA, V.; GHARE, P. M.; MOORE, J. M.
APPLICATIONS OF GRAPH THEORY ALGORITHMS.
COHE 1978 -1 COHEN, A. I.
ALGORITHM FOR SCHEDULING SURFACE COAL MINES, AN (REVISED VERSION).
DAMM 1978 -1 DAMM, E.
SHORTEST PATH IN A RECTANGULAR GRID, THE.
DENAA 1978 -1 DENARDO, E. V.; FOX, B. L.
BUCKETS, SHORTEST PATHS, AND INTEGER PROGRAMMING.
DENAA 1979 -1 DENARDO, E. V.; FOX, B. L.
SHORTEST-ROUTE METHODS: 1. REACHING, PRUNING, AND BUCKETS.
DENAA 1980 -1 DENARDO, E. V.; FOX, B. L.
ENFORCING CONSTRAINTS ON EXPANDED NETWORKS.
DEWI 1979 -1 DEWITT, H. K.; KRIEGER, M. M.
EXPECTED LENGTH OF SHORTEST PATHS AND ALGORITHM BEHAVIOR.
DIAL 1979 -1 DIAL, R.; GLOVER, F.; KARNEY, D.; KLINGMAN, D.
COMPUTATIONAL ANALYSIS OF ALTERNATIVE ALGORITHMS AND LABELING TECHNIQUES FOR FINDING SHORTEST PATH TREES, A.
DIAL 1980 -1 DIAL, R.; GLOVER, F.; KARNEY, D.; KLINGMAN, D.
SHORTEST PATH FOREST WITH TOPOLOGICAL ORDERING: AN ALGORITHM DESCRIPTION IN SDL.
DION 1978 -1 DIONNE, R.
ETUDE ET EXTENSION D'UN ALGORITHME DE MURCHLAND.
DODO 1977 -1 DODONOV, A. G.; CHERNYSHEV, JU. O.; SADOVOI, N. N.; SHCHETININ, A. M.
SOLUTION OF THE ASSIGNMENT PROBLEM BY REDUCING IT TO THE PROBLEM OF FINDING THE OPTIMAL PATH ON A GRAPH (RUSSIAN).
DREY 1977 -1 DREYFUS, S. E.; LAW, A. M.
ART AND THEORY OF DYNAMIC PROGRAMMING, THE.
DUBOA 1978 -1 DUBOIS, D.; PRADE, H.
ALGORITHMES DE PLUS COURTS CHEMINS POUR TRAITER DES DONNEES FLOUES.
ELAMA 1977 -1 ELAM, J.; KLINGMAN, D.; MULVEY, J. M.
EVALUATION OF MATHEMATICAL PROGRAMMING AND MINICOMPUTERS, AN.
ENGQ 1980 -1 ENGQUIST, M.
SUCCESSIVE SHORTEST PATH ALGORITHM FOR THE ASSIGNMENT PROBLEM, A.
ERMO 1976 -1 ERMOLEV, JU. M.; MELNIK, I. M.
SHORTEST PATHS IN STOCHASTIC GRAPHS.
FONL 1977 -1 FONLUPT, J.
AFFECTATION EXPONENTIELLE ET LE PROBLEME DU PLUS COURT CHEMIN DANS UN GRAPHE, L'.
FONL 1980 -1 FONLUPT, J.
AFFECTATION EXPONENTIELLE ET LE PROBLEME DU PLUS COURT CHEMIN DANS UN GRAPHE, L'.
FREI 1979 -1 FREIDENFELDS, J.; MAC LAUGHLIN, C. D.
HEURISTIC BRANCH-AND-BOUND ALGORITHM FOR TELEPHONE FEEDER CAPACITY EXPANSION, A.
FULK 1977 -1 FULKERSON, D. R.; HARDING, G. C.
MAXIMIZING THE MINIMUM SOURCE-SINK PATH SUBJECT TO A BUDGET CONSTRAINT.
GALLB 1980 -1 GALLO, G.
REOPTIMIZATION PROCEDURES IN SHORTEST PATH PROBLEMS.
GAULA 1978 -1 GAUL, W.; HARTUNG, J.
ZEIT- UND KOSTENOPTIMIERUNG VON BOTTLENECKWEGEN.
GEND 1977 -1 GENDREAU, M.
ETUDE SUR LA GENERATION DES RESEAUX ALEATOIRES.
GOLDD 1978 -1 GOLDEN, B. L.; BALL, M. O.
SHORTEST PATHS WITH EUCLIDEAN DISTANCES: AN EXPLANATORY MODEL.
GOND 1980 -1 GONDRAN, M.
CHEMINS ET CONNEXITE.
GONDA 1978 -1 GONDRAN, M.; MINOUX, M.
INDEPENDANCE LINEAIRE DANS LES DIOIDES, L'.
GONDA 1979 -1 GONDRAN, M.; MINOUX, M.
GRAPHES ET ALGORITHMES.
GOTO 1974 -1 GOTO, S.; OHTSUKI, T.
SIMPLEX ALGORITHM ON A LINEAR GRAPH - A UNIFIED VIEW OF THE EXTREMAL PATH AND CUTSET PROBLEMS ON A GRAPH, THE.
GOTOA 1978 -1 GOTO, S.; SANGIOVANNI-VINCENTELLI, A.
NEW SHORTEST PATH UPDATING ALGORITHM, A.
HACK 1979 -1 HACKBARTH, K.-D.
ALGORITHMEN ZUR BERECHNUNG MINIMALER DISJUNKTER WEGE IN NETZEN.
HADL 1979 -1 HADLOCK, F.
OPTIMUM PATHS IN LATTICE GRAPHS.
HAES 1979 -1 HAESSIG, K.
GRAPHENTHEORETISCHE METHODEN IN DER LOGISTIK.
HANDB 1980 -1 HANDLER, G. Y.; ZANG, I.
DUAL ALGORITHM FOR THE CONSTRAINED SHORTEST PATH PROBLEM, A.
HANSB 1980 -2 HANSEN, P.
O(M LOG D) ALGORITHM FOR SHORTEST PATHS, AN.
HITC 1968 -1 HITCHNER, L. E.
COMPARATIVE INVESTIGATION OF THE COMPUTATIONAL EFFICIENCY OF SHORTEST PATH ALGORITHMS, A.
HORN 1980 -1 HORNE, G. J.
FINDING THE K LEAST COST PATHS IN AN ACYCLIC ACTIVITY NETWORK.
HOUC 1977 -1 HOUCK, D. J.; PICARD, J.-C.; QUEYRANNE, M.; VEMUGANTI, R. R.
TRAVELLING SALESMAN PROBLEM AND SHORTEST N-PATHS, THE.
HOUC 1980 -1 HOUCK, D. J.; PICARD, J.-C.; QUEYRANNE, M.; VEMUGANTI, R. R.
TRAVELLING SALESMAN PROBLEM AS A CONSTRAINED SHORTEST PATH PROBLEM: THEORY AND COMPUTATIONAL EXPERIENCE, THE.
HULM 1979 -1 HULME, B.; WISNIEWSKI, J. A.
COMPARISON OF SHORTEST PATH ALGORITHMS APPPLIED TO SPARSE GRAPHS, A.
ITAIA 1977 -1 ITAI, A.; RODEH, M.
FINDING A MINIMUM CIRCUIT IN A GRAPH.
JARVB 1978 -1 JARVIS, J. J.; TUFEKCI, S.
DECOMPOSITION ALGORITHM FOR FINDING THE SHORTEST PATH BETWEEN A SOURCE AND A SINK NODE, A.
JOHNB 1978 -1 JOHNSON, D. S.; LENSTRA, J. K.; RINNOOY KAN, A. H. G.
COMPLEXITY OF THE NETWORK DESIGN PROBLEM, THE.

JOHND 1972 -1 JOHNSON, E. L.
ON SHORTEST PATHS AND SORTING.
JOHND 1978 -1 JOHNSON, E. L.
MATCHINGS AND BIDIRECTED GRAPHS.
KAIN 1978 -1 KAINEN, P. C.
LONG AND SHORT WALKS IN TREES.
KARPA 1981 -1 KARP, R. M.; ORLIN, J. B.
PARAMETRIC SHORTEST PATH ALGORITHMS WITH AN APPLICATION TO CYCLIC STAFFING.
KATO 1978 -1 KATOH, N.
O(KN**2) ALGORITHM FOR OBTAINING THE K-TH SHORTEST SIMPLE PATHS IN AN UNDIRECTED GRAPH WITH NON-NEGATIVE ARC LENGTH (JAPANESE), AN.
KAUFE 1977 -2 KAUFMANN, A.; PICHAT, E.
METHODES MATHEMATIQUES NON NUMERIQUES ET LEURS ALGORITHMES. TOME 2 ALGORITHMES DE RECHERCHE DE CHEMINS ET PROBLEMS ASSOCIES.
KELT 1978 -1 KELTON, W. D.; LAW, A. M.
MEAN-TIME COMPARISON OF ALGORITHMS FOR THE ALL-PAIRS SHORTEST-PATH PROBLEM WITH ARBITRARY ARC LENGTHS, A.
KLEEA 1979 -1 KLEE, V.; LARMAN, D.
USE OF FLOYD'S ALGORITHM TO FIND SHORTEST RESTRICTED PATHS.
KLINA 1978 -1 KLINGMAN, D.; MOTE, J.; WHITMAN, D.
IMPROVING FLOW MANAGEMENT AND CONTROL VIA IMPROVING SHORTEST PATH ANALYSIS.
KOEH 1979 -1 KOEHLER, A. B.; MAC CLURE, R. H.
USE OF ARCS AND NODES FOR THE DETERMINATION OF CRITICAL PATHS IN PERT/CPM NETWORKS, THE.
LANS 1981 -1 LANSDOWNE, Z. F.
RAIL FREIGHT TRAFFIC ASSIGNMENT.
LAWL 1979 -4 LAWLER, E. L.
SHORTEST PATH AND NETWORK FLOW ALGORITHMS.
LE 1979 -1 LE CONG THANH
ON THE PROBLEM OF FINDING SHORTEST PATHS IN FINITE GRAPHS (RUSSIAN).
LEVN 1971 -1 LEVNER, E. V.
SCHEDULING PROBLEM THAT CAN BE REDUCED TO A SHORTEST PATH PROBLEM (RUSSIAN), A.
LEWIB 1978 -1 LEWIS, H. R.; PAPADIMITRIOU, C. H.
EFFICACITE DES ALGORITHMES, L'.
LUSS 1980 -1 LUSS, H.
NETWORK FLOW APPROACH FOR CAPACITY EXPANSION PROBLEMS WITH TWO FACILITY TYPES, A.
MAHR 1978 -1 MAHR, B.
STRATEGIES AND ARITHMETIC COMPLEXITY OF PATHALGORITHMS.
MAHR 1981 -1 MAHR, B.
BIRD'S-EYE VIEW TO PATH PROBLEMS, A.
MALAA 1975 -1 MALATO DE SOUSA, J. A.
ON A PROBLEM OF SHORTEST PATHS IN GRAPHS (PORTUGUESE).
MAND 1978 -1 MANDL, C. E.
ALGORITHMS AND COMPUTER PROGRAMS IN DETERMINISTIC NETWORK OPTIMIZATION APPLIED TO PUBLIC SYSTEMS.
MARTA 1975 -1 MARTELLI, A.
SOME REMARKS ON THE COMPLEXITY OF HEURISTIC SEARCH ALGORITHMS.
MEGIC 1979 -1 MEGIDDO, N.; TAMIR, A.; ZEMEL, E.; CHANDRASEKARAN, R.
O(N(LOG N)(LOG N)) ALGORITHM FOR THE KTH LONGEST PATH IN A TREE WITH APPLICATIONS TO LOCATION PROBLEMS, AN.
MINI 1978 -1 MINIEKA, E.
OPTIMIZATION ALGORITHMS FOR NETWORKS AND GRAPHS.
MINO 1979 -1 MINOUX, M.
GENERALIZED PATH ALGEBRAS.
NIJE 1979 -1 NIJENHUIS, A.
MINIMAL-PATH ALGORITHM FOR THE "MONEY CHANGING PROBLEM", A.
NOSH 1978 -1 NOSHITA, K.; MASUDA, E.; MACHIDA, H.
ON THE EXPECTED BEHAVIOURS OF THE DIJKSTRA'S SHORTEST PATH ALGORITHM FOR COMPLETE GRAPHS.
ONAGA 1978 -1 ONAGA, K.; MURATA, T.
DT-POLYNOMIAL APPROACH TO DISCRETE TIME-VARYING NETWORK FLOW PROBLEMS, THE.
OREL 1977 -1 OREL, E. N.
FINDING A SHORTEST PATH IN A GRAPH USING THE MINORANT OF THE BELLMAN FUNCTION.
PICA 1978 -1 PICARD, J.-C.; QUEYRANNE, M.
TIME-DEPENDENT TRAVELING SALESMAN PROBLEM AND ITS APPLICATION TO THE TARDINESS PROBLEM IN ONE-MACHINE SCHEDULING, THE.
PINT 1978 -1 PINTO, P. A.; DANNENBERG, D. G.; KHUMAWALA, B. M.
HEURISTIC NETWORK PROCEDURE FOR THE ASSEMBLY LINE BALANCING PROBLEM, A.
QUEY 1977 -1 QUEYRANNE, M.
PROBLEME DU VOYAGEUR DE COMMERCE A COUTS VARIABLES ET QUELQUES APPLICATIONS, LE.
ROBIB 1976 -1 ROBINSON, D. W.
ANALYSIS OF A SHORTEST PATH ALGORITHM FOR TRANSPORTATION APPLICATIONS.
ROBID 1977 -1 ROBINSON, J. M.
DETERMINING THE K-TH SHORTEST PATH BY MATRIX METHOD (HUNGARIAN).
ROMAA 1980 -1 ROMANI, F.
SHORTEST-PATH PROBLEM IS NOT HARDER THAN MATRIX MULTIPLICATION.
ROSA 1979 -1 ROSA, M. S.
FINDING THE PATH WITH SMALLEST AVERAGE SPEED FROM A GIVEN SOURCE TO A GIVEN DESTINATION IN A DIRECTED NETWORK WITHOUT CYCLES.
SERD 1978 -1 SERDYUKOV, A. I.
SUR QUELQUES CHEMINS EXTREMAUX DANS LES GRAPHES (RUSSIAN).
SHEE 1977 -1 SHEE, S. C.
TABULAR ALGORITHMS FOR THE SHORTEST PATH AND LONGEST PATH.
SHIE 1979 -1 SHIER, D. R.
ON ALGORITHMS FOR FINDING THE K SHORTEST PATHS IN A NETWORK.
SHIEA 1980 -1 SHIER, D. R.; WITZGALL, C.
ARC TOLERANCES IN SHORTEST PATH AND NETWORK FLOW PROBLEMS.
THUE 1979 -1 THUENTE, D. J.
TWO ALGORITHMS FOR SHORTEST PATHS THROUGH MULTIPLE CRITERIA NETWORKS.
TUFEA 1981 -1 TUFEKCI, S.; TOLEDO, M.
COMPARISON OF DECOMPOSITION ALGORITHMS FOR SHORTEST PATH PROBLEMS, A.
VIDA 1978 -1 VIDAL, R. V. V.
DESIGN OF A PIPELINE ROUTE.
VLIE 1978 -1 VLIET, D. VAN
IMPROVED SHORTEST PATH ALGORITHMS FOR TRANSPORT NETWORKS.
WHIT 1979 -1 WHITE, G. M.; CHAN, P.-W.
TOWARDS THE CONSTRUCTION OF OPTIMAL EXAMINATION SCHEDULES.

****

WILLB 1980 -1 WILLIAMSON, S. G.
TREE OF PATHS OF A GRAPH, THE.
YOUNB 1979 -1 YOUNGER, D. H.
FROM SHORTEST PATHS TO DIRECTED CUT TRANSVERSALS.
ZAMF 1975 -1 ZAMFIRESCU, T.
GRAPHEN, IN WELCHEN JE ZWEI ECKPUNKTE VON EINEM LAENGSTEN WEG VERMIEDEN WERDEN.
ZIEL 1977 -1 ZIELINSKI, S.
SOLUTION OF LINEAR PROGRAMMING PROBLEMS IN ZERO-ONE VARIABLES.
ZIMM 1981 -1 ZIMMERMANN, U.
LINEAR AND COMBINATORIAL OPTIMIZATION IN ORDERED ALGEBRAIC STRUCTURES.
ZIMM 1981 -3 ZIMMERMANN, U.
SOME REMARKS ON ALGEBRAIC PATH PROBLEMS.

AGAS 1975 -1 AGASHE, S. D.
NEW CHARACTERIZATION OF TREES AND CO-TREES, A.
ANEJ 1980 -1 ANEJA, Y. P.
INTEGER LINEAR PROGRAMMING APPROACH TO THE STEINER PROBLEM IN GRAPHS, AN.
BARRA 1979 -1 BARR, R. S.; GLOVER, F.; KLINGMAN, D.
ENHANCEMENTS OF SPANNING TREE LABELING PROCEDURES FOR NETWORK OPTIMIZATION.
BENT 1978 -1 BENTLEY, J. L.
FAST ALGORITHMS FOR CONSTRUCTING MINIMAL SPANNING TREES IN COORDINATE SPACES.
BENT 1980 -1 BENTLEY, J. L.
PARALLEL ALGORITHM FOR CONSTRUCTING MINIMUM SPANNING TREES, A.
BOYCC 1977 -1 BOYCE, W. M.
IMPROVED PROGRAM FOR THE FULL STEINER TREE PROBLEM, AN.
BOYCD 1978 -1 BOYCE, W. M.; GAREY, M. R.; JOHNSON, D. S.
NOTE ON BISECTING MINIMUM SPANNING TREES, A.
CAHI 1978 -1 CAHIT, I.; CAHIT, R.
TRANSFORMATIONS ON SPANNING TREES.
CAME 1978 -1 CAMERINI, P. M.
MIN-MAX SPANNING TREE PROBLEM AND SOME EXTENSIONS, THE.
CAMEA 1980 -1 CAMERINI, P. M.; FRATTA, L.; MAFFIOLI, F.
K BEST SPANNING ARBORESCENCES OF A NETWORK, THE.
CAMEB 1980 -1 CAMERINI, P. M.; GALBIATI, G.; MAFFIOLI, F.
COMPLEXITY OF SPANNING TREE PROBLEMS: PART I.
CHAC 1979 -1 CHACHRA, V.; GHARE, P. M.; MOORE, J. M.
APPLICATIONS OF GRAPH THEORY ALGORITHMS.
CHANE 1981 -1 CHANDRASEKARAN, R.; ANEJA, Y. P.; NAIR, K. P. K.
MINIMAL COST-RELIABILITY RATIO SPANNING TREE.
CHIN 1978 -1 CHIN, F. Y.; HOUCK, D. J.
ALGORITHMS FOR UPDATING MINIMAL SPANNING TREES.
CHOUA 1978 -1 CHOUKHMANE, E.-A.
HEURISTIQUE POUR LE PROBLEME DE L'ARBRE DE STEINER, UNE.
CHRIF 1978 -1 CHRISTOFIDES, N.; MINGOZZI, A.; THOTH, P.
EXACT ALGORITHMS FOR THE VEHICLE ROUTING PROBLEM.
CHUNB 1978 -1 CHUNG, F. R. K.; HWANG, F. K.
LOWER BOUND FOR THE STEINER TREE PROBLEM, A.
CLAUB 1980 -1 CLAUSEN, J.; HANSEN, L. A.
FINDING K EDGE-DISJOINT SPANNING TREES OF MINIMUM TOTAL WEIGHT IN A NETWORK: AN APPLICATION OF MATROID THEORY.
COCK 1978 -1 COCKAYNE, E. J.; HARTNELL, B. L.; HEDETNIEMI, S. T.
LINEAR ALGORITHM FOR DISJOINT MATCHINGS IN TREES, A.
EBER 1980 -1 EBERT, J.
FINDING SPANNING FORESTS: A PROBLEM OF DATA MANIPULATION.
EPIH 1975 -1 EPIHIN, V. V.
ESTIMATION OF THE NUMBER OF TREES OF A GRAPH (RUSSIAN).
EVAN 1978 -1 EVANS, J. R.
NOTE ON THE SHORTEST SPANNING TREE PROBLEM, A.
FARR 1980 -3 FARRELL, E. J.
SPANNING TREES IN GRAPHS WITH CYCLOMATIC NUMBERS 2, 3, AND 4.
FLAM 1975 -1 FLAMENT, C.
ARETES MAXIMALES DES COCYCLES D'UN GRAPHE PREORDONNE.
FOUL 1978 -1 FOULDS, L. R.; GIBBONS, P. B.
BRANCH AND BOUND APPROACH TO THE STEINER PROBLEM IN GRAPHS, A.
GABOB 1978 -1 GABOW, H. N.
GOOD ALGORITHM FOR SMALLEST SPANNING TREES WITH A DEGREE CONSTRAINT, A.
GABOD 1978 -1 GABOW, H. N.; MYERS, E. W.
FINDING ALL SPANNING TREES OF DIRECTED AND UNDIRECTED GRAPHS.
HENDA 1980 -1 HENDY, M. D.; FOULDS, L. R.; PENNY, D.
PROVING PHYLOGENETIC TREES MINIMAL WITH L-CLUSTERING AND SET PARTITIONING.
HWAN 1978 -1 HWANG, F. K.
RECTILINEAR STEINER PROBLEM, THE.
HWAN 1979 -1 HWANG, F. K.
O(N LOG N) ALGORITHM FOR RECTILINEAR MINIMAL SPANNING TREES, AN.
ICHIA 1981 -1 ICHIMORI, T.; SHIODE, S.; ISHII, H.; NISHIDA, T.
MINIMUM SPANNING TREE WITH NORMAL VARIATES AS WEIGHTS.
JOHNB 1978 -1 JOHNSON, D. S.; LENSTRA, J. K.; RINNOOY KAN, A. H. G.
COMPLEXITY OF THE NETWORK DESIGN PROBLEM, THE.
KAME 1973 -1 KAMEDA, T.; TOIDA, S.
EFFICIENT ALGORITHMS FOR DETERMINING AN EXTREMAL TREE OF A GRAPH (EXTENDED ABSTRACT).
KANG 1977 -1 KANG, A. N. C.; LEE, R. C. T.; CHANG, C.-L.; CHANG, S. K.
STORAGE REDUCTION THROUGH MINIMAL SPANNING TREES AND SPANNING FORESTS.
KELM 1976 -1 KELMANS, A. K.
OPERATIONS OVER GRAPHS THAT INCREASE THE NUMBER OF THEIR TREES (RUSSIAN).
KORH 1979 -1 KORHONEN, P.
ALGORITHM FOR TRANSFORMING A SPANNING TREE INTO A STEINER TREE, AN.
KOU 1978 -1 KOU, L.; MARKOWSKY, G.; BERMAN, L.
FAST ALGORITHM FOR STEINER TREES, A.
LARS 1980 -1 LARSON, R. C.; LI, V. O. K.
FINDING MINIMUM RECTILINEAR DISTANCE PATHS IN THE PRESENCE OF BARRIERS.
LITW 1980 -1 LITWHILER, D. W. JR.; ALY, A. A.
STEINER'S PROBLEM AND FAGNANO'S RESULT ON THE SPHERE.
LOVA 1977 -2 LOVASZ, L.
HOMOLOGY THEORY FOR SPANNING TREES OF A GRAPH, A.
MALK 1978 -1 MALKEVITCH, J.
SPANNING TREES IN POLYTOPAL GRAPHS.
MALO 1978 -1 MALOJI, M. W.; UHRY, J.-P.
PRIMAL, ONE-PASS ALGORITHM FOR CONSTRUCTING A MINIMUM-WEIGHT ROOTED SPANNING ARBORESCENCE, A.
MAND 1978 -1 MANDL, C. E.
ALGORITHMS AND COMPUTER PROGRAMS IN DETERMINISTIC NETWORK OPTIMIZATION APPLIED TO PUBLIC SYSTEMS.
MEGI 1978 -2 MEGIDDO, N.
COST ALLOCATION FOR STEINER TREES.
MINI 1978 -1 MINIEKA, E.
OPTIMIZATION ALGORITHMS FOR NETWORKS AND GRAPHS.
MORO 1976 -1 MOROZOV, S. A.
ON THE PROBLEM OF FINDING THE SHORTEST CONNECTING TREE WITH CONSTRAINT (RUSSIAN).

SPANNING TREES

MOUS 1980 -1 MOUSTAKIDES, G.; BEDROSIAN, S. D.
FINDING THE GRAPH WITH THE MAXIMUM NUMBER OF SPANNING TREES.
NARUA 1980 -1 NARULA, S. C.; HO, C. A.
DEGREE-CONSTRAINED MINIMUM SPANNING TREE.
NOSH 1978 -1 NOSHITA, K.; MASUDA, E.; MACHIDA, H.
ON THE EXPECTED BEHAVIOURS OF THE DIJKSTRA'S SHORTEST PATH ALGORITHM FOR COMPLETE GRAPHS.
PAPA 1978 -2 PAPADIMITRIOU, C. H.
COMPLEXITY OF THE CAPACITATED TREE PROBLEM, THE.
ROHLA 1978 -1 ROHLF, F. J.
PROBABILISTIC MINIMUM SPANNING TREE ALGORITHM, A.
ROSH 1977 -1 ROSHCHIN, G. B.
ALGORITHM FOR DETERMINING THE MINIMAL SPANNING TREE OF AN INCREASING GRAPH (RUSSIAN), AN.
ROSH 1978 -1 ROSHCHIN, G. B.
DETERMINATION OF A MINIMUM SPANNING TREE OF A GRAPH (RUSSIAN).
SACH 1976 -1 SACHS, H.
ON THE NUMBER OF SPANNING TREES.
SLATA 1977 -1 SLATER, P. J.
FIBONACCI NUMBERS IN THE COUNT OF SPANNING TREES.
SMITE 1980 -1 SMITH, J. M.; LIEBMAN, J. S.
O(N**2) HEURISTIC ALGORITHM FOR THE DIRECTED STEINER MINIMAL TREE PROBLEM, AN.
SMOR 1976 -1 SMORODINSKI, JA. A.
TREES AND THE MANY-BODY PROBLEM (RUSSIAN).
SZAM 1979 -1 SZAMKOLOWICZ, L.
ON PROBLEMS RELATED TO CHARACTERISTIC VERTICES OF GRAPHS.
TAKA 1979 -1 TAKAHASHI, H.; MATSUYAMA, A.
APPROXIMATE SOLUTION FOR THE STEINER PROBLEM IN GRAPHS, AN.
TUTT 1977 -1 TUTTE, W. T.
ON THE SPANNING TREES OF SELF-DUAL MAPS.
VERGA 1971 -1 VERGNAS, M. LAS
SUR UNE PROPRIETE DES ARBRES MAXIMAUX DANS UN GRAPHE.
WIN 1979 -1 WIN, S.
ON A CONJECTURE OF LAS VERGNAS CONCERNING CERTAIN SPANNING TREES IN GRAPHS.
ZELI 1978 -1 ZELINKA, B.
NUMBER OF ISOMORPHISM CLASSES OF SPANNING TREES OF A GRAPH, THE.

AFANA 1978 -1 AFANAS'EV, M. JU.
EXAMPLE OF THE CYCLING OF A STOCHASTIC INTEGER ALGORITHM IN A BILEVEL MULTICOMMODITY PROBLEM (RUSSIAN), AN.
ANGLA 1977 -1 ANGLUIN, D.; VALIANT, L. G.
FAST PROBABILISTIC ALGORITHMS FOR HAMILTONIAN CIRCUITS AND MATCHINGS.
ARRO 1979 -1 ARROWSMITH, D. K.
PERCOLATION THEORY ON MULTIROOTED DIRECTED GRAPHS.
CLEE 1979 -1 CLEEF, H. J.; GAUL, W.
STOCHASTIC FLOW PROBLEM.
CLEE 1981 -1 CLEEF, H. J.; GAUL, W.
FLOWS IN GRAPHS AND STOCHASTIC PROGRAMMING.
COX 1980 -1 COX, J. T.
TIME CONSTANT OF FIRST-PASSAGE PERCOLATION ON THE SQUARE LATTICE, THE.
ERMO 1976 -1 ERMOLEV, JU. M.; MELNIK, I. M.
SHORTEST PATHS IN STOCHASTIC GRAPHS.
FONS 1979 -1 FONSO, R.
ON A STOCHASTIC TRANSPORTATION PROBLEM (ITALIAN).
FORTA 1979 -1 FORTUNE, S.; HOPCROFT, J. E.
NOTE ON RABIN'S NEAREST-NEIGHBOUR ALGORITHM, A.
FRANE 1978 -1 FRANK, O.
ESTIMATION OF THE NUMBER OF CONNECTED COMPONENTS IN A GRAPH BY USING A SAMPLED SUBGRAPH.
GEND 1977 -1 GENDREAU, M.
ETUDE SUR LA GENERATION DES RESEAUX ALEATOIRES.
GOLDB 1978 -2 GOLDEN, B. L.
STATISTICAL ESTIMATION IN COMBINATORIAL DECISION PROBLEMS.
HAMM 1979 -1 HAMMER, G.
RANDOMISIERTE HEURISTIKEN.
HAMMG 1980 -1 HAMMERSLEY, J. M.
GENERALIZATION OF MAC DIARMID'S THEOREM FOR MIXED BERNOULLI PERCOLATION, A.
HAST 1978 -1 HASTINGS, N. A. J.; MELLO, J. M. C.
DECISION NETWORKS.
IGEL 1979 -1 IGELMUND, G.; RADERMACHER, F. J.
PRESELECTIVE STRATEGIES FOR THE OPTIMIZATION OF STOCHASTIC PROJECT NETWORKS UNDER RESOURCE CONSTRAINTS (ABSTRACT).
JANS 1981 -1 JANSON, S.
UPPER BOUND FOR THE VELOCITY OF FIRST-PASSAGE PERCOLATION, AN.
KAER 1979 -1 KAERKES, R.
OPTIMIZATION OF (STOCHASTIC) NETWORKS UNDER RESOURCE CONSTRAINTS (ABSTRACT).
KAO 1978 -1 KAO, E. P. C.
PREFERENCE ORDER DYNAMIC PROGRAM FOR A STOCHASTIC TRAVELING SALESMAN PROBLEM, A.
KEOWA 1980 -1 KEOWN, A. J.; TAYLOR, B. W. III
CHANCE-CONSTRAINED INTEGER GOAL PROGRAMMING MODEL FOR CAPITAL BUDGETING IN THE PRODUCTION AREA, A.
KEST 1980 -1 KESTEN, H.
ON THE TIME CONSTANT AND PATH LENGTH OF FIRST-PASSAGE PERCOLATION.
LEIP 1978 -1 LEIPAELAE, T.
ON THE SOLUTIONS OF STOCHASTIC TRAVELING SALESMAN PROBLEMS.
LIEB 1981 -1 LIEBERHERR, K.
PROBABILISTIC COMBINATORIAL OPTIMIZATION.
LUEK 1978 -1 LUEKER, G. S.
MAXIMIZATION PROBLEMS ON GRAPHS WITH EDGE WEIGHTS CHOSEN FROM A NORMAL DISTRIBUTION.
LUEK 1979 -1 LUEKER, G. S.
OPTIMIZATION PROBLEMS ON GRAPHS WITH INDEPENDENT RANDOM EDGE WEIGHTS.
MAC B 1980 -1 MAC DIARMID, C.
CLUTTER PERCOLATION AND RANDOM GRAPHS.
MAC B 1981 -1 MAC DIARMID, C.
GENERAL PERCOLATION AND RANDOM GRAPHS.
MAC B 1980 -2 MAC DIARMID, C.
PERCOLATION ON SUBSETS OF THE SQUARE LATTICE.
MART 1979 -1 MARTEL, A.
HORAIRE DE TRAVAIL OPTIMAL FARE A UNE DEMANDE ALEATOIRE: LE CAS DES JEUX OLYMPIQUES DE MONTREAL.
NICO 1981 -1 NICOLAI, W.
TIME-ORIENTED ANALYSIS OF PROJECTS USING STOCHASTIC NETWORK TECHNIQUES.
RABI 1979 -1 RABIN, M. O.
PROBABILISTIC ALGORITHM FOR TESTING PRIMALITY.
RADE 1981 -1 RADERMACHER, F. J.
COST-DEPENDENT ESSENTIAL SYSTEMS OF ES-STRATEGIES FOR STOCHASTIC SCHEDULING PROBLEMS.
ROHLA 1978 -1 ROHLF, F. J.
PROBABILISTIC MINIMUM SPANNING TREE ALGORITHM, A.
SEYMA 1978 -1 SEYMOUR, P. D.; WELSH, D. J. A.
PERCOLATION PROBABILITIES ON THE SQUARE LATTICE.
SIMU 1978 -1 SIMUNDICH, T. M.
EFFICIENT ALGORITHM FOR SOLVING A STOCHASTIC, INTEGER PROGRAMMING PROBLEM ARISING IN RADIO NAVIGATION, AN.
SMYT 1978 -1 SMYTHE, R. T.; WIERMAN, J. C.
FIRST-PASSAGE PERCOLATION ON THE SQUARE LATTICE.
SNIE 1979 -1 SNIEDOVICH, M.
PREFERENCE ORDER ASSEMBLY LINE PROBLEM: A COUNTER EXAMPLE.
SNIE 1980 -1 SNIEDOVICH, M.
PREFERENCE ORDER STOCHASTIC KNAPSACK PROBLEMS: METHODOLOGICAL ISSUES.
SNIE 1979 -2 SNIEDOVICH, M.
PREFERENCE ORDER STOCHASTIC TRAVELING SALESPERSON PROBLEMS: A COUNTER EXAMPLE.
SNIE 1979 -3 SNIEDOVICH, M.
SOME COMMENTS ON PREFERENCE ORDER DYNAMIC PROGRAMMING MODELS.
STEWA 1980 -1 STEWART, W. R.; GOLDEN, B. L.
CHANCE-CONSTRAINED APPROACH TO THE STOCHASTIC VEHICLE ROUTING PROBLEM, A.
TOBI 1978 -1 TOBIAS, T.
KUHN-TUCKER CONDITIONS FOR THE TWO-PHASE STOCHASTIC PROGRAMMING PROBLEM WITH INTEGRAL CONSTRAINTS (RUSSIAN).
WALKB 1977 -1 WALKUP, D. W.
MATCHINGS IN RANDOM REGULAR BIPARTITE DIGRAPHS.
WALKB 1979 -1 WALKUP, D. W.
ON THE EXPECTED VALUE OF A RANDOM ASSIGNMENT PROBLEM.
WELS 1979 -2 WELSH, D. J. A.
STOCHASTIC OPTIMIZATION ON NETWORKS.

STOCHASTIC INTEGER PROGRAMMING, PROBABILISTIC ALGORITHMS
****

WOLL 1980 -1 WOLLMER, R. D.
INVESTMENT IN STOCHASTIC MINIMUM COST GENERALIZED MULTICOMMODITY NETWORKS WITH APPLICATION TO COAL TRANSPORT.
WOLL 1980 -2 WOLLMER, R. D.
TWO STAGE LINEAR PROGRAMMING UNDER UNCERTAINTY WITH 0-1 INTEGER FIRST STAGE VARIABLES.
ZIPK 1980 -2 ZIPKIN, P. H.
TRANSPORTATION PROBLEMS WITH AGGREGATED DESTINATIONS WHEN DEMANDS ARE UNCERTAIN.

ALI 1978 -1 ALI, A. I.; HELGASON, R. V.; KENNINGTON, J. L.
CONVEX COST NETWORK FLOW PROBLEM: A SURVEY OF ALGORITHMS, THE.

ALI A 1978 -1 ALI, A. I.; HELGASON, R. V.; KENNINGTON, J. L.; LALL, H. S.
PRIMAL SIMPLEX NETWORK CODES: STATE-OF-THE-ART IMPLEMENTATION TECHNOLOGY.

ARMSD 1977 -1 ARMSTRONG, R. D.; FROME, E.
SPECIAL PURPOSE LINEAR PROGRAMMING ALGORITHM FOR OBTAINING LEAST ABSOLUTE VALUE ESTIMATORS IN A LINEAR MODEL WITH DUMMY VARIABLES.

ASSA 1978 -1 ASSAD, A.
MULTICOMMODITY NETWORK FLOWS - A SURVEY.

AVON 1979 -1 AVONDO-BODINO, G.
GRAPH THEORY AND OPERATIONS RESEARCH.

BACH 1980 -1 BACHEM, A.
KOMPLEXITAETSTHEORIE IM OPERATIONS RESEARCH.

BACH 1980 -2 BACHEM, A.
THEOREMS OF THE ALTERNATIVE IN COMBINATORIAL PROGRAMMING.

BAKEC 1979 -1 BAKER, E.; BODIN, L. D.; FINNEGAN, W. F.; PONDER, R. J.
EFFICIENT HEURISTIC SOLUTIONS TO AN AIRLINE CREW SCHEDULING PROBLEM.

BALAA 1979 -1 BALAS, E.
BIVALENT PROGRAMMING BY IMPLICIT ENUMERATION.

BALAA 1979 -2 BALAS, E.
DISJUNCTIVE PROGRAMMING.

BALAH 1979 -2 BALAS, E.; PADBERG, M. W.
SET PARTITIONING - A SURVEY.

BARC 1978 -1 BARCELO, J.
STATE-OF-THE-ART SURVEY ABOUT ENUMERATIVE METHODS (SPANISH).

BEAL 1979 -1 BEALE, E. M. L.
BRANCH AND BOUND METHODS FOR MATHEMATICAL PROGRAMMING SYSTEMS.

BERG 1979 -2 BERGE, C.
PACKING PROBLEMS AND HYPERGRAPH THEORY: A SURVEY.

BERMD 1978 -1 BERMOND, J. C.
HAMILTONIAN GRAPHS.

BERMH 1981 -1 BERMOND, J. C.; THOMASSEN, C.
CYCLES IN DIGRAPHS - A SURVEY.

BIGG 1979 -2 BIGGS, N.
RESONANCE AND RECONSTRUCTION.

BLAZB 1978 -1 BLAZEWICZ, J.; WEGLARZ, J.
DETERMINISTIC TASK SCHEDULING PROBLEM ON PROCESSORS OF COMPUTER SYSTEMS WITH ALLOWANCE FOR ADDITIONAL RESOURCES (POLISH).

BOOKA 1980 -1 BOOKBINDER, J. H.; SETHI, S. P.
DYNAMIC TRANSPORTATION PROBLEM: A SURVEY, THE.

BRAU 1978 -1 BRAUN, H.
LITERATUR UEBER GRAPHEN-ISOMORPHIE, EINDEUTIGE STRUKTURBENENNUNG UND VERWANDTE THEMEN.

BROU 1979 -1 BROUWER, A. E.; SCHRIJVER, A.
UNIFORM HYPERGRAPHS.

BRUT 1969 -1 BRUTER, C.
SUR DIFFERENTS PROBLEMES POSES EN THEORIE DES MATROIDES.

BURK 1979 -3 BURKARD, R. E.
TRAVELLING SALESMAN AND ASSIGNMENT PROBLEMS: A SURVEY.

BURKJ 1980 -1 BURKARD, R. E.; ZIMMERMANN, U.
COMBINATORIAL OPTIMIZATION IN LINEARLY ORDERED SEMIMODULES: A SURVEY.

CATL 1979 -4 CATLIN, P. A.
SURVEY OF EXTENSIONS OF BROOKS' GRAPH COLORING THEOREM.

CHEU 1980 -1 CHEUNG, T.-Y.
COMPUTATIONAL COMPARISON OF EIGHT METHODS FOR THE MAXIMUM NETWORK FLOW PROBLEM.

CHRIB 1979 -1 CHRISTOFIDES, N.
TRAVELLING SALESMAN PROBLEM, THE.

CHRID 1979 -1 CHRISTOFIDES, N.; HEWINS, R. D.; SALKIN, G. R.
GRAPH THEORETIC APPROACHES TO FOREIGN EXCHANGE OPERATIONS.

CHRIG 1979 -1 CHRISTOFIDES, N.; MINGOZZI, A.; TOTH, P.
LOADING PROBLEMS.

CHRIG 1979 -2 CHRISTOFIDES, N.; MINGOZZI, A.; TOTH, P.
VEHICLE ROUTING PROBLEM, THE.

CHRIH 1978 -1 CHRISTOFIDES, N.; WHITLOCK, C.
GRAPH CONNECTIVITY AND VULNERABILITY, A SURVEY.

COLB 1978 -1 COLBOURN, C. J.
BIBLIOGRAPHY OF THE GRAPH ISOMORPHISM PROBLEM, A.

COOPB 1979 -2 COOPER, M. W.
SURVEY OF METHODS FOR PURE NONLINEAR INTEGER PROGRAMMING, A.

DEFR 1978 -1 DEFRENNE, A.
TIMETABLING PROBLEM: A SURVEY, THE.

EMMO 1978 -1 EMMONS, H.
SURVEY OF STATIC JOB SHOP SCHEDULING THEORY, A. (REVISED VERSION).

ERLE 1981 -1 ERLENKOTTER, D.
COMPARATIVE STUDY OF APPROACHES TO DYNAMIC LOCATION PROBLEMS, A.

FIAL 1978 -1 FIALA, F.
VEHICLE ROUTING PROBLEM.

FIOR 1978 -1 FIORINI, S.
BIBLIOGRAPHIC SURVEY OF EDGE COLORINGS, A.

FIORA 1978 -1 FIORINI, S.; WILSON, R. J.
EDGE-COLORINGS OF GRAPHS.

FISH 1978 -2 FISHER, M. L.
LAGRANGIAN RELAXATION METHODS FOR COMBINATORIAL OPTIMZATION (REVISED VERSION).

GARF 1979 -1 GARFINKEL, R. S.
BRANCH AND BOUND METHODS FOR INTEGER PROGRAMMING.

GATI 1979 -1 GATI, G.
FURTHER ANNOTATED BIBLIOGRAPHY ON THE ISOMORPHISM DISEASE.

GENS 1979 -1 GENS, G. V.; LEVNER, E. V.
COMPLEXITY OF APPROXIMATION ALGORITHMS FOR COMBINATORIAL PROBLEMS: A SURVEY.

GENS 1979 -4 GENS, G. V.; LEVNER, E. V.
PROBLEMES D'OPTIMISATION DISCRETE ET ALGORITHMES APPROCHES EFFECTIFS (REVUE) (RUSSIAN).

GIANC 1979 -1 GIANNESSI, F.; NICOLETTI, B.
CREW SCHEDULING PROBLEM: A TRAVELLING SALESMAN APPROACH, THE.

GILM 1979 -1 GILMORE, P. C.
CUTTING STOCK, LINEAR PROGRAMMING, KNAPSACKING, DYNAMIC PROGRAMMING AND INTEGER PROGRAMMING, SOME INTERCONNECTIONS.

SURVEYS, BIBLIOGRAPHIES

GODI 1978 -1 GODIN, V. B.
INTERACTIVE SCHEDULING: HISTORICAL SURVEY AND STATE OF THE ART.
GOND 1979 -2 GONDRAN, M.
OPTIMISATION COMBINATOIRE.
GRAHA 1978 -1 GRAHAM, R. L.; LAWLER, E. L.; LENSTRA, J. K.; RINNOOY KAN, A. H. G.
OPTIMIZATION AND APPROXIMATION IN DETERMINISTIC SEQUENCING AND SCHEDULING: A SURVEY.
GRAHA 1979 -1 GRAHAM, R. L.; LAWLER, E. L.; LENSTRA, J. K.; RINNOOY KAN, A. H. G.
OPTIMIZATION AND APPROXIMATION IN DETERMINISTIC SEQUENCING AND SCHEDULING: A SURVEY.
GROEB 1981 -1 GROETSCHEL, M.
APPROACHES TO HARD COMBINATORIAL OPTIMIZATION PROBLEMS.
GUAN 1979 -1 GUAN, M. G.
BRIEF SURVEY OF RESEARCH WORKS ON NETWORK THEORY BY CHINESE MATHEMATICIANS, A.
GUPTB 1980 -2 GUPTA, O. K.
NONLINEAR INTEGER PROGRAMMING ALGORITHMS: A SURVEY.
HAMMA 1979 -1 HAMMER, P. L.
BOOLEAN ELEMENTS IN COMBINATORIAL OPTIMIZATION.
HAMMD 1979 -1 HAMMER, P. L.; NGUYEN, S.
PARTIAL ORDER IN THE SOLUTION SPACE OF BIVALENT PROGRAMS, A.
HAND 1979 -1 HANDLER, G. Y.
COMPLEXITY AND EFFICIENCY IN MINIMAX NETWORK LOCATION.
HANSB 1979 -1 HANSEN, P.
METHODS OF NONLINEAR 0-1 PROGRAMMING.
HARTB 1977 -1 HARTMANN, K.
VERFAHREN ZUR LOESUNG GANZZAHLIGER NICHTLINEARER OPTIMIERUNGSPROBLEME.
HASA 1980 -1 HASANUDDIN AHMAD, S.
GROUP THEORETIC APPROACH OF INTEGER PROGRAMMING - A SURVEY.
HINX 1980 -1 HINXMAN, A. I.
TRIM-LOSS AND ASSORTMENT PROBLEMS: A SURVEY, THE.
HOFF 1979 -1 HOFFMAN, A. J.
ROLE OF UNIMODULARITY IN APPLYING LINEAR INEQUALITIES TO COMBINATORIAL THEOREMS, THE.
JEROB 1978 -1 JEROSLOW, R. G.
CUTTING PLANE THEORY: ALGEBRAIC METHODS.
JEROB 1979 -1 JEROSLOW, R. G.
INTRODUCTION TO THE THEORY OF CUTTING-PLANES, AN.
JEROB 1979 -3 JEROSLOW, R. G.
THEORY OF CUTTING-PLANES, THE.
JOHND 1979 -1 JOHNSON, E. L.
ON THE GROUP PROBLEM AND A SUBADDITIVE APPROACH TO INTEGER PROGRAMMING.
JOHND 1980 -1 JOHNSON, E. L.
INTEGER PROGRAMMING. FACETS, SUBADDITIVITY, AND DUALITY FOR GROUP AND SEMI-GROUP PROBLEMS.
KENN 1978 -1 KENNINGTON, J. L.
SURVEY OF LINEAR COST MULTICOMMODITY NETWORK FLOWS, A.
KINGA 1980 -2 KING, J. R.; SPACHIS, A. S.
SCHEDULING: BIBLIOGRAPHY AND REVIEW.
KLEE 1979 -1 KLEE, V.
COMBINATORIAL OPTIMIZATION: WHAT IS THE STATE OF THE ART?
KLEE 1980 -1 KLEE, V.
COMBINATORIAL OPTIMIZATION: WHAT IS THE STATE OF THE ART?
KORM 1979 -1 KORMAN, S. M.
GRAPH-COLOURING PROBLEM, THE.
KORTA 1979 -1 KORTE, B.
APPROXIMATIVE ALGORITHMS FOR DISCRETE OPTIMIZATION PROBLEMS.
KORTA 1979 -2 KORTE, B.
GANZZAHLIGE PROGRAMMIERUNG.
KORTD 1981 -2 KORTE, B.; SCHRADER, R.
SURVEY ON ORACLE TECHNIQUES, A.
KRAR 1979 -1 KRARUP, J.; PRUZAN, P. M.
SELECTED FAMILIES OF LOCATION PROBLEMS.
KRISB 1979 -1 KRISHNAMOORTHY, M. S.; SAKSENA, J. P.
ALGEBRA OF PROJECT NETWORKS.
LAGE 1979 -1 LAGEWEG, B. J.; LENSTRA, J. K.; RINNOOY KAN, A. H. G.
MINIMIZING MAXIMUM LATENESS ON ONE MACHINE: ALGORITHMS AND APPLICATIONS.
LANDA 1979 -1 LAND, A.; POWELL, S.
COMPUTER CODES FOR PROBLEMS OF INTEGER PROGRAMMING.
LAWL 1979 -4 LAWLER, E. L.
SHORTEST PATH AND NETWORK FLOW ALGORITHMS.
LENSA 1978 -2 LENSTRA, J. K.; RINNOOY KAN, A. H. G.
COMPUTATIONAL COMPLEXITY OF DISCRETE OPTIMIZATION PROBLEMS.
LENSA 1979 -2 LENSTRA, J. K.; RINNOOY KAN, A. H. G.
COMPLEXITY OF PACKING, COVERING AND PARTITIONING PROBLEMS.
LENSA 1980 -3 LENSTRA, J. K.; RINNOOY KAN, A. H. G.
INTRODUCTION TO MULTIPROCESSOR SCHEDULING, AN.
LENSA 1979 -4 LENSTRA, J. K.; RINNOOY KAN, A. H. G.
COMPUTATIONAL COMPLEXITY OF DISCRETE OPTIMIZATION PROBLEMS.
LEWIA 1978 -1 LEWIS, H. R.; CHRISTOS, H. P.
EFFICIENCY OF ALGORITHMS, THE.
LOVA 1979 -1 LOVASZ, L.
GRAPH THEORY AND INTEGER PROGRAMMING.
MADE 1979 -1 MADER, W.
CONNECTIVITY AND EDGE-CONNECTIVITY IN FINITE GRAPHS.
MAFF 1979 -1 MAFFIOLI, F.
COMPLEXITY OF COMBINATORIAL OPTIMIZATION ALGORITHMS AND THE CHALLENGE OF HEURISTICS, THE.
MAHR 1981 -1 MAHR, B.
BIRD'S-EYE VIEW TO PATH PROBLEMS, A.
MARTC 1979 -3 MARTELLO, S.; TOTH, P.
0-1 KNAPSACK PROBLEM, THE.
MATTA 1977 -1 MATTHEISS, T. H.; RUBIN, D. S.
SURVEY AND COMPARISON OF METHODS FOR FINDING ALL VERTICES OF CONVEX POLYHEDRAL SETS, A.
MOLE 1979 -1 MOLE, R. H.
SURVEY OF LOCAL DELIVERY VEHICLE ROUTING METHODOLOGY, A.
MULD 1979 -1 MULDER, H. M.
RAMSEY THEORY.
NARUB 1979 -1 NARULA, S. C.; KINDORF, J. R.
LINEAR 0-1 PROGRAMMING: A COMPARISON OF IMPLICIT ENUMERATION ALGORITHMS.
OSKOA 1968 -1 OSKOLKOVA, S. E.; OSKOLKOV, I. O.
APPLICATION OF CERTAIN HEURISTIC METHODS TO THE SOLUTION OF SCHEDULING PROBLEMS (SURVEY).

PADB 1979 -1 PADBERG, M. W.
COVERING, PACKING AND KNAPSACK PROBLEMS.
PADB 1979 -2 PADBERG, M. W.
NULL-EINS-ENTSCHEIDUNGSPROBLEME.
RATH 1977 -1 RATHMANN, D.
ZUR LOESUNG DISKRETER OPTIMIERUNGSPROBLEME MIT GRUPPENTHEORETISCHEN ANSAETZEN.
READ 1979 -1 READ, R. C.
ALGORITHMS IN GRAPH THEORY.
REVE 1981 -1 REVELLE, C.; COHON, J.; SHOBRYS, D.
MULTIPLE OBJECTIVES IN FACILITY LOCATION: A REVIEW.
SAHNC 1978 -1 SAHNI, S.; HOROWITZ, E.
COMBINATORIAL PROBLEMS: REDUCIBILITY AND APPROXIMATION.
SANDA 1979 -1 SANDI, C.
SUBGRADIENT OPTIMIZATION.
SAPOA 1977 -1 SAPOZENKO, A. A.; ASRATJAN, A. S.; KUZJURIN, N. N.
SURVEY OF SOME RESULTS IN COVERING PROBLEMS (RUSSIAN), A.
SCHMC 1980 -1 SCHMIDT, G.; STROEHLEIN, T.
TIMETABLE CONSTRUCTION - AN ANNOTATED BIBLIOGRAPHY.
SCHRD 1979 -1 SCHRIJVER, A.
FRACTIONAL PACKING AND COVERING.
SHAPA 1978 -1 SHAPIRO, J. F.
FUTURE DIRECTIONS OF LARGE SCALE MIXED INTEGER PROGRAMMING.
SHAPA 1979 -1 SHAPIRO, J. F.
SURVEY OF LAGRANGIAN TECHNIQUES FOR DISCRETE OPTIMIZATION, A.
SHAR 1978 -1 SHARMA, J. K.
EXTENSIONS AND SPECIAL CASES OF TRANSPORTATION PROBLEM: A SURVEY.
SKUR 1977 -1 SKURBA, V. V.; BELETSKIJ, S. A.
NUMERICAL METHODS IN THE SOLUTION OF THE ASSEMBLY LINE BALANCING PROBLEM. A SURVEY.
SLOW 1977 -1 SLOWINSKI, R.
OPTIMAL AND HEURISTIC PROCEDURES FOR PROJECT SCHEDULING WITH MULTIPLE CONSTRAINED RESOURCES - A SURVEY.
SPIE 1979 -1 SPIELBERG, K.
ENUMERATIVE METHODS IN INTEGER PROGRAMMING.
STEC 1979 -2 STECKHAN, H.
NETZFLUSS-ANALYSE.
THOMC 1979 -1 THOMASSEN, C.
LONG CYCLES IN DIGRAPHS WITH CONSTRAINTS ON THE DEGREES.
TIND 1979 -1 TIND, J.
BLOCKING AND ANTIBLOCKING POLYHEDRA.
WEID 1977 -1 WEIDE, B.
SURVEY OF ANALYSIS TECHNIQUES FOR DISCRETE ALGORITHMS, A.
WELS 1979 -1 WELSH, D. J. A.
COLOURING PROBLEMS AND MATROIDS.
WILSA 1978 -1 WILSON, R. J.
EDGE COLOURINGS OF GRAPHS - A SURVEY.
WOLS 1979 -1 WOLSEY, L. A.
CUTTING PLANE METHODS.
WOODA 1978 -1 WOODALL, D. R.
MINIMAX THEOREMS IN GRAPH THEORY.
ZION 1979 -1 ZIONTS, S.
SURVEY OF MULTIPLE CRITERIA INTEGER PROGRAMMING METHODS, A.

ANDR 1977 -1 ANDRASFAI, B.
INTRODUCTORY GRAPH THEORY.
BAZAB 1977 -1 BAZARAA, M. S.; JARVIS, J. J.
LINEAR PROGRAMMING AND NETWORK FLOWS.
BERG 1973 -1 BERGE, C.
INTRODUCTION A LA THEORIE DES HYPERGRAPHES.
BIRD 1976 -1 BIRD, R.
PROGRAMS AND MACHINES. AN INTRODUCTION TO THE THEORY OF COMPUTING.
BOHE 1977 -1 BOHEME, G.
ANWENDUNGSORIENTIERTE MATHEMATIK. BD. 4: AKTUELLE ANWENDUNGEN DER MATHEMATIK.
BRADB 1977 -1 BRADLEY, S. P.; HAX, A. C.; MAGNANTI, T. L.
APPLIED MATHEMATICAL PROGRAMMING.
CABO 1977 -1 CABOT, A. V.; HARNETT, D. L.
INTRODUCTION TO MANAGMENT SCIENCE, AN.
CHAC 1979 -1 CHACHRA, V.; GHARE, P. M.; MOORE, J. M.
APPLICATIONS OF GRAPH THEORY ALGORITHMS.
CHARC 1977 -1 CHARTRAND, G.
GRAPHS AS MATHEMATICAL MODELS.
COOP 1977 -1 COOPER, L.; BHAT, U. N.; LEBLANC, L. J.
INTRODUCTION TO OPERATIONS RESEARCH MODELS.
CVETA 1979 -1 CVETKOVIC, D. M.; DOOB, M.; SACHS, H.
SPECTRA OF GRAPHS. THEORY AND APPLICATION.
DREY 1977 -1 DREYFUS, S. E.; LAW, A. M.
ART AND THEORY OF DYNAMIC PROGRAMMING, THE.
DUEC 1977 -1 DUECK, W.
DISKRETE OPTIMIERUNG.
ECKE 1977 -1 ECKER, K.
ORGANISATION VON PARALLELEN PROZESSEN. THEORIE DETERMINISTISCHER SCHEDULES.
EVEN 1979 -1 EVEN, S.
GRAPH ALGORITHMS.
FIORA 1977 -1 FIORINI, S.; WILSON, R. J.
EDGE-COLOURINGS OF GRAPHS.
GOLU 1980 -1 GOLUMBIC, M. C.
ALGORITHMIC GRAPH THEORY AND PERFECT GRAPHS.
GONDA 1979 -1 GONDRAN, M.; MINOUX, M.
GRAPHES ET ALGORITHMES.
GRAV 1977 -1 GRAVER, J. E.; WATKINS, M. E.
COMBINATORICS WITH EMPHASIS ON THE THEORY OF GRAPHS.
HALI 1980 -1 HALIN, R.
GRAPHENTHEORIE I.
HANDA 1979 -1 HANDLER, G. Y.; MIRCHANDANI, P. B.
LOCATION ON NETWORKS - THEORY AND ALGORITHMS.
HART 1975 -1 HARTIGAN, J. A.
CLUSTERING ALGORITHMS.
HARTA 1976 -1 HARTLEY, R. V.
OPERATIONS RESEARCH: A MANAGERIAL EMPHASIS.
HAST 1978 -1 HASTINGS, N. A. J.; MELLO, J. M. C.
DECISION NETWORKS.
HORO 1978 -1 HOROWITZ, E.; SAHNI, S.
FUNDAMENTALS OF COMPUTER ALGORITHMS.
JENS 1980 -1 JENSEN, P. A.; BARNES, J. W.
NETWORK FLOW PROGRAMMING.
KAUFD 1977 -1 KAUFMANN, A.; HENRY-LABORDERE, A.
INTEGER AND MIXED PROGRAMMING. THEORY AND APPLICATIONS.
KAUFE 1977 -1 KAUFMANN, A.; PICHAT, E.
METHODES MATHEMATIQUES NON NUMERIQUES ET LEURS ALGORITHMES. TOME 1 ALGORITHMES DE RECHERCHE DES ELEMENTS MAXIMAUX.
KAUFE 1977 -2 KAUFMANN, A.; PICHAT, E.
METHODES MATHEMATIQUES NON NUMERIQUES ET LEURS ALGORITHMES. TOME 2 ALGORITHMES DE RECHERCHE DE CHEMINS ET PROBLEMS ASSOCIES.
LIU 1977 -2 LIU, C. L.
ELEMENTS OF DISCRETE MATHEMATICS.
MAND 1979 -1 MANDL, C. E.
APPLIED NETWORK OPTIMIZATION.
MEIS 1978 -1 MEISSNER, J.-D.
HEURISTISCHE PROGRAMMIERUNG.
MINI 1978 -1 MINIEKA, E.
OPTIMIZATION ALGORITHMS FOR NETWORKS AND GRAPHS.
NAUS 1979 -1 NAUSS, R. M.
PARAMETRIC INTEGER PROGRAMMING.
NEIT 1977 -1 NEITZEL, W.
TOURENPLANUNG. PROBLEMDARSTELLUNG UND LOESUNSVERFAHREN FUER EIN-DEPOT-PROBLEME.
PAULB 1978 -1 PAUL, W. J.
KOMPLEXITAETSTHEORIE.
PFAF 1976 -1 PFAFFENBERGER, R. C.; WALKER, D. A.
MATHEMATICAL PROGRAMMING FOR ECONOMICS AND BUSINESS.
PRIT 1979 -1 PRITSKER, A. A. B.
MODELING AND ANALYSIS USING Q-GERT NETWORKS.
ROBIA 1980 -1 ROBINSON, D. F.; FOULDS, L. R.
DIGRAPHS: THEORY AND TECHNIQUES.
SACK 1977 -1 SACKOV, V. N.
COMBINATORIAL METHODS OF DISCRETE MATHEMATICS (RUSSIAN).
SALK 1975 -1 SALKIN, H. M.
INTEGER PROGRAMMING.
SCHME 1978 -1 SCHMITZ, P.; SCHOENLEIN, A.
LINEARE UND LINEARISIERBARE OPTIMIERUNGSMODELLE SOWIE IHRE ADV-GESTUETZTE LOESUNG.
SCHO 1978 -1 SCHOCH, M.
ERWEITERUNGSPRINZIP UND SEINE ANWENDUNG ZUR ENTWICKLUNG VON ALGORITHMEN FUER DIE LOESUNG KOMBINATORISCHER OPTIMIERUNGSAUFGABEN, DAS.
STRE 1977 -1 STREET, A. P.; WALLIS, W. D.
COMBINATORIAL THEORY: AN INTRODUCTION.
TRUD 1976 -1 TRUDEAU, R. J.
DOTS AND LINES.
TUCK 1980 -1 TUCKER, A. C.
APPLIED COMBINATORICS.

****

WALT 1979 -1 WALTHER, H.
ANWENDUNGEN DER GRAPHENTHEORIE.
ZIMM 1981 -1 ZIMMERMANN, U.
LINEAR AND COMBINATORIAL OPTIMIZATION IN ORDERED ALGEBRAIC STRUCTURES.

BABA 1981 -1 BABAEV, A. A.; DRUGANOV, B. N.
METHOD OF BRANCH AND BOUND IN THE PROBLEM OF COMPOSING WEEKLY SCHEDULE OF STUDIES (RUSSIAN).
BARRB 1965 -1 BARRACLOUGH, E. D.
APPLICATION OF A DIGITAL COMPUTER TO THE CONSTRUCTION OF TIME-TABLES, THE.
CART 1979 -1 CARTER, M. W.
FINAL EXAMINATION SCHEDULING FOR CORRESPONDENCE STUDENTS.
CHRIA 1971 -1 CHRISTIE, A.
MULTI-DIMENSIONAL SCHEDULING ALGORITHMS.
CSER 1978 -1 CSERNY, L.
FORMULATION OF THE TIME-TABLE PROBLEM AND THE EXAMINATION OF ITS CONSISTENT SOLUTIONS. II (HUNGARIAN), THE.
CSIM 1965 -1 CSIMA, J.
INVESTIGATIONS ON A TIME-TABLE PROBLEM.
DEFR 1978 -1 DEFRENNE, A.
TIMETABLING PROBLEM: A SURVEY, THE.
DEMP 1968 -1 DEMPSTER, M. A. H.
ON THE GOTLIEB-CSIMA TIME-TABLING ALGORITHM.
DESR 1978 -1 DESROCHES, S.; LAPORTE, G.; ROUSSEAU, J.-M.
HOREX: A COMPUTER PROGRAM FOR THE CONSTRUCTION OF EXAMINATION SCHEDULES.
EARL 1968 -1 EARLY, S.
EVALUATING A TIME-TABLING ALGORITHM BASED ON GRAPH-RECOLOURING.
GRAN 1979 -1 GRANDON, G. M.
OPTIMIZING HIGH SCHOOL CURRICULUM ASSIGNMENTS.
JAHN 1979 -1 JAHNO, V. M.
CLASS OF LINEAR DYNAMIC TIMETABLE MODELS, A.
KONY 1978 -1 KONYA, I.; SOMOGYI, P.; SZABADOS, T.
METHOD OF TIME-TABLE CONSTRUCTION BY COMPUTER, A.
LASZ 1978 -1 LASZLO, C.
FORMULATION OF THE TIME-TABLE PROBLEM AND THE EXAMINATION OF ITS CONSISTENT SOLUTIONS I (HUNGARIAN), THE.
LAWRB 1973 -1 LAWRIE, N.; VEITCH, H.
TIME-TABLING IN SECONDARY SCHOOLS - A STUDY OF MANUAL AND COMPUTER METHODS.
LEWI 1961 -1 LEWIS, G. F.
SCHOOL TIME-TABLE, THE.
MART 1979 -1 MARTEL, A.
HORAIRE DE TRAVAIL OPTIMAL FARE A UNE DEMANDE ALEATOIRE: LE CAS DES JEUX OLYMPIQUES DE MONTREAL.
MICH 1970 -1 MICHALSEN, H.
WORKING STRATEGY FOR GENERAL SCHOOL SCHEDULING, A.
OAKF 1966 -1 OAKFORD, A. C.
SCHOOL SCHEDULING - PRACTICE AND THEORY.
PAPO 1976 -1 PAPOULIAS, D. B.
INVESTIGATION OF COMBINATORIAL TIME-TABLING SYSTEMS.
PAPO 1977 -1 PAPOULIAS, D. B.
ASSIGNMENT-TO-DAYS PROBLEM IN A SCHOOL TIME-TABLE, A HEURISTIC APPROACH, THE.
PAPO 1978 -1 PAPOULIAS, D. B.
ALGORITHM FOR SCHOOL TIME-TABLING SYSTEMS (PART II), AN.
PAPO 1980 -1 PAPOULIAS, D. B.
ASSIGNMENT-TO-DAYS PROBLEM IN A SCHOOL TIME-TABLE, A HEURISTIC APPROACH, THE.
SADY 1978 -1 SADYKOV, R. G.
OPTIMIZATION OF AN ALGORITHM FOR DEVISING A SCHEDULE OF EDUCATIONAL ACTIVITIES (RUSSIAN).
SCHMC 1974 -1 SCHMIDT, G.; STROEHLEIN, T.
SOME ASPECTS IN THE CONSTRUCTION OF TIMETABLES.
SCHMC 1980 -1 SCHMIDT, G.; STROEHLEIN, T.
TIMETABLE CONSTRUCTION - AN ANNOTATED BIBLIOGRAPHY.
SCHRC 1980 -1 SCHREUDER, J. A. M.
CONSTRUCTING TIMETABLES FOR SPORT COMPETITIONS.
SCOTA 1980 -1 SCOTT, J. L.
HEURISTIC ALGORITHM FOR EXAMINATION TIMETABLING, A.
TALA 1979 -1 TALANOV, V. A.; IL'ICEV, A. P.
THREE-INDEX TRANSPORTATION PROBLEMS AND COMPILING SCHOOL TIMETABLES (RUSSIAN).
WAJS 1978 -1 WAJS, W.
ON A CERTAIN ALGORITHM FOR ARRANGING TIME TABLES (POLISH).
WERR 1978 -1 WERRA, D. DE
GRAPHS, HYPERGRAPHS AND TIMETABLING.
WERR 1981 -2 WERRA, D. DE
REMARKS ON THE REQUIREMENT MATRIX OF SCHOOL TIMETABLE PROBLEMS AND REGULAR EMBEDDINGS OF GRAPHS.
WERR 1978 -4 WERRA, D. DE
SOME COMMENTS ON A NOTE ABOUT TIMETABLING.
WILLA 1968 -1 WILLIAMS, M. R.
GRAPH THEORY MODEL FOR THE SOLUTION OF TIMETABLES, A.

AHRE 1980 -1 AHRENS, J. H.; FINKE, G.
PRIMAL TRANSPORTATION AND TRANSSHIPMENT ALGORITHMS.
ALEKA 1981 -1 ALEKSEEV, O. G.; BABAEV, A. A.
ON HUNGARIAN METHOD EFFICIENCY IMPROVEMENT (RUSSIAN).
ALTA 1980 -1 ALTAR, M.
ALGORITHM FOR THE SOLUTION OF THE DYNAMIC PRODUCTION-TRANSPORTATION PROBLEM, AN.
ANEJB 1979 -1 ANEJA, Y. P.; NAIR, K. P. K.
BICRITERIA TRANSPORTATION PROBLEM.
ARMSE 1980 -1 ARMSTRONG, R. D.; KLINGMAN, D.; WHITMAN, D.
IMPLEMENTATION AND ANALYSIS OF A VARIANT OF THE DUAL METHOD FOR THE CAPACITATED TRANSSHIPMENT PROBLEM.
AVON 1979 -1 AVONDO-BODINO, G.
GRAPH THEORY AND OPERATIONS RESEARCH.
BAREA 1969 -1 BARENBAUM, F. B.
CERTAIN TRANSPORT PROBLEM WITH A CONCAVE TARGET FUNCTION (RUSSIAN), A.
BARR 1980 -1 BARR, R. S.; ELAM, J.; GLOVER, F.; KLINGMAN, D.
NETWORK AUGMENTING PATH BASIS ALGORITHM FOR TRANSSHIPMENT PROBLEMS, A.
BARRA 1977 -1 BARR, R. S.; GLOVER, F.; KLINGMAN, D.
ALTERNATING BASIS ALGORITHM FOR ASSIGNMENT PROBLEMS, THE.
BARRA 1978 -1 BARR, R. S.; GLOVER, F.; KLINGMAN, D.
GENERALIZED ALTERNATING PATH ALGORITHM FOR TRANSPORTATION PROBLEMS, THE.
BARRA 1979 -2 BARR, R. S.; GLOVER, F.; KLINGMAN, D.
NEW OPTIMIZATION METHOD FOR LARGE-SCALE FIXED CHARGE TRANSPORTATION PROBLEMS, A.
BELJ 1976 -1 BELJAEVA, L. V.; ZURBENKO, N. G.; SOR, N. Z.
NONLINEAR TRANSPORTATION PROBLEM (RUSSIAN), A.
BHATB 1978 -1 BHATIA, H. L.
SOLID TRANSPORTATION PROBLEM IN LINEAR FRACTIONAL PROGRAMMING.
BHATB 1979 -1 BHATIA, H. L.
NOTE ON A ZERO-ONE MINIMIZING TRANSPORTATION PROBLEM, A.
BHATC 1978 -1 BHATIA, H. L.; SWARUP, K.; PURI, M. C.
PROCEDURE FOR TIME MINIMIZATION TRANSPORTATION PROBLEM, A.
BHATC 1979 -1 BHATIA, H. L.; SWARUP, K.; PURI, M. C.
TIME ENUMERATION TECHNIQUE FOR TIME-COST TRADE-OFF IN A TRANSPORTATION PROBLEM.
BOFI 1976 -1 BOFILL, A.; DIAZ, A.
SENSITIVITY ANALYSIS FOR THE TRANSPORTATION PROBLEM IN LINEAR PROGRAMMING (SPANISH).
BOOKA 1980 -1 BOOKBINDER, J. H.; SETHI, S. P.
DYNAMIC TRANSPORTATION PROBLEM: A SURVEY, THE.
BRAN 1978 -1 BRANDT, A.; INTRATOR, J.
FAST ALGORITHMS FOR LONG TRANSPORTATION PROBLEMS.
BRANA 1978 -1 BRANMAN, J.
SHORT COMMUNICATION. A NOTE ON PIVOTING IN TRANSPORTATION CODES.
BRON 1979 -1 BRONSTEIN, M. L.; KIM, K. V.
ELIMINATION ON THE POSSIBILITY OF CYCLING IN THE PRIMAL NETWORK METHOD (RUSSIAN).
BURK 1978 -1 BURKARD, R. E.
GENERAL HUNGARIAN METHOD FOR THE ALGEBRAIC TRANSPORTATION PROBLEM, A.
BURK 1979 -2 BURKARD, R. E.
REMARKS ON SOME SCHEDULING PROBLEMS WITH ALGEBRAIC OBJECTIVE FUNCTIONS.
BURK 1979 -4 BURKARD, R. E.
UEBER EINE ANWENDUNG ALGEBRAISCHER TRANSPORTPROBLEME BEI REIHENFOLGEPROBLEMEN.
BURKJ 1980 -2 BURKARD, R. E.; ZIMMERMANN, U.
WEAKLY ADMISSIBLE TRANSFORMATIONS FOR SOLVING ALGEBRAIC ASSIGNMENT AND TRANSPORTATION PROBLEMS.
BUTA 1975 -1 BUTAN, E. I.; NECVAL, N. A.
ALGORITHMS FOR THE OPERATIONAL CONTROL OF ARRIVAL FLOWS IN A TRANSPORTATION NETWORK (RUSSIAN).
CHARB 1978 -1 CHARNES, A.; DUFFA, S.; RYAN, M. J.
DEGENERACY AND THE MORE-FOR-LESS PARADOX.
CHERC 1974 -1 CHERNYSHEV, JU. O.
REDUCTION OF THE BIVALENT PROGRAMMING PROBLEM TO THE TRANSPORT PROBLEM (RUSSIAN), THE.
CHERD 1977 -1 CHERNYSHEV, JU. O.; OSTROUH, E. N.
POSSIBILITY OF REDUCING A CERTAIN CLASS OF LINEAR PROGRAMMING PROBLEMS TO PROBLEMS OF TRANSPORT TYPE (RUSSIAN), THE.
DERI 1980 -2 DERIGS, U.
ENGPASS-ZIELFUNKTION UND ZEIT/KOSTEN - TRADE-OFFS BEIM TRANSPORTPROBLEM.
DERI 1980 -4 DERIGS, U.
METHODEN ZUR LOESUNG DES BOTTLENECK-TRANSPORTPROBLEMS.
DERIC 1979 -1 DERIGS, U.; ZIMMERMANN, U.
AUGMENTING PATH METHOD FOR SOLVING LINEAR BOTTLENECK TRANSPORTATION PROBLEMS, AN.
DIAZ 1978 -1 DIAZ, J. A.
SOLVING MULTIOBJECTIVE TRANSPORTATION PROBLEMS.
DIAZ 1979 -1 DIAZ, J. A.
FINDING A COMPLETE DESCRIPTION OF ALL EFFICIENT SOLUTIONS IN A MULTIOBJECTIVE TRANSPORTATION PROBLEM.
DINEA 1978 -1 DINESCU, C.; SAVULESCU, B.
NEW RESULTS IN THE FLOW TRANSPORT PROBLEM.
DJUK 1977 -1 DJUKANOV, V. G.
LIST REPRESENTATION FOR THE MACHINE SOLUTION OF AN ILL-POSED TRANSPORT PROBLEM (RUSSIAN).
DODU 1975 -1 DODU, J. C.
MODELE D'OPTIMISATION A LONG TERME D'UN RESEAU DE TRANSPORT.
DROE 1977 -1 DROESBEKE, F.; BERCKMANS, A.
TRANSPORTATION PROBLEM WITH CAPACITIES AND MIXED CONSTRAINTS, THE.
EMEL 1978 -1 EMELICHEV, V. A.; KRACKOVSKII, A. P.
ASYMPTOTIC PROPERTIES OF TRANSPORTATION POLYHEDRA (RUSSIAN).
EMELA 1977 -1 EMELICHEV, V. A.; KRAVTSOV, M. K.; KRACKOVSKII, A. P.
BEWEIS EINER HYPOTHESE VON BOLKER (RUSSIAN).
EMELA 1978 -1 EMELICHEV, V. A.; KRAVTSOV, M. K.; KRACKOVSKII, A. P.
MINIMAL NUMBER OF VERTICES OF A NONDEGENERATE TRANSPORTATION POLYTOPE WITH A FIXED NUMBER OF FACES (RUSSIAN), THE.
EMELA 1977 -2 EMELICHEV, V. A.; KRAVTSOV, M. K.; KRACKOVSKII, A. P.
ON A CONJECTURE ABOUT THE MAXIMAL NUMBER OF VERTICES OF A TRANPORTATION POLYTOPE (RUSSIAN).
EMELA 1978 -2 EMELICHEV, V. A.; KRAVTSOV, M. K.; KRACKOVSKII, A. P.
ON SOME CLASSES OF TRANSPORTATION POLYTOPES (RUSSIAN).
EMELB 1977 -1 EMELICHEV, V. A.; TRUKHANOVSKIJ, N. N.
SPECTRUM OF TRANSPORTATION POLYHEDRA (RUSSIAN), THE.
EMELC 1977 -1 EMELICHEVA, V. S.; KRAVTSOV, M. K.
FACES OF A DEGENERATE TRANSPORTATION POLYHEDRON (RUSSIAN), THE.

EREM 1978 -2 EREMENKO, I. V.; PHOVELISVILI, Z. I.
ON THE QUESTION OF PERFECTING A NUMERICAL SCHEME FOR THE SOLUTION OF A TRANSPORT PROBLEM BY THE HUNGARIAN METHOD (RUSSIAN).

EVAN 1979 -1 EVANS, J. R.
AGGREGATION IN THE GENERALIZED TRANSPORTATION PROBLEM.

EVAN 1978 -5 EVANS, J. R.
SOLVING MULTICOMMODITY TRANSPORTATION PROBLEMS THROUGH AGGREGATION.

EVANB 1977 -1 EVANS, J. R.; JARVIS, J. J.; DUKE, R. A.
GRAPHIC MATROIDS AND THE MULTICOMMODITY TRANSPORTATION PROBLEM.

FARK 1981 -1 FARKAS, Z. M.
SOLUTION OF A MODIFIED TRANSPORTATION PROBLEM WITH PENALTY FUNCTION BY THE METHOD "OPTIMIZATION WITH MINIMAL INFORMATION" ("OMI").

FEDE 1977 -1 FEDENJA, O. A.
POLYHEDRA OF A MULTI-INDEX PLANAR TRANSPORT PROBLEM WITH A MINIMAL NUMBER OF VERTICES I (RUSSIAN), THE.

FEDE 1977 -2 FEDENJA, O. A.
POLYHEDRA OF A MULTI-INDEX PLANAR TRANSPORT PROBLEM WITH A MINIMAL NUMBER OF VERTICES II (RUSSIAN), THE.

FIED 1979 -1 FIEDLER, M.
OPTIMIERUNG UND GRAPHENTHEORIE.

FINK 1978 -1 FINKE, G.
UNIFIED APPROACH TO RESHIPMENT, OVERSHIPMENT AND POST-OPTIMIZATION PROBLEMS, A.

FINKA 1978 -1 FINKE, G.; AHRENS, J. H.
VARIANT OF THE PRIMAL TRANSPORTATION ALGORITHM, A.

FISKA 1979 -1 FISK, J. C.; MAC KEOWN, P. G.
PURE FIXED CHARGE TRANSPORTATION PROBLEM, THE.

FONS 1979 -1 FONSO, R.
ON A STOCHASTIC TRANSPORTATION PROBLEM (ITALIAN).

FOUL 1980 -1 FOULDS, L. R.; GIBBONS, P. B.
NEW ALGORITHMS FOR THE BULK, ZERO-ONE TIME MINI-MAX TRANSPORTATION MODEL.

GABA 1979 -1 GABASOV, R. F.; KOSTJUKOVA, O. I.
ON AN ALGORITHM FOR SOLVING A NETWORK DISTRIBUTOR PROBLEM.

GART 1976 -1 GARTNER, N. H.; GOLDEN, B. L.; WONG, R. T.
MODELING AND OPTIMIZATION FOR TRANSPORTATION SYSTEMS PLANNING AND OPERATIONS.

GEND 1977 -1 GENDREAU, M.
ETUDE SUR LA GENERATION DES RESEAUX ALEATOIRES.

GERL 1978 -1 GERLOVIN, E. L.; SROGOVICH, E. B.
METHODS FOR SOLVING NONLINEAR NETWORK TRANSPORTATION PROBLEMS (RUSSIAN).

GLOVC 1970 -1 GLOVER, F.; KARNEY, D.; KLINGMAN, D.
DOUBLE-PRICING DUAL AND FEASIBLE START ALGORITHMS FOR THE CAPACITATED TRANSPORTATION (DISTRIBUTION) PROBLEM.

GLOVD 1978 -1 GLOVER, F.; KARNEY, D.; KLINGMAN, D.; RUSSELL, R.
SOLVING SINGLY CONSTRAINED TRANSSHIPMENT PROBLEMS.

GOLDG 1977 -1 GOLDFARB, D.
STEEPEST EDGE SIMPLEX ALGORITHMS FOR NETWORK FLOW PROBLEMS.

GRABB 1978 -1 GRABOWSKI, W.; LELENO, J.
PROBLEME DE SELECTION DES ITINERAIRES (POLISH).

GRIB 1978 -1 GRIBOV, A. B.
SOLUTION RECURSIVE DES PROBLEMES DE TRANSPORT DE LA PROGRAMMATION LINEAIRE (RUSSIAN).

GUDE 1978 -1 GUDEHUS, T.
TRANSPORTMATRIX UND FASSUNGSVERMOEGEN.

GUIGA 1979 -1 GUIGNARD, M.; SPIELBERG, K.
DIRECT DUAL APPROACH TO A TRANSSHIPMENT FORMULATION FOR MULTI-LAYER NETWORK PROBLEMS WITH FIXED CHARGES, A.

GUPTC 1977 -1 GUPTA, R.
TIME-COST TRANSPORTATION PROBLEM.

GUPTC 1979 -1 GUPTA, R.
SOLVING THE GENERALIZED TRANSPORTATION PROBLEM WITH CONSTRAINTS.

HALL 1978 -1 HALL, M. A.
PROPERTIES OF THE EQUILIBRIUM STATE IN TRANSPORTATION NETWORKS.

HARR 1978 -1 HARRIS, B.
NEW ALGORITHM FOR TREE MODIFICATION IN THE PRIMAL TRANSPORTATION PROBLEM, A.

HARR 1979 -1 HARRIS, B.
RAPID DUAL METHOD FOR THE HITCHCOCK PROBLEM, A.

HAYEA 1979 -1 HAYES, M.
BLOCKBUSTING: OR HOW TO HANDLE COMPLEX CONSTRAINTS IN THE TRANSPORTATION TABLEAU.

HINDB 1978 -1 HINDI, K. S.; BRAMELLER, A.; HAMAM, K. M.
SOLUTION OF FIXED COST TRANS-SHIPMENT PROBLEMS BY A BRANCH AND BOUND METHOD.

INTR 1980 -1 INTRATOR, J.; BERREBI, M.
AUXILIARY PROCEDURES FOR SOLVING LONG TRANSPORTATION PROBLEMS.

INTRA 1980 -1 INTRATOR, J.; ENGELBERG, A.
SENSITIVITY ANALYSIS AS A MEANS OF REDUCING THE DIMENSIONALITY OF A CERTAIN CLASS OF TRANSPORTATION PROBLEMS.

INTRB 1978 -1 INTRATOR, J.; PAROUSH, J.
IMPROVING LOOPS AND VANISHING VARIABLES IN LONG TRANSPORTATION PROBLEMS.

ISAE 1970 -1 ISAEVA, M. N.
LARGEST POSSIBLE NUMBER OF BASIS SOLUTIONS IN THE TRANSPORT PROBLEM, (RUSSIAN), THE.

ISER 1979 -1 ISERMANN, H.
ENUMERATION AF ALL EFFICIENT SOLUTIONS FOR A LINEAR MULTIPLE-OBJECTIVE TRANSPORTATION PROBLEM, THE.

JAKS 1981 -1 JAKSCH, H. J.
NECESSARY 0-1 CONDITIONS FOR THE EXISTENCE OF SOLUTIONS OF A TWO-COMMODITY TRANSPORT PROBLEM.

JEFF 1978 -1 JEFFERSON, T. R.; SCOTT, C. H.
GEOMETRIC PROGRAMMING APPLIED TO TRANSPORTATION PLANNING.

JUNGA 1970 -1 JUNGINGER, W.
UEBER DIE LOESUNG DES DREIDIMENSIONALEN TRANSPORTPROBLEMS.

JUNGA 1977 -1 JUNGINGER, W.
ALGORITHM FOR THE SOLUTION OF MULTI-INDEX TRANSPORTATION PROBLEMS, AN.

JUNGA 1978 -1 JUNGINGER, W.
KLASSIFIKATION DER MEHRDIMENSIONALEN TRANSPORTPROBLEME.

KABE 1980 -1 KABE, D. G.
DIRECT SOLUTIONS TO THE M-MEDIAN AND FRACTIONAL TRANSPORTATION PROBLEMS.

KACP 1980 -1 KACPRZYK, J.; KRAWCZAK, M.
ON AN INEXACT TRANSPORTATION PROBLEM.

KARN 1978 -1 KARNEY, D.; KLINGMAN, D.
NETGEN REVISITED: A PROGRAM FOR GENERATING LARGE SCALE (UN) CAPACITATED ASSIGNMENT, TRANPORTATION, AND MINIMUM COST FLOW NETWORK PROBLEMS.

KASS 1978 -1 KASSAY, F.
SENSITIVITY ANALYSIS OF A TRANSPORTATION PROBLEM. A CHANGE OF OBJECTIVE FUNCTION COEFFICIENTS-C(IJ) (CZECHOSLOVAKIAN).

KATSA 1979 -1 KATSNEL'SON, M. B.; KHRANOVICH, I. L.
TRANSPORT PROBLEM ON A NETWORK WITH AMPLIFICATION IN THE ARCS. I. THE SOLUTION METHOD.

KEMP 1979 -1 KEMPER, F. M.
ALGORITHM FOR FORMATION OF THE ESSENTIAL CONSTRAINTS OF A TRANSPORT PROBLEM WITH PROHIBITIONS (RUSSIAN), AN.

KERI 1978 -1 KERI, G.
ON THE POSSIBILITY OF CYCLING IN THE SIMPLEX ALGORITHM APPLIED TO THE TRANSPORTATION PROBLEM (HUNGARIAN).

KHAK 1978 -1 KHAKIMOV, A.
ADVANTAGE OF THE OPERATIVE METHOD OF MANAGING A TRANSPORTATION SYSTEM BETWEEN TWO POINTS (RUSSIAN).

KHRA 1979 -1 KHRANOVICH, I. L.
TRANSPORT PROBLEM ON A NETWORK WITH AMPLIFICATION IN THE ARCS. II. EFFECT OF PERTURBATIONS IN THE INITIAL DATA.

KLIN 1979 -1 KLINGMAN, D.; MOTE, J.
MULTI-PERIOD PRODUCTION, DISTRIBUTION, AND INVENTORY PLANNING MODEL, A.

KLUY 1979 -1 KLUYVER, C. A. DE
SOLVING THE MULTI-INDEX TRANSPORTATION PROBLEM BY DECOMPOSITION.

KONO 1971 -1 KONONENKO, A. M.
TRANSPORTATION POLYTOPES OF ORDER 2 X N (RUSSIAN).

KONOA 1979 -1 KONONENKO, A. M.; TRUKHANOVSKIJ, N. N.
CLASSES DE POLYEDRES DE TRANSPORT AVEC UN NOMBRE MAXIMAL DE SOMMETS (RUSSIAN).

KONOA 1978 -2 KONONENKO, A. M.; TRUKHANOVSKIJ, N. N.
POLYEDRES DE TRANSPORT AVEC UN NOMBRE MAXIMAL DE SOMMETS (RUSSIAN).

KORC 1979 -1 KORCHEMKIN, M. B.
PIECEWISE SOLUTION OF A CERTAIN CLASS OF TRANSPORTATION PROBLEMS, THE.

KORNB 1977 -1 KORNILOVA, L. E.; NGUYEN VAN VI
TRANSPORTATION PROBLEM WITH RESPECT TO THE TIME CRITERION (RUSSIAN).

KORNB 1977 -2 KORNILOVA, L. E.; NGUYEN VAN VI
TRANSPORTATION PROBLEM WITH RESPECT TO THE TIME CRITERION WITH AN ADDITIONAL CONSTRAINT (RUSSIAN).

KORT 1980 -1 KORTANEK, K. O.; YAMASAKI, M.
EQUALITIES IN TRANSPORTATION PROBLEMS AND CHARACTERIZATIONS OF OPTIMAL SOLUTIONS.

KRAC 1978 -1 KRACKOVSKII, A. P.
FORMULA FOR THE MAXIMUM NUMBER OF VERTICES OF A TRANSPORTATION POLYTOPE (RUSSIAN), A.

KRAC 1979 -1 KRACKOVSKII, A. P.
ASYMPTOTIC PROBLEM OF BOLKER (RUSSIAN), AN.

KRACA 1979 -1 KRACKOVSKII, A. P.; EMELICHEV, V. A.
ESTIMATION OF THE UPPER LIMIT FOR THE TRANSPORT POLYTOPE DIAMETER (RUSSIAN).

KRAF 1981 -1 KRAFFT, O.
NOTE ON A SPECIAL TRANSPORTATION PROBLEM, A.

KRAUA 1977 -1 KRAUSE, H.
MOEGLICHKEITEN ZUR LOESUNG VON ZWEISTUFIGEN TRANSPORTPROBLEMEN.

KRAVA 1979 -1 KRAVTSOV, M. K.
(D-2)-DIMENSIONAL FACES OF A TRANSPORT POLYHEDRON OF DIMENSION D (RUSSIAN).

KRAVA 1973 -2 KRAVTSOV, M. K.
ON THE QUESTION OF LOWERING THE DIMENSION OF A TRANSPORT PROBLEM (RUSSIAN).

KRAVB 1979 -1 KRAVTSOV, M. K.; EMELICHEV, V. A.
ESTIMATION PAR EXCES DU DIAMETRE D'UN POLYEDRE DE TRANSPORT (RUSSIAN).

KRAVB 1979 -2 KRAVTSOV, M. K.; EMELICHEV, V. A.
UPPER BOUND FOR THE DIAMETER OF A TRANSPORT POLYTOPE (RUSSIAN).

KRAVC 1979 -1 KRAVTSOV, M. K.; KORZNIKOV, A. D.
ENUMERATION PROBLEMS ON TRUNCATED TRANSPORT POLYTOPES (RUSSIAN).

KRIV 1979 -1 KRIVONOZKO, V. E.; PROPOI, A. I.
METHOD FOR THE SOLUTION OF DYNAMIC TRANSPORTATION PROBLEMS.

KURIA 1975 -1 KURIYAMA, S.; SHIMOSAKON, T.; NOSE, T.; TOKIOKA, H.
APPLICATION OF DYNAMIC PROGRAMMING TO OBTAIN AN OPTIMAL INVENTORY TRANSPORTATION SYSTEM FOR SEASONAL GOODS (AN N-STATION INVENTORY TRANSSHIPMENT MODEL) (JAPANESE), AN.

KUZN 1976 -1 KUZNETSOV, V. A.
METHOD FOR THE SOLUTION OF A TRANSPORTATION-PRODUCTION PROBLEM OF A SPECIAL FORM (RUSSIAN), A.

LEBL 1979 -2 LEBLANC, L. J.; ABDULAAL, M.
OPTIMIZATION METHODS FOR DESIGN OF MULTIMODEL NETWORKS.

LITV 1970 -1 LITVAK, B. G.; RAPPOPORT, A. M.
CONDITIONS FOR THE REDUCIBILITY OF LINEAR PROGRAMMING PROBLEMS TO TRANSPORTATION PROBLEMS (RUSSIAN).

LOS 1979 -1 LOS, M.
DISCRETE-CONVEX PROGRAMMING APPROACH TO THE SIMULTANEOUS OPTIMIZATION OF LAND USE AND TRANSPORTATION, A.

MAC E 1978 -1 MAC GINNIS, L. F.
IMPLEMENTATION AND TESTING OF A PRIMAL-DUAL ALGORITHM FOR ASSIGNMENT PROBLEM.

MAC I 1978 -1 MAC KEOWN, P. G.
SOME COMPUTATIONAL RESULTS OF USING THE AHRENS-FINKE METHOD FOR HANDLING DEGENERACY IN FIXED CHARGE TRANSPORTATION PROBLEMS.

MAC I 1980 -1 MAC KEOWN, P. G.
SOLVING INCREMENTAL QUANTITY DISCOUNTED TRANSPORTATION PROBLEMS BY VERTEX RANKING.

MAGR 1978 -1 MAGRUPOVA, D. A.
MATRIX-DIAGONAL METHOD OF SOLVING A CLASS OF TRANSPORT PROBLEMS OF LINEAR PROGRAMMING (RUSSIAN), THE.

MARL 1979 -1 MARLIN, P. G.
APPLICATION OF THE TRANSPORTATION MODEL TO A LARGE SCALE "DISTRICTING" PROBLEM.

MASC 1980 -1 MASCH, V. V.
CYCLIC METHOD OF SOLVING THE TRANSSHIPMENT PROBLEM WITH AN ADDITIONAL LINEAR CONSTRAINT, THE.

MELA 1979 -1 MELAMED, I. J.; PLOTINSKIJ, Y. M.
ALGORITHME HEURISTIQUE DE RESOLUTION DU PROBLEME DE LIVRAISON GENERALISE (RUSSIAN).

MIRC 1979 -1 MIRCHANDANI, P. B.; ODONI, A. R.
LOCATING NEW PASSENGER FACILITIES ON A TRANSPORTATION NETWORK.

MISRA 1981 -1 MISRA, S.; DAS, C.
THREE-DIMENSIONAL TRANSPORTATION PROBLEM WITH CAPACITY RESTRICTION.

MITS 1978 -1 MITSUMORI, S.
MINIMUM NUMBER OF VEHICLES TO MEET DYNAMIC TRANSPORTATION DEMAND.
MOOR 1978 -1 MOORE, L. J.; TAYLOR, B. W. III; LEE, S. M.
ANALYSIS OF A TRANSSHIPMENT PROBLEM WITH MULTIPLE CONFLICTING OBJECTIVES.
MORIB 1978 -1 MORITZ, A.
MATHEMATISCHES MODELL FUER DIE ERRECHNUNG DER MINIMALEN TRANSPORTKOSTEN IM UNGARISCHEN BINNENHANDEL.
MULV 1978 -1 MULVEY, J. M.
PIVOT STRATEGIES FOR PRIMAL-SIMPLEX NETWORK CODES.
NAGE 1980 -1 NAGELHOUT, R. V.; THOMPSON, G. L.
SINGLE SOURCE TRANSPORTATION ALGORITHM, A.
NAGE 1980 -2 NAGELHOUT, R. V.; THOMPSON, G. L.
STUDY OF THE BOTTLENECK SINGEL SOURCE TRANSPORTATION PROBLEM, A.
NEEB 1978 -1 NEEBE, A. W.
BRANCH AND BOUND ALGORITHM FOR THE P-MEDIAN TRANSPORTATION PROBLEM, A.
NEIT 1977 -1 NEITZEL, W.
TOURENPLANUNG. PROBLEMDARSTELLUNG UND LOESUNSVERFAHREN FUER EIN-DEPOT-PROBLEME.
NGUY 1978 -1 NGUYEN VAN VI
TRANSPORT TIME CRITERION PROBLEM WITH ADDITIONAL LIMITATIONS.
NOVO 1979 -1 NOVOKRESHCHENOVA, L. D.; EPSHTEIN, G. L.
FORMATION OF AGGREGATES IN PARALLEL SOLUTION OF A TRANSPORT PROBLEM (RUSSIAN).
OHSE 1978 -1 OHSE, D.
ZEIT-UMLADE- ODER BOTTLENECK-TRANSSHIPMENTPROBLEM, DAS.
PARS 1973 -1 PARSONS, J. E.
TRANSPORTATION PROBLEM: ANOTHER APPROXIMATION METHOD, THE.
PETEB 1980 -1 PETERSON, B. E.
CUT-FLOW PROCEDURE FOR TRANSPORTATION NETWORK OPTIMIZATION, A.
PIME 1978 -1 PIMENTEL, R. F.
COMPARATIVE ANALYSIS OF SOME TECHNIQUES TO SOLVE THE GENERALIZED TRANSPORTATION PROBLEM (SPANISH).
PINS 1978 -1 PINSKER, A. G.
TRANSPORTATION PROBLEM IN FUNCTION SPACES, THE.
PITF 1979 -1 PITFIELD, D. E.; SENIOR, M.
ALGORITHM 7: OBTAINING SHADOW PRICES FROM THE NAG TRANSPORTATION PROBLEM PRIMAL.
PODD 1980 -1 PODDUBNY, G. V.
OPTIMIZATIONAL PROBLEM OF TRANS-SHIPMENTS IN PORTS (RUSSIAN).
POGA 1978 -1 POGANY, Z.
ALGORITHM FOR SOLVING THE GENERALIZED TRANSPORTATION PROBLEM, AN.
PORO 1977 -1 POROCKII, S. M.
TWO-STEP STOCHASTIC PROBLEMS OR THE TRANSPORT TYPE.
PRAG 1954 -1 PRAGER, W.
PROBLEMS OF TRAFFIC AND TRANSPORTATION.
RAMAB 1980 -1 RAMAKRISHNAN, K. G.
SOLVING TWO-COMMODITY TRANSPORTATION PROBLEMS WITH COUPLING CONSTRAINTS.
RAO B 1980 -1 RAO, R. C.; SHAFTEL, T. L.
COMPUTATIONAL EXPERIENCE ON AN ALGORITHM FOR THE TRANSPORTATION PROBLEM WITH NONLINEAR OBJECTIVE FUNCTIONS.
RAO B 1981 -1 RAO, R. C.; SHAFTEL, T. L.
CAPACITATED TRANSPORTATION PRODUCTION PROBLEM: COMPUTATIONAL EXPERIENCE, THE.
RARDA 1979 -1 RARDIN, R. L.; CHOE, U.
TIGHTER RELAXATIONS OF FIXED CHARGE NETWORK FLOW PROBLEMS.
REMK 1980 -1 REMKE, W.
LOESUNG EINES DREISTUFIGEN TRANSPORTPROBLEMS MIT HILFE VON SUBGRADIENTENVERFAHREN.
RIIV 1979 -1 RIIVES, K.
DETERMINATION OF THE VERTICES OF TRANSPORT POLYTOPES (RUSSIAN), A.
ROSSA 1979 -1 ROSS, G. T.; ZOLTNERS, A. A.
WEIGHTED ASSIGNMENT MODELS AND THEIR APPLICATION.
RYAN 1980 -1 RYAN, M. J.
MORE ON THE MORE FOR LESS PARADOX IN THE DISTRIBUTION MODEL.
SABA 1975 -1 SABAU, A.
ON THE SOLUTION OF A TRANSPORTATION PROBLEM ON AN INTERVAL (ROMANIAN).
SAHAA 1979 -1 SAHA, T.
ON A TRI-CRITERION TRANSPORTATION PROBLEM.
SAPIA 1970 -1 SAPIRO, V. R.
ON THE QUESTION OF THE STATISTICAL ESTIMATION OF VARIOUS METHODS FOR SOLVING THE TRANSPORT PROBLEM (RUSSIAN).
SCHEB 1979 -1 SCHENK, G.; THIERS, G.
COMPARISON OF SOME ALGORITHMS AND HEURISTICS FOR SOLVING THE HITCHCOCK-KOOPMANS TRANSPORTATION PROBLEM, A.
SCHIB 1975 -1 SCHIEBEL, W.; UNGER, G.
DUALE ENTARTUNG IN DER LINEAREN OPTIMIERUNG, TRANSPORTPROBLEM MIT ZUSAETZLICHEN NEBENBEDINGUNGEN UND RUNDREISEPROBLEM.
SCHMA 1978 -1 SCHMID, H. J.
GEOMETRICAL INTERPRETATION OF THE HUNGARIAN METHOD, A.
SCHME 1978 -1 SCHMITZ, P.; SCHOENLEIN, A.
LINEARE UND LINEARISIERBARE OPTIMIERUNGSMODELLE SOWIE IHRE ADV-GESTUETZTE LOESUNG.
SCHN 1978 -1 SCHNIEDERJANS, M. J.; KWAK, N. K.
SIMULATED TRANSPORTATION PROBLEM FOR IMPROVED OPERATIONAL PLANNING: AN APPLICATION IN THE TRUCKING INDUSTRY, A.
SESH 1980 -1 SESHAN, C. R.; ACHARY, K. K.
BRANCH AND BOUND ALGORITHM FOR A TRANSPORTATION TYPE PROBLEM WITH PIECEWISE LINEAR CONVEX OBJECTIVE FUNCTION, A.
SESHA 1980 -2 SESHAN, C. R.; TIKEKAR, V. G.
ON SHARMA-SWARUP ALGORITHM FOR TIME MINIMIZING TRANSPORTATION PROBLEMS.
SGUR 1977 -1 SGUREV, V. S.; VASILEV, V. S.
DECOMPOSITION METHOD FOR THE SOLUTION OF A CLASS OF INTEGER PROGRAMMING PROBLEMS (BULGARIAN), A.
SGUR 1980 -1 SGUREV, V. S.; VASILEV, V. S.
OPTIMIZATION OF A CLOSED DYNAMIC TRANSPORTATION SYSTEM WITH LIMITED CAPACITY (BULGARIAN).
SHAF 1978 -1 SHAFTEL, T. L.
COMPUTATIONAL EXPERIENCE ON AN ALGORITHM FOR THE TRANSPORTATION PROBLEM WITH NON-LINEAR OBJECTIVE FUNCTIONS.
SHAR 1978 -1 SHARMA, J. K.
EXTENSIONS AND SPECIAL CASES OF TRANSPORTATION PROBLEM: A SURVEY.
SHAR 1978 -2 SHARMA, J. K.
NOTE ON THE TIME MINIMIZING SOLID TRANSPORTATION PROBLEM, A.

SHARB 1977 -1 SHARMA, J. K.; SWARUP, K.
TIME MINIMIZING TRANSPORTATION PROBLEMS.
SHARC 1970 -1 SHARP, J. F.; SNYDER, J. C.; GREENE, J. H.
DECOMPOSITION ALGORITHM FOR SOLVING THE MULTIFACILITY PRODUCTION-TRANSPORTATION PROBLEM WITH NONLINEAR PRODUCTION COSTS, A.
SHIMA 1978 -1 SHIMSHAK, D. G.; KASLIK, J. A.; BARCLAY, T. D.
EFFECTIVE HEURISTIC FOR VOGELS'S APPROXIMATION METHOD.
SHVA 1978 -1 SHVARTIN, S. M.
STUDY OF STABILITY OF TRANSPORTATION PROBLEMS (RUSSIAN).
STANA 1978 -1 STANCU-MINASIAN, I. M.
ON THE TRANSPORTATION PROBLEM WITH MULTIPLE OBJECTIVE FUNCTIONS.
STEW 1979 -1 STEWART, T. J.; ITTMANN, H. W.
TWO-STAGE OPTIMIZATION IN A TRANSPORTATION PROBLEM.
SWAR 1966 -1 SWARUP, K.
TRANSPORTATION TECHNIQUE IN LINEAR FRACTIONAL FUNCTIONAL PROGRAMMING.
SZWAA 1979 -1 SZWARC, W.; POSNER, M. E.
TRIDIAGONAL TRANSPORTATION PROBLEM, THE.
TABA 1973 -1 TABAK, D.
APPLICATION OF MODERN CONTROL AND OPTIMIZATION TECHNIQUES TO TRANSPORTATION SYSTEMS.
TALA 1979 -1 TALANOV, V. A.; IL'ICEV, A. P.
THREE-INDEX TRANSPORTATION PROBLEMS AND COMPILING SCHOOL TIMETABLES (RUSSIAN).
TRUK 1979 -1 TRUKHANOVSKIJ, N. N.
CONDITIONS DE RESOLUBILITE D'UNE CLASSE DE PROBLEMES DE TRANSPORT PLANAIRES A PLUSIEURS INDICES (RUSSIAN).
VASIA 1979 -1 VASILEVA, E. M.; LEVIT, B. JU.; LIVSIC, V. N.
CHOICE OF OPTIMAL TRAJECTORY IN THE DEVELOPMENT OF A TURNPIKE TRANSPORTATION NETWORK (RUSSIAN), THE.
VLIE 1978 -1 VLIET, D. VAN
IMPROVED SHORTEST PATH ALGORITHMS FOR TRANSPORT NETWORKS.
VOLP 1978 -1 VOLPENTESTA, A.
ON THE INTEGER MULTICOMMODITY TRANSPORTATION PROBLEM. AN APPLICATION TO CREW SCHEDULING PROBLEMS.
WALK 1980 -1 WALK, M.
DUALITAET EINES VERALLGEMEINERTEN TRANSPORT- UND POTENTIALPROBLEMS.
WALT 1979 -1 WALTHER, H.
ANWENDUNGEN DER GRAPHENTHEORIE.
WOLT 1979 -1 WOLTERS, J. A. M.
MINIMISING THE NUMBER OF AIRCRAFT FOR A TRANSPORTATION NETWORK.
WUES 1978 -1 WUESTEFELD, A.
EINPARAMETRISCHE OPTIMIERUNG FUER DIE P-NORM ZIELFUNKTION BEIM TRANSPORTPROBLEM.
WUESA 1980 -1 WUESTEFELD, A.; ZIMMERMANN, U.
NONLINEAR ONE-PARAMETRIC LINEAR PROGRAMMING AND T-NORM TRANSPORTATION PROBLEMS.
YOUS 1978 -1 YOUSSEF, M. Y.
METHODES ET PROGRAMMES D'OPTIMISATION DANS LES PROBLEMES NON LINEAIRES DE FLOT ET DE TRANSPORT.
ZARY 1977 -1 ZARYAN, L. L.; LEBEDEV, S. S.; MESTETSKIJ, L. M.
SOLUTION OF INTEGER TRANSPORTATION PROBLEMS BY GENERALIZED LAGRANGE MULTIPLIERS (RUSSIAN).
ZIMM 1979 -1 ZIMMERMANN, U.
DUALITY PRINCIPLES AND THE ALGEBRAIC TRANSPORTATION PROBLEM.
ZIPK 1980 -2 ZIPKIN, P. H.
TRANSPORTATION PROBLEMS WITH AGGREGATED DESTINATIONS WHEN DEMANDS ARE UNCERTAIN.

ABDU 1980 -1 ABDUL-KADER, I.
CERTAINES PROPRIETES DES TOURNOIS AYANT UN CIRCUIT HAMILTONIEN UNIQUE.
AINO 1979 -1 AINOUCHE, A.; CHRISTOFIDES, N.
ON THE EXISTENCE OF HAMILTONIAN CIRCUITS IN UNDIRECTED GRAPHS.
AJZE 1978 -1 AJZENSHTAT, V. S.; MAXIMOVICH, E. P.
CERTAIN CLASS OF PROBLEMS OF A TRAVELLING SALESMAN (RUSSIAN).
AKL 1979 -1 AKL, S. G.
LOWER BOUND ON THE MAXIMUM NUMBER OF CROSSING-FREE HAMILTON CYCLES IN A RECTILINEAR DRAWING OF K(N), A.
ALI B 1980 -1 ALI, A. I.; KENNINGTON, J. L.
M-TRAVELLING SALEMEN PROBLEM, THE.
ALI B 1980 -2 ALI, A. I.; KENNINGTON, J. L.
M-TRAVELLING SALESMEN PROBLEM: A DUALITY BASED BRANCH-AND-BOUND ALGORITHM, THE.
ALIP 1978 -1 ALIPOV, N. V.; SHUMEJKO, N. A.
SUR UN ALGORITHME DE RESOLUTION DU PROBLEME DE CONNEXION DES FILS DE MONTAGE SOUS FORME DE CIRCUIT FERME (RUSSIAN).
ALSP 1979 -2 ALSPACH, B.
HAMILTONIAN CYCLES IN VERTEX-TRANSITIVE GRAPHS OF ORDER 2P.
ANGLA 1977 -1 ANGLUIN, D.; VALIANT, L. G.
FAST PROBABILISTIC ALGORITHMS FOR HAMILTONIAN CIRCUITS AND MATCHINGS.
ASAN 1981 -1 ASANO, T.; KIKUCHI, S.; SAITO, N.
EFFICIENT ALGORITHM TO FIND A HAMILTONIAN CIRCUIT IN A 4-CONNECTED MAXIMAL PLANAR GRAPH, AN.
ATRI 1978 -1 ATRI, G. D'
IMPROVED LOWER BOUNDS TO THE TRAVELLING SALESMAN PROBLEM.
ATRI 1980 -1 ATRI, G. D'
NOTE ON HEURISTICS FOR THE TRAVELING SALESMAN PROBLEM, A.
BALAC 1979 -1 BALAS, E.; CHRISTOFIDES, N.
RESTRICTED LAGRANGEAN APPROACH TO THE TRAVELING SALESMAN PROBLEM, A.
BARE 1980 -1 BAREFOOT, C. A.; ENTRINGER, R. C.
EXTREMAL MAXIMAL UNIQUELY HAMILTONIAN GRAPHS.
BARRC 1978 -1 BARRER, J. N.
CERTAIN PERMUTATION PROBLEMS AND THEIR RELATION TO THE ASSIGNMENT PROBLEM.
BERE 1979 -1 BERENGUER, X.
CHARACTERIZATION OF LINEAR ADMISSIBLE TRANSFORMATIONS FOR THE M-TRAVELLING SALESMAN PROBLEM, A.
BERMO 1978 -1 BERMOND, J. C.
HAMILTONIAN GRAPHS.
BIGAB 1979 -1 BIGALKE, A.; KOEHLER, N.
ANTIGERICHTETE HAMILTONLINIEN IN VOLLSTAENDIG GERICHTETEN GRAPHEN.
BIXBB 1978 -1 BIXBY, R. E.; WANG, D.-L.
ALGORITHM FOR FINDING HAMILTONIAN CIRCUITS IN CERTAIN GRAPHS, AN.
BOND 1972 -1 BONDY, J. A.
VARIATIONS ON THE HAMILTONIAN THEME.
BOND 1978 -1 BONDY, J. A.
HAMILTON CYCLES IN GRAPHS AND DIGRAPHS.
BURDB 1979 -1 BURDJUK, V. J.; DEINEKO, V. G.
SOLVABLE CASES OF THE TRAVELLING SALESMAN PROBLEM WITH SEVERAL SALESMEN (RUSSIAN).
BURK 1979 -3 BURKARD, R. E.
TRAVELLING SALESMAN AND ASSIGNMENT PROBLEMS: A SURVEY.
BURKF 1980 -1 BURKARD, R. E.; HAMMER, P. L.
NOTE ON HAMILTONIAN SPLIT GRAPHS, A.
CAMEA 1975 -1 CAMERINI, P. M.; FRATTA, L.; MAFFIOLI, F.
TRAVELLING SALESMAN PROBLEM: HEURISTICALLY GUIDED SEARCH AND MODIFIED GRADIENT TECHNIQUES.
CARP 1977 -1 CARPANETO, G.; TOTH, P.
NEW ALGORITHM FOR THE TRAVELLING SALESMAN PROBLEM WITH DUEDATES, A.
CASTB 1979 -1 CASTELLANI, G.; GIANNESSI, F.
DECOMPOSITION OF MATHEMATICAL PROGRAMS BY MEANS OF THEOREMS OF ALTERNATIVE FOR LINEAR AND NONLINEAR SYSTEMS.
CHAL 1977 -1 CHALKOV, V. D.
EFFECTIVE APPROXIMATE ALGORITHM FOR THE SOLUTION OF THE TRAVELLING SALESMAN PROBLEM (BULGARIAN), AN.
CHAL 1978 -1 CHALKOV, V. D.
APPROXIMATE ALGORITHM FOR SOLVING THE TRAVELLING SALESMAN PROBLEM WITH GROUPED POINTS (BULGARIAN).
CHRIB 1979 -1 CHRISTOFIDES, N.
TRAVELLING SALESMAN PROBLEM, THE.
CHRIH 1978 -2 CHRISTOFIDES, N.; WHITLOCK, C.
LP-BASED TSP ALGORITHM, AN.
CIOBA 1978 -1 CIOBOTARU, S.
ON THE ENUMERATION OF HAMILTONIAN ROADS AND CIRCUITS IN CERTAIN PARTIAL GRAPHS OF K(N).
CLAU 1978 -1 CLAUS, A.
SIMULTANEOUS ENUMERATION APPROACH TO THE TRAVELLING SALESMAN PROBLEM, A.
CORND 1981 -1 CORNUEJOLS, G.; PULLEYBLANK, W. R.
CRITICAL GRAPHS, MATCHINGS AND TOURS - A HIERARCHY OF RELAXATIONS FOR THE TRAVELLING SALESMAN PROBLEM.
CORND 1980 -3 CORNUEJOLS, G.; PULLEYBLANK, W. R.
TRAVELLING SALESMAN POLYTOPE AND (0,2)-MATCHINGS, THE.
CROWB 1979 -1 CROWDER, H. P.; PADBERG, M. W.
SOLVING LARGE-SCALE SYMMETRIC TRAVELLING SALESMAN PROBLEMS TO OPTIMALITY.
CRUY 1978 -1 CRUYSSEN, P. VAN DER; RIJCKAERT, M. J.
HEURISTIC FOR THE ASYMMETRIC TRAVELLING SALESMAN PROBLEM.
CUTL 1980 -1 CUTLER, M.
EFFICIENT SPECIAL CASE ALGORITHMS FOR THE N-LINE PLANAR TRAVELING SALESMAN PROBLEM.
DEMI 1978 -1 DEMIDENKO, V. M.
ON THE OPTIMIZATION OF THE VALUE V(A,T) ON THE SET OF CYCLES (RUSSIAN).
DEMI 1979 -1 DEMIDENKO, V. M.
TRAVELING SALESMAN PROBLEM WITH NON-SYMMETRIC MATRICES (RUSSIAN).
DEMI 1980 -1 DEMIDENKO, V. M.
SPECIAL CASES OF THE TRAVELLING SALESMAN PROBLEM WITH A SYMMETRIC MATRIX (RUSSIAN).
DERI 1981 -2 DERIGS, U.
ON SOME EXPERIMENTS WITH A COMPOSITE HEURISTIC FOR SOLVING TRAVELLING SALESMAN PROBLEMS.
DIRA 1973 -1 DIRAC, G. A.
NOTE ON HAMILTON CIRCUITS AND HAMILTON PATHS.
DREY 1977 -1 DREYFUS, S. E.; LAW, A. M.
ART AND THEORY OF DYNAMIC PROGRAMMING, THE.

DRIS 1979 -1 DRISCOLL, W. C.; EMMONS, H.
VEHICLE ROUTING FOR MINIMUM COST.
EA 1978 -1 EA, K.
EXTENSION DU PROBLEME DU VOYAGEUR DE COMMERCE: LE PROBLEME DU RAMASSAGE SCOLAIRE, UNE.
EREM 1978 -1 EREMENKO, I. V.; PHOVELISVILI, Z. I.
APPROXIMATE AND EXACT METHOD FOR SEARCHING THE HAMILTONIAN CYCLE OF MINIMAL LENGTH (RUSSIAN), AN.
FABI 1979 -2 FABIAN, C.
DUE-DATE RESTRICTIONS IN TRAVELLING SALESMAN PROBLEM.
FIAL 1978 -1 FIALA, F.
VEHICLE ROUTING PROBLEM.
FISHB 1978 -2 FISHER, M. L.; JAIKUMAR, R.
DECOMPOSITION ALGORITHM FOR LARGE-SCALE VEHICLE ROUTING, A.
FISHC 1979 -1 FISHER, M. L.; NEMHAUSER, G. L.; WOLSEY, L. A.
ANALYSIS OF APPROXIMATIONS FOR FINDING A MAXIMUM WEIGHT HAMILTONIAN CIRCUIT, AN.
FOUQ 1978 -1 FOUQUET, J.-L.
PROBLEMES HAMILTONIENS DANS LES PUISSANCES DE GRAPHES ORIENTES.
FOUQA 1978 -1 FOUQUET, J.-L.; JOLIVET, J.-L.
GRAPHES HYPOHAMILTONIENS ORIENTES.
FOX B 1980 -1 FOX, K. R.; GAVISH, B.; GRAVES, S. C.
N-CONSTRAINT FORMULATION OF THE (TIME-DEPENDENT) TRAVELING SALESMAN PROBLEM, AN.
FREDA 1976 -1 FREDERICKSON, G. N.; HECHT, M. S.; KIM, C. E.
APPROXIMATION ALGORITHMS FOR SOME ROUTING PROBLEMS.
FRIED 1979 -2 FRIEZE, A. M.
ON THE WORST-CASE PERFORMANCE OF SOME ALGORITHMS FOR THE ASYMMETRIC TRAVELLING SALESMAN PROBLEM.
FRIED 1979 -4 FRIEZE, A. M.
WORST-CASE ANALYSIS OF ALGORITHMS FOR TRAVELLING SALESMAN PROBLEMS.
GABO 1970 -1 GABOVICH, E. J.
TRAVELLING SALESMAN PROBLEM, THE.
GARFA 1978 -1 GARFINKEL, R. S.; GILBERT, K. C.
BOTTLENECK TRAVELING SALESMAN PROBLEM: ALGORITHMS AND PROBABILISTIC ANALYSIS, THE.
GAVIB 1979 -1 GAVISH, B.; SHLIFER, E.
APPROACH FOR SOLVING A CLASS OF TRANSPORTATION SCHEDULING PROBLEMS, AN.
GAVIC 1980 -1 GAVISH, B.; SRIKANTH, K.
OPTIMAL SOLUTION METHOD FOR THE MULTIPLE TRAVELLING SALESMAN PROBLEM, AN.
GENS 1979 -2 GENS, G. V.; LEVNER, E. V.
COMPUTATIONAL COMPLEXITY OF APPROXIMATION ALGORITHMS FOR COMBINATORIAL PROBLEMS.
GENSA 1978 -1 GENSCH, D. H.
INDUSTRIAL APPLICATION OF THE TRAVELING SALESMAN'S SUBTOUR PROBLEM, AN.
GIANC 1979 -1 GIANNESSI, F.; NICOLETTI, B.
CREW SCHEDULING PROBLEM: A TRAVELLING SALESMAN APPROACH, THE.
GOLDB 1978 -2 GOLDEN, B. L.
STATISTICAL ESTIMATION IN COMBINATORIAL DECISION PROBLEMS.
GOLDC 1978 -1 GOLDEN, B. L.; ALT, F. B.
INTERVAL ESTIMATION OF A GLOBAL OPTIMUM FOR LARGE COMBINATORIAL PROBLEMS.
GOLDE 1980 -1 GOLDEN, B. L.; BODIN, L. D.; DOYLE, T.; STEWART, W. R.
APPROXIMATE TRAVELING SALESMAN ALGORITHMS.
GOND 1978 -1 GONDRAN, M.
DEUX TRANSFORMATIONS IDEALES POUR REGULARISER LES PROBLEMES COMBINATOIRES.
GOUY 1978 -1 GOUYOU-BEAUCHAMPS, D.
ALGORITHME DE RECHERCHE DE CIRCUIT HAMILTONIEN DANS LES GRAPHES 4-CONNEXES PLANAIRES, UN.
GRAB 1978 -1 GRABOWSKI, J.
ALGORITHM FOR THE SOLUTION OF THE TRAVELING SALESMAN PROBLEM VIA DISJUNCTIVE GRAPHS (POLISH), AN.
GROEB 1978 -1 GROETSCHEL, M.
HYPO-HAMILTONIAN FACETS OF THE SYMMETRIC TRAVELLING SALESMAN POLYTOPE.
GROEB 1980 -1 GROETSCHEL, M.
ON THE MONOTONE SYMMETRIC TRAVELLING SALESMAN PROBLEM: HYPOHAMILTONIAN/ HYPOTRACEABLE GRAPHS AND FACETS.
GROEB 1980 -2 GROETSCHEL, M.
ON THE SYMMETRIC TRAVELLING SALESMAN PROBLEM: SOLUTION OF 120-CITY PROBLEM.
GROEE 1979 -1 GROETSCHEL, M.; PADBERG, M. W.
ON THE SYMMETRIC TRAVELLING SALESMAN PROBLEM I: INEQUALITIES.
GROEE 1979 -2 GROETSCHEL, M.; PADBERG, M. W.
ON THE SYMMETRIC TRAVELLING SALESMAN PROBLEM II: LIFTING THEOREMS AND FACETS.
GROEF 1981 -1 GROETSCHEL, M.; PULLEYBLANK, W. R.
CLIQUE TREES AND THE TRAVELLING SALESMAN PROBLEM.
GROEH 1978 -1 GROETSCHEL, M.; WAKABAYASHI, Y.
HYPOTRACEABLE DIGRAPHS.
GROEH 1980 -1 GROETSCHEL, M.; WAKABAYASHI, Y.
HYPOHAMILTONIAN DIGRAPHS.
GROEH 1981 -1 GROETSCHEL, M.; WAKABAYASHI, Y.
ON THE STRUCTURE OF THE MONOTONE ASYMMETRIC TRAVELLING SALESMAN POLYTOPE I: HYPOHAMILTONIAN FACETS.
GROEH 1981 -2 GROETSCHEL, M.; WAKABAYASHI, Y.
ON THE STRUCTURE OF THE MONOTONE ASYMMETRIC TRAVELLING SALESMAN POLYTOPE II: HYPOTRACEABLE FACETS.
GRUN 1978 -1 GRUNDMANN, W.; KRAUSE, H.
BEITRAG ZUR LOESUNG SPEZIELLER TOURENPROBLEME MIT SYMMETRISCHER ENTFERNUNGSMATRIX, EIN.
GUPT 1978 -1 GUPTA, J. N. D.
SEARCH ALGORITHM FOR THE TRAVELING SALESMAN PROBLEM, A.
HAEG 1979 -1 HAEGGKVIST, R.
ON F-HAMILTONIAN GRAPHS.
HAMI 1979 -1 HAMIDOUNE, Y. O.
SUR LES PARCOURS HAMILTONIENS DANS LES GRAPHES ORIENTES.
HARTF 1978 -1 HARTWIG, A.; TERNO, J.
TRANSFORMATION VON REIHENFOLGEPROBLEMEN AUF RUNDREISEPROBLEME.
HAUP 1980 -1 HAUPTMANN, H.
STATISTIC FOR JUDGING SOLUTIONS OF THE TRAVELLING SALESMAN PROBLEM, A.
HETY 1975 -1 HETYEI, G.
ON THE 1-FACTORS AND THE HAMILTONIAN CIRCUITS OF COMPLETE N-COLORABLE GRAPHS (HUNGARIAN).
HONGA 1977 -1 HONG, S.; PADBERG, M. W.
ON THE SOLUTION OF TRAVELLING SALESMAN PROBLEMS.
HORAA 1979 -1 HORAK, P.; TOVAREK, L.
ON HAMILTONIAN CYCLES OF COMPLETE N PARTITE GRAPHS.

HOUC 1977 -1 HOUCK, D. J.; PICARD, J.-C.; QUEYRANNE, M.; VEMUGANTI, R. R.
TRAVELLING SALESMAN PROBLEM AND SHORTEST N-PATHS, THE.
HOUC 1980 -1 HOUCK, D. J.; PICARD, J.-C.; QUEYRANNE, M.; VEMUGANTI, R. R.
TRAVELLING SALESMAN PROBLEM AS A CONSTRAINED SHORTEST PATH PROBLEM: THEORY AND COMPUTATIONAL EXPERIENCE, THE.
HURR 1980 -1 HURRION, R. D.
VISUAL INTERACTIVE (COMPUTER) SOLUTIONS FOR THE TRAVELLING SALESMAN PROBLEM.
IVAN 1981 -1 IVANEK, J.; MORAVEK, J.
HEURISTIC IMPROVEMENT OF THE DYNAMIC PROGRAMMING TREATMENT OF THE TRAVELLING SALESMAN PROBLEM.
JACK 1979 -1 JACKSON, B.
EDGE-DISJOINT HAMILTON CYCLES IN REGULAR GRAPHS OF LARGE DEGREE.
JACK 1980 -1 JACKSON, B.
HAMILTON CYCLES IN REGULAR 2-CONNECTED GRAPHS.
JACK 1979 -2 JACKSON, B.
HAMILTON CYCLES IN REGULAR TWO-CONNECTED GRAPHS.
JENKA 1979 -2 JENKYNS, T. A.
GREEDY TRAVELLING SALESMAN'S PROBLEM, THE.
JEROA 1980 -1 JEROMIN, B.; KOERNER, F.
UEBER DIE CHRISTOFIDES SCHRANKE FUER DAS TRAVELING SALESMAN PROBLEM.
JEROA 1980 -2 JEROMIN, B.; KOERNER, F.
VERSCHAERFUNG DER CHRISTOFIDES SCHRANKE FUER DAS TRAVELING SALESMAN PROBLEM, EINE.
JONK 1978 -1 JONKER, R.; DELEVE, G.; VANDERVELDE, J. A.; VOLGENANT, A.
SOLVING SYMMETRIC TRAVELING SALESMAN PROBLEMS ASYMMETRICALLY.
JONK 1980 -1 JONKER, R.; DELEVE, G.; VANDERVELDE, J. A.; VOLGENANT, A.
ROUNDING SYMMETRIC TRAVELING SALESMAN PROBLEMS WITH AN ASYMMETRIC ASSIGNMENT PROBLEM.
JONKA 1980 -1 JONKER, R.; KAAS, R.; VOLGENANT, T.
DATA-DEPENDENT BOUNDS FOR HEURISTICS TO FIND A MINIMUM WEIGHT HAMILTONIAN CIRCUIT.
KANE 1978 -1 KANELLAKIS, P. C.
ALGORITHMS FOR A SCHEDULING APPLICATION OF THE ASYMMETRIC TRAVELING SALESMAN PROBLEM.
KANEA 1980 -1 KANELLAKIS, P. C.; PAPADIMITRIOU, C. H.
LOCAL SEARCH FOR THE ASYMMETRIC TRAVELING SALESMAN PROBLEM.
KAO 1978 -1 KAO, E. P. C.
PREFERENCE ORDER DYNAMIC PROGRAM FOR A STOCHASTIC TRAVELING SALESMAN PROBLEM, A.
KARP 1979 -1 KARP, R. M.
PATCHING ALGORITHM FOR THE NONSYMMETRIC TRAVELING-SALESMAN PROBLEM, A.
KARP 1978 -2 KARP, R. M.
PROBABILISTIC ANALYSIS OF PARTITIONING ALGORITHMS FOR THE TRAVELING-SALESMAN PROBLEM IN THE PLANE.
KAZA 1974 -1 KAZAKOVA, M. F.
PROBLEM OF FINDING THE PARETO OPTIMA IN A POLYMATRIX TRAVELLING SALESMAN PROBLEM (RUSSIAN), THE.
KOER 1980 -3 KOERNER, F.
ZUR SUBTORELIMINATION BEIM TRAVELING SALESMAN PROBLEM.
KORO 1966 -1 KOROBKOV, V. K.; KRICHEVSKII, R. E.
ALGORITHMS FOR THE TRAVELING SALESMAN PROBLEM (RUSSIAN).
KORS 1977 -1 KORSHUNOV, A. D.
SOLUTION OF A PROBLEM OF P. ERDOES AND A. RENYI ON HAMILTONIAN CYCLES IN NON-ORIENTED GRAPHS (RUSSIAN).
KUBO 1975 -1 KUBO, H.; OKINO, N.
NEW SOLUTION OF THE SYMMETRIC TRAVELLING SALESMAN PROBLEM, A.
KUBO 1976 -1 KUBO, H.; OKINO, N.
NEW PRACTICAL SOLUTION FOR LARGE-SCALE TRAVELING SALESMAN PROBLEMS (JAPANESE), A.
KUBO 1975 -2 KUBO, H.; OKINO, N.
PRACTICAL APPROACHES TO THE TRAVELLING SALESMAN PROBLEM (JAPANESE).
LAHR 1979 -1 LAHRICHI, A.
COUTS MOYENS DE CIRCUITS HAMILTONIENS DE K(N).
LAND 1979 -1 LAND, A.
SOLUTION OF SOME 100-CITY TRAVELLING SALESMAN PROBLEMS, THE.
LAPO 1978 -1 LAPORTE, G.
SERIATION PROBLEM AND THE TRAVELLING SALESMAN PROBLEM, THE.
LAPOB 1980 -1 LAPORTE, G.; NOBERT, Y.
CUTTING PLANES ALGORITHM FOR THE M-SALESMEN PROBLEM, A.
LAPOD 1981 -1 LAPORTE, G.; NORBERT, Y.; MERCURE, H.
MULTI-DEPOT TRAVELLING SALESMAN PROGRAM, THE.
LEIP 1978 -1 LEIPAELAE, T.
ON THE SOLUTIONS OF STOCHASTIC TRAVELING SALESMAN PROBLEMS.
LENSA 1979 -1 LENSTRA, J. K.; RINNOOY KAN, A. H. G.
CHARACTERIZATION OF LINEAR ADMISSIBLE TRANSFORMATIONS FOR THE M-TRAVELLING SALESMAN PROBLEM: A RESULT OF BERENGUER, A.
LENSA 1978 -3 LENSTRA, J. K.; RINNOOY KAN, A. H. G.
ON THE EXPECTED PERFORMANCE OF BRANCH-AND-BOUND ALGORITHMS.
LEONA 1973 -1 LEONT'EV, V. K.
STUDY OF AN ALGORITHM FOR SOLVING TRAVELING SALESMAN PROBLEM (RUSSIAN).
LESN 1977 -1 LESNIAK-FOSTER, L. M.
ON CRITICALLY HAMILTONIAN GRAPHS.
LESN 1978 -1 LESNIAK-FOSTER, L. M.
ON N-DISTANT HAMILTONIAN LINE GRAPHS.
LEWIA 1978 -1 LEWIS, H. R.; CHRISTOS, H. P.
EFFICIENCY OF ALGORITHMS, THE.
LIES 1979 -1 LIESEGANG, D. G.
"TUBE-PASSING PROBLEM" AND THE TRAVELLING SALESMAN PROBLEM, THE.
LIOU 1978 -1 LIOUVILLE, B.
PROBLEME DU VOYAGEUR DE COMMERCE DANS UN PRODUIT CARTESIEN DE DEUX GRAPHES, LE.
LOKI 1979 -1 LOKIN, F. C. J.
PROCEDURES FOR TRAVELLING SALESMAN PROBLEMS WITH ADDITIONAL CONSTRAINTS.
LUGAA 1979 -1 LUGACHEV, M. I.; SHUBINA, L. Y.
OPERATIVE PLANNING PROBLEM FOR A DISCRETE PRODUCTION PROCESS WITH REGARD TO EQUIPMENT READJUSTMENT (RUSSIAN), AN.
MAKAA 1975 -1 MAKAROV, I. P.; YAVORSKII, V. V.
ONE GENERALIZATION OF THE TRAVELING SALESMAN PROBLEM.
MAND 1978 -1 MANDL, C. E.
ALGORITHMS AND COMPUTER PROGRAMS IN DETERMINISTIC NETWORK OPTIMIZATION APPLIED TO PUBLIC SYSTEMS.
MARTF 1979 -1 MARTINEC, I.
COMBINATORIAL ALGORITHM FOR M-TOUR TRAVELLING SALESMAN PROBLEMS (CZECHOSLOVAKIAN), A.

MATT 1978 -1 MATTHAEUS, F.
TOURENPLANUNG - VERFAHREN ZUR EINSATZDISPOSITION VON FUHRPARKS.
MILI 1976 -1 MILIOTIS, P.
ALL-INTEGER ARITHMETIC LP-CUTTING PLANES CODE APPLIED TO THE TRAVELLING SALESMAN PROBLEM, AN.
MILI 1978 -1 MILIOTIS, P.
USING CUTTING PLANES TO SOLVE THE SYMMETRIC TRAVELING SALESMAN PROBLEM.
MINI 1978 -1 MINIEKA, E.
OPTIMIZATION ALGORITHMS FOR NETWORKS AND GRAPHS.
MINIA 1975 -1 MININA, T. R.; PEREKREST, V. T.
CERTAIN WAY OF APPROXIMATING THE SOLUTIONS OF THE TRAVELING SALESMAN PROBLEM (RUSSIAN), A.
MOLL 1979 -1 MOLLUZZO, J. C.
SOME HAMILTONIAN COUNTEREXAMPLES.
MONI 1980 -1 MONIEN, B.; URMETZER, N.; VORNBERGER, O.
CONSIDERATION OF THE TRAVELLING SALESMAN PROBLEM USING THE ASSIGNMENT PROBLEM, A.
NEIT 1977 -1 NEITZEL, W.
TOURENPLANUNG. PROBLEMDARSTELLUNG UND LOESUNSVERFAHREN FUER EIN-DEPOT-PROBLEME.
NICU 1979 -3 NICULESCU, S.
ALGORITHM TO FIND HAMILTONIAN PATHS IN GRAPHS, AN.
NIKO 1976 -1 NIKOGOSJAN, Z. G.
THEOREMS ON HAMILTONIAN CYCLES AND SKELETONS (RUSSIAN).
NORB 1979 -1 NORBACK, J. P.; LOVE, R. F.
HEURISTIC FOR THE HAMILTONIAN PATH PROBLEM IN EUCLIDEAN TWO-SPACE.
OBER 1979 -1 OBERLY, D. J.; SUMNER, D. P.
EVERY CONNECTED, LOCALLY CONNECTED NONTRIVIAL GRAPH WITH NO INDUCED CLAW IS HAMILTONIAN.
PADBA 1980 -1 PADBERG, M. W.; HONG, S.
ON THE SYMMETRIC TRAVELLING SALESMAN PROBLEM: A COMPUTATIONAL STUDY.
PANN 1978 -1 PANNY, W.
VERFAHREN ZUR LOESUNG DES TRAVELLING-SALESMAN-PROBLEMS UNTER BESONDERER BERUECKSICHTIGUNG DER METHODE "BRANCH-AND-BOUND".
PAPA 1976 -1 PAPADIMITRIOU, C. H.
COMPLEXITY OF COMBINATORIAL OPTIMIZATION PROBLEMS, THE.
PAPA 1978 -1 PAPADIMITRIOU, C. H.
ADJACENCY RELATION ON THE TRAVELLING SALESMAN POLYTOPE IS NP-COMPLETE, THE.
PAPAB 1978 -1 PAPADIMITRIOU, C. H.; STEIGLITZ, K.
SOME EXAMPLES OF DIFFICULT TRAVELING SALESMAN PROBLEMS.
PAUN 1979 -1 PAUN, G.
ON SOME VARIANTS OF THE TRAVELLING SALESMAN PROBLEM. A MATHEMATICAL LINGUISTIC APPROACH (ROMANIAN).
PICA 1978 -1 PICARD, J.-C.; QUEYRANNE, M.
TIME-DEPENDENT TRAVELING SALESMAN PROBLEM AND ITS APPLICATION TO THE TARDINESS PROBLEM IN ONE-MACHINE SCHEDULING, THE.
PIOT 1976 -1 PIOTROVSKI, M.
CLASS OF HAMILTONIAN GRAPHS (RUSSIAN), A.
PIOT 1976 -2 PIOTROVSKI, M.
SOME PROPERTIES OF HAMILTONIAN GRAPHS (RUSSIAN).
PITA 1978 -1 PITACCO, E.
ON A GENERALIZATION OF THE TRAVELING SALESMAN PROBLEM (ITALIAN).
PLES 1979 -1 PLESNIK, J.
NP-COMPLETENESS OF THE HAMILTONIAN CYCLE PROBLEM IN PLANAR DIGRAPHS WITH DEGREE BOUND TWO, THE.
POLJA 1972 -1 POLJANSKII, S. V.
TRAVELING SALESMAN PROBLEM AND PBIB(2)-DESIGNS (RUSSIAN), THE.
PRIC 1978 -1 PRICE, W. L.
ALGORITHM WHICH GENERATES THE HAMILTONIAN CIRCUITS OF A CUBIC PLANAR MAP, AN.
PULL 1979 -3 PULLEYBLANK, W. R.
POLYHEDRAL OPTIMIZATION AND THE TRAVELLING SALESMAN PROBLEM.
QUEY 1977 -1 QUEYRANNE, M.
PROBLEME DU VOYAGEUR DE COMMERCE A COUTS VARIABLES ET QUELQUES APPLICATIONS, LE.
RAO A 1980 -1 RAO, M. R.
NOTE ON THE MULTIPLE TRAVELING SALESMEN PROBLEM, A.
RYANA 1979 -1 RYANG, S. Y.; RYU, H. D.
NEW METHOD OF DECIDING HAMILTONIAN CIRCLES AND SPANNING PARTIAL GRAPHS, (KOREAN), A.
SAHNB 1975 -1 SAHNI, S.; GONZALEZ, T.
P-COMPLETE APPROXIMATION PROBLEMS.
SAHNC 1978 -1 SAHNI, S.; HOROWITZ, E.
COMBINATORIAL PROBLEMS: REDUCIBILITY AND APPROXIMATION.
SCHEA 1979 -1 SCHEITHAUER, G.; TERNO, J.
NEW EXTENSION PRINCIPLE ALGORITHM FOR THE TRAVELING SALESMAN PROBLEM, A.
SCHEA 1979 -2 SCHEITHAUER, G.; TERNO, J.
TSPE - AN ALGOL PROCEDURE FOR SOLVING THE TRAVELING SALESMAN PROBLEM.
SCHIA 1979 -1 SCHIEBEL, W.; TERNO, J.; UNGER, G.
BEITRAG ZUR KLASSIFIZIERUNG VON RUNDREISEPROBLEMEN, EIN.
SCHIB 1975 -1 SCHIEBEL, W.; UNGER, G.
DUALE ENTARTUNG IN DER LINEAREN OPTIMIERUNG, TRANSPORTPROBLEM MIT ZUSAETZLICHEN NEBENBEDINGUNGEN UND RUNDREISEPROBLEM.
SCHME 1978 -1 SCHMITZ, P.; SCHOENLEIN, A.
LINEARE UND LINEARISIERBARE OPTIMIERUNGSMODELLE SOWIE IHRE ADV-GESTUETZTE LOESUNG.
SERD 1978 -2 SERDYUKOV, A. I.
TRAVELING SALESMAN PROBLEM IN THE PRESENCE OF EXCLUSIONS (RUSSIAN), THE.
SHOC 1979 -1 SHOCK, R. C.
EXACT ALGORITHM FOR THE SMALL SCALE TRAVELLING SALESMAN PROBLEM, AN.
SIMM 1979 -1 SIMMONS, G. J.; SLATER, P. J.
GENERALIZED PETERSEN GRAPHS G(N,4) ARE HAMILTONIAN FOR ALL N NOT = 8, THE.
SKUP 1974 -1 SKUPIEN, Z.
HAMILTONIAN CIRCUITS AND PATH COVERINGS OF VERTICES IN GRAPHS.
SKUP 1977 -1 SKUPIEN, Z.
ON EXTENDING PATH SYSTEMS AND (Q, R)-EDGE HAMILTONIAN GRAPHS.
SKUPA 1974 -1 SKUPIEN, Z.; WOJDA, A. P.
ON HIGHLY HAMILTONIAN GRAPHS.
SMITH 1980 -1 SMITH, T. H. C.
LIFO IMPLICIT ENUMERATION ALGORITHM FOR THE ASYMMETRIC TRAVELLING SALESMAN PROBLEM USING A ONE-ARBORESCENCE RELAXATION, A.
SMITI 1975 -1 SMITH, T. H. C.; THOMPSON, G. L.
COMPARISON OF TWO DIFFERENT LAGRANGEAN RELAXATIONS OF THE TSP, A.

SNIE 1979 -2 SNIEDOVICH, M.
PREFERENCE ORDER STOCHASTIC TRAVELING SALESPERSON PROBLEMS: A COUNTER EXAMPLE.
STEI 1978 -1 STEIN, D. M.
ASYMPTOTIC, PROBABILISTIC ANALYSIS OF A ROUTING PROBLEM, AN.
STINA 1977 -1 STINSON, J. P.
HEURISTIC ALGORITHM FOR OBTAINING AN INITIAL SOLUTION FOR THE TRAVELING SALESMAN PROBLEM, A.
SVES 1978 -1 SVESTKA, J. A.
CONTINUOUS VARIABLE REPRESENTATION OF THE TRAVELING SALESMAN PROBLEM, A.
SYSL 1977 -1 SYSLO, M. M.
BISECTION METHOD FOR THE TRAVELING SALESMAN PROBLEM, A.
SYSL 1980 -1 SYSLO, M. M.
GENERALIZATIONS OF THE STANDARD TRAVELLING SALESMAN PROBLEM.
SYSLB 1977 -1 SYSLO, M. M.; SKUPIEN, Z.
APPLIED GRAPH THEORY. III. EULER AND HAMILTONIAN GRAPHS. THE TRAVELING SALESMAN PROBLEM (POLISH).
TELE 1978 -1 TELEMTAEV, M. M.
OPTIMALITY CONDITION FOR A HAMILTONIAN CYCLE (RUSSIAN).
THOMC 1979 -1 THOMASSEN, C.
LONG CYCLES IN DIGRAPHS WITH CONSTRAINTS ON THE DEGREES.
TIMO 1976 -1 TIMOFEEV, E. A.
LOWER BOUND FOR THE TRAVELING SALESMAN PROBLEM (RUSSIAN), A.
TIMO 1979 -1 TIMOFEEV, E. A.
MINMAX DOUBLY CONNECTED SUBGRAPHS AND THE TRAVELLING SALESMAN PROBLEM FOR "WEAK POINTS" (RUSSIAN).
VAND 1976 -1 VANDENMEERENDONK, H. W.
SINGLE MACHINE MULTI-PRODUCT PLANNING PROBLEMS.
VANDB 1979 -1 VANDERVELDE, J. A.; JONKER, R.; DELEVE, G.; VOLGENANT, A.
LOWER BOUNDS FOR TRAVELING SALESMAN PROBLEMS WITH KNOWN RELATIVE ORDER FOR A PART OF THE CITIES.
VOLG 1978 -1 VOLGENANT, A.; JONKER, R.; DELEVE, G.
NON-OPTIMAL TRAVELING SALESMAN TRAJECTORIES 1: THE SYMMETRIC CASE (IN DUTCH).
WALS 1976 -1 WALSH, A. M.
POLYNOMIAL ALGORITHMS FOR CERTAIN GRAPH-THEORETIC PROBLEMS.
WALT 1979 -1 WALTHER, H.
ANWENDUNGEN DER GRAPHENTHEORIE.
WEST 1978 -1 WEST, D. B.
PAIRS OF ADJACENT HAMILTONIAN CIRCUITS WITH SMALL INTERSECTION.
WHITB 1980 -1 WHITE, G. P.; SWEENEY, D. J.
USING MULTIDIMENSIONAL SCALING TO SOLVE TRAVELING SALESMAN AND MACHINE SCHEDULING PROBLEMS.
WHITC 1977 -1 WHITE, G. P.; WILLIAMS, T. A.
HEURISTIC SOLUTION TECHNIQUES FOR MULTIPLE TRIP TIME-CONSTRAINED TRAVELING SALESMAN PROBLEMS.
YAMA 1978 -1 YAMAMOTO, Y.
HELD-KARP ALGORITHM AND DEGREE-CONSTRAINED MINIMUM 1-TREES, THE.
ZARE 1979 -1 ZARETZKY, L. S.
TRAVELLING SALESMAN AND DELIVERY PROBLEMS SOLVING BY METHOD OF STATE FUNCTIONS CORRECTION (RUSSIAN).
ZEPS 1980 -1 ZEPS, D. A.
EXHAUSTIVE SEARCH ALGORITHM FOR FINDING HAMILTONIAN CYCLES (RUSSIAN), AN.

ANAS 1977 -1 ANASTASJAN, J. G.
CERTAIN PROPERTIES OF BIPARTITE HYPERGRAPHS (RUSSIAN).
BERG 1973 -1 BERGE, C.
INTRODUCTION A LA THEORIE DES HYPERGRAPHES.
BERG 1978 -1 BERGE, C.
MULTICOLORING OF A GRAPH.
BERG 1980 -1 BERGE, C.
BALANCED MATRICES AND PROPERTY (G).
BLANA 1979 -1 BLAND, R. G.; HUANG, H.-C.; TROTTER, L. E. JR.
GRAPHICAL PROPERTIES RELATED TO MINIMAL IMPERFECTION.
BRUY 1979 -1 BRUYNEEL, G.
SOME APPLICATIONS OF MINIMAL BALANCED SETS IN GRAPH THEORY.
BUCK 1980 -1 BUCKINGHAM, M. A.
CIRCLE GRAPHS.
BURL 1980 -1 BURLET, M.; UHRY, J.-P.
PARITY GRAPHS.
CHERC 1974 -1 CHERNYSHEV, JU. O.
REDUCTION OF THE BIVALENT PROGRAMMING PROBLEM TO THE TRANSPORT PROBLEM (RUSSIAN), THE.
CUNN 1981 -3 CUNNINGHAM, W. H.
POLYHEDRA FOR COMPOSED INDEPENDENCE SYSTEMS.
GOLU 1980 -1 GOLUMBIC, M. C.
ALGORITHMIC GRAPH THEORY AND PERFECT GRAPHS.
GRAV 1977 -1 GRAVER, J. E.; WATKINS, M. E.
COMBINATORICS WITH EMPHASIS ON THE THEORY OF GRAPHS.
GROED 1981 -1 GROETSCHEL, M.; LOVASZ, L.; SCHRIJVER, A.
ELLIPSOID METHOD AND ITS CONSEQUENCES IN COMBINATORIAL OPTIMIZATION, THE.
GROED 1981 -2 GROETSCHEL, M.; LOVASZ, L.; SCHRIJVER, A.
POLYNOMIAL ALGORITHMS FOR PERFECT GRAPHS.
GRUE 1978 -1 GRUENBAUM, B.; SHEPHARD, G. C.
PERFECT COLORINGS OF TRANSITIVE TILINGS AND PATTERNS IN THE PLANE.
HOFF 1979 -1 HOFFMAN, A. J.
ROLE OF UNIMODULARITY IN APPLYING LINEAR INEQUALITIES TO COMBINATORIAL THEOREMS, THE.
HSU A 1979 -1 HSU, W.-L.
HOW TO COLOR CLAW-FREE PERFECT GRAPHS.
HSU B 1979 -1 HSU, W.-L.; NEMHAUSER, G. L.
ALGORITHMS FOR MINIMUM COVERINGS BY CLIQUES AND MAXIMUM CLIQUES IN CLAW-FREE PERFECT GRAPHS.
JOLI 1975 -1 JOLIVET, J.-L.
GRAPHES PARFAITS POUR UNE PROPRIETE P.
KARA 1976 -1 KARAPETJAN, I.A.
CRITICAL AND ESSENTIAL EDGES IN PERFECT GRAPHS (RUSSIAN).
KRES 1980 -1 KRESS, M.; TAMIR, A.
USE OF JACOBI'S LEMMA IN UNIMODULARITY THEORY, THE.
MAURC 1978 -1 MAURRAS, J. F.
GOOD ALGORITHMS, OLD IDEAS.
MONMC 1979 -1 MONMA, C. L.; TROTTER, L. E. JR.
ON PERFECT GRAPHS AND POLYHEDRA WITH (0,1)-VALUED EXTREME POINTS.
PELE 1978 -1 PELED, U. N.
MATROIDAL GRAPHS.
RAO D 1977 -1 RAO, S. B.; RAVINDRA, G.
CHARACTERIZATION OF PERFECT TOTAL GRAPHS, A.
RAVI 1975 -1 RAVINDRA, G.
ON BERGE'S CONJECTURE CONCERNING PERFECT GRAPHS.
SCHRD 1979 -1 SCHRIJVER, A.
FRACTIONAL PACKING AND COVERING.
TRUE 1978 -1 TRUEMPER, K.
ALGEBRAIC CHARACTERIZATIONS OF UNIMODULAR MATRICES.
TUCK 1979 -1 TUCKER, A. C.
BERGE'S STRONG PERFECT GRAPH CONJECTURE.
WERR 1981 -1 WERRA, D. DE
ON SOME CHARACTERIZATIONS OF TOTALLY UNIMODULAR MATRICES.
WESS 1977 -1 WESSEL, W.
SOME COLOR-CRITICAL EQUIVALENTS OF THE STRONG PERFECT GRAPH CONJECTURE.
WOODA 1978 -1 WOODALL, D. R.
MINIMAX THEOREMS IN GRAPH THEORY.

ARTEA 1980 -1 ARTEMENKO, V. I.; SERGIENKO, I. V.
METHOD FOR SOLVING LINEAR PROGRAMMING PROBLEMS WITH BOOLEAN VARIABLES (RUSSIAN), A.

ATRI 1978 -2 ATRI, G. D'
IMPROVED LOWER BOUNDS TO 0/1 PROBLEMS VIA LAGRANGEAN RELAXATION.

BABAD 1979 -1 BABAEV, DZ. A.; VELIEV, G. P.; MAMEDOV, K. S.
A PRIORI DETERMINATION OF OPTIMAL VARIABLE VALUES IN DISCRETE PROGRAMMING PROBLEMS, THE.

BALAF 1980 -1 BALAS, E.; MARTIN, C. H.
PIVOT AND COMPLEMENT - A HEURISTIC FOR 0-1 PROGRAMMING.

BALAG 1980 -1 BALAS, E.; MAZZOLA, J. B.
LINEARIZING NONLINEAR 0-1 PROGRAMS.

BALAG 1980 -2 BALAS, E.; MAZZOLA, J. B.
VALID INEQUALITIES FOR 0-1 PROGRAMMING POLYTOPES.

BEAL 1980 -1 BEALE, E. M. L.
FRACTIONAL PROGRAMMING WITH ZERO-ONE VARIABLES.

BENZ 1980 -2 BENZAKEN, C.; HAMMER, P. L.; SIMEONE, B.
SOME REMARKS ON CONFLICT GRAPHS OF QUADRATIC PSEUDO-BOOLEAN FUNCTIONS.

BITR 1979 -1 BITRAN, G. R.
THEORY AND ALGORITHMS FOR LINEAR MULTIPLE OBJECTIVE PROGRAMS WITH ZERO-ONE VARIABLES.

BLAI 1975 -2 BLAIR, C. E.
TOPICS IN INTEGER PROGRAMMING.

BORT 1977 -1 BORTOT, P.
SOME PROPERTIES OF A SET OF NON LINEAR BOOLEAN INEQUATIONS.

BUZY 1978 -1 BUZYCKII, P. L.; VOTJAKOV, A. A.
ALGORITHMIC CRITERION OF OPTIMALITY IN INTEGER PROGRAMMING, AN.

CARLB 1979 -1 CARLSON, R. C.; SHUKLA, P. R.
ROBUSTNESS OF THE INTERACTIVE ALGORITHM FOR MULTICRITERION ZERO-ONE VARIABLE PROBLEMS UNDER PROBABILISTIC TRADEOFFS.

CARLC 1979 -1 CARLSON, R. C.; SHUKLA, P. R.; BAUM, S.
INTERACTIVE SOLUTION OF DISCRETE MULTICRITERION PROBLEMS: AN ALGORITHM AND COMPUTATIONAL RESULTS FOR THE BINARY VARIABLE CASE.

CART 1980 -1 CARTER, M. W.
INDEFINITE ZERO-ONE QUADRATIC PROBLEM, THE.

CHERC 1974 -1 CHERNYSHEV, JU. O.
REDUCTION OF THE BIVALENT PROGRAMMING PROBLEM TO THE TRANSPORT PROBLEM (RUSSIAN), THE.

DESP 1974 -1 DESPONTIN, M.; OUDHEUSDEN, D. VAN; HANSEN, P.
CHOIX DE MEDIAS PAR PROGRAMMATION QUADRATIQUE EN VARIABLES 0-1.

FERL 1979 -1 FERLAND, J. A.; FLORIAN, M.
SUB-OPTIMAL ALGORITHM TO SOLVE A LARGE SCALE 0-1 PROGRAMMING PROBLEM, A.

GIOR 1975 -1 GIORDANO, F. R.
HEURISTIC FOR THE CONSTRUCTION OF SURROGATE CONSTRAINTS FOR THE SOLUTION OF THE LINEAR ZERO-ONE INTEGER PROBLEM, A.

GLOVC 1977 -1 GLOVER, F.; KARNEY, D.; KLINGMAN, D.
STUDY OF ALTERNATIVE RELAXATION APPROACHES FOR A MANPOWER PLANNING PROBLEM, A.

GLOVH 1980 -1 GLOVER, F.; MULVEY, J. M.
EQUIVALENCE OF THE 0-1 INTEGER PROGRAMMING PROBLEM TO DISCRETE GENERALIZED AND PURE NETWORKS.

GRANA 1980 -2 GRANOT, D.; GRANOT, F.
MINIMAL COVERS, EXTENSIONS OF MINIMAL COVERS AND FACETS OF A POSYNOMIAL INEQUALITY IN 0-1 VARIABLES.

GRANB 1979 -1 GRANOT, D.; GRANOT, F.; KALLBERG, J.
COVERING RELAXATION FOR POSITIVE 0-1 POLYNOMIAL PROGRAMS.

GRANC 1980 -1 GRANOT, D.; GRANOT, F.; VAESSEN, W.
ACCELERATED COVERING RELAXATION ALGORITHM FOR SOLVING 0-1 POSITIVE POLYNOMIAL PROGRAMS, AN.

GRAND 1978 -1 GRANOT, F.
EFFICIENT HEURISTIC ALGORITHMS FOR POSITIVE 0-1 POLYNOMIAL PROGRAMMING PROBLEMS.

GRAVC 1980 -1 GRAVES, S. C.; LAMAR, B. W.
INTEGER PROGRAMMING PROCEDURE FOR ASSEMBLY SYSTEM DESIGN PROBLEMS, AN.

GROP 1978 -1 GROPPEN, V. O.
ENHANCEMENT OF OPERATING SPEED OF RANDOMIZED ALGORITHMS FOR COMBINATORIAL PROBLEMS WITH BOOLEAN VARIABLES.

GROP 1978 -2 GROPPEN, V. O.
IMPROVING BRANCH-AND-BOUND METHODS FOR DISCRETE PROBLEMS WITH BOOLEAN VARIABLES.

GUIGA 1981 -1 GUIGNARD, M.; SPIELBERG, K.
LOGICAL REDUCTION METHODS IN ZERO-ONE PROGRAMMING (MINIMAL PREFERRED VARIABLES).

HANNA 1979 -1 HANNAN, E. L.; MAC KEOWN, P. G.
MATCHING SWIMMERS TO EVENTS IN A CHAMPIONSHIP SWIMMING MEET.

HANSB 1974 -1 HANSEN, P.
PROGRAMMES MATHEMATIQUES EN VARIABLES 0-1.

HANSB 1979 -1 HANSEN, P.
METHODS OF NONLINEAR 0-1 PROGRAMMING.

HAUSC 1978 -1 HAUSMANN, D.; KORTE, B.
COLOURING CRITERIA FOR ADJACENCY ON 0-1-POLYHEDRA.

HENR 1979 -1 HENRY-LABORDERE, A.
RESOLUTION D'UN PROGRAMME QUADRATIQUE EN VARIANTES BIVALENTES PAR DECOMPOSITION. APPLICATION AU PLACEMENT DE COMMUTATEURS DANS UN RESEAU.

HOAN 1978 -1 HOANG HAI HOC
SOLVING AN INTEGER PROGRAMMING PROBLEM.

JACQ 1980 -1 JACQMIN, N. E.
BINARY INTEGER LINEAR PROGRAMMING: A HYBRID IMPLICIT ENUMERATION APPROACH.

JAMB 1978 -1 JAMBEKAR, A. B.; STEINBERG, D. I.
COMPUTATIONAL EXPERIENCE WITH AN ALGORITHM FOR 0-1 INTEGER PROGRAMMING.

JOHNE 1980 -1 JOHNSON, E. L.; PADBERG, M. W.
DEGREE-TWO INEQUALITIES, CLIQUE FACETS, AND BIPEFECT GRAPHS.

JOHNG 1980 -1 JOHNSON, E. L.; SUHL, U.
EXPERIMENTS IN INTEGER PROGRAMMING.

KAREA 1979 -1 KARELIN, V. P.; KALASHNIKOV, V. A.
UTILISATION DE LA METHODE DE LA PROGRAMMATION BIVALENTE POUR RESOUDRE QUELQUES PROBLEMES DE PROJET TECHNIQUE (RUSSIAN).

KEOW 1978 -1 KEOWN, A. J.; MARTIN, J. D.
CAPITAL BUDGETING IN THE PUBLIC SECTOR: A ZERO-ONE GOAL PROGRAMMING APPROACH.

KLEIA 1980 -1 KLEIN, D.; HANNAN, E. L.
BRANCH AND BOUND ALGORITHM FOR THE MULTIPLE OBJECTIVE ZERO-ONE LINEAR PROGRAMMING PROBLEM, A.

KOSTB 1980 -1 KOSTREVA, M. M.
ADAPTIVE ESTIMATES IMPROVE BINARY PROGRAMMING.

KRAR 1981 -1 KRARUP, J.; PRUZAN, P. M.
REDUCIBILITY OF MINIMAX TO MINISUM 0-1 PROGRAMMING PROBLEMS.
KRARA 1981 -1 KRARUP, J.; PRUZAN, P. M.; BURKARD, R. E.
EFFICIENCY AND OPTIMALITY IN MINISUM, MINIMAX 0-1 PROGRAMMING PROBLEMS.
LEVID 1979 -1 LEVIN, V. I.
BLOCK LOGICAL CONSTRUCTIONS IN SOME PROBLEMS OF DISCRETE OPTIMIZATION.
LIEB 1980 -1 LIEBERHERR, K.
P-OPTIMAL HEURISTICS.
LIU B 1978 -1 LIU, Y. P.
MODULO-2 PROGRAMMING AND PLANAR EMBEDDINGS (CHINESE).
LYSK 1980 -1 LYSKA, W.; MUELLER, H.
ALGORITHMUS ZUR LOESUNG EINER KLASSE LINEARER 0-1 OPTIMIERUNGSAUFGABEN MIT SPEZIELLER STRUKTUR, EIN.
MAZZ 1980 -1 MAZZOLA, J. B.
PROCEDURE FOR GENERATING THE CONVEX HULL OF A 0-1 PROGRAMMING POLYTOPE WITH POSITIVE COEFFICIENTS, A.
PADB 1979 -2 PADBERG, M. W.
NULL-EINS-ENTSCHEIDUNGSPROBLEME.
PATTA 1976 -1 PATTERSON, J. M.
ZERO-ONE INTEGER PROGRAMMING: A STUDY IN COMPUTATIONAL EFFICIENCY AND A STATE-OF-THE-ART SURVEY.
PIRY 1979 -1 PIRYANOVICH, V. A.
COMPUTER EXPERIMENTS ON SOLVING INTEGER LINEAR PROGRAMMING PROBLEMS BY LOCALLY STOCHASTIC ALGORITHMS.
SALC 1973 -1 SALCEDO, E.
METHODS OF PARTIAL ENUMERATION FOR THE SOLUTION OF DISCRETE OPTIMIZATION PROBLEMS (SPANISH), THE.
SCHOA 1978 -1 SCHOCH, M.; LYSKA, W.
KOMBINATORISCHE ALGORITHMEN ZUR LOESUNG SPEZIELLER NICHTLINEARER 0-1 OPTIMIERUNGSAUFGABEN.
SCHOA 1978 -2 SCHOCH, M.; LYSKA, W.
WEITERER KOMBINATORISCHER ALGORITHMUS FUER 0-1-OPTIMIERUNGSAUFGABEN, EIN.
SERGA 1980 -1 SERGIENKO, I. V.; LEBEDEVA, T. T.; ROSHCHIN, V. A.
APPROXIMATE METHODS FOR THE SOLUTION OF DISCRETE OPTIMIZATION PROBLEMS (RUSSIAN).
SHCH 1976 -1 SHCHERBINA, O. A.
OPTIMAL PARTITIONING INTO BLOCKS OF A QUASIBLOCK PROBLEM OF BOOLEAN PROGRAMMING (RUSSIAN).
SHCH 1980 -1 SHCHERBINA, O. A.
SUR UN ALGORITHME LOCAL POUR LES PROBLEMES D'OPTIMISATION A VALEURS ENTIERES (RUSSIAN).
SIME 1979 -2 SIMEONE, B.
QUADRATIC 0-1 PROGRAMMING, BOOLEAN FUNCTIONS AND GRAPHS.
SOYS 1978 -1 SOYSTER, A. L.; LEV, B.; SLIVKA, W.
ZERO-ONE PROGRAMMING WITH MANY VARIABLES AND FEW CONSTRAINTS.
SPIEA 1980 -1 SPIELBERG, K.; SUHL, U.
EXPERIMENTAL SOFTWARE SYSTEM FOR LARGE SCALE 0-1 PROBLEMS WITH EFFICIENT DATA STRUCTURES AND ACCESS TO MPSX/370, AN.
TAHA 1971 -1 TAHA, H.
HYPERBOLIC PROGRAMMING WITH BIVALENT VARIABLES.
TCHE 1980 -1 TCHERBINA, O. A.
ON LOCAL ALGORITHM OF INTEGRAL OPTIMIZATION (RUSSIAN).
TINH 1980 -1 TINHOFER, G.
GRAPHSACK PROBLEM, THE.
TRUBA 1981 -1 TRUBIN, V. A.; VOITISHIN, YU. V.
ALGORITHM FOR SOLVING A SET-DIVISION PROBLEM (RUSSIAN), AN.
TRYP 1979 -1 TRYPIA, M. N.
BINARY TREE SEARCH METHOD FOR THE 0-1 LINEAR PROGRAMMING PROBLEM, A.
TSAR 1977 -1 TSAROUCHIS, N.
SIMPLEX-TYPE ALGORITHM FOR A HYBRID ZERO-ONE PROGRAMMING PROBLEM, A.
ULA 1979 -1 ULA, N.
ANALOGUE COMPUTER SOLUTION OF CERTAIN ZERO-ONE INTEGER PROGRAMMING PROBLEMS.
VIZV 1978 -1 VIZVARI, B.
LAGRANGE MULTIPLIERS IN INTEGER PROGRAMMING.
WILS 1977 -1 WILSON, J. M.
METHOD FOR REDUCING COEFFICIENTS IN ZERO-ONE LINEAR INEQUALITIES, A.
WOLS 1977 -1 WOLSEY, L. A.
VALID INEQUALITIES AND SUPERADDITIVITY OF 0-1 INTEGER PROGRAMS.
YUKH 1979 -1 YUKHIMENKO, B. I.
ON CERTAIN SOLUTION ALGORITHMS FOR PROBLEMS OF LINEAR PROGRAMMING WITH BOOLEAN VARIABLES (RUSSIAN).
ZAK 1977 -1 ZAK, JU. A.
ON A CLASS OF INTEGER LINEAR PROGRAMMING PROBLEMS WITH BOOLEAN VARIABLES (RUSSIAN).
ZEME 1978 -1 ZEMEL, E.
FUNCTIONS FOR MEASURING THE QUALITY OF PROXIMATE SOLUTIONS TO ZERO-ONE PROGRAMMING PROBLEMS.
ZEME 1978 -2 ZEMEL, E.
LIFTING THE FACETS OF ZERO-ONE POLYTOPES.
ZERN 1976 -1 ZERNAK, A. N.
METHOD OF SOLVING QUASILINEAR INTEGER PROGRAMMING PROBLEMS (RUSSIAN), A.
ZORY 1977 -1 ZORYCHTA, K.
ON CONVERTING THE 0-1 LINEAR PROGRAMMING PROBLEM TO A SET-COVERING PROBLEM.
ZUFR 1979 -1 ZUFRYDEN, F. S.
ZIPMAP - A ZERO-ONE INTEGER PROGRAMMING MODEL FOR MARKET SEGMENTATION AND PRODUCT POSITIONING.

PART 3

LIST OF AUTHORS

BURR, S. A.
BURR 1976 -1
BURSCHEID, H. J.
BURS 1979 -1
BURSHTEJN, M. I.
BURSA 1976 -1; BURSA 1979 -1; BURSA 1979 -2
BUSHELL, G.
FLORA 1976 -1
BUSOLINI, D. T.
BUSO 1978 -1; BUSO 1978 -2
BUTAN, E. I.
BUTA 1975 -1
BUTZ, L.
BUTZ 1980 -1; BUTZ 1981 -1; BUTZ 1982 -1
BUZYCKII, P. L.
BUZY 1978 -1
CABOT, A. V.
CABO 1977 -1
CAHIT, I.
CAHI 1978 -1
CAHIT, R.
CAHI 1978 -1
CAI, M. C.
CHU 1974 -1; LIU C 1980 -1; MA 1980 -1
CAIE, J.
CAIE 1978 -1; CAIE 1980 -1; CAIEA 1979 -1
CALAMAI, P.
CALA 1980 -1
CALVILLO, G.
CALV 1980 -1
CAMERINI, P. M.
CAME 1978 -1; CAMEA 1975 -1; CAMEA 1979 -1
CAMEA 1980 -1; CAMEA 1980 -2; CAMEB 1980 -1
CAMEC 1978 -1; CAMEC 1978 -2; CAMEC 1979 -1
CAMEC 1980 -1; CAMEC 1980 -2
CAMERON, K.
CAMED 1979 -1
CAMERON, P. J.
CAMEE 1975 -1
CAMION, P.
CAMI 1975 -1
CANI, P. DE
CANI 1978 -1; SMIT 1980 -1
CAREY, M.
BRES 1980 -1
CARLITZ, L.
CARL 1976 -1
CARLSON, R. C.
CARLA 1979 -1; CARLB 1979 -1; CARLC 1979 -1
SHUK 1979 -1
CARNEIRO RIBEIRO, C. DA C.
CARN 1978 -1
CARPANETO, G.
CARP 1977 -1
CARRE, B.
CARR 1979 -1
CARSTENS, H. G.
ABEL 1979 -1
CARTER, M. W.
BAKEE 1979 -1; CART 1979 -1; CART 1980 -1
CARTER, P. L.
CARTA 1978 -1
CASTAGNA, F.
CAST 1972 -1
CASTELLANI, G.
CASTA 1975 -1; CASTB 1979 -1
CATLIN, P. A.
CATL 1978 -1; CATL 1978 -2; CATL 1979 -1
CATL 1979 -2; CATL 1979 -3; CATL 1979 -4
CAVANAGH, R. A.
CAVA 1975 -1
CAZANESCU, V.-E.
CAZA 1978 -1
CEGOLINA, E. P.
GORDA 1977 -1
CERNYSOVA, G. D.
KAPL 1973 -1
CHACHRA, V.
CHAC 1979 -1
CHAIKEN, J. M.
CHAI 1978 -1; CHAI 1978 -2
CHALKOV, V. D.
CHAL 1977 -1; CHAL 1978 -1
CHALMET, L. G.
CHALA 1981 -1; CHALB 1977 -1; CHALC 1981 -1
NAMB 1979 -1
CHAMBER, M. T.
CHAM 1979 -1
CHAN, A. W.
CHAN 1979 -1
CHAN, P.-W.
WHIT 1979 -1
CHANARATNA, V.
LIEBA 1977 -1
CHAND, M.
AGRAA 1978 -1; AGRAA 1979 -1; AGRAA 1980 -1
CHANDRA, A.
CHANA 1979 -1
CHANDRA, A. K.
CHANB 1978 -1; CHANC 1978 -1
CHANDRA, S.
CHAND 1979 -1; CHAND 1979 -2; CHAND 1980 -1
CHAND 1980 -2
CHANDRAMOHAN, M.
CHAND 1979 -1; CHAND 1979 -2; CHAND 1980 -1
CHAND 1980 -2
CHANDRASEKARAN, R.
CHANE 1981 -1; CHANF 1978 -1; CHANF 1981 -1
CHANG 1980 -1; CHANH 1978 -1; CHANH 1980 -1
MEGIC 1979 -1
CHANG, C.-L.
KANG 1977 -1
CHANG, Q. L.
CHANI 1978 -1
CHANG, S. K.
KANG 1977 -1; MARUA 1977 -1
CHANG, T.-S.
BRIC 1978 -1
CHAO, C. Y.
CHAO 1979 -1
CHAPLEAU, L.
DESRA 1980 -1
CHARALAMBOUS, C.
CALA 1980 -1
CHARIN, V. S.
PROT 1977 -1; PROT 1979 -1
CHARLES, O.
PANW 1978 -1
CHARNES, A.
ARMSA 1979 -1; CHAR 1961 -1; CHARA 1977 -1
CHARB 1978 -1
CHARTRAND, G.
BEHZA 1967 -1; CHARC 1977 -1; CHARD 1969 -1
CHARE 1979 -1; CHARF 1979 -1
CHARYEV, G.
AKHM 1979 -1
CHATY, G.
CHAT 1979 -1
CHEBOTAREV, A. S.
CHEB 1976 -1
CHEIN, M.
CHAT 1979 -1
CHELNOKOV, V. M.
CHEL 1976 -1
CHEN, C. C.
CHEN 1979 -1
CHEN, D.-S.
CHENA 1978 -1
CHEN, I.-N.
CHENB 1979 -1
CHEN, K.-Y.
CHENC 1976 -1
CHEN, N.-F.
CHEND 1975 -1
CHEN, P. Y.
CHENB 1979 -1
CHEN, R.
CHENE 1978 -1
CHEN, Y. H.
CHENF 1973 -1; LABA 1977 -1
CHEN, Z.
DAS D 1978 -1; DAS E 1979 -1
CHERENKOV, A. P.
CHER 1979 -1
CHERKASHIN, A. M.
RUBIB 1980 -1; RUBIB 1980 -2
CHERKASSKII, B. V.
CHERA 1977 -1; CHERA 1977 -2
CHERNIKOVA, N. V.
CHERB 1978 -1; NGUEA 1981 -1
CHERNJAK, A. A.
TYSHA 1979 -1
CHERNYSHEV, JU. O.
CHERC 1970 -1; CHERC 1974 -1; CHERC 1977 -1
CHERD 1977 -1; DODO 1977 -1
CHERVAK, JU. JU.
CHERE 1978 -1
CHEUNG, T.-Y.
CHEU 1978 -1; CHEU 1980 -1; CHEU 1980 -2
CHIEN, R. T.
CHIE 1964 -1
CHIN, F. Y.
ACHU 1981 -1; CHIN 1978 -1
CHO, Y.
SAHNA 1979 -1; SAHNA 1979 -2; SAHNA 1980 -1
CHOBELJICH, S. N.
JOVA 1973 -1
CHOE, U.
RARDA 1979 -1
CHONG, P. S. C.
ZOLTA 1979 -1

CHOU, T.-W. J.
CHOU 1979 -1
CHOUDUM, S. A.
PART 1975 -1
CHOUKHMANE, E.-A.
CHOUA 1978 -1
CHRISTEN, C. A.
CHRI 1979 -1
CHRISTIE, A.
CHRIA 1971 -1
CHRISTOFIDES, N.
AINO 1979 -1; BALAC 1979 -1; CHRIB 1971 -1
CHRIB 1979 -1; CHRIC 1979 -1; CHRID 1979 -1
CHRIE 1979 -1; CHRIF 1978 -1; CHRIG 1979 -1
CHRIG 1979 -2; CHRIG 1980 -1; CHRIG 1980 -2
CHRIH 1978 -1; CHRIH 1978 -2
CHRISTOS, H. P.
LEWIA 1978 -1
CHU, Y. C.
CHU 1974 -1
CHUNG, F. R. K.
CHUN 1980 -1; CHUNA 1978 -1; CHUNB 1978 -1
CHUNG, S.-J.
CHUNC 1979 -1; CHUNC 1979 -2; CHUNC 1980 -1
CHUNC 1980 -2
CHUNGPHAISAN, V.
CHUND 1978 -1
CHURCH, R. L.
CHUR 1978 -1; SCHIC 1979 -1
CHVATAL, V.
AVISA 1978 -1; CHVA 1979 -1; CHVA 1980 -1
CHVAA 1979 -1
CINI, M.
BIAN 1980 -1
CIOBANU, G.
CIOB 1977 -1; CIOB 1981 -1
CIOBOTARU, S.
CIOBA 1978 -1
CIOFFI, G.
CIOF 1979 -1
CIUREA, E.
CIUR 1979 -1; CIUR 1979 -2
CLARK, G. M.
CLAR 1980 -1
CLARK, L.
CLARA 1980 -1
CLAUS, A.
CLAU 1978 -1; CLAUA 1981 -1; KLEIE 1972 -1
CLAUSEN, J.
CLAUB 1980 -1
CLAYTON, R. E.
LEE B 1978 -1
CLEEF, H. J.
CLEE 1979 -1; CLEE 1981 -1
CLIMACO, J. C. N.
CLIM 1981 -1
CLOCOTICI, V.
CLOC 1976 -1
COBHAM, A.
COBH 1963 -1
COBIAN, J. M.
COBI 1981 -1
COCKAYNE, E. J.
COCK 1978 -1; COCKA 1978 -1; HOLY 1979 -1
MITC 1979 -1
CODY, R. A.
COFFA 1977 -1
COELHO, J. D.
COEL 1981 -1
COFFMAN, E. G. JR.
BAKEA 1980 -1; COFF 1978 -1; COFFA 1977 -1
COFFB 1978 -1; COFFC 1980 -1; COFFD 1979 -1
COFFE 1976 -1; COFFF 1977 -1; COFFF 1978 -1
COFFG 1977 -1; COFFG 1978 -1; COFFH 1976 -1
COGIS, O.
COGI 1979 -1
COHEN, A. I.
COHE 1978 -1
COHON, J.
REVE 1981 -1; SCHIC 1979 -1
COLBOURN, C. J.
COLB 1978 -1; COLB 1979 -1; COLBA 1979 -1
COLBB 1978 -1
COLBOURN, M. J.
COLBB 1978 -1
COLIJN, A. W.
BERMA 1977 -1; COLI 1973 -1
COLLIER, J. B.
COLL 1978 -1
COLLINS, M.
COLLA 1978 -1
COLLOMB, P.
COLLB 1977 -1
COMBOT, J.-P.
COMB 1979 -1
COMPANYS, R.
COMP 1975 -1; CORO 1977 -1
CONCA, C.
ETCH 1978 -1
CONLEY, W.
CONL 1978 -1; CONLA 1977 -1
CONNER, J. L.
CONN 1971 -1; CONN 1972 -1; CONN 1973 -1
CONN 1973 -2
CONRADT, D.
CONR 1978 -1; CONR 1979 -1; PAPEB 1979 -1
COOK, W. D.
ARMSB 1979 -1; ARMSC 1979 -1; COOK 1980 -1
COOKA 1979 -1
COOPER, J. K.
BEHZA 1967 -1
COOPER, L.
COLLA 1978 -1; COOP 1977 -1; COOPA 1977 -1
KATZ 1979 -1
COOPER, M. W.
COOPB 1979 -1; COOPB 1979 -2
COOPER, W. W.
CHAR 1961 -1; CHARA 1977 -1
COPPINS, R. J.
COPP 1980 -1
CORDOVIL, R.
CORD 1979 -1; CORD 1980 -1; CORD 1980 -2
CORDA 1979 -1
CORKINDALE, D.
CORK 1978 -1
CORLEY, H. W.
CORL 1980 -1
CORNEIL, D. G.
CORN 1978 -1
CORNUEJOLS, G.
CORNA 1978 -1; CORNA 1979 -1; CORNB 1979 -1
CORNC 1980 -1; CORNC 1980 -2; CORND 1980 -1
CORND 1980 -2; CORND 1980 -3; CORND 1981 -1
CORNE 1979 -1; CORNE 1980 -1
COROMINAS, A.
CORO 1977 -1
CORT, J. D.
CORT 1978 -1
COURCELLE, B.
BOAS 1977 -1
COURTILLOT, M.
COUR 1965 -1
COX, J. T.
COX 1980 -1
CRAMER, J.
CRAM 1979 -1
CRAMER, M.
CRAMA 1977 -1
CRAPO, H. H.
CRAP 1970 -1
CROITORU, C.
CROI 1979 -1; CROI 1980 -1
CROWDER, H. P.
CHENE 1978 -1; CROW 1978 -1; CROWA 1978 -1
CROWB 1979 -1
CRUM, R. L.
CRUM 1979 -1
CRUSE, A. B.
CRUS 1979 -1
CRUYSSEN, P. VAN DER
CRUY 1978 -1
CSERNY, L.
CSER 1978 -1
CSIMA, J.
CSIM 1965 -1
CULL, P.
CULL 1980 -1
CULLEN, F. H.
CULLA 1980 -1
CULVER, W. D.
MAC F 1978 -1
CUMMINGS, L. J.
CUMM 1977 -1
CUNINGHAME-GREEN, R. A.
CUNI 1979 -1; CUNI 1981 -1
CUNNINGHAM, W. H.
BIXBA 1979 -1; BIXBA 1980 -1; CUNN 1979 -1
CUNN 1979 -2; CUNN 1981 -1; CUNN 1981 -2
CUNN 1981 -3; CUNN 1981 -4; CUNN 1982 -1
CUNNA 1980 -1; CUNNB 1981 -1; CUNNC 1978 -1
CUNTO, E.
CUNT 1978 -1
CUTLER, M.
CUTL 1980 -1; CUTLA 1978 -1
CVETKOVIC, D. M.
CVET 1972 -1; CVETA 1979 -1
CZAPNIK, J.
CZAP 1977 -1
DABROWSKI, J.
KUBA 1978 -1

****

HASTINGS, N. A. J.
HAST 1978 -1
HATTORI, Y.
NAKAC 1979 -1
HAUPTMANN, H.
HAUP 1980 -1
HAUSMANN, D.
GILEA 1979 -1; HAUS 1978 -1; HAUS 1978 -2
HAUS 1979 -1; HAUS 1980 -1; HAUS 1980 -2
HAUS 1981 -1; HAUSA 1980 -1; HAUSB 1979 -1
HAUSB 1979 -2; HAUSB 1981 -1; HAUSC 1978 -1
HAUSC 1978 -2; HAUSC 1978 -3; HAUSC 1978 -4
HAUSC 1980 -1; HAUSC 1980 -2; HAUSC 1981 -1
HAX, A. C.
BITRA 1977 -1; BRADB 1977 -1
HAYES, G. M. JR.
HAYE 1979 -1
HAYES, M.
HAYEA 1979 -1
HAYS, R.
HAYS 1967 -1
HEARN, D. W.
BARTD 1979 -1
HECHT, M. S.
FREDA 1976 -1
HEDETNIEMI, S. T.
COCK 1978 -1; COCKA 1978 -1; FARL 1979 -1
MITC 1979 -1; MITCA 1979 -1
HEICKEN, K.
HEIC 1980 -1
HEINHOLD, M.
HEIN 1978 -1
HEINRICH, K.
HEINA 1976 -1; HEINA 1977 -1; HEINB 1978 -1
HEINRICH, P.
HEINC 1979 -1; HEIND 1979 -1
HELGASON, R. V.
ALI 1978 -1; ALI A 1978 -1; ALI A 1980 -1
COLLA 1978 -1; HELG 1976 -1; HELG 1978 -1
HELG 1979 -1
HELL, P.
HELL 1981 -1; HELL 1981 -2; KIRKA 1978 -1
HEMGESBERG, G.
EVERA 1977 -1
HEMMINGER, R. L.
BONDA 1978 -1
HENDERSON, P. B.
HEND 1975 -1
HENDRICK, T. E.
SEWA 1978 -1
HENDRICKSON, C.
BRES 1980 -1
HENDY, M. D.
HENDA 1980 -1
HENRY-LABORDERE, A.
HENR 1979 -1; KAUFD 1977 -1
HEPPES, A.
HEPP 1976 -1
HERMAN, R.
HERM 1979 -1
HERMANN, P. P.
HERMA 1973 -1
HERROELEN, W. S.
ASSC 1979 -1; ELMAB 1980 -1
HESKE, A.
DERIA 1980 -1
HESSELBACH, J.
HESS 1977 -1
HETYEI, G.
HETY 1974 -1; HETY 1975 -1
HEWINS, R. D.
CHRID 1979 -1
HEY, A.
CHRIE 1979 -1
HEYDEMANN, M. C.
BERME 1979 -1; BERMF 1978 -1; HEYD 1980 -1
HILL, E. JR.
HILL 1978 -1
HILLIER, F. S.
FAAL 1979 -1; HILLA 1977 -1; HILLB 1979 -1
HILLSMAN, E. L.
ROSI 1979 -1
HILTON, A. J. W.
GELL 1974 -1; HILT 1975 -1; HILT 1977 -1
HILT 1977 -2; HILT 1978 -1
HIMELWRIGHT, P. E.
HIME 1974 -1
HINDELANG, T. J.
HIND 1979 -1
HINDERER, K.
HINDA 1977 -1
HINDI, K. S.
HINDB 1978 -1
HINE, J. H.
HINE 1978 -1

HINTEREGGER, J.
HINT 1976 -1
HINXMAN, A. I.
BOFF 1979 -1; BOFFA 1979 -1; HINX 1980 -1
HIRATA, T.
HIRA 1979 -1
HIRAYAMA, H.
YATS 1972 -1
HIRSCHBERG, D. S.
CHANB 1978 -1; HIRS 1978 -1; HIRSA 1979 -1
HIRSHFIELD, D. S.
SHEPA 1979 -1
HITCHNER, L. E.
HITC 1968 -1
HITOMI, K.
YOSH 1978 -1; YOSH 1979 -1; YOSHA 1978 -1
HMELEVSKII, JU. I.
FRIO 1976 -1; FRUMA 1980 -1
HO, A. C.
BALAD 1980 -1; HO 1979 -1
HO, C. A.
NARUA 1980 -1
HO, Y. C.
HO A 1980 -1
HOANG HAI HOC
HOAN 1978 -1; HOAN 1979 -1
HOBBS, A. M.
BOLLA 1978 -1; FLEI 1976 -1; HOBB 1979 -1
HOBB 1979 -2; HOBB 1979 -3
HOCHBAUM, D.
FISHA 1978 -1; FISHA 1978 -2; HOCH 1979 -1
HOCH 1979 -2; HOCH 1979 -3; HOCH 1980 -1
HOCH 1980 -2
HODGSON, M. J.
HODG 1978 -1; HODG 1981 -1
HODGSON, T. J.
MAC C 1980 -1
HODZAEV, F. Z.
HODZ 1978 -1
HODZINSKII, A. N.
HODZA 1978 -1
HOEDE, C.
HOED 1978 -1; HOED 1979 -1; HOEDA 1981 -1
HOENEMANN, F.
HOEN 1979 -1
HOENERLOH, H.
HOENA 1979 -1
HOFFER, J.
DEAK 1981 -1
HOFFMAN, A. J.
BERGA 1978 -1; BUCKB 1979 -1; HOFF 1978 -1
HOFF 1979 -1; HOFFA 1970 -1
HOFFMAN, F.
HADLA 1979 -1
HOFRI, M.
HOFR 1980 -1
HOGG, G. L.
DESSB 1975 -1; GLAN 1978 -1
HOLLOWAY, C. A.
HOLL 1972 -1
HOLM, S.
HOLM 1978 -1; KLEIB 1979 -1
HOLMBERG, G.
HOLMA 1976 -1
HOLST, O.
HOLS 1979 -1
HOLYER, I. J.
HOLY 1979 -1
HOMENKO, N. P.
HOME 1977 -1; HOMEA 1976 -1; HOMEB 1977 -1
HONDA, N.
OKAW 1979 -1
HONG, J. W.
HONG 1979 -1
HONG, S.
HONGA 1977 -1; PADBA 1980 -1
HOPCROFT, J. E.
AHO 1973 -1; FORTA 1979 -1; FORTB 1980 -1
HORAK, P.
HORA 1979 -1; HORAA 1979 -1
HORAK, V.
HORAB 1978 -1
HORNE, G. J.
HORN 1980 -1
HOROWITZ, E.
FINN 1979 -1; HORO 1978 -1; SAHNC 1978 -1
HORST, R.
HORS 1980 -1
HOSHI, M.
SATO 1978 -1
HOSIOS, A. J.
HOSI 1980 -1
HOUCK, D. J.
CHIN 1978 -1; HOUC 1977 -1; HOUC 1980 -1
HOUCA 1979 -1

Vol. 101: W. M. Wonham, Linear Multivariable Control. A Geometric Approach. X, 344 pages. 1974.

Vol. 102: Analyse Convexe et Ses Applications. Comptes Rendus, Janvier 1974. Edited by J.-P. Aubin. IV, 244 pages. 1974.

Vol. 103: D. E. Boyce, A. Farhi, R. Weischedel, Optimal Subset Selection. Multiple Regression, Interdependence and Optimal Network Algorithms. XIII, 187 pages. 1974.

Vol. 104: S. Fujino, A Neo-Keynesian Theory of Inflation and Economic Growth. V, 96 pages. 1974.

Vol. 105: Optimal Control Theory and its Applications. Part I. Proceedings 1973. Edited by B. J. Kirby. VI, 425 pages. 1974.

Vol. 106: Optimal Control Theory and its Applications. Part II. Proceedings 1973. Edited by B. J. Kirby. VI, 403 pages. 1974.

Vol. 107: Control Theory, Numerical Methods and Computer Systems Modeling. International Symposium, Rocquencourt, June 17–21, 1974. Edited by A. Bensoussan and J. L. Lions. VIII, 757 pages. 1975.

Vol. 108: F. Bauer et al., Supercritical Wing Sections II. A Handbook. V, 296 pages. 1975.

Vol. 109: R. von Randow, Introduction to the Theory of Matroids. IX, 102 pages. 1975.

Vol. 110: C. Striebel, Optimal Control of Discrete Time Stochastic Systems. III. 208 pages. 1975.

Vol. 111: Variable Structure Systems with Application to Economics and Biology. Proceedings 1974. Edited by A. Ruberti and R. R. Mohler. VI, 321 pages. 1975.

Vol. 112: J. Wilhelm, Objectives and Multi-Objective Decision Making Under Uncertainty. IV, 111 pages. 1975.

Vol. 113: G. A. Aschinger, Stabilitätsaussagen über Klassen von Matrizen mit verschwindenden Zeilensummen. V, 102 Seiten. 1975.

Vol. 114: G. Uebe, Produktionstheorie. XVII, 301 Seiten. 1976.

Vol. 115: Anderson et al., Foundations of System Theory: Finitary and Infinitary Conditions. VII, 93 pages. 1976

Vol. 116: K. Miyazawa, Input-Output Analysis and the Structure of Income Distribution. IX, 135 pages. 1976.

Vol. 117: Optimization and Operations Research. Proceedings 1975. Edited by W. Oettli and K. Ritter. IV, 316 pages. 1976.

Vol. 118: Traffic Equilibrium Methods, Proceedings 1974. Edited by M. A. Florian. XXIII, 432 pages. 1976.

Vol. 119: Inflation in Small Countries. Proceedings 1974. Edited by H. Frisch. VI, 356 pages. 1976.

Vol. 120: G. Hasenkamp, Specification and Estimation of Multiple-Output Production Functions. VII, 151 pages. 1976.

Vol. 121: J. W. Cohen, On Regenerative Processes in Queueing Theory. IX, 93 pages. 1976.

Vol. 122: M. S. Bazaraa, and C. M. Shetty,Foundations of Optimization VI. 193 pages. 1976

Vol. 123: Multiple Criteria Decision Making. Kyoto 1975. Edited by M. Zeleny. XXVII, 345 pages. 1976.

Vol. 124: M. J. Todd. The Computation of Fixed Points and Applications. VII, 129 pages. 1976.

Vol. 125: Karl C. Mosler. Optimale Transportnetze. Zur Bestimmung ihres kostengünstigsten Standorts bei gegebener Nachfrage. VI, 142 Seiten. 1976.

Vol. 126: Energy, Regional Science and Public Policy. Energy and Environment I. Proceedings 1975. Edited by M. Chatterji and P. Van Rompuy. VIII, 316 pages. 1976.

Vol. 127: Environment, Regional Science and Interregional Modeling. Energy and Environment II. Proceedings 1975. Edited by M. Chatterji and P. Van Rompuy. IX, 211 pages. 1976.

Vol. 128: Integer Programming and Related Areas. A Classified Bibliography. Edited by C. Kastning. XII, 495 pages. 1976.

Vol. 129: H.-J. Lüthi, Komplementaritäts- und Fixpunktalgorithmen in der mathematischen Programmierung. Spieltheorie und Ökonomie. VII, 145 Seiten. 1976.

Vol. 130: Multiple Criteria Decision Making, Jouy-en-Josas, France. Proceedings 1975. Edited by H. Thiriez and S. Zionts. VI, 409 pages. 1976.

Vol. 131: Mathematical Systems Theory. Proceedings 1975. Edited by G. Marchesini and S. K. Mitter. X, 408 pages. 1976.

Vol. 132: U. H. Funke, Mathematical Models in Marketing. A Collection of Abstracts. XX, 514 pages. 1976.

Vol. 133: Warsaw Fall Seminars in Mathematical Economics 1975. Edited by M. W. Loś, J. Loś, and A. Wieczorek. V. 159 pages. 1976.

Vol. 134: Computing Methods in Applied Sciences and Engineering. Proceedings 1975. VIII, 390 pages. 1976.

Vol. 135: H. Haga, A Disequilibrium – Equilibrium Model with Money and Bonds. A Keynesian – Walrasian Synthesis. VI, 119 pages. 1976.

Vol. 136: E. Kofler und G. Menges, Entscheidungen bei unvollständiger Information. XII, 357 Seiten. 1976.

Vol. 137: R. Wets, Grundlagen Konvexer Optimierung. VI, 146 Seiten. 1976.

Vol. 138: K. Okuguchi, Expectations and Stability in Oligopoly Models. VI, 103 pages. 1976.

Vol. 139: Production Theory and Its Applications. Proceedings. Edited by H. Albach and G. Bergendahl. VIII, 193 pages. 1977.

Vol. 140: W. Eichhorn and J. Voeller, Theory of the Price Index. Fisher's Test Approach and Generalizations. VII, 95 pages. 1976.

Vol. 141: Mathematical Economics and Game Theory. Essays in Honor of Oskar Morgenstern. Edited by R. Henn and O. Moeschlin. XIV, 703 pages. 1977.

Vol. 142: J. S. Lane, On Optimal Population Paths. V, 123 pages. 1977.

Vol. 143: B. Näslund, An Analysis of Economic Size Distributions. XV, 100 pages. 1977.

Vol. 144: Convex Analysis and Its Applications. Proceedings 1976. Edited by A. Auslender. VI, 219 pages. 1977.

Vol. 145: J. Rosenmüller, Extreme Games and Their Solutions. IV, 126 pages. 1977.

Vol. 146: In Search of Economic Indicators. Edited by W. H. Strigel. XVI, 198 pages. 1977.

Vol. 147: Resource Allocation and Division of Space. Proceedings. Edited by T. Fujii and R. Sato. VIII, 184 pages. 1977.

Vol. 148: C. E. Mandl, Simulationstechnik und Simulationsmodelle in den Sozial- und Wirtschaftswissenschaften. IX, 173 Seiten. 1977.

Vol. 149: Stationäre und schrumpfende Bevölkerungen: Demographisches Null- und Negativwachstum in Österreich. Herausgegeben von G. Feichtinger. VI, 262 Seiten. 1977.

Vol. 150: Bauer et al., Supercritical Wing Sections III. VI, 179 pages. 1977.

Vol. 151: C. A. Schneeweiß, Inventory-Production Theory. VI, 116 pages. 1977.

Vol. 152: Kirsch et al., Notwendige Optimalitätsbedingungen und ihre Anwendung. VI, 157 Seiten. 1978.

Vol. 153: Kombinatorische Entscheidungsprobleme: Methoden und Anwendungen. Herausgegeben von T. M. Liebling und M. Rössler. VIII, 206 Seiten. 1978.

Vol. 154: Problems and Instruments of Business Cycle Analysis. Proceedings 1977. Edited by W. H. Strigel. VI, 442 pages. 1978.

Vol. 155: Multiple Criteria Problem Solving. Proceedings 1977. Edited by S. Zionts. VIII, 567 pages. 1978.

Vol. 156: B. Näslund and B. Sellstedt, Neo-Ricardian Theory. With Applications to Some Current Economic Problems. VI, 165 pages. 1978.

Vol. 157: Optimization and Operations Research. Proceedings 1977. Edited by R. Henn, B. Korte, and W. Oettli. VI, 270 pages. 1978.

Vol. 158: L. J. Cherene, Set Valued Dynamical Systems and Economic Flow. VIII, 83 pages. 1978.

Vol. 159: Some Aspects of the Foundations of General Equilibrium Theory: The Posthumous Papers of Peter J. Kalman. Edited by J. Green. VI, 167 pages. 1978.

Vol. 160: Integer Programming and Related Areas. A Classified Bibliography. Edited by D. Hausmann. XIV, 314 pages. 1978.

Vol. 161: M. J. Beckmann, Rank in Organizations. VIII, 164 pages. 1978.

Vol. 162: Recent Developments in Variable Structure Systems, Economics and Biology. Proceedings 1977. Edited by R. R. Mohler and A. Ruberti. VI, 326 pages. 1978.

Vol. 163: G. Fandel, Optimale Entscheidungen in Organisationen. VI, 143 Seiten. 1979.

Vol. 164: C. L. Hwang and A. S. M. Masud, Multiple Objective Decision Making – Methods and Applications. A State-of-the-Art Survey. XII, 351 pages. 1979.

Vol. 165: A. Maravall, Identification in Dynamic Shock-Error Models. VIII, 158 pages. 1979.

Vol. 166: R. Cuninghame-Green, Minimax Algebra. XI, 258 pages. 1979.

Vol. 167: M. Faber, Introduction to Modern Austrian Capital Theory. X, 196 pages. 1979.

Vol. 168: Convex Analysis and Mathematical Economics. Proceedings 1978. Edited by J. Kriens. V, 136 pages. 1979.

Vol. 169: A. Rapoport et al., Coalition Formation by Sophisticated Players. VII, 170 pages. 1979.

Vol. 170: A. E. Roth, Axiomatic Models of Bargaining. V, 121 pages. 1979.

Vol. 171: G. F. Newell, Approximate Behavior of Tandem Queues. XI, 410 pages. 1979.

Vol. 172: K. Neumann and U. Steinhardt, GERT Networks and the Time-Oriented Evaluation of Projects. 268 pages. 1979.

Vol. 173: S. Erlander, Optimal Spatial Interaction and the Gravity Model. VII, 107 pages. 1980.

Vol. 174: Extremal Methods and Systems Analysis. Edited by A. V. Fiacco and K. O. Kortanek. XI, 545 pages. 1980.

Vol. 175: S. K. Srinivasan and R. Subramanian, Probabilistic Analysis of Redundant Systems. VII, 356 pages. 1980.

Vol. 176: R. Färe, Laws of Diminishing Returns. VIII, 97 pages. 1980.

Vol. 177: Multiple Criteria Decision Making-Theory and Application. Proceedings, 1979. Edited by G. Fandel and T. Gal. XVI, 570 pages. 1980.

Vol. 178: M. N. Bhattacharyya, Comparison of Box-Jenkins and Bonn Monetary Model Prediction Performance. VII, 146 pages. 1980.

Vol. 179: Recent Results in Stochastic Programming. Proceedings, 1979. Edited by P. Kall and A. Prékopa. IX, 237 pages. 1980.

Vol. 180: J. F. Brotchie, J. W. Dickey and R. Sharpe, TOPAZ – General Planning Technique and its Applications at the Regional, Urban, and Facility Planning Levels. VII, 356 pages. 1980.

Vol. 181: H. D. Sherali and C. M. Shetty, Optimization with Disjunctive Constraints. VIII, 156 pages. 1980.

Vol. 182: J. Wolters, Stochastic Dynamic Properties of Linear Econometric Models. VIII, 154 pages. 1980.

Vol. 183: K. Schittkowski, Nonlinear Programming Codes. VIII, 242 pages. 1980.

Vol. 184: R. E. Burkard and U. Derigs, Assignment and Matching Problems: Solution Methods with FORTRAN-Programs. VIII, 148 pages. 1980.

Vol. 185: C. C. von Weizsäcker, Barriers to Entry. VI, 220 pages. 1980.

Vol. 186: Ch.-L. Hwang and K. Yoon, Multiple Attribute Decision Making – Methods and Applications. A State-of-the-Art-Survey. XI, 259 pages. 1981.

Vol. 187: W. Hock, K. Schittkowski, Test Examples for Nonlinear Programming Codes. V. 178 pages. 1981.

Vol. 188: D. Bös, Economic Theory of Public Enterprise. VII, 142 pages. 1981.

Vol. 189: A. P. Lüthi, Messung wirtschaftlicher Ungleichheit. IX, 287 pages. 1981.

Vol. 190: J. N. Morse, Organizations: Multiple Agents with Multiple Criteria. Proceedings, 1980. VI, 509 pages. 1981.

Vol. 191: H. R. Sneessens, Theory and Estimation of Macroeconomic Rationing Models. VII, 138 pages. 1981.

Vol. 192: H. J. Bierens: Robust Methods and Asymptotic Theory in Nonlinear Econometrics. IX, 198 pages. 1981.

Vol. 193: J. K. Sengupta, Optimal Decisions under Uncertainty. VII, 156 pages. 1981.

Vol. 194: R. W. Shephard, Cost and Production Functions. XI, 104 pages. 1981.

Vol. 195: H. W. Ursprung, Die elementare Katastrophentheorie: Eine Darstellung aus der Sicht der Ökonomie. VII, 332 pages. 1982.

Vol. 196: M. Nermuth, Information Structures in Economics. VIII, 236 pages. 1982.

Vol. 197: Integer Programming and Related Areas. A Classified Bibliography. 1978 – 1981. Edited by R. von Randow. XIV, 338 pages. 1982.

GPSR Compliance

The European Union's (EU) General Product Safety Regulation (GPSR) is a set of rules that requires consumer products to be safe and our obligations to ensure this.

If you have any concerns about our products, you can contact us on ProductSafety@springernature.com

In case Publisher is established outside the EU, the EU authorized representative is:

Springer Nature Customer Service Center GmbH
Europaplatz 3
69115 Heidelberg, Germany

Batch number: 10844827

Printed by Printforce, the Netherlands